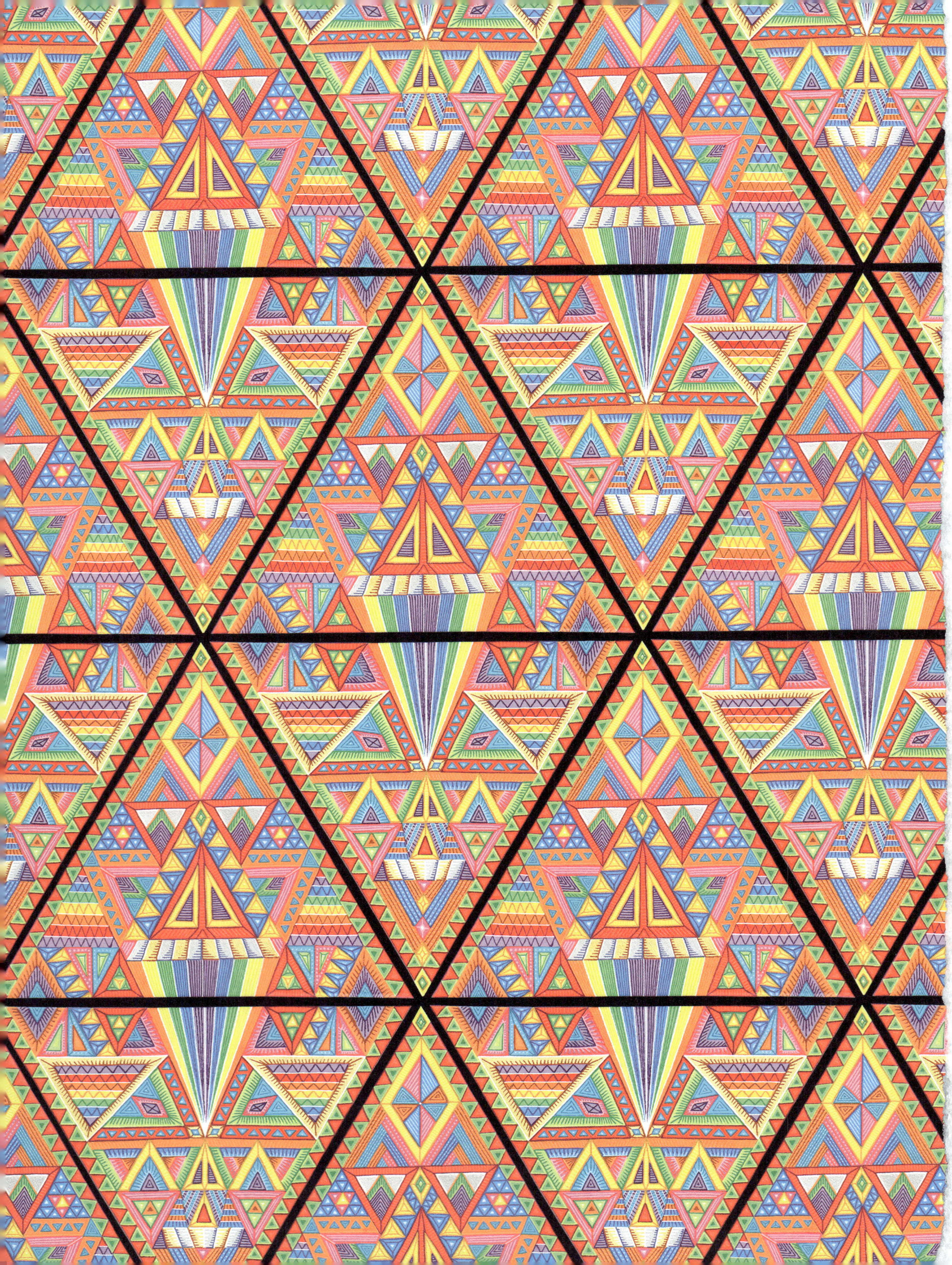

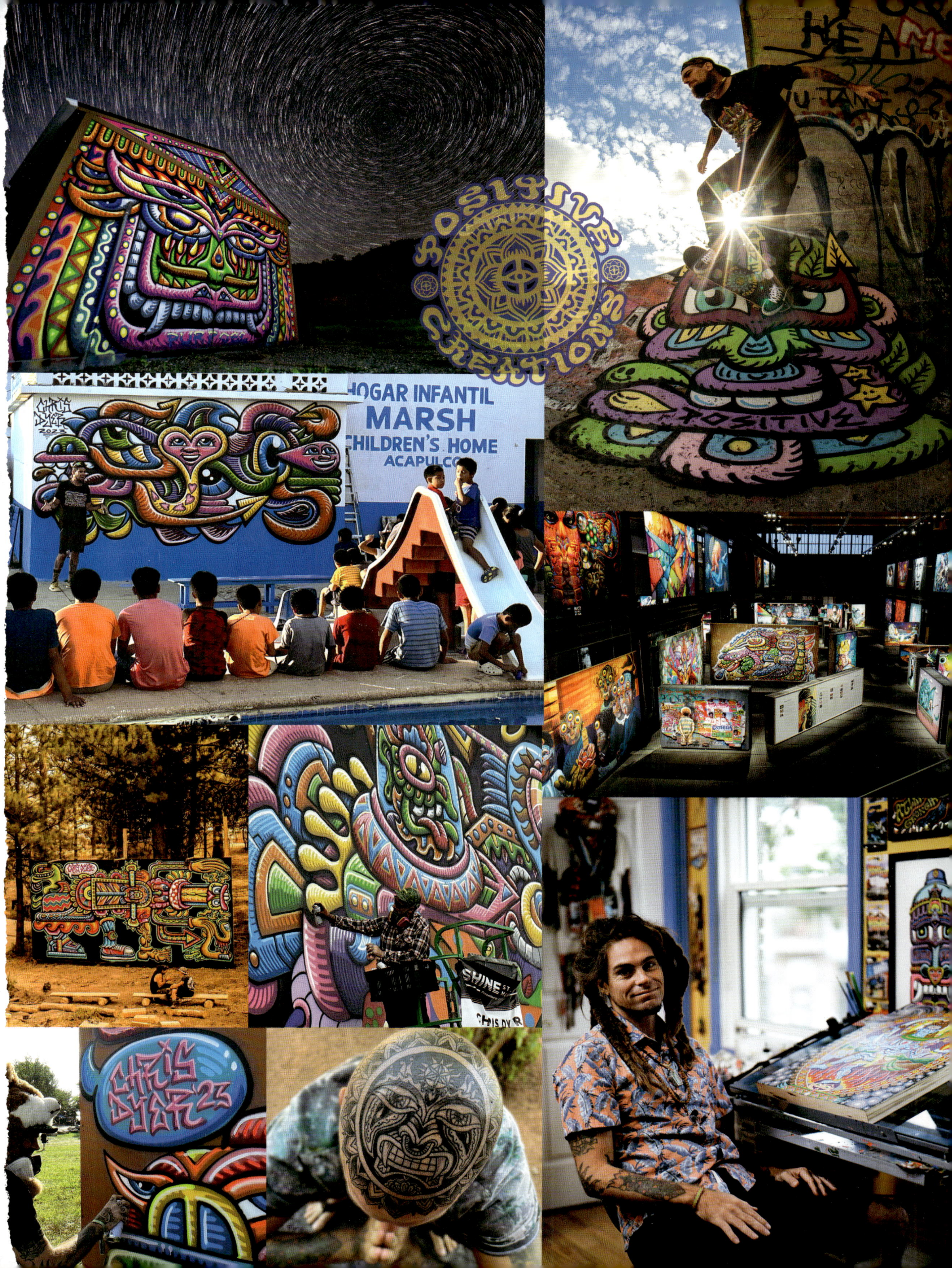
HOGAR INFANTIL
MARSH
CHILDREN'S HOME
ACAPULCO
POSITIVE
CHRIS DYER23

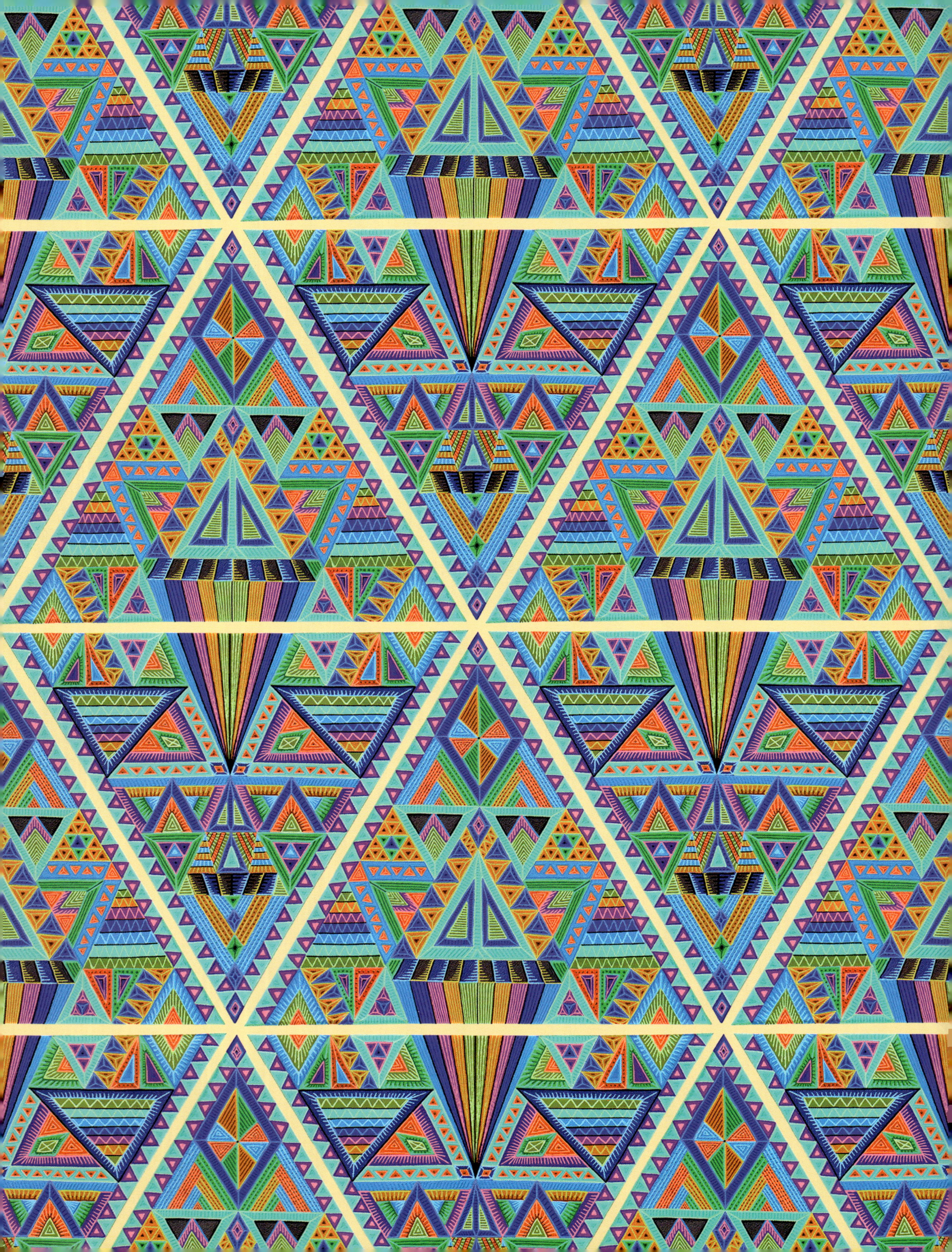

SHAMANIC JOURNEY

THE ART OF CHRIS DYER

2011 TO 2023

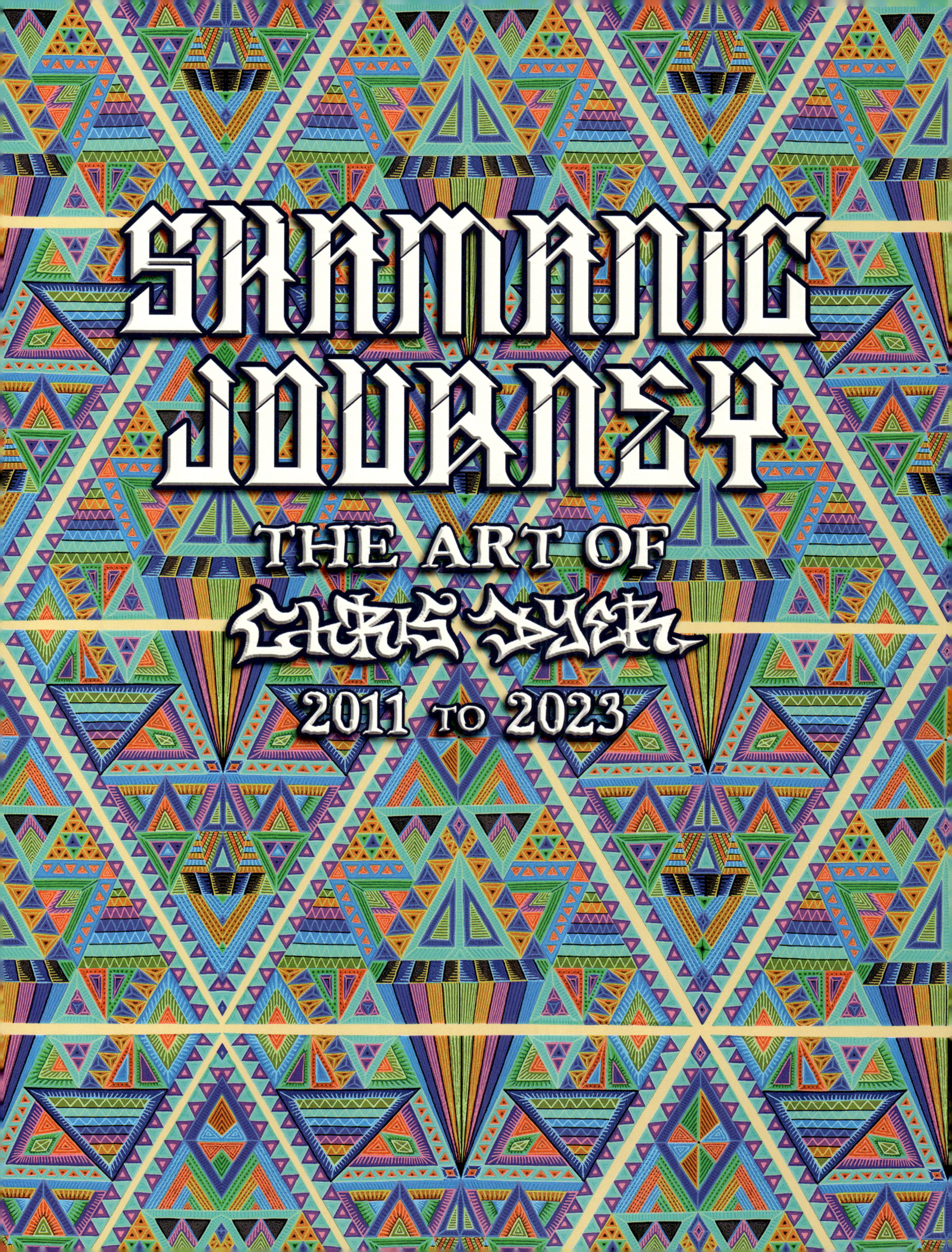

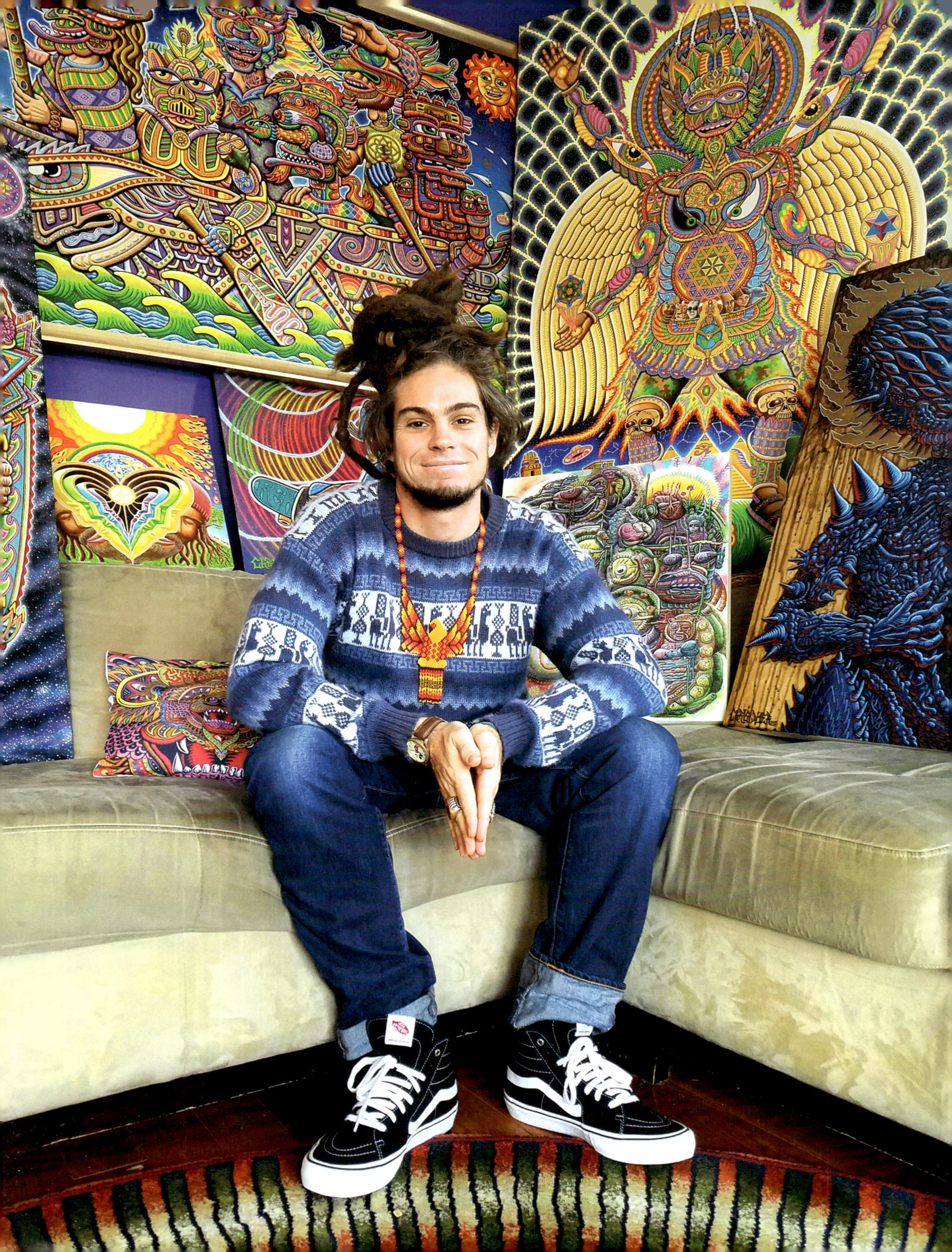

FOREWORDS

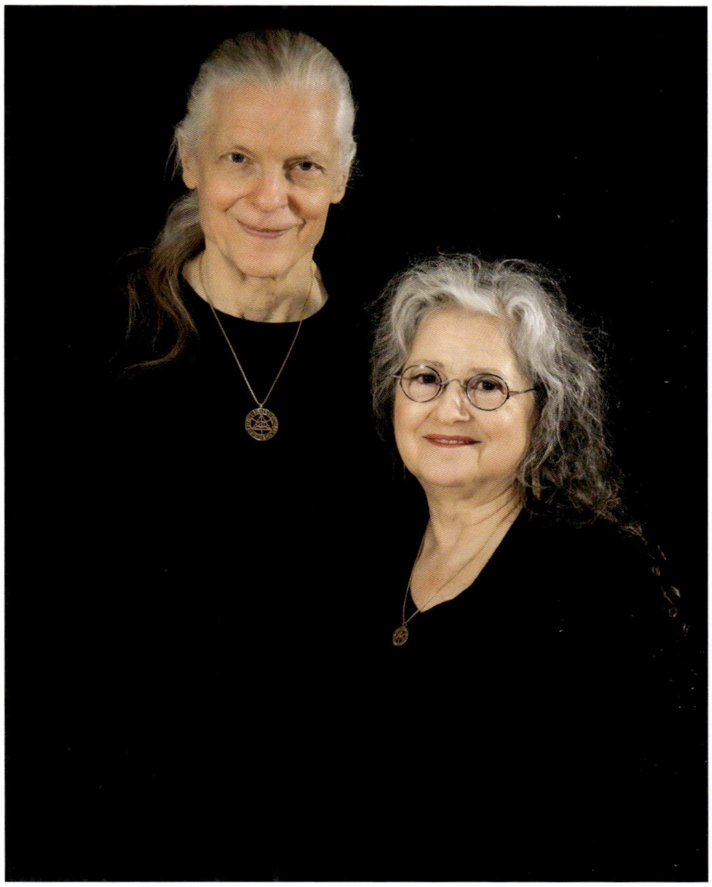

Chris Dyer is an extraordinary and unique Visionary Artist. Through his highly imaginative, labor intensive paintings of wild and strangely beautiful creatures, Chris reveals positive dimensions of consciousness while acknowledging shadow beings and the complexities of multidimensional realities. He has become an important muralist and live painter on stages throughout the world. His natural agility and courage as a skateboarder translates into work that continues to evolve, jumping into new mediums from coloring books to digital animation.

As a faculty member at CoSM, Chris has been a great inspiration to the many artists who have taken his art workshops. Sharing his deep spiritual faith with raw power, Chris channels vividly colored beings and environments, graphically bold and iconic art for the street and galleries. The cheerful monsters appearing in Dyer's work echo psychedelic beings depicted in "Chavín de Huantar," cave statuary created 3,500 years ago in Peru. Some of these invisible beings may have accompanied Chris on his journey from his Peruvian homeland to his beloved residence in Saint Petersburg, Florida.

-**Alex Grey** and **Allyson Grey**, Visionary Artists

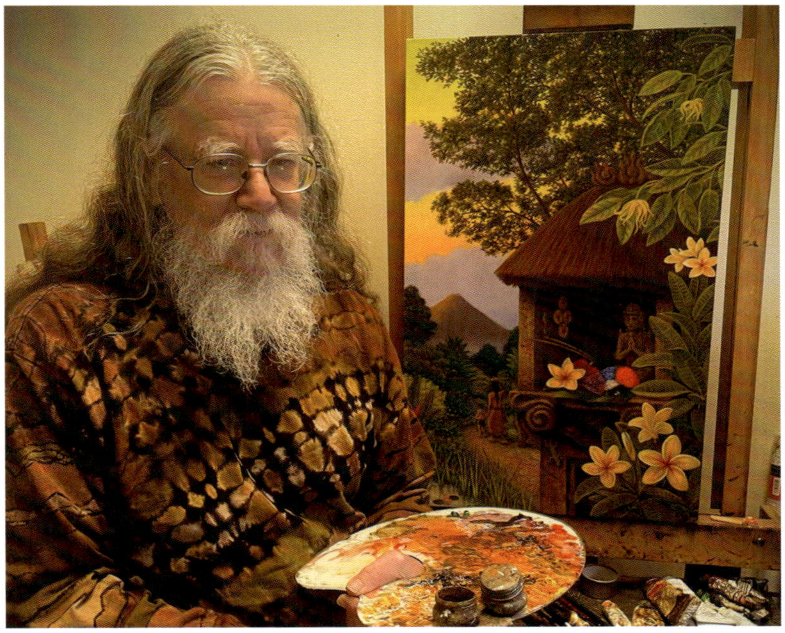

I have known Chris for quite a while now. When we first met he was an up-and-comer to the visionary art scene, but he already had plenty of experience in the graffiti/skate world to expand from. I've always been inspired by his never- ending positive energy and strong work ethic, the man never stops! Not only is he an excellent artist with a unique style, he is also a talented writer and puts together many interesting and provocative interviews with our art colleagues. He adds a lot to the flow in the river of culture we all swim in. Thank you Chris, and I wish you all the best as you continue on the path!

-**Mark Henson**, Visionary Artist

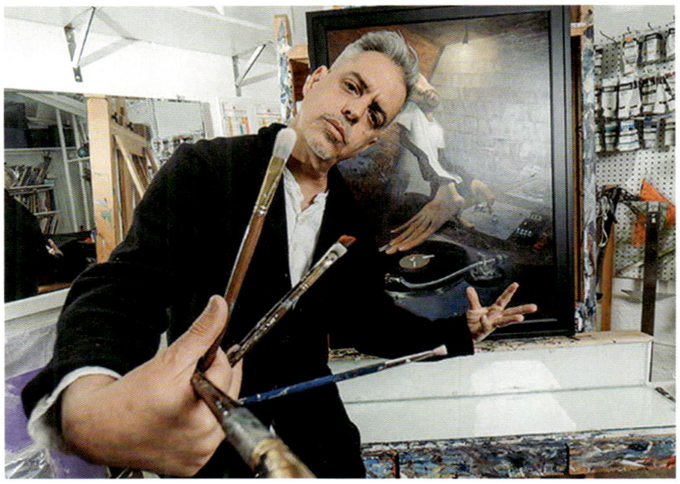

Dyer's unique work carries a message of unity and interconnectedness. In a world that often seems divided, his art serves as a reminder of our shared humanity and the underlying oneness that connects us all. His vibrant, kaleidoscopic visions and his kind heart are a call to embrace diversity and celebrate the beauty of our differences. His art serves as a bridge between the conscious and subconscious, inviting viewers to explore the depths of their own minds. His own deep healing is evident in his work and this is what makes Dyer a true artist.

-**Justin Bua**, Artist

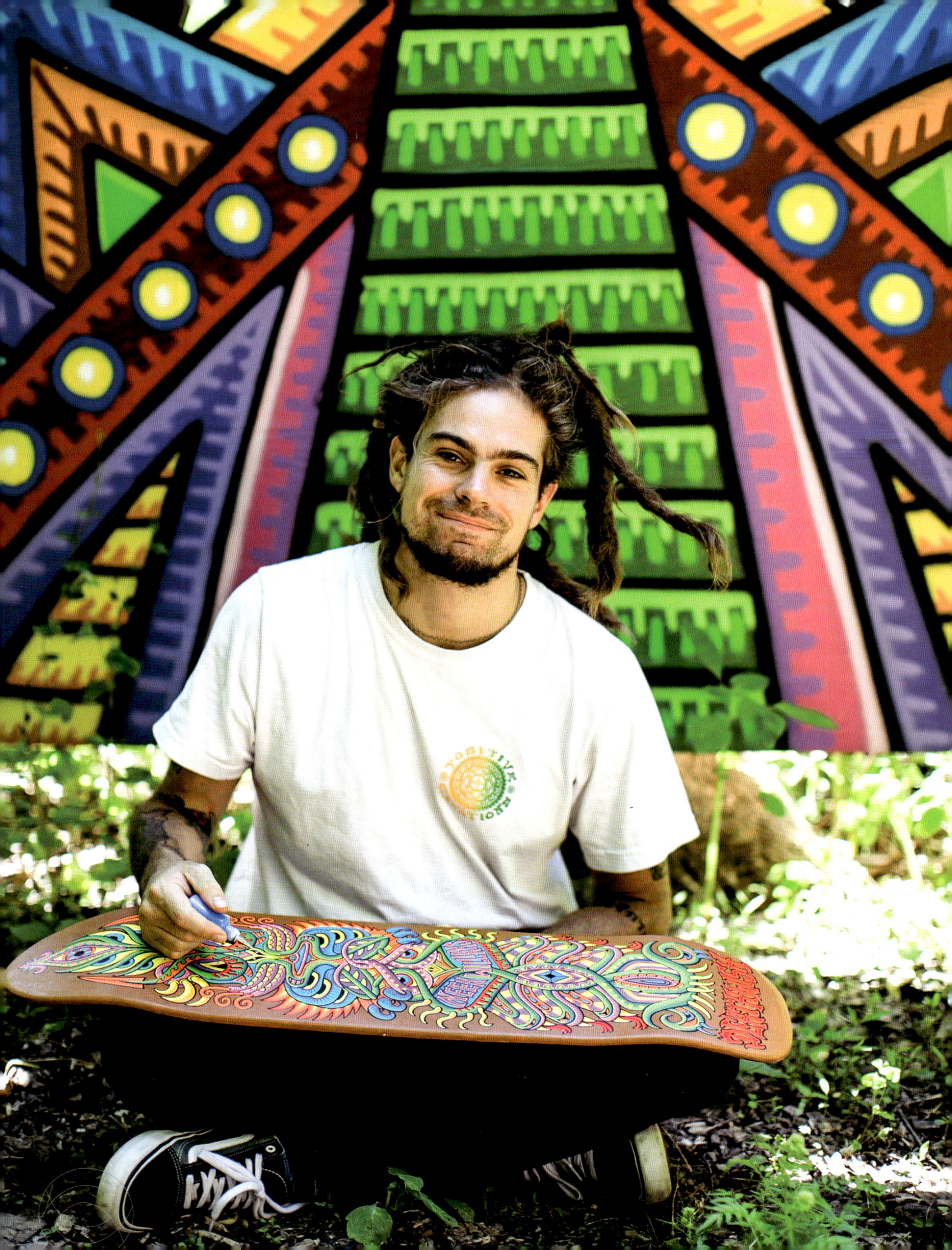

INTRO

Hi! Much Gratitude for picking up my second Art Book! It has been thirteen years since I released my last one, “Positive Creations”, and so much has continually changed! Seems like I have died and been reborn so many times that I don’t try to hold on anymore. As per usual, my hyper-expressive self is here to tell you all of the stories!

As the planet’s spiritual evolution has sped up and intensified, so has mine. A lot of my stories involve intense Love and heartbreak. There is medicine in both seasons of joy and pain, so I welcome them in my process of growth. Some people who were good friends in earlier chapters of this books ended up letting me down, so I had to purge them from my life. I’ve asked myself if I should remove these people entirely, but decided to keep them in, as they where part of my history. Blessings to all who provided potent lessons on my journey.

As the awakening of humanity advances, we continue facing harder and harder struggles, individually and collectively. The art I create reflects my personal process and I hope many others will find resonance in these images and worlds. I work hard at my craft and try to keep exploring and expressing through a variety of mediums and styles. Most importantly, I try my best to remain authentic through it all, so my soul can touch yours.

Negativity is a valuable teacher in this dualistic school of life. I value its role in the contrast we need to expand. This said, I would rather focus on the positive side of things. In the face of all the hardships of life, I try to stay Optimistic so I can keep striving for improvement, when sometimes it seems easier to just give up. The world desperately needs this energy these days, as the dark forces are progressively throwing harder challenges at us. These sick people are doing all they can to disempower humanity, but it’s too late, we are waking up! Ironically, their efforts for total domination on the soul of humanity is actually speeding up the awakening! More and more we are seeing reality past manufactured divisions and evolving into a better version of ourselves!

In this new book offering, I share myself with you, in all openness and honesty. Through my art and words, you will see and feel all my ups and downs, my stories of Love as well as Heartbreak. I will also take you around this beautiful planet, to explore new lands and show you the art I created in those journeys. Most importantly, in my partnership with Shamanic Medicines, I have brought back some visions of magical alien dimensions, waiting for us past this one. I hope these pages will uplift your vibration and inspire you on your own path of self-discovery and creation. Much Love!

Chris Dyer

CHAPTER ONE
THE MARRIED

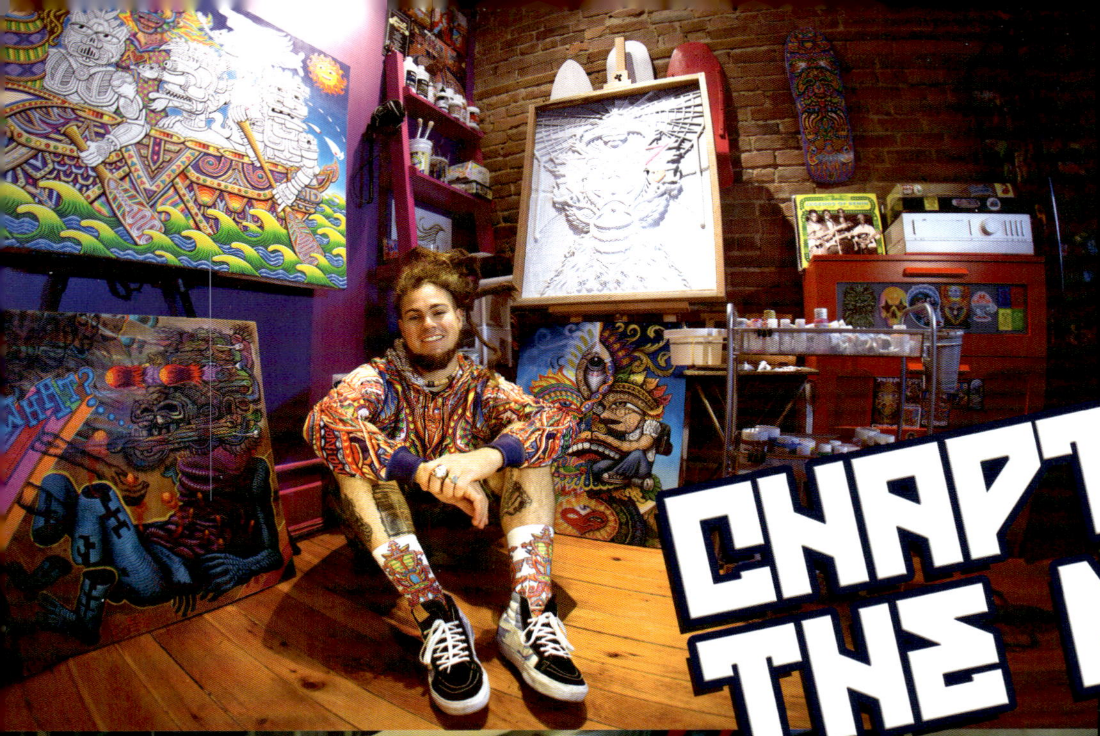

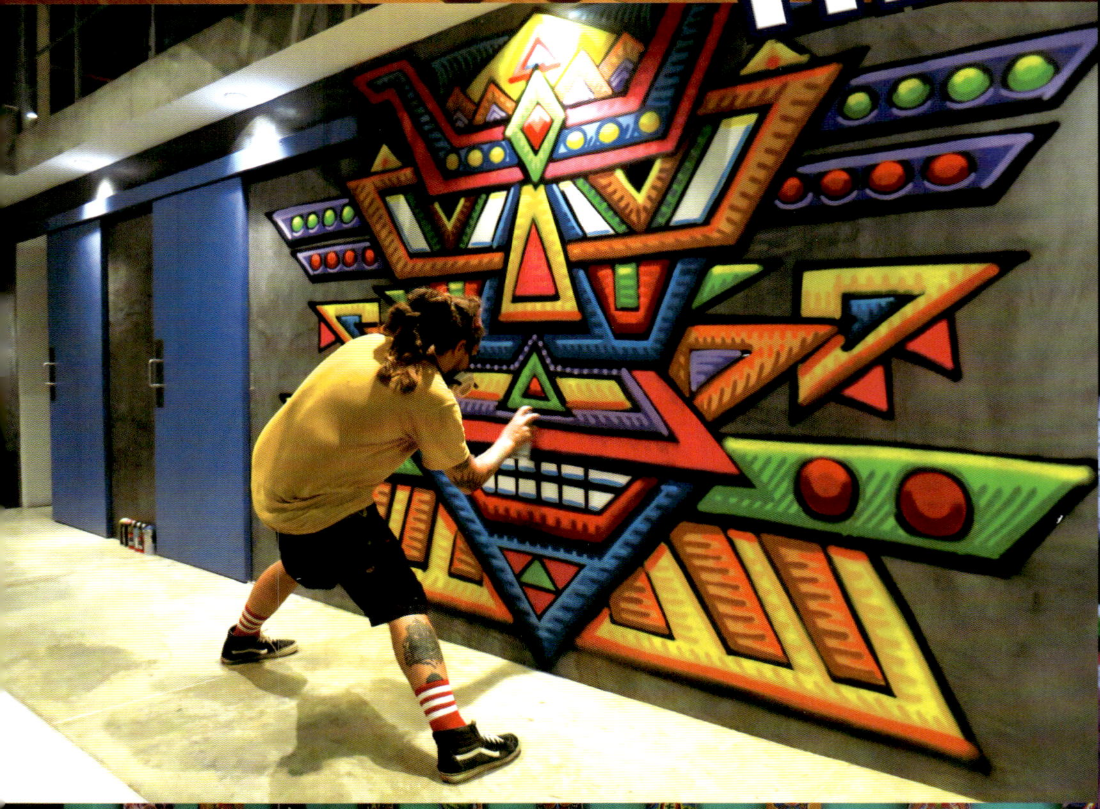

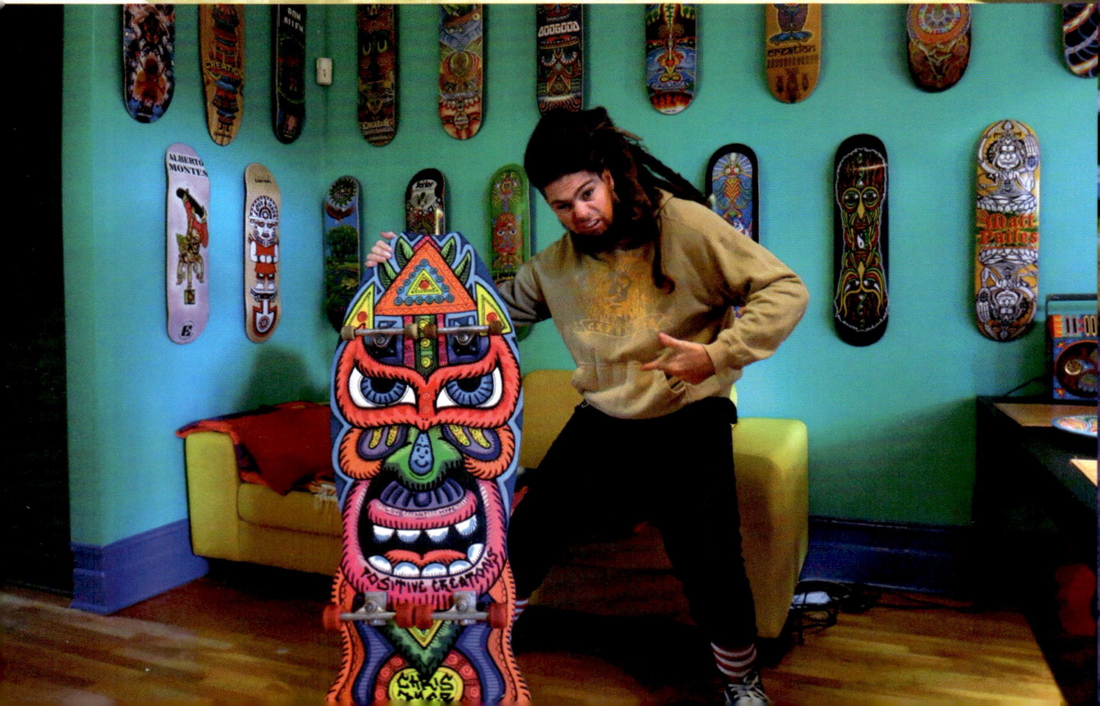

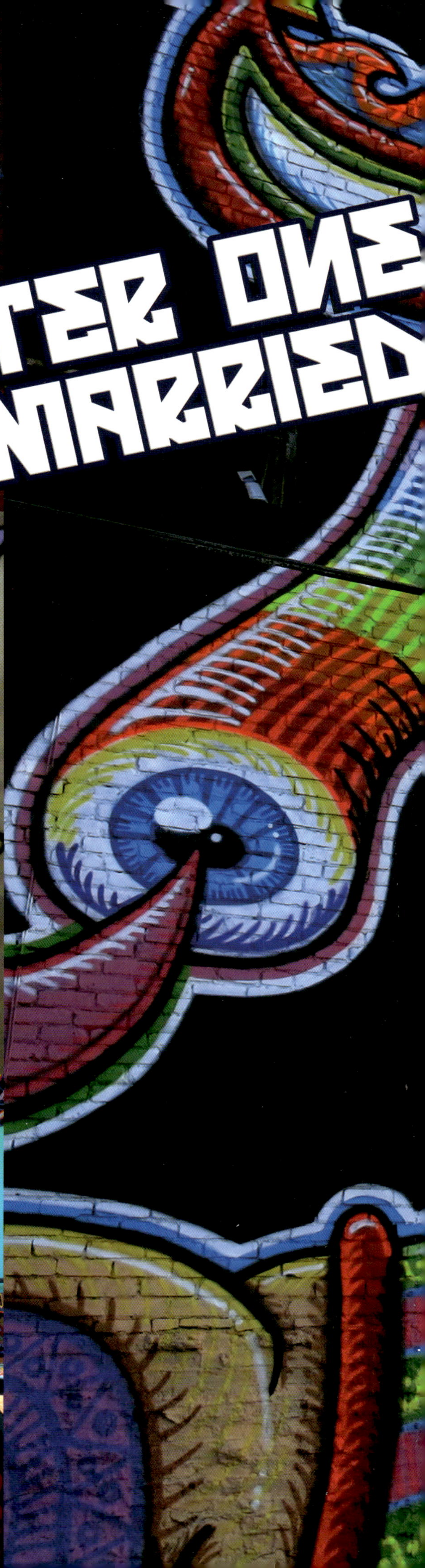

YEARS

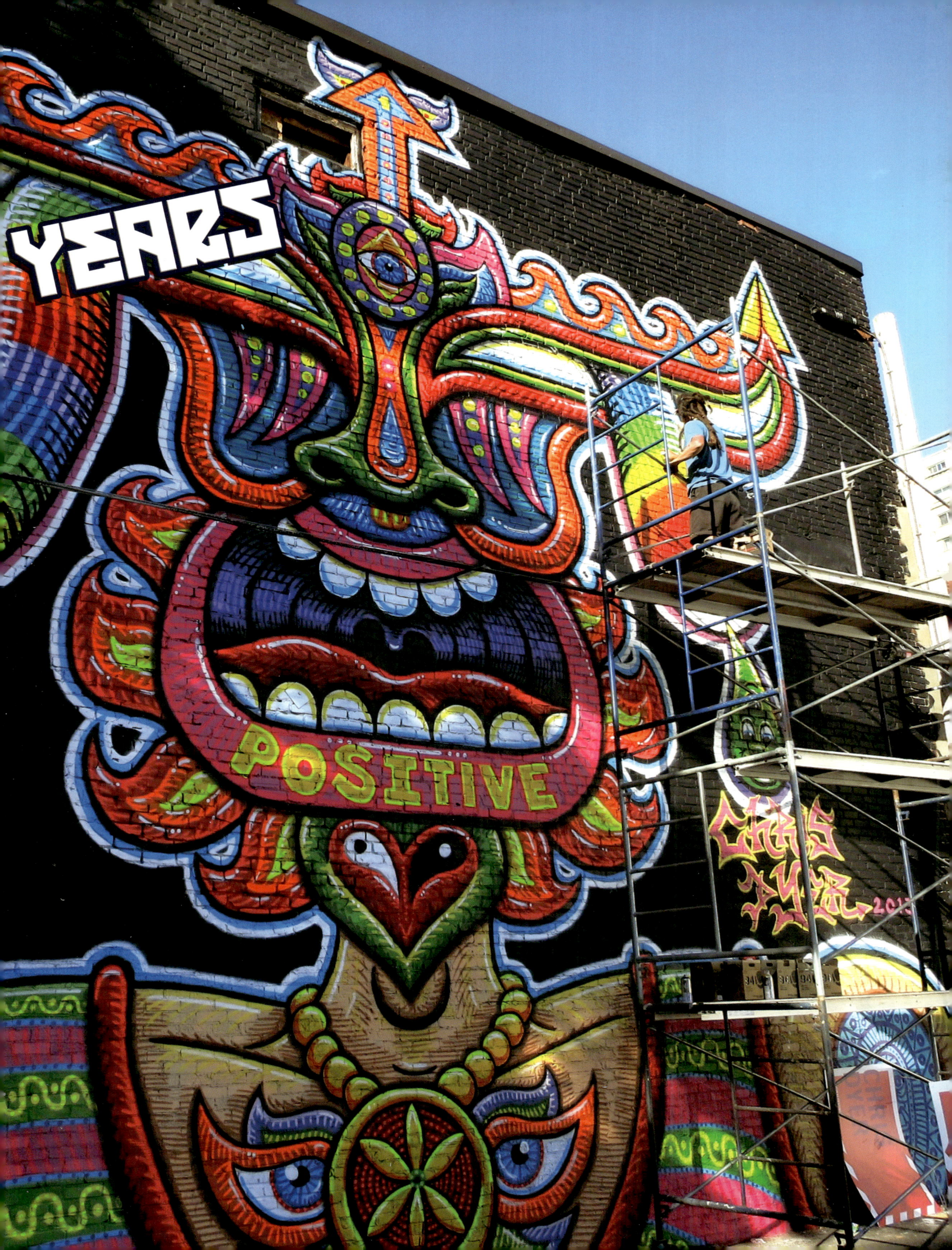

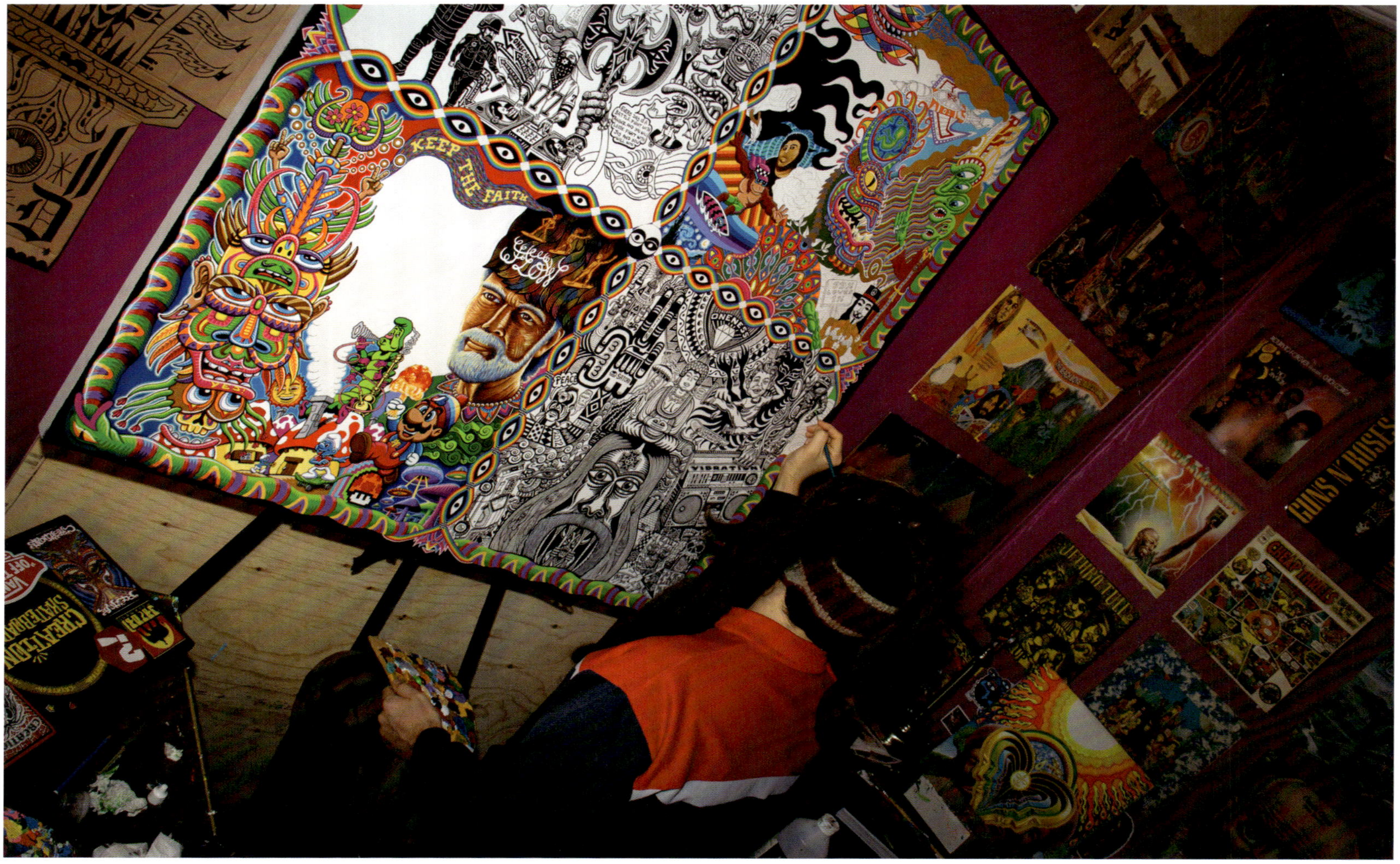

After I finished my last coffee table book in 2011, I felt the relaxation that comes from delivering a potent offering of soul expressions. So I was able to allow myself the time to dive into this ambitious painting, which blossomed little by little, over the lapse of two years. Usually, I meticulously plan out my paintings, from subject matter to composition, but on this one I let myself just flow spontaneously, allowing different sections to appear organically. It was like painting 100 paintings in one, with no particular theme. I did brake it up in four quadrants though, two in color and two without. Although those were chill years of home life, the world had a spike in chaos, especially during the “Occupy Movement” city takeovers. So a few political points of view were expressed in the mix, which wasn’t very common in my work. It was fun to play with a wide range of styles and topics, like a collaborative jam with different aspects of myself. In a way the piece ended up being a random mess of expressions, but at the same time it still has a cohesive order, just like life. Everything is meant to be. Sometimes the mess of the world seems unbearable, yet if we can appreciate the elegant dance of its energy, we can observe order coming out of the chaos.

A big influence on this piece was the art of **Ron English**, not only his unique painting style, but in his approach of remixing pop culture icons into social commentary, as to “Jam” our corrupt society. I actually got to meet Ron at his home studio in New York state at that time, thanks to **Alex** and **Allyson Grey** who took me there. Becoming friends with all these legends has been extremely encouraging to my path.

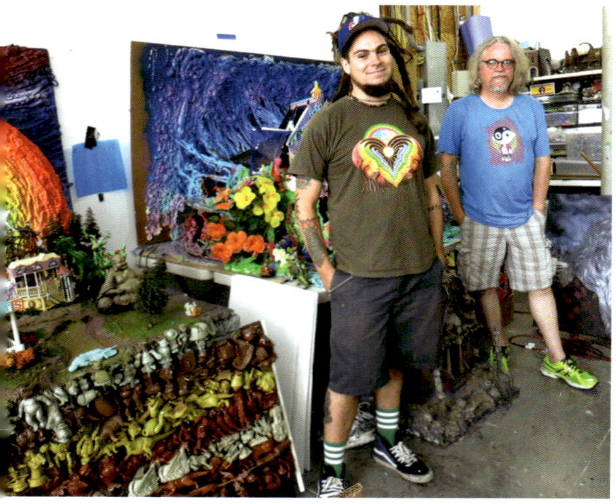

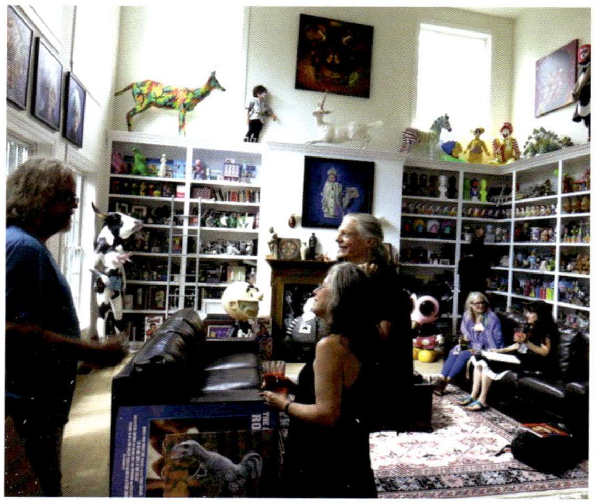

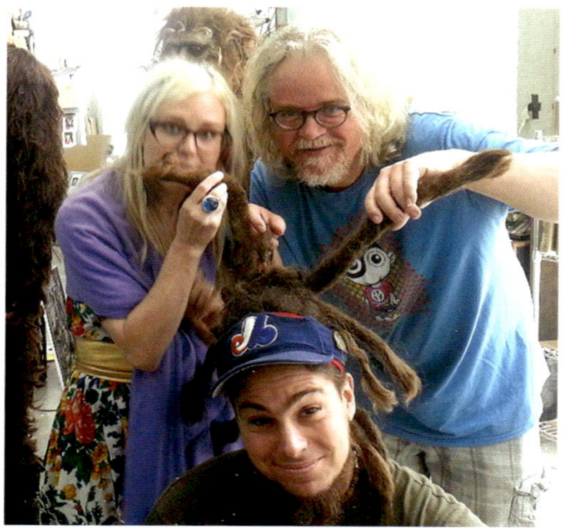

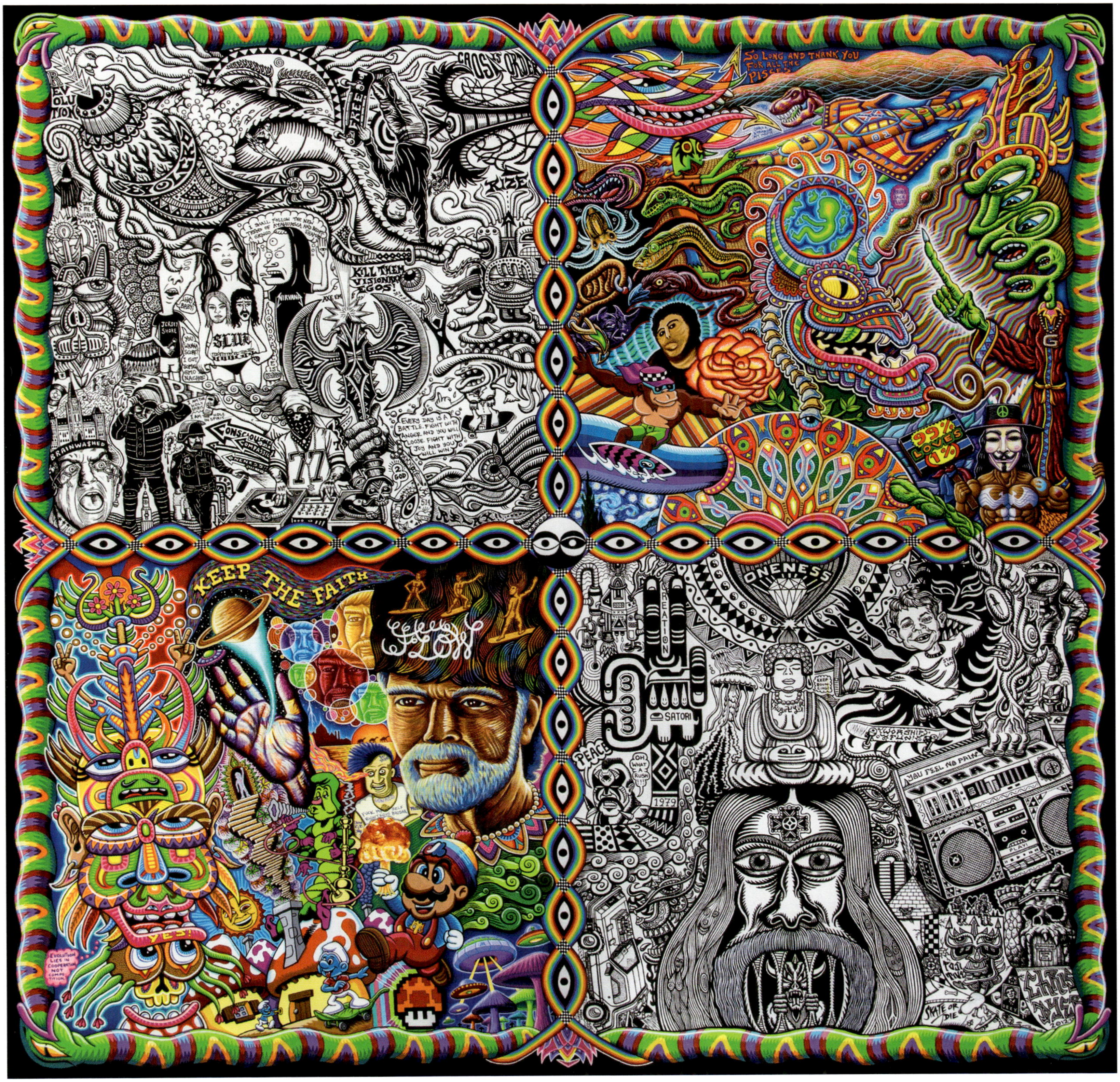

"Chaos Culture Jam" Acrylics on Canvas, 2012-2013

"EXPERIENCED WITH AN OPEN MIND, CHRIS DYER'S ART IS A PORTAL INTO A NEW DIMENSION OF INFINITE POSSIBLE REALITIES. HE IS THE UNDISPUTED LEADER OF THE PSYCHEDELIC ART MOVEMENT OF HIS GENERATION. SO PROUD OF THIS BROTHER WHO IS KILLING IT."

-RON ENGLISH, POP SURREALIST STREET ARTIST

MIAMI

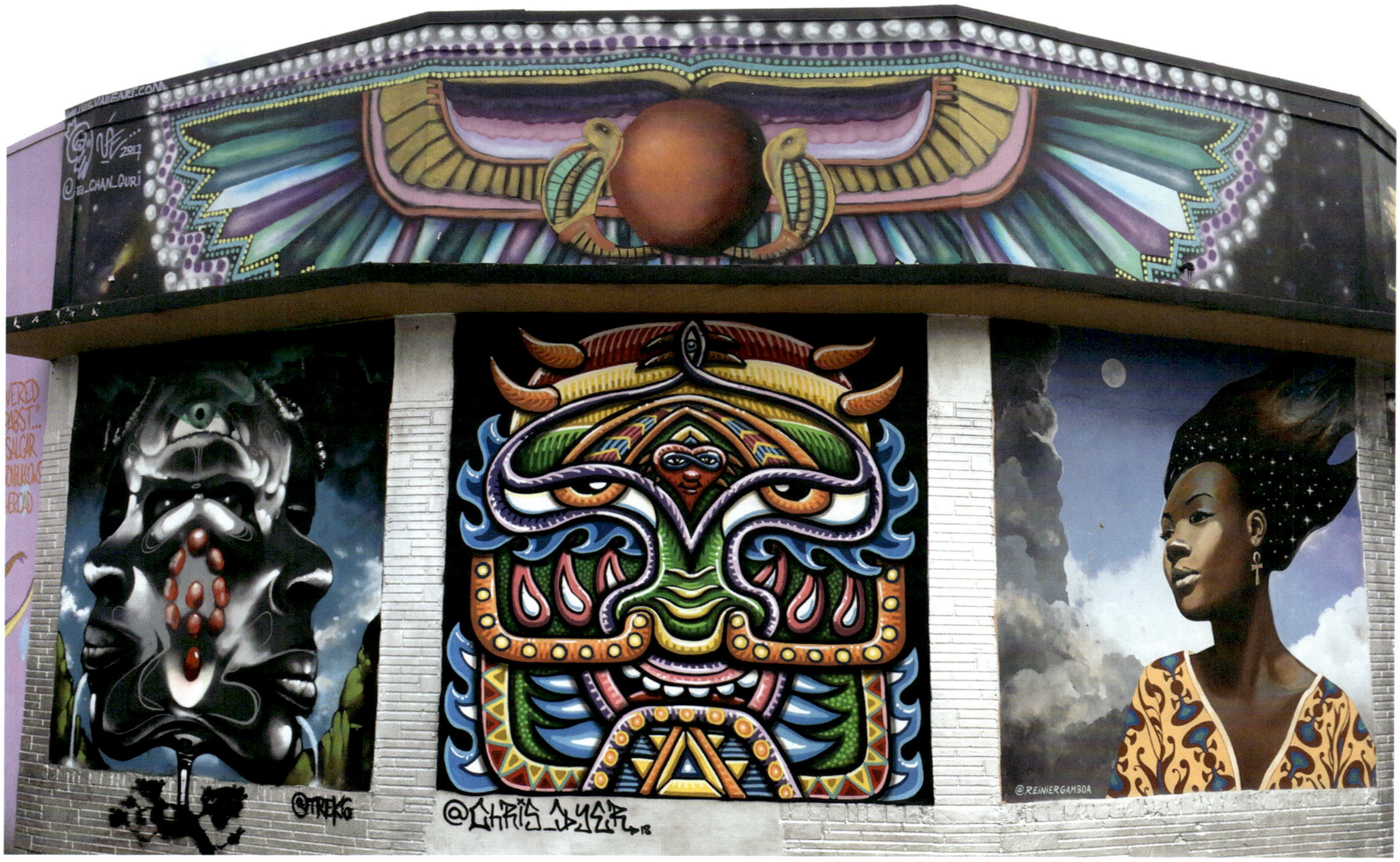

The **"Moksha Family"** is an conscious Art Collective from Miami, Florida, who have been holding down the good vibes for over 20 years. They have invited me to participate at their Art Basel events several times, which is always a really special time with beautiful people. Every year they commission a different visionary artist do a version of their symbol, and 2011 was the year they chose me.

There were are a few things I had to include in this symbol, like the use of the mushroom cap hat, ecstatic eyes, fire tongue and fiery 3rd eye. Since they are big supporters of the psychedelic movement, I also included some extra medicine on the character's tongue. I was asked to make it a kind of "Higher-self Self-portrait" too, so I added in my classic dreads n beard. I also gave him plenty of tears to show the intense emotions of the transcendental state. And since Miami is such a sexual city, I made the Mushroom hat look like the head of an ejaculating penis, with an energy vagina third eye.

Anyways, I really appreciate Moksha's organizer **Ray Orraca**, who's become a good friend over the years, as well as the beautiful community that supports positive spiritual art and music in that fun city.

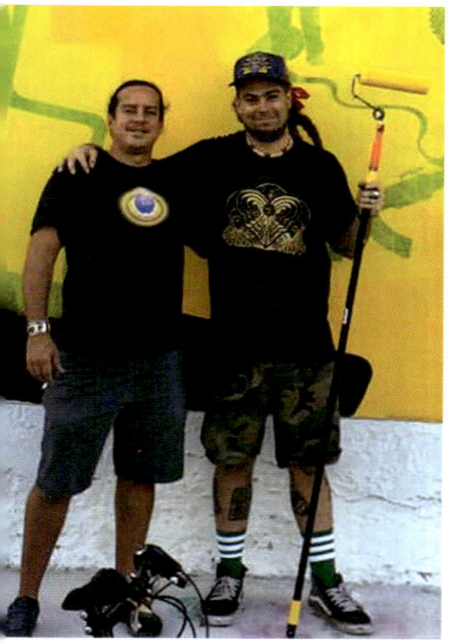

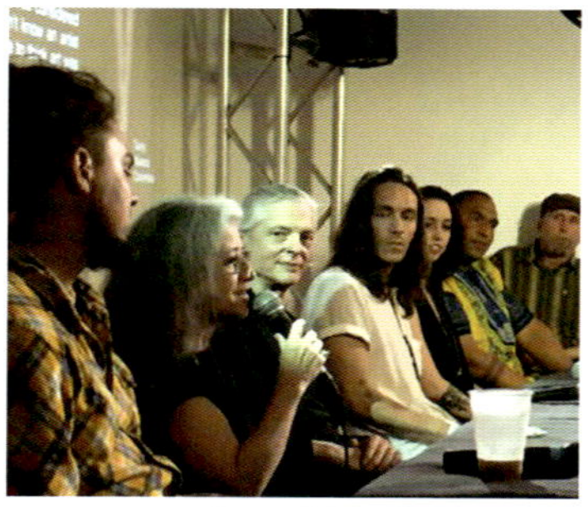

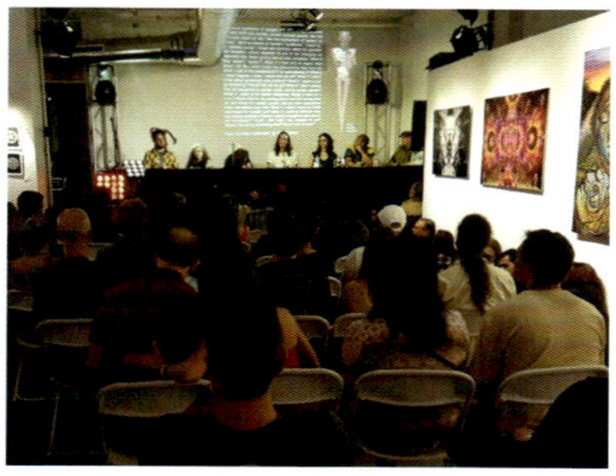

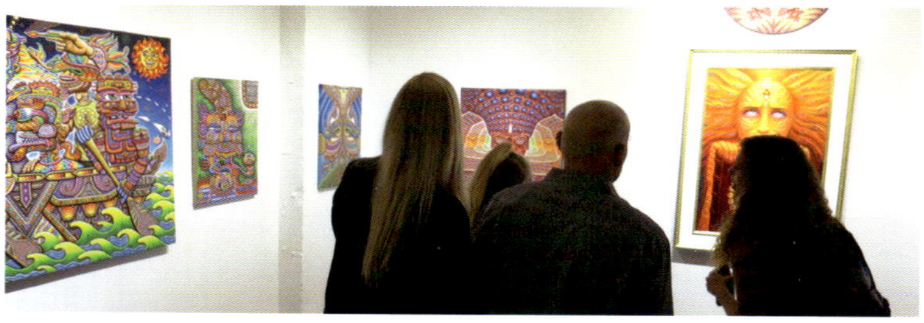

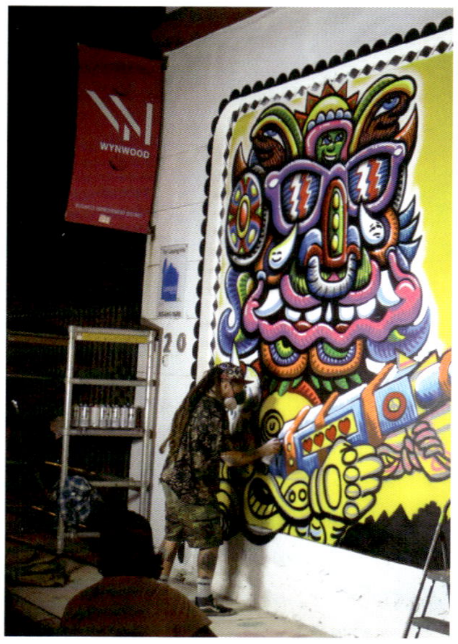

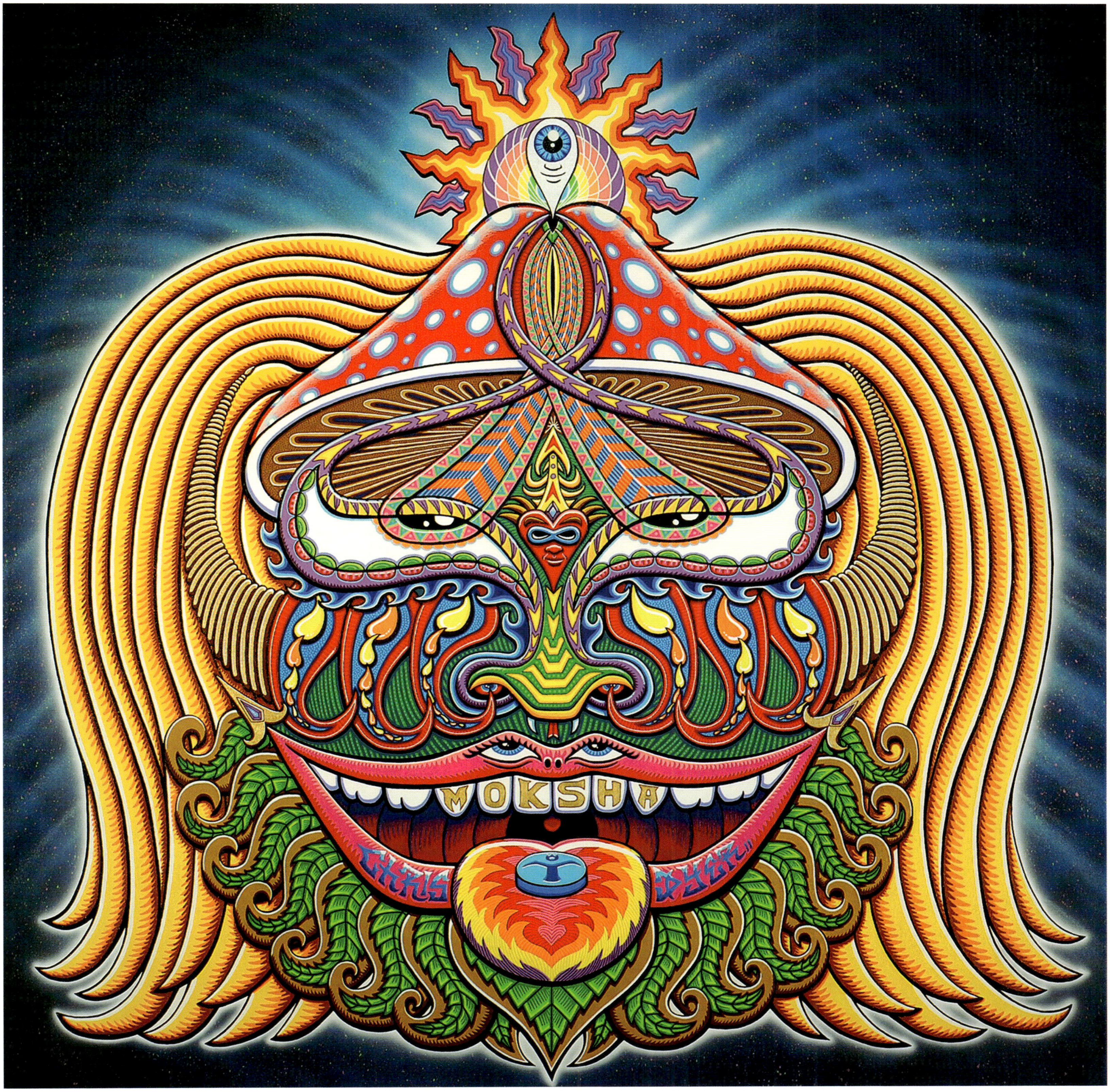

"Moksha Master" Acrylics and spray paint on canvas, 2011

Previous Page: Mural at the current Moksha Family headquarters, along artists **El Chan Guri**, **Trek 6**, and **Rainier Gamboa**.

ITALY

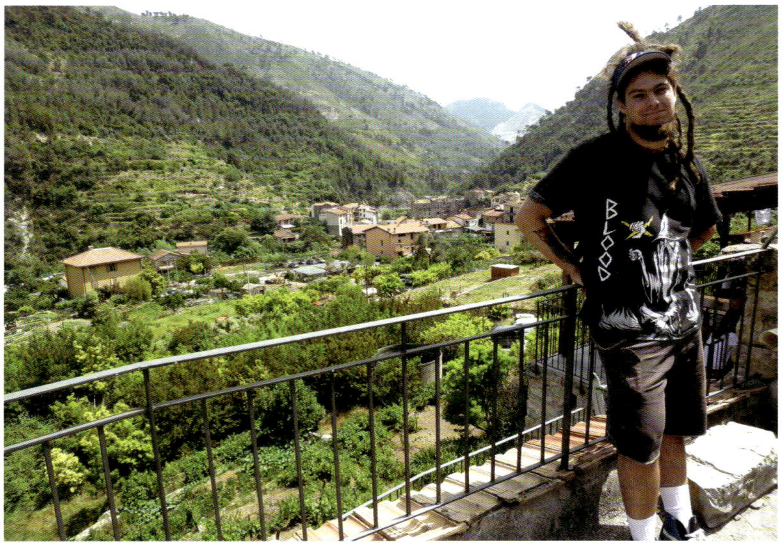

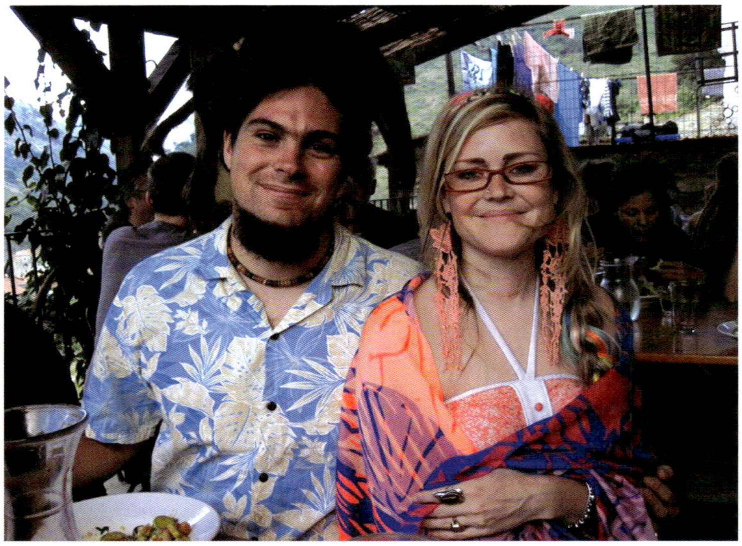

On the first few years of my marriage, my wife Valerie had been growing a nodule over her thyroid gland. We were hoping it would shrink and disappear, but instead it became a more obvious growth in her beautiful neck. So eventually we went to Belgium, where she is originally from, to have it removed. To our great sadness, once they took it out, along her thyroid, they found cancer in it, so she had to be radiated...

This whole situation left my beloved quite weak and depressed, so to cheer her up and inject positivity back into our lives, I took her to Italy for a three week long painting workshop! The workshop took place at "Torri Superiore", which was a gorgeous little eco-village in middle of the countryside mountains. Our teachers were peers and friends from the visionary art movement: **Amanda Sage**, **Maura Holden**, **Andrew Gonzalez**, and **Laurence Caruana**. Andrew taught us airbrushing skills and the other three teachers taught us an ancient painting technique called "Mische", consisting of laying layers of egg tempera or casein and glassing them with layers of oil paint. It is a long meticulous process but it had great results.

We felt so blessed on those healing weeks, hanging out with our new artist friends from around the world. We mostly spent our days painting, but also enjoyed some pretty nature hikes, ate delicious food, and drank lots of wine. We also took a day trip to **"Damanhur"**, which is a super trippy spiritual temple that was secretly carved inside a mountin over a period of 20 years!

The first painting I did at this workshop was called **"Humanitree"**. As the title suggests, it is some kind of tree creature expressing the self-destructive essence of humanity. But in a way, this semi-aggressive interdimentional entity also expressed the way Life was working Valerie and me. She burned and pushed us into growth through the path of suffering. Valerie's essence was never really the same after that process which slowly changed the dynamics of our relationship. All we could do was surrender and flow into wherever that might take us.

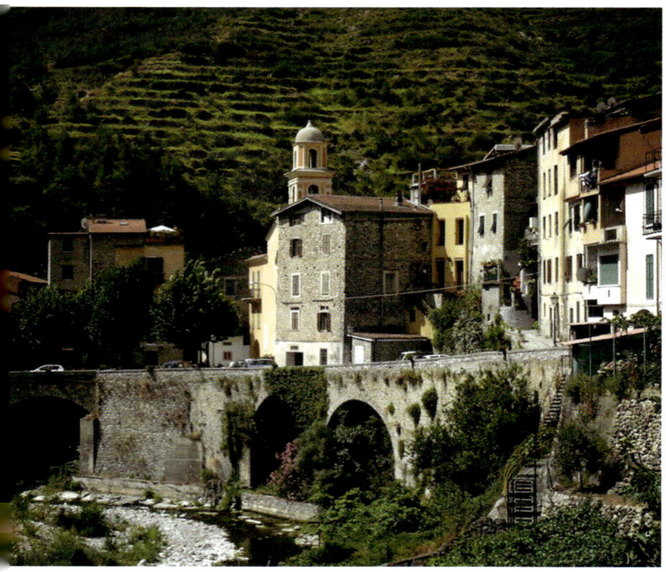

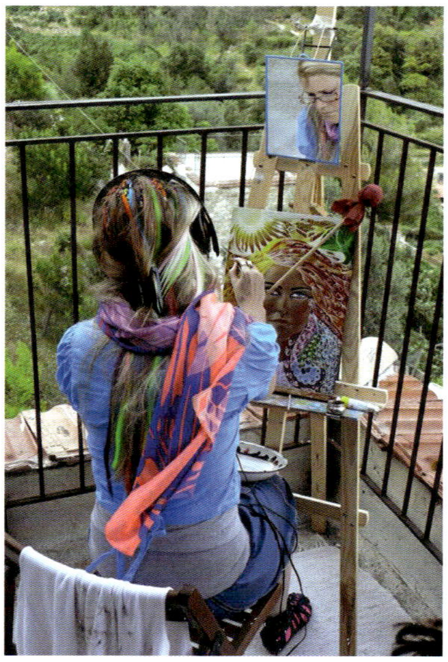

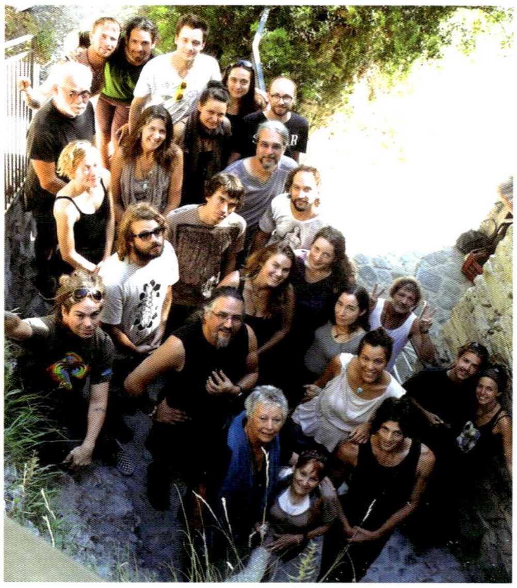

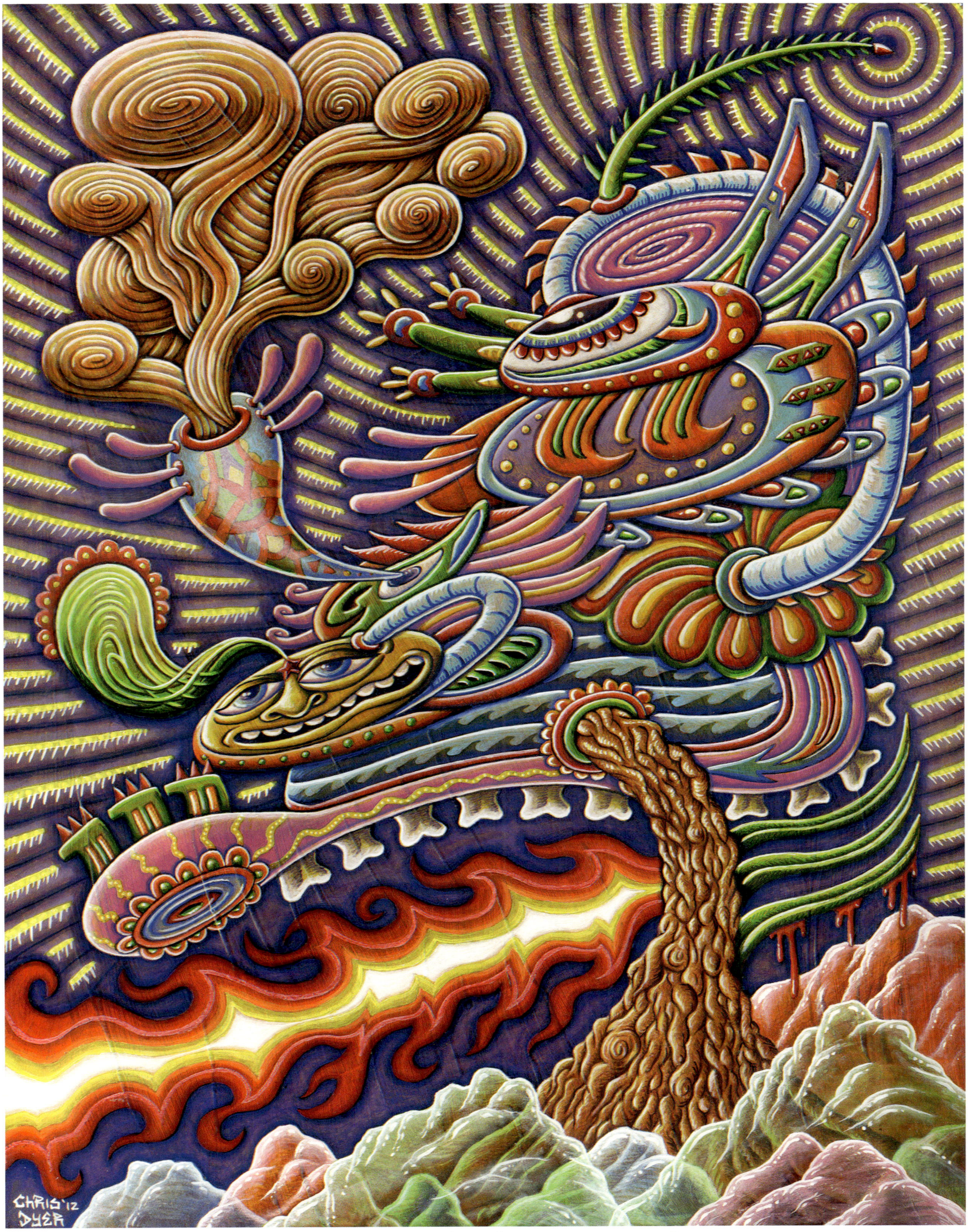

"Humanitree" Oil and casein on wood, 2012

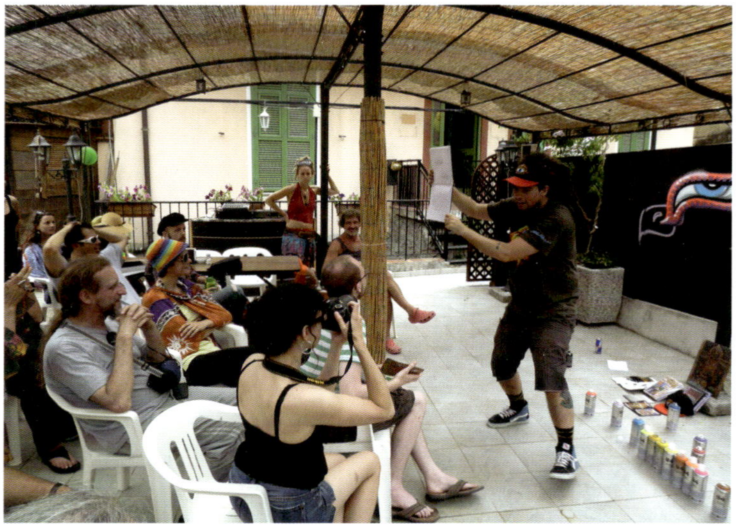

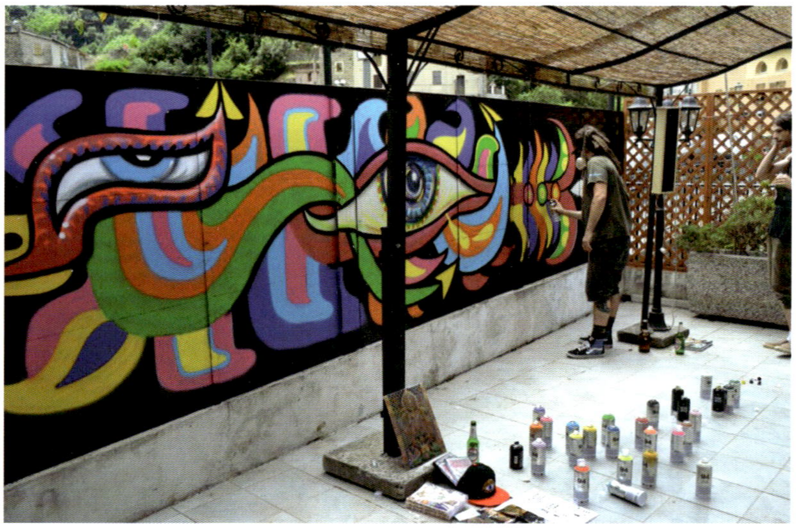

Something that became really special to me at this workshop, was that I was given the chance to teach a class of my own. Until that point I had only taught art to kids in elementary and high schools in Montreal and Ottawa. I never felt that I was skilled enough to teach adult artists. But seeing Amanda teach us inspired me to give it a shot! So one chill afternoon, I taught a spray painting class, where I explained the steps to creating a mural and gave a demonstration on how to use the cans. It was the beginning of a whole new branch of my career, since that was the inception of an array of art classes and workshops, which I taught all around the world! So I was so grateful for the opportunity to get my feet wet in Italy! Lesson is, if you don't try new things, you can't learn how to master new skills! This trip also became the subject matter of the first webisode of my **"Artventures"**. This was a traveling video series I launched on YouTube, which lasted several years. Truly the beginning of a new era!

The second painting I did at that workshop was a self portrait, which was something all students of the class had to paint. Usually I don't like painting myself so much, as I try to detach from the over-identification of my human vehicle. But it definitely was a great exercise in realism, especially when using the mische technique and mediums that aren't my strength. I called it **"The Listener"** because I used this painting to humble and calm down my competitive nature. **Amanda Sage** is my artistic peer in the Visionary Art scene. I see her as an equal, who is of a similar age, with powerful intentions of healing the planet through community and quality artistic skill. Stylistically though it seems like we're singing opposite songs, so preference is a question of personal taste. Those initial years, when the North American Visionary Art scene was just getting started, I would get paired with Amanda at a lot of events. Unfortunately, I always felt I was second in importance next to her. This inequality annoyed my ego, as I didn't feel inferior, just different. I knew this was all silly human insecurities, so to tackle this issue I placed myself as her student in this workshop. Amanda guided me a lot with his piece, as she is so good with portraits and this technique she learnt from masters like **Ernst Fuch**. I am very grateful and our friendship has authentically grown stronger through the years!

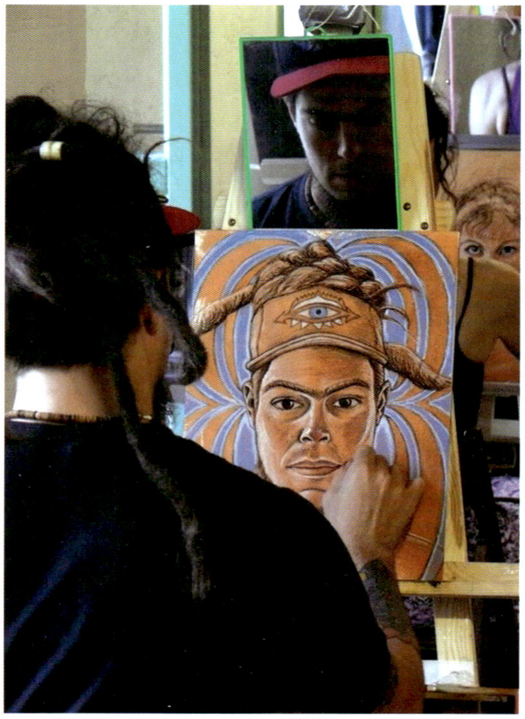

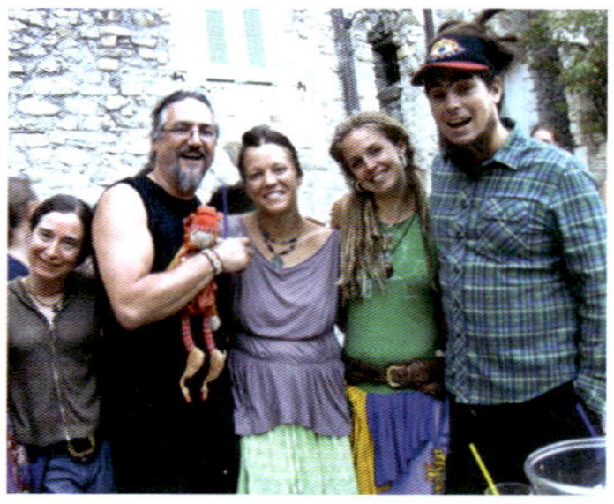

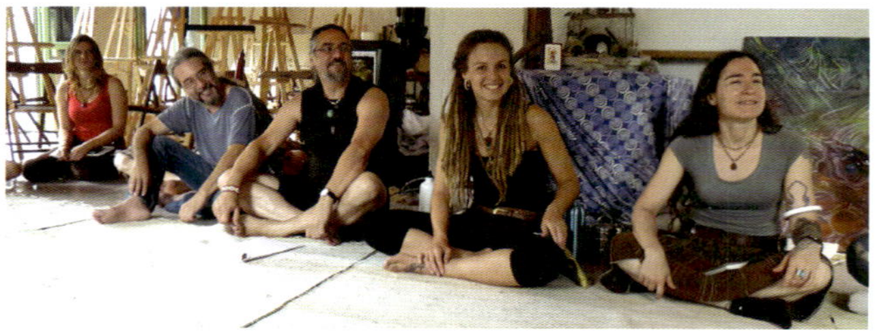

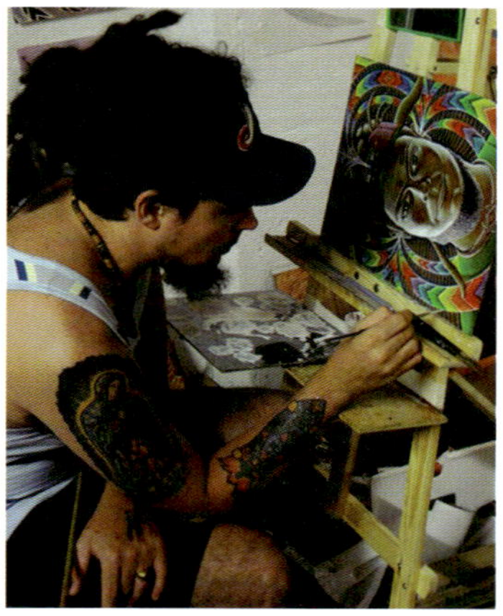

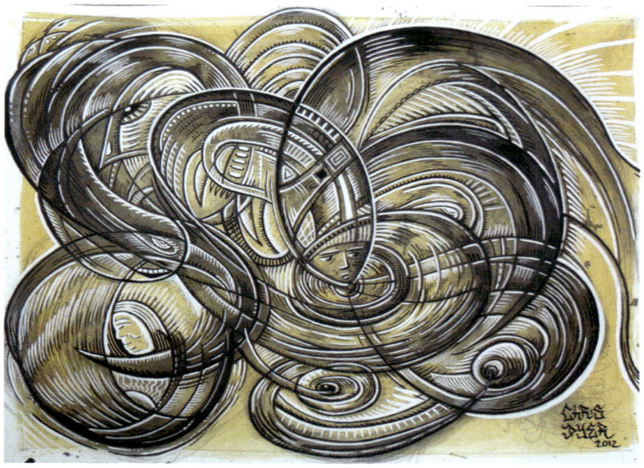

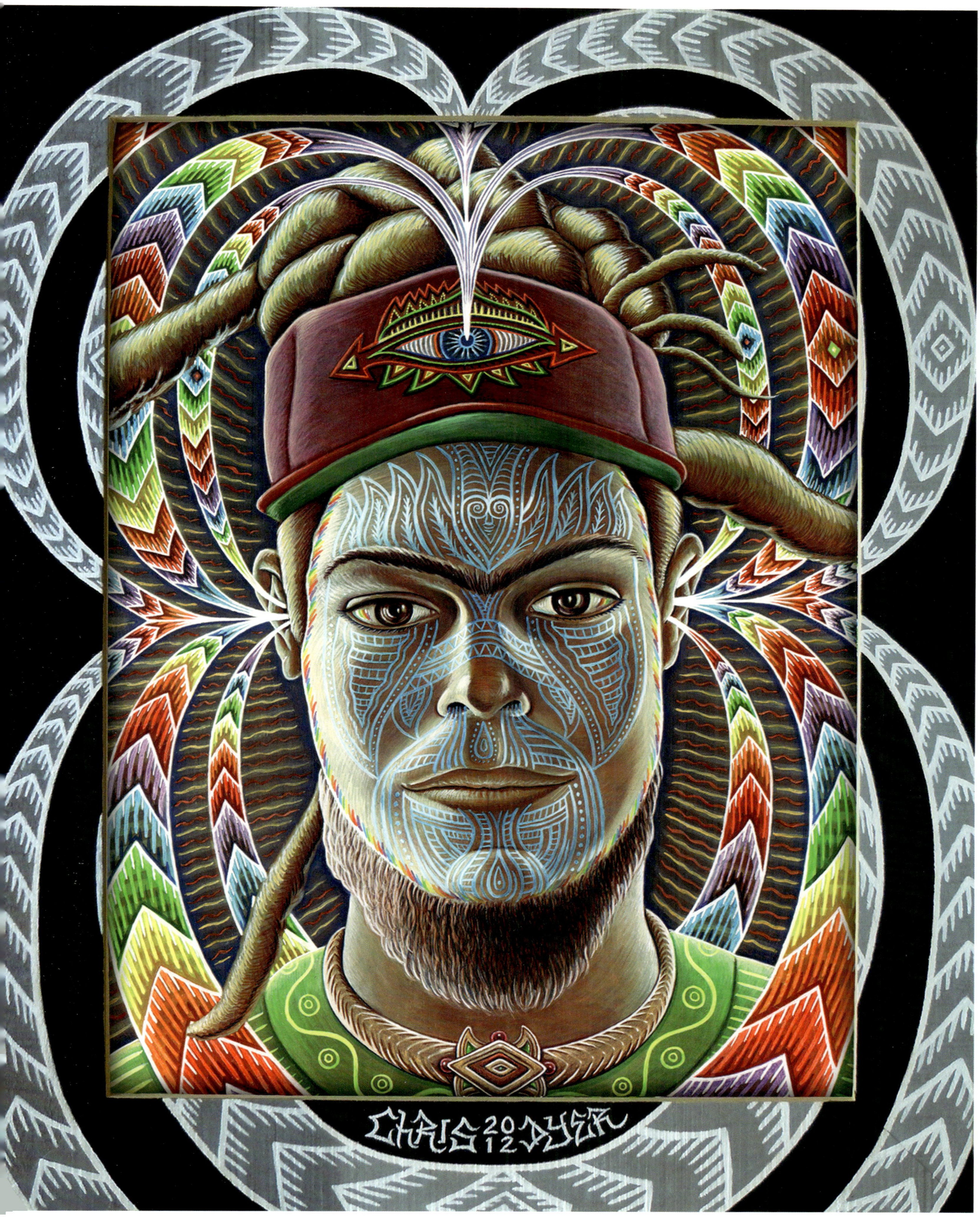

"The Listener" Oil and egg tempera on wood, 2012

AUSTRALIA

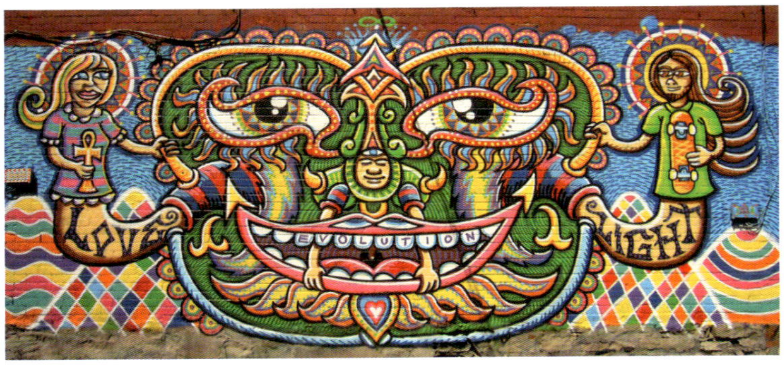

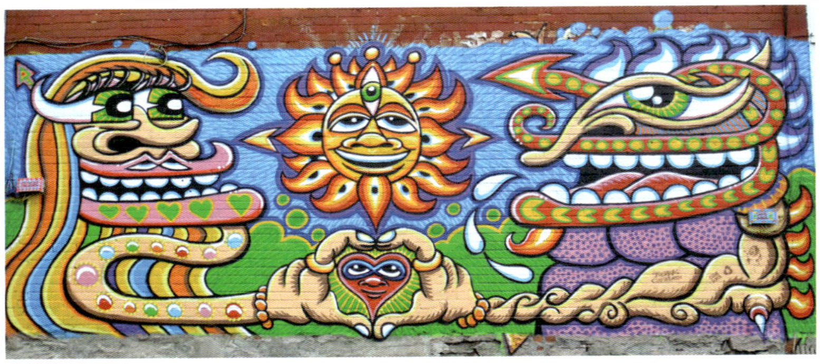

Later that same hyped up 2012 year, I got invited to exhibit and Live Paint at the **Eclipse Festival** in northern Australia. Though Valerie's health still wasn't doing well, I couldn't resist performing in that far away land, along many of my artist friends. I felt guilty about leaving Valerie alone at home, so I made the point to paint something that would call in some healing vibes for her.

Back at the Italian workshop I had taken in summer, my artist friend **Amanda Sage** and I had talked about doing a collaboration painting. Since we both would be in Australia, I prepared a collabo that Amanda could easily bat out of the park. On an egg shaped canvas, I painted the framing for a portrait of Valerie, yet left the face drawing unpainted, along with a flat background. At the festival Amanda worked her magic and didn't even need a reference picture to do a killer job! As for the background, she did her classic energy line work, as well as the full solar eclipse we all witnessed that week. That celestial alignment was very powerful for me and I believe it invited in a new chapter for my life, to hit me in the coming years. These shifts are never easy, but always necessary for growth.

Anyways, Valerie loved the painting and her health did improve quite a bit the next few years. This is one of those paintings that I couldn't sell, as it was only right that she would keep it for herself.

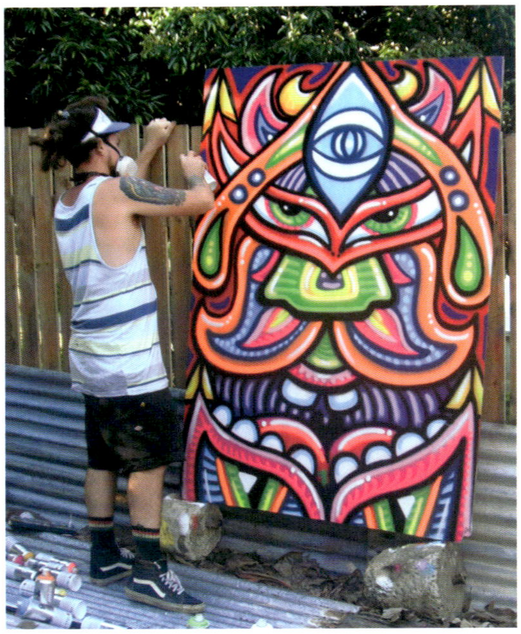

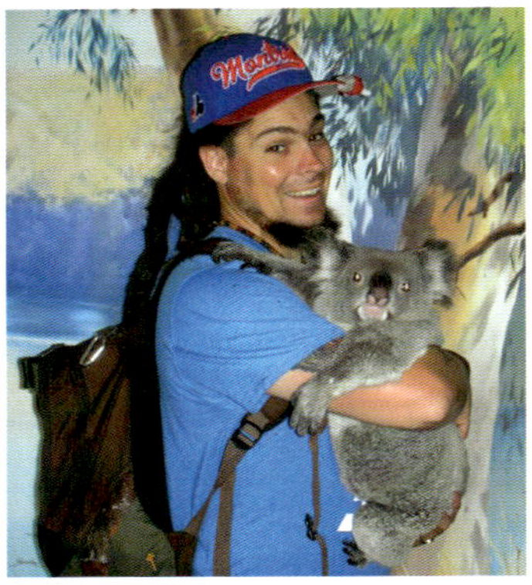

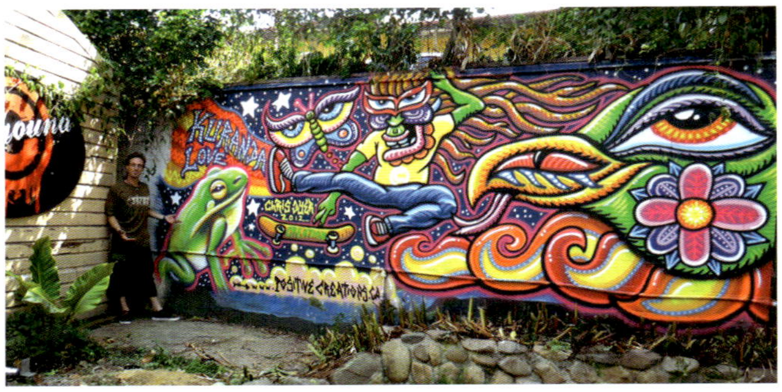

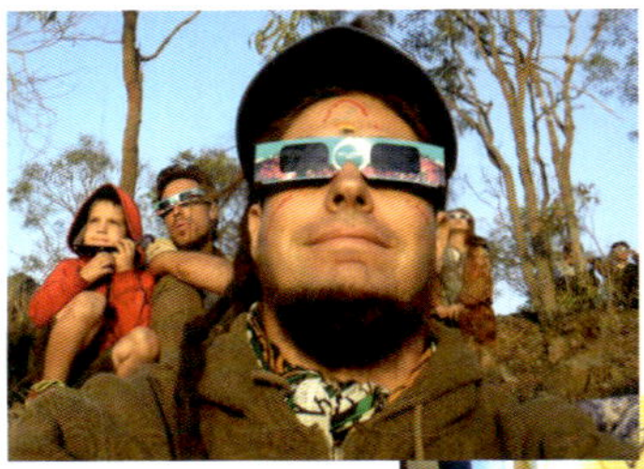

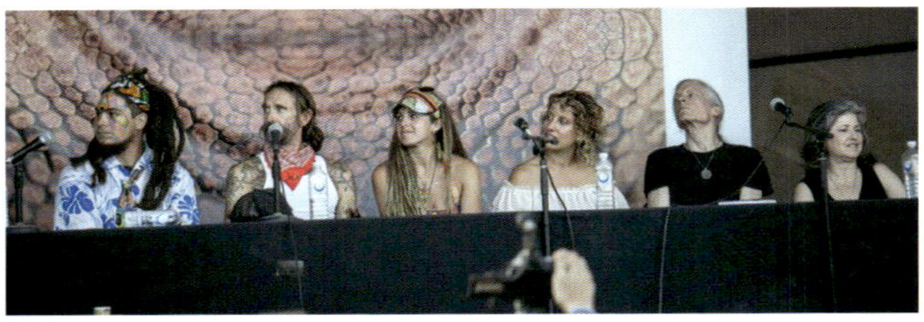

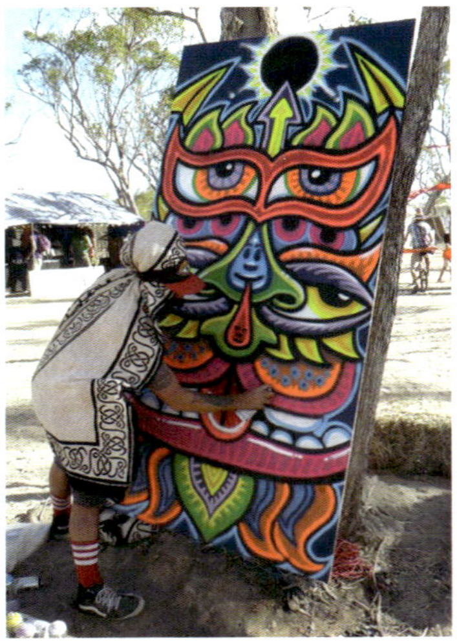

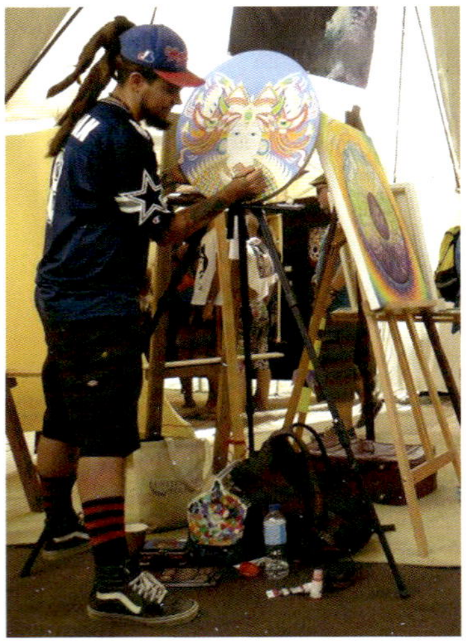

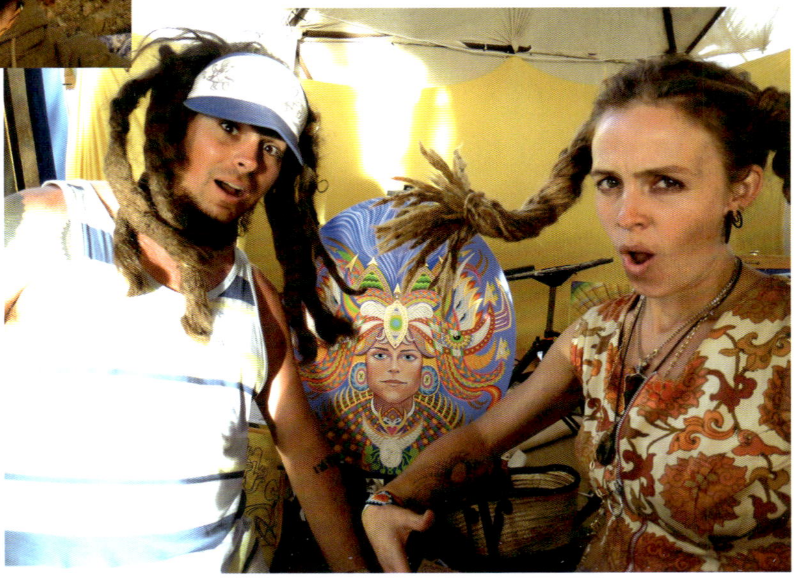

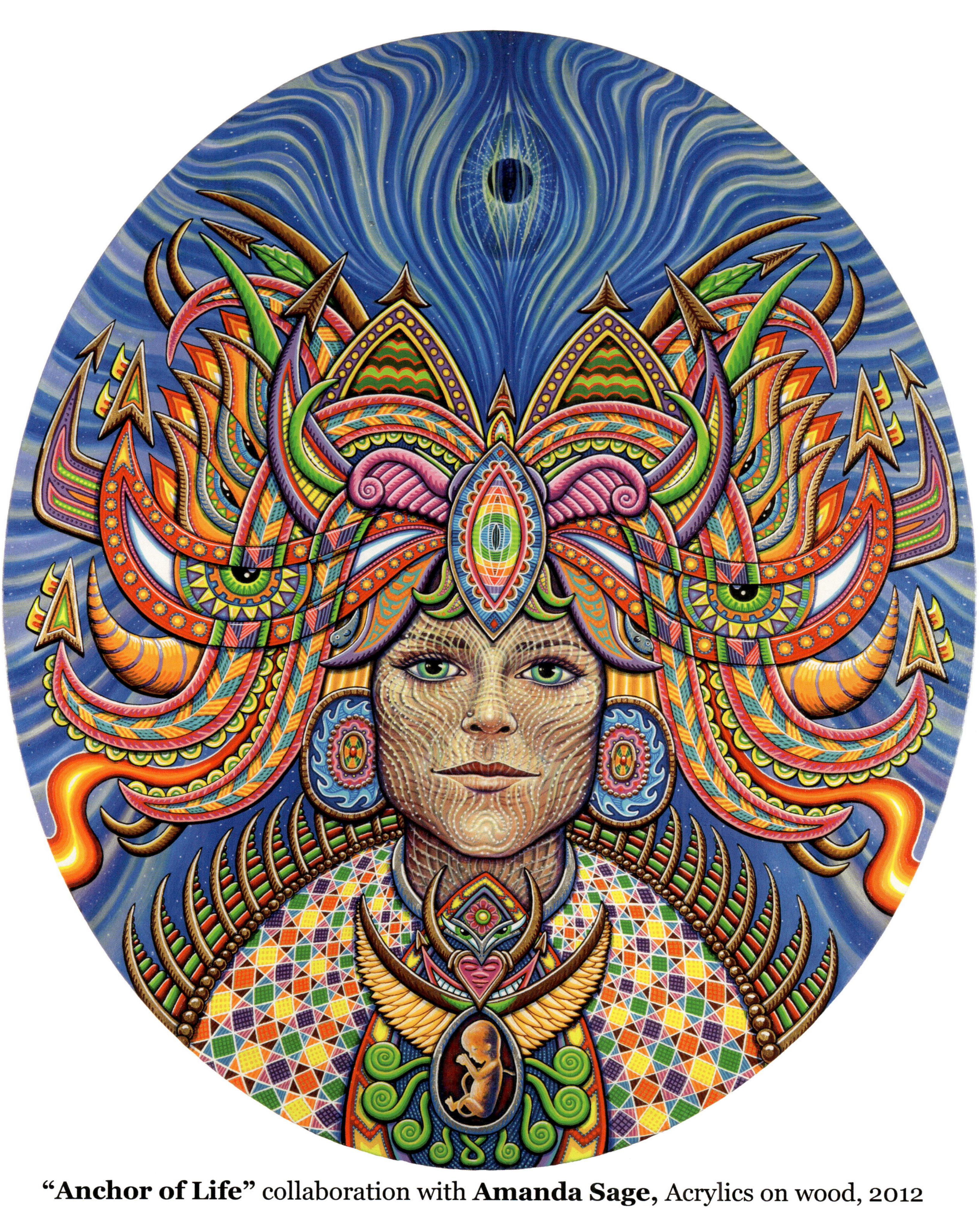

"Anchor of Life" collaboration with **Amanda Sage,** Acrylics on wood, 2012

"CHRIS INSPIRES ME THROUGH THE DEDICATION TO HIS ART, CONSISTENCY IN MESSAGE AND HIS BIG OPEN HEART. HE IS AUTHENTICALLY HIMSELF AND ALWAYS AMAZES ME WITH HIS NEWEST CREATIONS TO MAKE THE WORLD A MORE VIBRANT AND BEAUTIFUL PLACE." -AMANDA SAGE, VISIONARY ARTIST

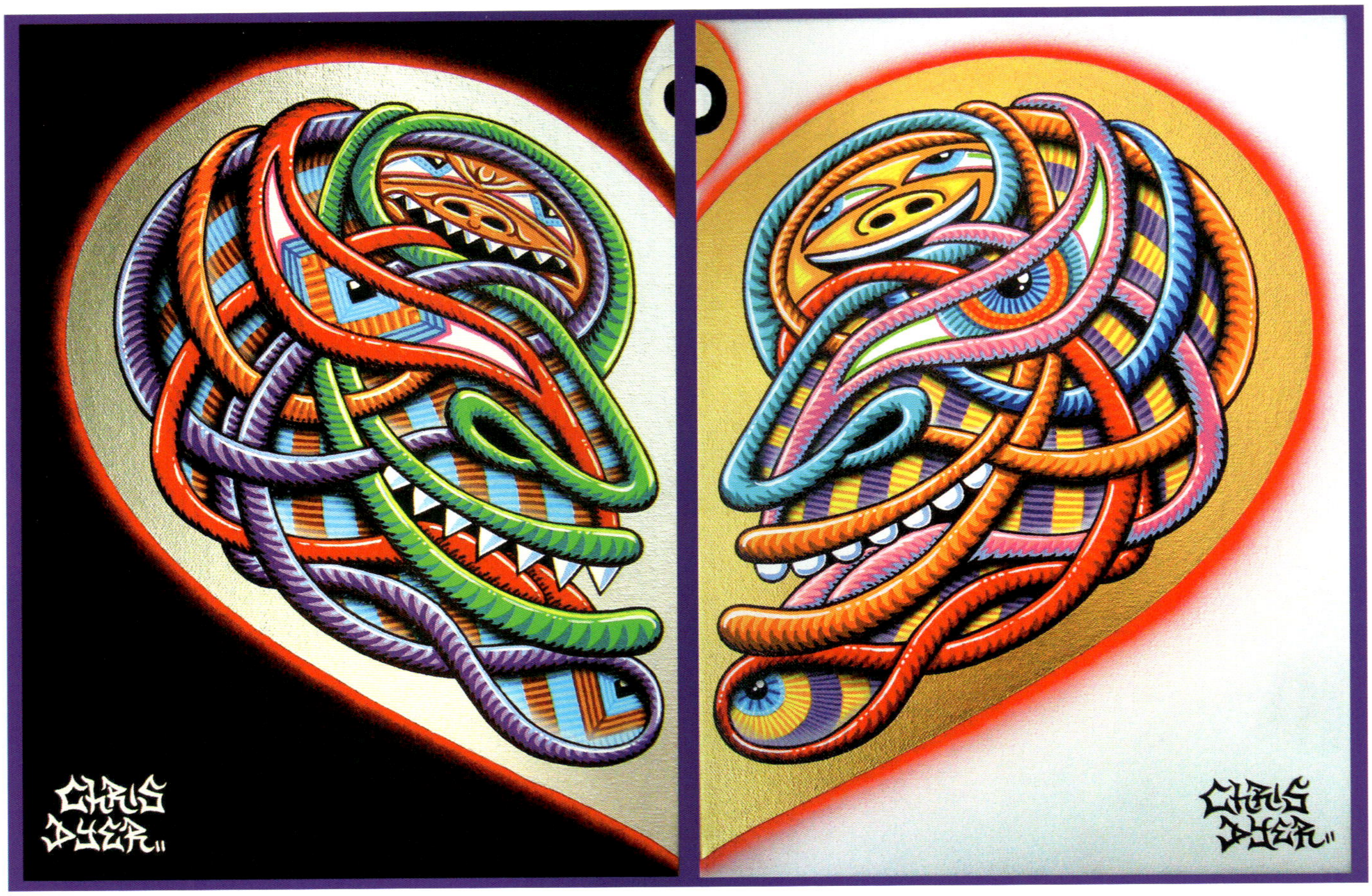

"United Heart" Acrylics on two canvases, 2011

The fact that we live in a dimension of Duality is a beautiful thing, because despite it's challenges, this dance of creation and destruction teaches us about contrast. Most people live in a tug of war between our complicated minds and our divine loving hearts. Depending on the day, we can operate from either of these centers, until we learn to balance and connect the gap between spirit and matter. The ideal is to spiral up higher frequency versions, back home to our Source. Humanity as a whole experiences similar divisions of self. We are all one race, who just want to be happy and safe. But we can't seem to agree on the path towards that, so we divide in our perspectives, opinions and actions. Instead of appreciating our superficial differences, we use these to divide and splinter into endless factions. Deep inside we all yearn to become the united Love of the original Creation Consciousness, but are totally confused about how to realize that. This dense physical plane has so many masks, illusions and tricks. I'm of the opinion that we should embark on the path of healing the wounds of our own broken hearts, as individuals and as a collective. Our video game seems to be getting more difficult with time, but we are actually working things out to be resolved once and for all. I Stay optimistic and hopeful that the future of our planet is of Love, Unity, Peace, Forgiveness, Compassion and Spiritual Understanding.

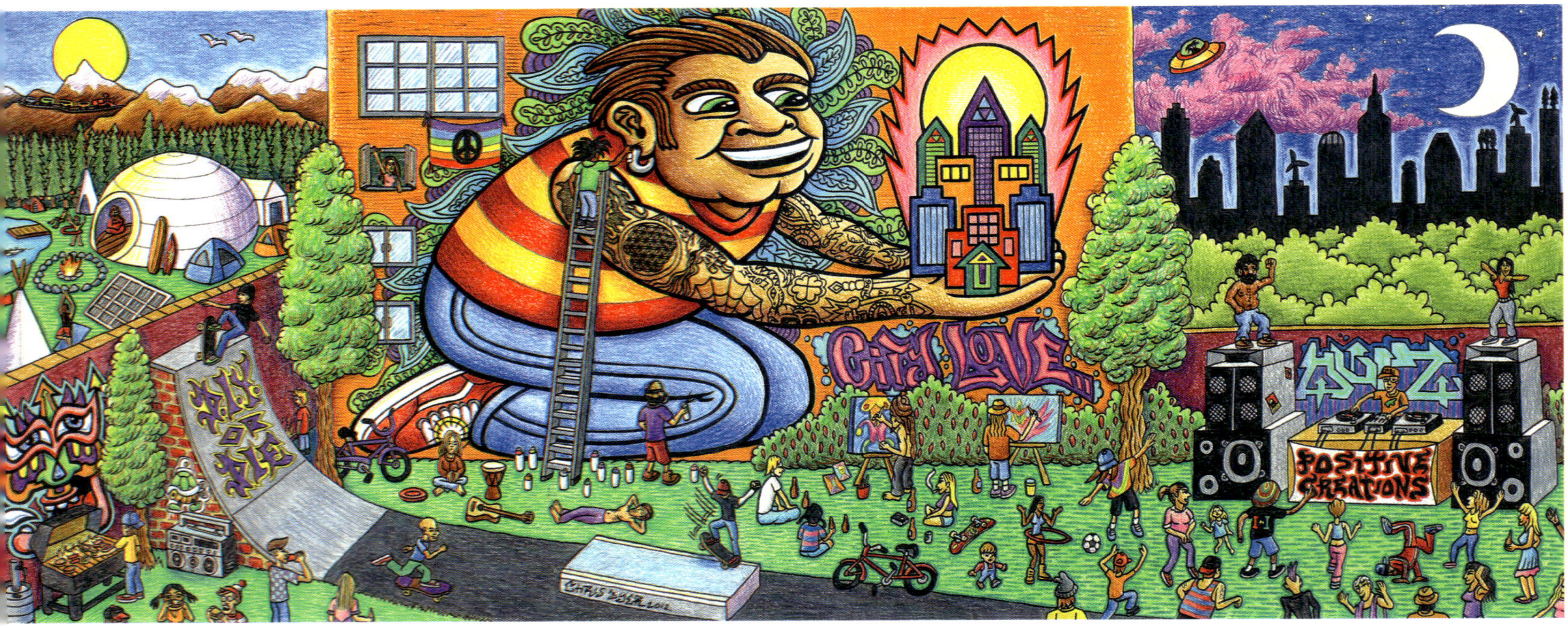

"City Love Utopia" Color Pencils, 2012

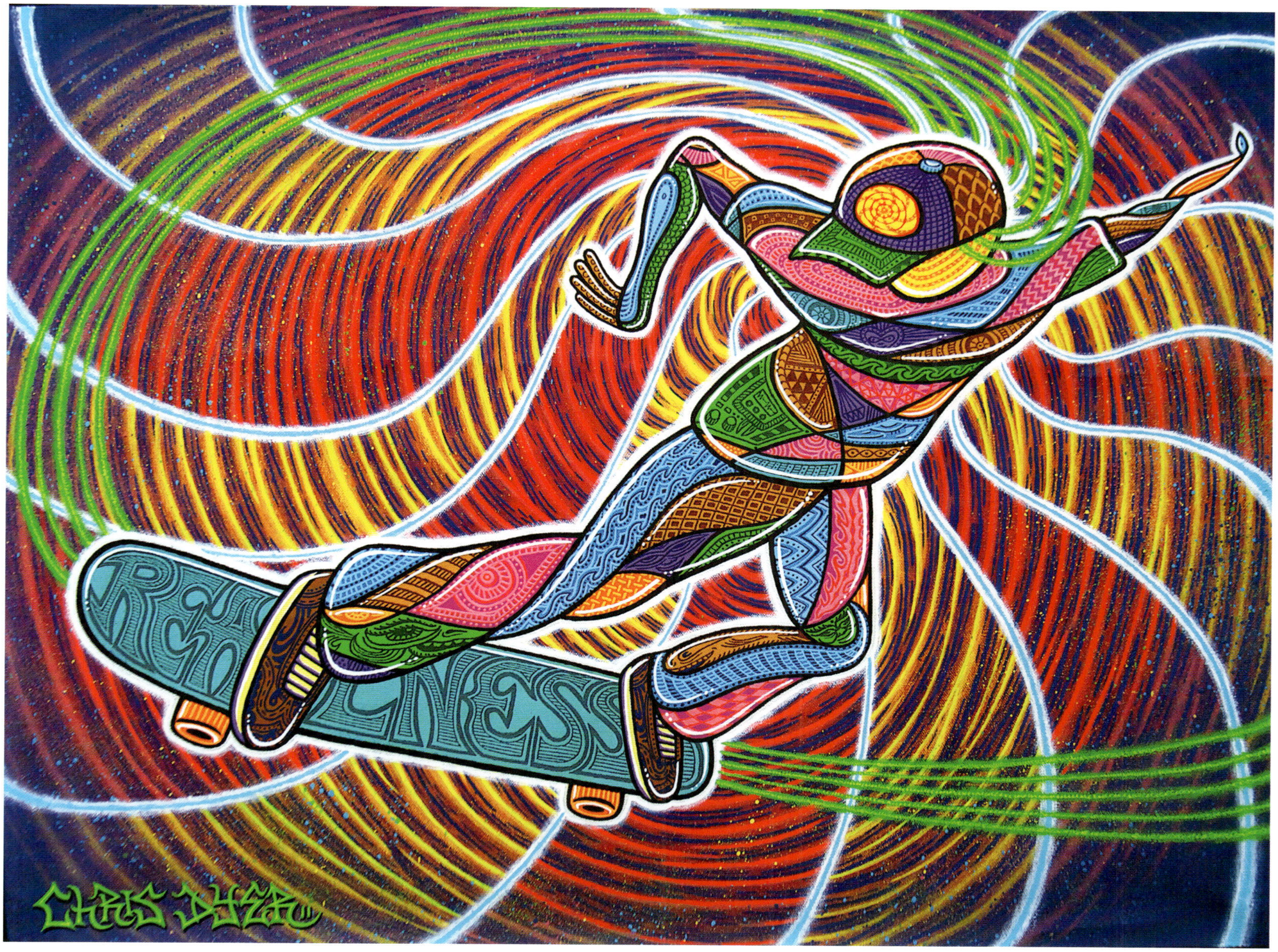

"Feeble-grinding the Vortex of Ascention" Acrylics on canvas, 2011

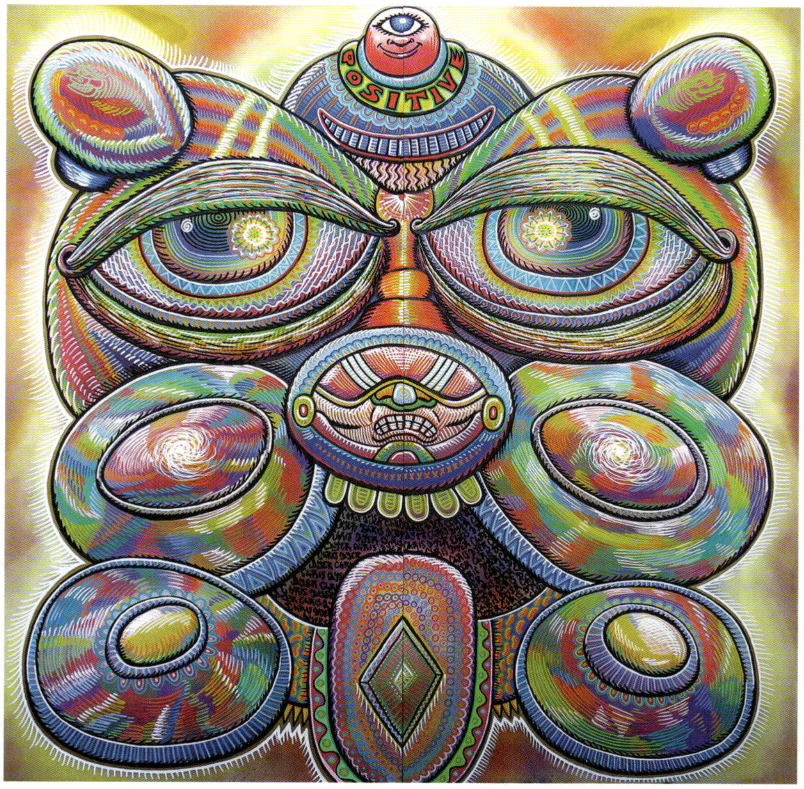

"Catalyst" Paint Markers, 2013

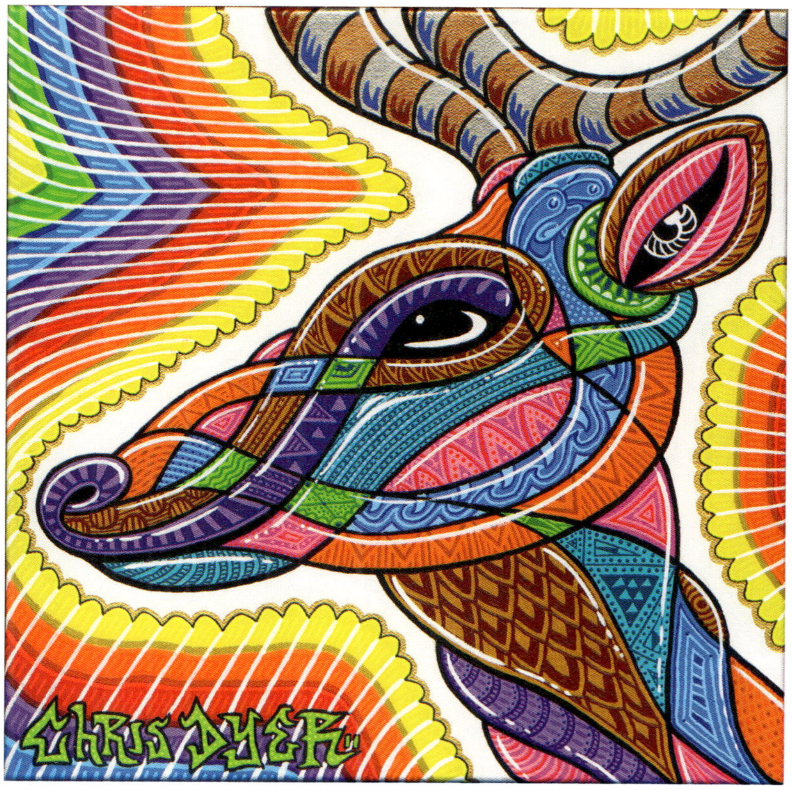

"Clear Deer" Acrylics on canvas, 2011

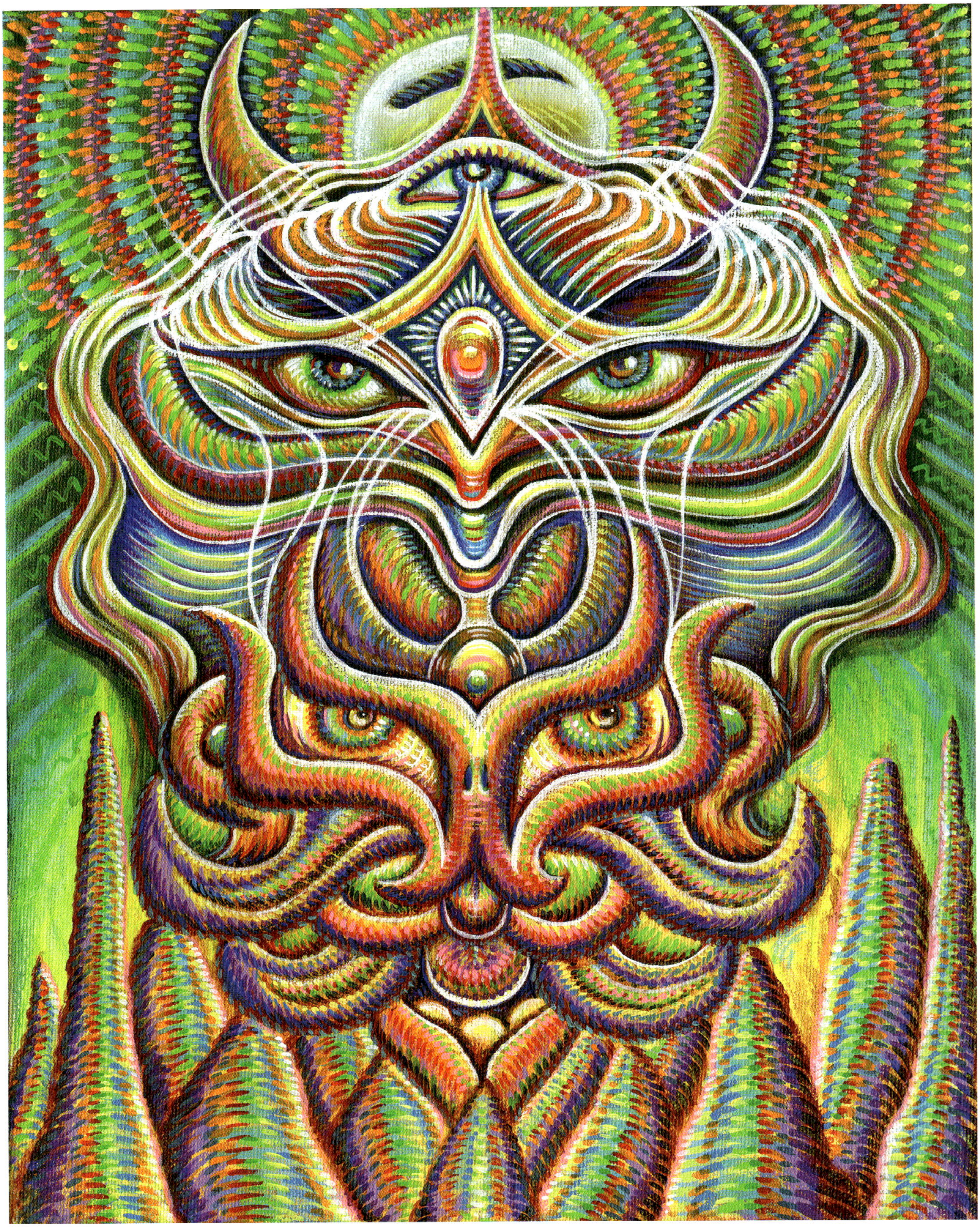

"Starseeds" collabo with **Jennifer McEuen** and **Matt Degrado**,
Acrylics on canvas, 2013

I Love to collaborate with my artist friends! It is so fun to see what happens when different talents and styles are combined to create something new! Here are a few energy combinations with three of the friends that I met at the painting workshop in Italy: **Jack Shure**, **Jenn McEuen** and **Matt Degrado**. Then there is one with my friend **Turtle Caps**, who is a street artist from NYC who lived in Montreal for some years. And then of course there was that time that time that I went to paint a piece with **Skinner** in his fun California studio! We even filmed a funny skit about it for his YouTube channel.

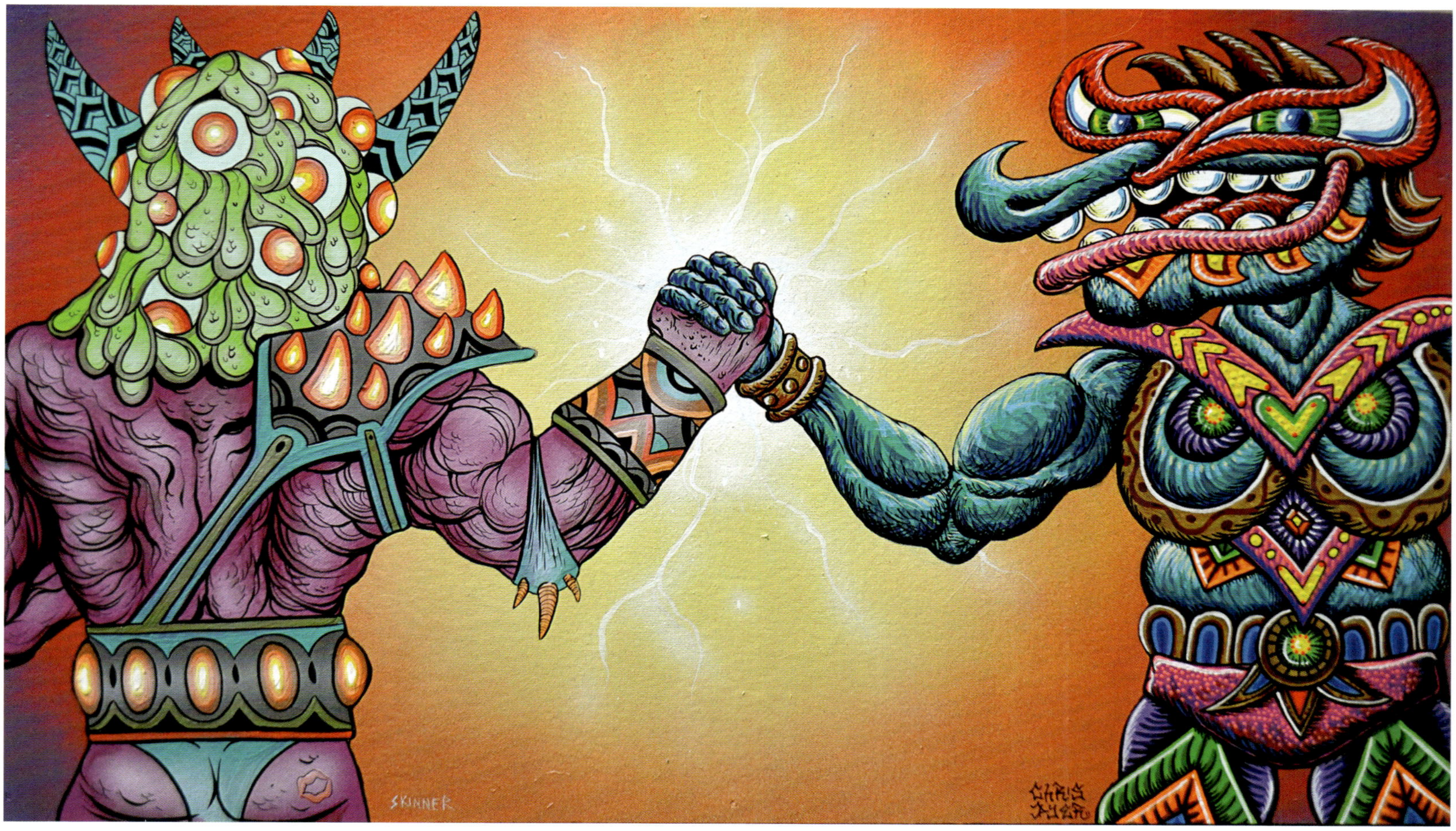

"You Son of a Bitch!" collabo with Skinner, Acrylics on wood, 2011

"CHRIS DYER IS A PSYCHEDELIC JOURNEYMAN WHO BRINGS US VISIONS OF LOVE AND PEACE THROUGH THE COURAGE OF HIS TRAVELS! A TRUE REMINDER OF THE POSITIVITY THAT WE ALL NEED!"

-SKINNER, PSYCHEDELIC NIGHTMARE ARTIST

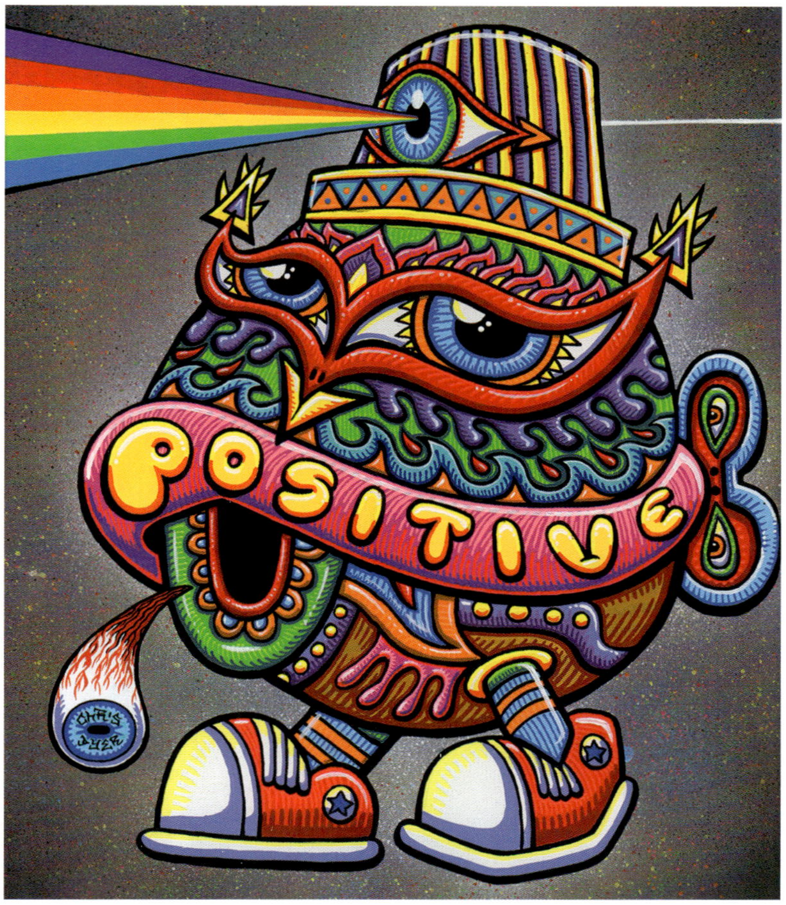

"Activated" collabo with **Turtle Caps**, Acrylics, 2013

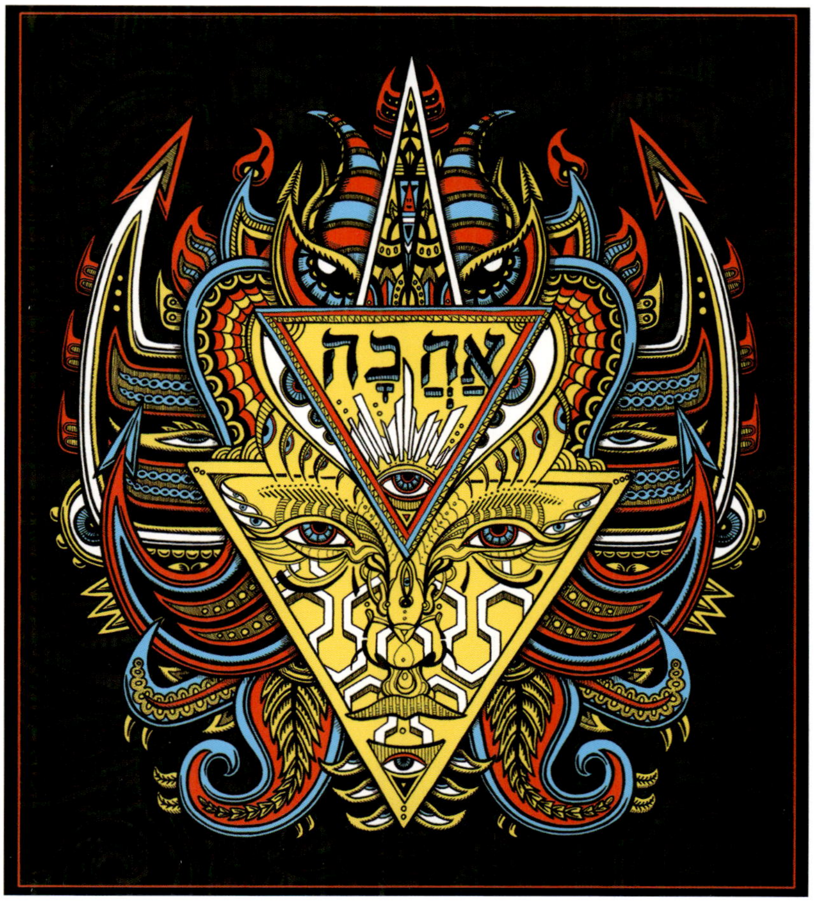

"Love" collabo with **Jack Shure**, Ink, 2013

MONTREAL

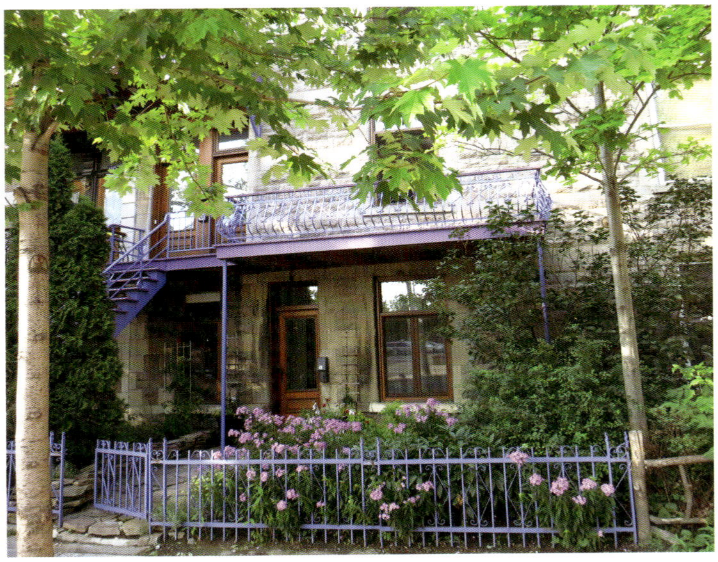

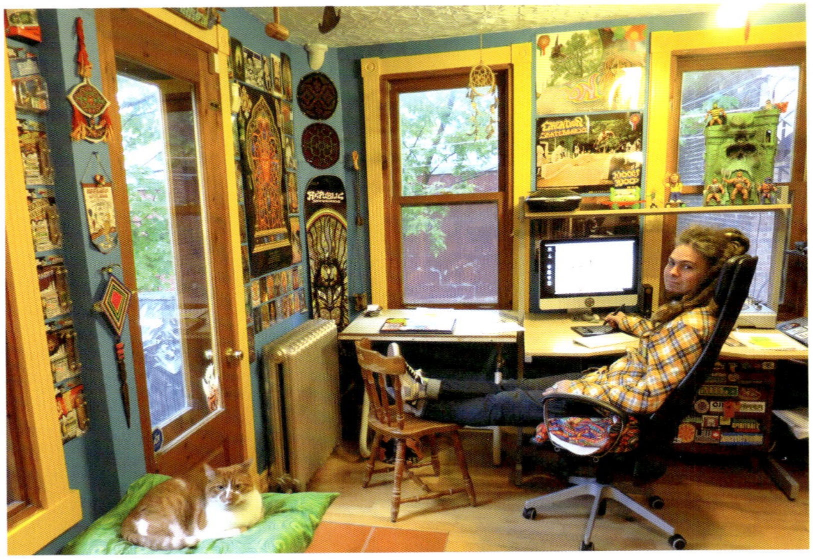

2012 was a very hyped up year, which was supposed to bring us either an Apocalypse or a Spiritual Ascension. Yet as it passed, nothing obvious seemed to of happened. To me, a portal of positivity had opened up and the following year brought great upgrades to our life. Out of nowhere, Valerie's parents, who had always objected to our union, bought us a big nice apartment right by one of Montreal's nicest parks! So we moved to a beautiful new neighborhood and were able to expand our creative space. At that same time, my art career finally caught on fire! For many years I had a credit debt I could never seem to clear, but all of a sudden I erased it and then even managed to build capital for my business. It was the stability I had been working so hard for since I finished college a decade before! Valerie's health was improving, but I still made the point to travel less, as to be a good husband that takes care of his wife. Home life of creation and Love was really special. I was grateful for this happy period of my life!

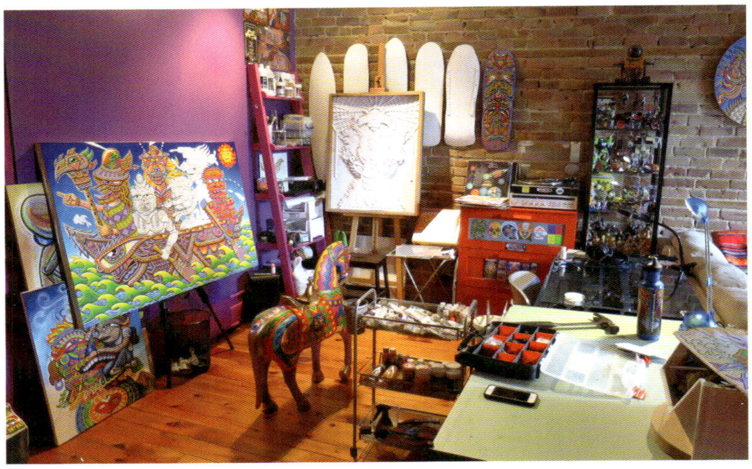

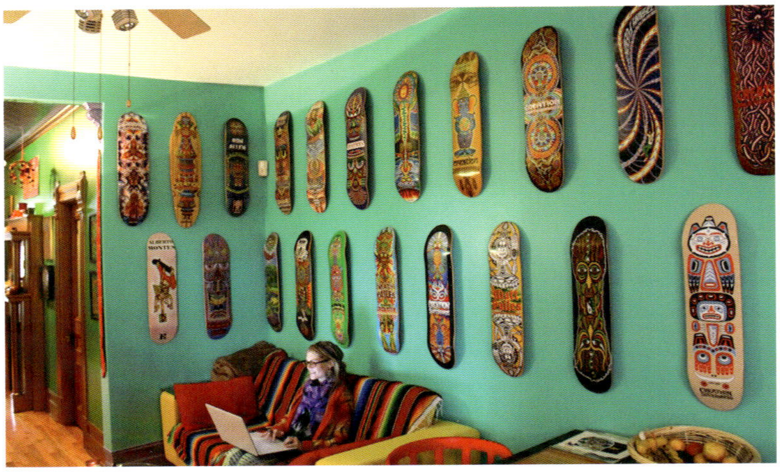

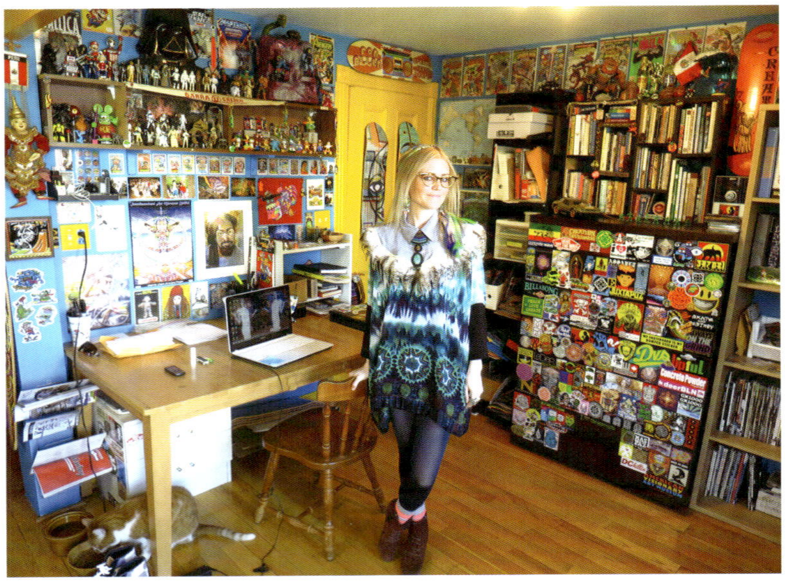

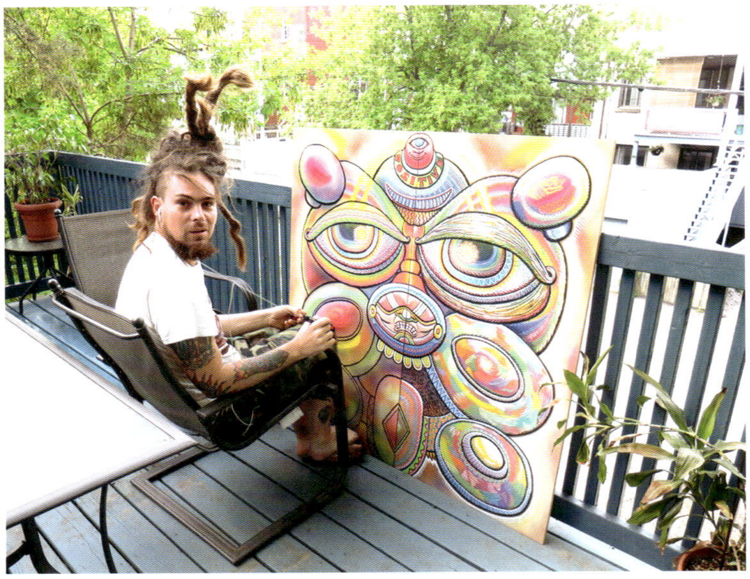

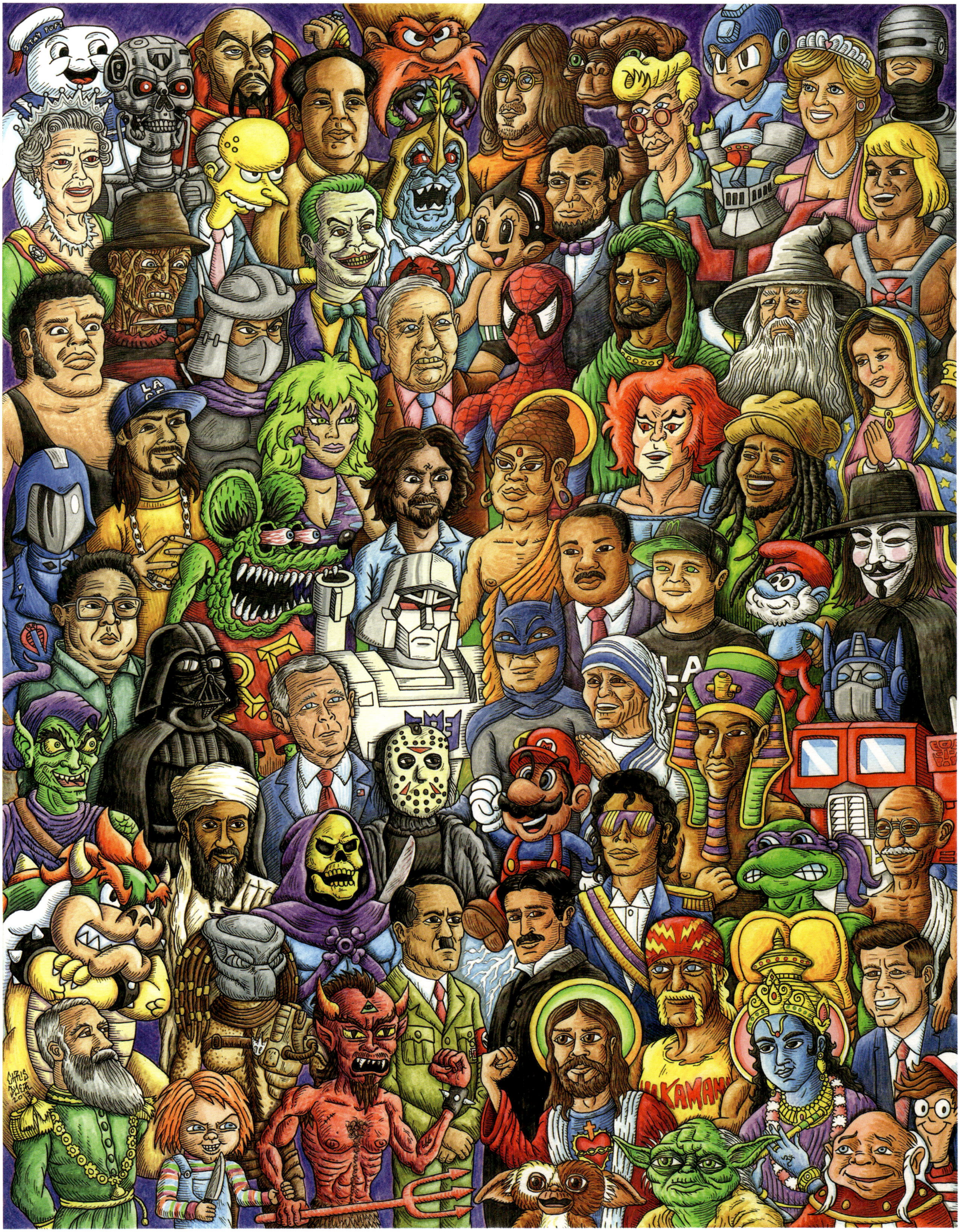

"Evil vs. Good" Watercolours, 2013

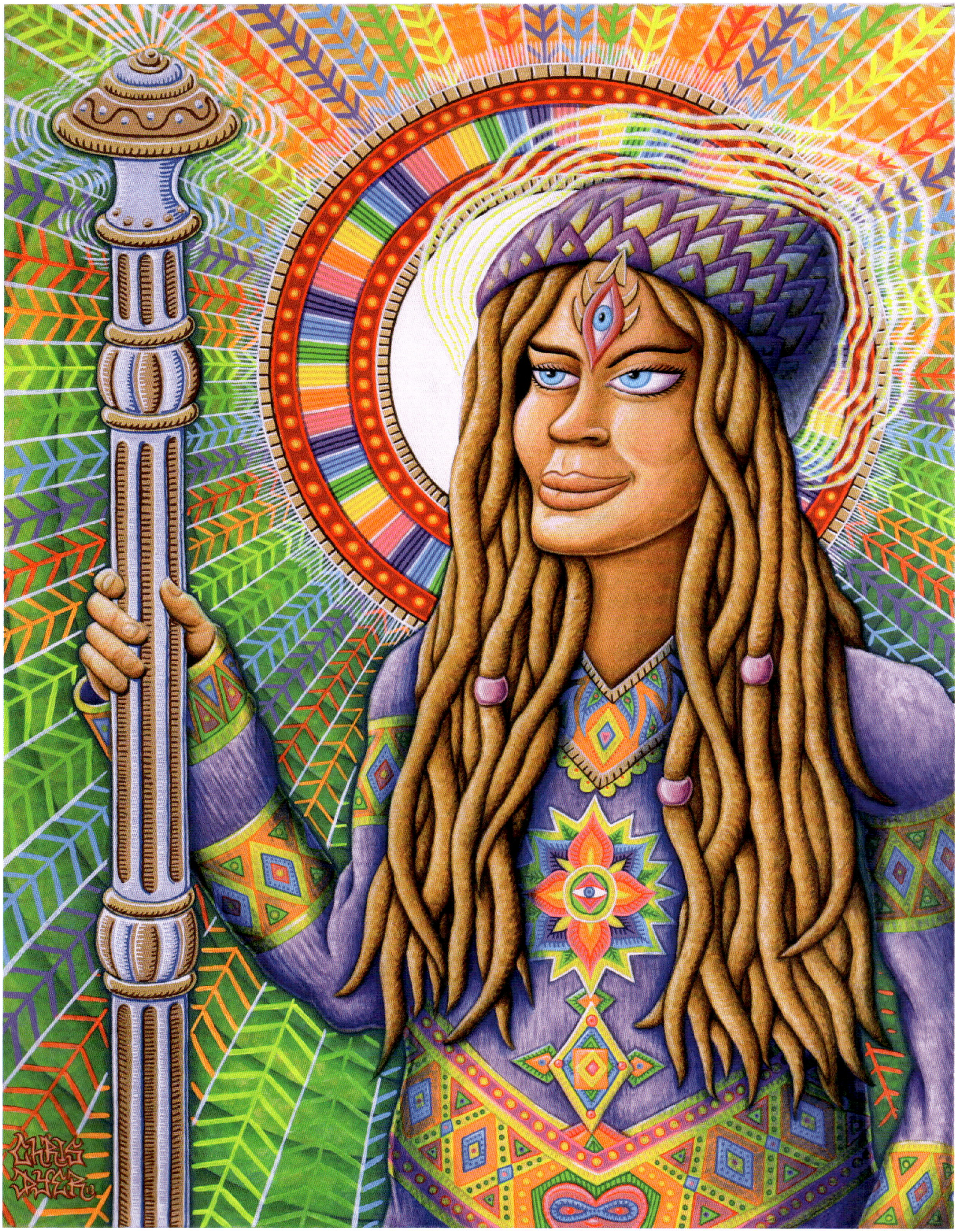

“Shayana” Acrylics on canvas, 2013

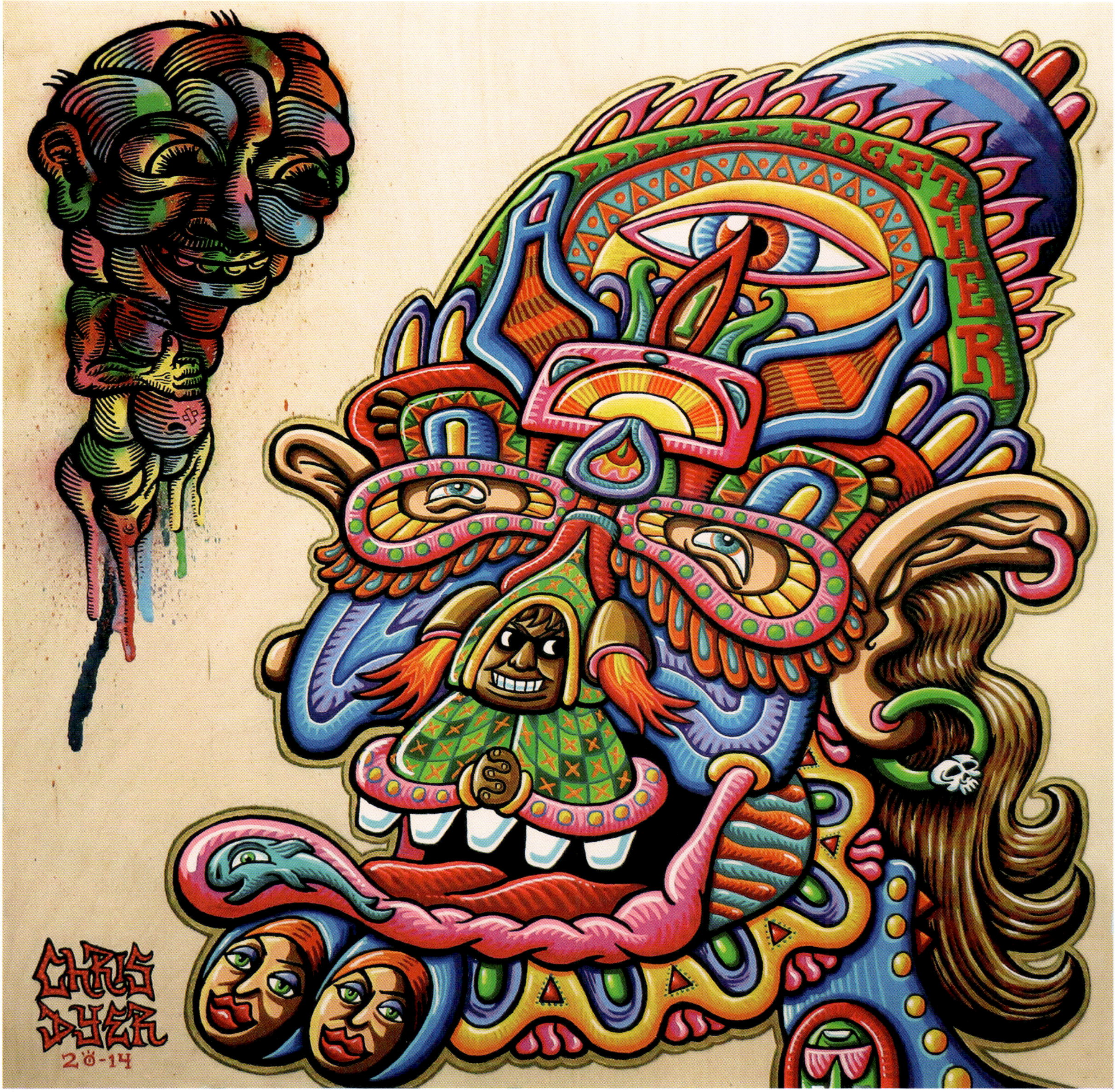

"Message from Beyond" Acrylics on wood, 2014

Painting commissions are not really my favorite, as I would rather just paint for myself. I was taking plenty these days though. The piece seen in the previous spread, **"Evil vs. Good"**, was a concept requested by the popular San Diego brand **"Sk8 Mafia"**. The painting was supposed to be used on skateboards for their Pros **Peter Smolik** and **Jake Brown**. After all the work I did for it, they decided not to use it because of the amount of copyright liabilities in the piece. Sadly they didn't feel they had to pay me either. Luckily, Peter and Jake eventually left that brand and used that graphic on **"Real Life Pillage"**.

The little painting seen above here "Message from Beyond" was requested by the popular Montreal street art Gallery **"Station 16"**. After a fun group show it sold to a solid collector in our city.

The piece to the left was done for a psychedelics store from the Netherlands. They asked me to make my personal interpretation of their character **"Shayana"** who they described as "*a shamaness and handmaiden priestess healer of The Bright One.*" When I delivered this empowered forest nymph, they said they wanted some sexy bikini mushroom babe instead. This experience made me question if I wanted to keep taking painting commissions and with the years I eventually stopped.

COSM, NEW YORK

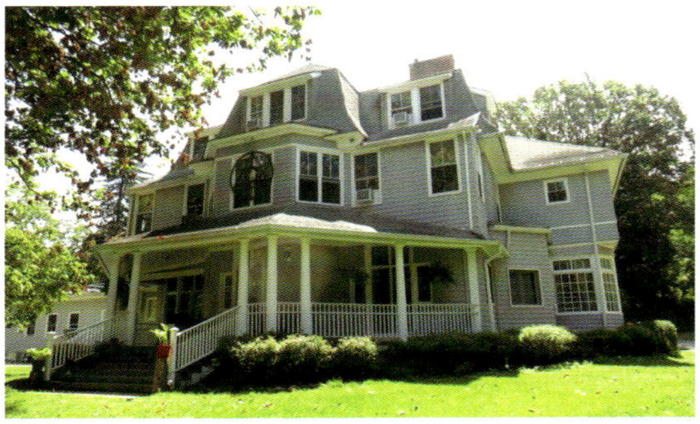

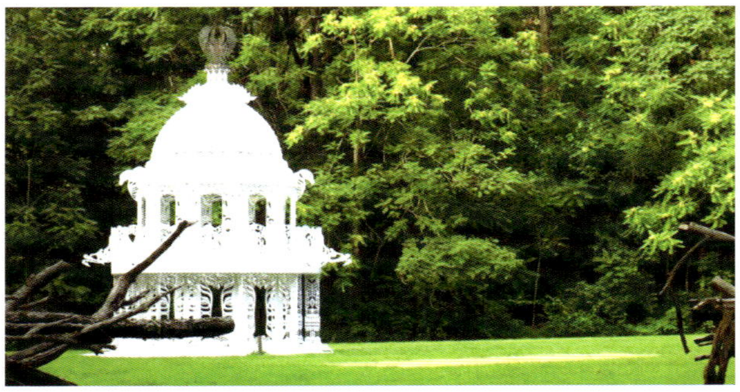

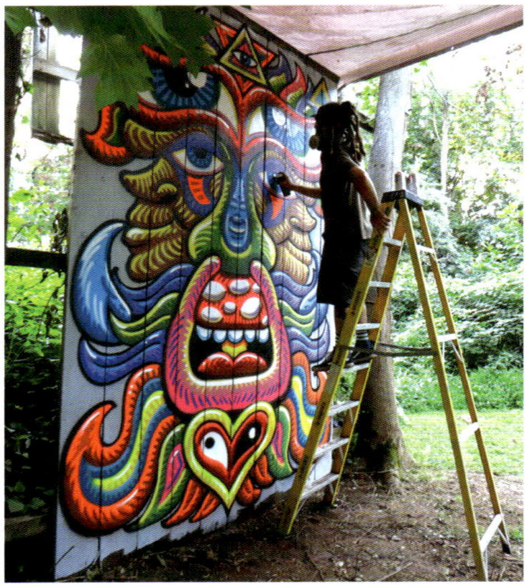

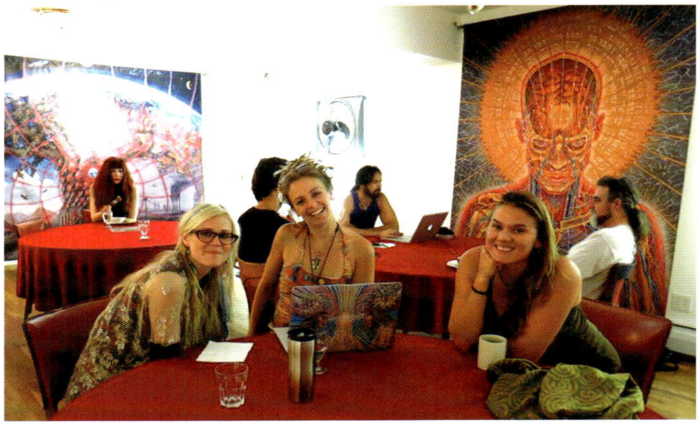

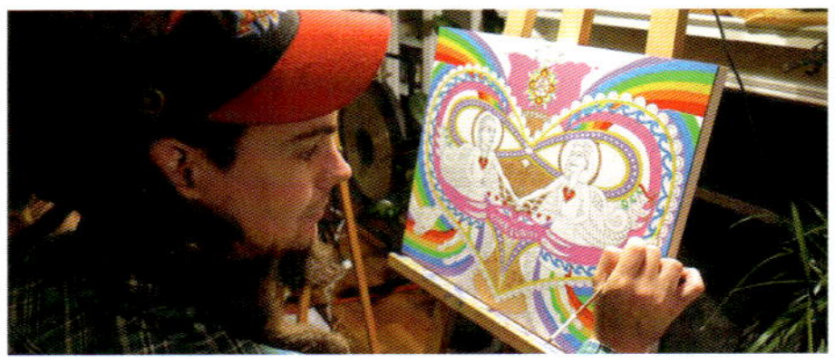

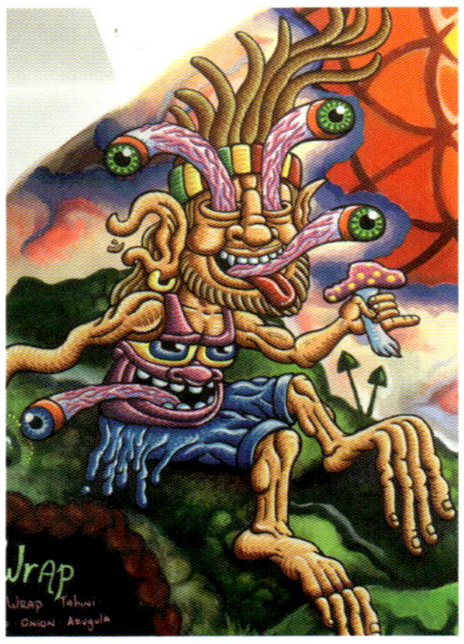

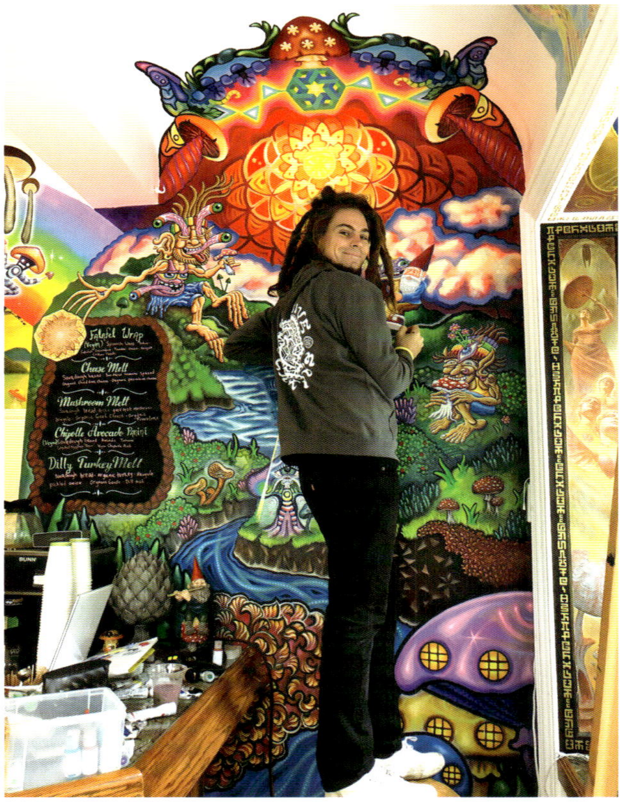

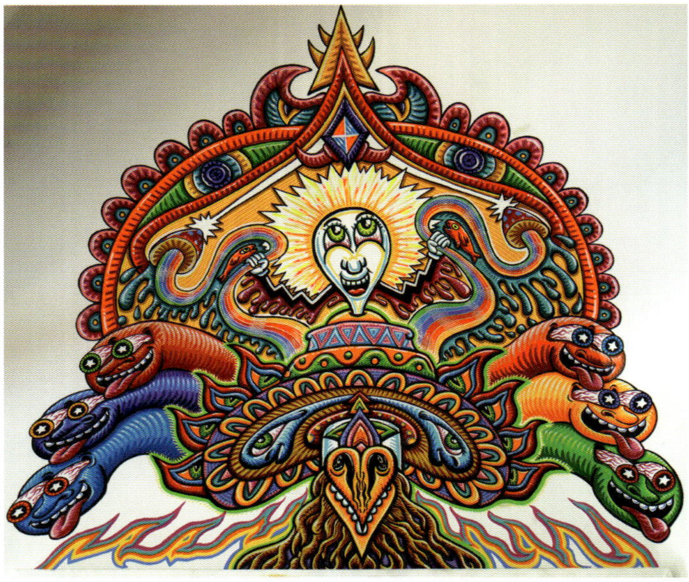

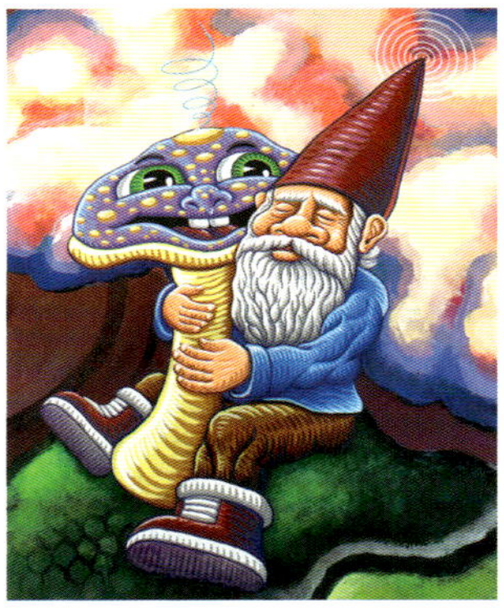

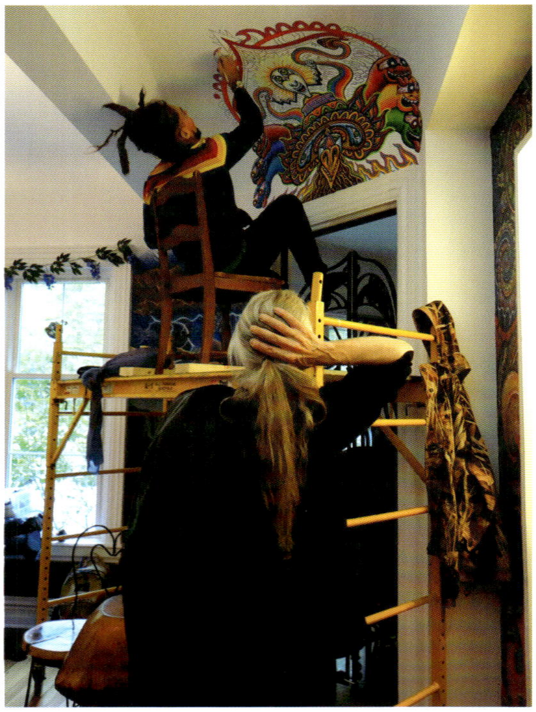

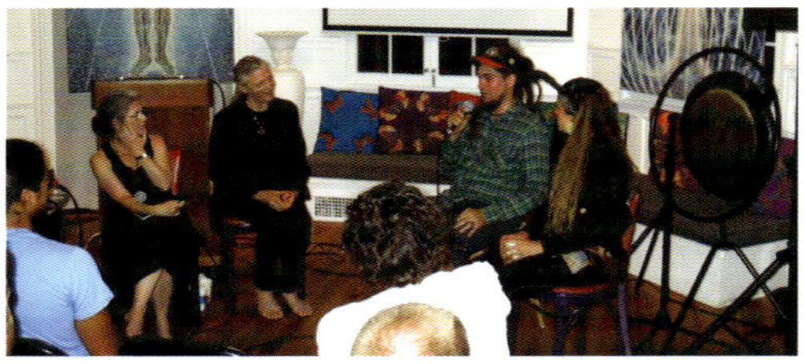

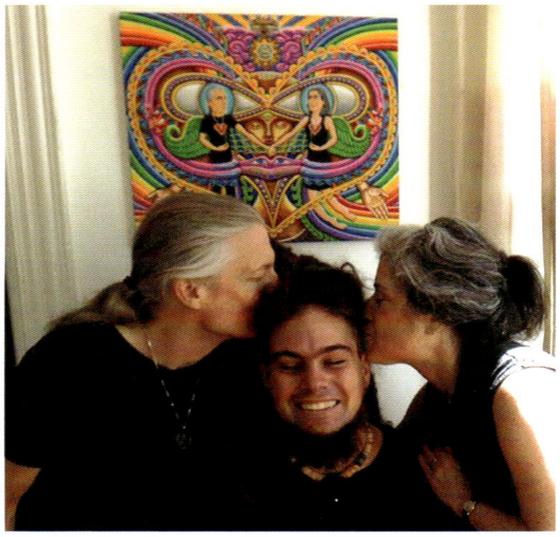

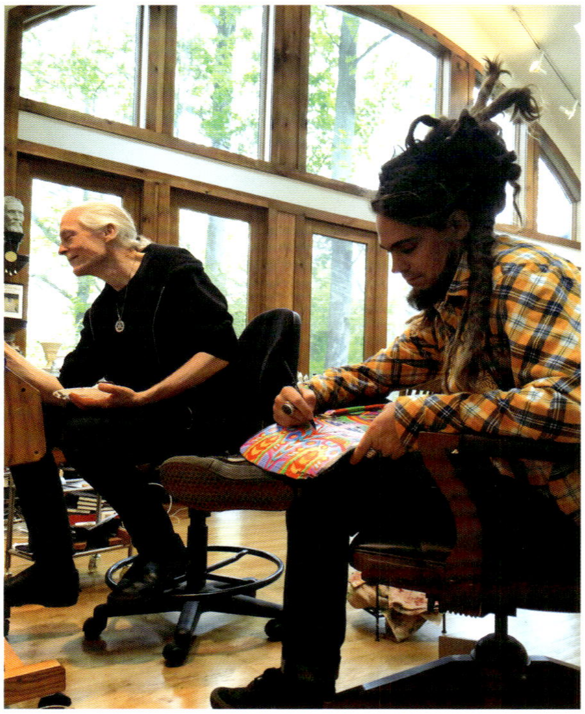

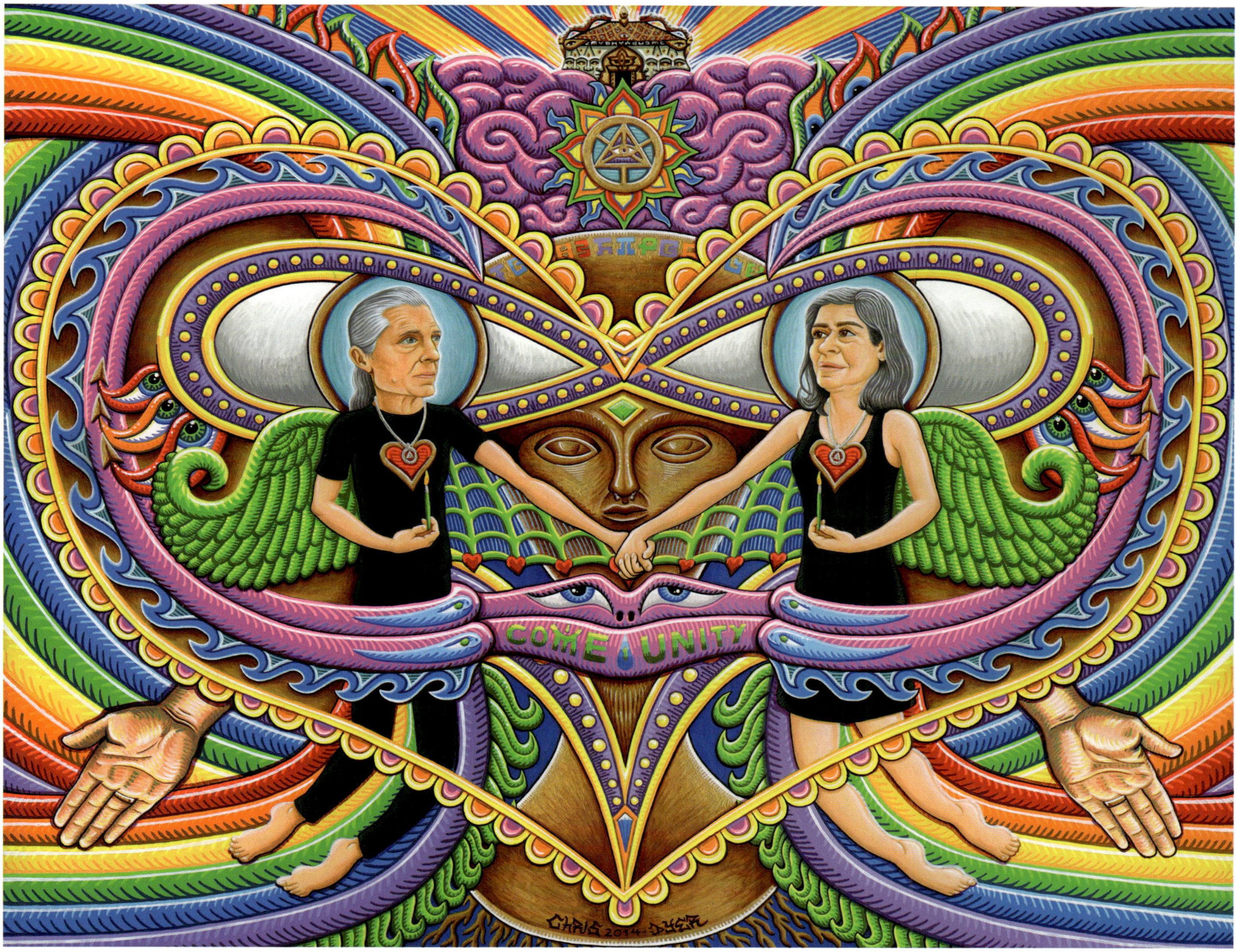

"CoSM-Unity Inte-Grey-tion" Acrylics on wood, 2013 - 2014

Ever since I discovered the art of **Alex Grey** in 2003, he has been a huge inspiration. So in early 2008 I took a train down to Manhattan to meet him at one of his Full Moon Ceremonies. We then saw each other many times over the years, at events we participated in around the world. By the time we did the panel discussion at the 2012 Eclipse Festival in Australia, he and his artist wife Allyson had gained appreciation for my own work. So the following year they invited me to teach at the new location of their **"Chapel of Sacred Mirrors"** in upstate New York. To my great honor, I was invited to be their assistant, along with Amanda Sage, during their yearly painting workshop. That was a super fun time, jamming with so many talented artist students that took the class!

Going to CoSM was a very inspiring experience, since it was a whole community created around the spiritual art that unites all religions and cultures. It is a beautiful place in nature where they can share their work, do meaningful events, and nurture thousands of spiritual artists. There, one can be open-hearted and use art as a path to get closer to God. So in the painting I did at their workshop I expressed my admiration towards Alex and Allyson, their love for each other and their community. I don't usually give away paintings, as they take so long to make, but I couldn't resist gifting this to them.

Anyways, on that first visit in 2013 I started painting the walls of their **"Mushroom Café"**, where so many great Visionary artists have collaborated. I continue to work on my pieces there every visit. That initial visit I also taught my first workshop there, which then became a yearly event. I will talk more about these workshops later in this book, along all the spray paint pieces I've done for them at **"Chris' Corner"**. I'm showing the first mural here though, which didn't live long as it got struck by lightning!

Super grateful to Alex and Allyson, who have become important mentors and friends on my path.

PERU

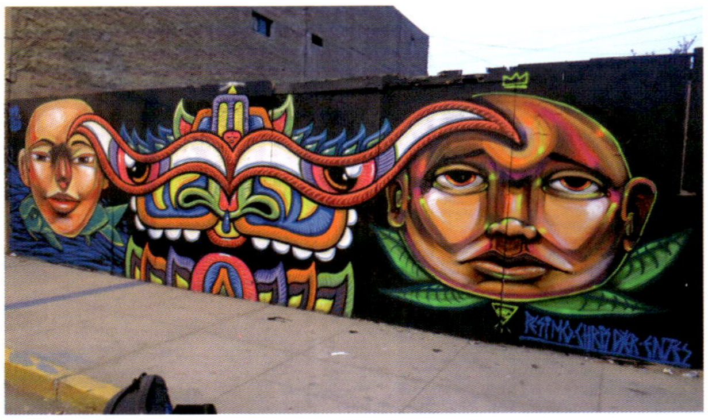
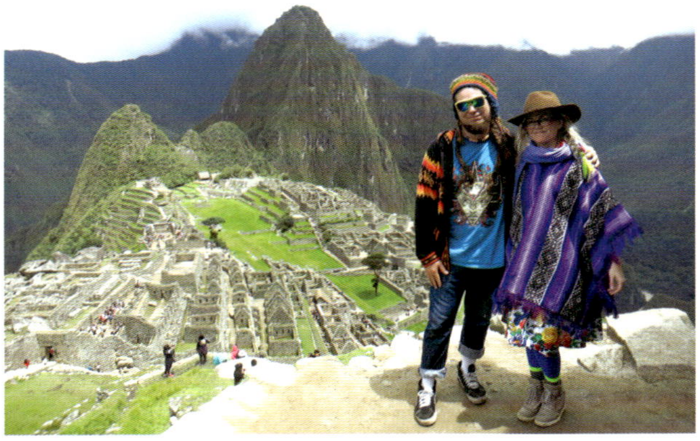
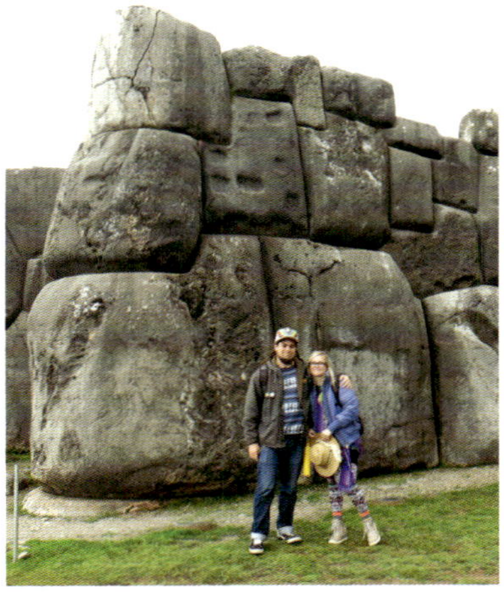

At the end of 2013, I finally took Valerie to my original country of Peru. For two months we travelled all around this mystical land and enjoyed many of its cultural and natural blessings. We also stayed with my parents in Lima, so I took the opportunity to do a big solo exhibition there. The opening party got packed with family, friends and fans and a local shaman, **Herbert Quinteros** offered to play live music for it. Though we knew each other for years on Facebook, that was the first time we met in person. He invited me to visit him in the jungle to meet **Ayahuasca**. I had actually not done psychedelics in several years, but I agreed to meet him at the end of my trip.

This painting tries to describe a small fragment of what I experienced in my two initiation ceremonies with the Ayahuasca medicine. This magical entity crowned me with blissful light, in reward for all the hard work I had been doing for myself and Gaia. She told me that my life was my Ayahuasca ceremony, and that from now on our alliance would be more clear and powerful. It's impossible for me to describe all she showed me that night, but it was extremely deep, ancient and beyond this planet or dimension! I realized I still had so many things to learn and remember! Herbert was an amazing guide, orchestrating the vibe of the ceremony so well with his beautiful "icaros" and music, so I placed him driving the spaceship-hat of Mother Aya, in my painting.

Though my first Ceremony was incredibly positive, I also managed to throw up and realized the gift that was. I saw how she could physically remove some of my accumulated negative energy, demons and parasites (as seen in the lower part of the painting, where I'm hugging my bucket for dear life!). So in my second ceremony, I allowed myself to struggle more and enjoy less. I asked her to remove some of my anger. This time I didn't get any visuals, instead, I was lit on fire. It felt like she was scanning through my body as little snakes, gathering the dirt I stored in different corners and then would bring that to my belly, which had turned into a furnace. I experienced this burning feeling for a long time, but Herbert didn't come to rescue me because he knew that it was the process I had to endure. After a few hours he saw I had enough and called me in front of him. His connection with the medicine is so strong that he played me a specific song which made me projectile puke into my bucket! He then said "Ahi salio la rabia!", which means "There goes your anger!", which was crazy, because I had not told him my initial intention. It really confirmed the reality of this intelligent anti-virus process.

On the technical side, this piece started as a drawing in 2014. When I shared it on Instagram, a fan asked me if I would want that as a 3D canvas and of course I agreed. Later that year, that kind soul, **Michael Clotherthy** from **"Cerebral Concepts"** attended my first COSM skate art workshop and gifted me this beautiful CNC-carved canvas! I was so stoked about it, yet it took me a while to properly paint its shaped complexion.

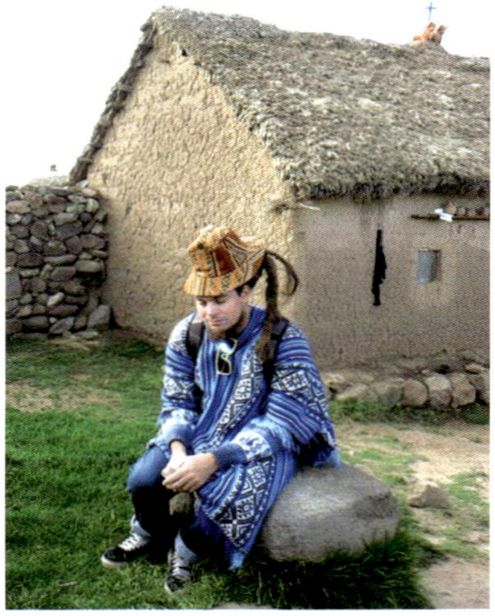
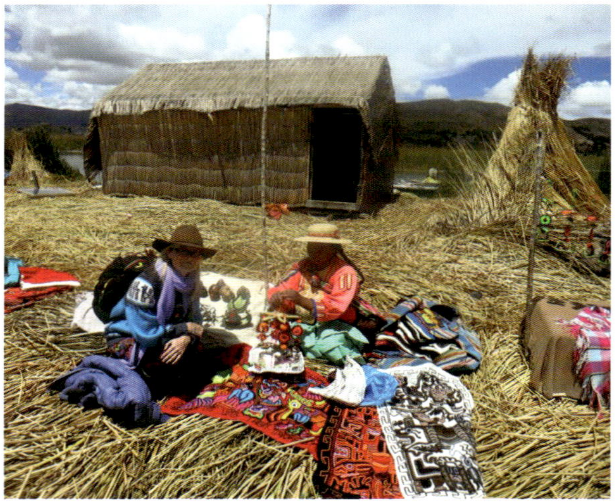
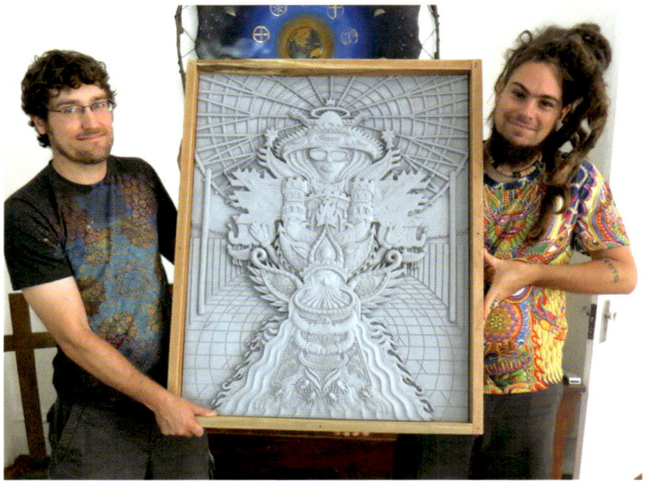

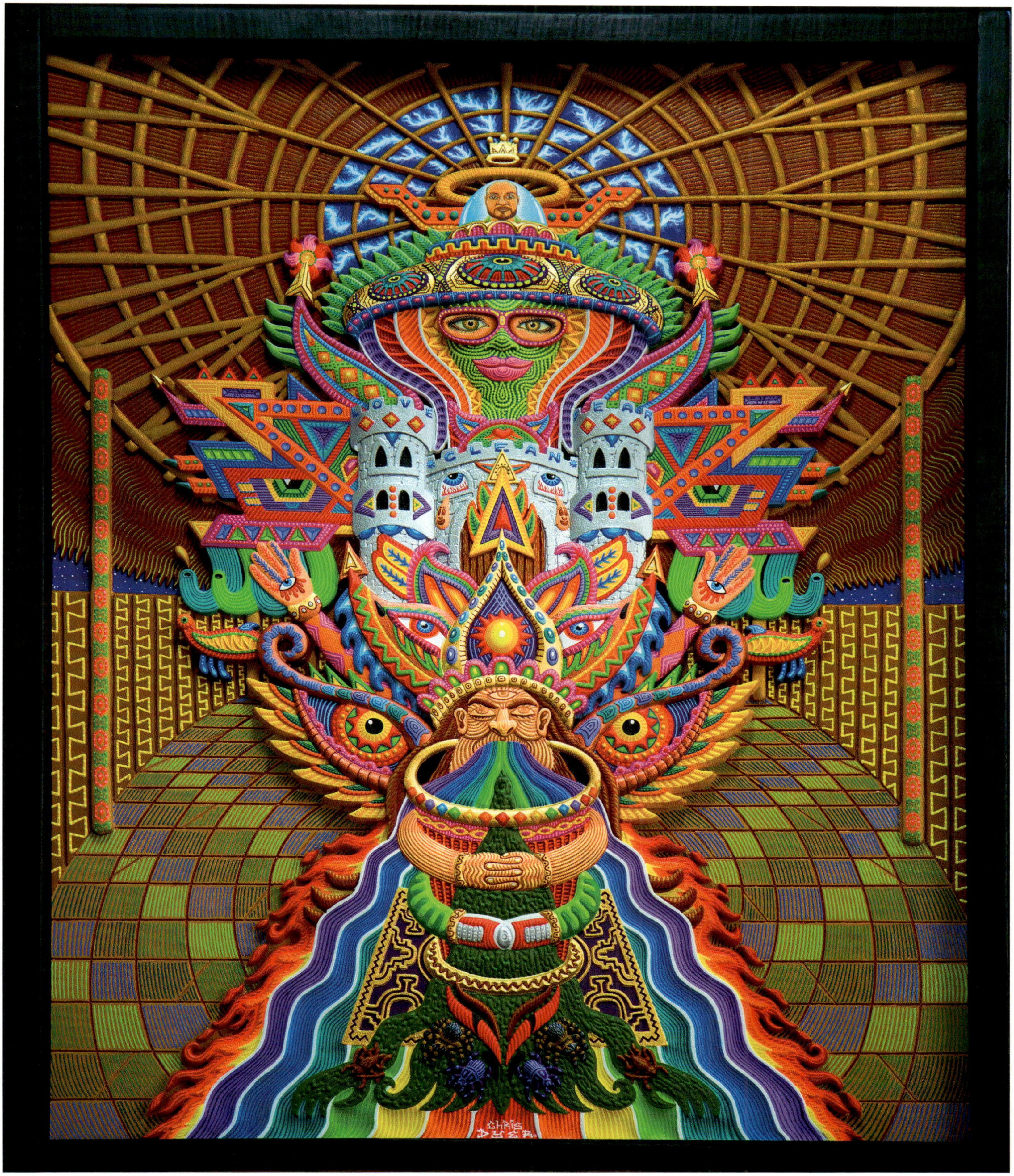

"The Purge" Acrylics on 3D canvas, 2014- 2016

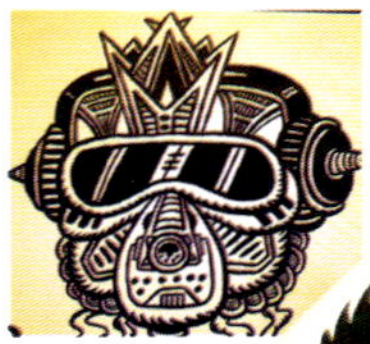

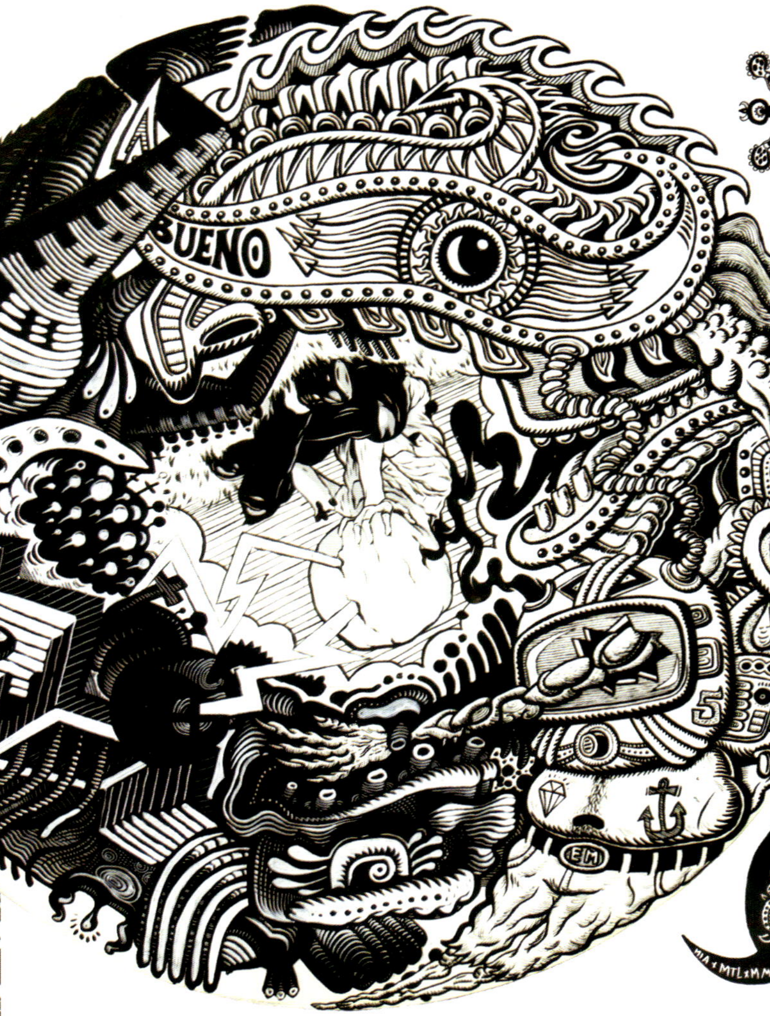
BUENO

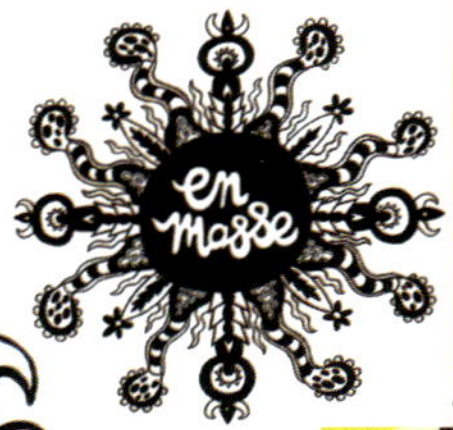
en masse

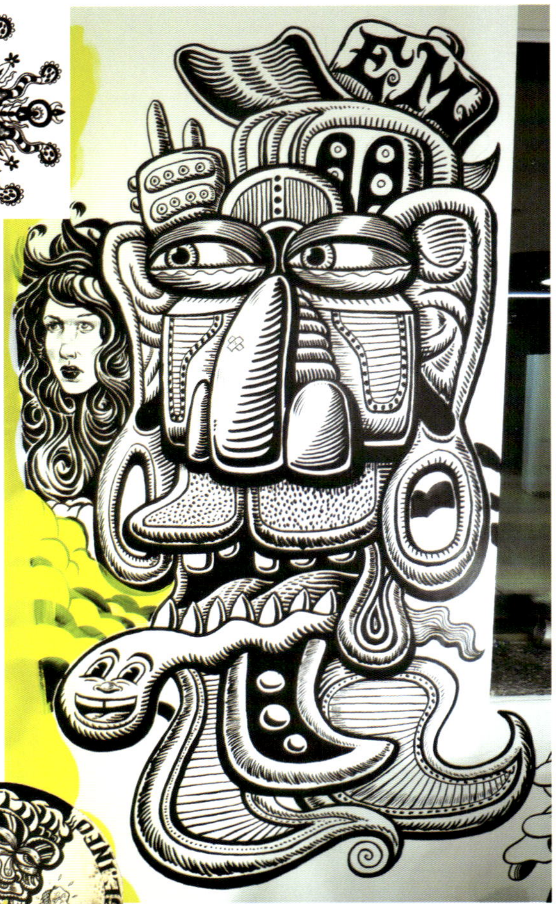
EM

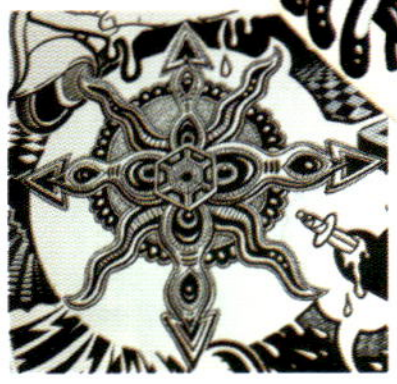

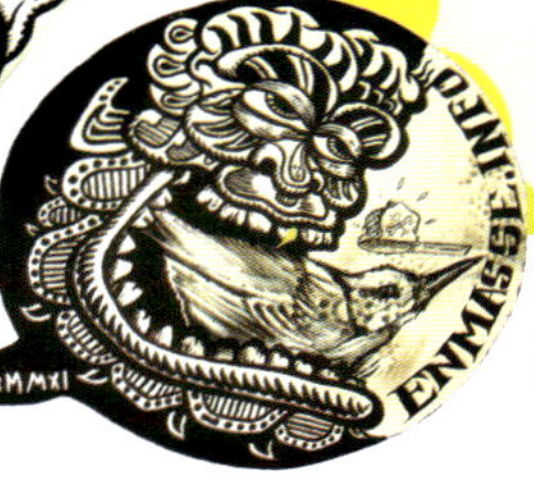

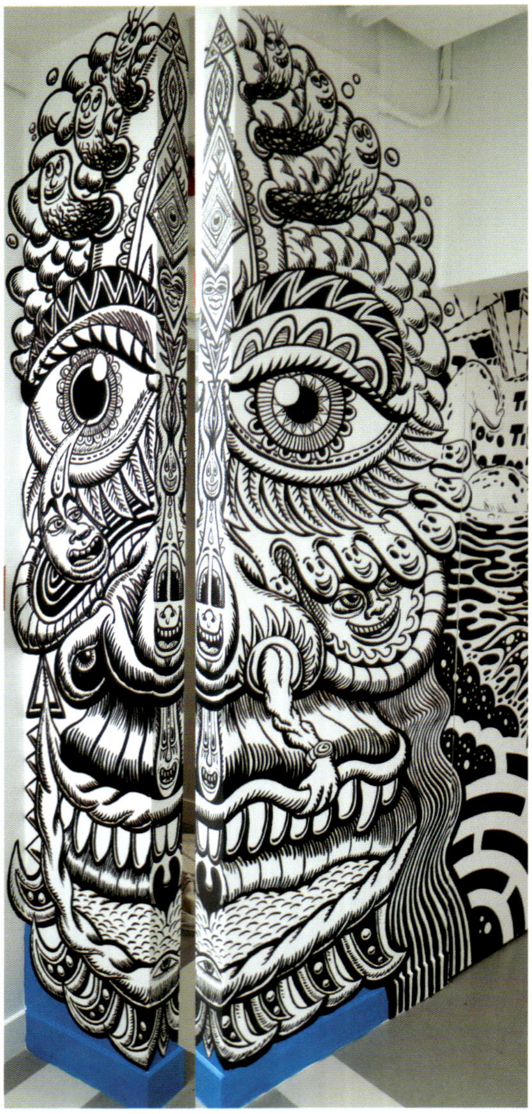

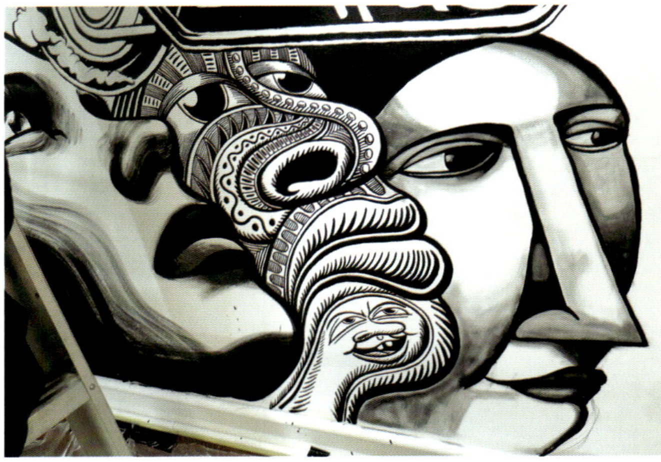

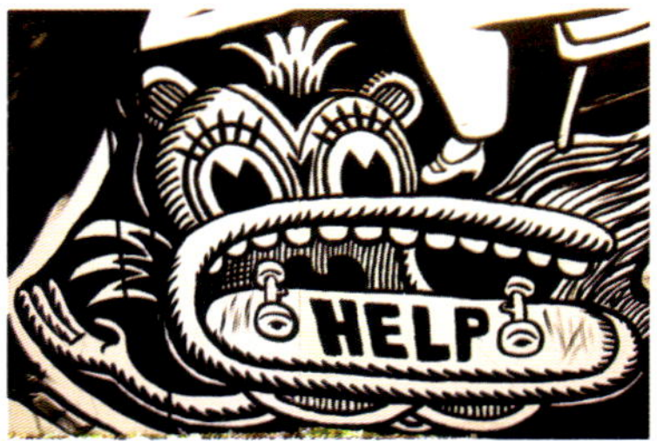
HELP

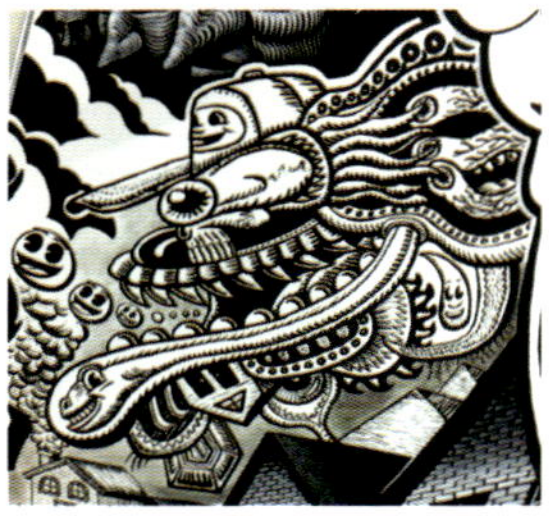

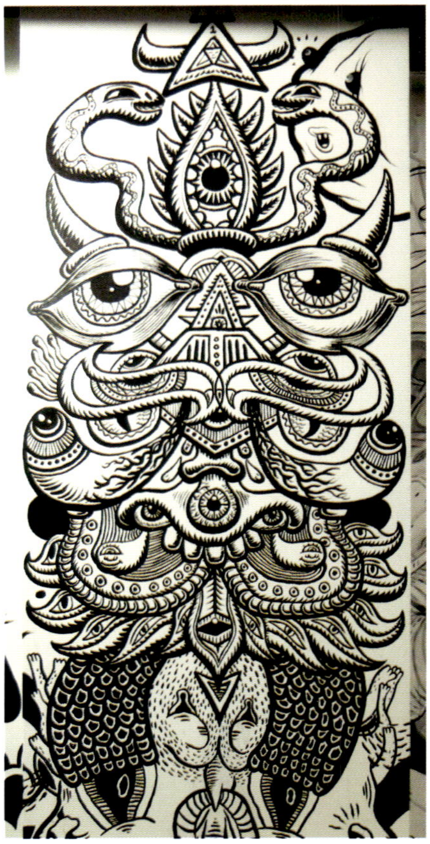

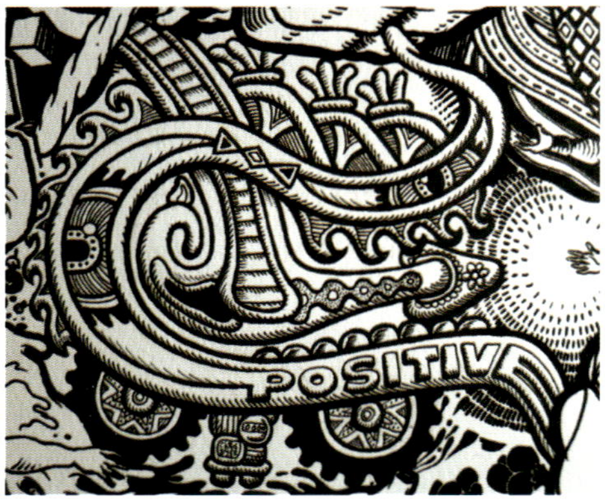
POSITIVE

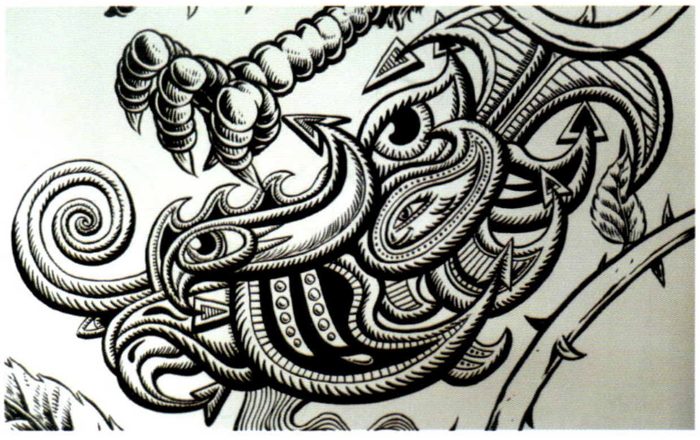

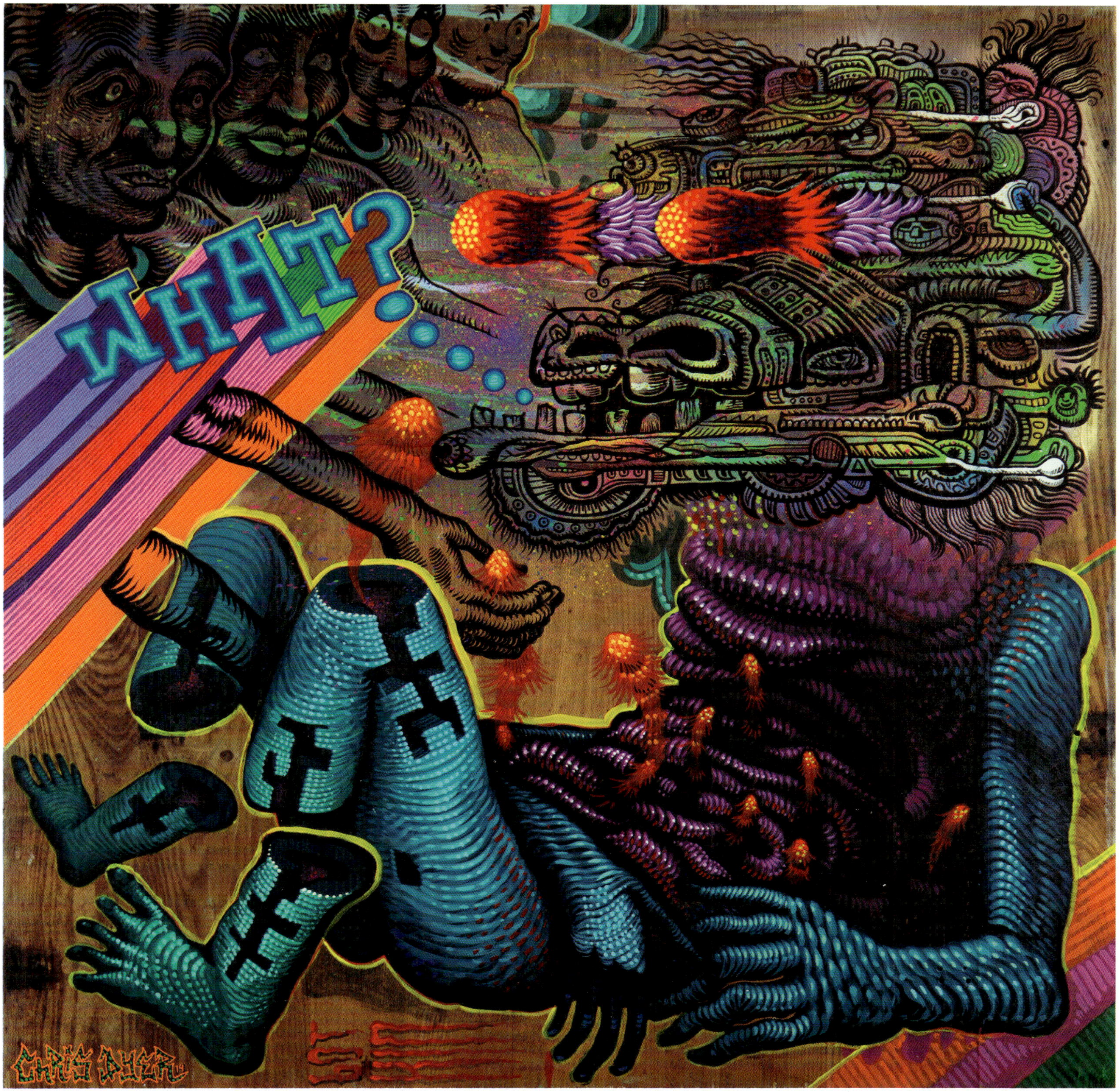

"What?" collaboration with **Jason Botkin**,
Acrylics and spray paint on wood, 2014

Jason Botkin is an old artist friend of mine from the Montreal community. He is the organizer of a collective called **"En Masse"** where he gathers the city's most talented artists to paint black and white murals. Here are some of the most recent freestyles with this collective. Anyways, Jason has a really trippy style, so when he asked me to combine forces on something really weird, it was my great pleasure. As somebody confused on what reality is truly about, I depicted this interdimensional entity questioning it too!

"CHRIS IS A KALEIDOSCOPIC CREATIVE FORCE OF NATURE, PARADOXICALLY DEFYING AND DEFINING WHAT IT MEANS TO BE AN ARTIST IN OUR PRESENT TIME AND SPACE. HIS ART STUBBORNLY ELUDES ALL ATEMPTS AT CATEGORIZATION, AS HE STEADILY MARCHES AROUND THIS WIDE WORLD, PAINTING TO THE BEAT OF HIS OWN SHAMANIC HEART'S DRUM."

-JASON BOTKIN, ARTIST

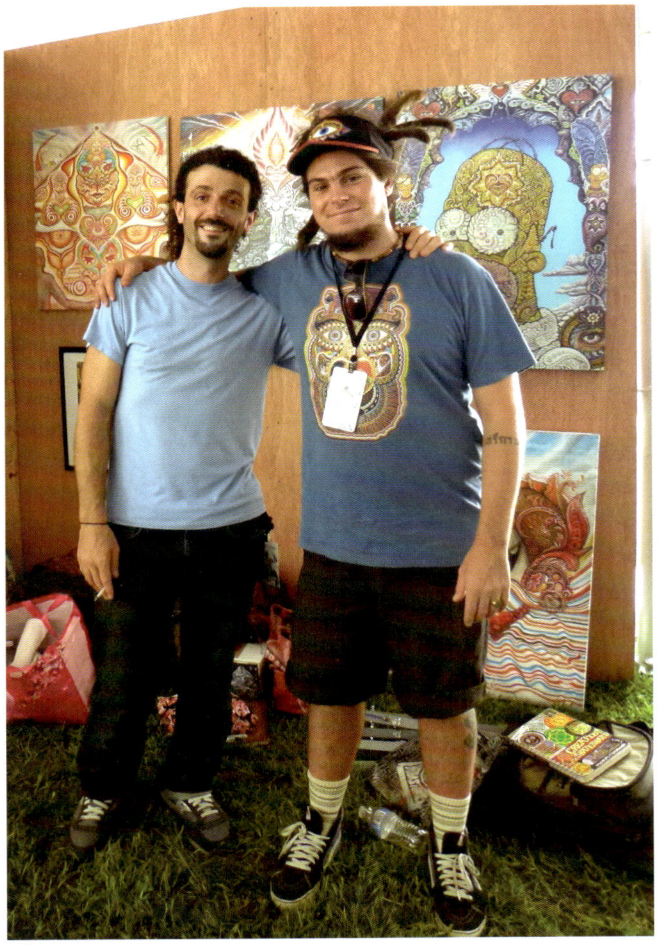
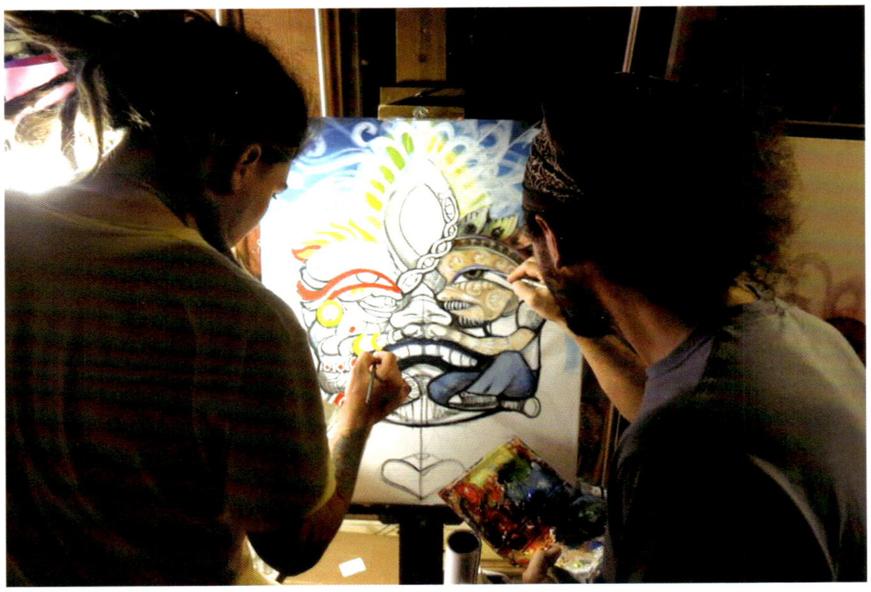
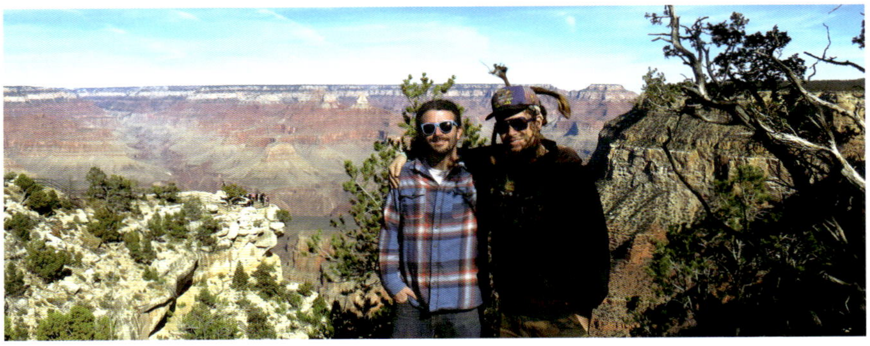

Back in the day, cartoony visionary art was a rare style in the Visionary scene, so I felt kinda lonely expressing in that flavor. But there was this guy in New York, **Randal Roberts**, who was doing a really cool version of that. I was a fan, so we became friends online and I tried to get him in group shows. Eventually he moved to California and started showing his work at Music Festivals and it didn't take long before he became a strong staple of our movement! We finally met in person in 2012, at the classic **Rootwire Music Festival**, where I connected with so many of the next generation of this spiritual art movement. Randal and I hit it off and he's been one of my best friends since. For years I would stay with him and his then girlfriend Morgan Mandala's Boulder home, whenever visiting Colorado. So it was a must to collaborate on a canvas on one of my stays, and naturally we made it about our own friendship. The painting is a frontal face view of an ecstatic creature we both resonated with. It is about uniting forces, magnifying each other's powers by the loving (non-sexual) relationship of two men. We also included our then lands (Montreal and Boulder) in the bottom corners. I Love this painting we did together, my Colorado visits, my friend Randal, and also the cool Dr. Strange painting I bought off him after a gig he had done for Marvel! Grateful!

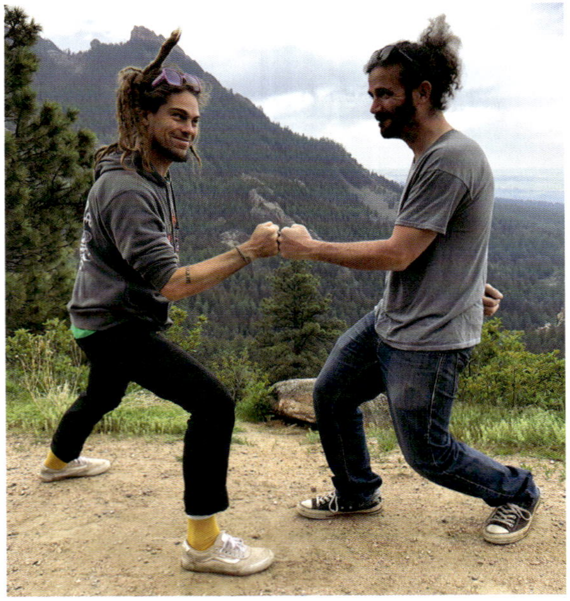
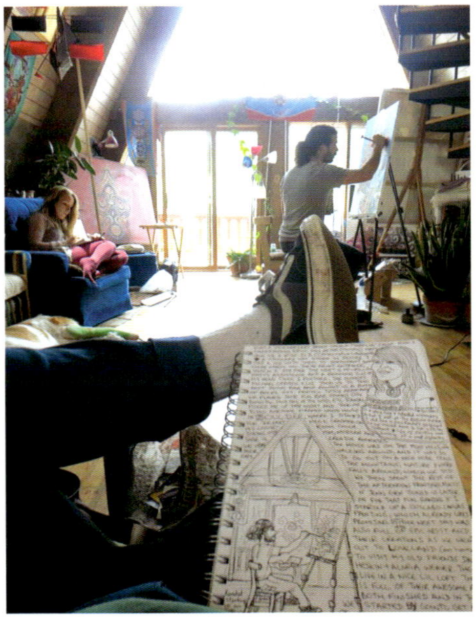
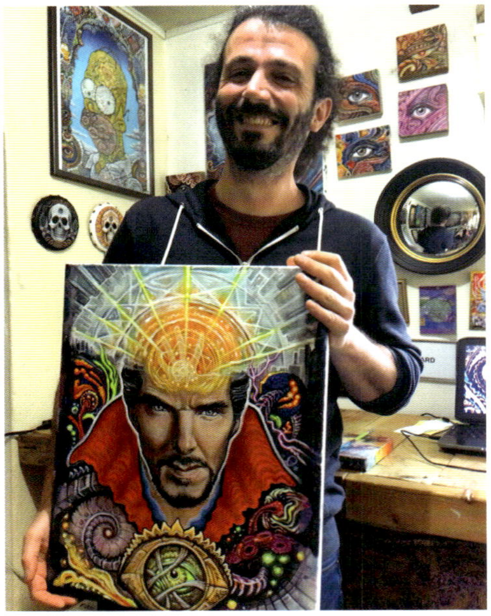

Next Page: **"Bromance"** collabo with **Randal Roberts**, Acrylics on canvas, 2015

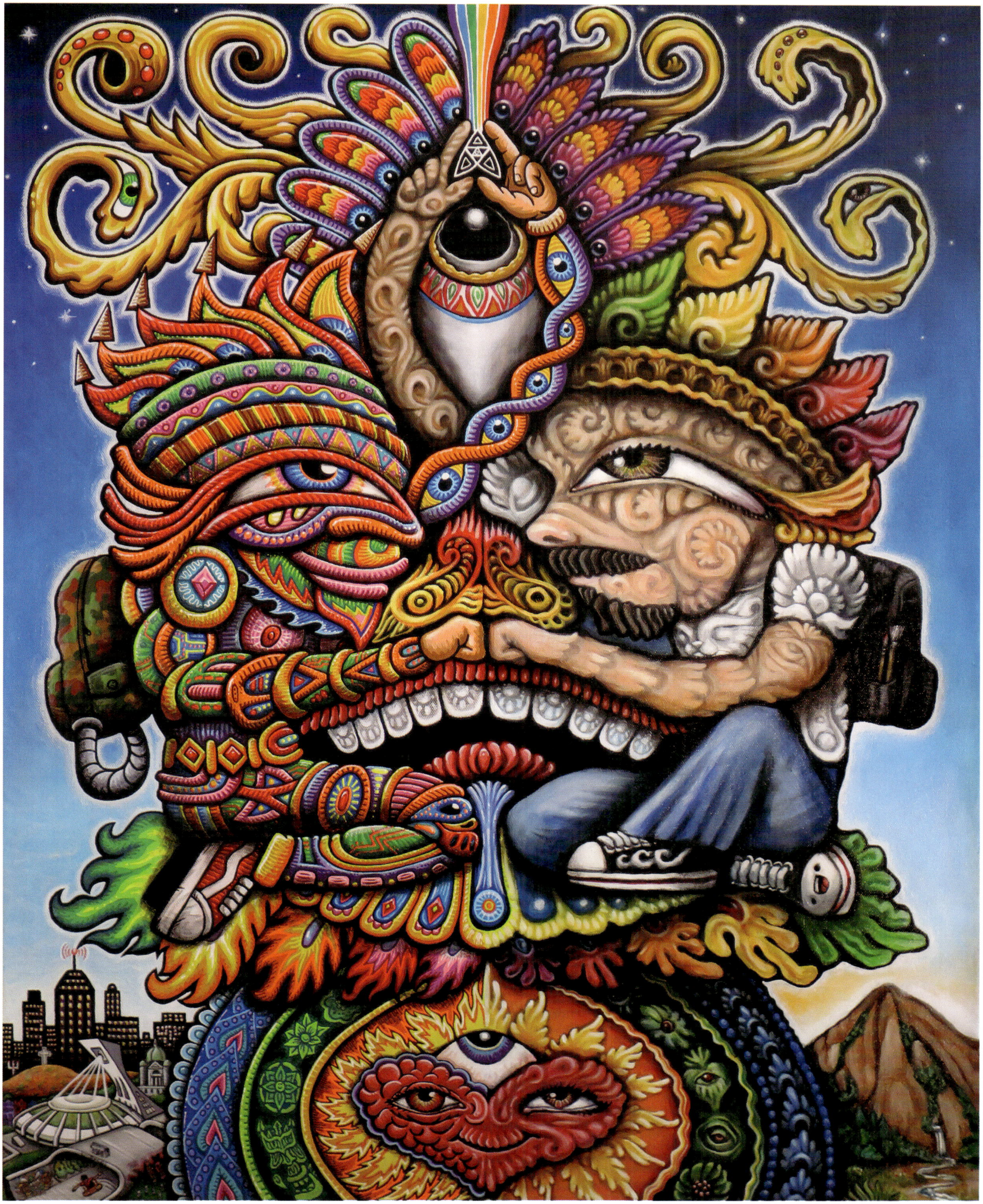

"SOME RARE ELECTRIC JUJU COURSES THROUGH CHRIS. HE IS AN ART MACHINE. HE'S BEEN A BROTHER-IN-ART TO ME FOR OVER A DECADE AND I WOULDN'T EVEN WANT TO IMAGINE A WORLD WITHOUT HIM IN IT."

-RANDAL ROBERTS, VISIONARY ARTIST

BELGIUM

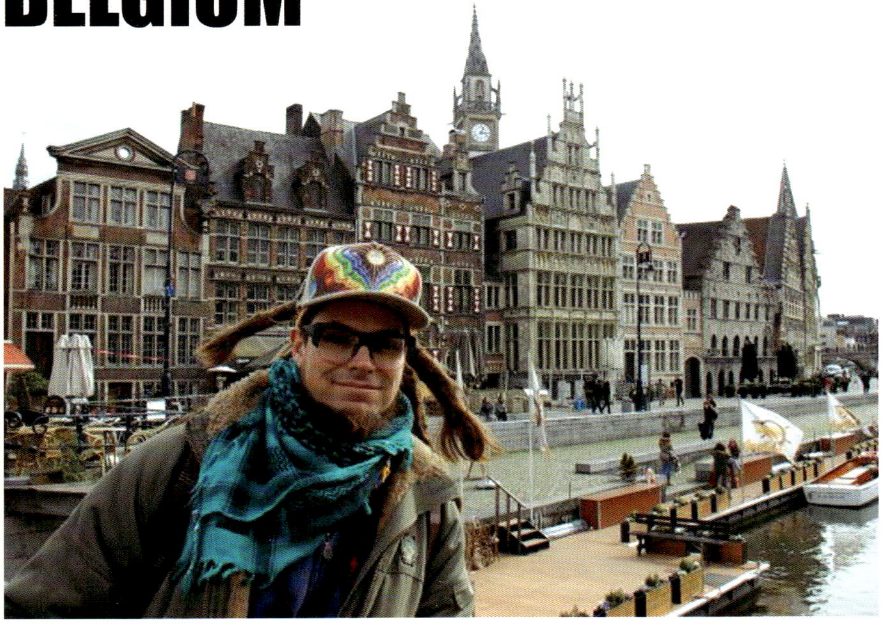

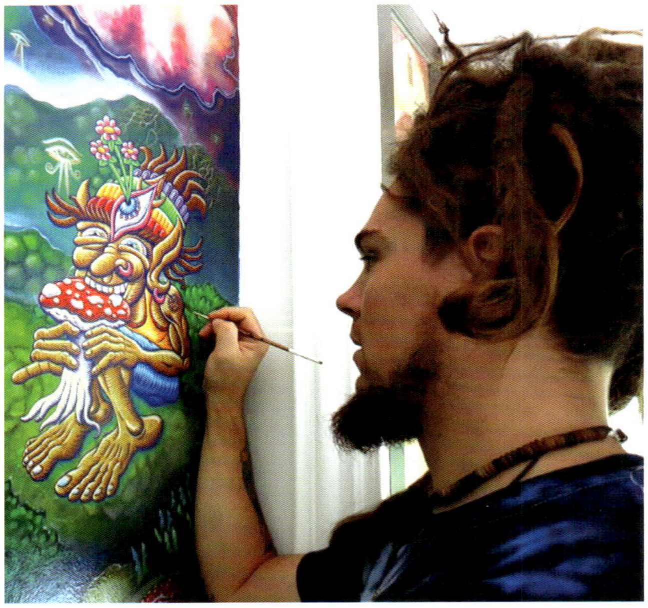

By the end of 2014 Valerie and I were doing super good. Her health was strong, and my finances too, so we decided we where ready to have a kid! For that, I planned for us to travel the world over winter, getting romantic in exotic locations. But before that, we decided to go to Belgium for a couple of weeks, to spend Christmas with her parents. Two weeks turned into four months, as both of Valerie's childhood pets died the week we arrived and then she fell very sick. I don't really want to get into the specifics of Valerie's struggles, but she suffered a lot from it and there was nothing I could do other than give her my support. It was very hard to see my beloved suffer day after day, constantly cancelling our flights back home. It was also frustrating to be living with my parents in law for so long... My only distraction was to go to the city of Ghent once in a while to spray paint murals, but most of the time I was in Valerie's childhood room painting canvases.
The first commission I did was for a good artist friend Sebastian Wahl and his wife Anastasia from NYC. They loved the Mushroom-eating gnome I had painted on the walls of Cosm's "Mushroom Café" and requested a polished version. It was really fun to recreate that cute trippy creature into his magical environment.

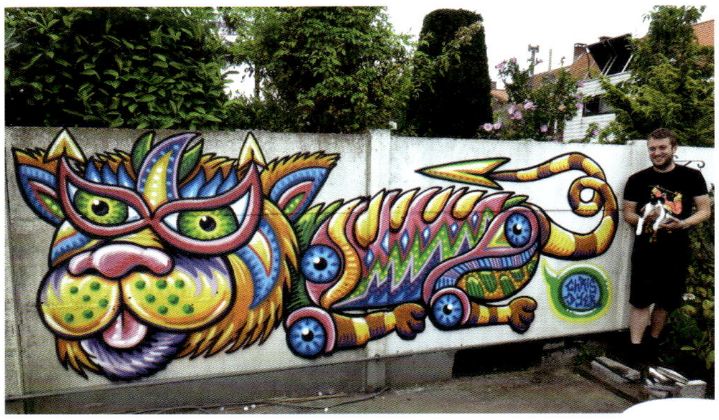

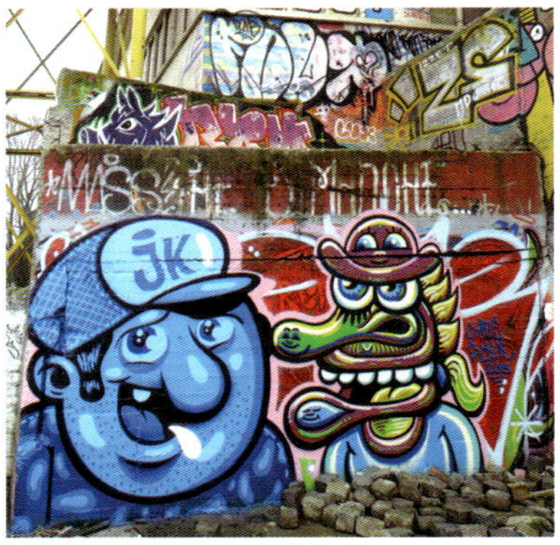

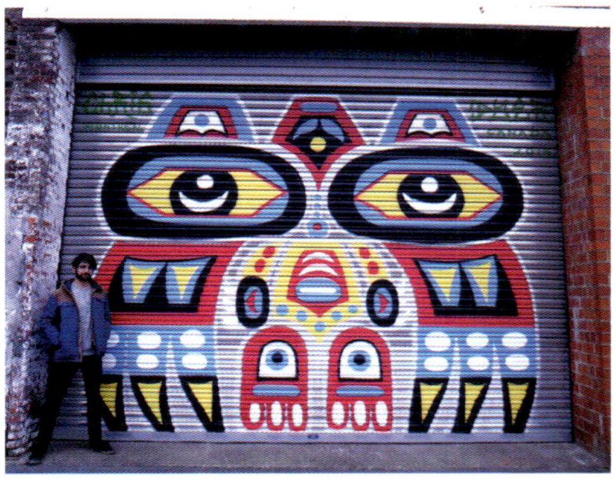

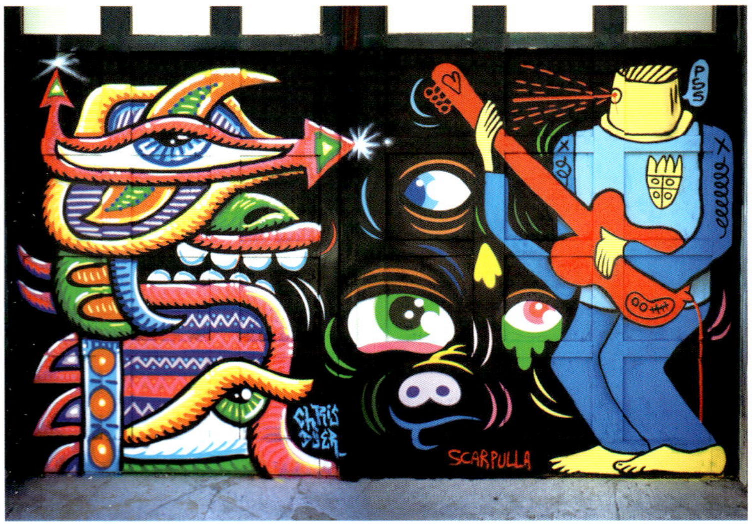

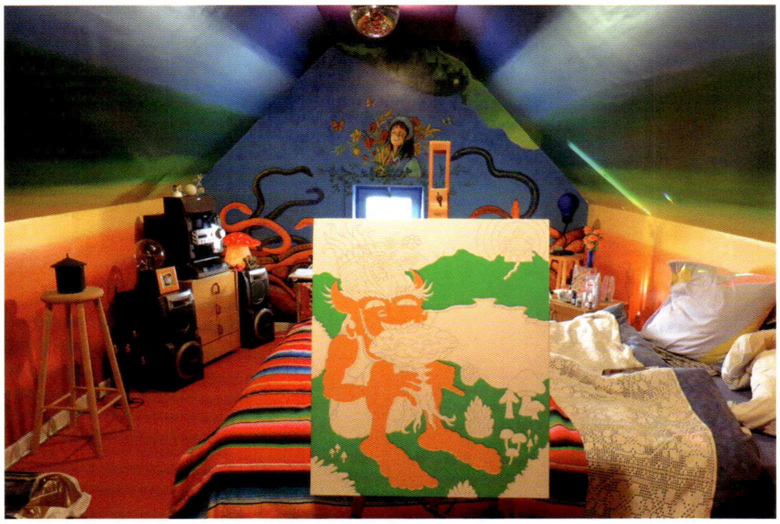

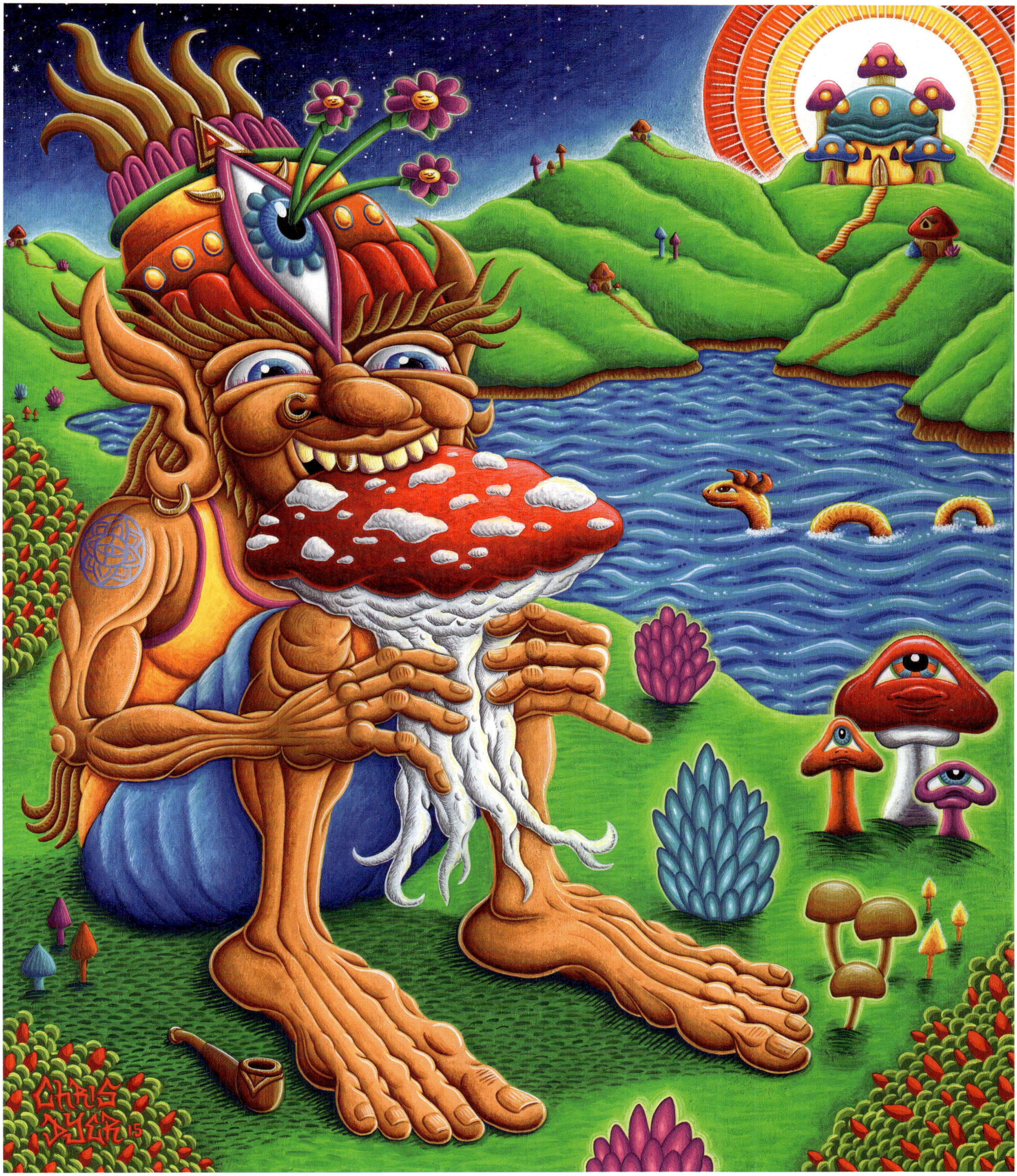

"The Muncher of Mushroomland" Acrylics on wood, 2015

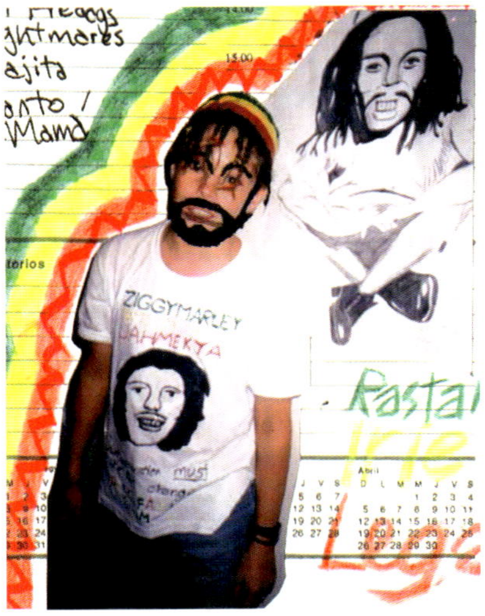
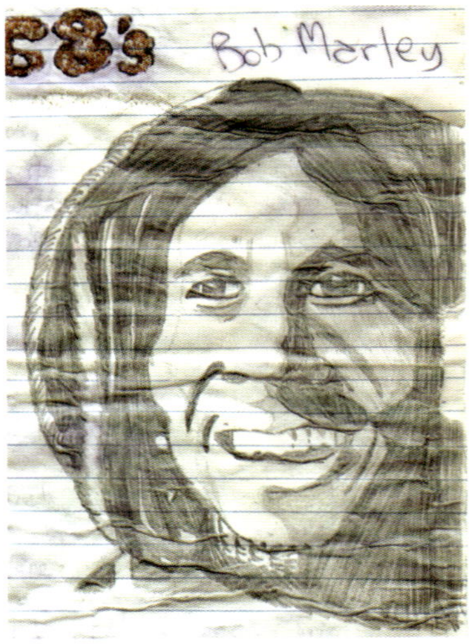

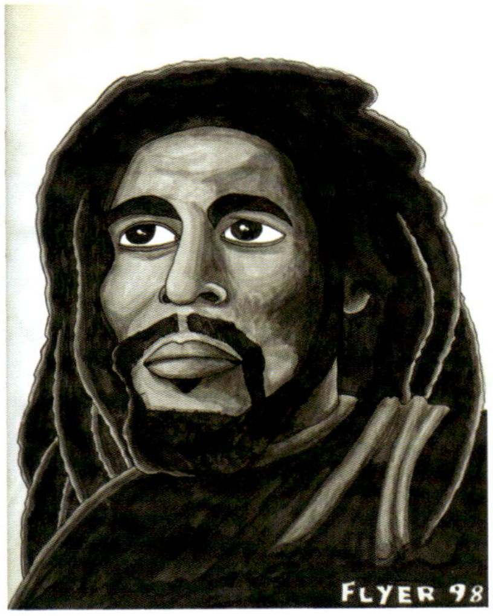

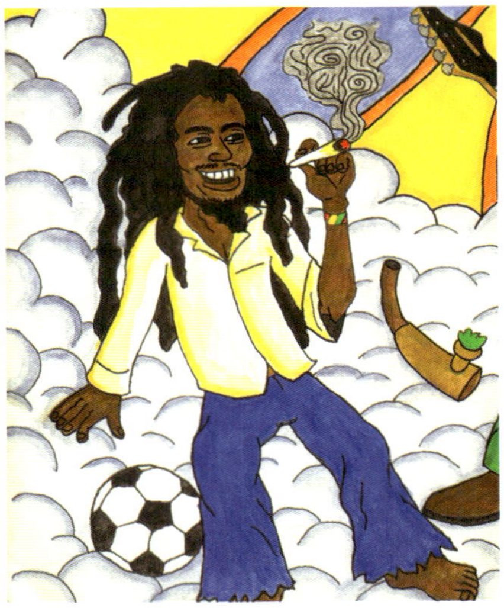

Some past Portraits of **Bob Marley** I've done back in 1991, 1992, 1998 and 1999.

The next commission painting I tackled during that time in Belgium was for the **"Reggae Festival Guide"**. This is an annual magazine that is printed and distributed widely at most reggae festivals worldwide, so I was stoked! That year was Bob Marley's 80th birthday, so they asked me to make a portrait of him for their cover. I've actually been making Bob Marley portraits ever since I was twelve years old, so it was a dream job! I am such a big fan of Bob and his soulful music. His message of Love, while standing up against the bullshit of Babylon, always resonates and helps me on my journey. I wonder how the world would be different if he was still around speaking his powerful voice! Since his life history and spiritual views are so potent, to complement the central portrait, I also illustrated a bunch of drawings of that all around him, displaying these important episodes and people. Doing realistic portraits isn't really my favorite approach, but always a fun challenge to achieve. This particular portrait of one of my biggest heroes later opened the doors for further collaborations with his family and in that way, contribute my own vibration to his mission of uniting the world as one! Shout outs to all Roots Rastas out there going against the New World Order programming! Big Ups to the Marley family who keep spreading the message of One Love past cultural limitations.

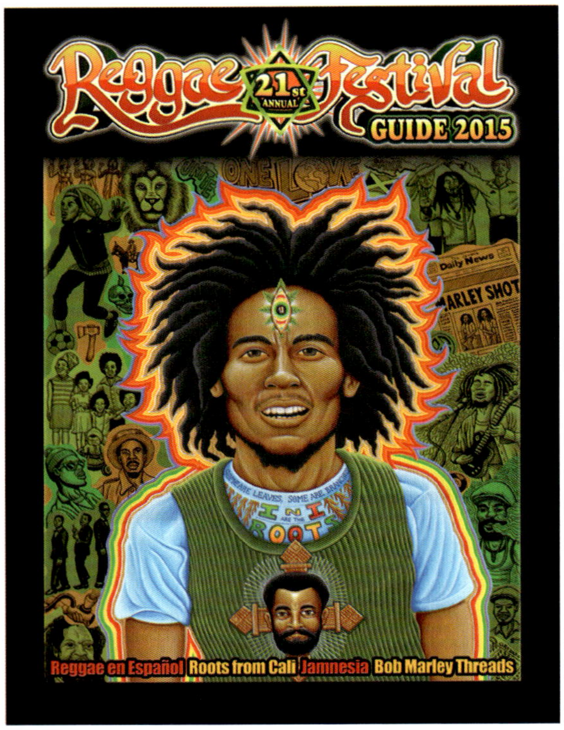

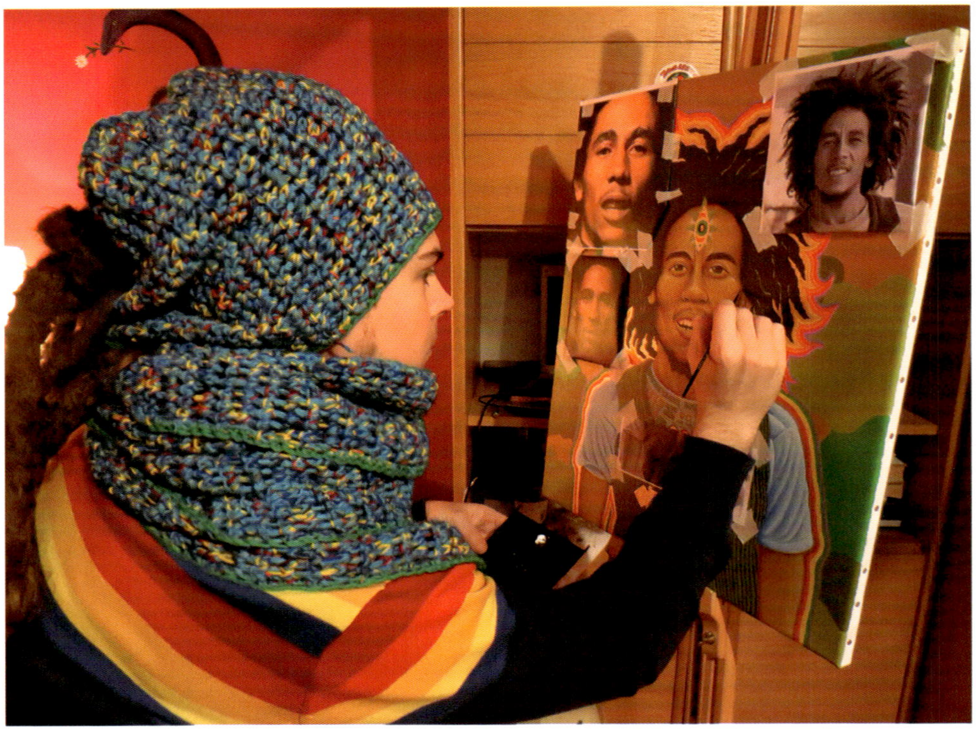

"CHRIS DYER'S WORK IS REALLY A PERFECTION. ART IS LIFE TO ME, YOU KNOW. THE FIRST ARTIST IS JAH, SO TO BE A CREATOR IS TO BE A REFLECTION OF HIM. CHRIS' ART IS BEAUTIFUL AND VERY POWERFUL! I LOVE IT! -JULIAN MARLEY, GRAMMY AWARD WINNING MUSICIAN AND BOB MARLEY'S SON

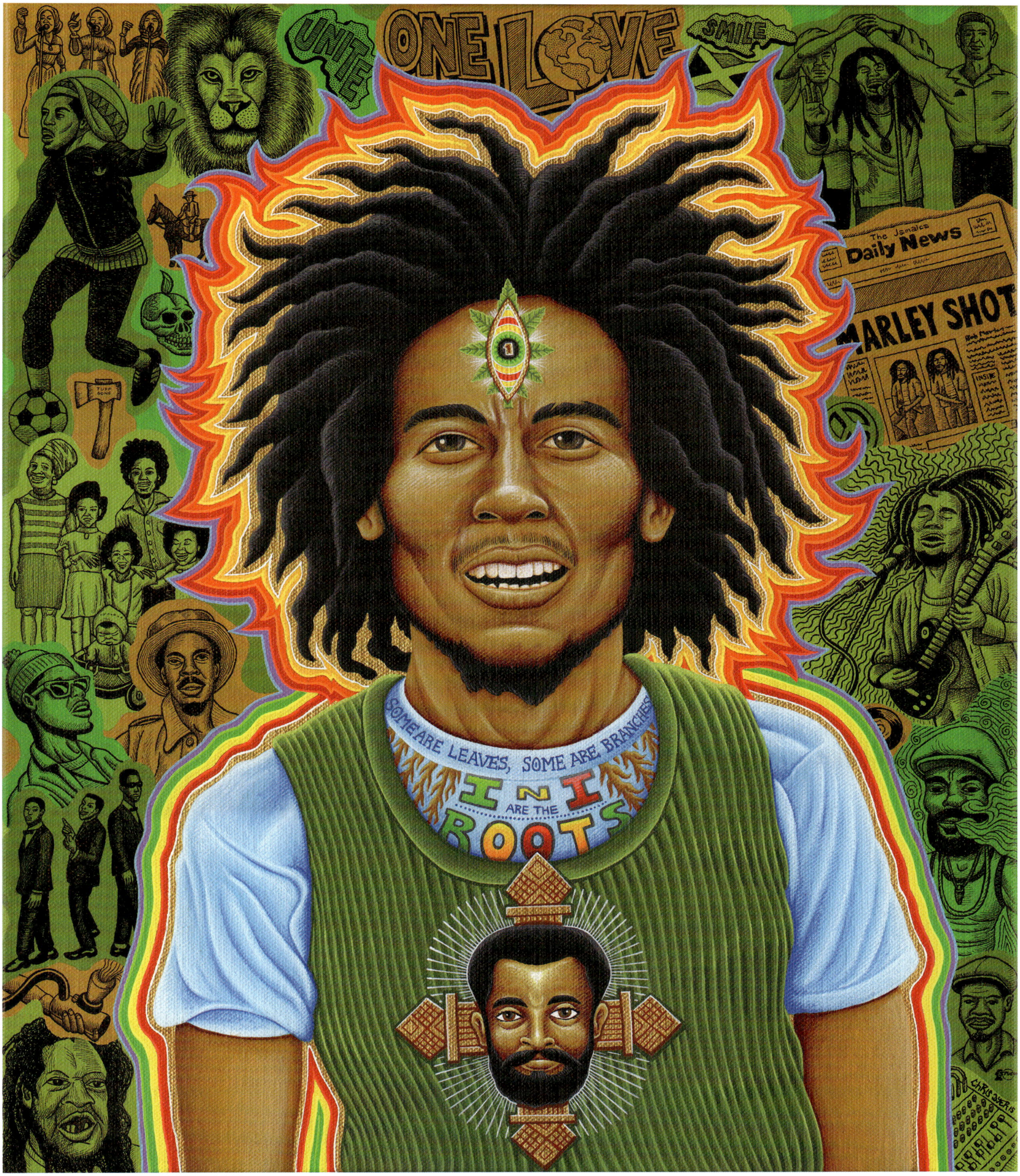

"Marley's Roots" Acrylics and Ink on Canvas, 2015

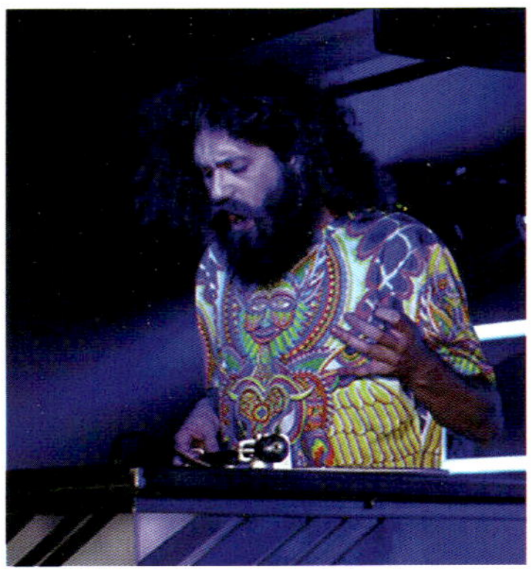

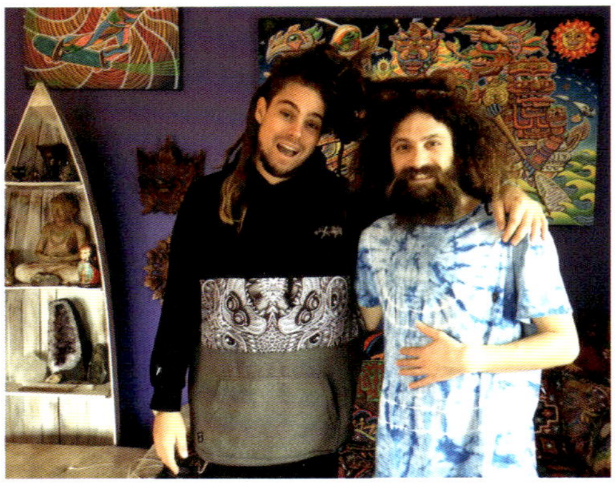

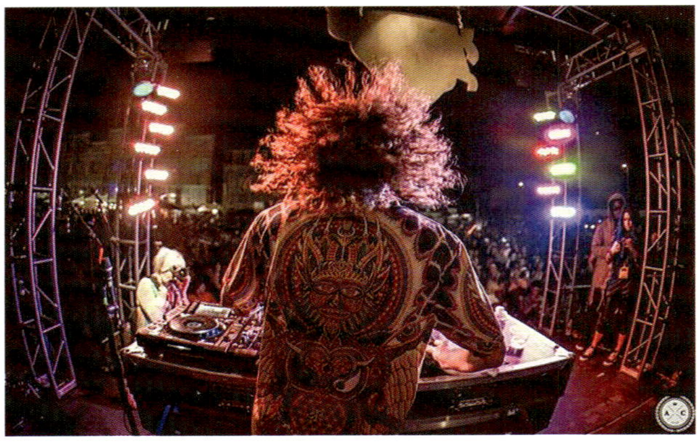

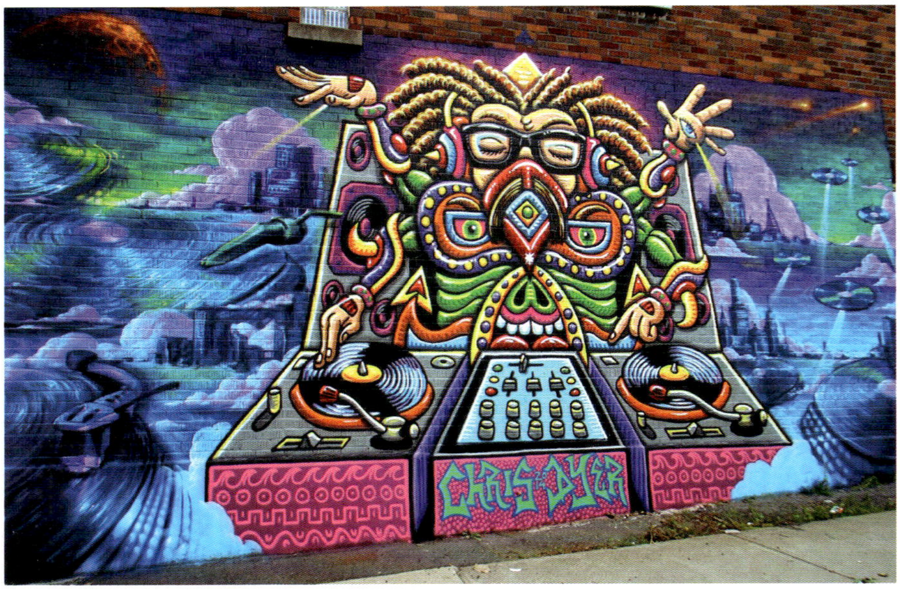

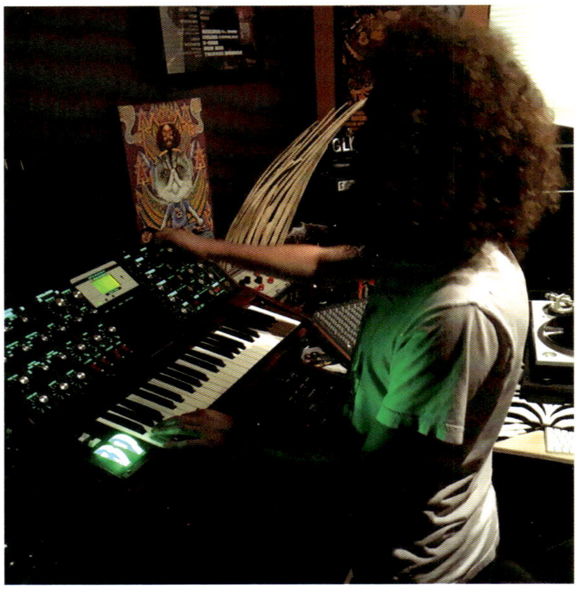

I Love music in all of its diversity and power. Good cultural vibrations uplift my soul as well as the masses. I have been collecting vinyl records ever since my dad gave me his old record player and LPs in the year 2000. Back then, you could go to any pawn shop and buy the best records for a buck each. Eventually I bought myself some proper "Technique 1200" turntables, so I could to learn how to play my favourite gems at art shows. As my alter-ego **"Selector El Flyer"**, I enjoy making Mixtapes where I can tell a story through the songs that I domino, and then share these on the Positive Creations Soundcloud.

One day I spotted pics of **"The Gaslamp Killer"** rocking my clothing at his performances. He's a DJ/Producer from LA who I was a big fan of, so I bigged him up with a nice mural in Montreal (a collabo piece with my homie **Monk-e**). GLK (his real name is Will) then hits me up out of nowhere and commissioned me to do a portrait of his cute cat Charlie. Cat portraits are not really something I do, but I was stoked to get hired by him and just did my magic, including his turntablism vibes into it too! Will loved it and we've become good friends through the years, always visiting each other when in town, to share quality conversations and new tunes.

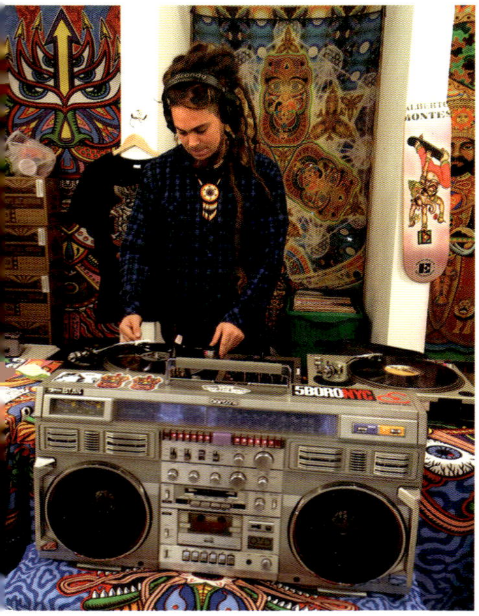

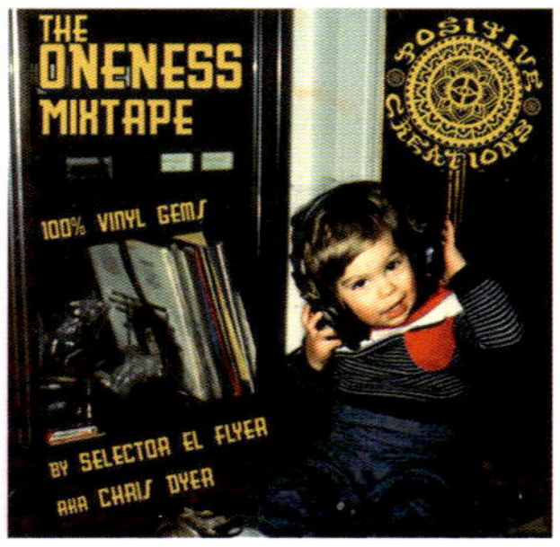

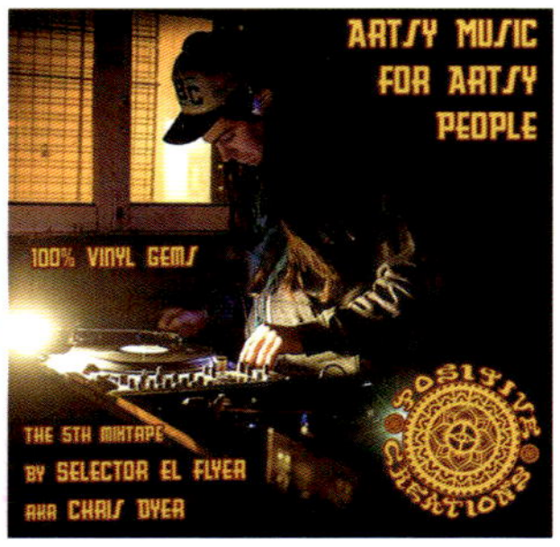

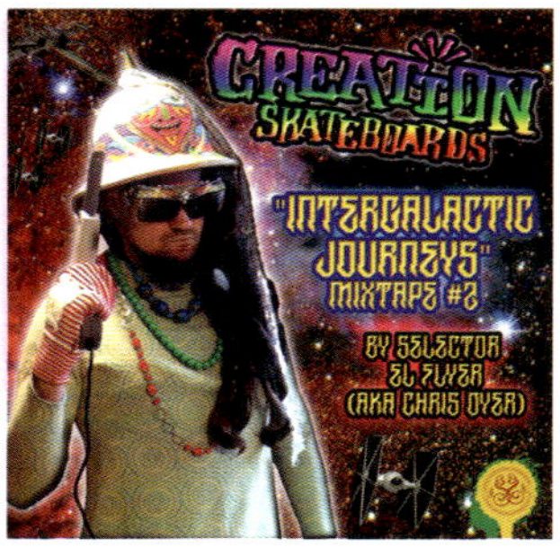

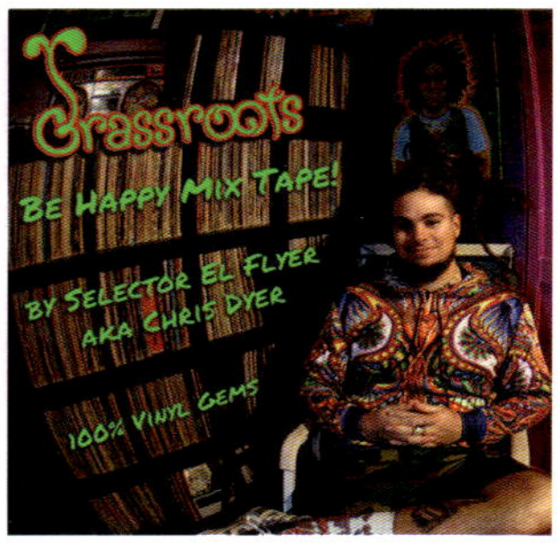

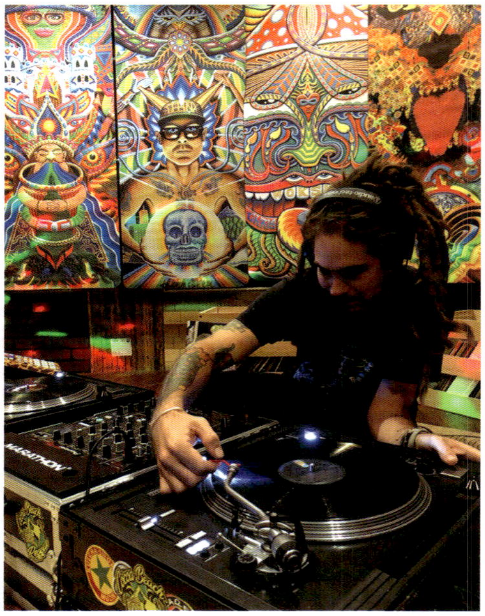

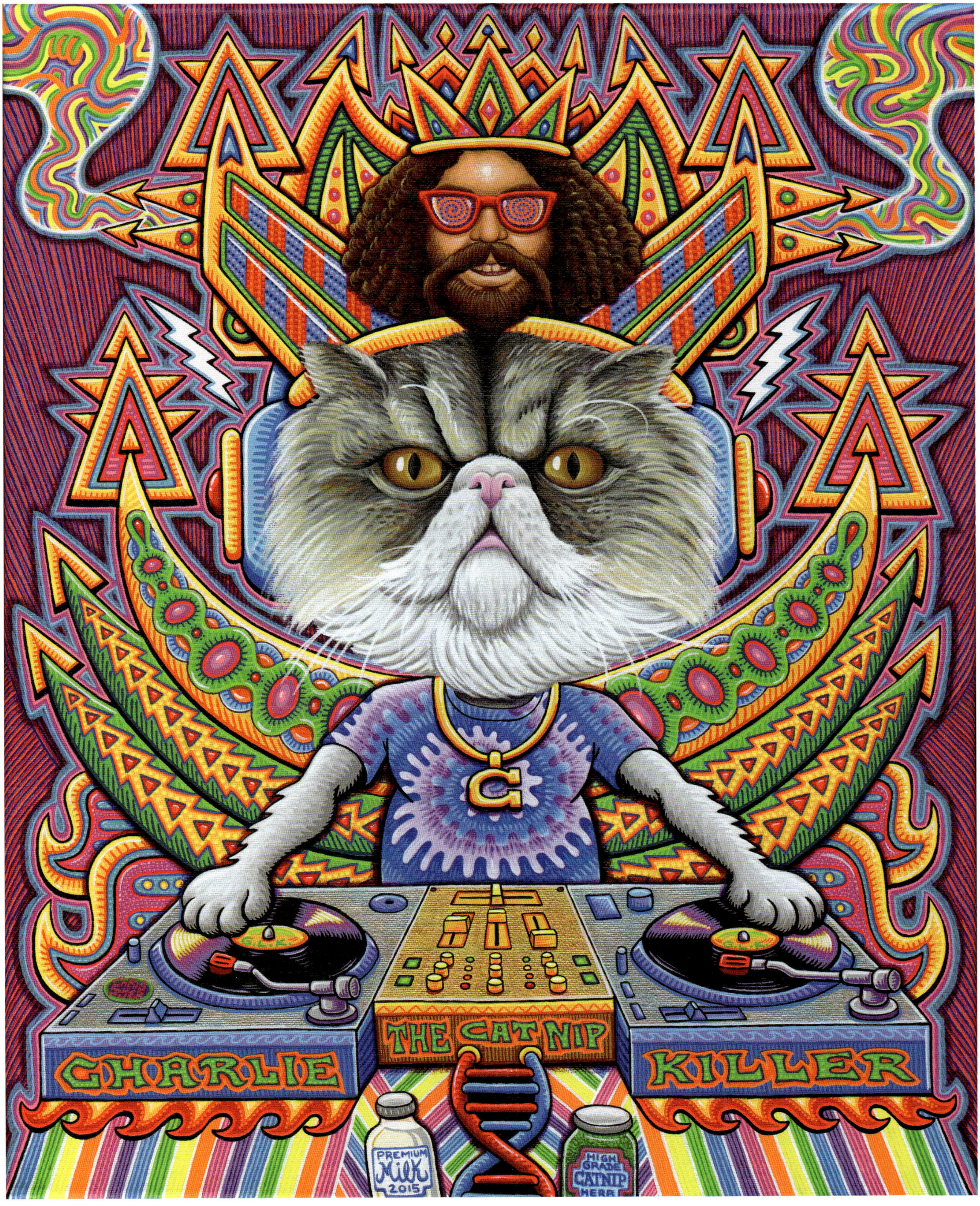

"Charlie The Catnip Killer" Acrylics on canvas, 2015

ATLANTIC OCEAN

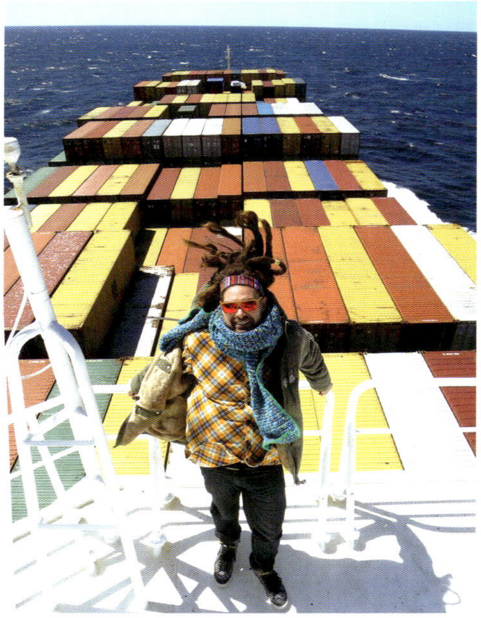

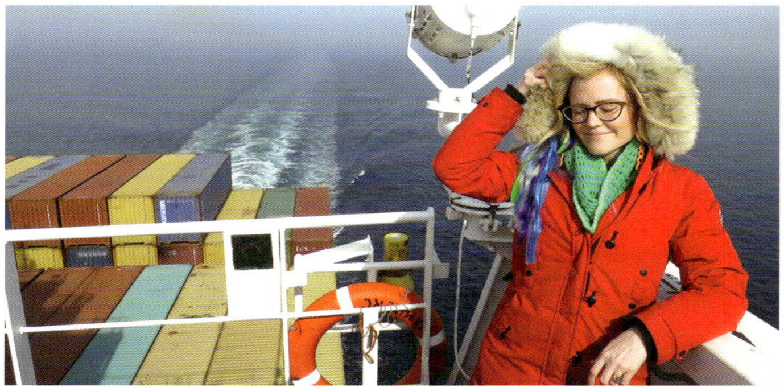

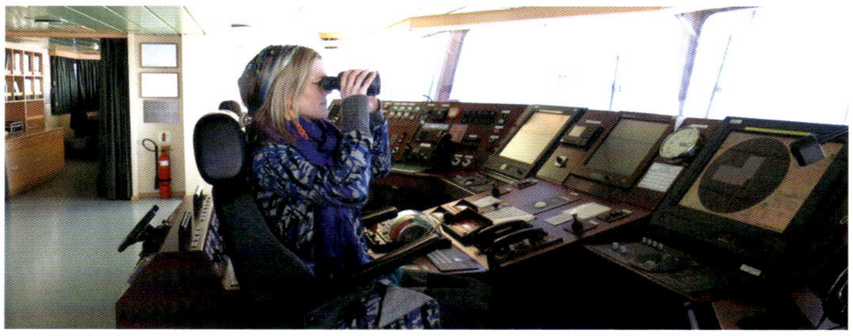

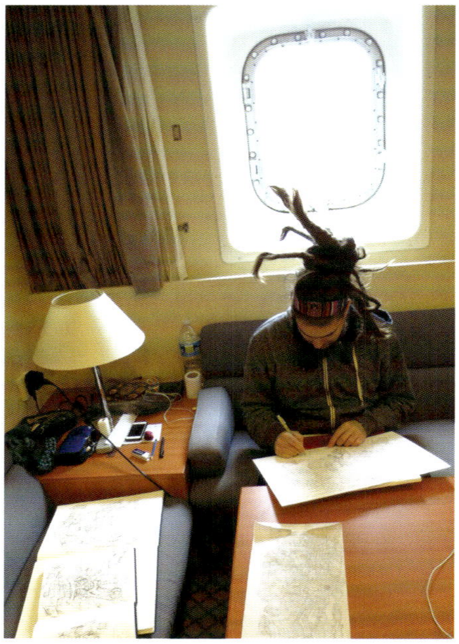

So after four months of staying at Valerie's parents' Belgian home I was going crazy. My beloved was a bit better, but physically unable to take a flight back home. So our escape plan was to get a room in a cargo boat and cross the Atlantic Ocean in ten days. The "MSC Ilona" was a German ship bigger than the Titanic, carrying two thousand containers, twenty Filipino workers and five civilian passengers. Crossing an endless ocean was scary at first, but then became relaxing. It was pure nature, with no boundaries, politics, or internet. I spent most of my time in our suite drawing up this illustration for a client, based on a trippy drawing I did back in 1998. I made some structural changes to it, and improved the line-work, but it was still about a sedated soul, entrapped on an intense voyage to nowhere.

Leaving Europe in this way was a good slow transition out of our disappointing winter. The ocean vibrations cooled down our broken hearts. I was sad that Valerie no longer felt like she was up to having a child. Yet we were so happy and relieved once we saw the New York skyline in our horizon, as that meant we were close to our Canadian home, ready for a new chapter of healing.

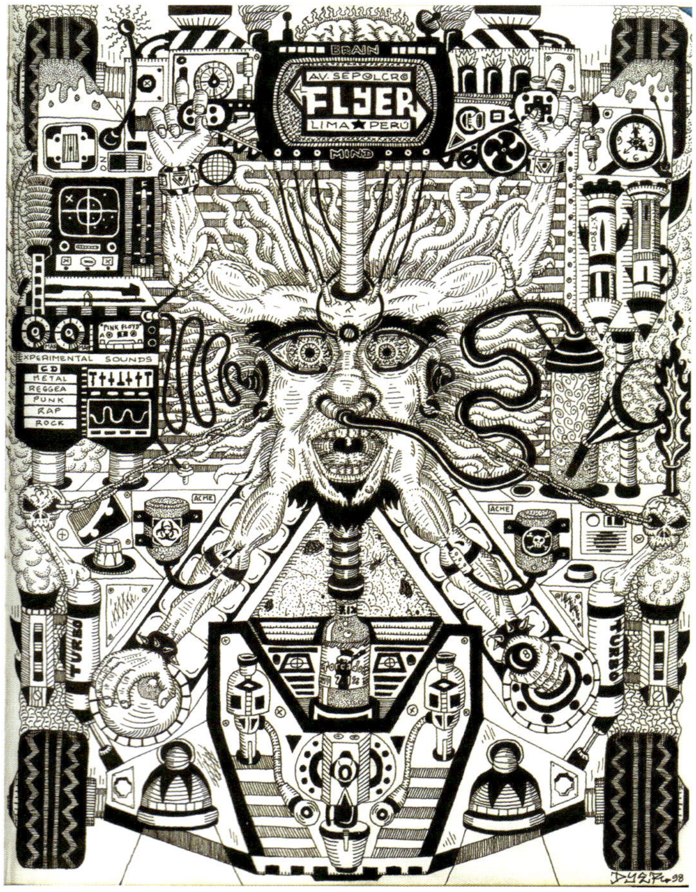

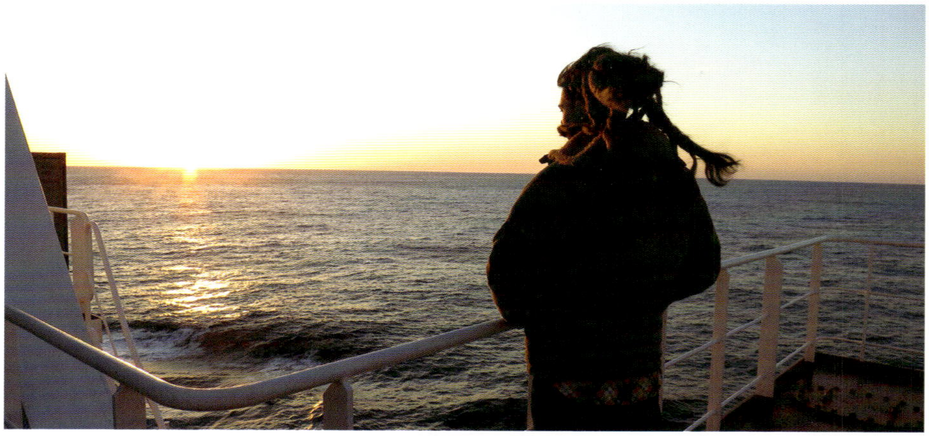

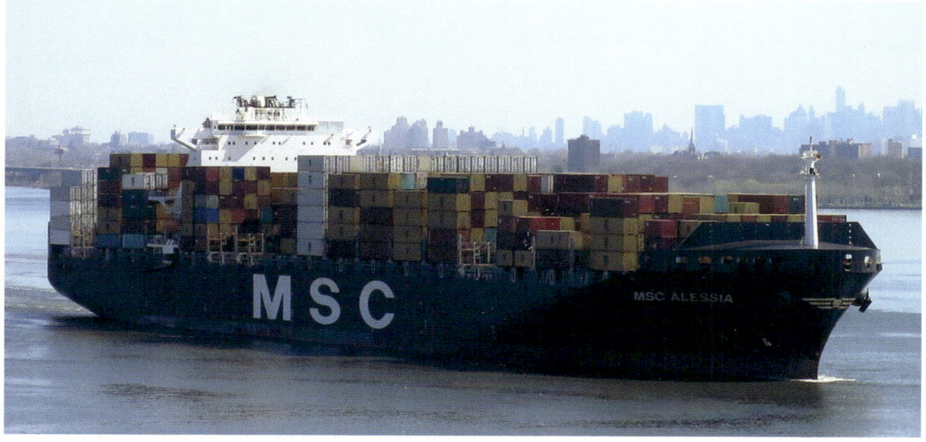

Next Page: **"Sedated Slave-Ship"** Ink and Photoshop, 2015

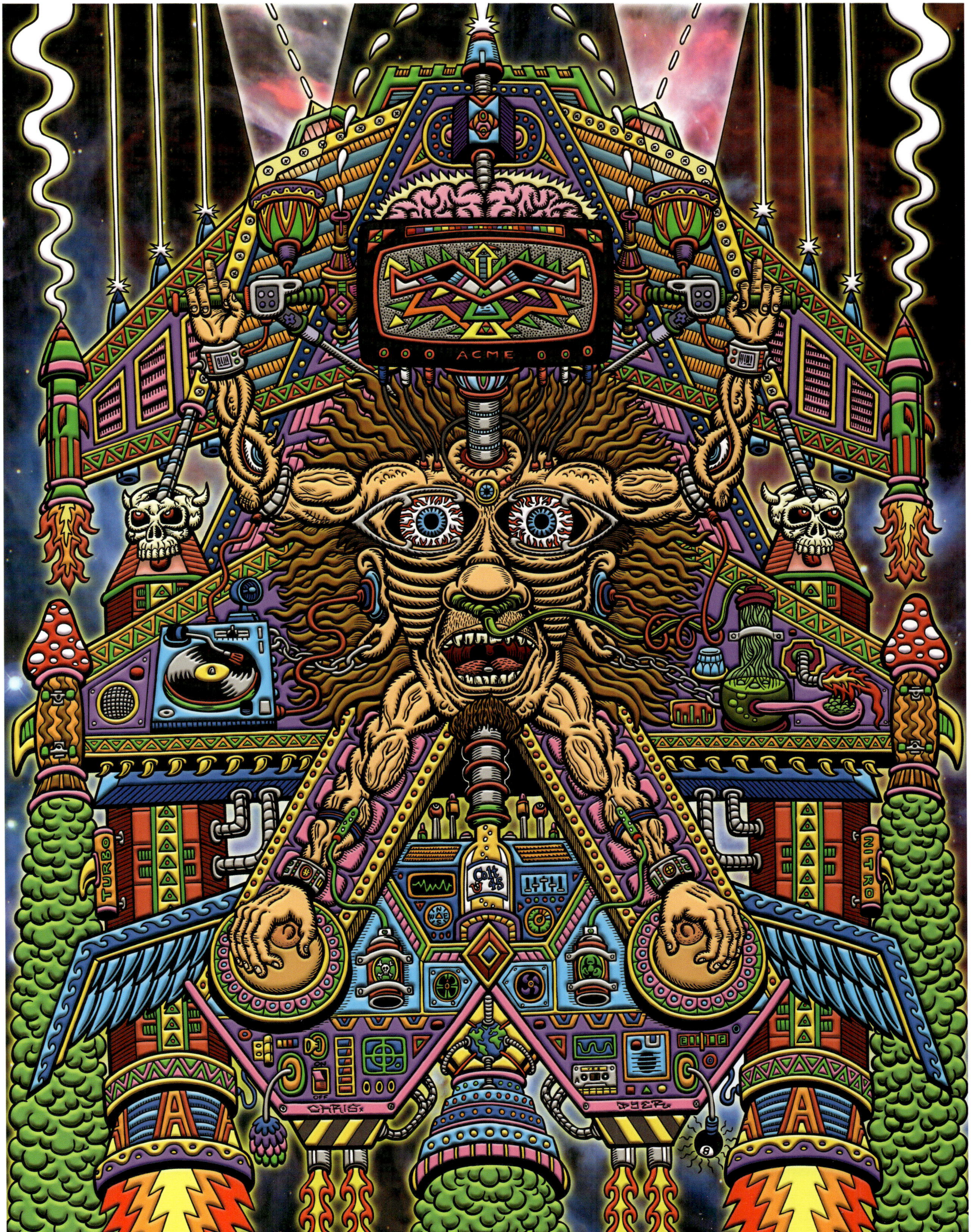
ACME
TURBO
NITRO
ON
OFF
CHRIS
DYER

Being back in Montreal was great, especially during summer, where I did so much street art with friends. My parents visited us from Peru and we even had our friends Alex and Allyson Grey come over for dinner one night, while in town for an event. Valerie couldn't fly or travel anymore, but she understood I couldn't keep turning down out of town jobs. So she gave me the green light to accept more gigs abroad, which was good for my career, but bad for our relationship. She felt a bit abandoned and stopped loving me in the same way. This led me into a depression, so I started to smoke weed again, as to feel better in the moment. It had been five years since I had quit smoking, for a few different reasons, but now it was back with a vengeance! The piece to the right, **"The Divine Comedian"** came out of that stoner year, which was weird, confusing and kinda funny. It's about keeping a good attitude, despite the absurdity of life. It is also about the hidden wisdom of people who play the "Clown" or "Heyoka" role, as to lift up moods.

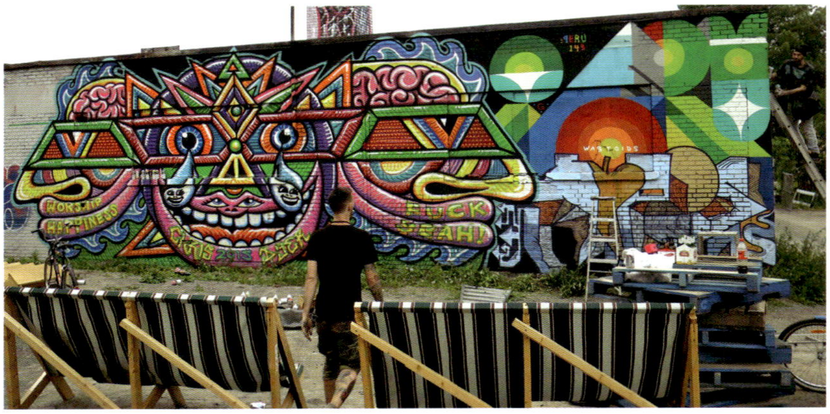

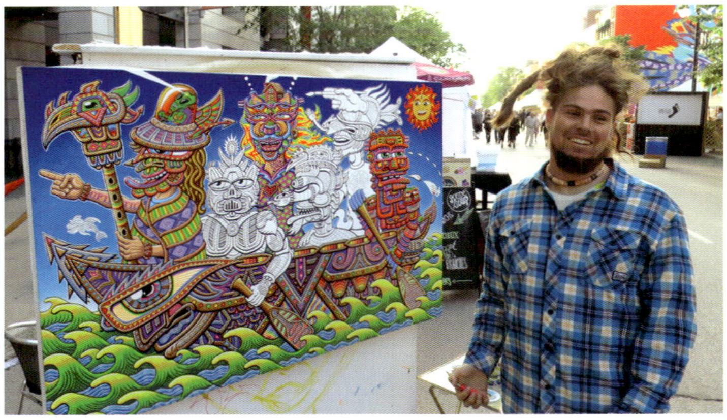

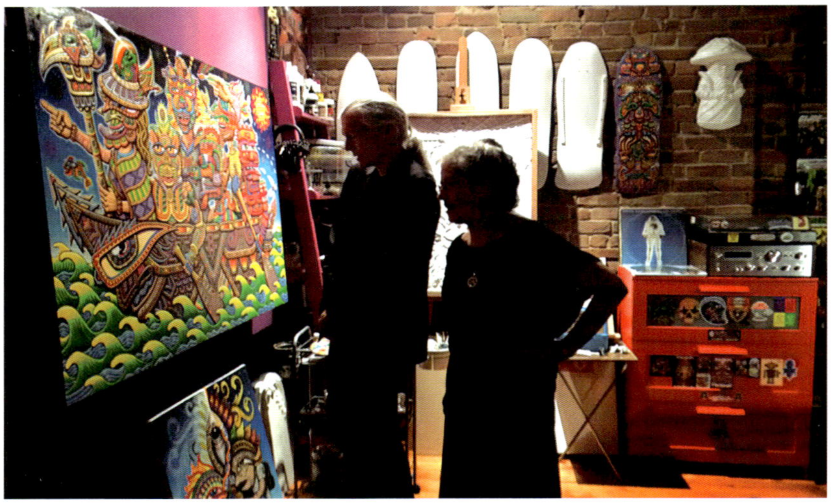

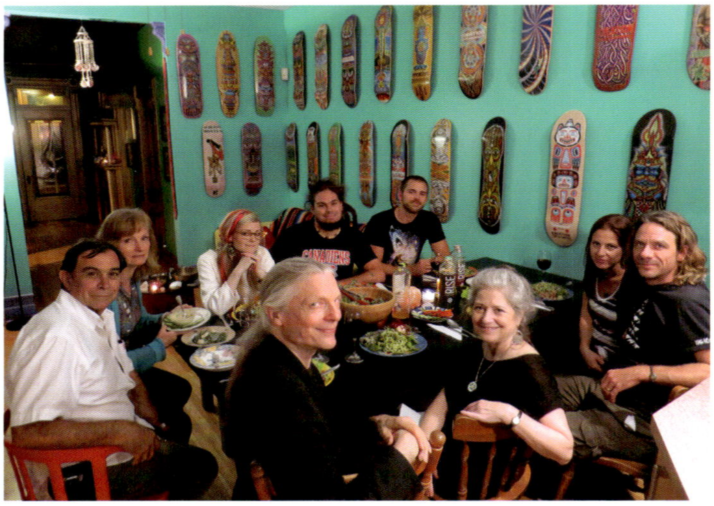

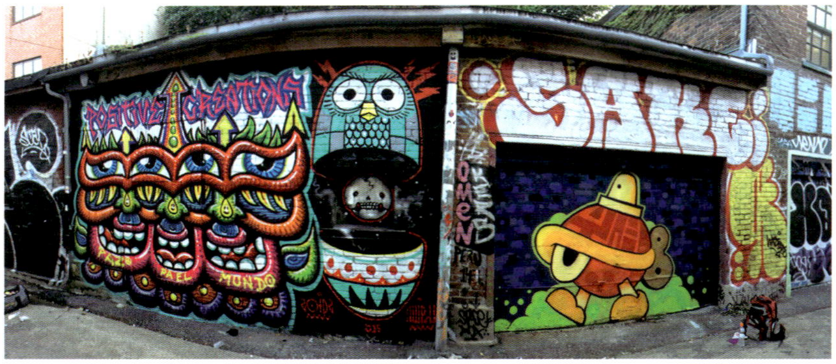

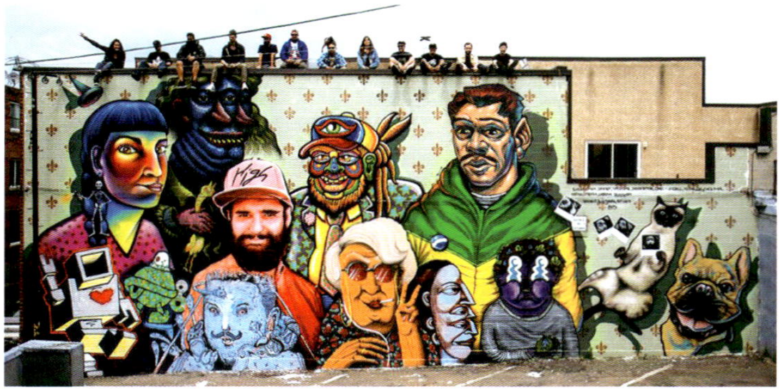

But the painting I mostly focused on in 2015 was the ambitious **"Optimystics Journey"**. That piece is a "Hero's Journey", inspired by a little "Haida" native drawing I saw in the Civilization Museum of Ottawa. In my own narrative, it is about a group of archetypal characters, traveling through the Ocean of Imagination, from a chaotic self-destructive world, towards a harmonious, clean and peaceful world. It can also be seen as a metaphor for the journey of an individual person transforming from corruption into balance. The Archetypes I chose to include in the boat are (from left to right) the shaman leader, the warrior soldier, the housewife mama, the rejected freak, the visionary artist and the hater troll (a negative human trait we can't seem to shake, even when moving forward). Each character is a reflection of aspects of myself and the people in my life at this time, like Valerie and our cat Leon. Also, they are reflections of aspects all humanity carries inside its journey of self realization.

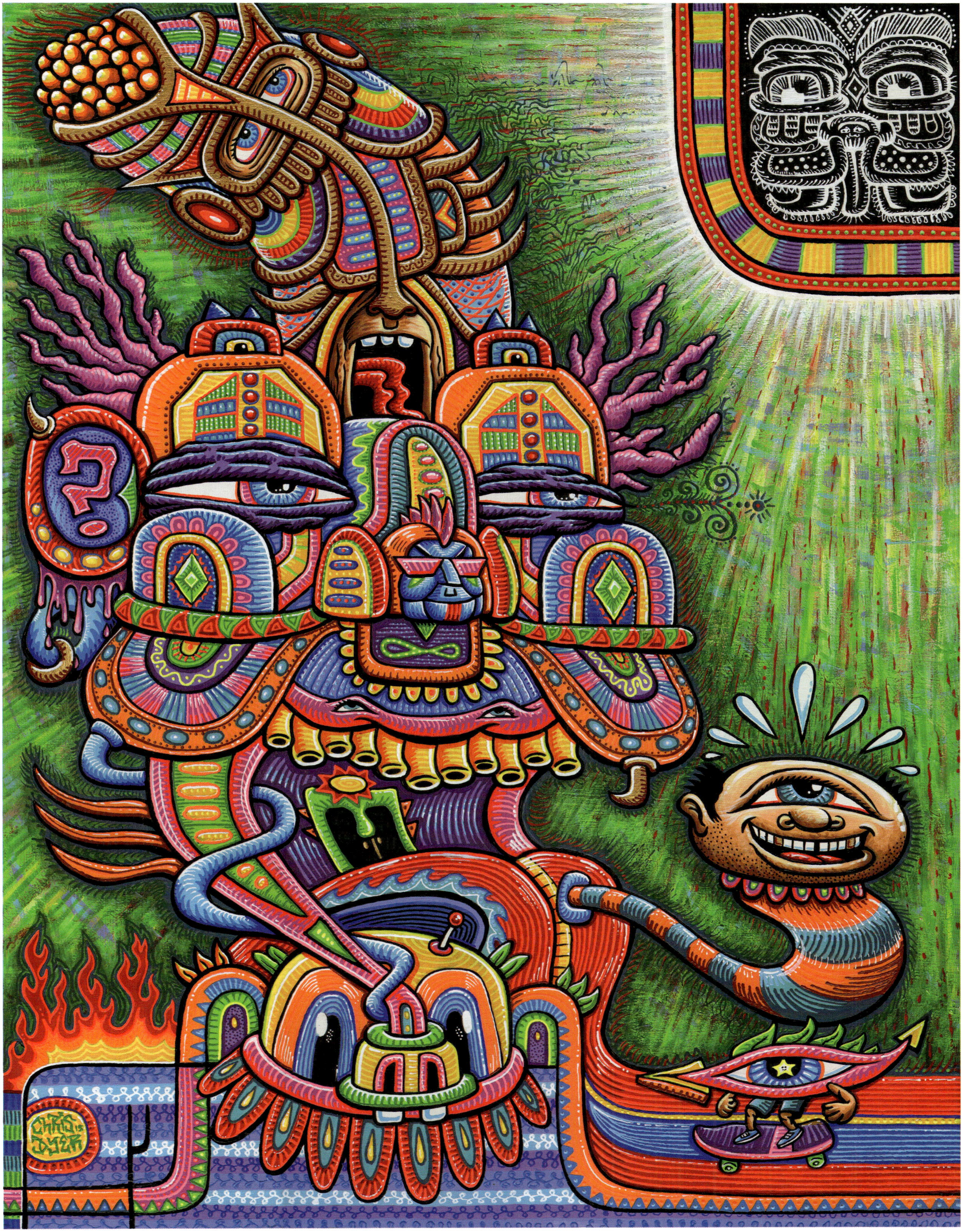

"The Divine Comedian" Acrylics on wood, 2015

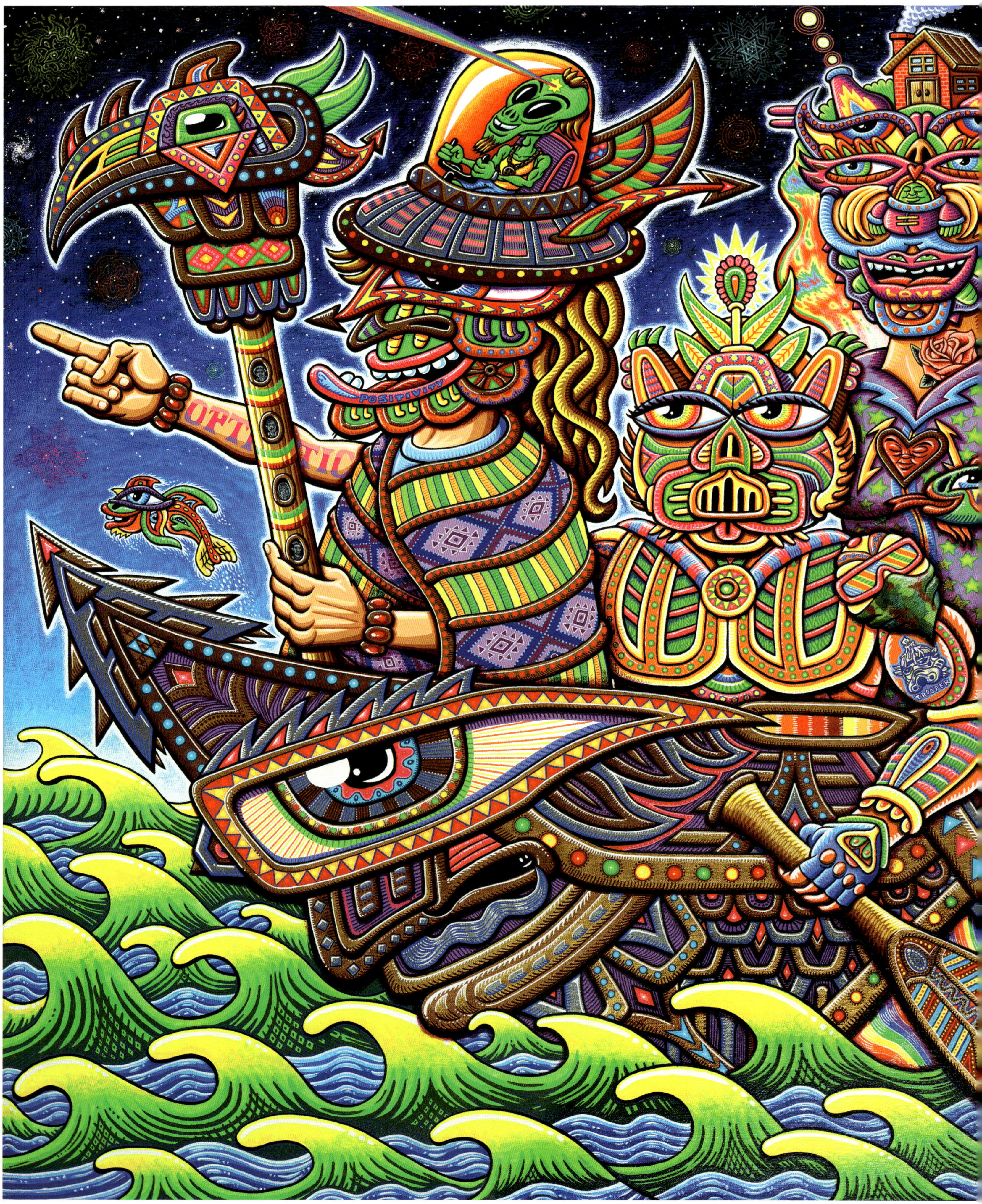

POSITIVITY
LOVE

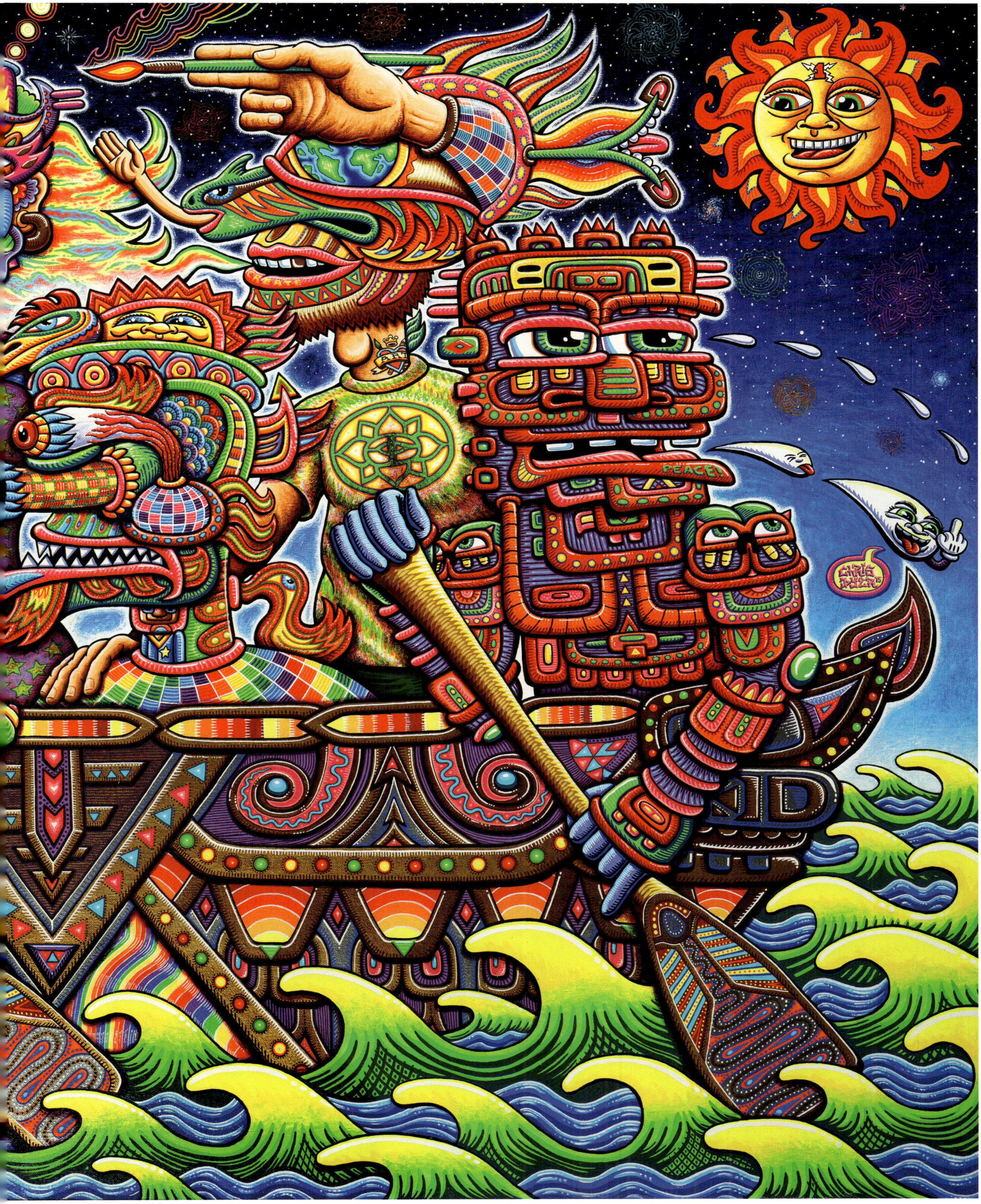

"Optimystics Journey" Acrylics on canvas, 2015

TARAPOTO

By the end of 2015 I was burnt out and my marriage was falling apart. Valerie was unhappy when I would leave on art missions and I would be unhappy when I would decline them, to stay home for her. So we started fighting a lot and separating emotionally. By then I was smoking so much weed that my throat and lungs where raw, my paranoia levels where up and my mental sharpness was down. I wanted to quit smoking, but I was just too addicted to the comforting buzz that medicine gave me.

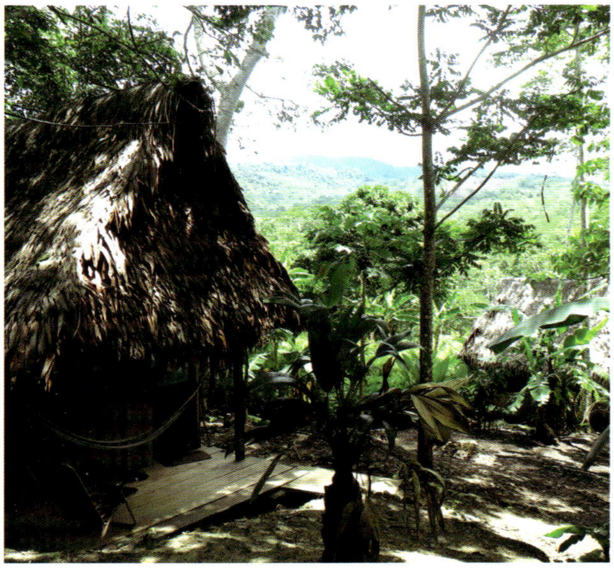

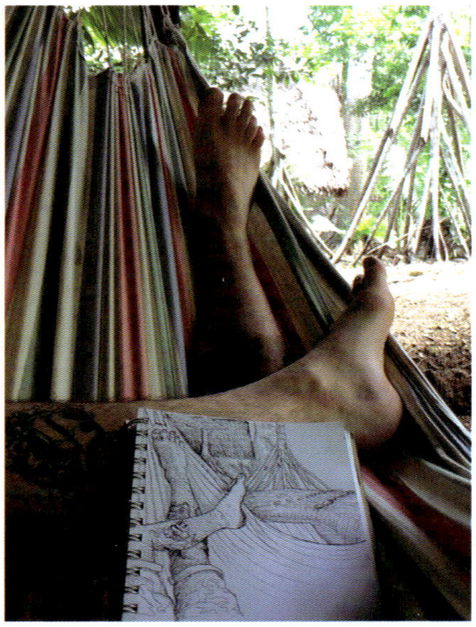

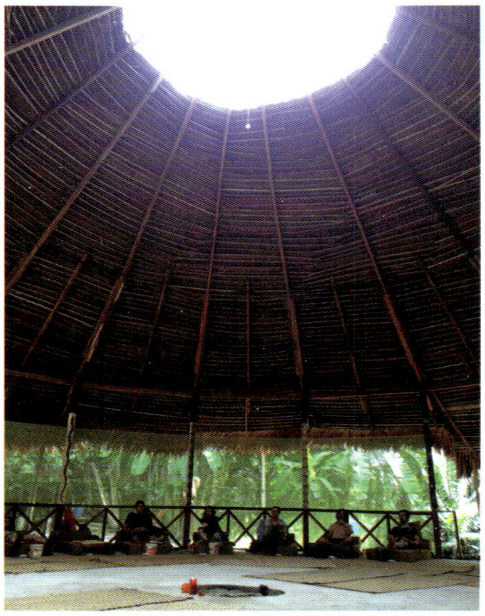

So my solution to this was to go back to the jungle of Peru, to the new center (Katari) that my shaman Herbert Quinteros had just opened in Tarapoto. Herbert made me do a "dieta" (diet) of a power plant called **"Ajo Sacha"**, as to detoxify my body and get more connected with my heart. We also did a couple of **Ayahuasca** ceremonies, that where violent/painful exorcisms of the entity I needed to clean out. I learned so much from Aya's wisdom in those sessions, but I mostly wanted to know if I should stay married or not. She said that the world is in trouble, with a need for all spiritual warriors like me to be out spreading medicine. If I would stay married I might help heal one person, but if I separate, I could go out and fulfill my destiny, spreading good vibrations and healing with thousands of people. So she said I had to do the painful sacrifice of divorcing, as to be of better service to the world.

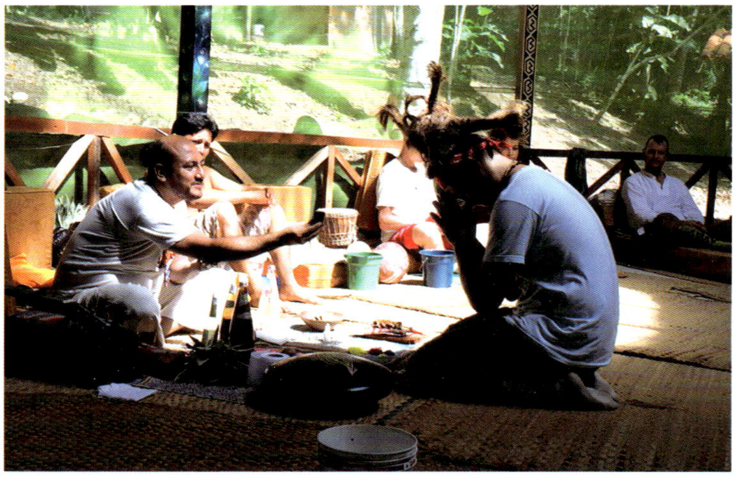

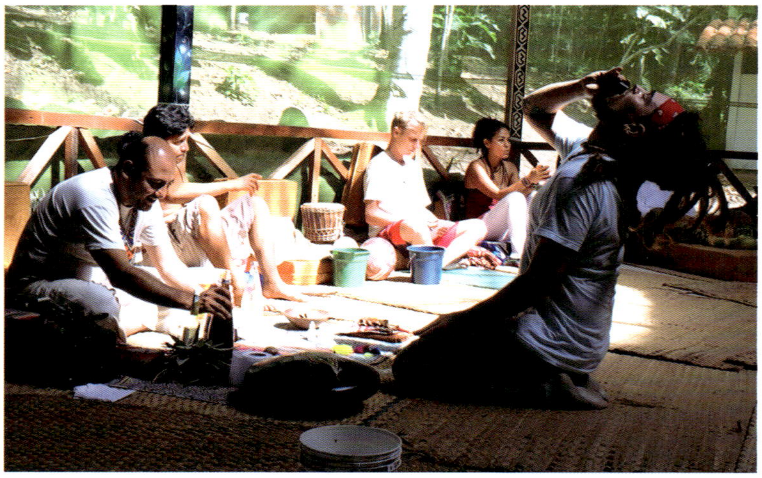

This was a difficult revelation and I cried a lot that week, thinking of how I was about to lose my wife, home and the life I loved. Once I returned to Montreal, I cancelled all my out of town jobs, as to try to make it work with Valerie. But one day she just told me she felt our karmic contract had concluded, and I agreed. We cried together for some days, and a month later I moved out to an apartment of my own, close by, to start a new chapter of my life.

The piece that I expressed in this period, **"Ayalupe Trinity"**, is about trusting the divine mother and surrendering to her wisdom. It is also an ode to Peru, which went from being the land that traumatized me as a kid, into the one that was healing me as an adult. The three virgins represent the different regions of Peru: the jungle, Andes and the desert coast, with the colors of our flag behind them. Also, the Virgin is actually the icon Peruvians used to secretly honor "Pachamama" (Mother Earth) once Christianity was imposed onto the conquered Inca Empire.

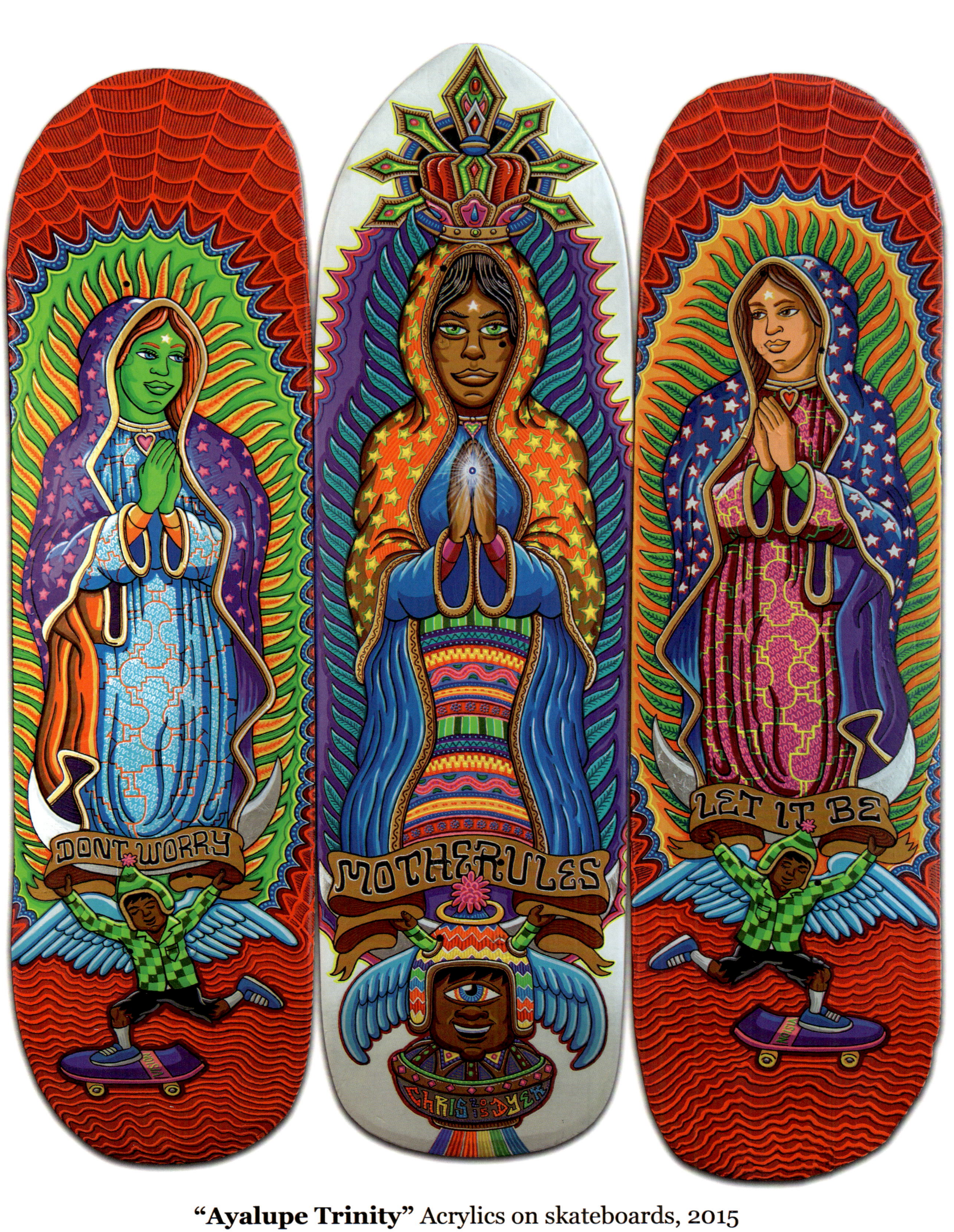

"Ayalupe Trinity" Acrylics on skateboards, 2015

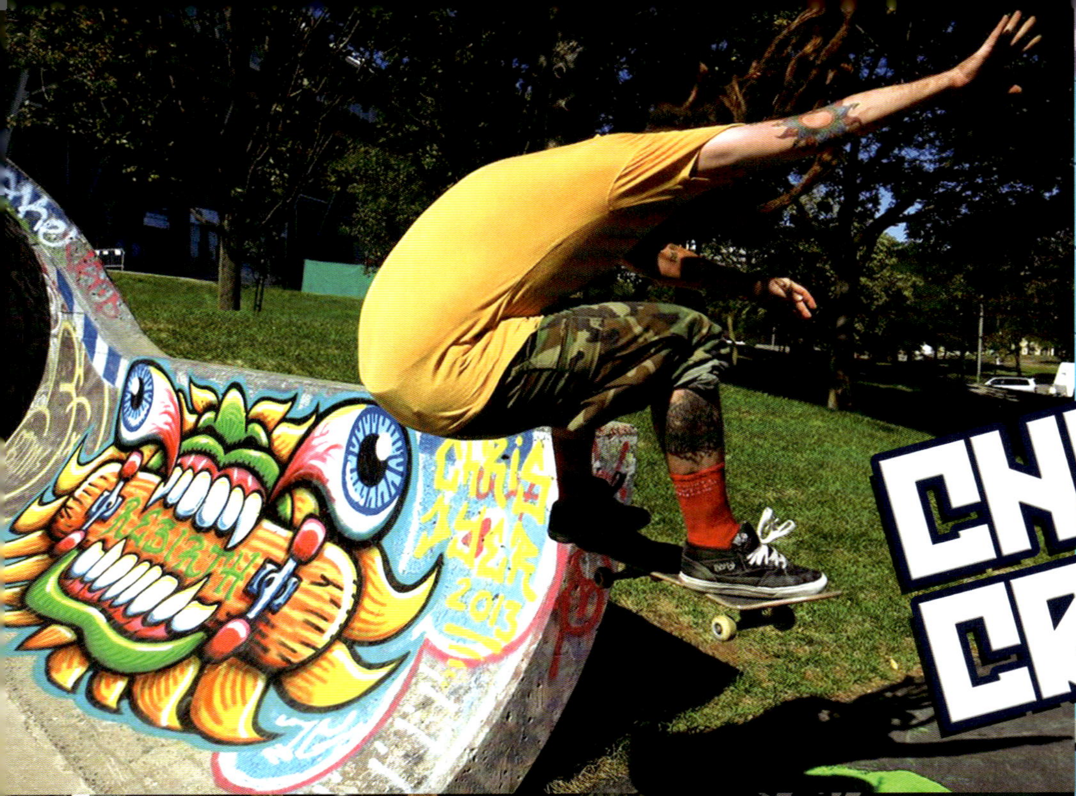

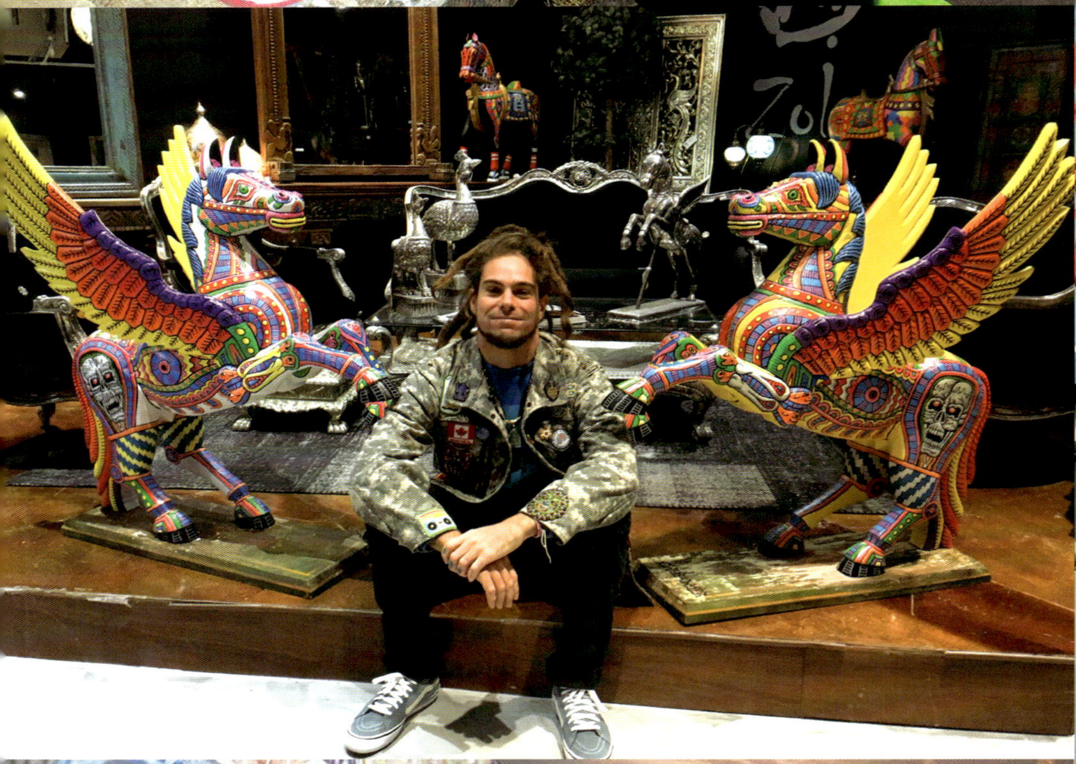

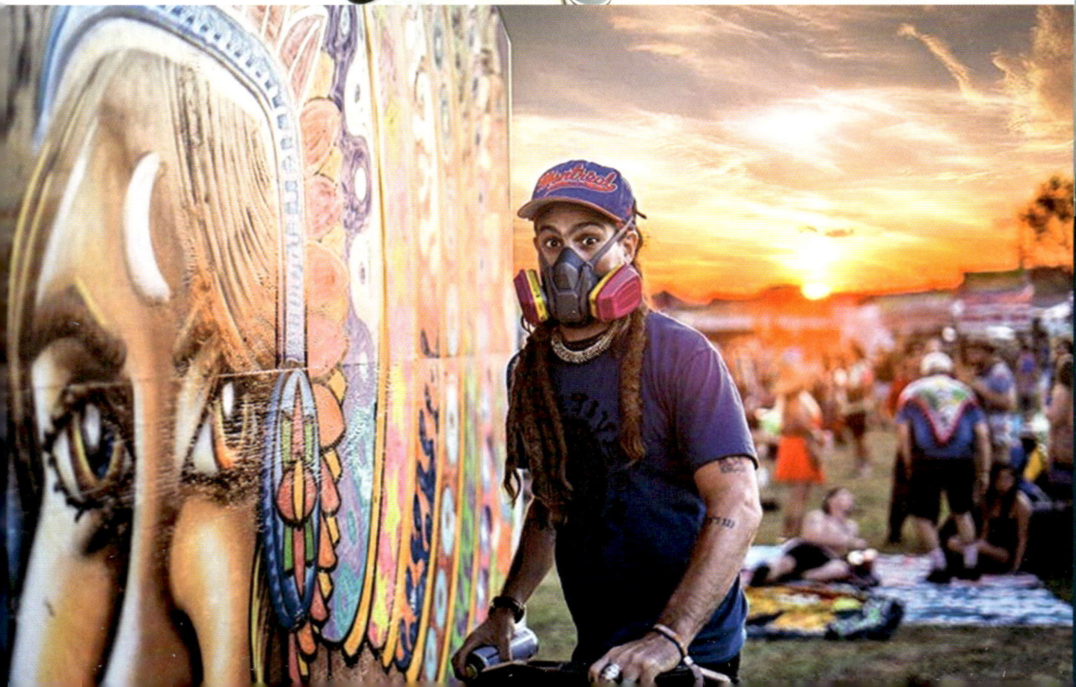

CHAPTER T
CREATIONS

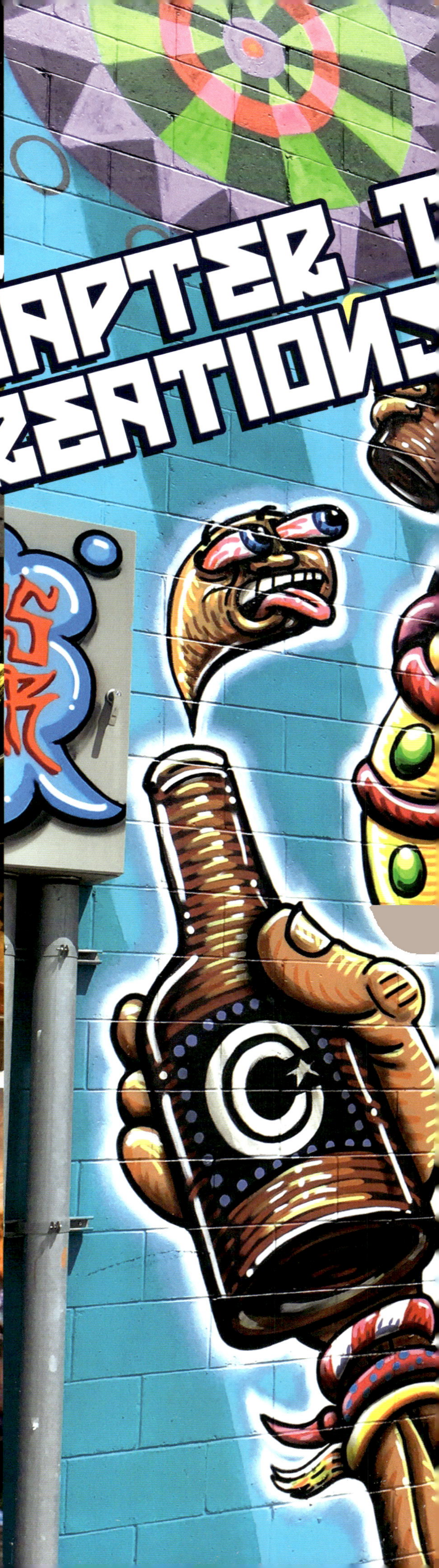

ND IN BETWEEN

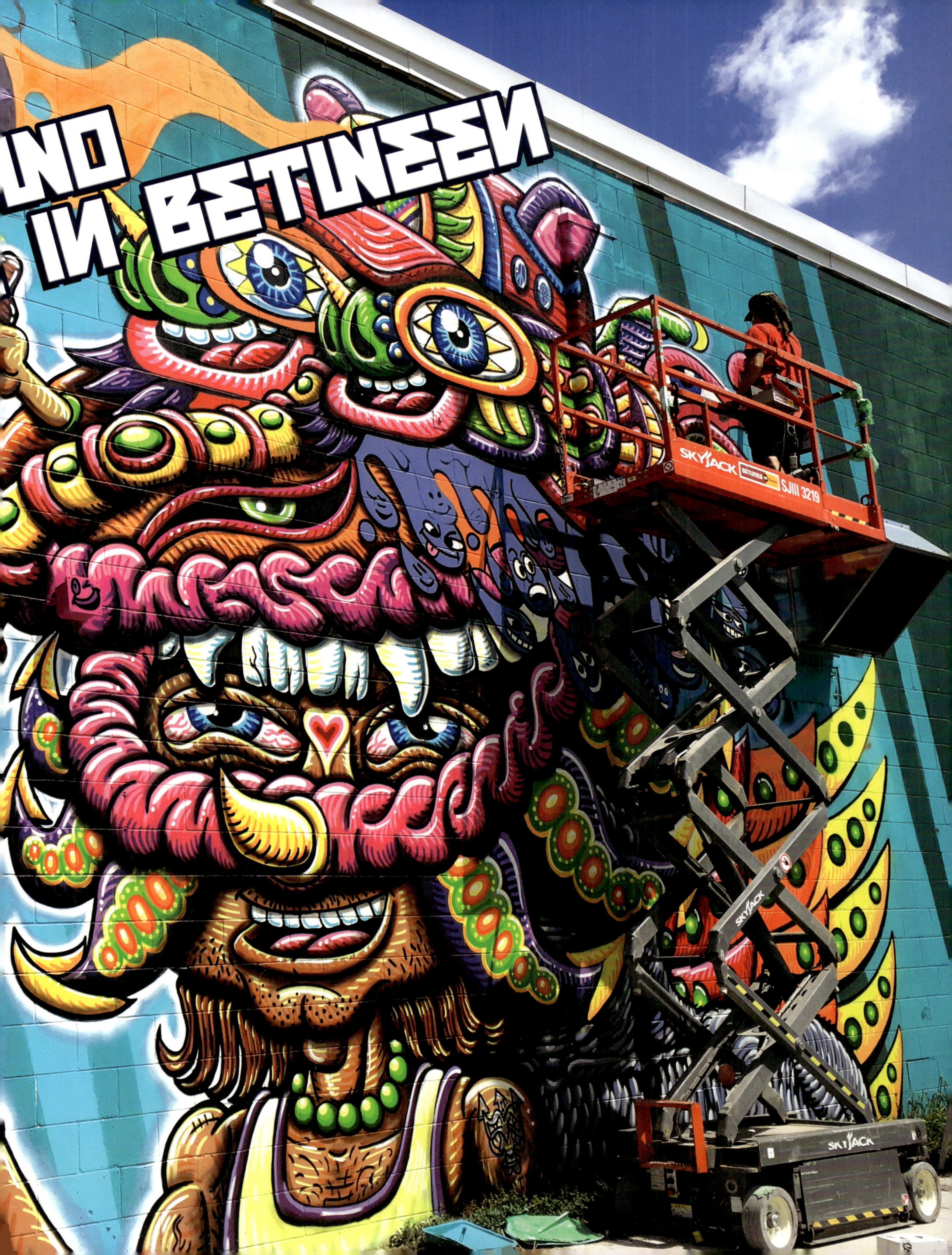

SKATEBOARD ART

As you might have read in my last book, I've been skating since 1986 and still do today. My favorite spot will always be **"The Big O"** in the Montreal Olympic Stadium complex. Once I became an environmentalist in my twenties, I was mostly painting on broken skateboards, as to reuse the wood of boards that would have ended in a landfill. Eventually I had to move on to bigger canvases, as to be able to say more, but I did continue to paint a few boards a year, mostly on my own used ones, which have collected my own concentrated energy.

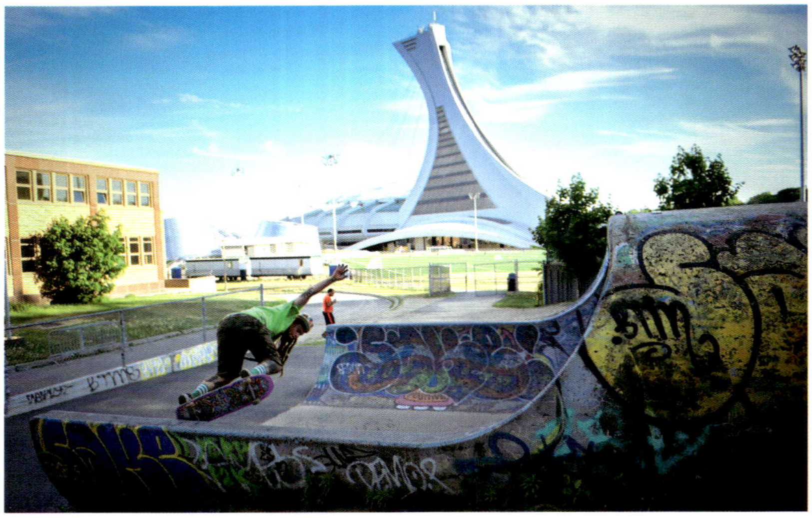

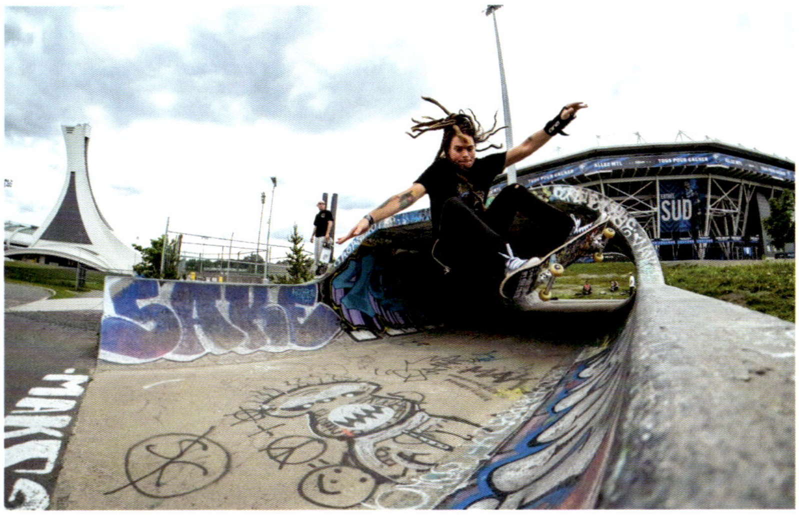

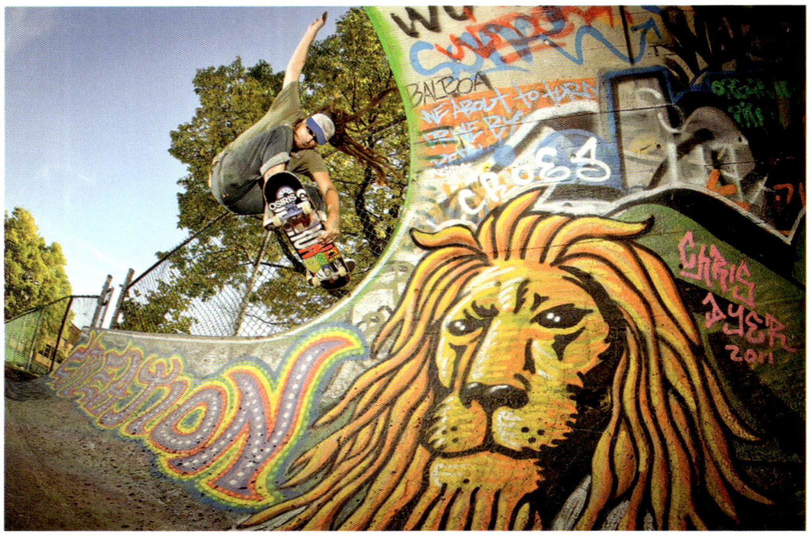

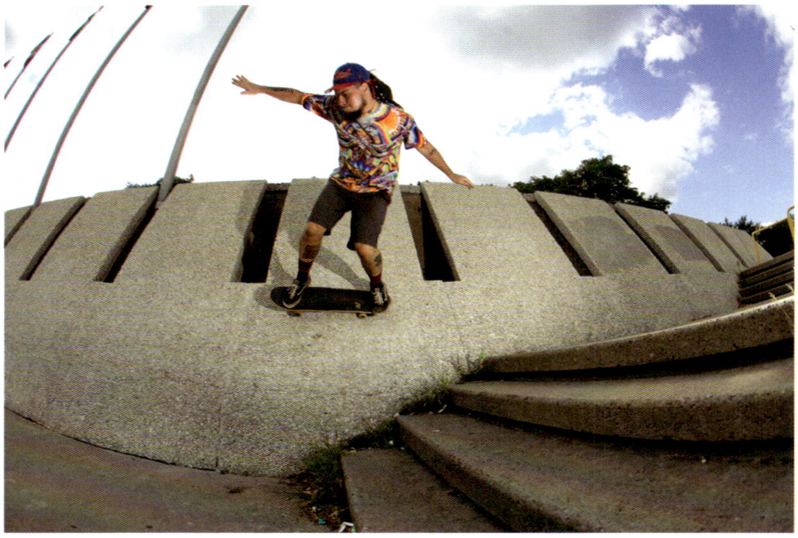

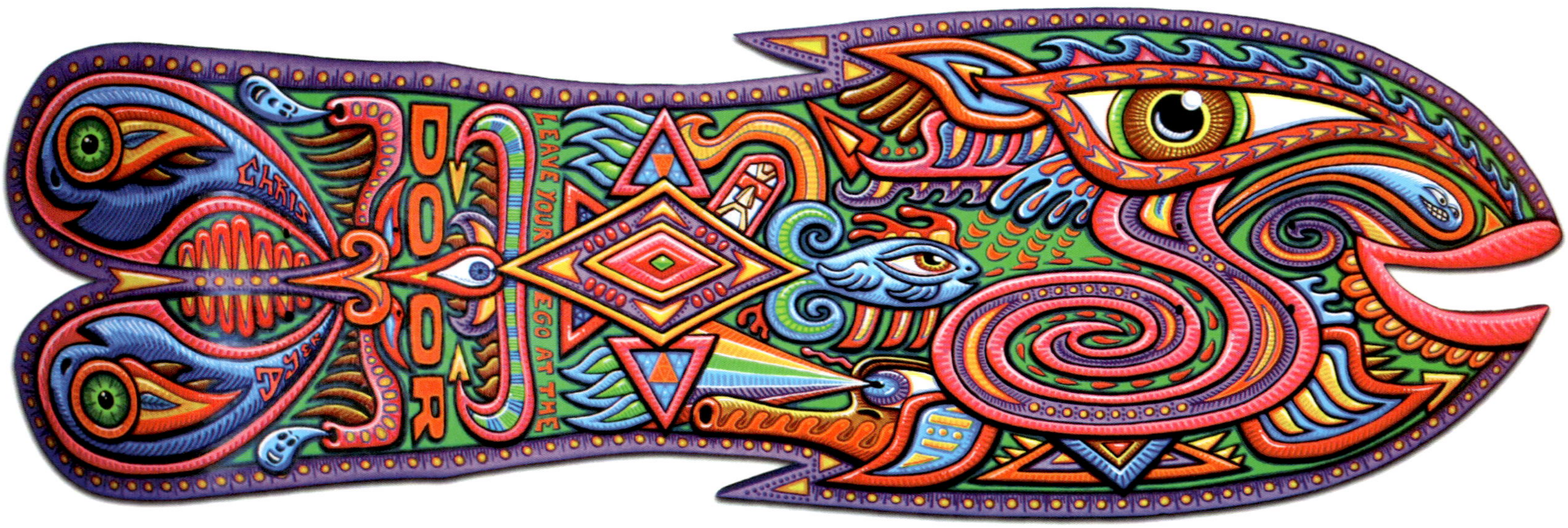

"Pez Pinga" Acrylics, 2014

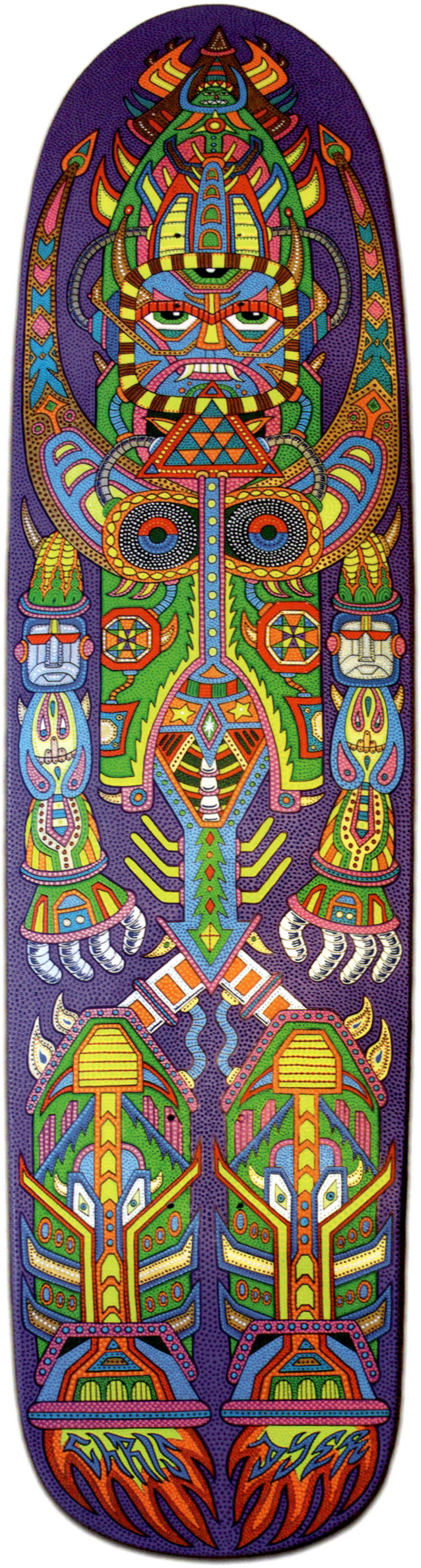

"Freklebot"
Acrylics
2011

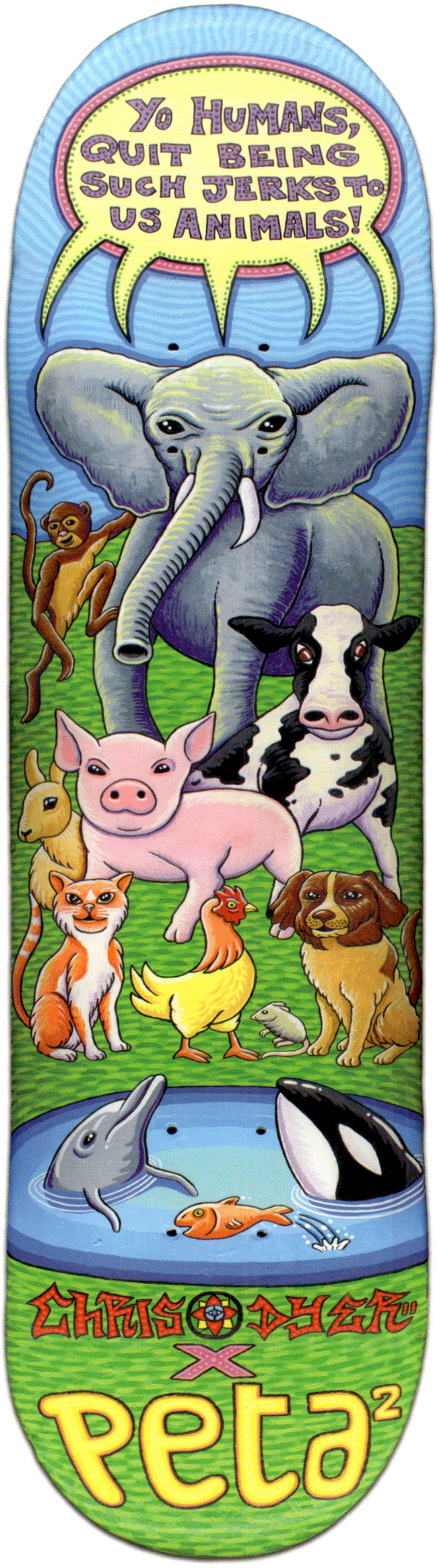

"Please Respect Animals"
Acrylics
2011

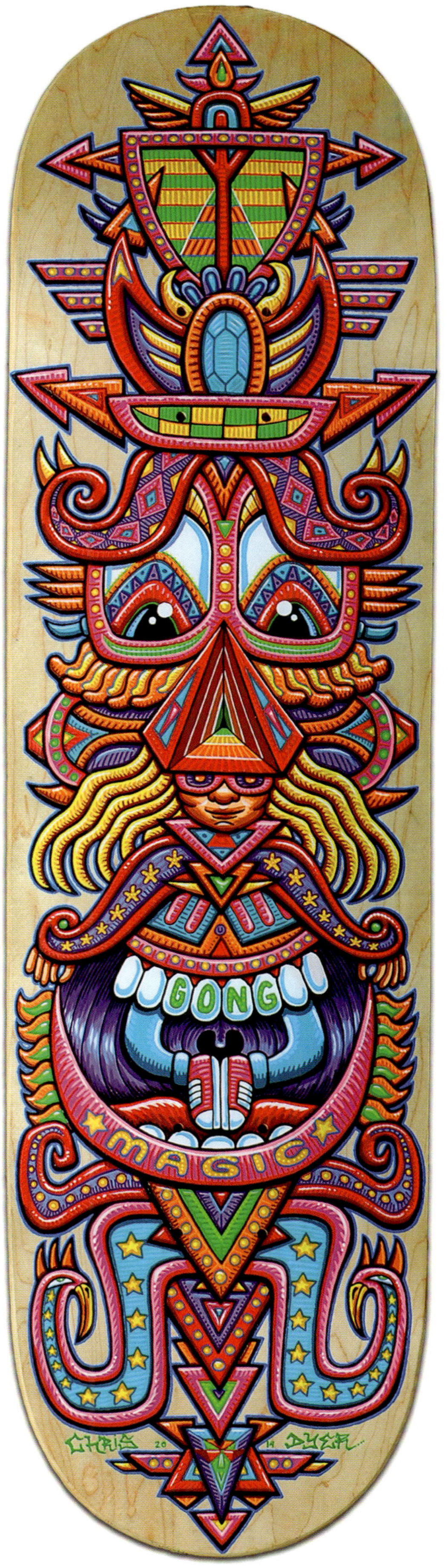

"Gong Show"
Acrylics
2014

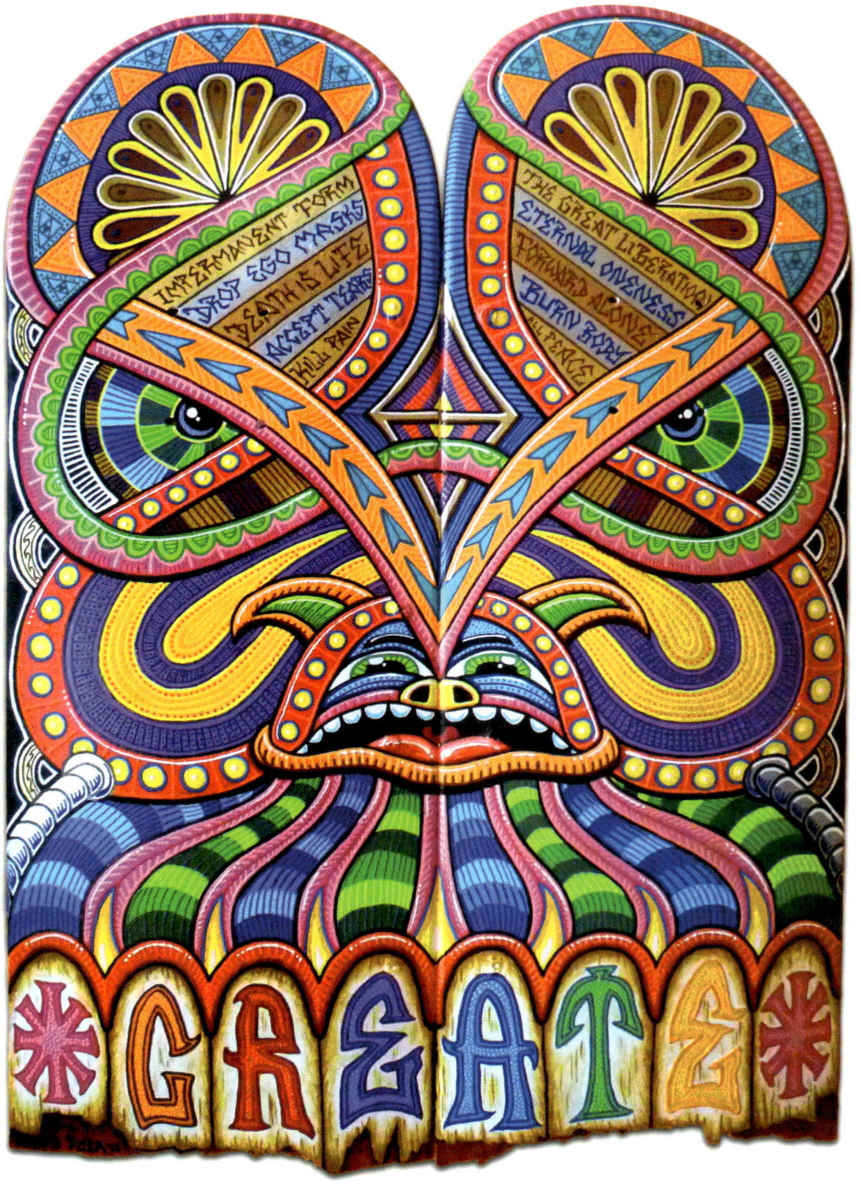

"Create" Acrylics, 2012

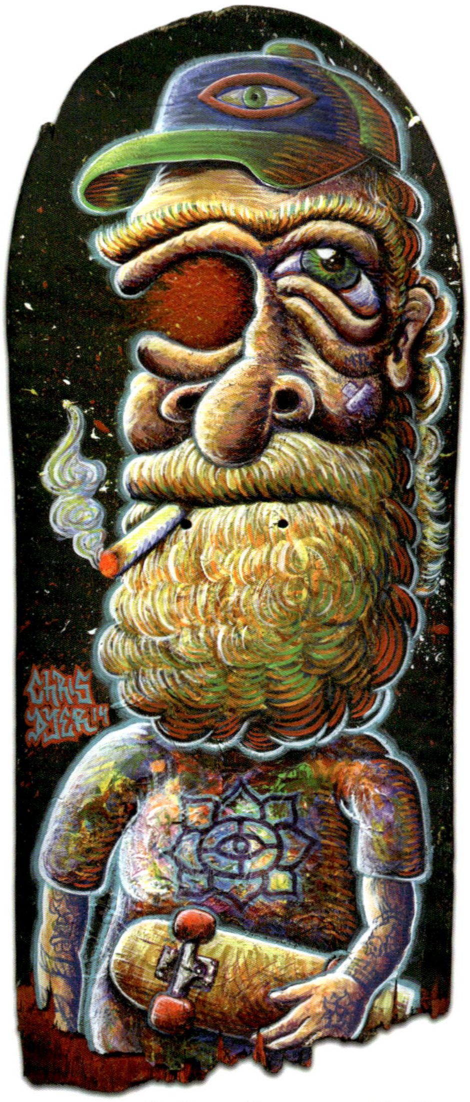

"Tarnished Goods"
Collaboration with **Peter Smolik**
Acrylics, 2014

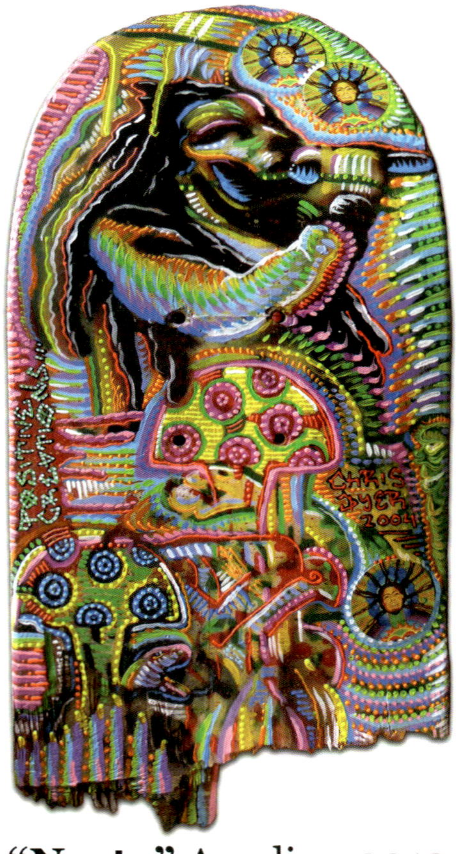

"Nesta" Acrylics, 2012

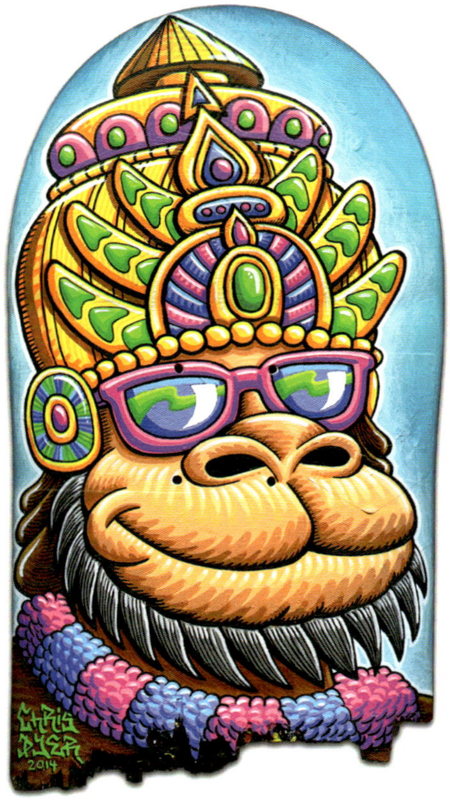

"Trilla Hanuman"
Acrylics, 2014

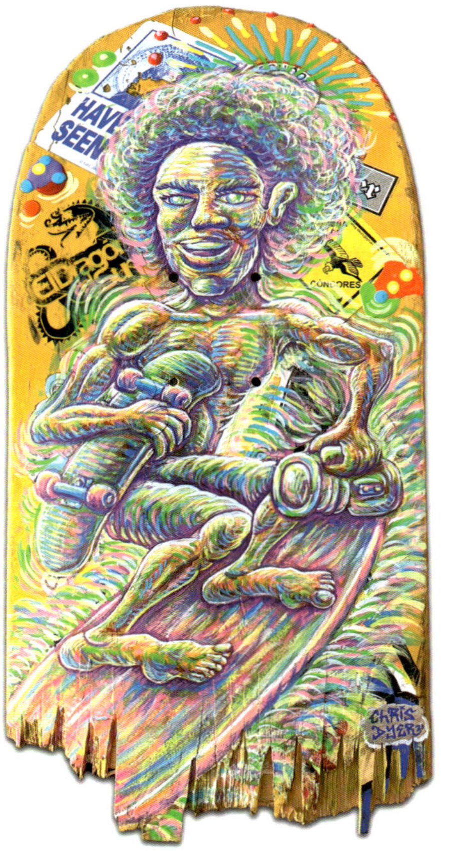

"Ben Zion" Acrylics, 2021

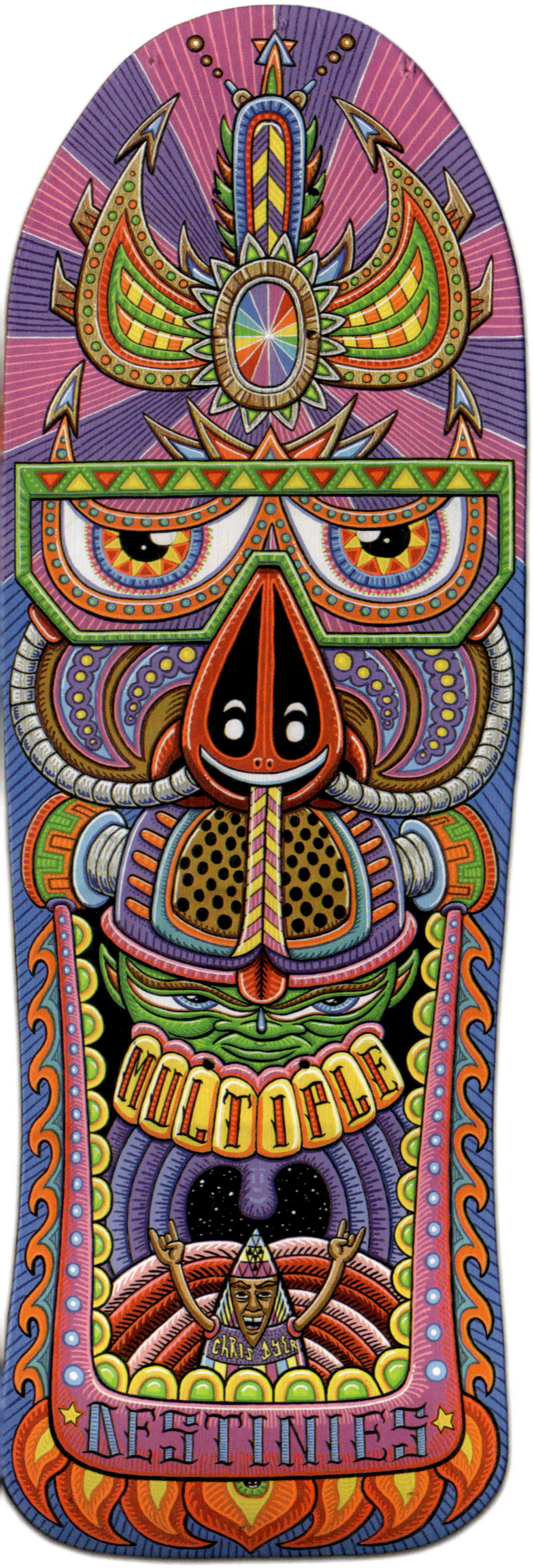

"Multiple Destinies"
Acrylics
2013

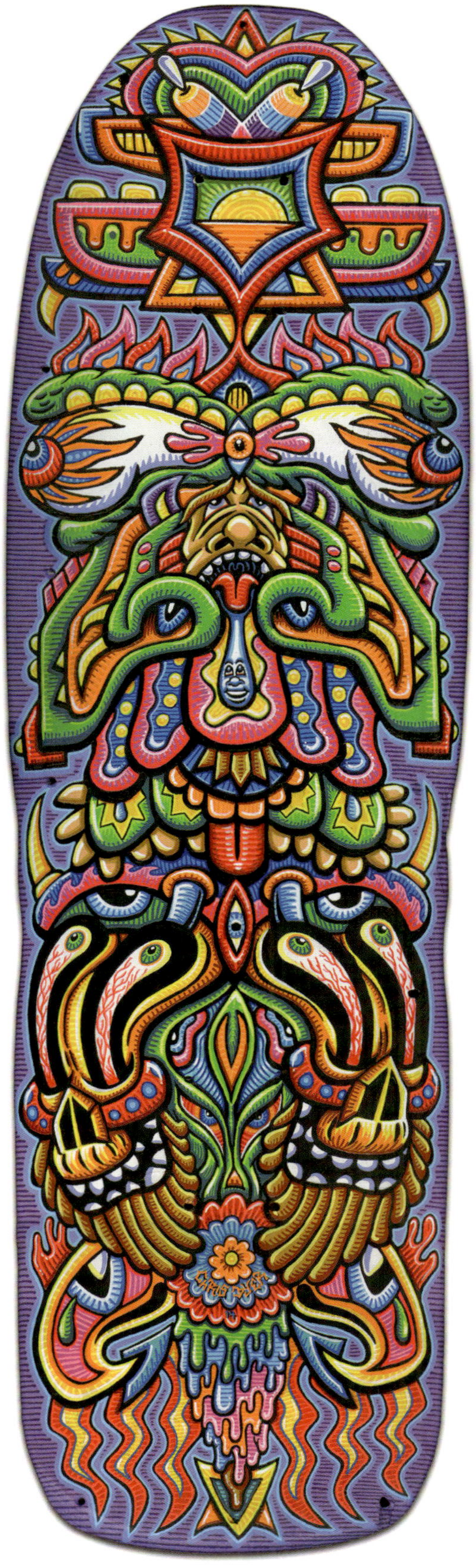

"Strange Ways"
Acrylics
2014

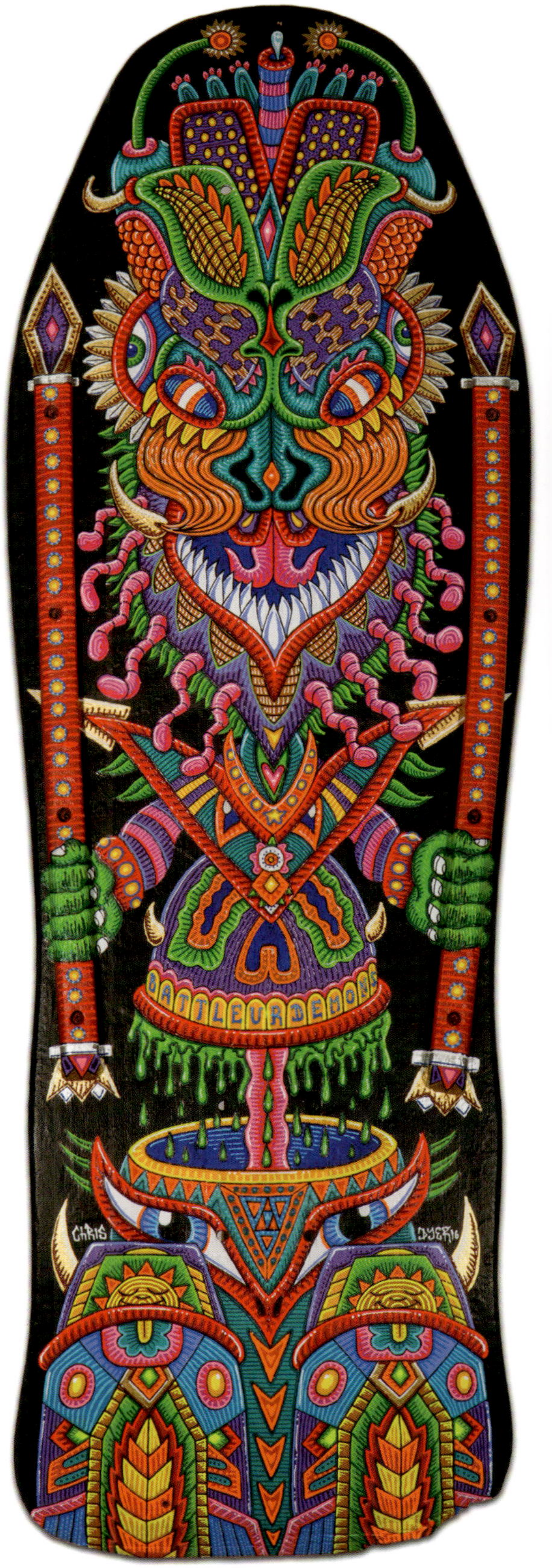

"Face your Demons"
Acrylics
2016

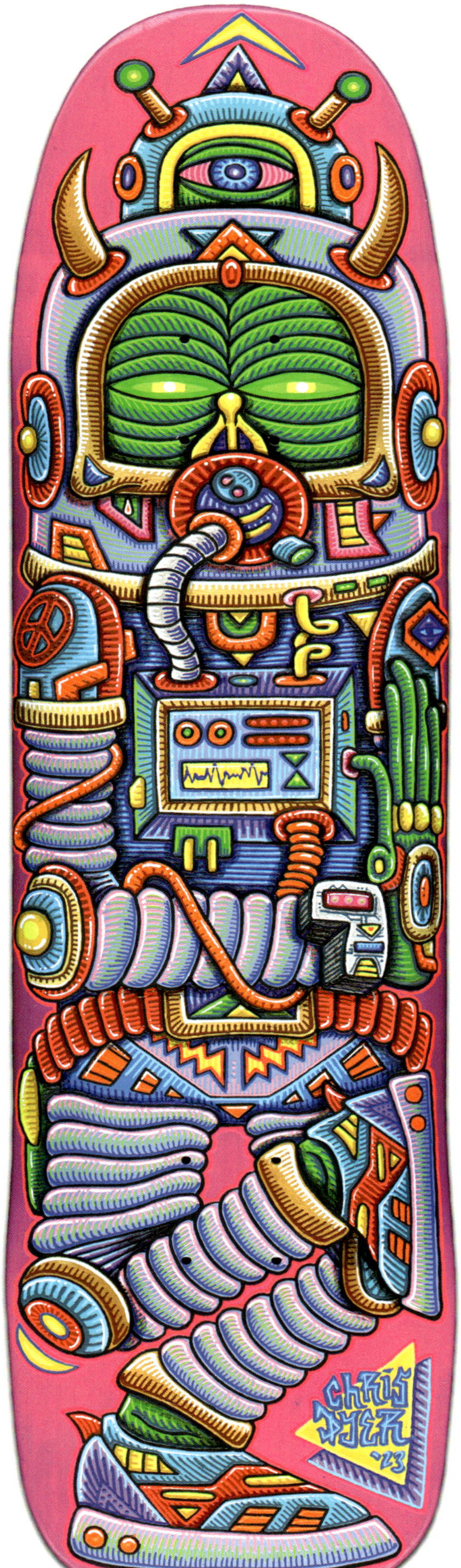

"Psychonaut"
Acrylics
2023

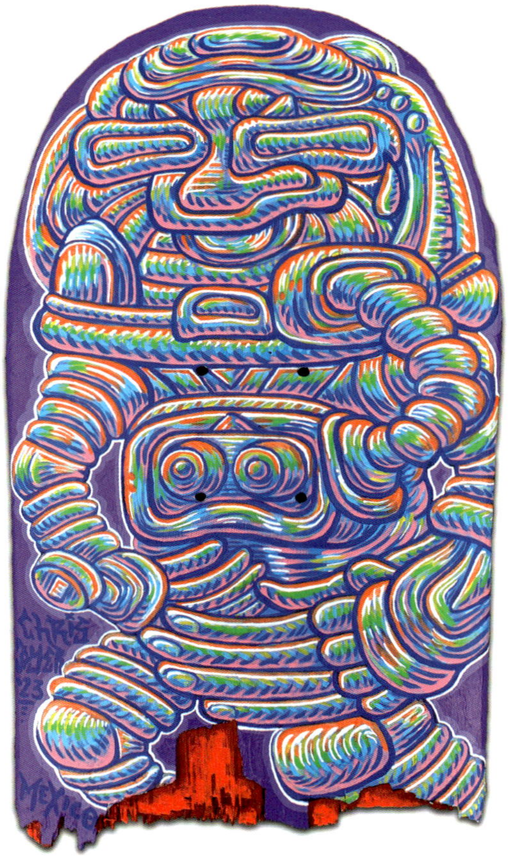

"12th Monkey"
Acrylics, 2023

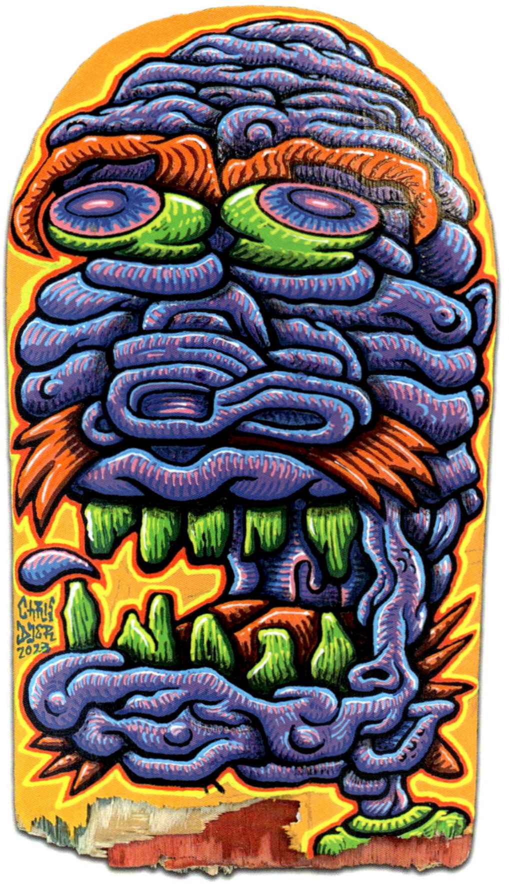

"Adicted to Pain"
Acrylics, 2023

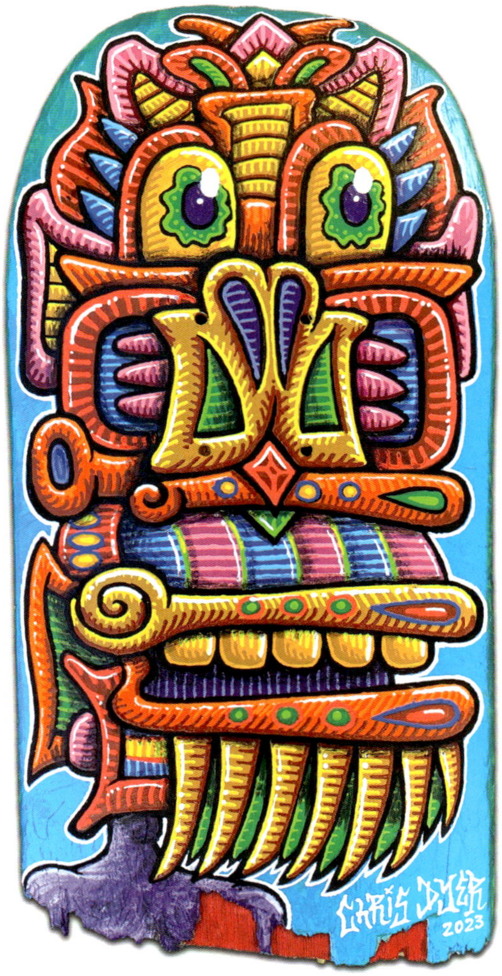

"Irie"
Acrylics, 2023

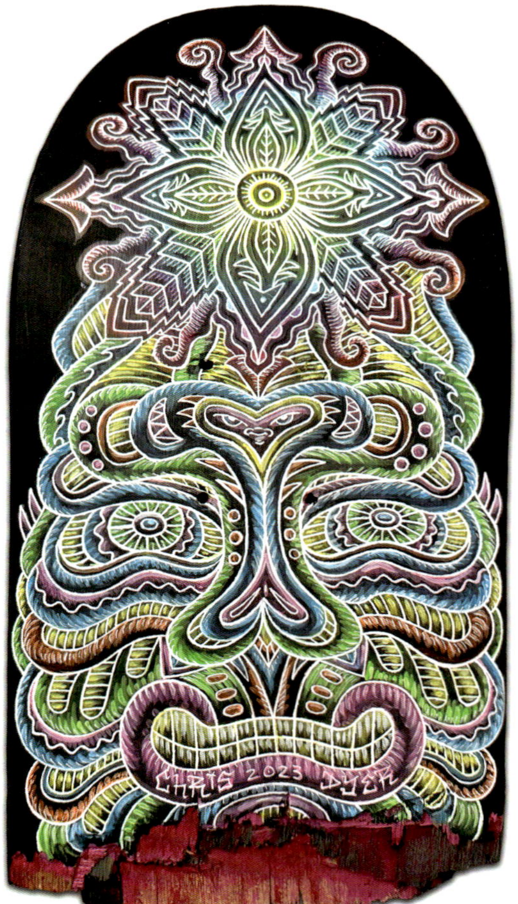

"Happy Heart"
Acrylics, 2023

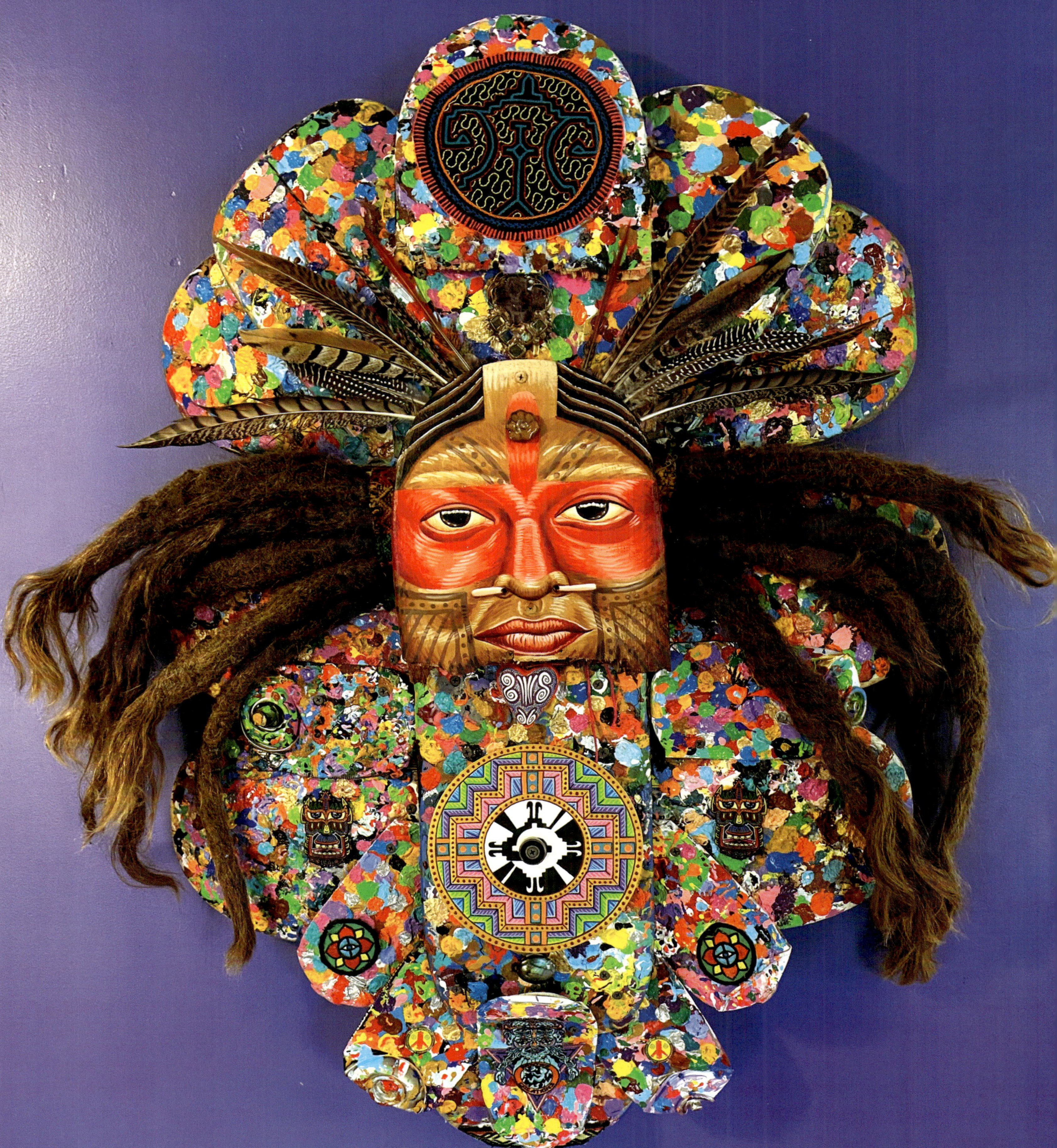

"Urban Tribal Revival"
Broken skateboards and crushed spray cans that I used as palletes, acrylics, a 45 vinyl record, mystic crystals, patches and feathers
2021

SKATE GRAPHICS

"Creation Skateboards" from California was my main commercial skateboard graphics client since I first did a series for them in 2005. After eight years of helping form the brand's esthetic, it's owner **Craig Nejedly**, who was too busy with his Humboldt Herb farm, asked me to be the **Brand Manager** and **Art Director**. That was a great honor and my chance to bridge even more visionary art into this industry! For four years I did everything in my power to improve the brand. I beefed up the team by adding legendary Pros and talented Ams, along with connecting international family that would represent the brand in their own countries. I also used all of my Visionary and Street Art connections to make sure each graphic was of the highest quality! The catalogues that came out those years are something I am still very proud of. We also became the first brand to use recycled wood for our boards. In that period I also directed an awesome skate video for the brand called **"Soul Harmonics"**. The skating by our team was awesome, and trippy animations of my art gave it a unique style. Unfortunately, our small brand didn't have the budget to advertise in big magazines or blogs, so all of these quality products and media I was grinding to produce, didn't really reach enough eyes. Eventually I was so frustrated about this, that I quit the brand entirely. Creation didn't last much longer after I left unfortunetly. I distanced myself from the whole skate industry in general, which I now perceived as a pissing contest between cool boys. As years passed, I eventually went back to doing graphics though, for a number of legendary brands that I've always loved like **Santa Cruz**, **H-Street**, **Deathwish**, **Plan B**, **Darkstar**, etc. Grateful!

CREATION SKATEBOARDS

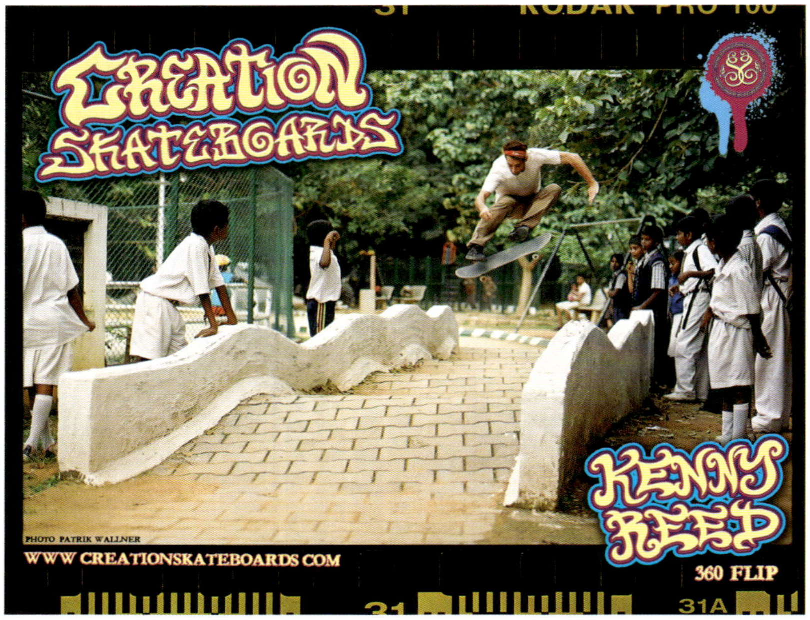

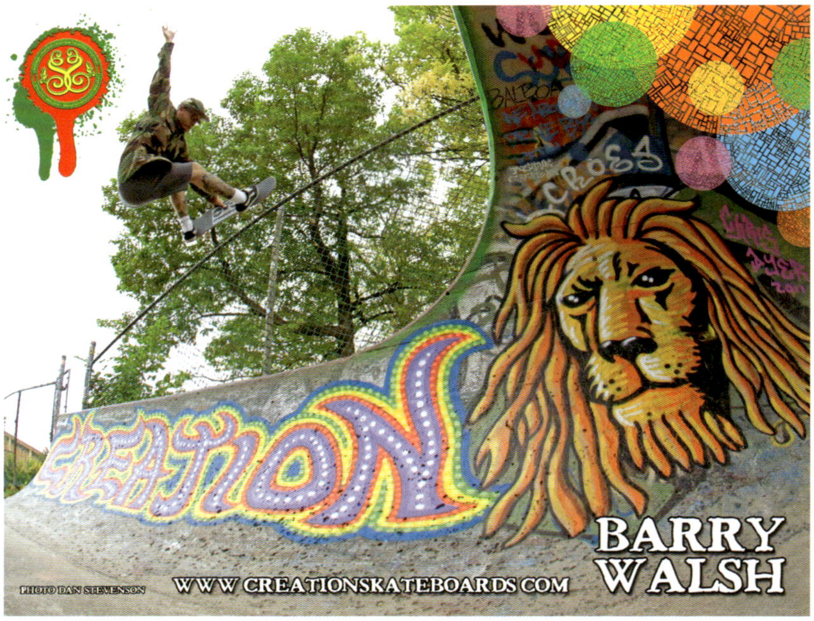

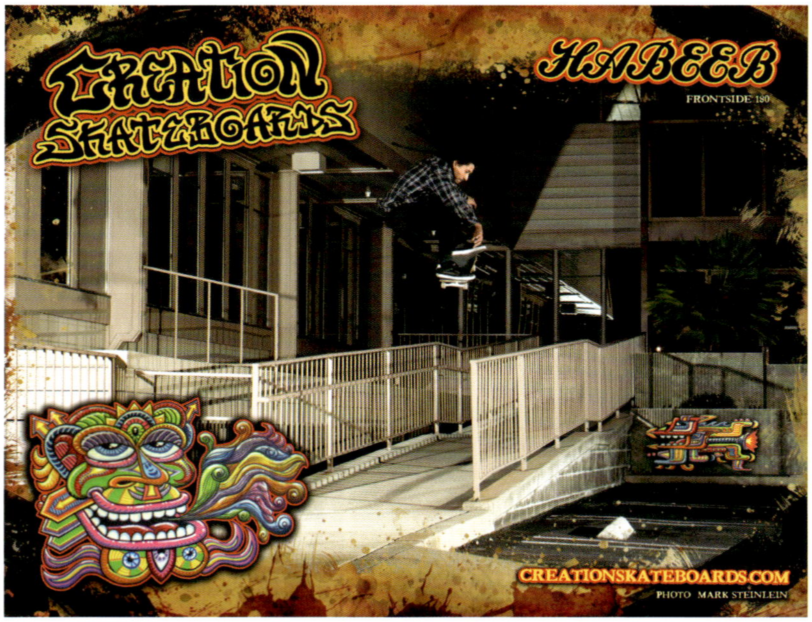

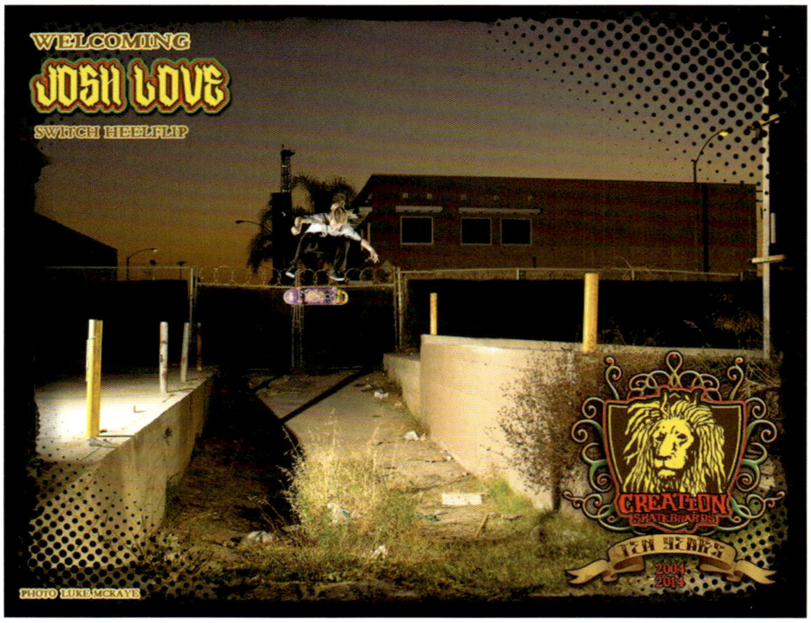

Creation Skateboards Catalogue Posters. Next Page: Creation Skateboard Graphics 2011-2015

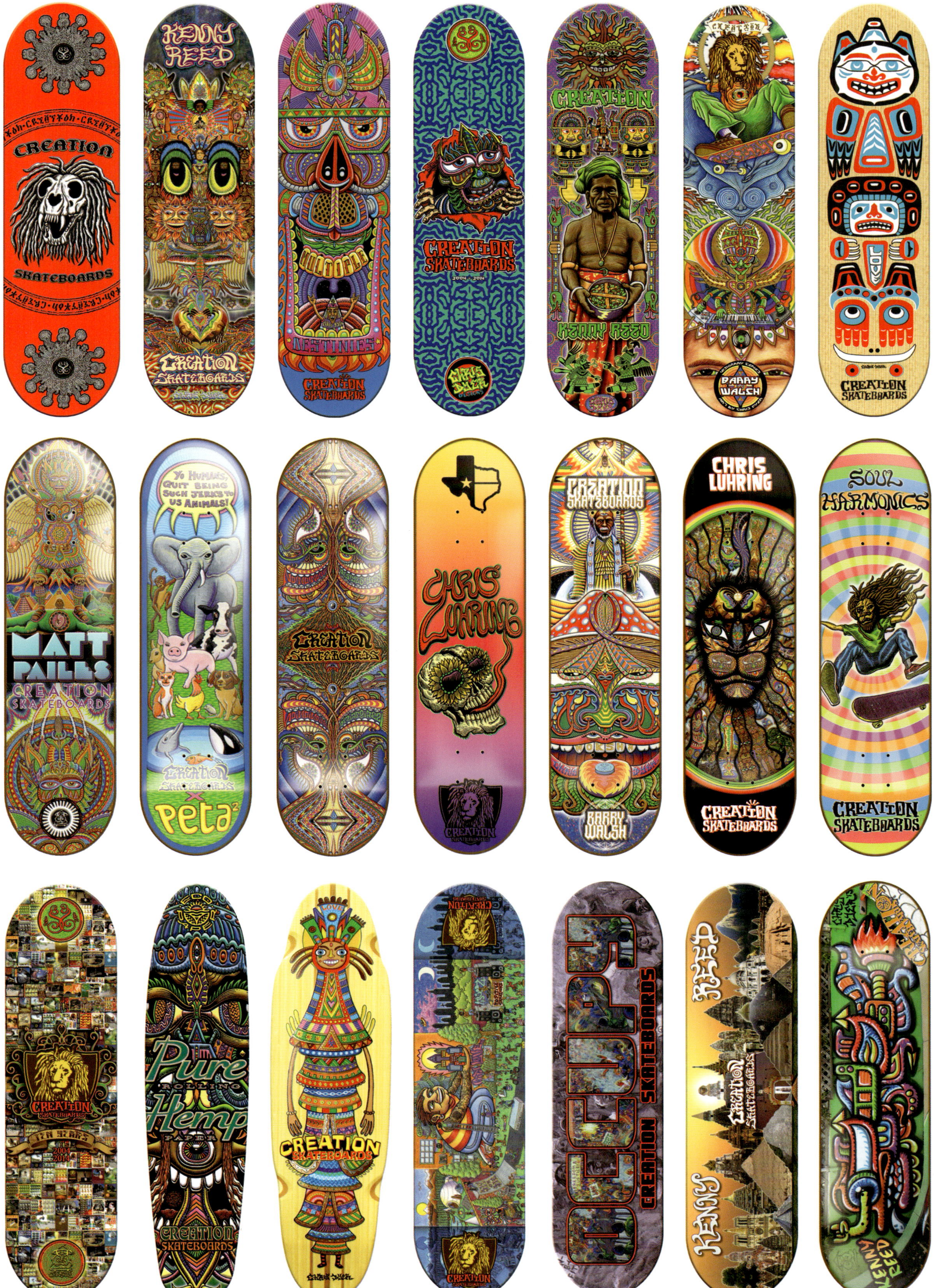
CREATION
SKATEBOARDS
KENNY REED
CREATION SKATEBOARDS
CREATION SKATEBOARDS
CREATION SKATEBOARDS
2004 – 2014
CREATION
KENNY REED
BARRY WALSH
LOVE
CREATION SKATEBOARDS
MATT PAILES
CREATION SKATEBOARDS
YO HUMANS! QUIT BEING SUCH JERKS TO US ANIMALS!
CREATION SKATEBOARDS
X
peta2
CREATION SKATEBOARDS
CHRIS LUHRING
CREATION SKATEBOARDS
CREATION SKATEBOARDS
BARRY WALSH
CHRIS LUHRING
CREATION SKATEBOARDS
SOUL HARMONICS
CREATION SKATEBOARDS
CREATION SKATEBOARDS
Pure Rolling Hemp Paper
CREATION SKATEBOARDS
CREATION SKATEBOARDS
CREATION SKATEBOARDS
OCCUPY
CREATION SKATEBOARDS
KENNY REED
CREATION SKATEBOARDS
KENNY REED

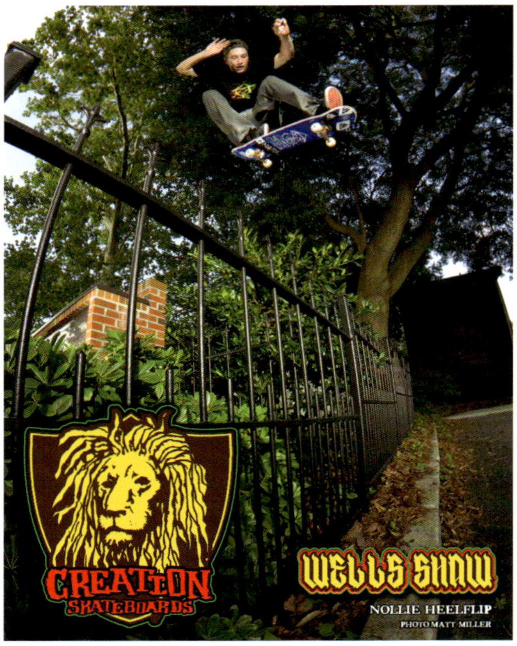

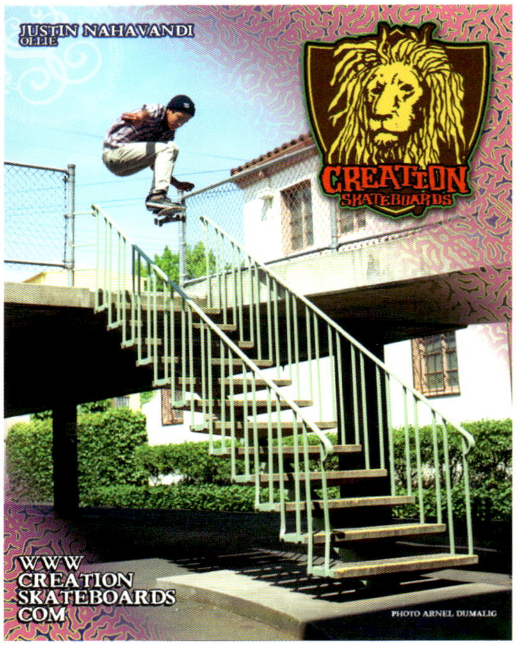

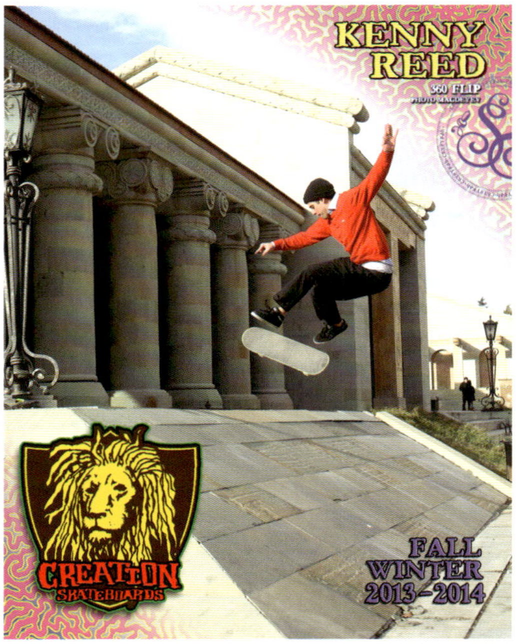

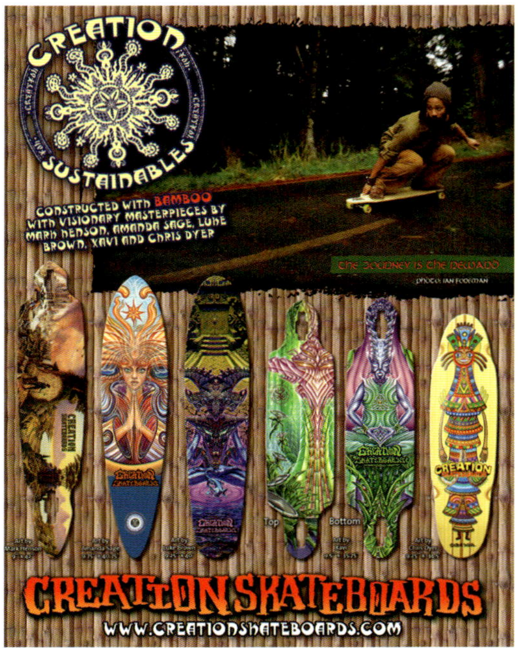

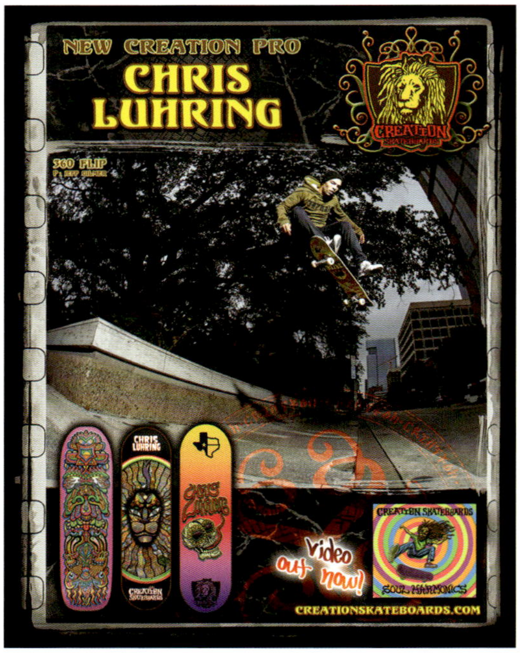

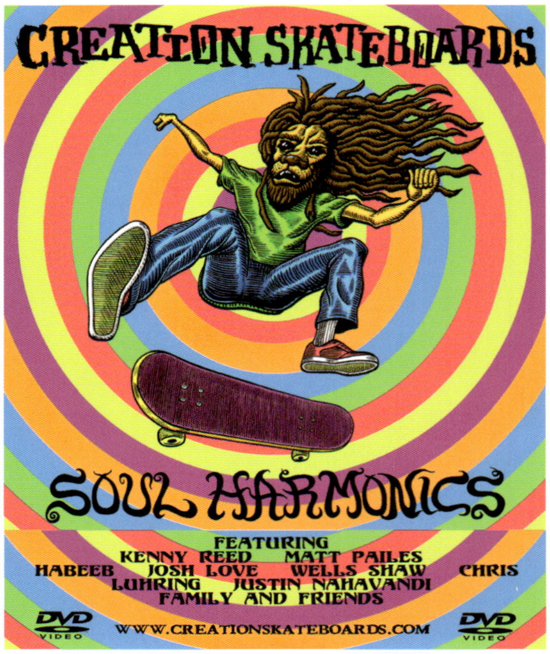

Magazine advertizements, catalogue covers and **“Soul Harmonics”** DVD cover

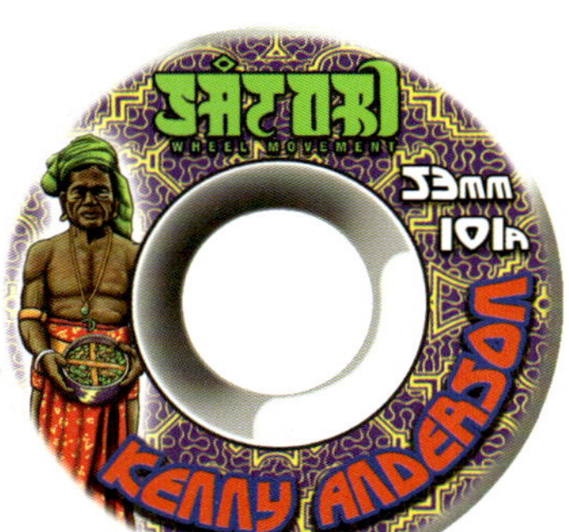

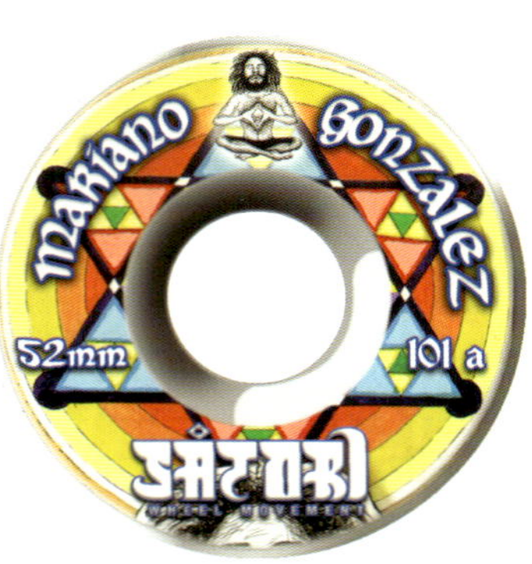

SATORI
WHEEL MOVEMENT

“Satori Movement” is the wheel and sustainable clothing brand which is part of the same distribution house (**“High Grade”**) as Creation Skateboards. These years I was so busy taking care of everything to do with the boards, that I only had the chance to do a couple of wheel designs, for Pro Skaters **Kenny Anderson** and **Mariano Gonzalez**. The other commission that I was asked to do was a hemp t-shirt design for **“Long Distance Revolutionary”**, which was a documentary about political prisoner **Mumia Abu-Jamal**. I was a big fan of his conscious speeches from death row, so it was a great honor to make that design! Love it when my art is used for good causes!

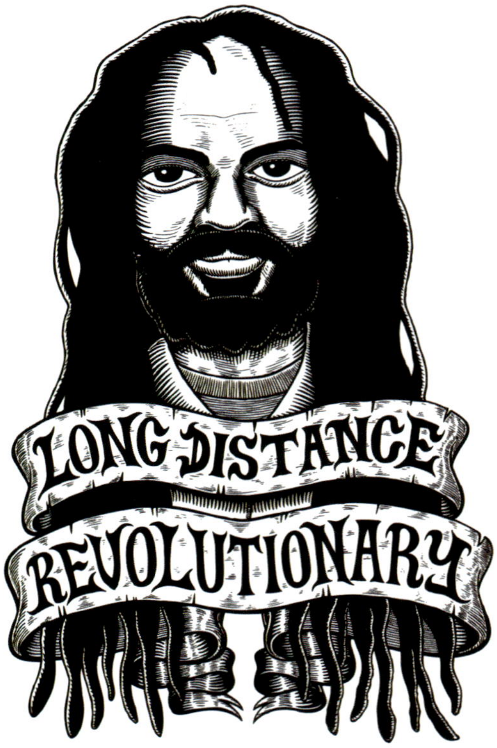

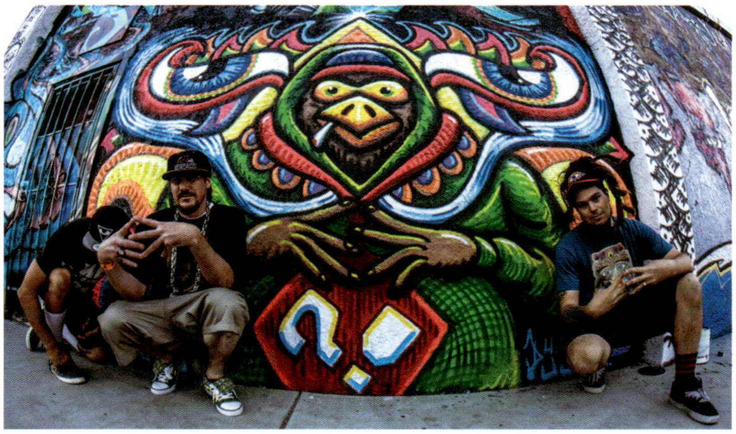

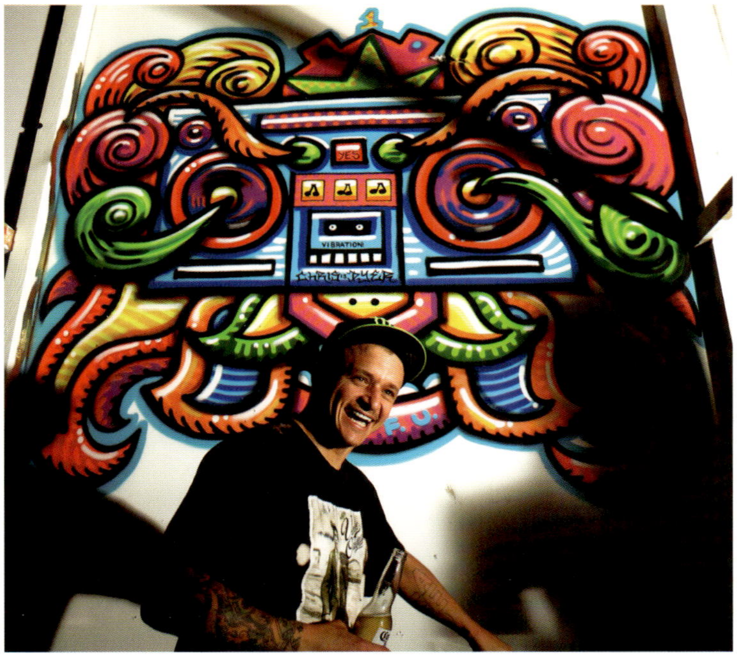

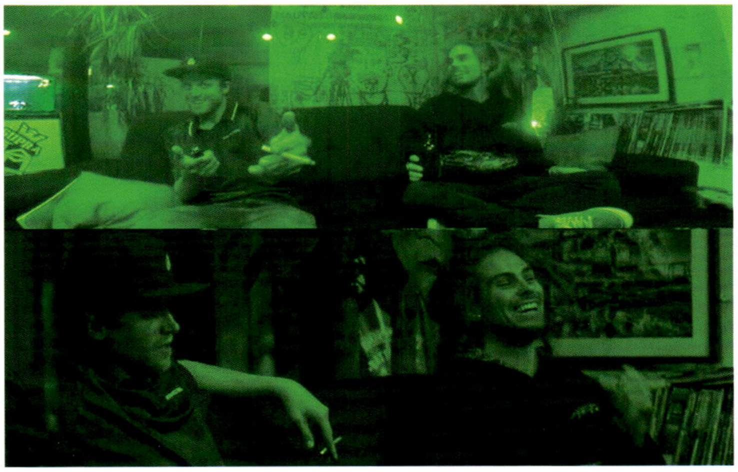

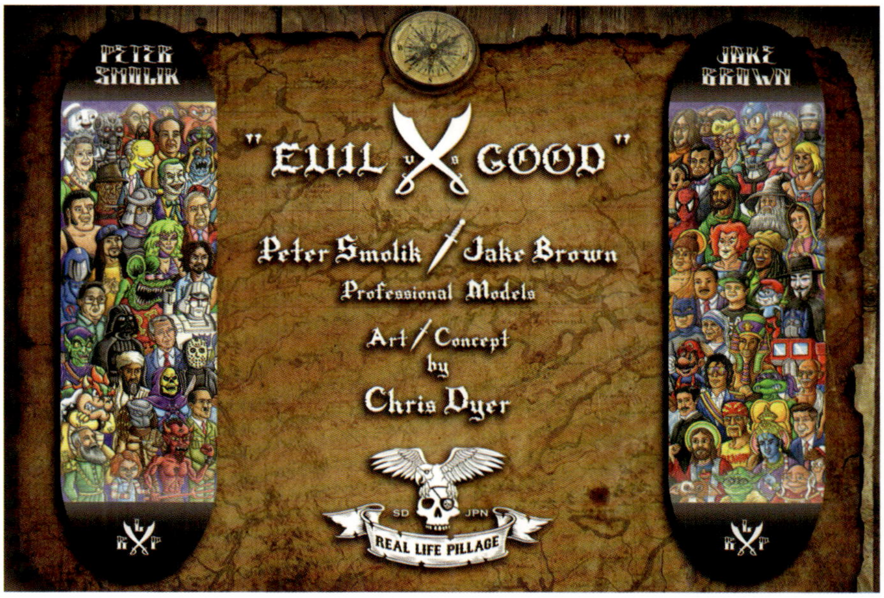

In 2013 I had a solo exhibition in **San Diego**. While I was there I got to meet the legendary Pro Skaters **Peter Smolik** and **Jake Brown**. I was a bit intimidated by them at first, but they ended being real nice gangstas. Peter took me to skate a rad backyard mini ramp one afternoon and we later collaborated on a broken deck painting (he had shot paint with a bb gun). Jake was kind enough to DJ at my art exhibition and also took me to his production studio, inside the huge DC/Monster ramp, so I painted him a lil piece there. I eventually did some artwork for different brands they owned like **"Paradox"** grip-tape, **"Laced"** clothing and **"DoogooD"** charity boards. Both of them skated for **"Sk8 Mafia"**, which Peter co-founded, so the owner hired me to do a graphic for them. That was the "Evil vs. Good" illustration I showed you previously in this book. Peter is in the "Bad" side and Jake in the "Good" side. As I mentioned before, these boards where never made with Sk8 Mafia because of possible copyright infringements and sadly they felt they didn't have to pay me for my work either. Years later, Peter and Jake weren't vibing with situations like this so they left that brand to go create **"Real Life Pillage"**. Finally this graphic got printed and nobody got in trouble.

That same year I was on a Montreal Podcast show called "The Dank Tank" to be interviewed along Thrasher SOTY **Wes Kremer**. We got really stoned during the interview, which was unusual for me, but the whole joke of the show. Wes and I got along real good so he ended gifting me a signed Sk8 Mafia pro deck of his, which took away the bad taste I had left from that brand. Nice people healing old industry wounds.

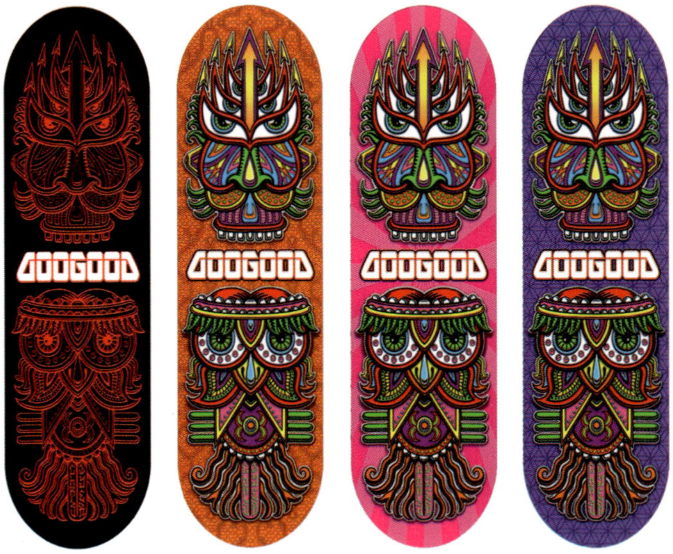

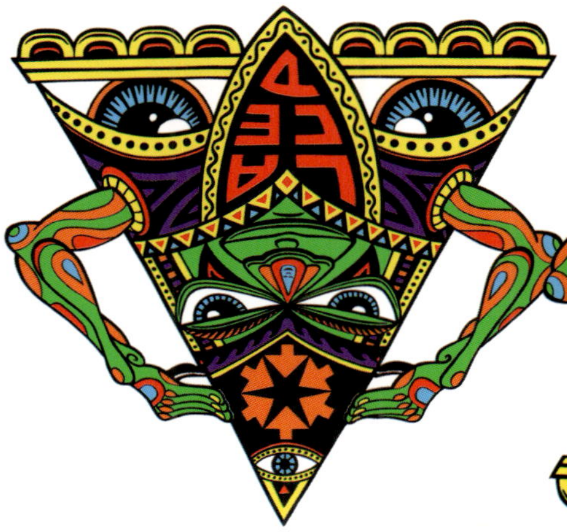

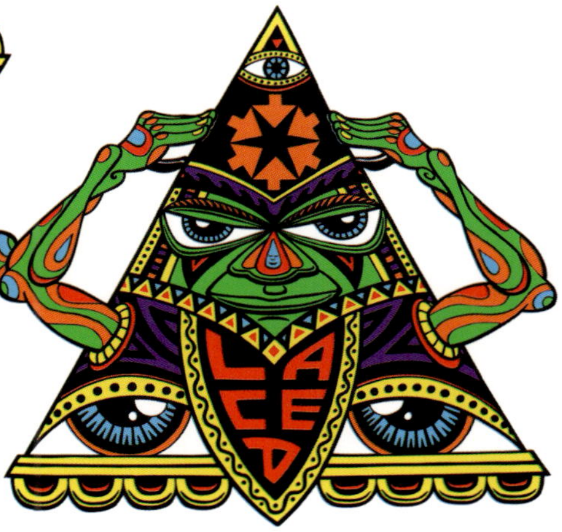

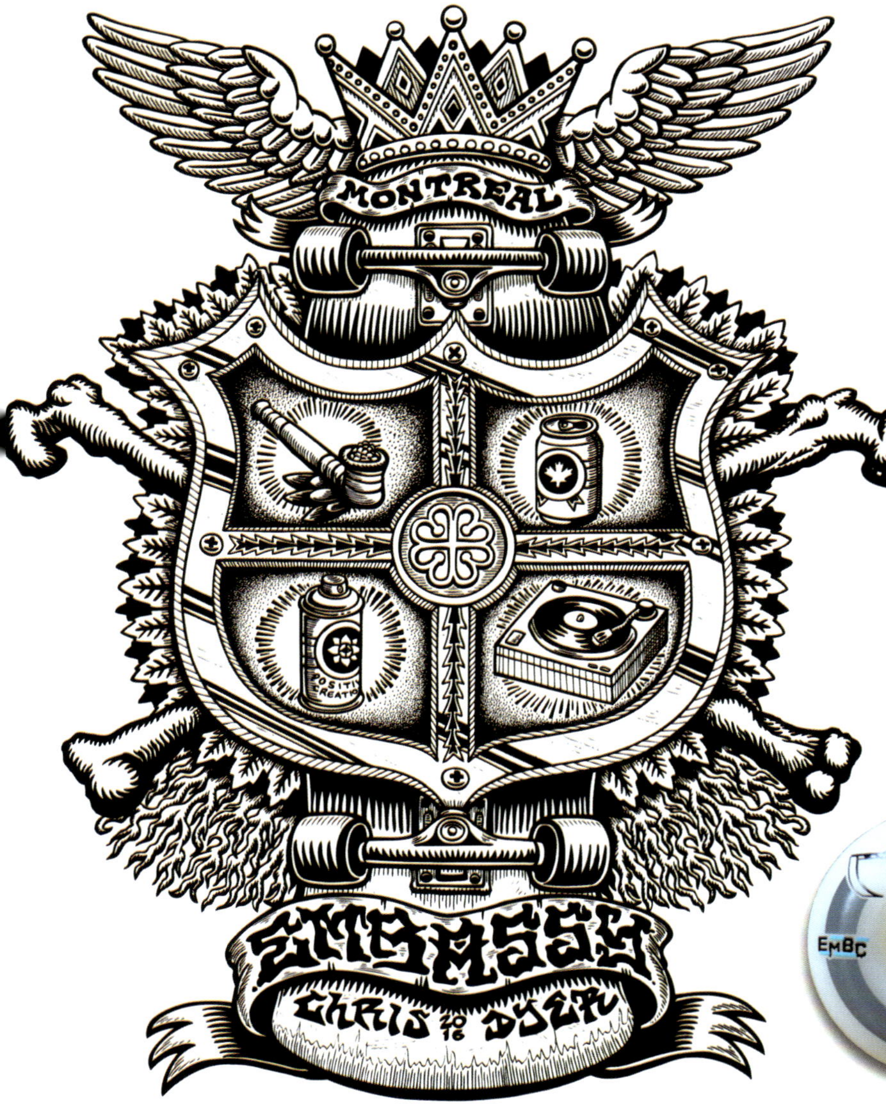

EMBC
MONTREAL

"Embassy" is our Montreal crew of Street Culture Pioneers, which includes OG skateboarders, artists, bombers, DJs, musicians, BMX riders, etc. At one point it was also a lifestyle clothing brand directed by my homie, legendary Canadian pro skater **Barry Walsh**. As part of the crew, I helped Barry do some initial products like hats, wheels and t-shirt designs. Always down to support the Roots Rock Skate movements of Urban Rasta Punks!

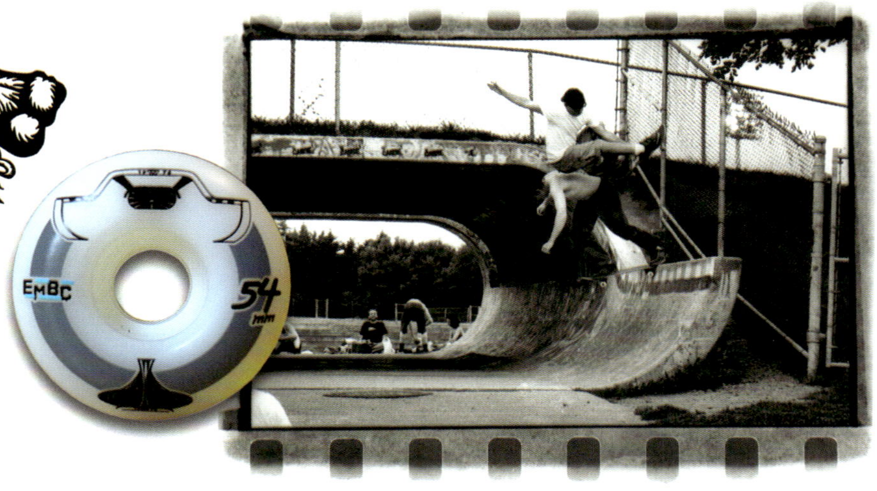

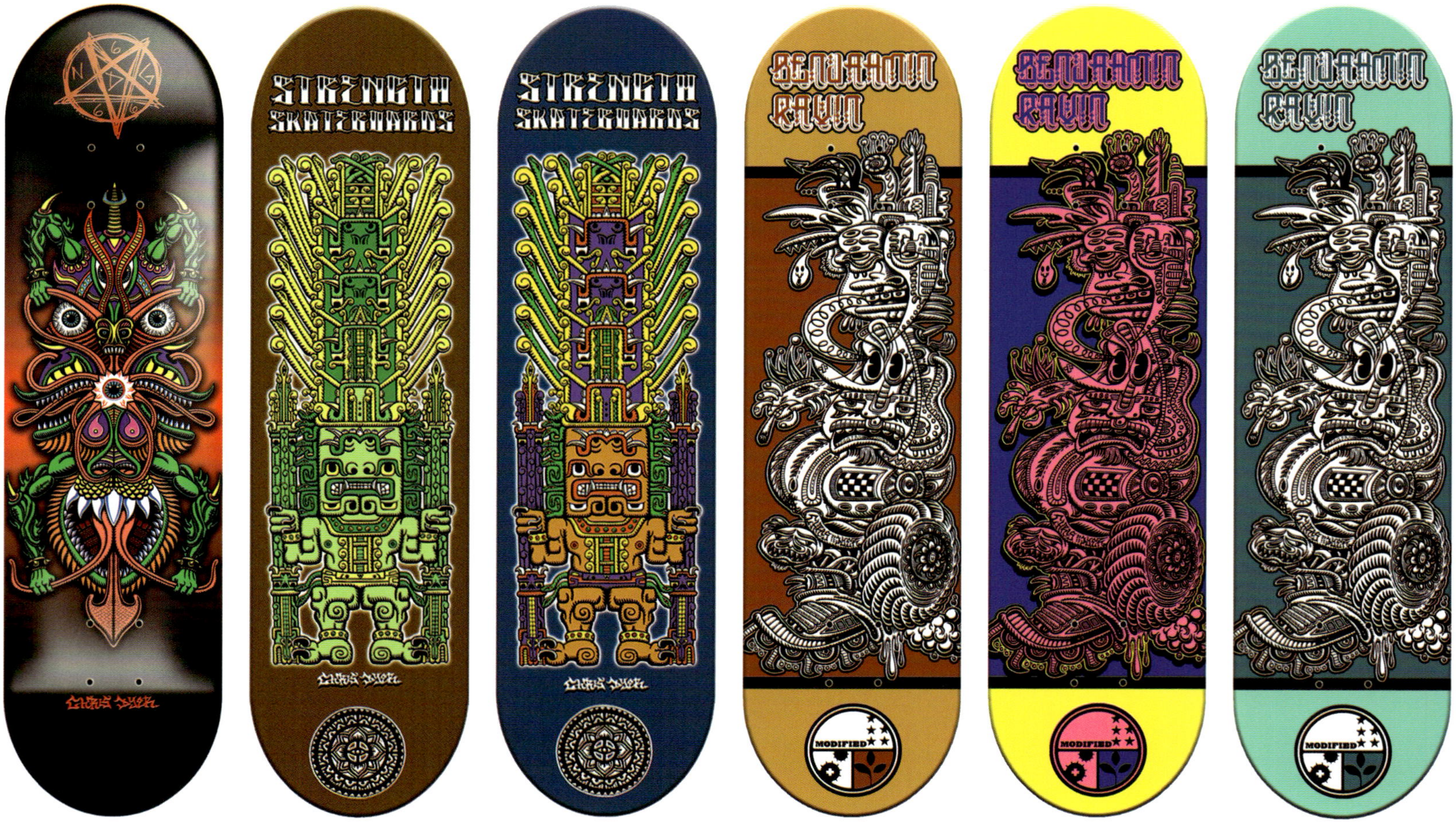

Some other skate graphics I did for underground brands like **"No Damn Good"**, **"Strength"** and **"Modified"**

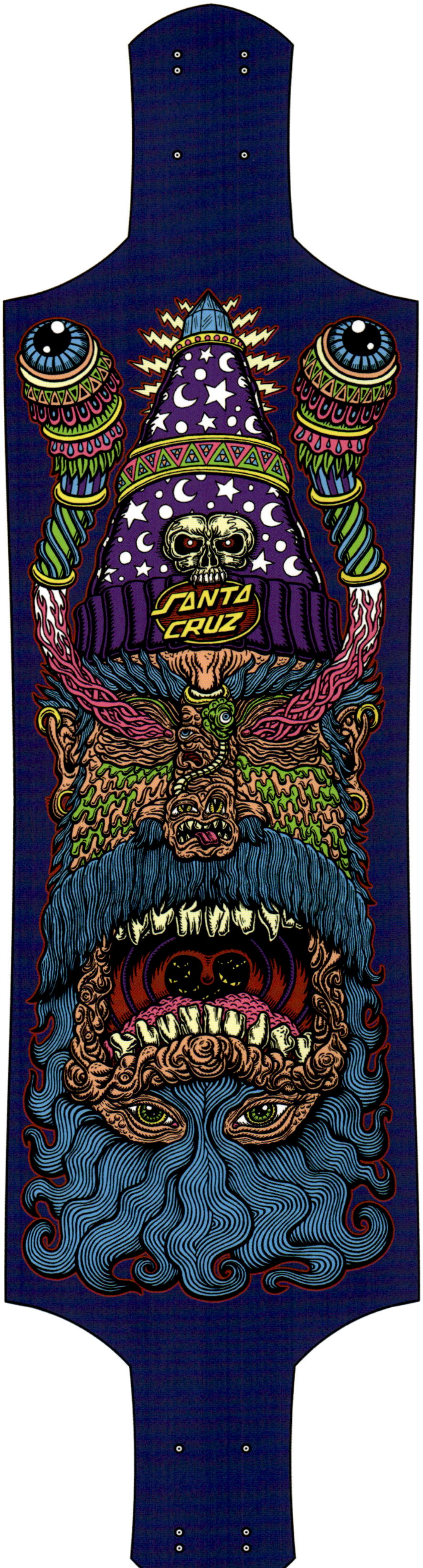

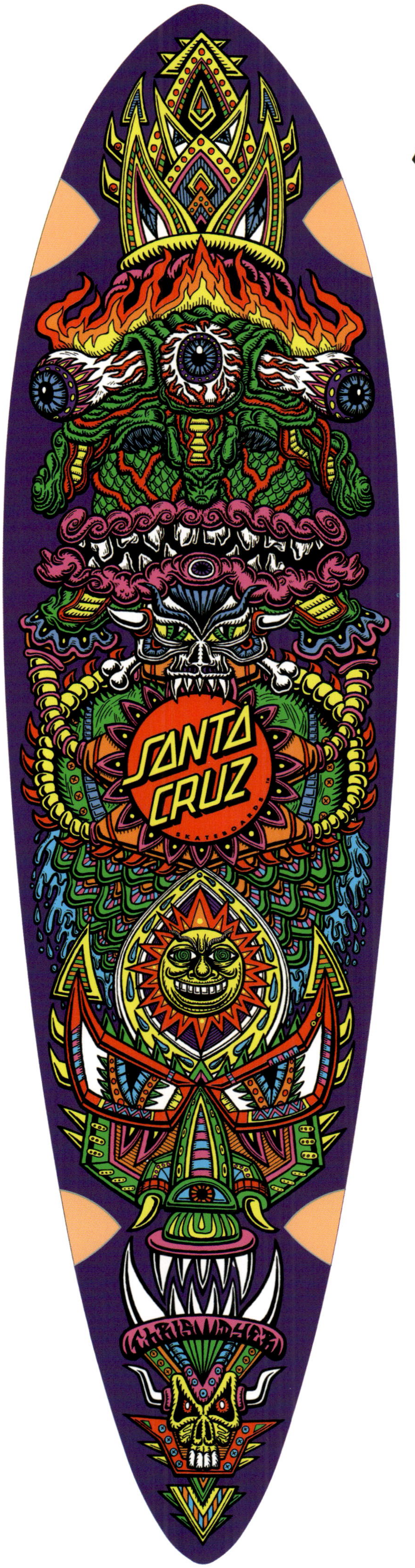

SANTA CRUZ SKATEBOARDS

Doing graphics for **Santa Cruz skateboards** was a childhood dream come true! One of my biggest art inspirations is **Jim Phillips**, who made most of their most iconic graphics in the 80's. Usually I make an effort to hide how much he's influenced my style, but on this gig I could just allow myself to fully express myself in his general language! The boards came out looking so good and they even glowed under black light! Grateful!

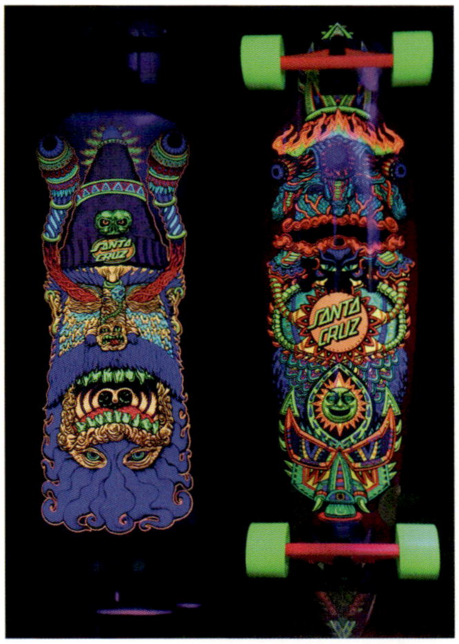

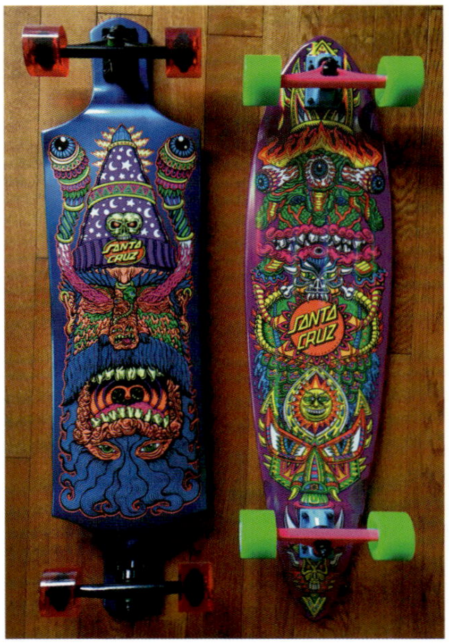

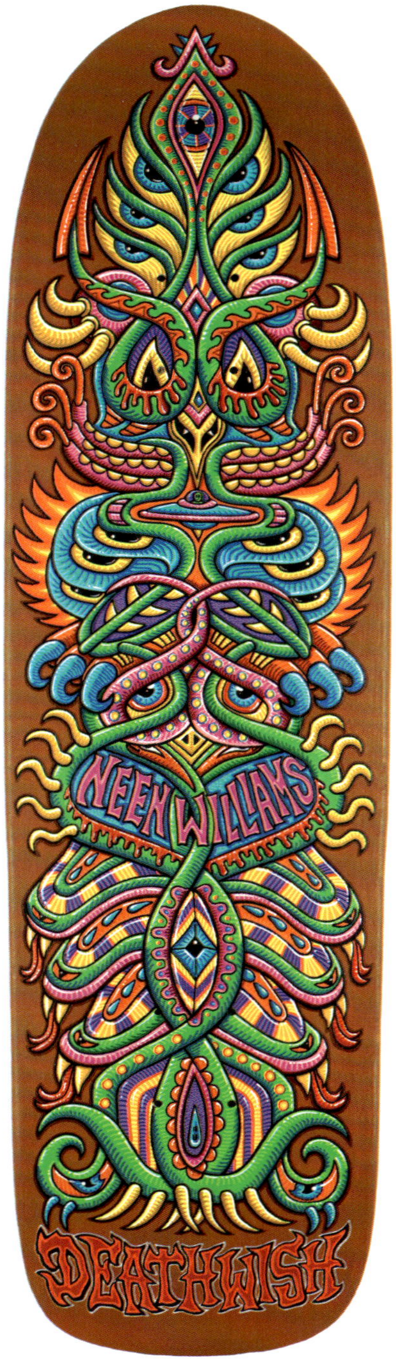

DEATHWISH

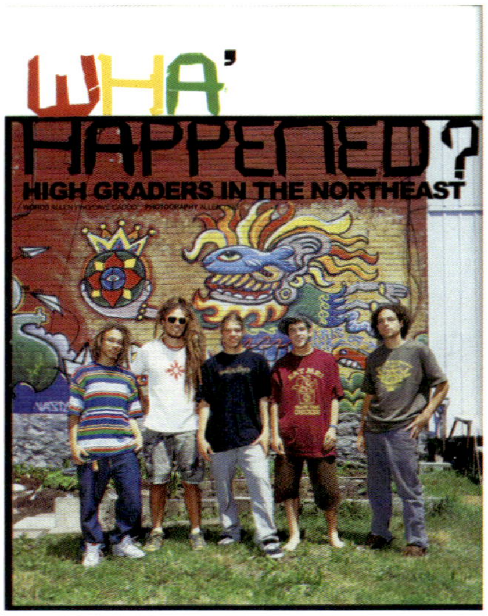

I met **Neen Williams** back in 2006, when he was a young amateur skater. He was sponsored by **"Satori"** wheels back then and crashed at my place when the team was touring through Canada. Neen was so chill and talented that it didn't take him long to get scooped by a huge brand like **"Deathwish"**, who eventually made him Pro. I was stoked for him and even more when I saw him transform into a positive role-model in the skate scene. I was stoked to do this graphic for him and pass along my medicine through his platforms.

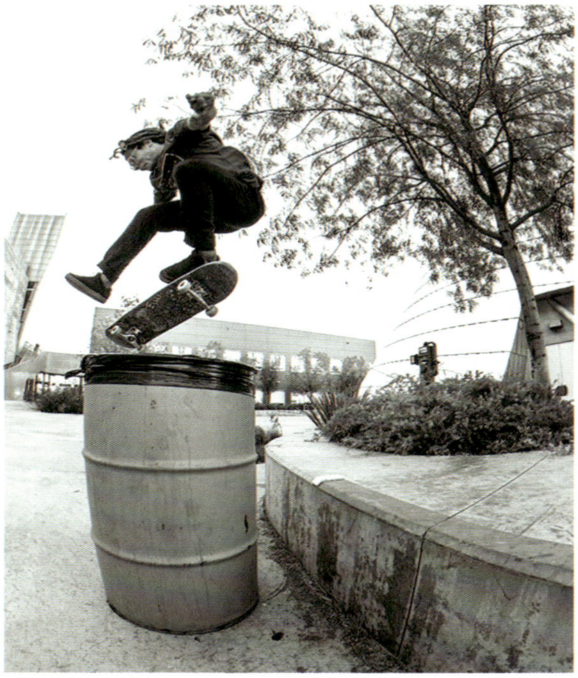

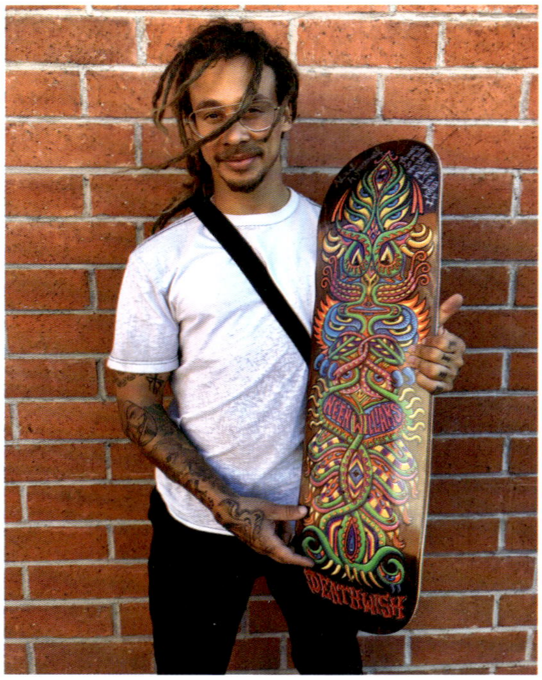

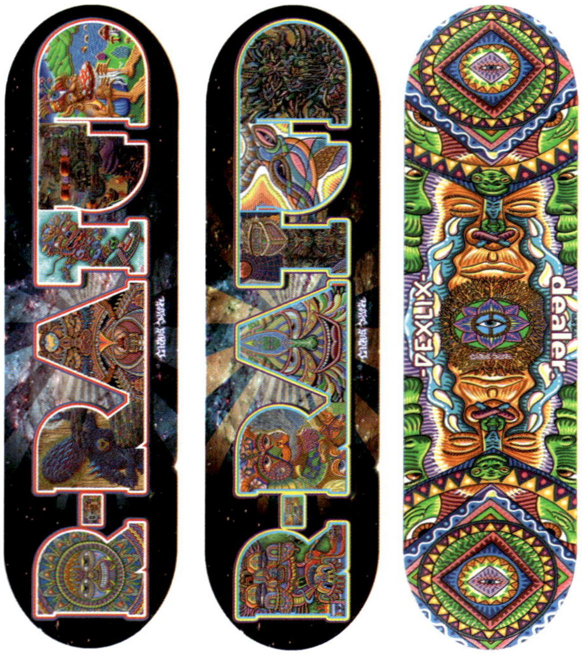

Some other skate graphics I did for the brands like **"R-Rated"** and **"Dealer"**.

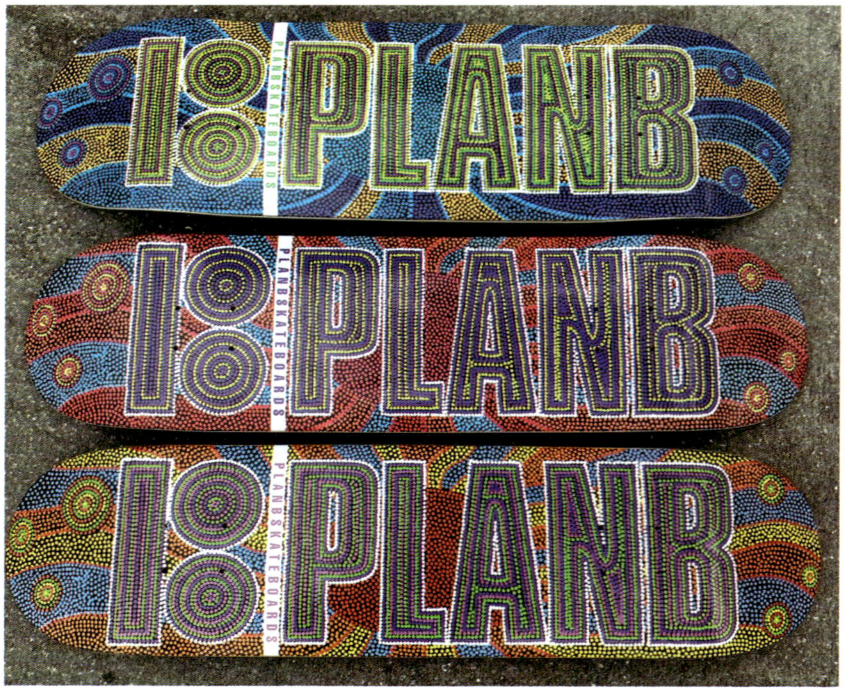

"Plan B" Australian series I did under the direction of **Colin Mckay**.

H-STREET

I met legendary Pro Skater **Tony Magnusson** in 2021, when my friend **Jake Brown** took me over to his Southern California home for a fun skate sesh. While we ripped his mountain-top Bowl, he invited me to do a series for his classic skate brand **H-Street**! So this gave me the chance to draw these sweet graphics for some very legendary Pro skaters including **Tony**, **Jake, Matt Hensley** and **Danny Way**! Such an honor!

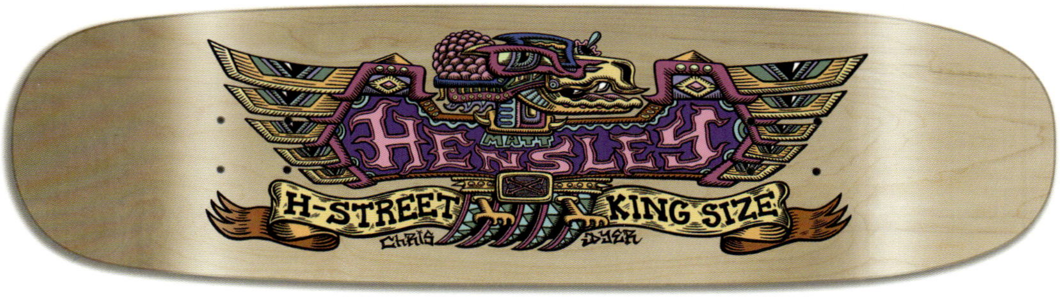

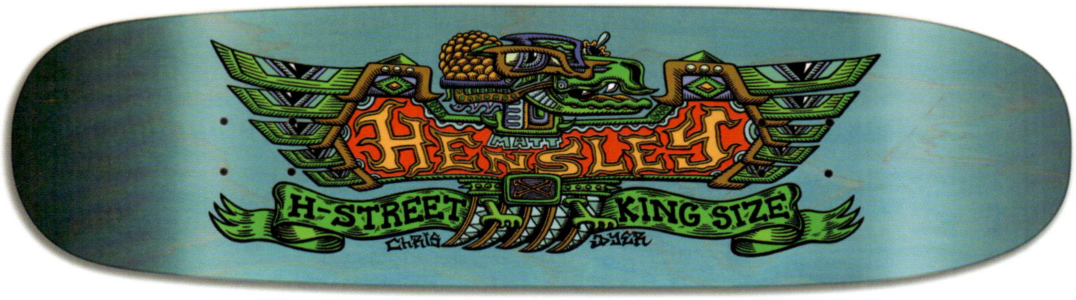

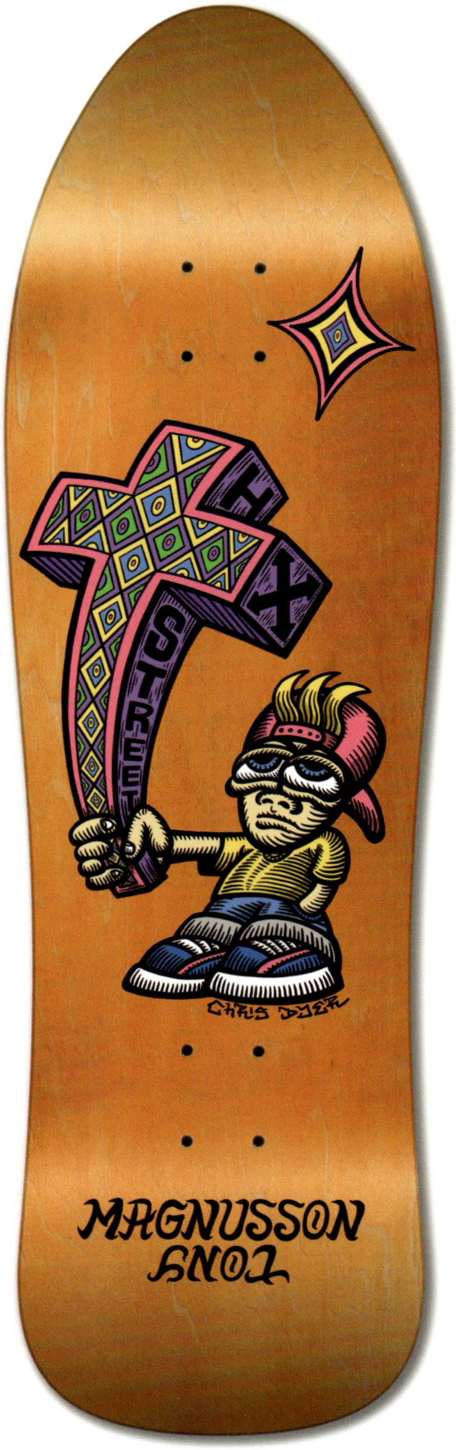

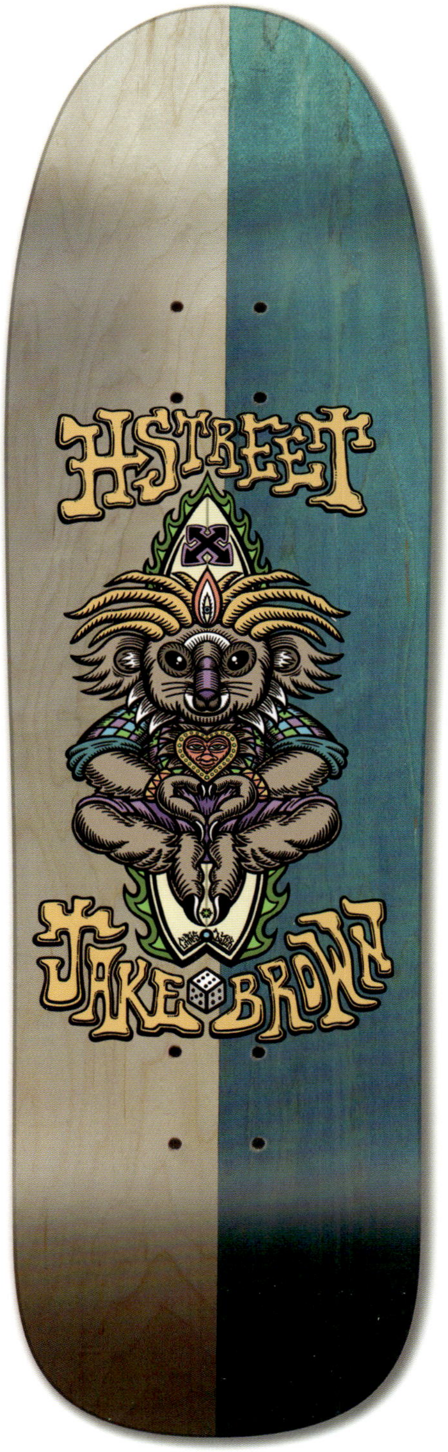

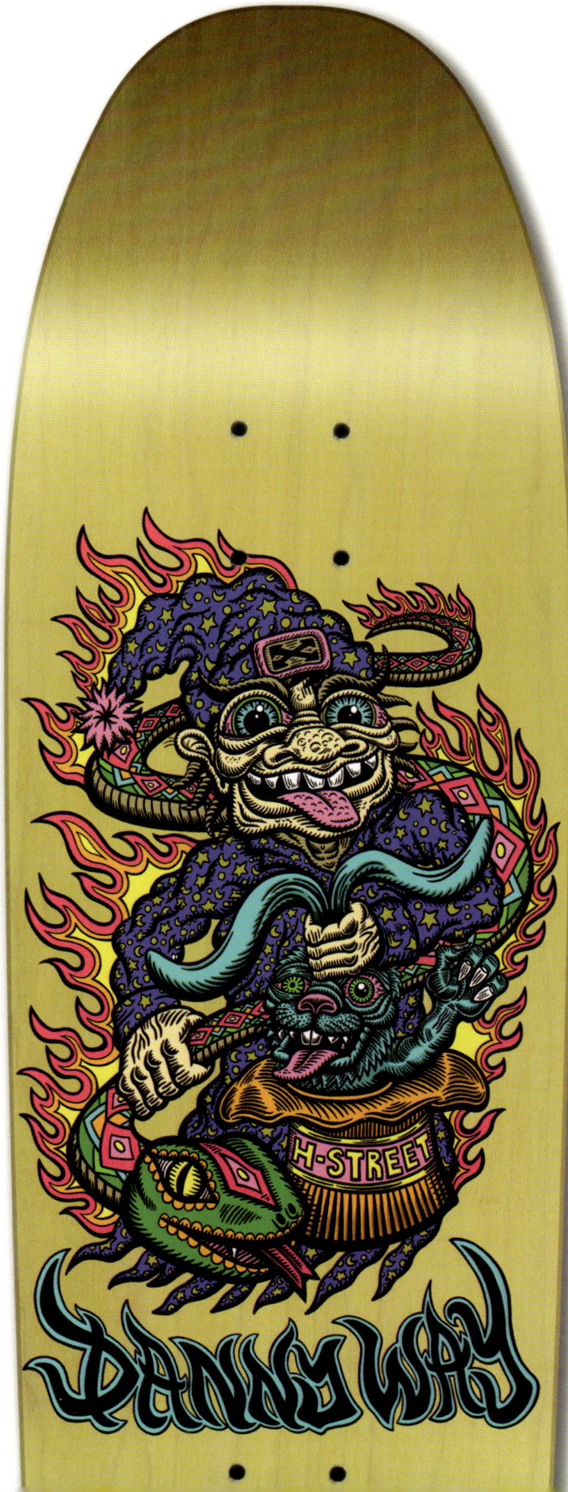

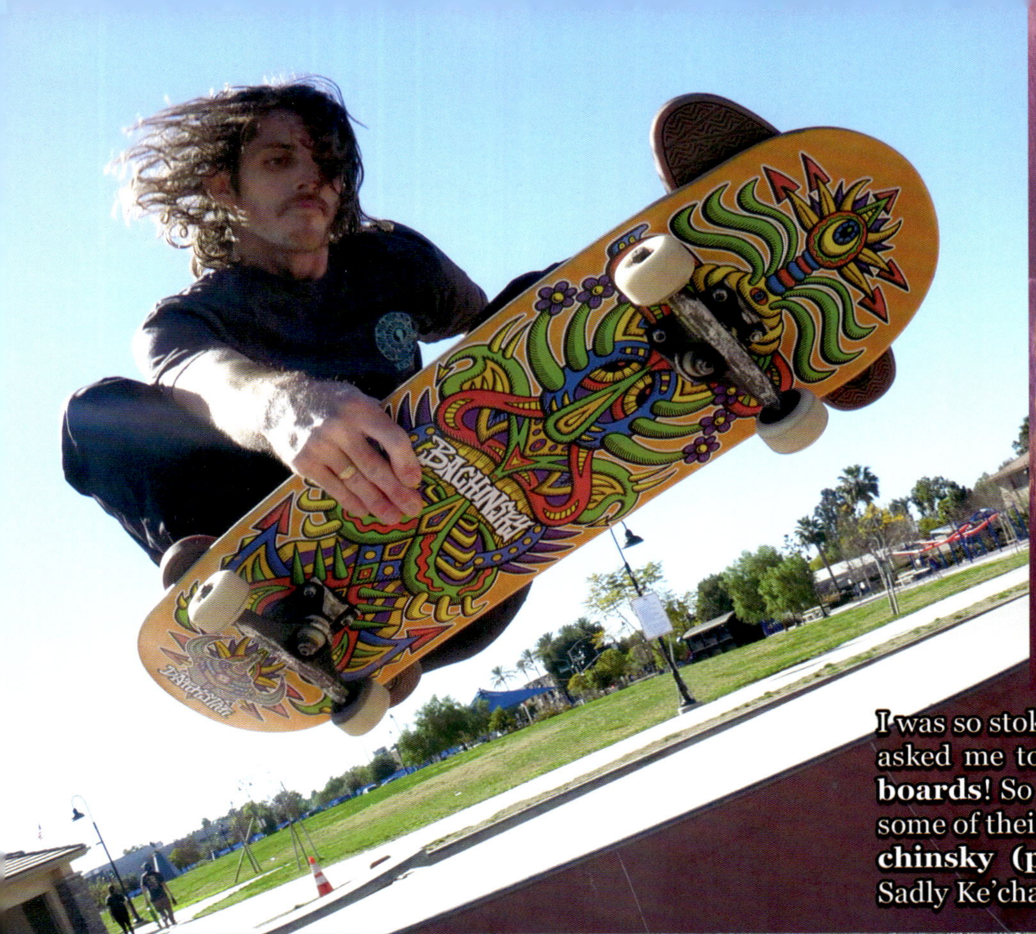

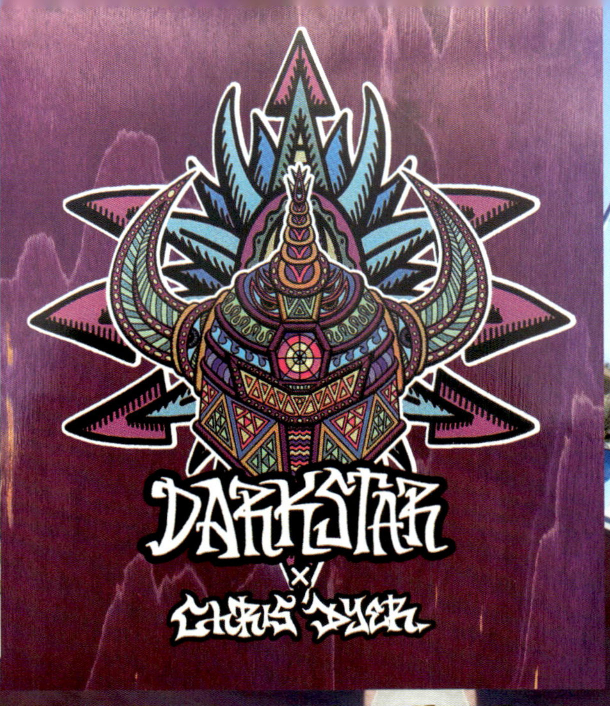

I was so stoked when legendary pro skater **Chet Thomas** asked me to make some graphics for **Darkstar Skateboards**! So I created the **'Tribal Series"** which featured some of their biggest pros like **Ryan Decenzo, Dave Bachinsky (pictured here)** and **Ke'chaud Johnson**! Sadly Ke'chaud passed recently... Rest In Power man!

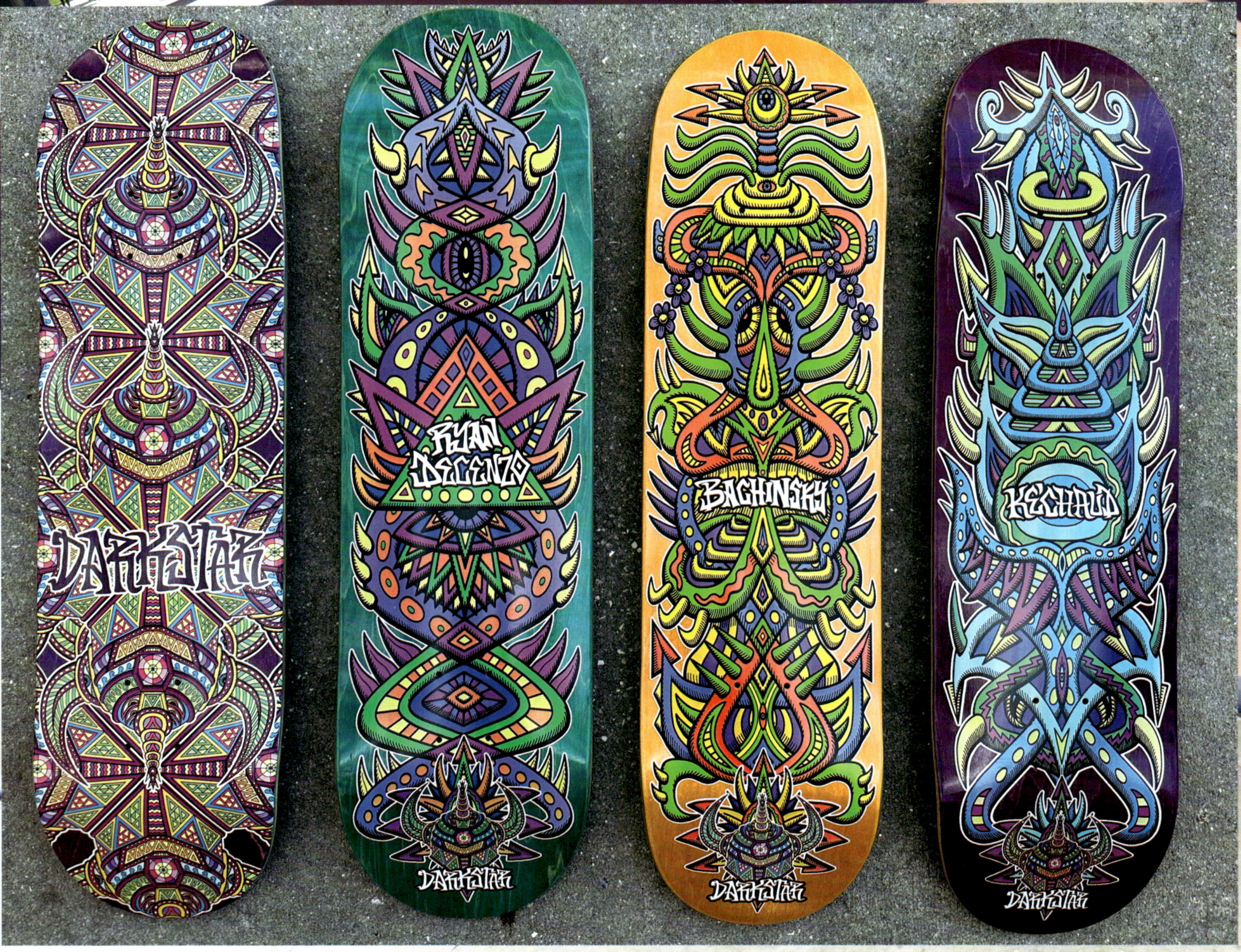

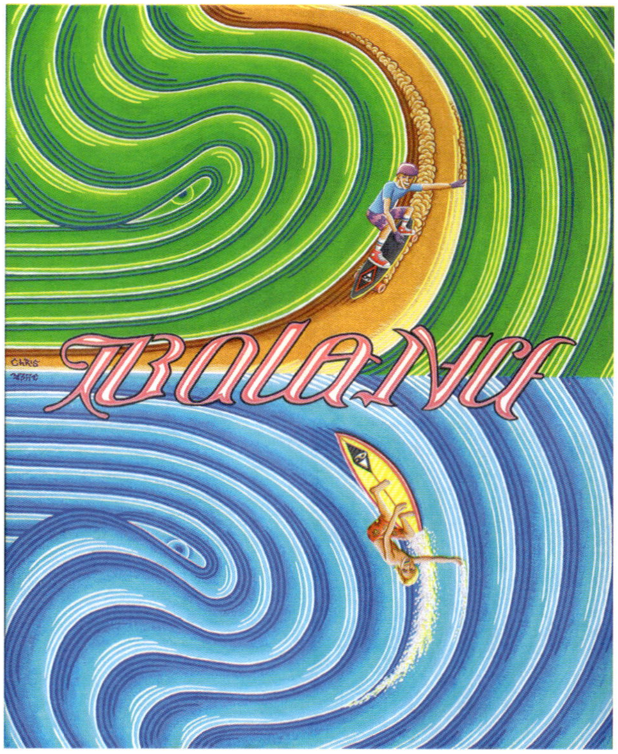

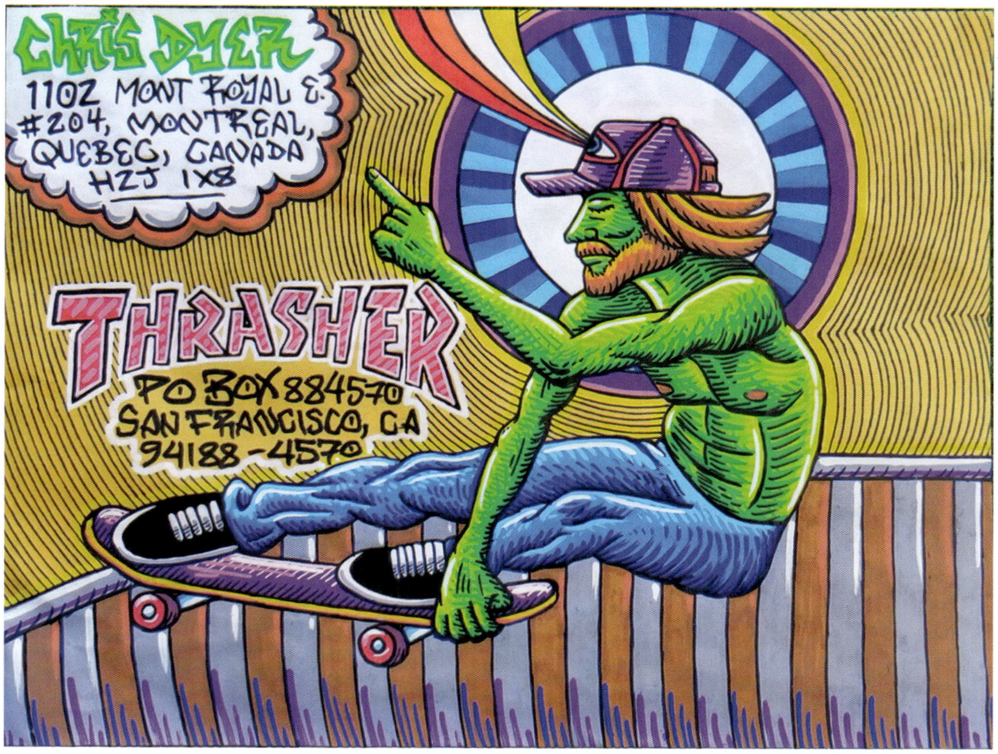

Here are a few more jobs I've done for the skate industry in the last ten years. Top left is some flyer artwork I did for **Concrete Wave** magazine. Beside it is the envelope artwork I did at the request of **Thrasher Magazine**, for their **"Mail Drop"** Art book. Bottom left is one of the 10 Limited Edition burnt graphics for **Teaken Skateboards** from Australia. To the right are some Insoles I did for **"Remind"**, along a rad pic of legendary pro skater **Chris Cole** holding one. And bottom right is a mural commission I did for **Vans** shoes in Canada, who sponsored me since 2012. It was done at a D.I.Y. skatepark in Montreal called **"Project 45"**.

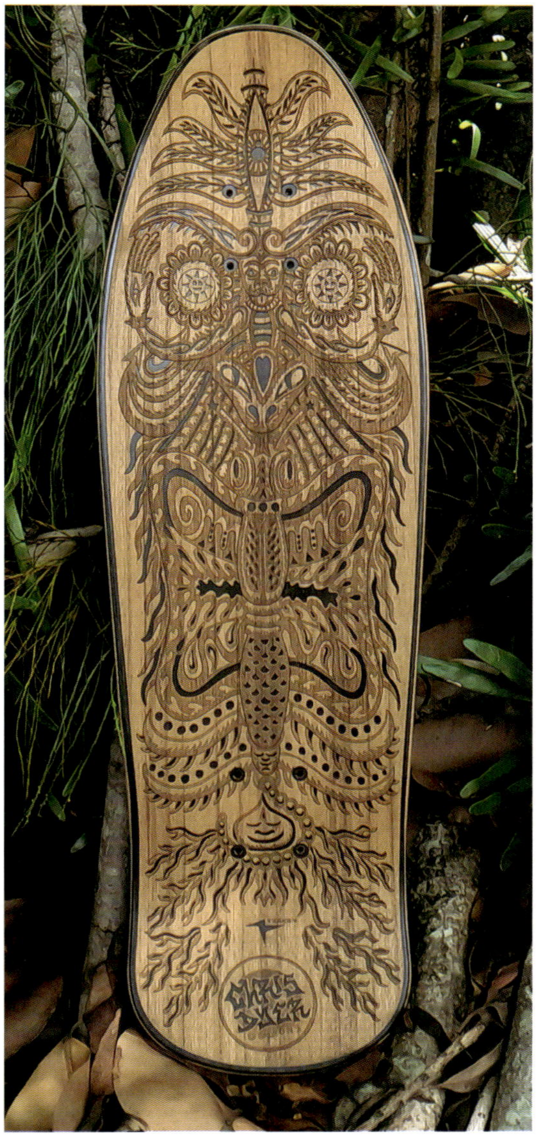

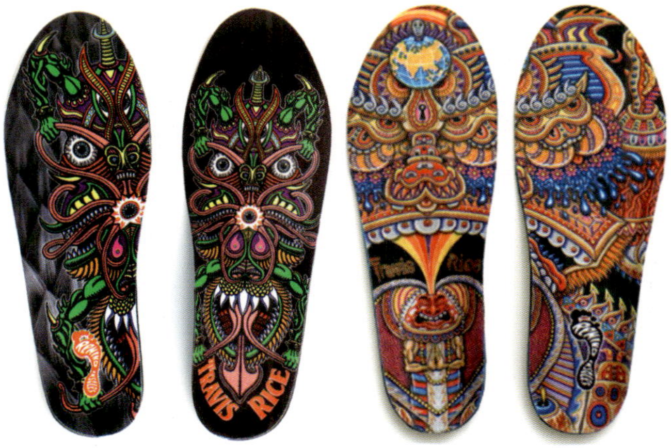

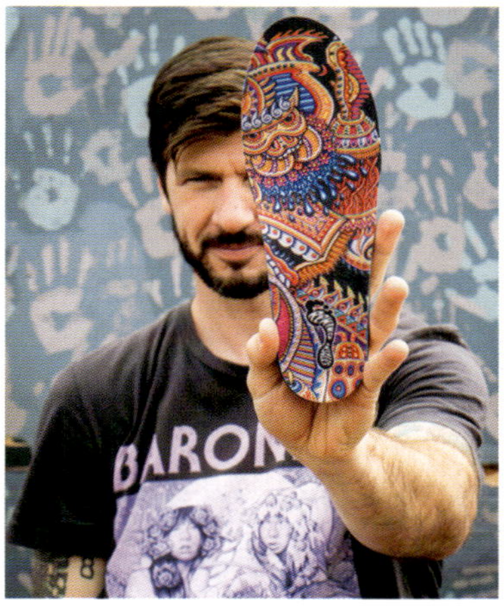

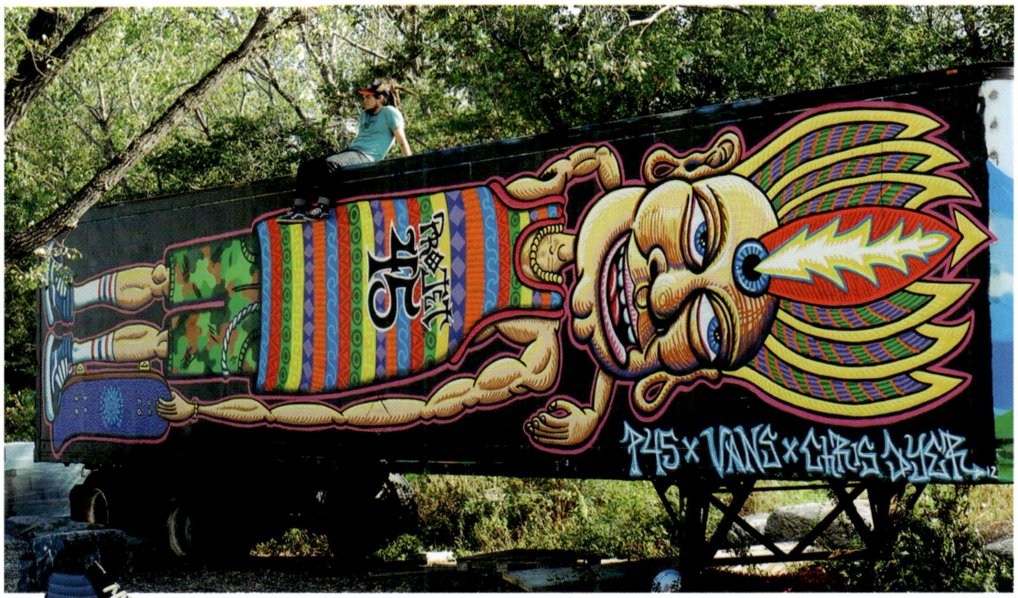

LOGOS

In these next few pages I'll be showing you some graphics I've been hired to do for a variety of clients. Though they are works for commercial purposes, they still make for some fun images and art that reaches the masses far and wide.

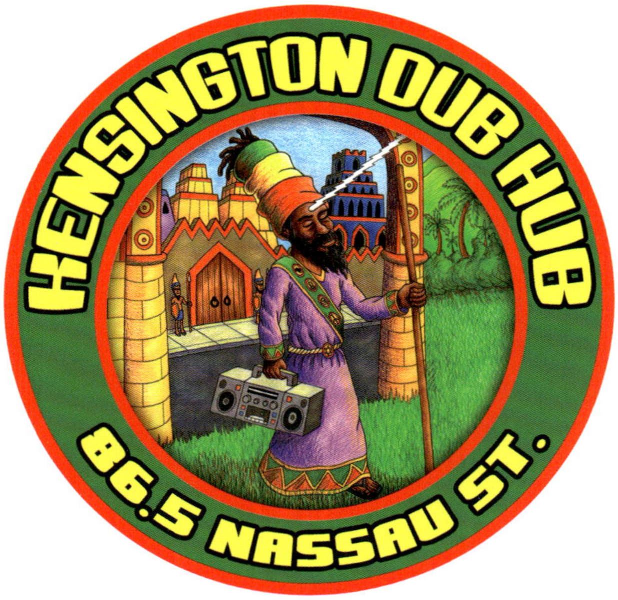

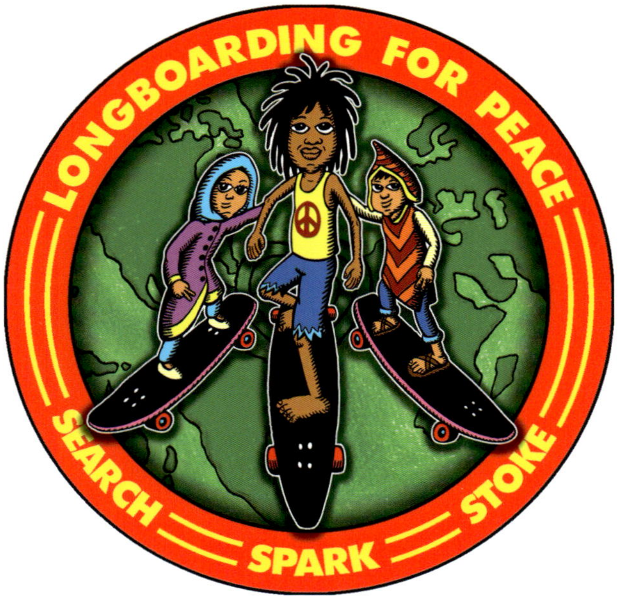

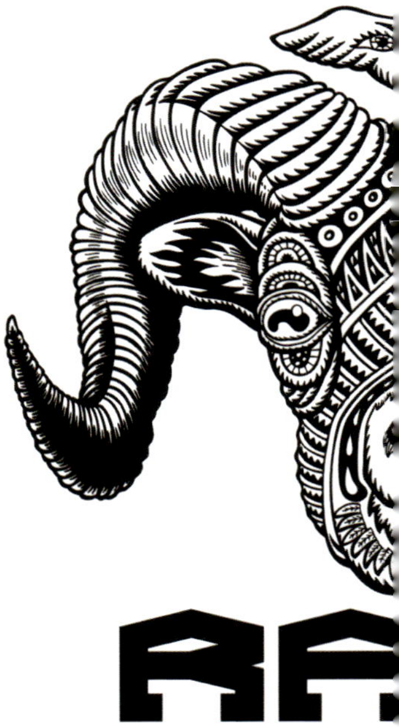

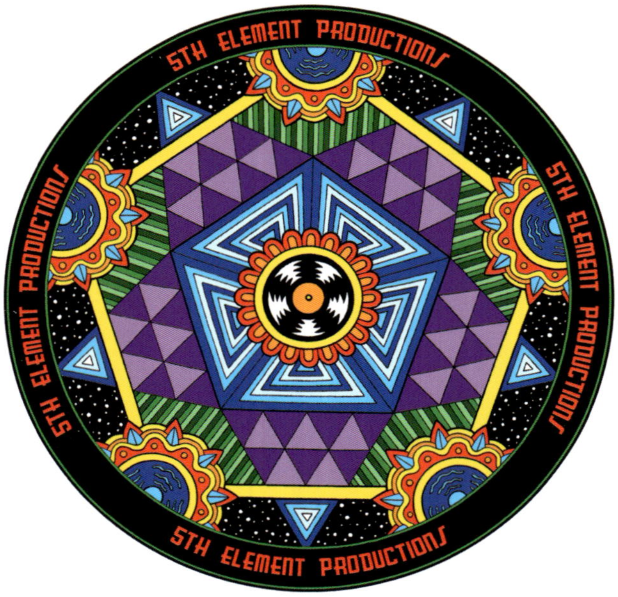

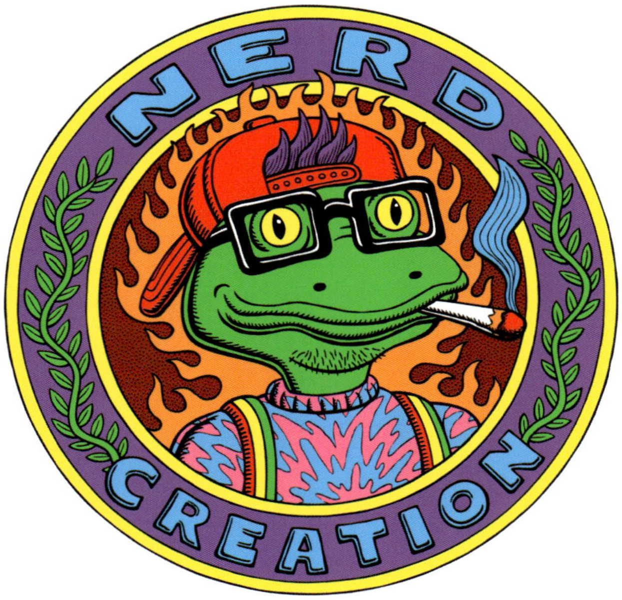

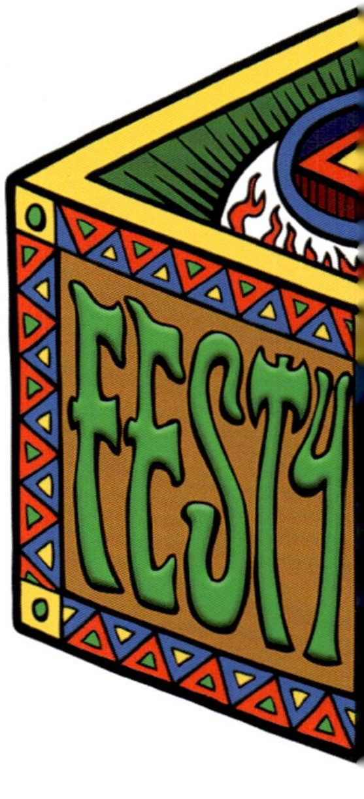

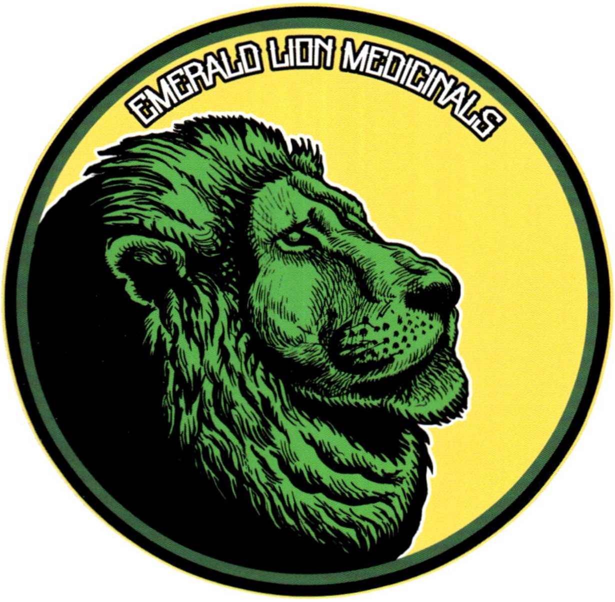

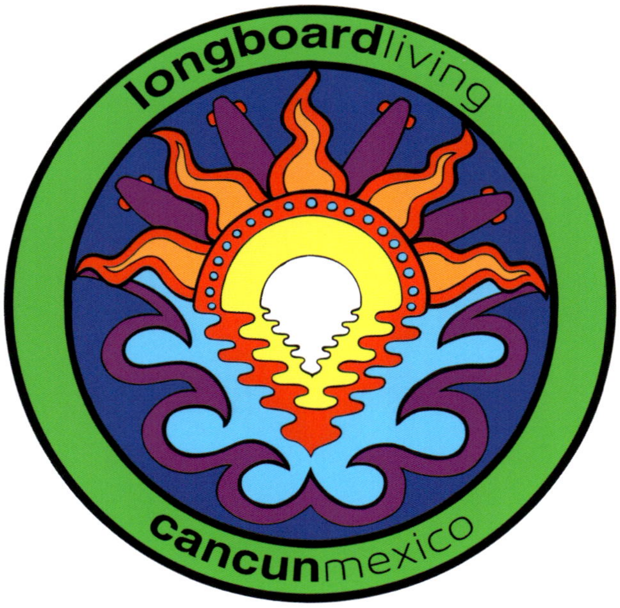

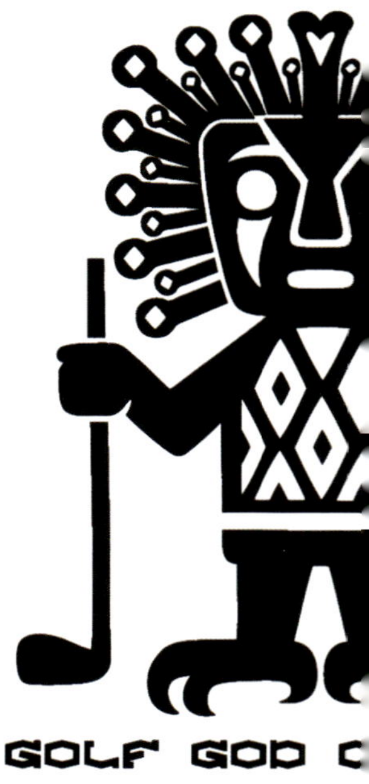

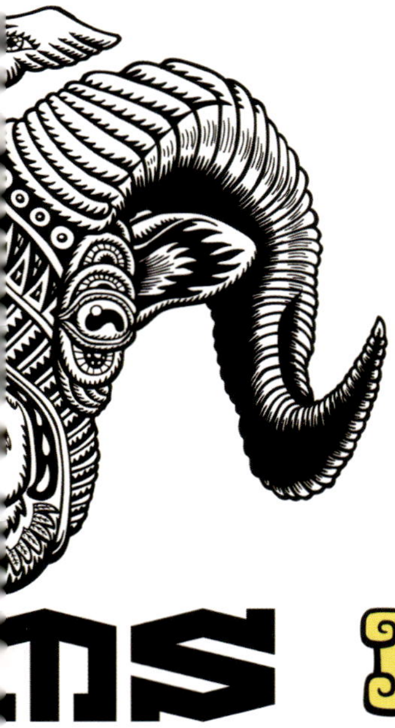

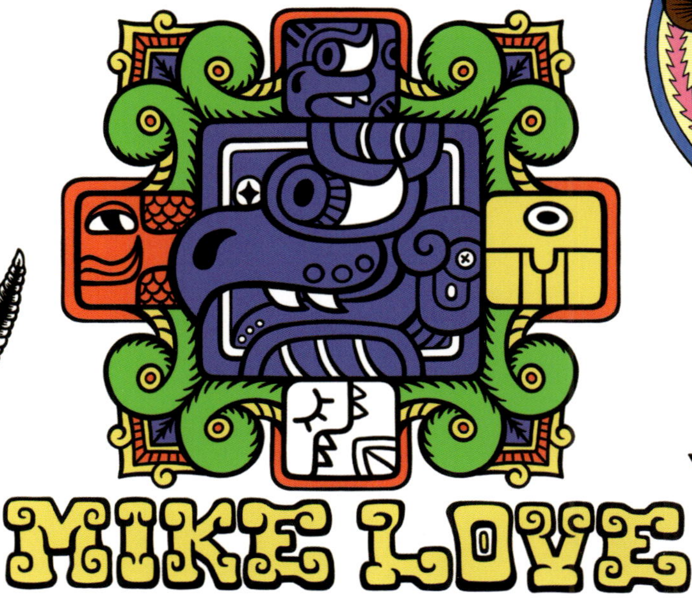
MIKE LOVE

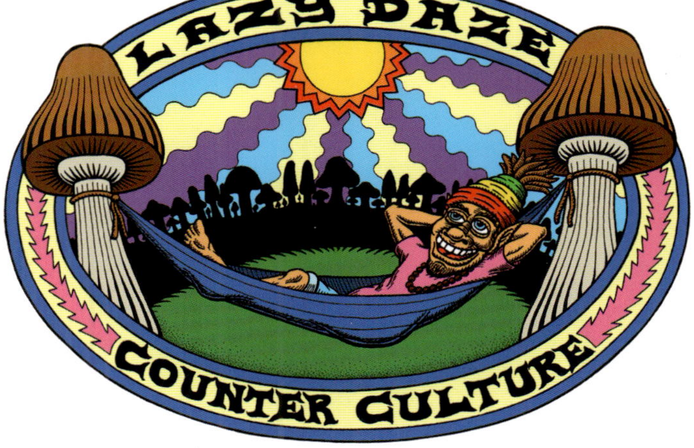
LAZY DAZE
COUNTER CULTURE

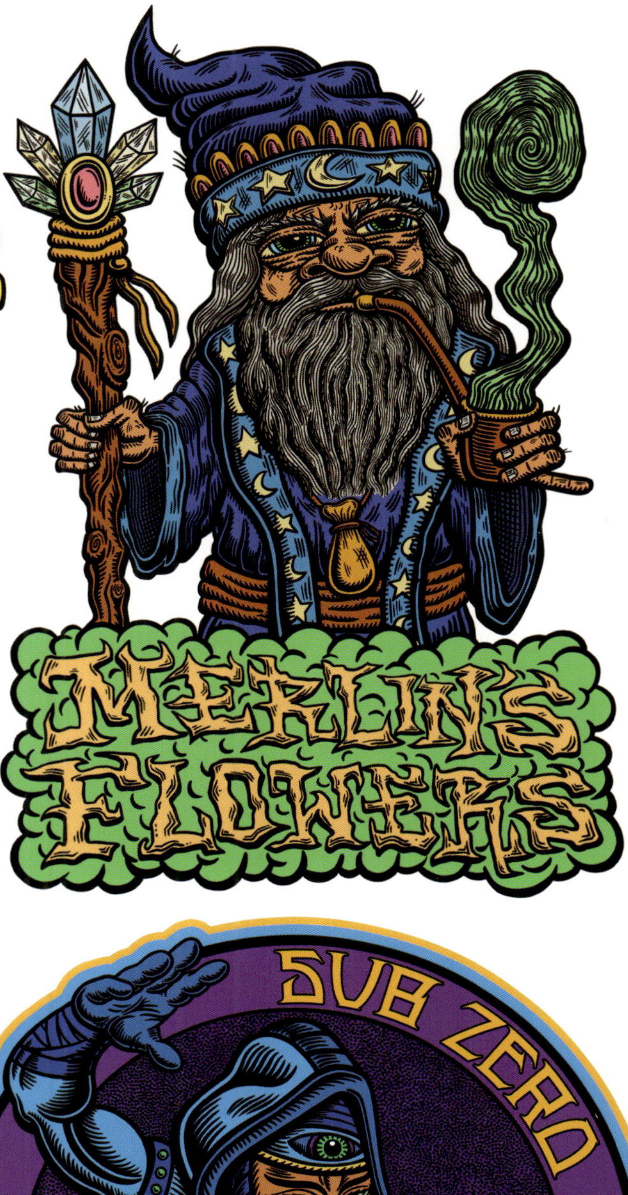

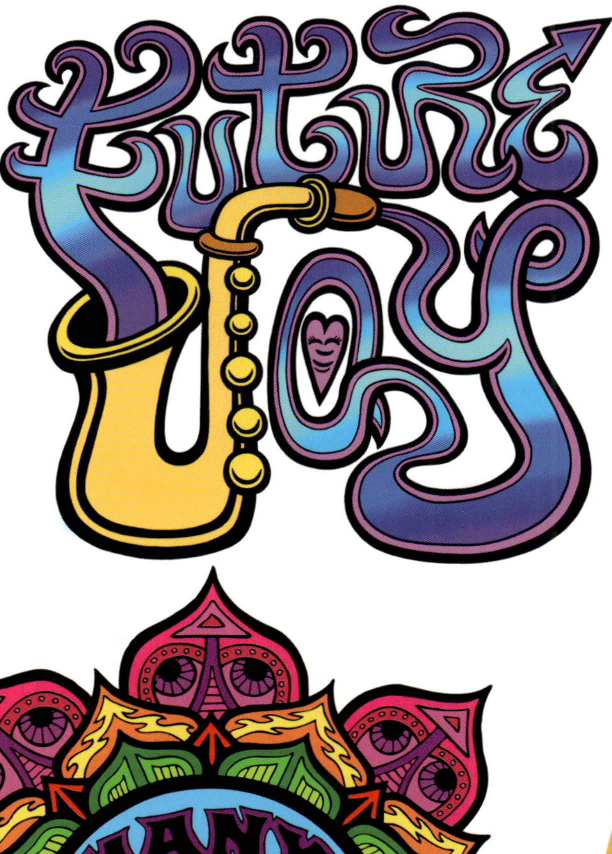
MERLINS FLOWERS

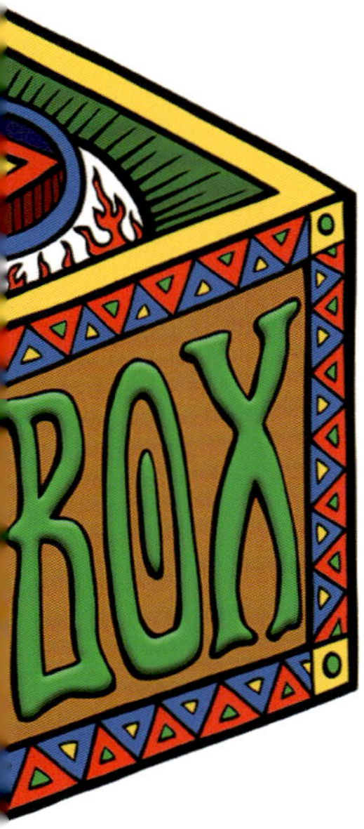
BOX

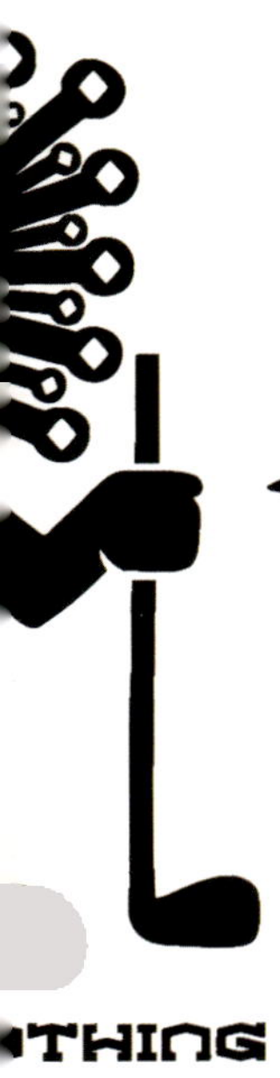

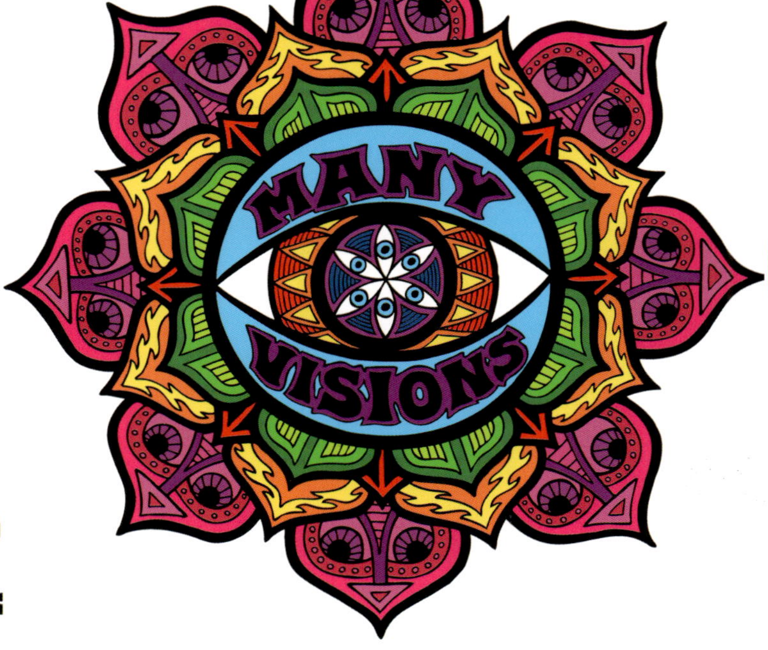
MANY
VISIONS

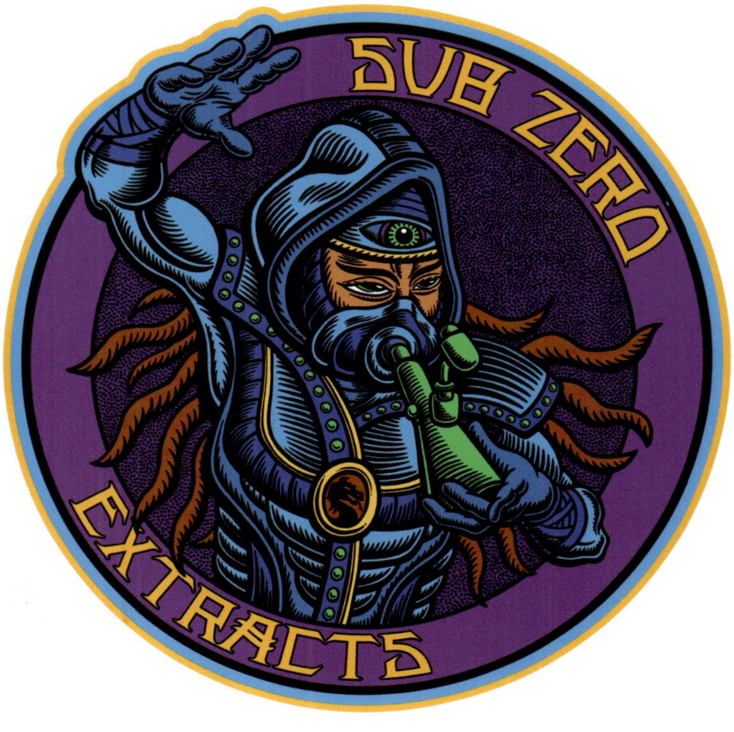
SUB ZERO
EXTRACTS

TEE SHIRT DESIGNS

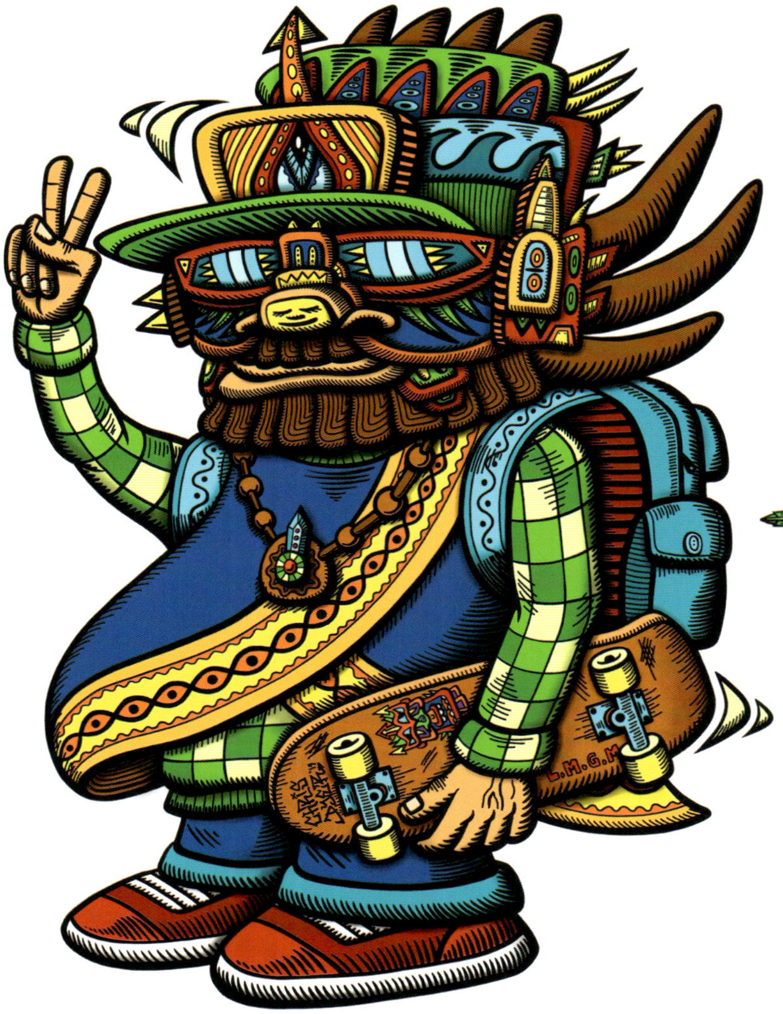

For **“Live More, Give More”** (New York)

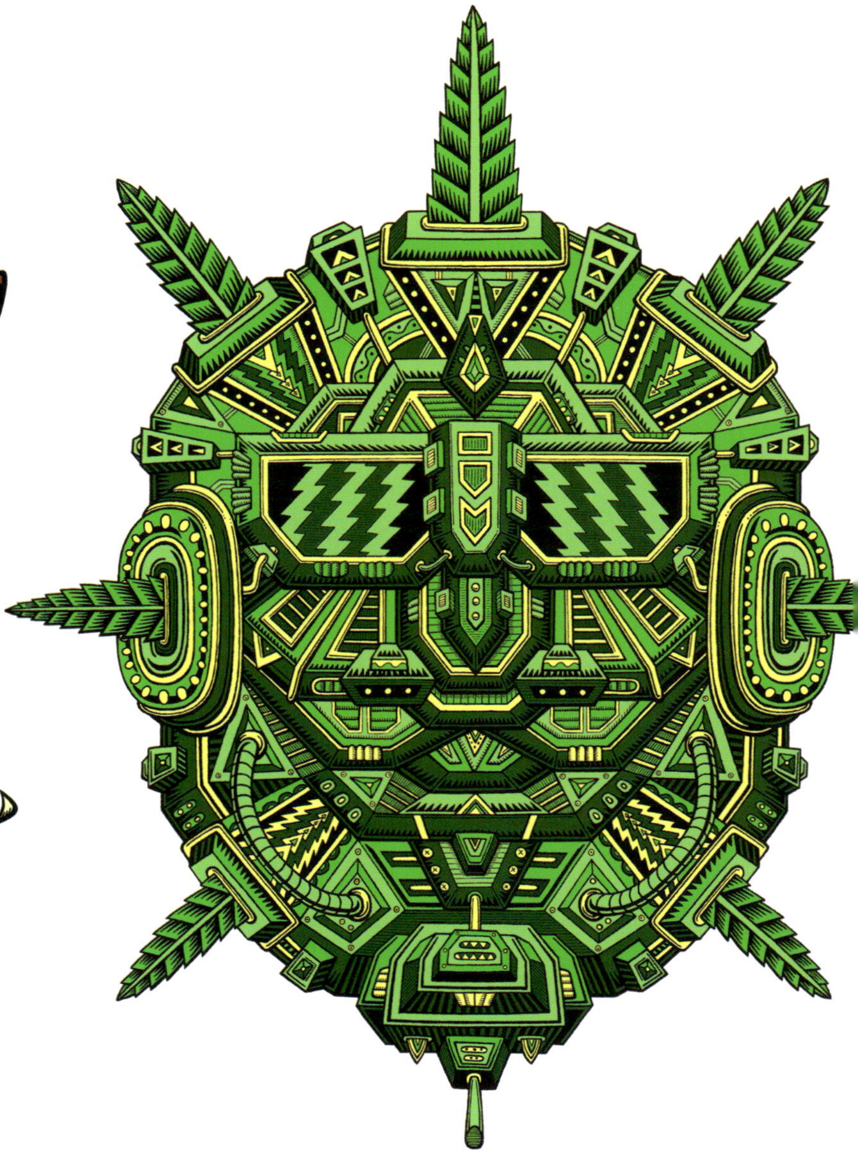

For **“Nugatron”** (Chicago)

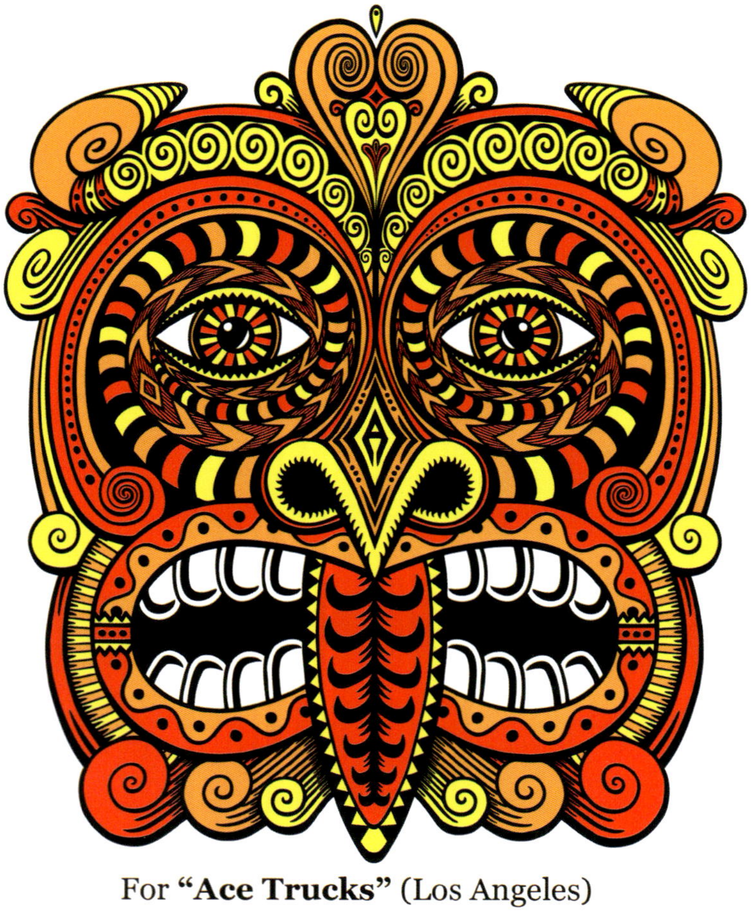

For **“Ace Trucks”** (Los Angeles)

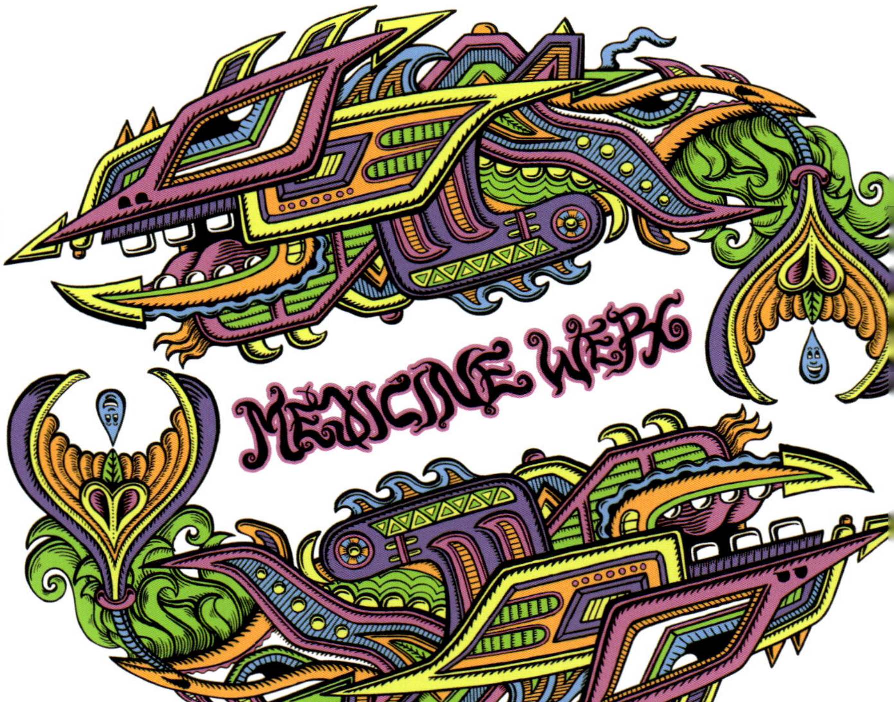

For **“Medicine Werx”** (Colorado)

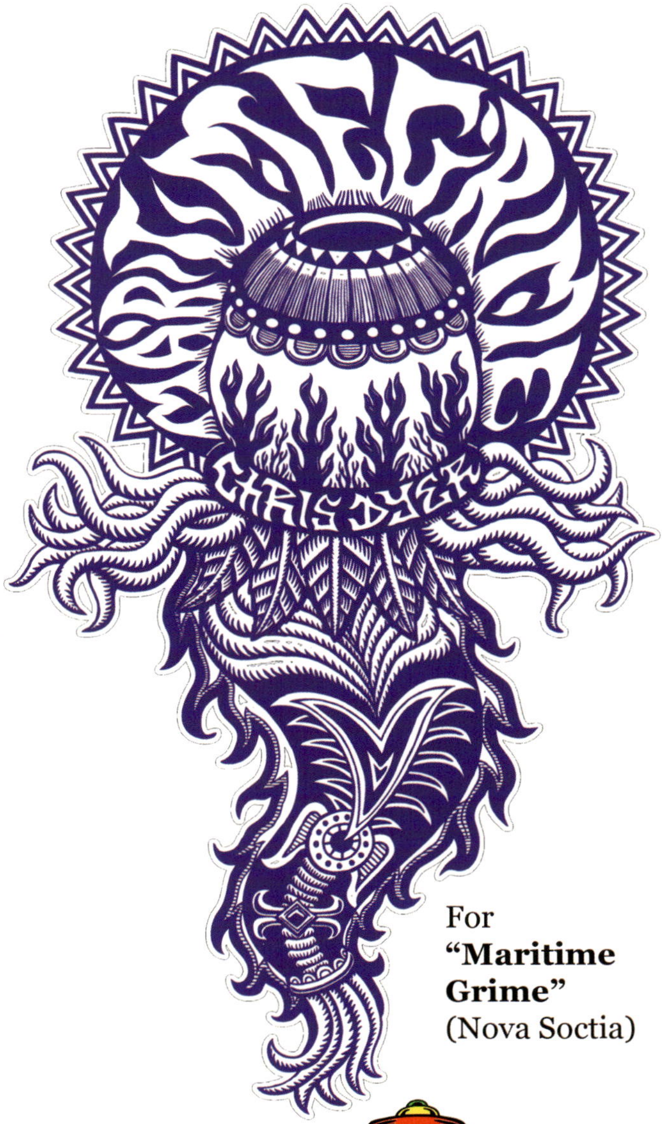

For **“Maritime Grime”** (Nova Soctia)

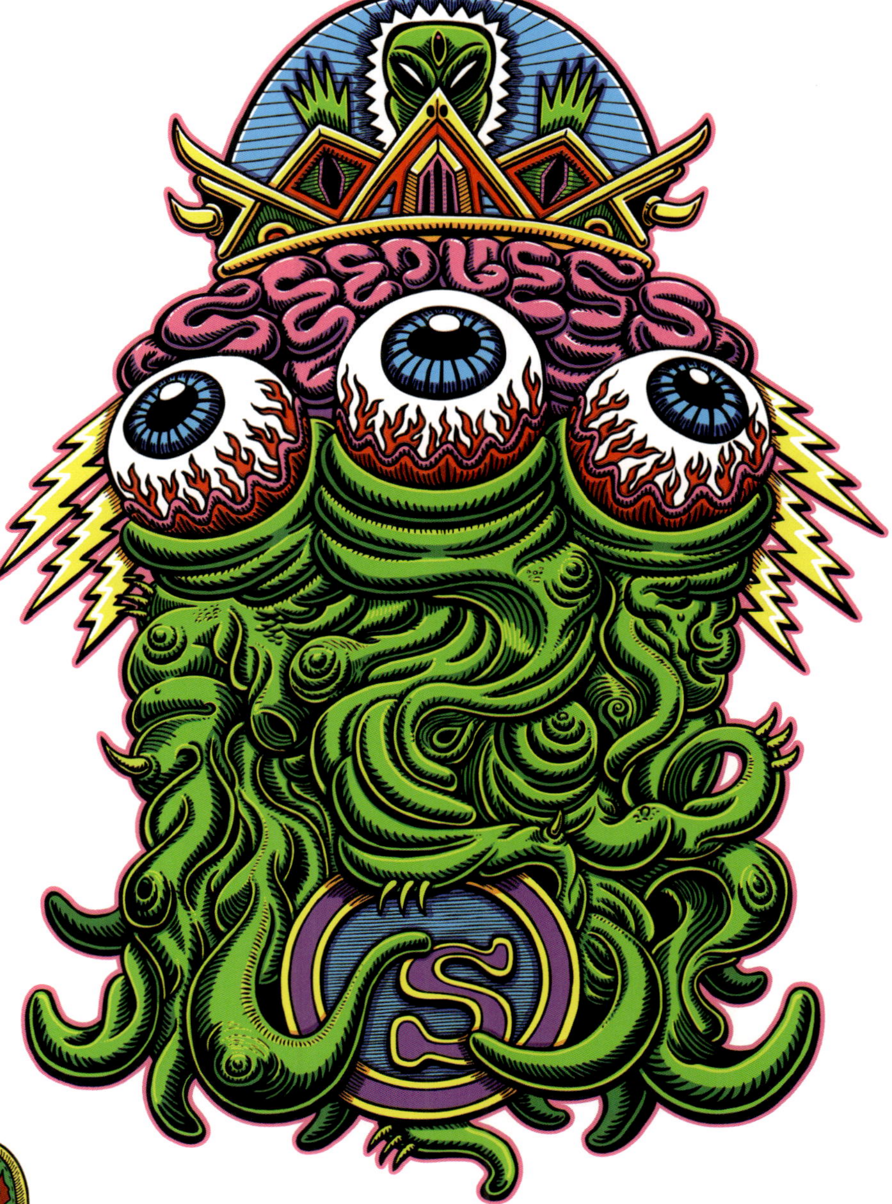

For **“Seedless Clothing”** (San Diego)

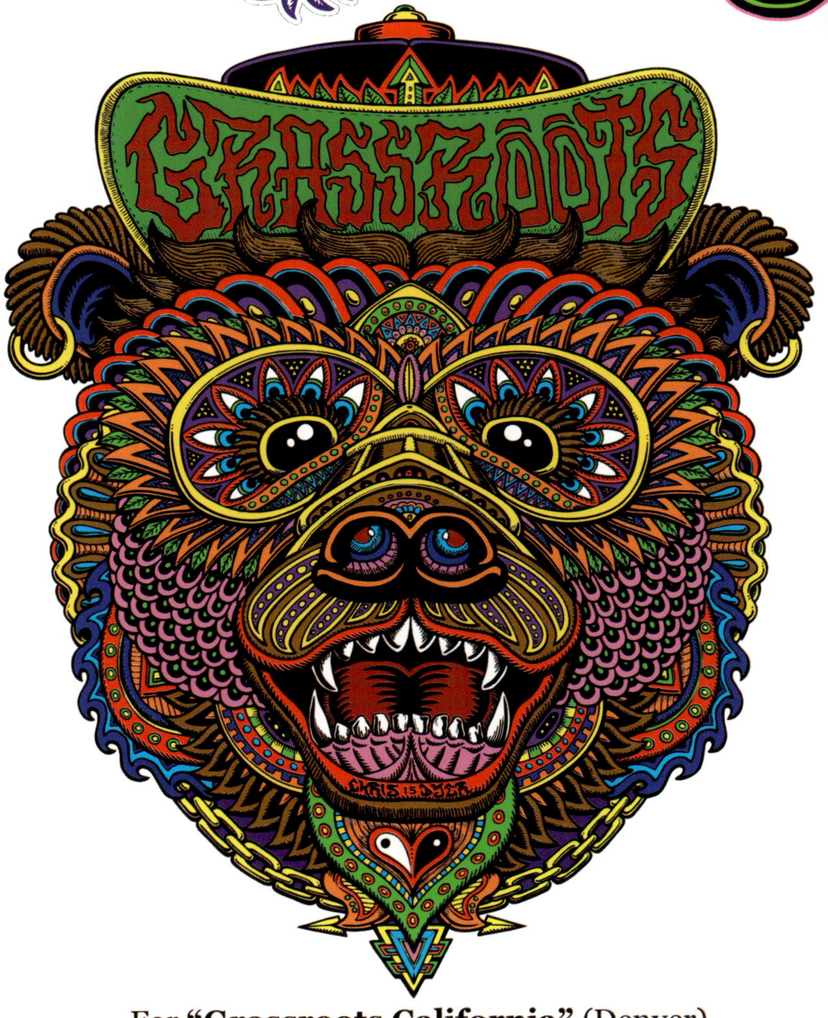

For **“Grassroots California”** (Denver)

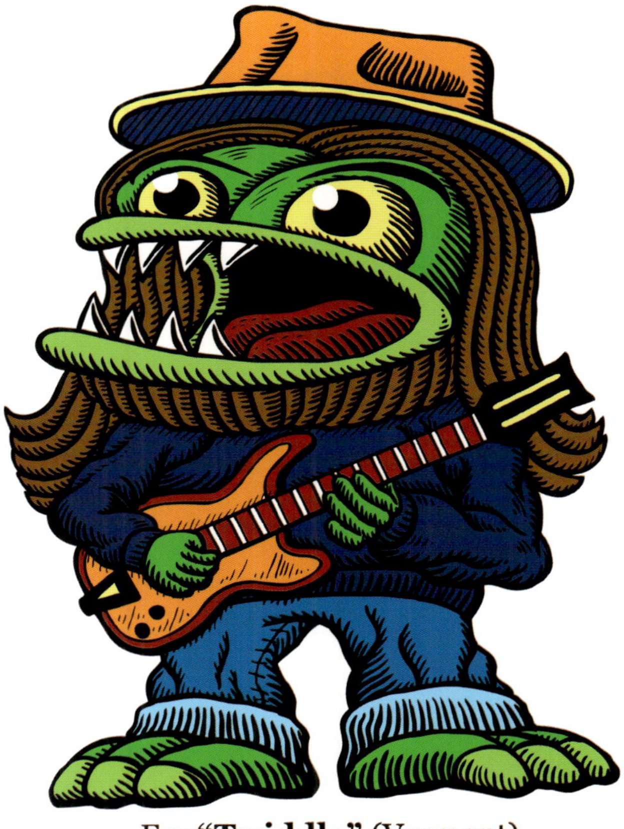

For **“Twiddle”** (Vermont)

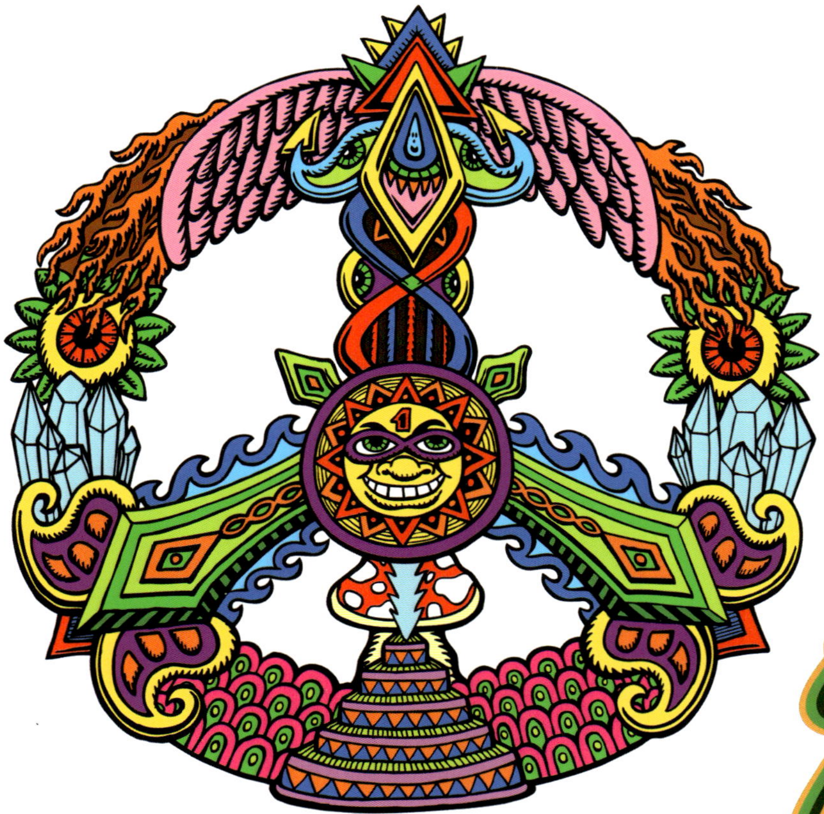

For **"Happy Daze"** (Australia)

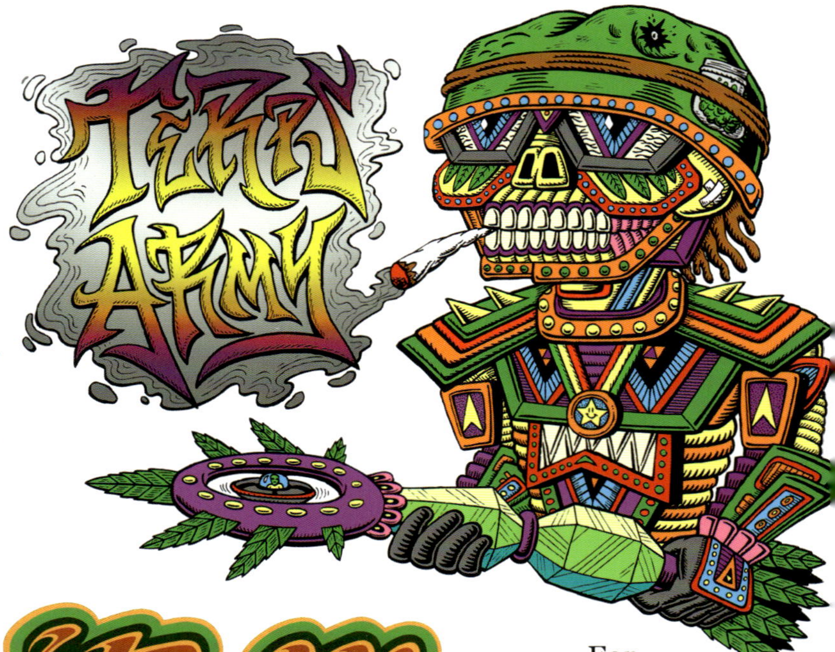

For
"Terps Army"
(Barcelona)

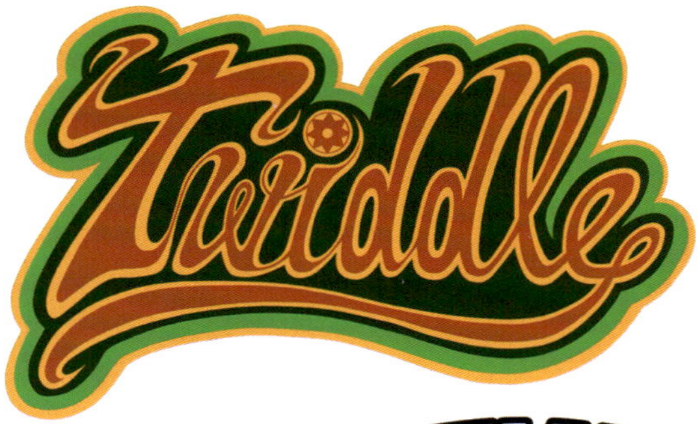

For
"Twiddle"
(Vermont)

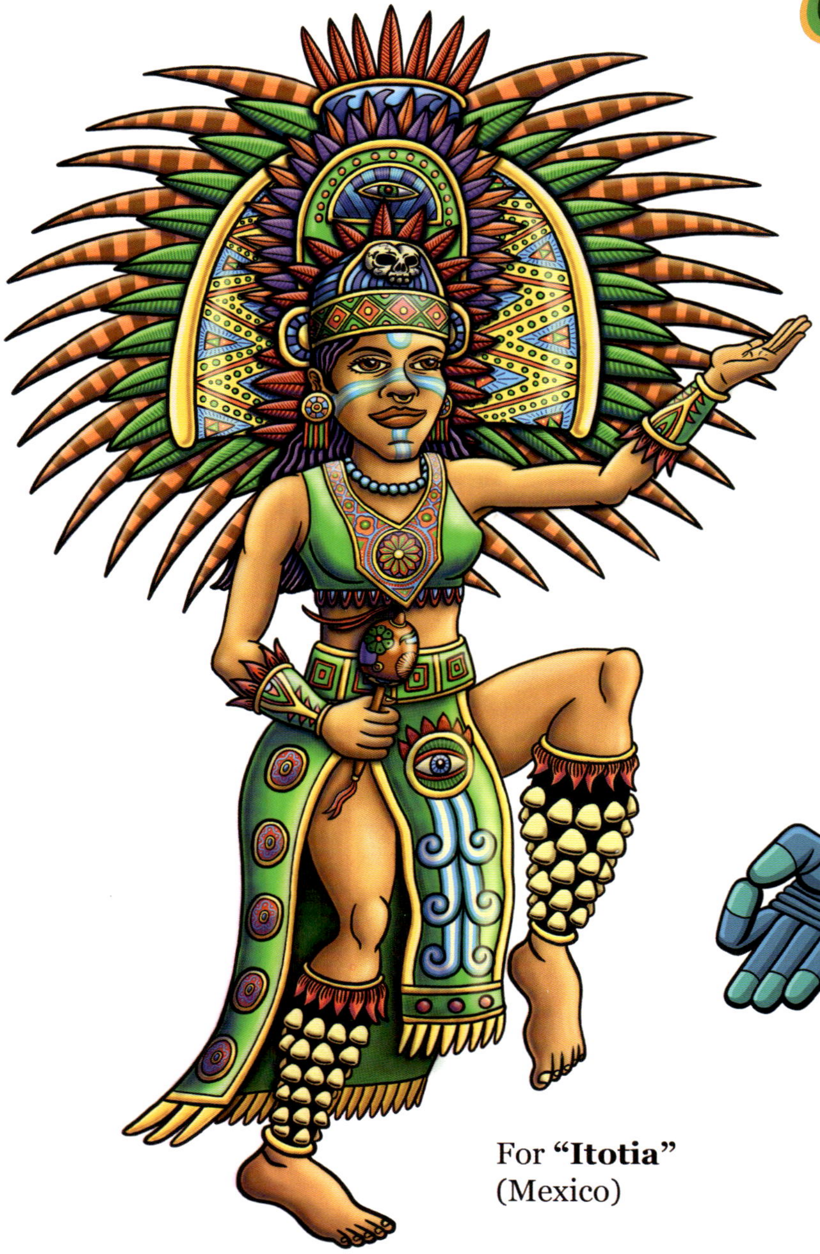

For **"Itotia"**
(Mexico)

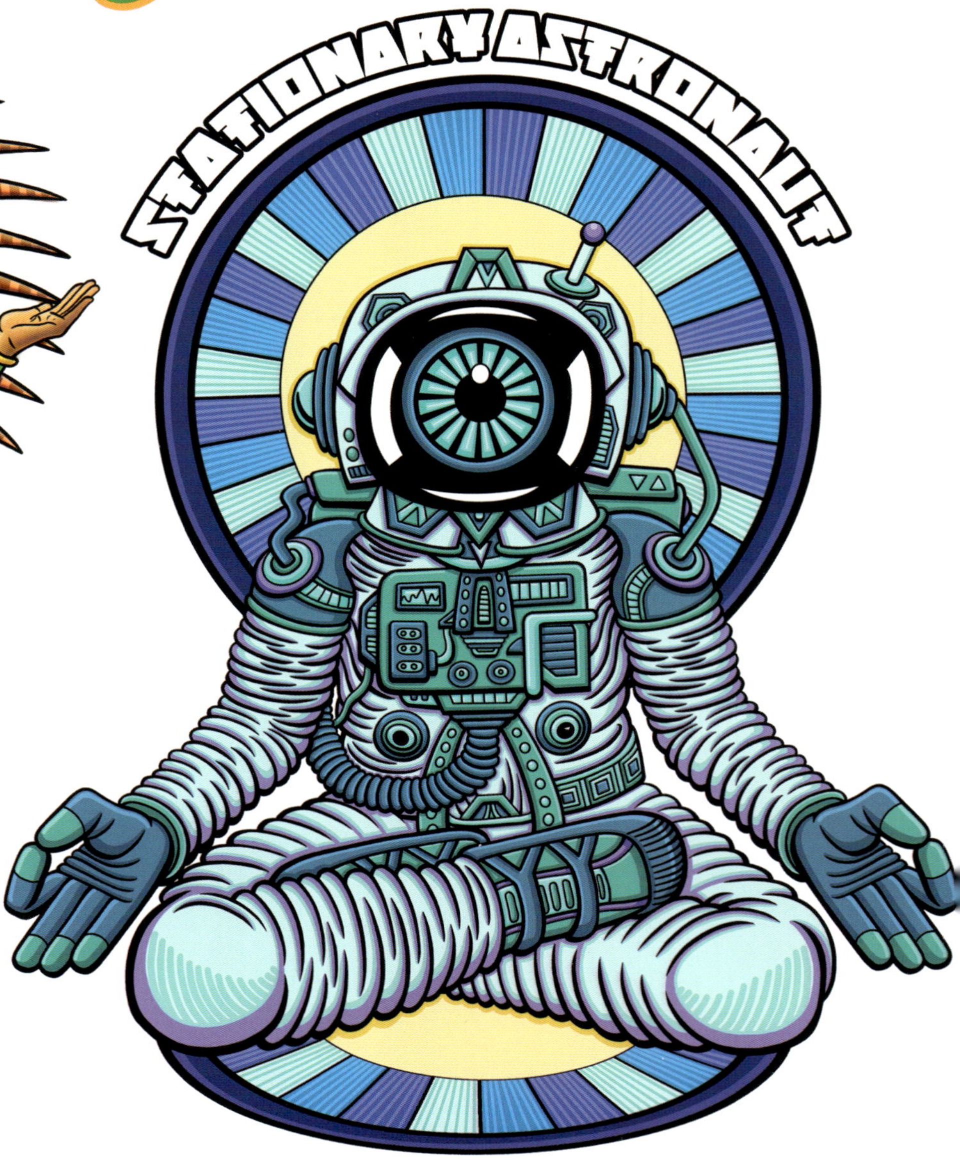

For **"Stationary Astronaut"** (Minnesota)

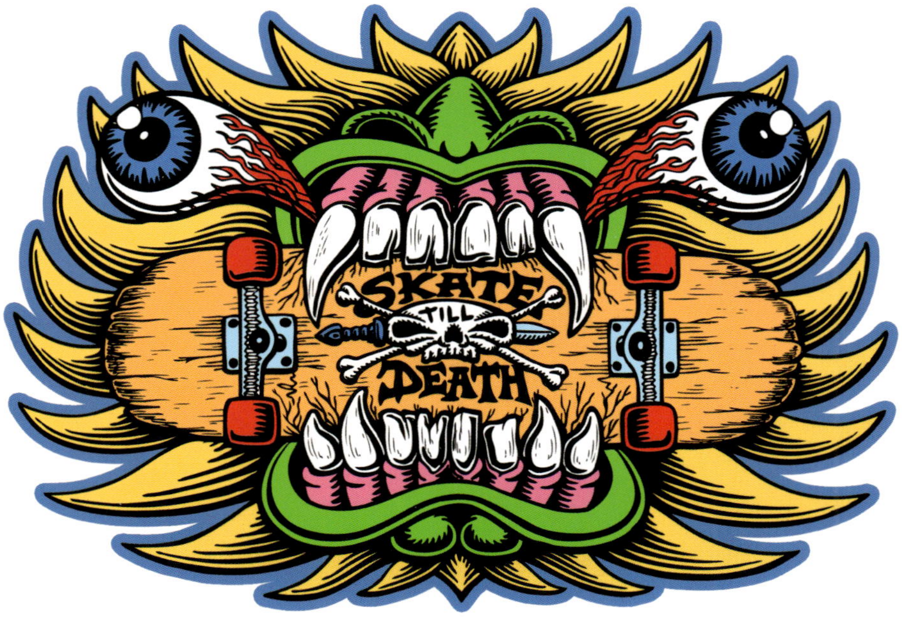

For **"Festy Box"** (Philladelphia)

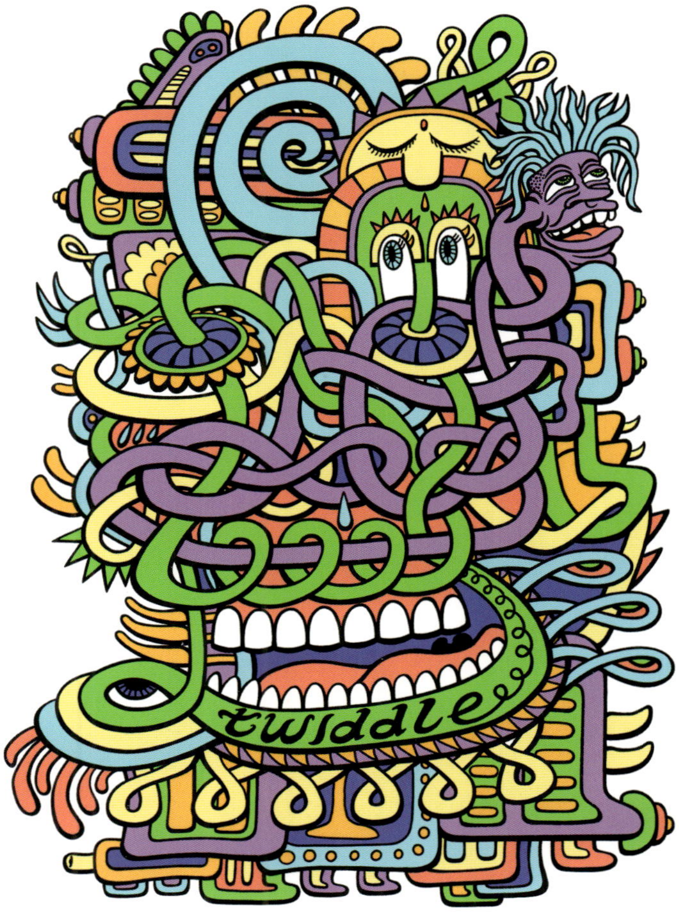

For **"Twiddle"** (Vermont)

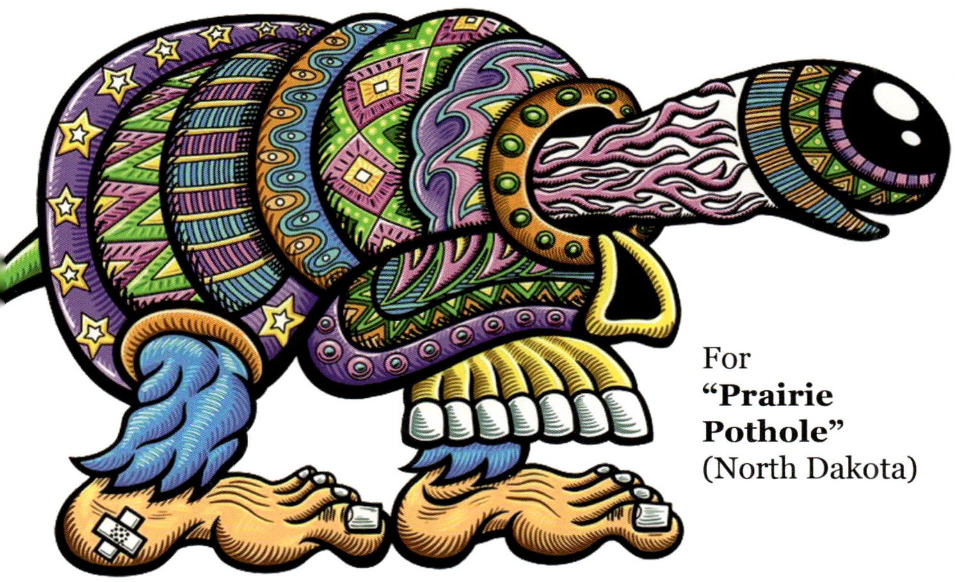

For **"Prairie Pothole"** (North Dakota)

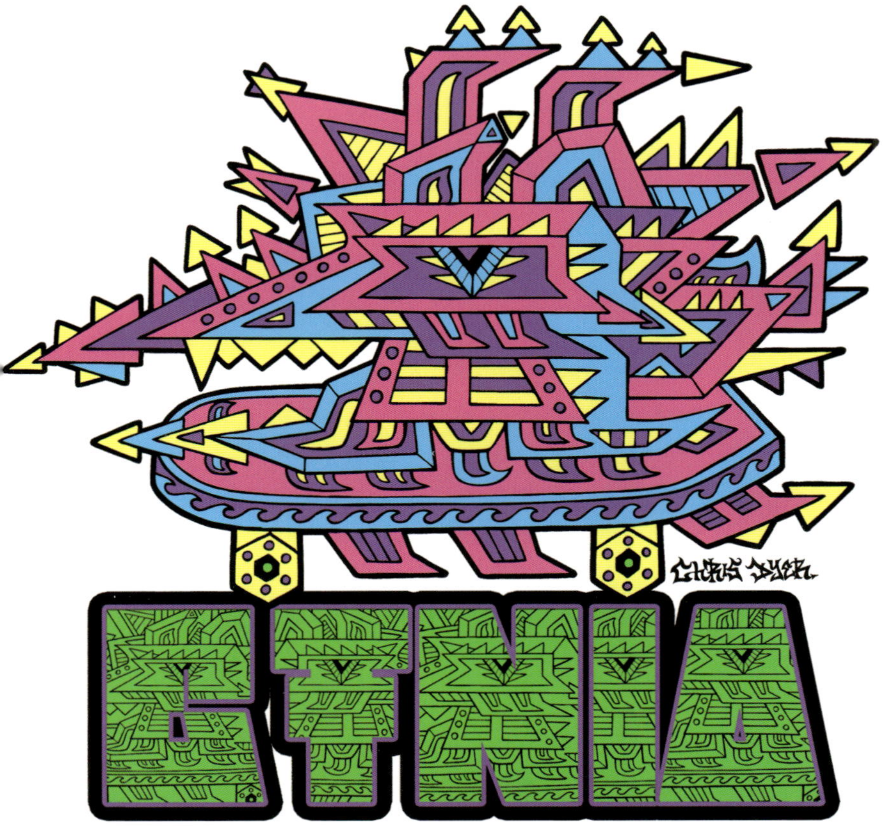

For **"Etnia"** (Costa Rica)

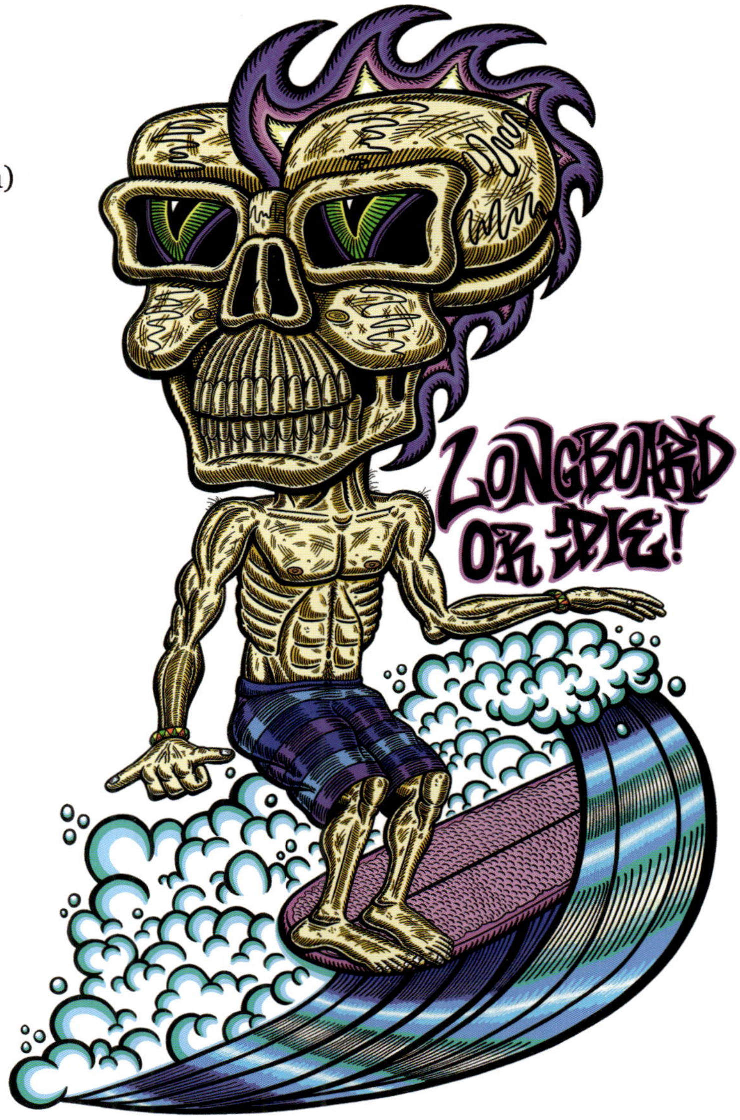

For **"Longboard or Die"** (Peru)

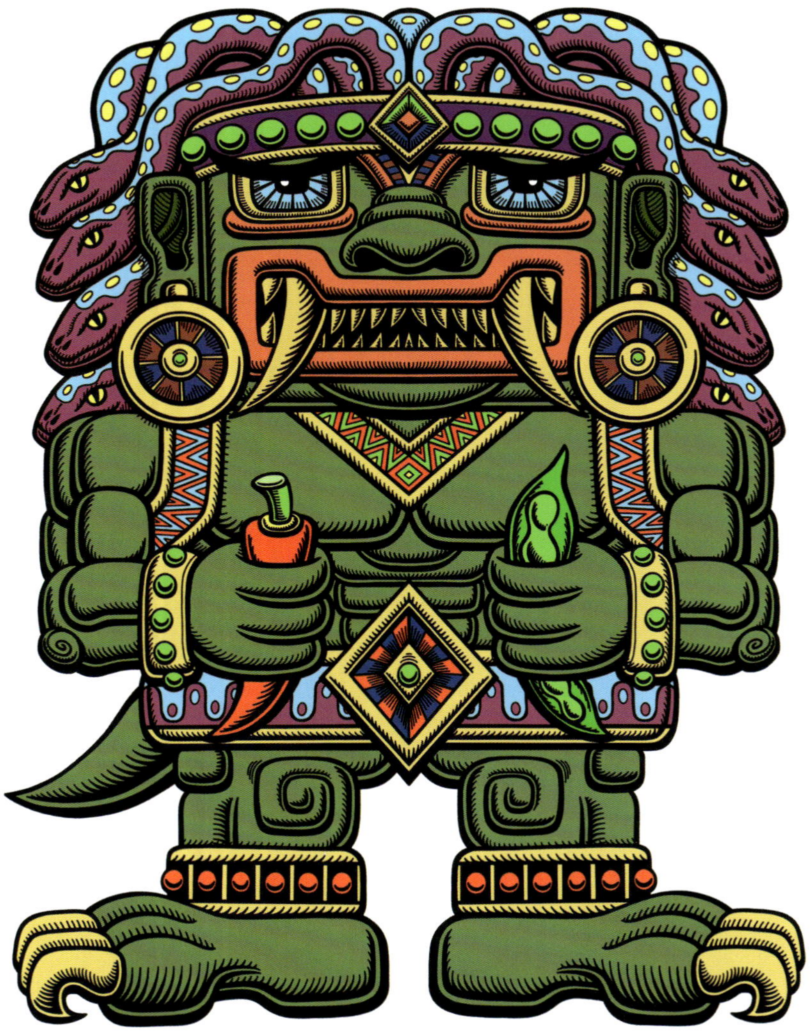

For **"Tonka Visionas"** (England)

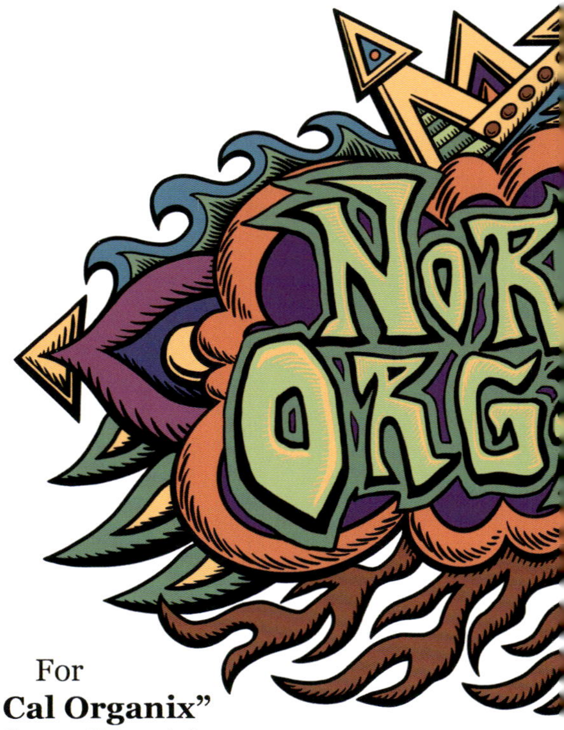

For
"Nor Cal Organix"
(Mendo, California)

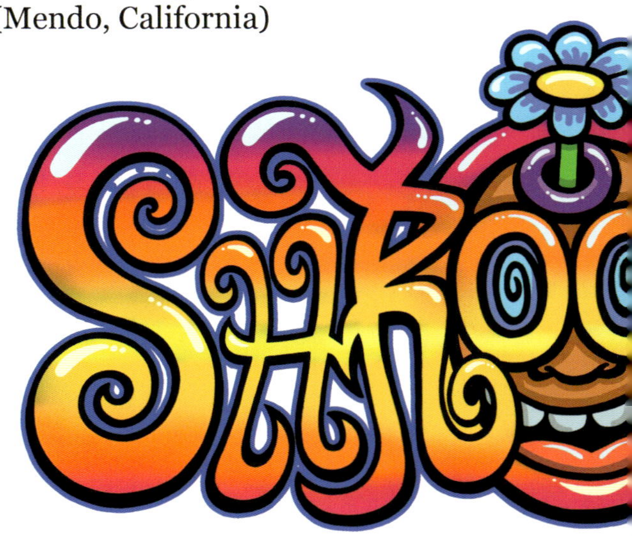

For
"Shroomski Magazine"
(Denver, Colorado)

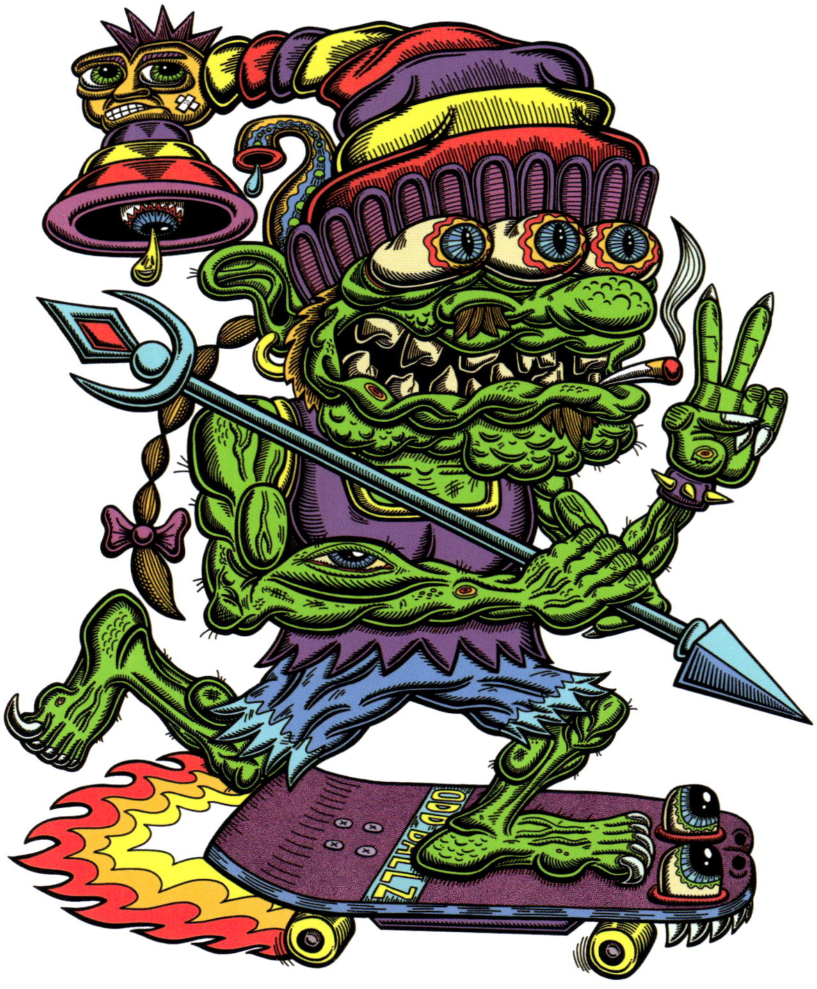

For **"Oddballz Skateshop"** (Austin, Texas)

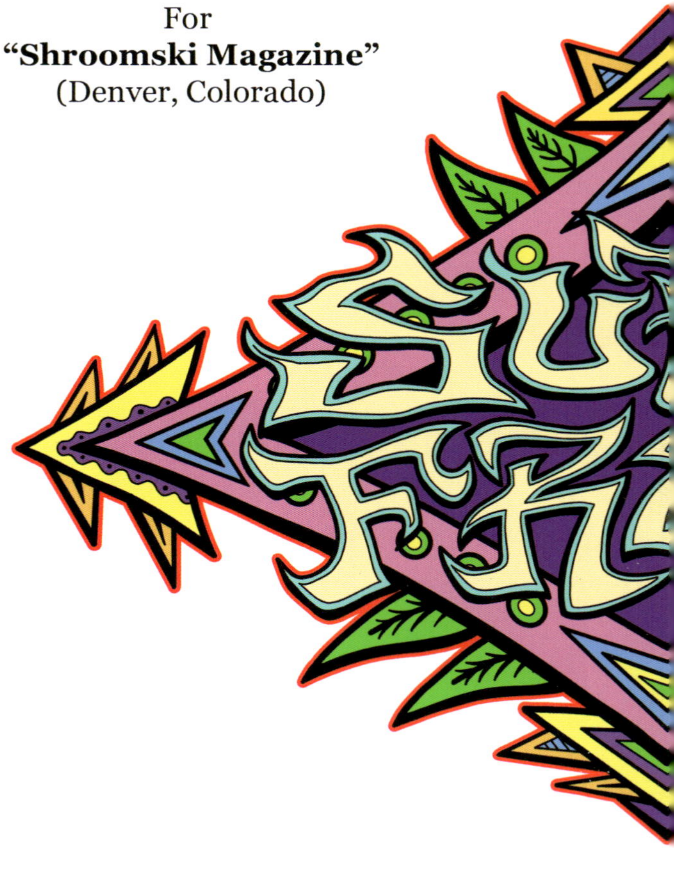

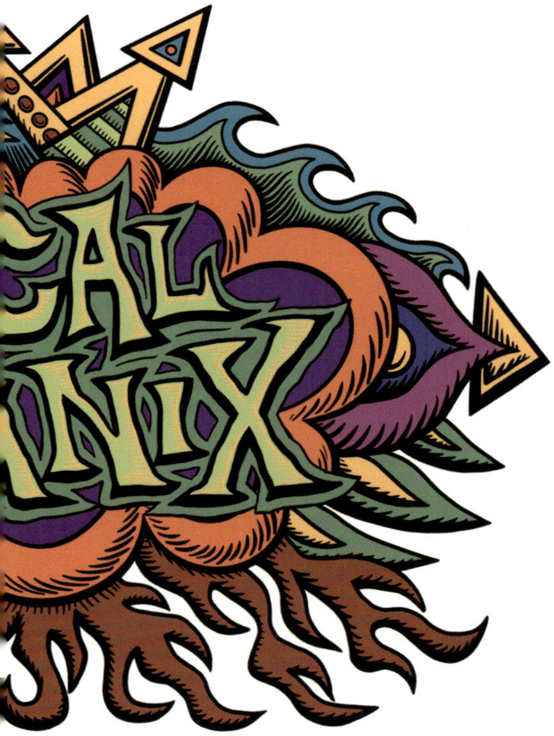

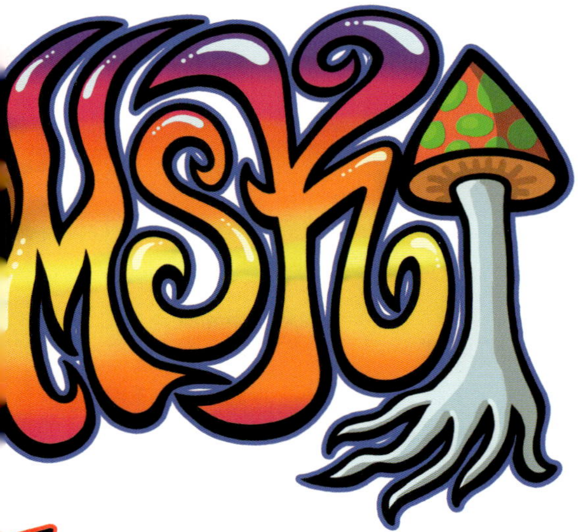

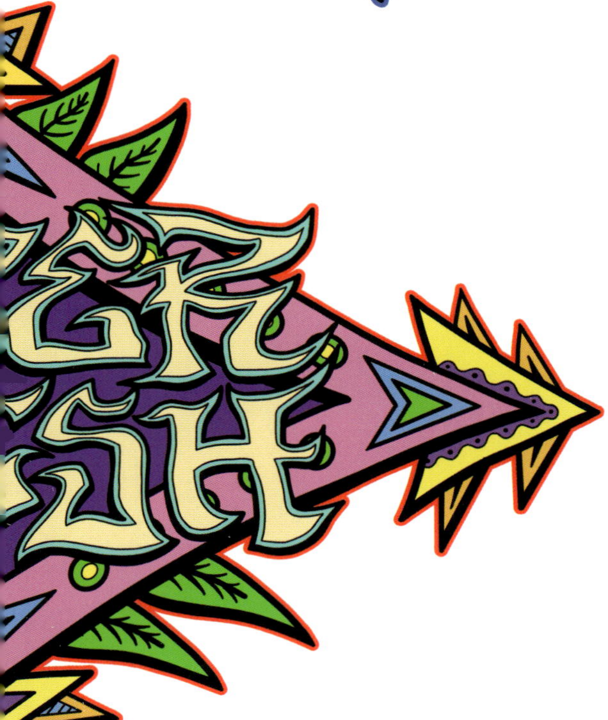

For **"Super Fresh"**
(San Clemente, California)

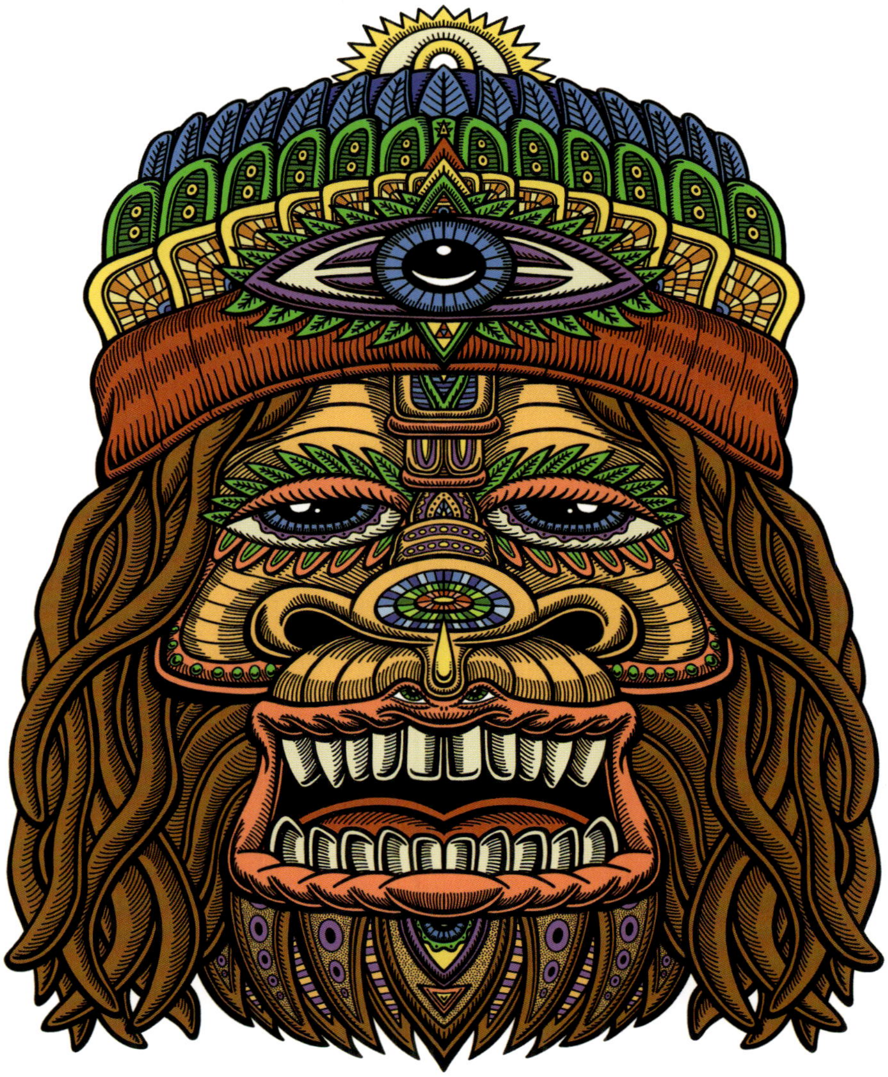

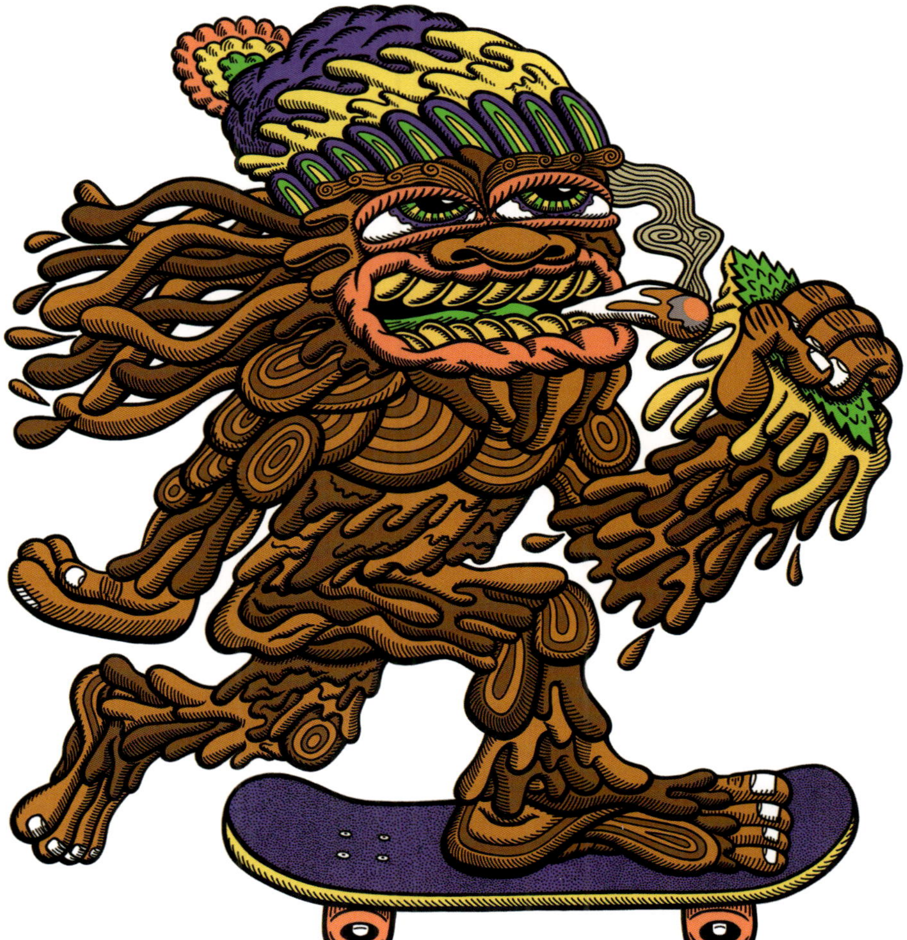

For **"Sasquash Rosin Press"** (California)

POSITIVE CREATIONS BRAND

In my last book I told you all about the roots of my artsy clothing and accessories brand **Positive Creations** which I started in 2004. I've had many partners, managers and set ups over the years, but as the demand grew and I was constantly on the road, I just hired fulfillment houses to run it. I've been lucky to have popular festival brands like **Grassroots California**, **The Headspace** and **Harmoneyez Visions** run my own merch situation at different points. The later brand, lead by **Cory Ponz** was a real nice fit for around 5 years. In that alliance we had our own brand house in Denver, which included our own printing setup and storage. We also where able to offer fun Pop-Up Booths of my products at several Music Festivals and events. I am very grateful to all the nice people who have worked for Positive Creations over the years and so happy that we've been able to offer quality products of my art for 20 years already!

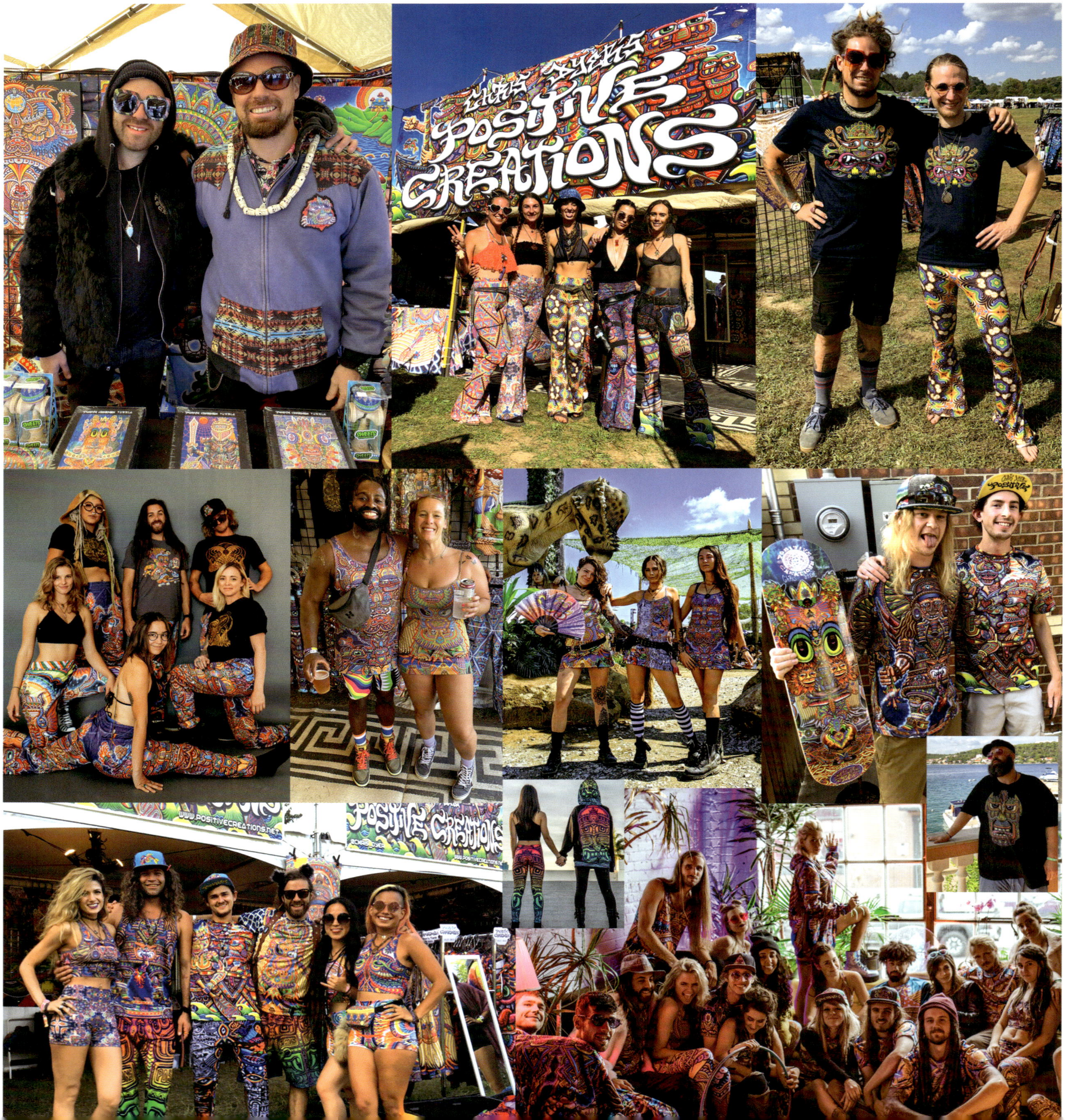

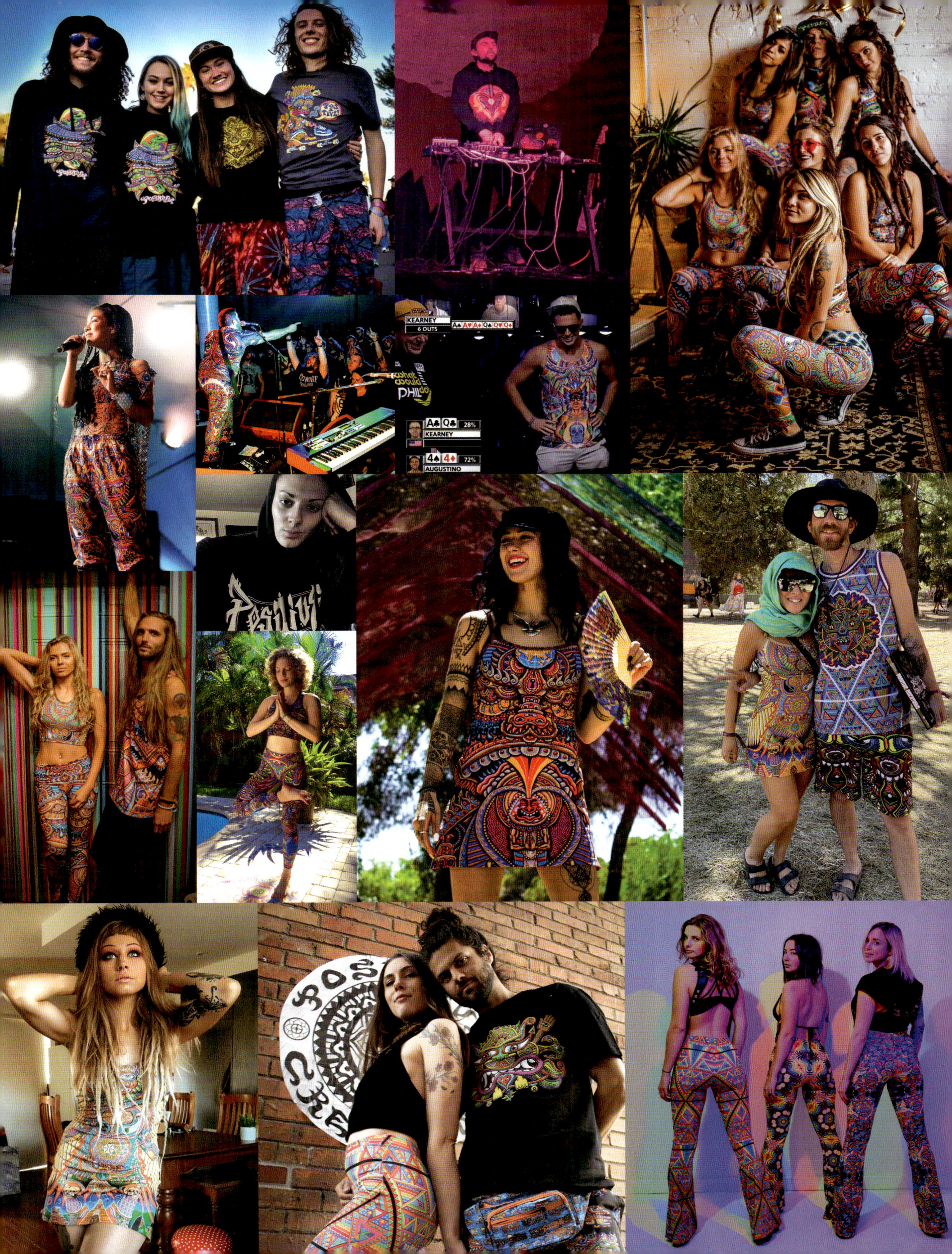
KEARNEY
6 OUTS
KEARNEY 28%
AUGUSTINO 72%

PC GRAPHICS

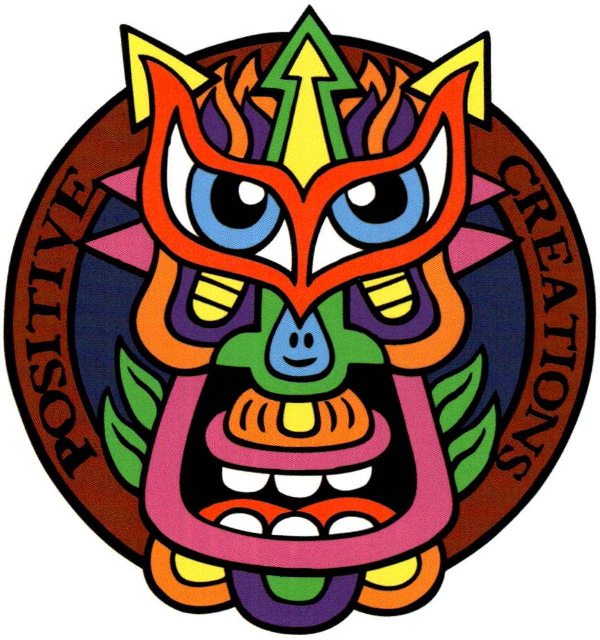

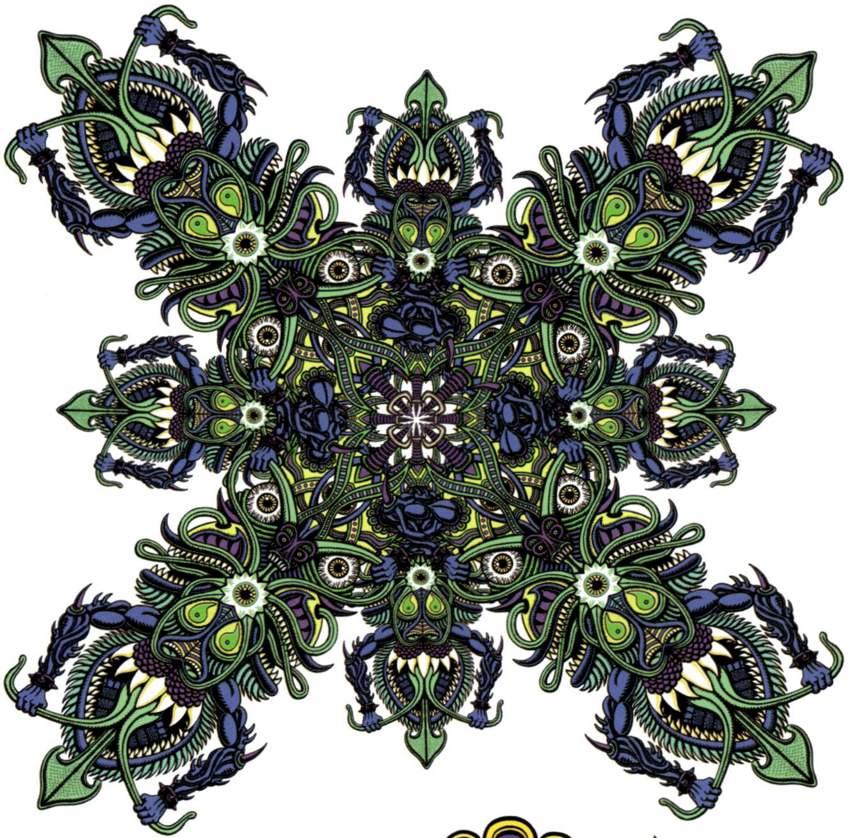

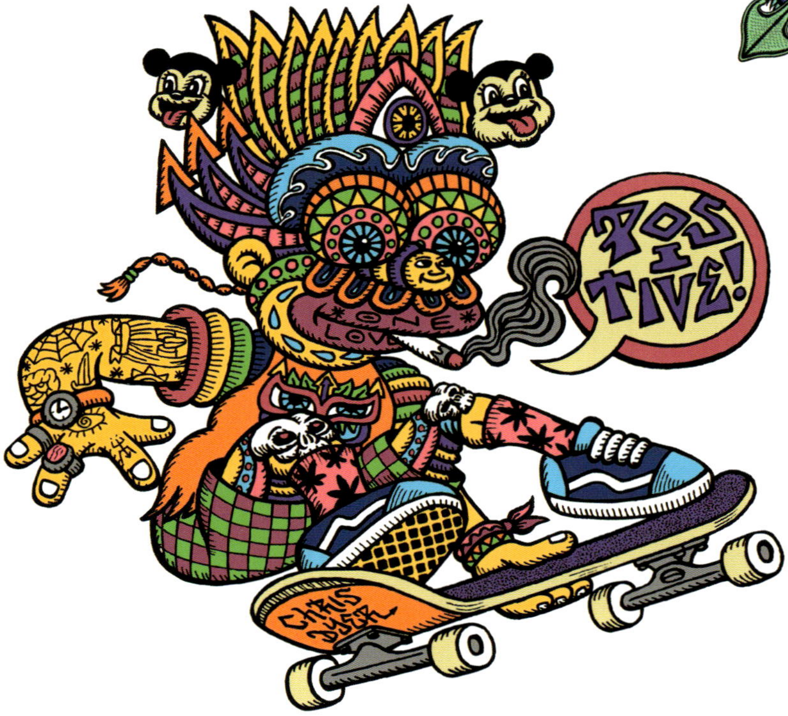

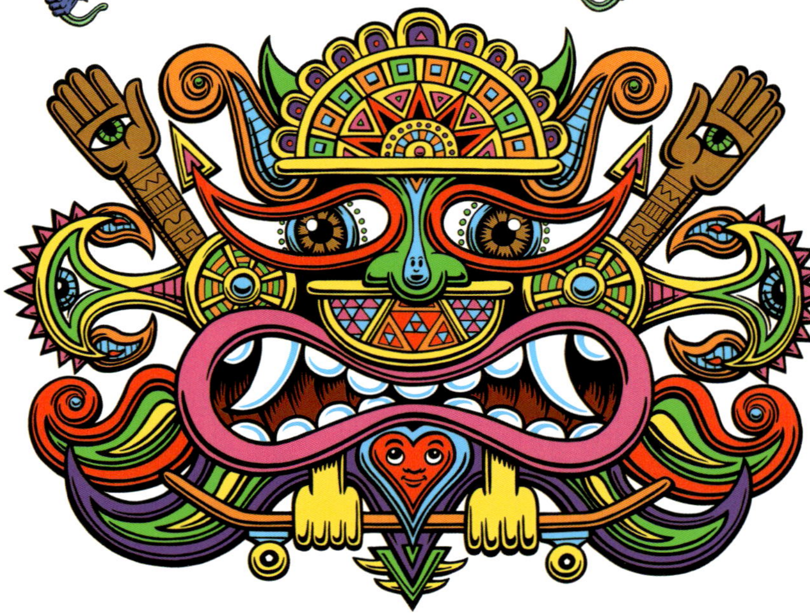

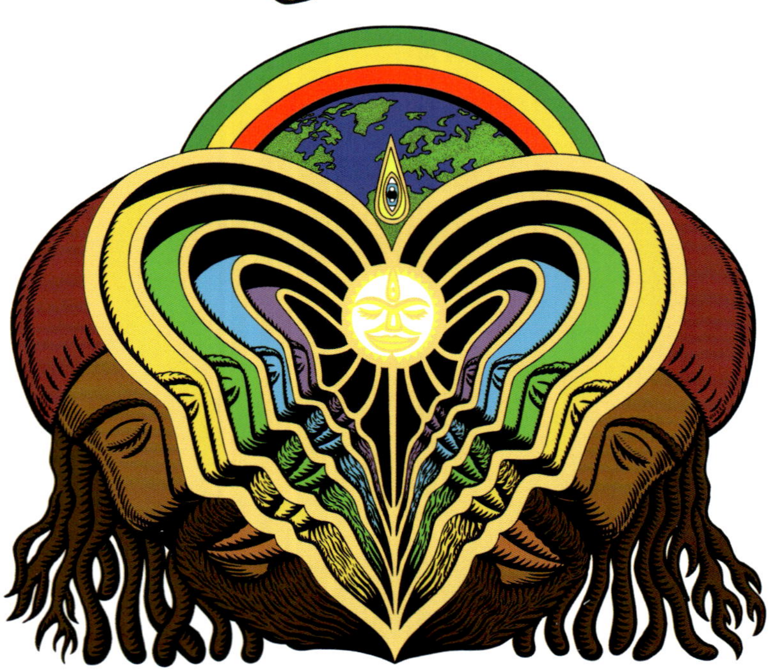

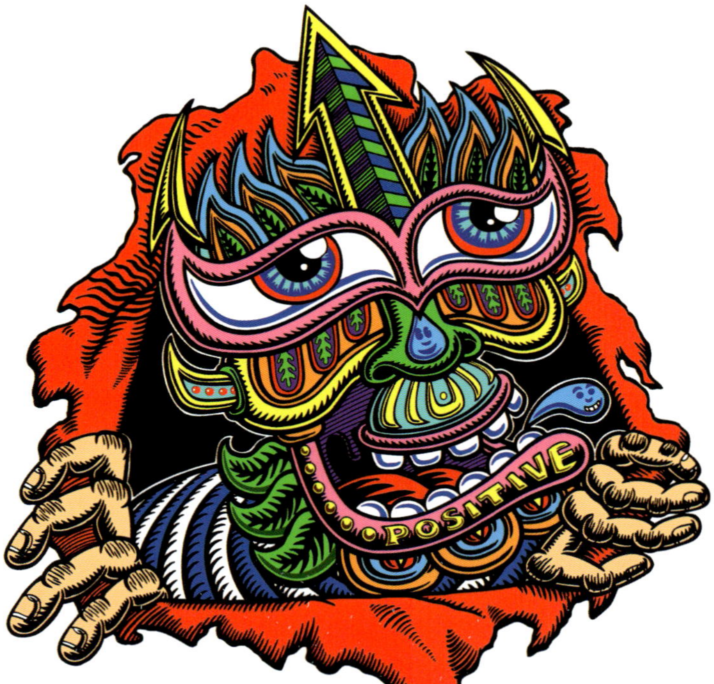

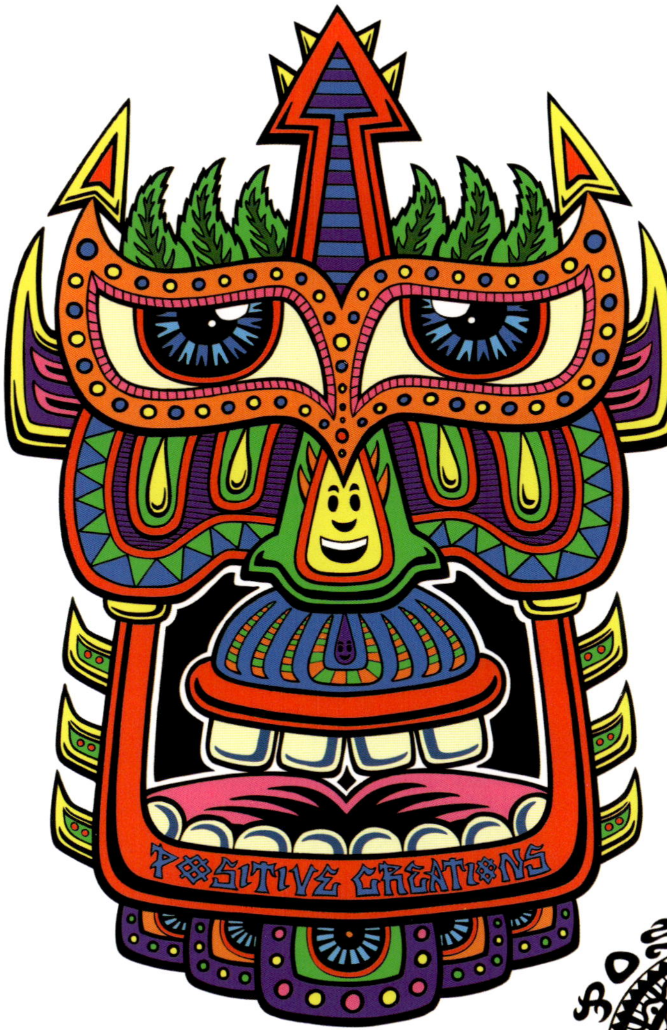
POSITIVE CREATIONS

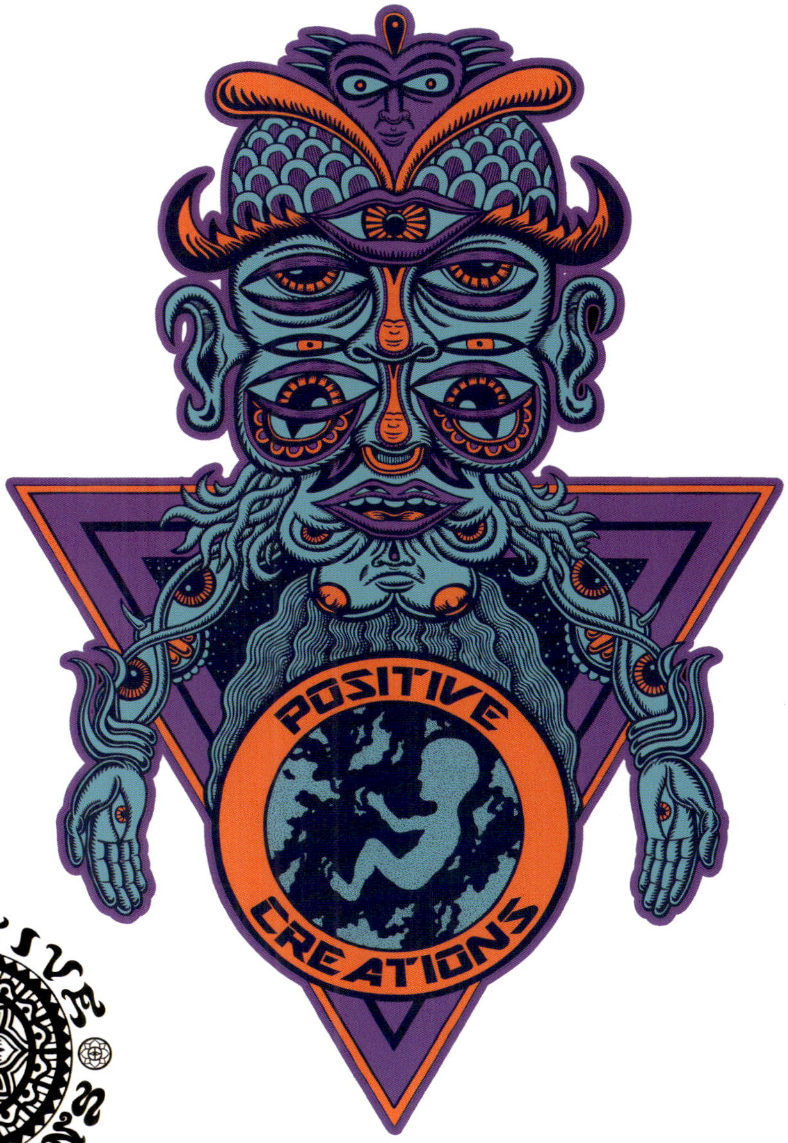
POSITIVE
CREATIONS

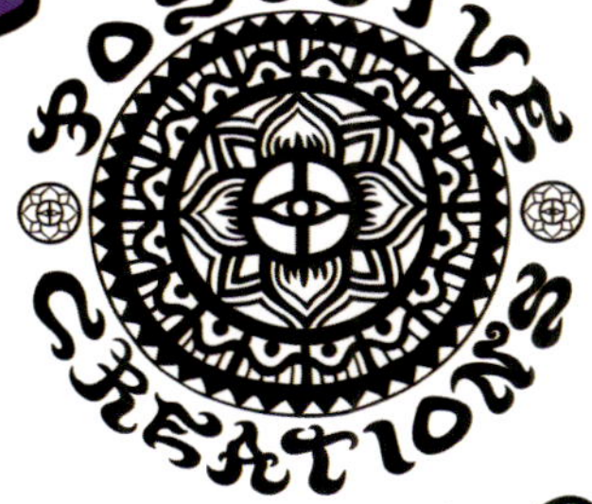
POSITIVE
CREATIONS

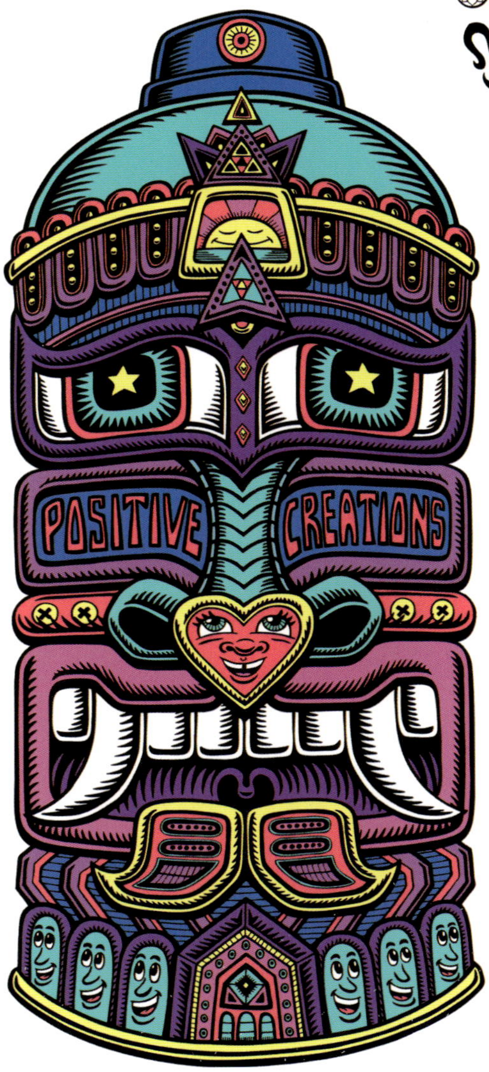
POSITIVE
CREATIONS

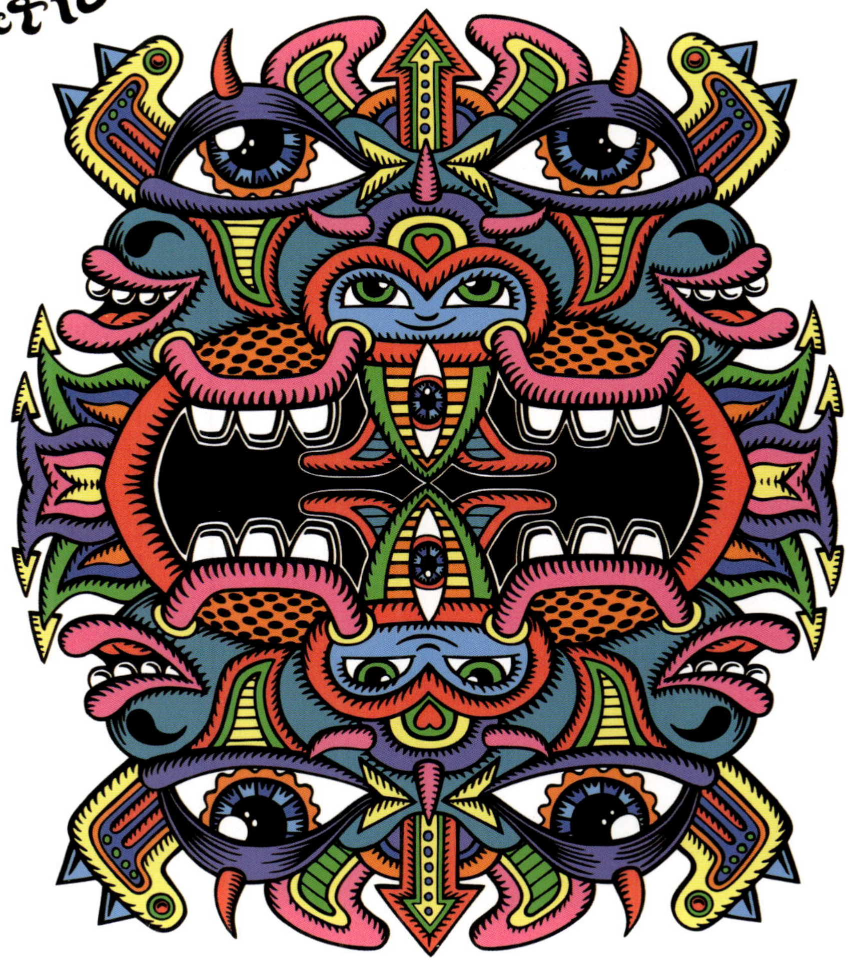

ALBUM COVERS

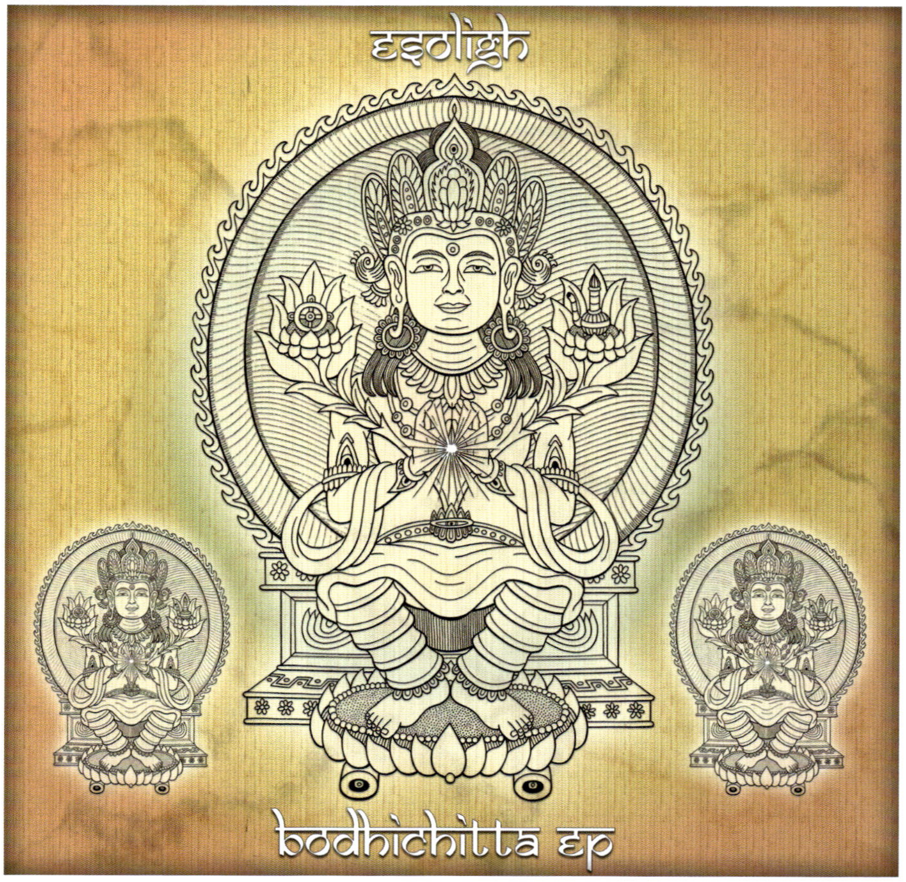

"Esoligh" - Bodhichitta EP (New Zealand)

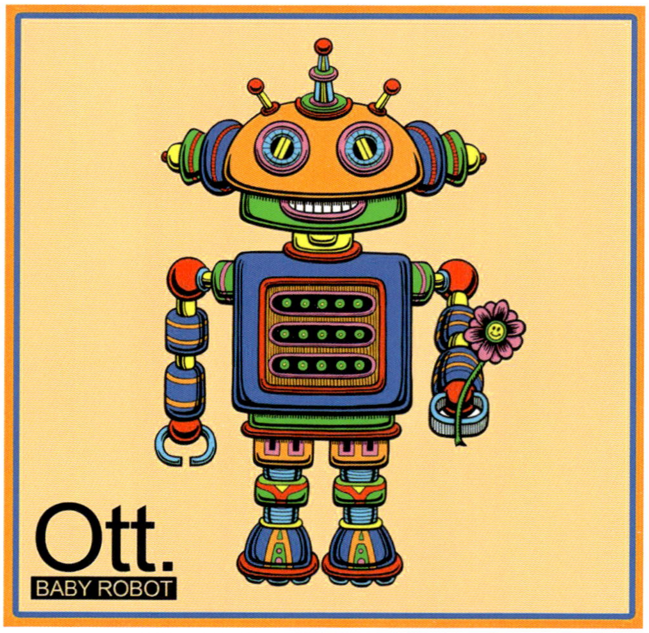

"Ott." - Baby Robot (England)

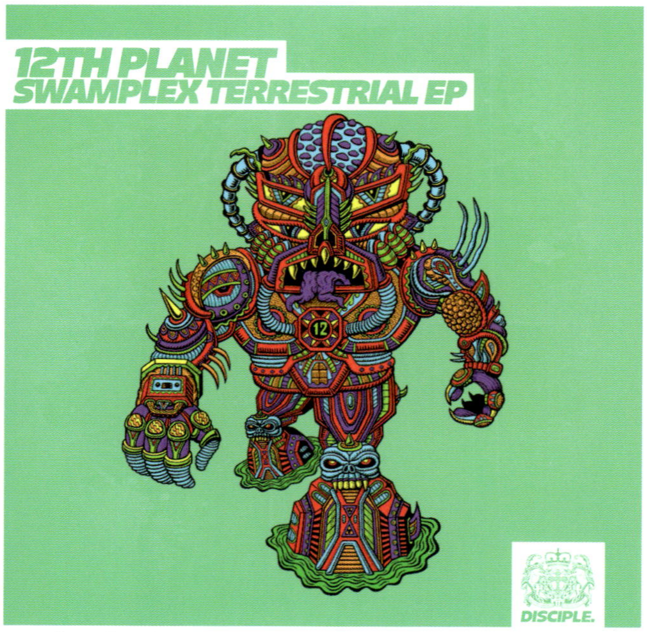

"12th Planet" - Swamplex Terrestrial (LA)

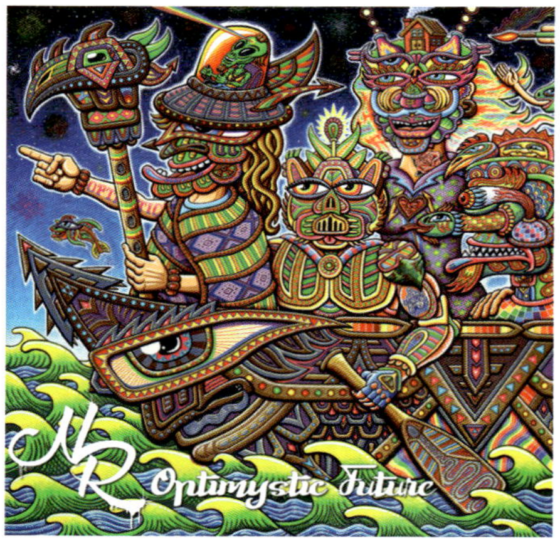

"New Reb"
- Optimystic Future (Oregon)

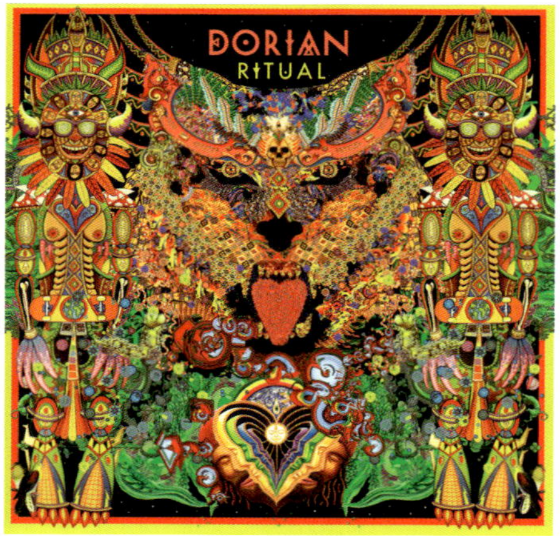

"Dorian"
- Ritual (Spain)

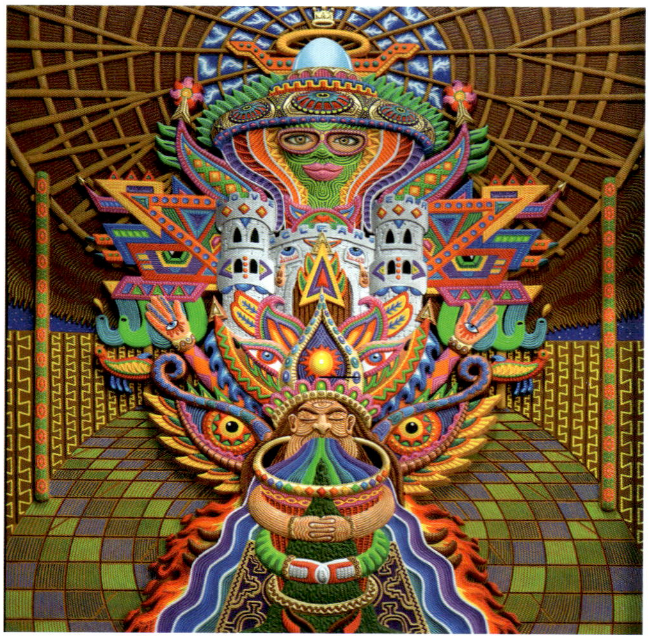

"Illuminati Congo" - Stupid Fresh Wisdom (Chicago)

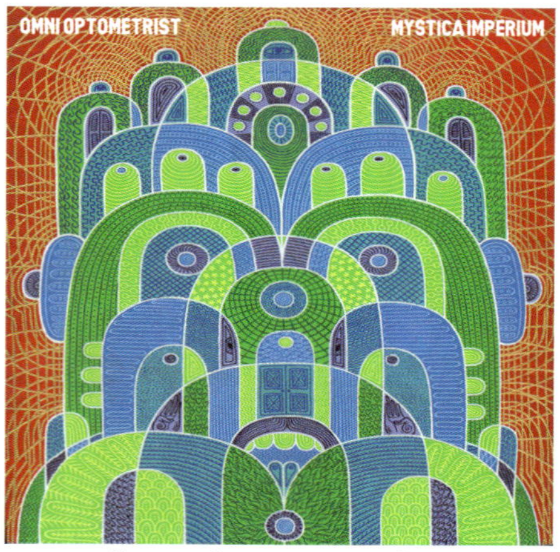

"Omni Optometrist"
- Mystica Imperium (Pennsylvania)

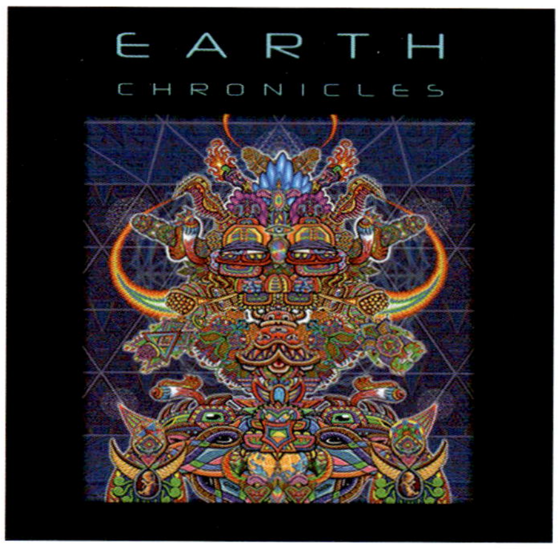

"Earth Chronicles"
- Self titled (Montreal)

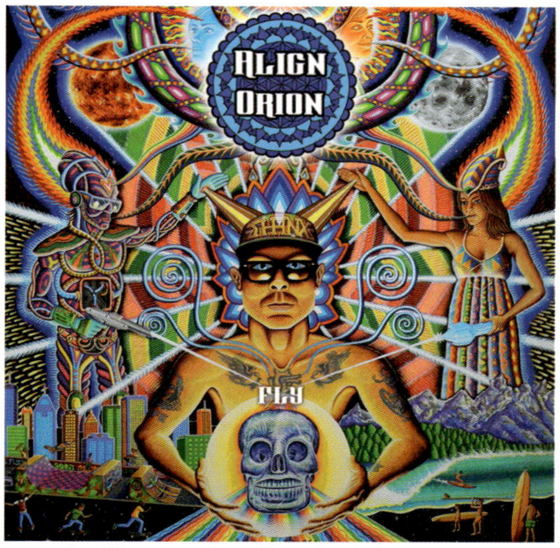

"Align Orion" - Fly (Chicago)

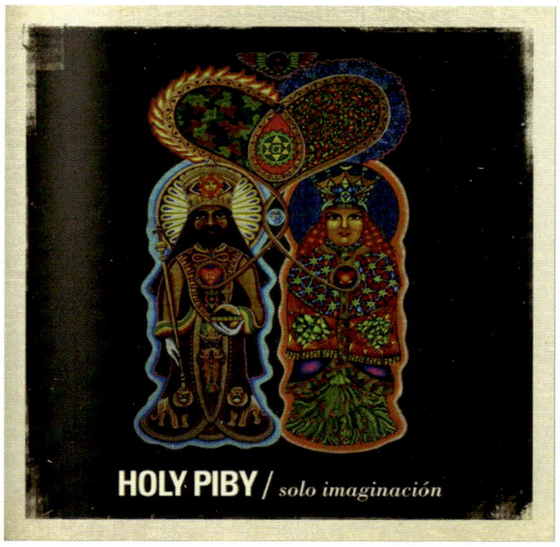

"Holy Piby" - Solo Imaginacion (Argentina)

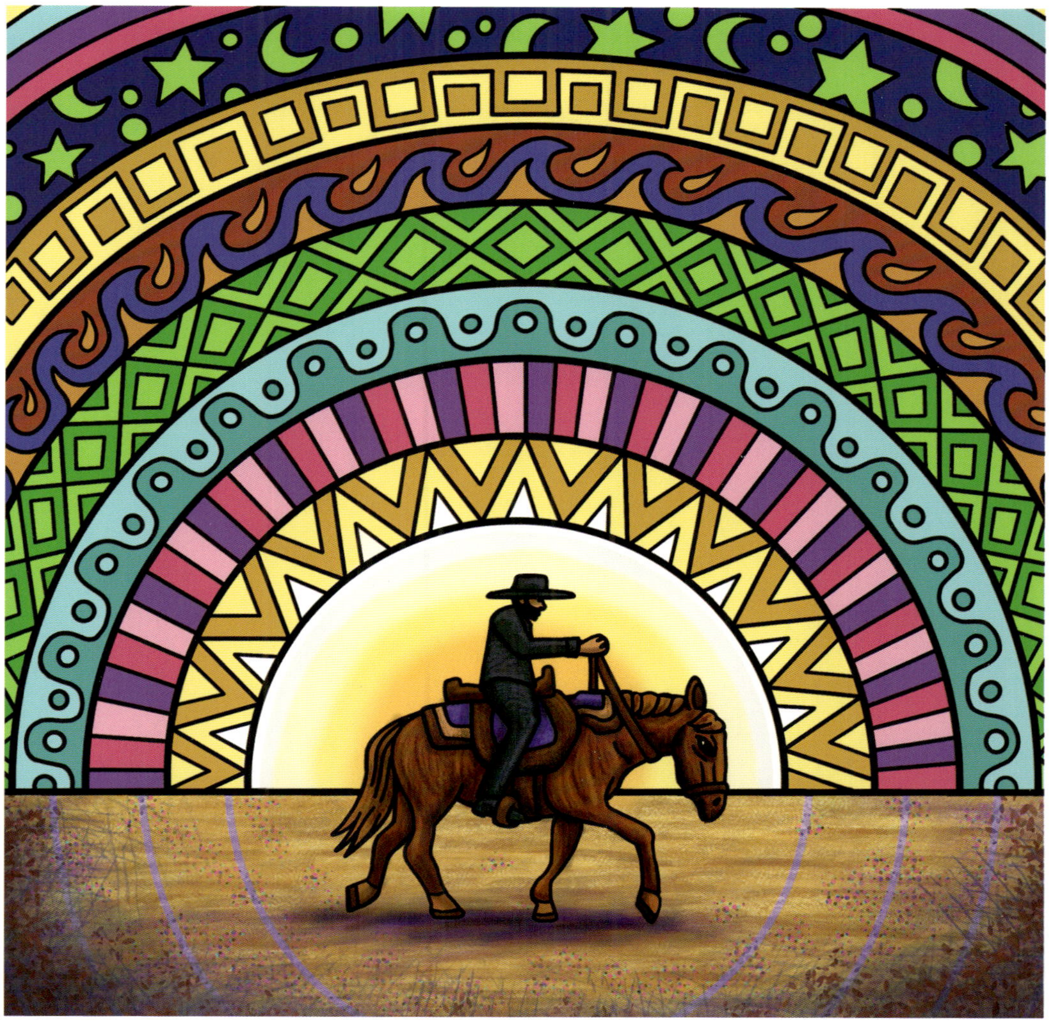
"Dirtwire" - The Horse with No Name (California)

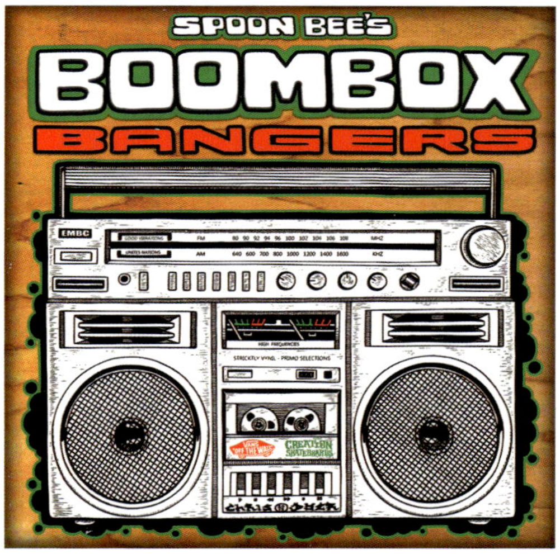

"Spoon Bee"-Boombox Bangers (Montreal)

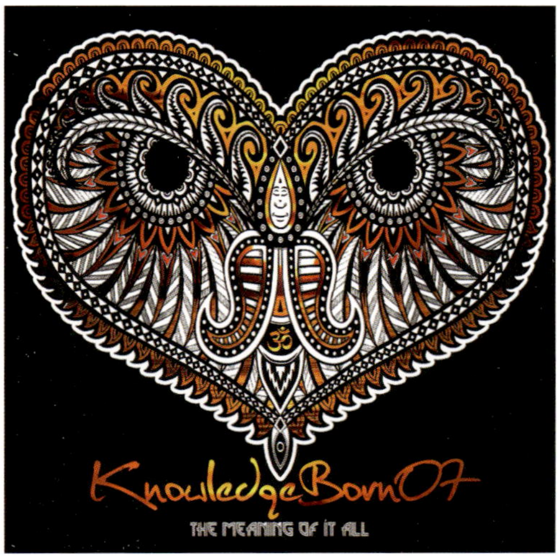

"KB07" -The Meaning of it All (Chicago)

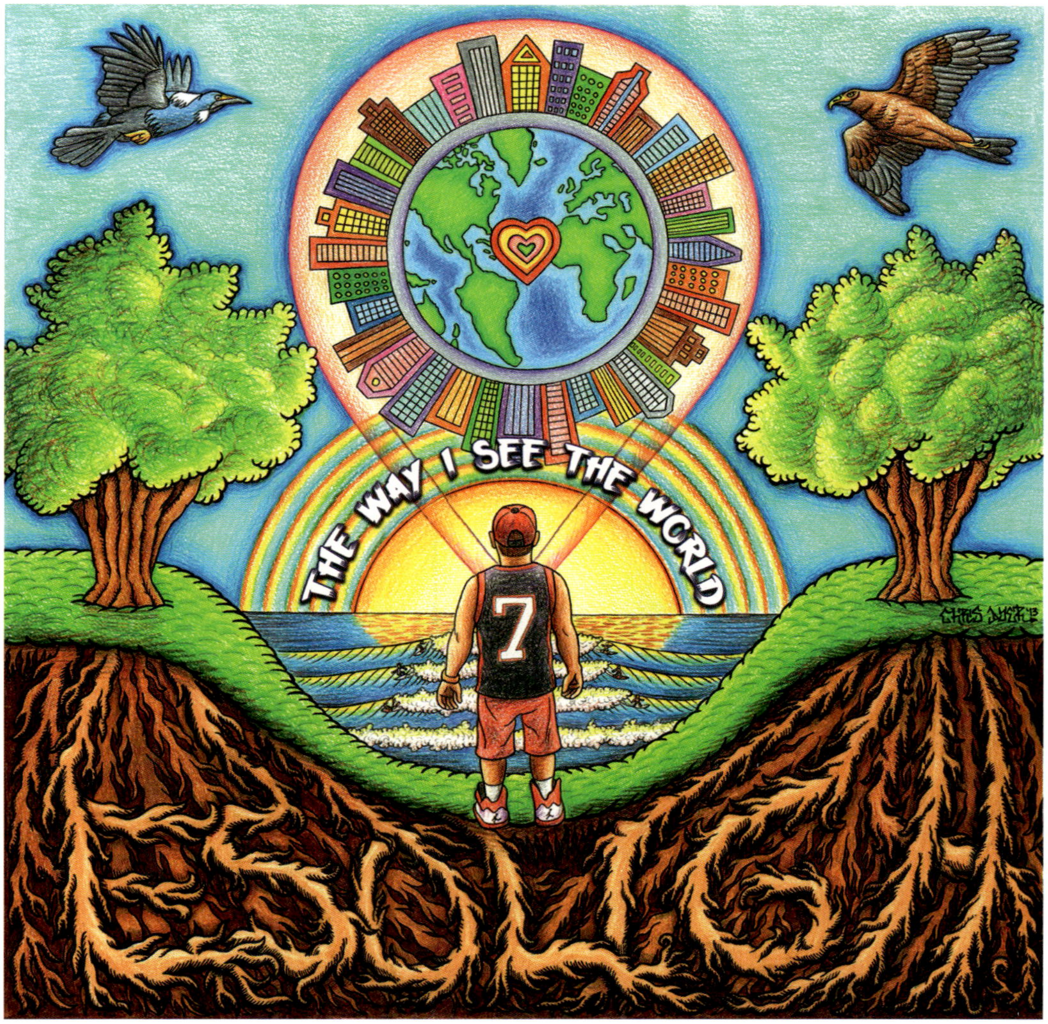

"Esoligh" - The way I see the World (New Zealand)

MAGAZINE COVERS

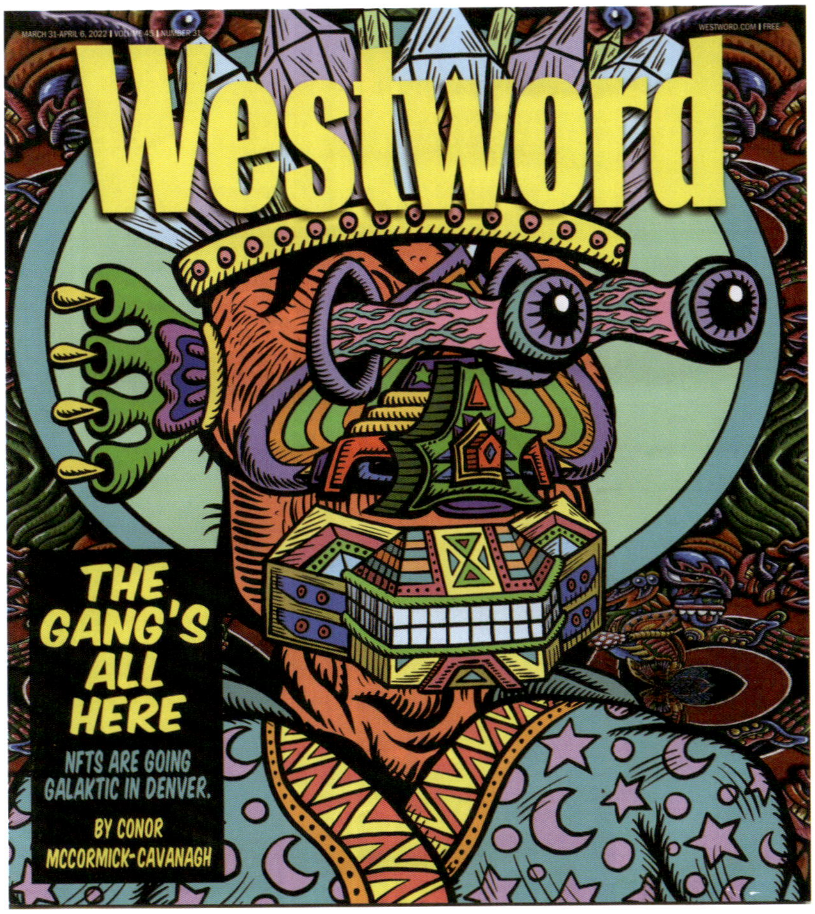

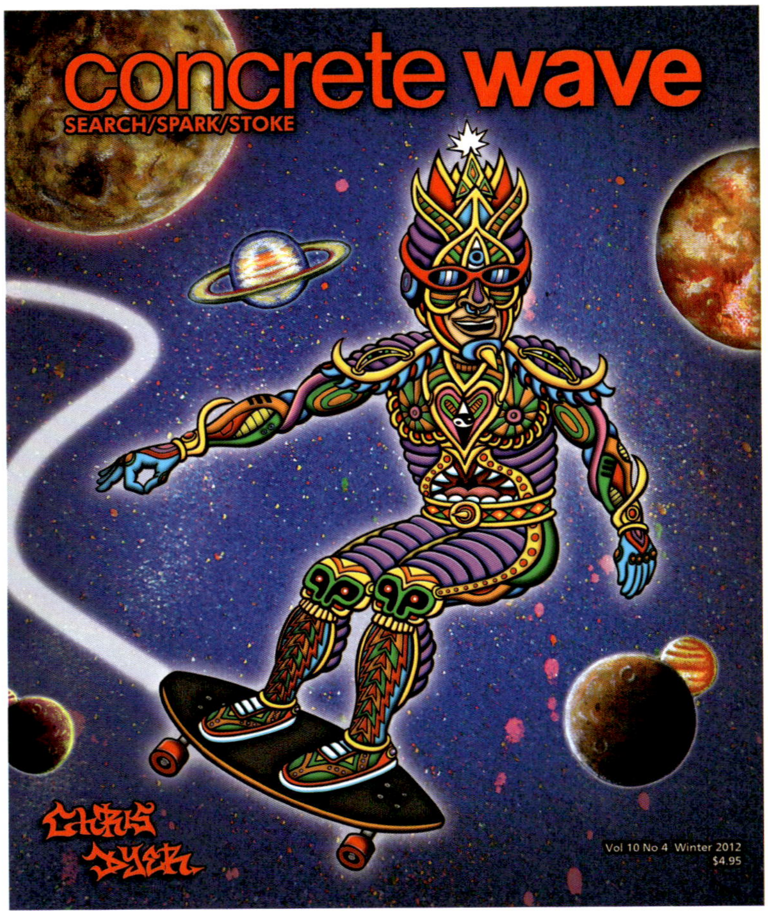

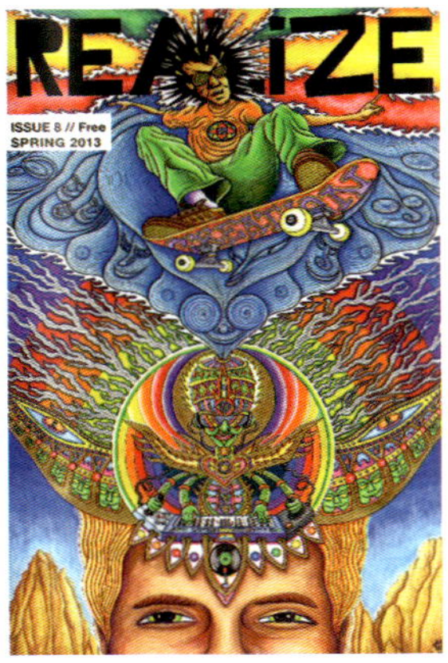

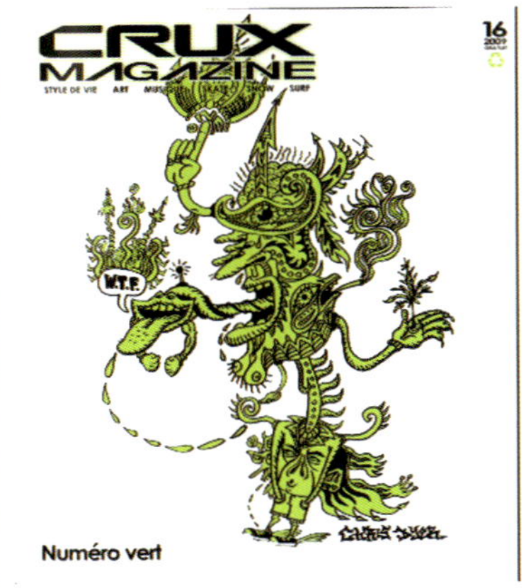

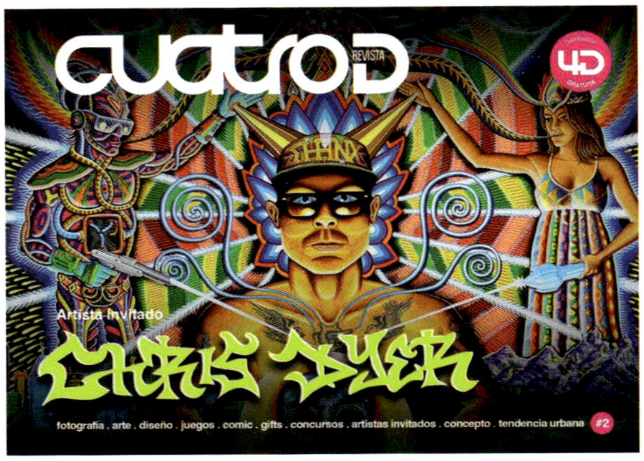

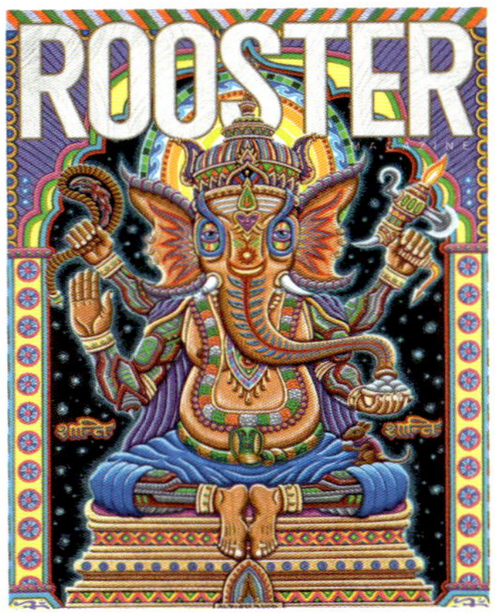

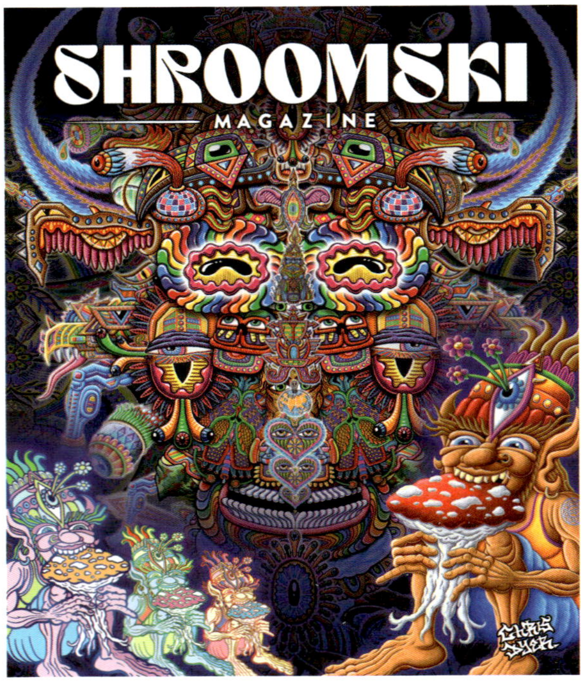

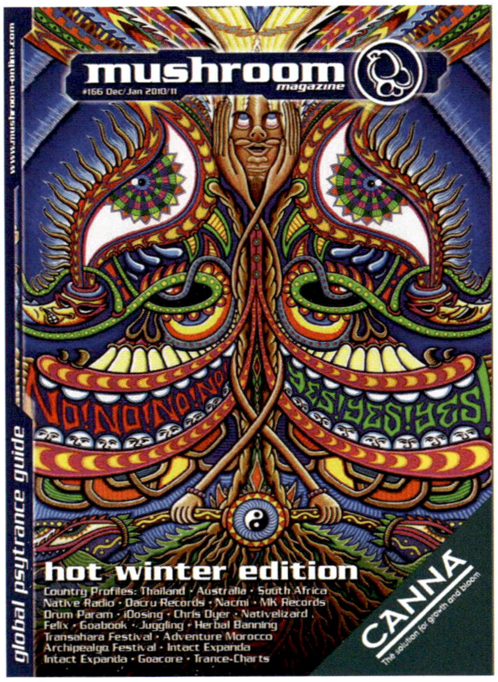

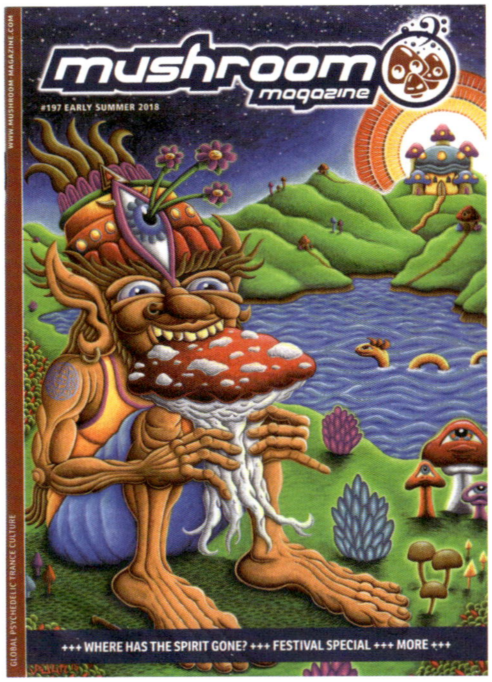

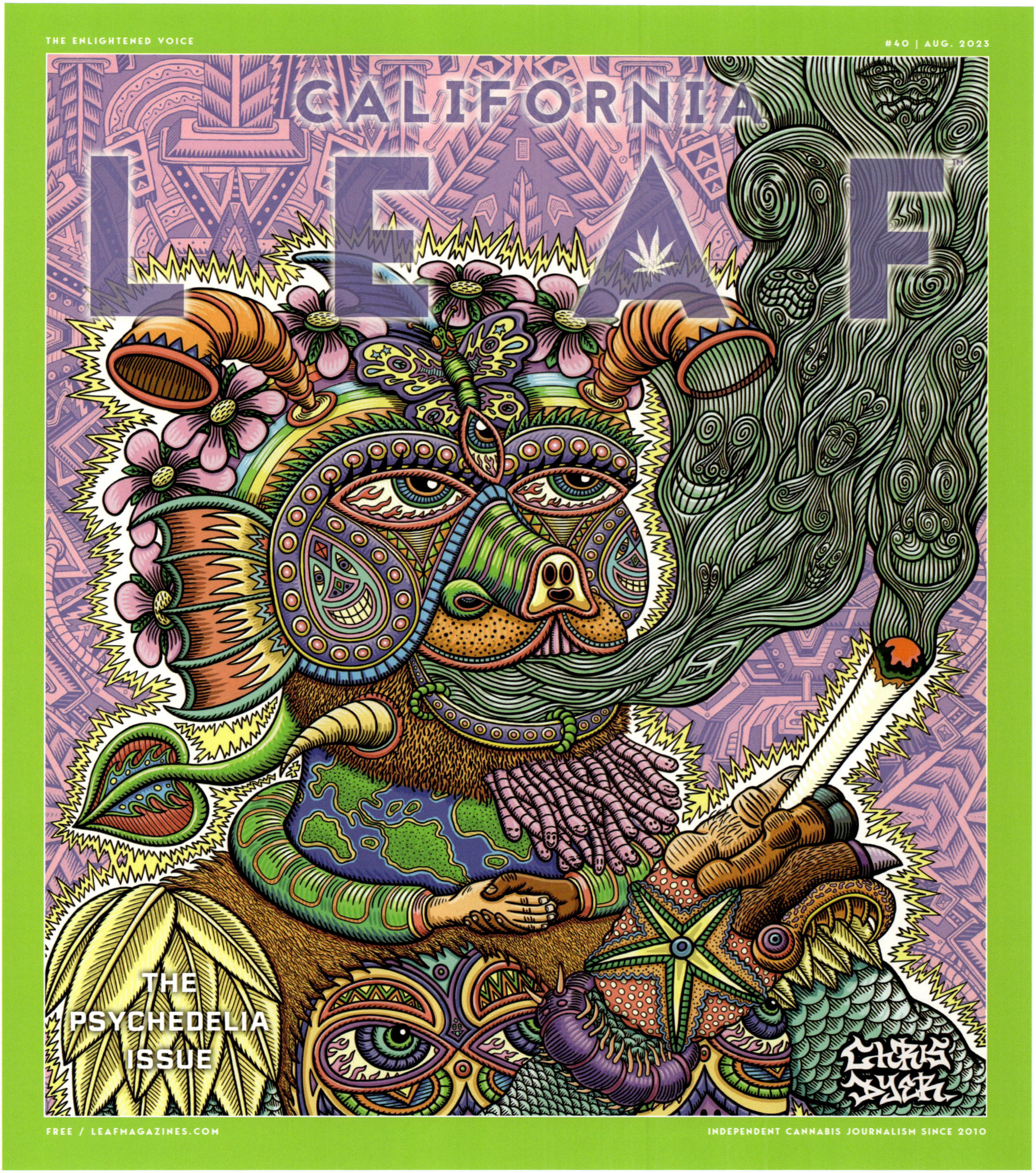

Magazine cover illustrations for **Westword** (Denver 2022), **Concrete Wave** (Ontario, 2012), **Realize** (California, 2013), **Crux** (Montreal, 2009), **Cuatro D** (Argentina, 2013), **Rooster** (Denver, 2020), **Shroomski** (Denver, 2023), **Mushroom** (Germany, 2010 and 2018) and **Leaf** (California, 2023)

PINS

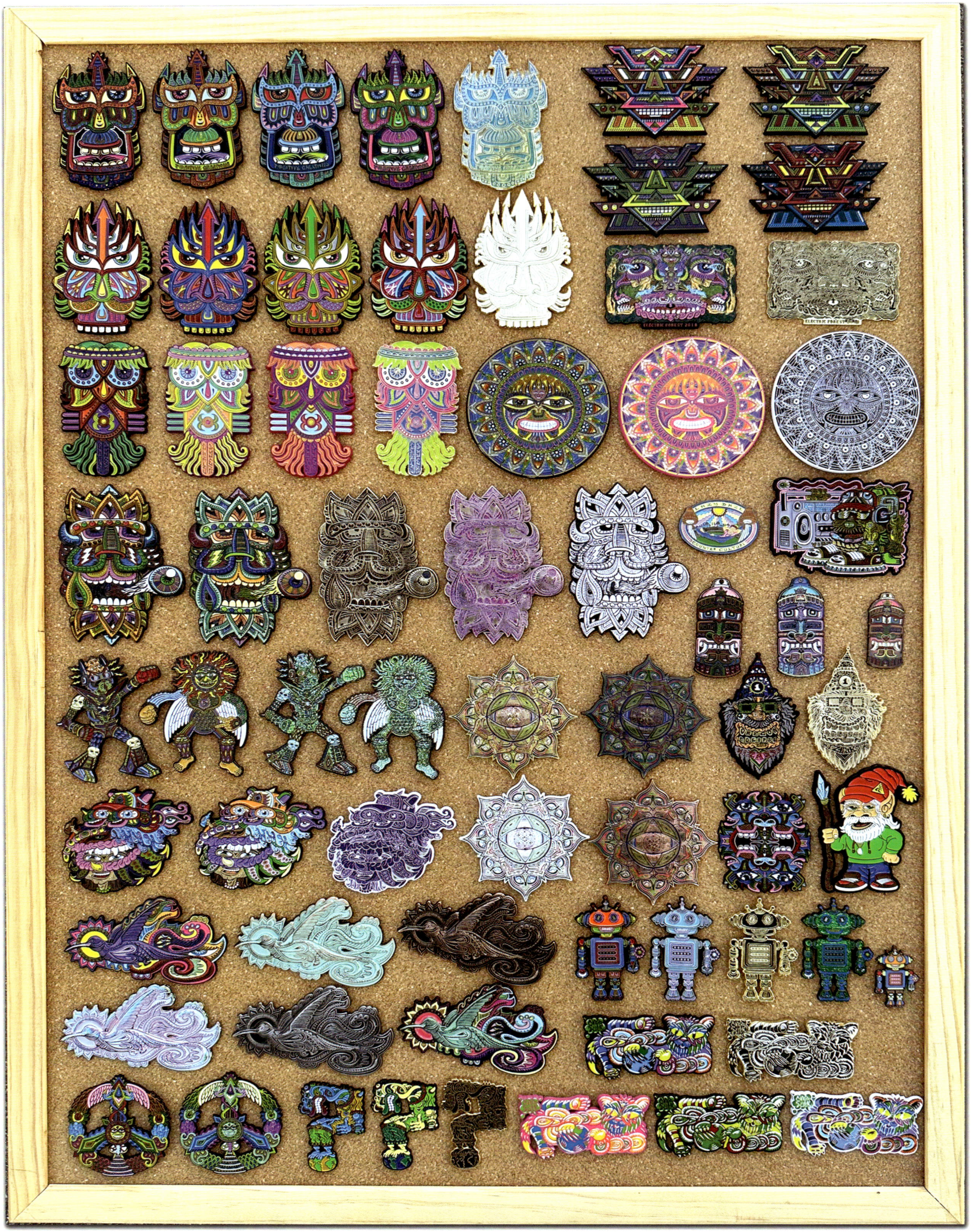

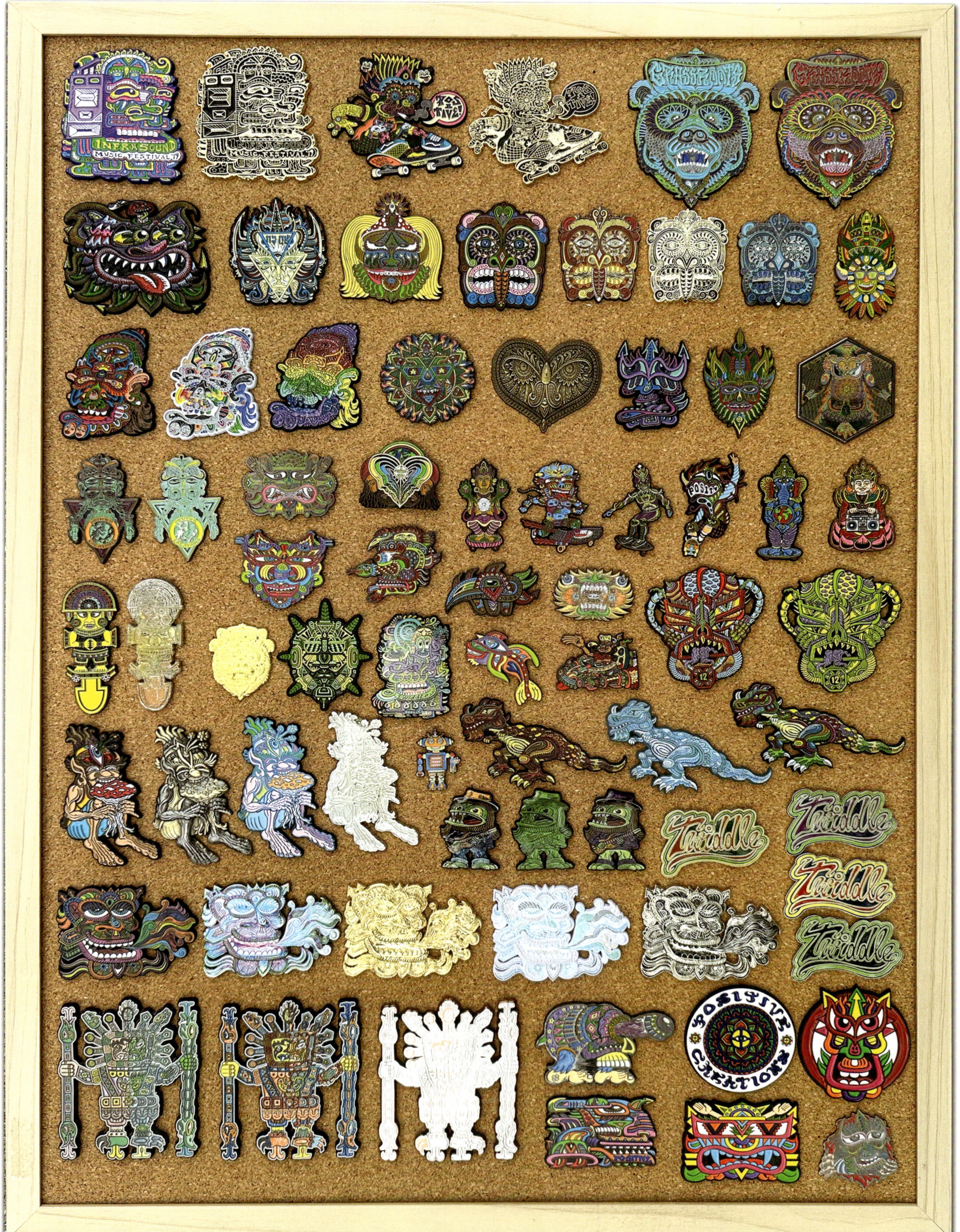

INFRASOUND
Twiddle
Twiddle
Twiddle
Twiddle
POSITIVE CREATIONS

TATTOOS

I love getting tattoos! I have had too many negative experiences designing tattoo commissions for others so I've stopped doing that. That said, I love it when fans get tattoos of my existing art! I prefer when they are well made, but I'm still stoked and honored even if they aren't polished. I've never learned how to tattoo myself, but somehow, I've still been convinced to badly scratch some friend's skins permanently, haha.

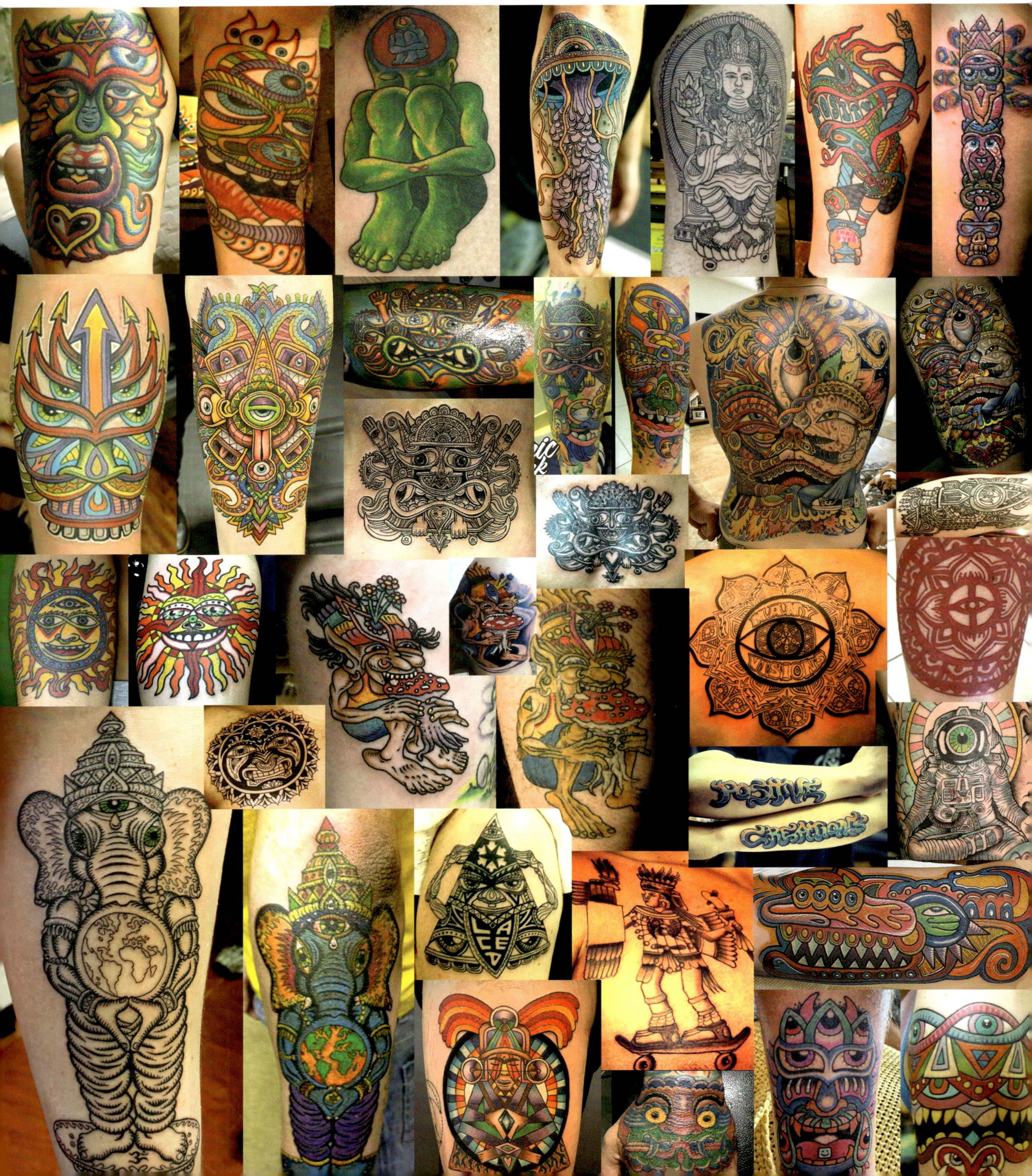

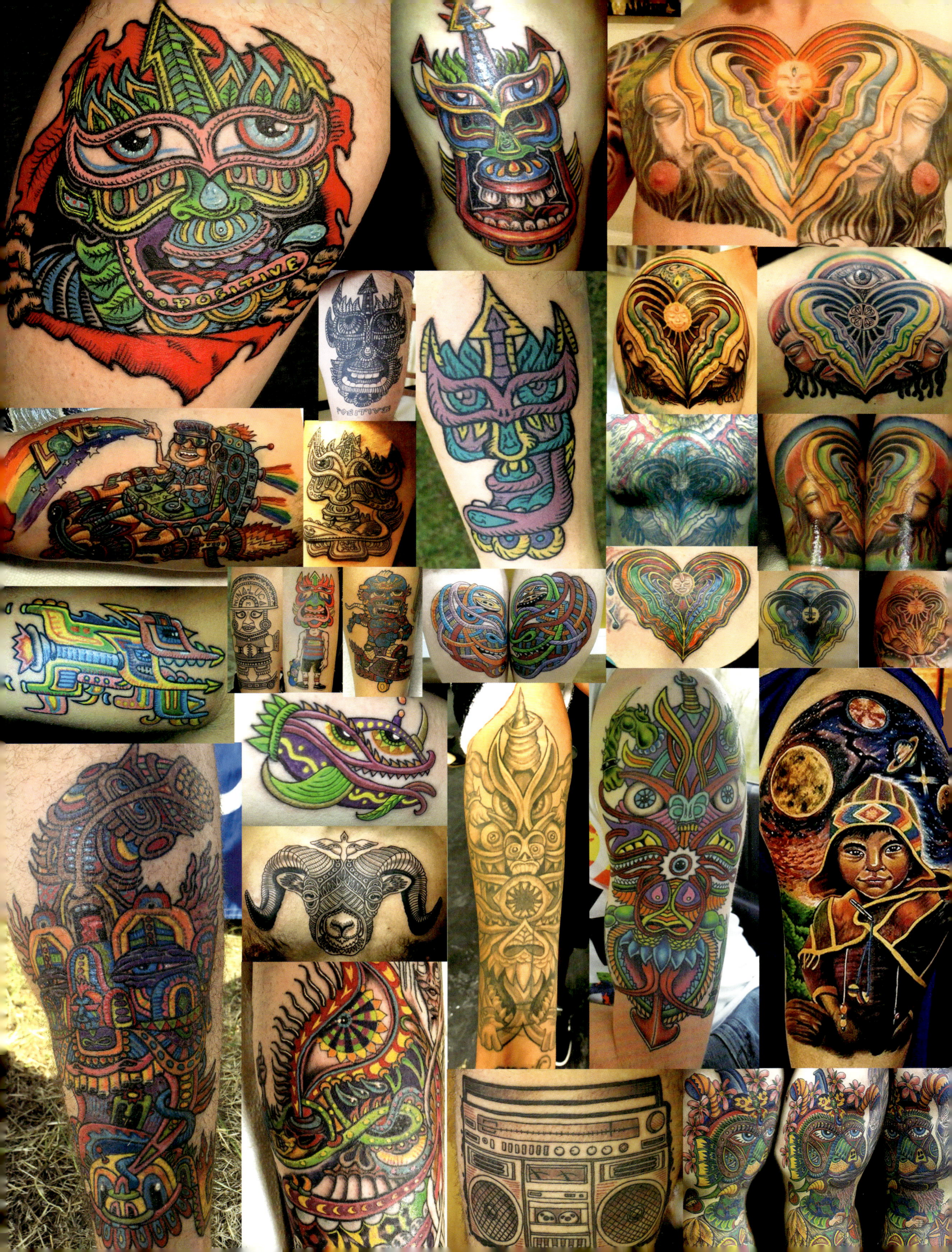
POSITIVE
LOVE

EVENT POSTERS

I love cool event posters, especially from the 60's hippie era. So these last few years I have been accepting a few more of those commissions, which has been fun, especially when I am a fan of the musicians!

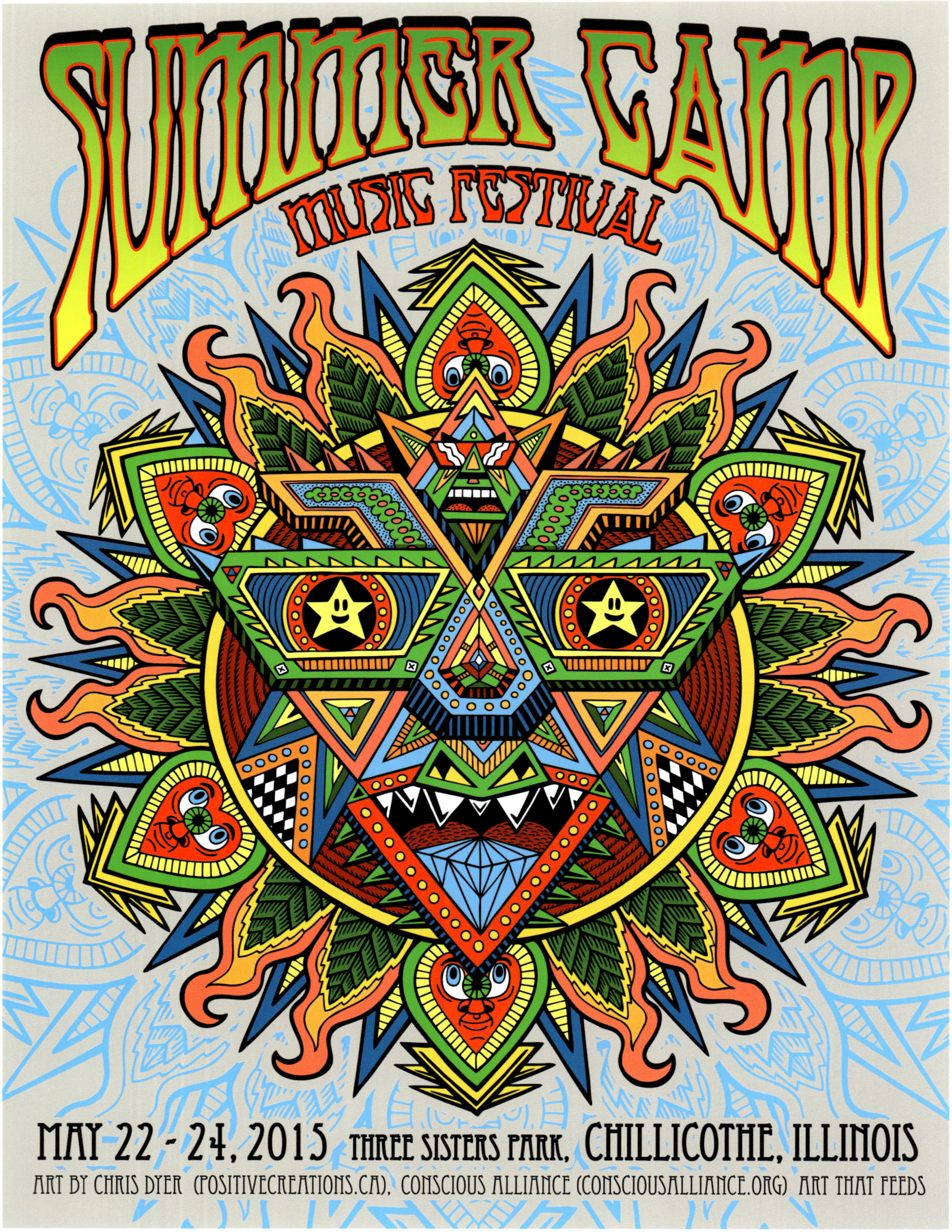

Posters for **"Summer Camp"** Music Festival and **"The String Cheese Incident"**

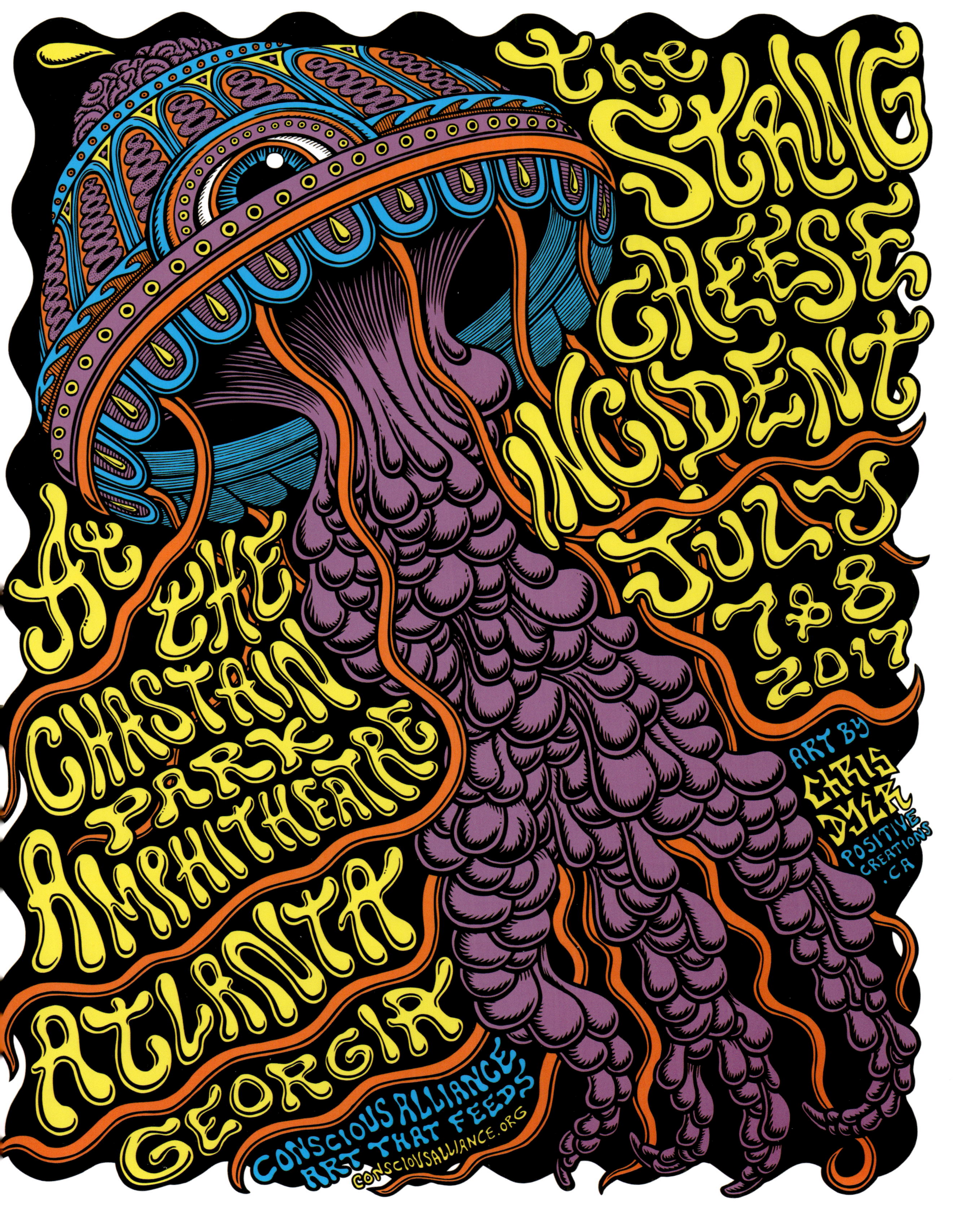

The String Cheese Incident
July 7 & 8 2017
At the Chastain Park Amphitheatre
Atlanta Georgia
Art by Chris Dyer
Positive Creations .ca
Conscious Alliance
Art That Feeds
consciousalliance.org

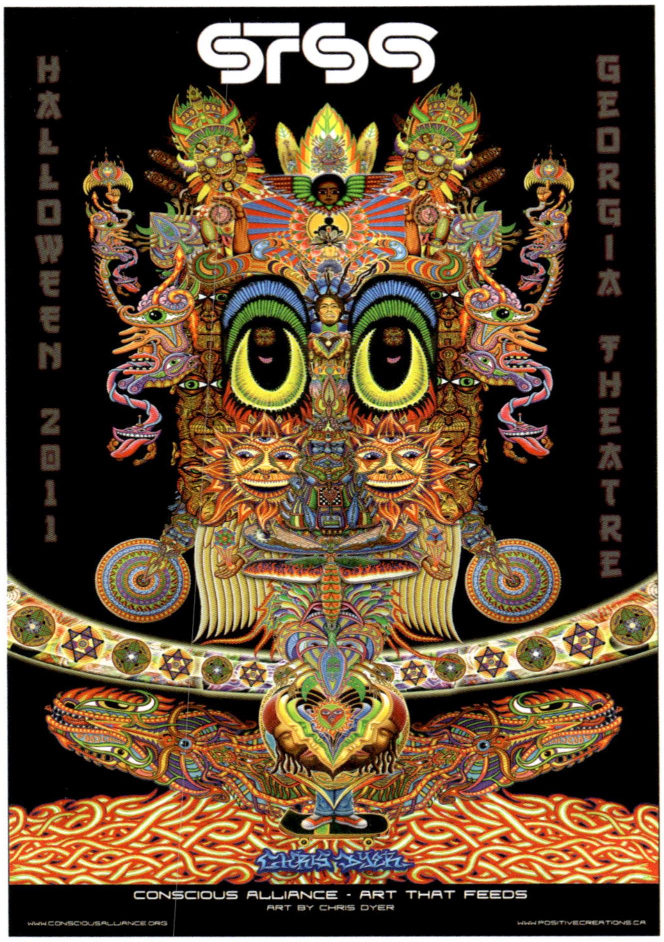

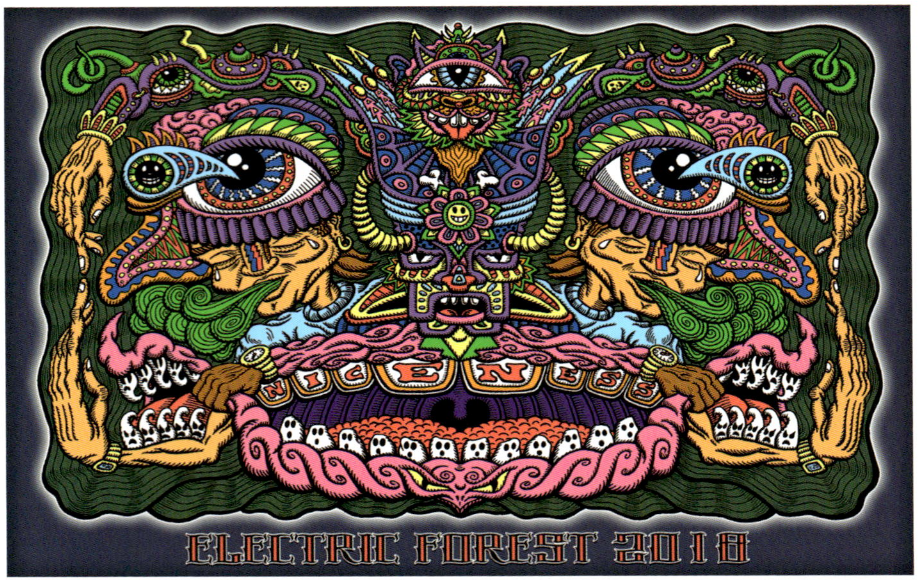

Event Posters for **"Sound Tribe Sector Nine"** (2011 and 2013), **"Electric Forest " Music Festival** (2018) and **Lettuce's "Rage Rocks"** (2017).

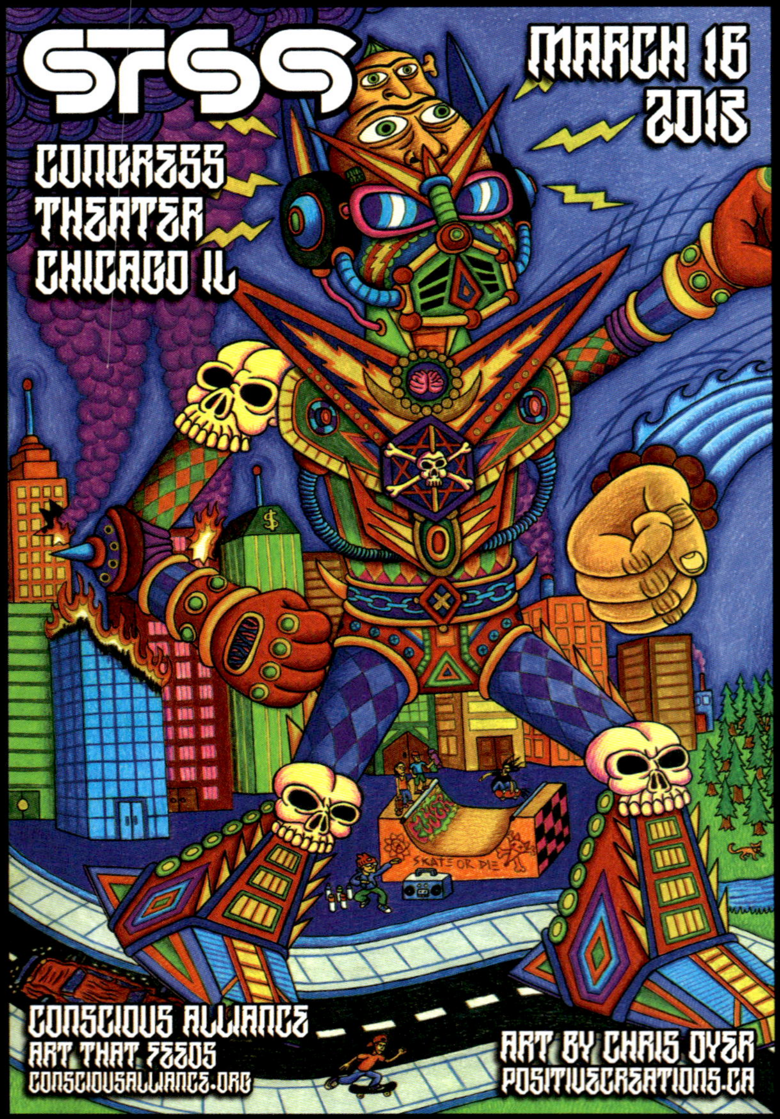

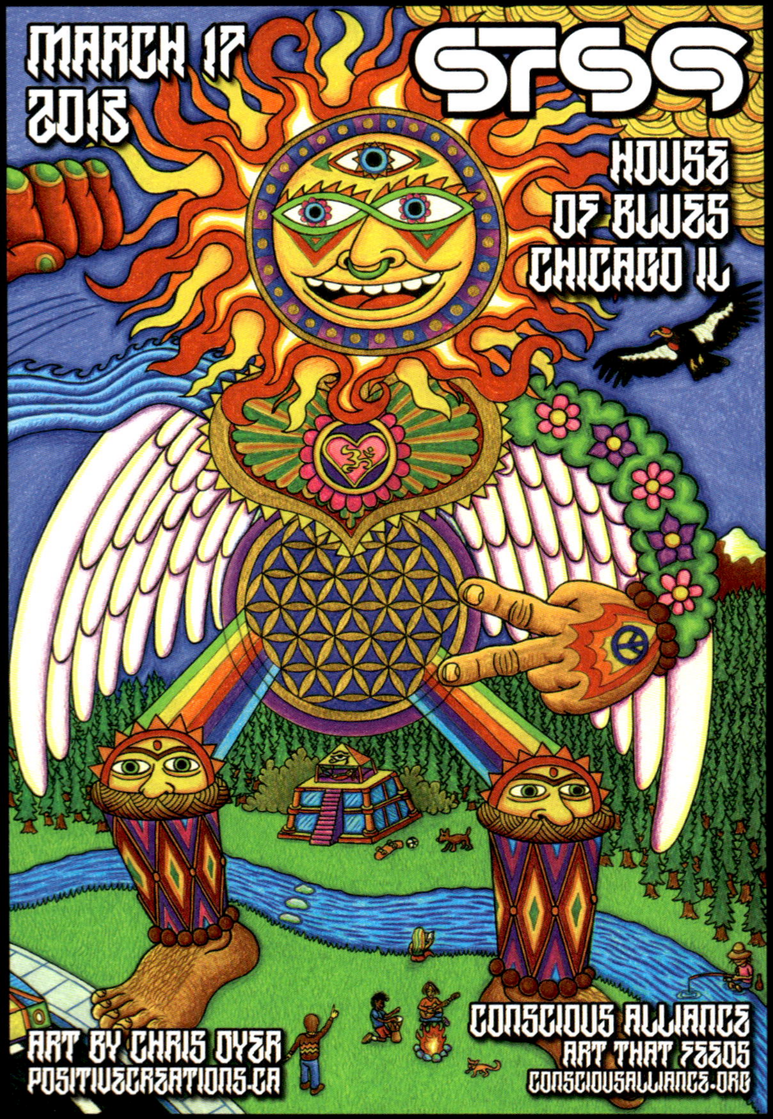

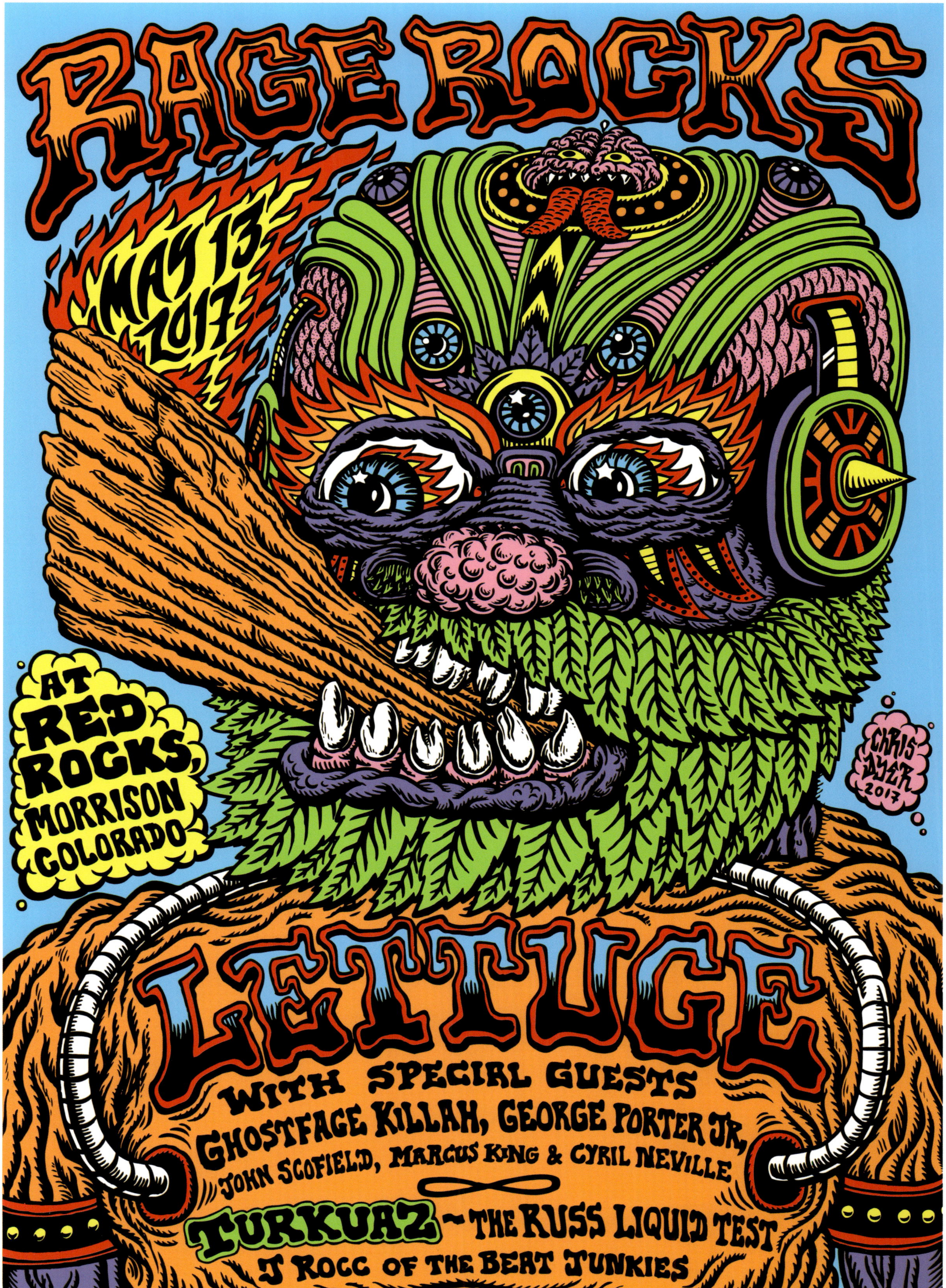
RAGE ROCKS
MAY 13 2017
AT RED ROCKS, MORRISON COLORADO
CHRIS DYER 2017
LETTUCE
WITH SPECIAL GUESTS
GHOSTFACE KILLAH, GEORGE PORTER JR,
JOHN SCOFIELD, MARCUS KING & CYRIL NEVILLE
TURKUAZ ~ THE RUSS LIQUID TEST
J ROCC OF THE BEAT JUNKIES

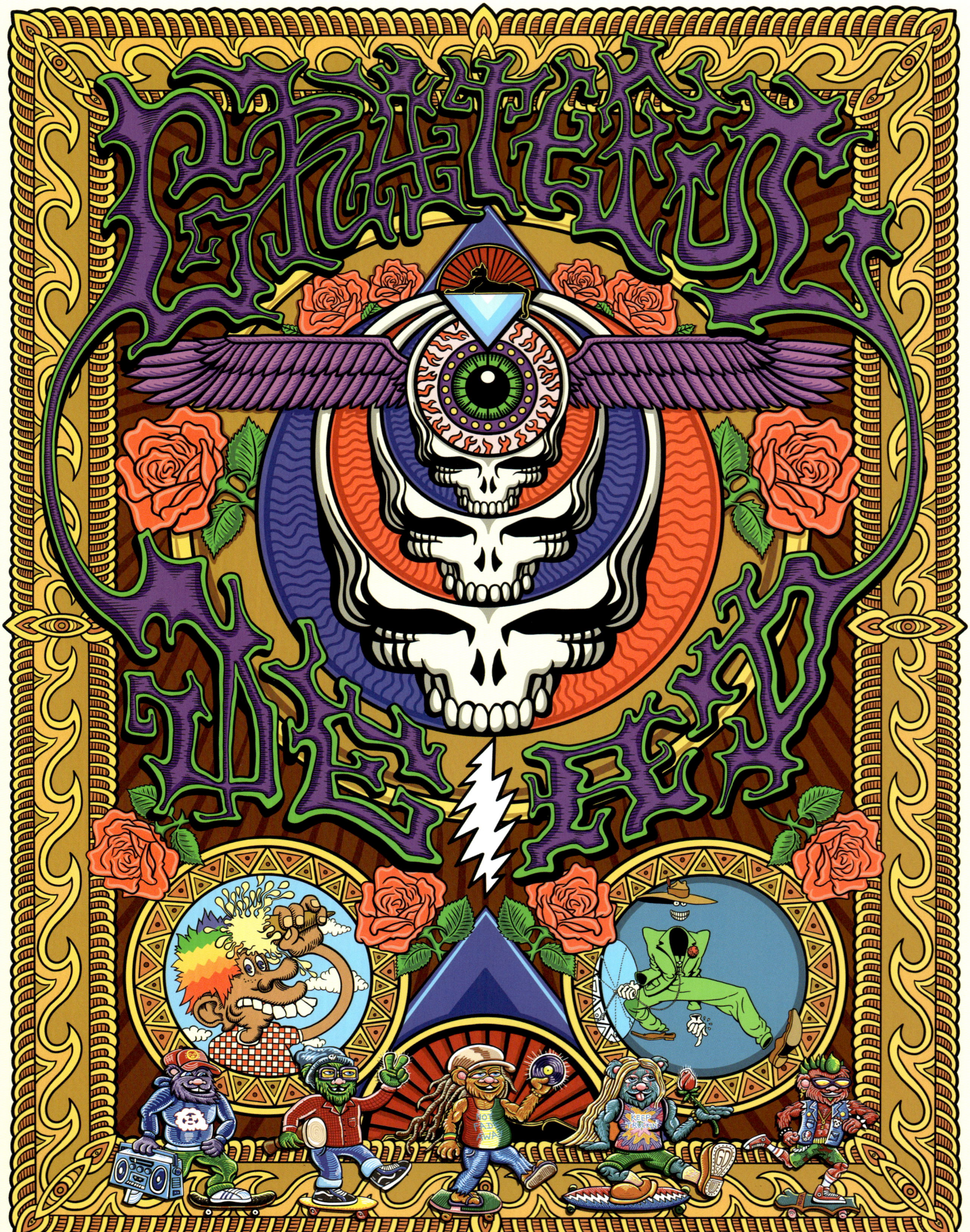
GRATEFUL DEAD

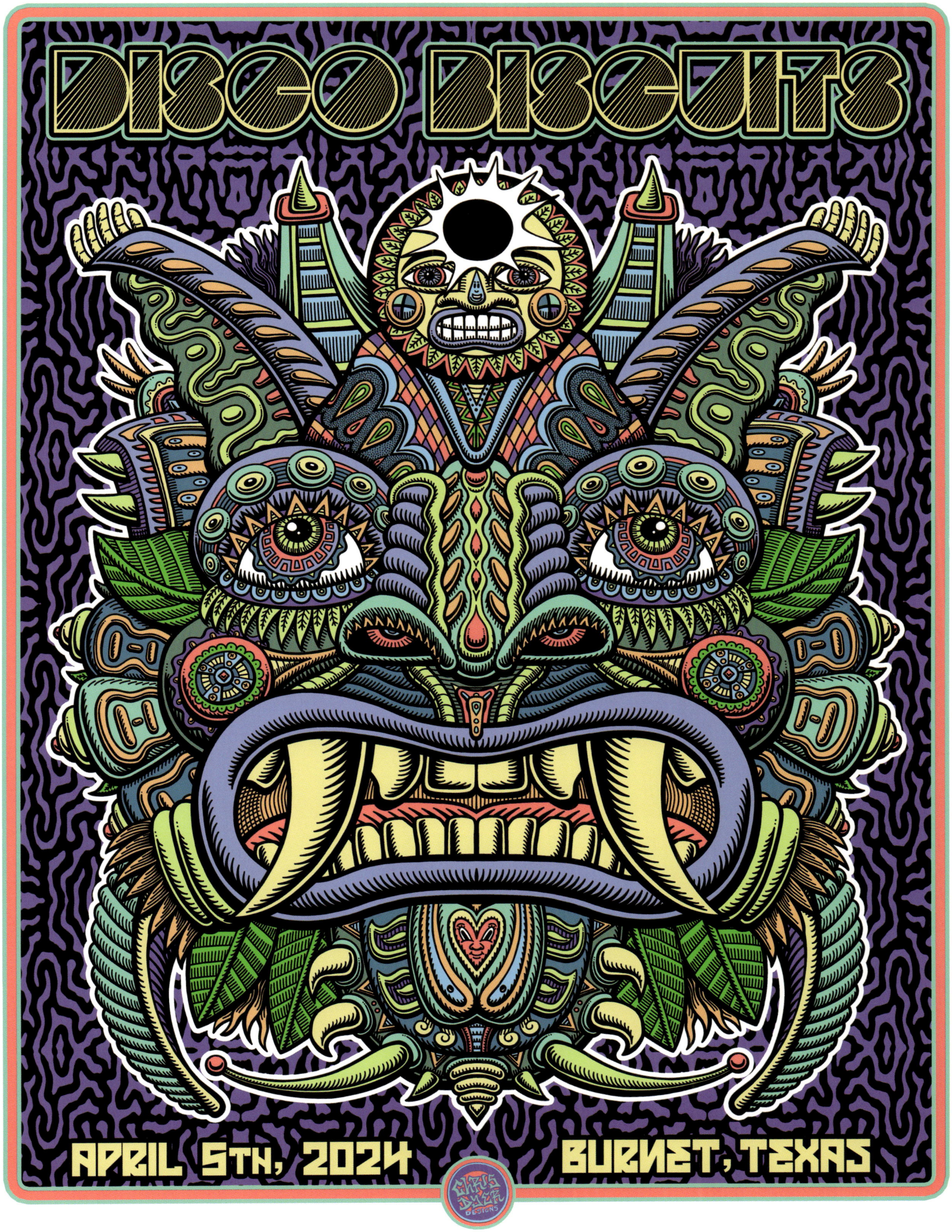

Posters for **"Grateful Dead"** via **Bottleneck Gallery** and for **"The Disco Biscuits "**

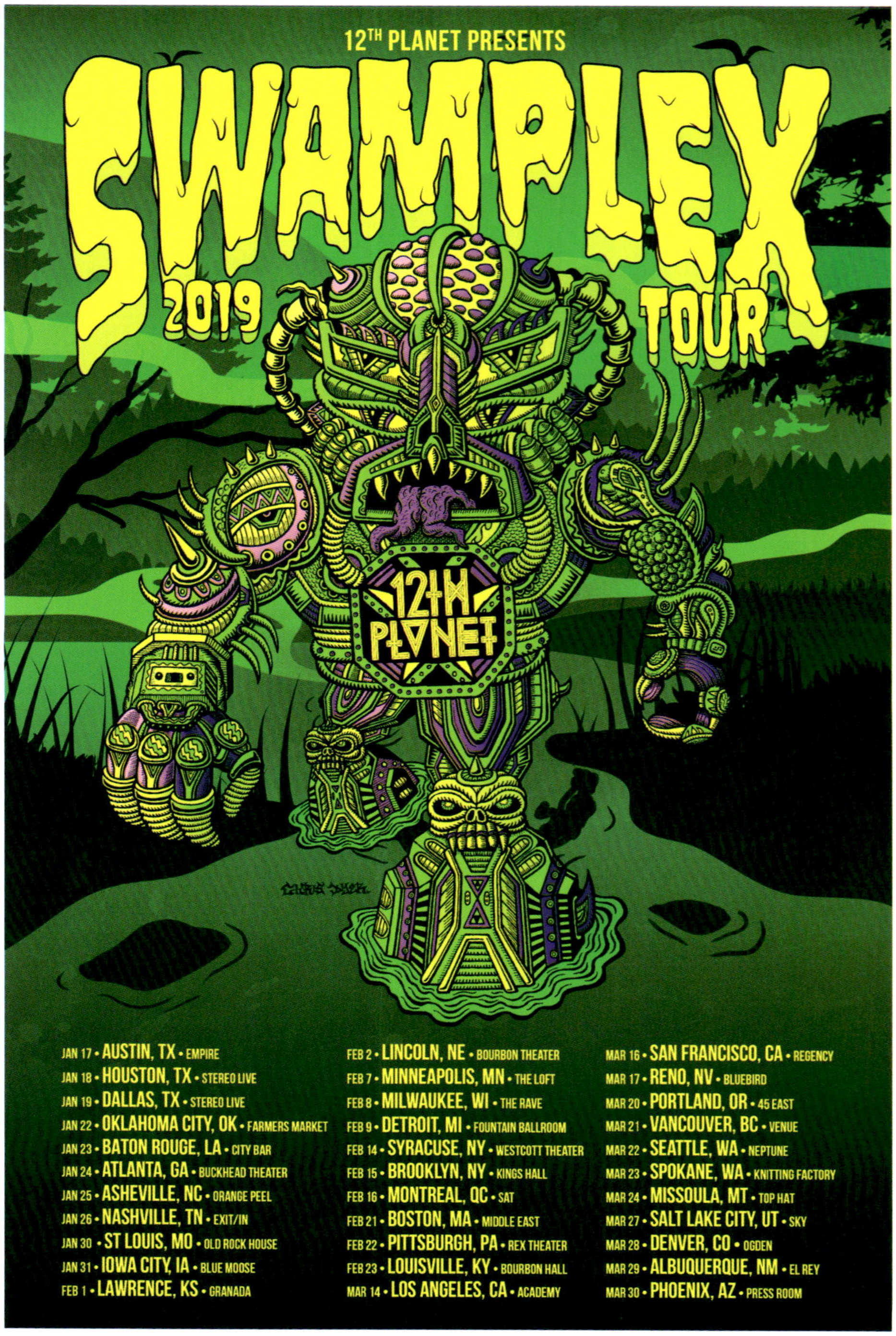

My friend from LA John **"12th Planet"** is one of the biggest Dubstep producers of our times! I'm stoked to have done art for his tour posters, which were laid out by **"Immanent VJ"**, who also animates my art for their live performance visuals. The "Swamplex" monster I drew quickly became a classic and even made an appearance on the popular video game **"Minecraft"**. And then my friends at **"Electrifly"** transformed him into a 3D animated being, activated by their lapel pins as well as an Instagram Face filter. Love it when my art comes alive like that!

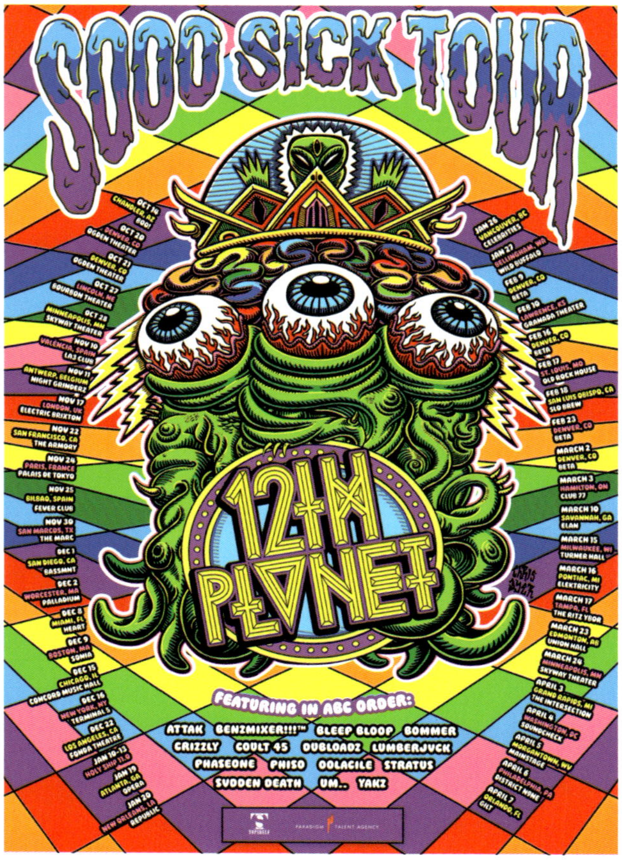

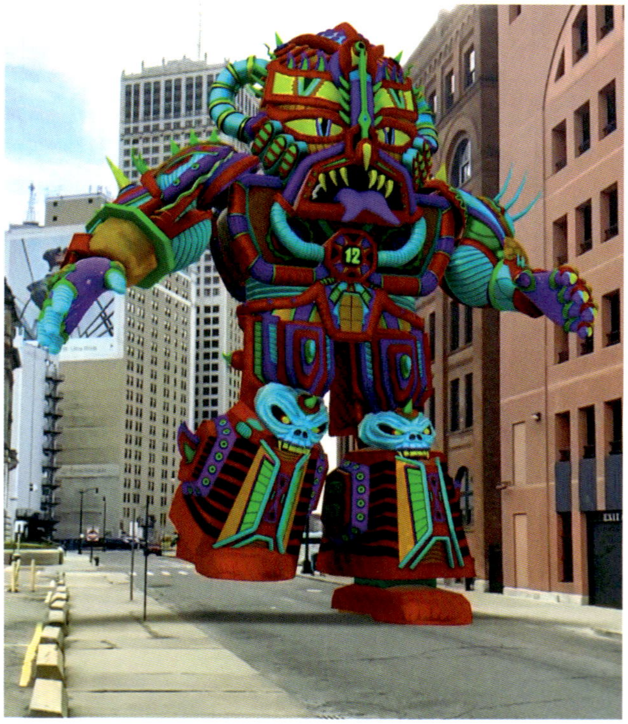

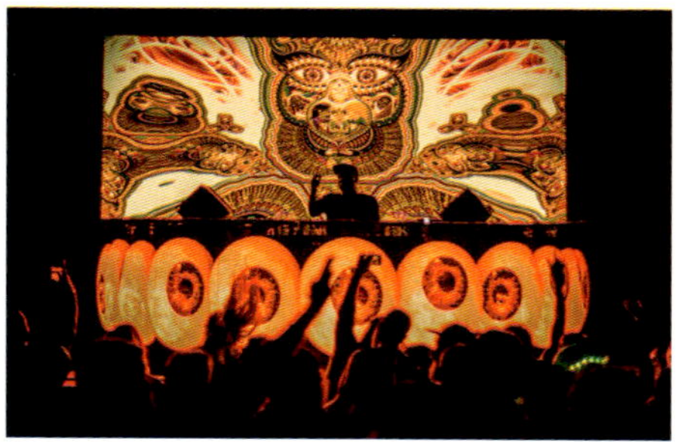

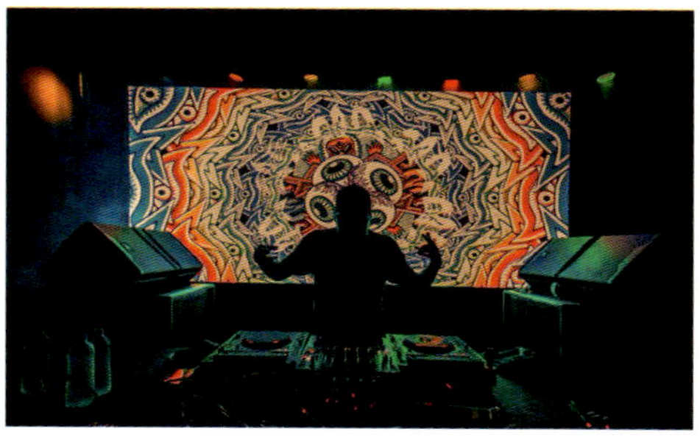

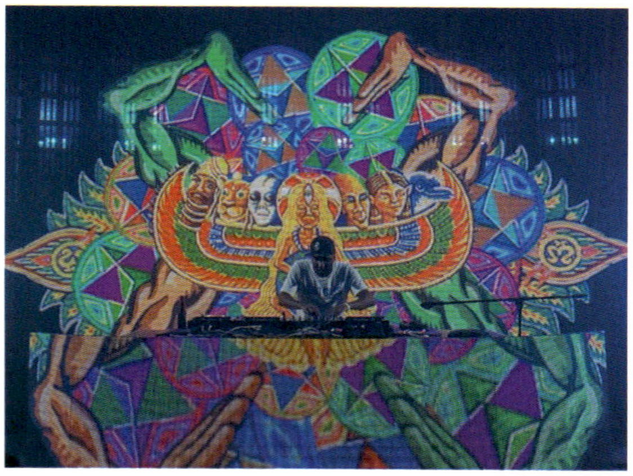

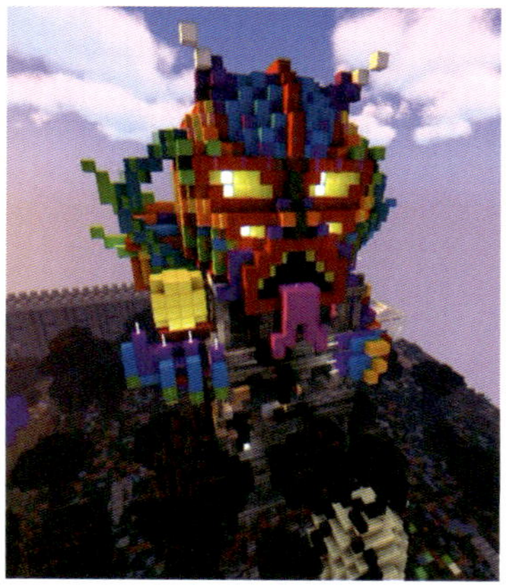

LIVE PAINTING

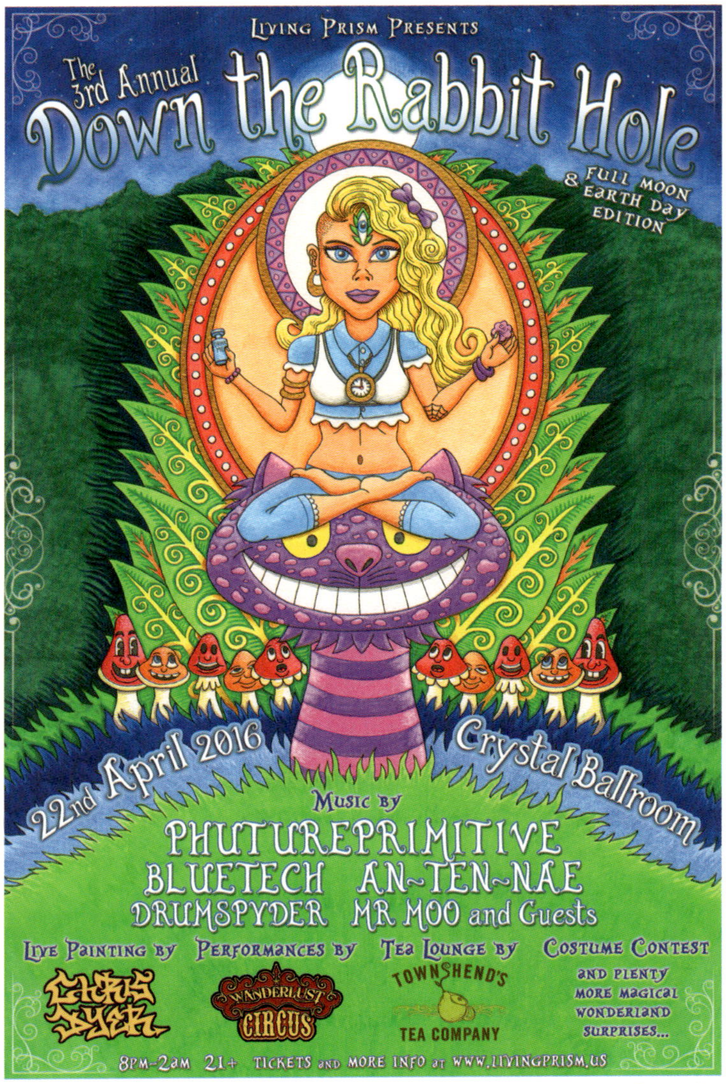

Performances for **"Down the Rabbit Hole"** in Portland (2016) and **"Deep Breath"** in Baltimore

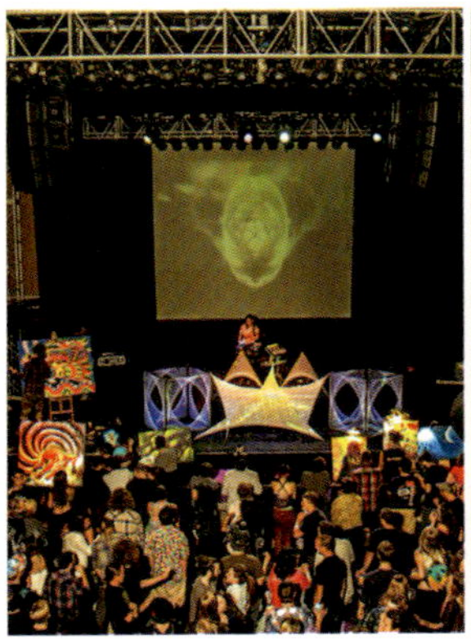

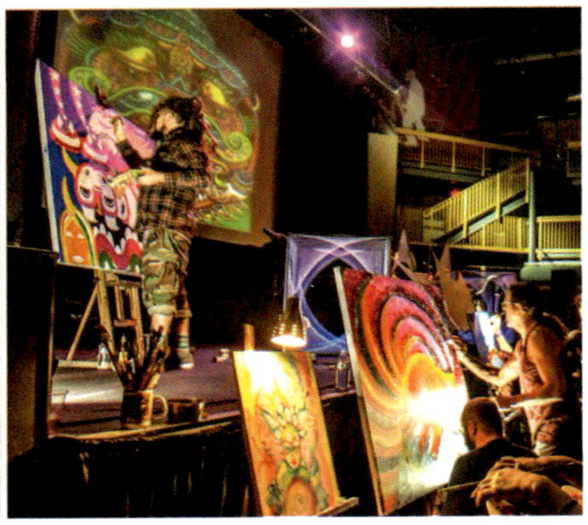

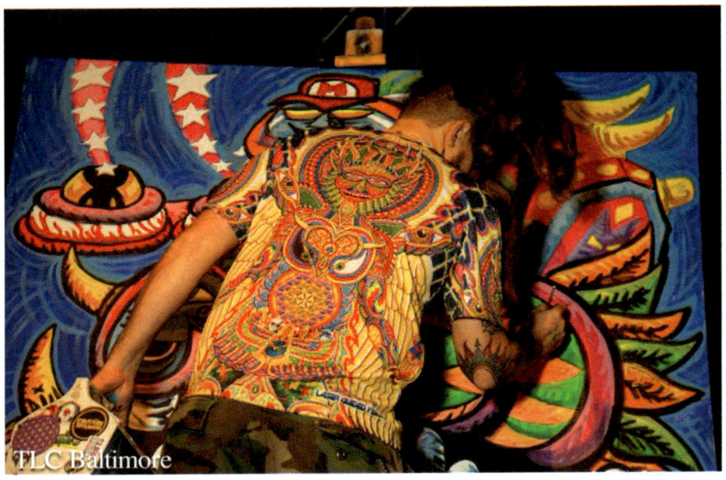

Painting canvases on stage, while musicians blast their vibrations is a super fun service I've done in the last decade. It can be nerve racking and hard to create a painting so quick, but once I get in my grove I feel like a rock star! Here a couple of my first performances, along the posters I designed for them.

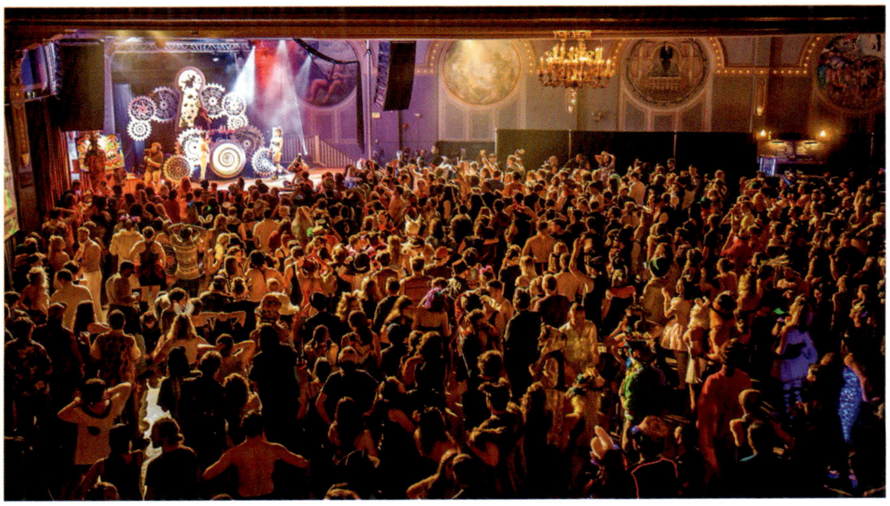

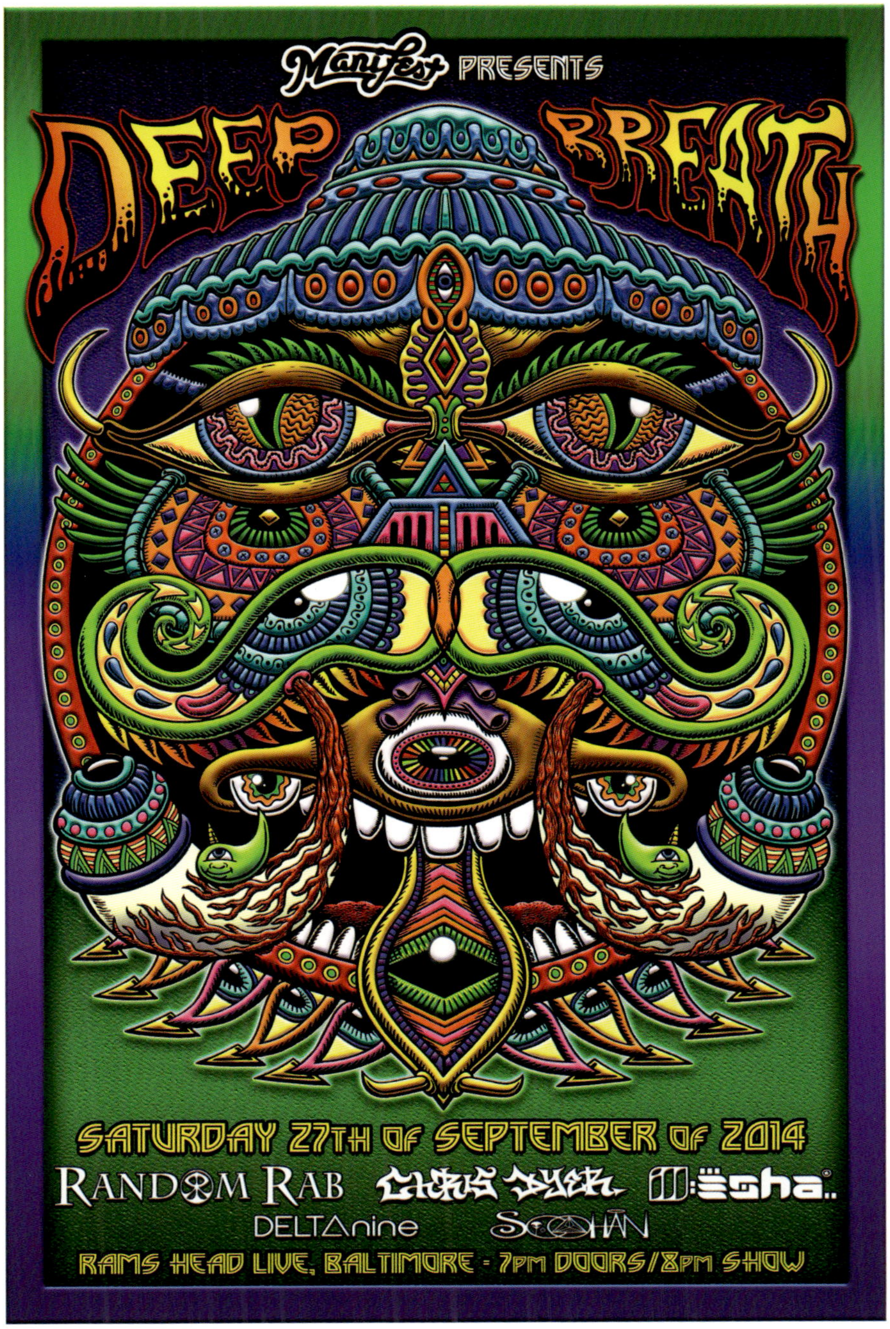

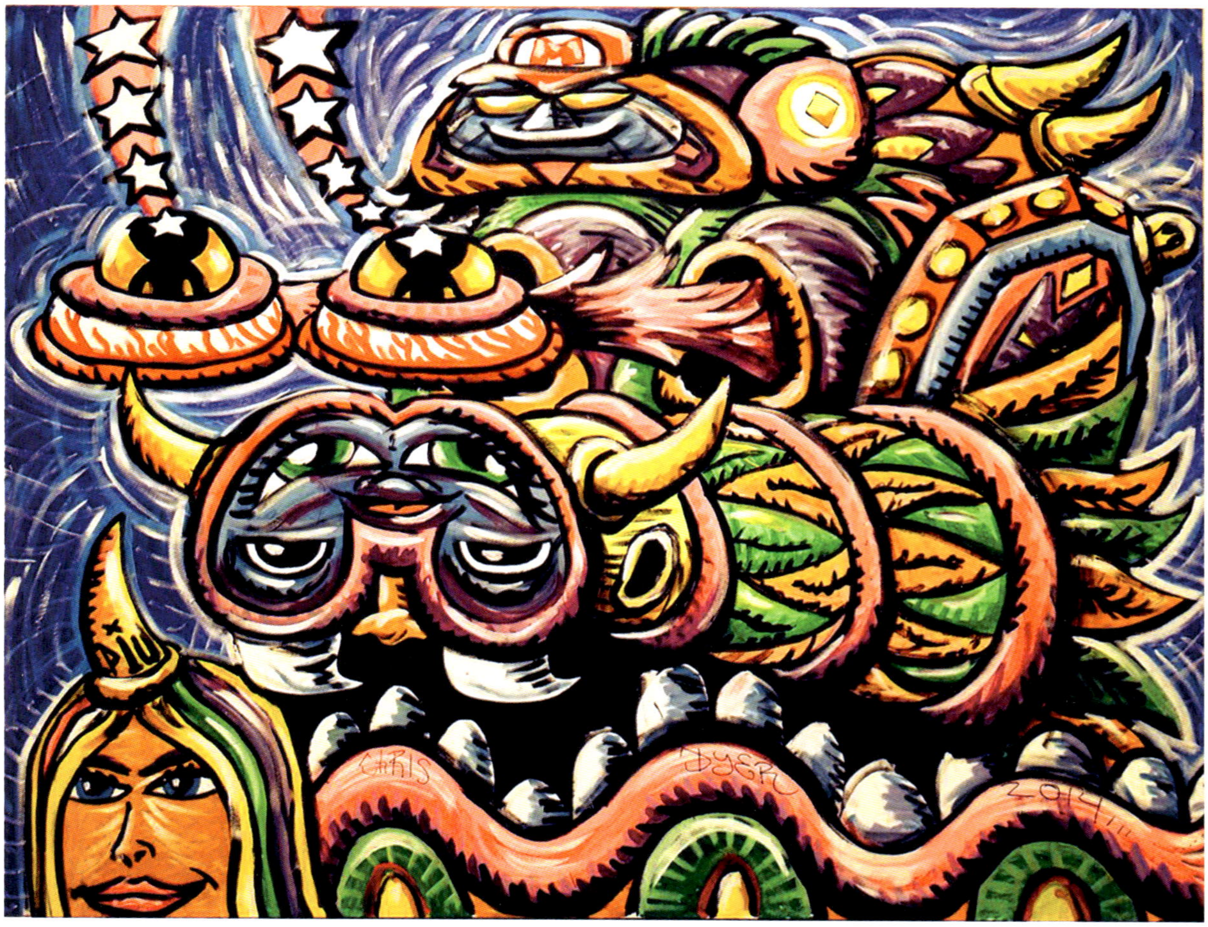

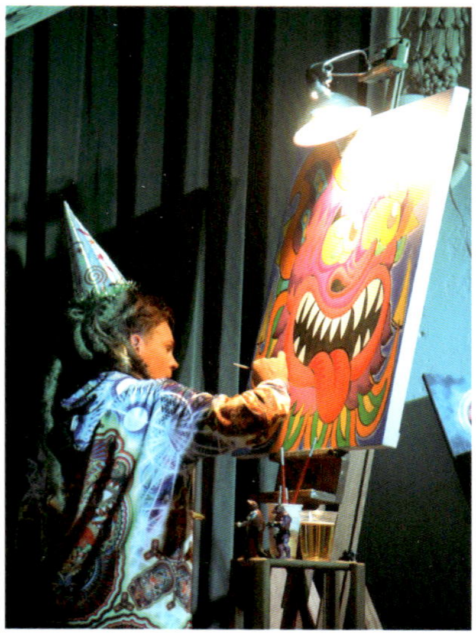

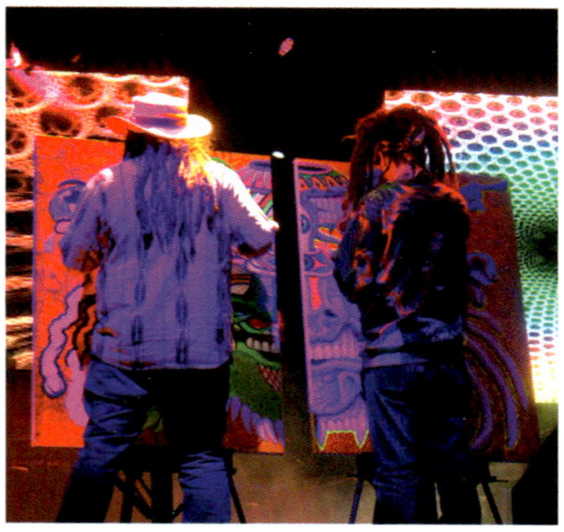

"Be More" Acrylics on canvas, 2014 (Baltimore) and **"Cheshire Cat"** Acrylics on canvas, 2016 (Portland)

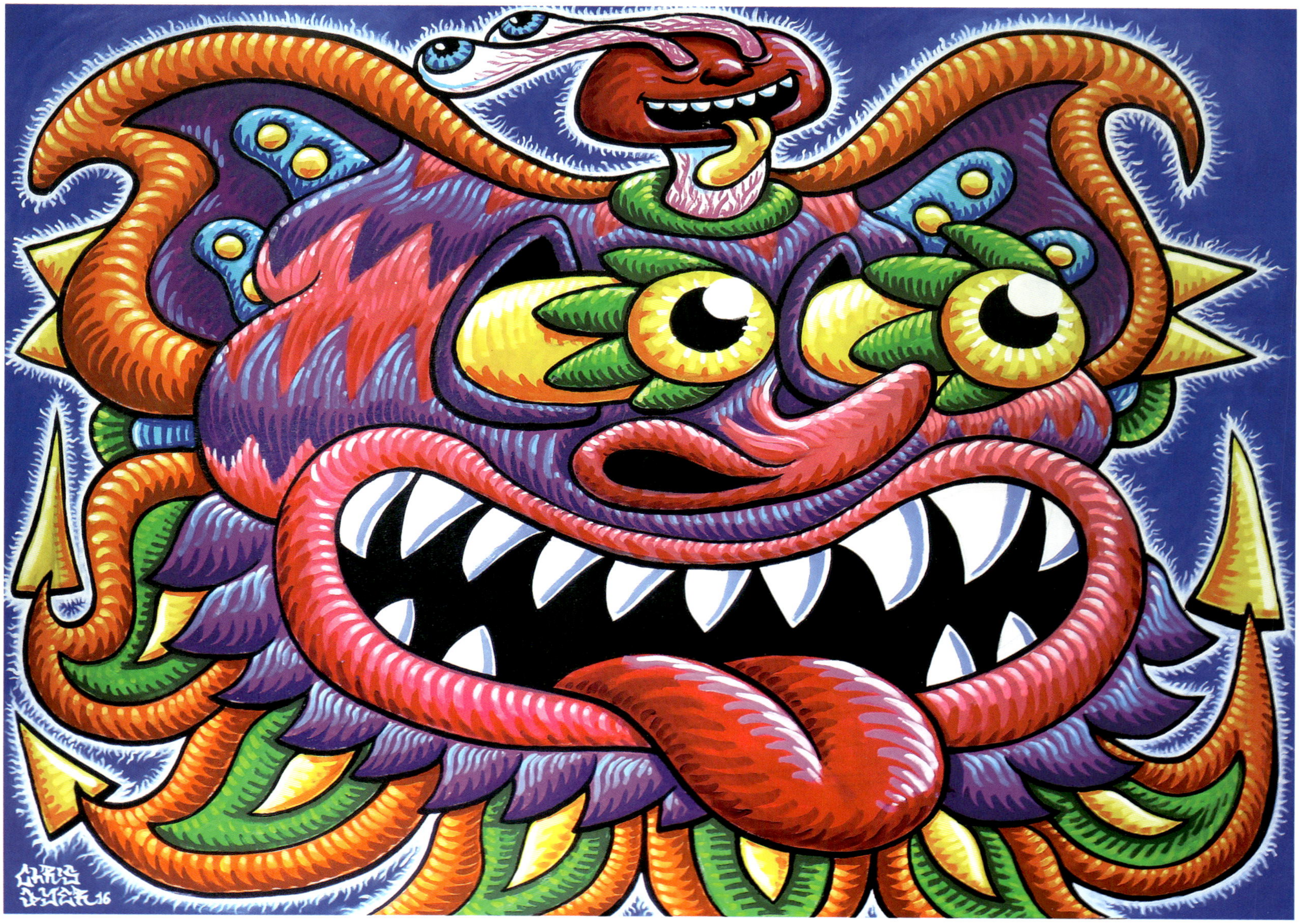

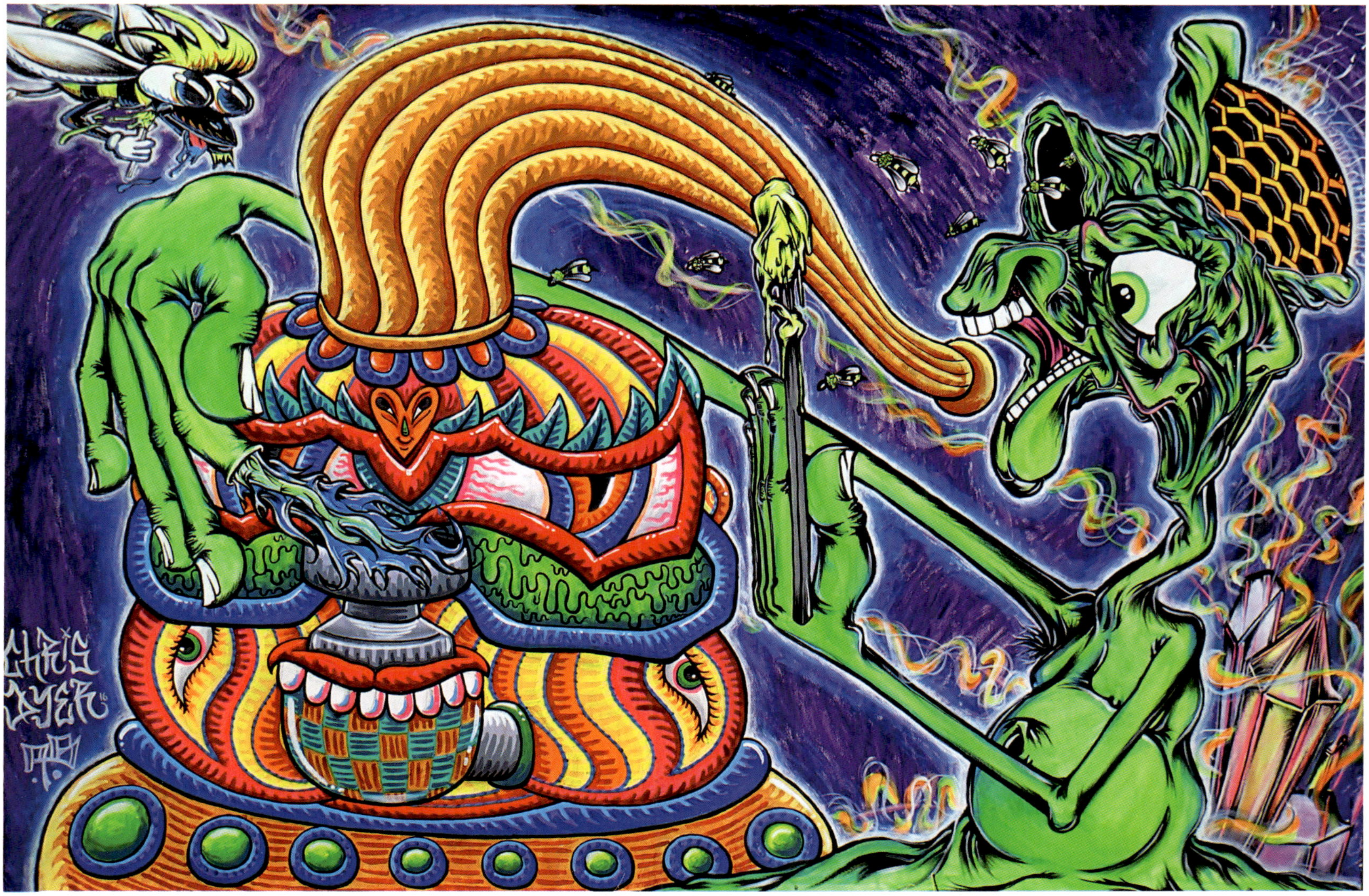

“The Dab Dance” Acrylics on canvas, 2016 and **“Uncle Rico”** Acrylics on two canvases, 2017.
Both are collaboration paintings with my friend **Aaron Brooks**, we did at **“Gem and Jam”** Festival in Arizona.

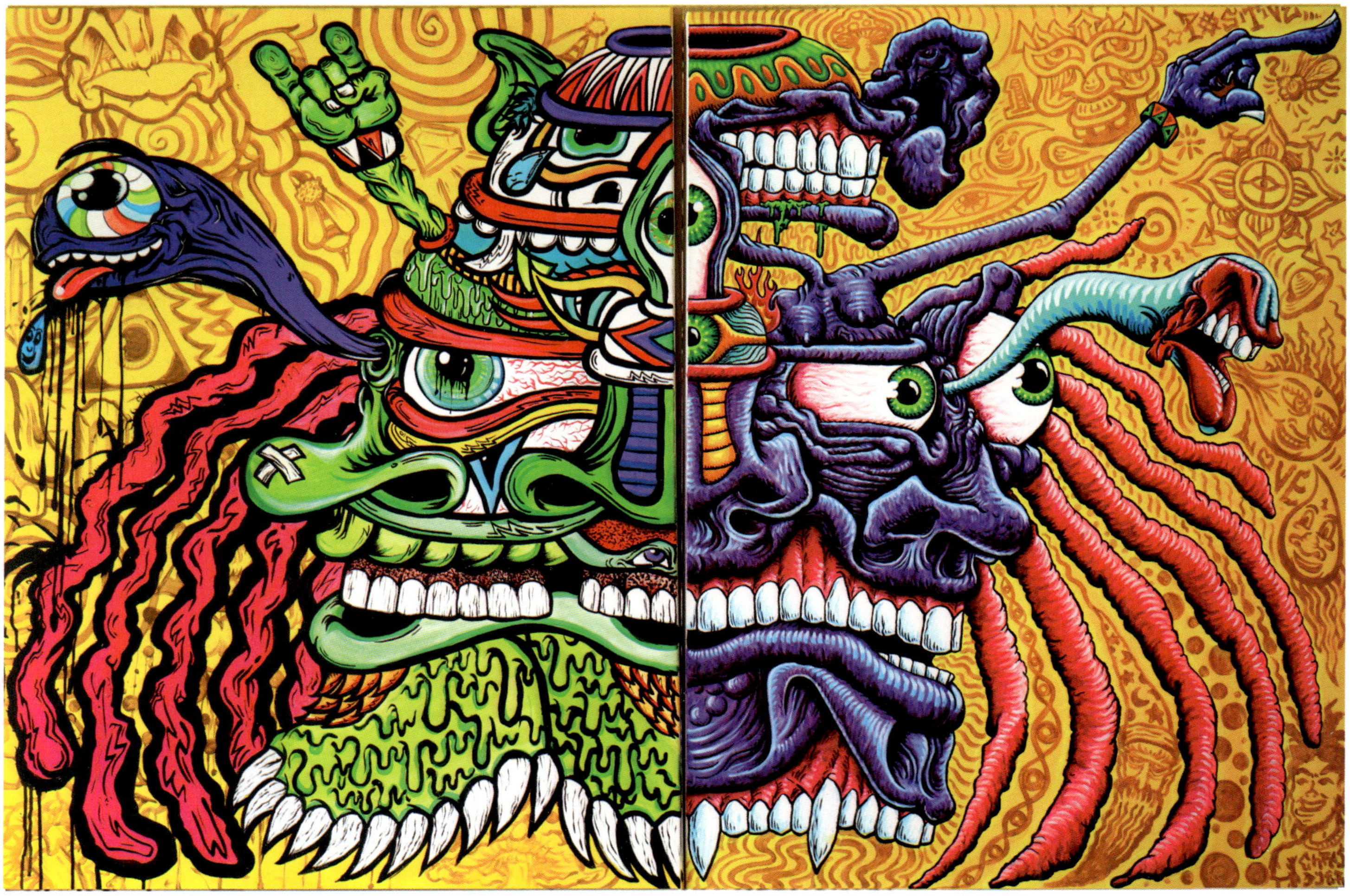

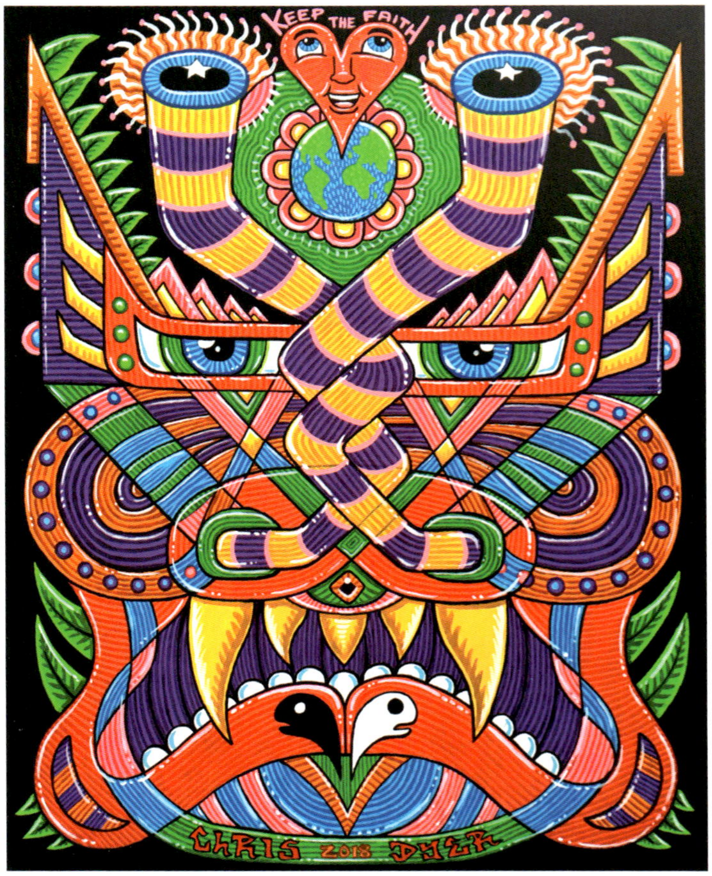

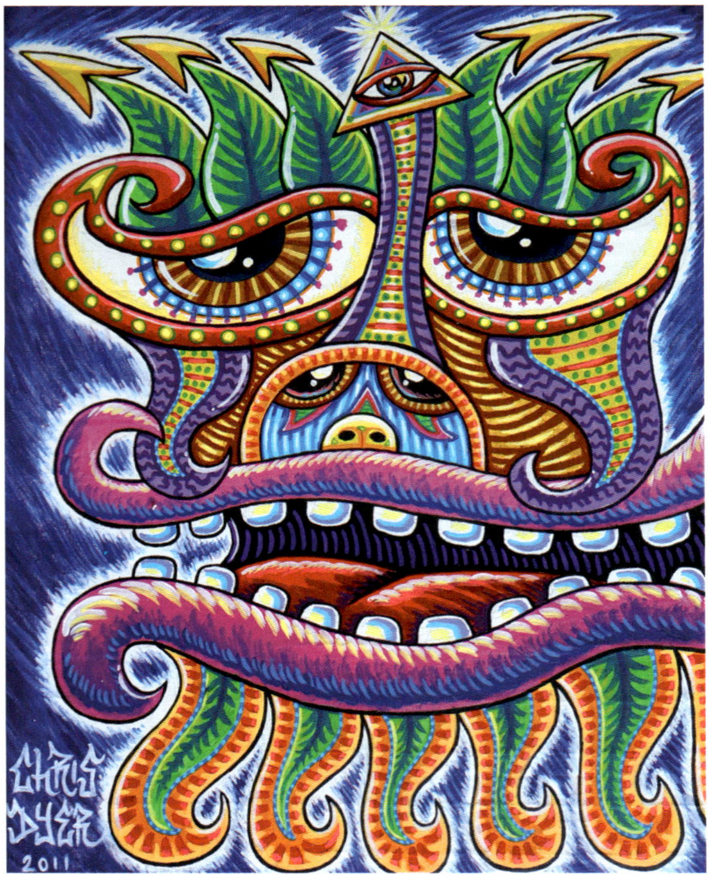

"Keep the Faith" Acrylics on canvas, at **"Earth Frequency Festival"** (Australia, 2018), **"Love the Life you Live"** Acrylics on canvas (for **"Midnite"** concert in Oakland, 2011) and **"Ugly but Happy"** Acrylics on canvas, at **"Present Perfect Festival"** (Saint Petersbourg, Russia 2016)

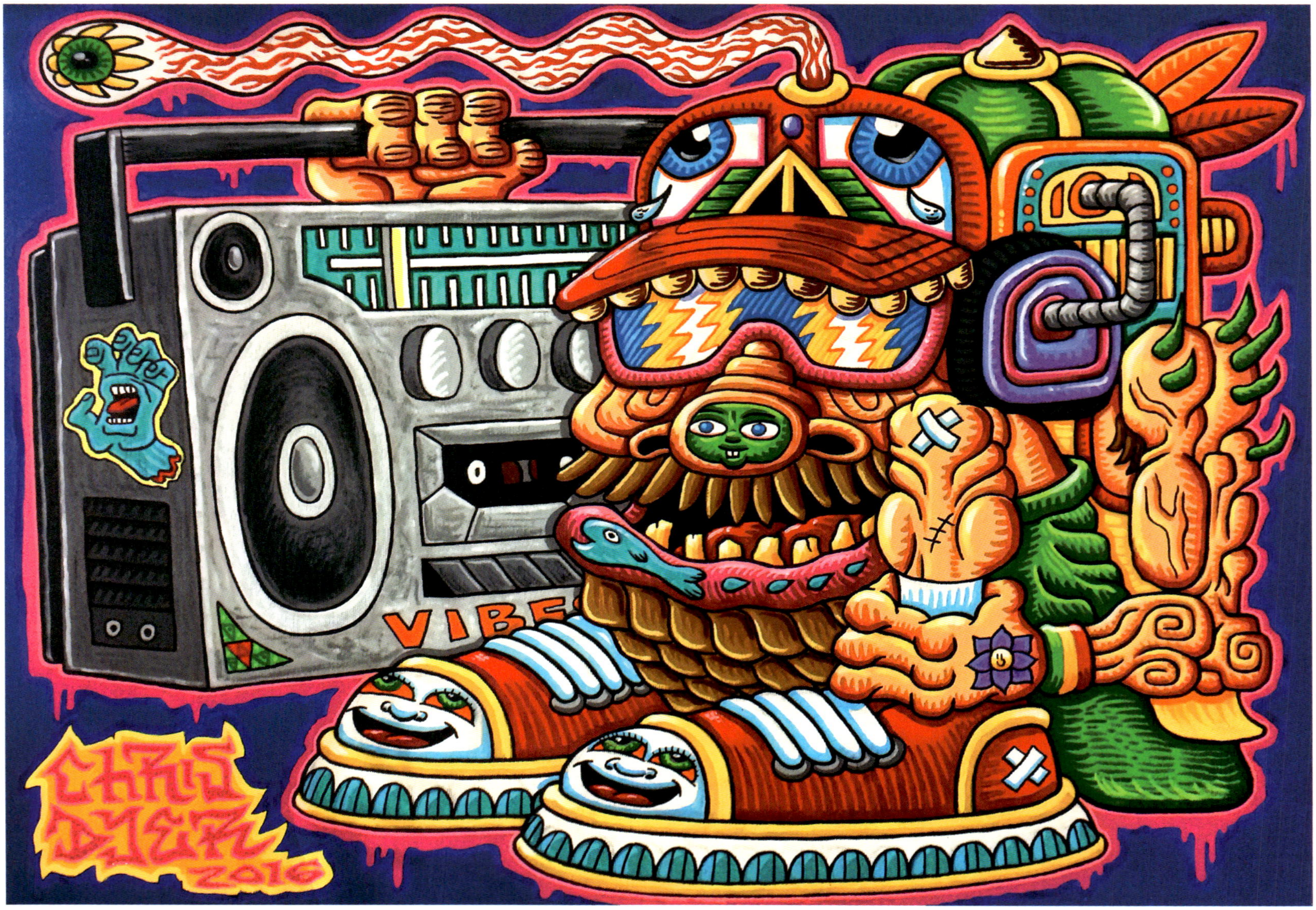

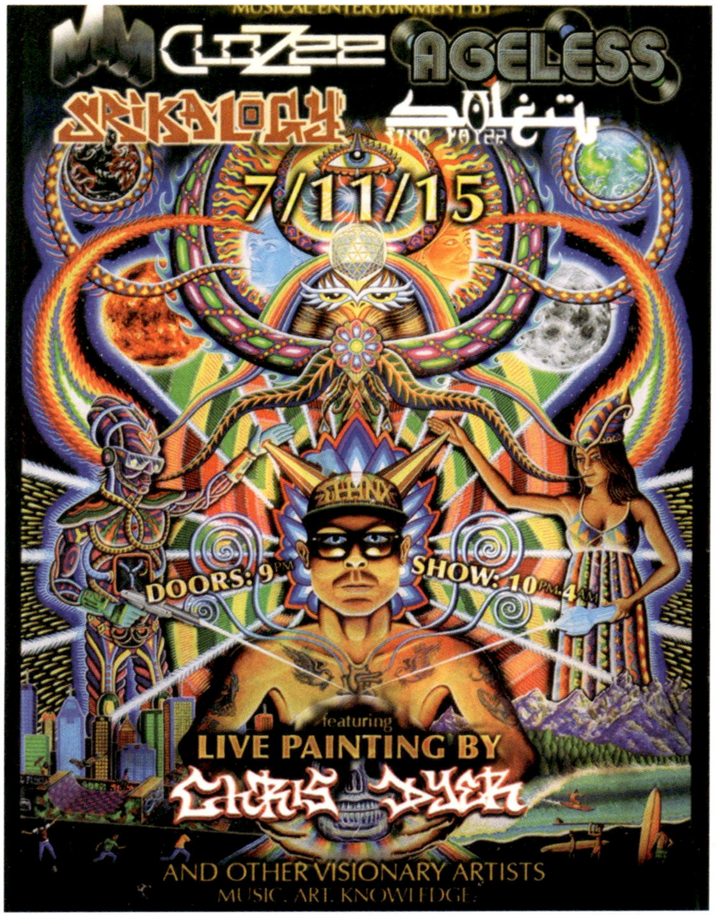

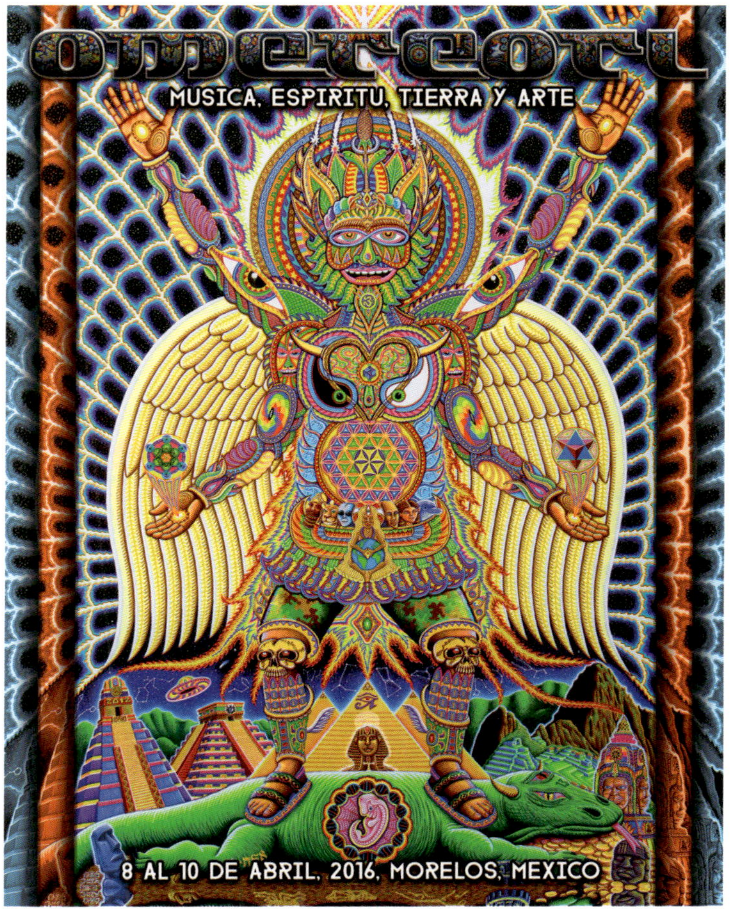

Above: Live Painting Posters for **"Nirvanity"** (Brooklyn, NY, 2015) and **"Ometeotl"** (Mexico, 2016)
Below: Event Poster and Acrylics Live Painting, at **"Todo el Mundo dice Aho!"** (Miami, 2023)

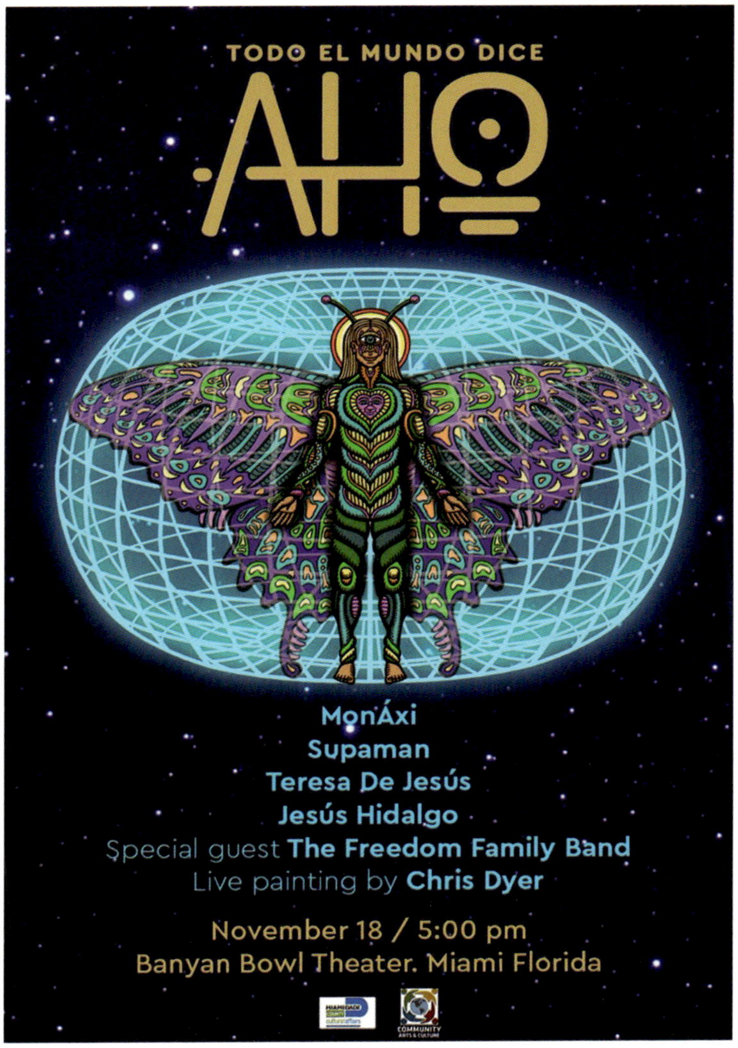

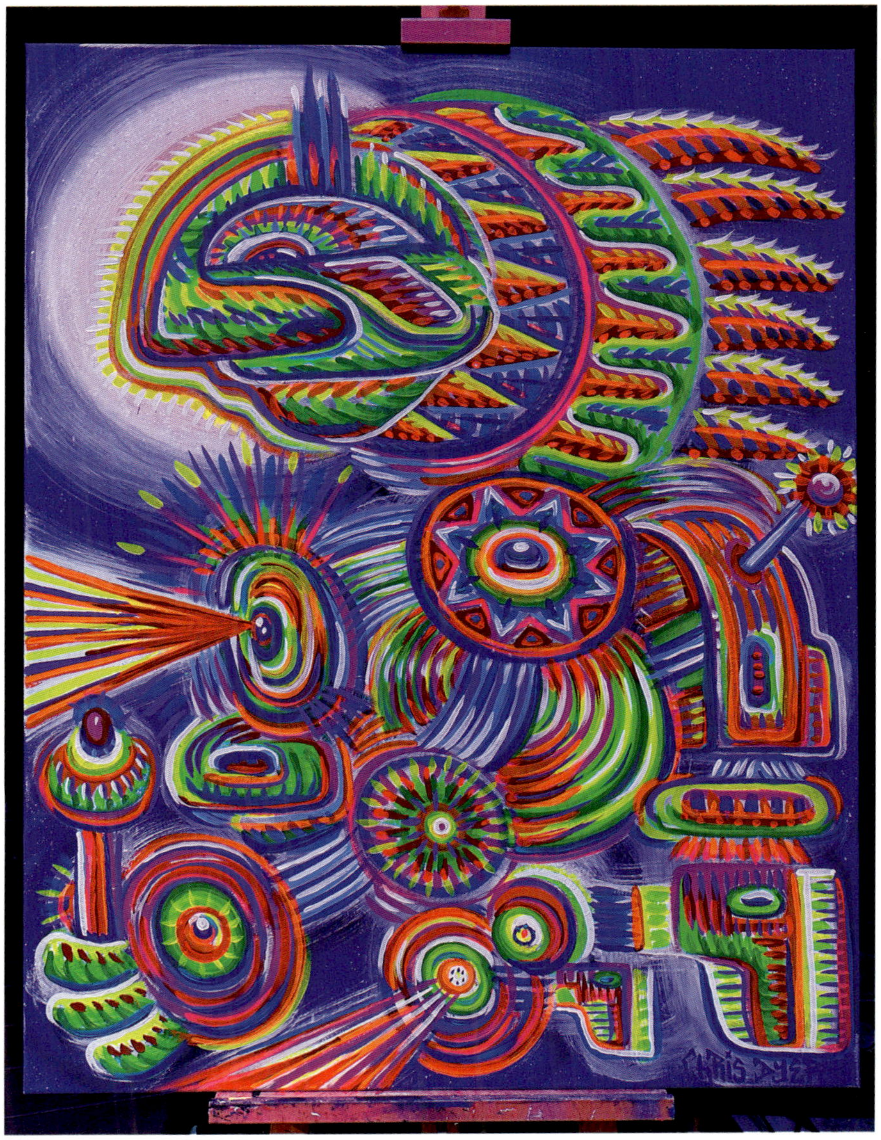

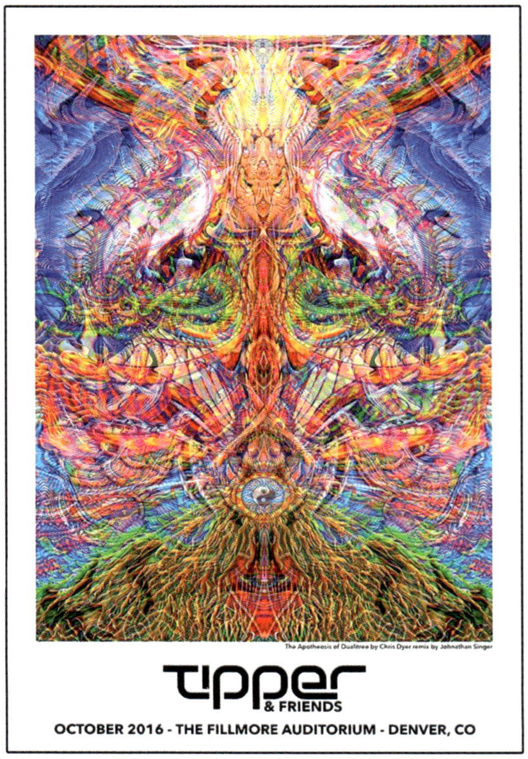

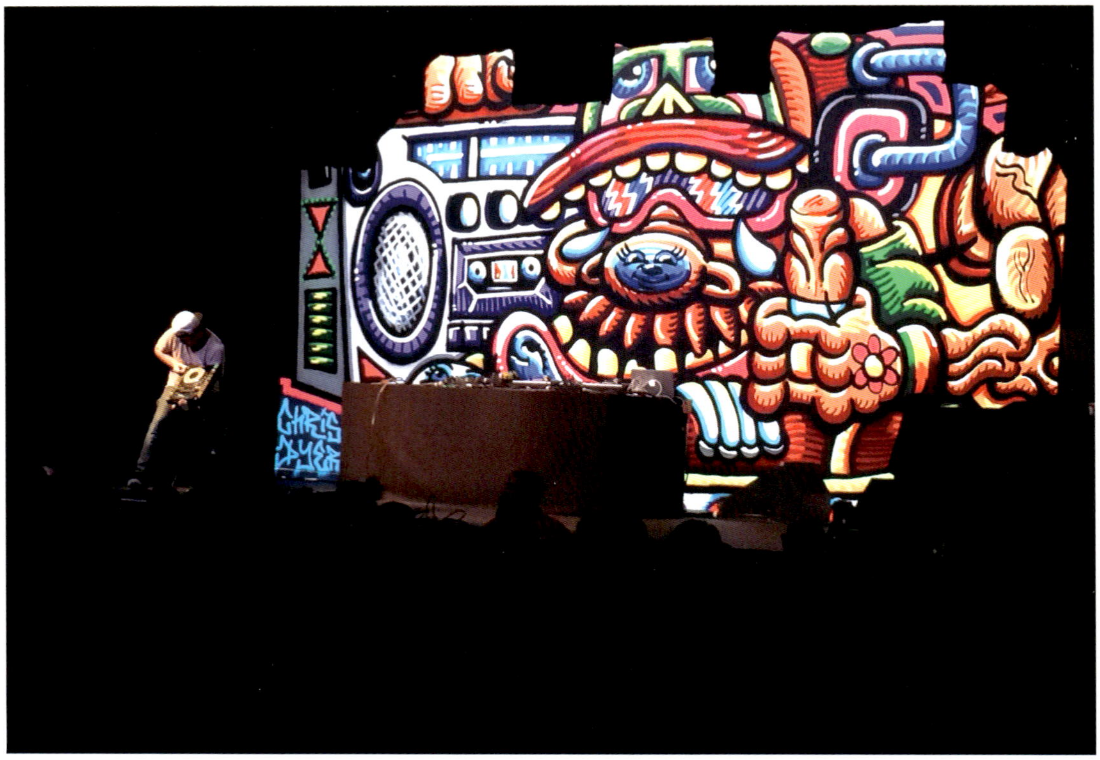

This live painting gig was a special three day event at the legendary **"Fillmore"** of **Denver**. The headliner was the super popular producer **"Tipper"**, with **"Cut Chemist"** and **"LTJ Bukem"** as opening acts. Then we also had my friend **Jonathan Singer** on the visuals, and who also made our collaboration event poster. I had a blast on stage, dancing and blasting this painting that is a big up to all positive DJs in the world!

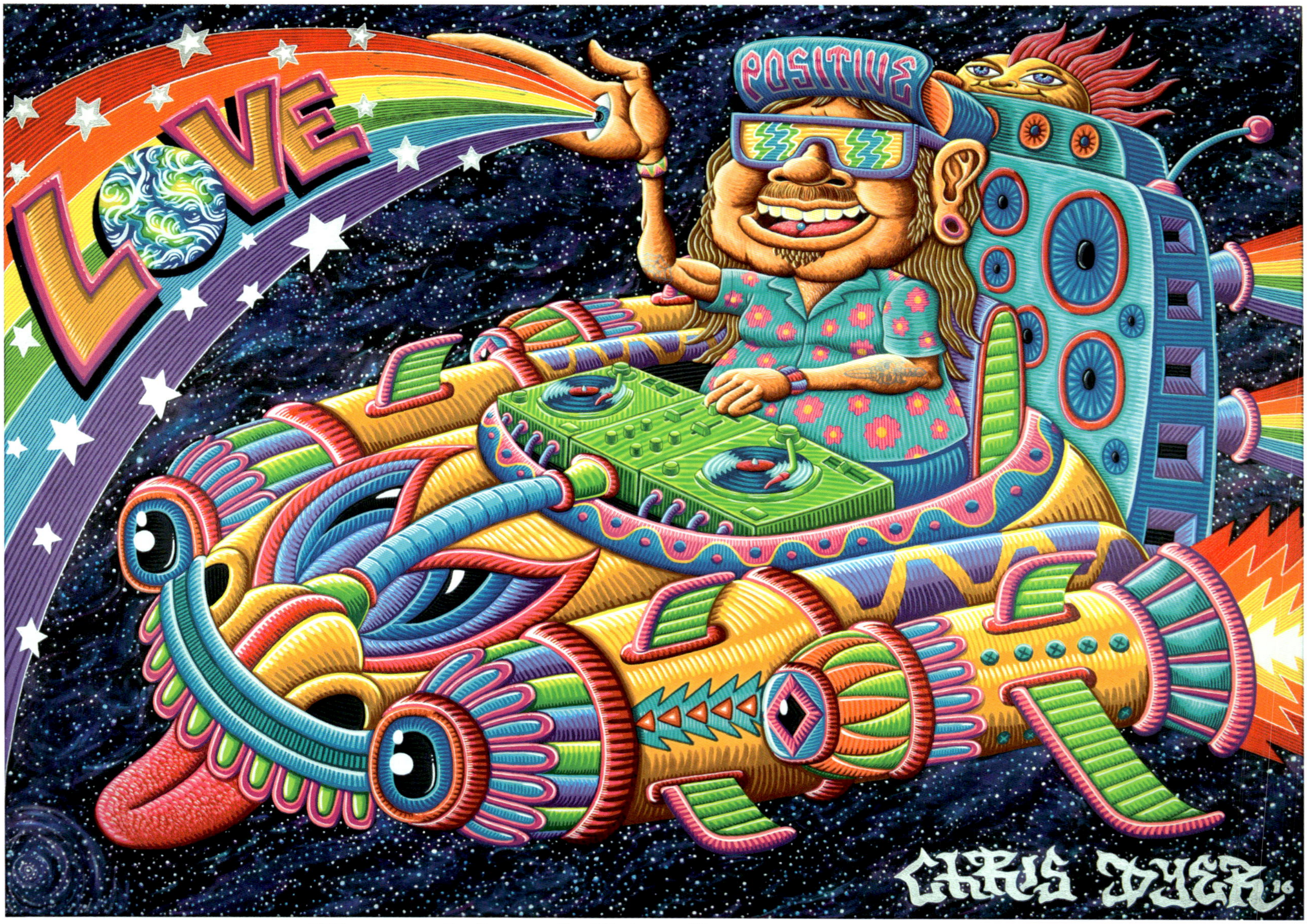

"Space Selectah!" Acrylics on canvas, 2016

MUSIC FESTIVAL LIVE MURALS

Once I got the hang of spray painting murals, I was able to take my live painting performances to the next level. I could go bigger and faster with that medium, so I've been hired to do my magic trick at many amazing music festivals all around the planet! On top of it, I've had the pleasure of performing for musicians I really enjoy like Immortal Technique, Reggie Watts, Mix Master Mike, Beats Antique, Nahko Bear, Diplo, Mike Love, Rising Appalachia, Trevor Hall and many more!

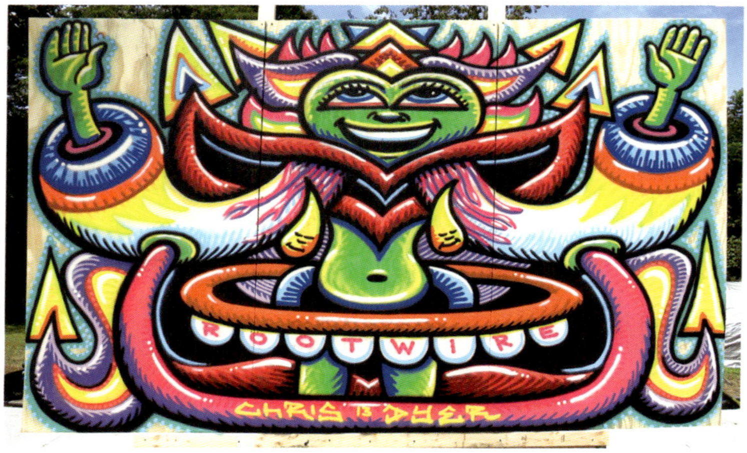

"Rootwire Festival" Ohio, 2013

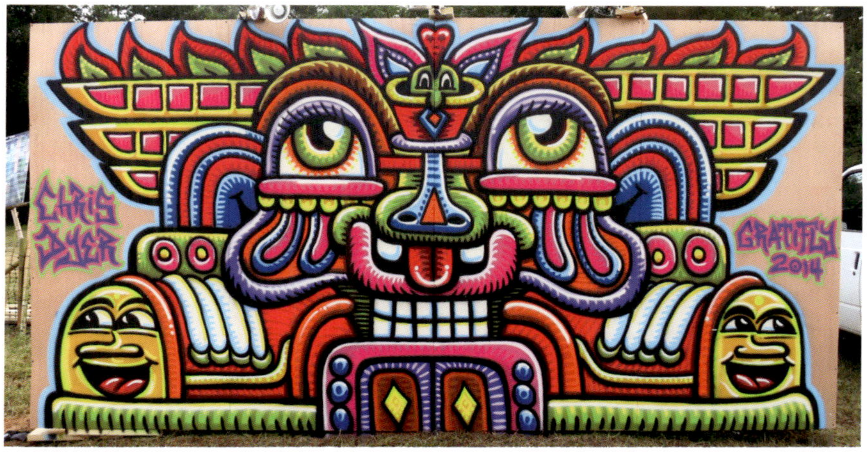

"Gratifly Festival" North Carolina, 2014

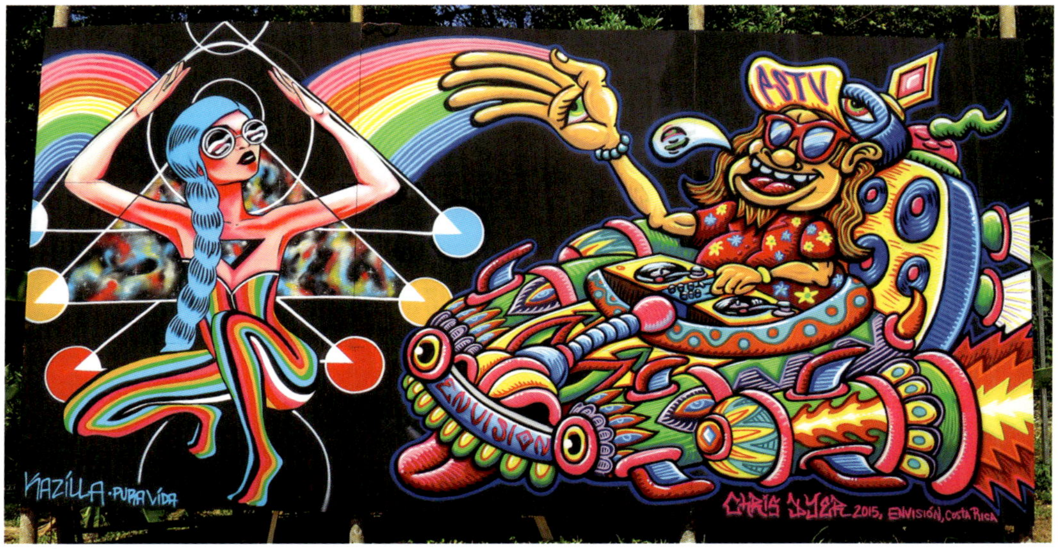

"Envision Festival" Costa Rica, 2015 (with **Kazilla**)

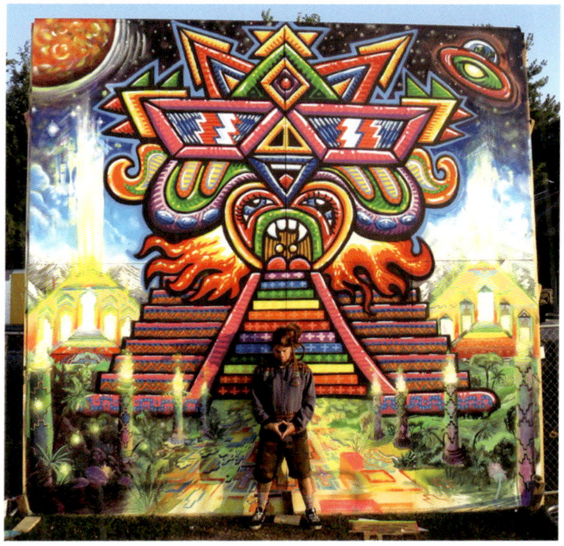

"Great North Festival" Maine, 2015 (with **Jonathan Solter**)

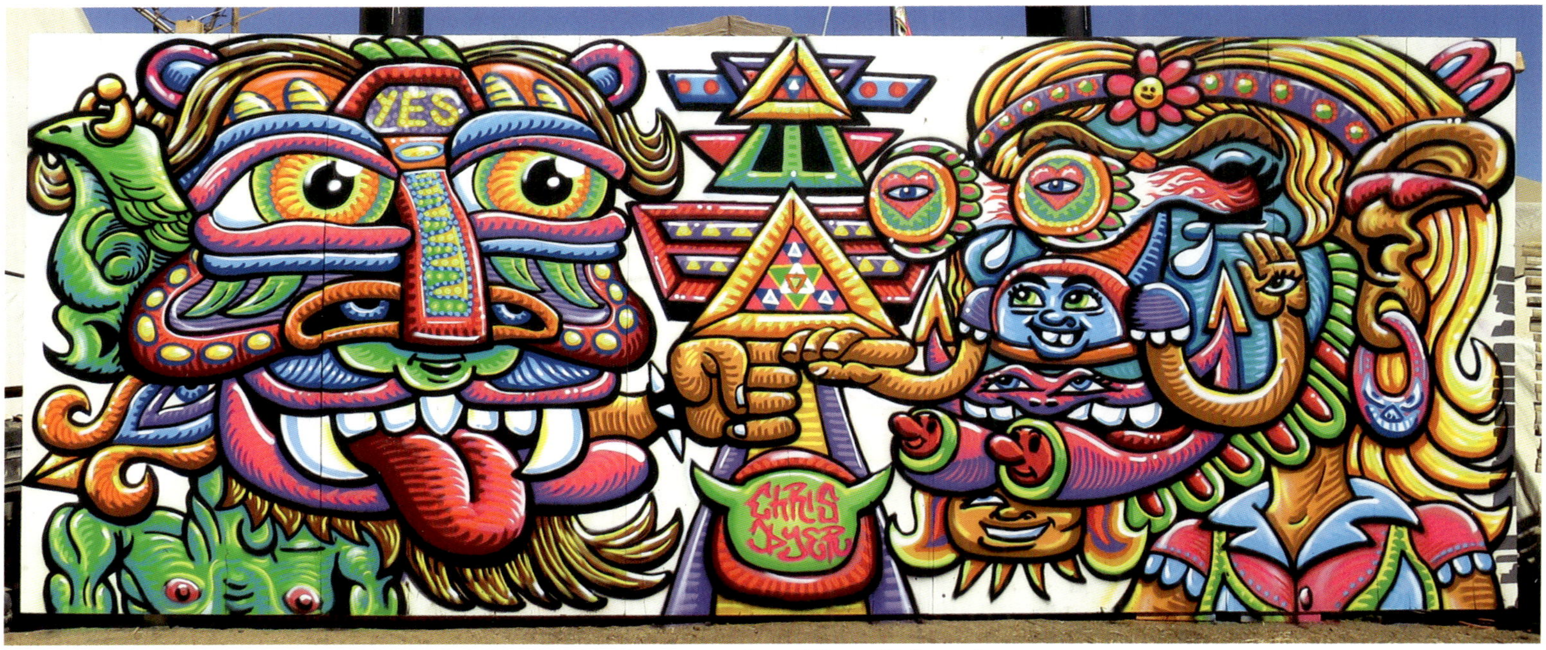

"Symbiosis Festival" California, 2015

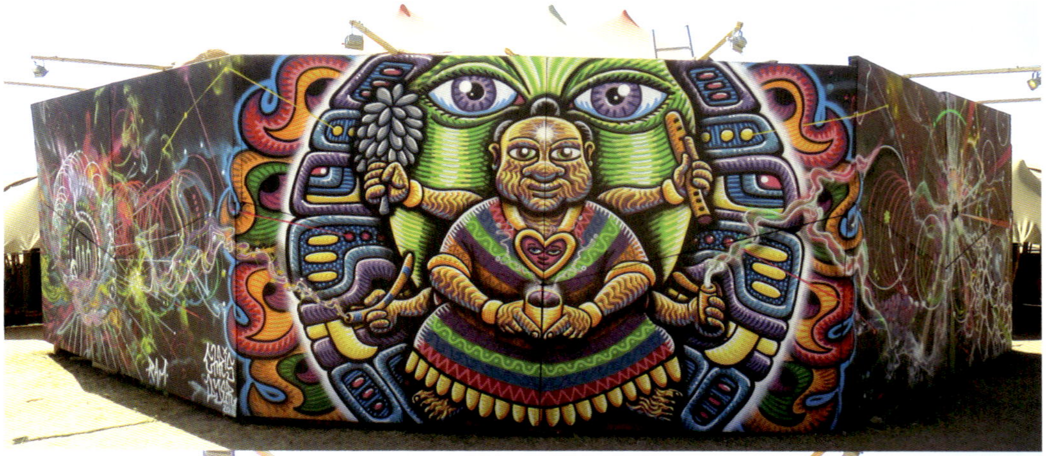

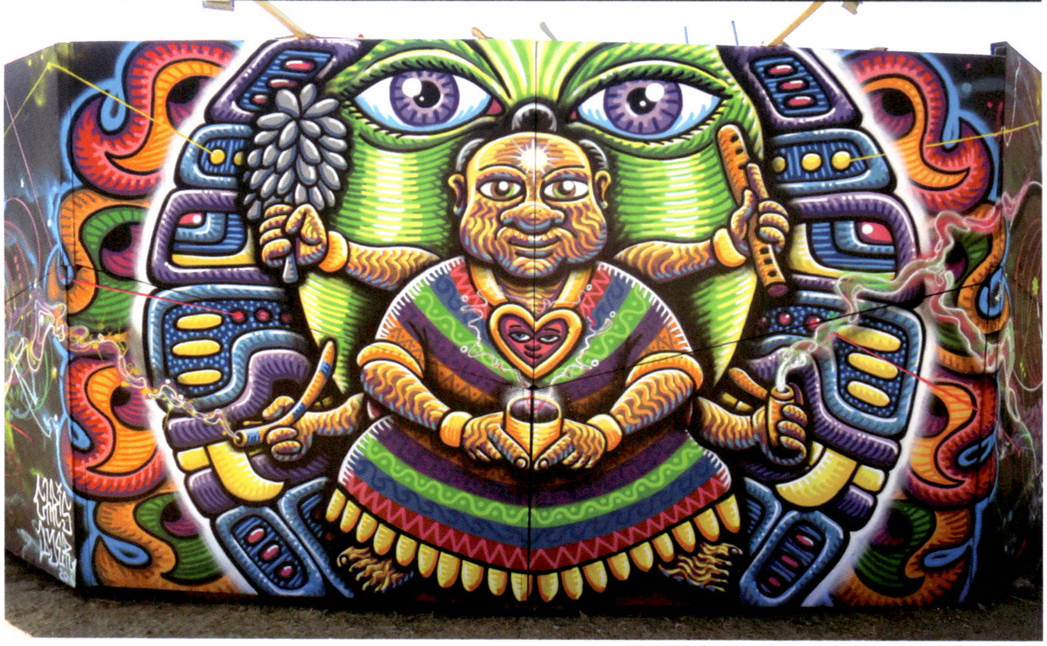

"Boom Festival" Portugal, 2016 (with **Ram Libson**)

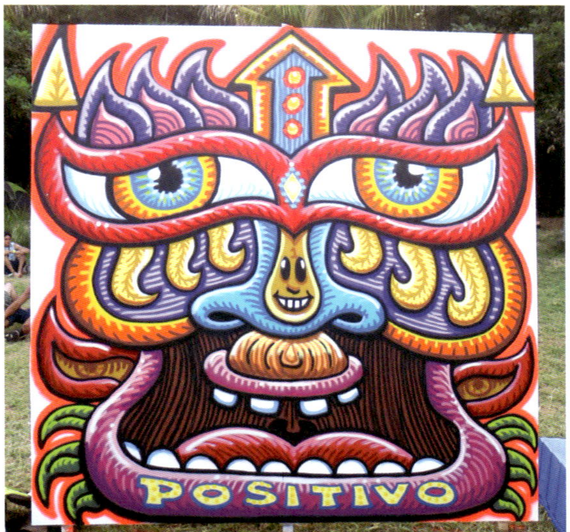

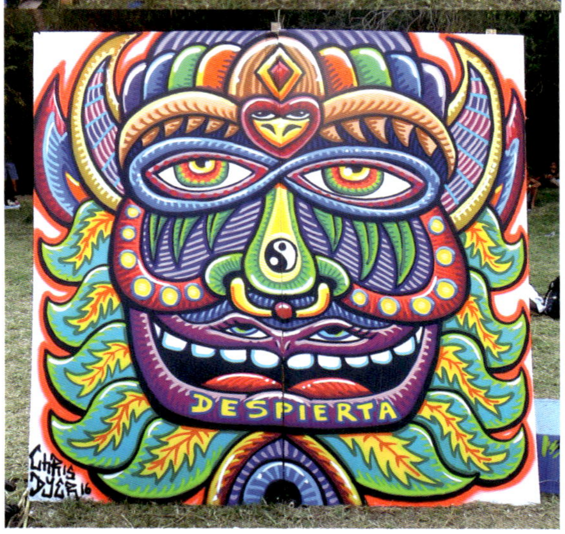

"Ometeotl Festival"
Mexico, 2016

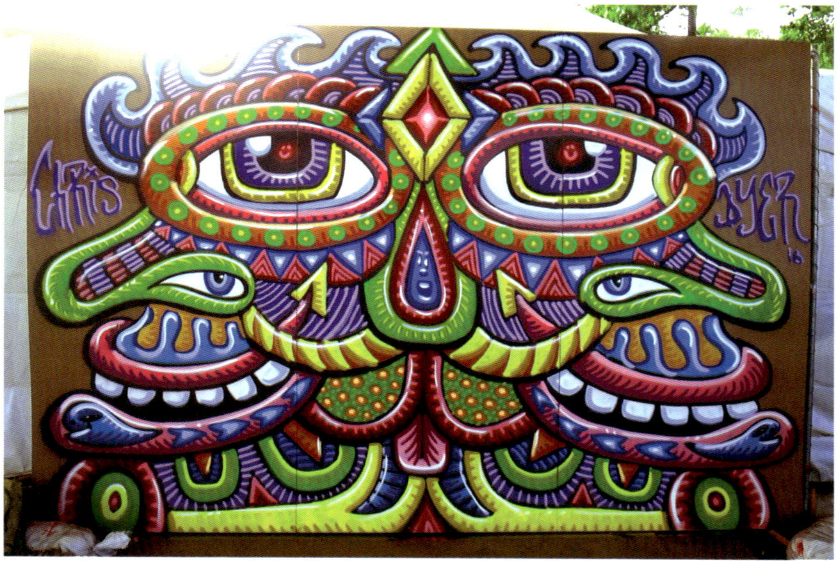

"North Coast Festival" Chicago, 2016

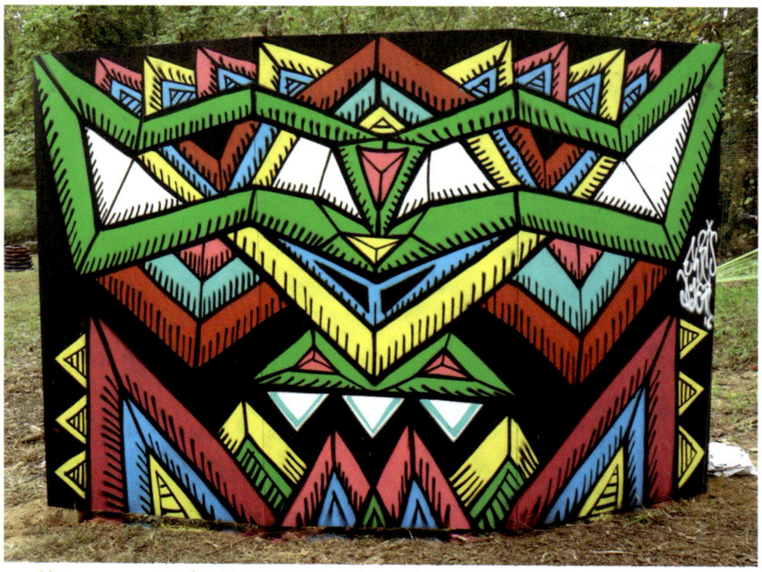

"Luna Light Festival" Maryland, 2016

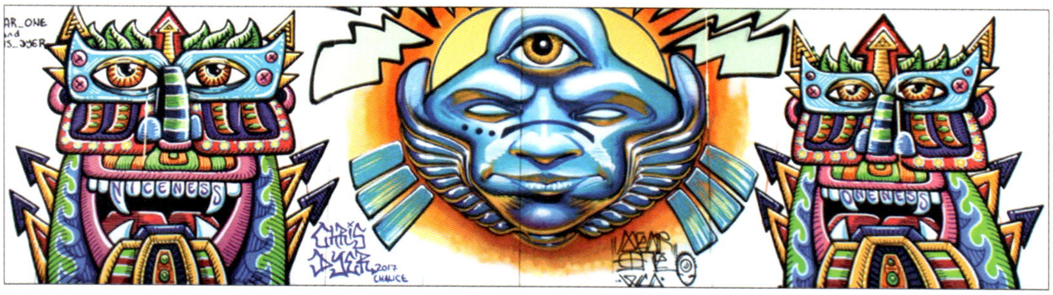

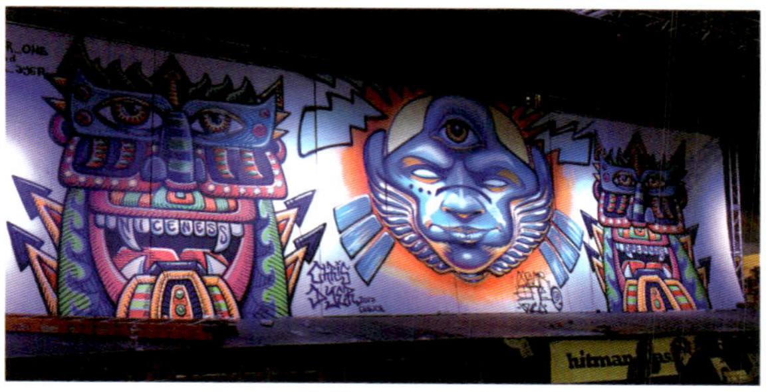

"Chalice Festival" Los Angeles, 2017 (with **Mear One**)

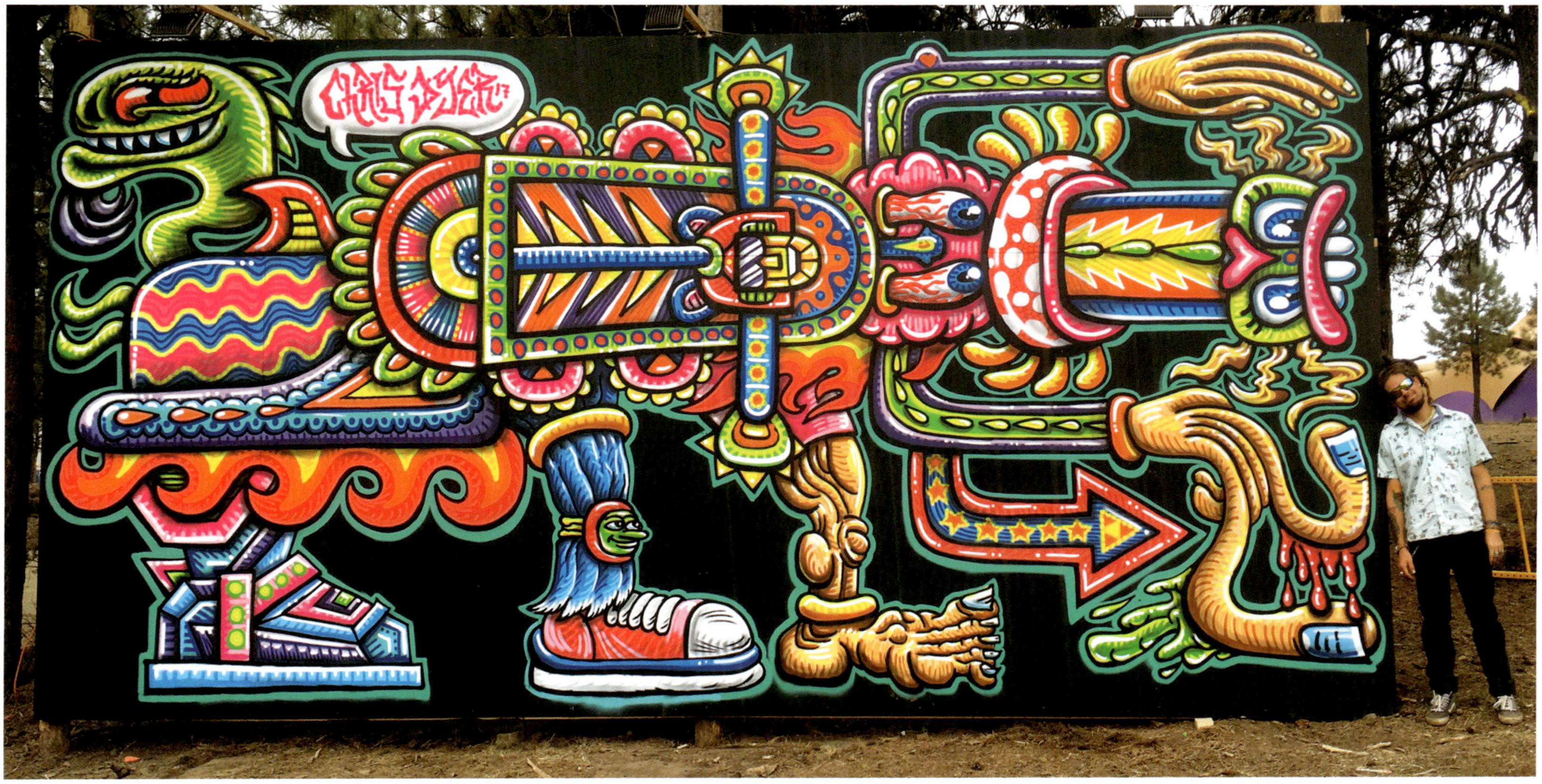

"Global Eclipse Festival" Oregon, 2017

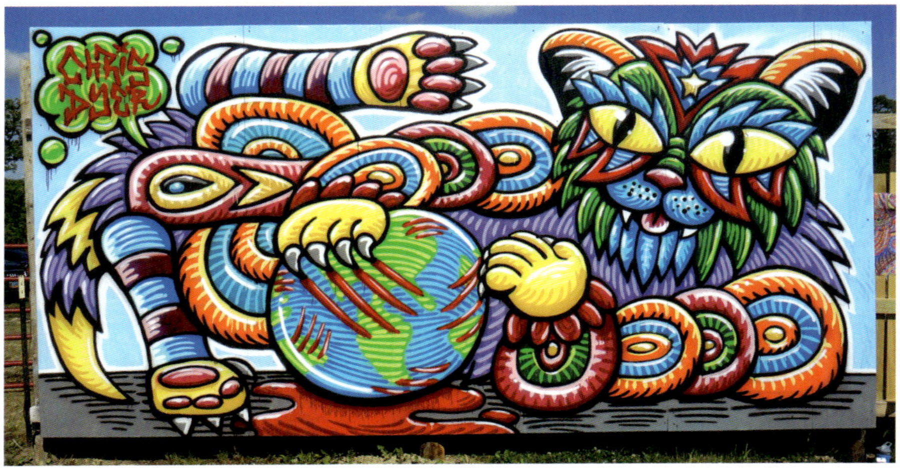

"Earth Rythms Festival" Minnesota, 2017

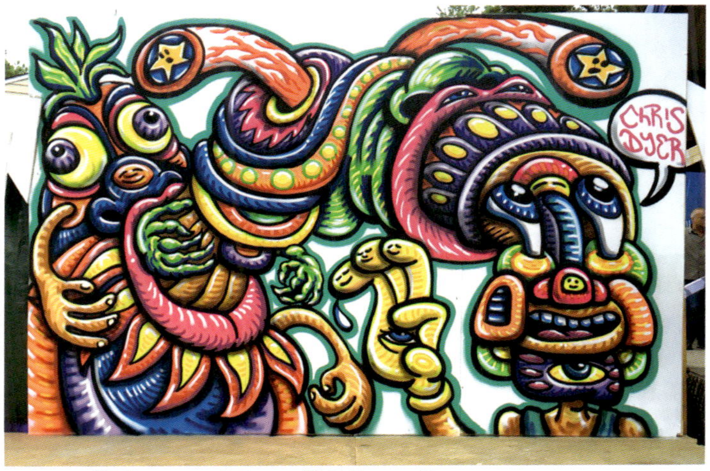

"Farm Fest" New Jersey, 2017

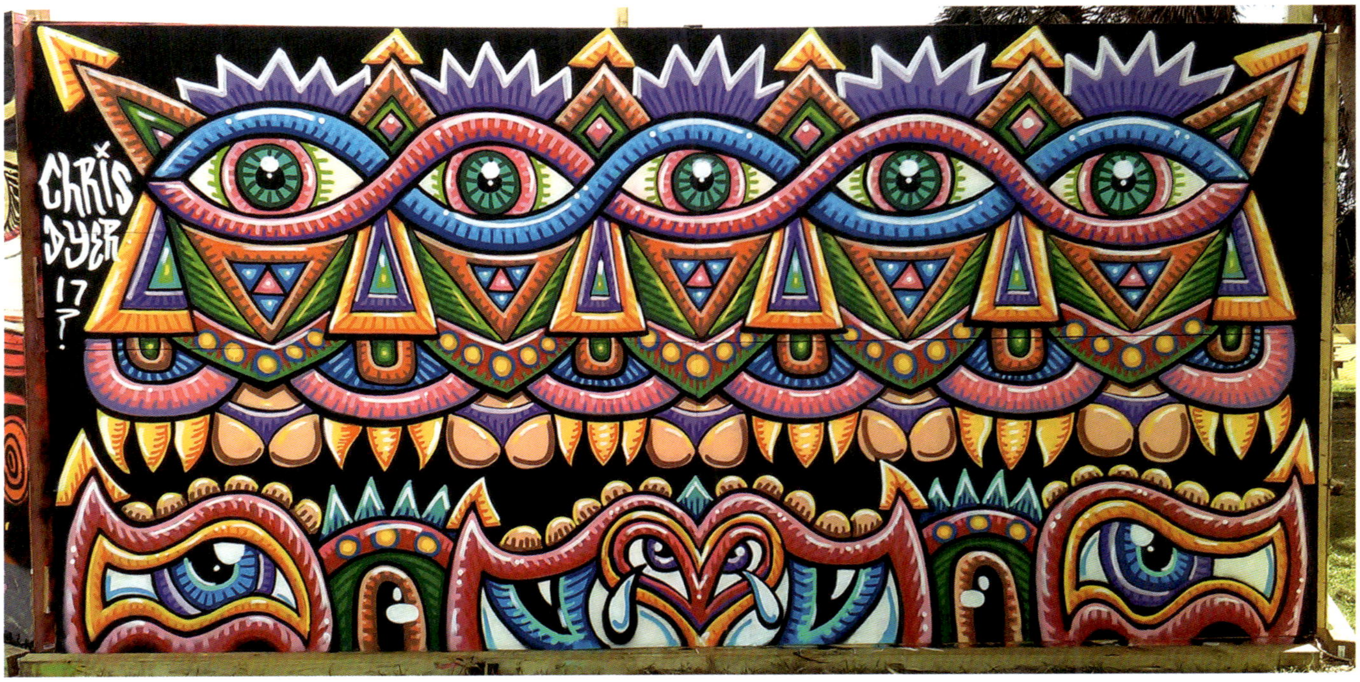

"Okeechobee Festival" Florida, 2017

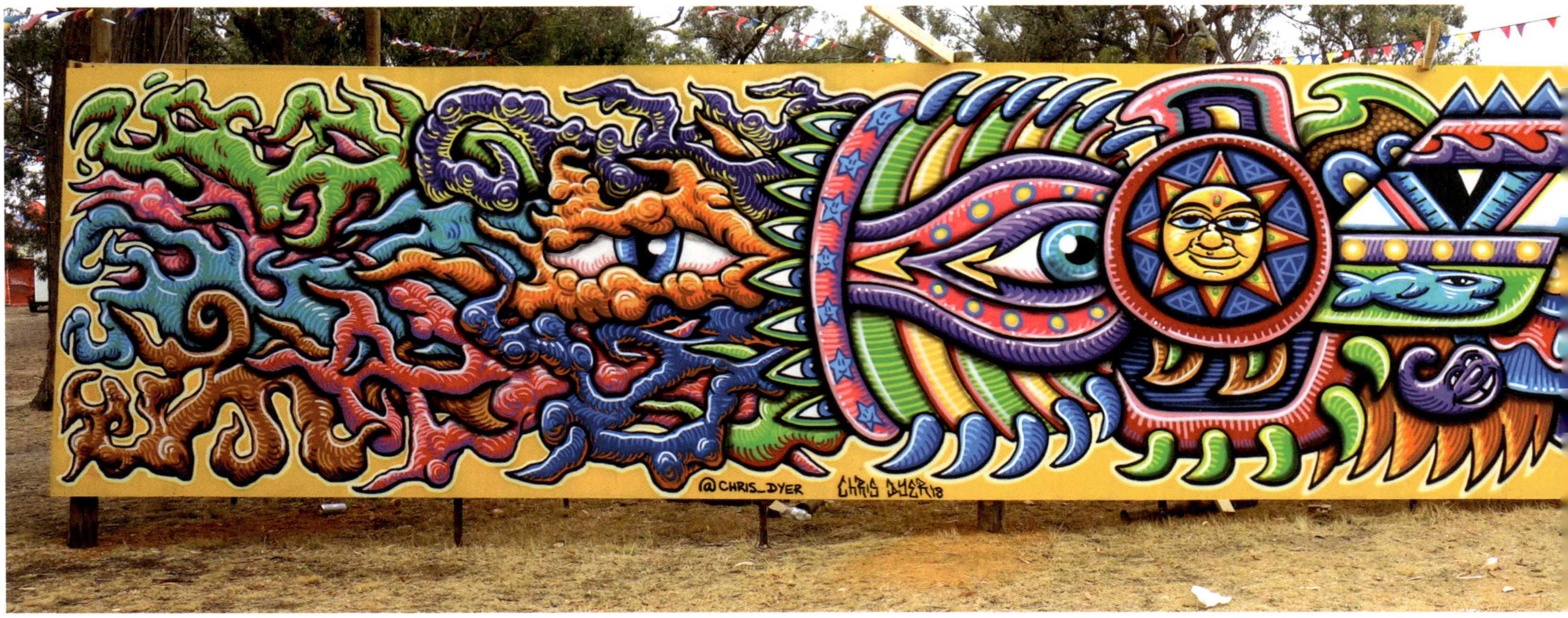

"Rainbow Serpent Festival" Australia, 2018

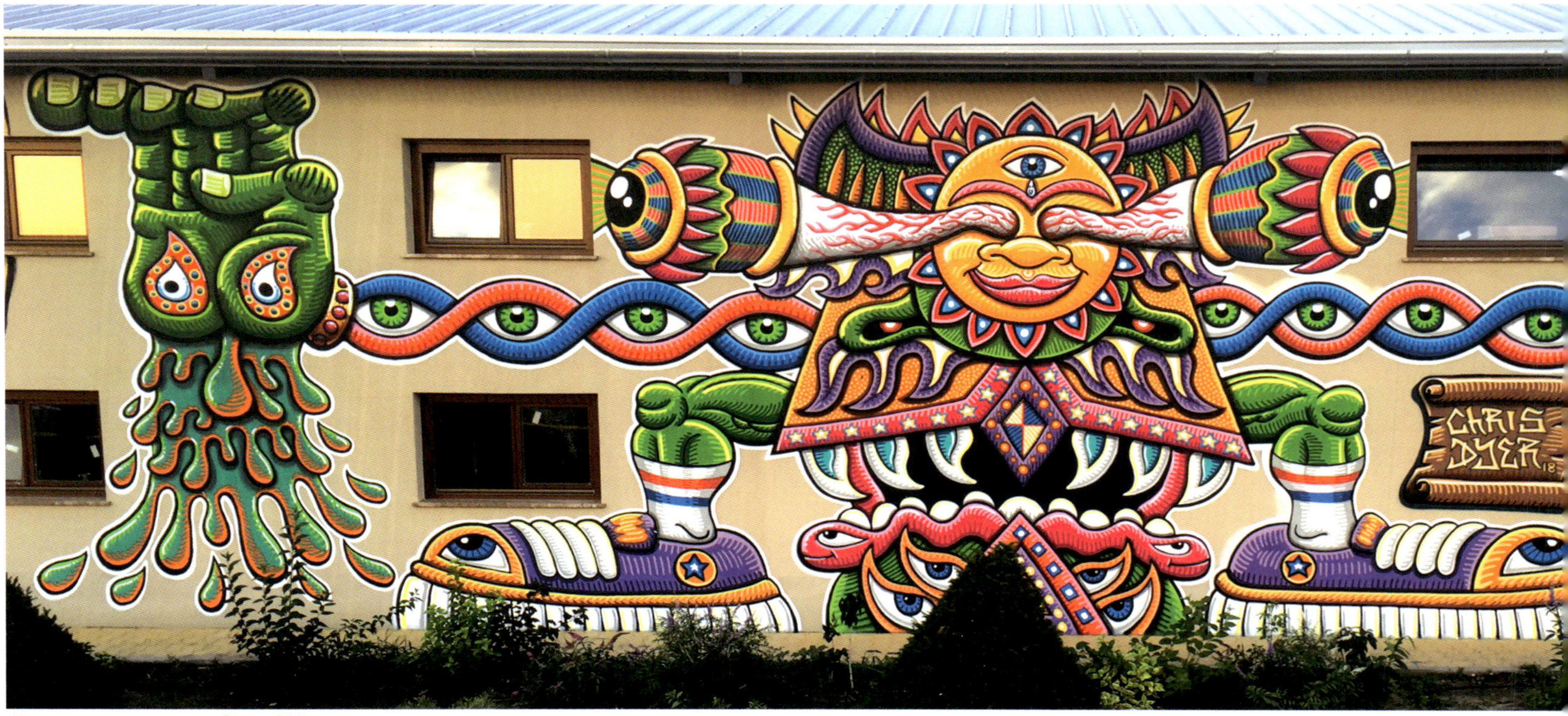

"Ozora Festival" Hungary, 2018

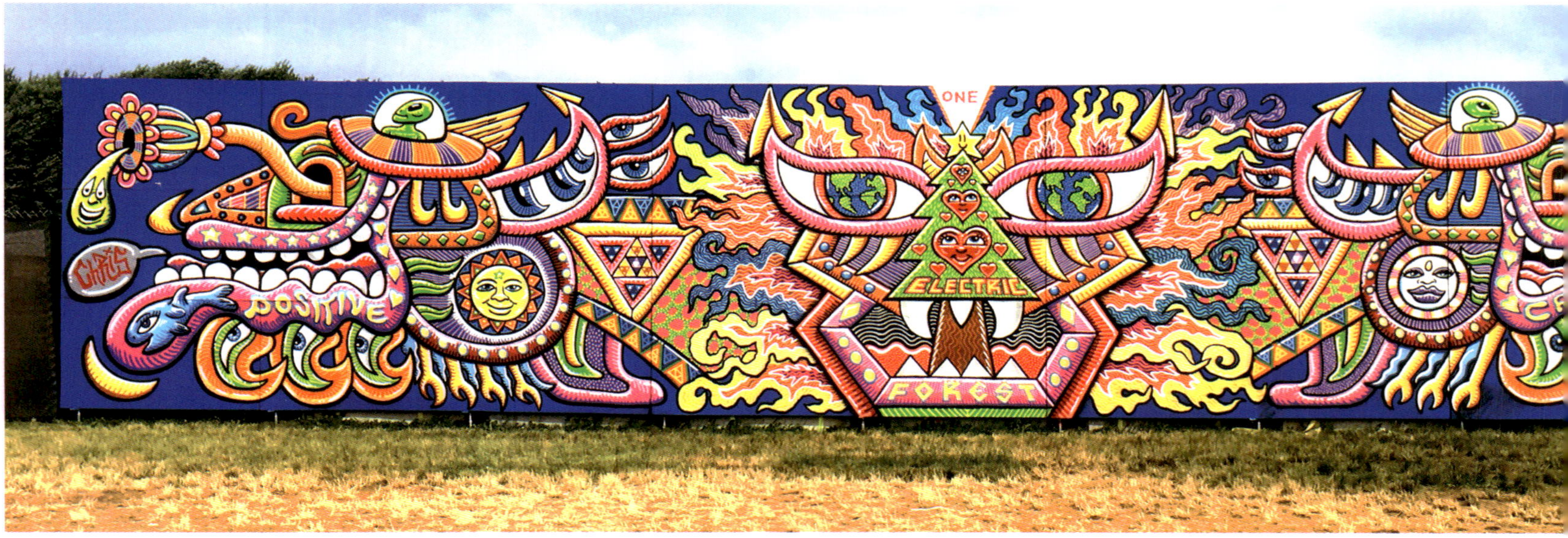

"Electric Forest" Michigan, 2018

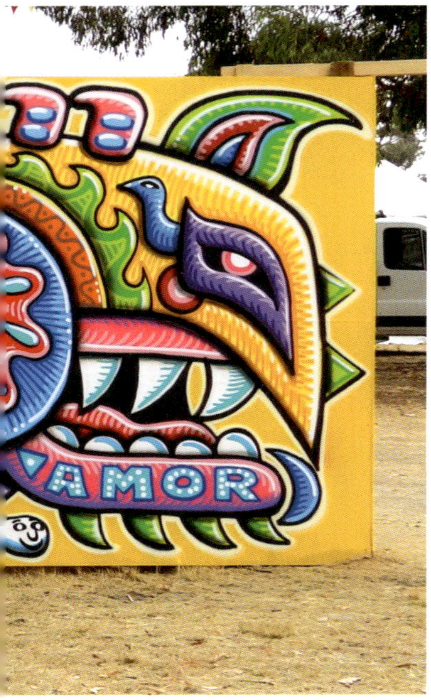

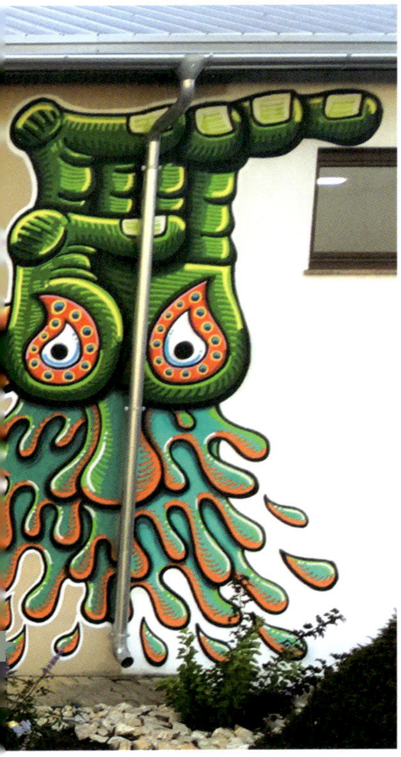

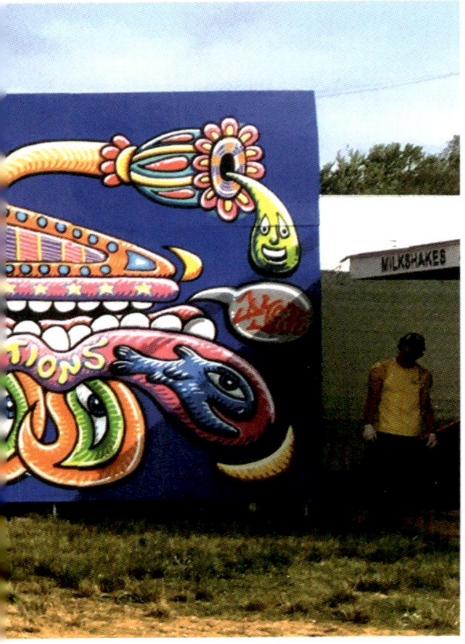

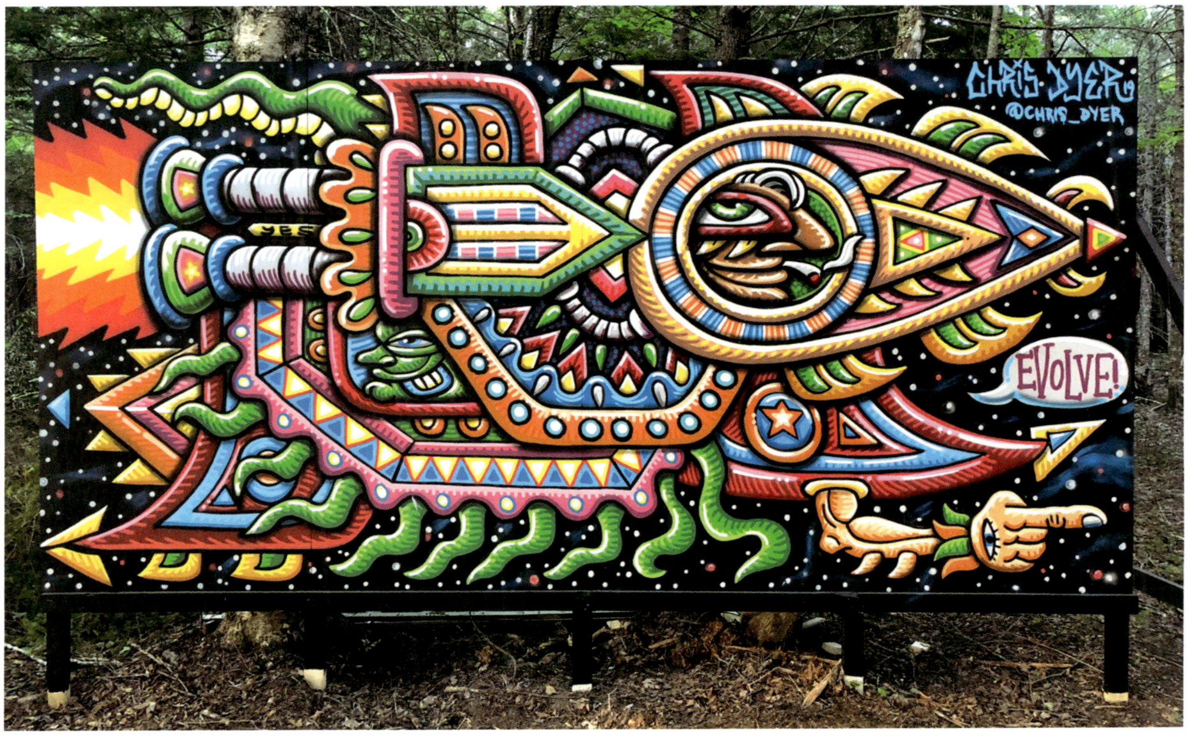

"Evolve Festival" New Brunswick, Canada, 2019

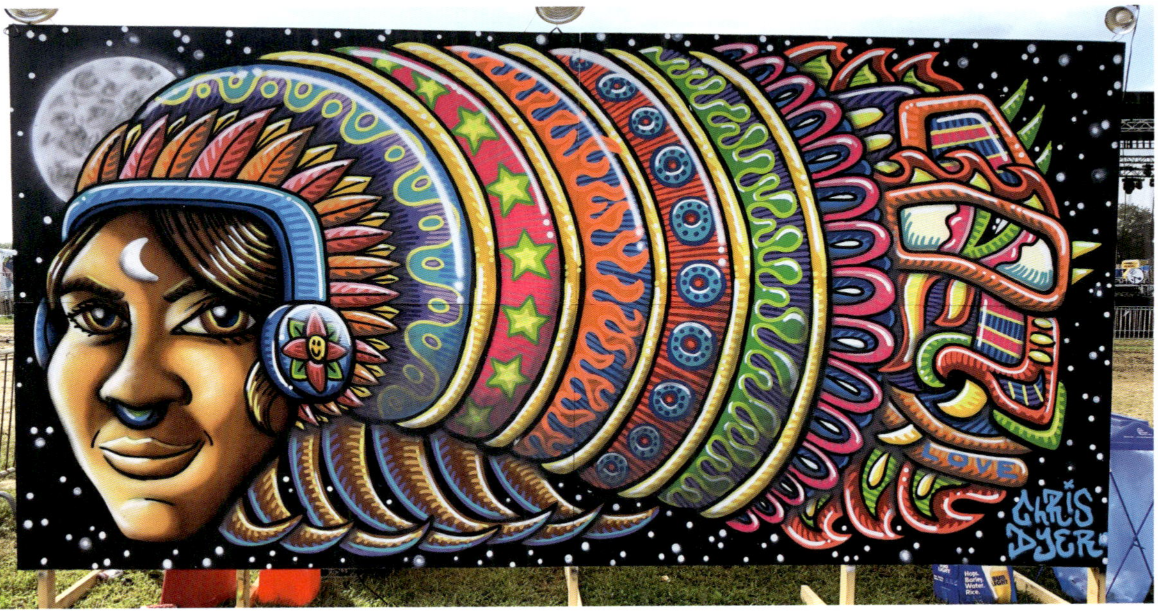

"Resonance Festival" Ohio, 2019

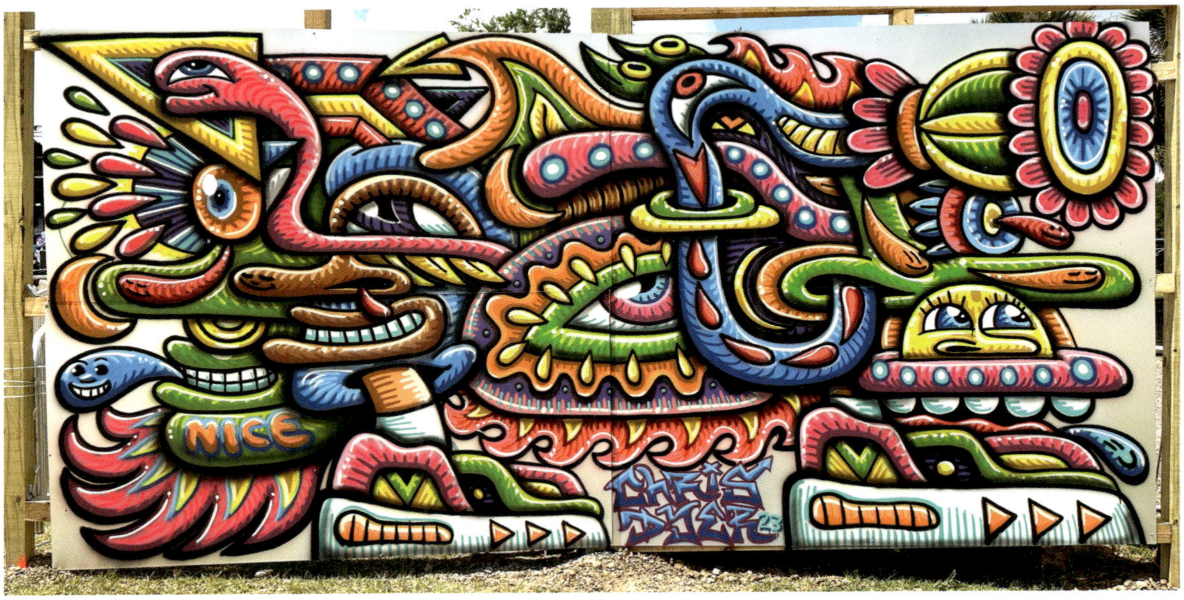

"Sol Festival" Alabama, 2023

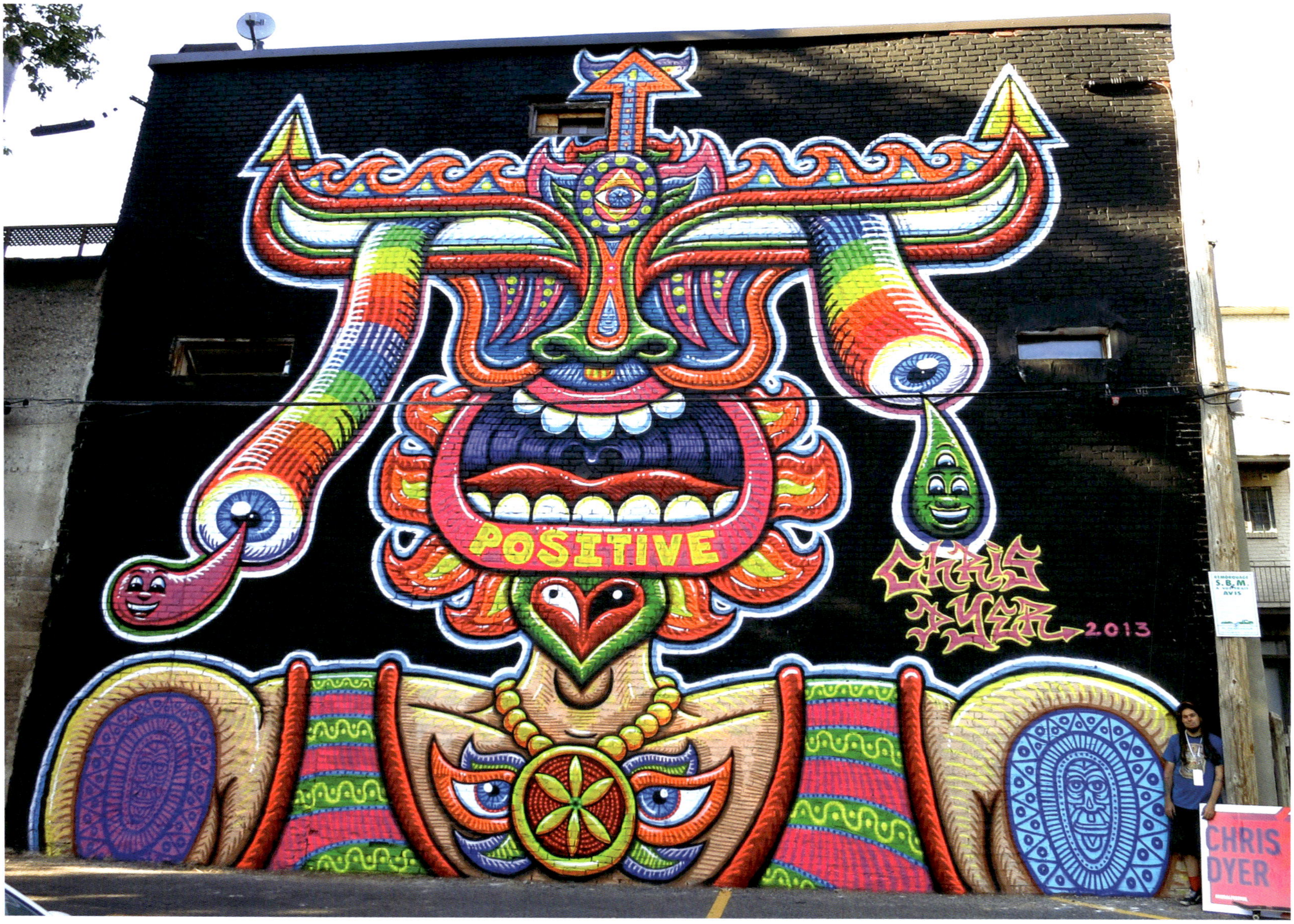

“Mural Festival” Montreal, 2013

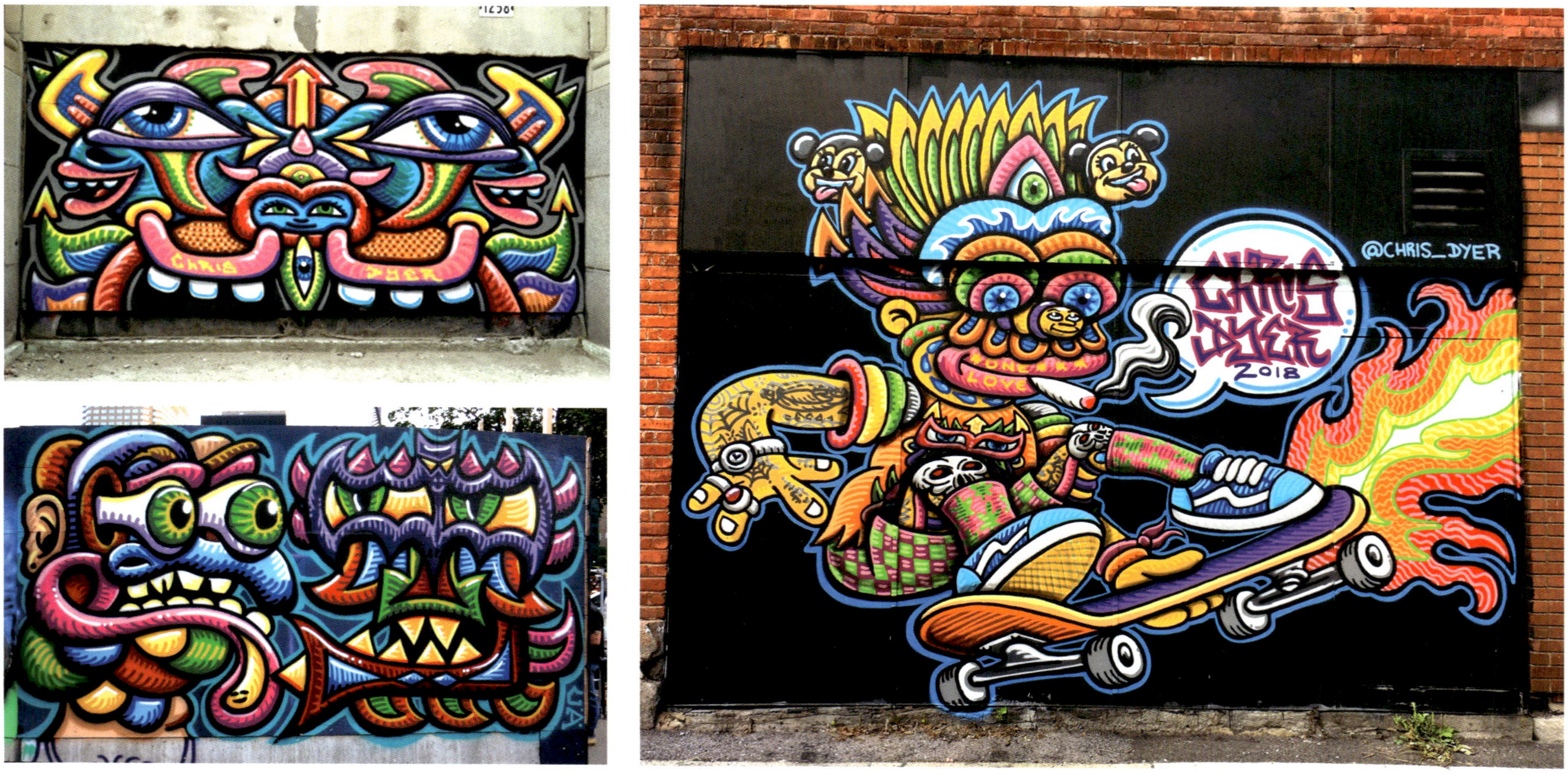

“Under Pressure Graffiti Festival” Montreal, 2013, 2014 & 2018

STREET MURALS

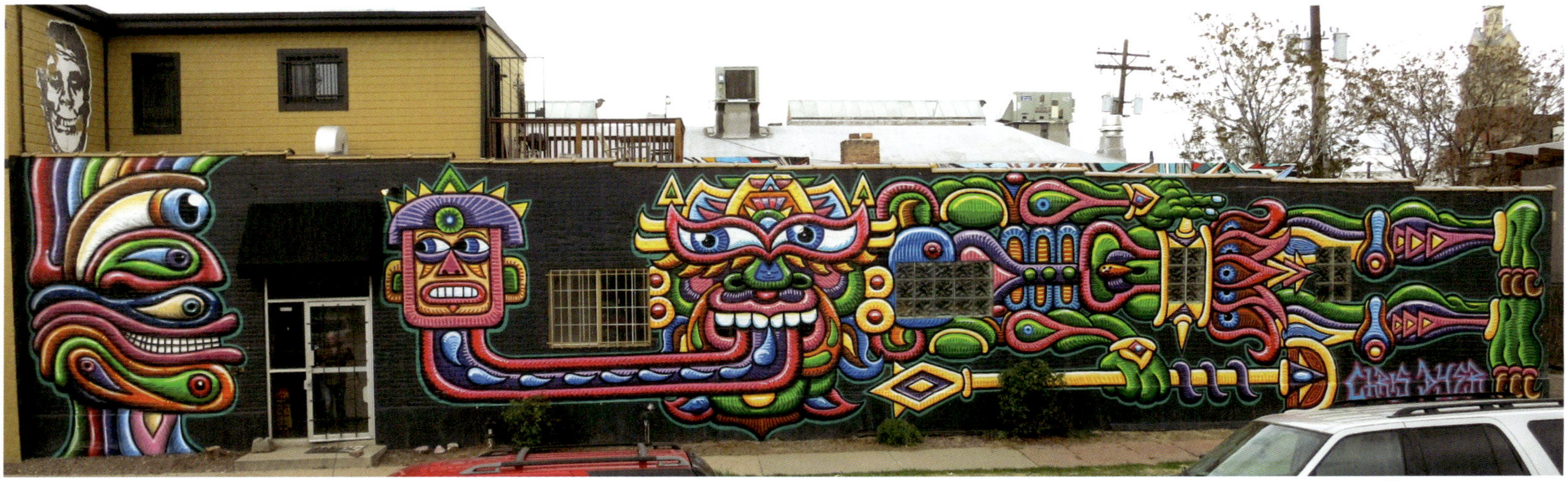

Denver, 2013

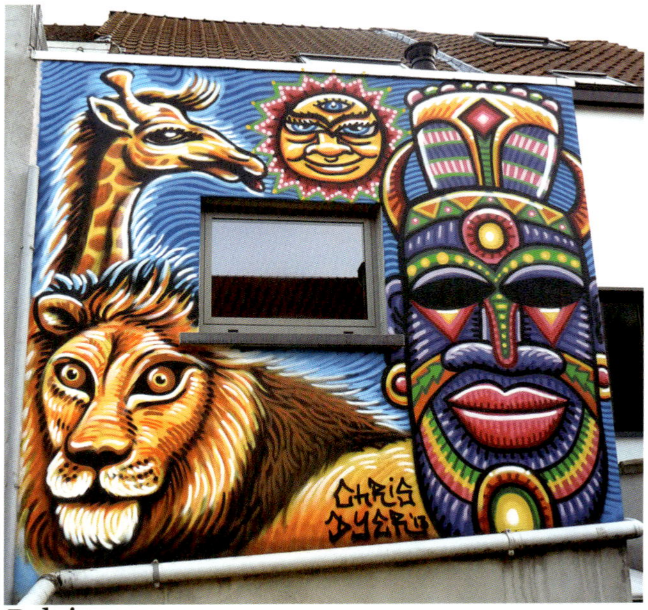

Belgium, 2013

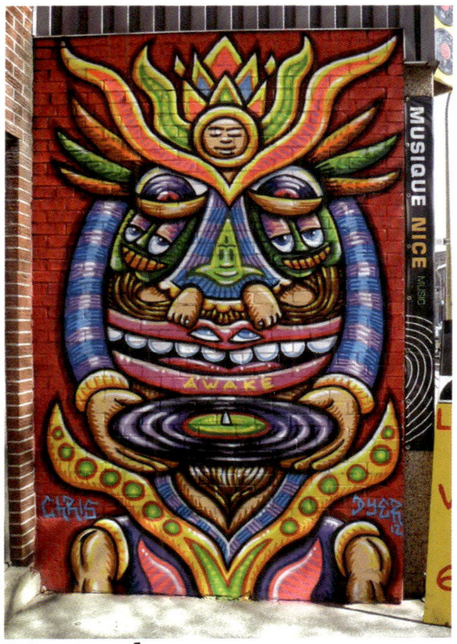

Montreal, 2012

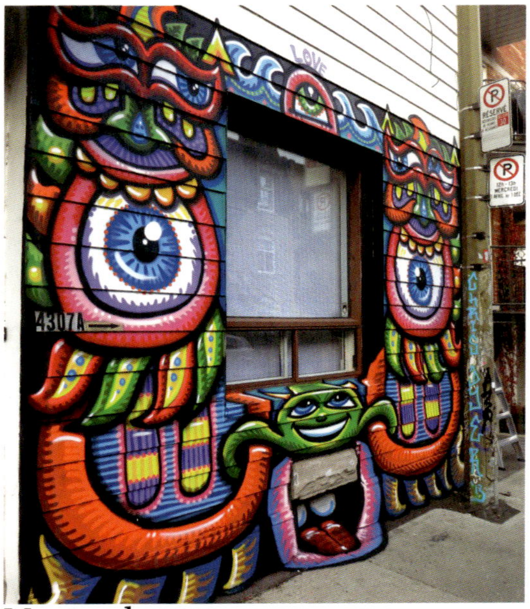

Montreal, 2013

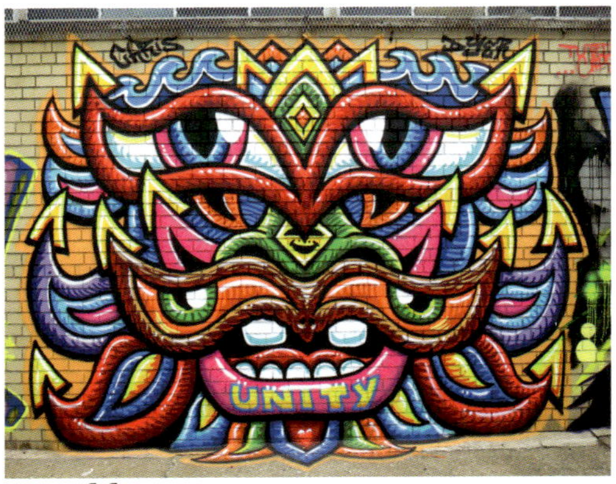

Brooklyn, 2014

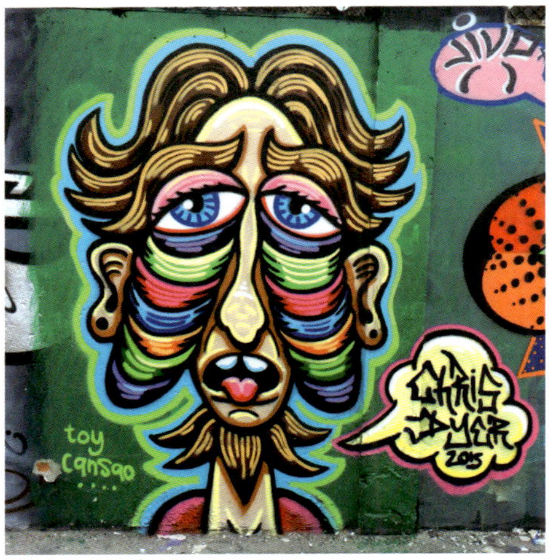

Costa Rica, 2014

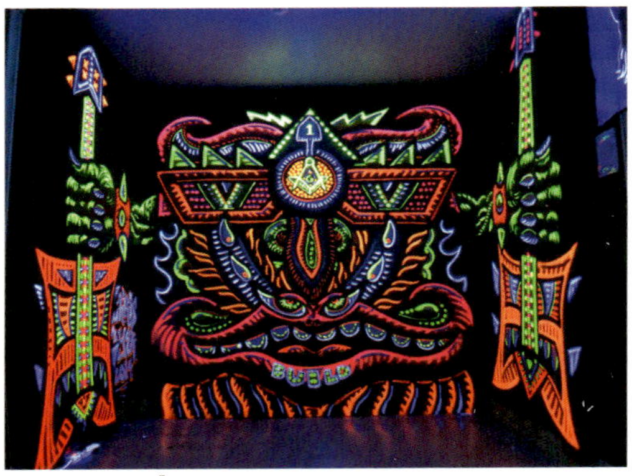

Montreal, 2014

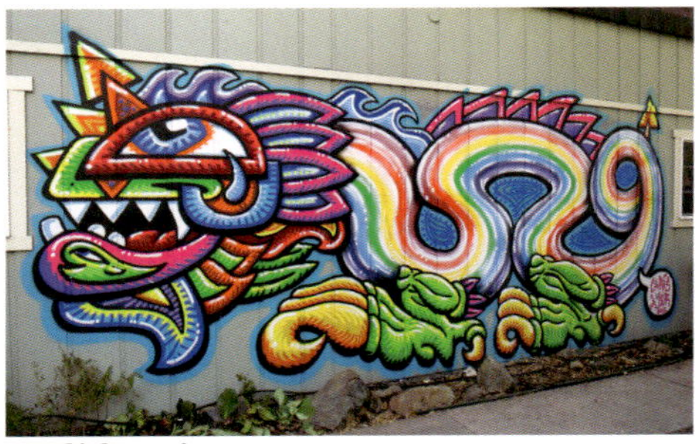

California, 2014

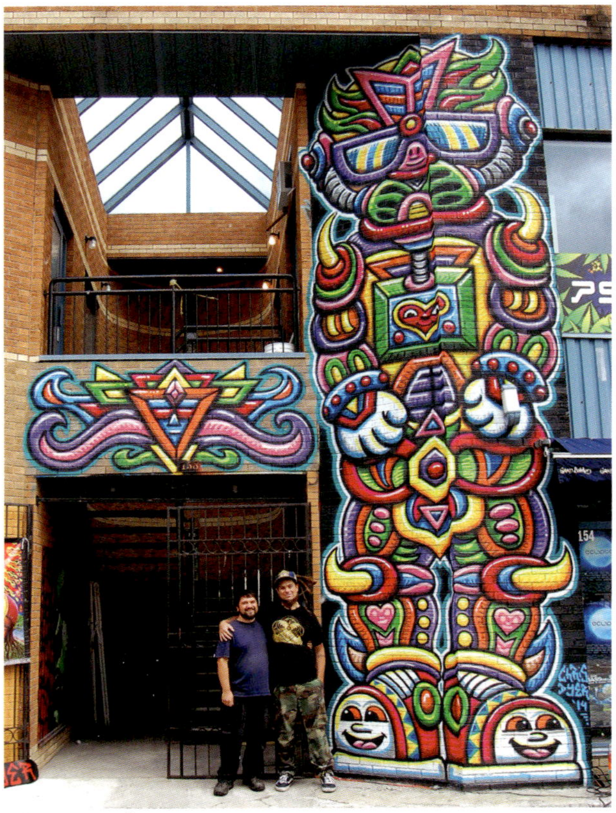

Montreal, 2014

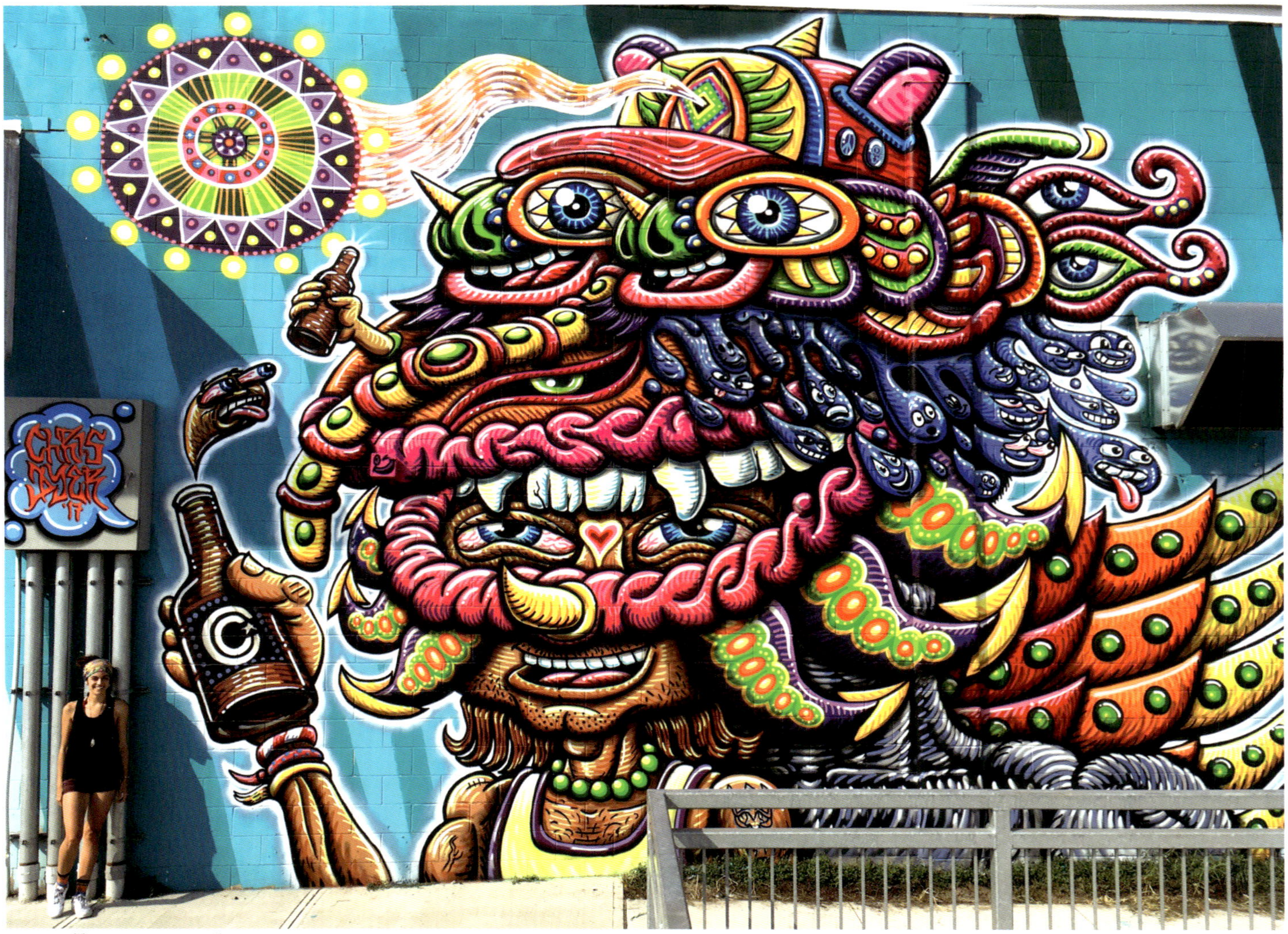

Hamilton, Canada, 2017

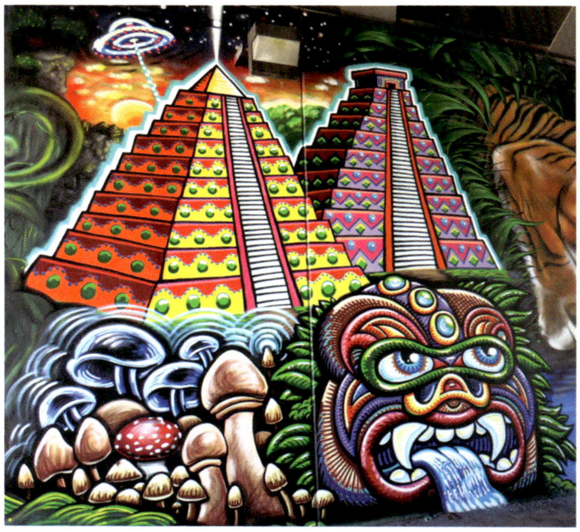

Toronto, 2014

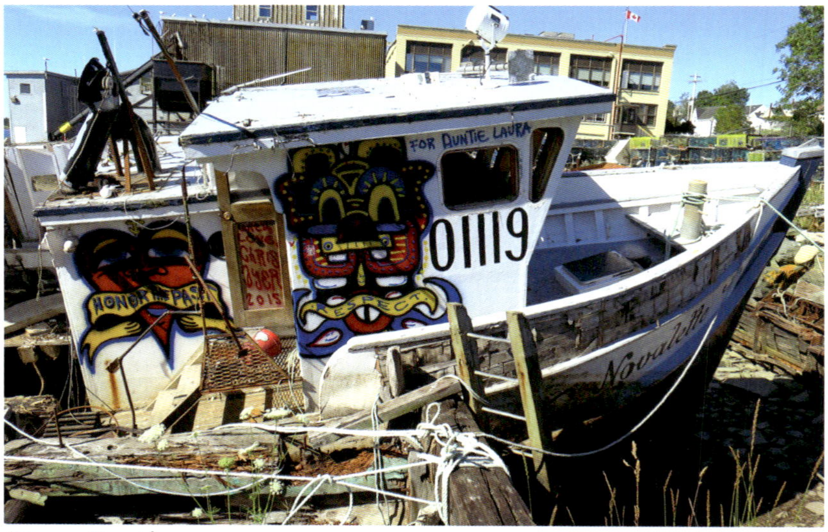

Nova Scotia, 2015

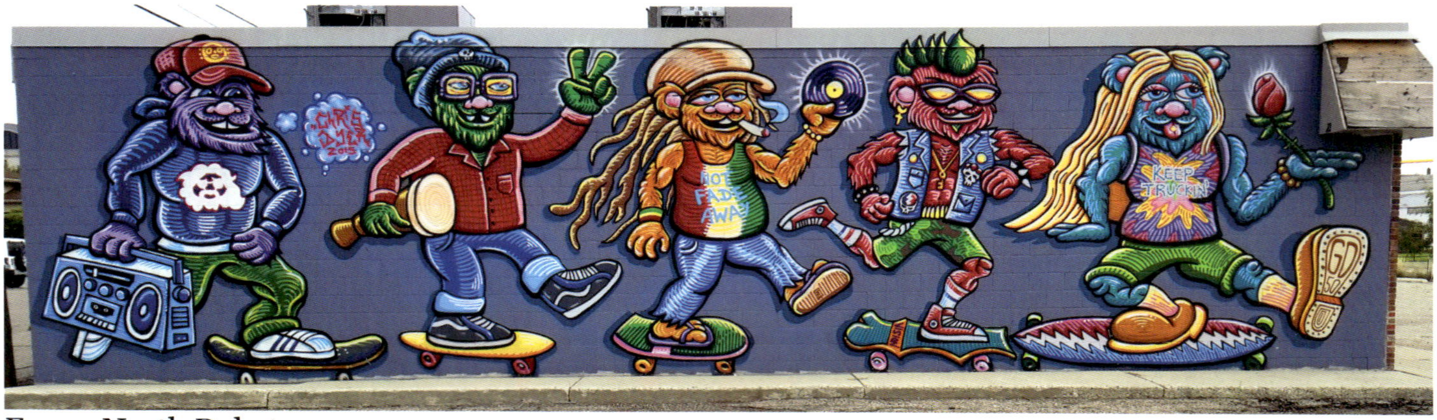

Fargo, North Dakota, 2015

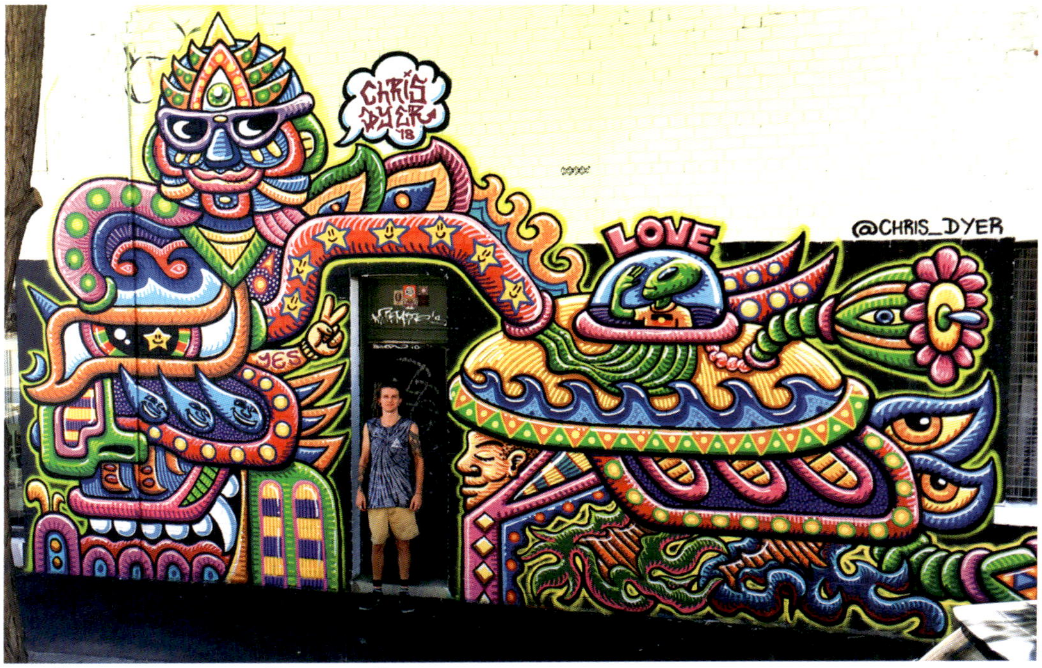

Melbourne, Australia, 2018

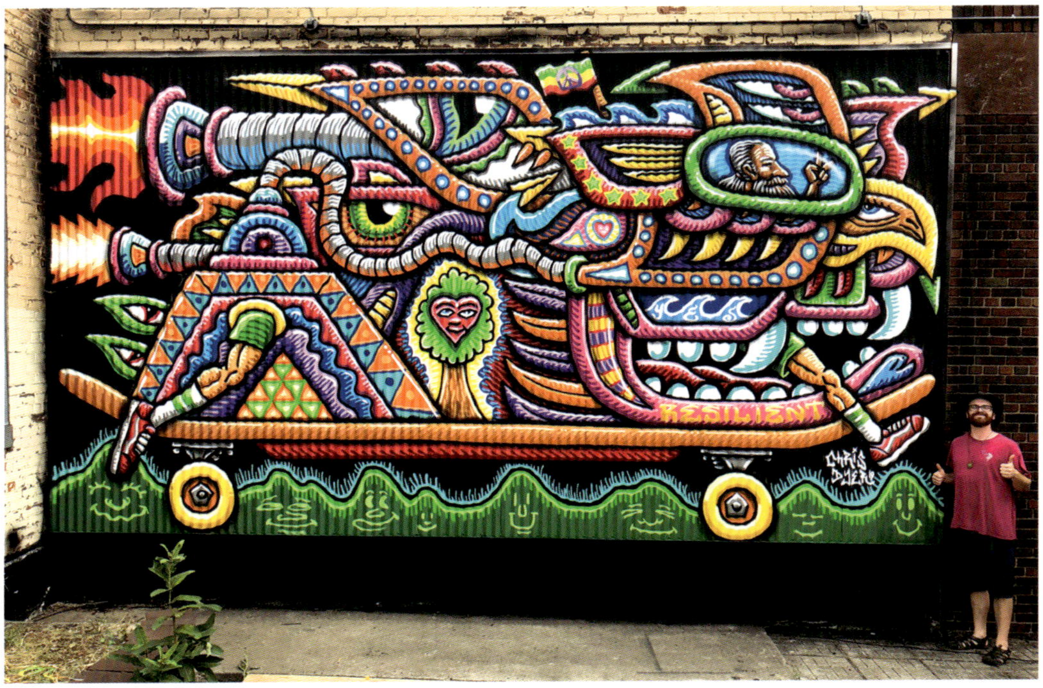

Detroit, Michigan, 2019

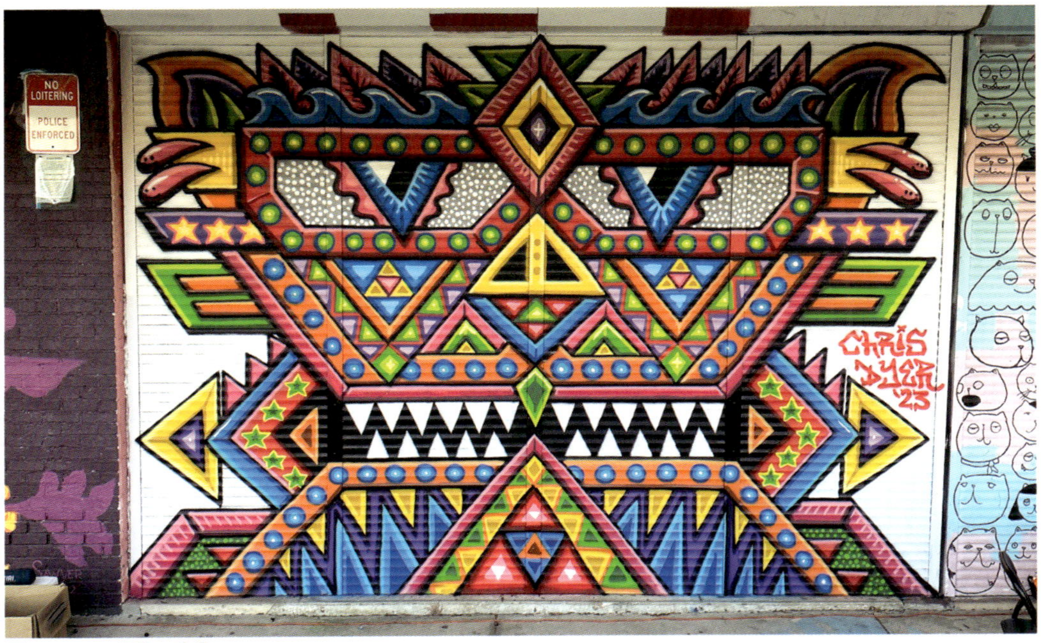

Tampa, Florida, 2023

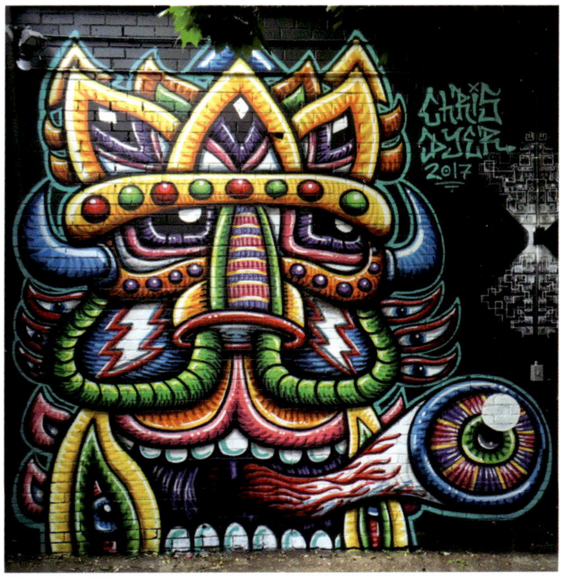

Denver, 2017

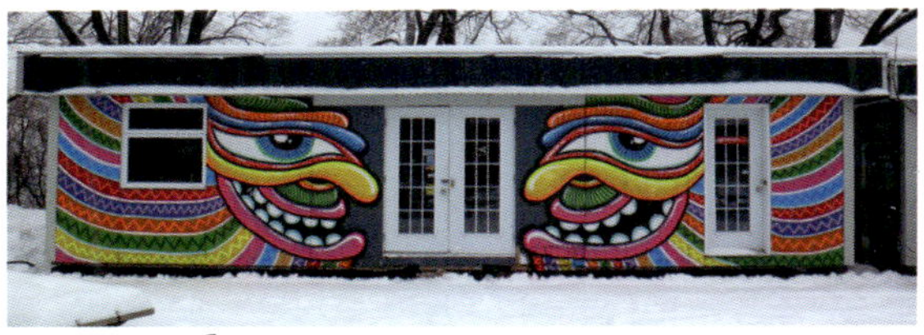

Montreal, 2012

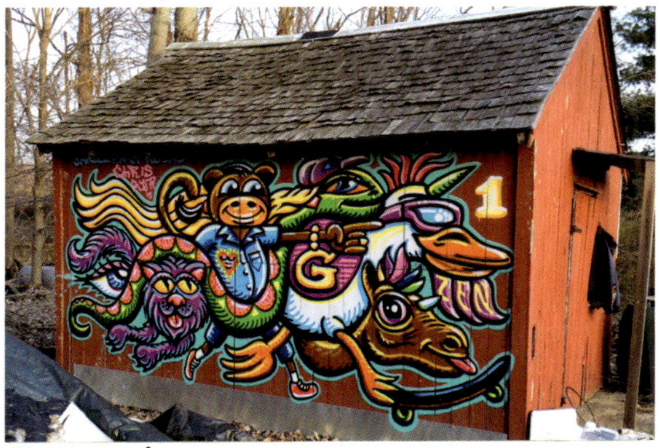

Connecticut, 2015

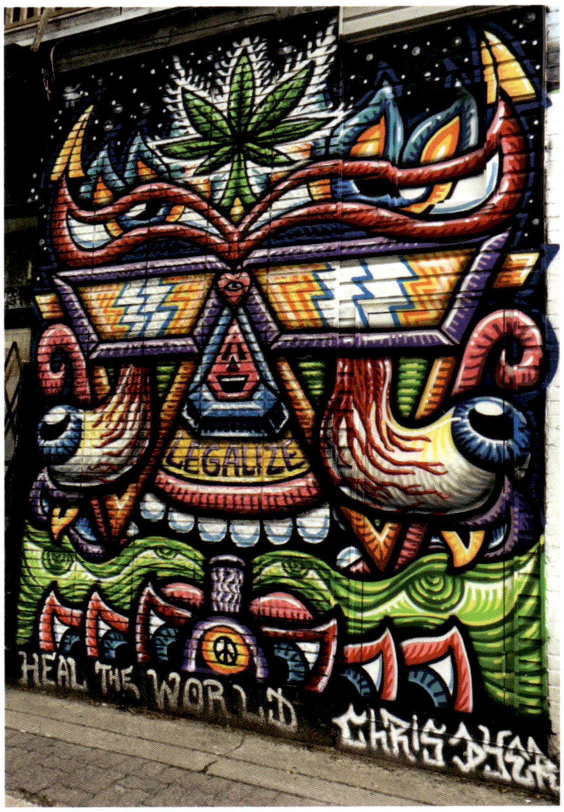

Montreal, 2017

STREET COLLABORATIONS

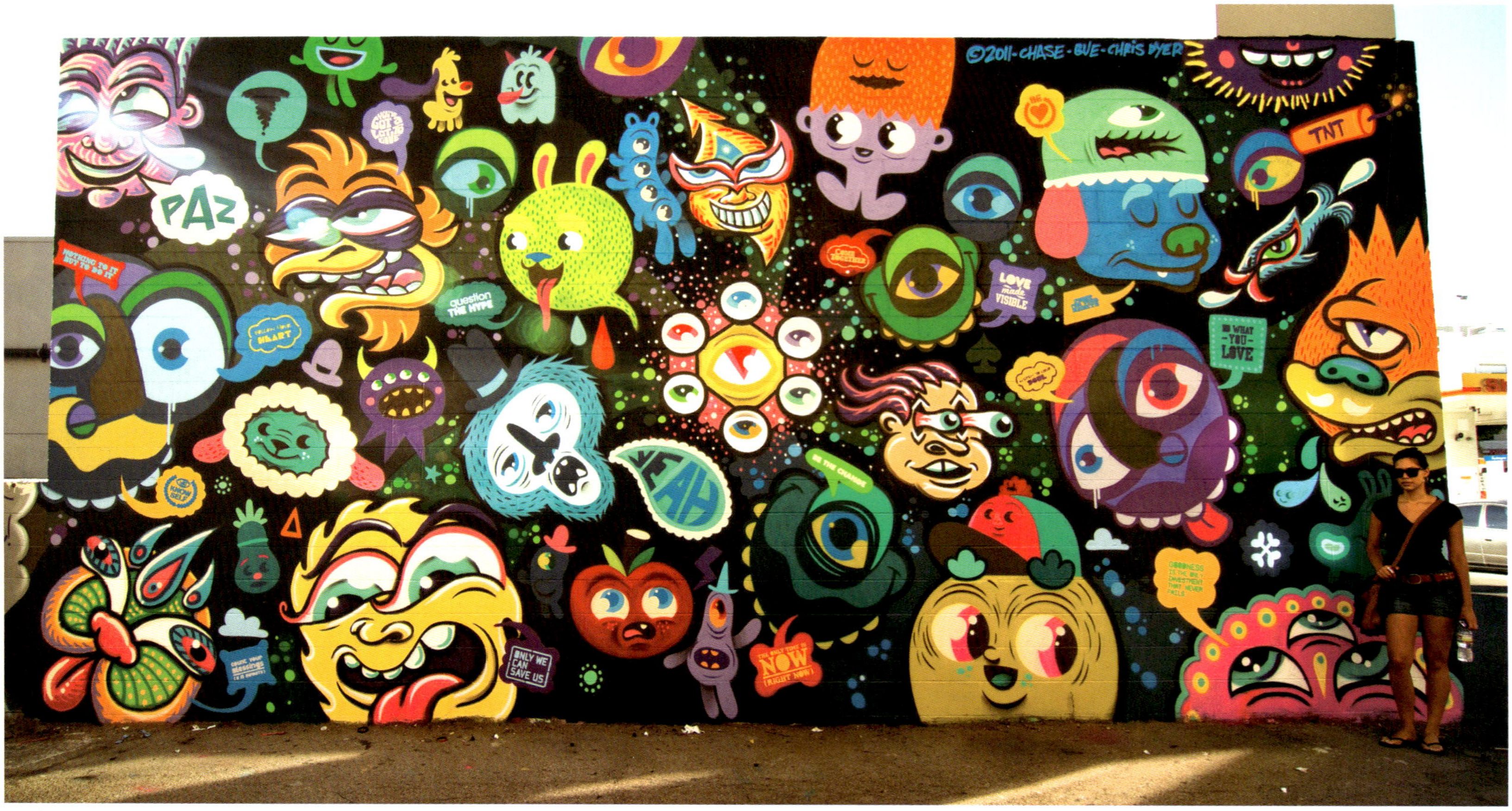

With **Chase** and **Bue the Warrior** (Los Angeles, California, 2011)

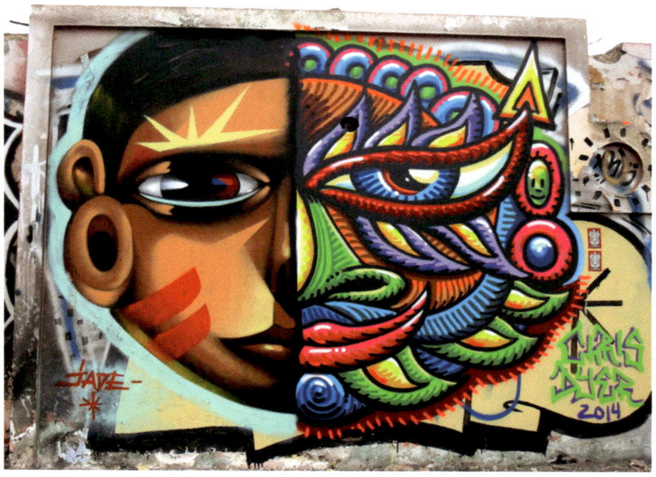

With **Jade Riviera** (Lima, Peru, 2013)

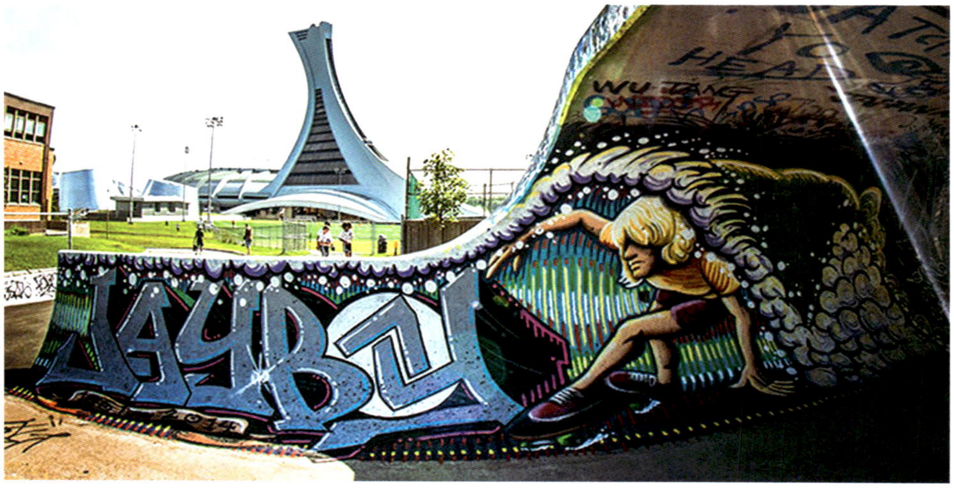

With **Quiz 71** (Montreal, 2014)

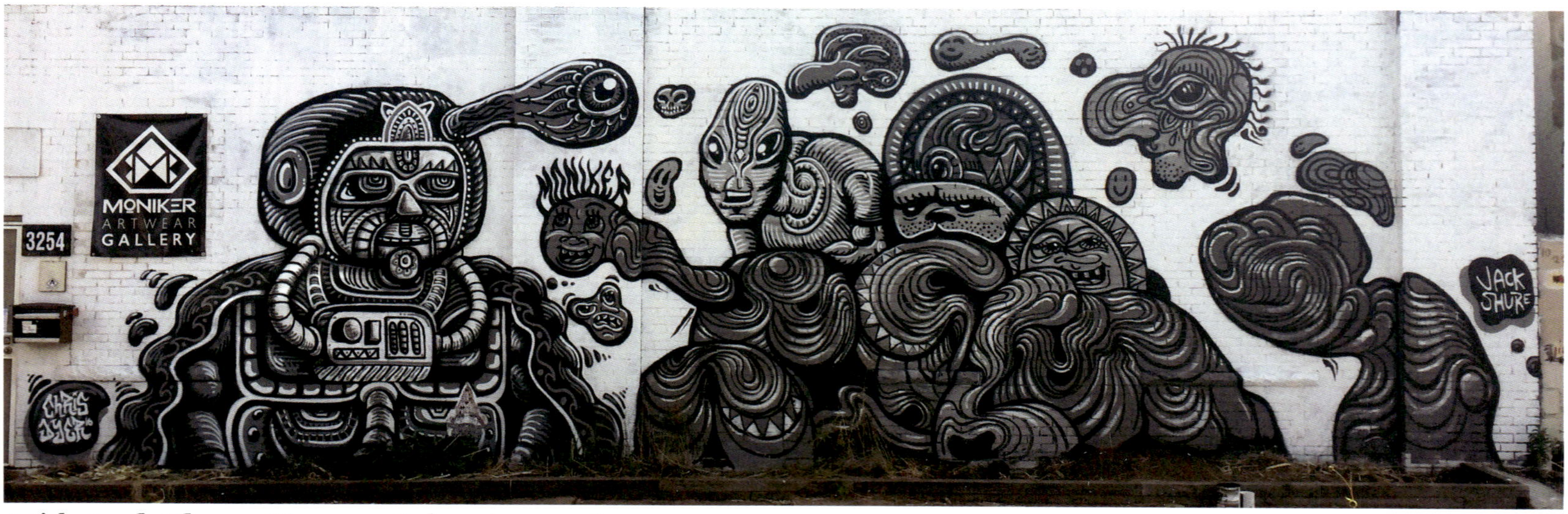

With **Jack Shure** (Denver, Colorado, 2016)

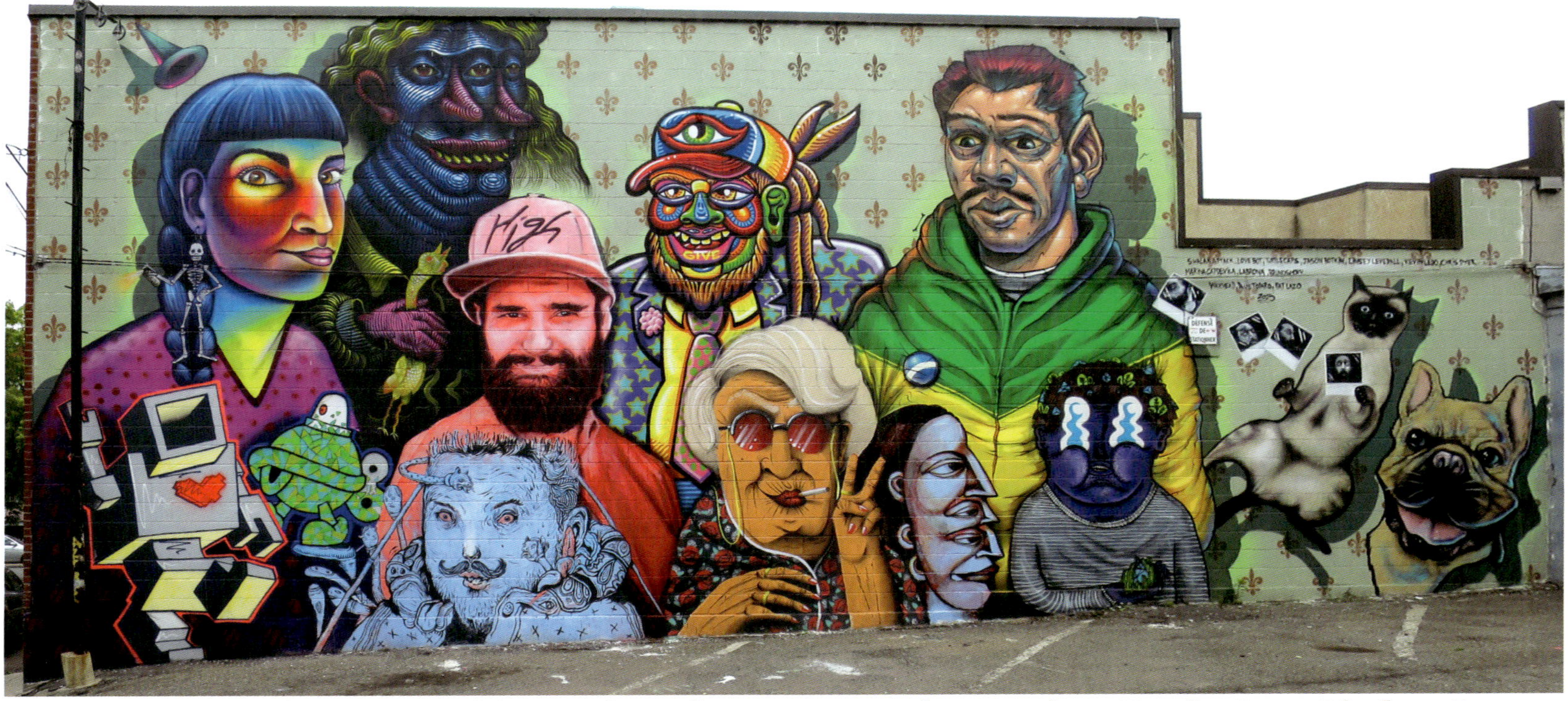

With **Shalak Attack**, **Jason Botkin**, **Kevin Ledo**, **Bruno Smoky**, **Lovebot**, **Turtle Caps**, **Lindsey Levendall**, **Marina Capdevilla**, **Labrona**, **Waxhead**, **Dave Todaro** and **Pat Lazo** (Montreal, 2015)

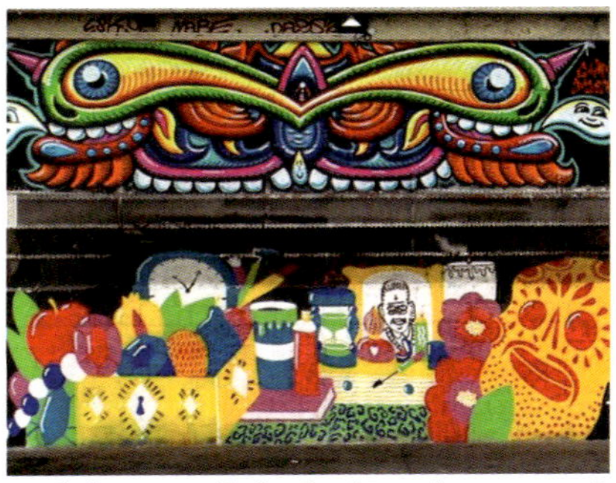

With **Kashink** (Paris, 2015)

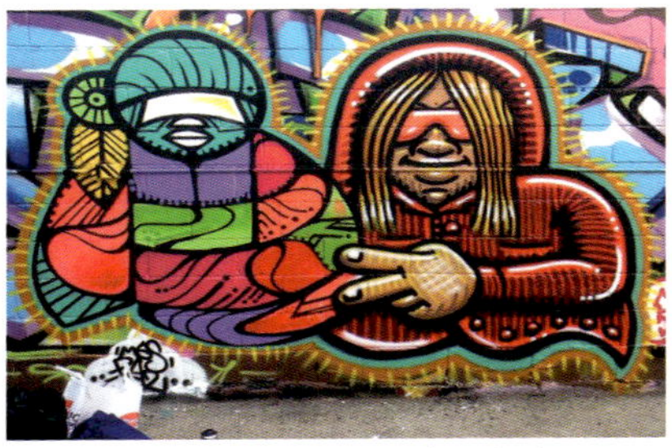

With **Mas Paz** (Virginia, 2014)

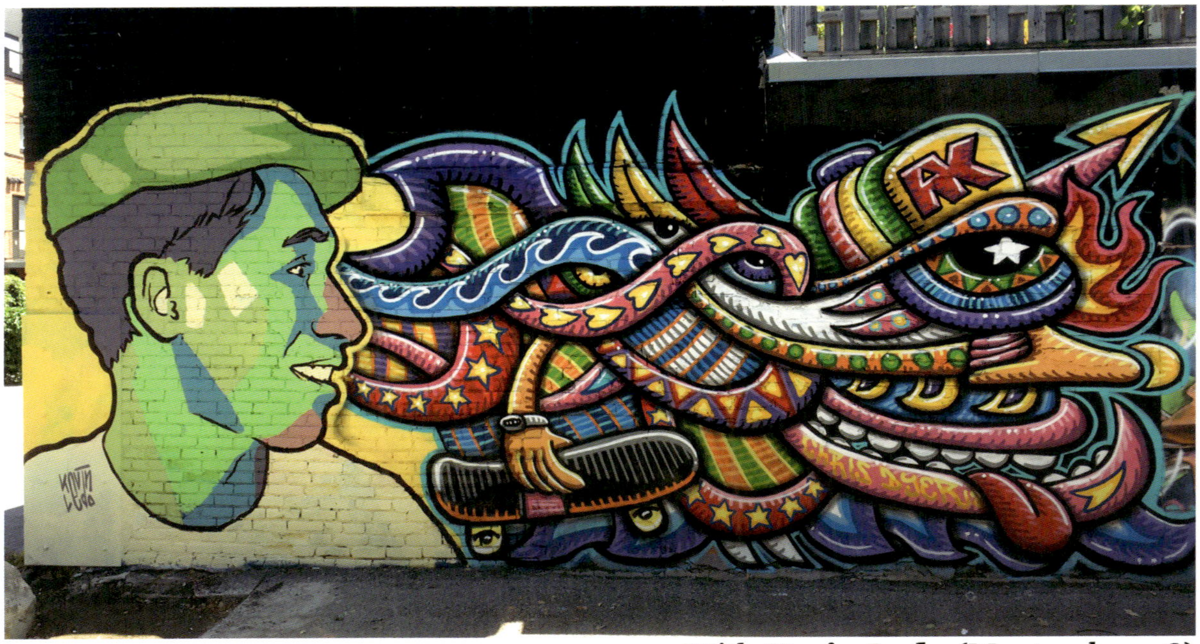

With **Kevin Ledo** (Montreal, 2018)

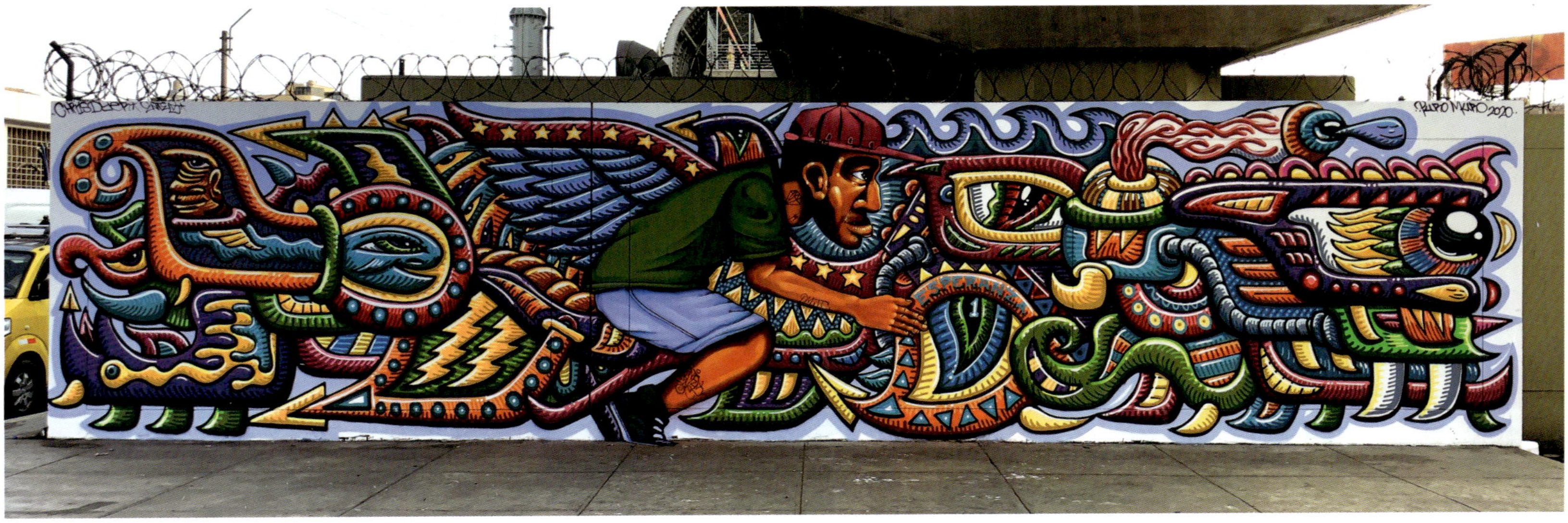

With **Entes** (La Victoria, Lima, Peru, 2020)

PAINTED VEHICLES

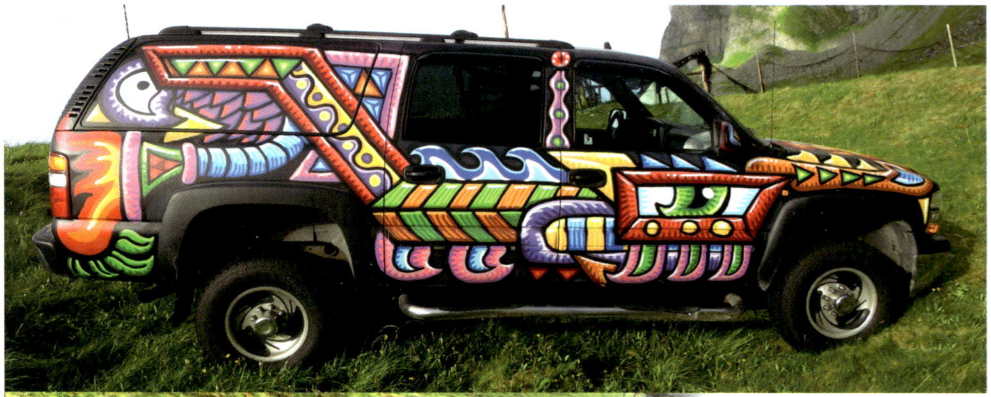

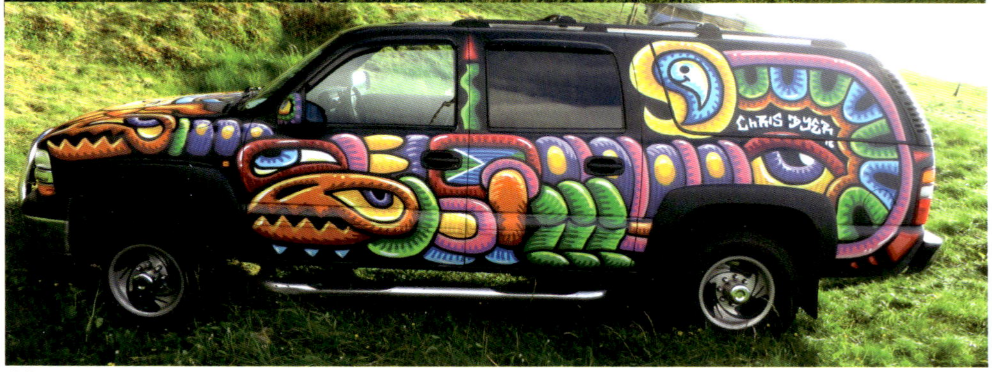

Norway, 2016

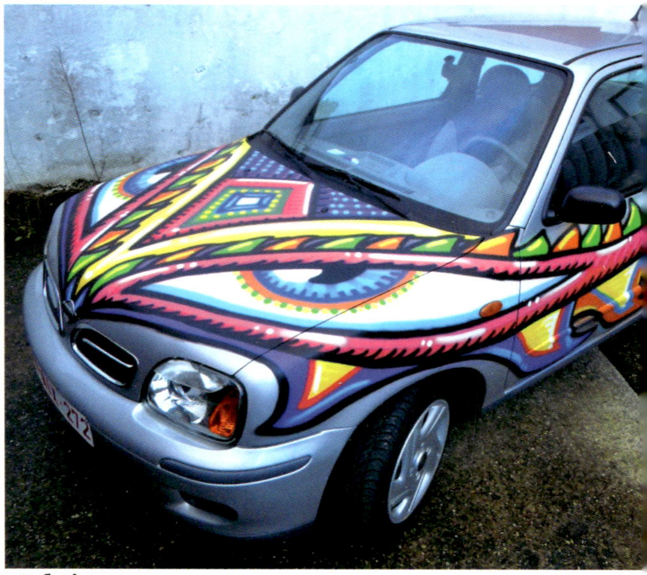

Belgium, 2013

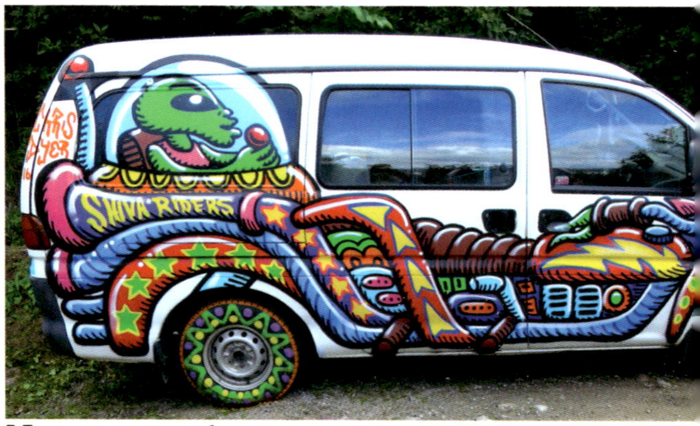

Norway, 2016

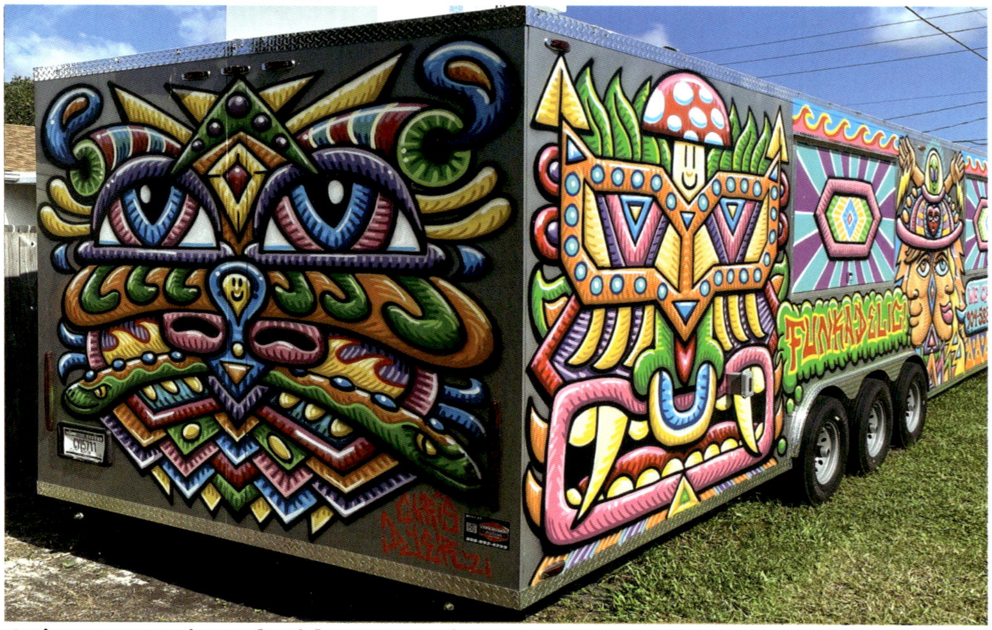

Saint Augustine Florida, 2021 (for "Funkadelic")

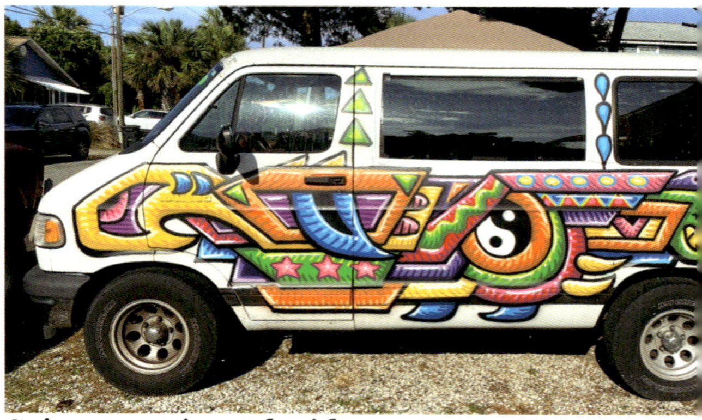

Saint Agustine, Florida, 2021

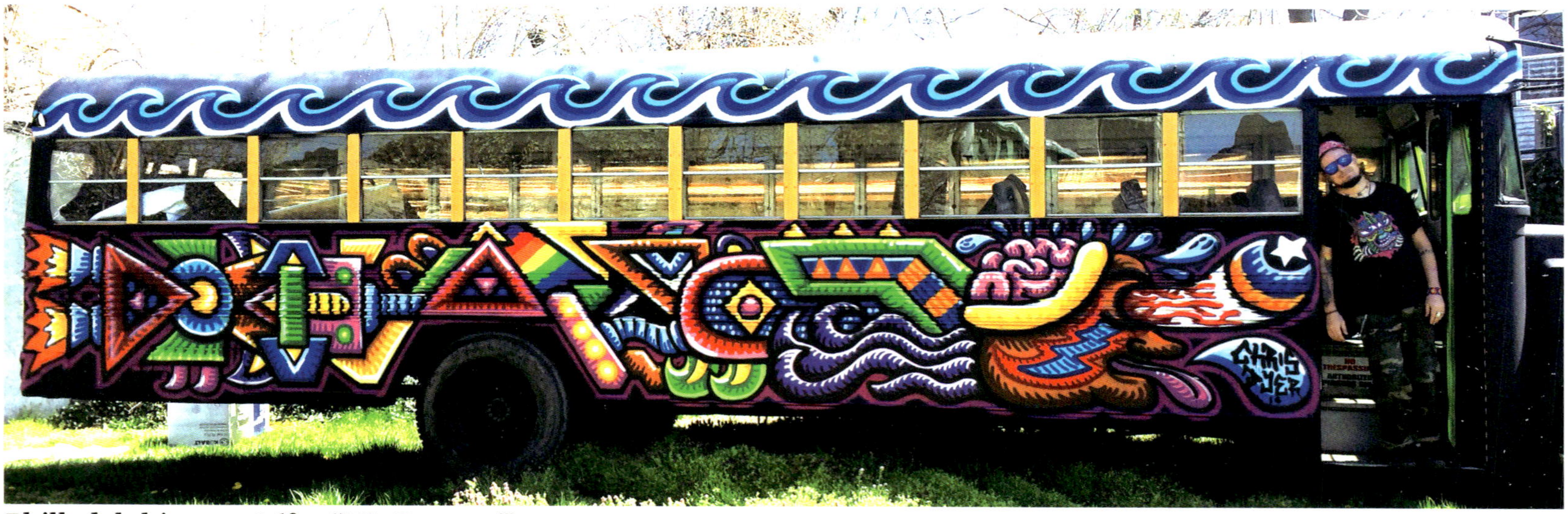

Philladelphia, 2016 (for "We Present")

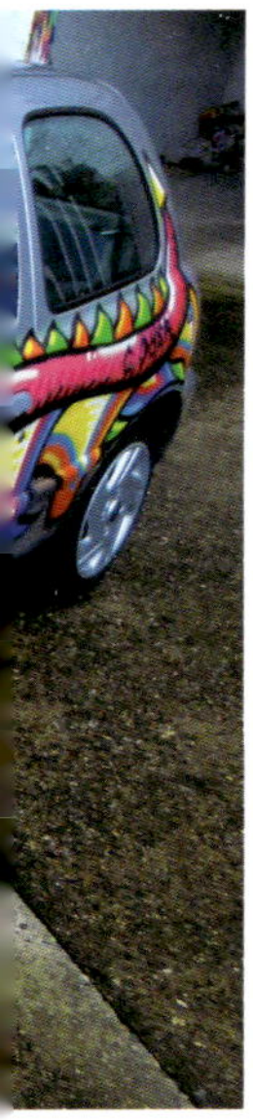

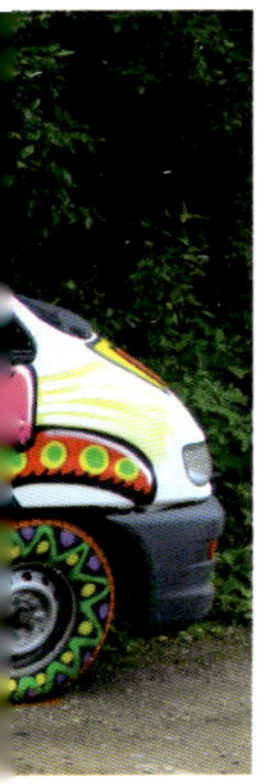

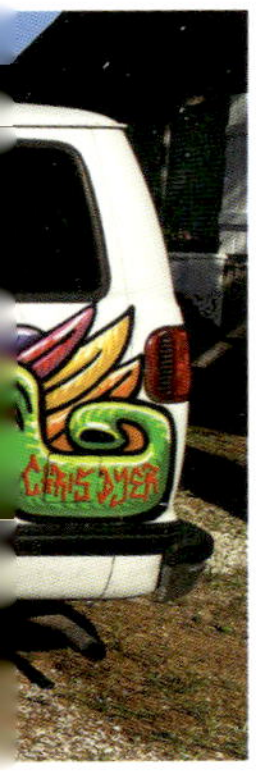

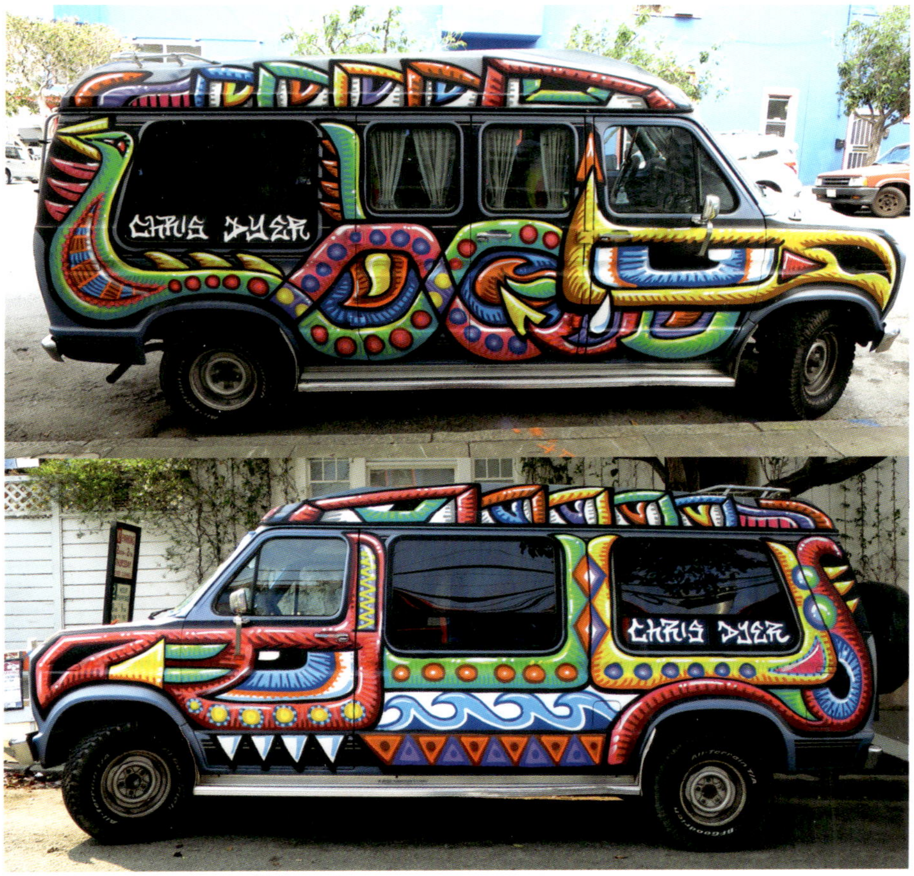

San Francisco, California, 2015

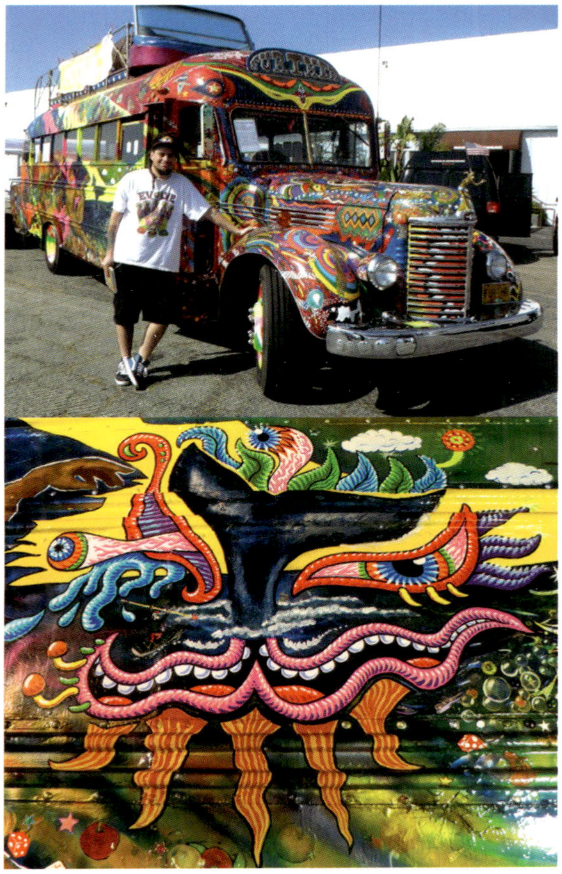

Eugene, Oregon, 2015
(on Ken Keysey's legendaray
Merry Prankster's bus **"Further"**)

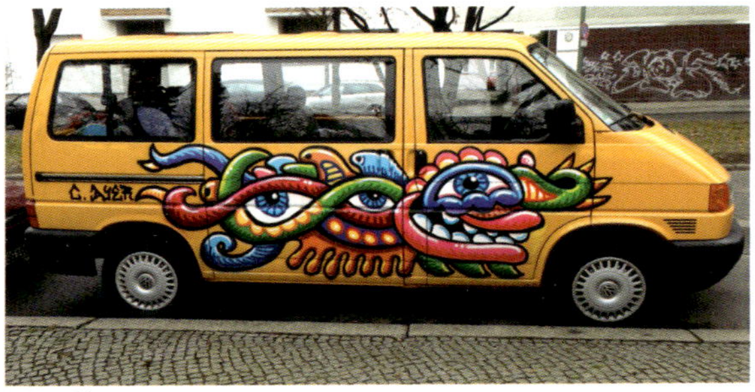

Berlin, Germany, 2013

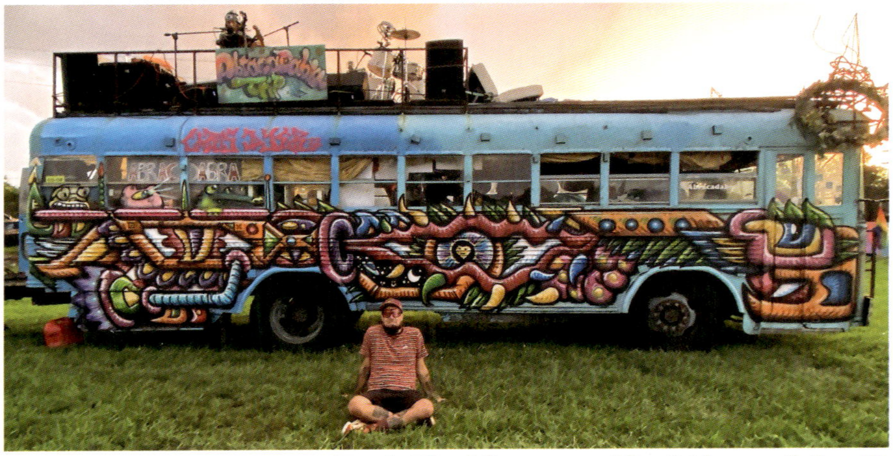

Miami, Florida, 2022 (for "Abracadabra")

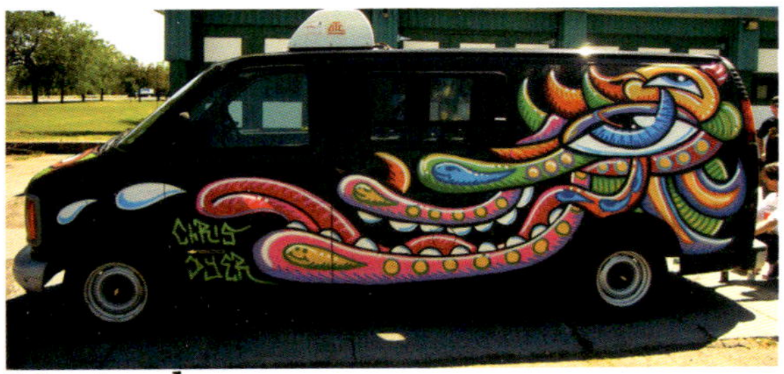

Montreal, 2011

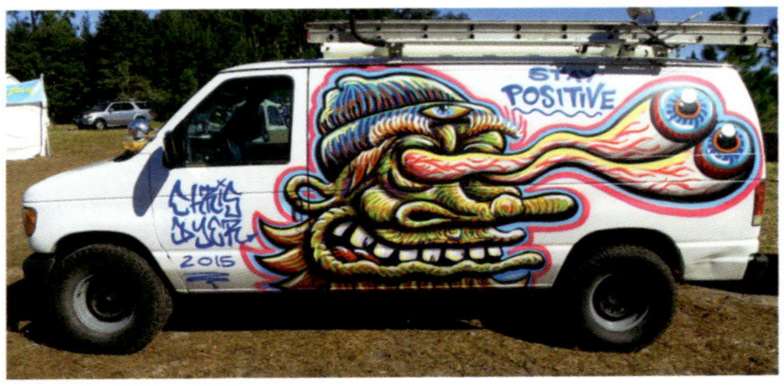

Orlando, Florida, 2015

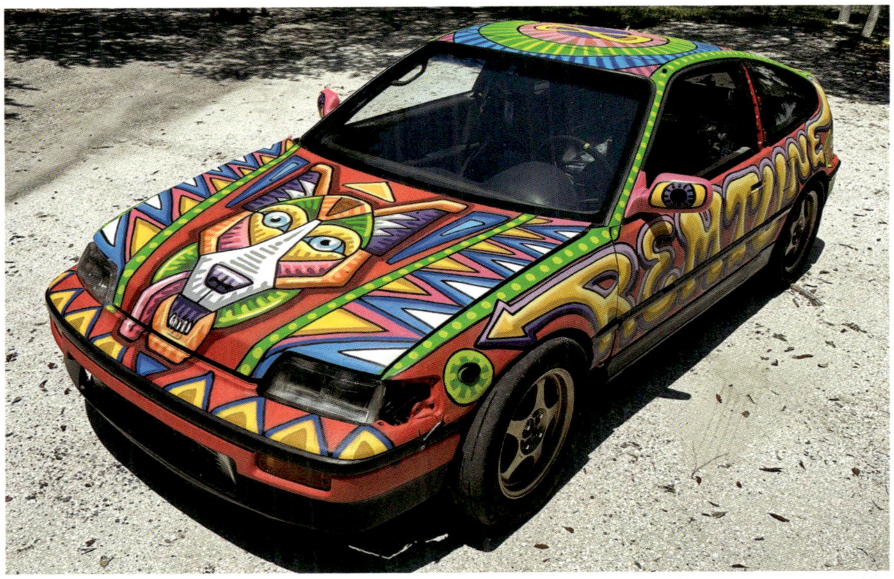

Saint Petersburg, Florida, 2023 (for "Remtune")

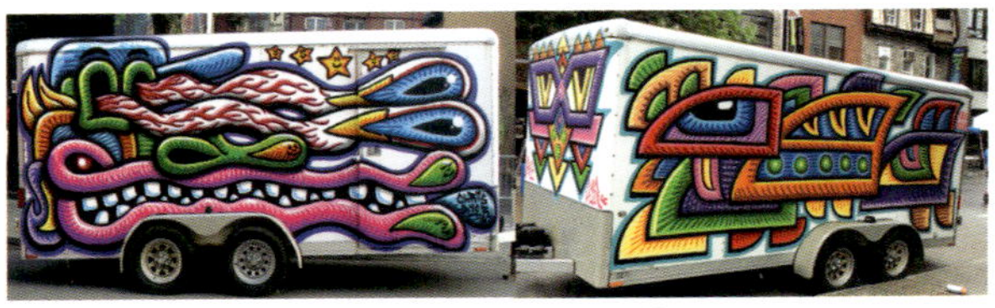

Montreal, 2016 (for "Rams")

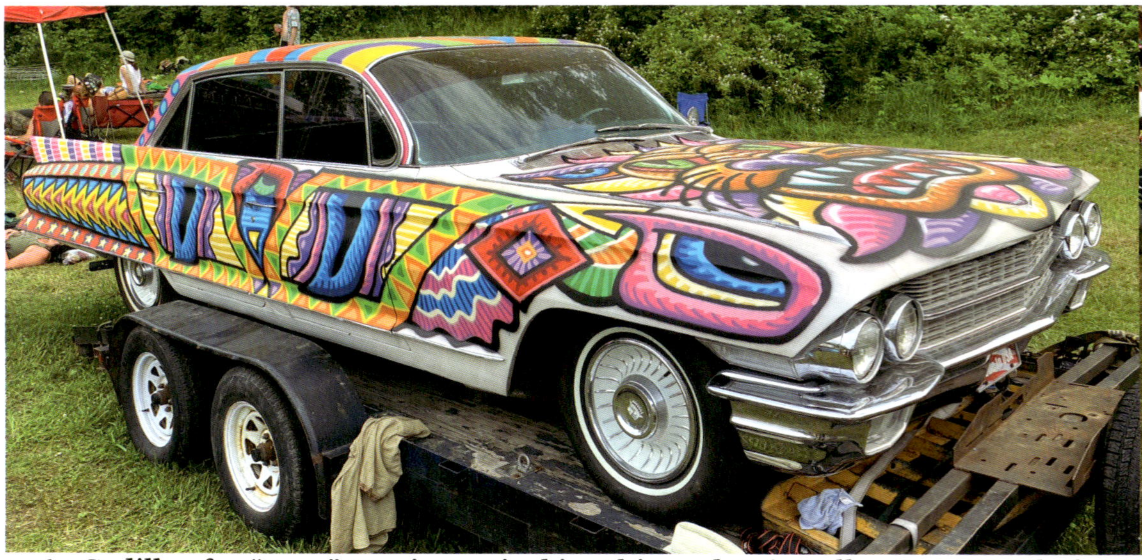

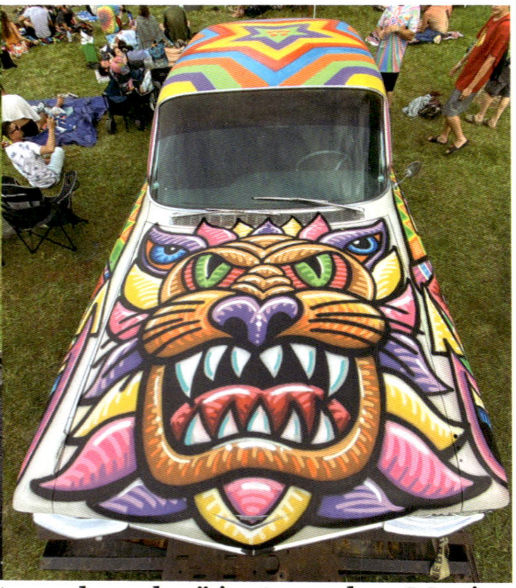

1963 Cadillac for "Pyro" Music Festival in Ohio and 80's Volkswagen Beetle for "Anarchapulco" in Acapulco, Mexico

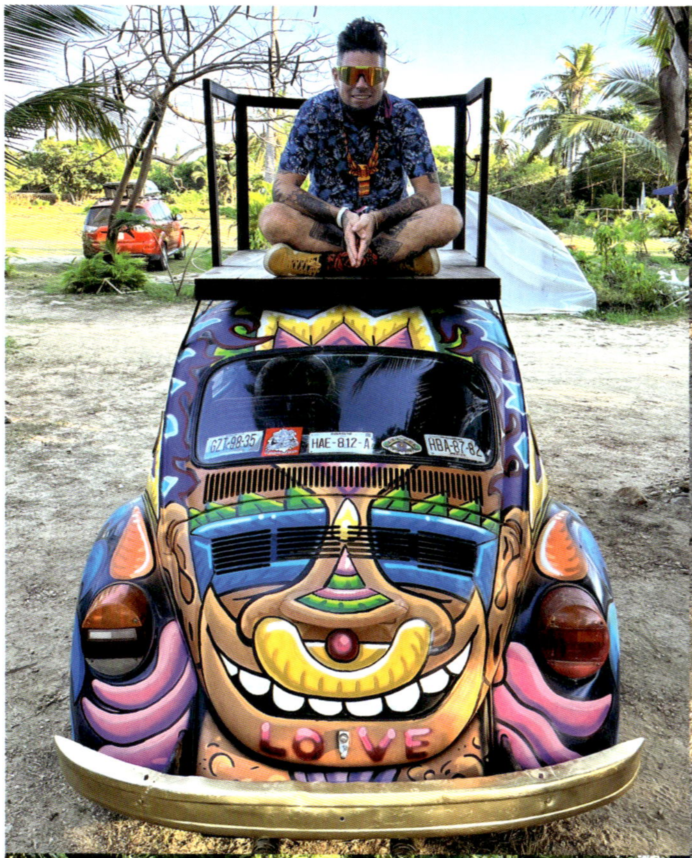

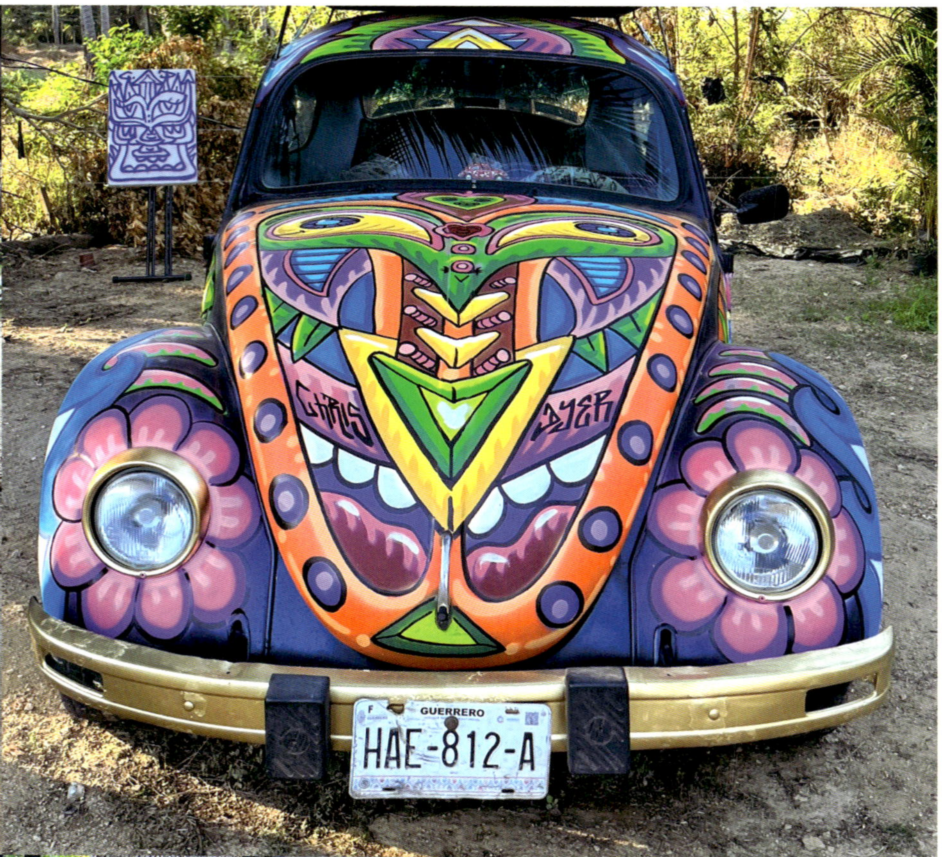

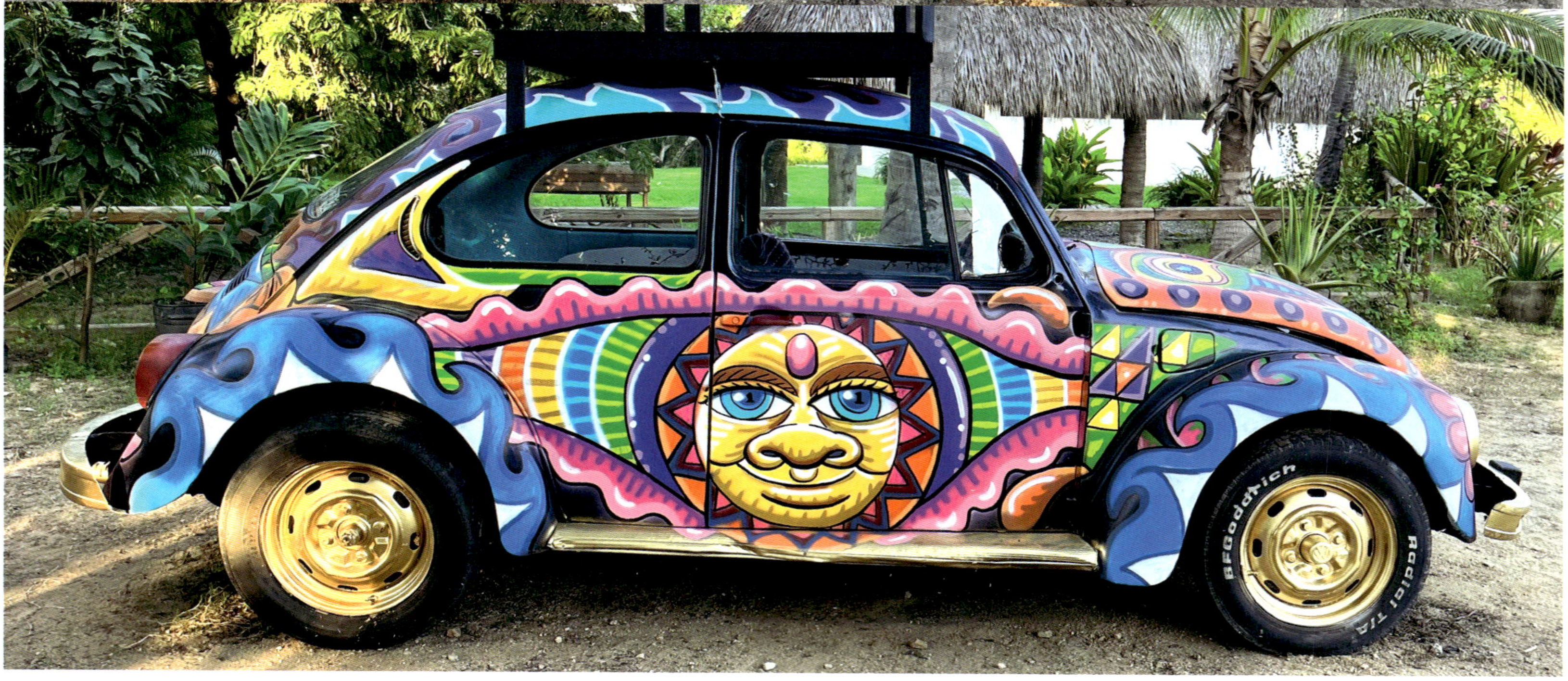

FISHBOMBS

As a collector, I have made a little game with myself where I try to spray paint different kinds of fish in different locations of this beautiful planet. I've always been impressed by God's amazing artistry and the amount of trippy fishes it has created. So as a reflection of the creator, I invent my own fish. Here a few of them.

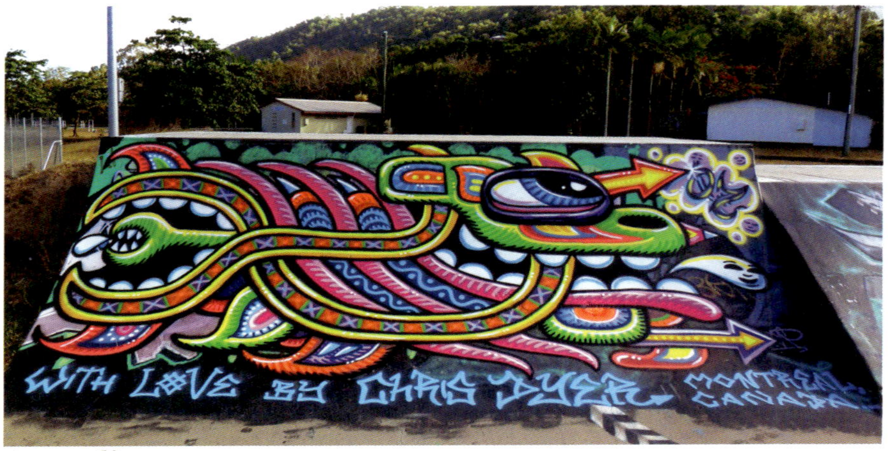

Australia, 2012

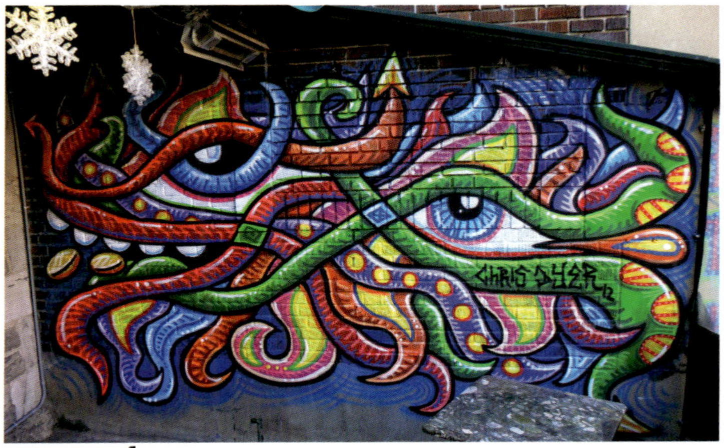

Montreal, 2012

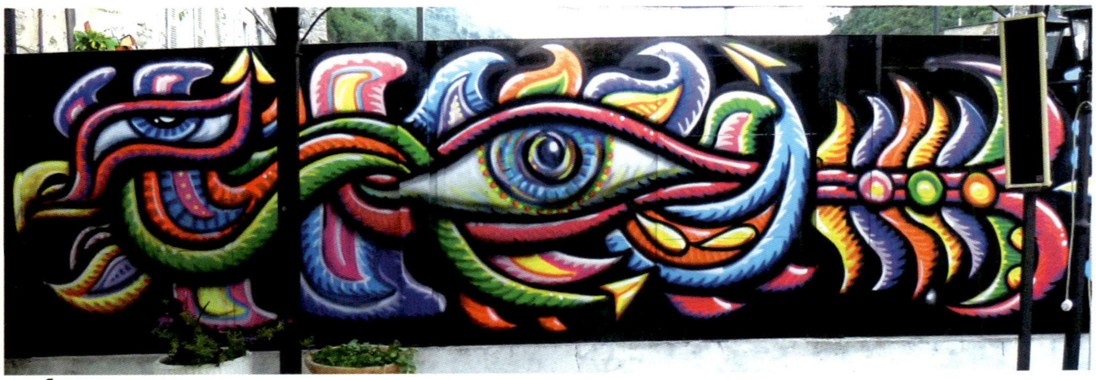
Italy, 2012

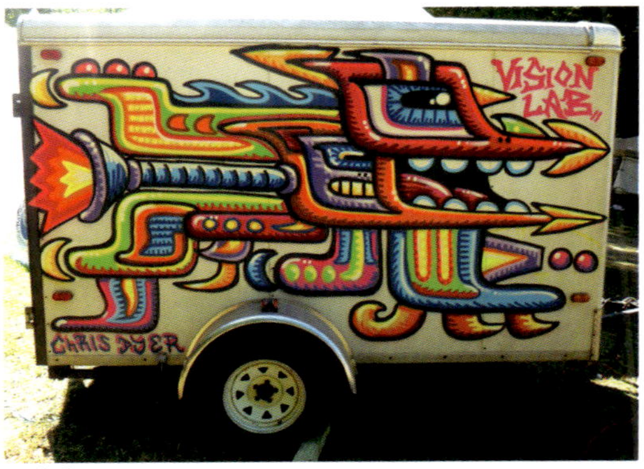

Ohio, 2012

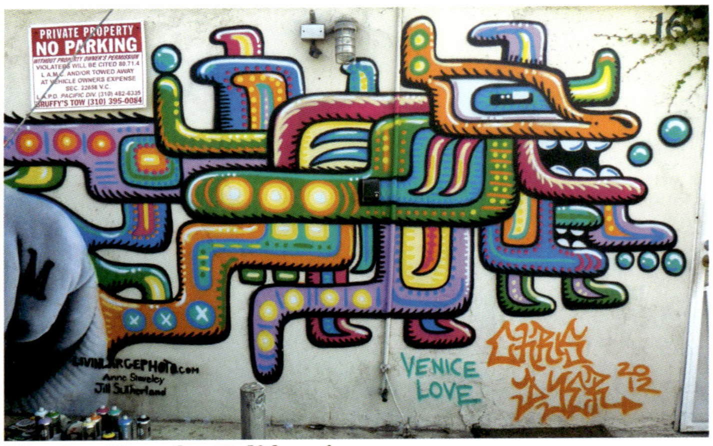

Venice Beach, California, 2012

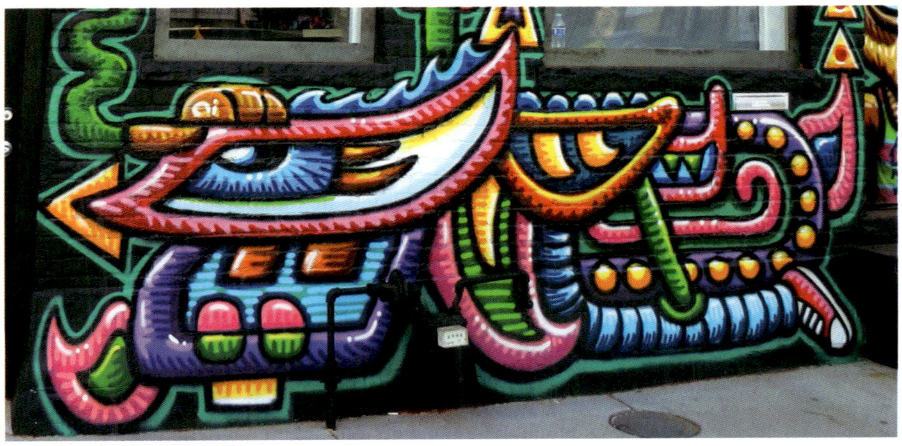
Denver, Colorado, 2014

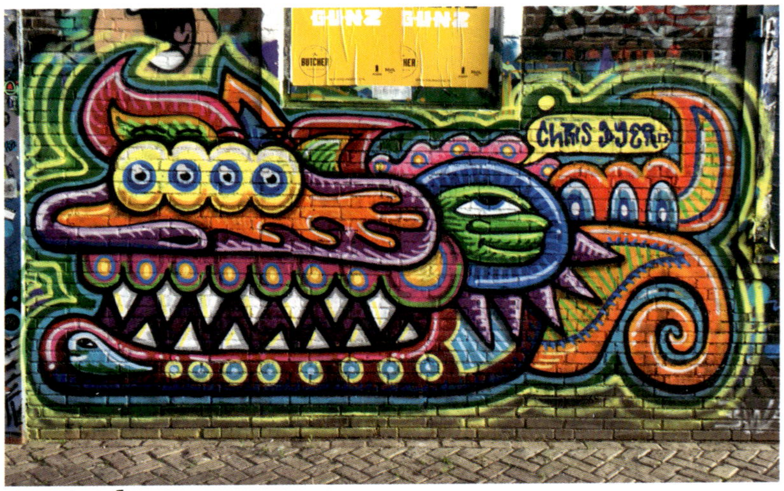

Amsterdam, 2017

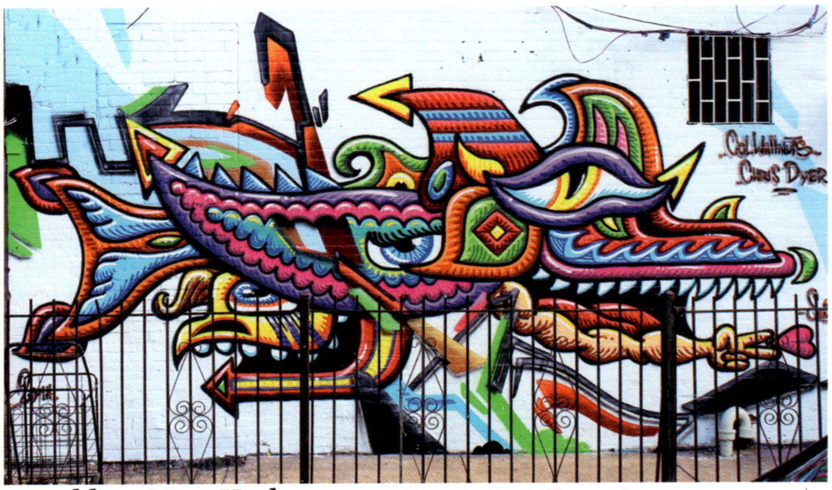

Brooklyn, New York, 2014 (with **Col Wallnuts**)

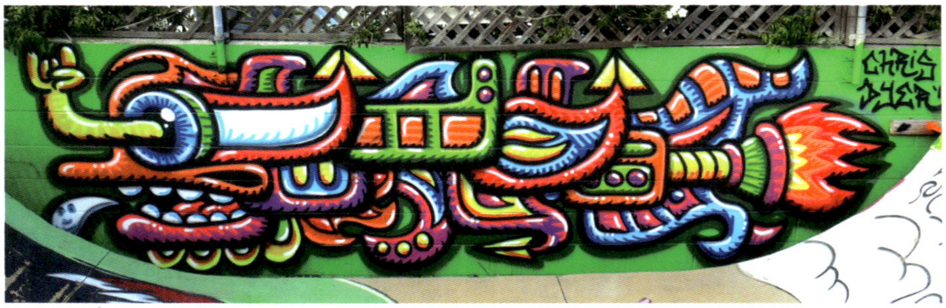

San Diego, 2013

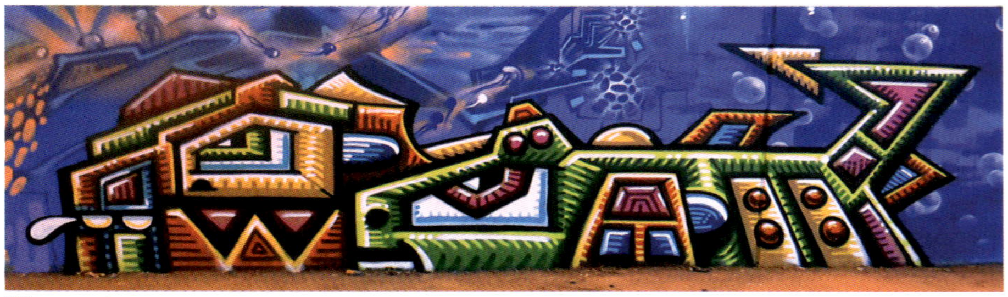

Toronto, 2014

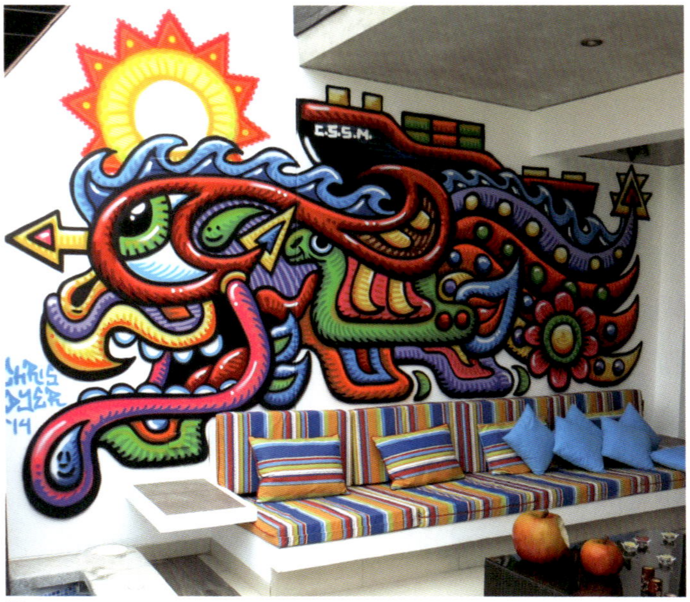

Peru, 2014

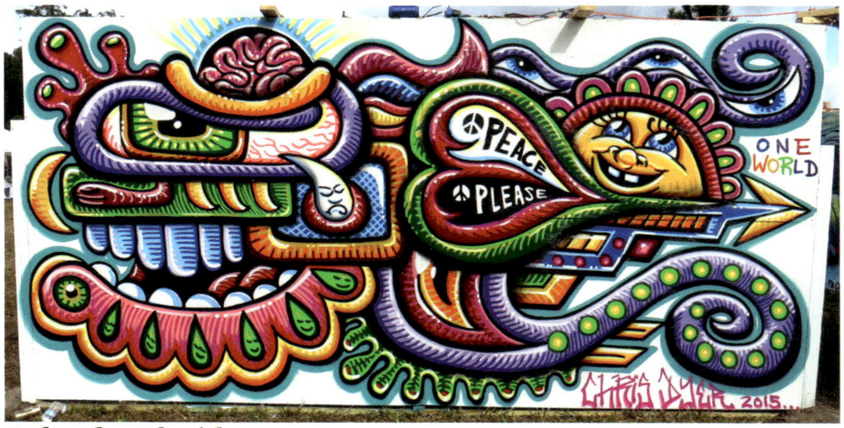

Orlando, Florida, 2015

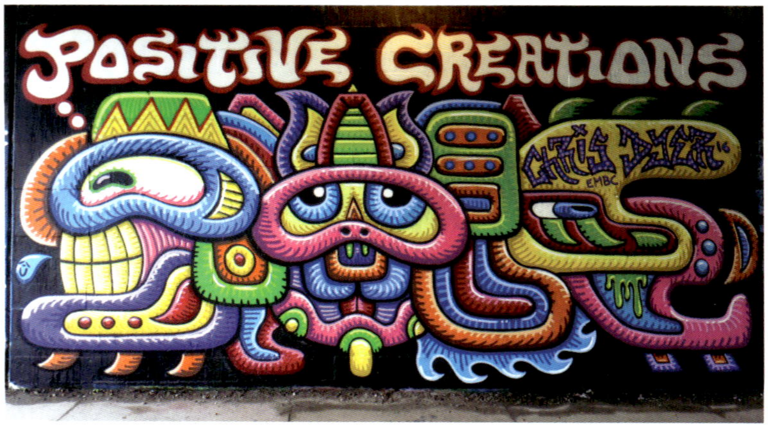

Chicago, 2016

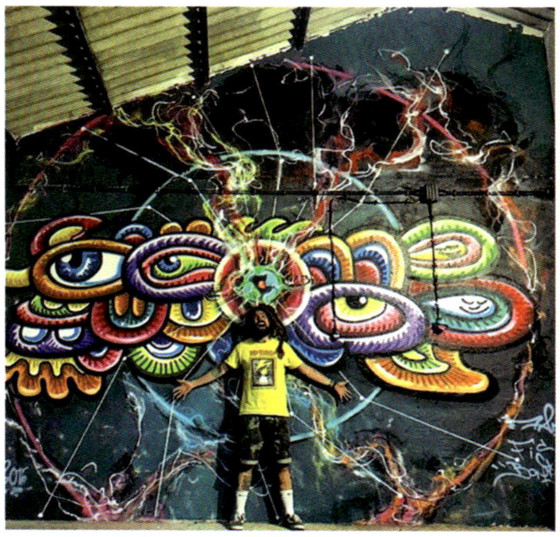

Portugal, 2016 (with **Ram Lisbon**)

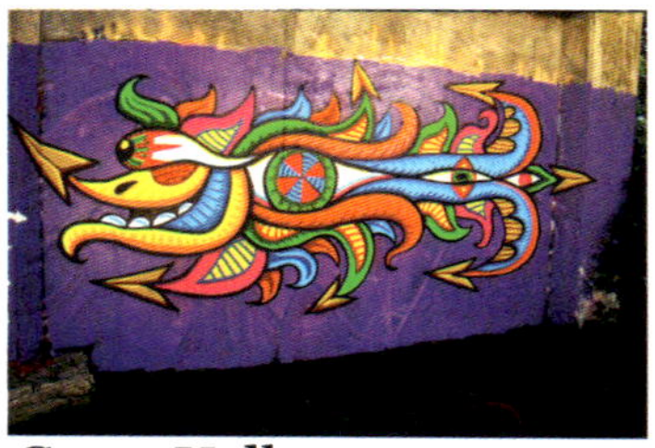

Grass Valley, 2011

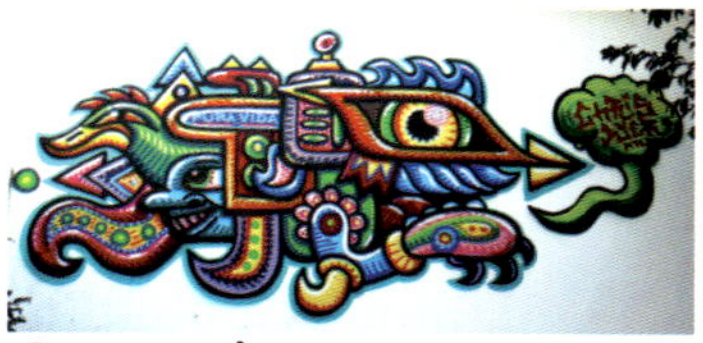

Costa Rica, 2015

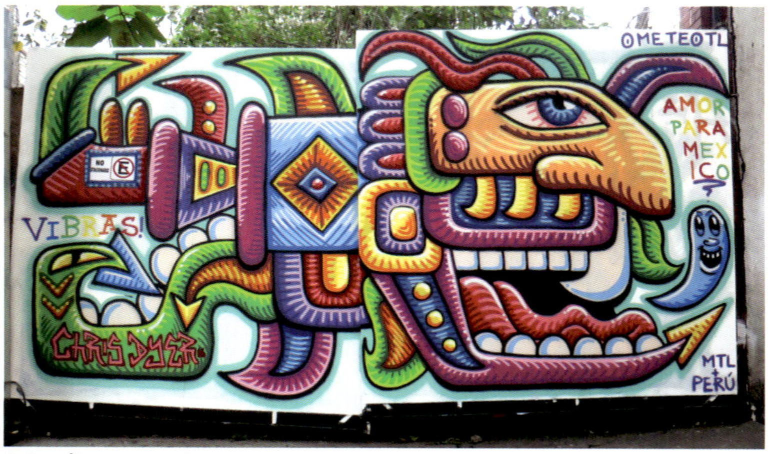

Mexico, 2016

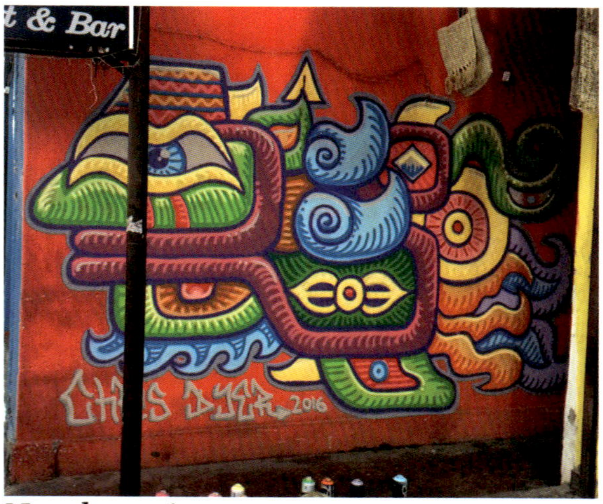

Nepal, 2016

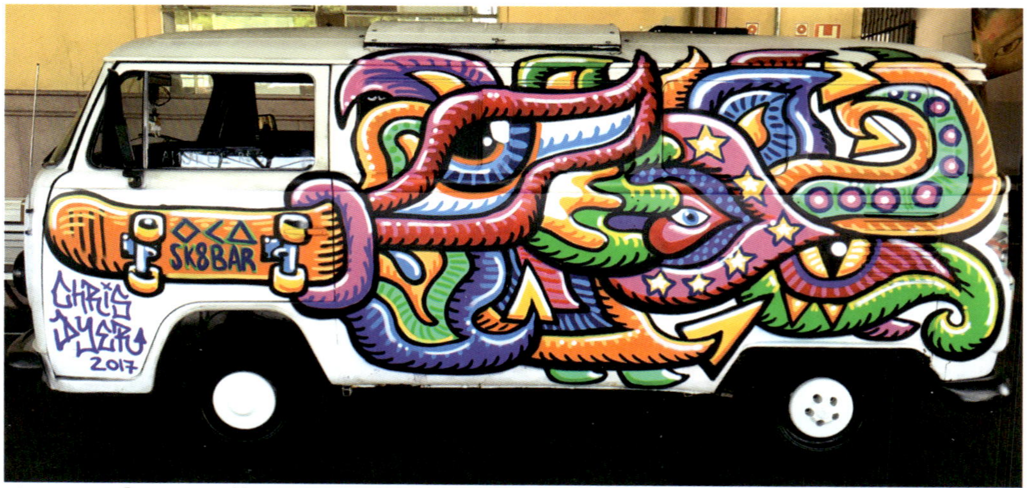

Sao Paulo, Brazil, 2017

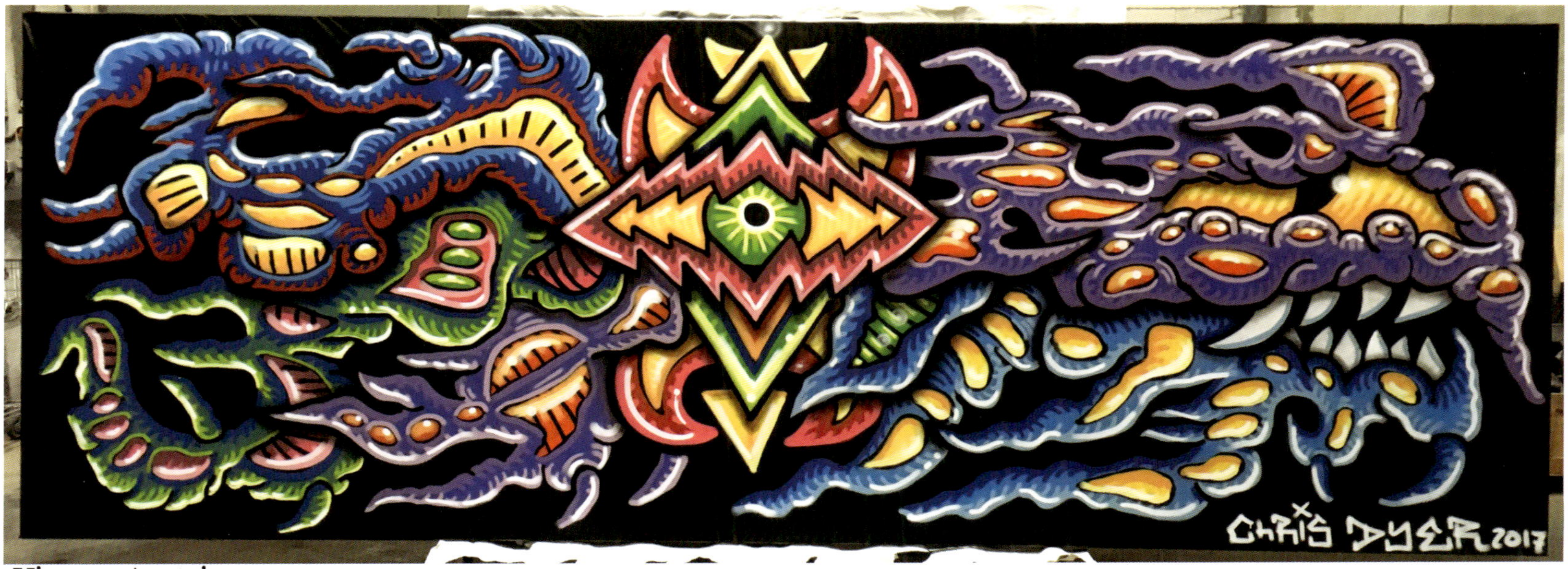

Vienna, Austria, 2017

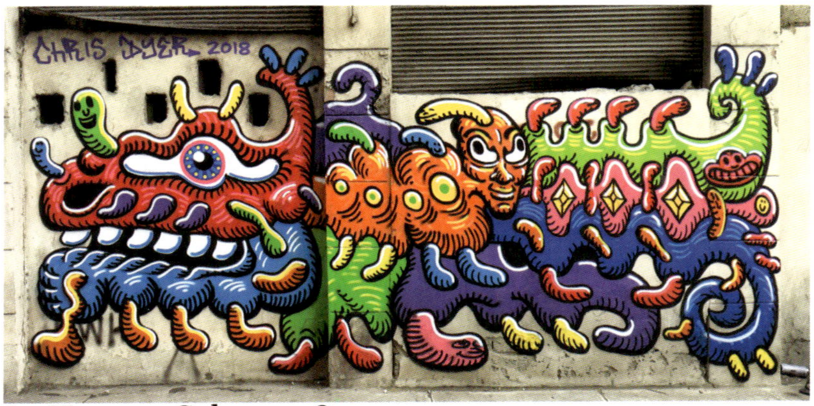

La Havana, Cuba, 2018

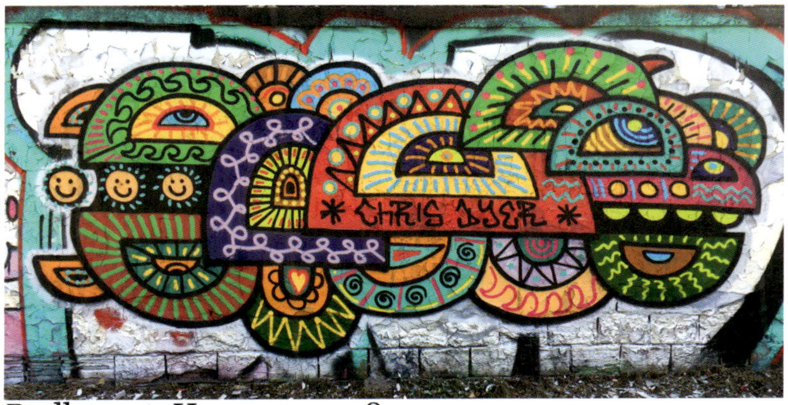

Budhapest, Hungary, 2018

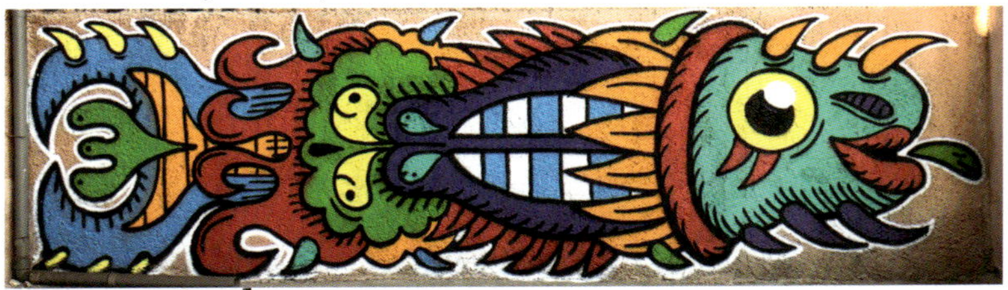
Amman, Jordan, 2019

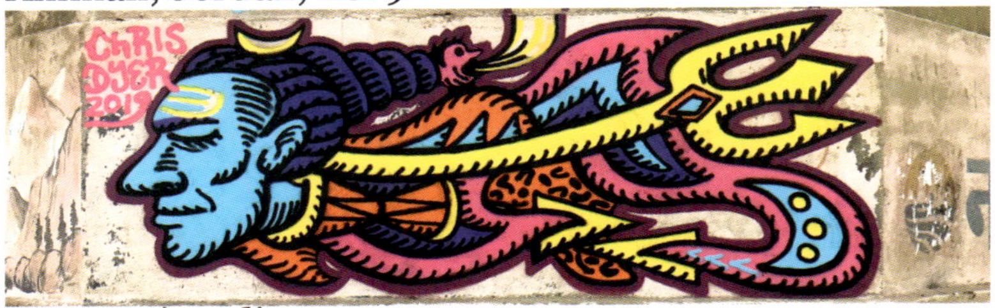

Varanasi, India, 2019

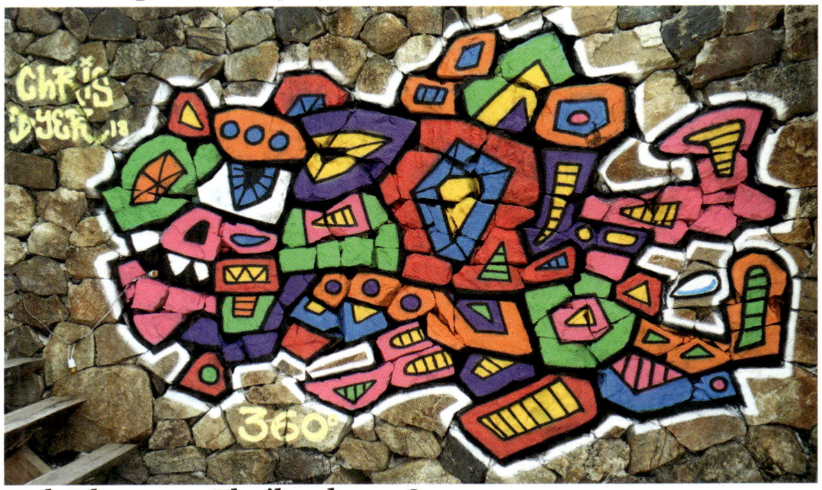

Koh Phangan, Thailand, 2018

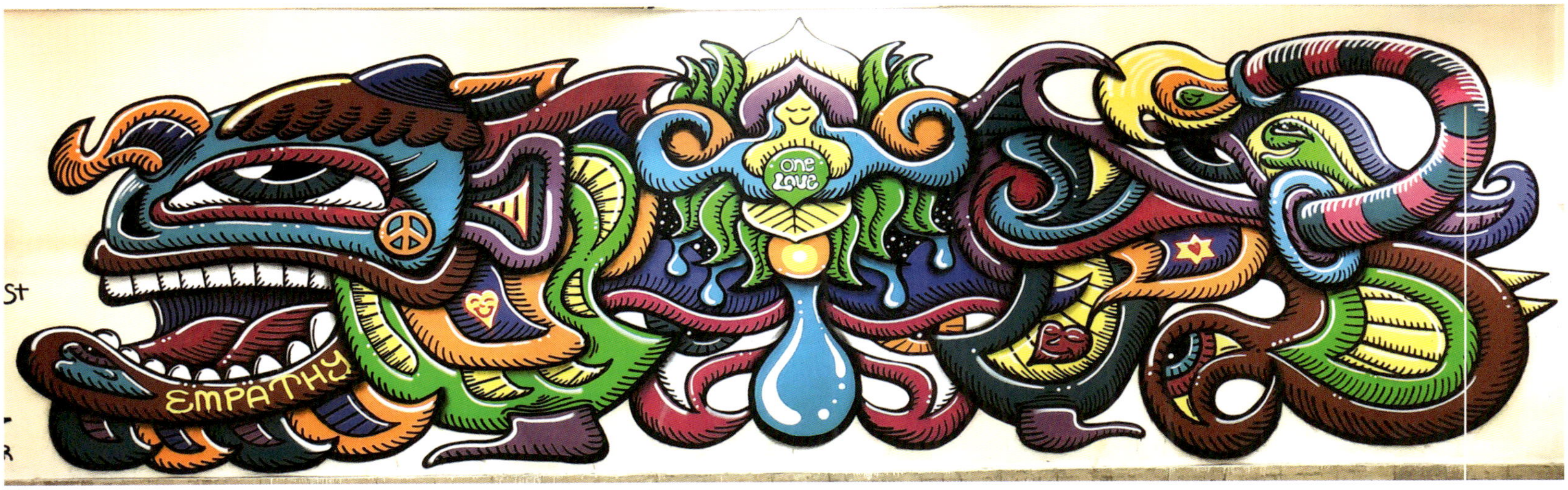

Tel Avive, Israel, 2019 (with **Arianne The Metanoist**)

GALAKTIC DUDES

When I released my last book, I had to sign many of them and I wanted to include a quick character to go along that. So I invented the "Galaktic Dude", who is an interdimentional cartoon of myself. A spiritual joker, skater who paints magic in his urban landscape. Here some of my favorite versions from around the world.

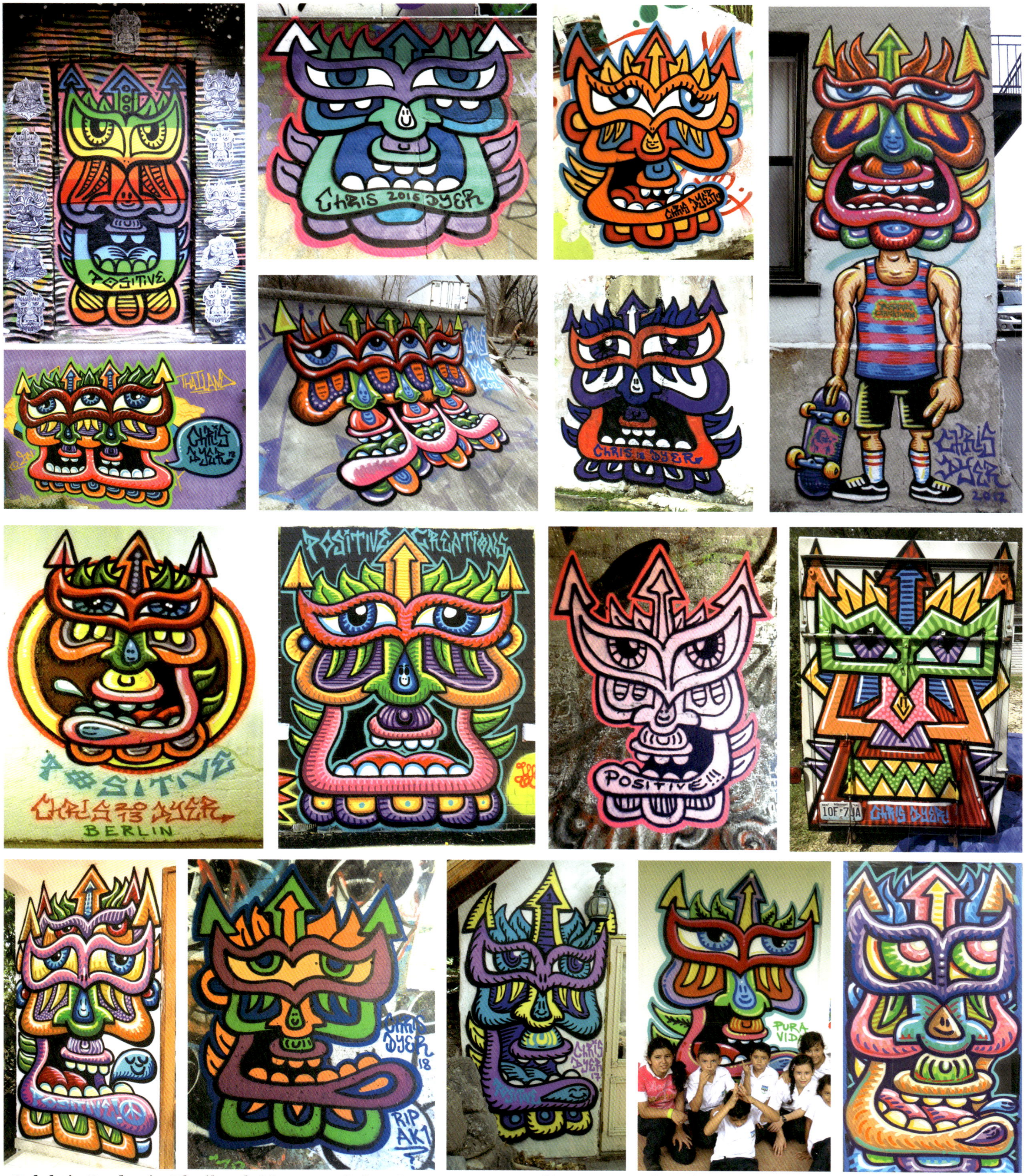

Galaktic Dudes in Thailand, Norway, Cuba, Germany, Australia, Peru, Colorado, Costa Rica, Jamaica, Mexico, etc.

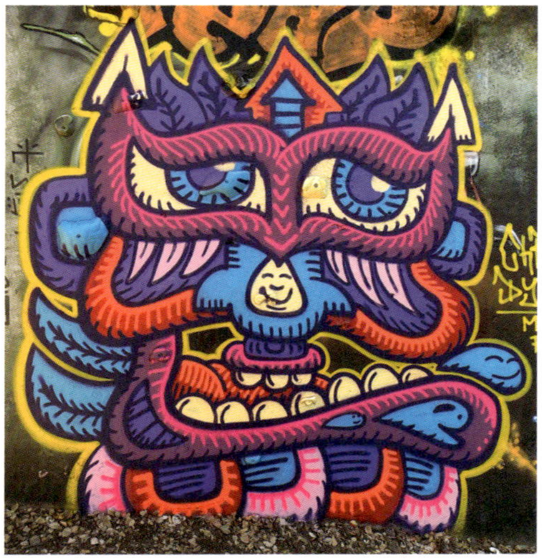

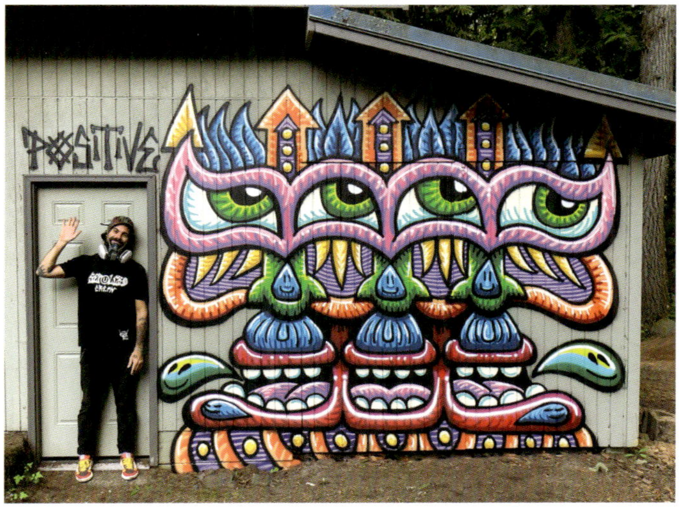
POSITIVE

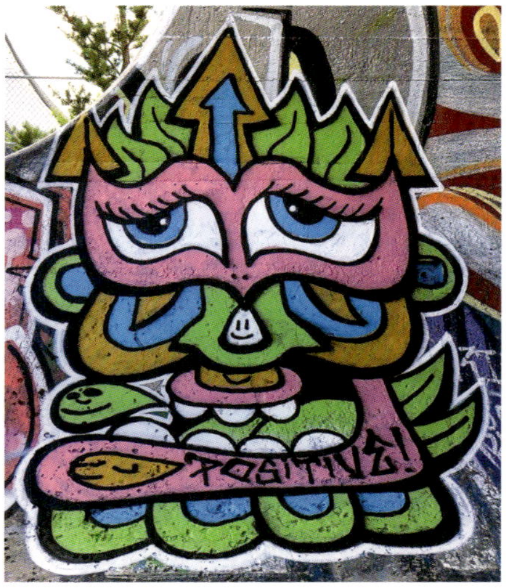
POSITIVE!

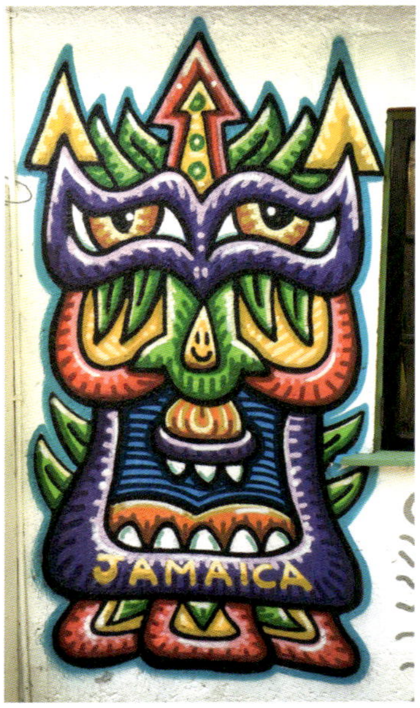
JAMAICA

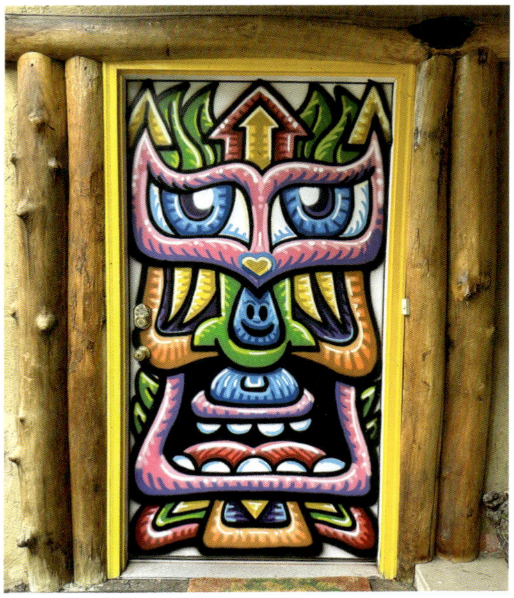

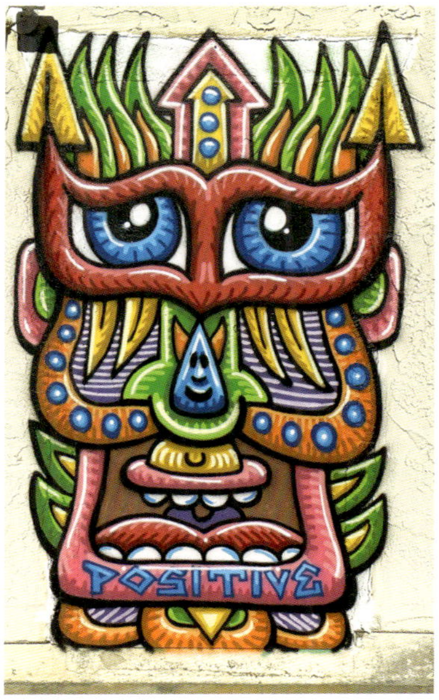
POSITIVE

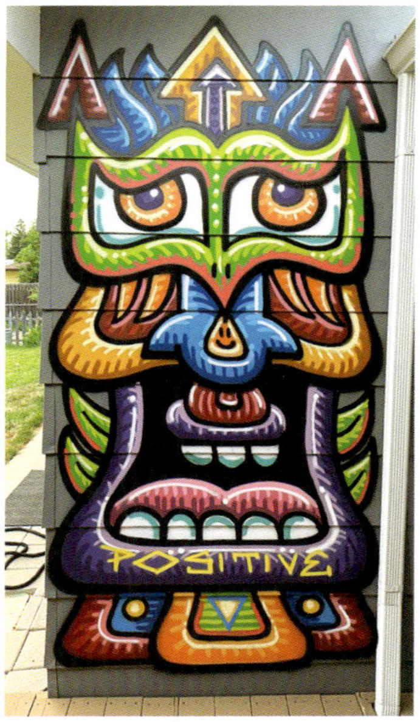
POSITIVE

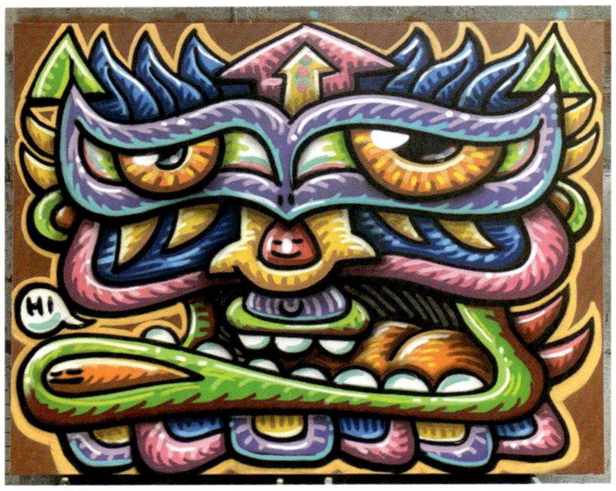
HI

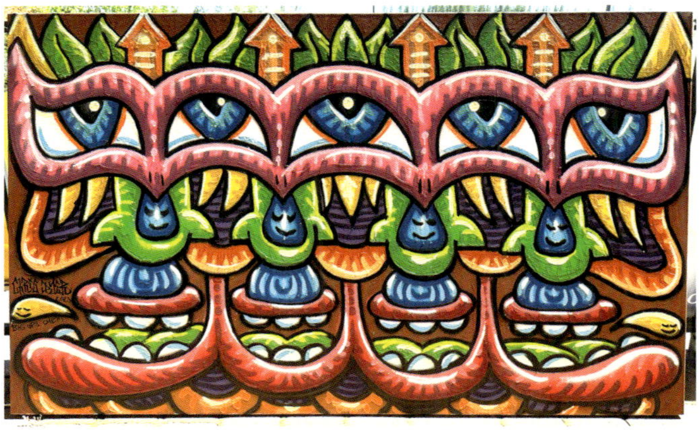

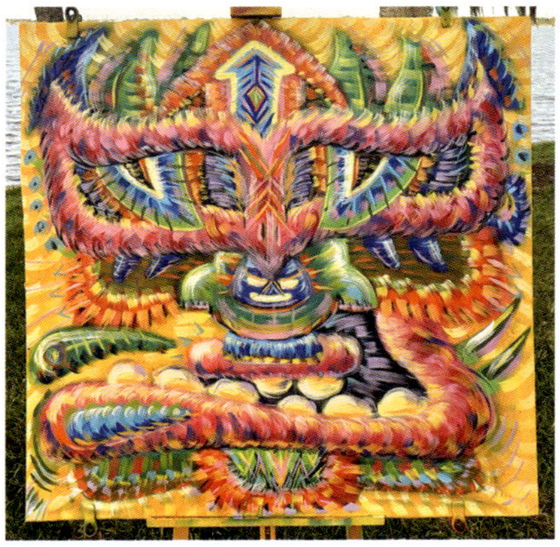

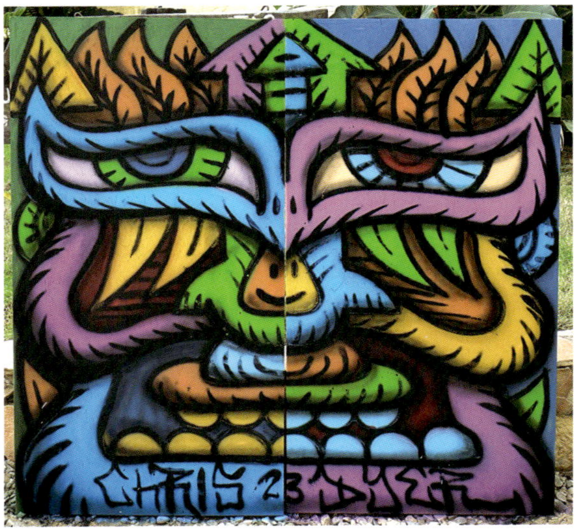
CHRIS 23 DYER

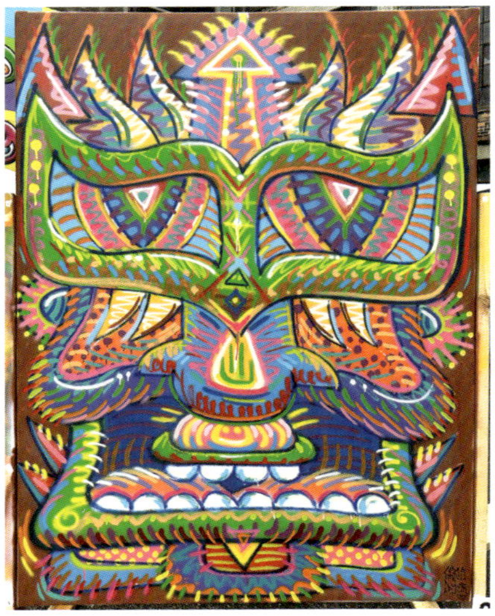

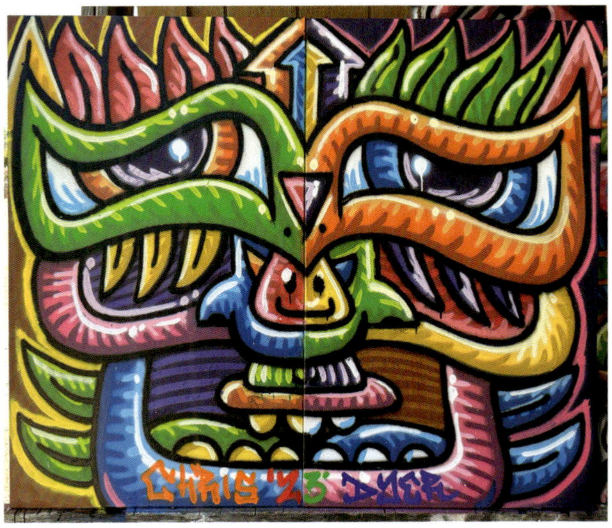
CHRIS '23 DYER

CHRIS' CORNER at COSM

By now I have been several times to Alex and Allyson Grey's **"Chapel of Sacred Mirrors"** to teach workshops. Though I teach about skate art, I also give my students a spray paint demonstration. It is an honor to have been given a little spot on their land to paint some creatures, usually wood cut installations in nature, which is different from my pieces on urban structures. I hope you get a chance to get irie out there one day!

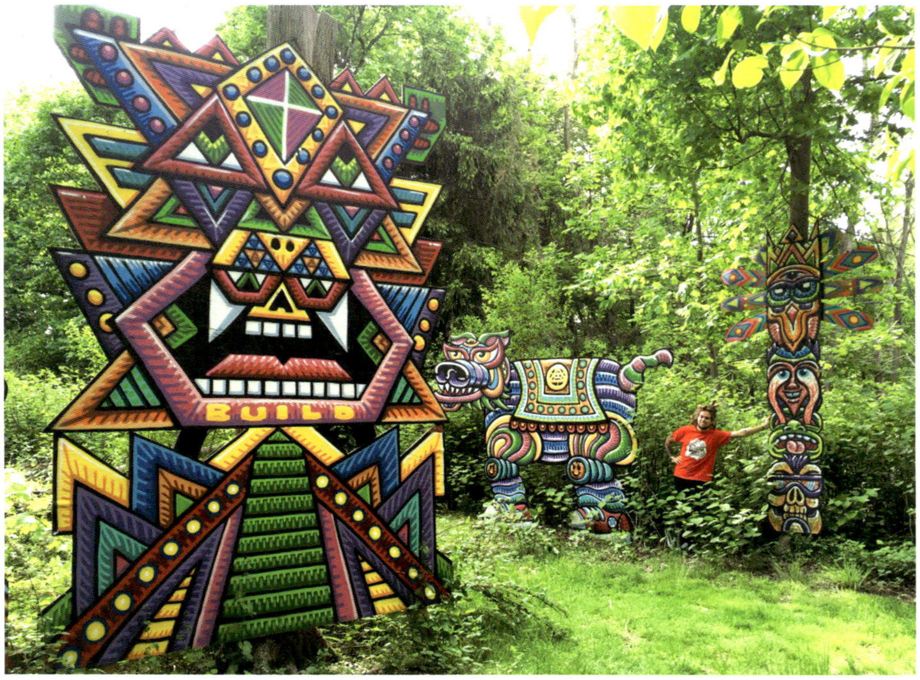

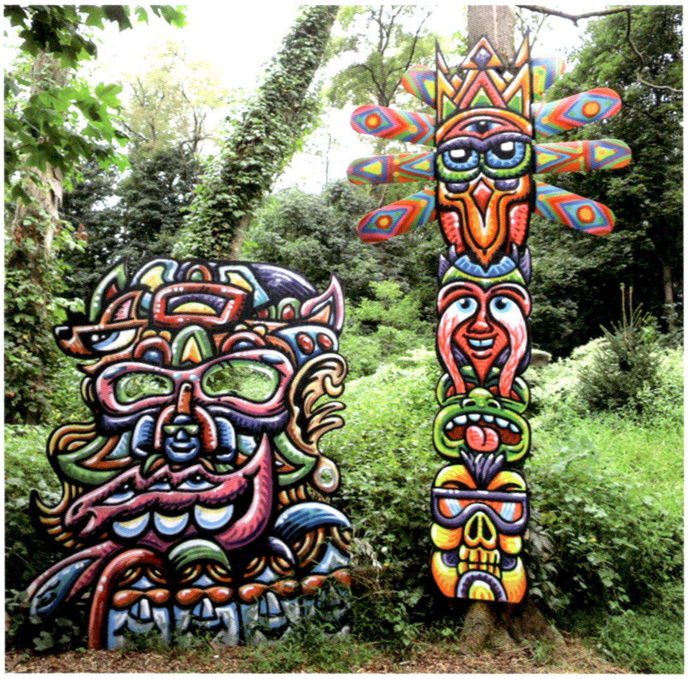

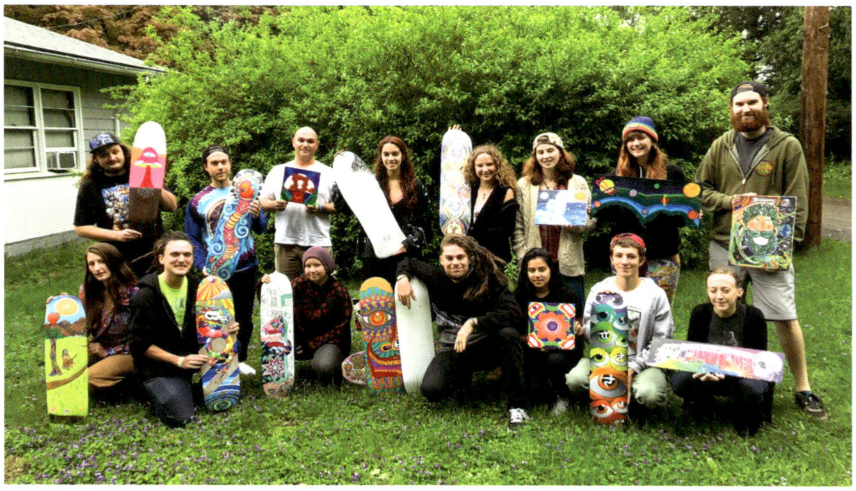

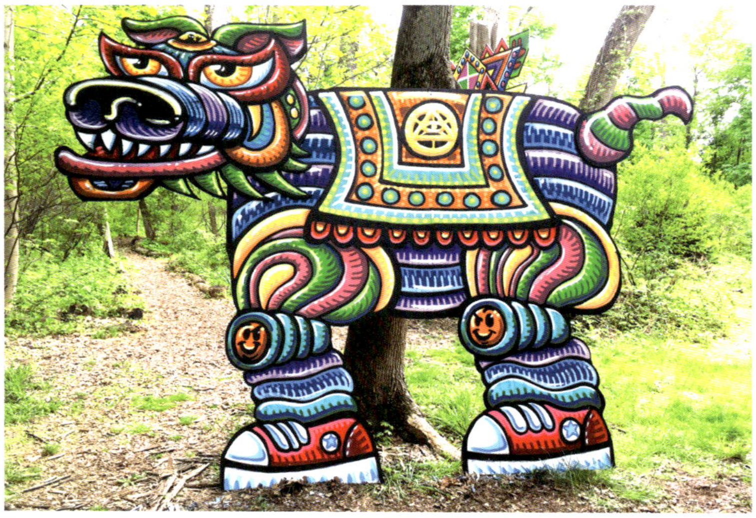

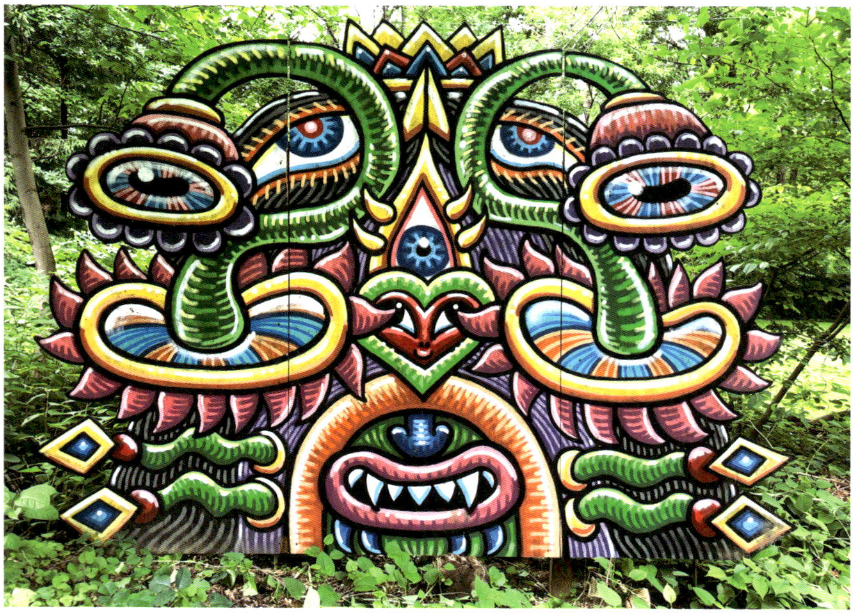

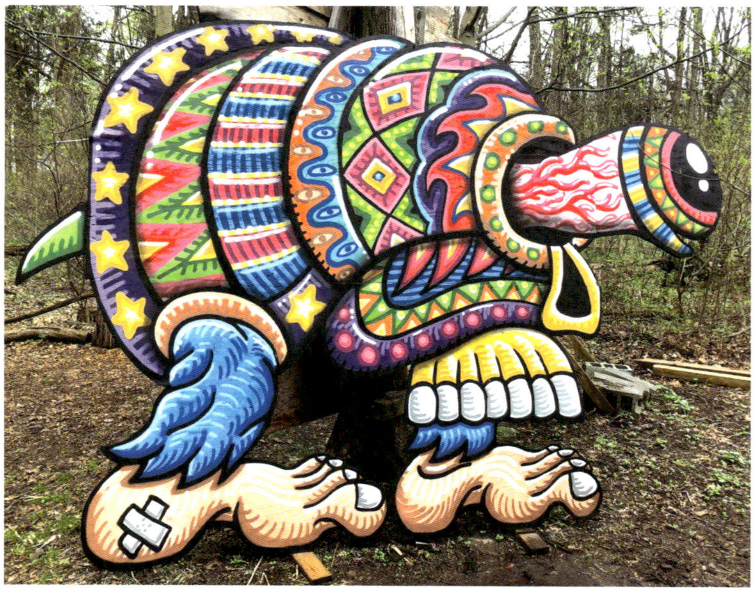

MIAMI ART BASEL

Every first week of December is Miami's big **"Art Week"**, better known as "Basel". It is an urban explosion of art, including street murals being blasted left and right, especially in the **Wynwood** district. I have been going there since 2011 and am like a pig in shit! Here some of the pieces I've sprayed at events or scored walls over the years.

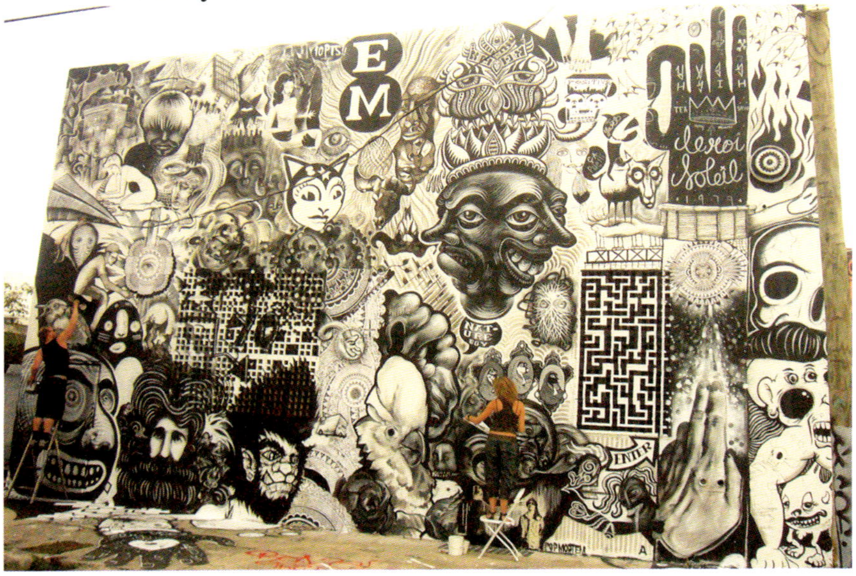

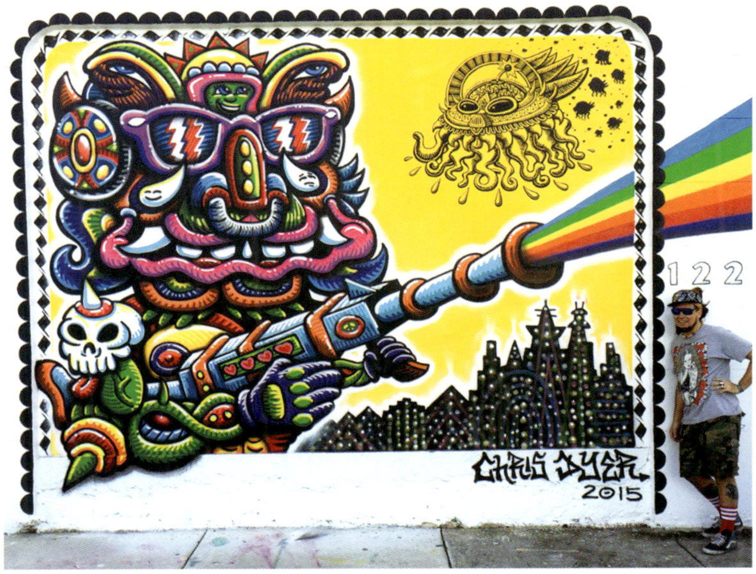

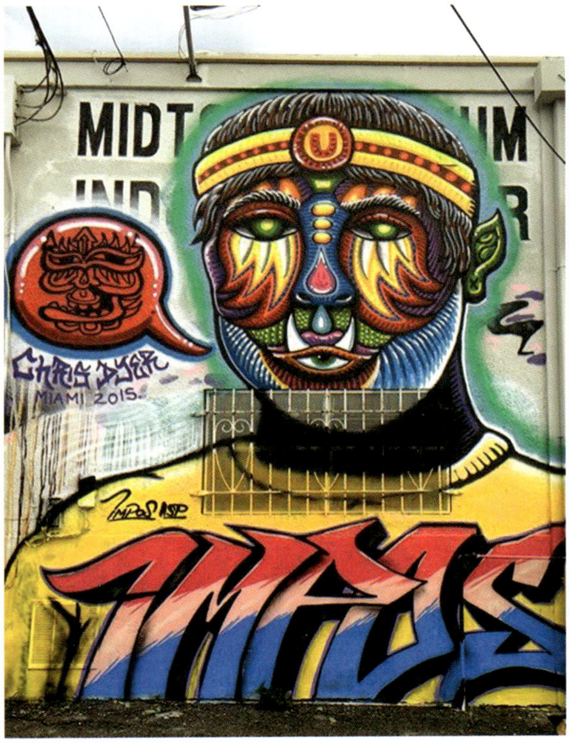

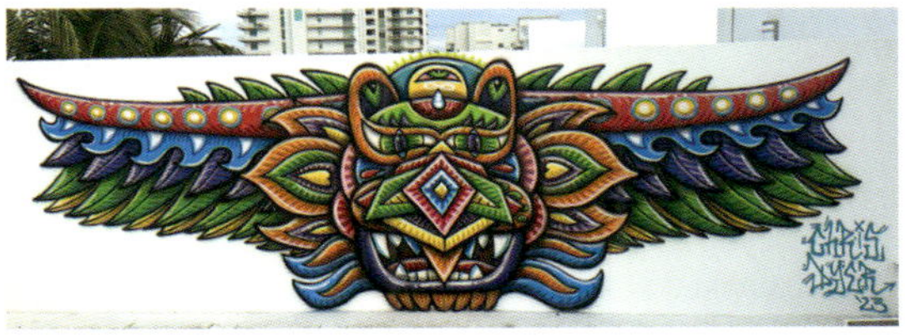

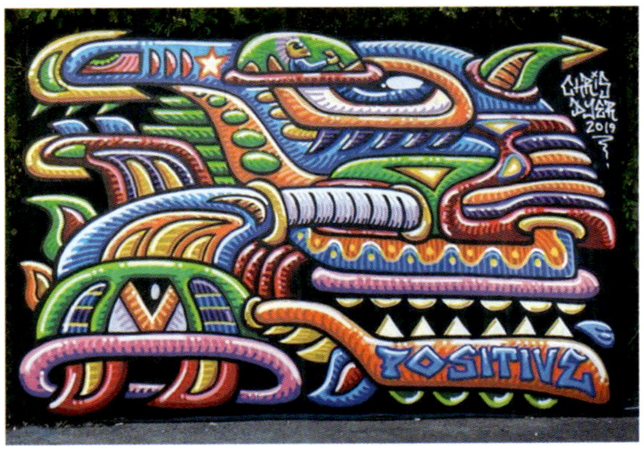

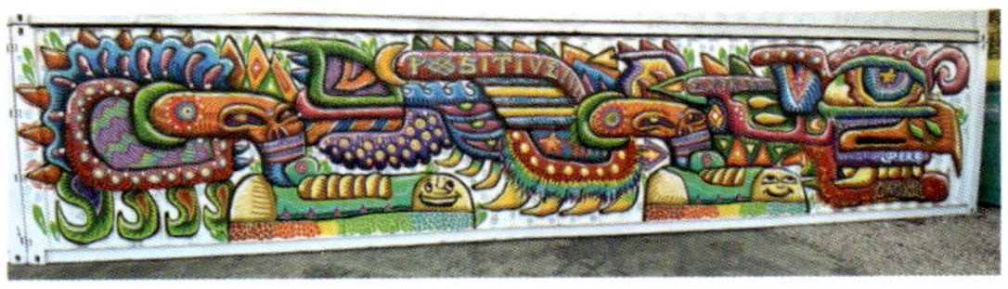

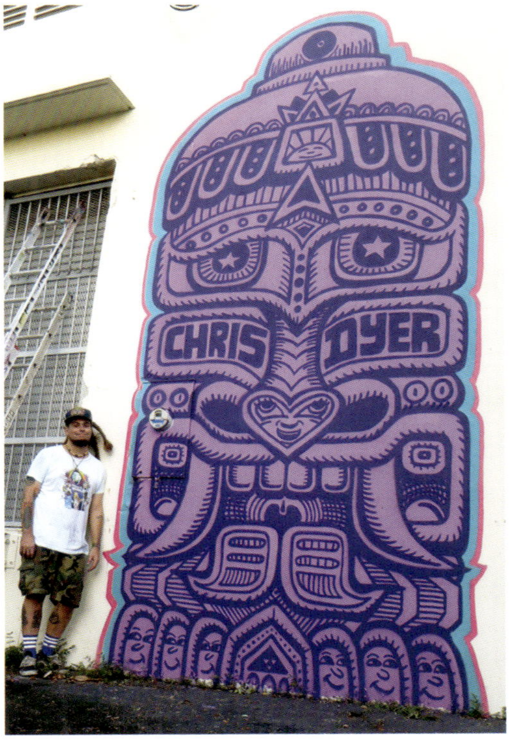

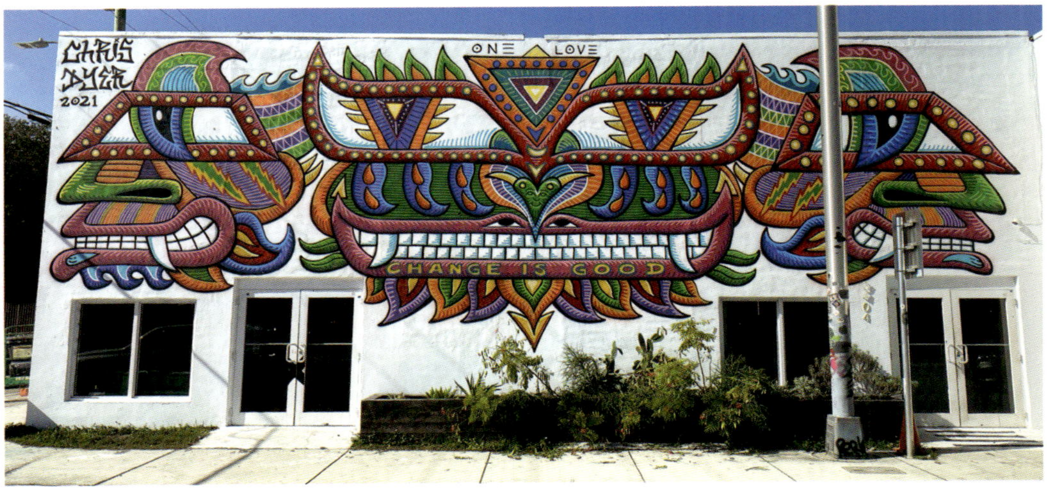

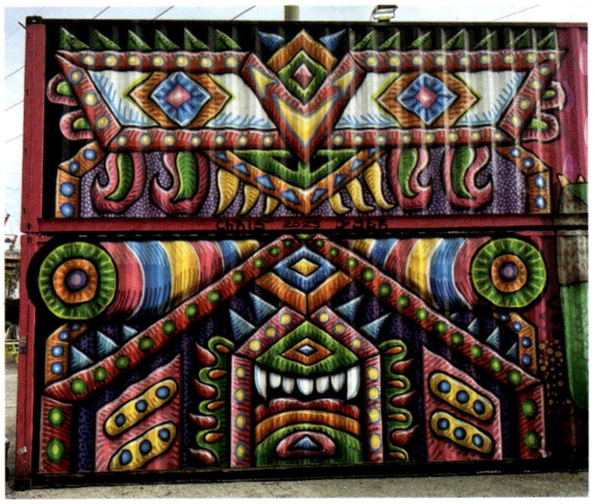

COLORING BOOK PARTIES

In 2016, the legendary San Francisco Publisher **"Last Gasp"** published the first of two volumes of my **"Kick-Ass Coloring Book for Rad Adults and Cool Kids"**. It has been such a fun way for my fans to collaborate with me and re-interpret my art! I also organized "Coloring Book Parties" in different major cities where fans could show me their skills live! Creative community building is crucial!

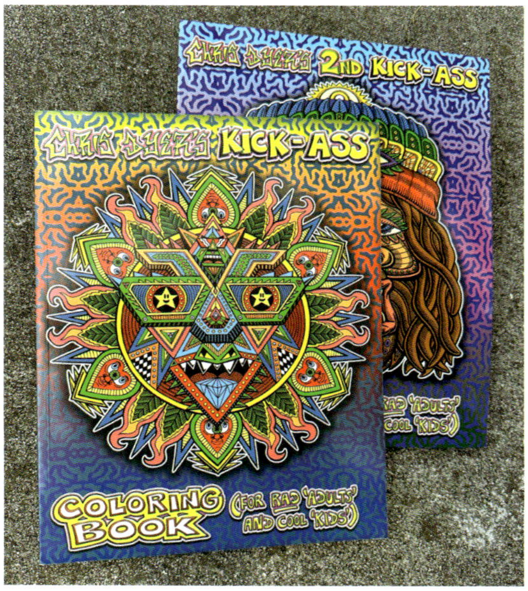

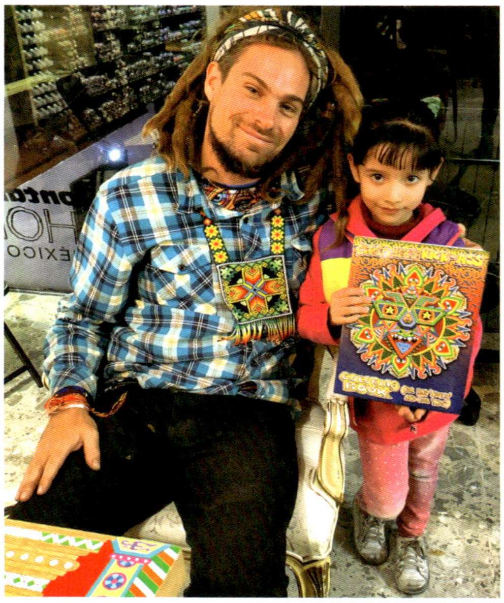

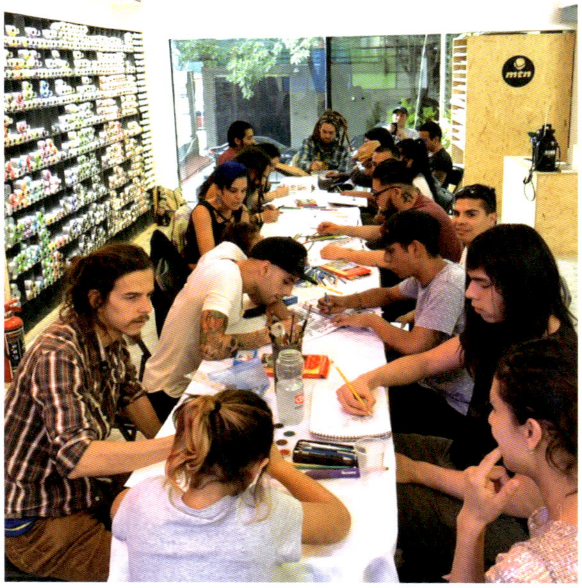

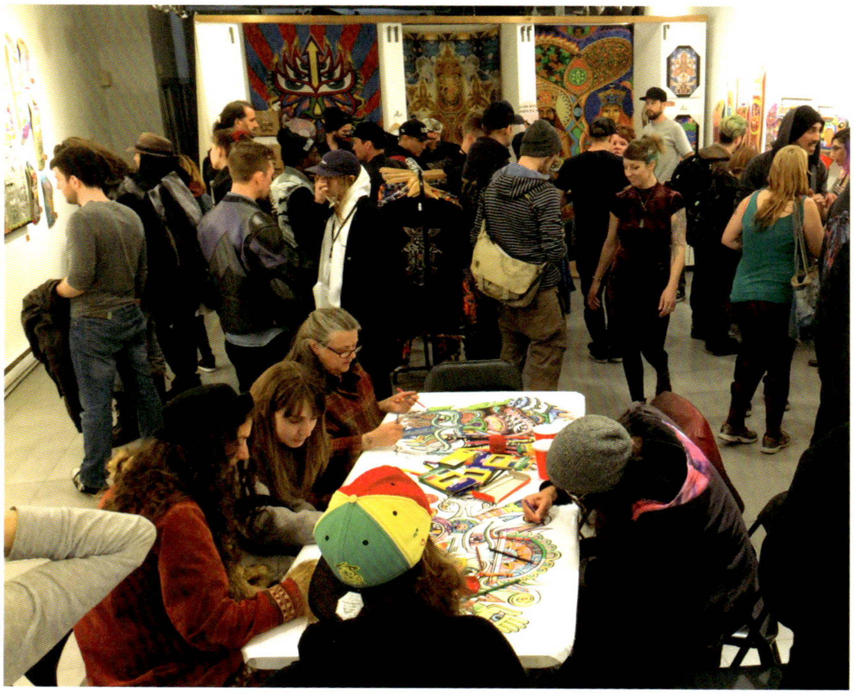

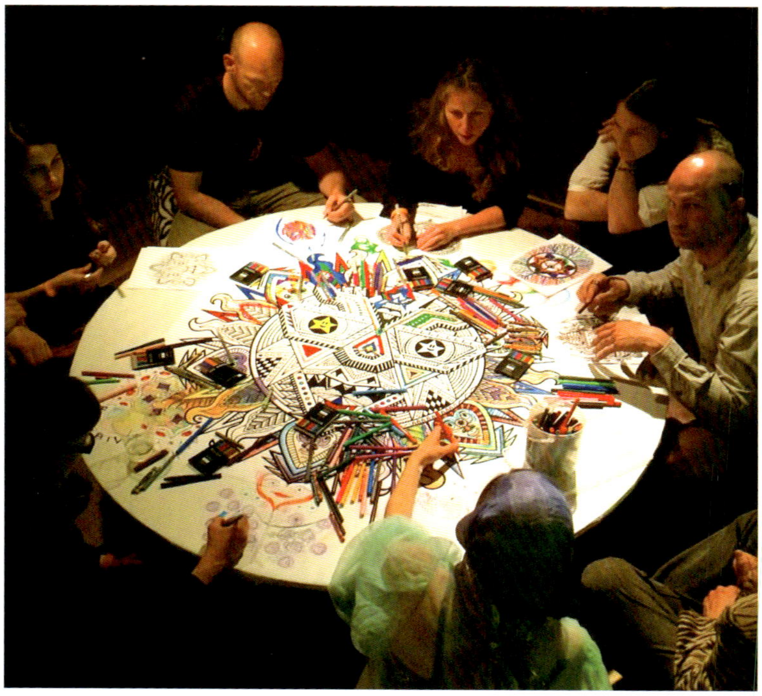

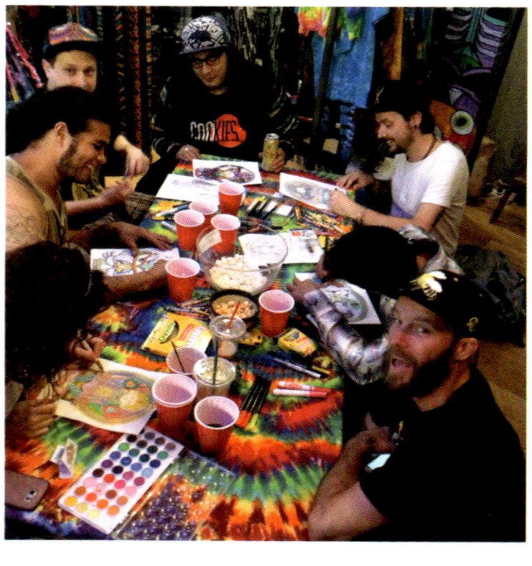

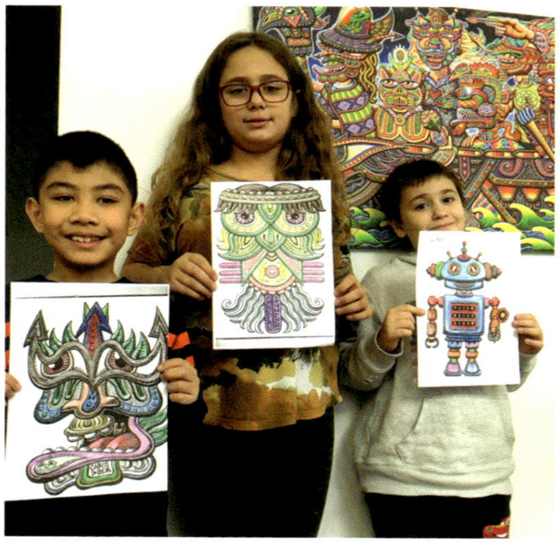

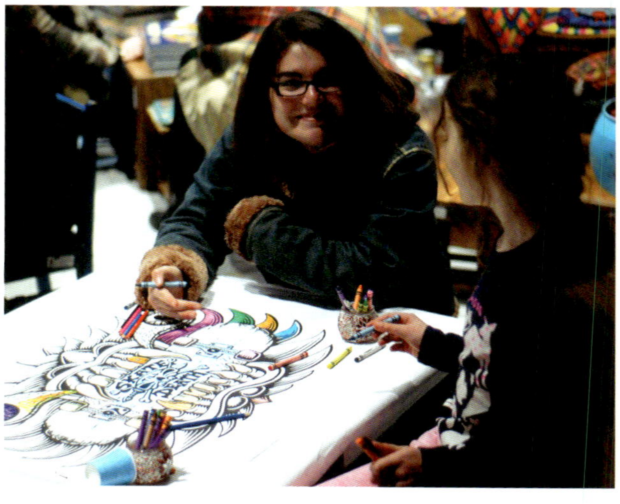

THE SUNLIGHT CHRONICLES

The “Sunlight Chronicles” is a journal project that I’ve been drawing and writing since 2002. I draw these live renditions of my reality with black ink, so there are plenty of mistakes, along my usual atrocious spelling. This makes for a very authentic reflection of my imperfect life. Here are some of my favorite pages from the different sketch books I’ve worked on in the last decade.

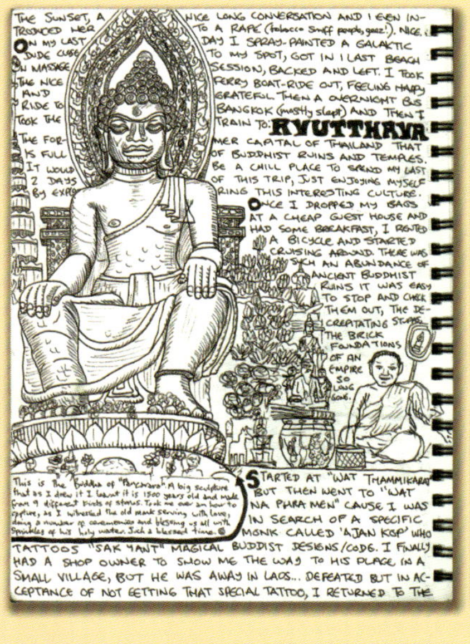

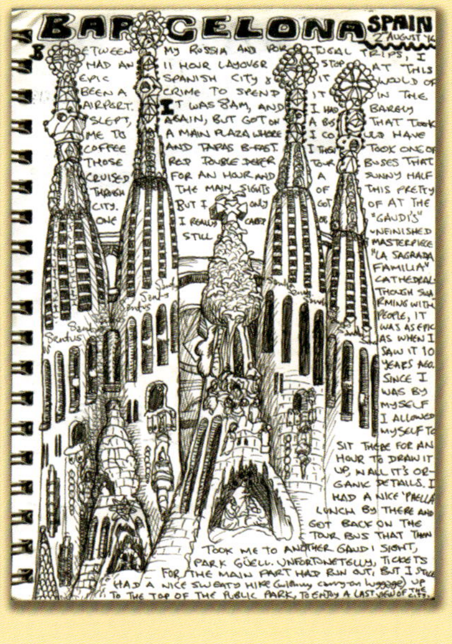

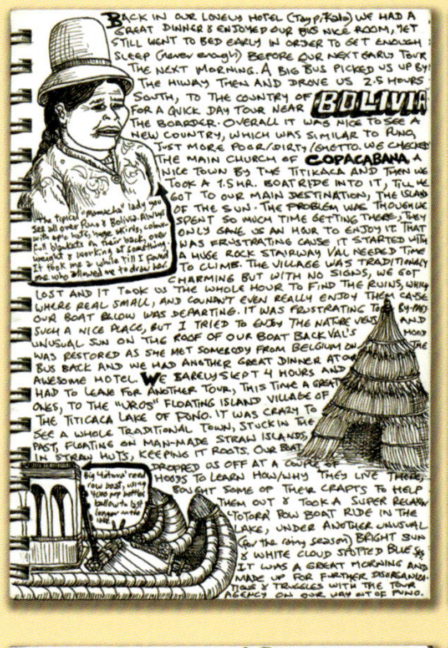

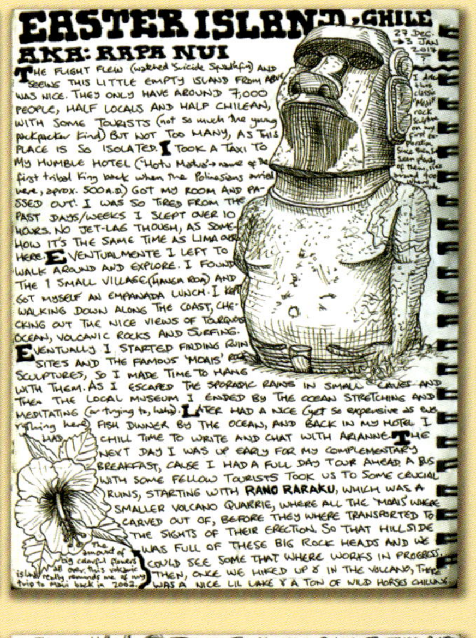

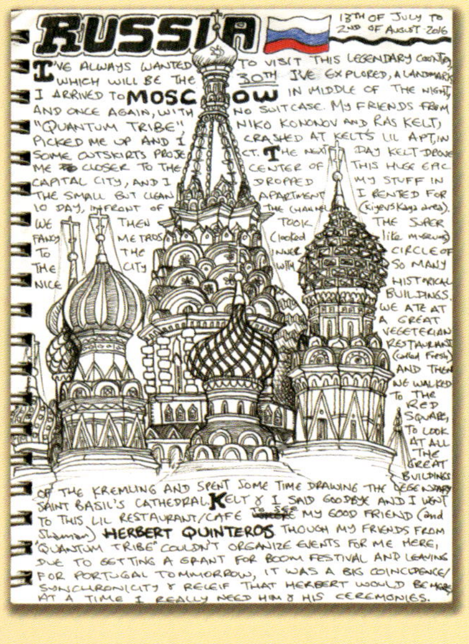

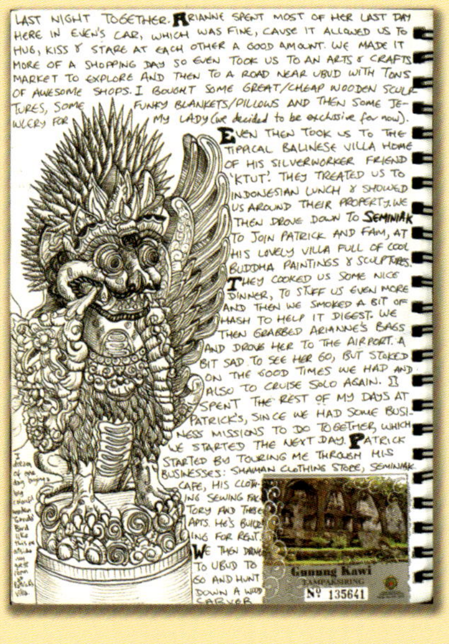

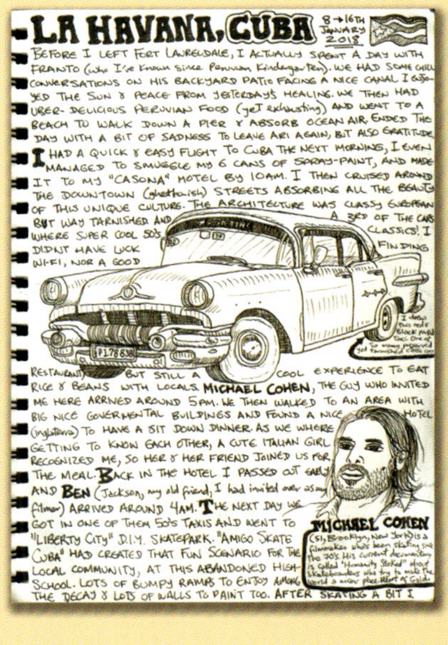

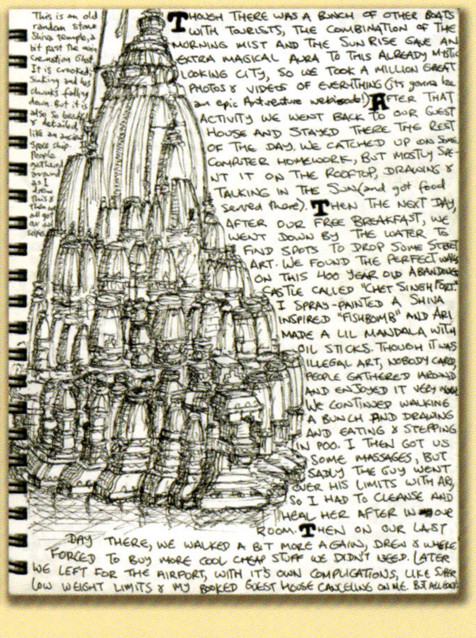

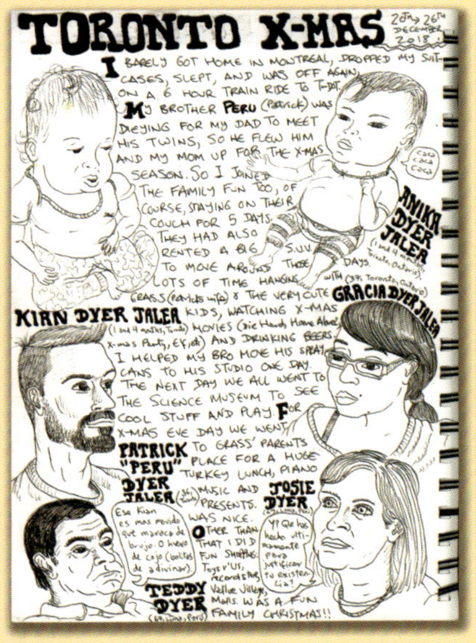

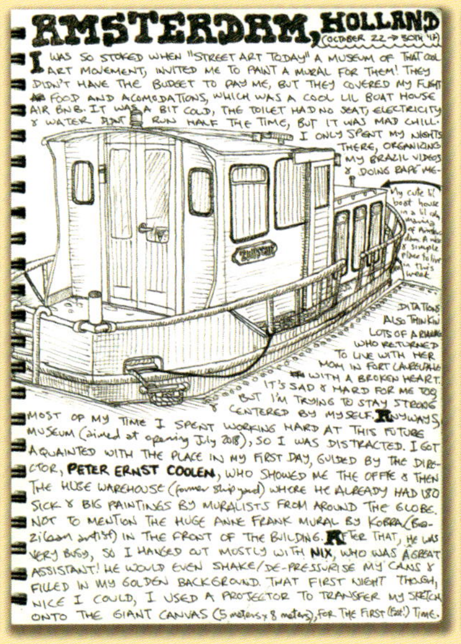

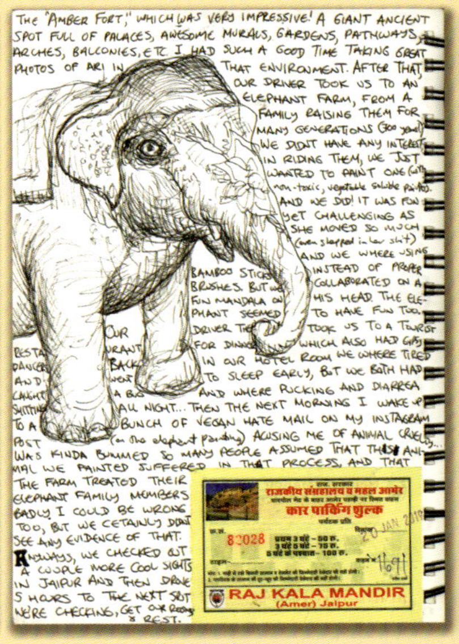

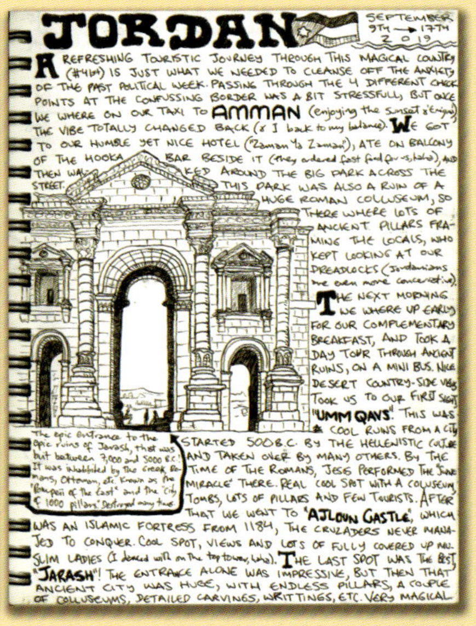

“CHRIS ONCE GAVE ME A COPY OF HIS FIRST PUBLISHED “SUNLIGHT CHRONICLES” BOOK. READING ABOUT THE HARD WORK IT TAKES TO PLANT TREES AND KNOWING ABOUT THE EFFORT THAT GOES INTO HELPING OUT MOTHER NATURE INSPIRED ME TO CREATE MY PAINTING “RESTORING THE FUTURE”. ” -MARK HENSON, VISIONARY ARTIST

SCULPTURES

Sculptures are a super fun way of expressing myself in this 3D world of ours! Some I can do with my own 2 hands, but usually I have to collaborate with different artists who are better at realizing all these concepts I come up with. I love what the unity of forces can do to bring my art into the next level of life!

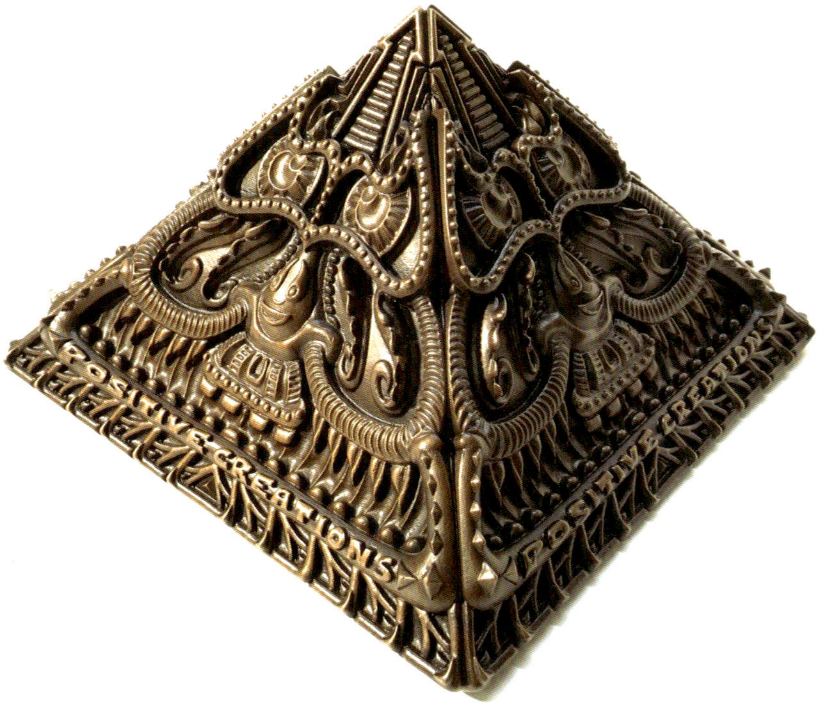

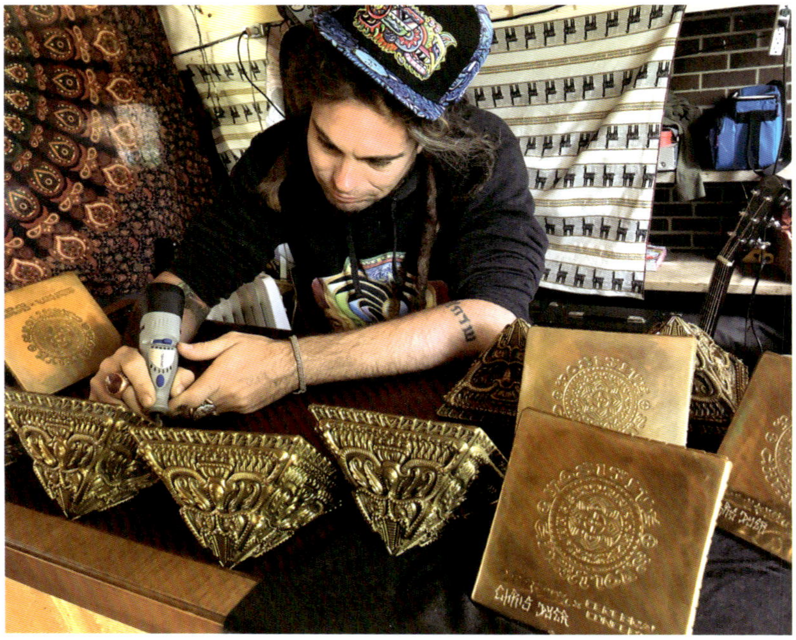

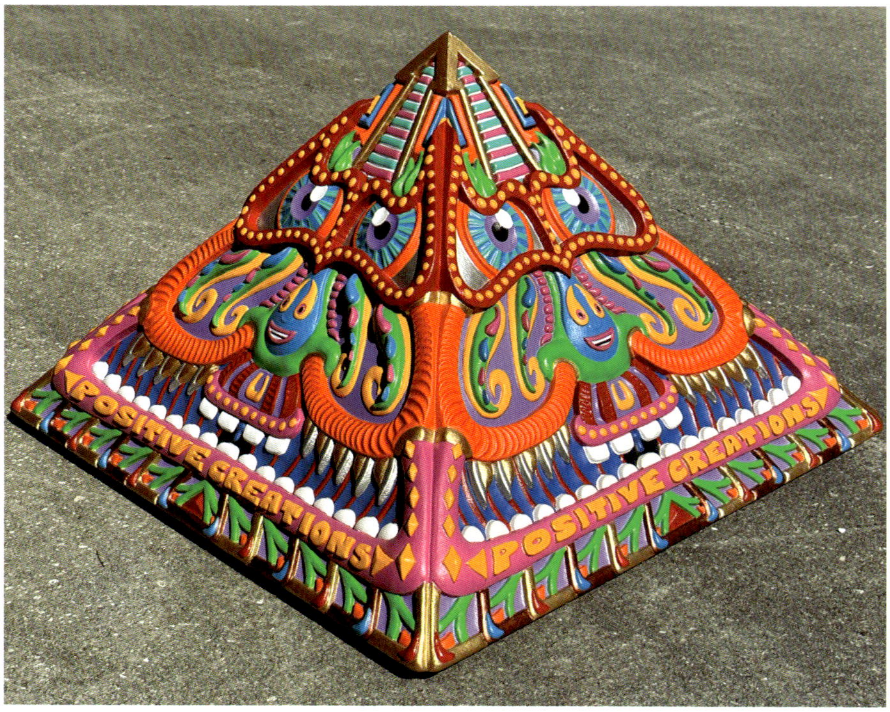

"The Positive Pyramid" 2017

For this project I designed a tribal pyramid that then **Michael Clotherthy** from "**Cerebral Concepts**" rendered out as a 3D scuplture. Our first offering of these sculptures where in Bronze a Limited Edition of 25. The next offering was an "Organite" collaboration with **Branch Ellison** with Lapis and Malachite accents under the resin that glowed in the dark! Later on Michael also made me a huge one I could paint in acrylics over the years! And then there was also a medium sized version that was painted by different artist friends **Sw33t Sat0r1, Sean Zenner, Max Paularena** and **DomE Moon.**

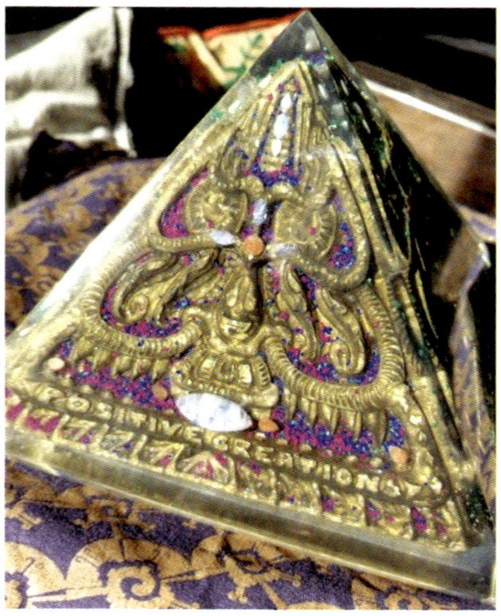

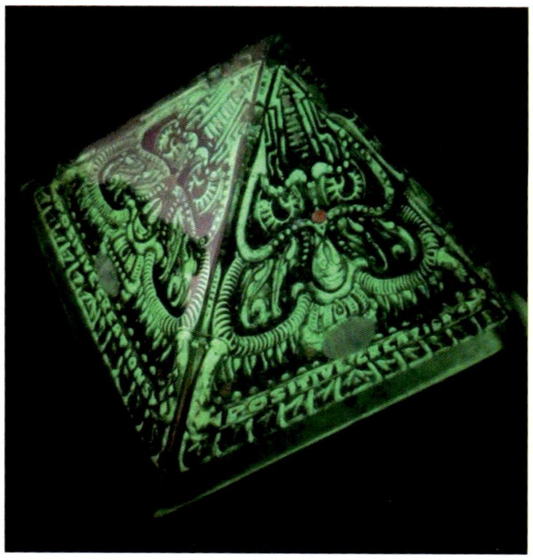

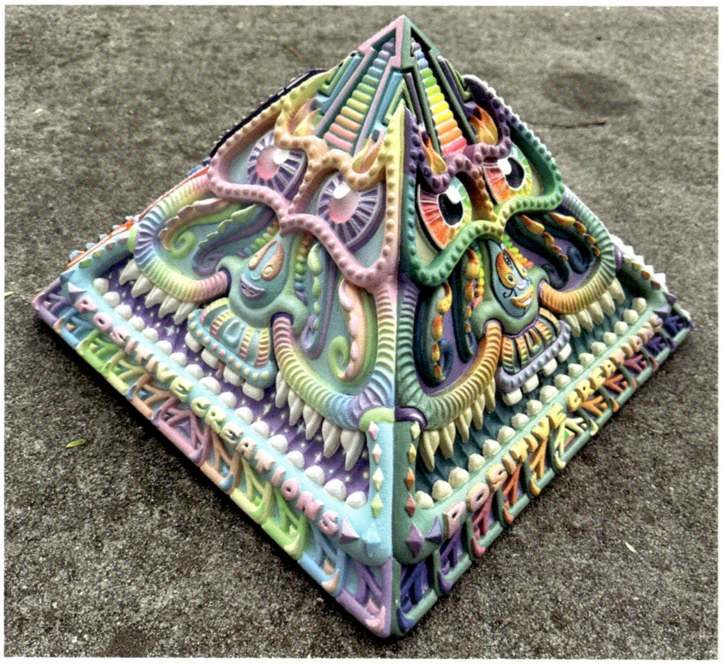

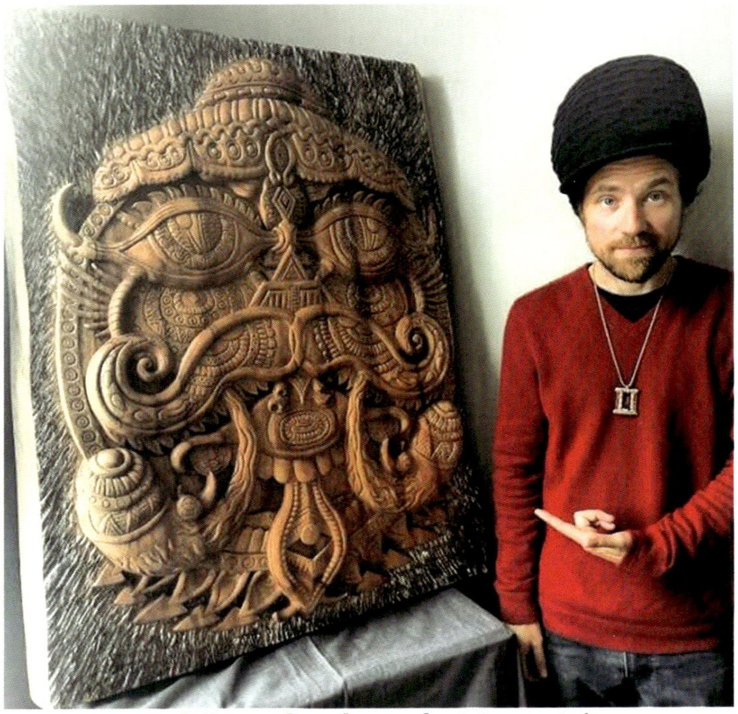

"Deep Breath" Wood sculpture by Wayan Ariawan, 2017

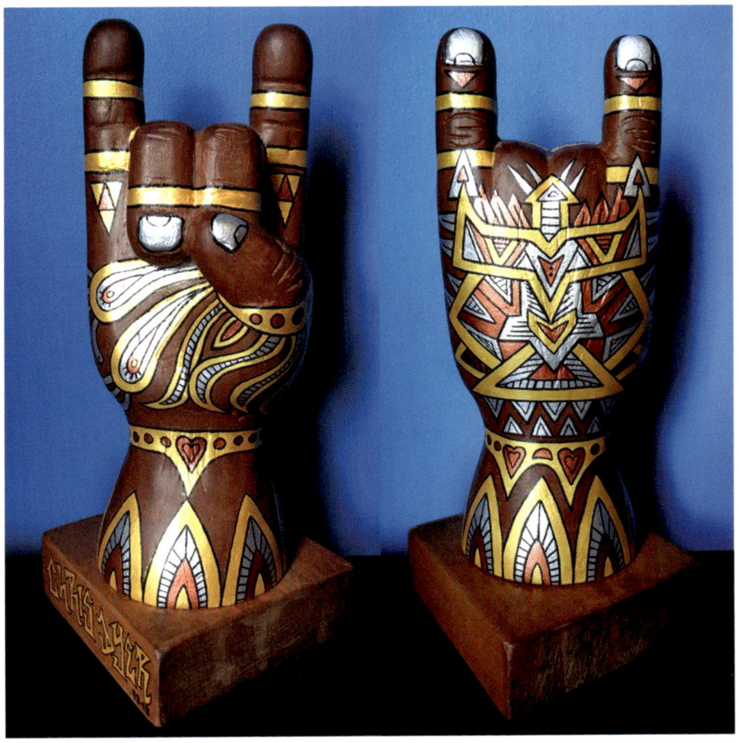

"Tribal Metal" Acrylics on wood, 1998-2018

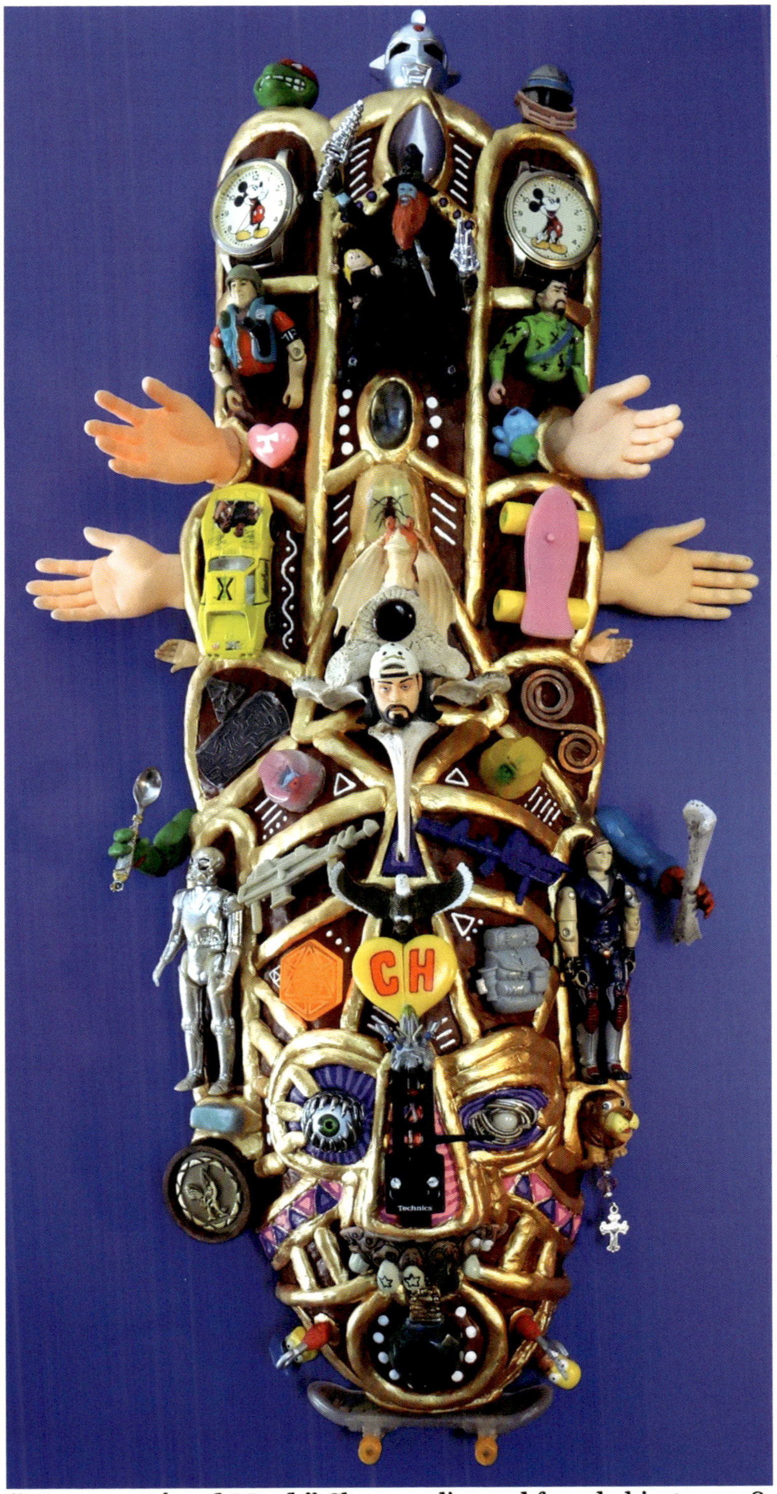

"Mystery Ritual Mask" Clay, acrylics and found objects, 2018

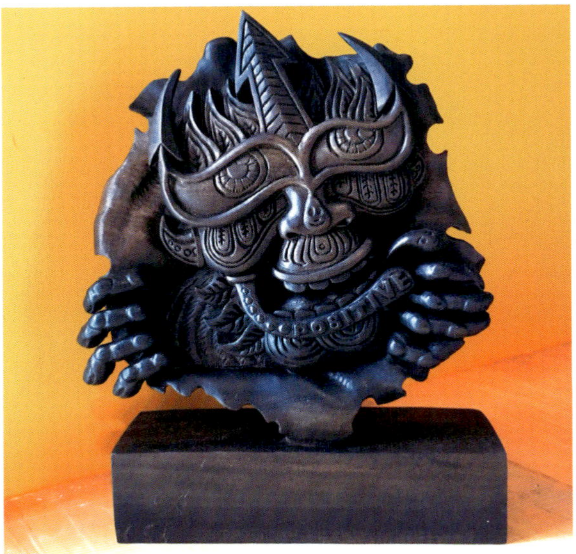

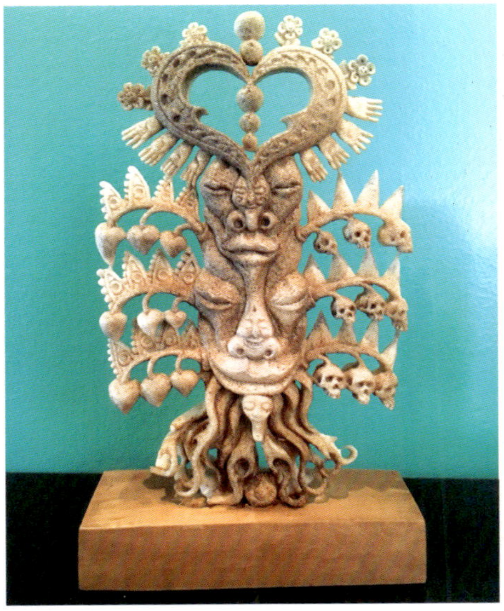

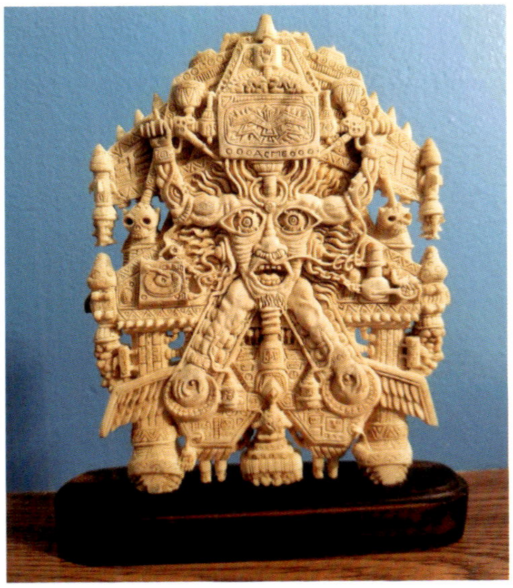

"Galaktic Ripper", **"Death Tree"** and **"Sedated Slaveship"** by the **Geriya Brothers** in Wood and Moose Antlers, 2017

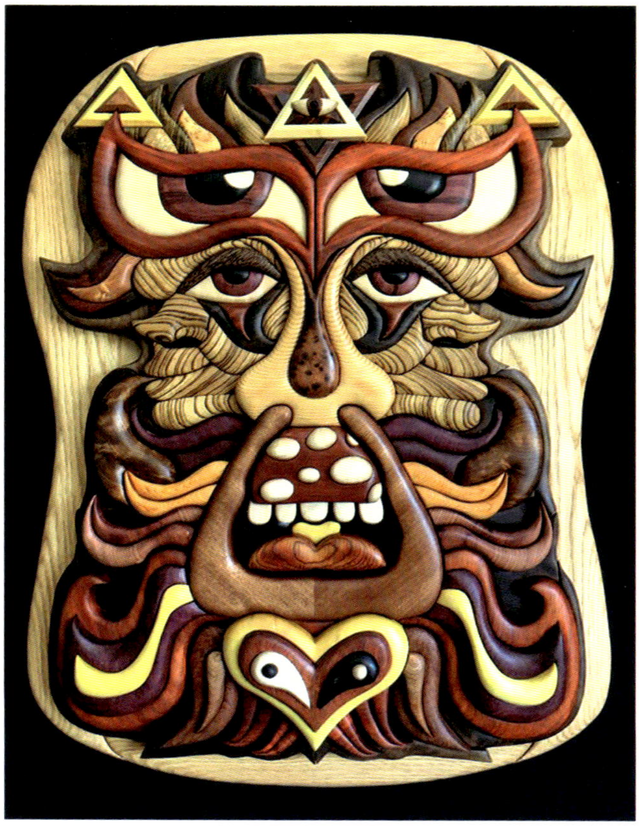

"Garden Guardian"
by **Kyle Vibes** - Woods, 2017

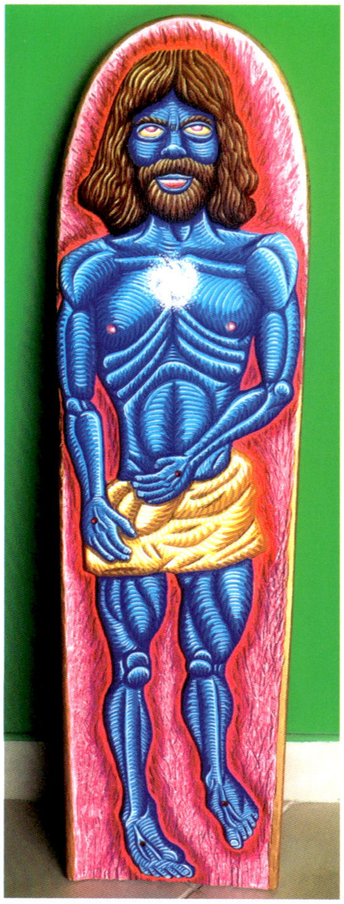

"Blueprint to Resurrection"
Acrylics on Wood, 1999 & 2021

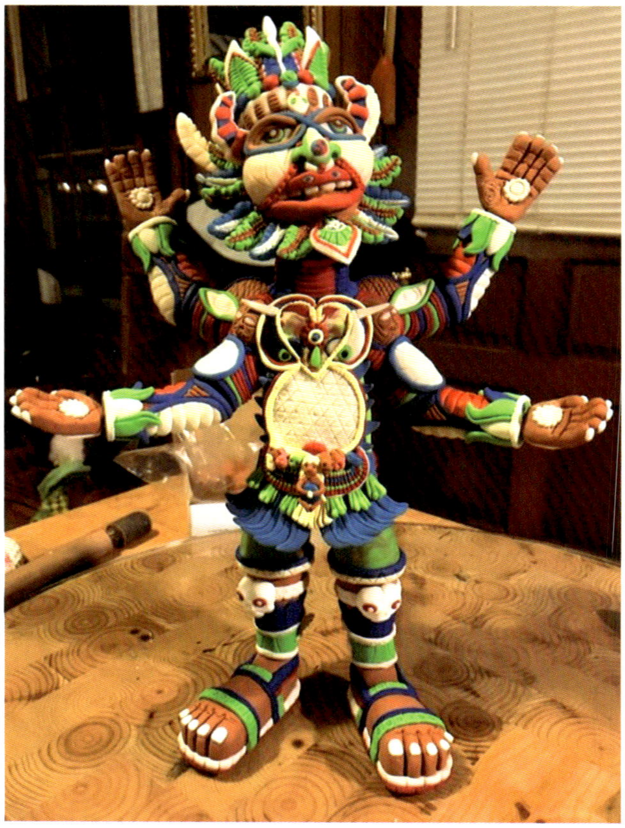

"Neo Human Evolution"
by **Gypsy Marsh** - Clay, 2016

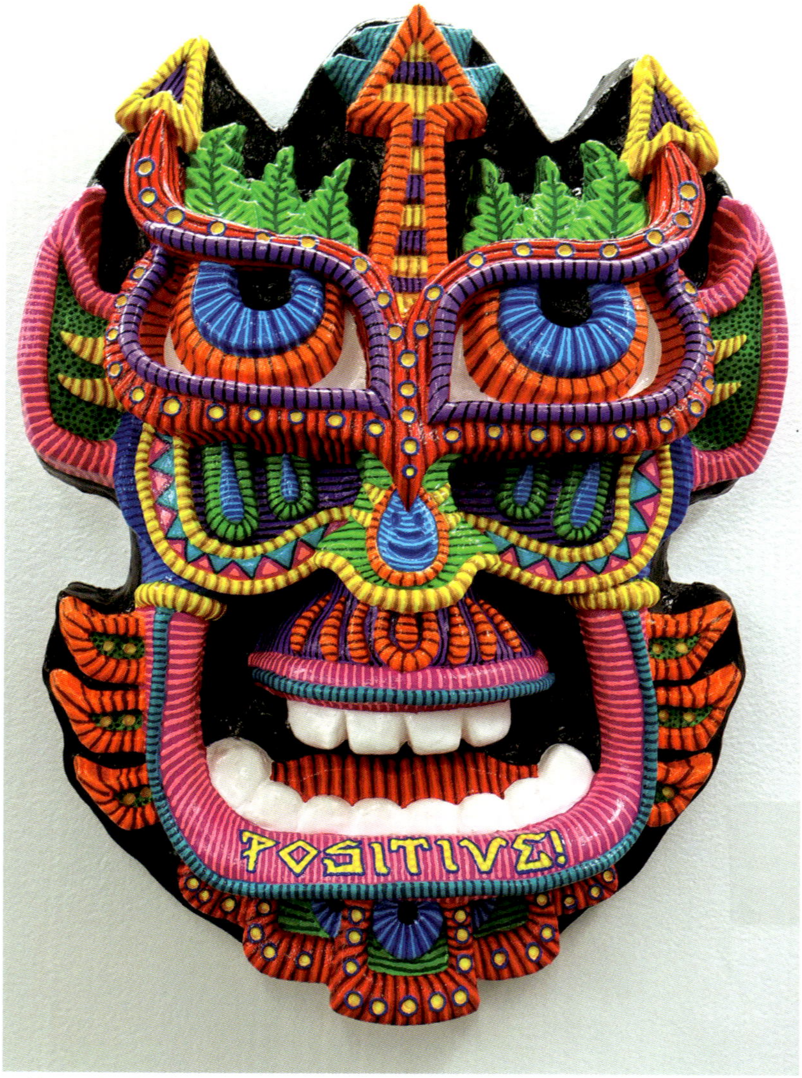

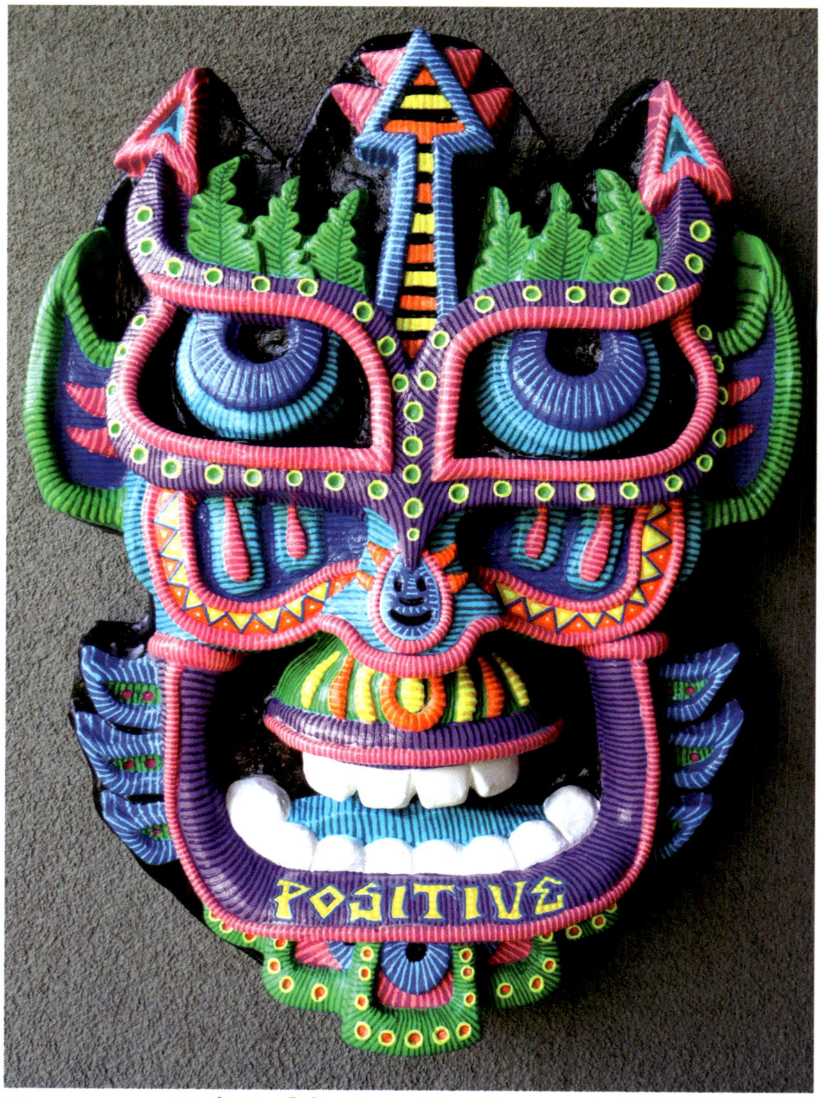

"Galaktic Dude Mask" by **John Shook** - Plaster, 2017. Painted in Acrylics by myself in 2018

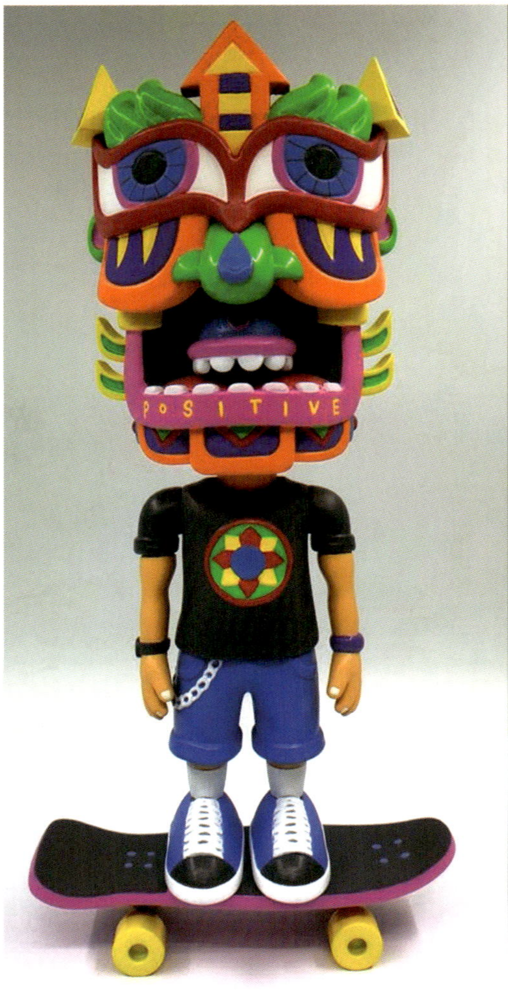

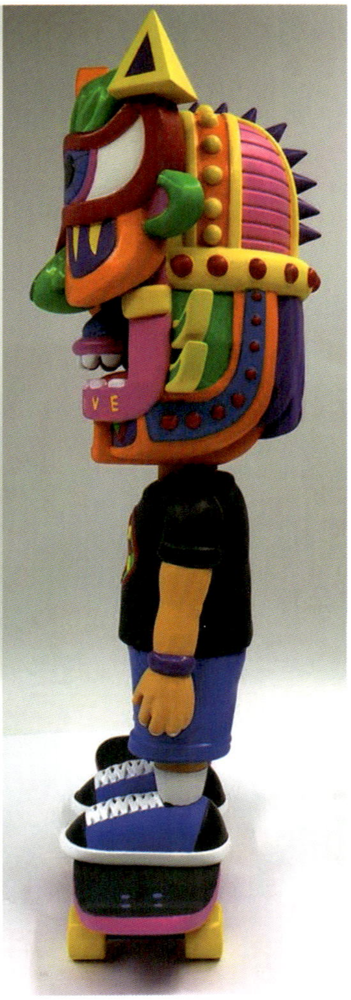

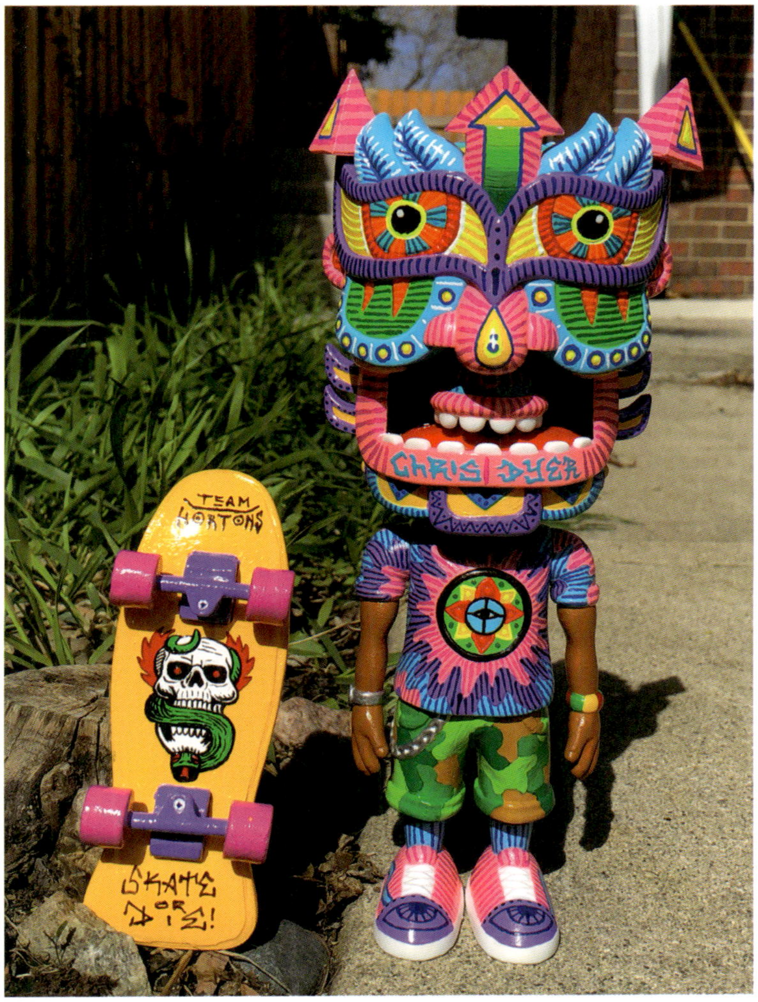

"The Galaktic Dude Toy" Acrylics on Vinyl, 2019

As an action figure collector, I always dreamt of having my own toy. Instead of waiting endlessly for a company to come and hire me to do that, I just went straight to a manufacturer and created a Galaktic Dude figure! He was ten inches tall, full color, had movable parts and came with an accessory skateboard! I was able to order a hundred of them and I was stoked when they sold out! Since I had the moulds, I also ordered a hundred blanks, which could be cheaper and a way for people to paint them too. Once I received those, I gave thirty of them to my favorite artist friends to custom paint and we then had an amazing group exhibition at **"Phil Lewis Gallery"** in Boulder, Colorado! Top right is my own custom job and below are the amazing ones from my friends.

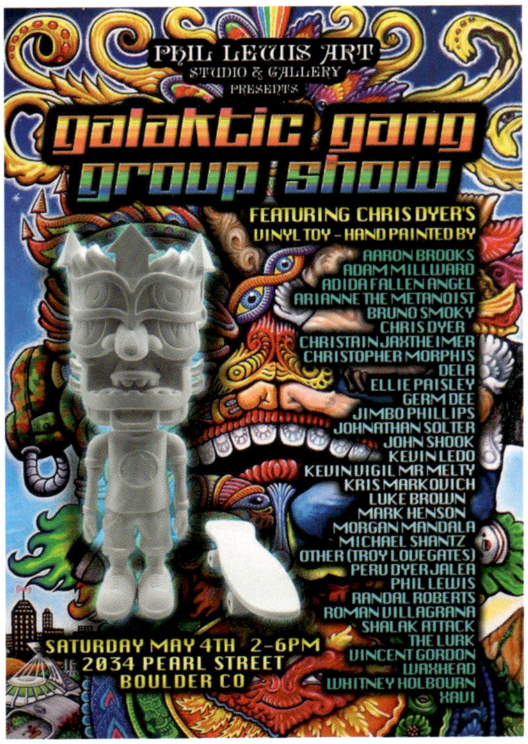

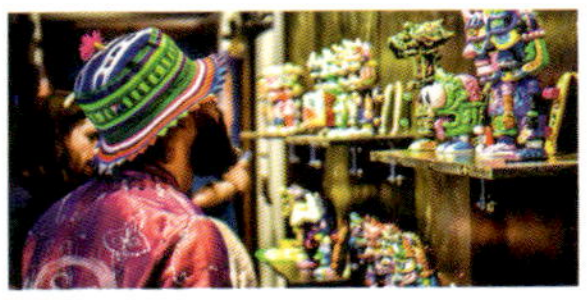

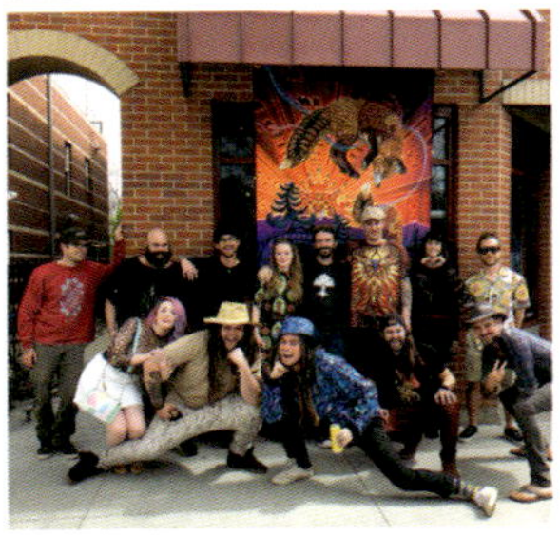

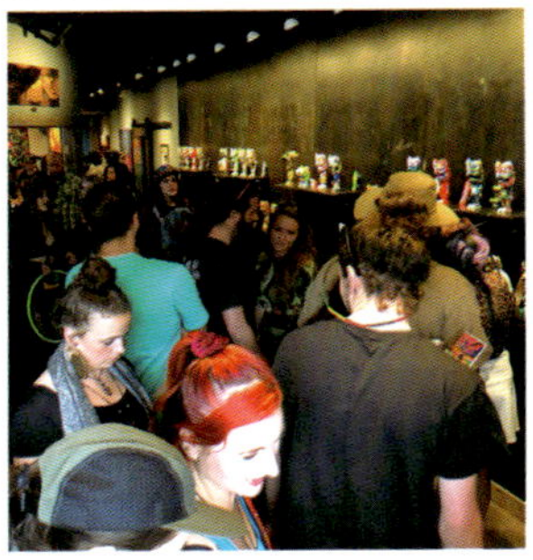

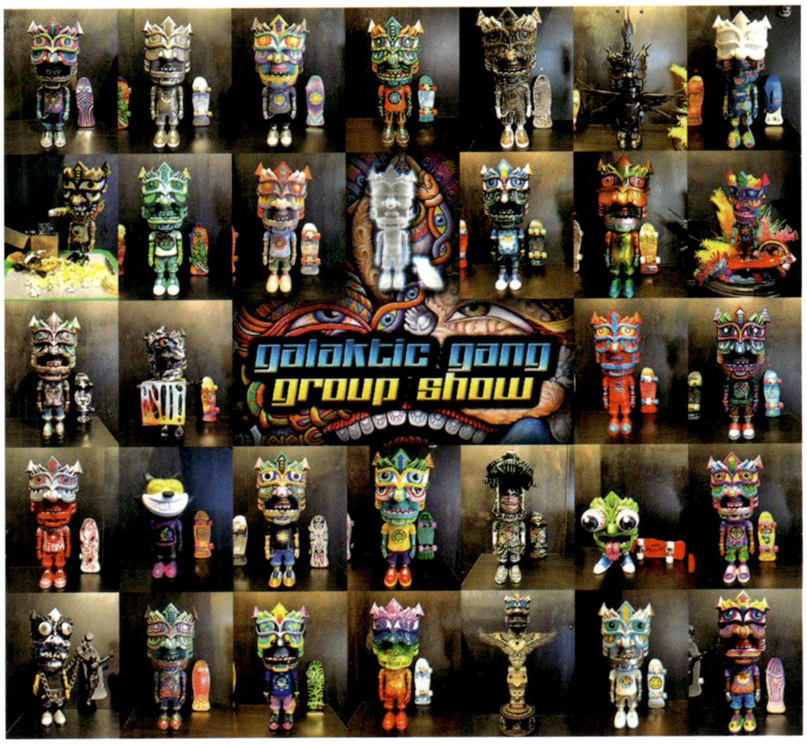

DIGITAL SCULPTURES

Here are some collaborations with digital artists that sculpt my art on their computers for different offerings!

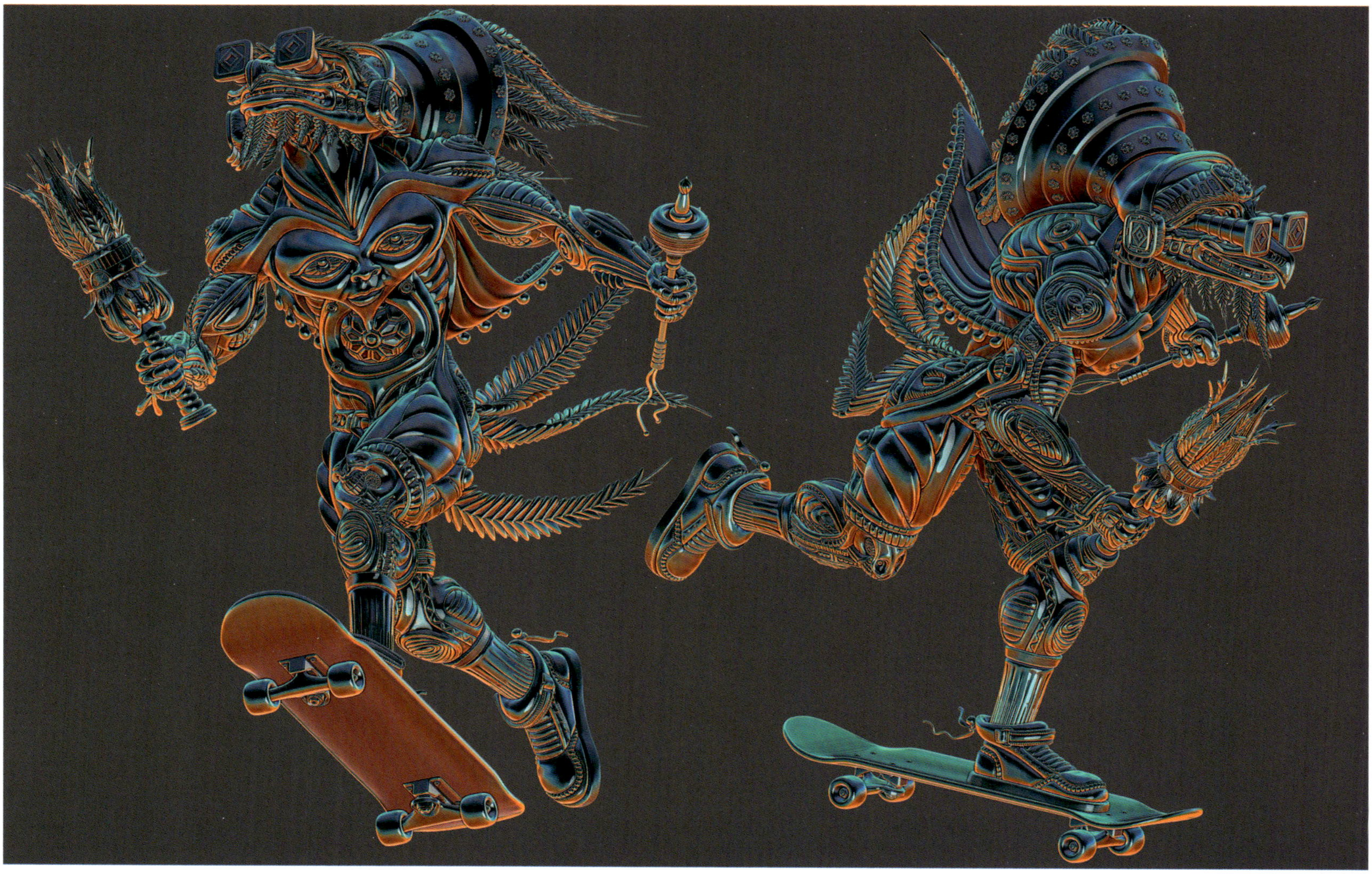

"Keep Pushing Forward" 3D Sculpt by **Hexsual**, 2023

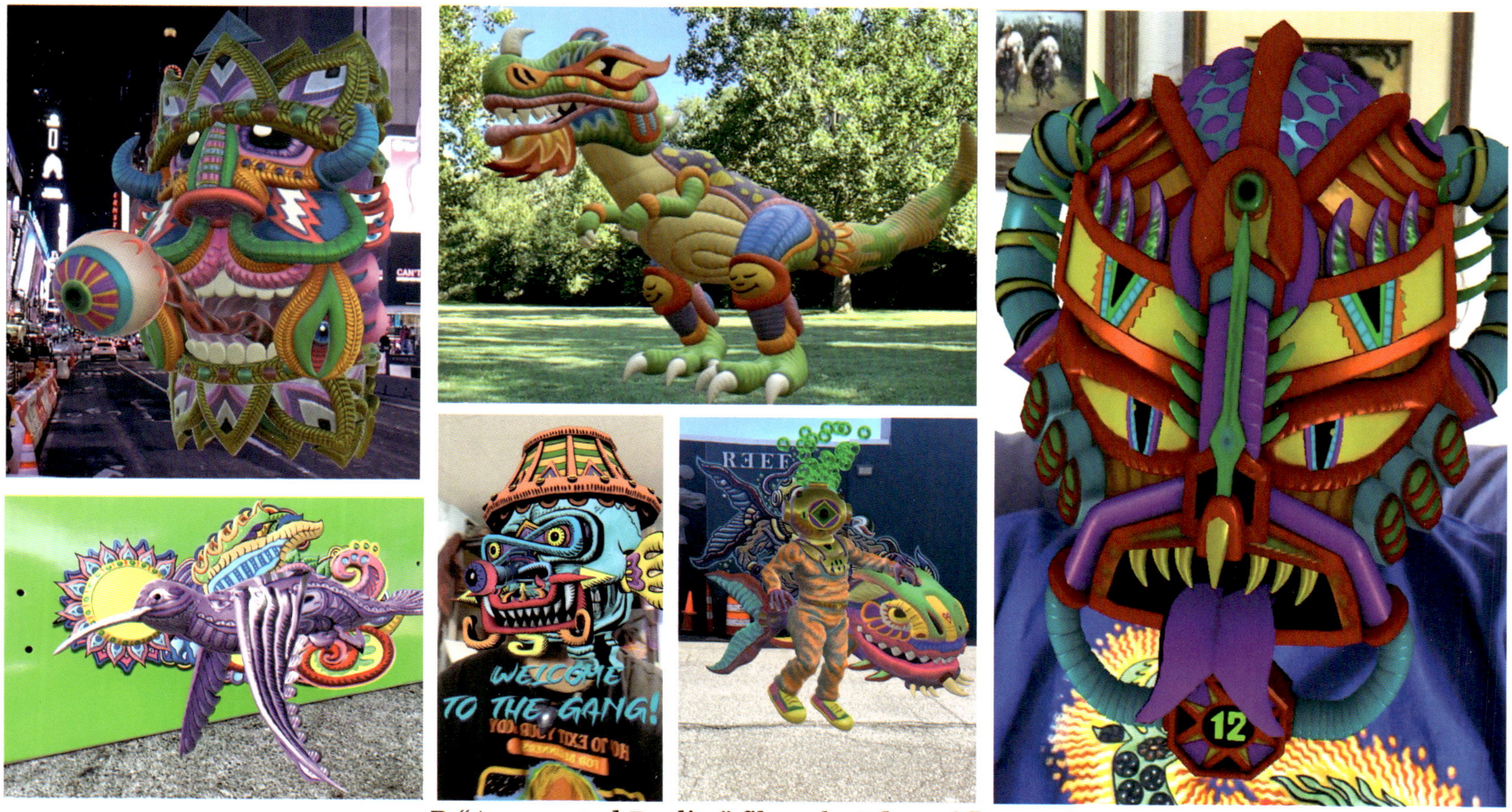

3D "Augmented Reality" filters by **Electrifly**, 2018-22

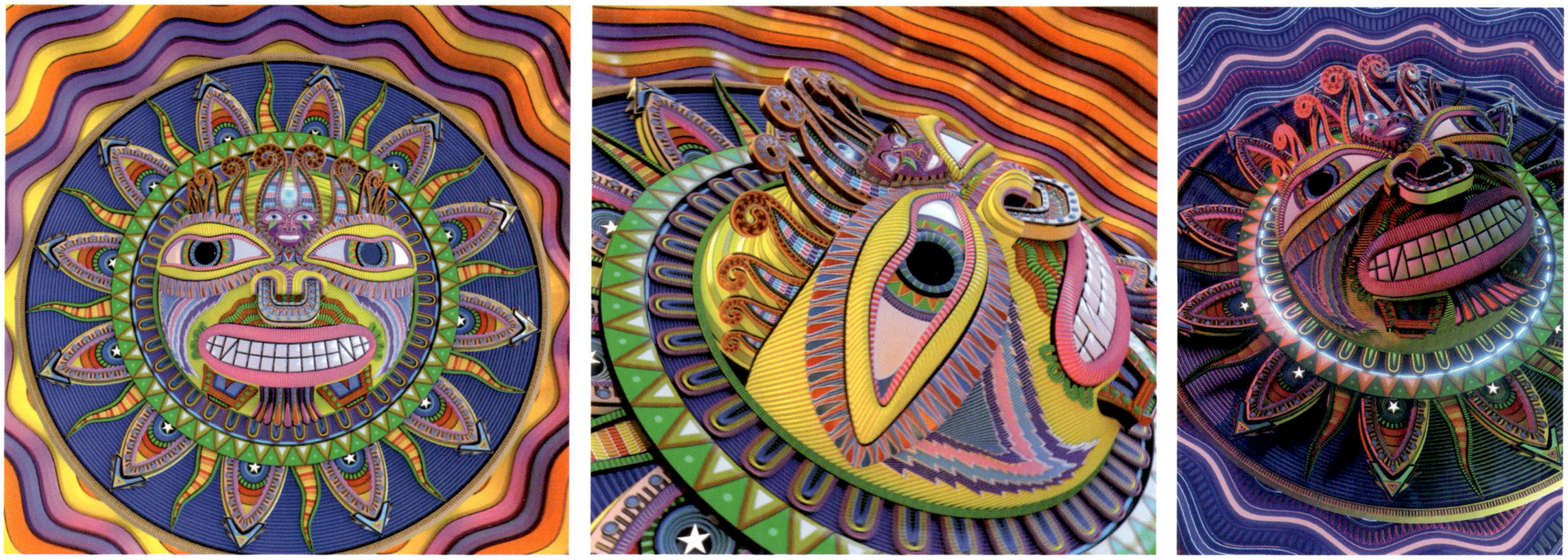

"**Taita Inti**" NFT with a 3D animation by **Hexsual** and music by **Chancha via Circuito**, 2022

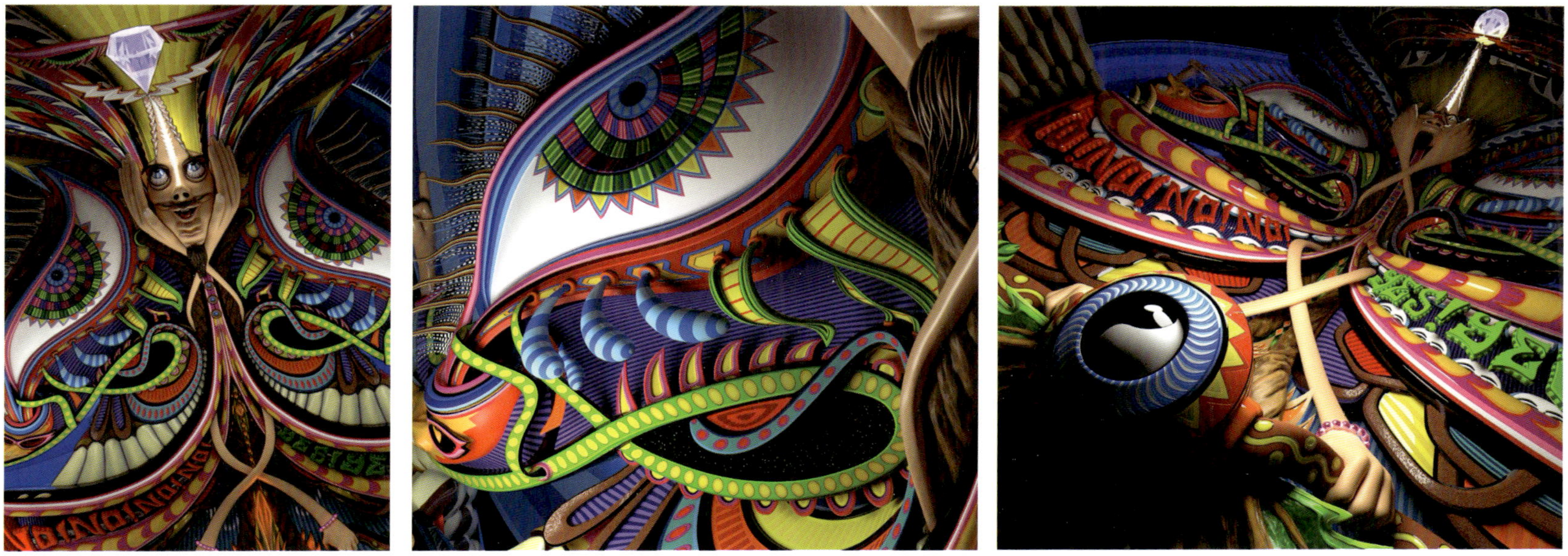

"**Apotheosis**" NFT with a 3D animation by **Hexsual** and music by **Roots of Creation**, 2024

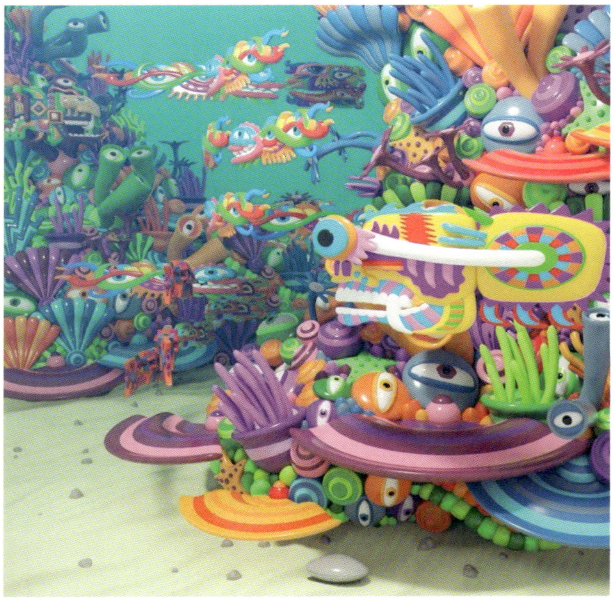

Above: "**Fishbomb Pond**"
3D animation by **Keana Sears, 2023**

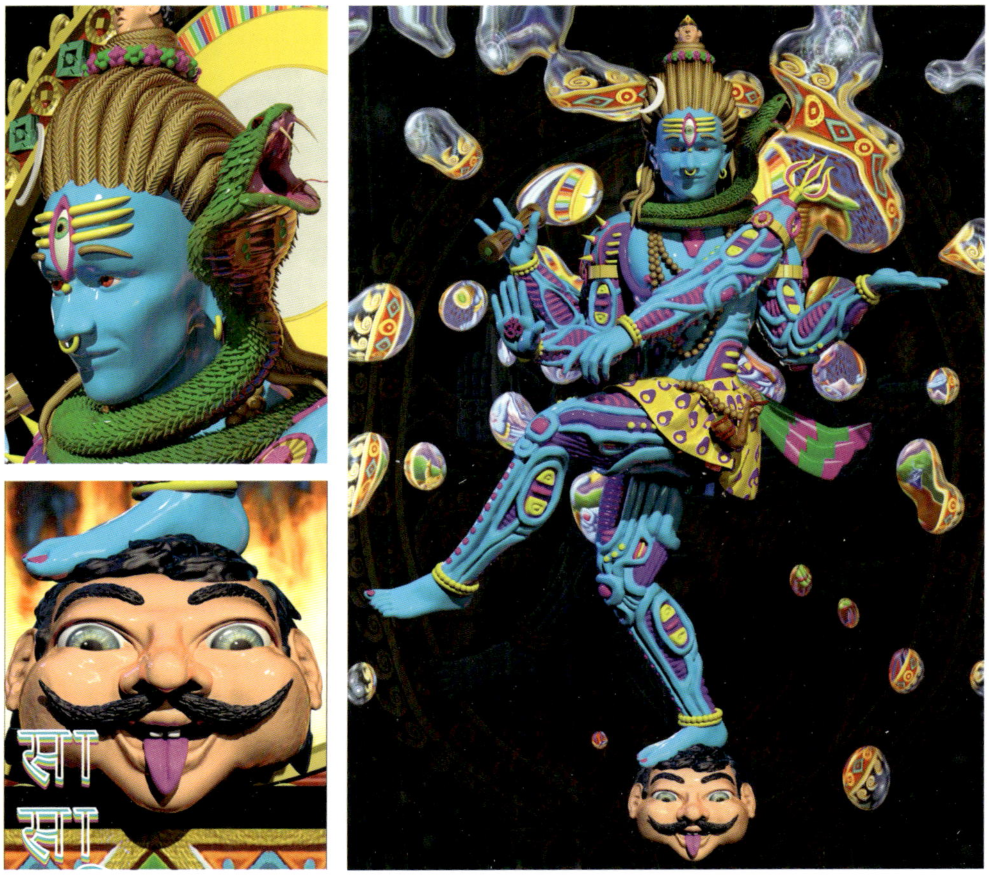

Right: "**Nataraja Shiva**"
NFT with 3D animation by **Zip Visuals**,
and Music by **MC Yogi**, 2021

GLASS SCULPTURES

Though I have never learnt how to sculpt with Glass myself, I have made so many friends in that fun artistic community, that it became natural to have these talented sculptors collaborate with my images! Hope you will get high from one of these unique pieces by Masters of that scene!

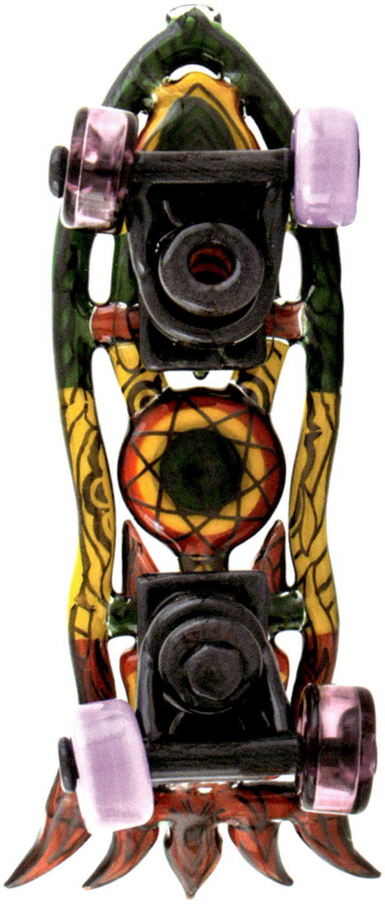

"Cosmic Skate Pipe" by **Tristan Hodges,** 2017

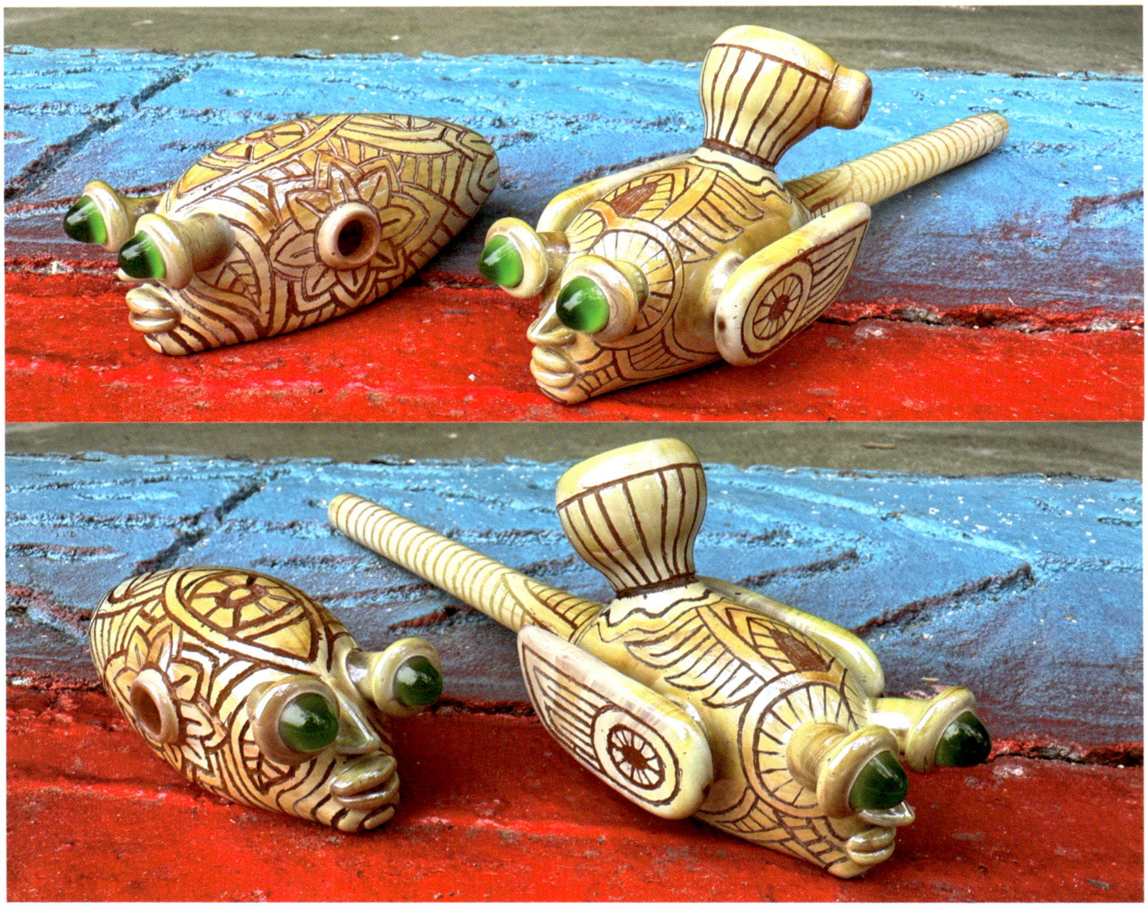

"Heady Mamas" caving over pipes by **Banjo Glass,** 2024

"CHRIS' VIBRANT ART AND LOVING SPIRIT ARE ABSOLUTELY INSEPARABLE AND HAVE BEEN A MAJOR INSPIRATION TO MY CREATIVE PATH FOR MANY YEARS. HE HAS A PURE HEART. THE HONESTY OF HIS SOUL'S EXPRESSIONS RIPPLE OUT ENDLESSLY INTO INFINITY BOTH AS MEDICINE AND AS A BEACON TO ALL SEEKERS OF LOVE AND TRUTH." -BANJO, ARTIST

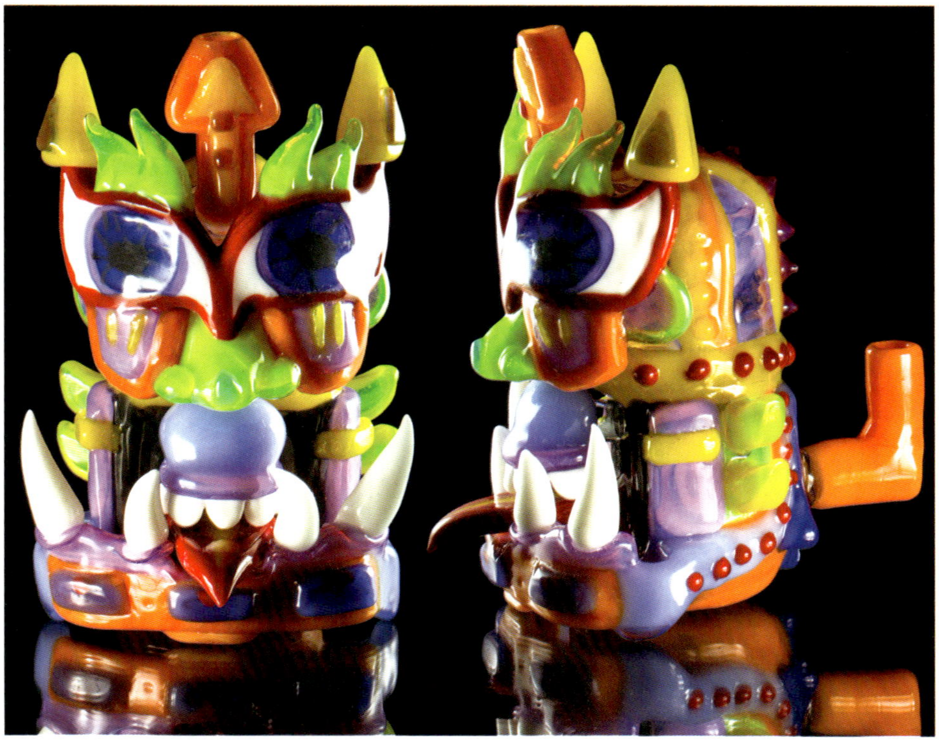

"Fukushima Galaktic Dude" by **Oak Locoboro,** 2024

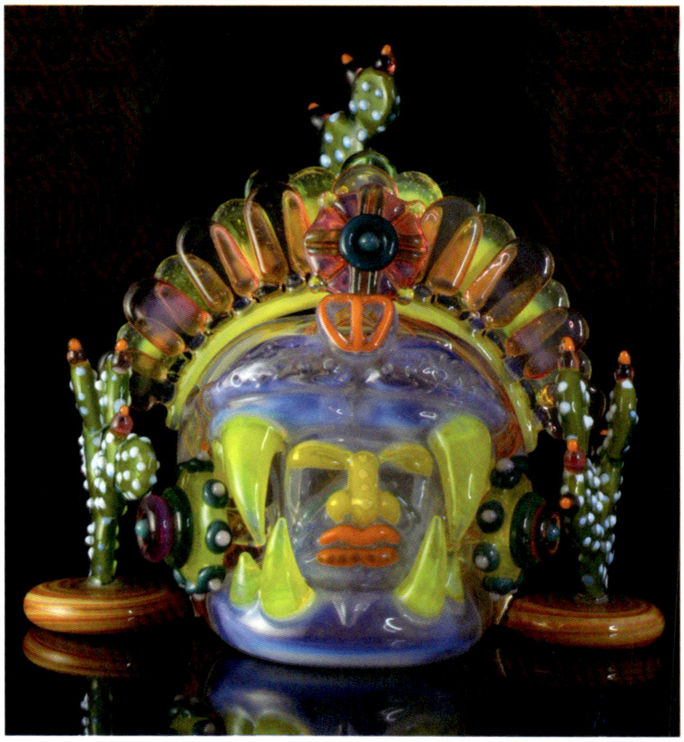

"Pachamago" by **Pinky Brewtz,** 2021

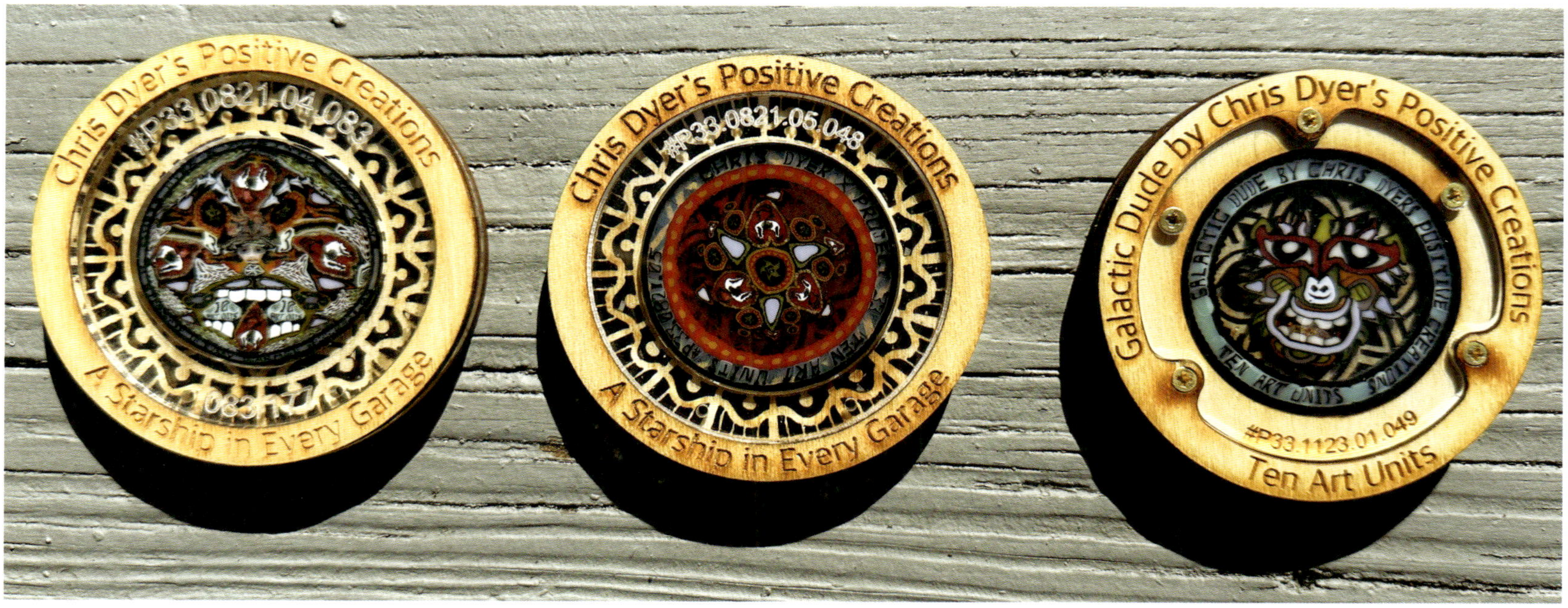

Three different Glass coins of my art created by **Marcel Braun's "Starship in Every Garage"** studios. 2021-23

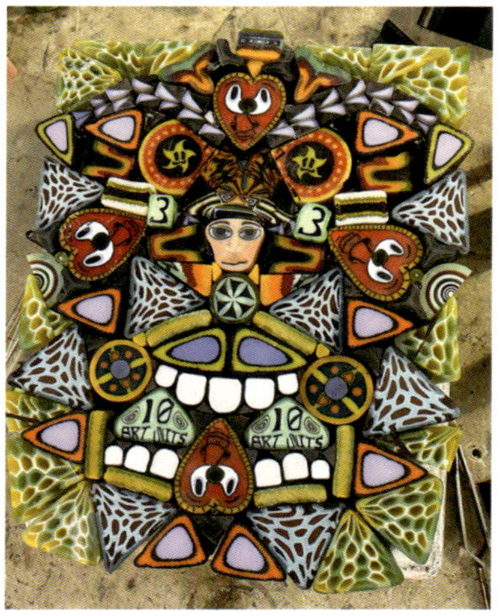

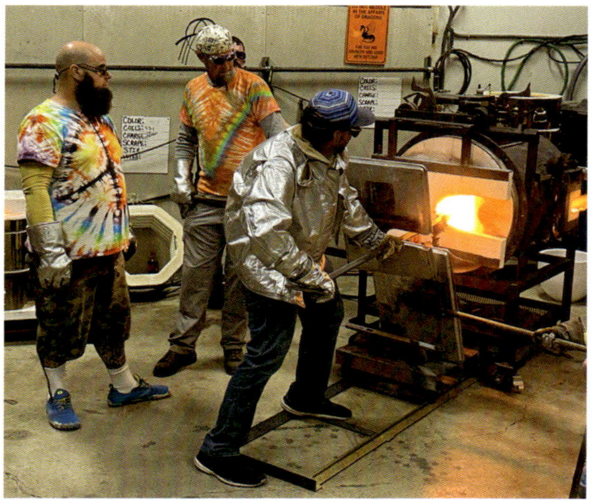

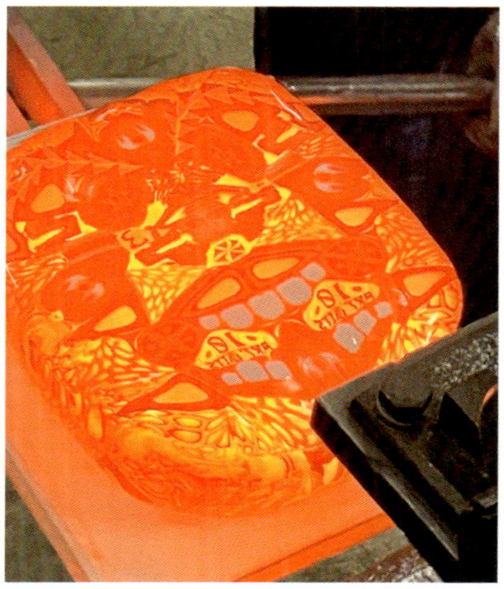

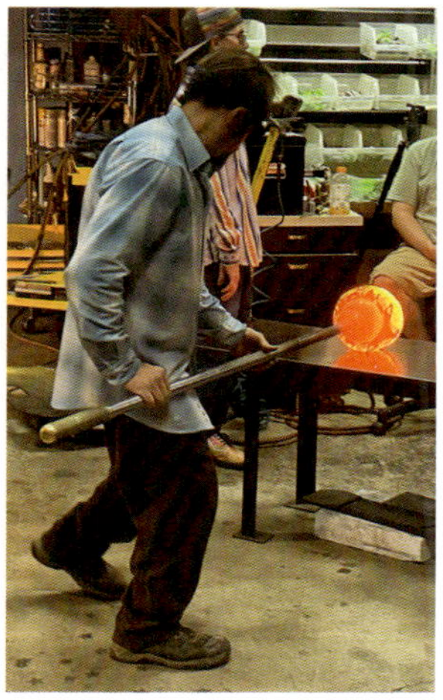

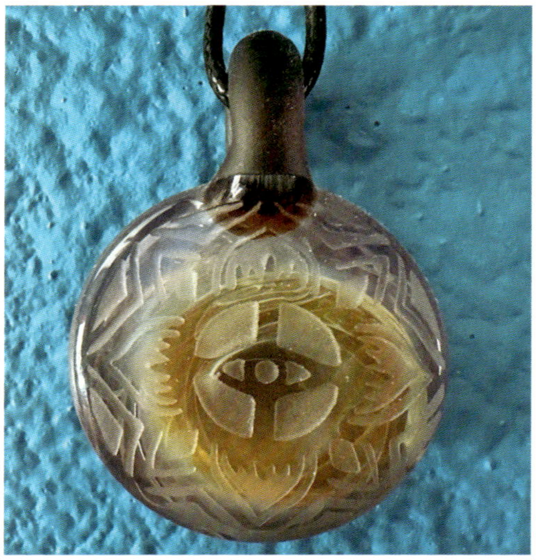

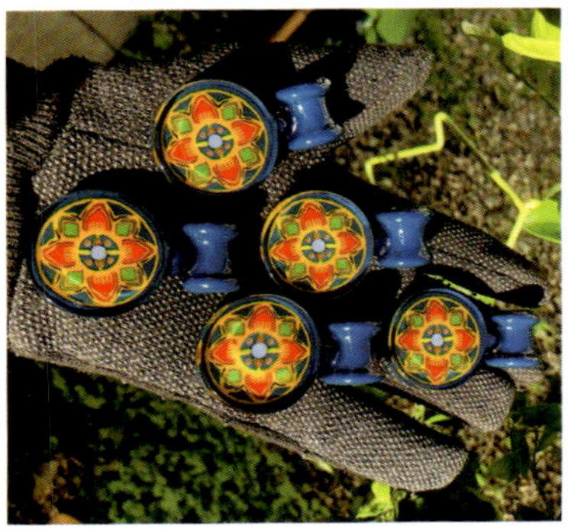

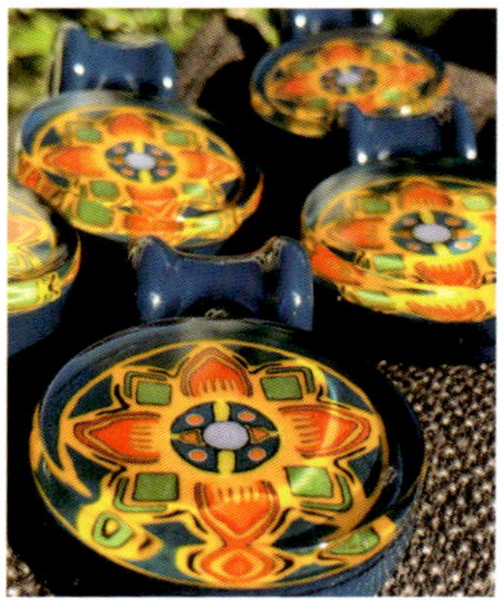

"Positive Creations Pendants"
by **Kyle Morton and Grimm Glass,** 2020

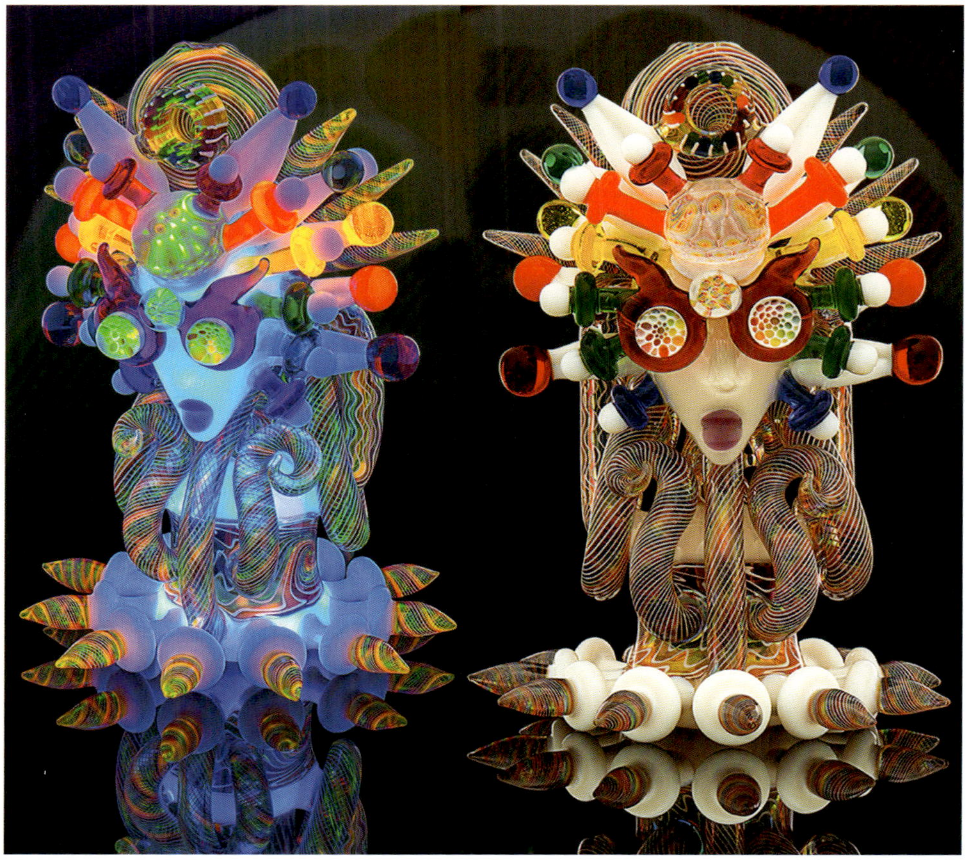

"Rainbro Bright" a dab rig by **LaceFace** and **Karma Glass**,
inspired by my painting "Anchor of Light", 2023

PAINTED OBJECTS

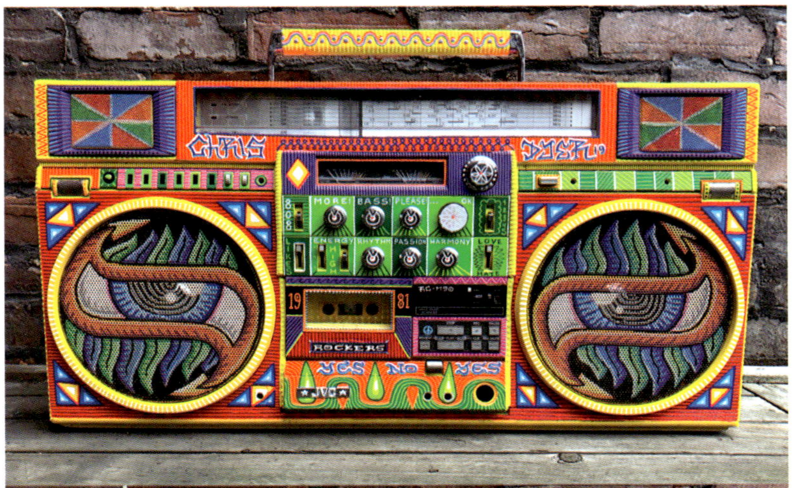

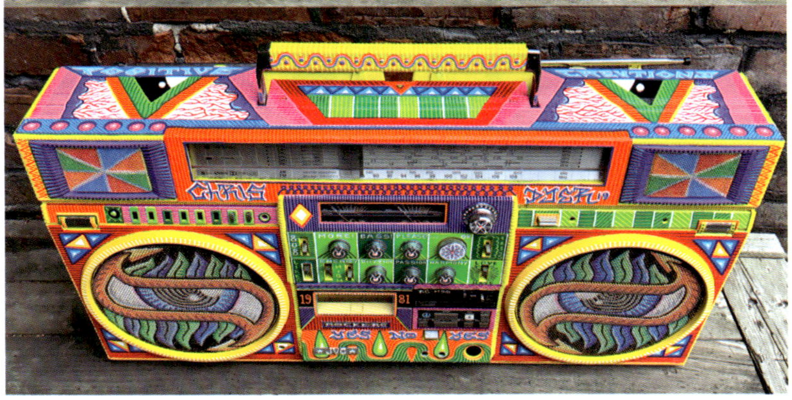

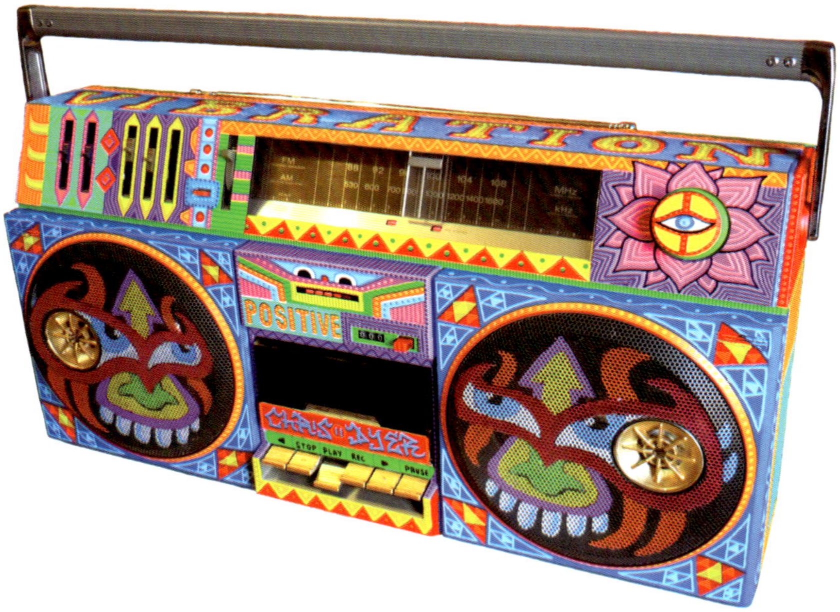

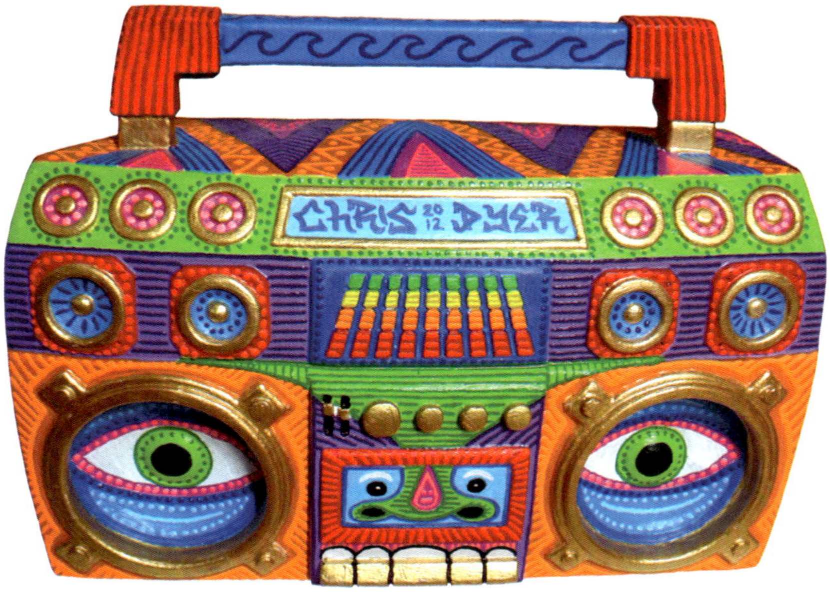

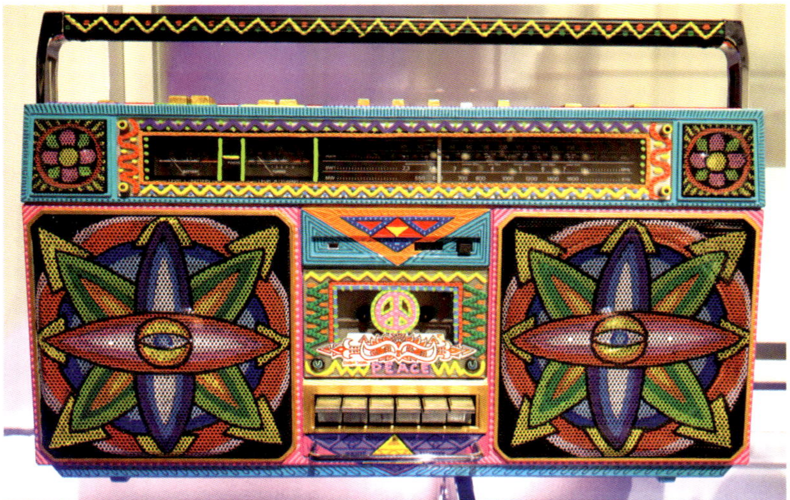

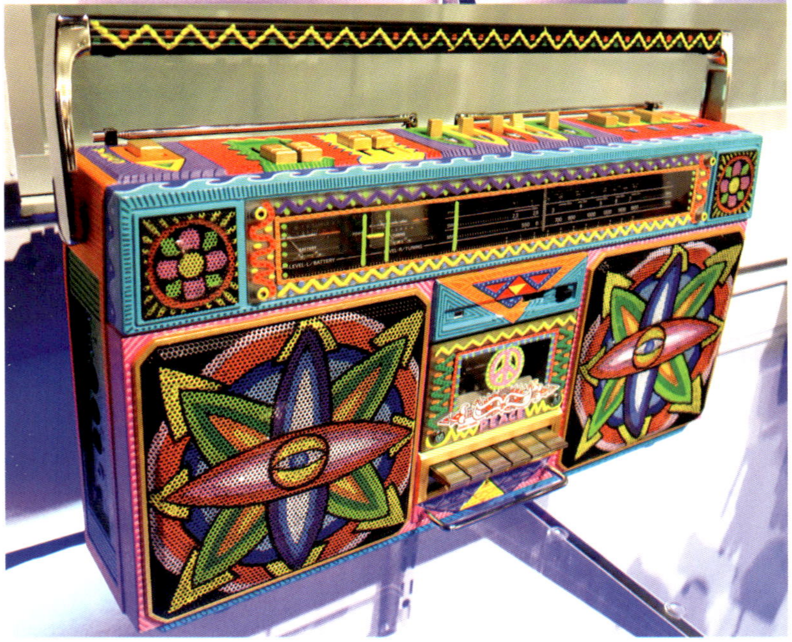

"Painted Boom Boxes"
Acrylics and paint markers, 2011 to 2019
My good friend **Barry Walsh** is a big collector of classic Boom Boxes. Through the years he's sold me some of his pieces, which have such great aesthetics. Most stay in my own personal collection, but a few end up with a funky paint job! Here some of my favorite ones! I Love art that plays music!

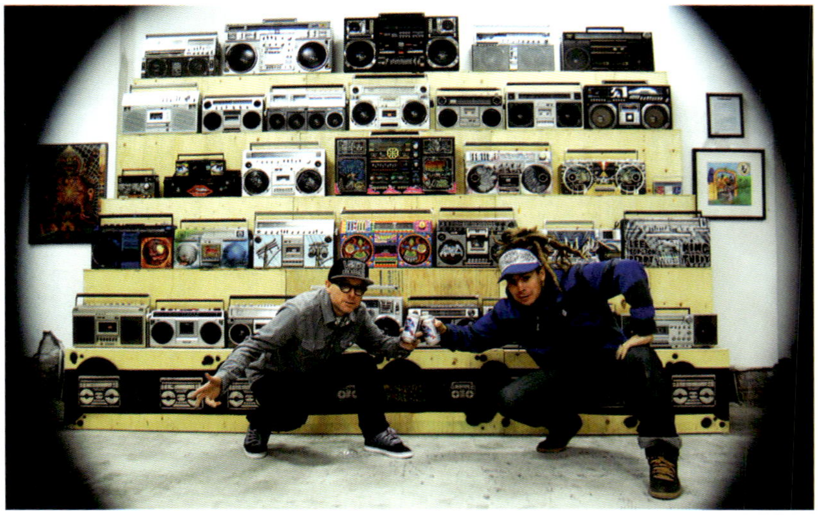

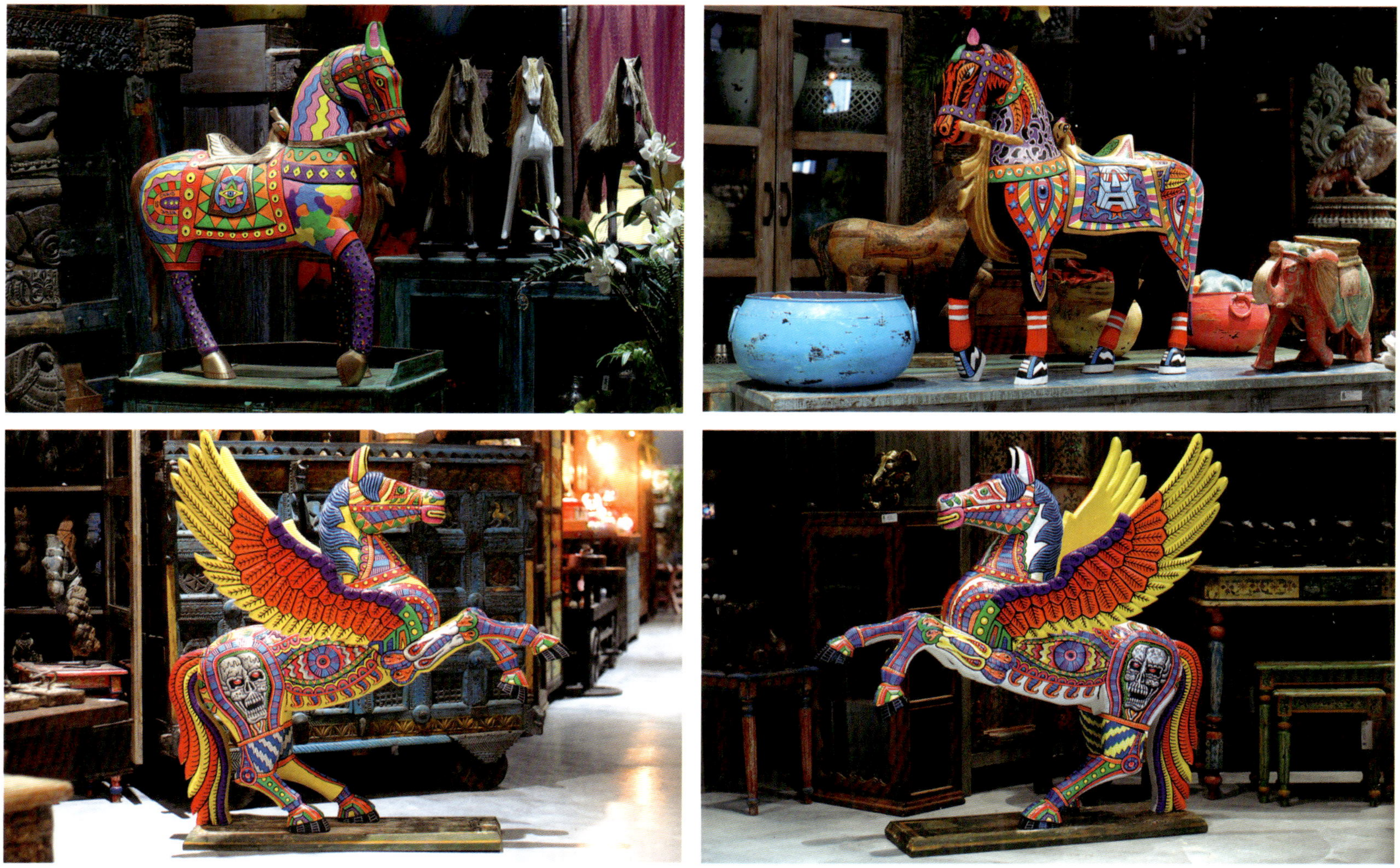

"High Horses"Acrylics and paint markers on wooden sculptures, 2015 to 2018

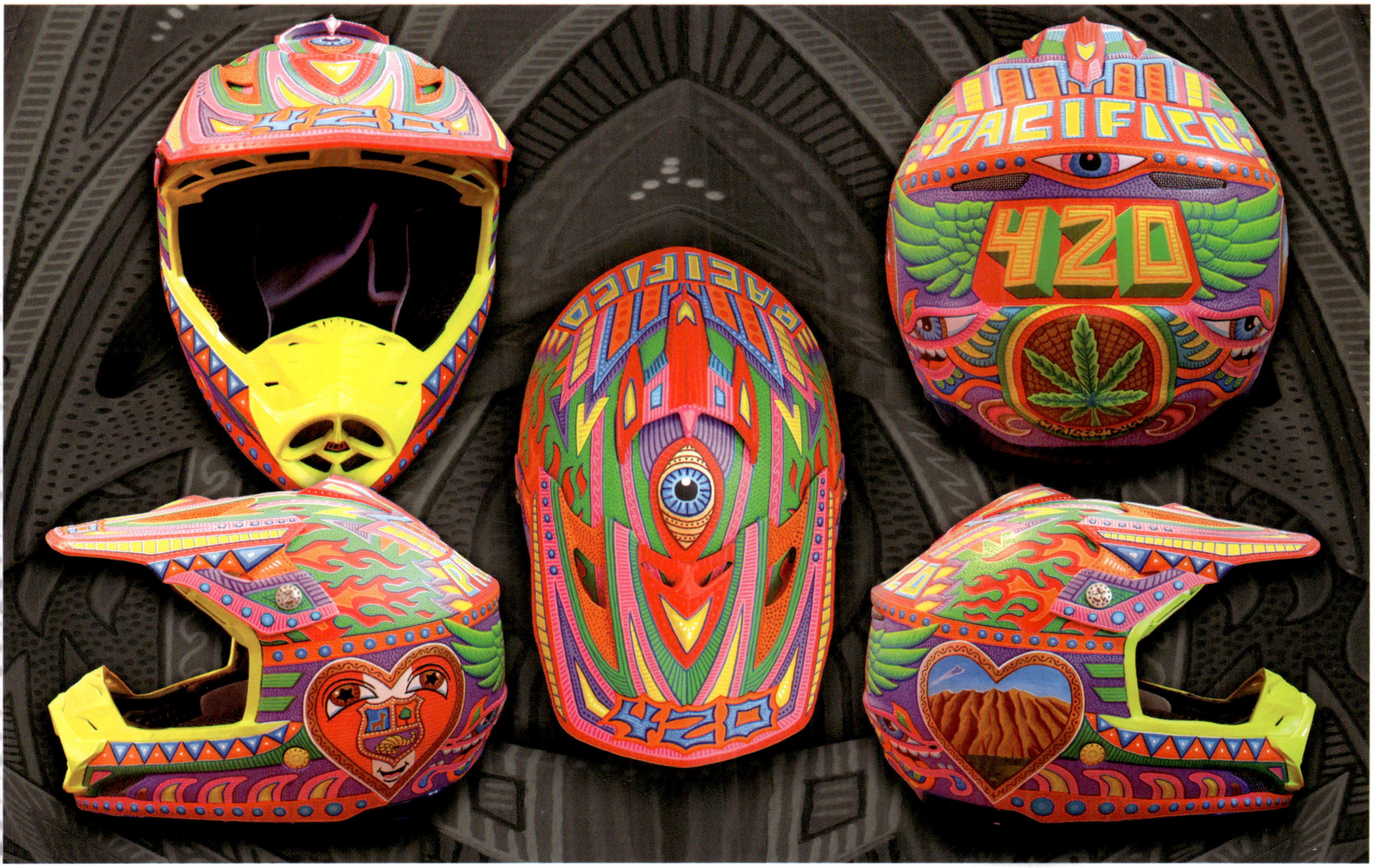

"Pacifico 420" Acrylics on Bike Helmet, 2014

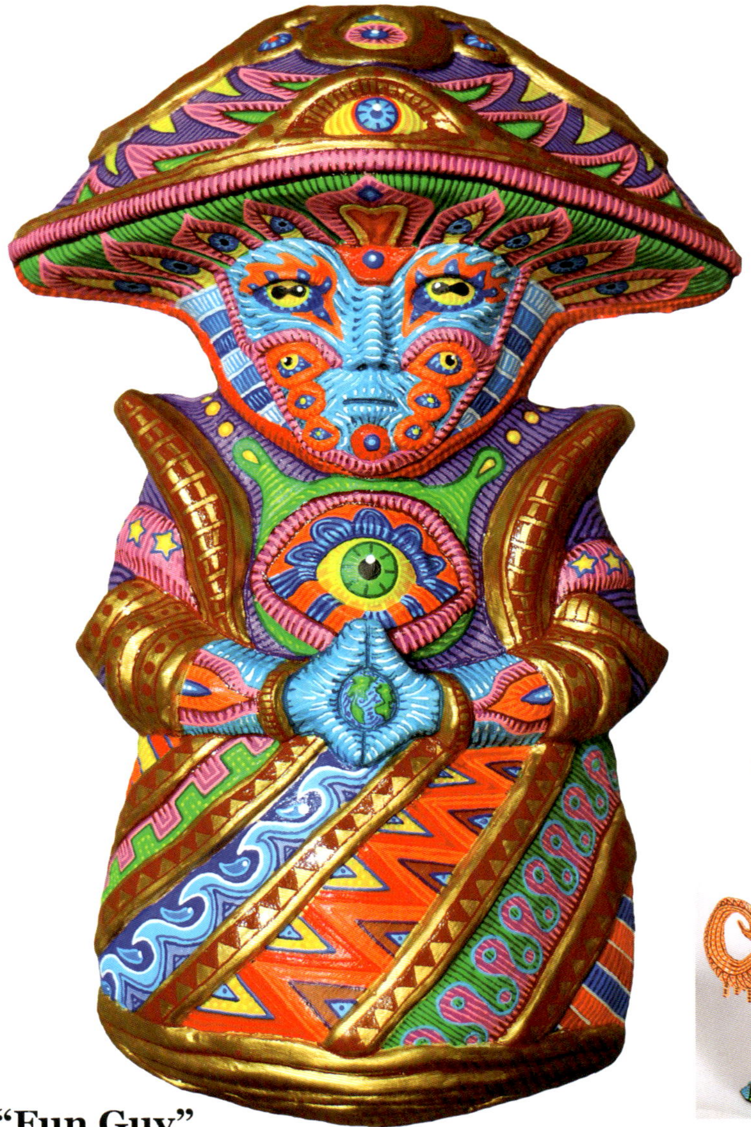

"Fun Guy"
Acrylics on plaster sculpture by **John Shook**, 2017

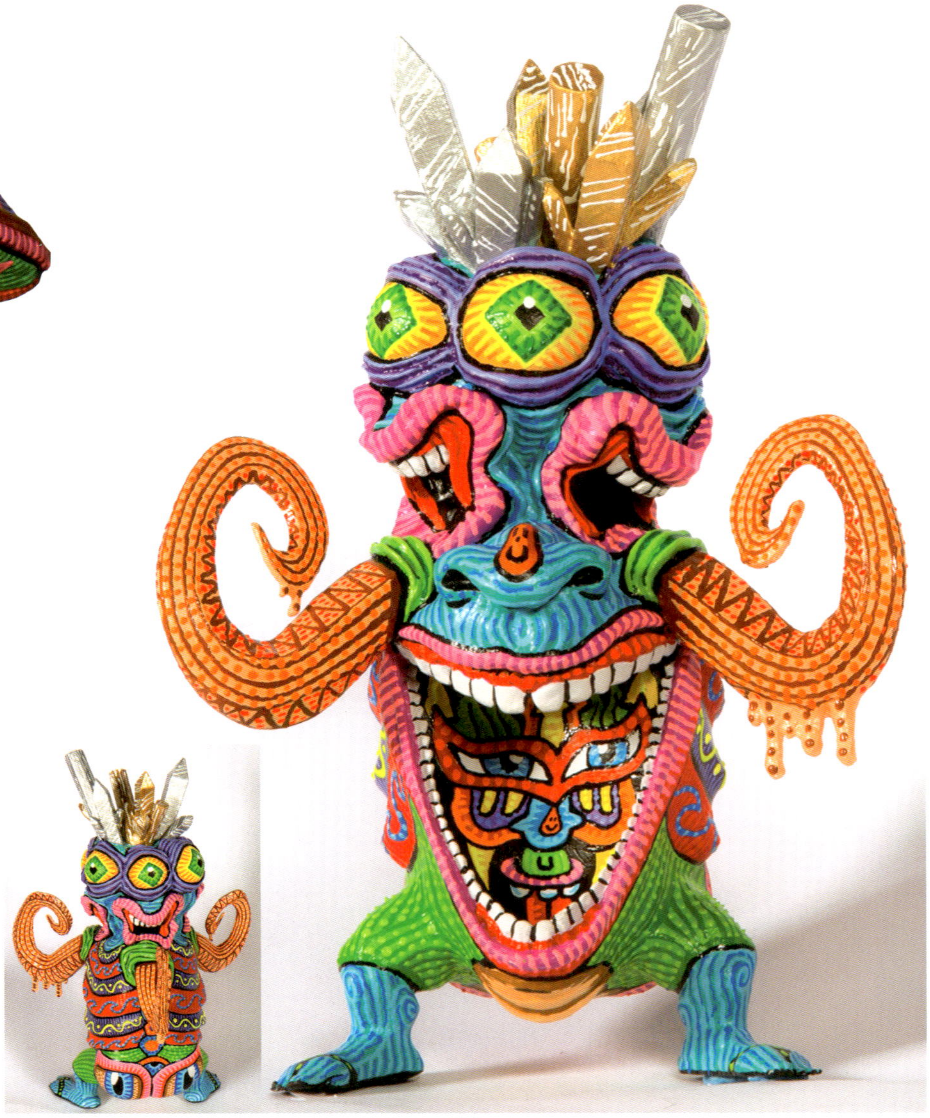

"Crystal God"
Acrylics on vinyl sculpture
by **Aaron Brooks**, 2017

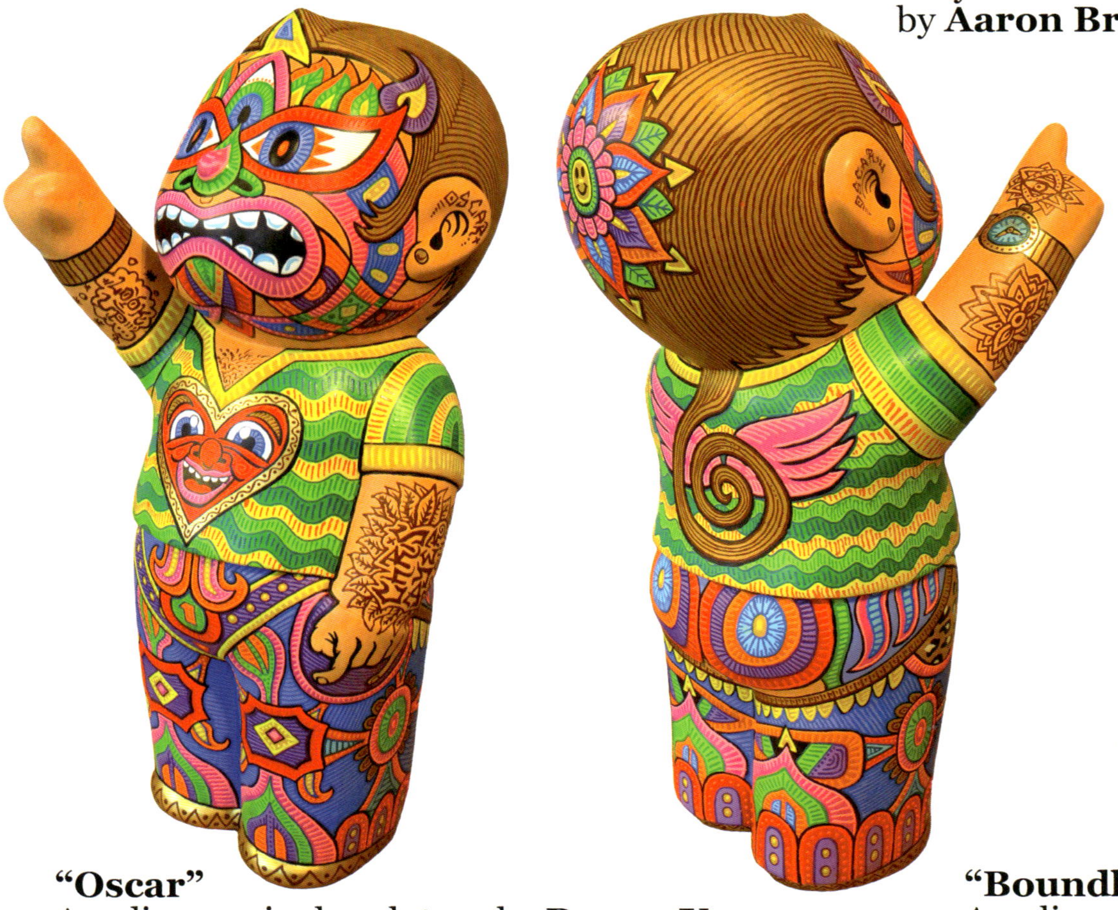

"Oscar"
Acrylics on vinyl sculpture by **Danny Yung**, 2015

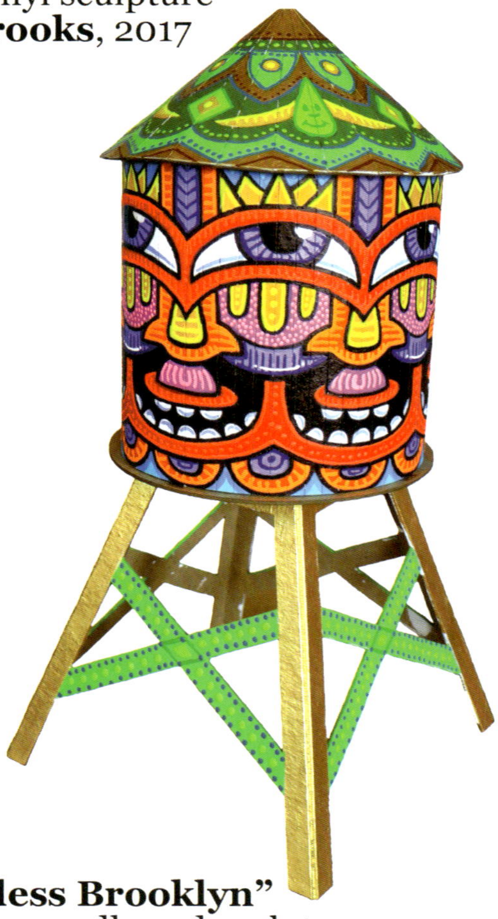

"Boundless Brooklyn"
Acrylics on cardboard sculpture, 2014

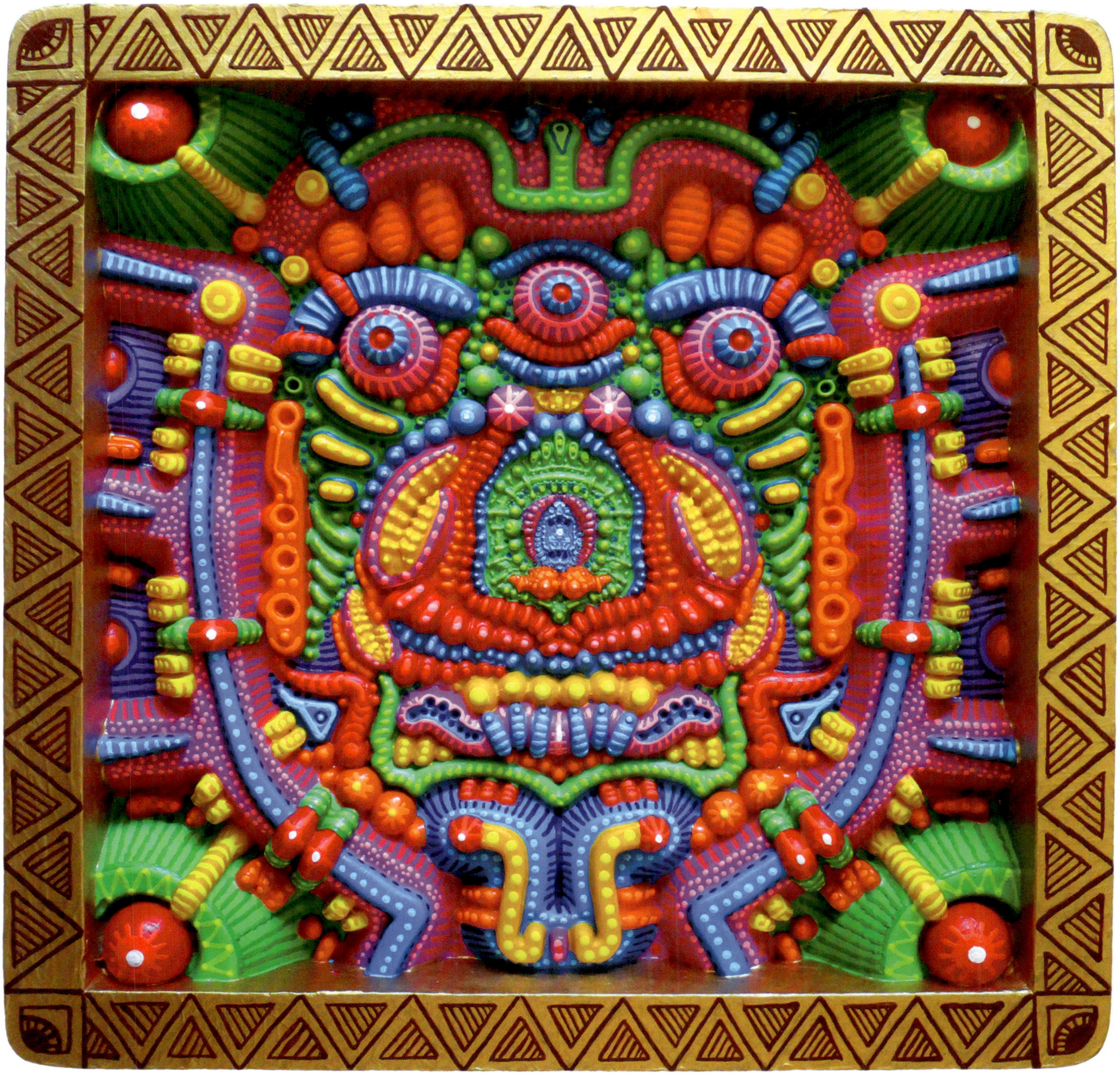

"Space Cake" Acrylics on vinyl sculpture by **Ben Ridgeway**, 2015

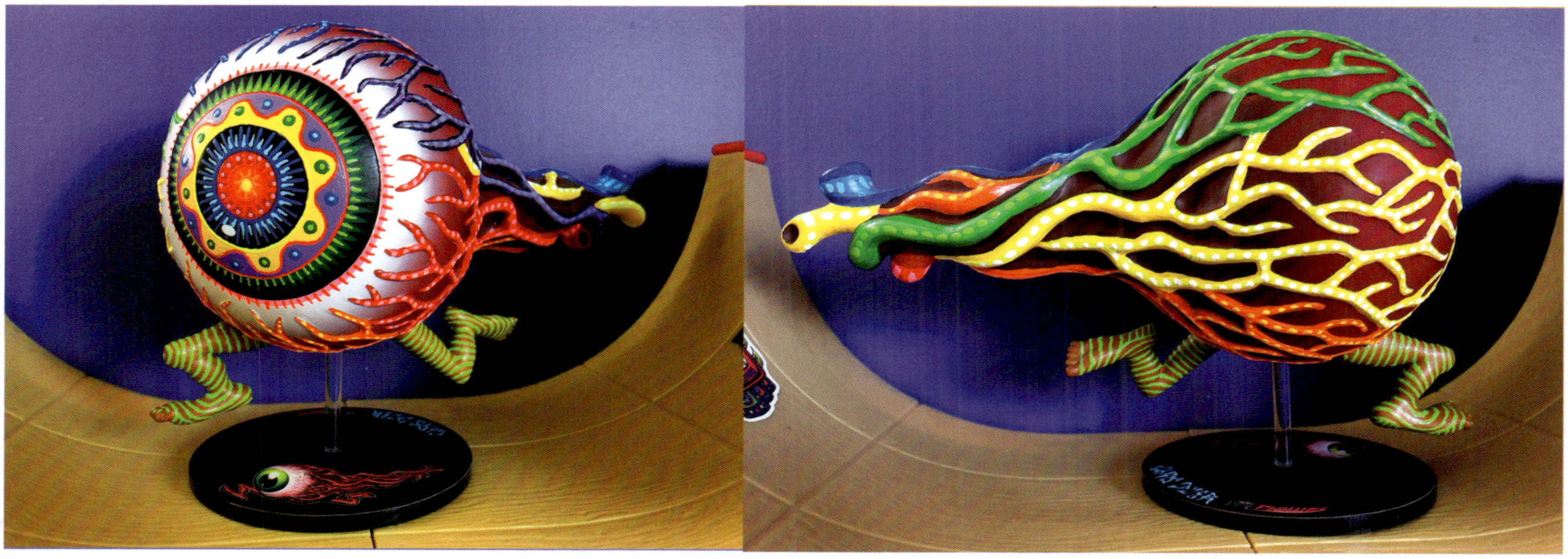

"Running Eye" Acrylics on vinyl sculpture by **Jim Phillips**, 2019

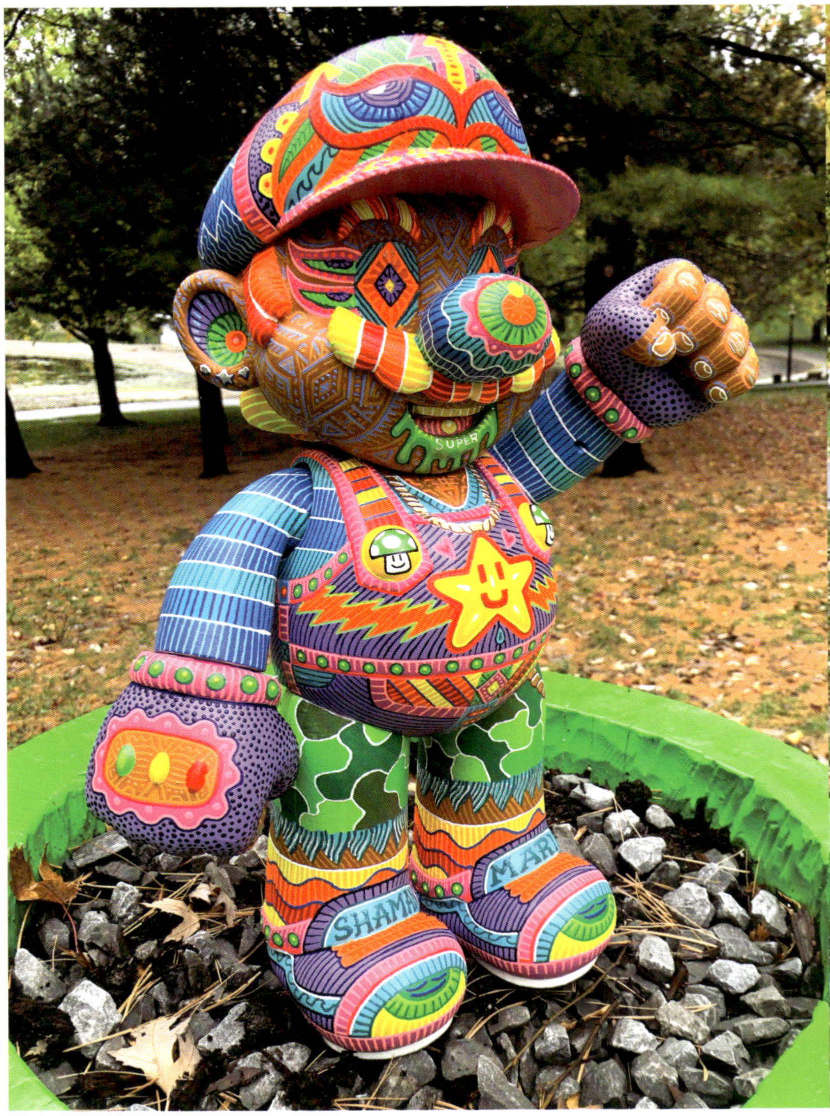

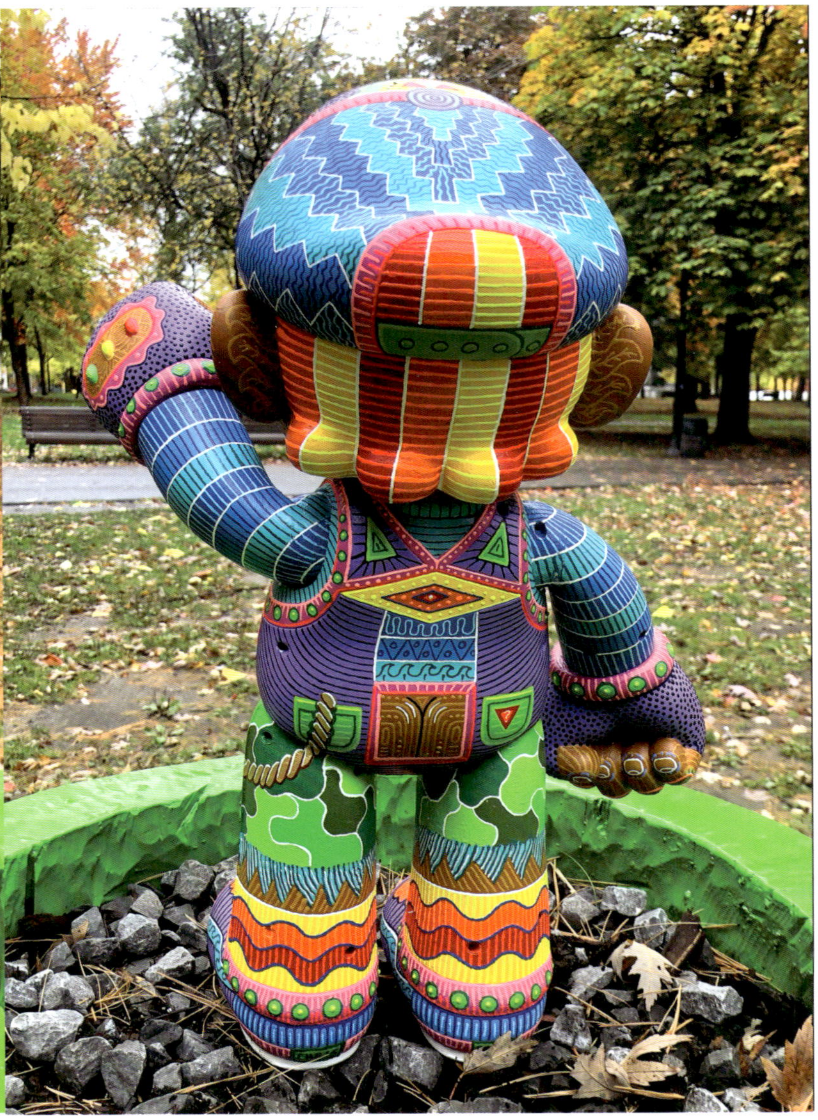

"Shroomed Mario" Acrylics on toy, 2020

"Junkyard Joe"Acrylics on Carousel Pony, 2020

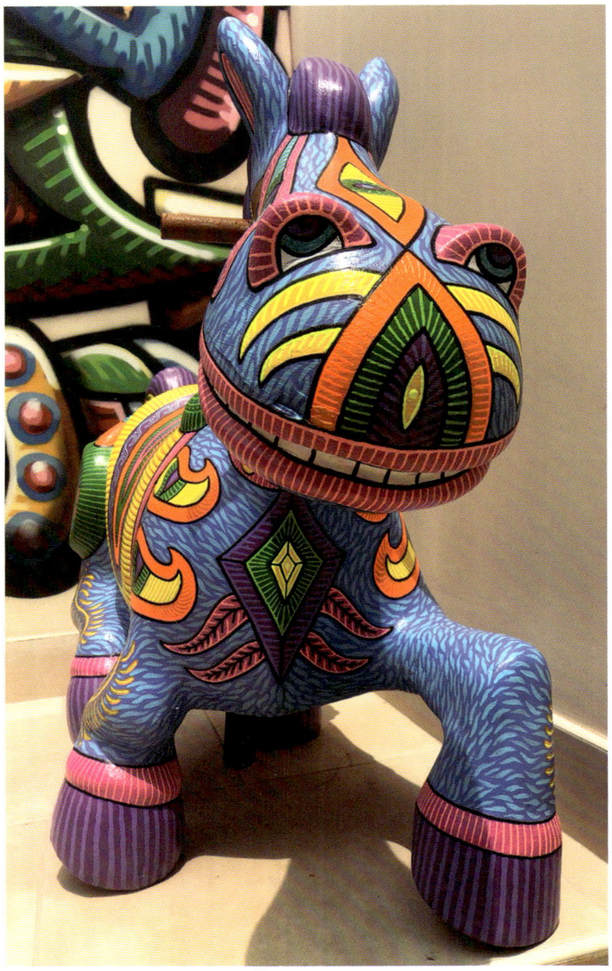

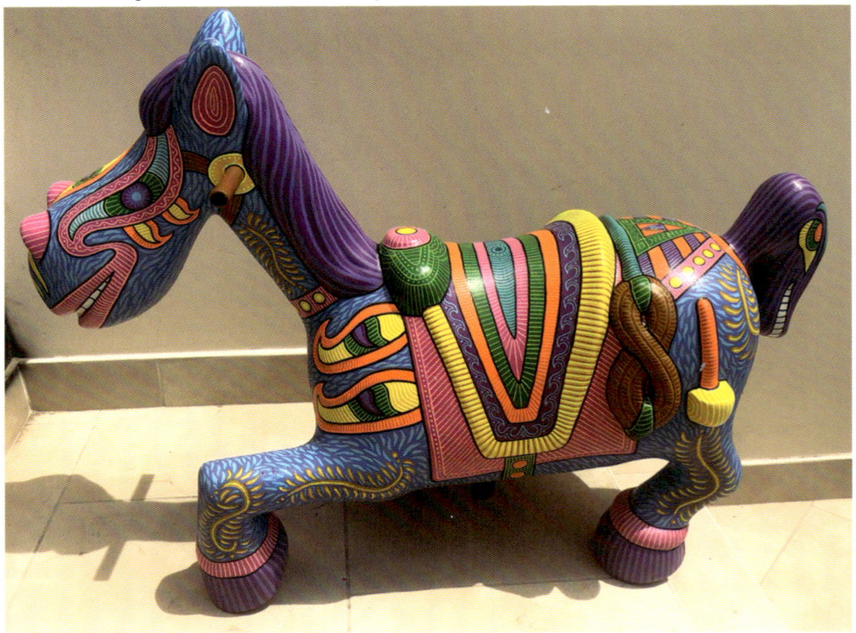

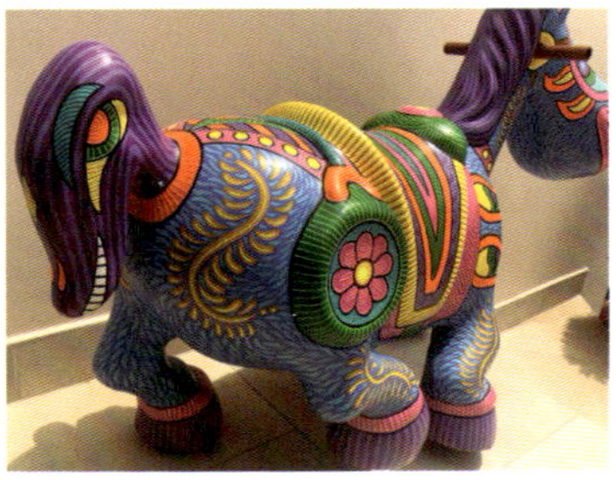

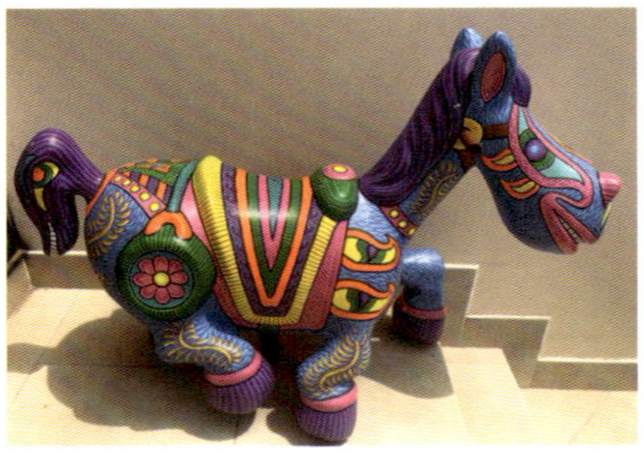

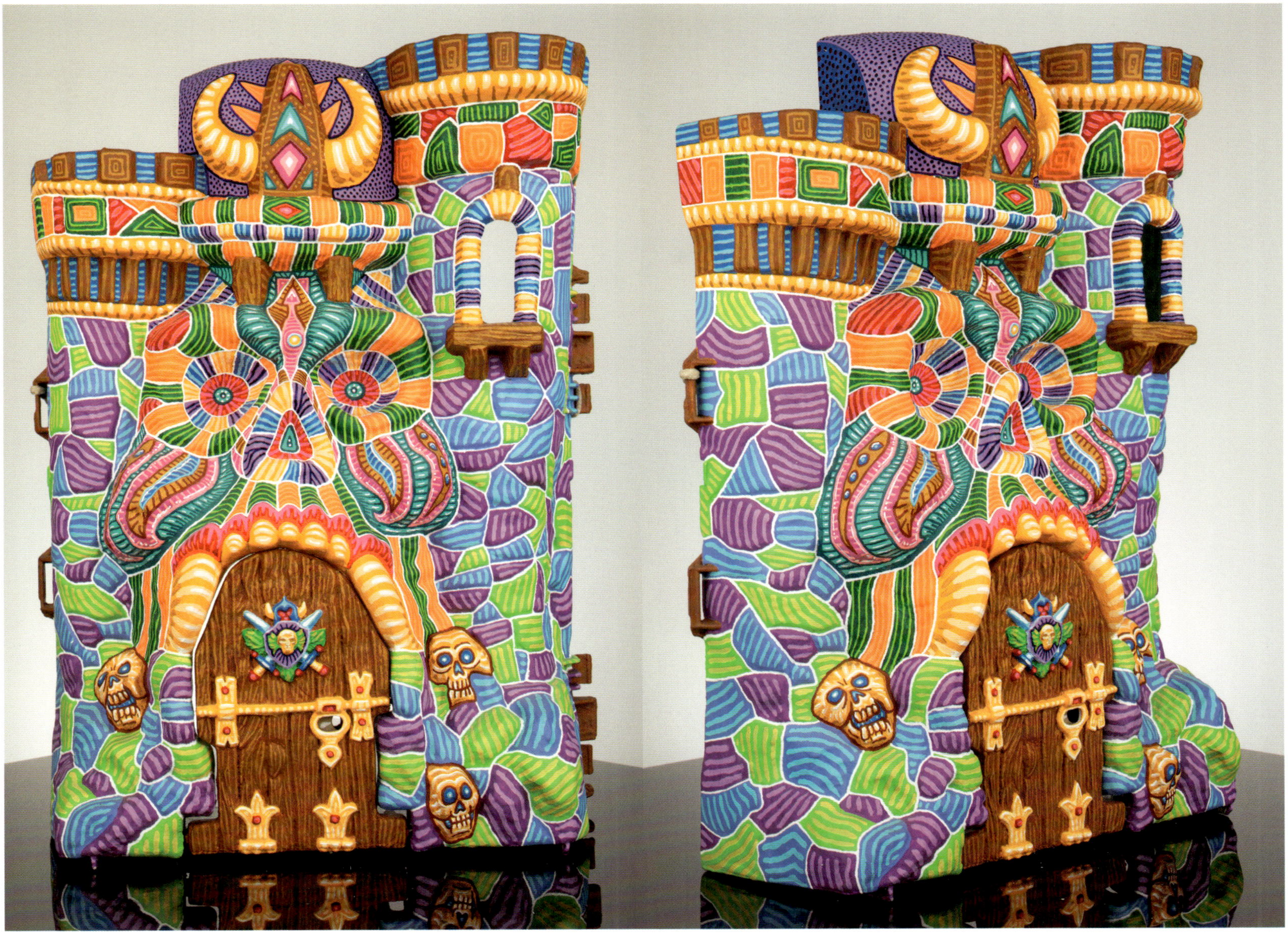

“Castle Rainbow-Skull” Acrylics on 80’s Plastic Toy, 2021

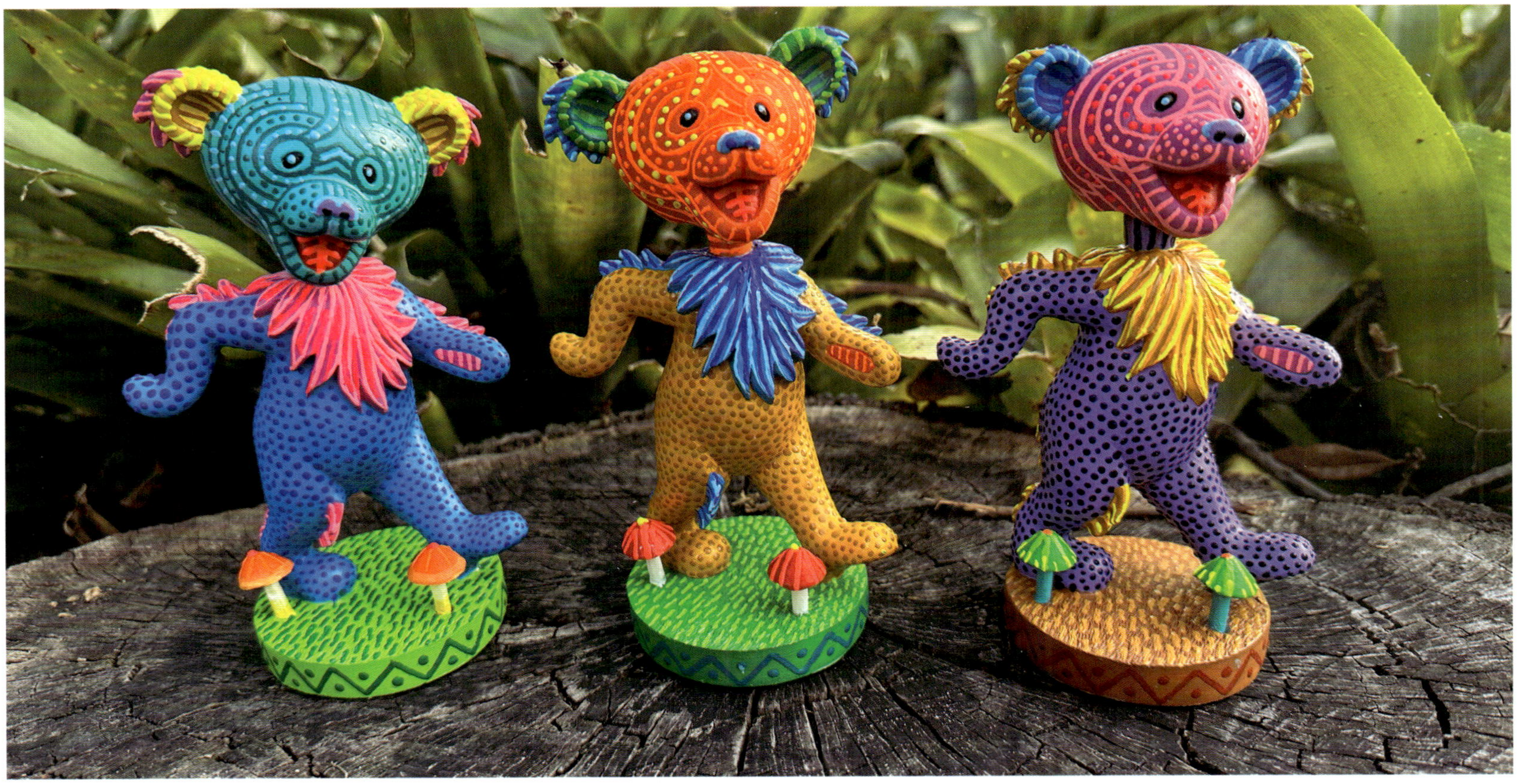

“Trippin’ Bears” Acrylics on Bobble-heads, 2023

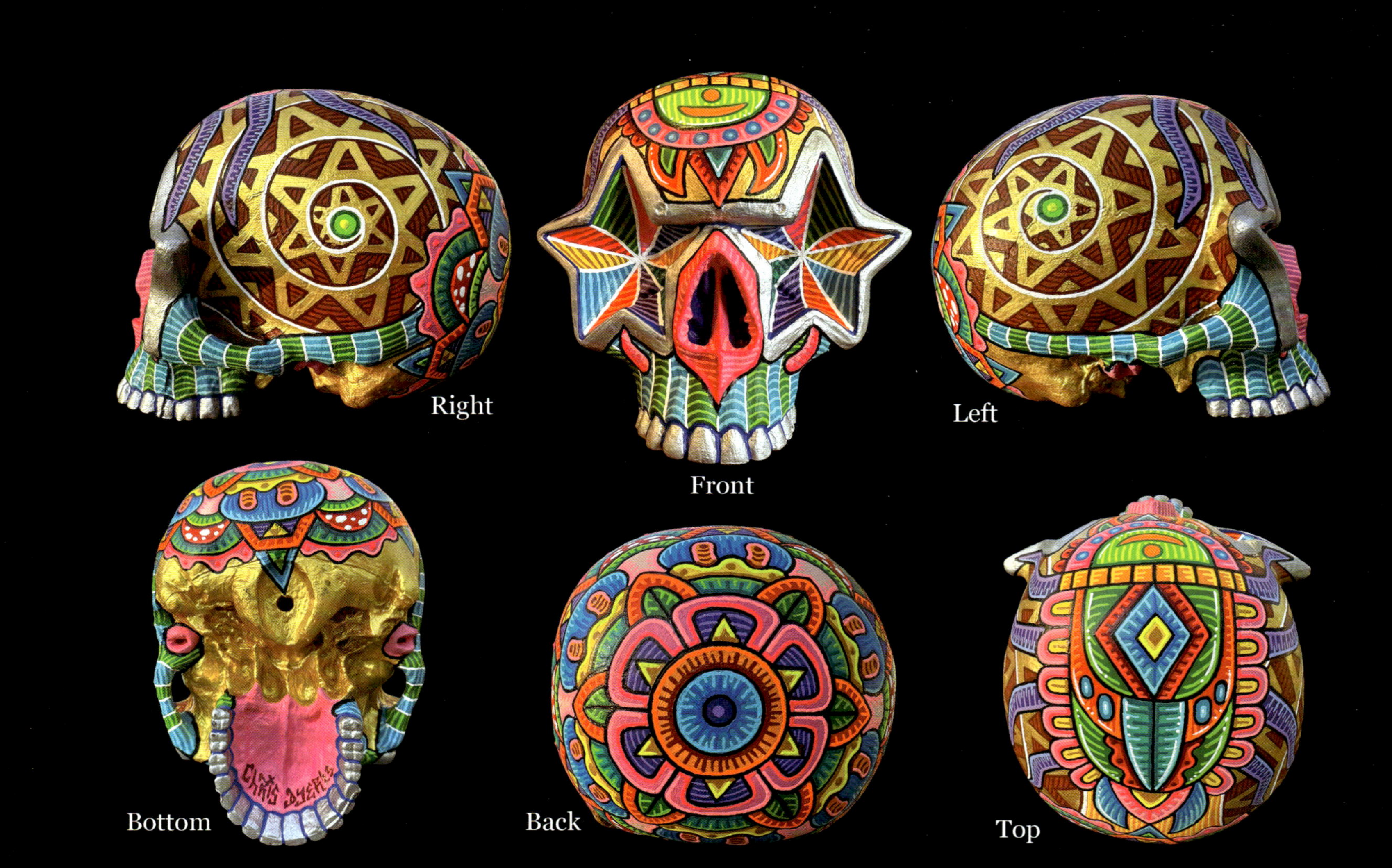

"Activated Star Skull" Acrylics on sculpture by **Ron English**, 2023

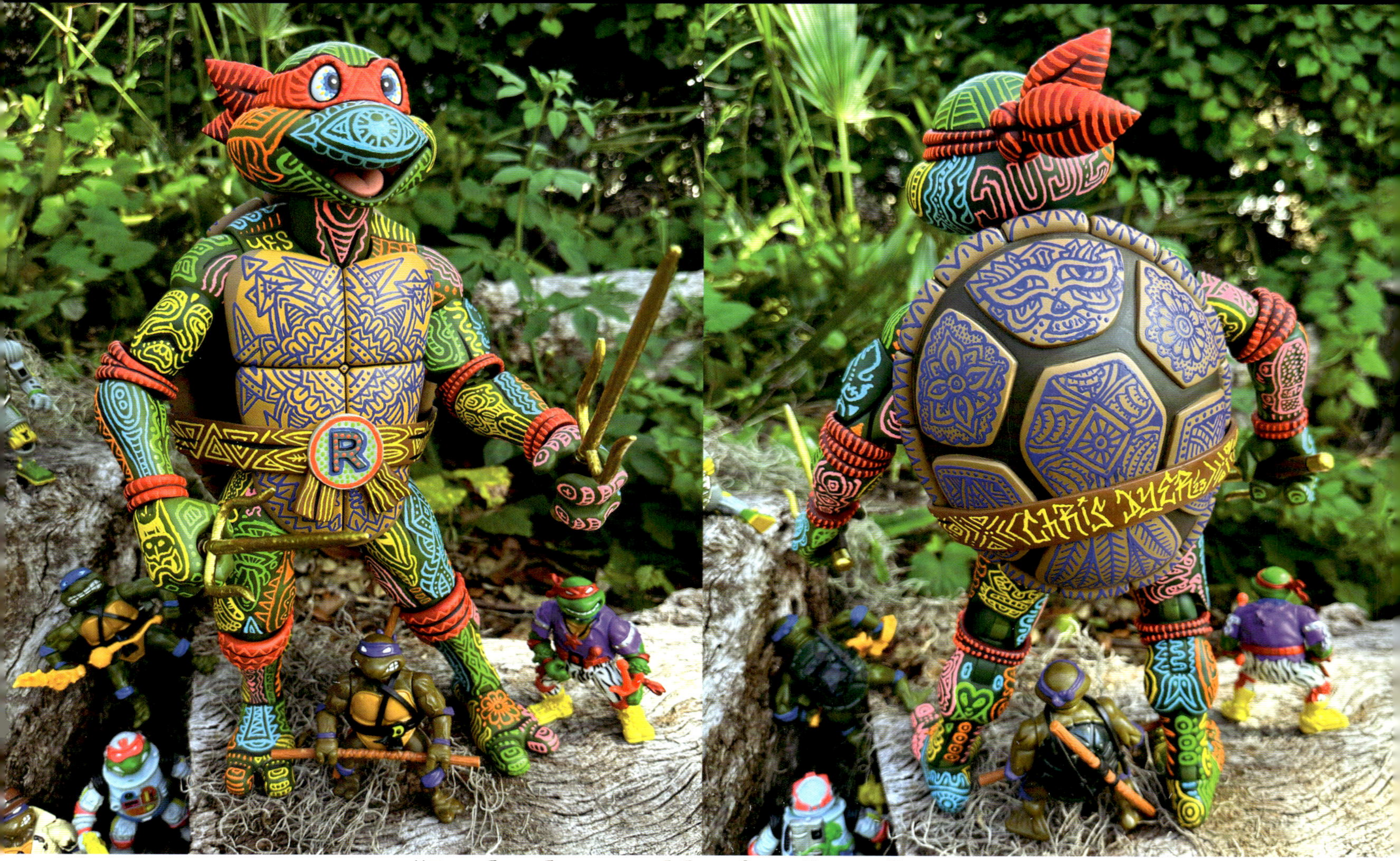

"Raphael on Moldy Pizza" Acrylics on Toy, 2023

SURFBOARDS

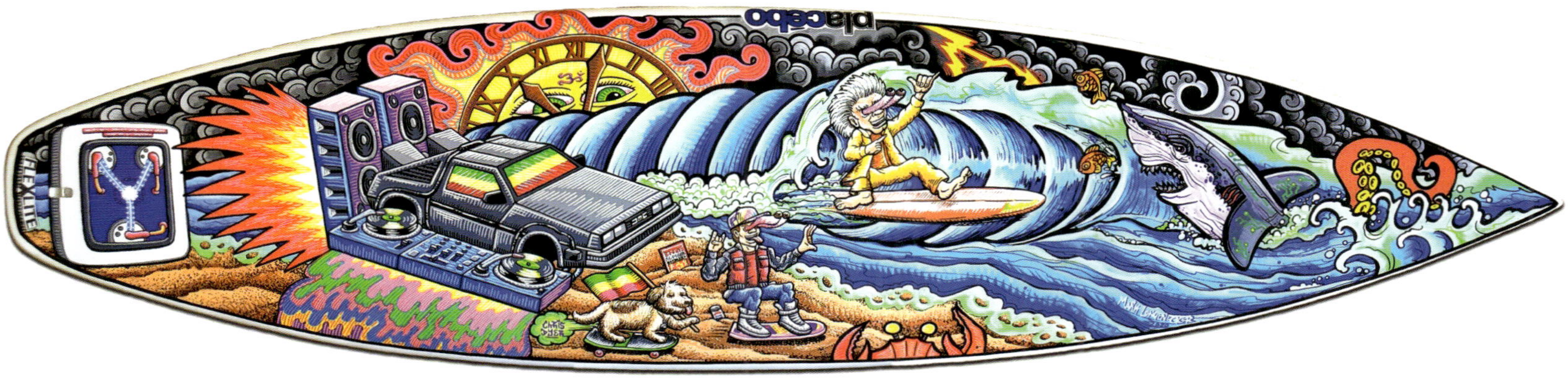

"Back to the Surfer Future" collaboration with **Mark Longnecker**, Paint Markers, 2019

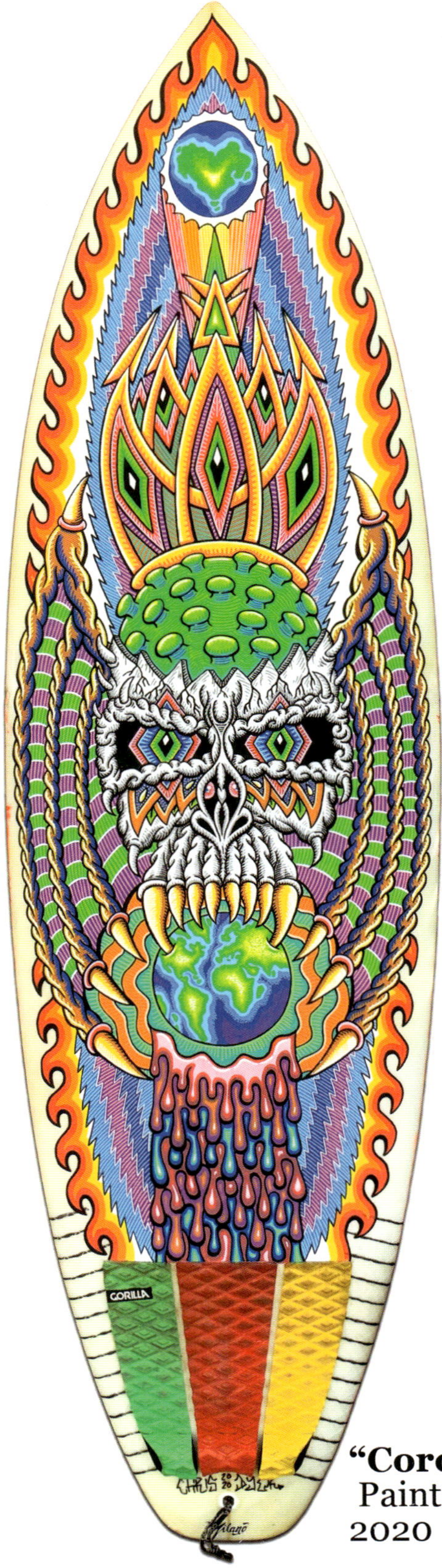

"Coronation"
Paint Markers,
2020

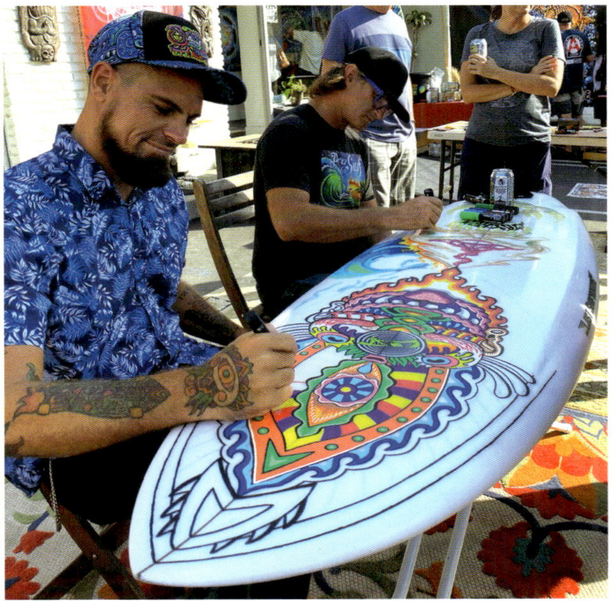

"COLLABORATIONS ARE SO EPIC TO SEE UNFOLD. WE ARE ALL STANDING ON THE SHOULDERS OF THE ONES WHO CAME BEFORE US AND INSPIRE US. TO WORK WITH AN ARTIST LIKE CHRIS WHILE WE ARE AT OUR BEST IS AN EPIC MOMENT RECORDED IN ART."
-DREW BROPHY, SURF ARTIST

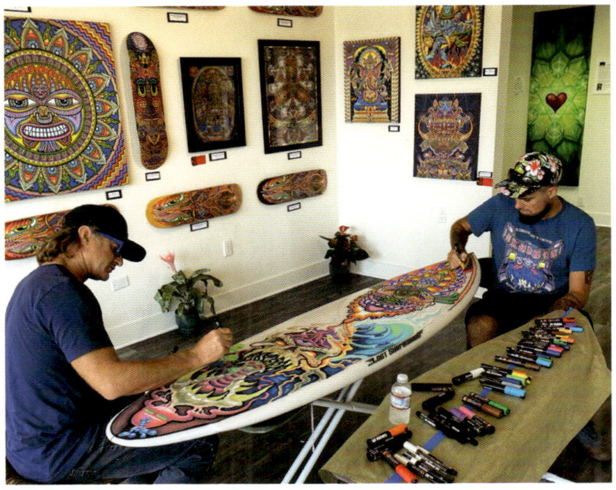

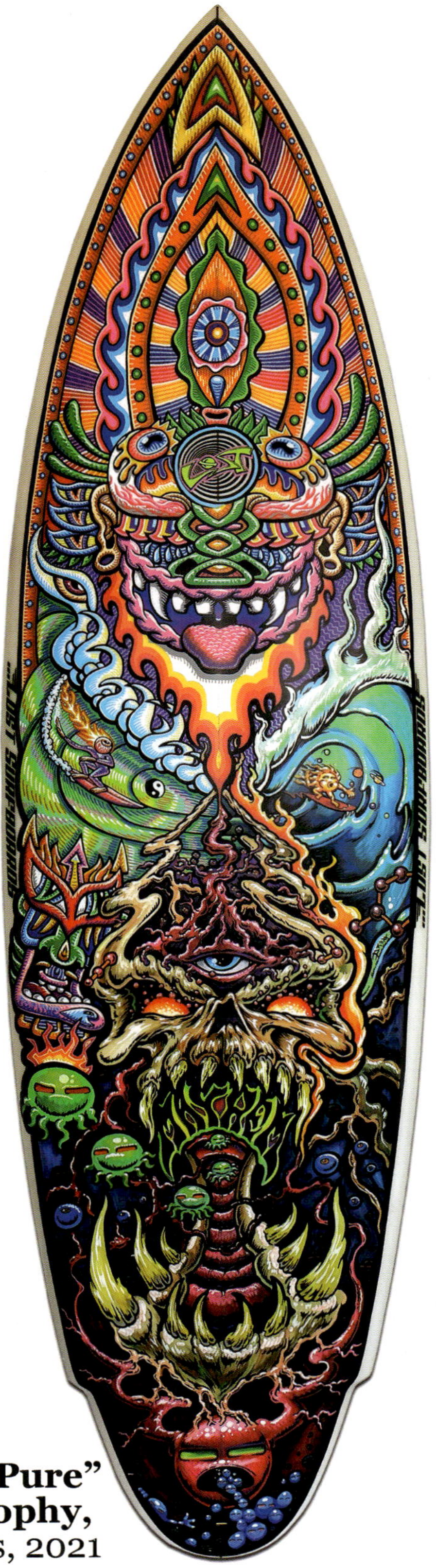

"Keeping it Pure"
Collabo with **Drew Brophy,**
Paint Markers, 2021

CHAPTER T
DEATHS A

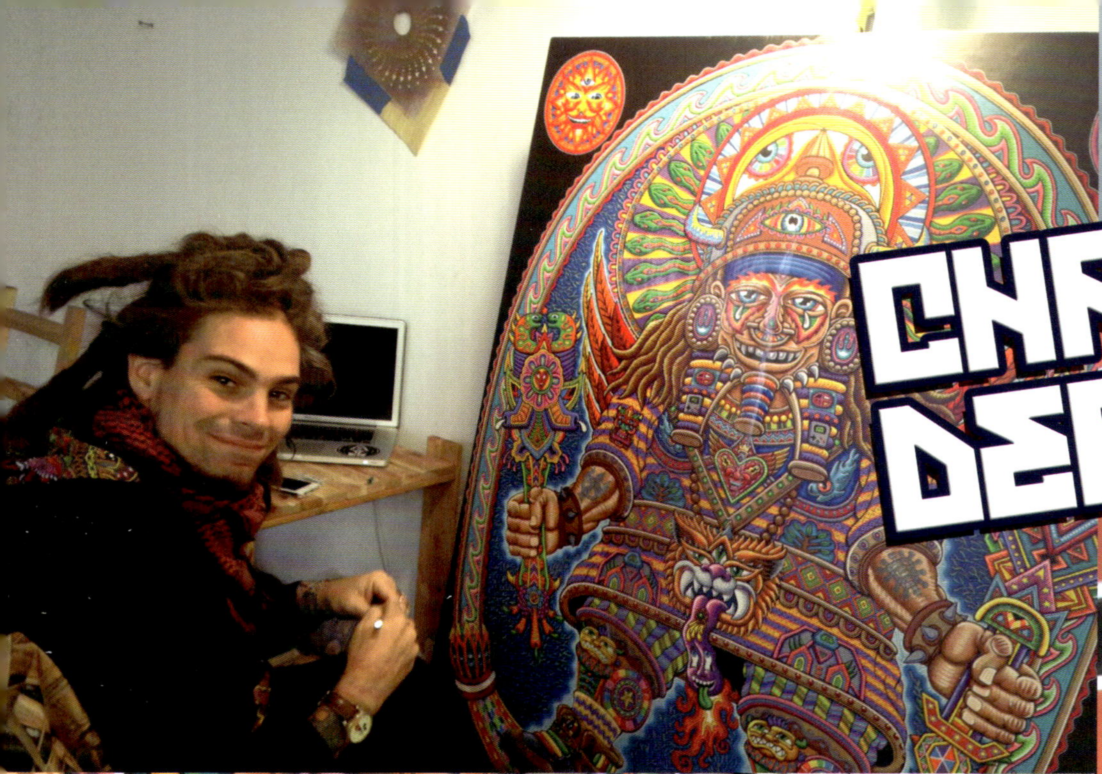

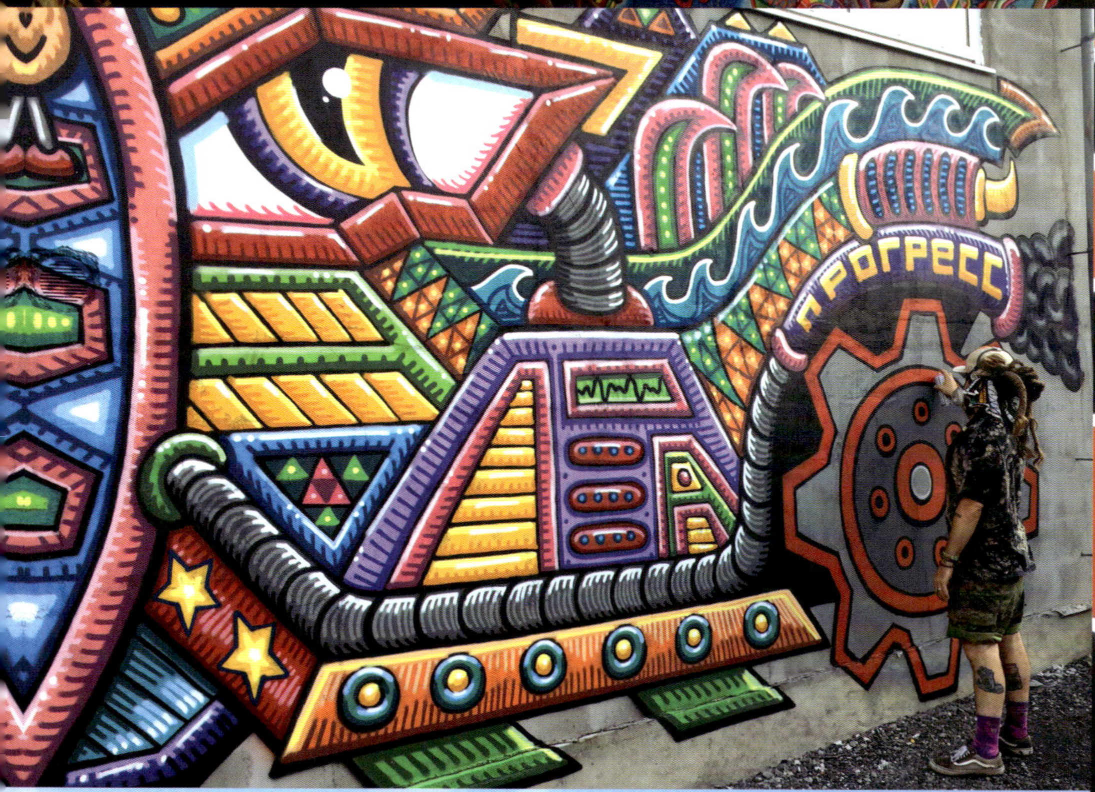

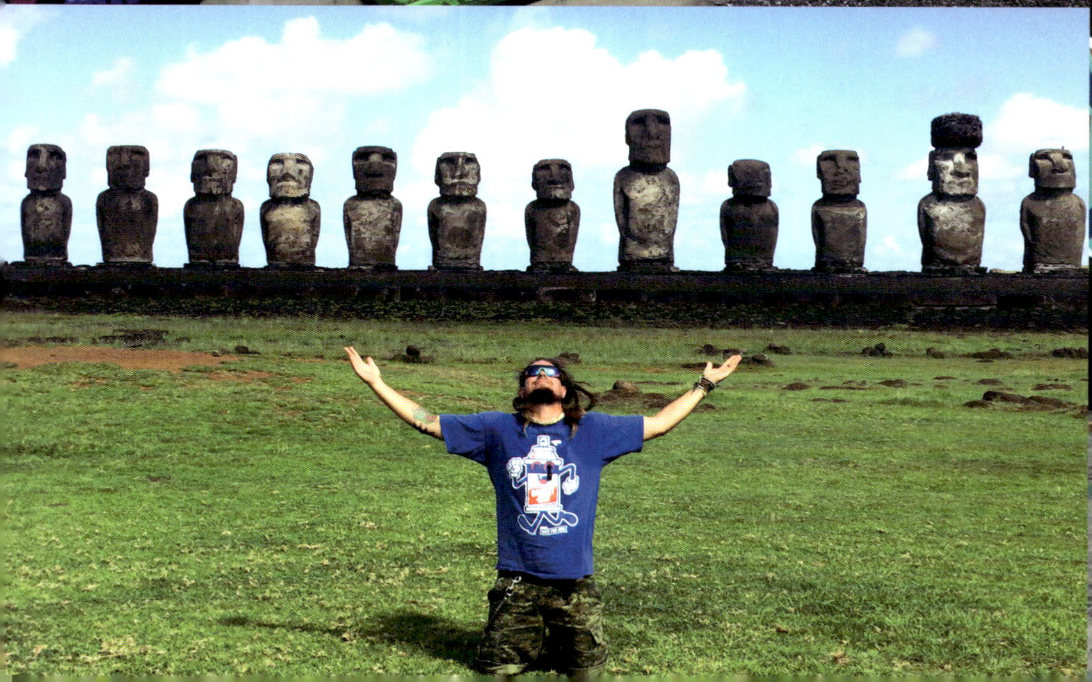

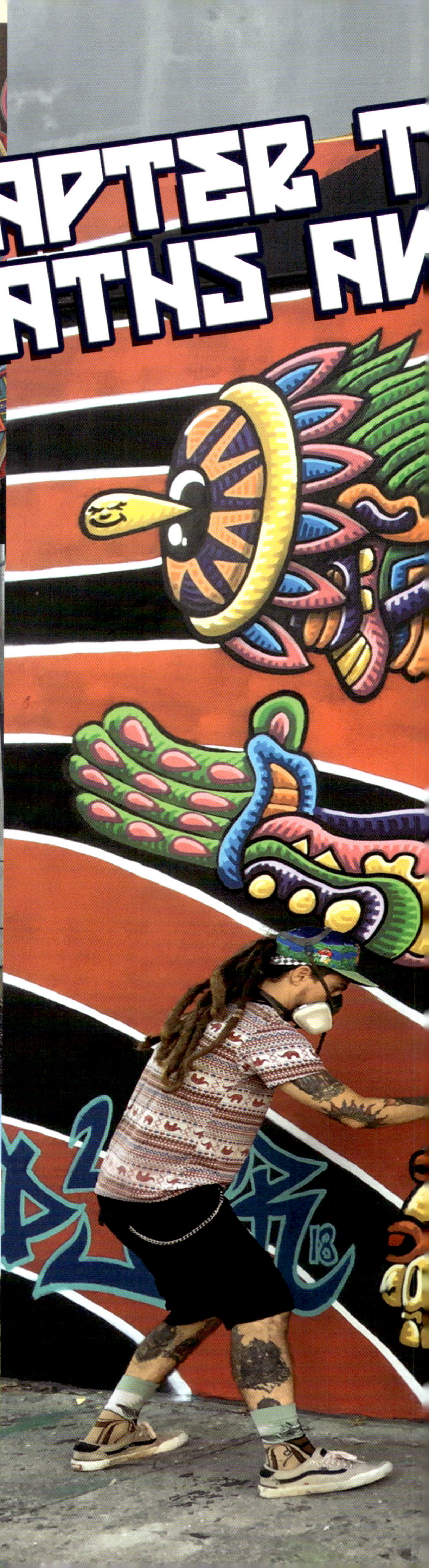

HREE
D REBIRTHS

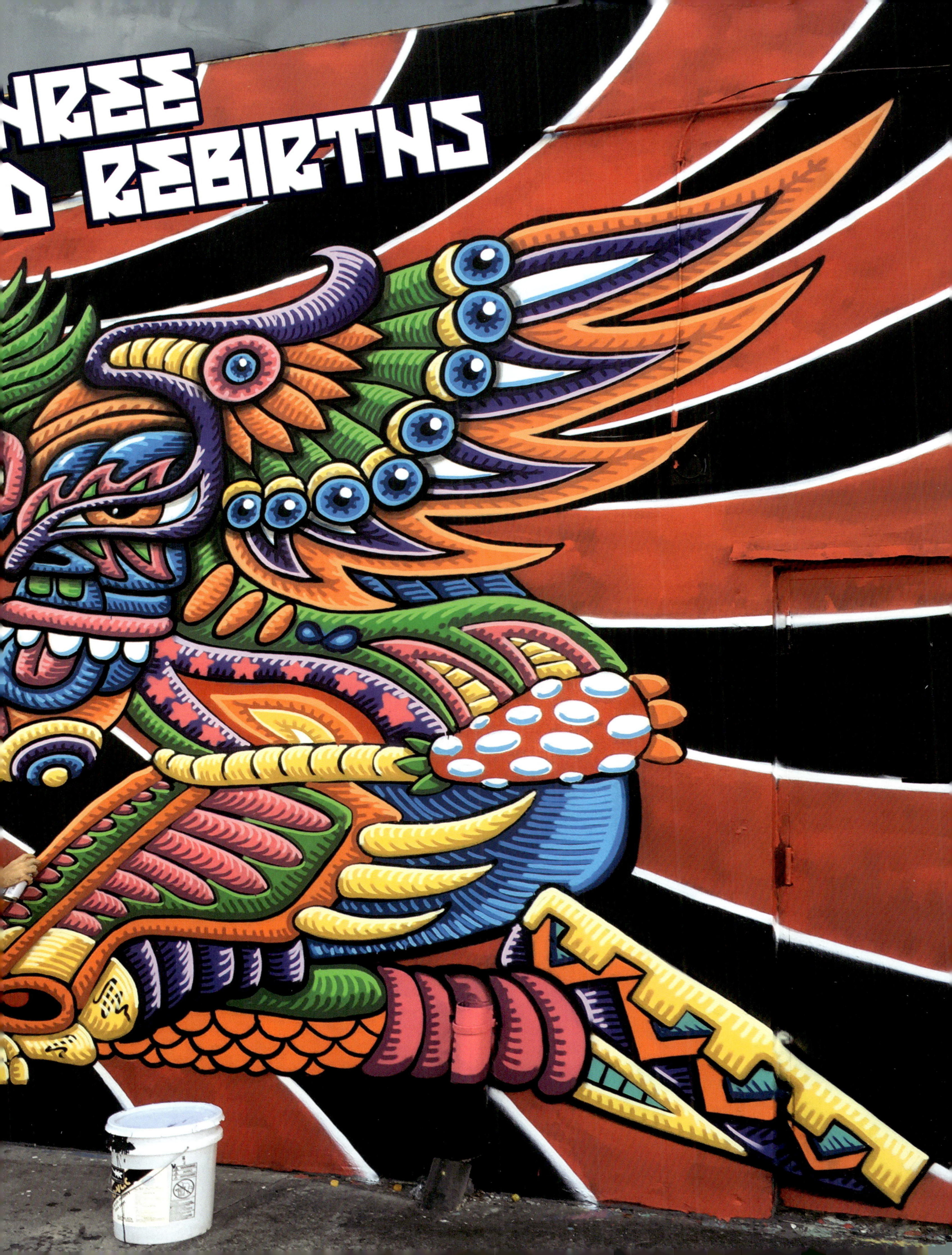

NORWAY

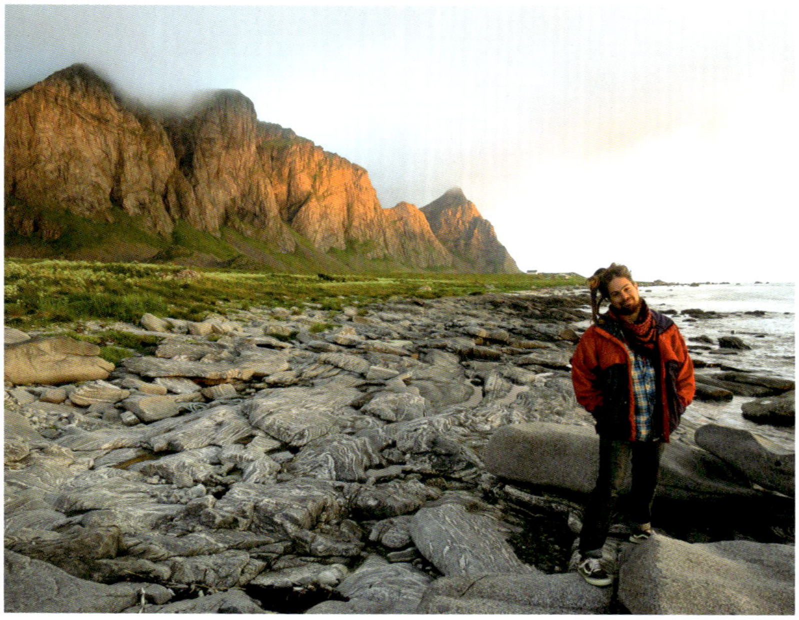

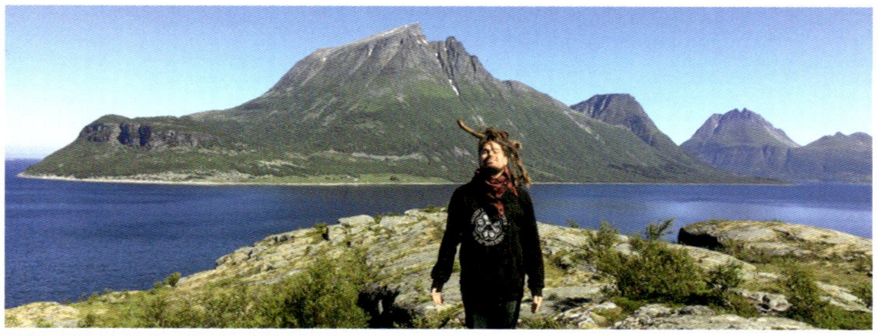

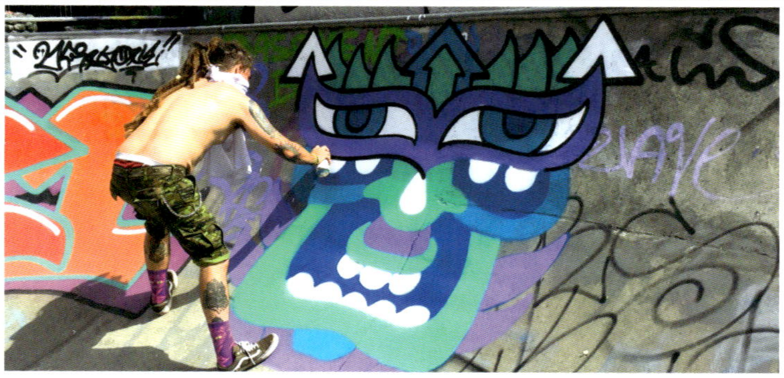

After I divorced Valerie, I found myself to be an out of shape 37 year old man, facing solitude and depression. But at least now I had the freedom to travel the world, in search of a brighter future. So I started accepting cool jobs that I had deflected in the past. The first one was for an old hippie from Oslo, who wanted me to paint his vehicles. **Even** was a former Hells Angel madman and hash smuggler, but also a sweetheart. He ended becoming a great friend, who I've travelled many the parts of the world with. On arrival we hung out at his beautiful country cabin by the fjords, and then we took a gorgeous five day road trip to the top of Norway. The destination was a little island in the Arctic Circle called **Vaeroy**, with a population of seven hundred people. There I live painted his truck at a trippy Psy-Trance Music Festival called **"Midnight Sun"**. It was so north that the sun never actually went under the horizon, hovering at midnight for a very long sunset, before rising again!

All in all it was a beautiful experience, but I was still very sad inside. I painted this piece to express how I was trying to escape my issues, yet couldn't, as they were inside me. Who was I without my wife or home to validate me? The beautiful views gave me some comfort, but there was much work to be done.

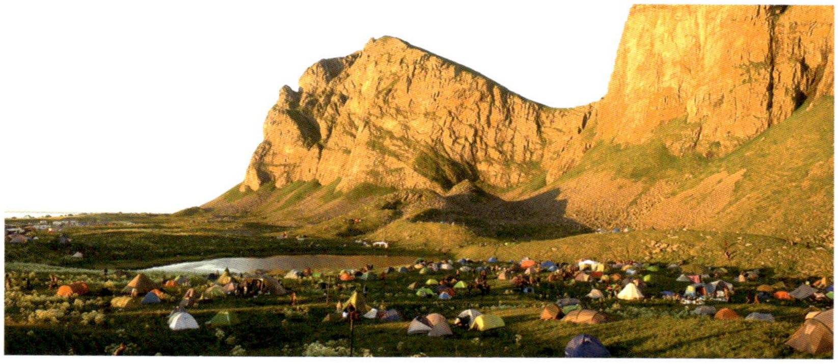

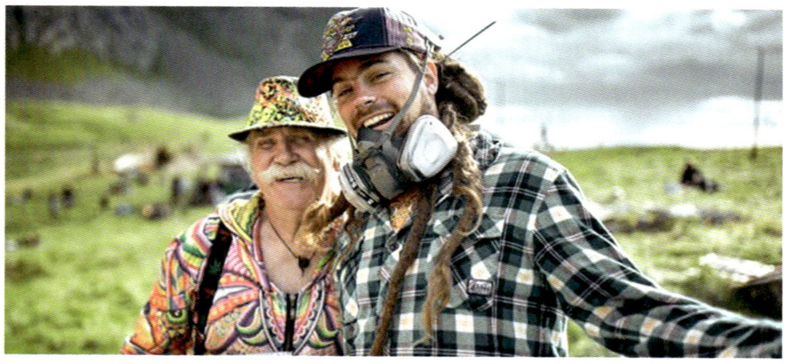

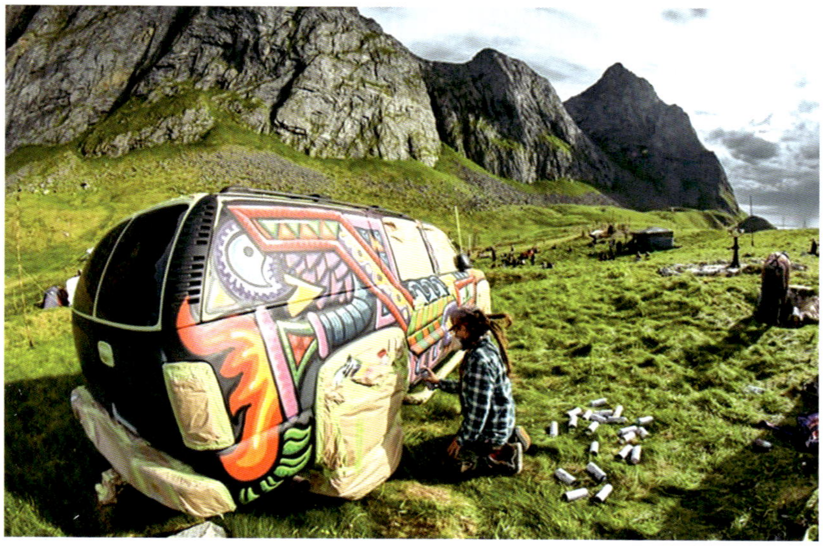

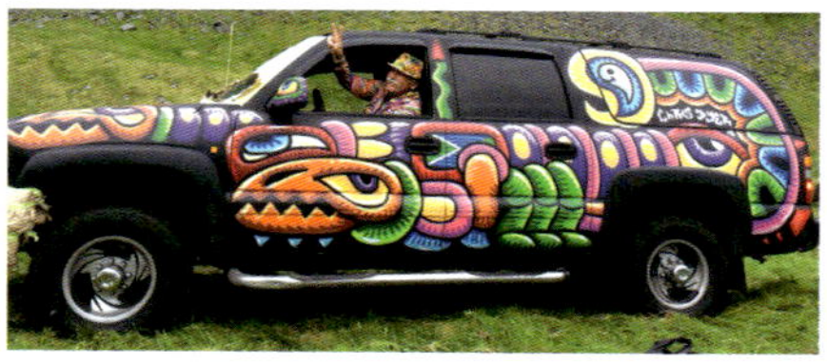

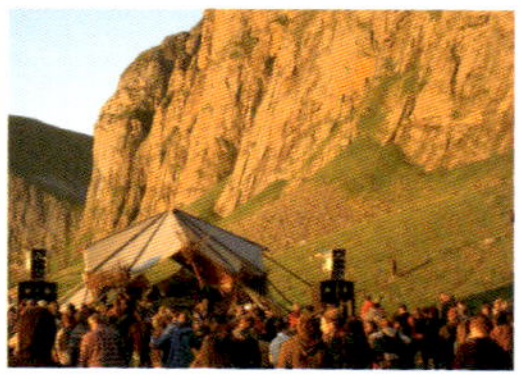

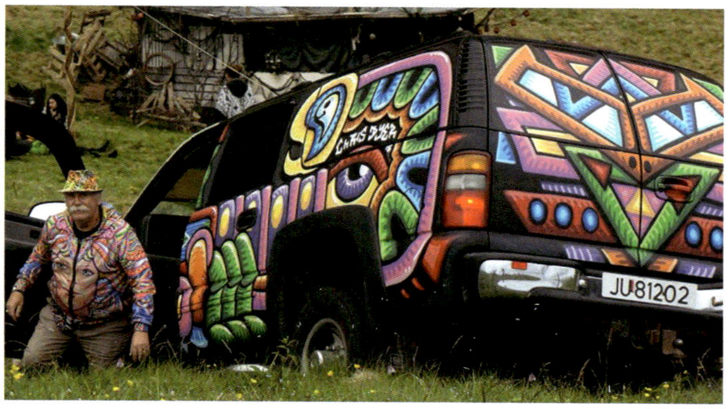

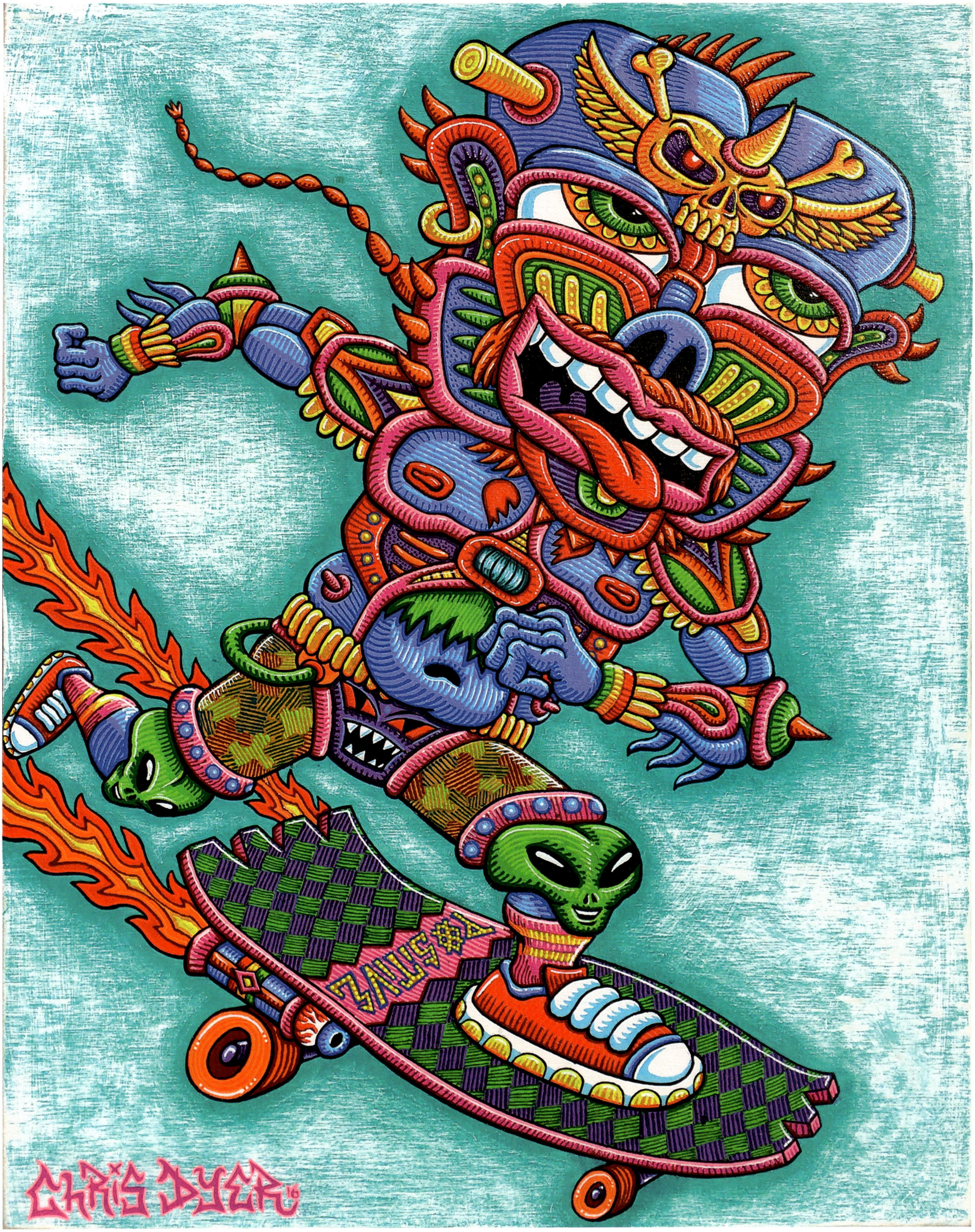

"Skating away from my Problems" Acrylics on wood, 2016

RUSSIA

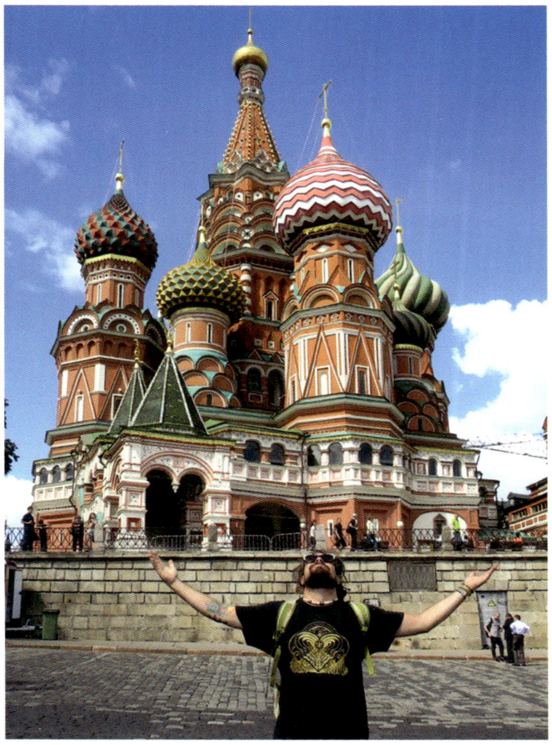

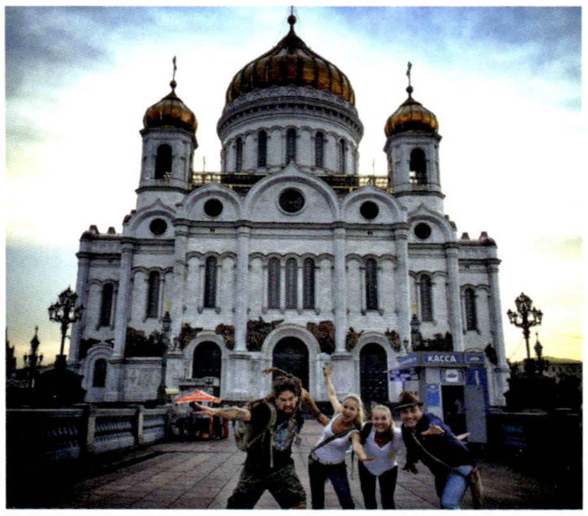

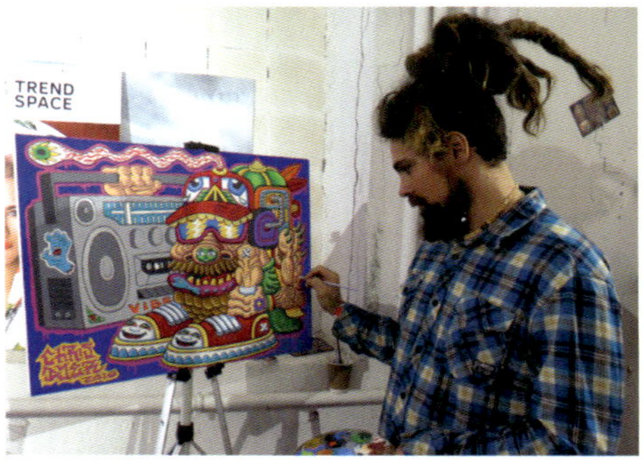

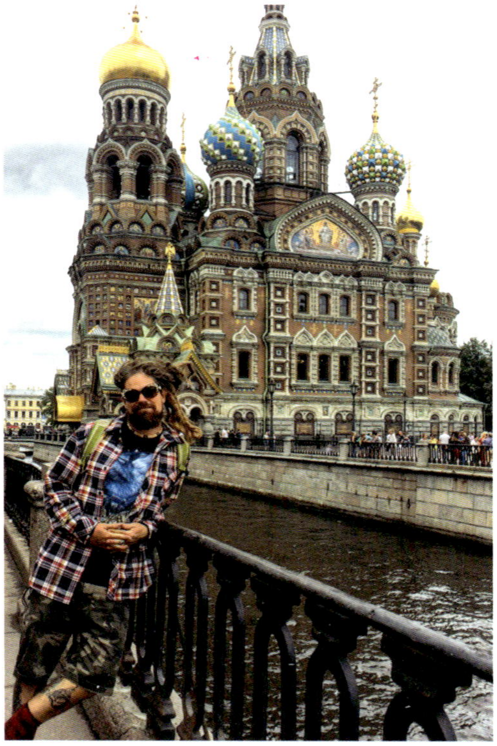

My next destination was the epic city of **Moscow**. Just as I arrived, my live painting project fell through, so I called my shaman friend **Herbert Quinteros** to see if he had any local contacts. By huge coincidence/synchronicity he told me that he was supposed to arrive and leave Moscow on the same days as me! So I pretty much spent the whole week checking out sights with him, but also got to do some very needed Medicine Ceremonies. Doing Ayahuasca in a Russian yoga studio was certainly different than doing it in the Peruvian jungle, but still very potent. It helped me let go of Valerie enough to turn the page, and keep her as a friend. The painting that I expressed from this was called **"Healing Medicine"**, which is less subjective and more about the energy of my transformation.

After that, I took a train to the super cool city of **Saint Petersbourg**, to do an art internship at **"The Street Art Museum"**. For a week I lived in their building and spray painted them a big mural for their collection. I also live painted them a canvas at a fun hipster Music Festival they did.

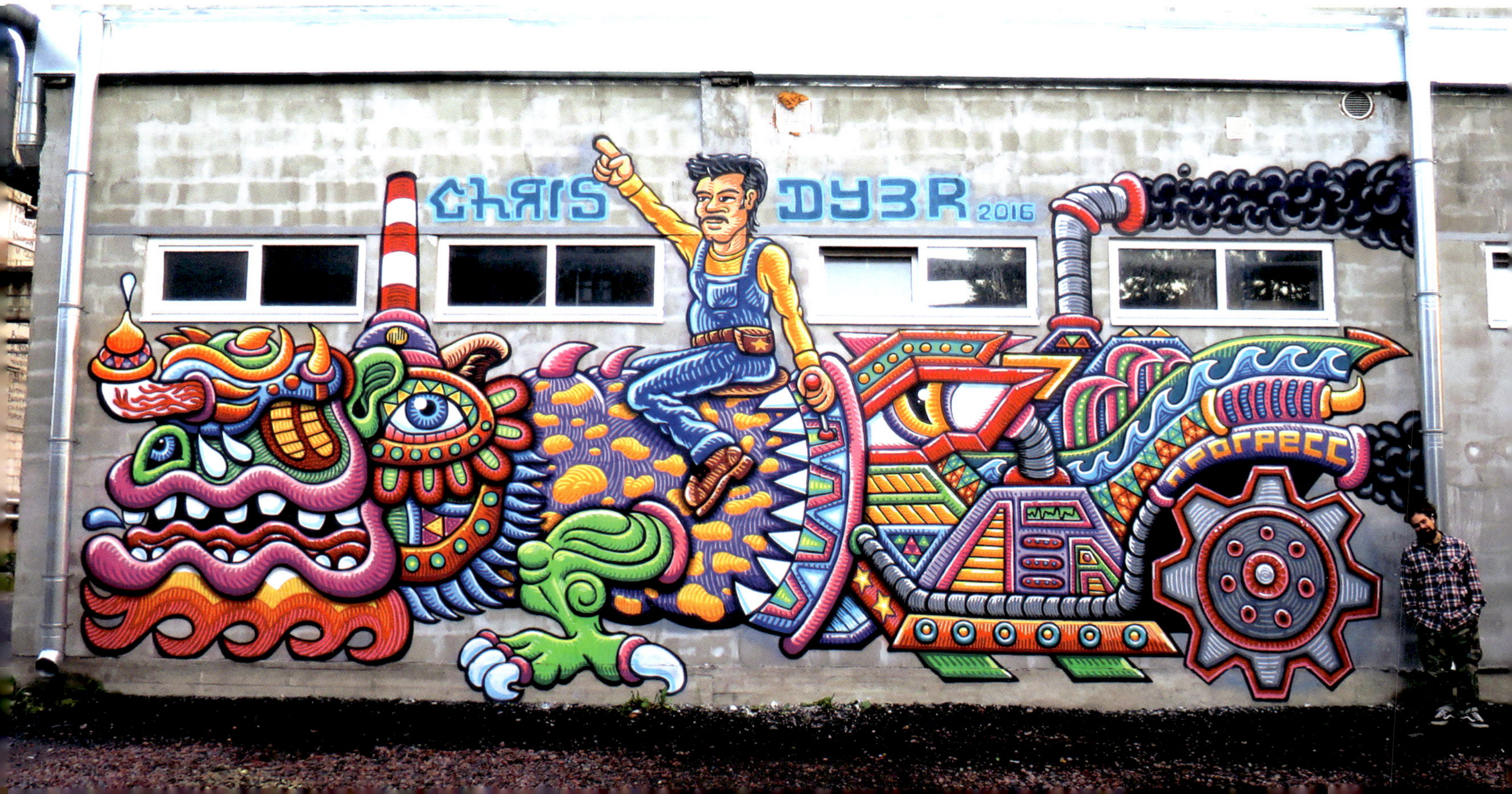

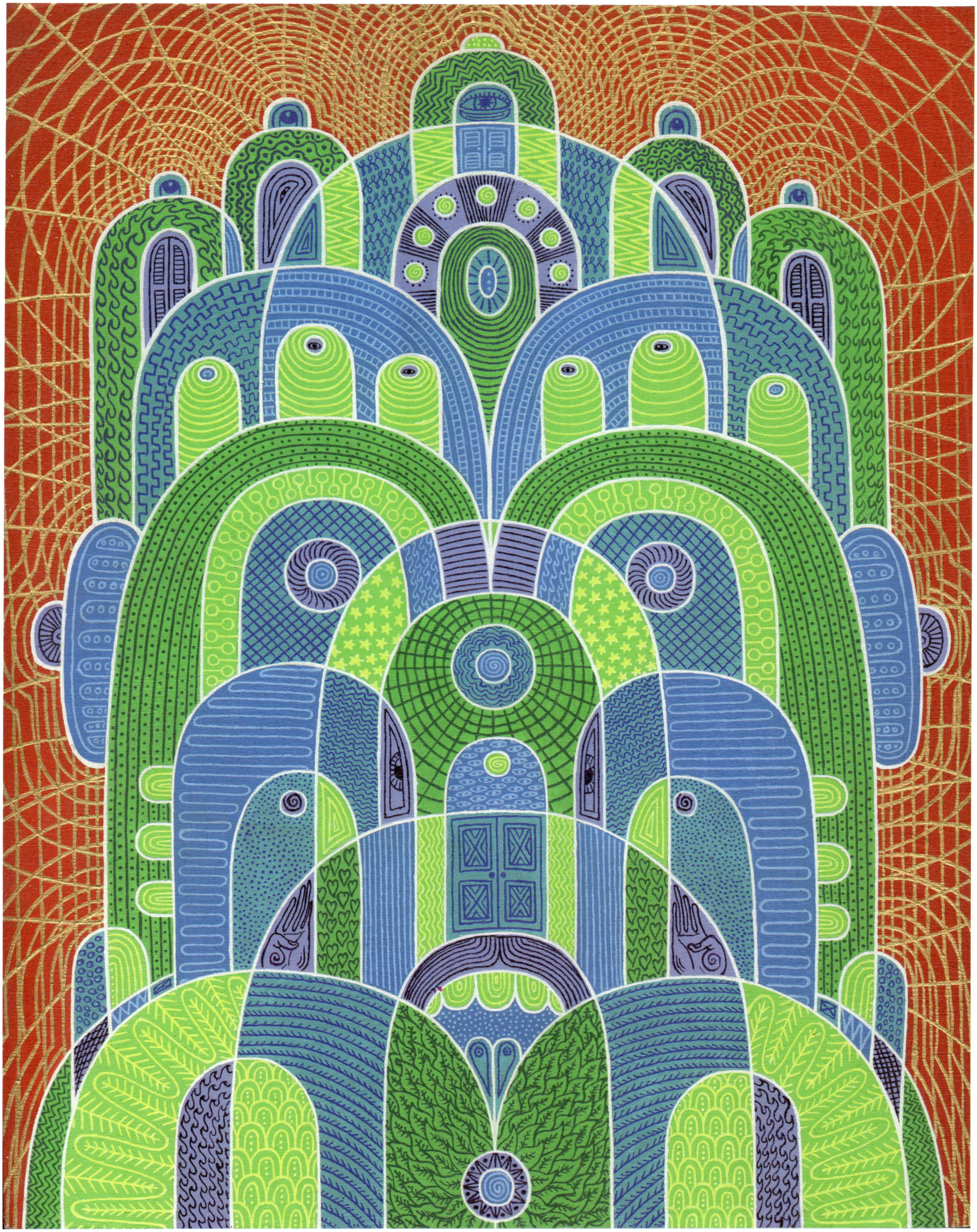

"Healing Medicine" Acrylics on wood, 2016

PORTUGAL

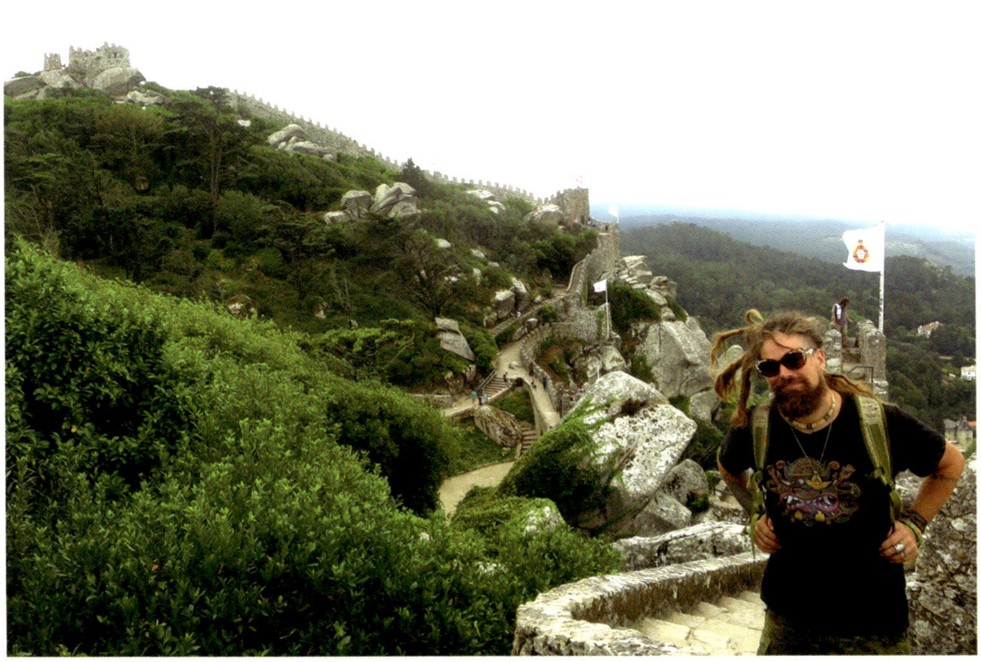

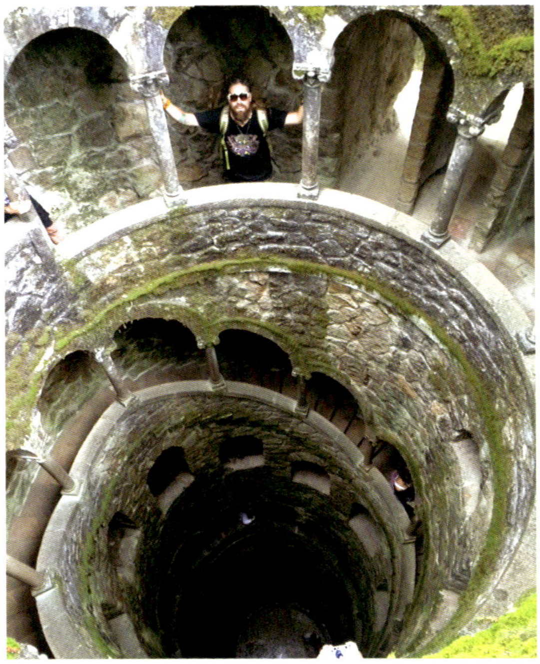

After Russia I flew to Portugal. **"Boom Music Festival"** had been inviting me to perform for them many times, so I finally accepted to live paint, exhibit and talk. It was a huge event packed with interesting people from all over the world. Including set-up time, it lasted a few weeks so I was able to connect with some very nice people. The theme of that year's festival was "The Shaman" so I painted Herbert in my mural, which was one of the two collabo pieces I did with local street artist **Ram Lisbon**. A lot of my visionary art family was there too and after the festival I kept adventuring through that beautiful country with my artist friend **Johnathan Solter**.

The triangular canvases I painted while I was there, **"DMT Diamond"** where also about integrating my last Ayahuasca Ceremonies from Russia. Once again, I didn't go very subjective, keeping the art about energy manifesting and transforming through shapes, in this case triangles of rainbow light.

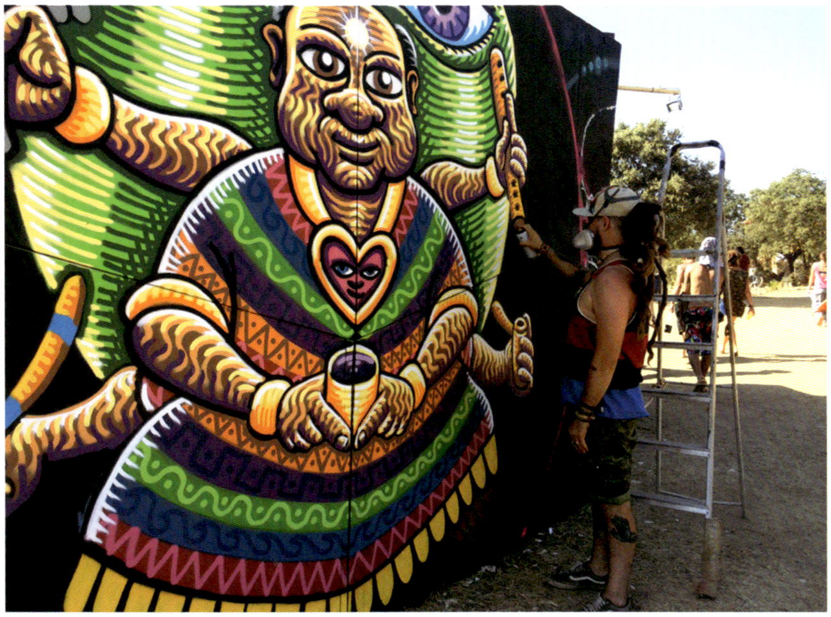

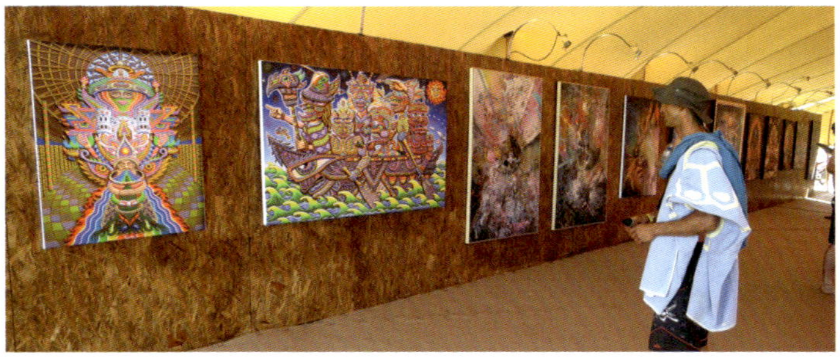

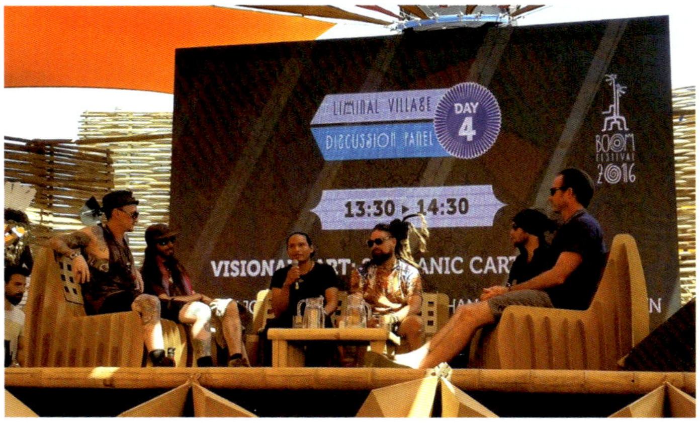

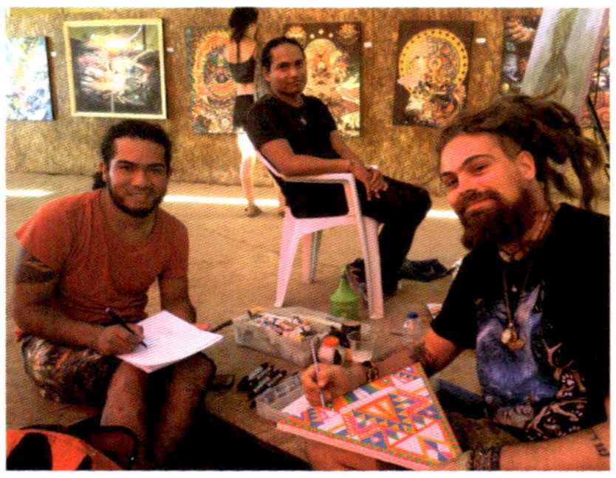

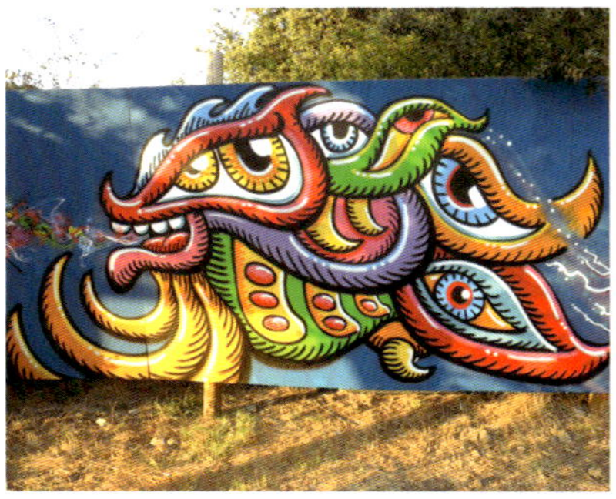

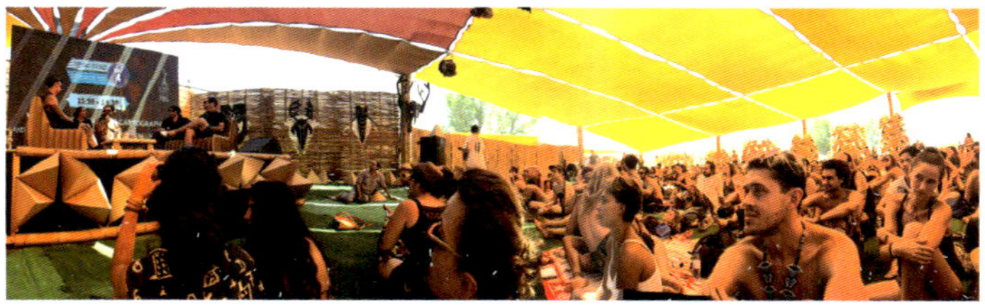

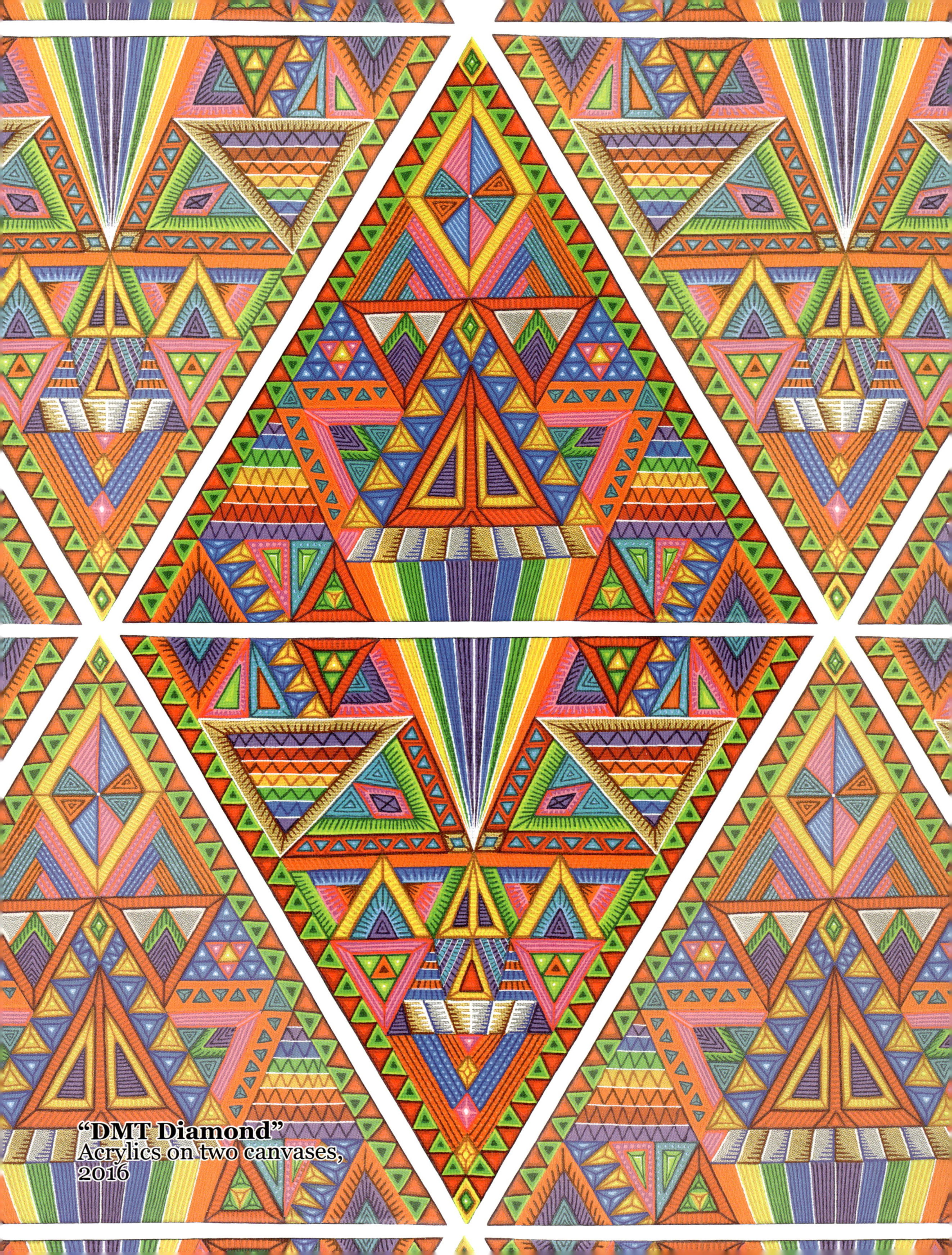

“DMT Diamond”
Acrylics on two canvases,
2016

USA TOUR 2016

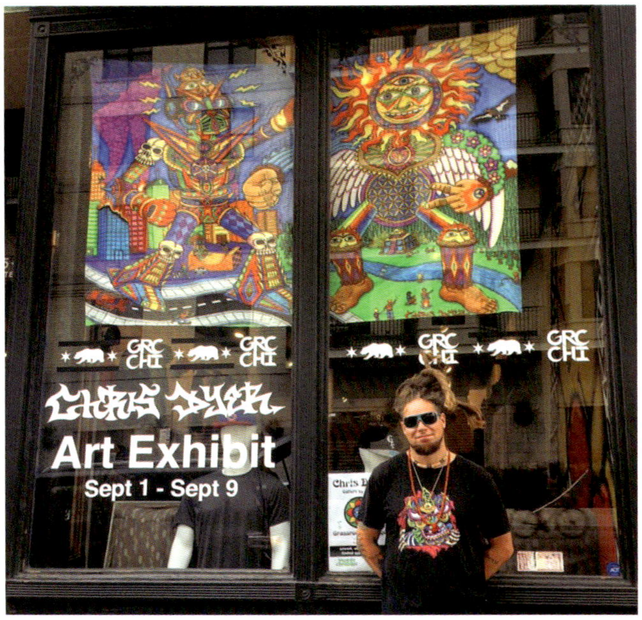

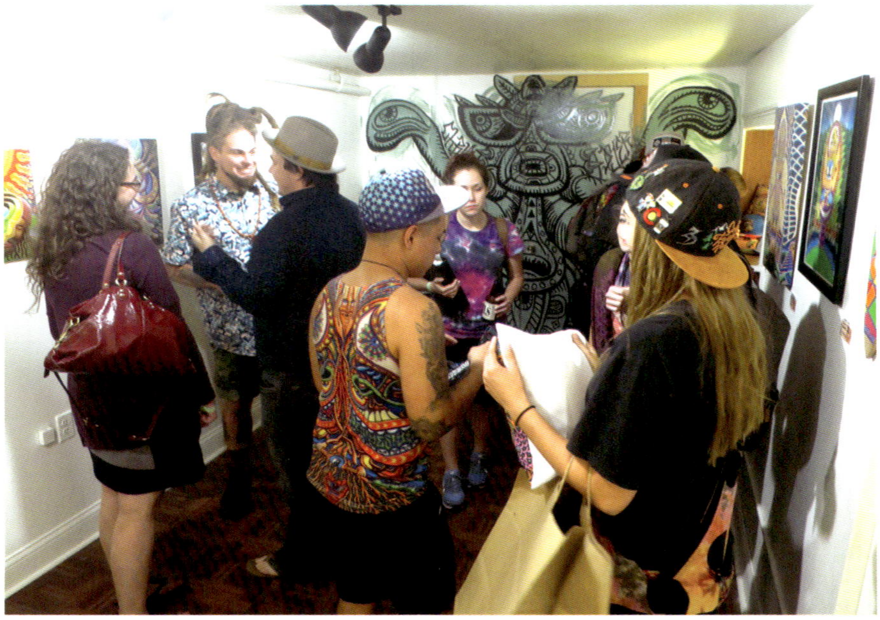

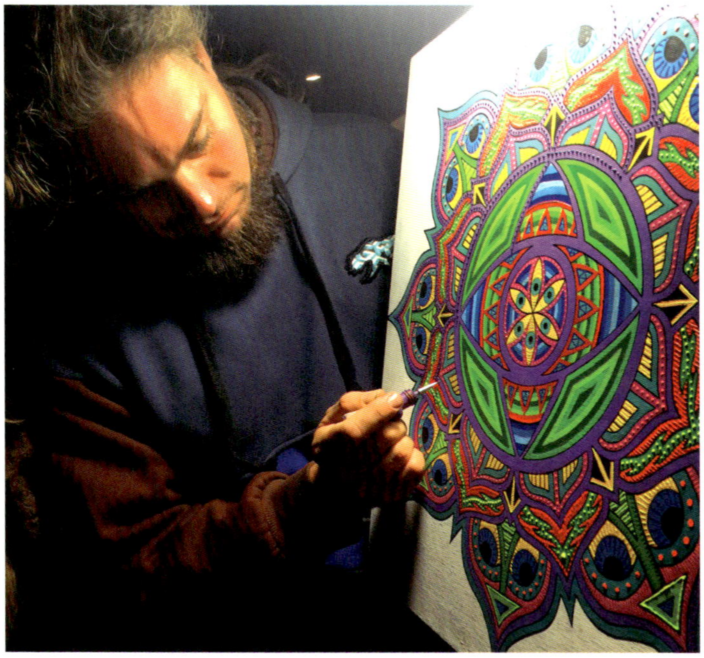

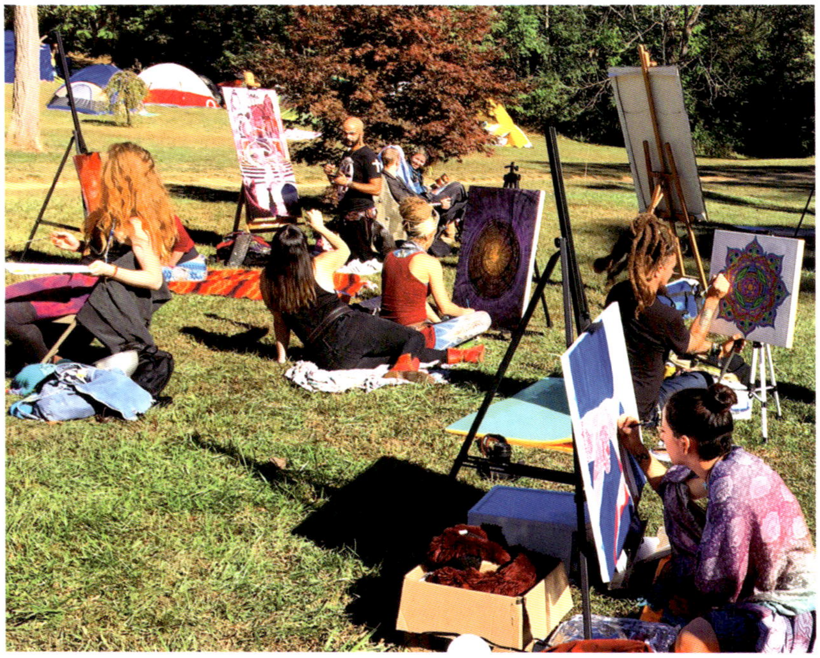

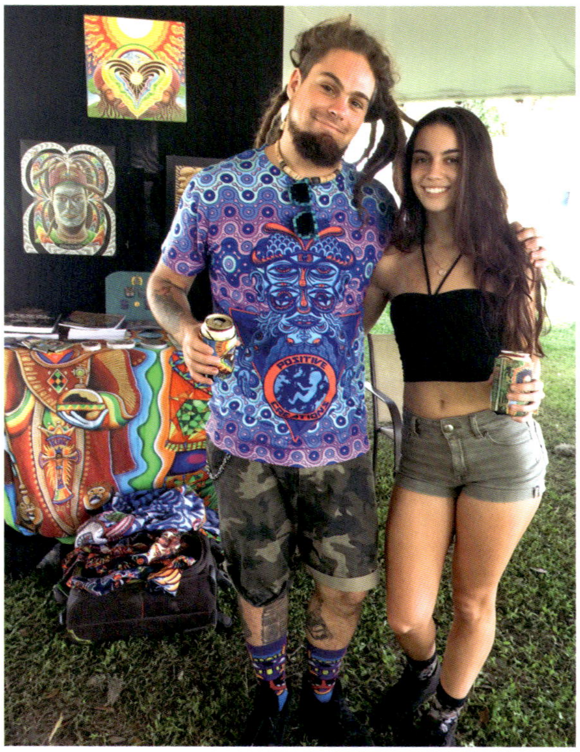

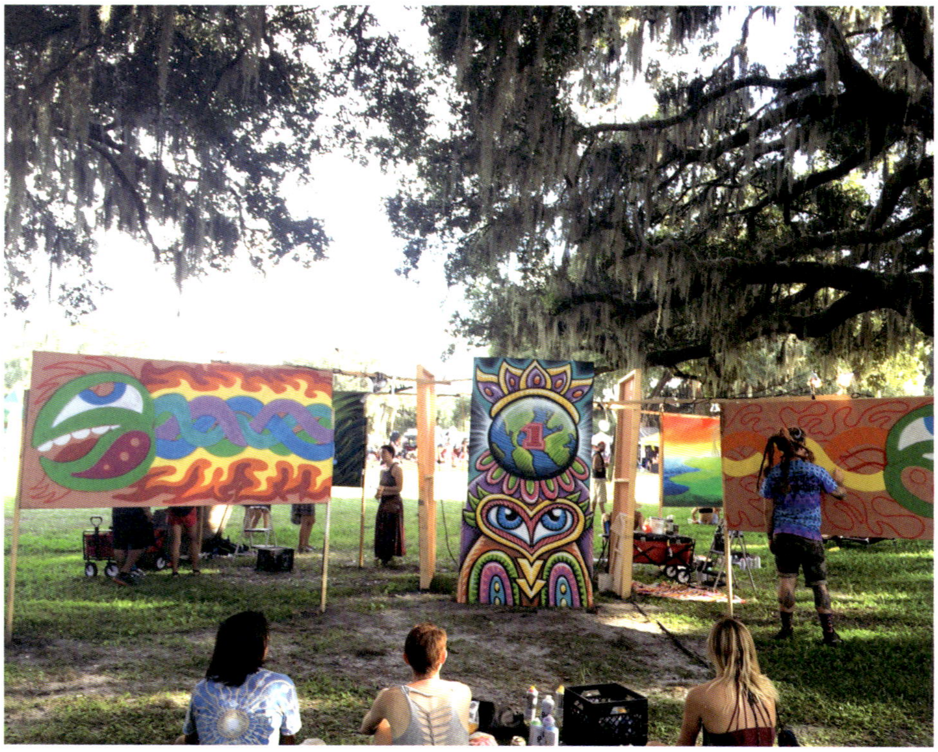

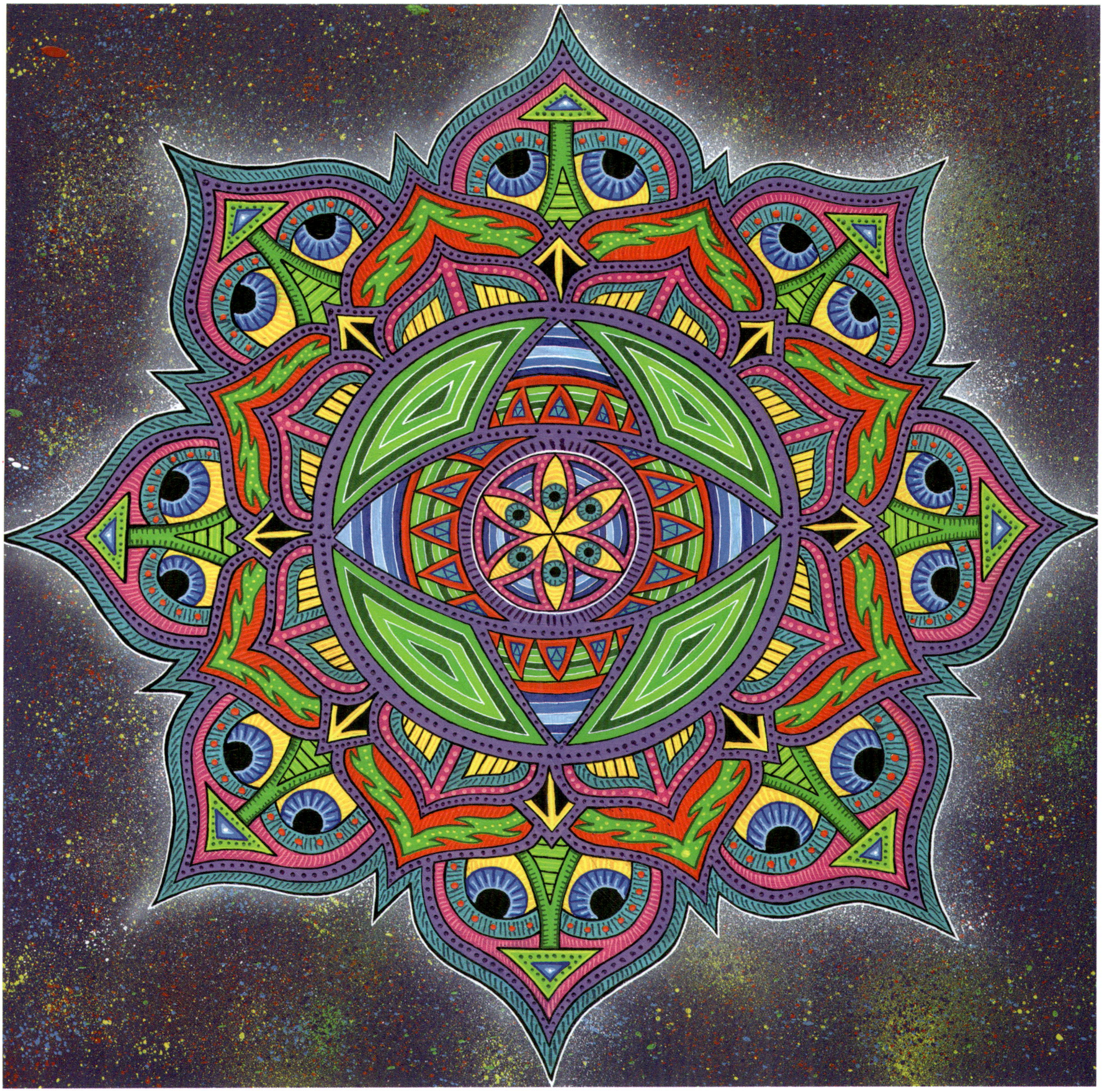

"Many Visions" Acrylics on wood, 2016

Once I was back in North America, I barely had time to rest at my new apartment before I was back on the road, touring the United States for a month. In that late summer journey I performed and exposed at different festivals and events in **Chicago**, **Florida**, **Colorado** and **Maryland**. As opposed to the shows I had just done across the pond, in the States I actually have a big fan base, which was good for my hurting emotional self-esteem. I was finally recuperating from my divorce and got to meet nice girls who resonated with me. One girl stood out though. Her name was **Arianne Cardoso**, and she came to volunteer at my merch table, while I live painted at **"Earthdance Music Festival"** in Florida. She was beautiful spiritual star-seed soul who painted and skateboarded. She was my kind of lady, but also nineteen years younger than me, so I tried my best to stay away from her. Yet through the festival our mutual attraction was too strong and connected pretty well!

The canvas I was painting those days was a mandala commission for my friend Bobby, who runs a clothing brand called **'Many Visions"**. It was fitting for this time, both cause it continued the non-subjective vibe I was doing and also because the girl I ended attracting was a mandala painter.

NEPAL

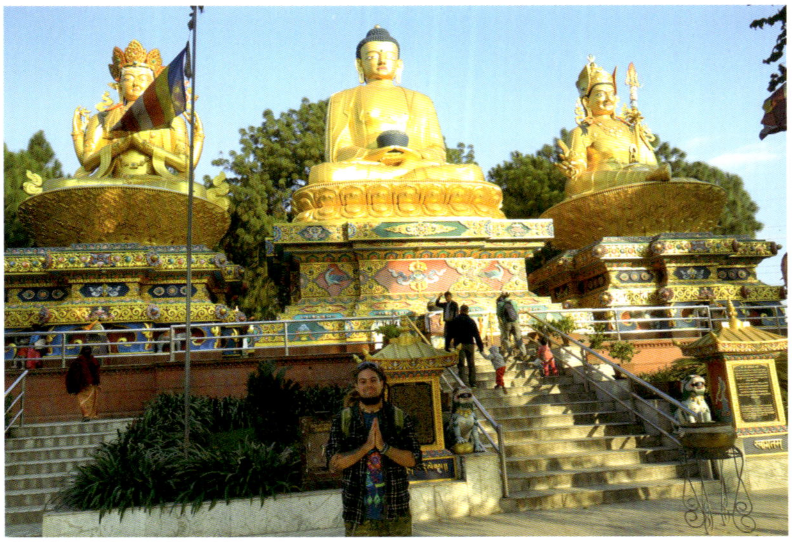

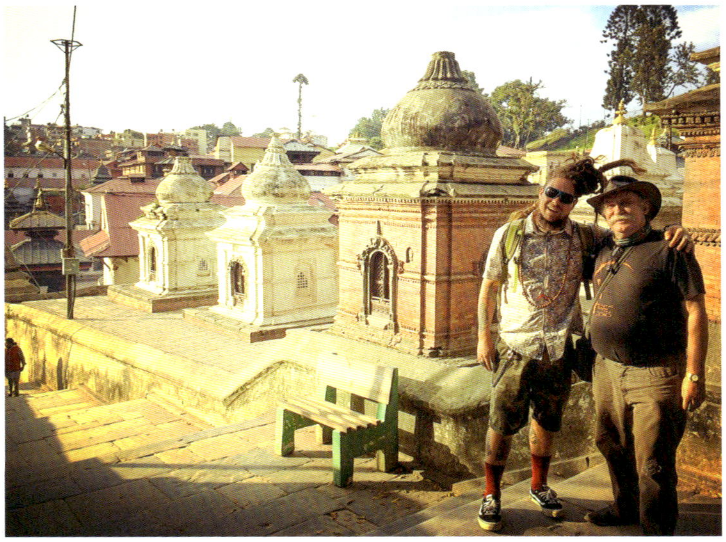

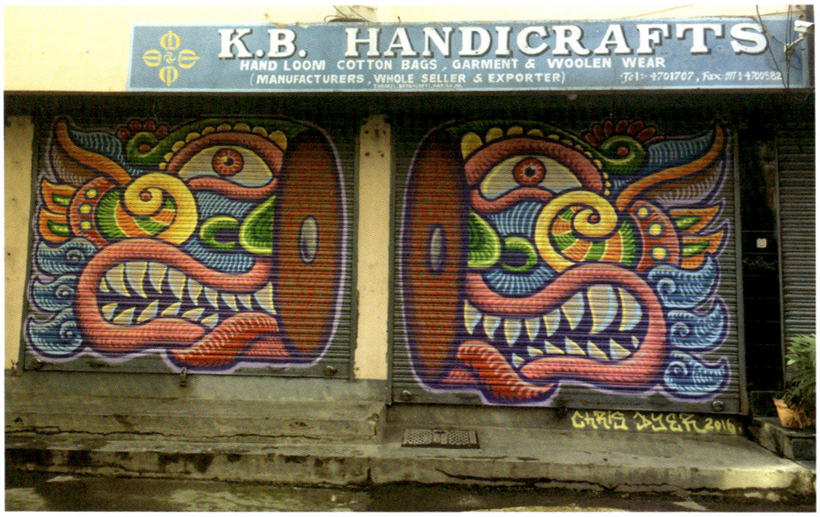
K.B. HANDICRAFTS
HAND LOOM COTTON BAGS, GARMENT & WOOLEN WEAR
(MANUFACTURERS, WHOLE SELLER & EXPORTER)
CHRIS DYER 2016

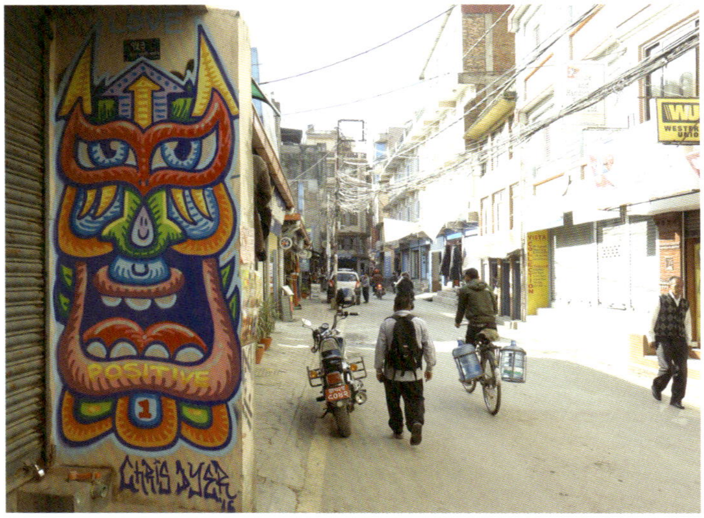
POSITIVE
1
CHRIS DYER

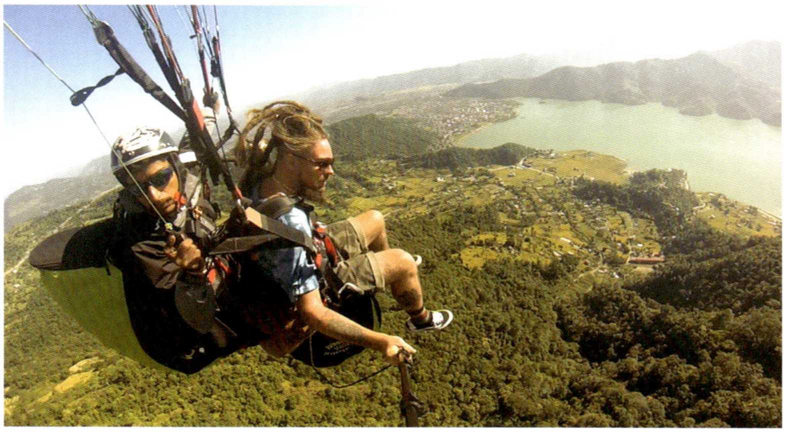

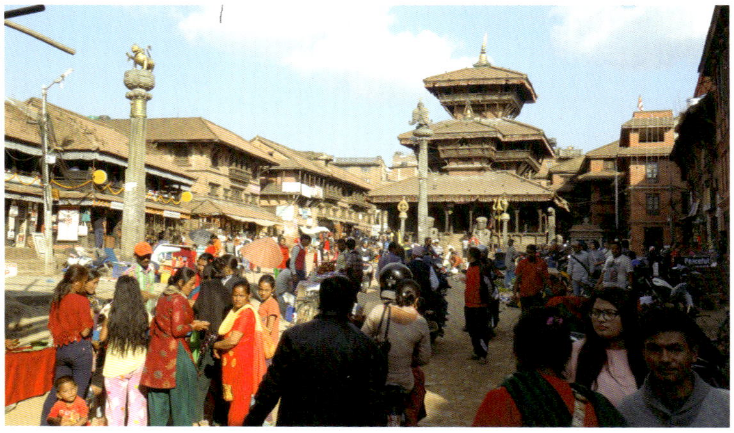

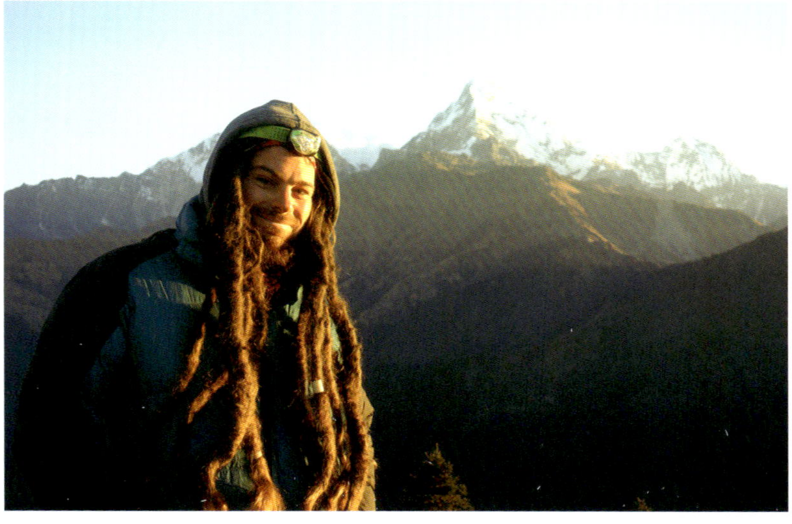

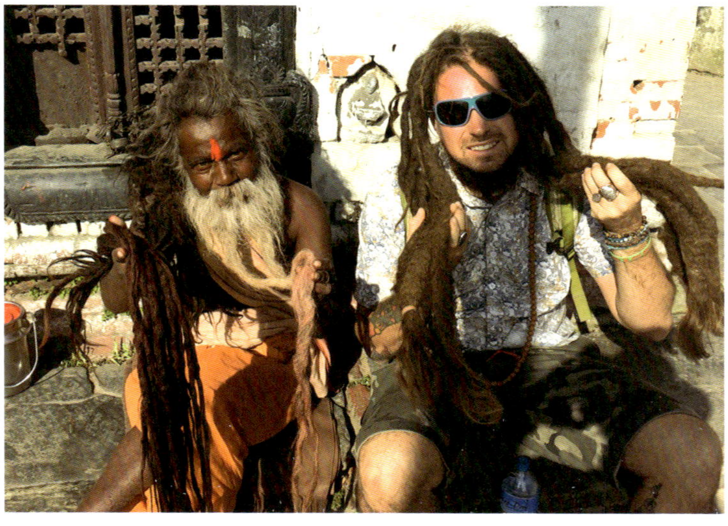

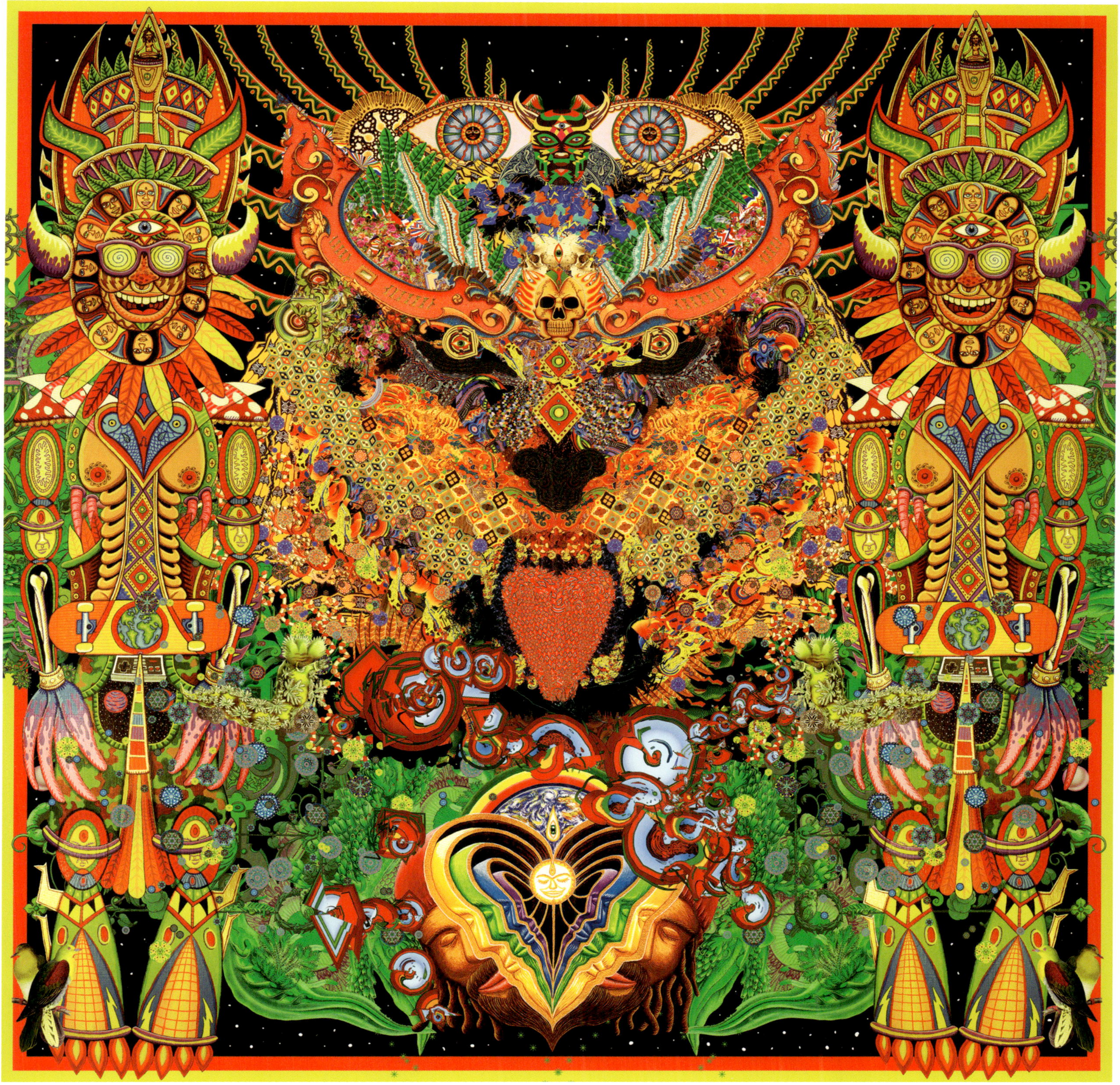

"Cumbia Cosmica" collabo with **La Prisa Mata**, Photoshop, 2016

Though I spray painted a few pieces while I was there, my mystic journey through Nepal was for my own healing and enjoyment. I met up with my new Norwegian friend Even in **Kathmandu** and had a lot of fun exploring the beautiful Buddhist sites of that special city. I later parted ways with him to spend some time alone in the beautiful nature of **Pokhara** village. The deepest part of the trip was hiking a trail of the **Himalayas**. Though I had a local guide showing the way, I felt like I was walking those days alone and went through a bunch of emotions. Those mountains have an intense energy that worked me like potent shamanic medicine. Through tears and laughter they helped me get over the last remainders of my divorce's pain and opened me up for the next chapter of Love in my life. I was grateful to have given myself that time and space to process these things properly.

BALI

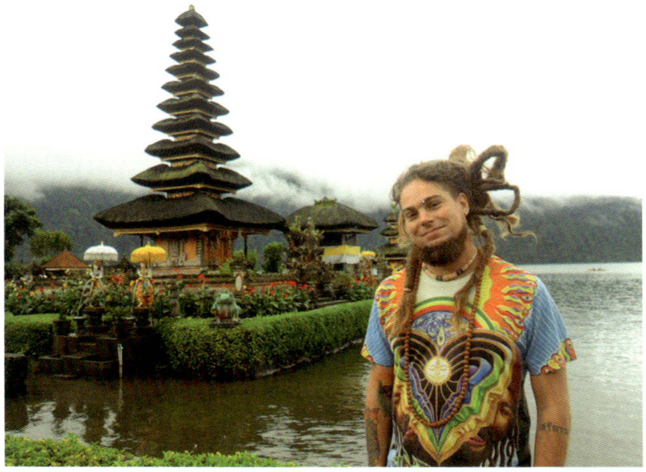

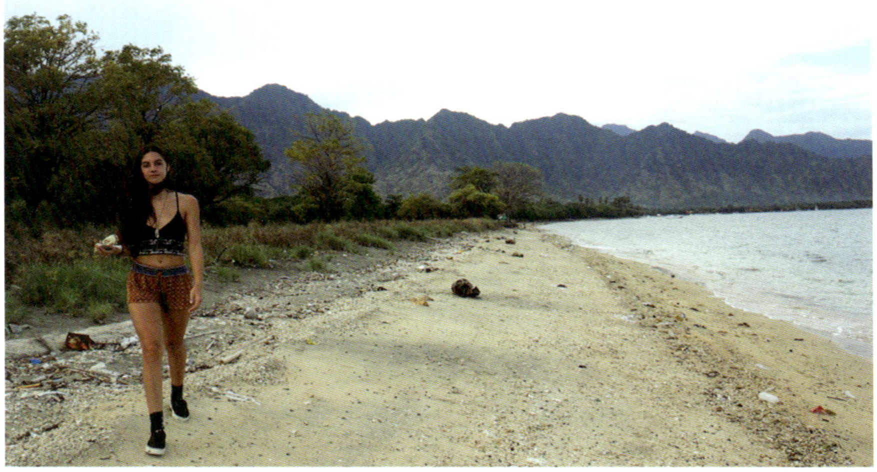

After meeting **Arianne** at that festival in Florida, we kept good communication. I wanted to see more of her, but my unconventional lifestyle didn't allow for going out on normal dates. So I just flew her out to my next destination, Bali, to enjoy a very romantic week of cultural explorations and creativity. Arianne arrived in middle of an art workshop I was teaching at a gorgeous hotel in **Ubud**. There we had the chance to enjoy all the beautiful natural and cultural sights of that lovely area. After the workshop ended, we crossed to the other side of the island to spend time at a more desolate beach area, where we could have calm moments painting by the ocean. Our time together was like a magical dream, like being in heaven.
The painting I expressed in that journey, **"Kundalini Rising"**, is about reawakening my sexual dragon, which had gone quite dormant in my complicated married life. Arianne was a kind mystical Scorpio who shared beautiful energetical healing and brought me back to full power. I was grateful.

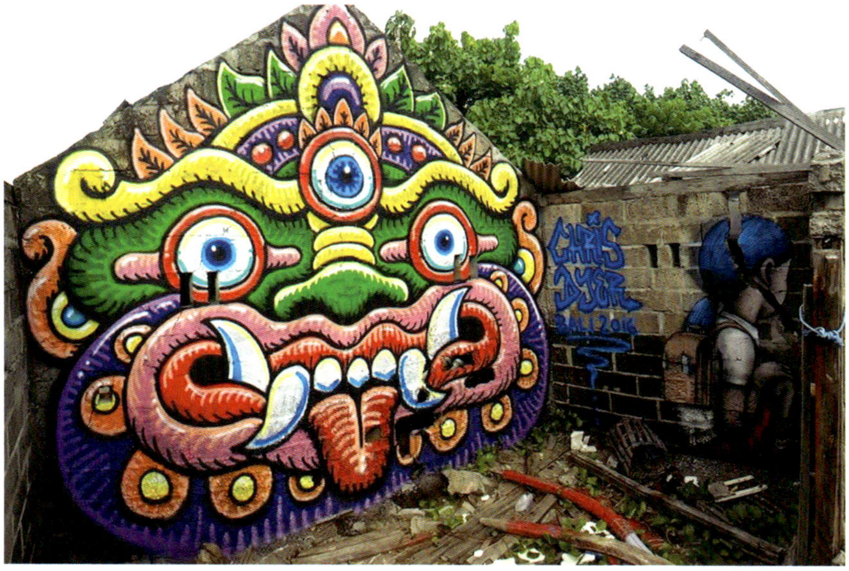

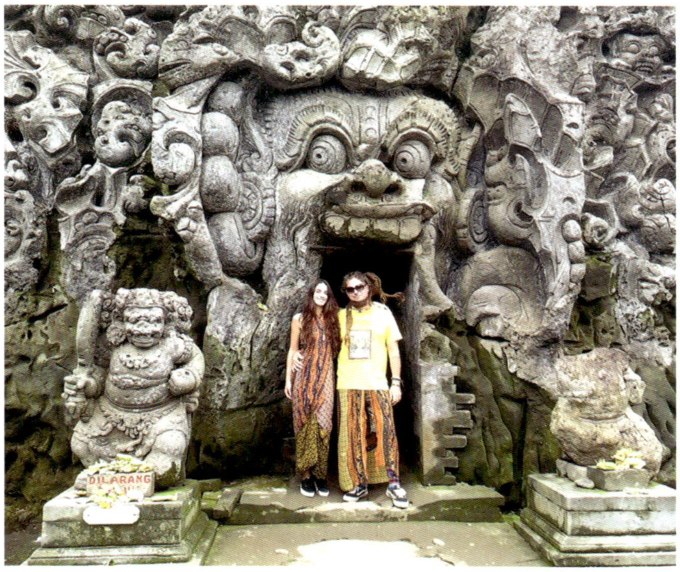

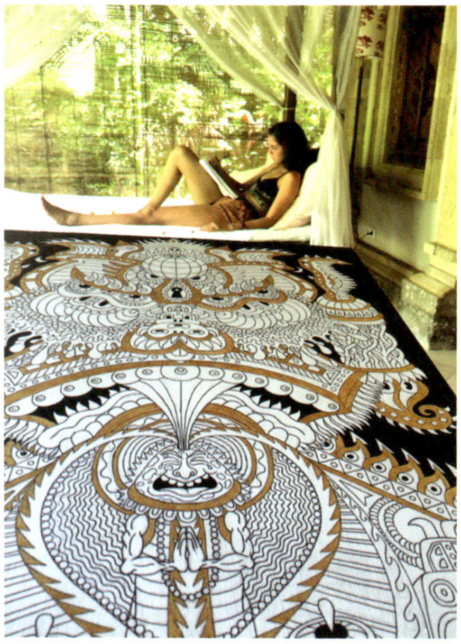

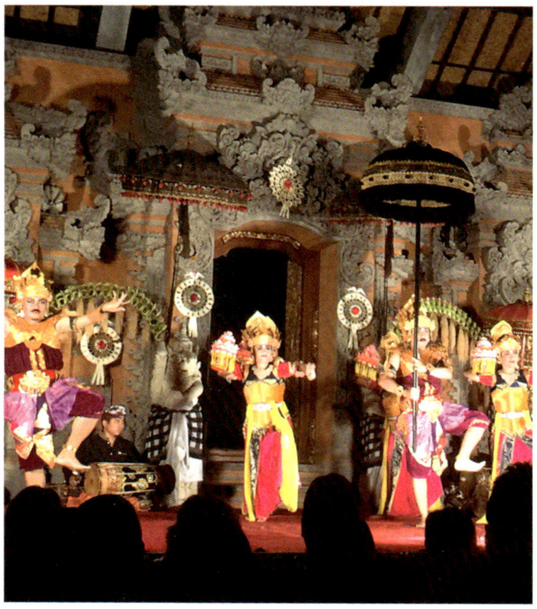

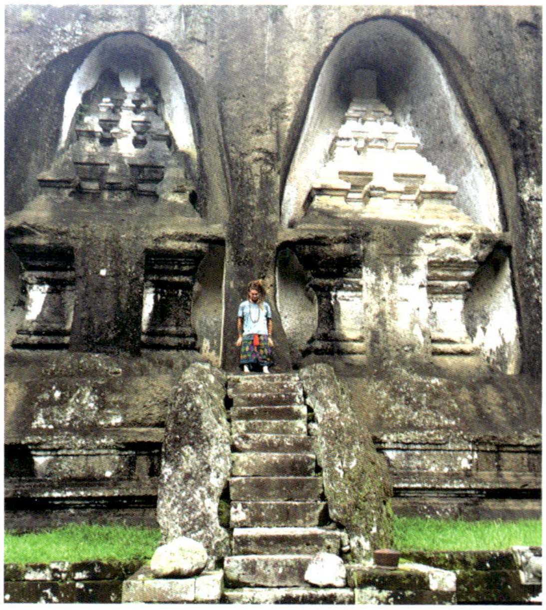

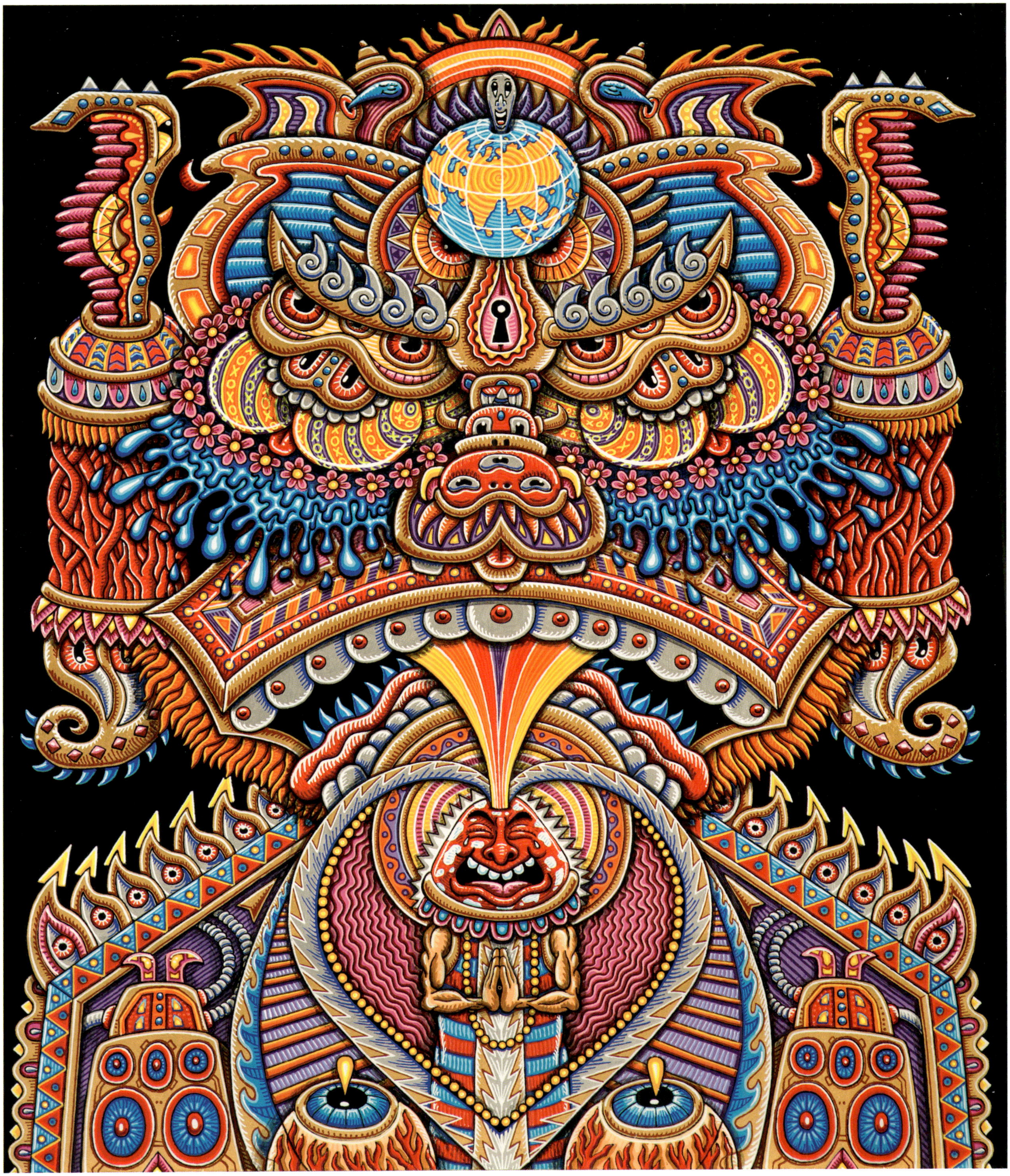

"Kundalini Awakening" Acrylics on wood, 2016

PERU

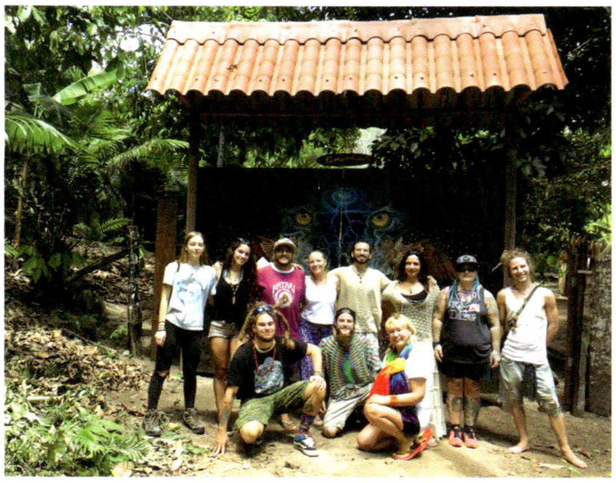
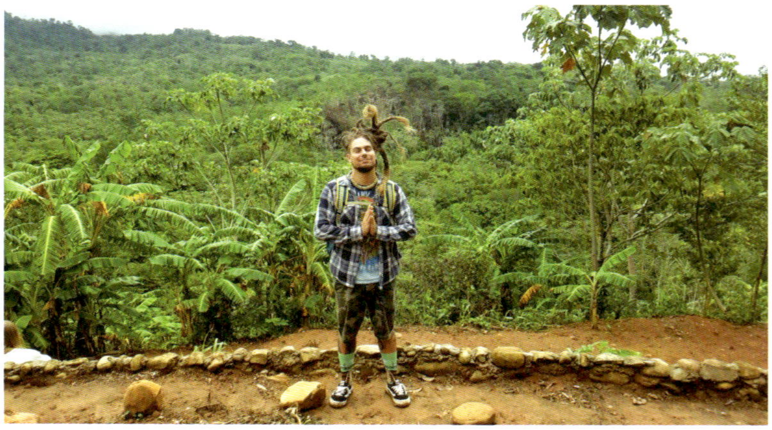
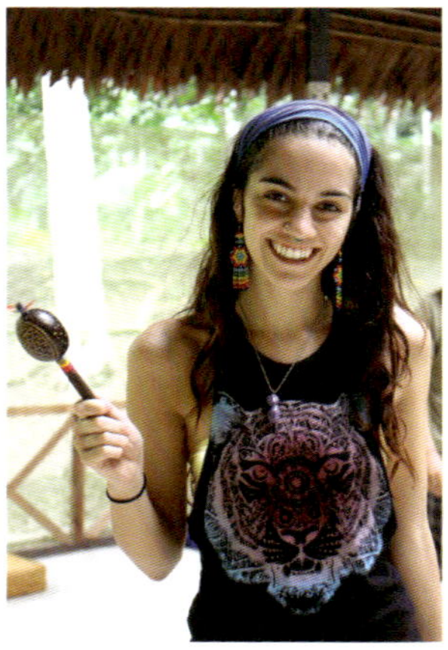

The following month I was back in Peru. After my last healing visit, I had decided I would go to Peru every December to spend Christmas with my parents and got to the jungle to do my medicine recalibrations. It was important to stay close to my aging parents, my original country and keep doing my inner work of becoming light. Earlier that year, Herbert had offered me to do one of my Art Workshops at **"Katari"**, his healing center in **Tarapoto**. I didn't know if adding Ayahuasca ceremonies to my classes would flow or even be safe, but I felt it was worth giving it a try. Naturally, I wanted to see more of Arianne, so I flew her down to join me on this adventure. She is actually from a Brazilian family, which had a shaman of their own, so she had already been working with the medicine since she was thirteen years old (thus why she was so spiritually awake and mature). Anyways, a lovely group of artists from around the world joined me in the jungle to do our art and healing work. Any worry I might have had melted away, as we had such a magical time! Everyone left empowered and with big smiles on their faces. So at the request of the grandmother medicine, this retreat would become a yearly affair!
After our jungle purges, to celebrate Christmas and my blessed comeback, I took Arianne and my parents to **Cuzco** for a vacation. We all had the best time. Life was back to being great, and I was grateful!
Anyways, this painting I started at the jungle retreat is called **"Wise Child Love Story"** and it is obviously about how I fell in Love with Arianne. She is a woman that worships the moon, so I painted it behind her alien version portrait. The composition is fragmented like classic Ayahuasca paintings from the **"Pablo Amaringo"** lineage, but obviously in my own style. I also show the first three journeys we did together (Arizona being the third).

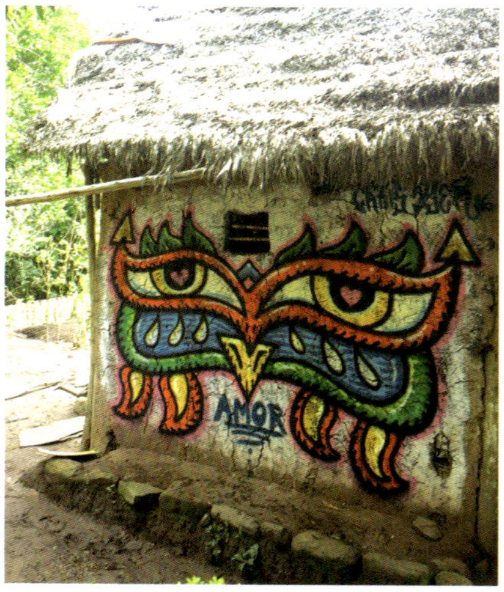

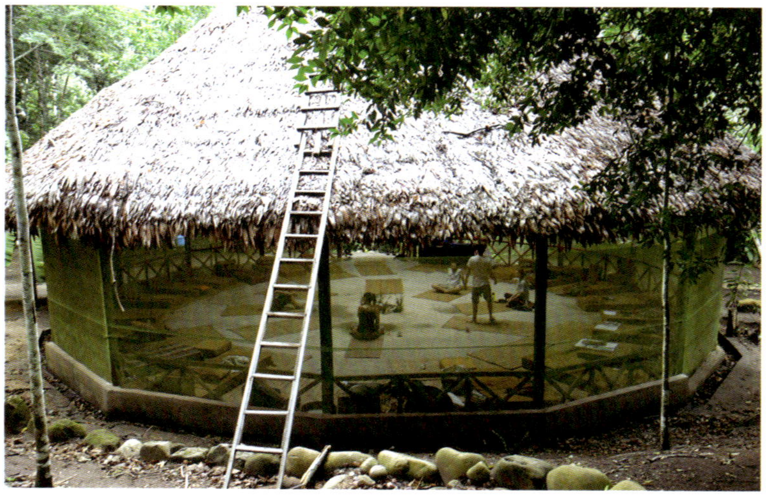
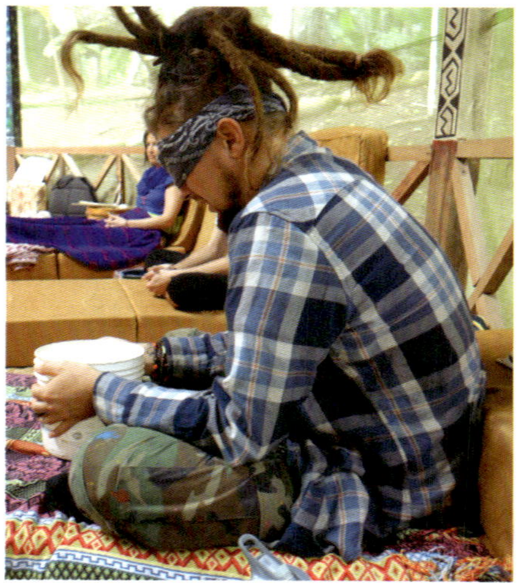

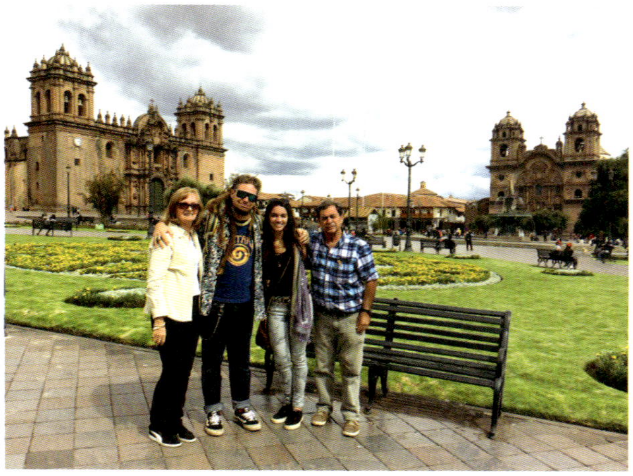
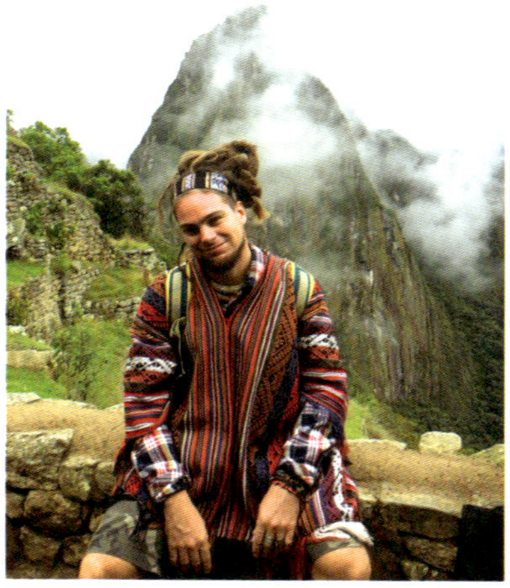
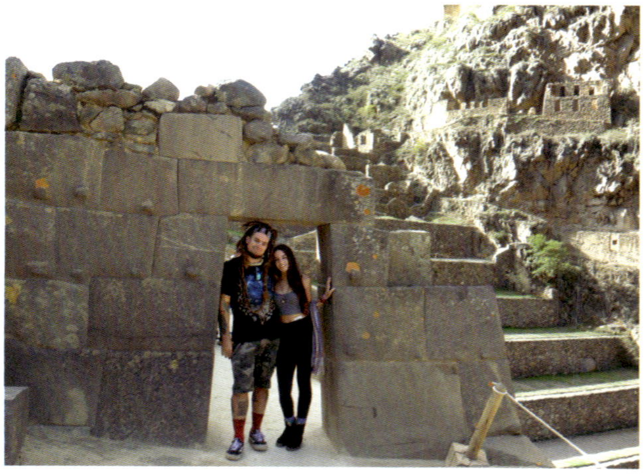

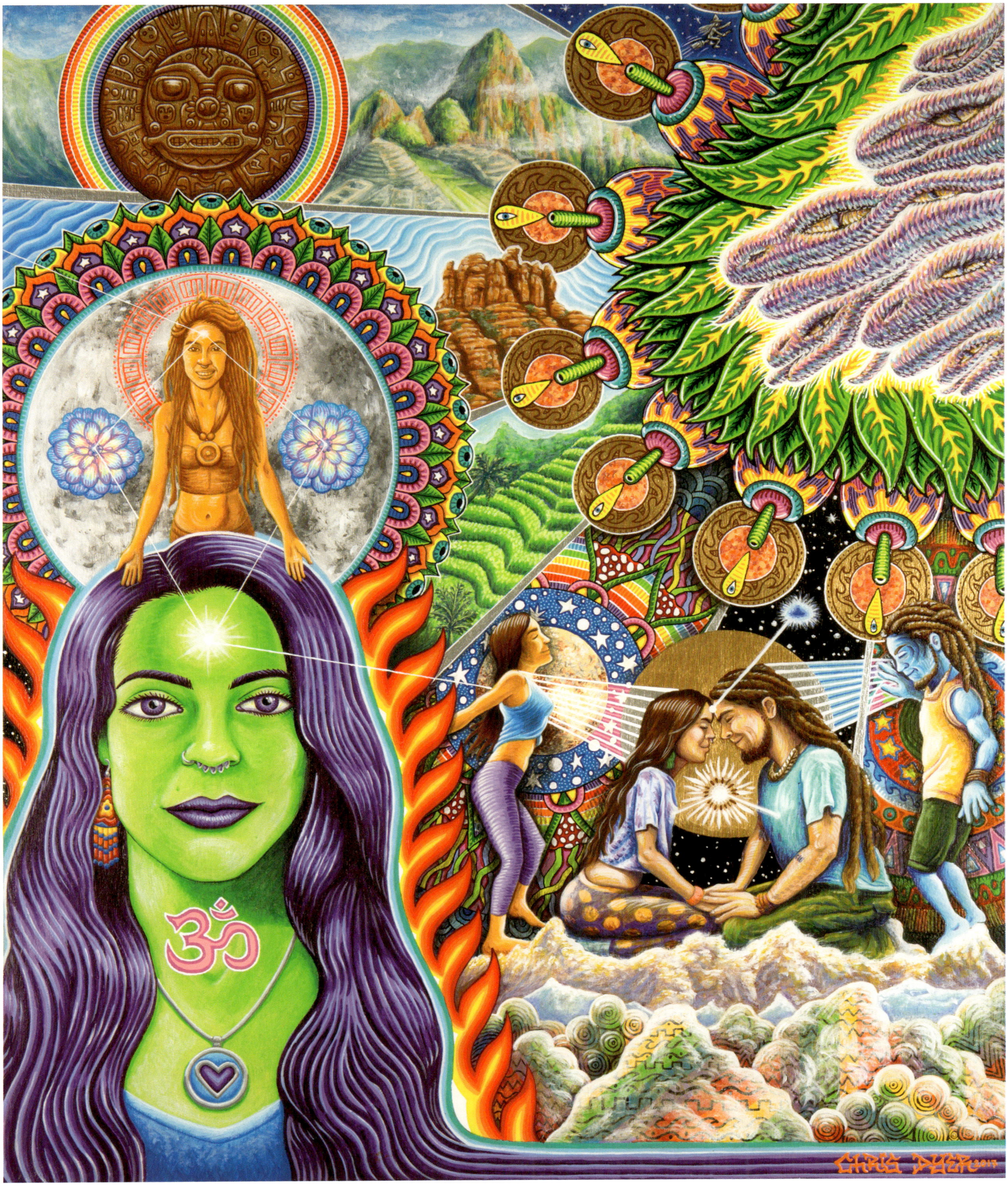

"Wise Child Love Story" Acrylics on wood, 2016-2017

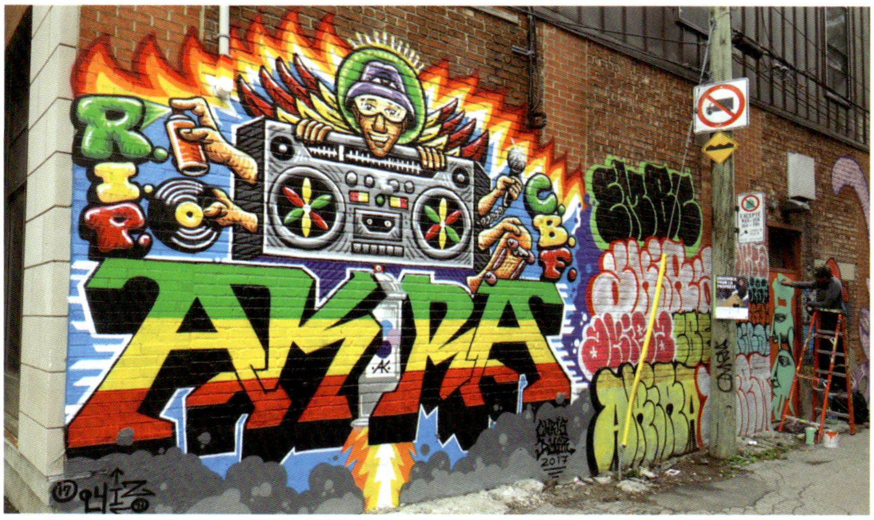

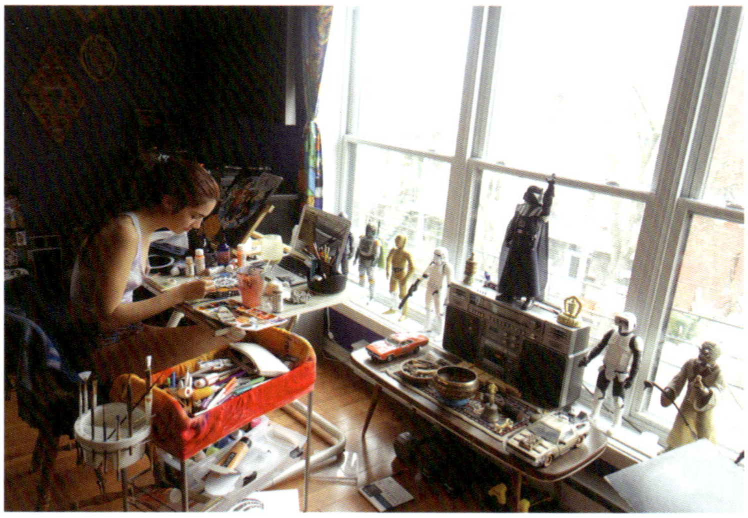

After those lovely journeys, Arianne decided to quit her costly Art College to move to Montreal with me. I took her under my wing and taught her all I could about the art path. While we enjoyed all the blessings of my beautiful island city, I taught her how to spray paint, run an art business, promotion and whatever else would give her career momentum. She enriched my life greatly and we had a blast and a half. I also got motivated enough to start going to the Gym and loose my fat! These are some quick little canvases I hit in that period, among other projects. Trump came into office the day Arianne moved up and it seemed like something extra weird was happening in American Politricks, that usually is all theatre.

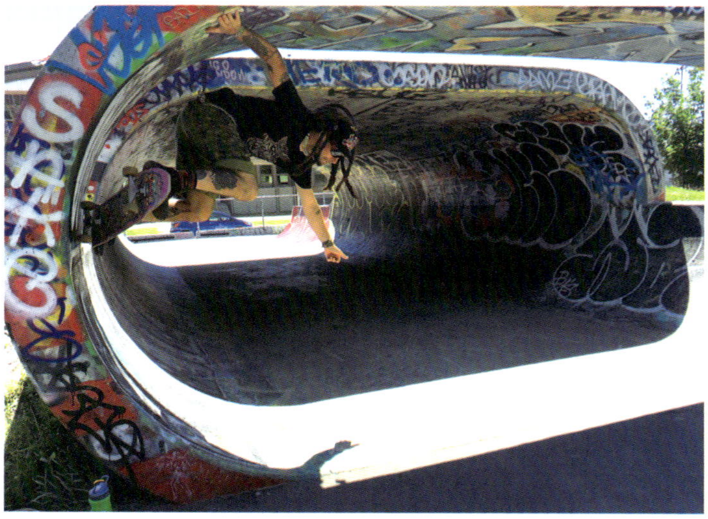

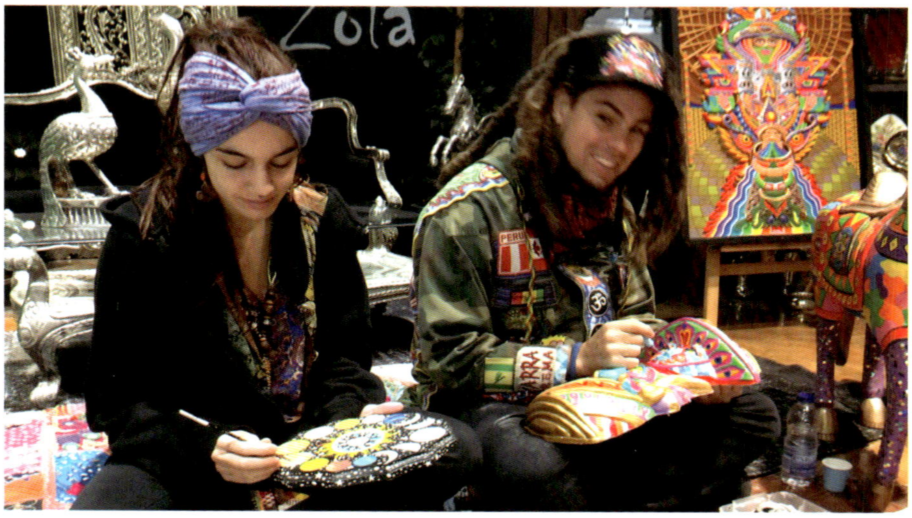

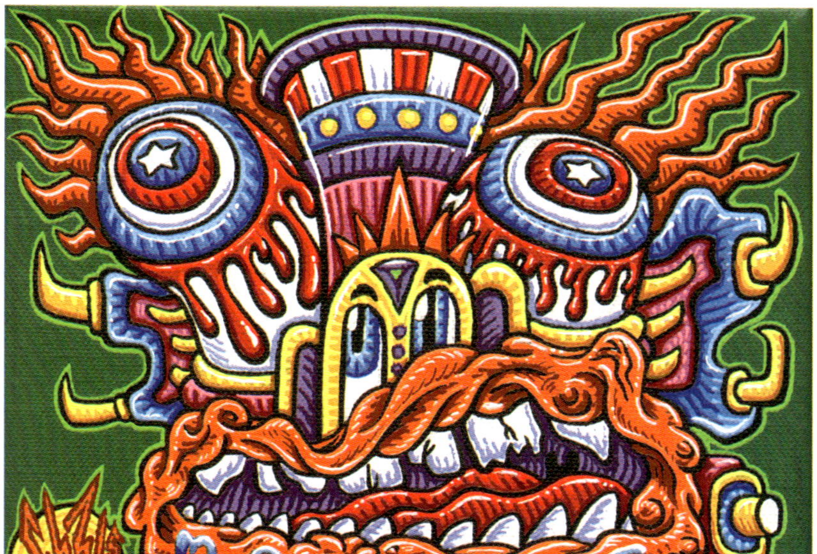

"Political Insanity" Acrylics on canvas, 2017

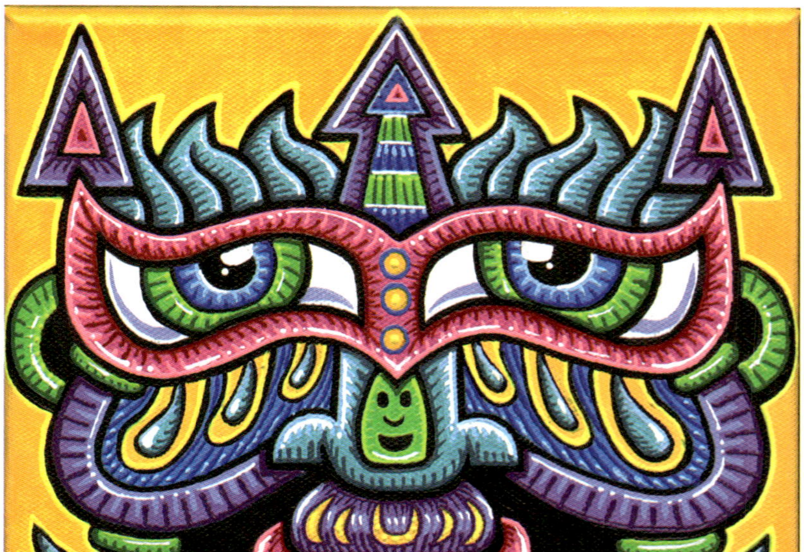

"Galaktic Dude" Acrylics on canvas, 2017

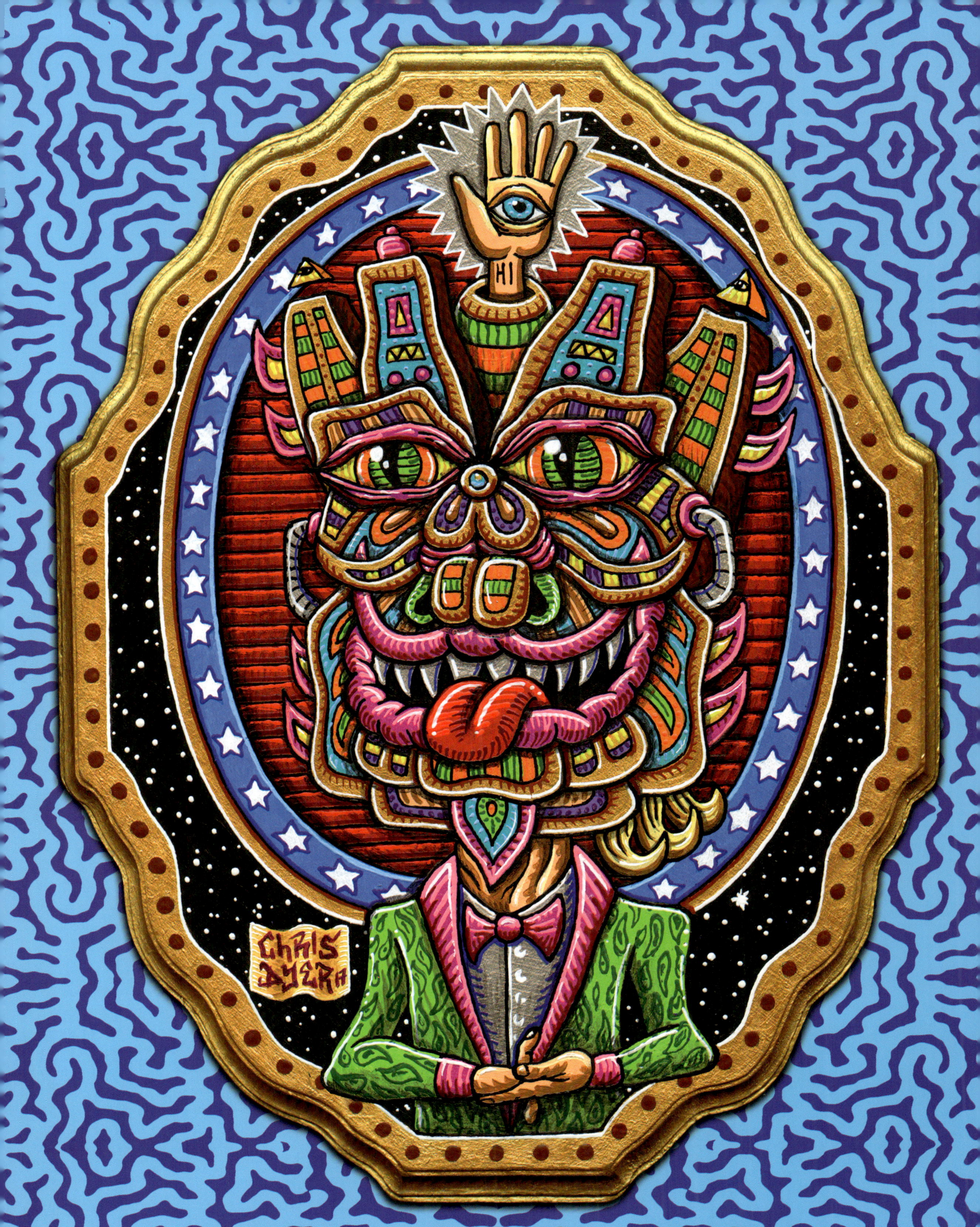

"Master of Puppets" Acrylics on wood, 2017

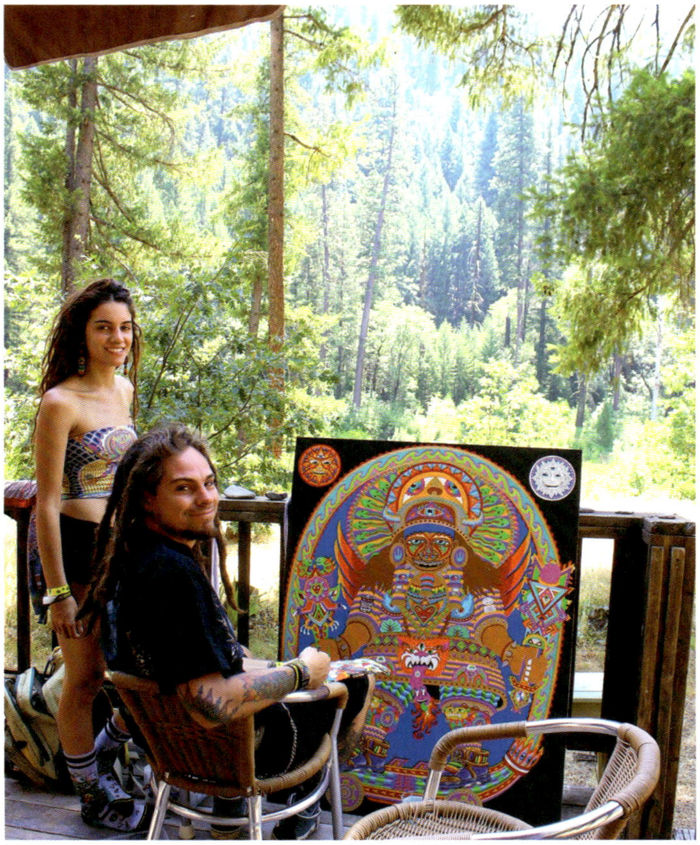

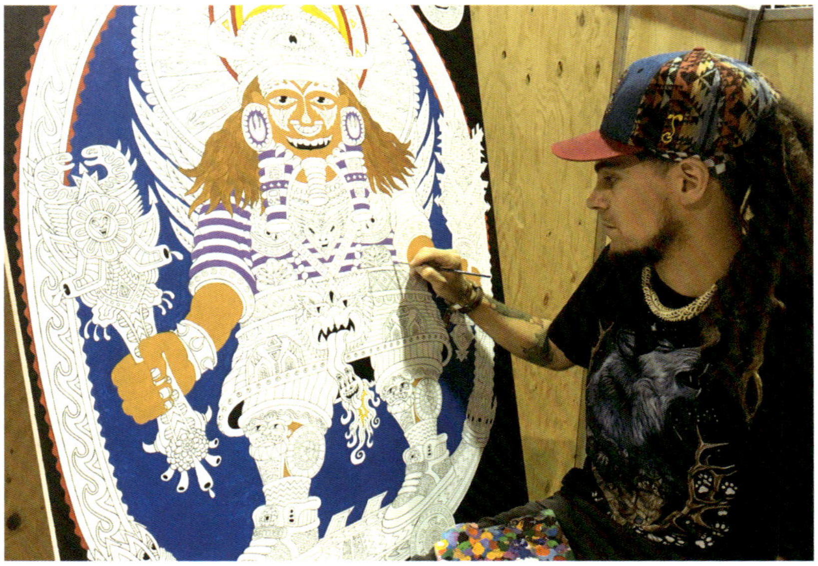

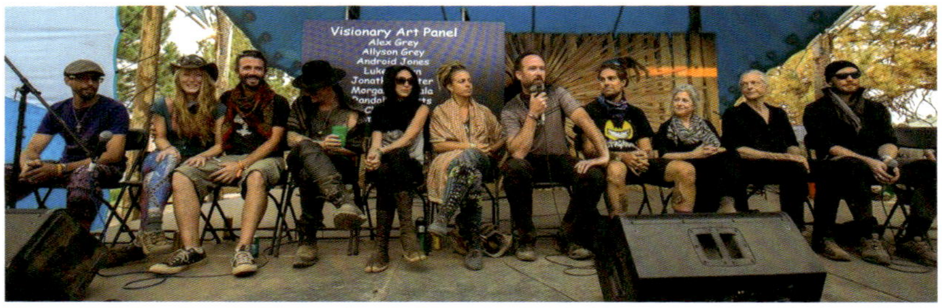

That summer I went on tour full force and Arianne was the perfect partner, she was down for the road missions, was supportive of my own work and was also creative on her own side. In 2017 we performed at many events in **Arizona, Florida, New York, Minnesota, Los Angeles, San Francisco, Nor Cal, New Jersey, Toronto, Oregon** and **Colorado**. It was super fun, but also hard work that wore us down as individuals and partners...

The big canvas that I difficultly carried around with me was **"The Ultimate Spiritual Warrior!"**. He is an archetype that represents the Peaceful Warrior in me and my brotherhood, equipped with the weapons of Love and Mindfulness. Culturally speaking, this tribal elder leans closer to an Inca, but as usual, he is an amalgamation of several different cultures, creating Oneness. He is a wise healer, an angel, a shaman, a courageous leader, a teacher, a creator, etc. He is all the positive archetypes and qualities I strive to grow into, so I can serve my community better. I also custom designed the 3D frame for this royal piece.

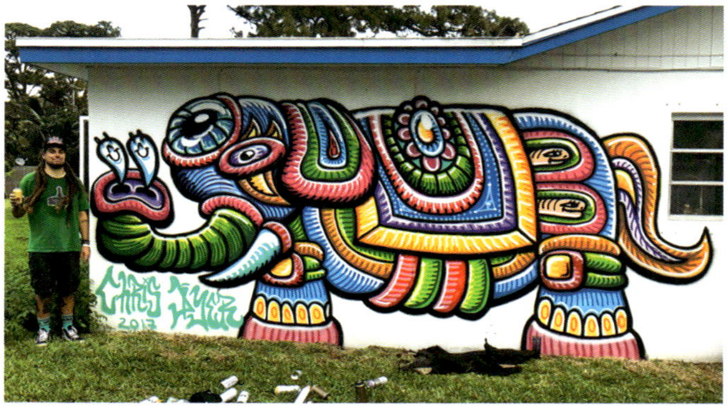

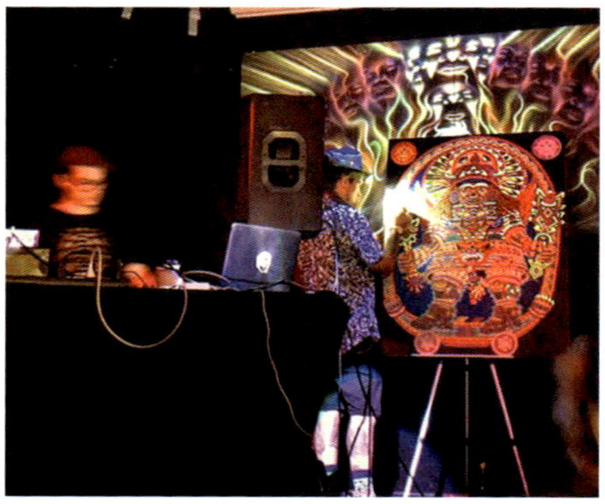

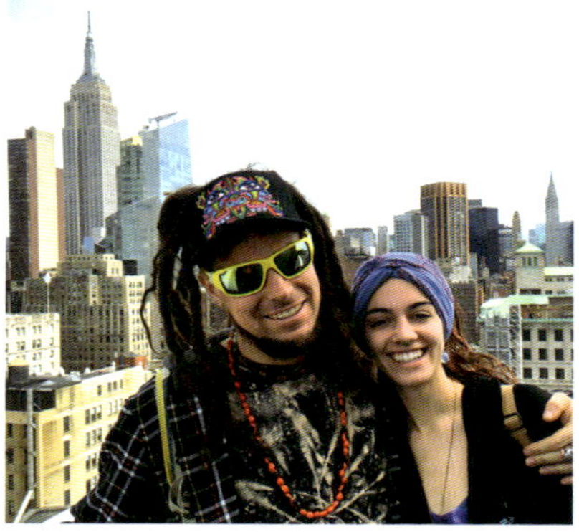

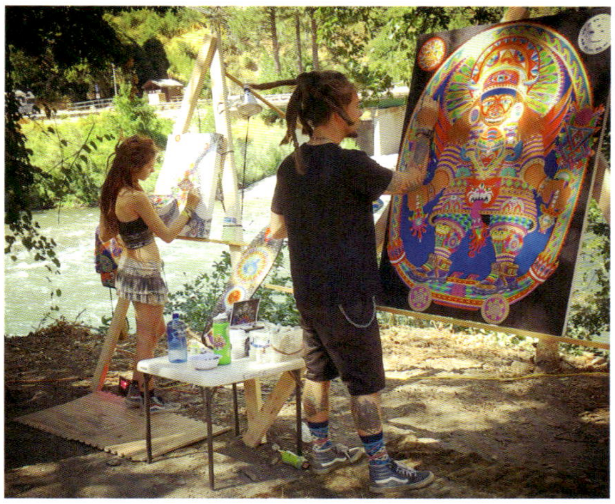

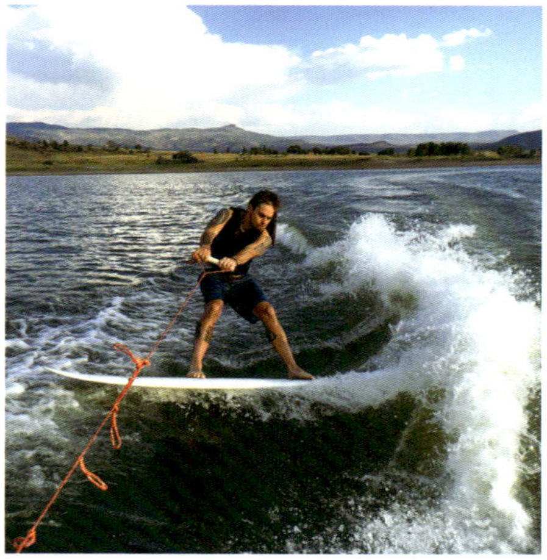

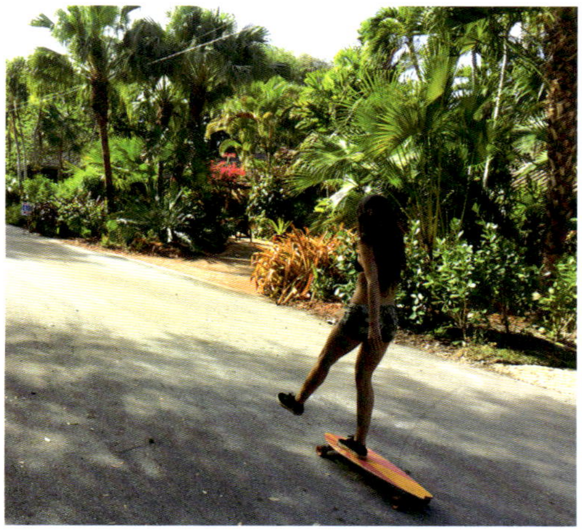

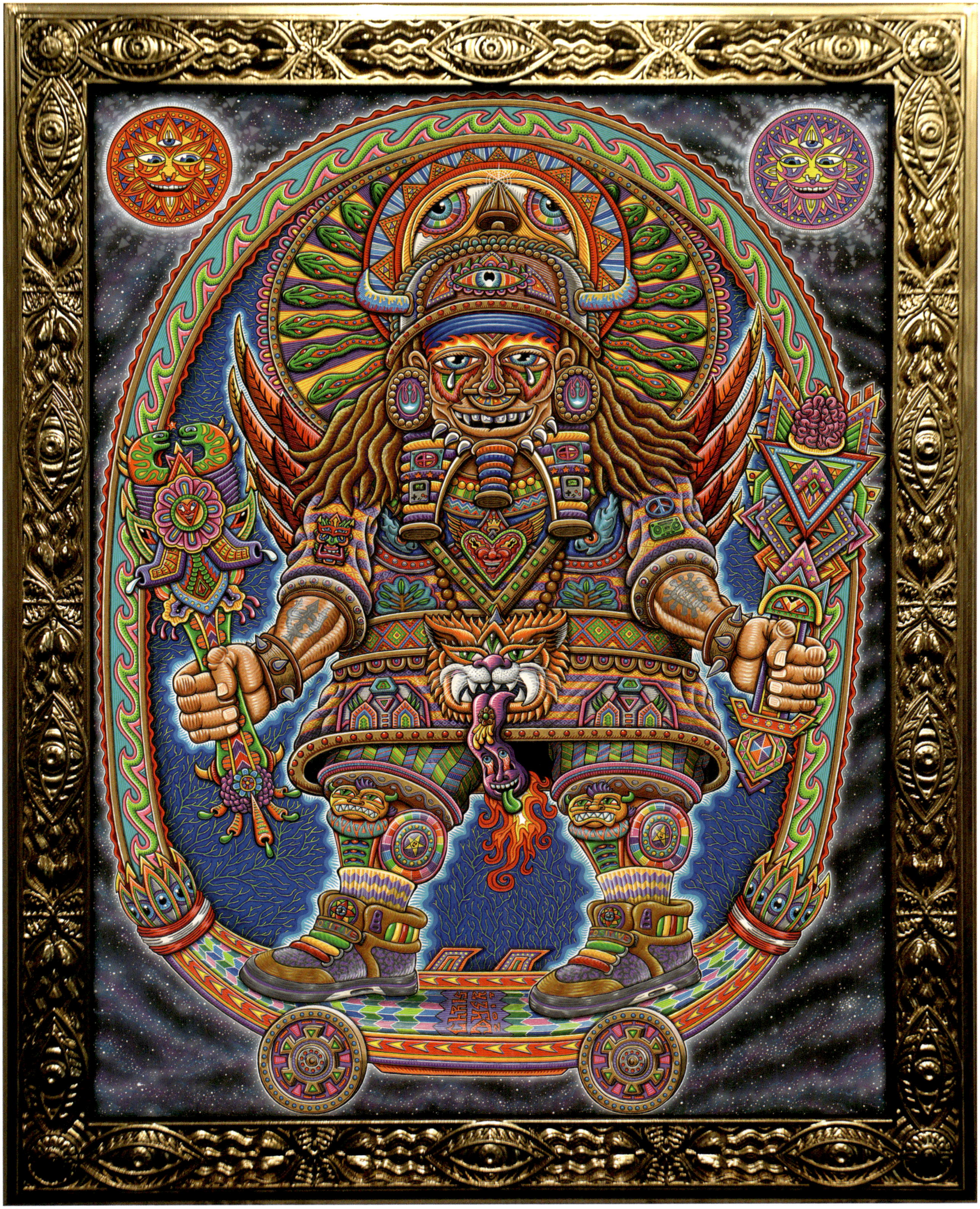

"The Ultimate Spiritual Warrior!" Acrylics on wood, 2017

BRAZIL

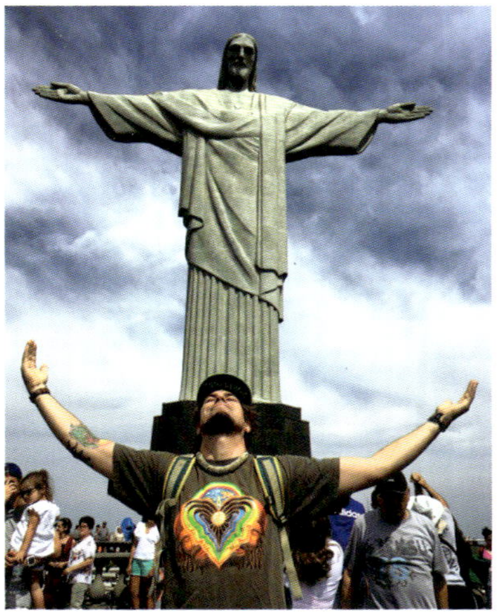
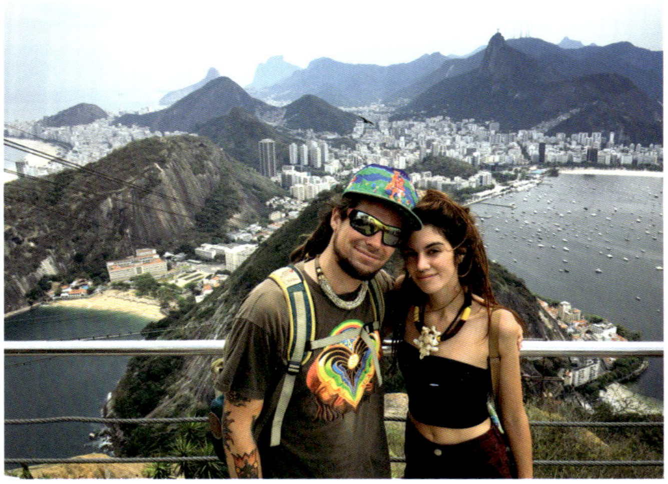
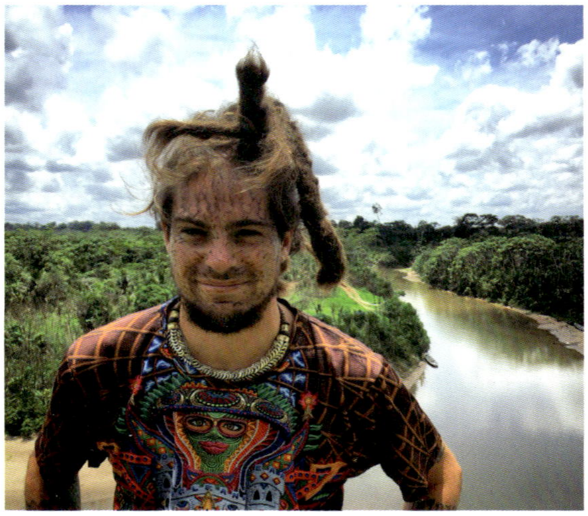

In October of that year, I got invited to paint and give talks at the **"Psychedelic Art Biennale"** in **Sao Paulo**. First though, we started by exploring the legendary city of **Rio**. By synchronicity, Herbert was also in Brazil that month. He was getting married to his Canadian girlfriend Acacia in the middle of the rainforest, and it was important I was part of that special moment. So we flew deep into the Amazonian jungle and then took a skinny motor-boat for 9 hours down a river, until we arrived to **Nova Esperanza** village. This was the home of the **Yawanawa tribe**, who paint their faces, and use feathers to express their divinity. Herbert's wedding was very nice and was followed by an Ayahuasca ceremony, which was very different to the Peruvian ones I was used to. Holding hands and chanting in a circle around the fire was cool, but I was uncertain if I was going to purge right there in front of everyone. I was also going through some emotional struggles, as I was going to break up with Arianne at the end of the trip. I still loved her much, but felt I needed time alone to find my personal strength and confidence, without another long term relationship as a safety net. It was a difficult decision but I had to follow my intuition. The ceremony did end in magic though, with a good purge, while I enjoyed the trippy sights of feathered Yawanawans dancing and singing.

The painting that I did on that trip, **"Shamanic Journey"** started as a bunch of random spray paint shapes, which I drew on top with ink and then shaded with acrylics. I had briefly tried this approach before, but this was a deeper dive into this approach, allowing more flow of subconscious expression. I feel like I am the small guy at the bottom left of the painting, trying to clear my aura from the mental demons around me. **Rapé** tobacco snuff, which the Yawanawans where masters of, was the daily meditative medicine I started using for that.

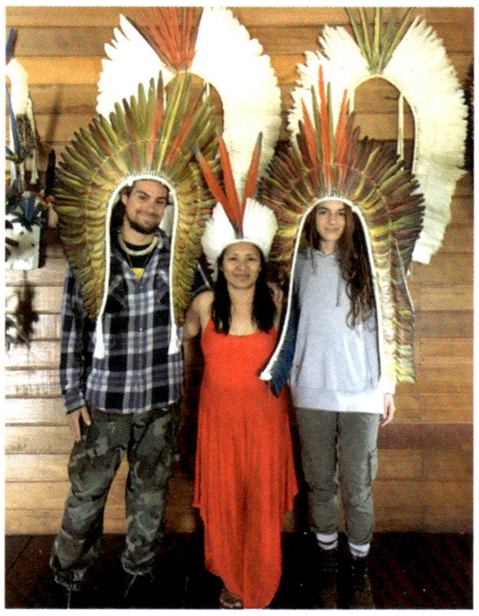
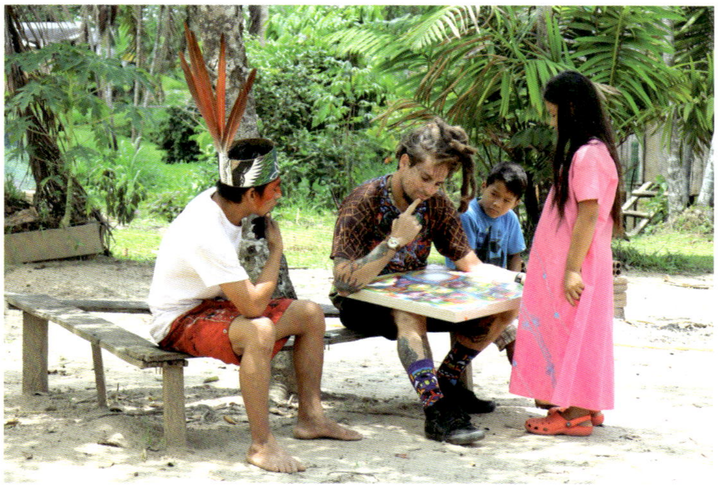
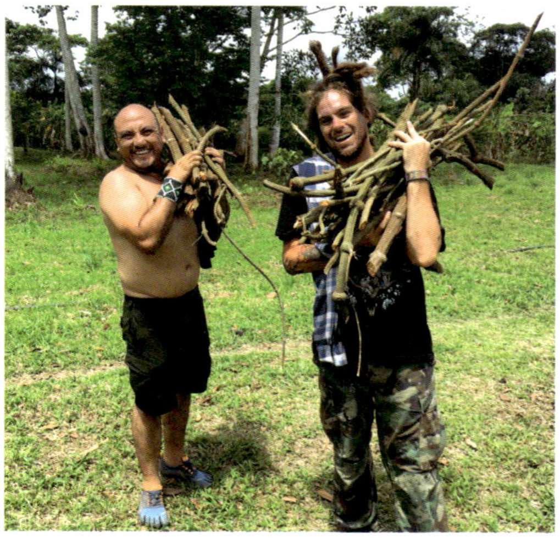
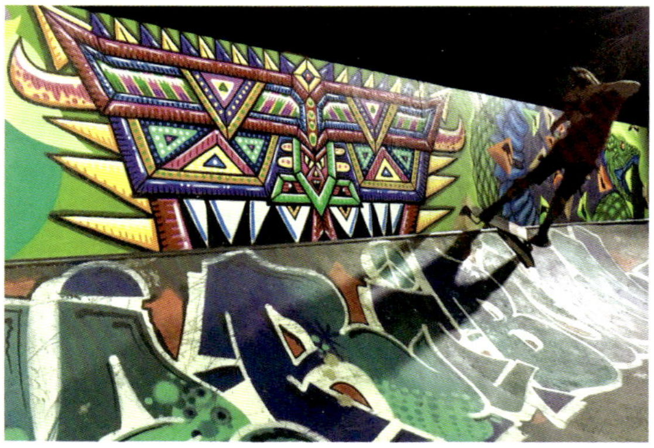
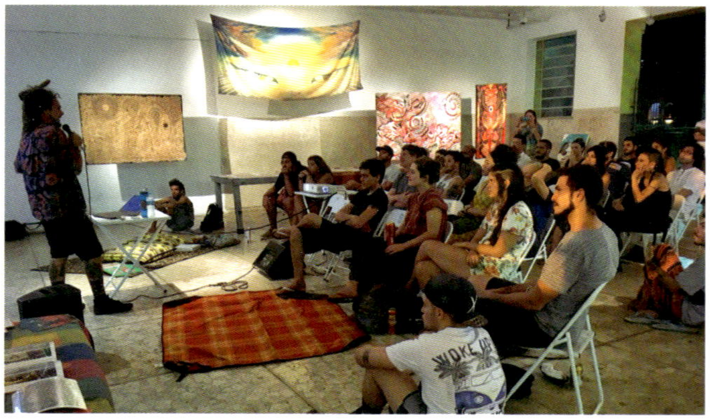
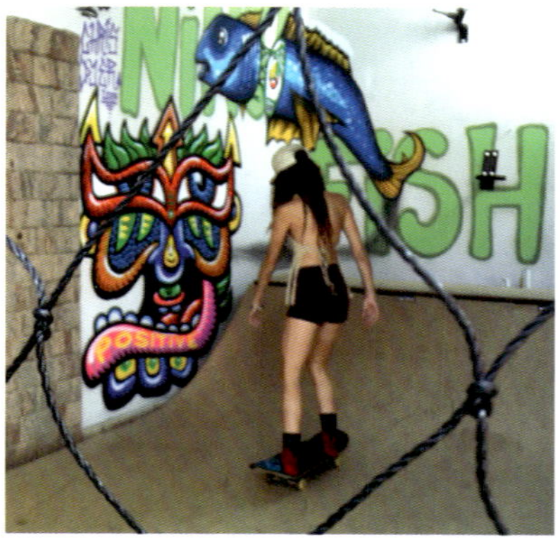

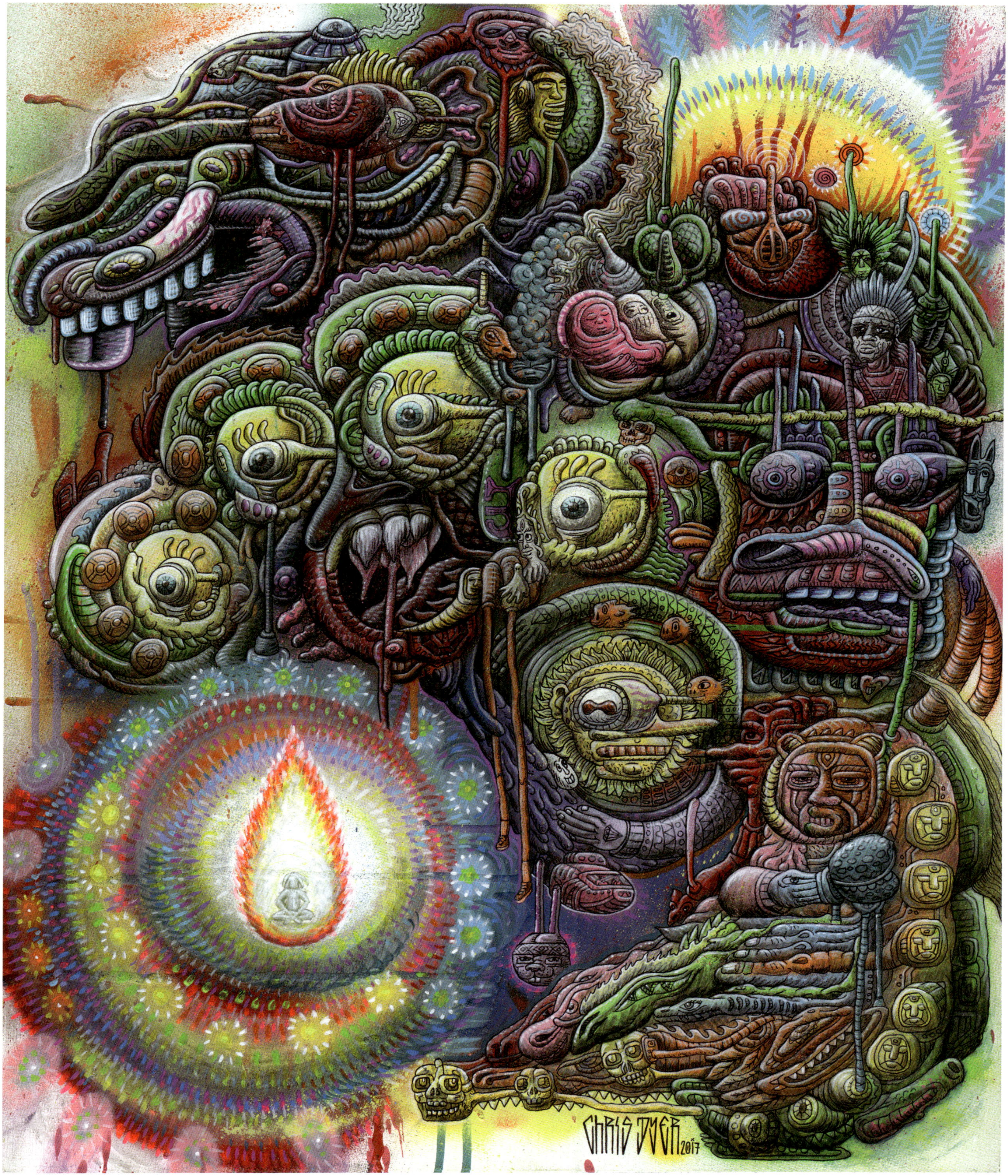

"Shamanic Journey" Acrylics on wood, 2017

AMSTERDAM & VIENNA

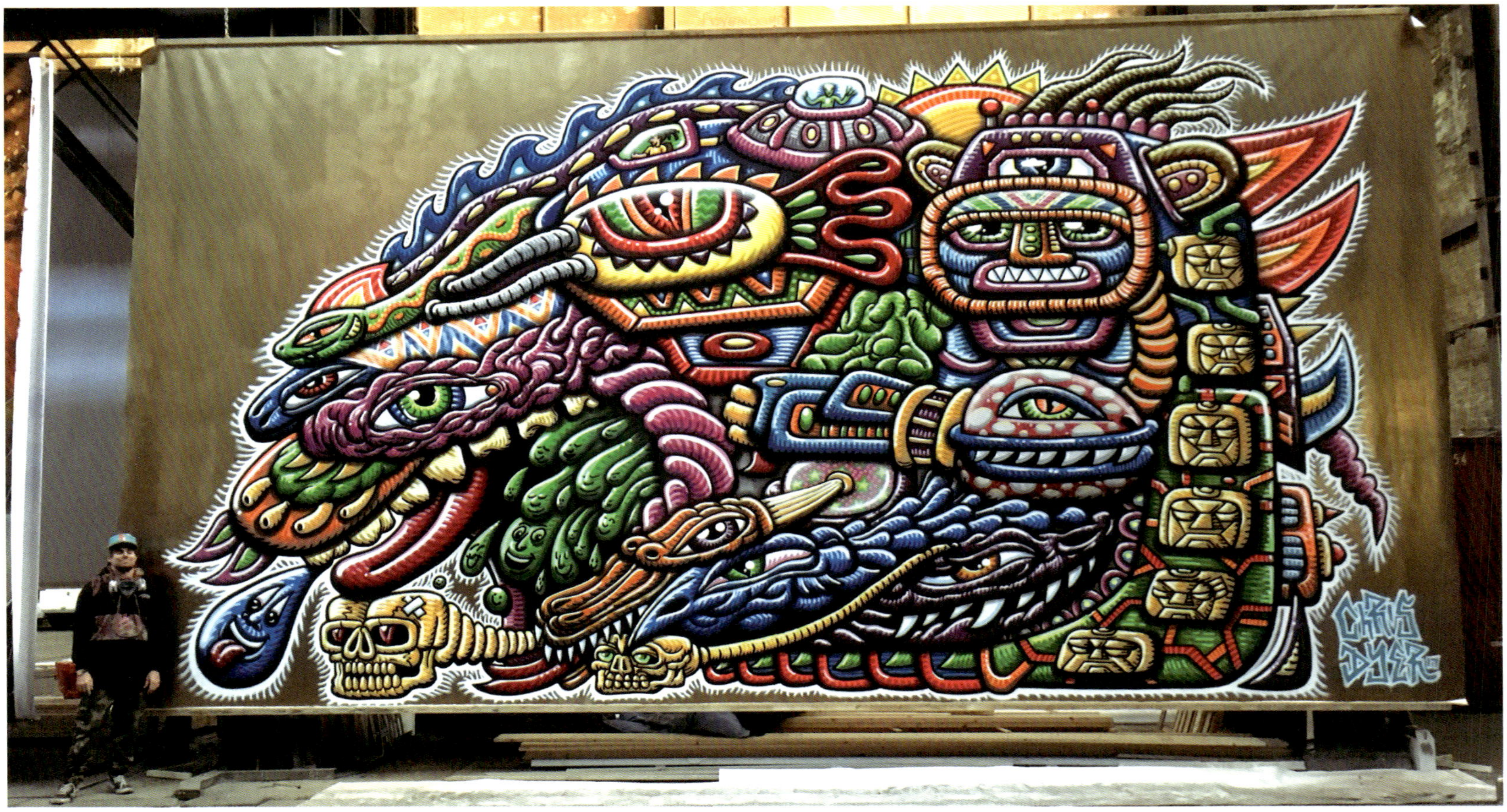

A week after that trip, Arianne and me split up. She returned to her mom's home in Florida and I continued on to my next art mission in **Amsterdam**. There, the upcoming **"Straat Museum"** gave me a boat house airbnb to stay at and a giant canvas to paint for their collection. That huge spray painting was based on sections of the new canvas I had just completed in Brazil, as a way to keep integrating those experiences.

Next, I flew to **Austria**, where I was going to stay for five weeks, teaching at the **"Vienna Academy of Visionary Art"**. The academy's directors **Laurence Caruana** and his wife **Florence Menard** gave me an apartment to live at during that Trimester. It was a nice experience to teach an international group of students for longer than usual, in a city with such impressive architecture and amazing art museums. But I also fell in a deep depression from letting go of Arianne. The dark, cold and rainy weather of Vienna's winter didn't help either, nor did the unfriendly vibes of the locals. To make things even harder on myself, I decided to go on a **"Master Cleanse"** which is a diet where you only drink juices for 11 days, as to purify your intestines from parasites.

The painting I did those weeks is a visual representation of my negative side, shadow, pain, fears, anger, paranoia, judgement, insecurities, etc. All these mind parasites I want to get rid of. I don't think one can actually kill one's shadow, as it's part of the dualistic human condition, formed by traumas of the past. So my intention was to allow it to purge, as to make it weaker and less in control. All the little characters coming out of his mouth and belly are supposed to be people who've hurt me, so I can release the resentment towards them. I approached it differently, with an unusual two-light source, used gold leaf for the first time and kept exploring with my spray paint decalcomania style. It was a very difficult painting to feel out, but it was definitely a healing process too!

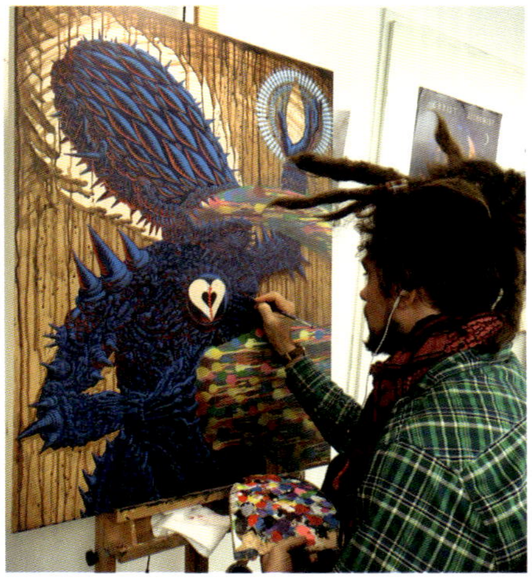

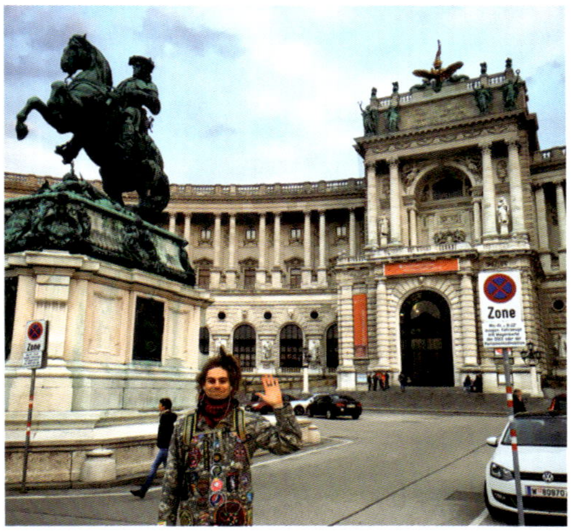

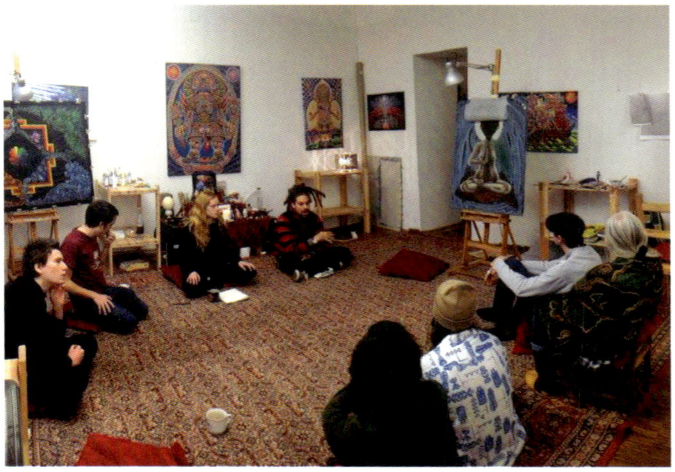

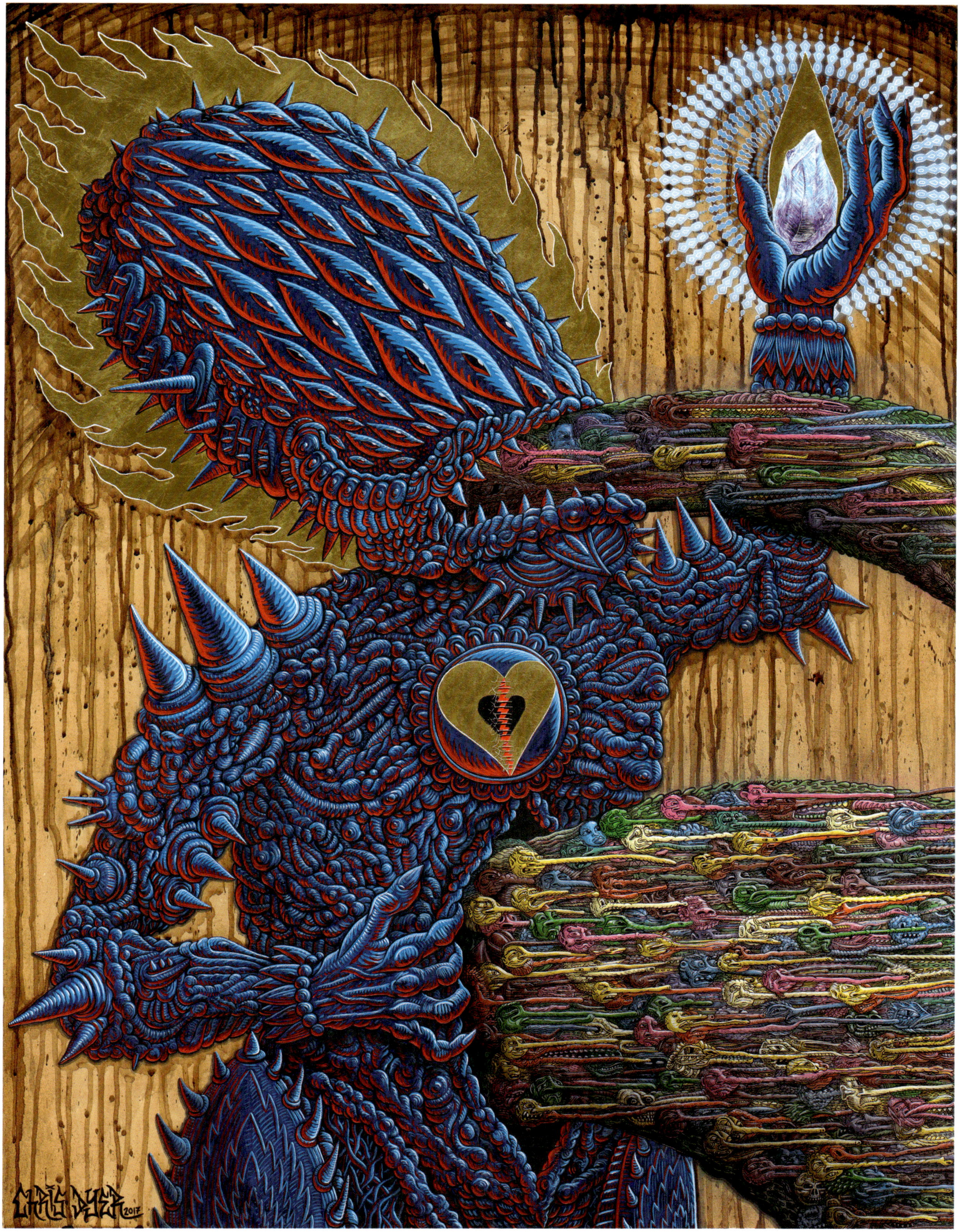

"Shadow Work" Acrylics, spray paint & gold leaf, 2017

TARAPOTO

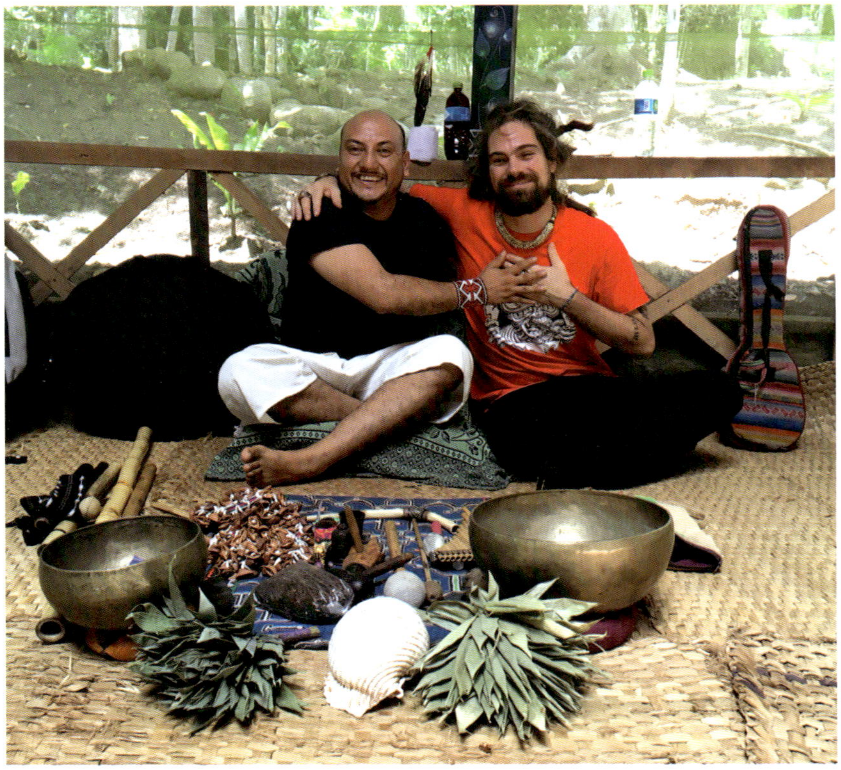

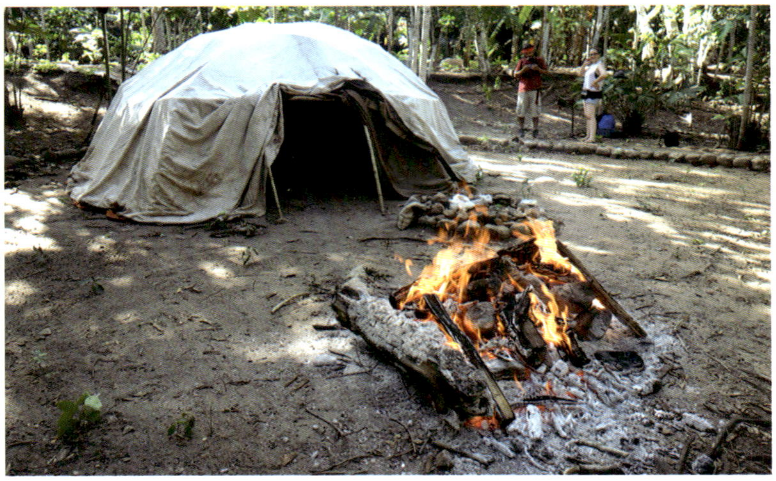

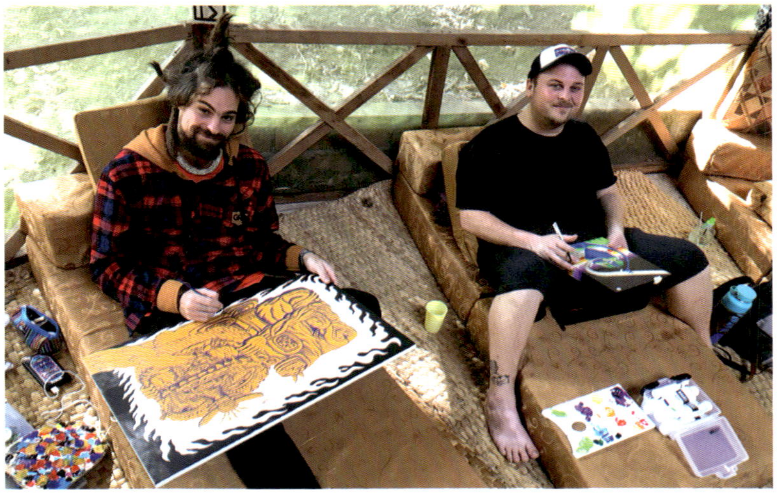

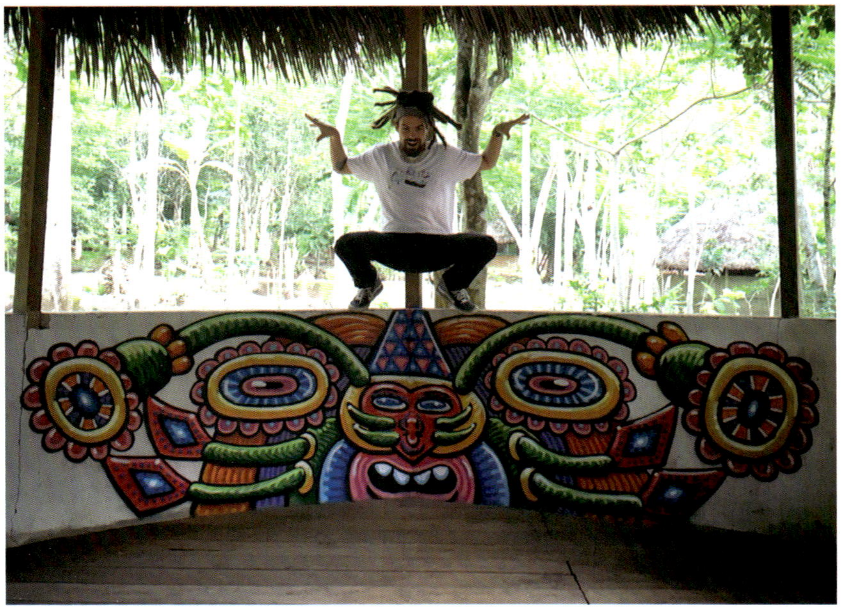

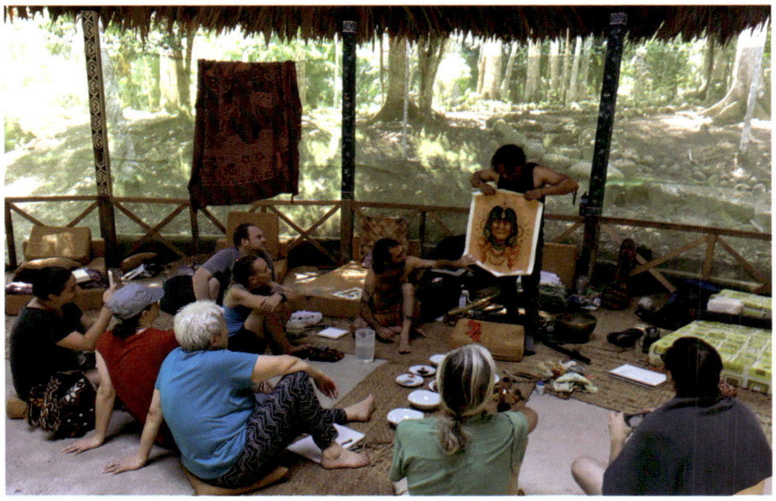

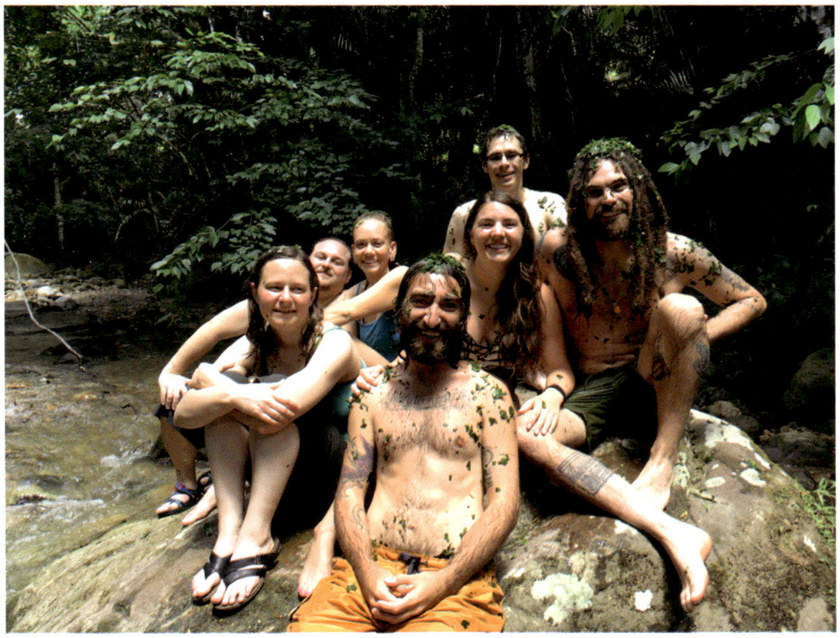

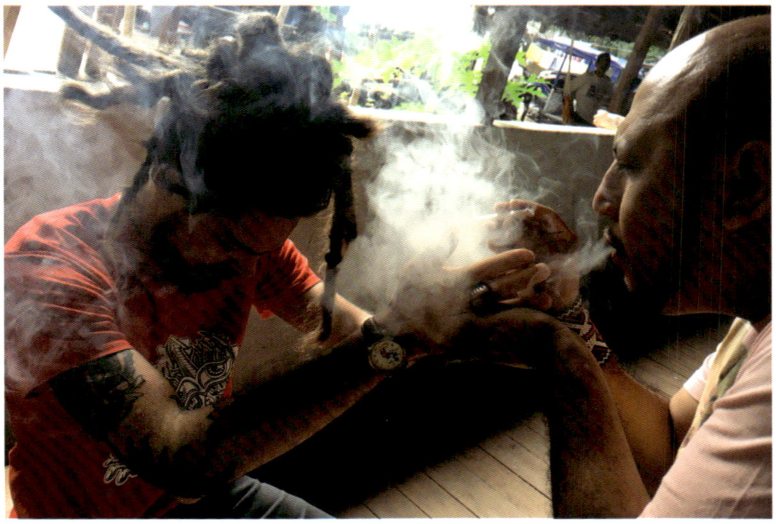

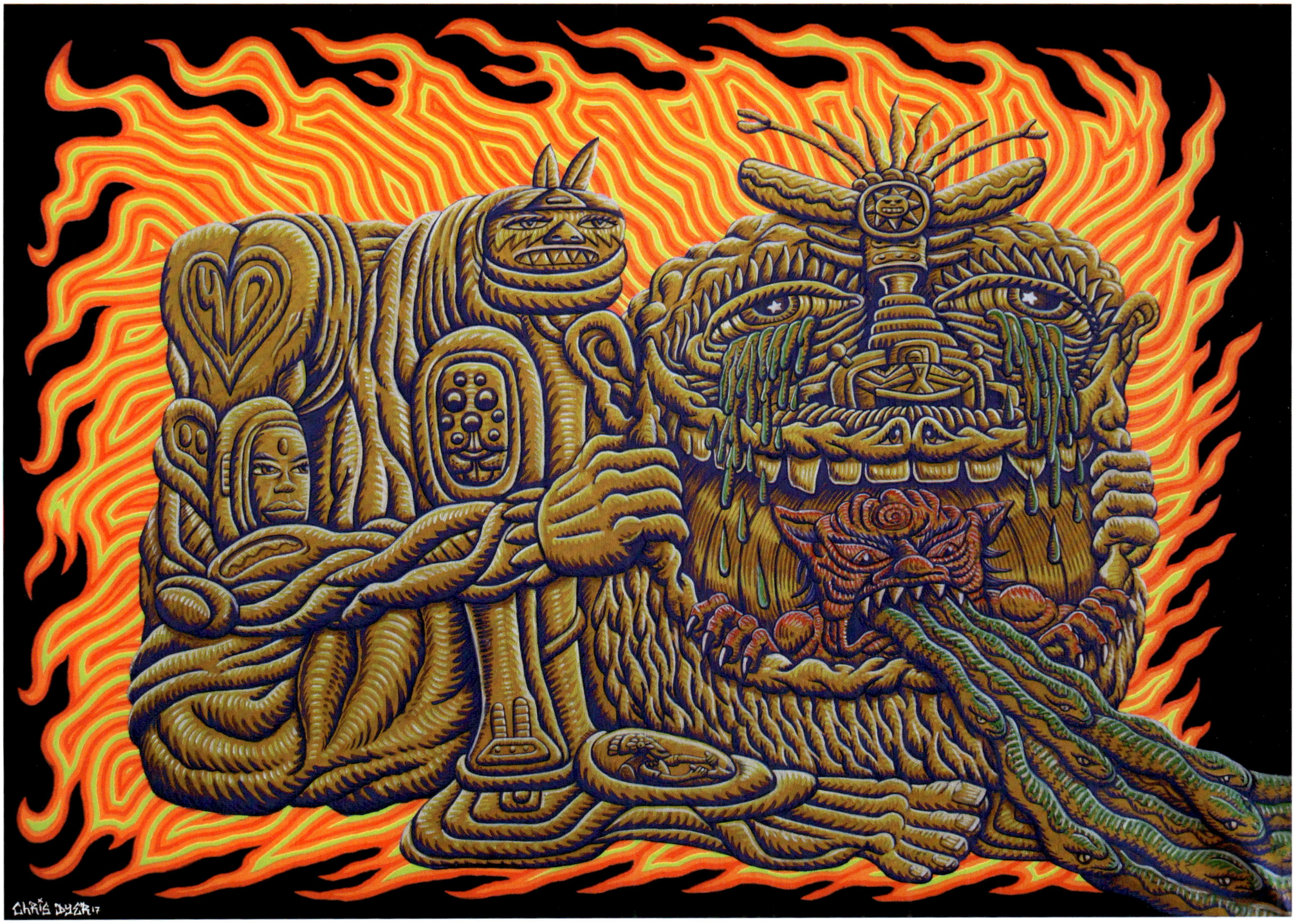

"Golden Boy Let it Go!" Acrylics on Canvas, 2017

My next stop was going back to the jungle of **Peru**, for my second **"Healing Visions"** Art and Medicine Retreat, at Katari Center in Tarapoto. There I welcomed another lovely group of spiritual artists from around the world, to teach and learn from. It was the perfect place to keep healing. During that time I also did a **"Bobinsana"** Master Plant Diet, which made me extra sensitive. It activated a very psychic aspect of myself, yet it made it a lot more challenging to fulfill the role of a teacher. The Ayahuasca Ceremonies were all very potent too, especially after all the shadow-work I had done in Vienna. A bunch of the pain that I had accumulated from the break-up was released like an electrocution. I also got in touch with some deep knowledge from the Akashic Tree library. By the end of the retreat I felt I was ready to go back to Arianne, but then I saw her hanging out with a new dude on Instagram, which really hurt my feelings. I realized I still had a lot of work to find my self-love, where I can truly be happy by myself, no matter what.

At this retreat I started this painting called **"Golden Boy, Let it Go!"**, which was my mantra for that process. I needed to let go of Arianne along with the negativity of my demons. The fire around this purging patient represents the pain I endured in the ceremony, where the universe was trying to teach me to surrender to whatever is. One step at a time, but always a nice to lighten the load.

CUBA

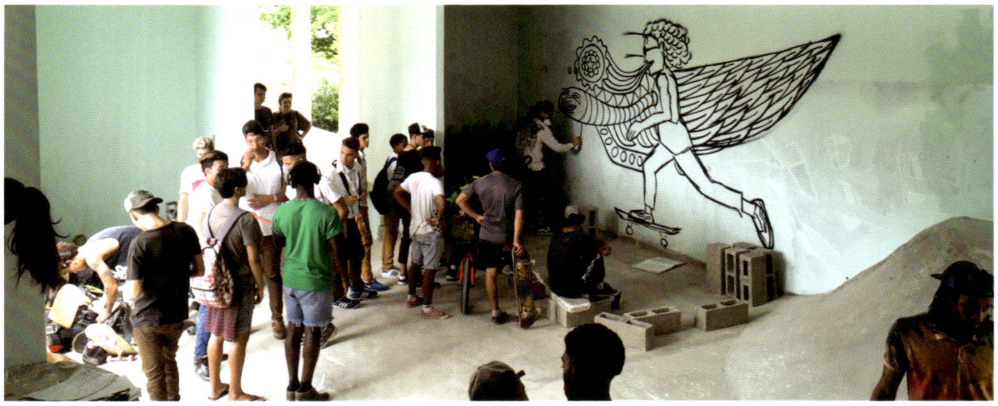

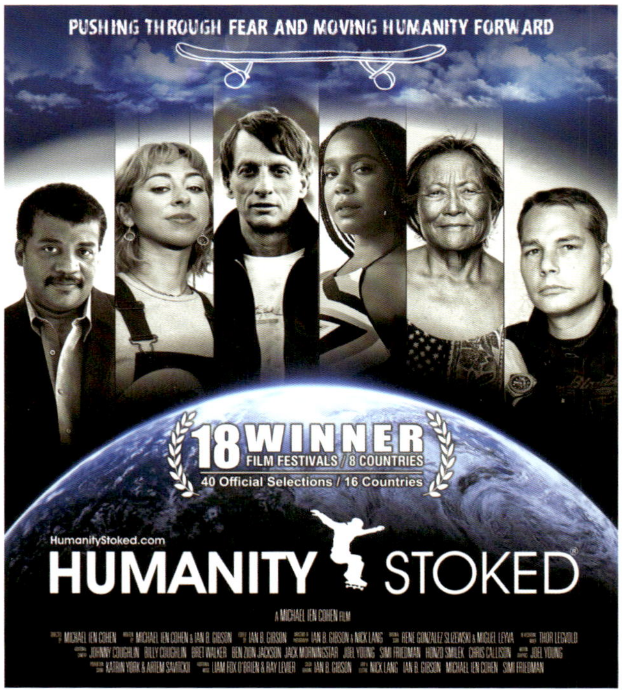

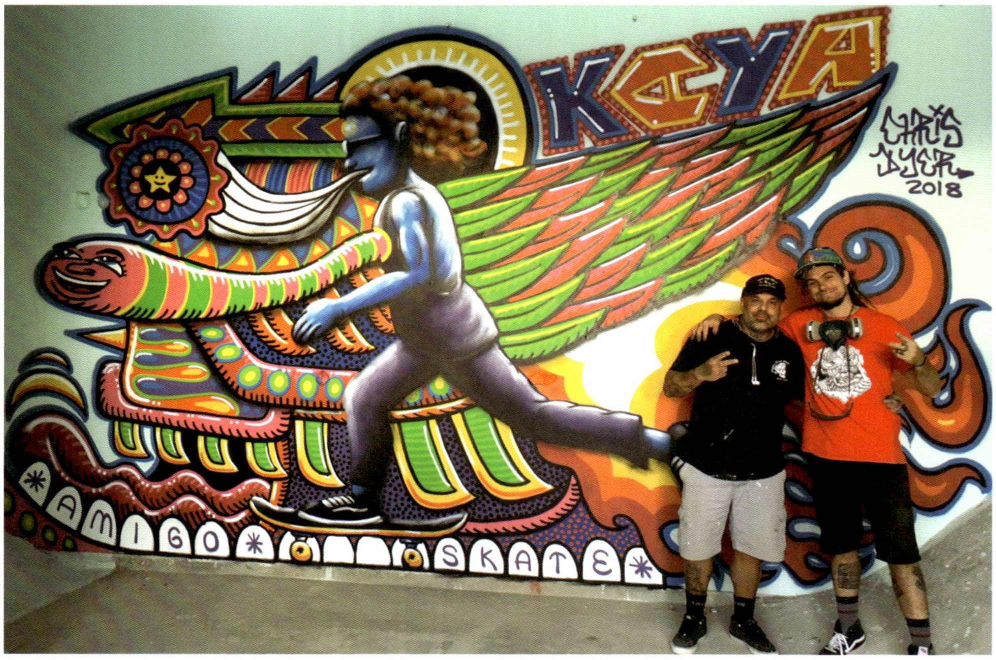

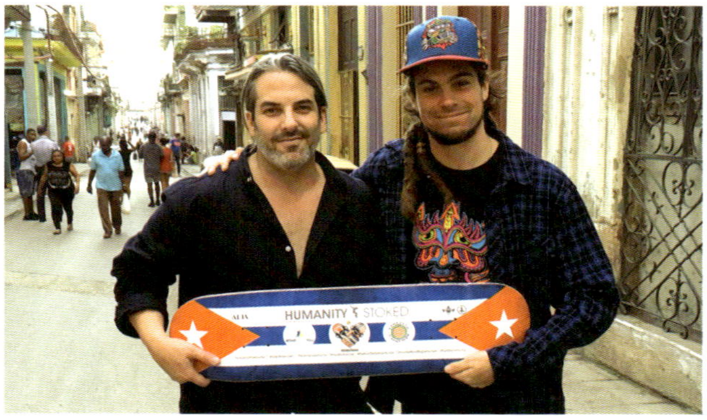

Still recuperating from my very sensitive Plant Diet and ceremonies, I jumped into the next scheduled art mission! I always wanted to visit the island of Cuba and this was the perfect opportunity. Movie producer **Michael Ean Cohen** had invited me to volunteer at some free events for skaters in the capital city of **La Habana**. The communist nature of this country made it that skaters there couldn't access any equipment, nor have proper facilities to play. So we teamed up with a charity organization called "**Amigo Skate**" to bring them some boards and throw some cool events for them! This happened at a D.I.Y. skatepark at an abandoned school. I managed to smuggle some spray paint cans into the country and was going to paint a mural for the park. This ended being a portrait of **Kaya**, who was the recently deceased son of the "Amigo Skate" organizer **Rene Lecour**. I wanted to honor his eternal spirit and even managed incorporate some of Kaya's ashes into the mural. It was an honor for me and he was very touched! At these skate jam events we had some world renowned musicians playing and I also managed to teach a quick skate-painting workshop for the kids. It was mad chaotic but very fun! All of this was actually captured for Michael's documentary **"Humanity Stoked"** which ended having a long list of famous personalities involved and won a bunch of awards!

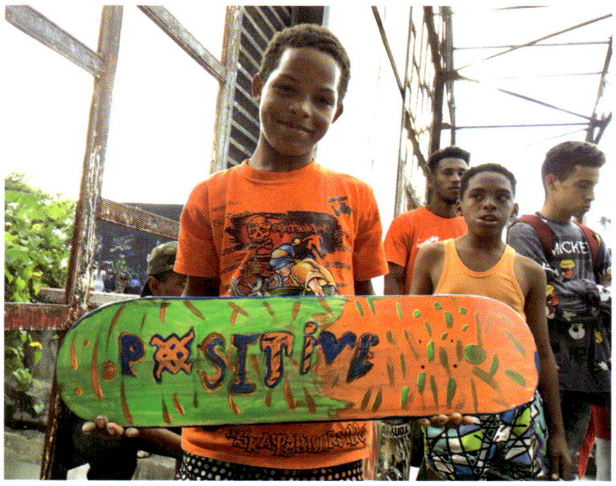

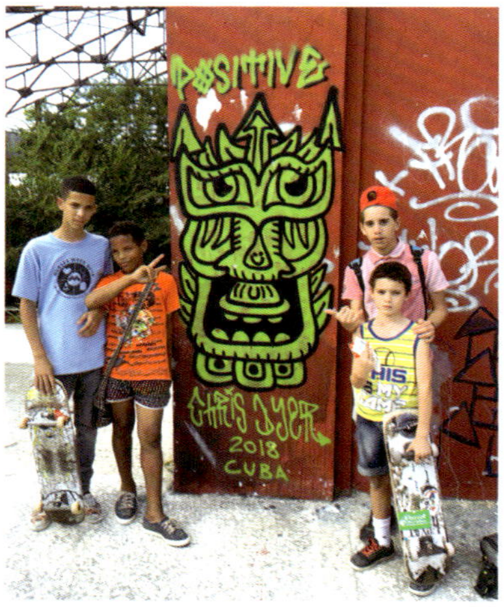

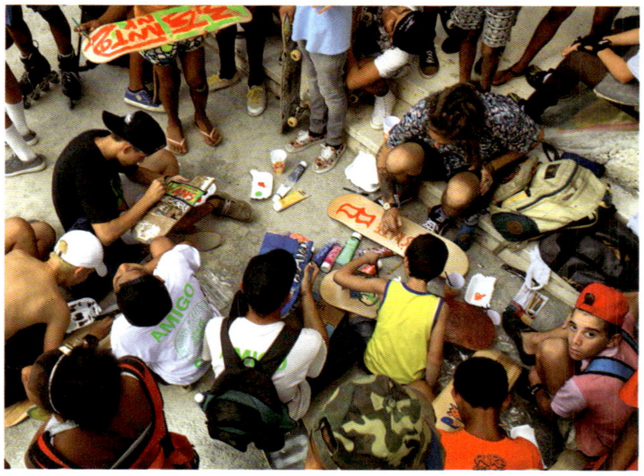

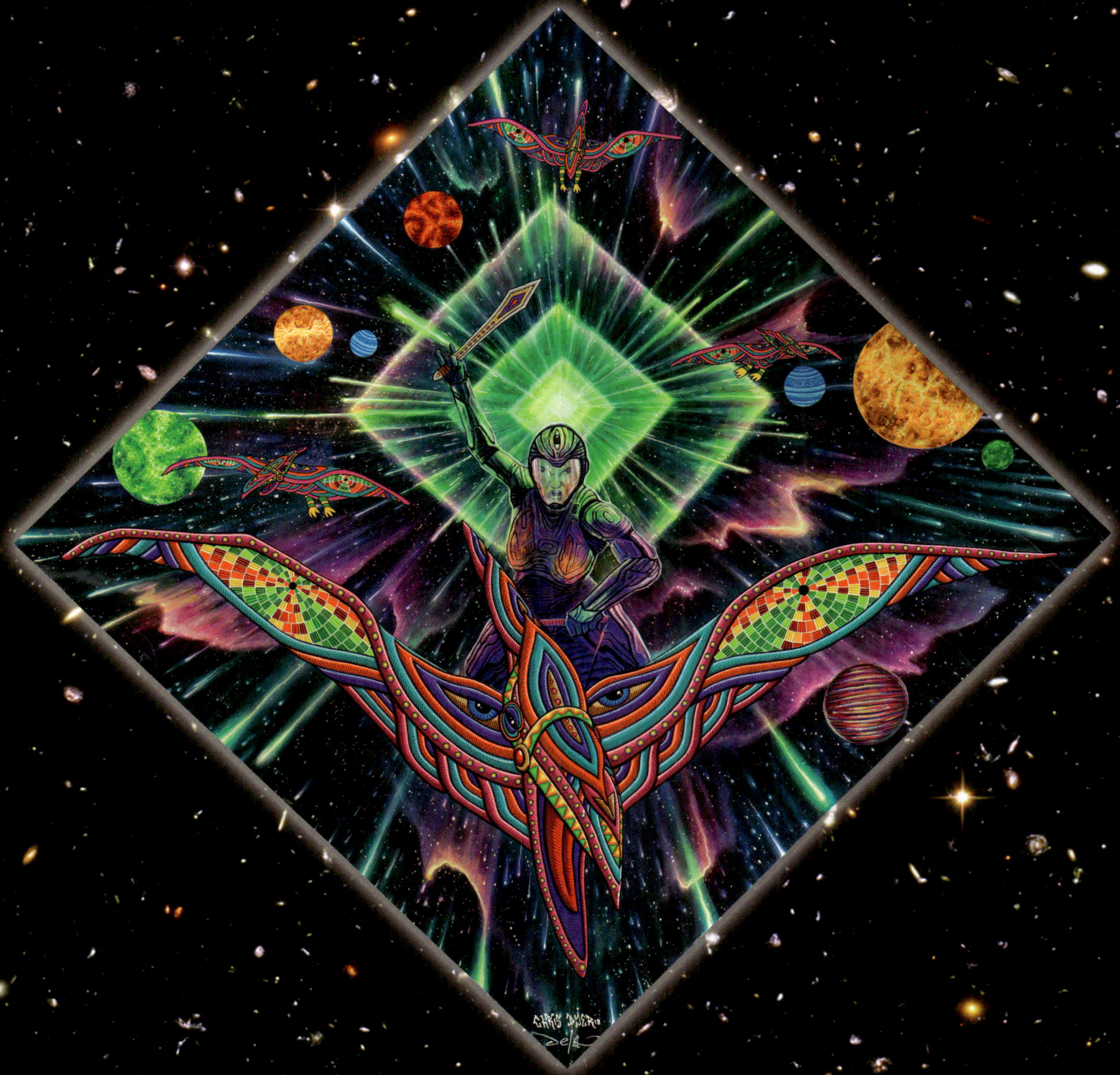

"Masters of the Parallel Universe"
Acrylics on Canvas, collaboration with **Dela**, 2018

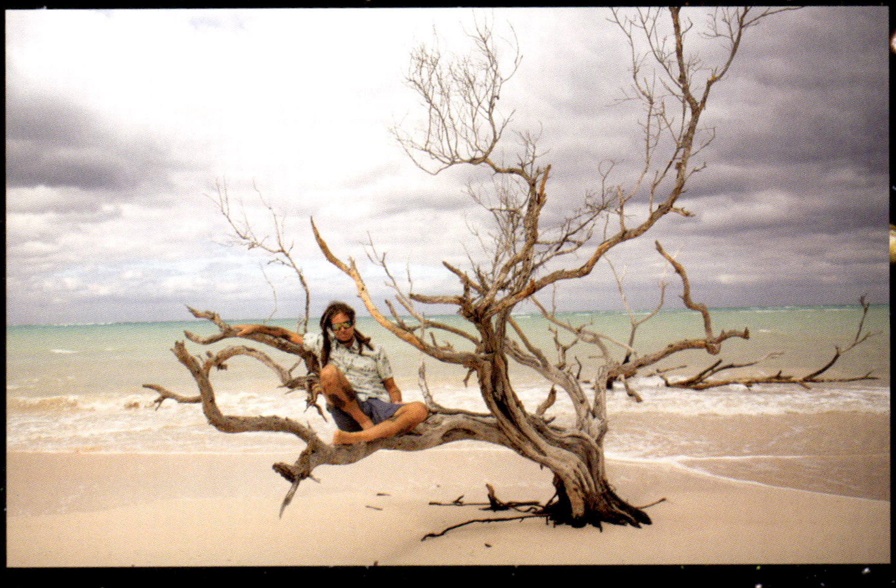

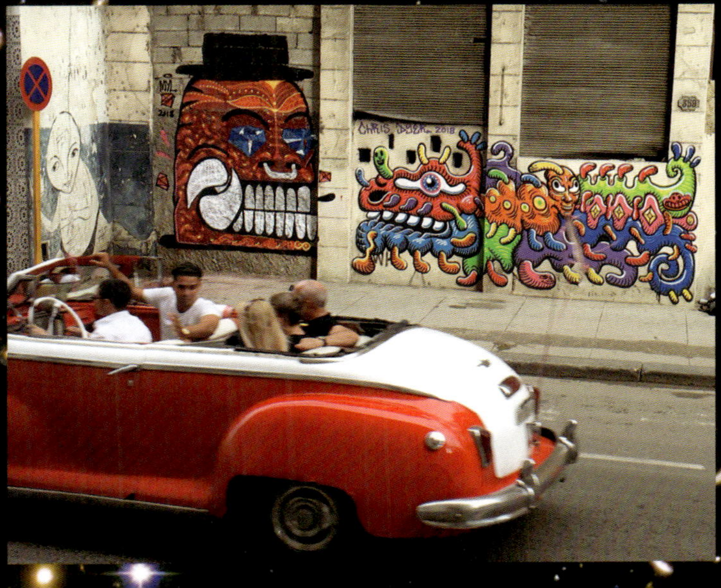

AUSTRALIA

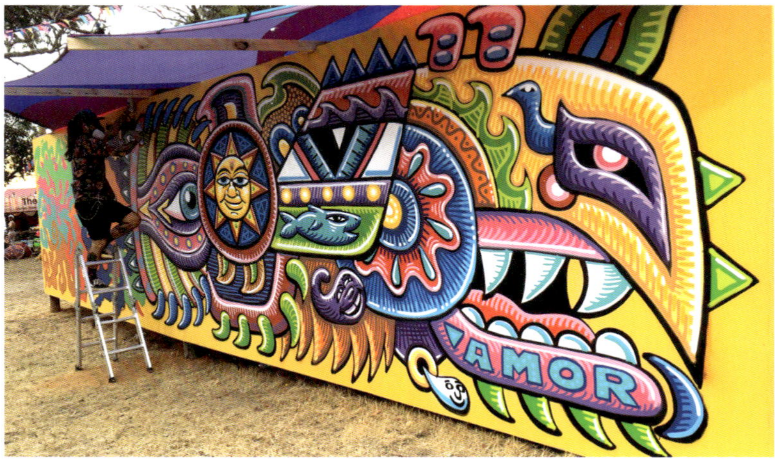

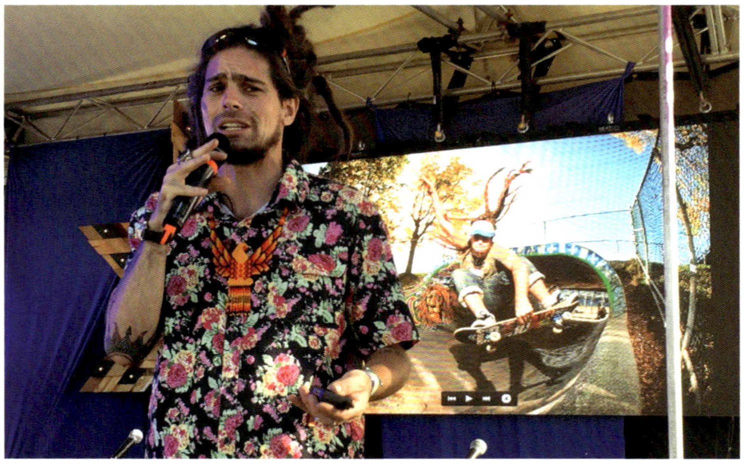

I returned to Australia in 2018 for a month long tour. I performed at **"Rainbow Serpent"** music festival, live painting a big mural and giving some speeches. It was hard work under the hot sun but I also enjoyed good times with artist friends. After that I went to the fun artsy city of **Melbourne**, which I loved. I taught a workshop there and also painted a big mural. After that I flew out to the **Byron Bay** area to live paint at **"Earth Frequency"** Music Festival and then teach another fun art workshop at a gorgeous retreat center called **"Paradise One"**. The experiences there were generally good, but the energy of the place really worked me emotionally, squeezing a bunch of emotional pain out of my being. My text communications with Arianne had gotten worse and worse, as her aloofness was hurting me. So I stopped writing her during this trip, which was a needed sanity break.

This painting, **"The King of Swords"** came out of that process of moving forward away from her energy. The character is inspired by the Tarot deck archetype, who has a healthy level of emotional detachment. Moving away into his own space, so that he doesn't become a "Wounded Lion" who hurts others because he is hurt himself. He focuses on the practical aspects of life and cuts from people who don't give him the respect he deserves. He doesn't mean to be hurtful, Love is always there, but he has to act from a place of inner truth and personal integrity. He reminds me I'm doing fine by honoring my challenging path. Sometimes it is healthy to keep your energy for yourself. This selfish world tends to take more than it gives and one has to know when to make a stand for oneself. I also added a magical super blood full moon, that I witnessed on mushrooms one night of many tears. This purge was helpful too.

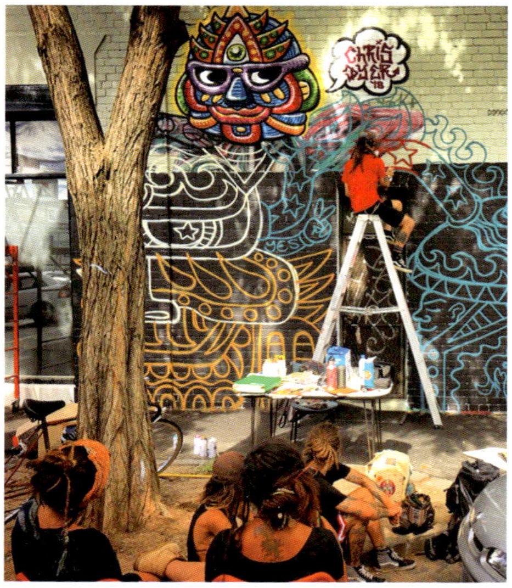

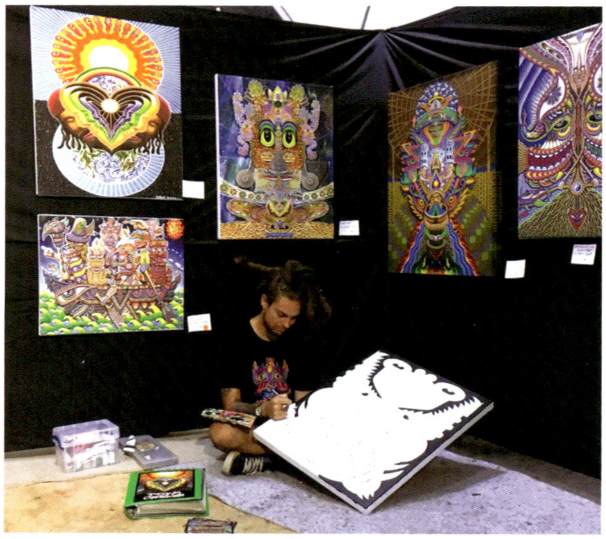

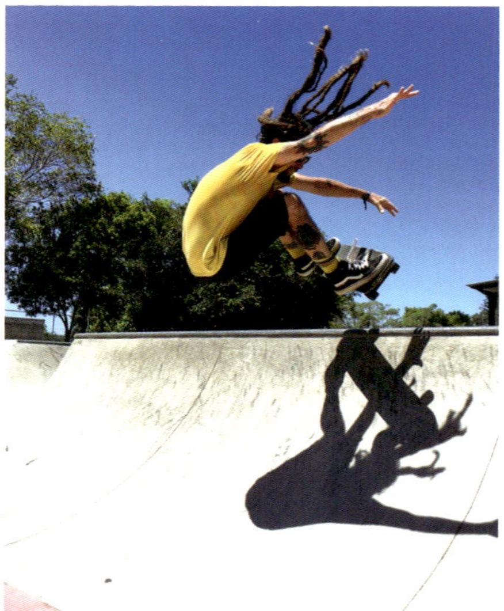

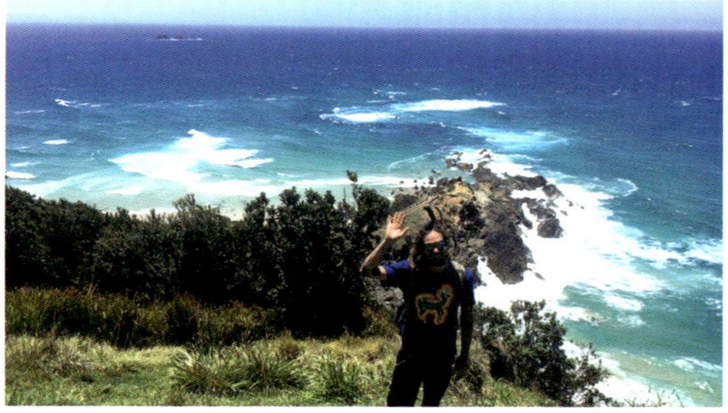

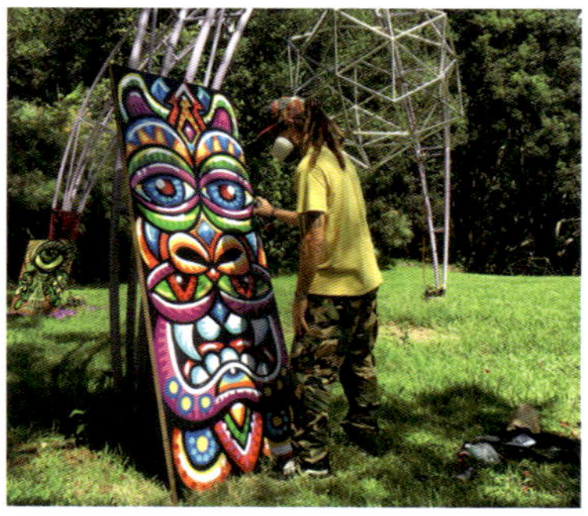

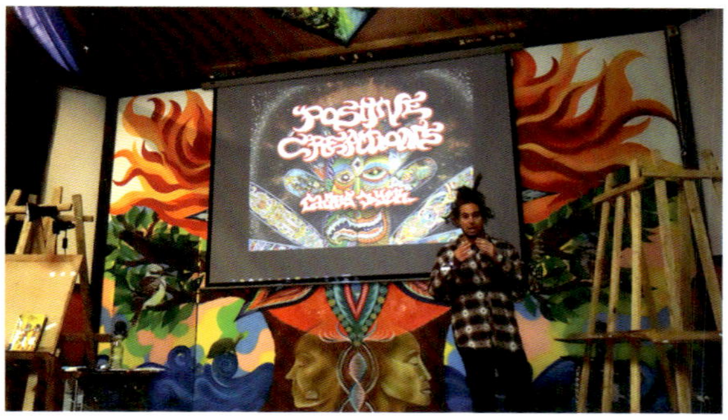

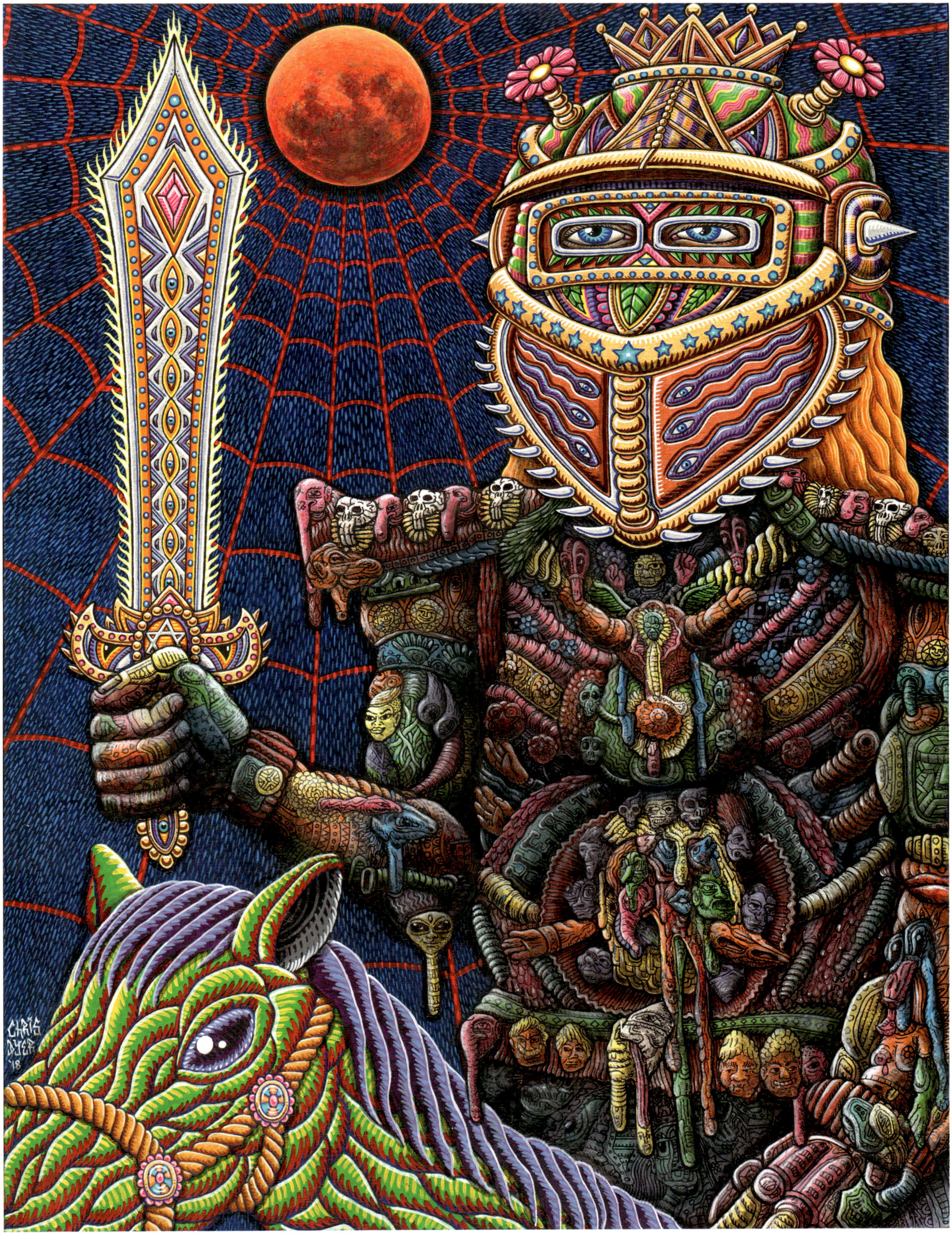

"King of Swords" Acrylics and spray paint on wood, 2018

THAILAND

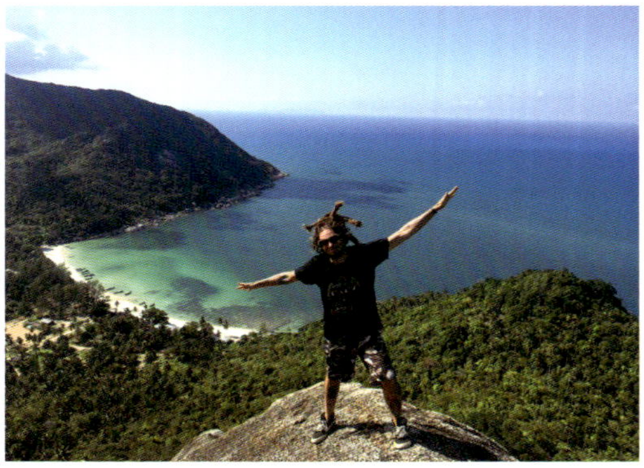
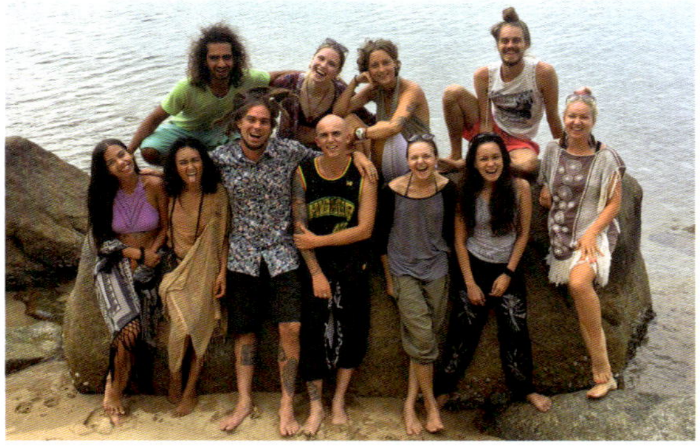
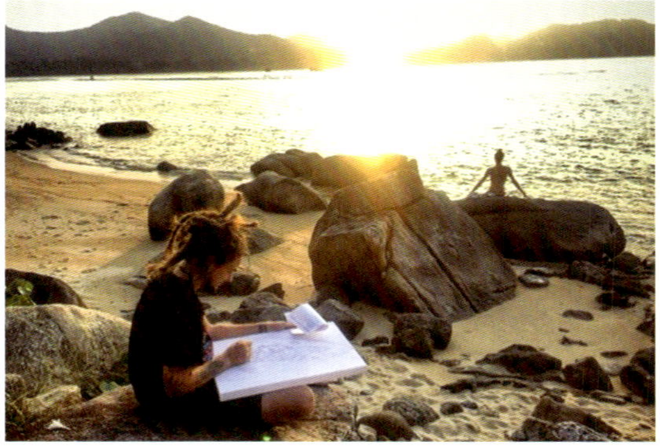

Since I was in the neighborhood, I jumped over to the amazing Kingdom of Thailand. I met up with my Norwegian friend **Even**, who had an apartment in **Bangkok** and we had fun cruising that crazy city for a couple of days. I then went to the spiritual side of **Koh Phangan** island, where a Russian friend, **Nirvana**, had organized me a **"Healing Visions"** art and medicine workshop. A really nice group of students joined me at a seaside restaurant to take my art classes and do potent Ayahuasca ceremonies at night. Unfortunately Herbert couldn't make it, because his wife was pregnant, but the local shaman we used did a good enough job. Either way the medicine succeeded at moving me further on my road to happiness. I also did some **"Kambo"** frog ceremonies with a German practitioner I met there. Kambo is frog venom that when applied (in little burn holes) makes your body go into a high pressure fever. That forces you to purge all the physical and energetic dirt in your body, while also boosting your immune system. In the past I usually did four "dots" of that medicine, but this practitioner applied twelve, which truly felt like I was dying, yet it purified me completely. Before I left the country I spent a bit more alone time in the ancient city of **Ayutthaya**, to explore plenty of Buddhist temples and ruins. I also managed to find a monk who gave me a magical (and very painful) **"Sak Yat"** protection tattoo. Despite all the hard initiations I went through, I flew back home feeling like gold and so in love with myself!

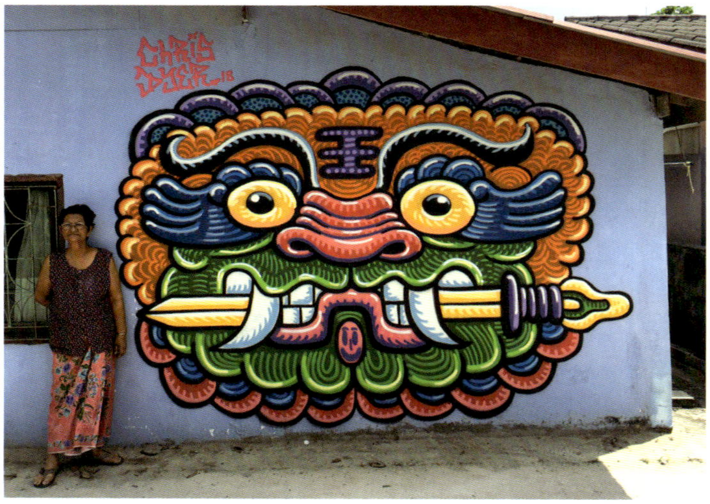
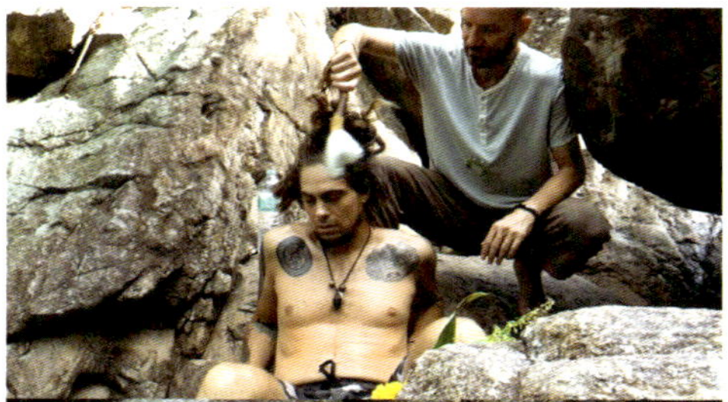
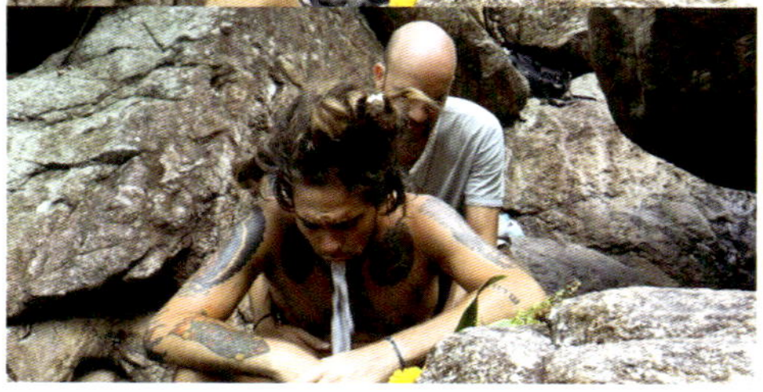
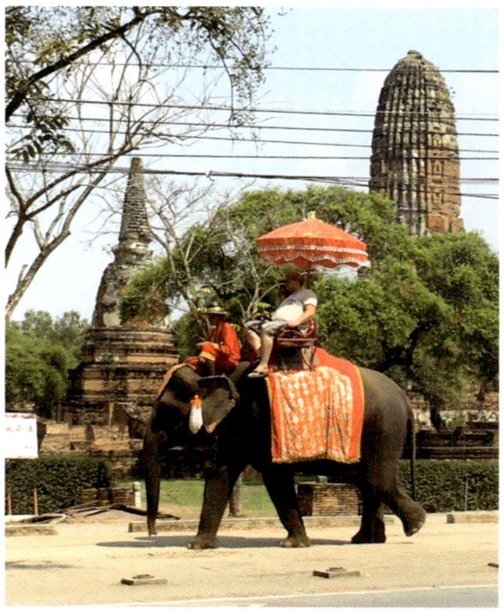

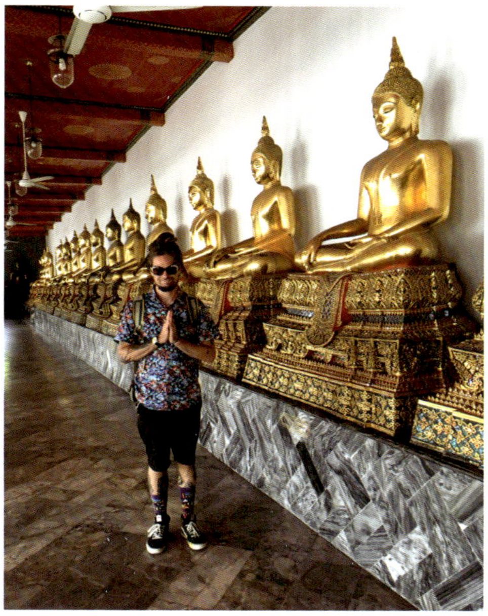
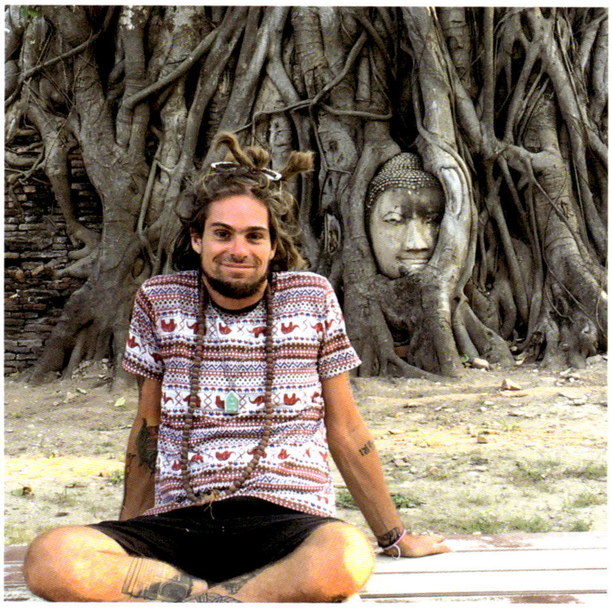
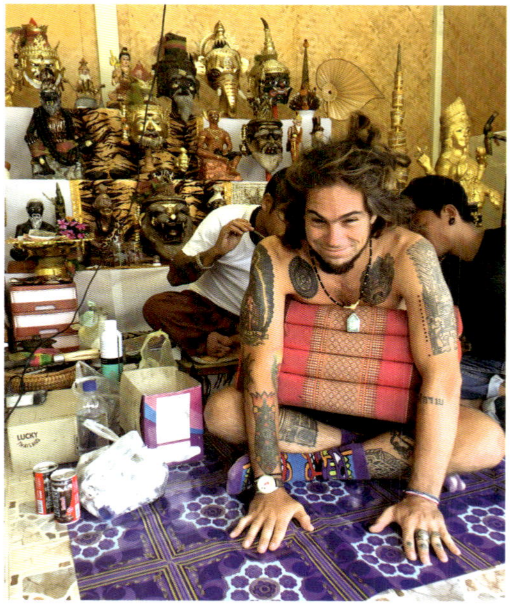

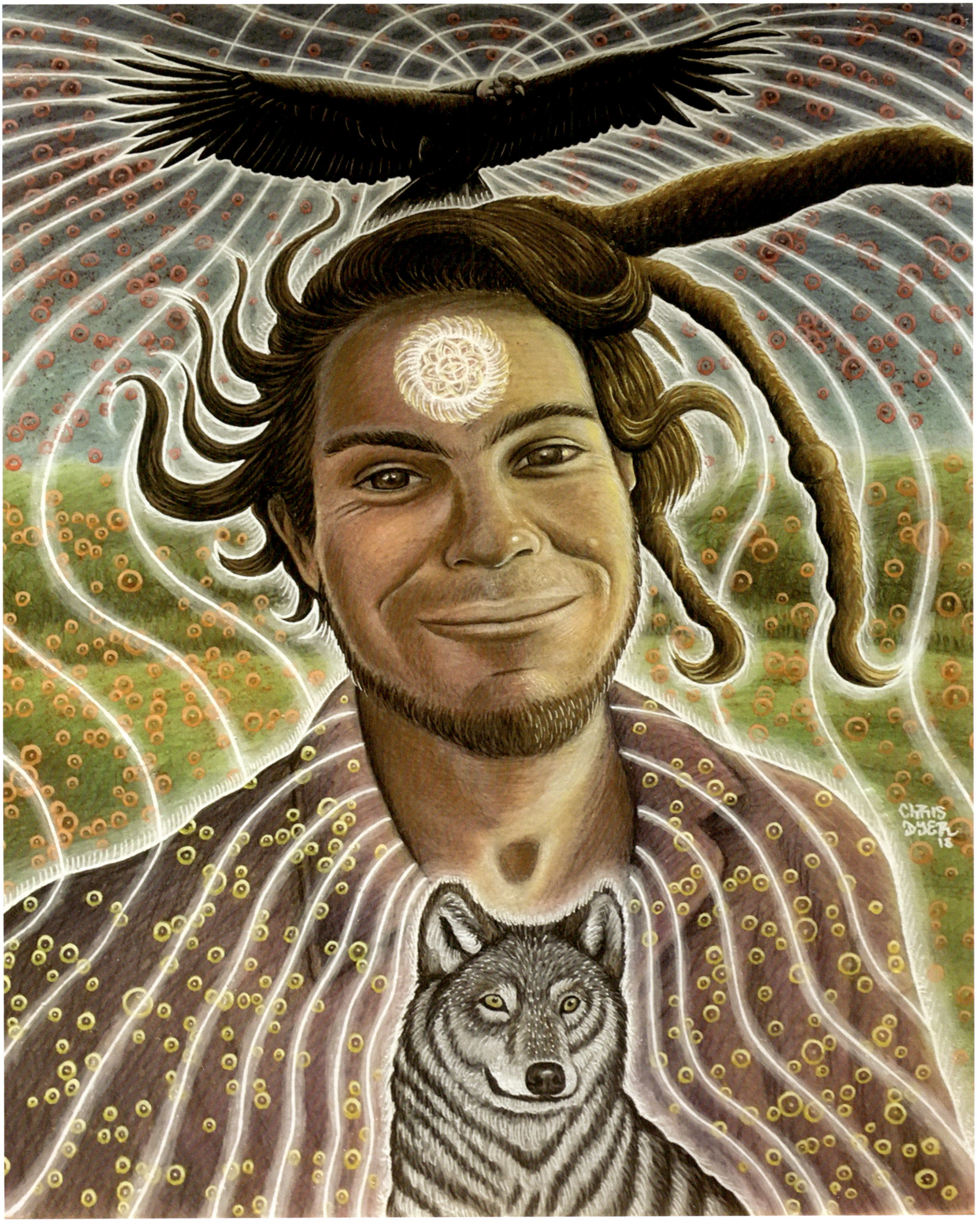

"Guides Grattitude" Colour pencils, markers and pastels on paper, 2018

CALIFORNIA

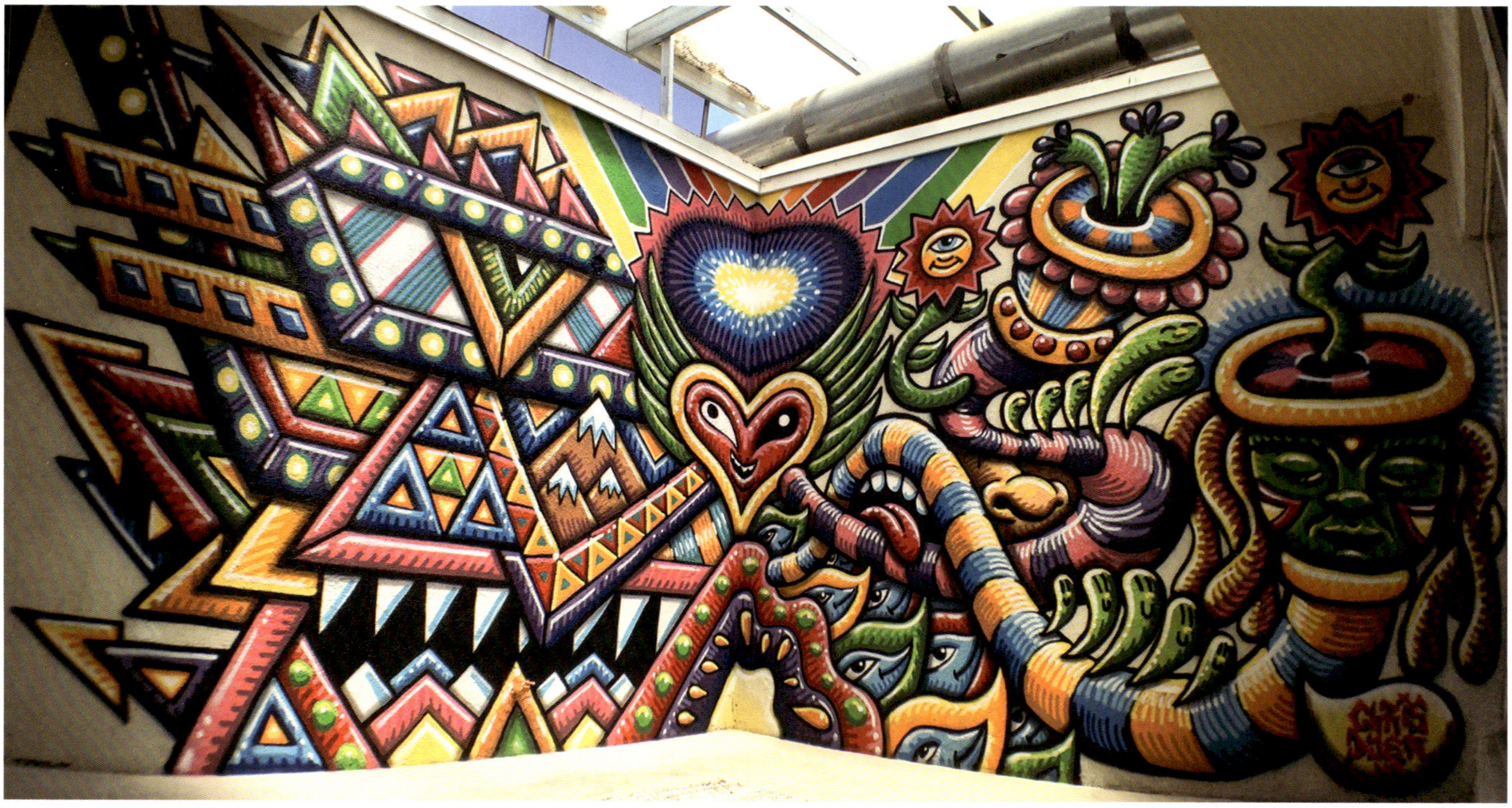

As spring rolled in I started touring again and I returned to good old California. My first gig there was a mural at a private home in **Los Angeles**. My clients where a nice spiritual couple who had done ceremonies with Herbert before, so we became instant family. They also had some shamanic medicines themselves, for their personal ceremonies. So to get in the vibe of the mural I joined them on a couple of journeys. The first ceremony was lovely and empowering, but on the second one they gave me three different kinds of medicines, which crossed each other out in me, inducing a dark effect (not necessarily a bad trip though). As I went to bed, I couldn't stop hallucinating twisted and bizarre monsters. It reminded me of the importance of using these delicate technologies with better guidance and respect. The painting that I started there, **"Cruzado"** captures the darker vibe of the astral plane when your psychic wires cross.

The second mission was a workshop I taught in the infamous **Humboldt County** of Nor Cal. The owner of a little Cannabis Farm invited me to paint a piece on her barn and then teach local kids inside it. It sounded kinda sketchy at first, but I went for it anyways and we all had a great time! Each student was happy to receive a big bag of herb as a complementary class material, haha. The real bonus though, was that we raised funds for a non-profit (Epic) that protects the giant redwoods of that area!

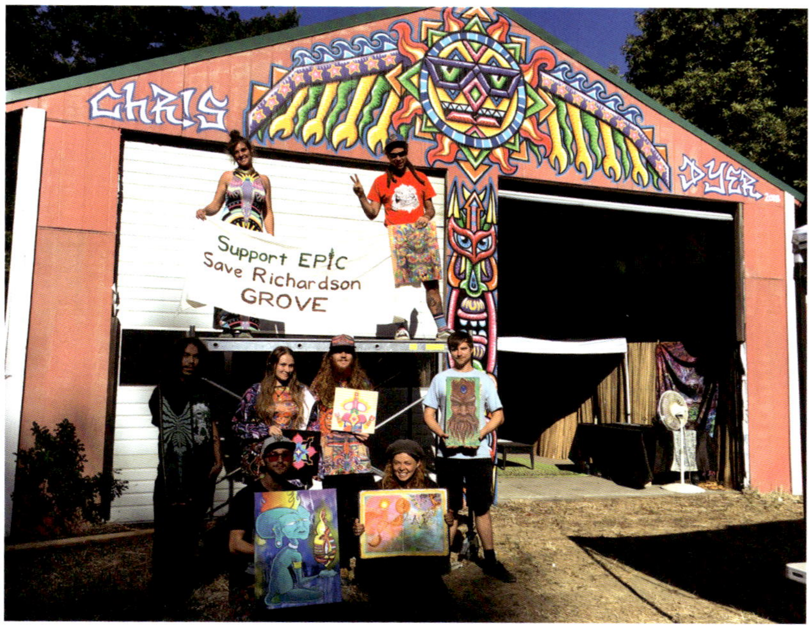

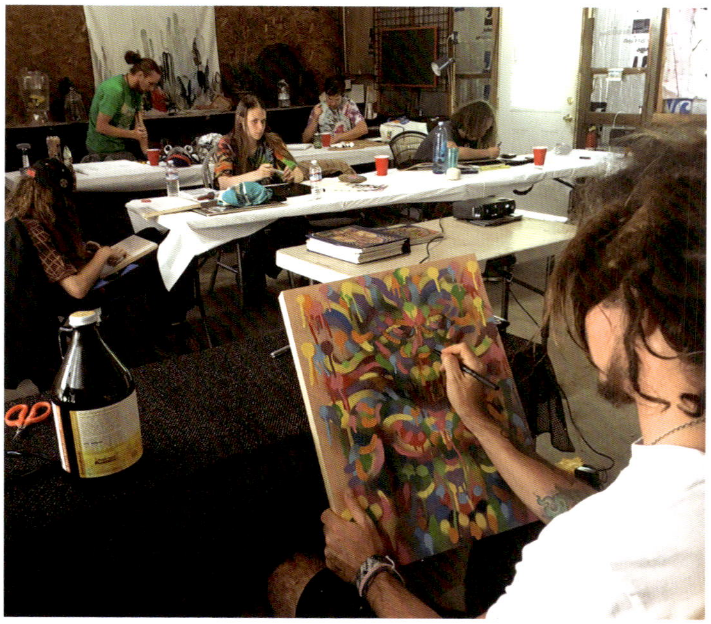

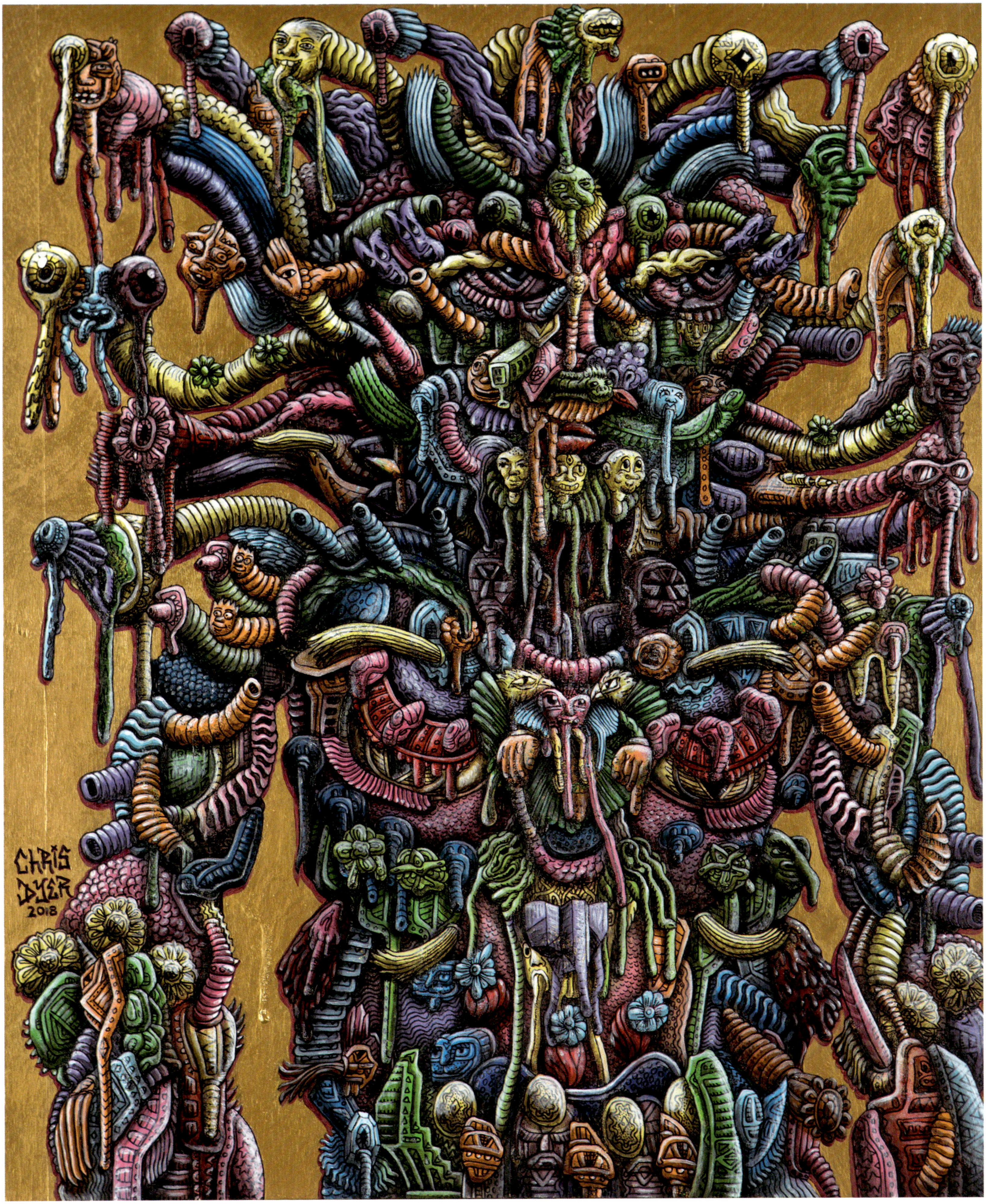

"Cruzado" Spray paint and acrylics on wood, 2018

MONTREAL

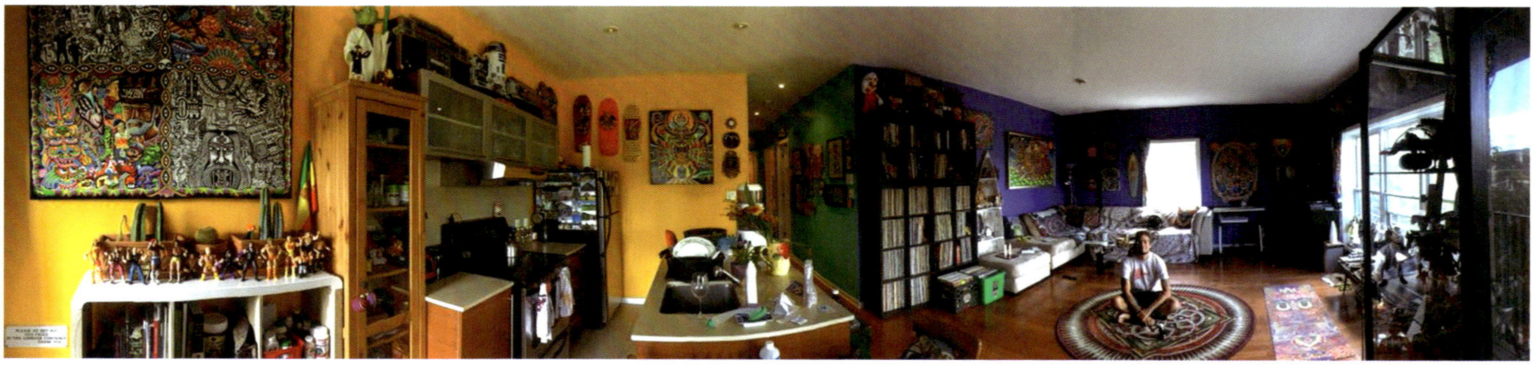

That Montreal summer with the homies was fun as always. I was stoked by a new little romance with another artist from Florida I had met on my spring tour. Her name was **Tiffany "Molasses" Tompkins** and she was a happy Leo (a sun sign) who painted lots of suns. She flew up to visit me in Montreal a couple of times and we had a really good time together. But I had learnt my lesson from dating Arianne, to not disrupt someone else's path so they can follow mine. So instead of asking her to quit art school to move countries and live my life, we broke up. It was a bit sad but this time I was less attached and held nothing but gratitude for the healing vibration we shared with each other.

I made this painting that summer. I have always loved painting sun characters, as a way to visually represent God. The Incas called their Father Sun **"Taita Inti"** so I also used this potent name. Other than giving it up to God and the bright warmth of summer, this painting was also a way to thank the energy of Tiffany the sun painter, who I represented as a little lion heart in the third eye region of the sun.

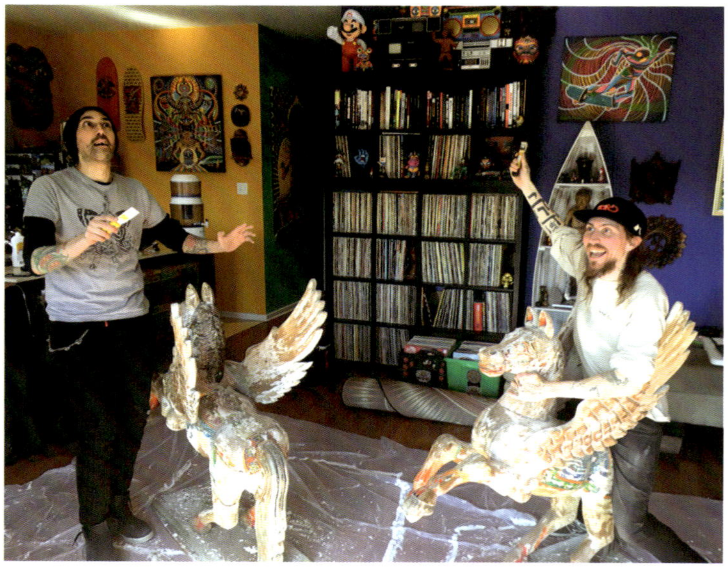

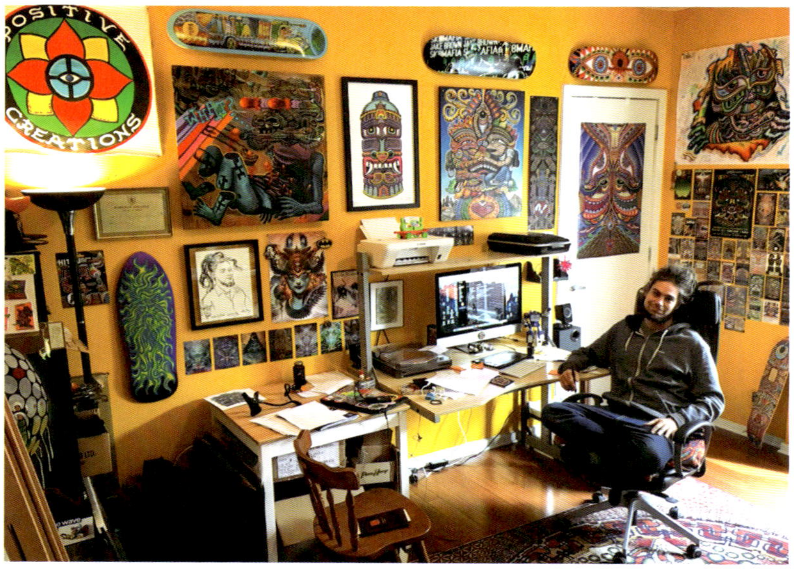

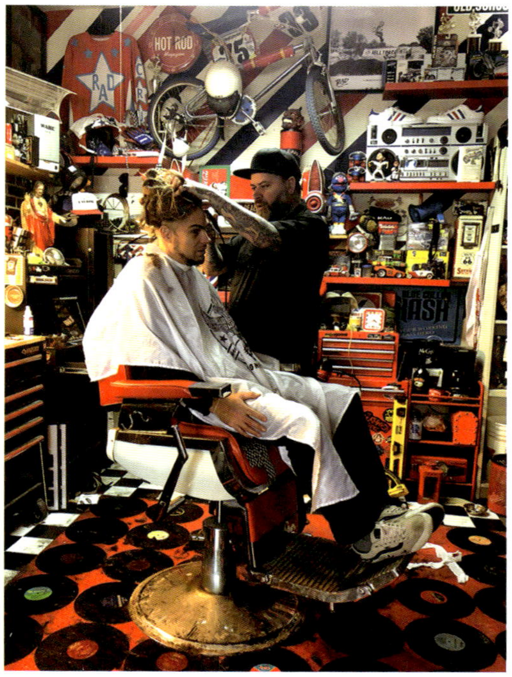

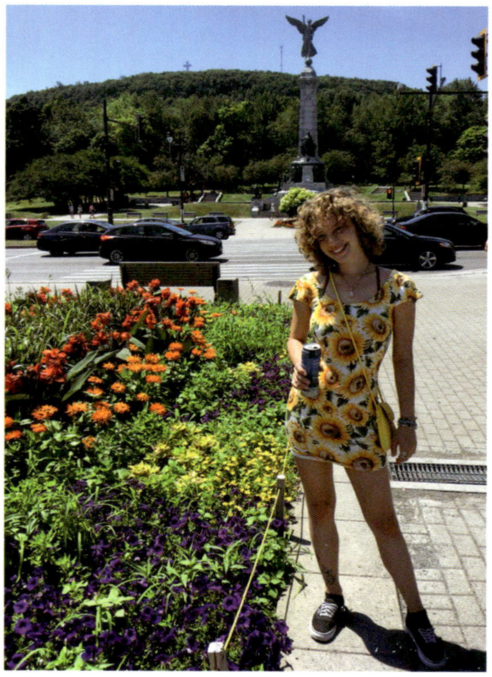

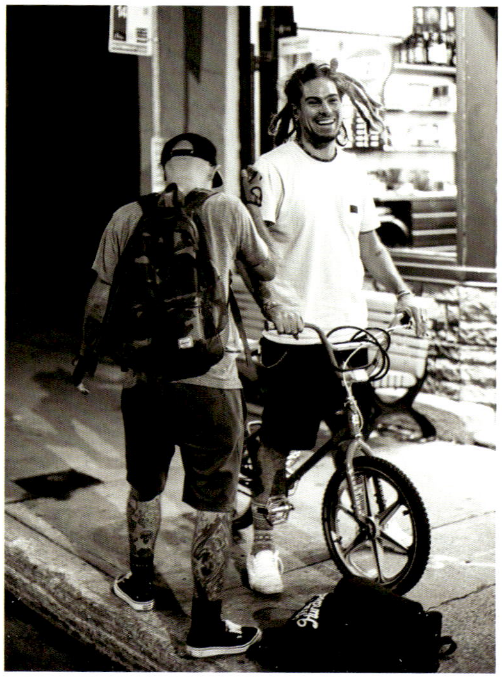

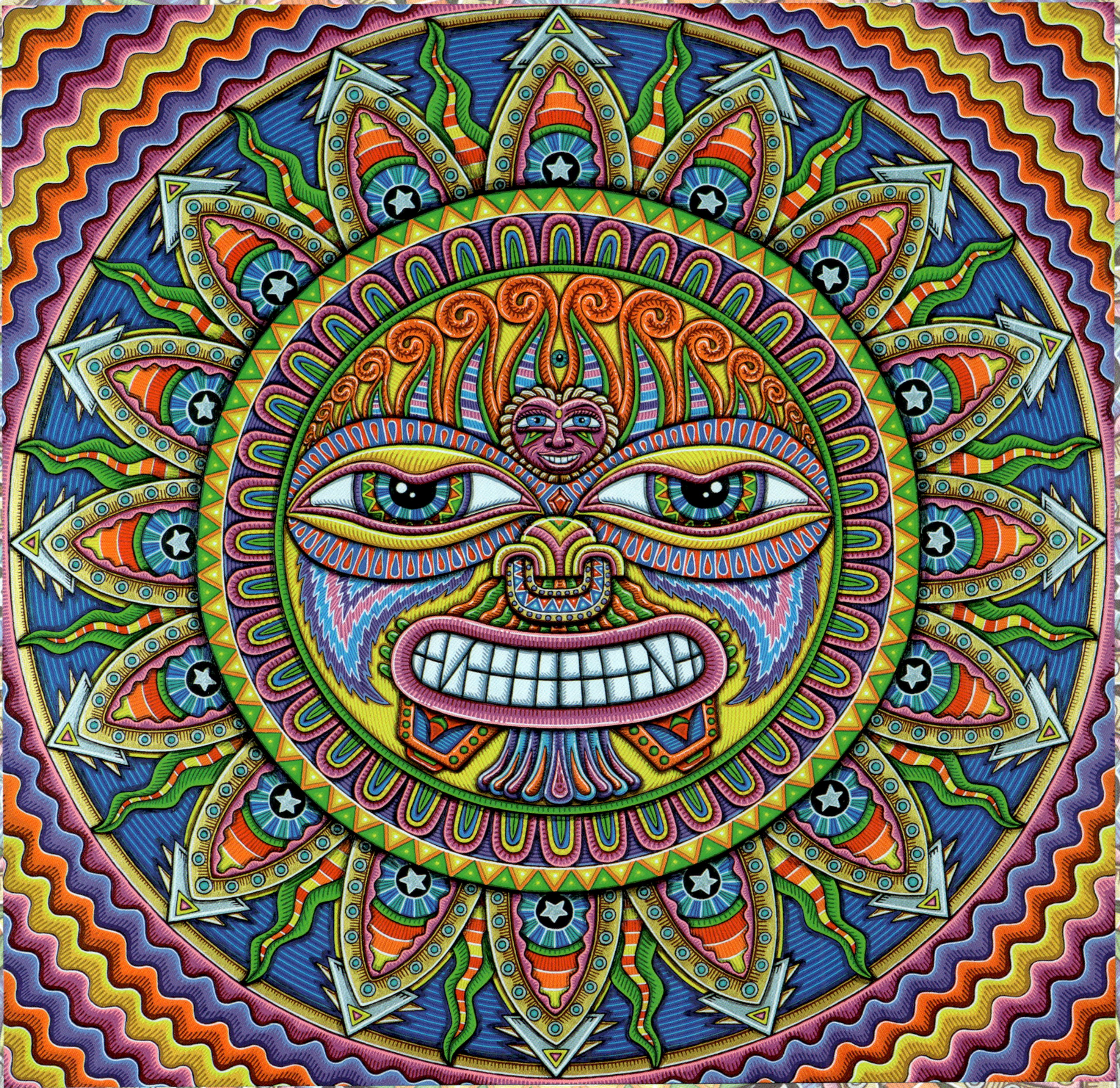

"Taita Inti" Acrylics on wood, 2018

HUNGARY

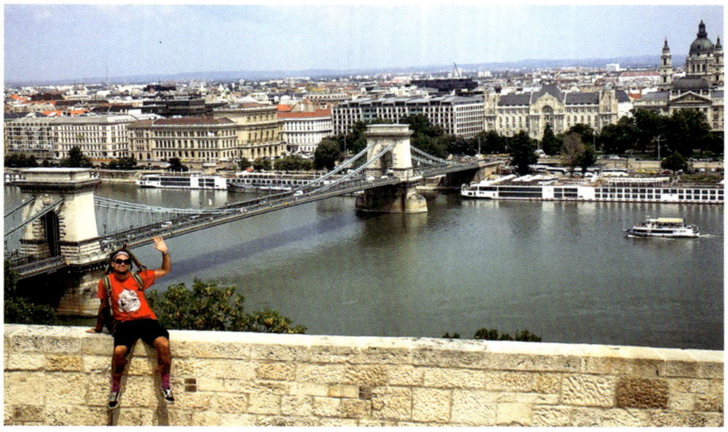

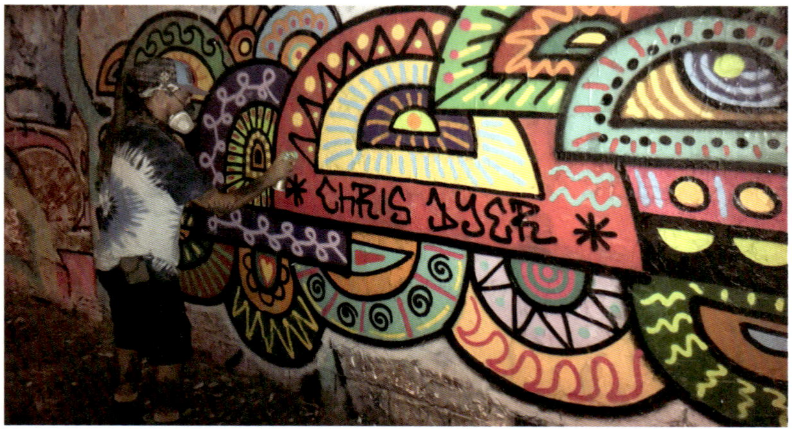

That summer I also got invited to perform at **"Ozora"** Music Festival in the Eastern European country of Hungary. I started my journey in the capital city of **Budapest**, which had beautiful architecture, art galleries and relaxing thermal baths. Once I got to the festival I spent a week spray painting a large mural on one of their permanent buildings and then I spent another week working on a canvas at the Visionary Art Gallery of the event. The non-stop Psytrance music was exhausting on my system, but I had a lot of fun with artist friends from around the world. I also taught a little workshop.

The title of the piece I made there pretty much explains what it is about. The angelic super-hero artist needs to stay focused on his process, at this stage of his life. After a few years of wrestling and purging a lot of my demons (shown on the right side), my intention was to shield myself from them by projecting a pyramid of light force-field that wouldn't allow them back into my influence. On the left side are three angels, also shown as temptation sirens, who had captured my heart at different parts of my voyage, but who I also had to push out of my life. At the bottom is my ex-wife Valerie, and on the top part are Arianne and Tiffany. I had a lot of great Love for each one of them, yet they weren't fitting into my life at this moment. It was a bittersweet situation with so much appreciation, yet I had to Love myself first and be alone. I was to be of service to my community for now, so relationships became secondary. The path of the traveling artist can be a lonely one, yet I was grateful for this part of the process.

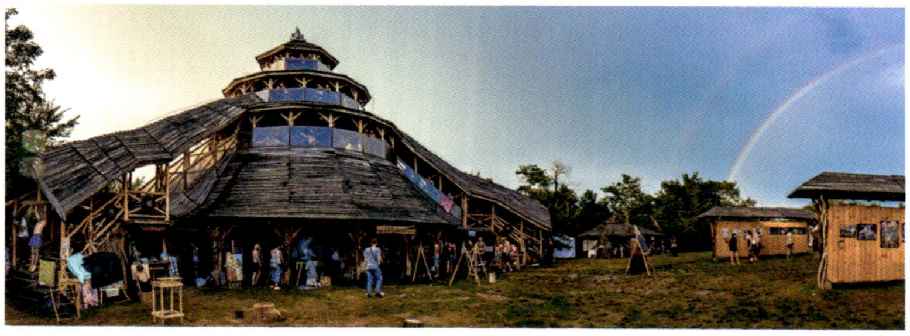

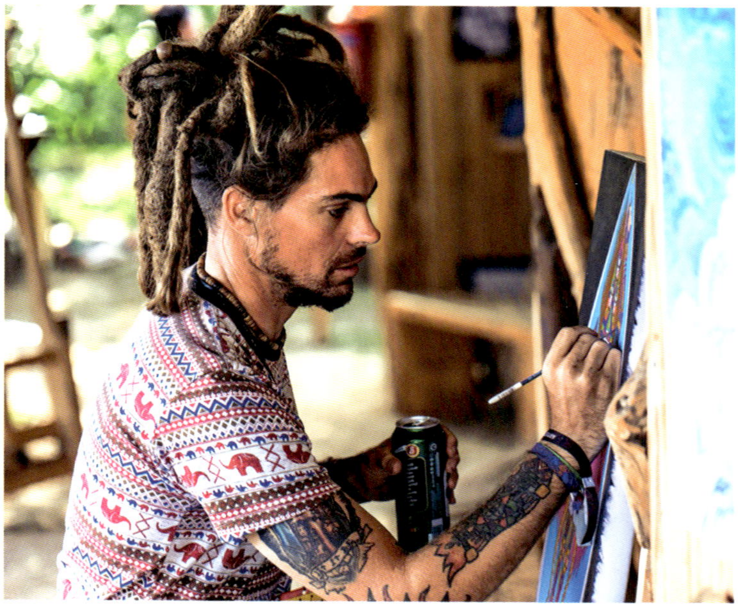

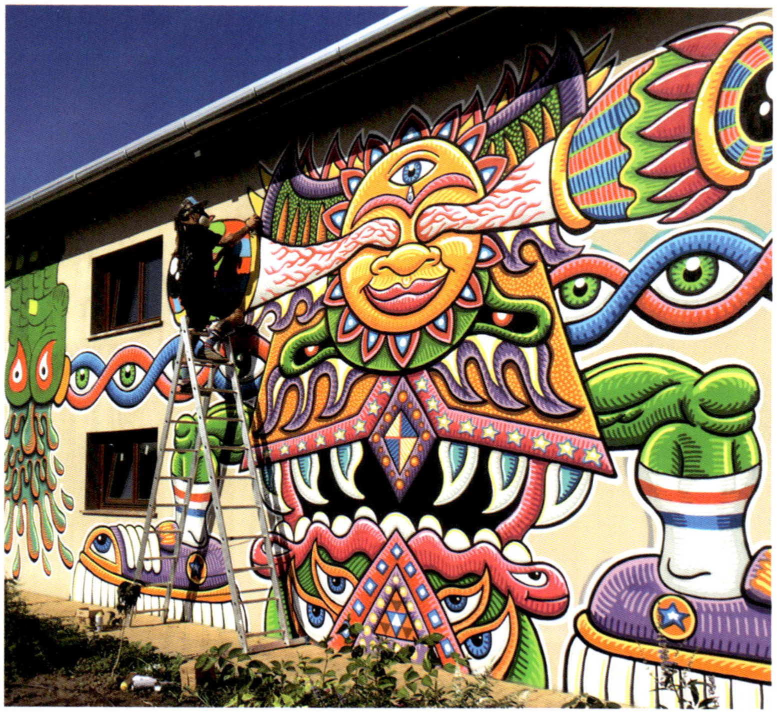

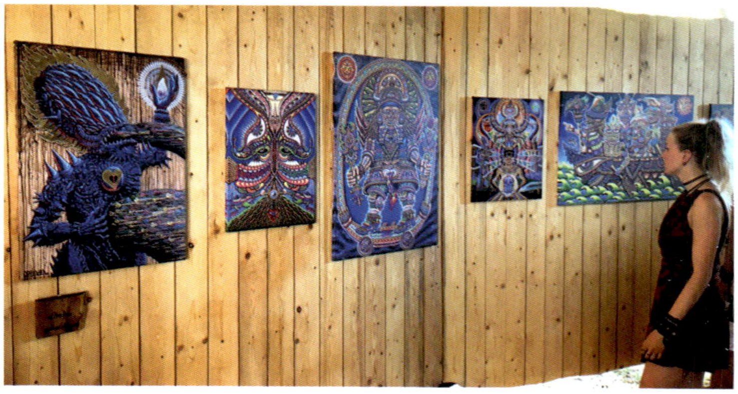

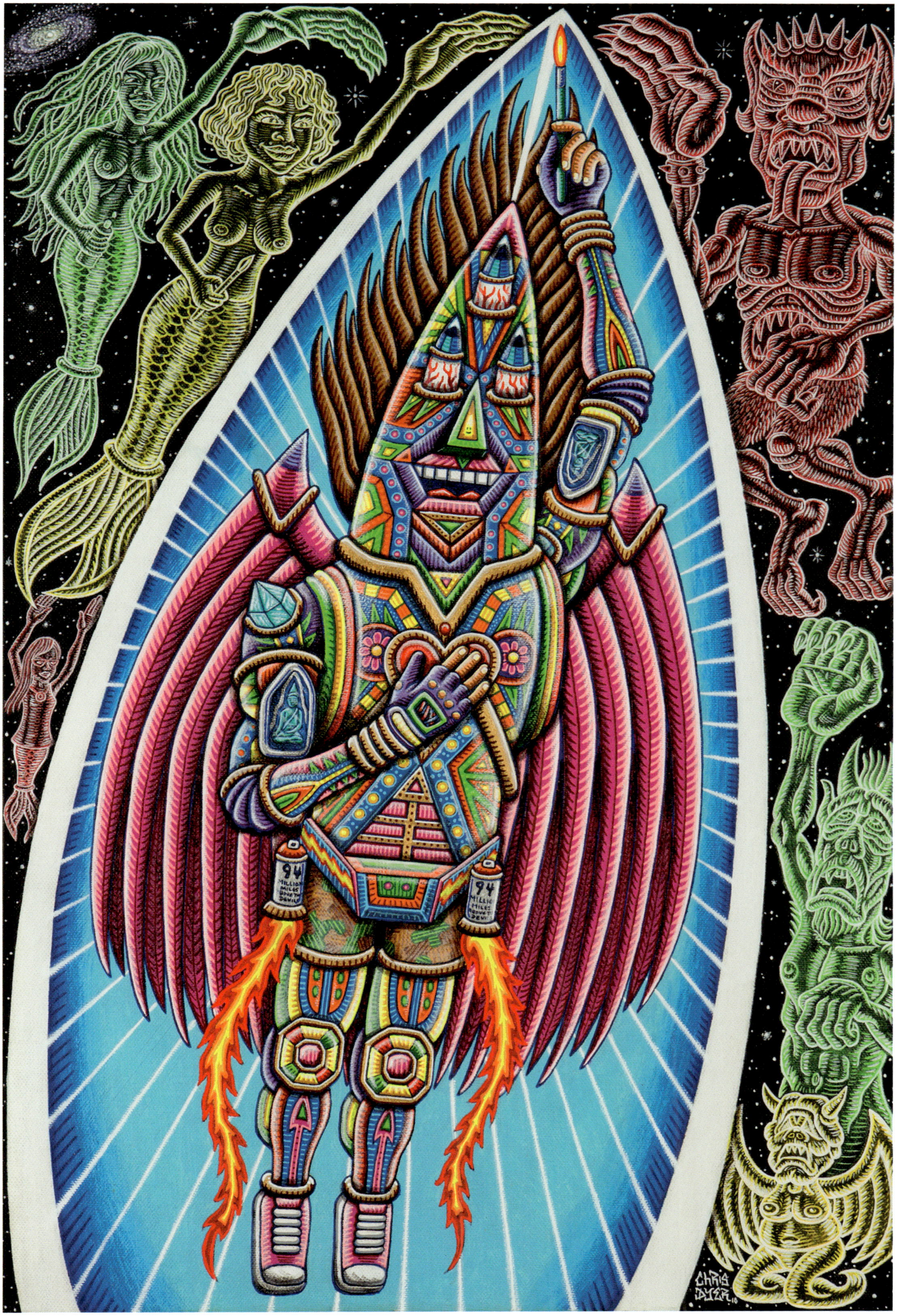

“Artist Superhero Focused on his Mission” Acrylics on canvas, 2018

MIAMI

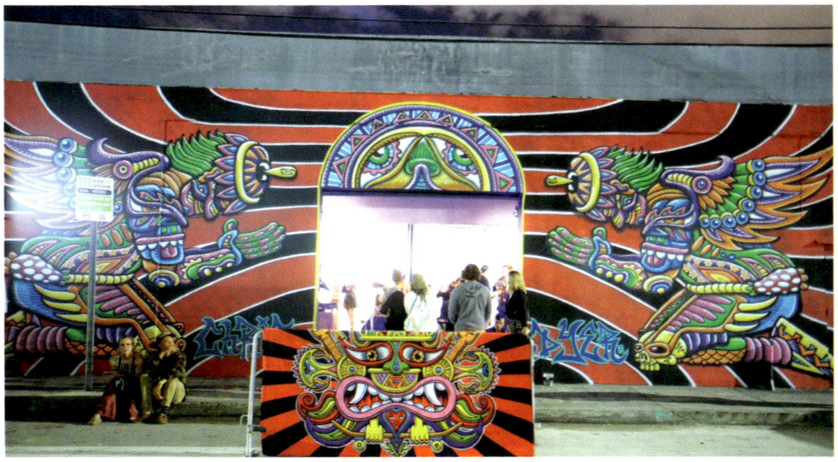

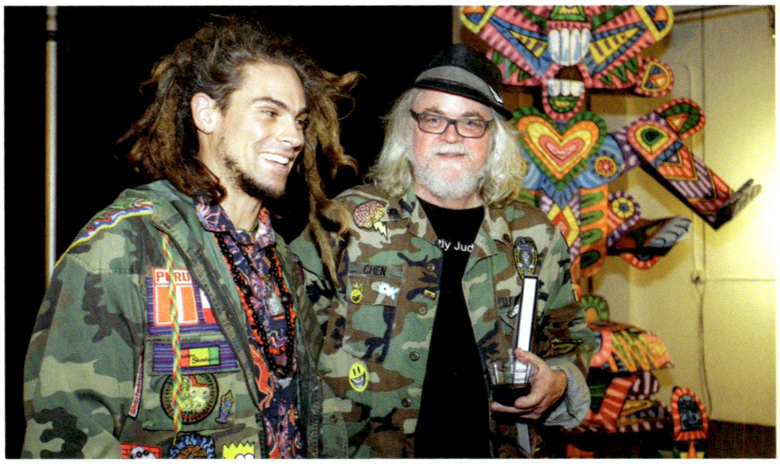

As I mentioned before, Miami's **"Art Week"**, also known as "Basel" is a time every December where the Art Scenes of the world descend to show their goods. I had been many times to exhibit and paint murals, as to get more exposure and business. But for 2018 I decided to throw down big, as to make a proper statement, while also sharing my personal medicine with the community. I teamed up with my friends at **"Moksha Family"** and **"Saturnlight Studios"** to produce my biggest solo exhibition yet, called **"Higher Reflections"**. It was a huge investment of my resources and time, but a fun gamble. We rented a big warehouse in **Wynwood** (the cool street art district), transformed it into a classy gallery, painted a giant mural in the entrance, built a huge skateboard robot, flew all of my art down from Canada, advertised in Juxtapoz magazine, etc. My brand manager Cory and team drove our product from Denver to set up a pop-up shop, and I also flew down my Montreal assistants, Germ and Martine, for extra support. I even taught a workshop on that week leading up, to help alleviate costs. By the time we had our opening party I was exhausted, but got quickly energized by all the amazing people who came to enjoy my art, including artist friends I really love and admire. The event lasted many days, where I got to give speeches, play a vinyl record DJ set and live paint during the different parties we offered. We had amazing musical performers share their vibrations and I even got to see my old friend Arianne again, who live painted for us one night too. In the end it was a very successful event that shared so many good moments and I also made some of my biggest sales yet. Super grateful!

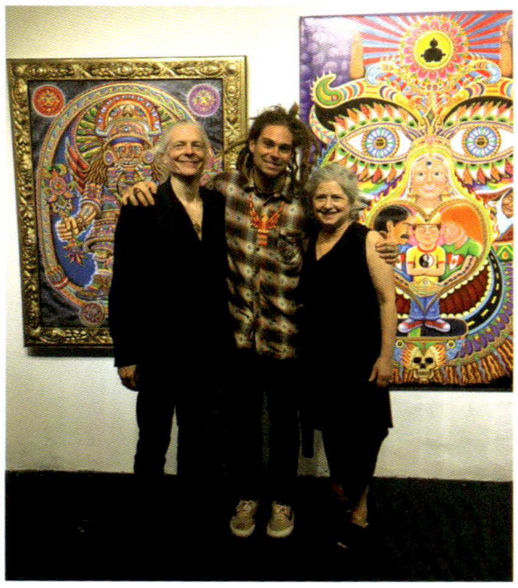

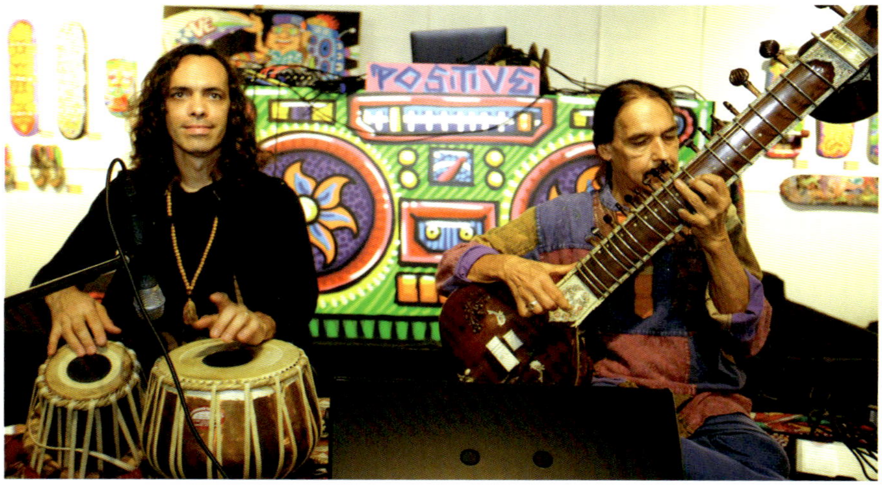

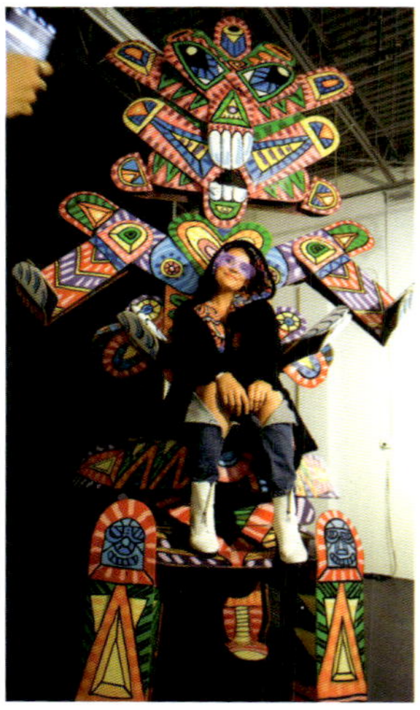

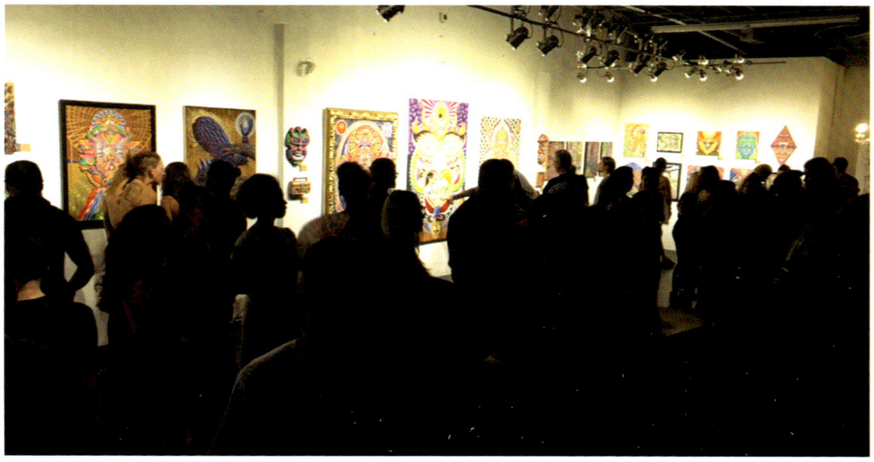

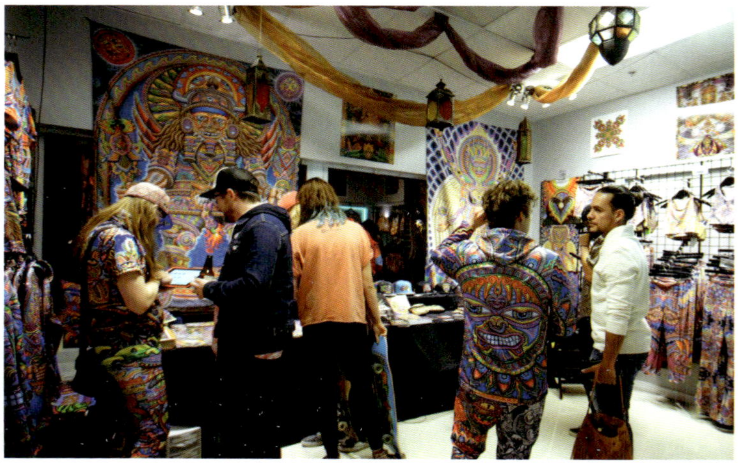

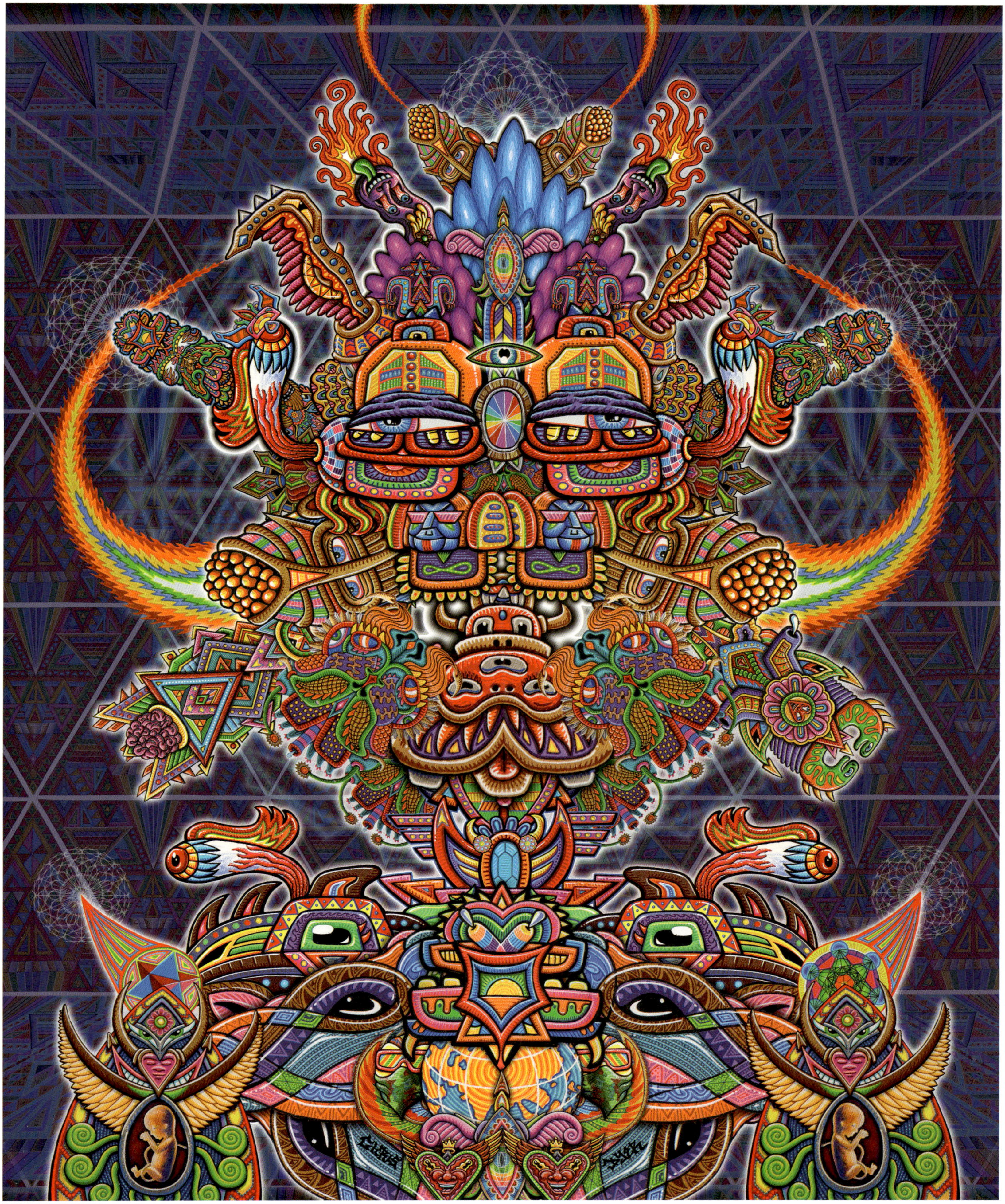

"Interdimentional Rebel" Photoshop of pieces of my paintings, 2018

JAMAICA

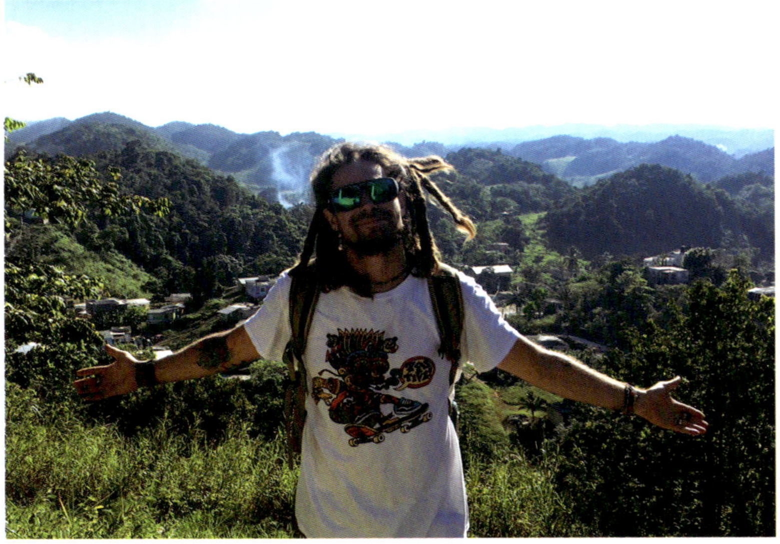

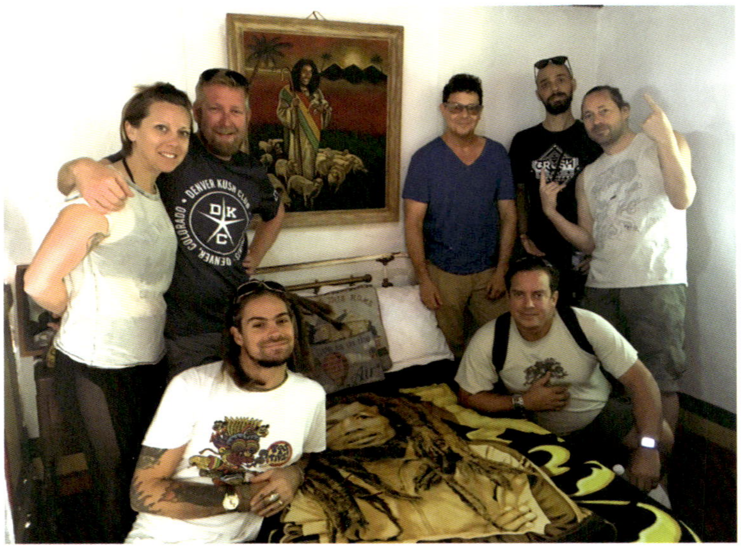

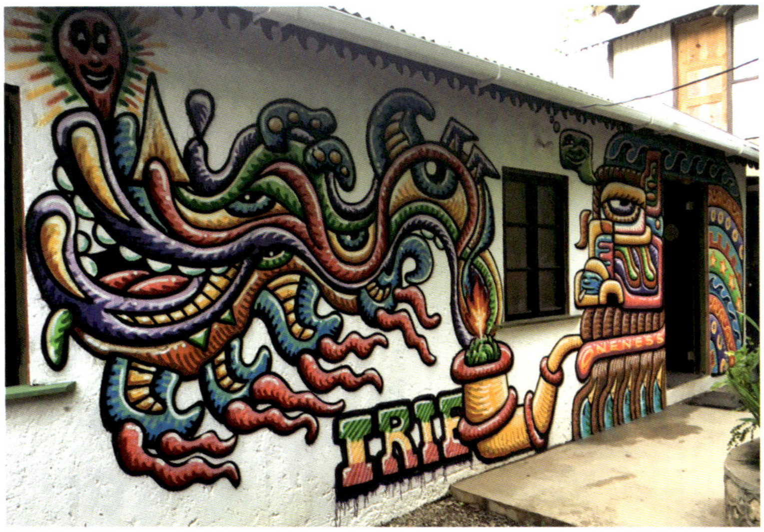
IRIE

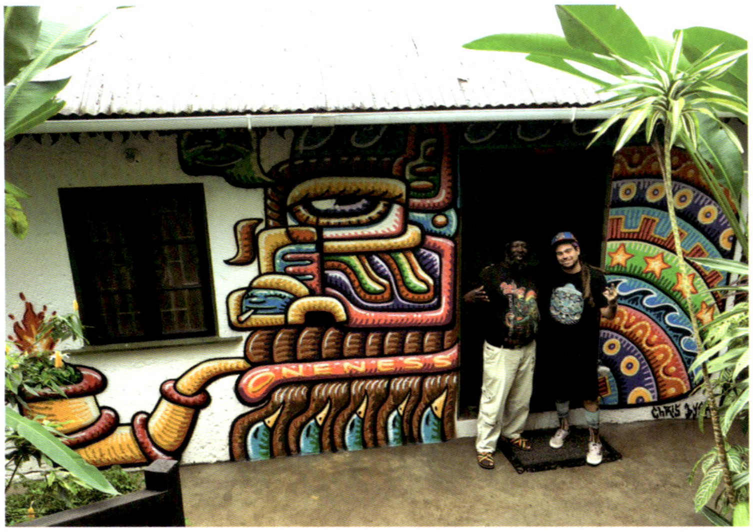

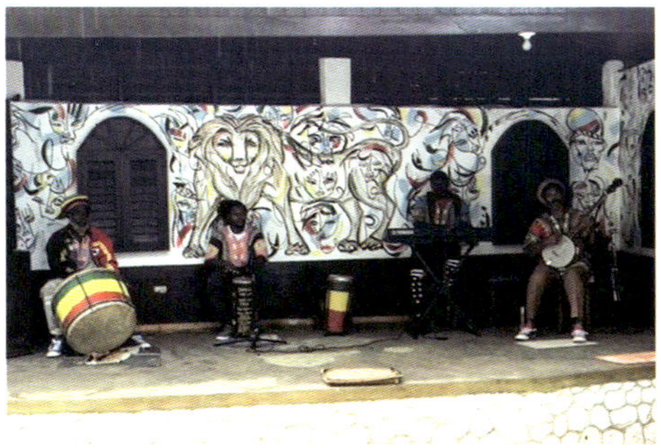

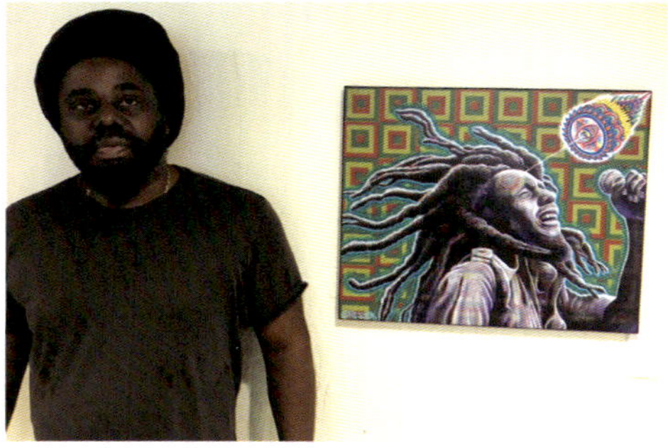

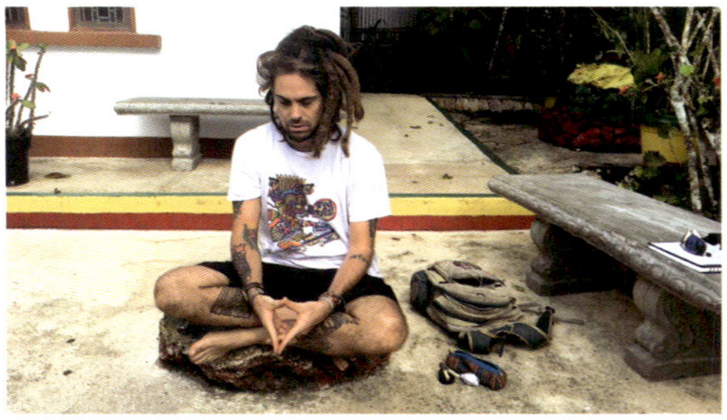

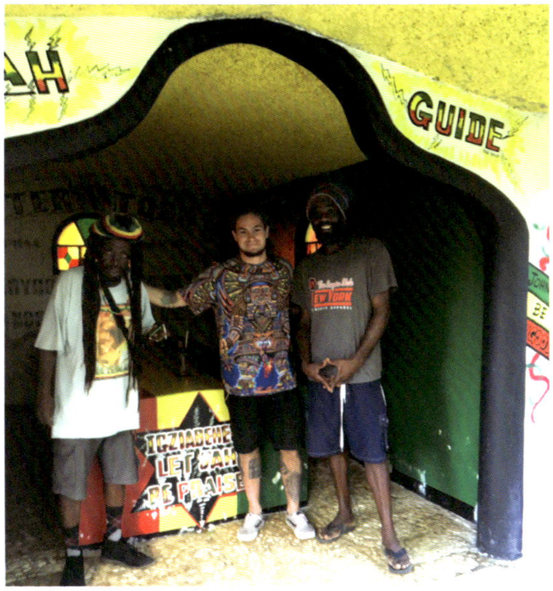
GUIDE

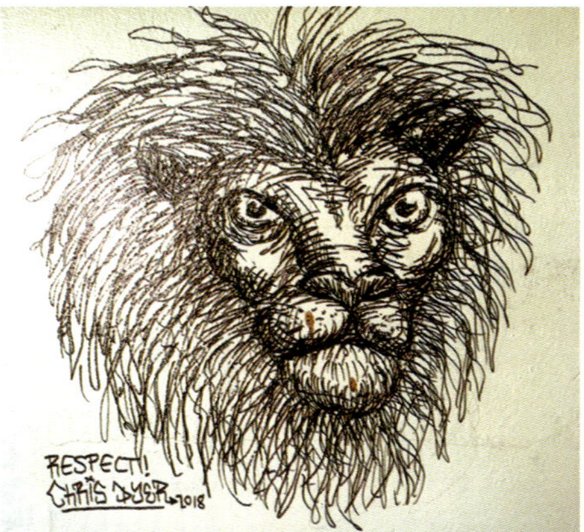
RESPECT!
CHRIS DYER 2018

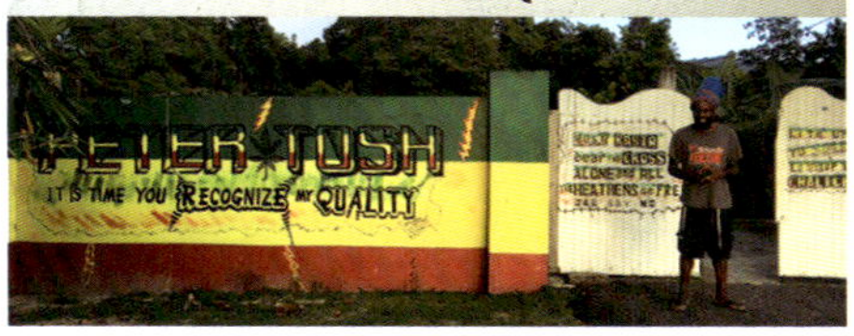
PETER TOSH
IT IS TIME YOU RECOGNIZE QUALITY

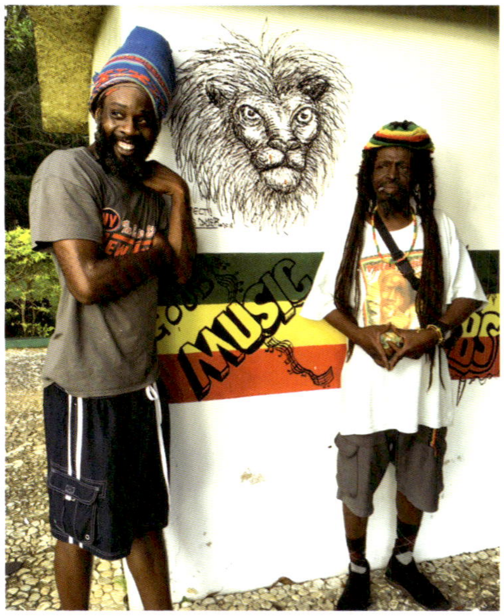
MUSIC

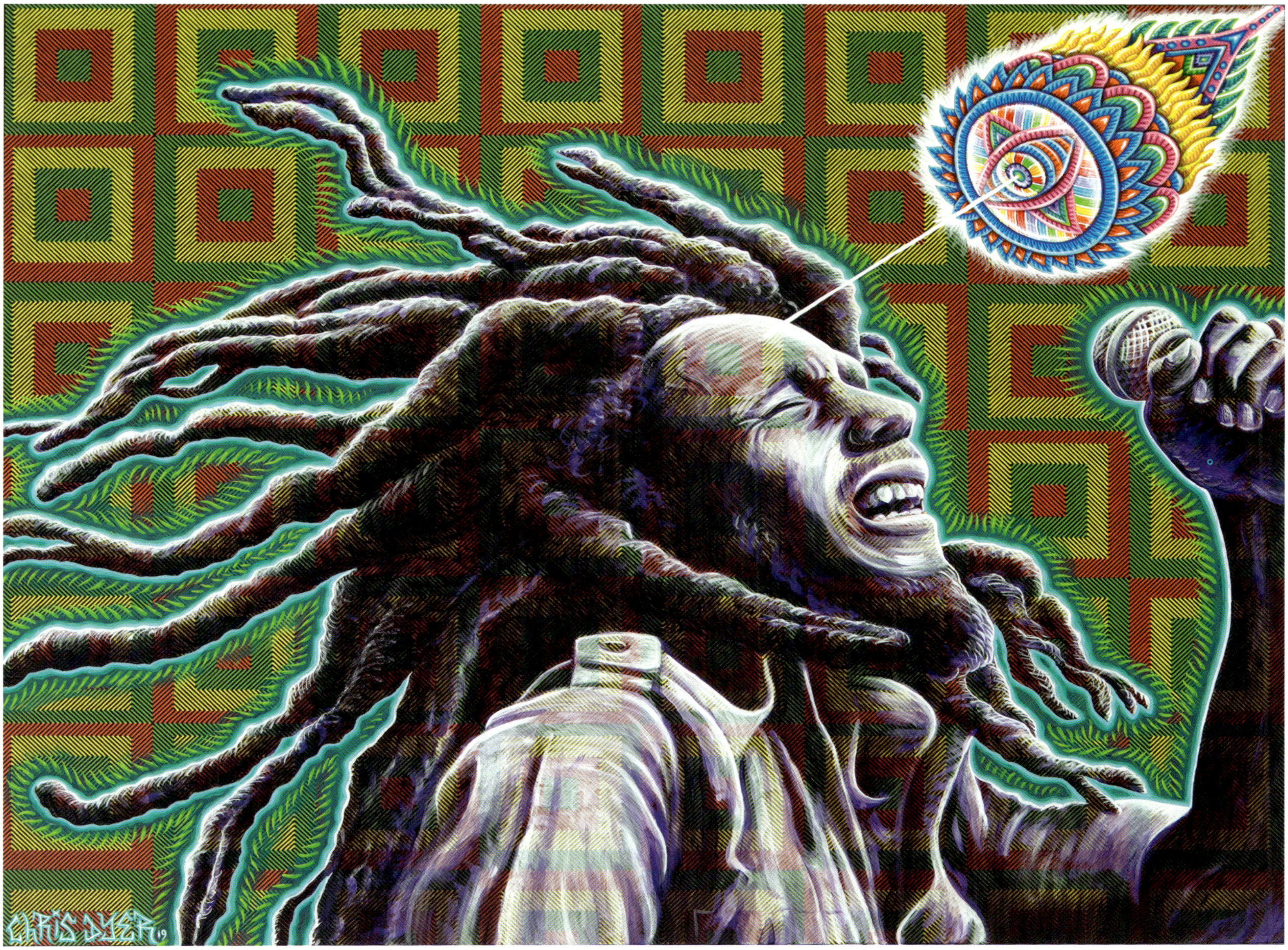

"Marley's Mystic Connection" Acrylics on wood, 2019

During my Miami show, I had the honor to be invited to paint at **Bob Marley's Mausoleum** by his brother, **Richie Booker**. So the day after my show ended, with barely a chance to stressfully pack my exhibition, I flew down to Jamaica! The other street artists invited to paint there were **"The London Police"** and **"Lindz and Lamb"**. Then my companion and assistant on this trip was my friend **Ray Orraca** from **"Moksha Family"**. Once on the island we were taken to **"Nine Mile"** in the countryside mountains of the island where Bob had grown up in a small shack and then was later buried in a chapel-like mausoleum. It was magical to see those historical structures of one of my biggest heroes, alongside hanging with his cousins and meditating on his classic rock. This place is now a complex that welcomes several daily tourists, so it had a museum, a restaurant, a live band and a gift shop. It was a dream come true to add a mural to one of their walls! I was also asked to paint a canvas for their museum, which I did a couple of months later, representing his connection with the consciousness from the other dimension.
After that fun mission, we cruised over to **Negril**, to enjoy some seaside natural beauty for a few more days. The Italian owner of the hostel we stayed at (Banana Shout) was actually a fan of mine, so was happy to take me around to record shops and beautiful beaches. He also told me that the mortal remains of **Peter Tosh**, another reggae hero of mine, were coincidentally in this area. So I made a point to go and pay my respects! The place was run by one of Peter's cousins, who was impressed by the chronicles drawings I was doing and invited me to put something up on the mausoleum! I undoubtedly accepted, but he only art material I had in my backpack was a sharpie marker, so I gave my best effort to draw them a nice Lion of Judah. They where stoked and I was grateful!

"THANK YOU FOR THIS BEAUTIFUL AND COLORFUL TRIBAL ARTWORK. ITS VIVID COLOURS AND INTRICATE DESIGNS ARE ABSOLUTELY CAPTIVATING AND REFLECT A DEEP CULTURAL RICHNESS." -RICHIE BOOKER, MUSICIAN AND BOB MARLEY'S BROTHER

INDIA

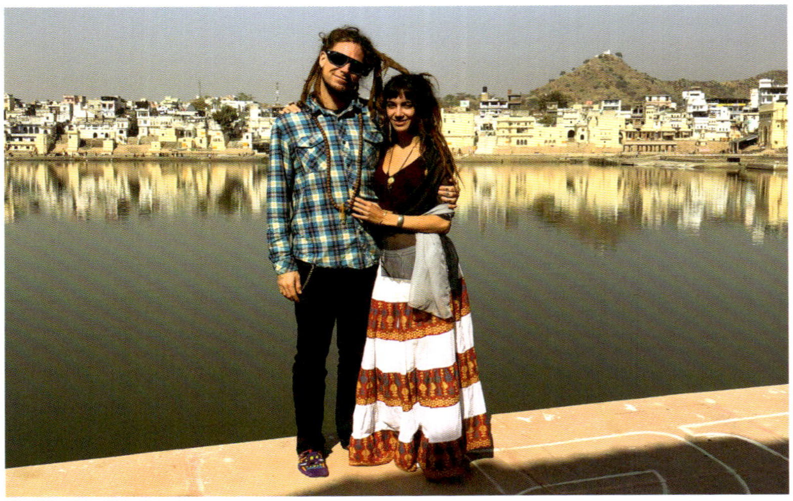

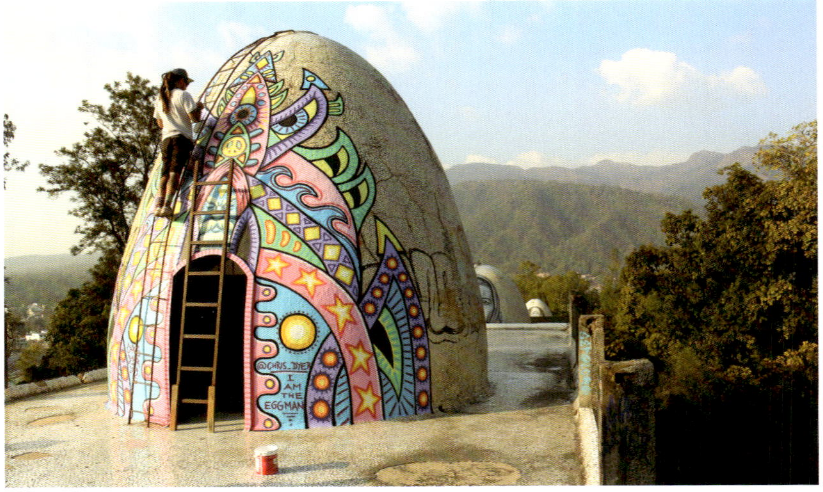

After my big art show, I felt my ego was satisfied and had less to prove, so it allowed me (the soul) to go and take a fun vacation to chill out. I've wanted to travel to India all my life, so I took this chance to finally explore many locations of that awesome country for a whole month. I had re-connected with Arianne during my Florida show, so I invited her to join me and give our relationship a fresh chance. It didn't take long till we fell back in Love and that made me real happy. On our trip we journeyed through **Delhi**, **Pushkar**, **Jaipur**, **Agra**, **Rishikesh**, **Varanasi**, **Hampi** and **Goa**. The only job I had scheduled for myself was at the end of the trip, a painting workshop in Goa. Other than that we just made a bunch of art for the fun of it. The highlight of that creation rampage was when we got to the abandoned **"Maharishi Ashram"** in Rishikesh, which the **Beatles** had visited him in the late 60's. The trippy buildings are now ruins being taken over by nature and street art. I was only able to smuggle a couple of spray paints into the country, so I mostly used low quality house paint to decorate an old Meditation Dome. It was so fun!!

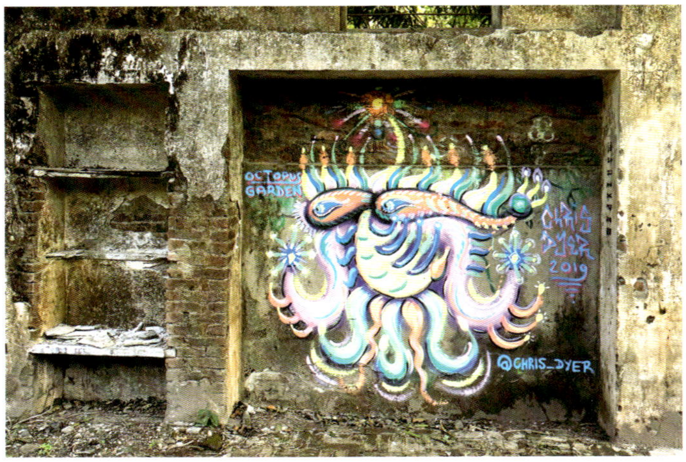

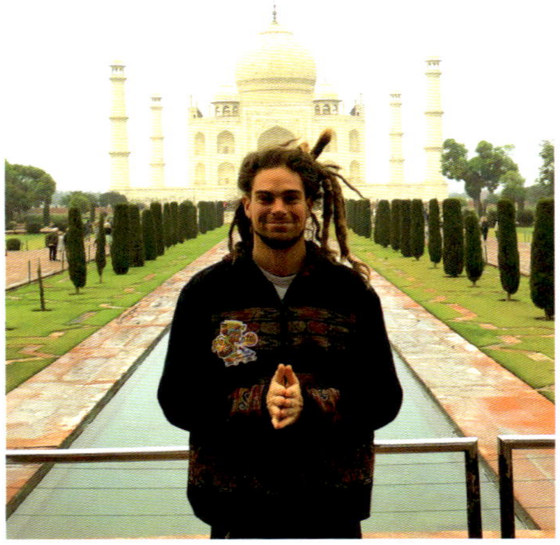

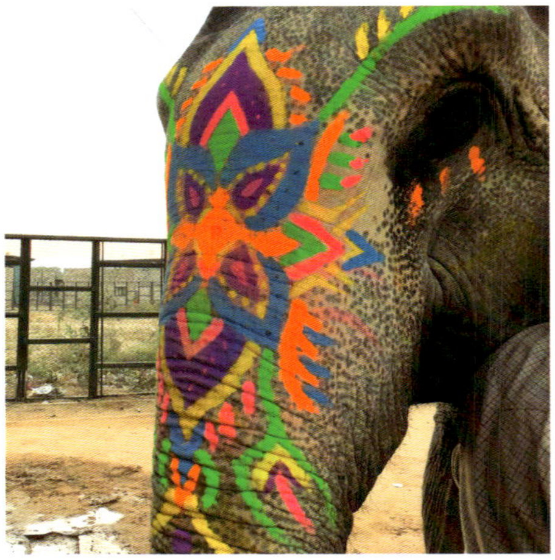

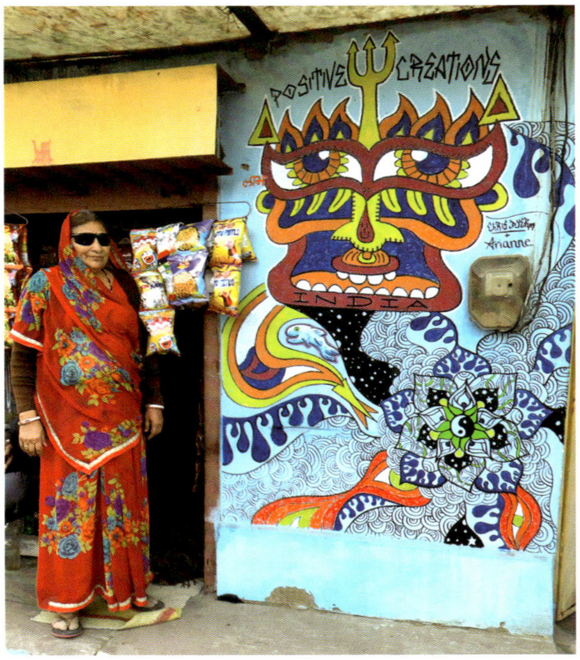

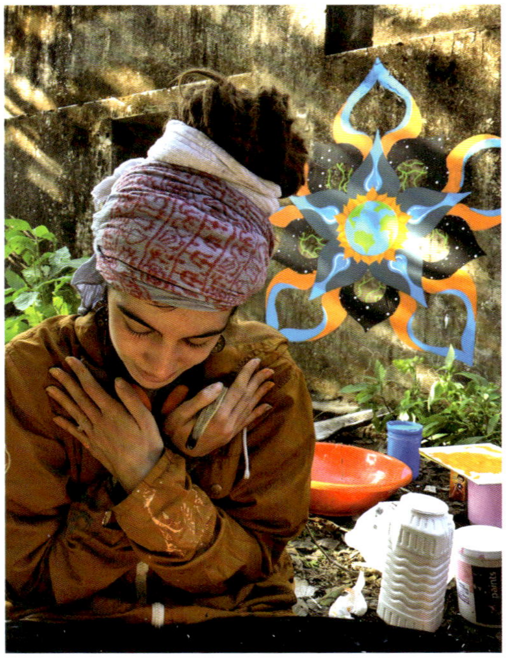

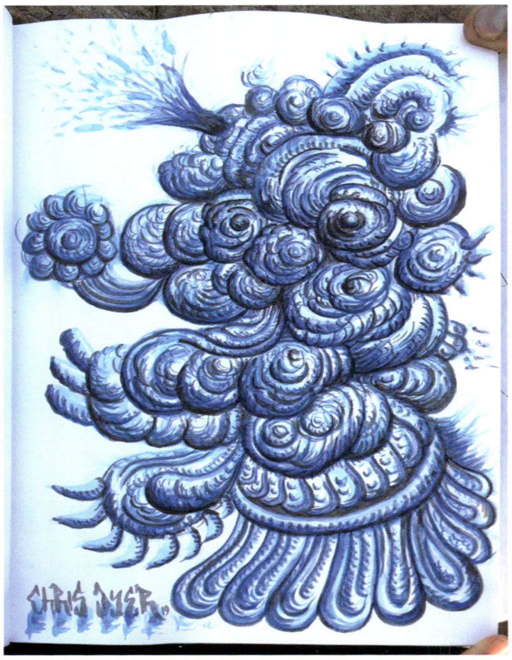

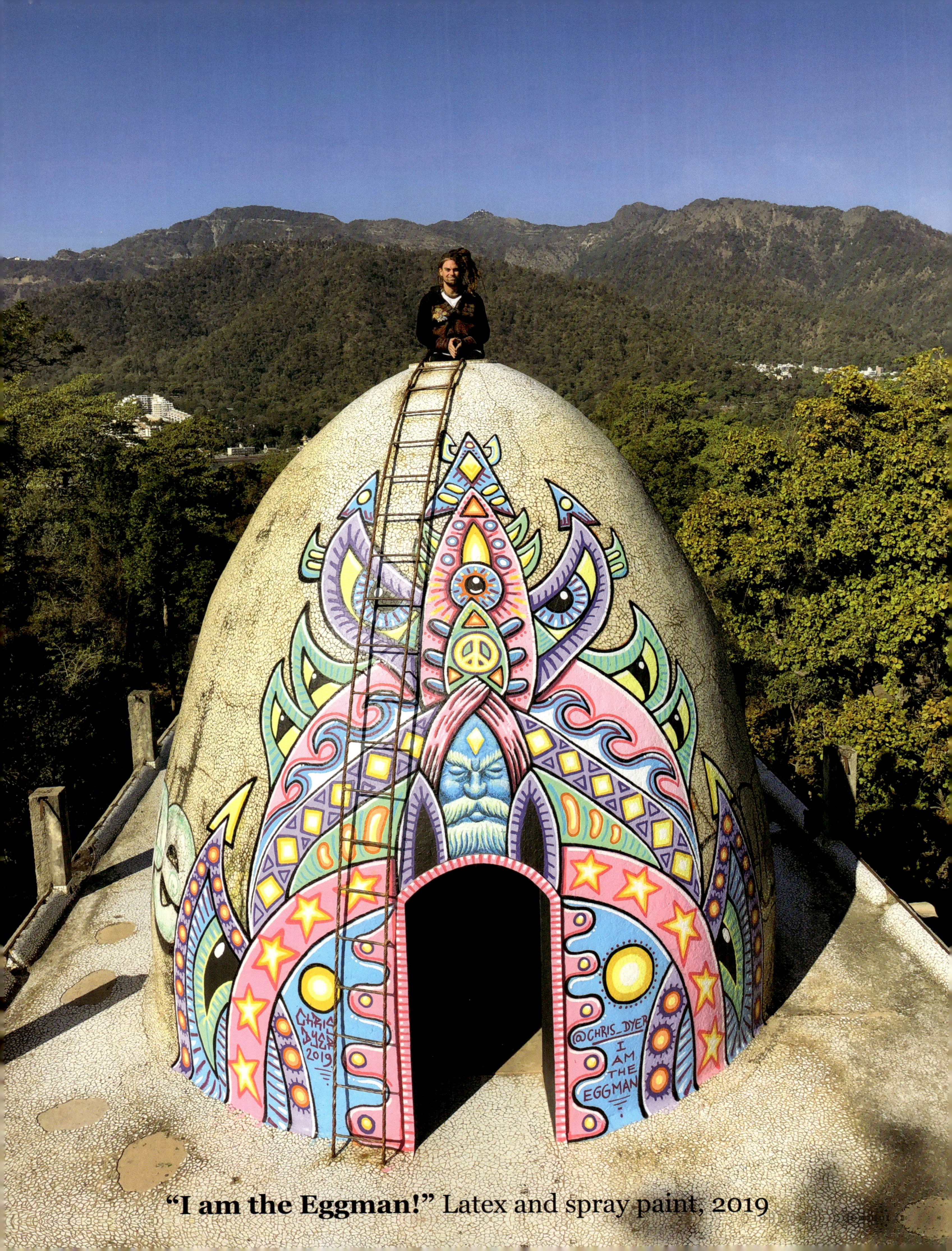

"I am the Eggman!" Latex and spray paint, 2019

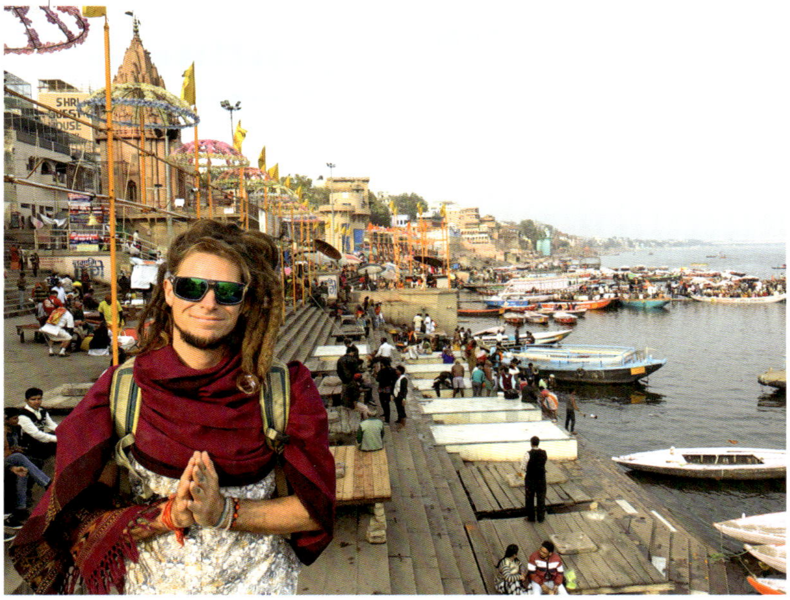

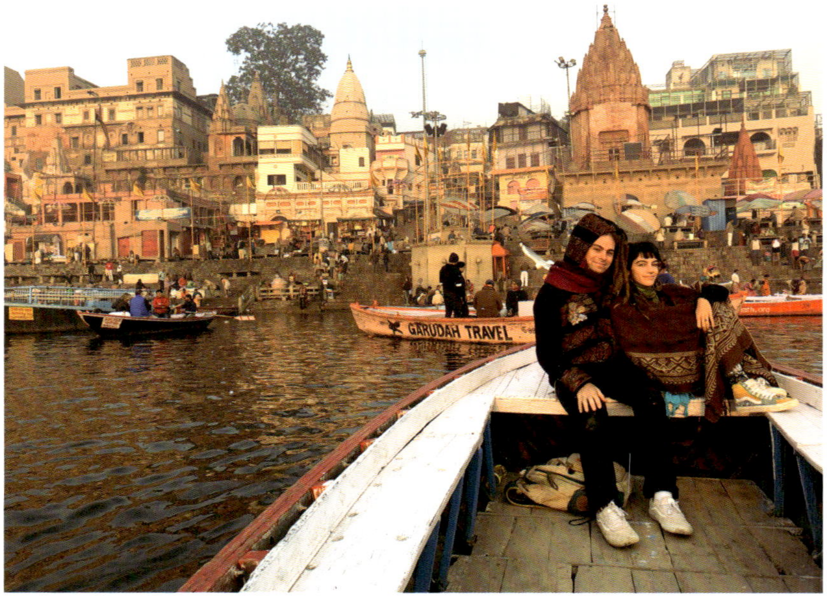

On this journey we got to see so many beautiful places, eat so much delicious food, enjoy nature and enjoy loving times. The painting I expressed on this trip is obviously about the Hindu deity **Ganesha**, who is said to remove obstacles. I had painted him previously so I was feeling like doing a Shiva instead, but we just really felt like honoring Ganesha after saving our asses so much, mostly from motorcycle accidents. The "Horn Please" and icons on the top part of the arch where things that I saw painted on the many inspiring trucks we saw on the road. And just to clarify, the Swastika symbol on his hand has nothing to do with Nazis, it's a divine symbol of good fortune for Hindus, Buddhists and Jains.

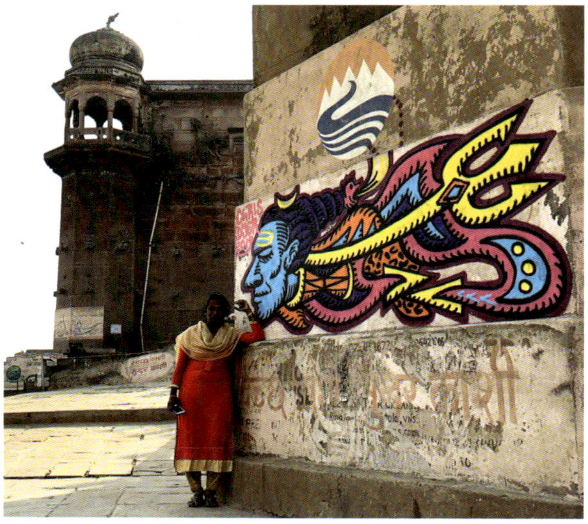

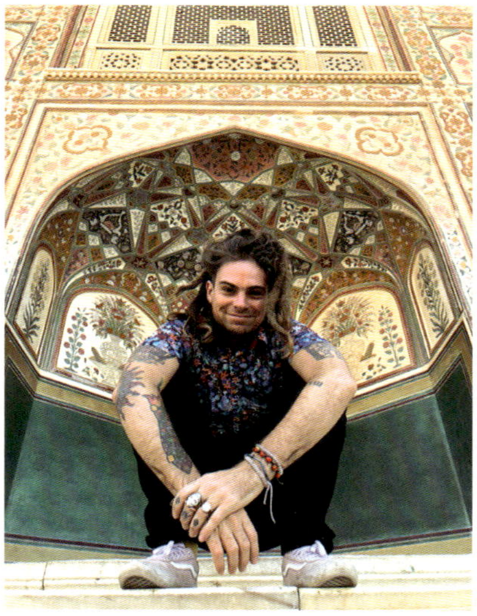

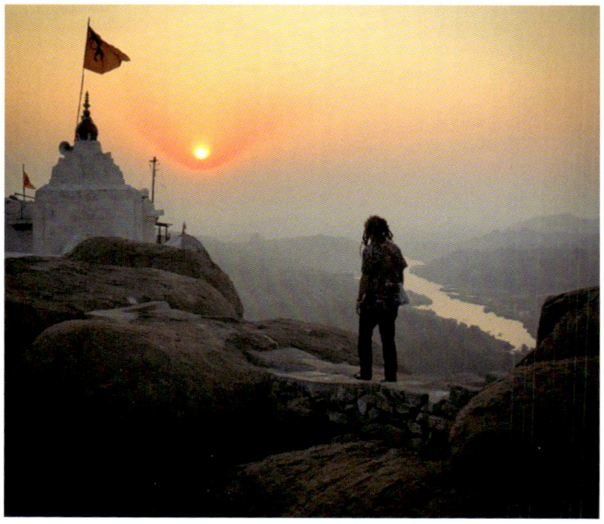

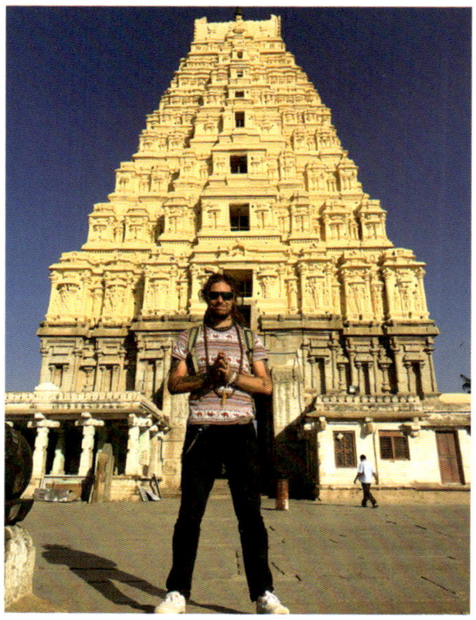

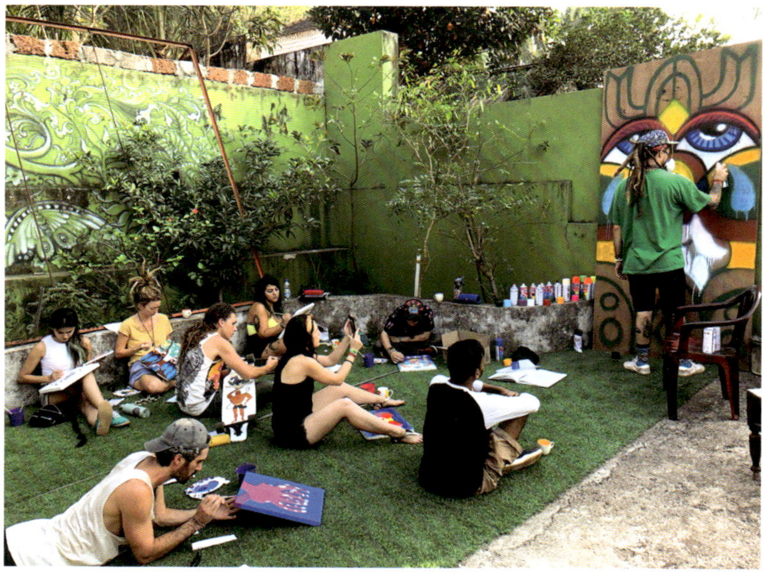

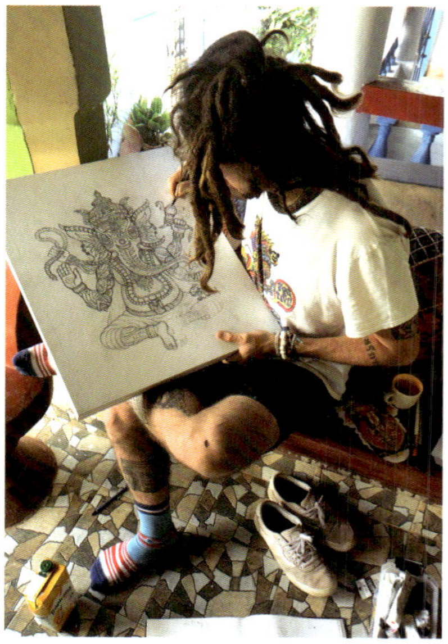

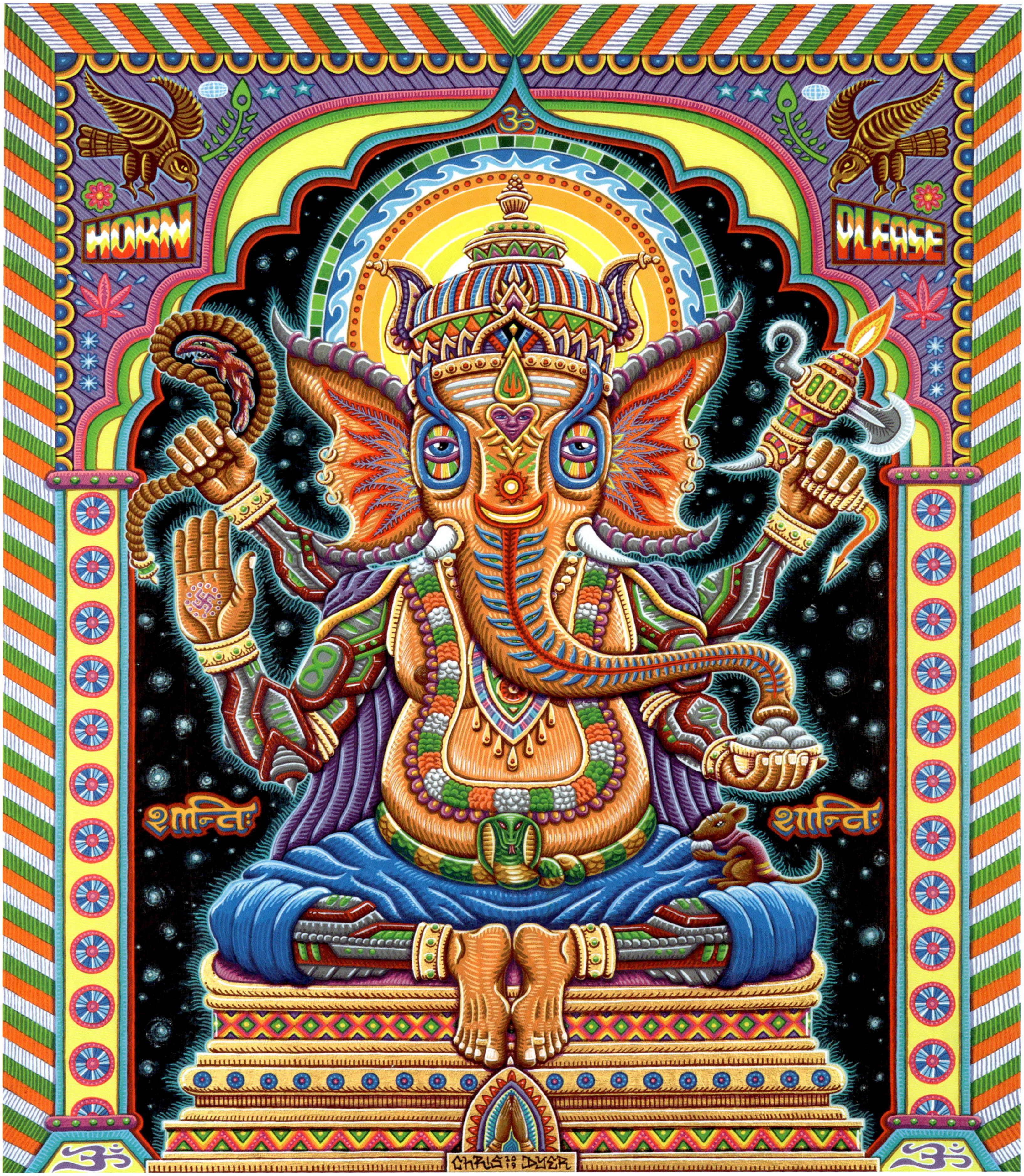

"Jai Ganesha" Acrylics on wood, 2019

MEXICO

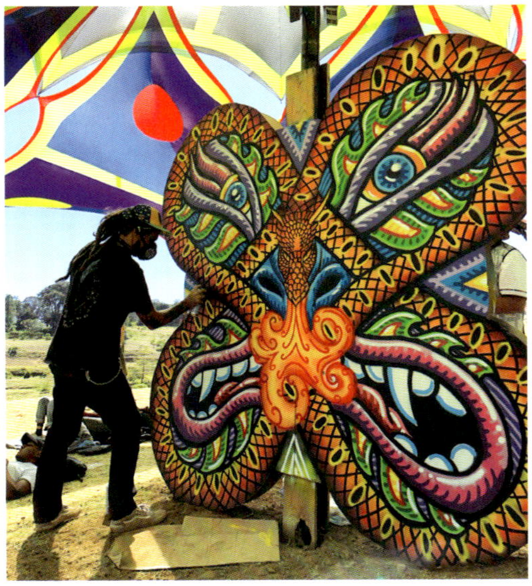

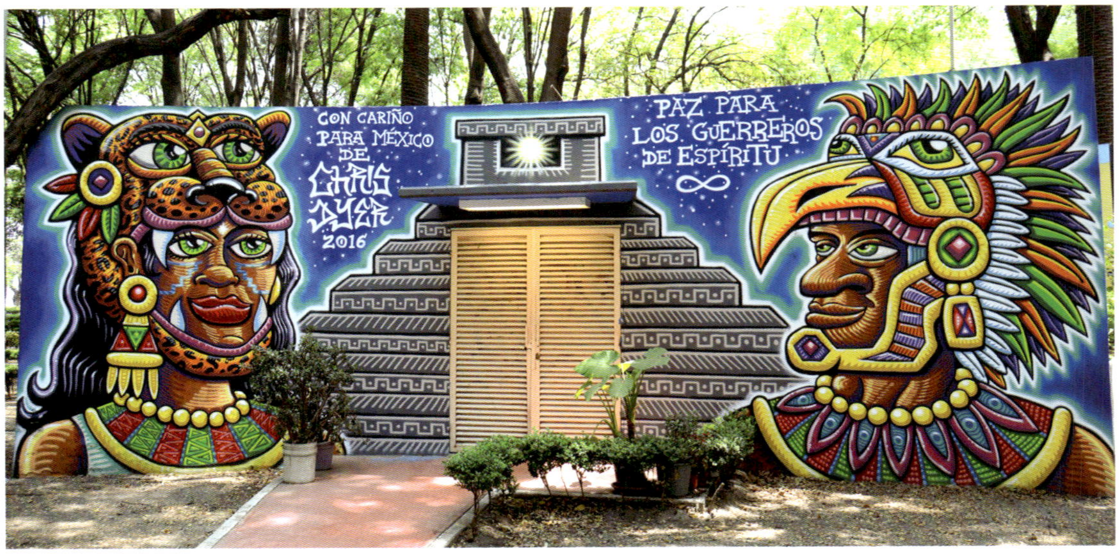

After India I flew straight to **Mexico City**, where I had a live painting performance at a music Festival. Once it was done I was invited to paint a piece at **"Pachamoma" Art Museum** in **Irapuato**. The director of the museum, **Fernando Barba**, was also a shaman who had trained under the "Seri" tribe of the Sonora Dessert. The medicine from that area is the **"Bufo Alvarious"** toad, 5-meo-DMT, which is four times stronger than "normal" DMT. As somebody who had gotten used to surrendering to that strong chemical on my Ayahuasca journeys, I was up to smoking it, but it ended being an extremely intense experience. The initial session might have only lasted fifteen minutes, but it was an absolute disintegration of my being, as if the sun exploded in me. It was a total ego death experience, which erased me and allowed me to become everything, in the white light body of the absolute. It was an amazing activation, blissful at points, but also terrifying for my mind and shocking to my nervous system. This brought flashbacks all day, and then panic attacks that first sleepless night, feeling like I would die (sucked into the void of nothingness) if I fell asleep. The next day, all my biggest fears came to the surface at once, which was a very hard time for me... Luckily some local shamanic healers ceremoniously closed up my psychic body, which was left way too open, and sucked out (and then vomited) a lot of my negative energy. Once I started "sleeping" at night again, I would have these incredibly interesting and potent visits from alien entities, repairing and teaching me feelings I had never had before. These lucid "dreams" happened every night for a week and then sporadically, for months after. The painting I did was based on those interdimentional night sessions, which I never saw, only felt, and I still don't really understand them. It did feel like I got expanded and schooled though. This sharp experience humbled me and taught me that I don't have to do a medicine unless it really calls me.

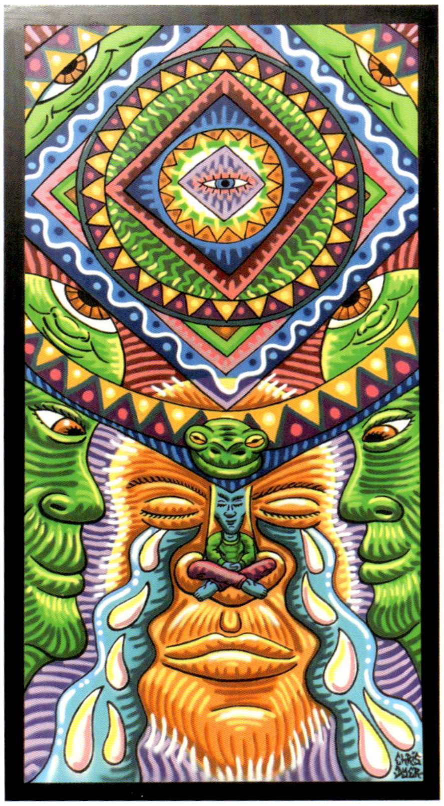

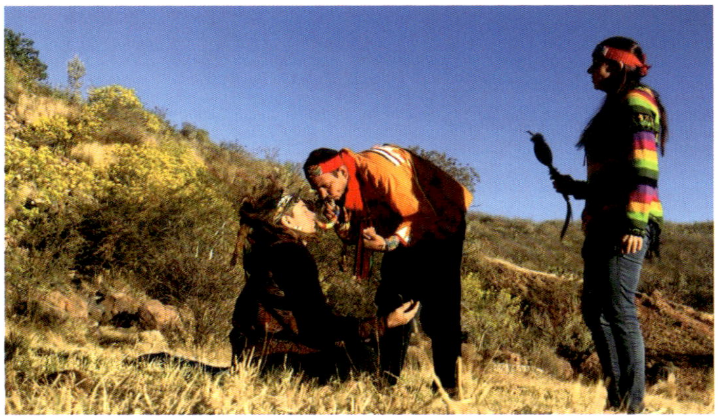

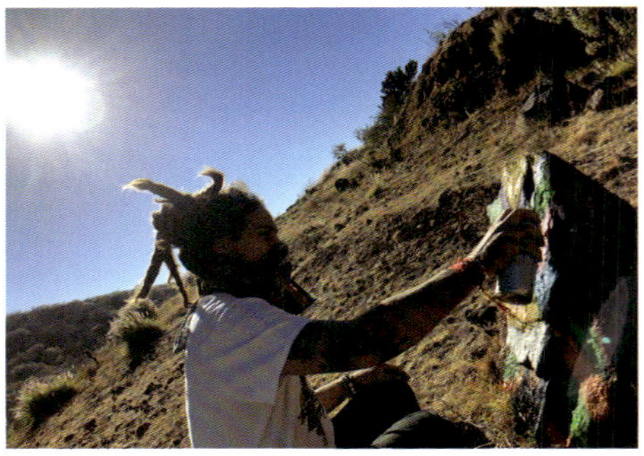

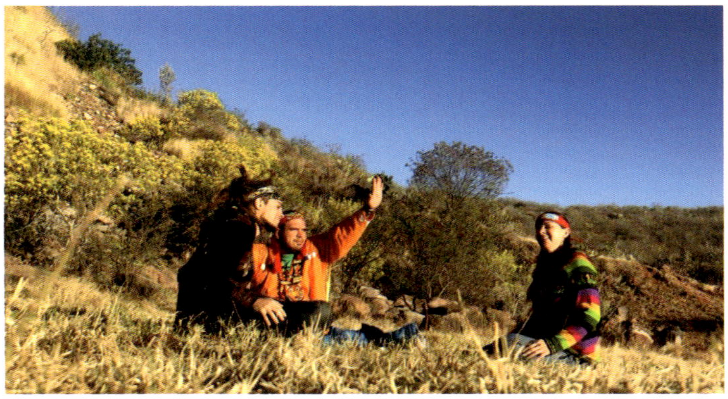

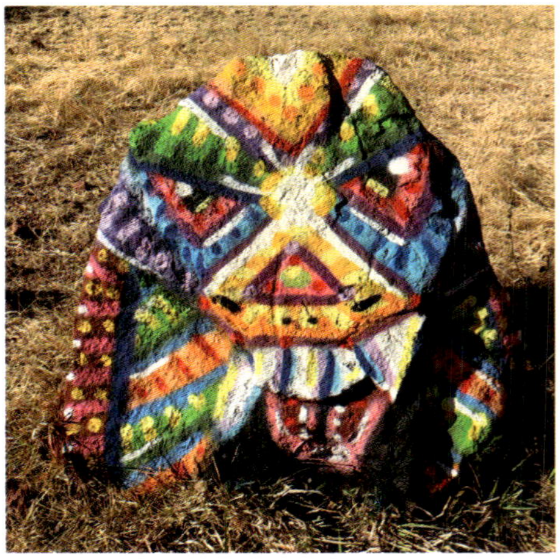

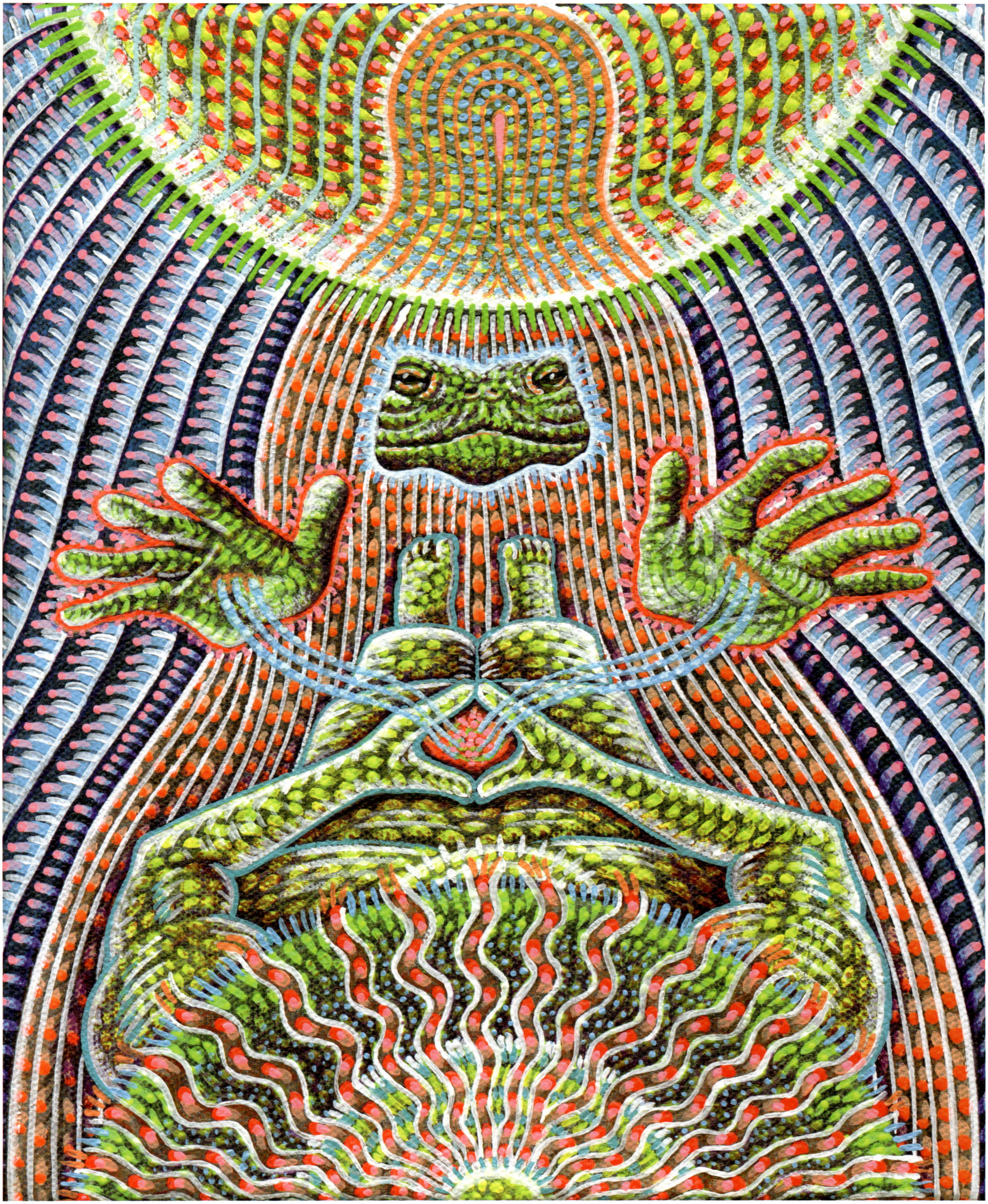

“Bufo the Midnight Visitor” Acrylics on canvas, 2019

FLORIDA

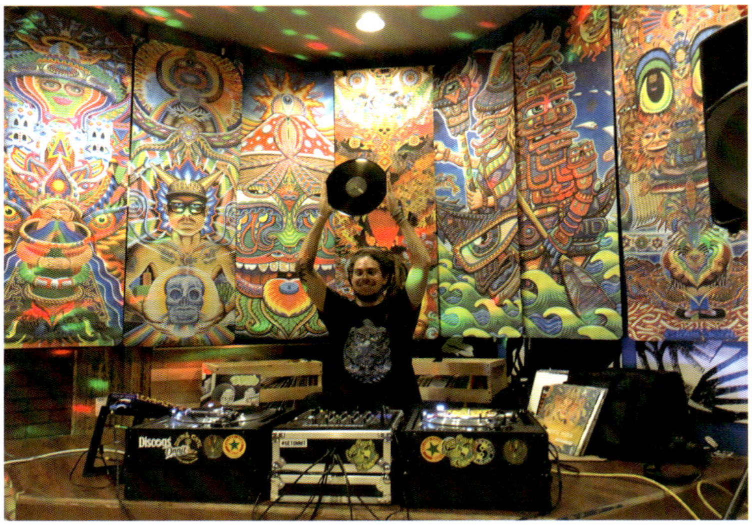

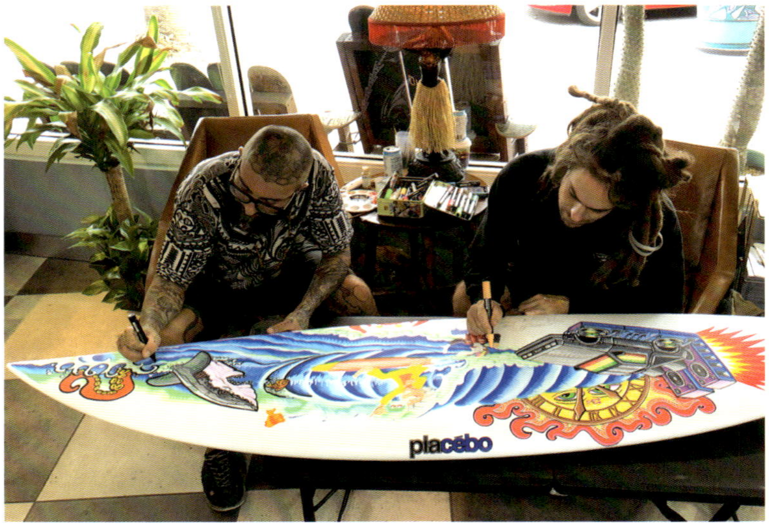

After Mexico and some integration time in Montreal, I met back up with Arianne in South Florida. She was getting ready to move back to my place so needed help. In that period, my shamanic family of **Miami** was doing a medicine retreat I was Live Painting at. Though I wasn't really ready to do psychedelics again so soon after my Mexico activations, I was already scheduled for this event, so I partook on the Kambo, Sananga and Ayahuasca ceremonies. Herbert was the shaman they flew up from Peru for this, so he continued working on the closing up of my process with the Bufo and then Aya gave me a wild Galactic ride. During those journeys Herbert sang a fun song that went **"Bribribribribribribribribri"**, which was so joyous, like liquid rainbow light that I had to interpret as a happy character sketch the next morning. Shortly after I had a DJ gig at a "Yoga Mat Art Show" up north in **Cocoa Beach**. It was for an awesome tattoo artist called **Mark Longnecker** and we ended up collaborating on a surfboard painting. Close by, in **Jacksonville**, I scored a quick mural gig and it was my chance to spray paint the joyous character I had recently met. It came out so dope that I then live-painted him on a canvas the following month, at a **"Charles the First"** and **"Off the Trees"** show I performed at in North Carolina.

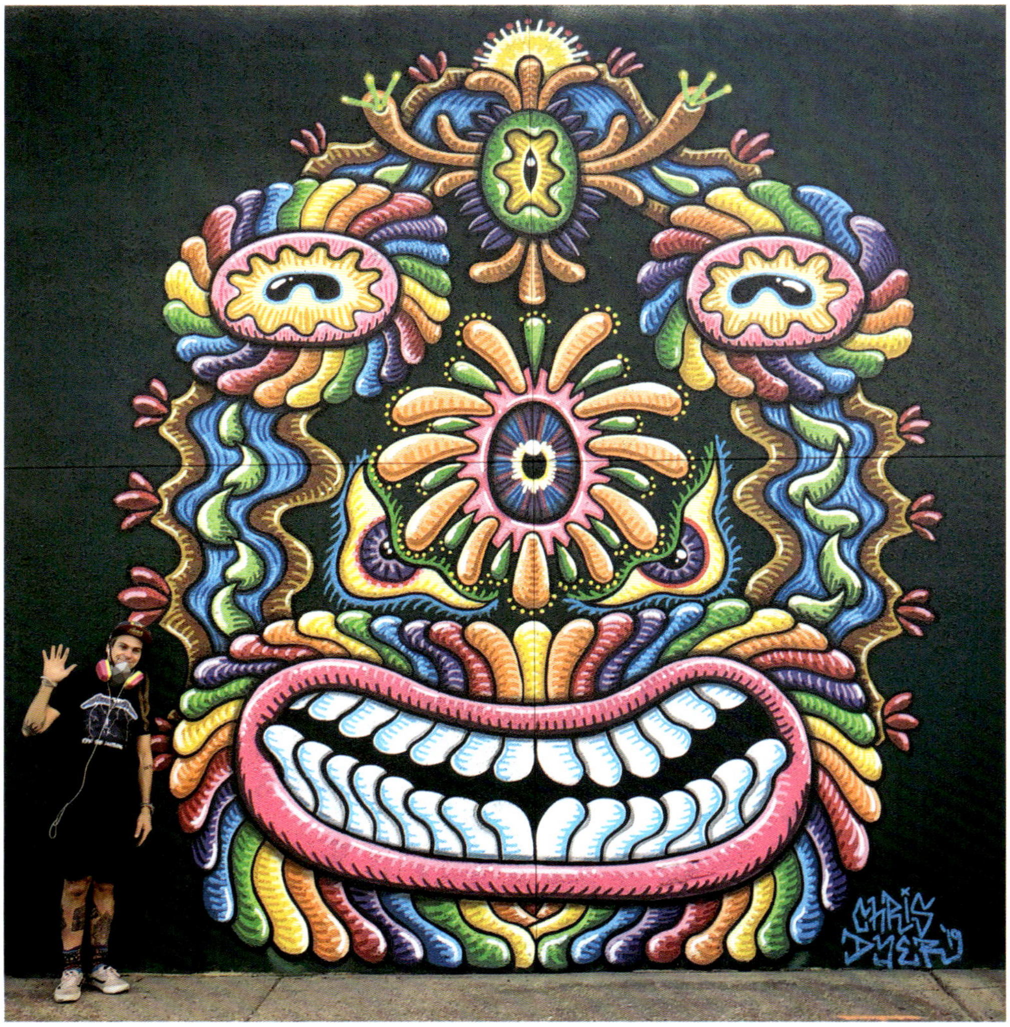

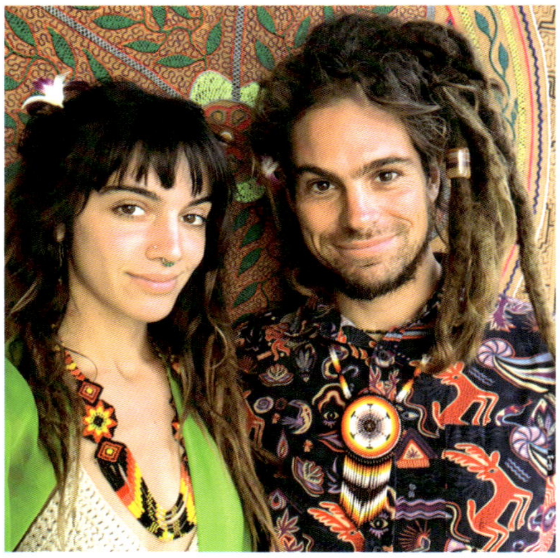

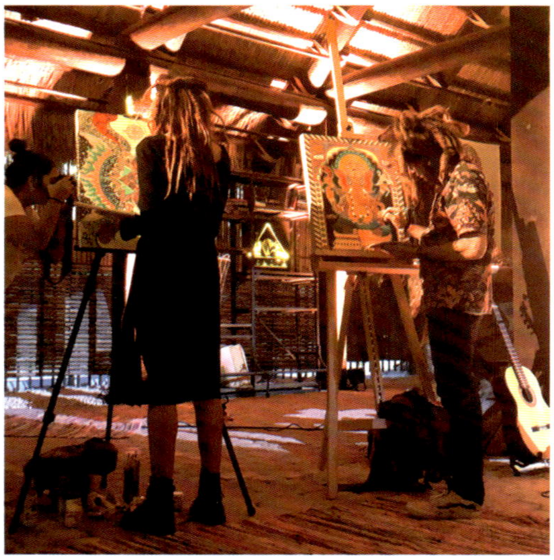

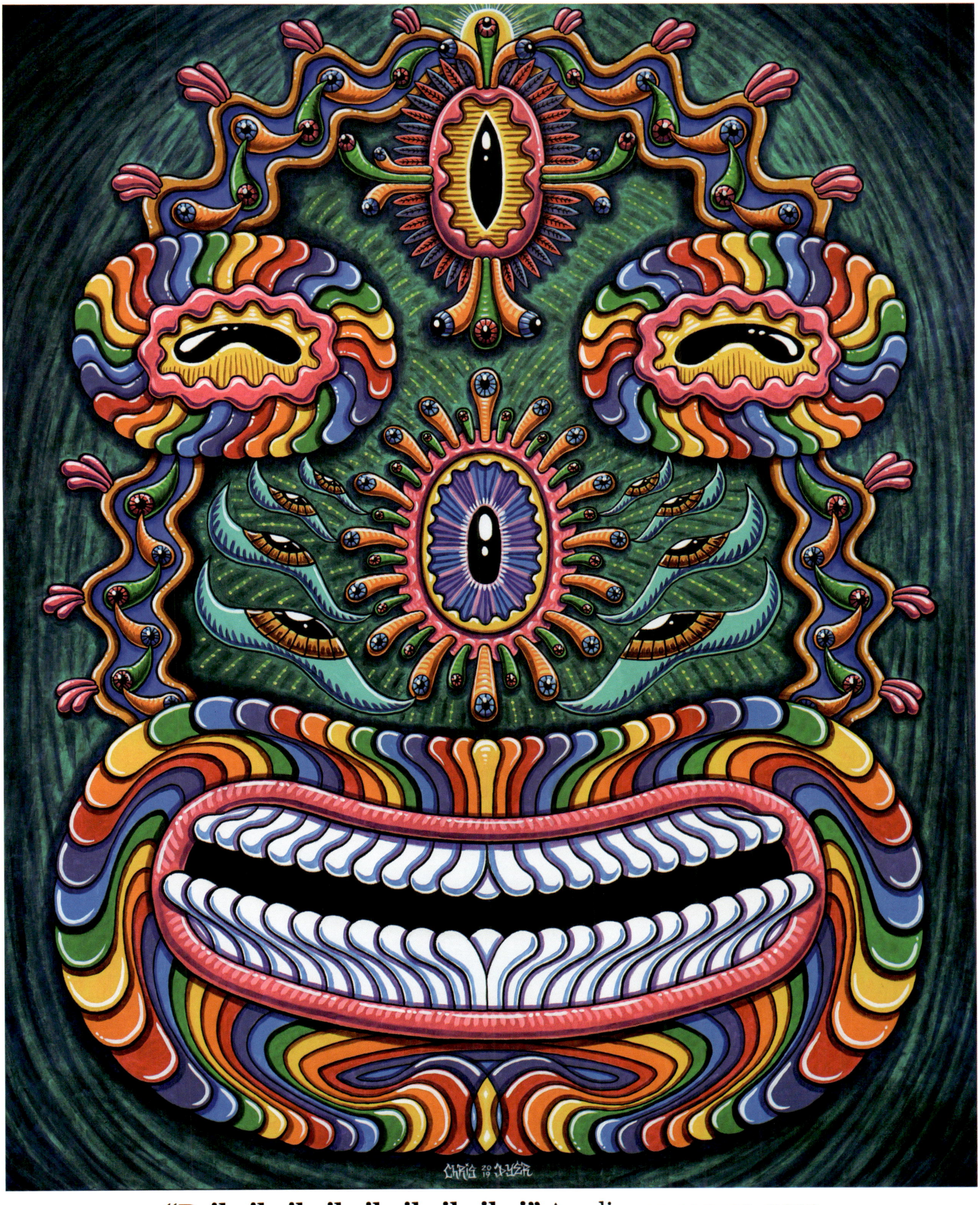

“Bribribribribribribribribribri” Acrylics on canvas, 2019

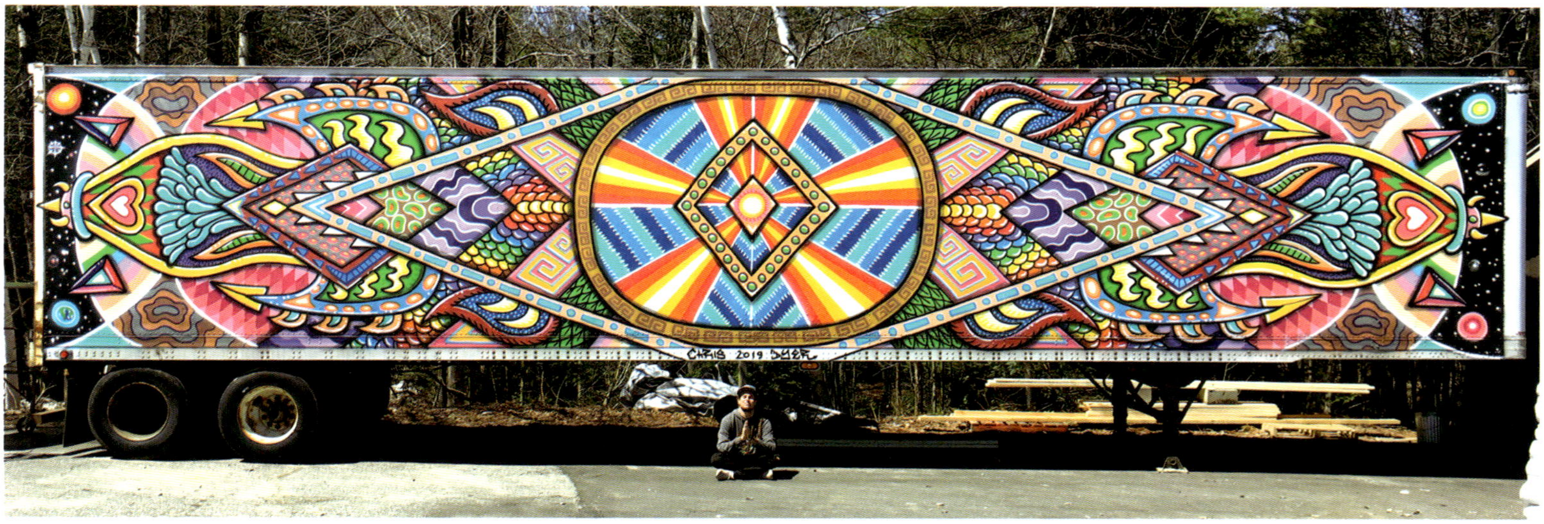

That year was awesome, with lots of touring around North America, to perform and paint murals. Also, after years of saving up I had enough capital to finally buy an apartment of my own! The place had a good amount of space, including studios for both Arianne and me. It was located in my favorite neighbourhood of Montreal (Le Plateau), a block away from our favorite park (Lafontaine). Painting the walls of the place and moving in was a lot of work, but so rewarding. I also painted a mural at my entrance, which kinda got me in trouble with the building, haha. Those lovely summer months, as I decorated my new place, I allowed myself plenty of time to integrate the lessons from the medicine work of the beginning of the year. This painting, done for a Montreal street art show, was one of the expressions that helped me visually express the inner work I had done. Art helps me digest and process all this evolving energy that I hold.

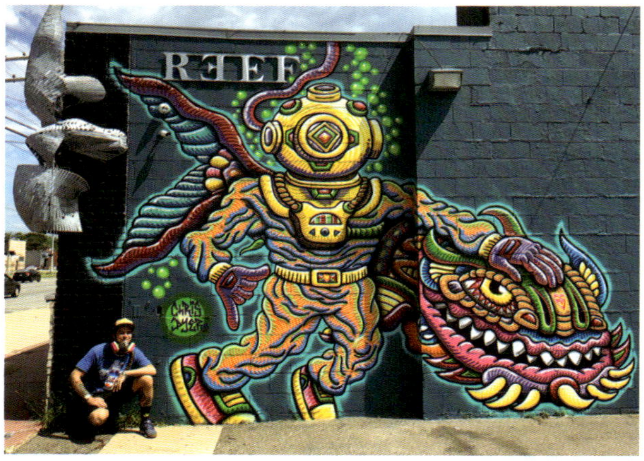

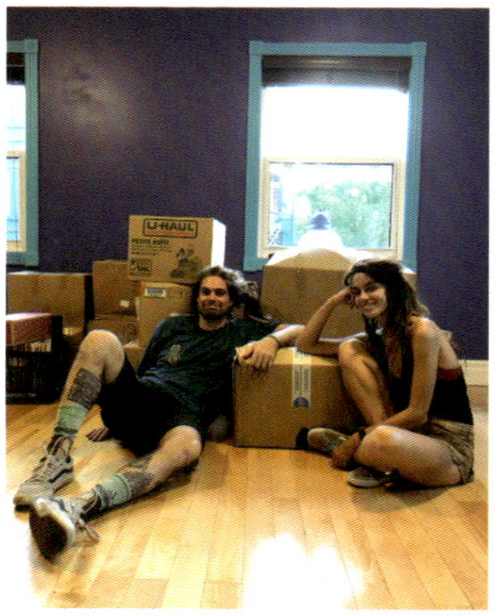

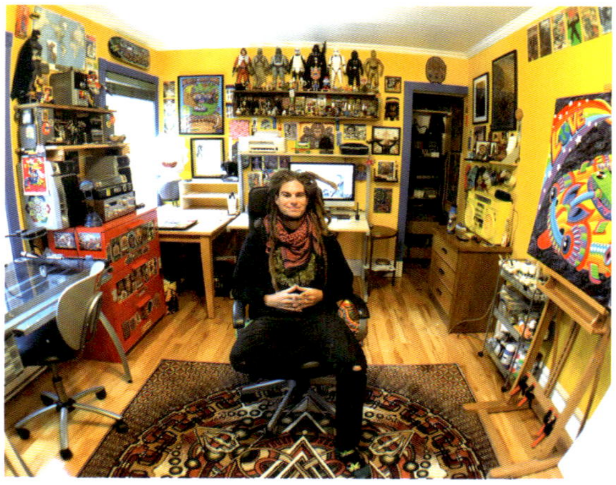

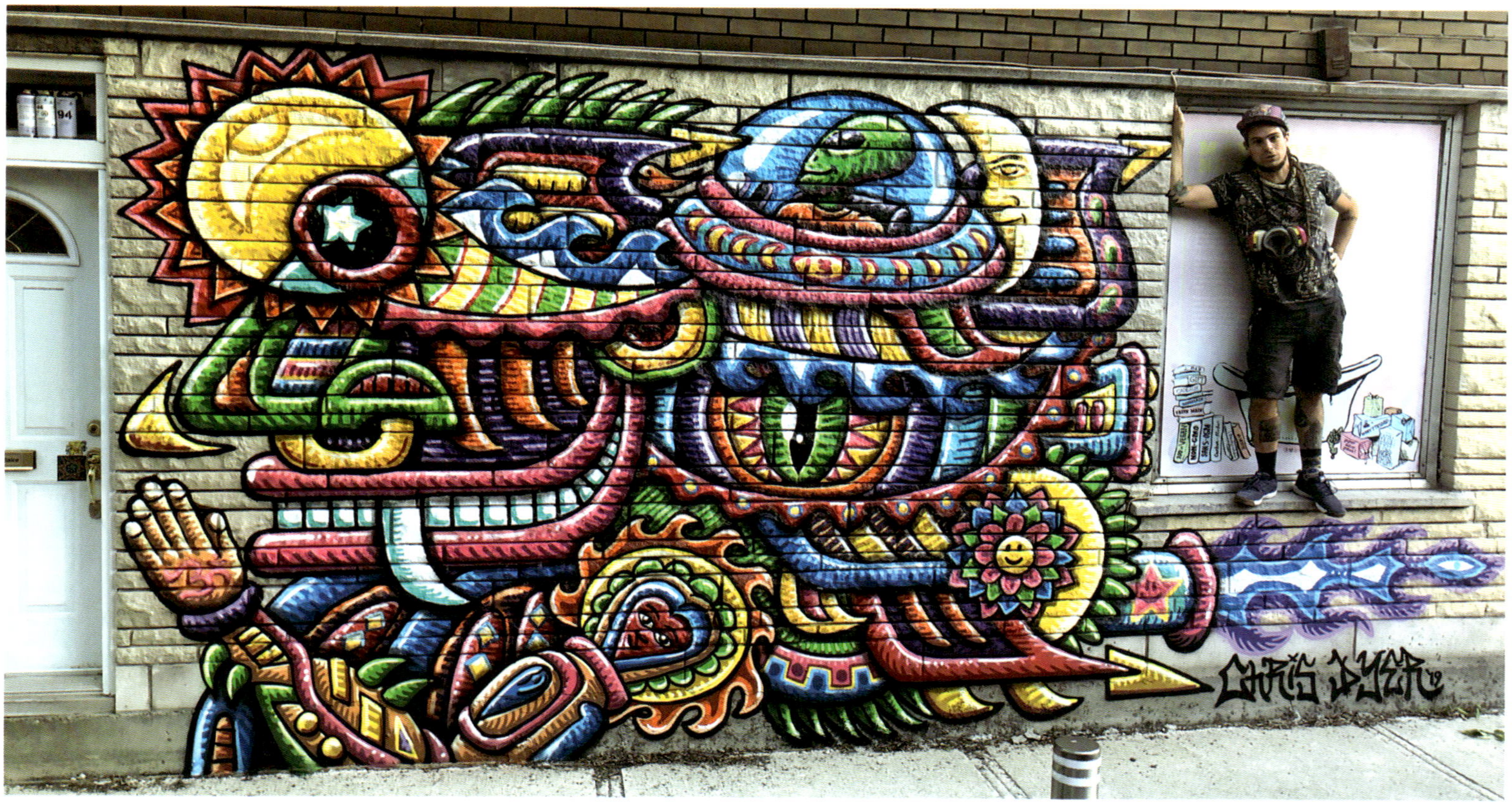

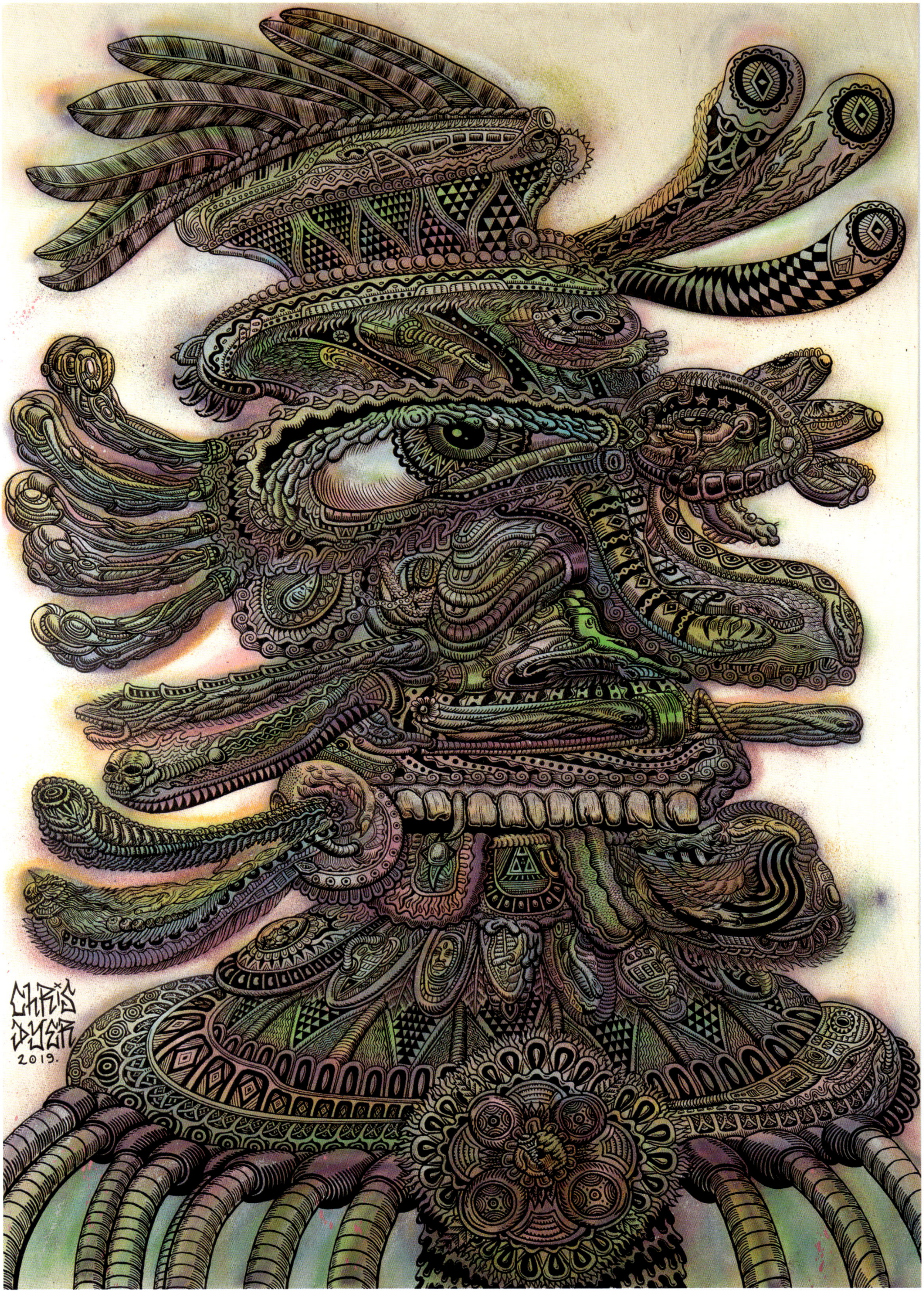

"Integration" Spray paint and ink on canvas, 2019

PALESTINE

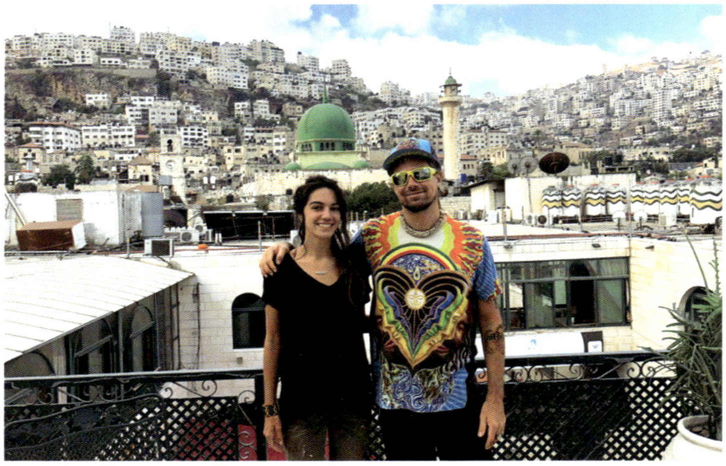

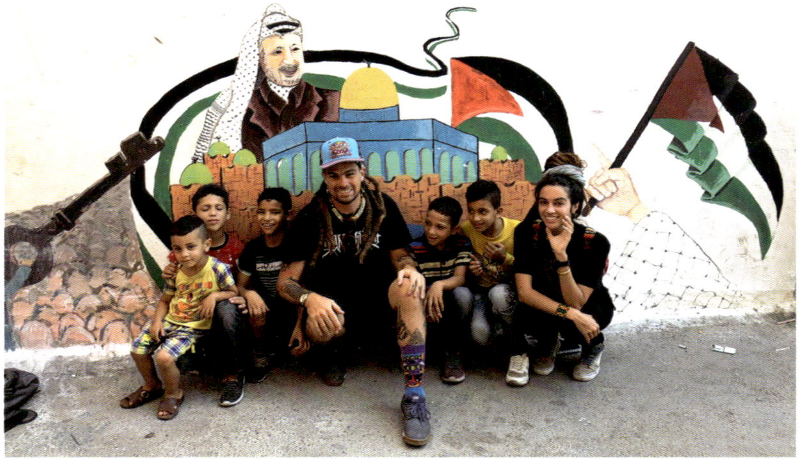

At the end of that summer, Arianne and I accepted an invitation to go and do some volunteer work in what is left of the country of Palestine. A non-profit called **"Beyond Us"** flew in a small group of international street artists to paint murals in **"Balata"**, the largest and most dangerous refugee camp of the **West Bank**. It was a really interesting, intense and heart breaking experience, as we had to learn firsthand about the harsh conditions of this occupied land. Art was all we could offer to cheer up these people, mostly children, who where kinda confused of what we were doing. My favorite part was the art workshop I did with the kids, who had fun painting some characters I had spray painted for them. Then on our day off, we cruised over to the ancient city of **Bethlehem**, where the Major had us over his office to congratulate us for our efforts. We then checked out the spot where Jesus was born and also Banksy's "Walled off Hotel". There we got to see the giant division wall and I had the chance to paint a little peace sign on it. I so wish Israel and Palestine could live in harmony once again, so that no more people have to suffer anymore. Yet the politricks are so damn complicated in that region and emotions high... I don't know what the solution is for all of that but I do know it involves lots of empathy, compassion, understanding and forgiveness.

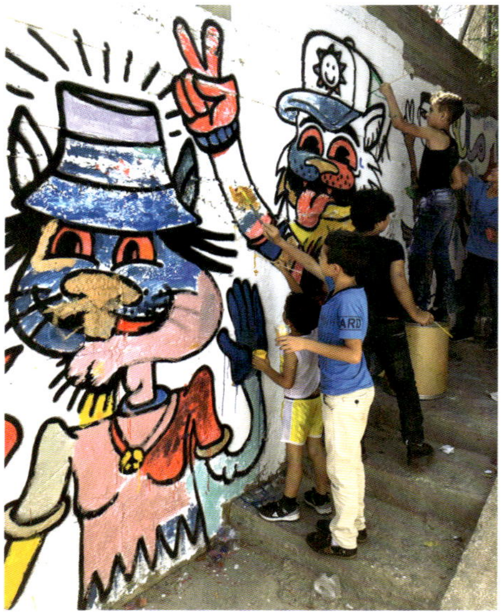

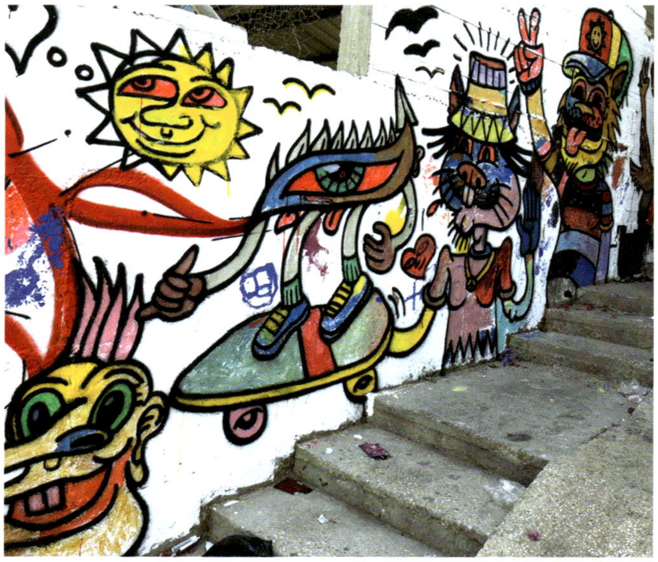

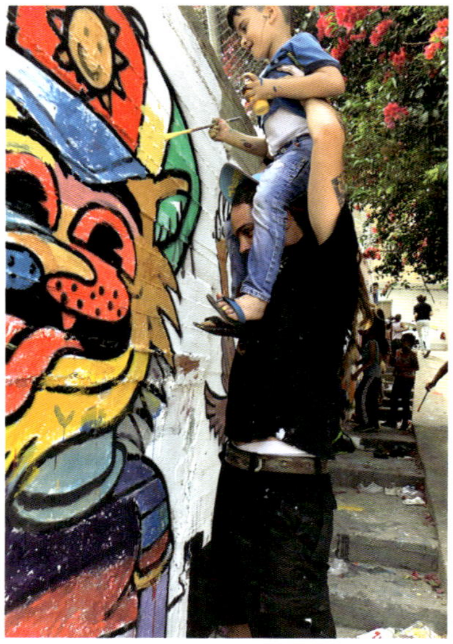

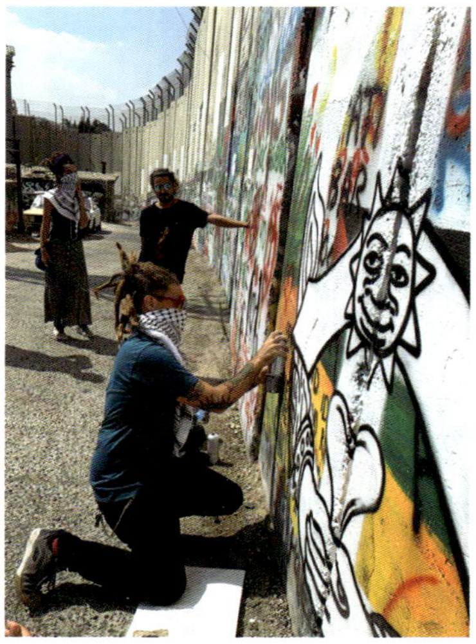

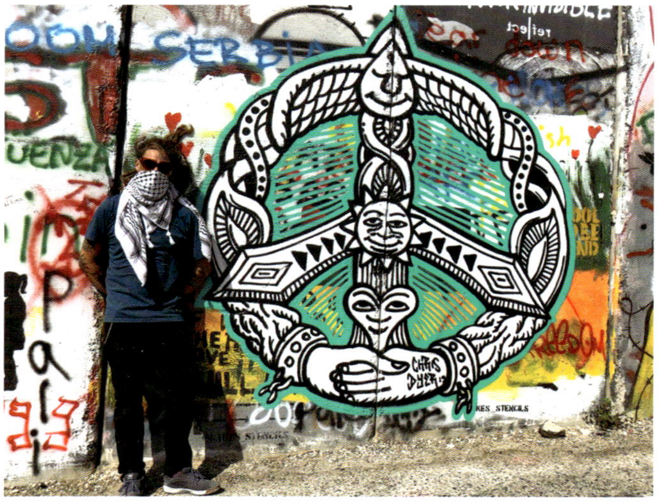

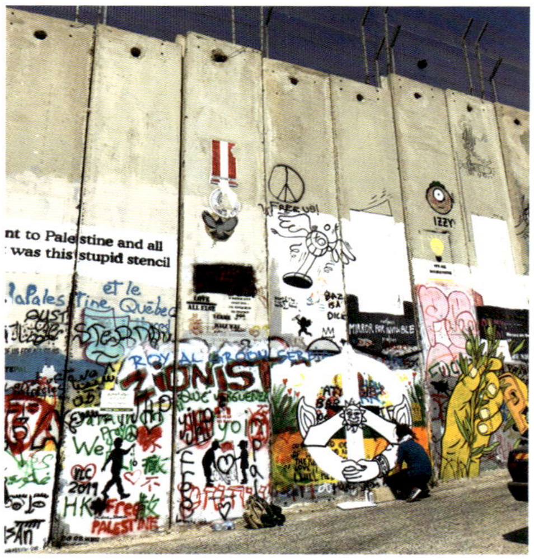

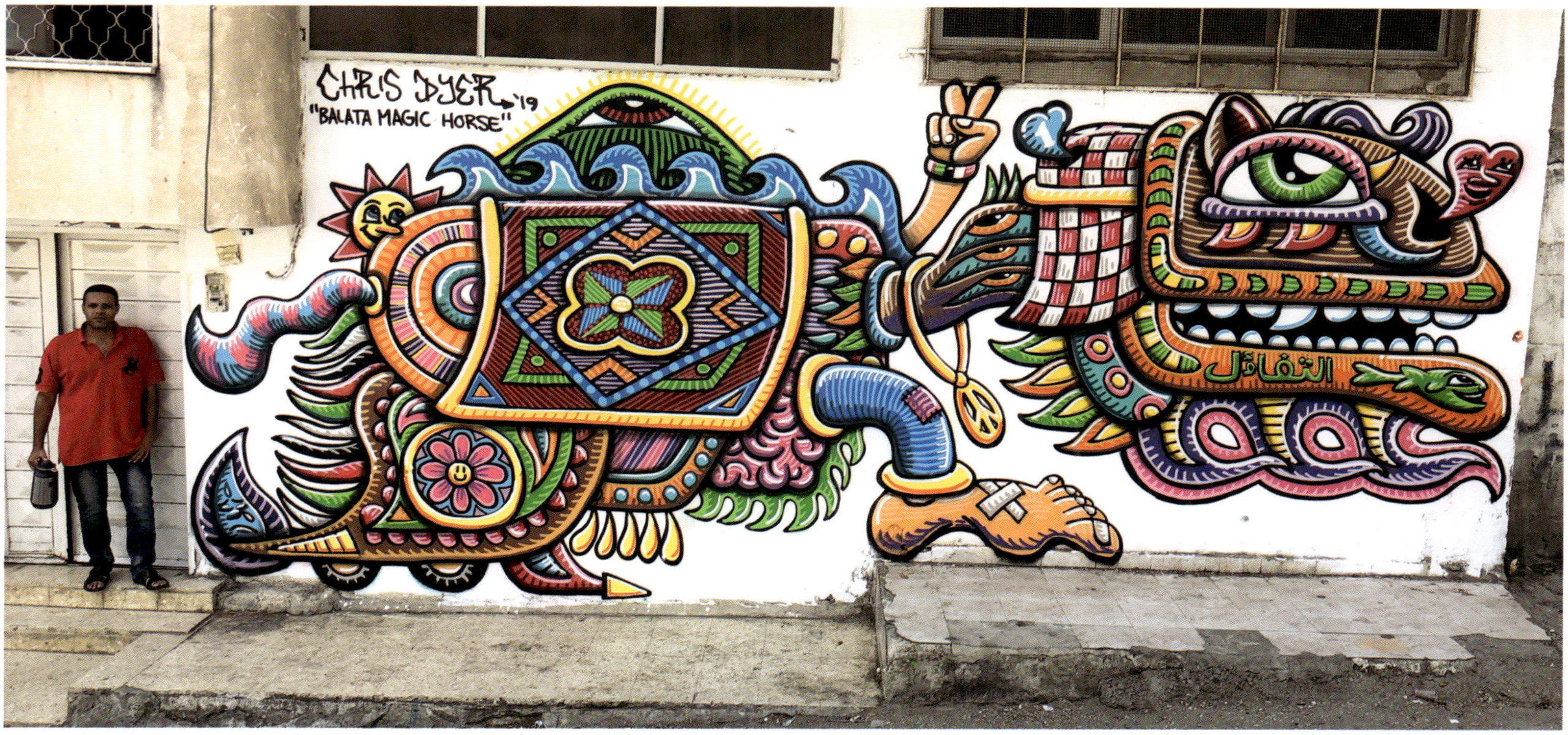

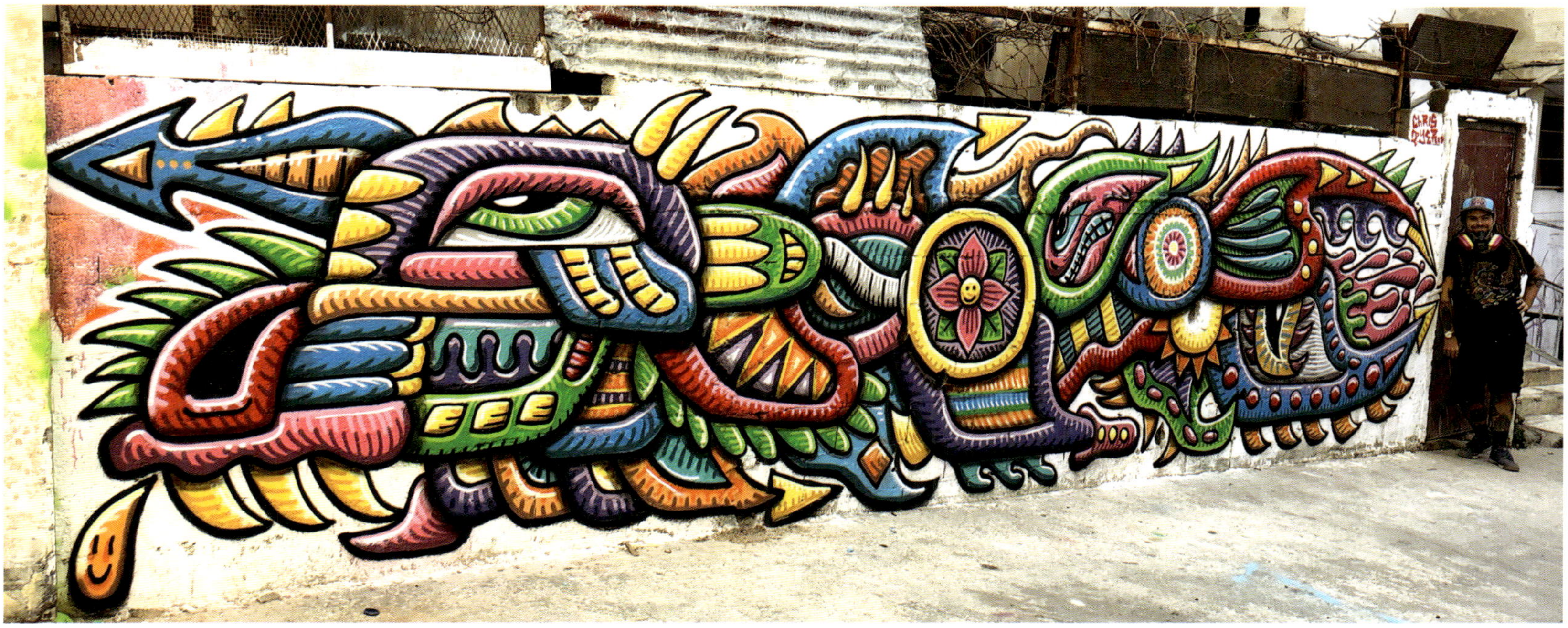

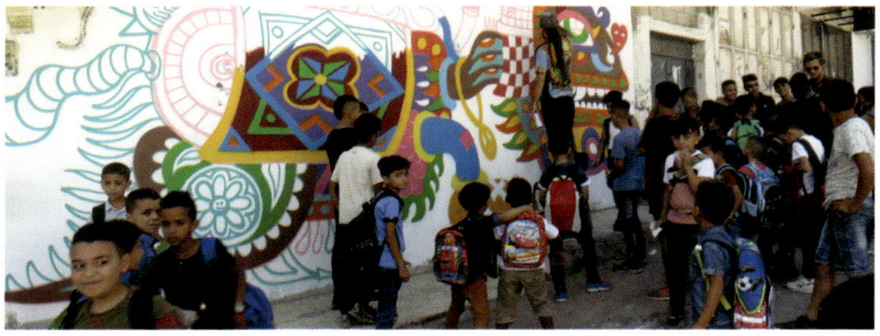

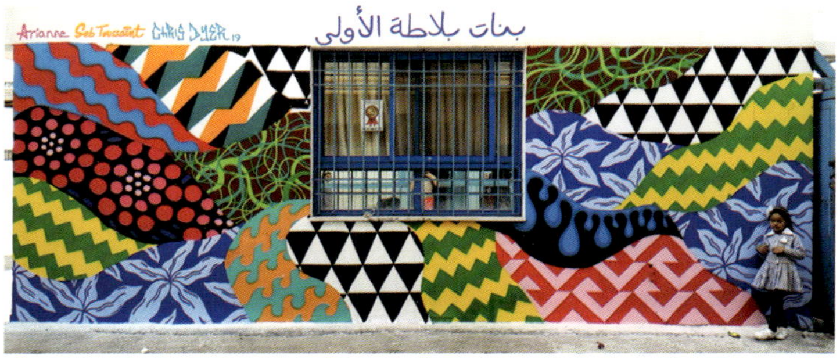

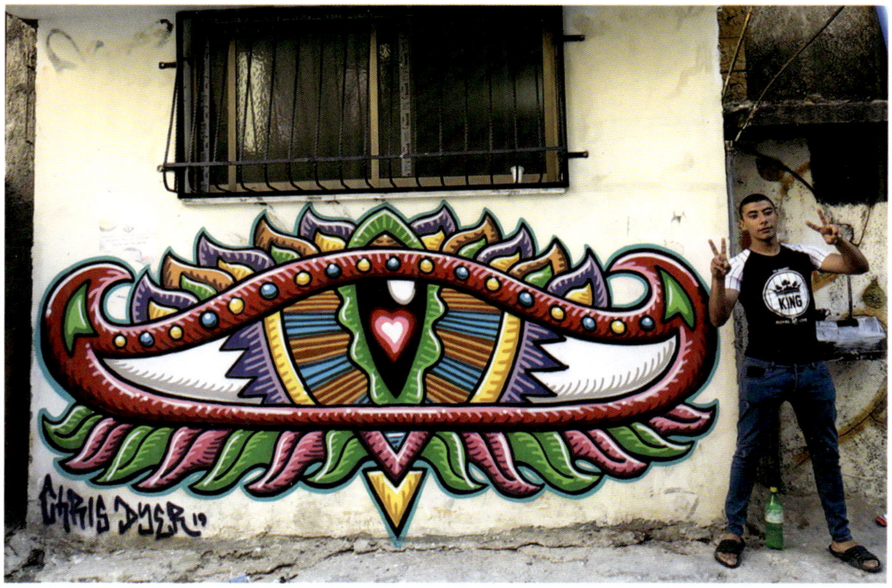

"Balata Refugee Camp Murals" Spray paint, 2019

JORDAN

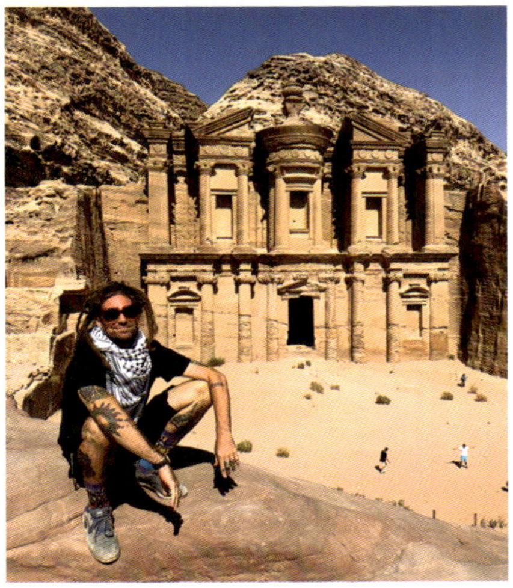

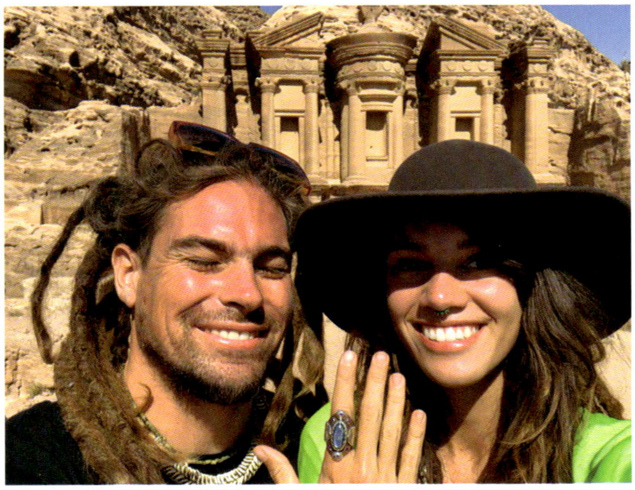

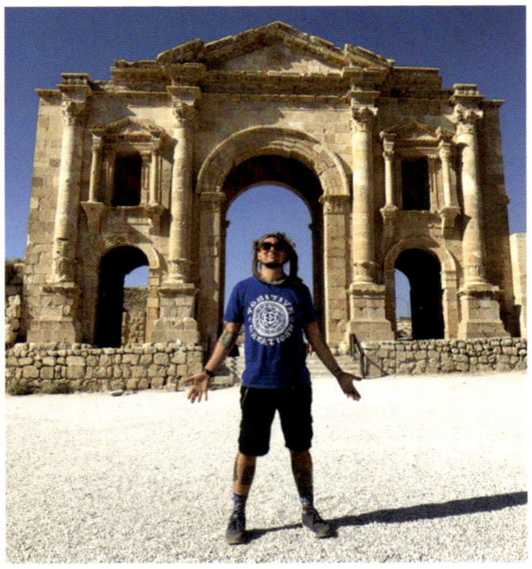

Entering the neighboring country of Jordan, was like a breath of fresh air, after our time in the high anxiety vibration of Palestine. For years I have wanted to see the impressive ruins of Petra, and since we where so close to them, it was inevitable to take a lil vacation through this ancient country. We arrived in the capital city of **Amman**, where our hostel was right in front of these gorgeous Roman ruins, with a big coliseum, surrounded by tall pillars! For the next days we checked out the super interesting biblical ruins of **"Unm Qavs"** and **"Jarash"**. We then rented a car and cruised down to the epic desert of **"Wadi Rum"** where we stayed with the Bedouins and explored through the super trippy rock formations of that area. It was quite magical and surreal! And then of course we went to spend some time at the incredible ruins of **Petra**, which are several thousand years old. There, in front of the amazing view of **"The Monastery"** carved into a mountain, I got on my knee, presented Arianne with an engagement ring and asked her to marry me! She was so surprised and shocked by my proposal, that it took her a minute to say yes in tears! Such a happy way to end this special Middle East journey!

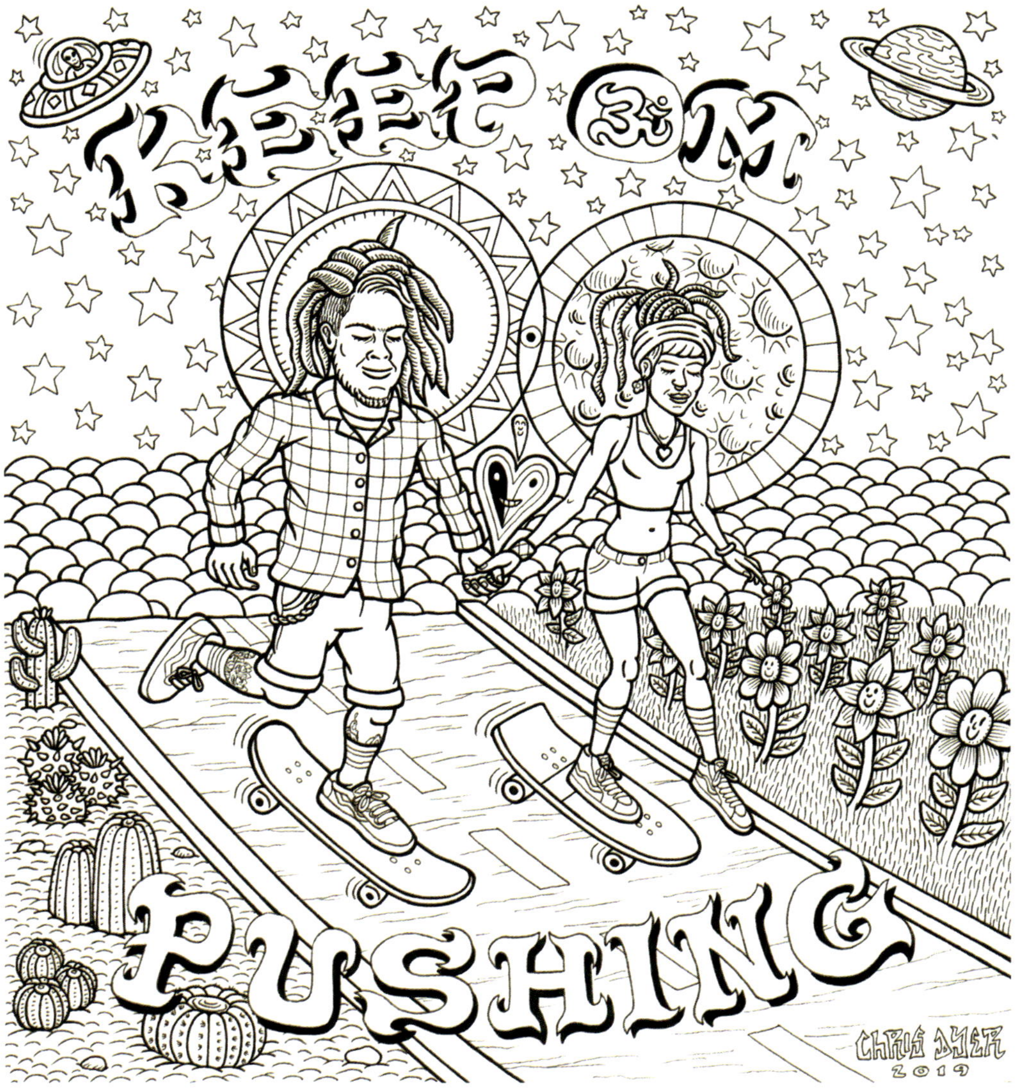

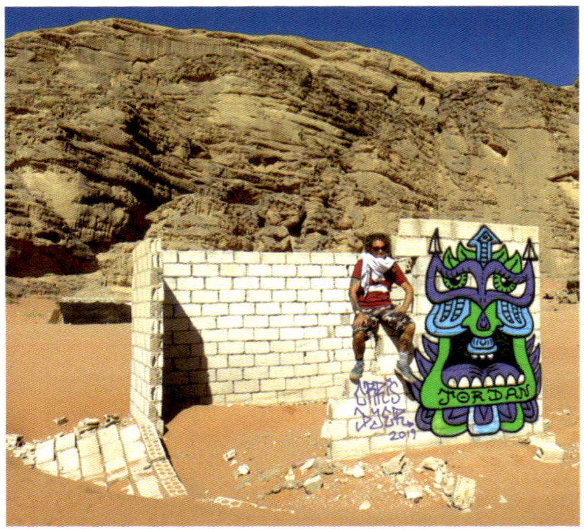

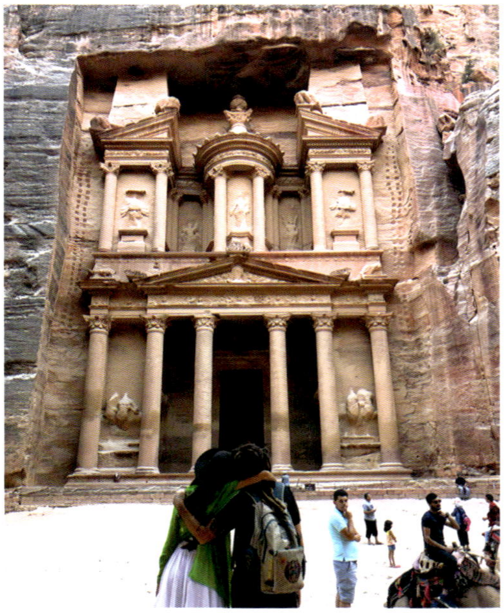

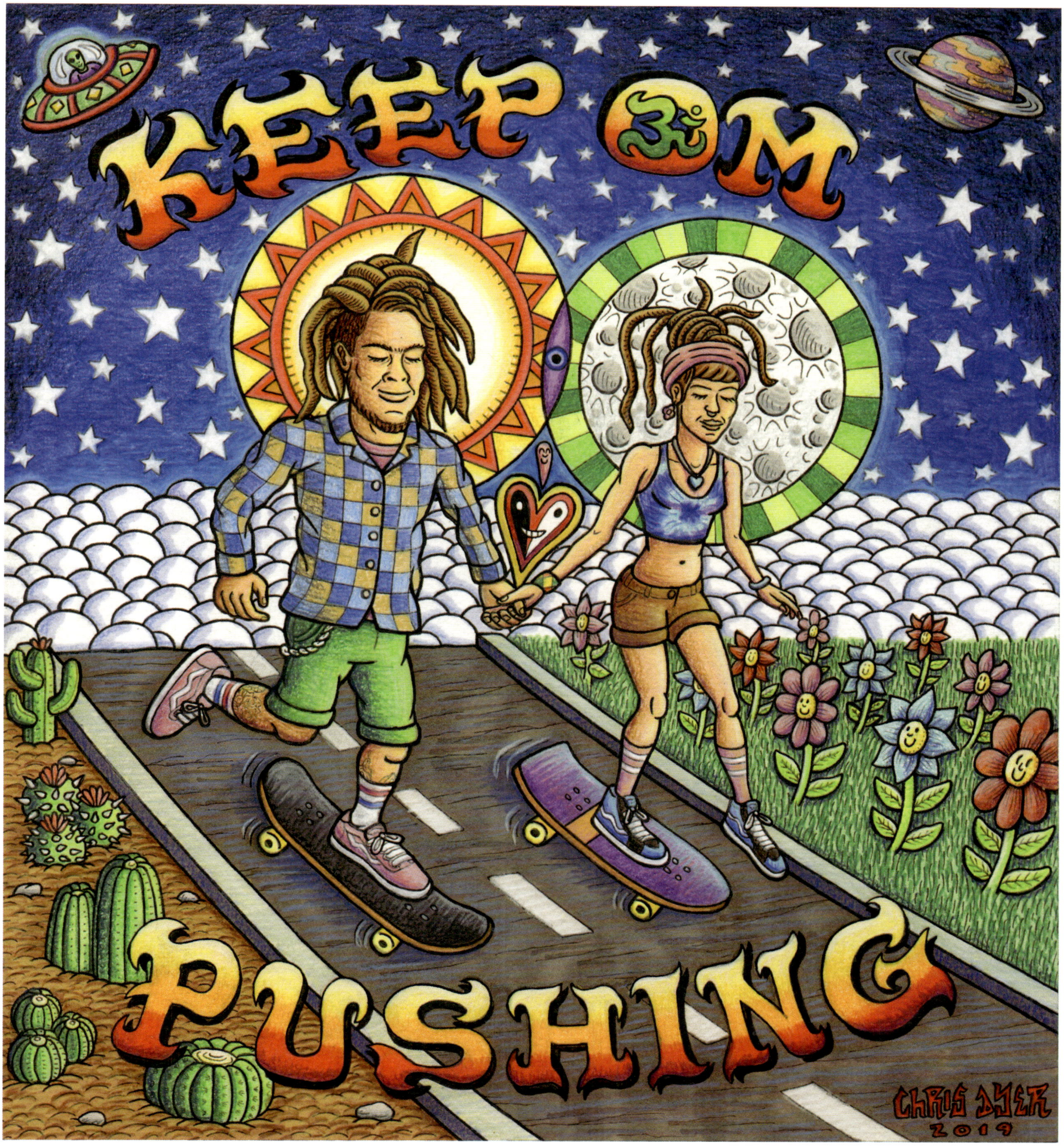

"Keep OM Pushing" Markers and color pencils, 2019-20

TARAPOTO

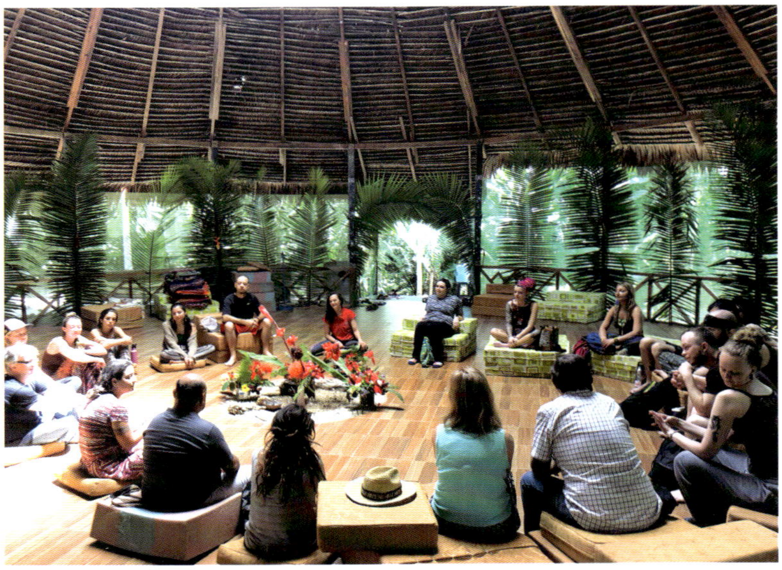

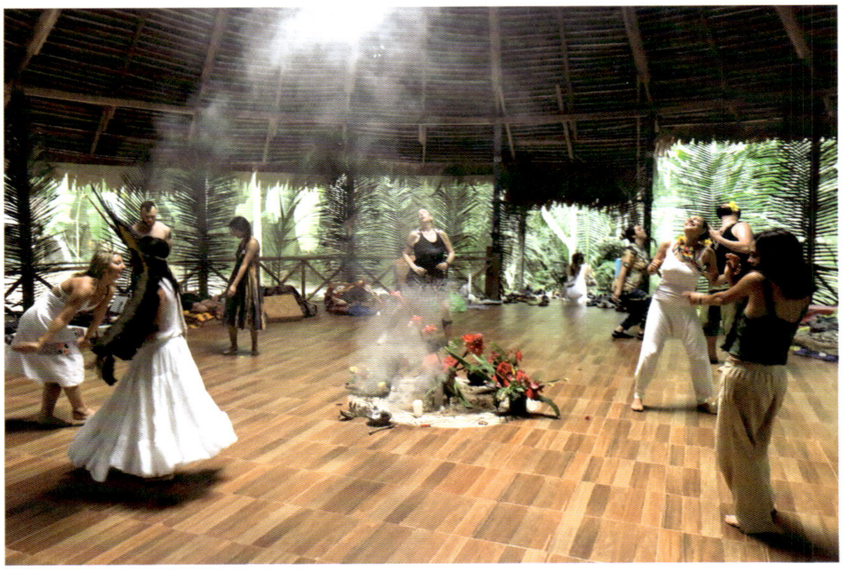

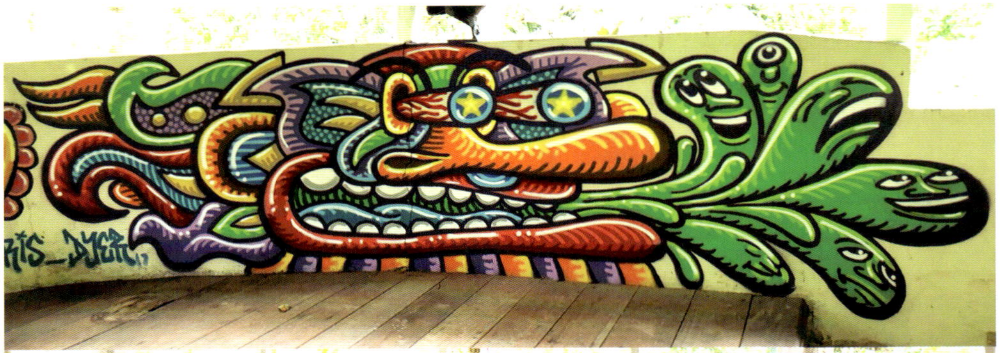

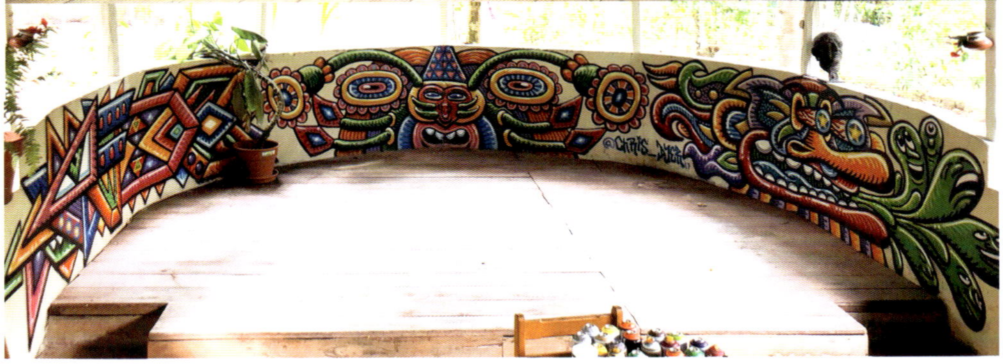

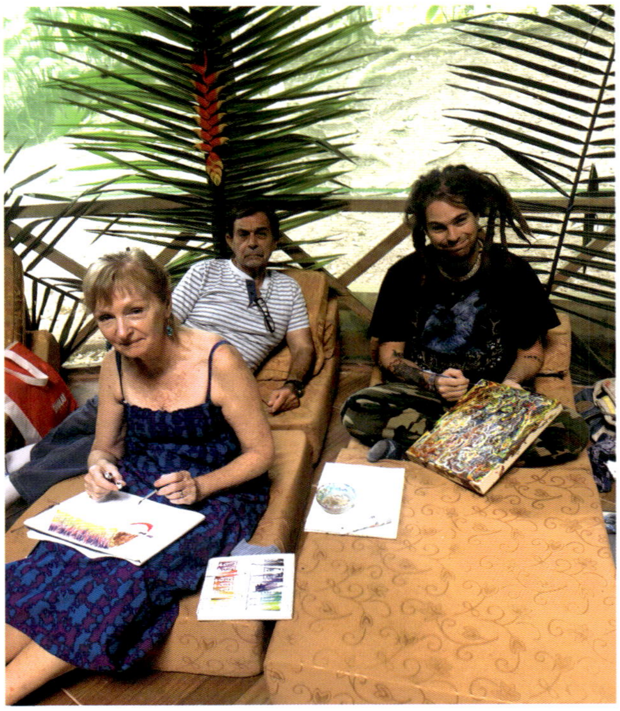

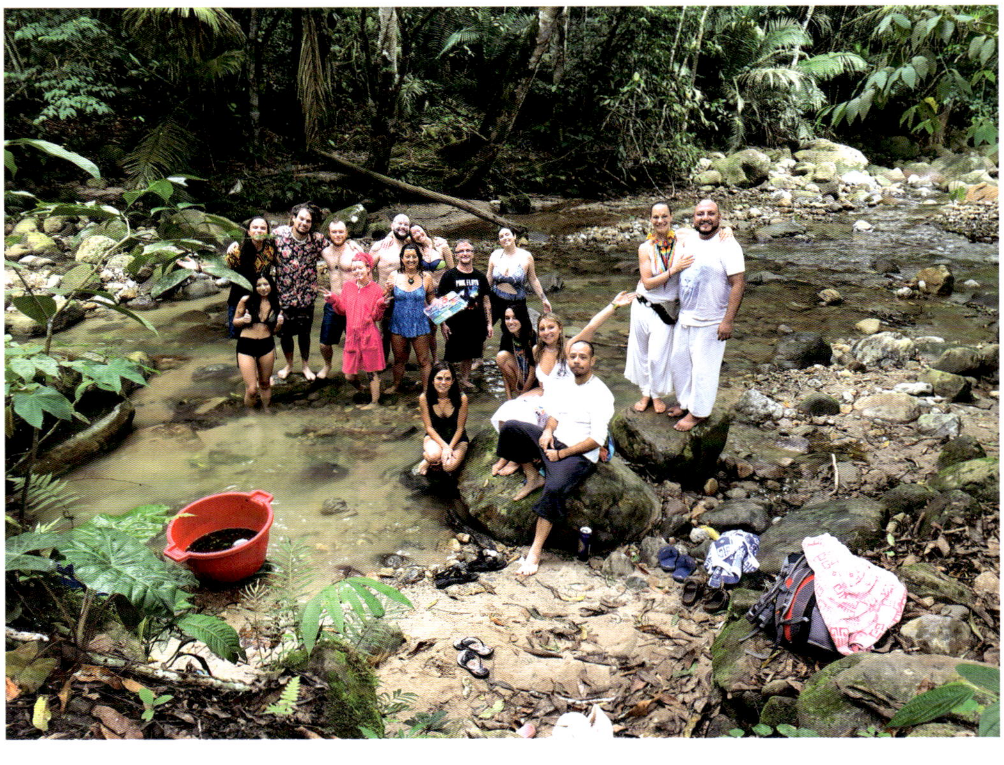

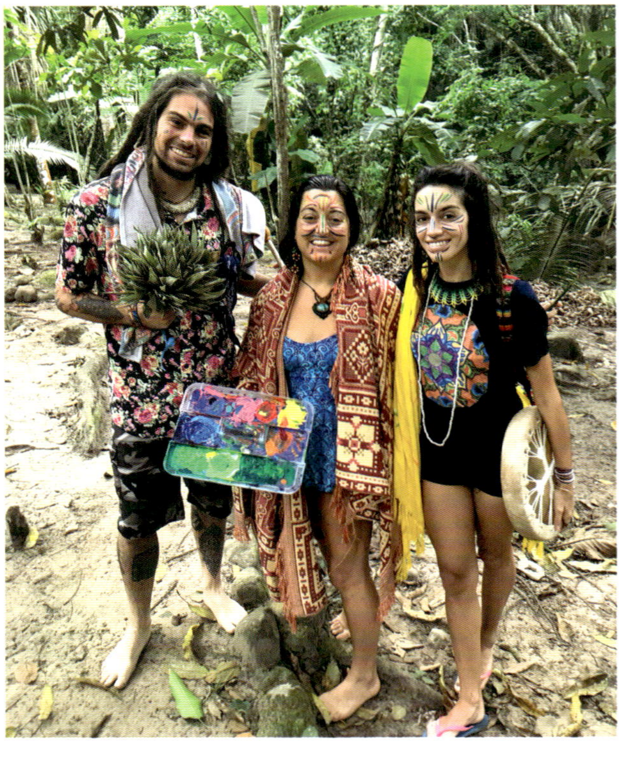

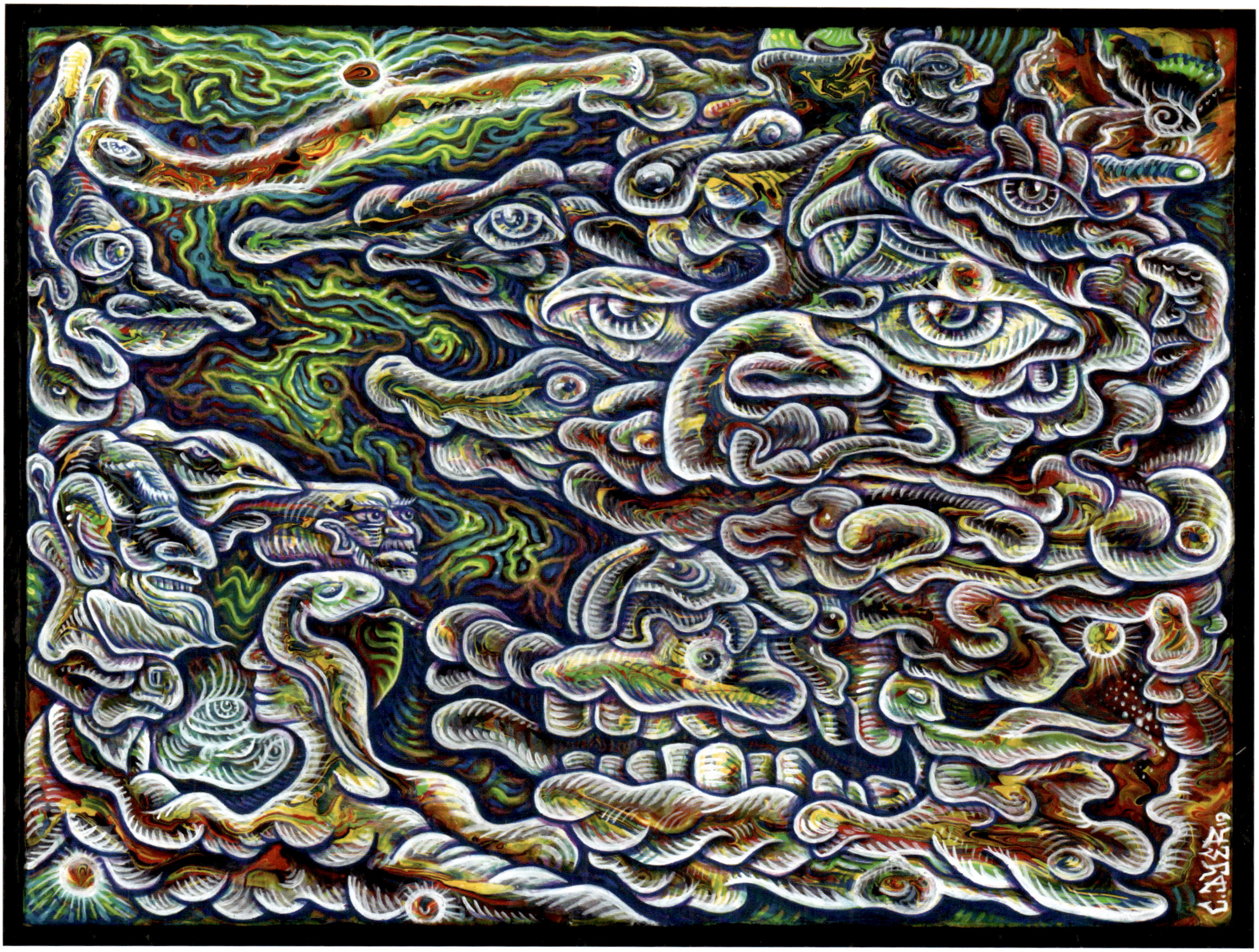

“Surrender to the Flow” Acrylics on wood, 2019

At the end of the year we went back to the Peruvian jungle so I could teach my forth **“Healing Visions”** Art and Medicine Retreat. We welcomed our biggest international group yet, and had some really potent ceremonies, especially with the addition of a couple of **“Yawanawa”** tribe shamans, who joined us from Brazil. The second ceremony was on a full moon and became an intense group activation. The medicine moved me higher and higher through the astral plane until I let go and dissolved into everythingness, probably the same unity light dimension of existence where Bufo launched me earlier that year. It was very expanding and as always, left me feeling full of Love! Another awesome thing about this retreat is that I finally convinced my seventy year old parents, **Teddy** and **Josie**, to join it! Herbert gave them smaller dosages, but my dad did purge quite a bit, as well as seeing panthers made out of gems. Then my mom said she saw lots of colorful stars, cobwebs and galactic flowers. They had a positive experience with the medicine and I was so happy to share this tribal side of me with them.

The painting I did during the retreat was a freestyle, fleshed out on a drip technique canvas I had prepared. I just flowed with the colorful shapes to find my characters. It reflects the flowing and surrender that the medicine teaches me about constantly.

QUILMANA

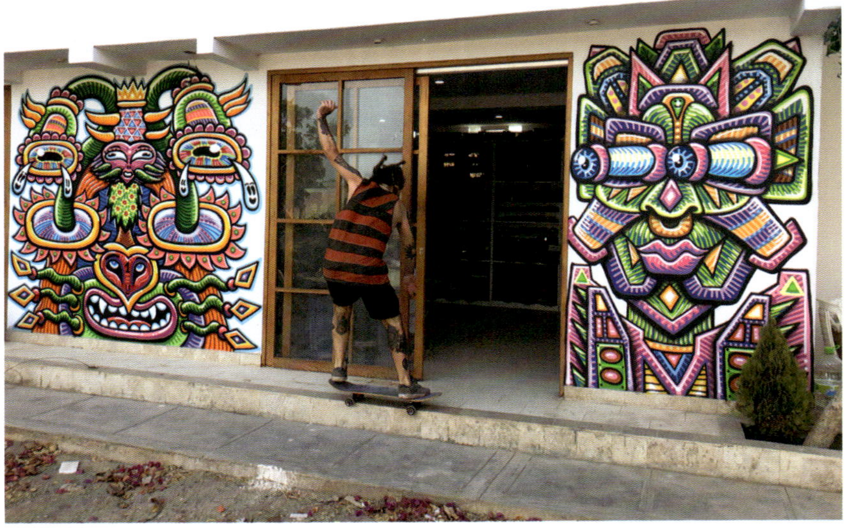
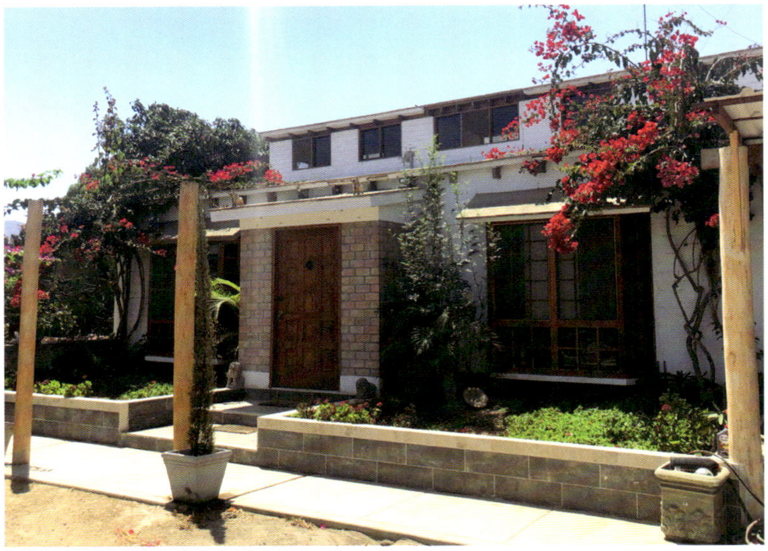

After the retreat, we went to stay with my parents in **Peru** for three months. In 2012 they bought an acre of land in a little valley village called **Quilmana**, two hours south of **Lima** and close to the famous surfing break, **Cerro Azul**. Surrounded by mountains, it's as rural as it gets. With a large Andean population, it is full of farms, dirt roads, donkey carts slowly going by, fresh air, sun every day, peace and quiet. For the past eight years my parents had slowly built their dream retirement house and were finally moving in. While they were at it, they also built a gallery for my dad's toy car collection, and a studio apartment for my yearly visits. This property also has an orchard with over three-hundred fruit trees, mostly avocados, but also lucumas, grapes, passion fruit, bananas, etc. There is still lots of work before this project is completed, so my dad is always busy building, while my mom takes care of us all. We call our land **"Muyawasi"**, which means "Orchard House" in Quechua language. My brother **"Peru 143"** and I have already been spray painting murals here and Arianne had the chance to add one too. My dream plan was to have a bunch of my artist friends visit throughout the years and add their own painting contributions to this magical place. It was great to escape Canadian winter, as it was summer here, and spend our days painting, eating delicious healthy food, and enjoying quality family time. I spent those three months painting this big canvas I brought. It was an interdimentional portrait of my friend and healer, **Herbert Quinteros,** who guided me through so many ceremonies and rebirths. **"Kausaipak"** is the word he says before he hands you an ayahuasca cup, which means "For Life".

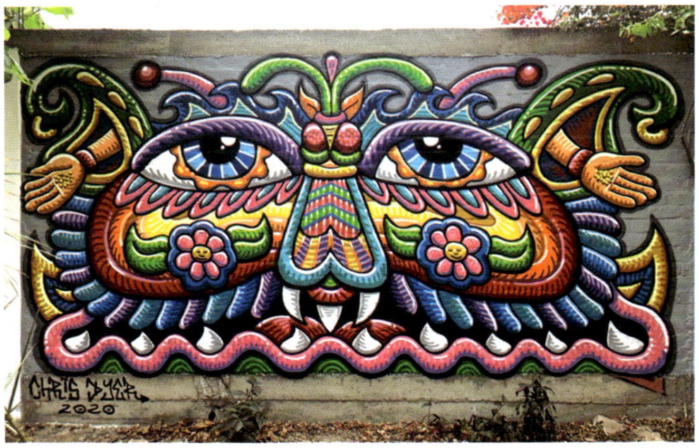
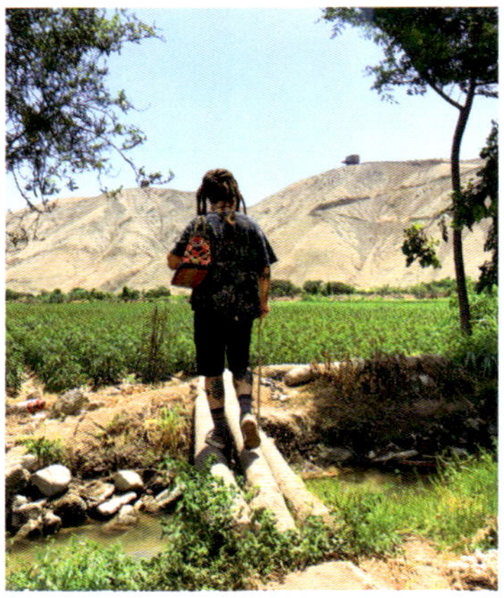
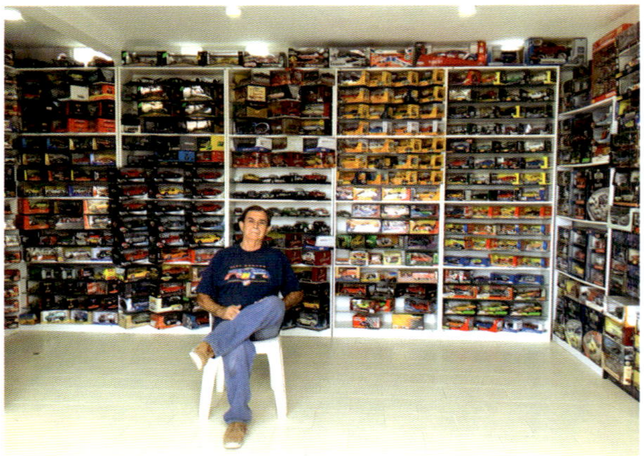
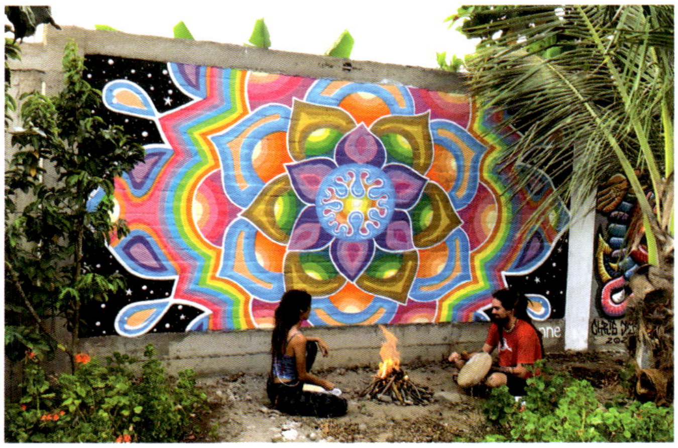
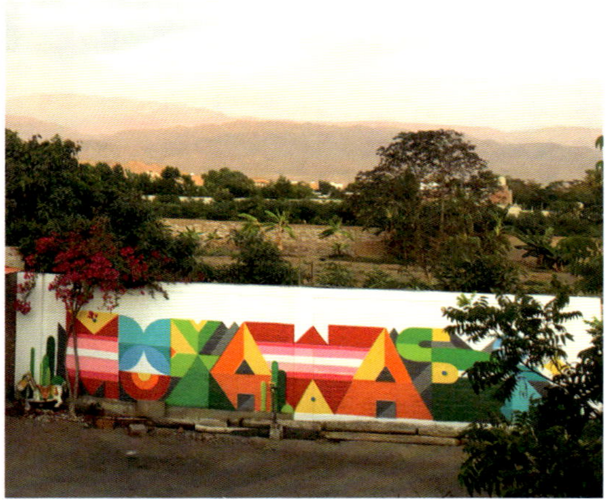
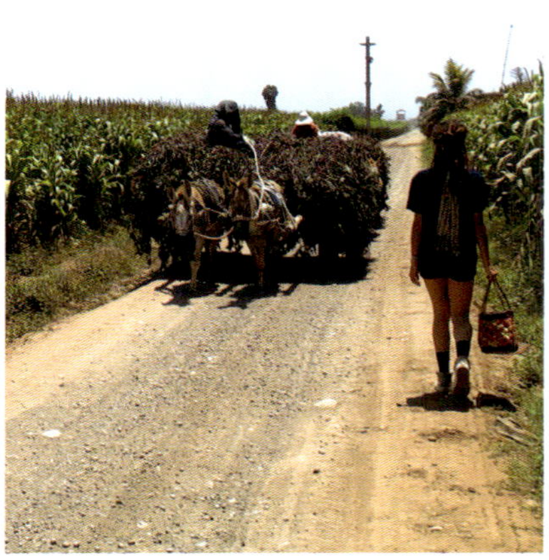

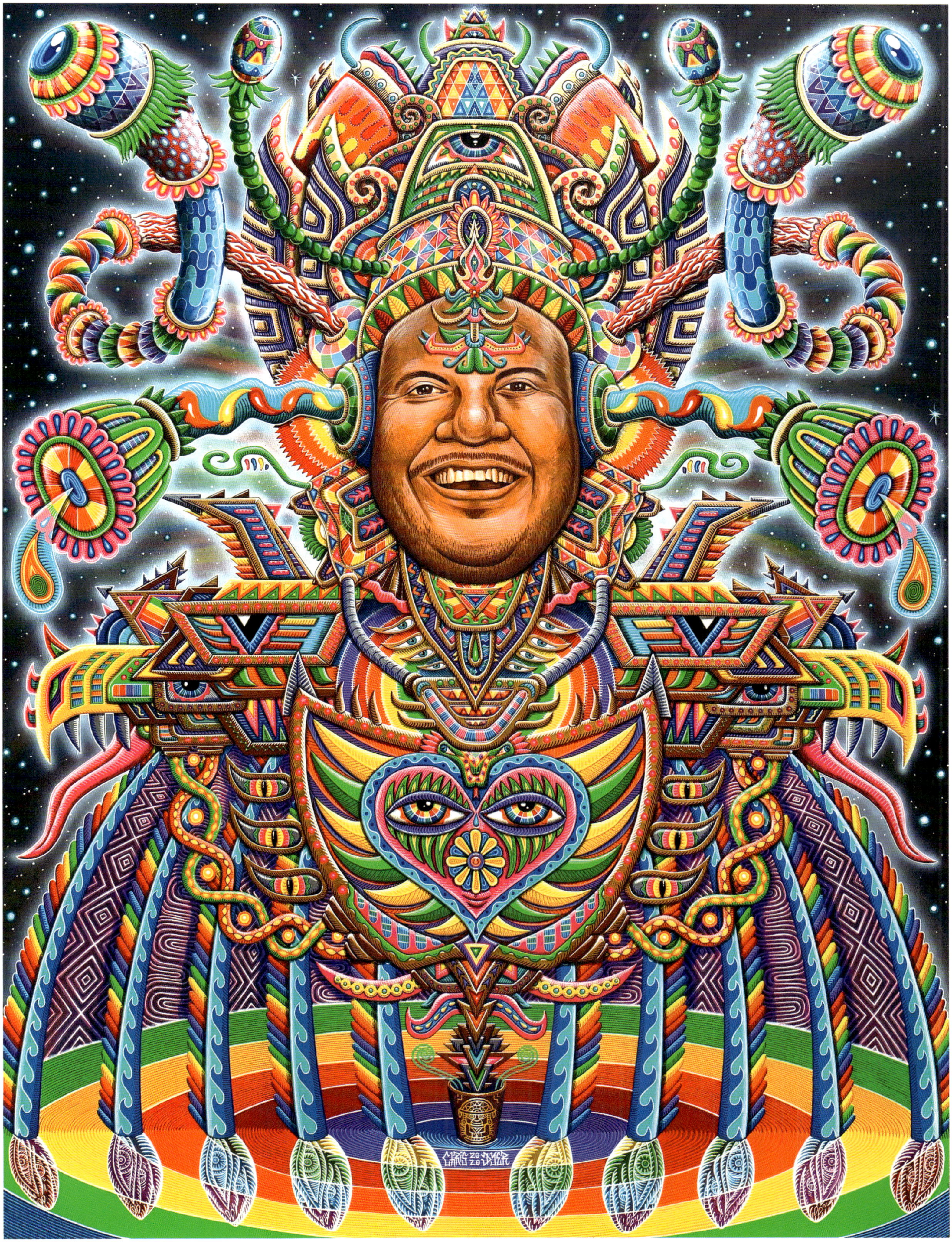

"Kausaipak" Acrylics on wood, 2020

CORONA QUARANTINE

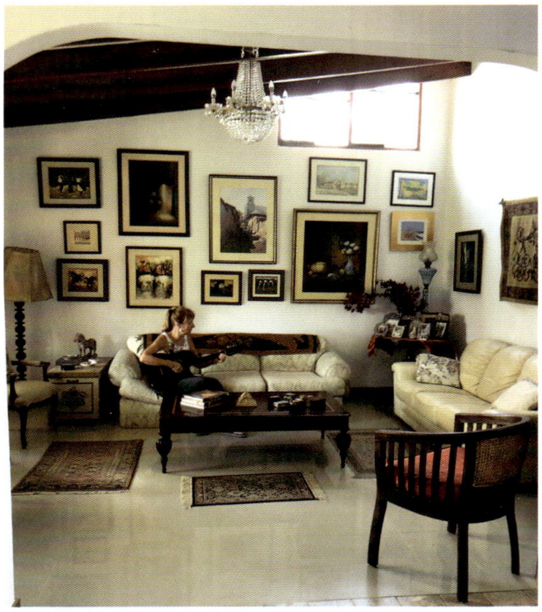
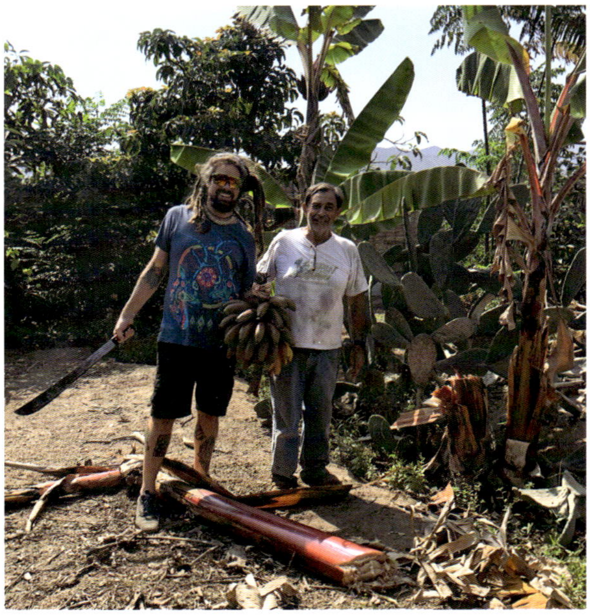
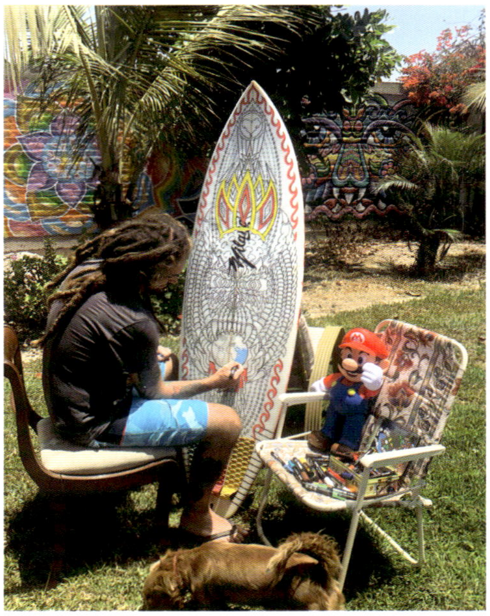

The 3rd of March of 2020 was my 41st Birthday. That night I was supposed to fly to Florida with Arianne to spend a couple of weeks at her mom's, before going back to our Montreal home. Unfortunately Spirit Airlines didn't allow us to fly with more than one luggage piece, so I decided to stay behind and let her go alone. I would stay an extra 2 weeks, do some final touches to my new painting and meet her home with all of our luggage. A day before taking that flight to reunite with her though, Peru declared their State of Emergency against the new **Covid-19** Virus spreading across the world. No flights went in or out of Peru for the next few months after that, so I ended spending four extra months with my parents! The Quarantine was very strict in Peru. Nobody could leave their homes for months, under punishment of jail. It was stressful not knowing when I could go back home and reunite with my beloved, so I grounded myself in making art and creating videos to help my followers stay optimistic through the strange times. My now long-distance relationship with Arianne didn't go well though. She seemed to use this physical separation to emotionally disconnect from me and move on to new life experiences and people. That, along some pretty low quality communications resulted in us breaking up... I was crushed and felt like a caged animal. So I ran a lot, almost every day inside our land, which helped me get back in shape, think lots and relieve stress. I had never spent so much time with my parents so I feel our adult relationship deepened too. The main art piece I painted was called **"Nobody Moves, Nobody gets Hurt"** after a "Yellowman" song. It was done with the few left over art materials I still had there and expressed my general frustration with how things went down. Eventually by June, the Government of Canada "Repatriated" me, flying me back home from a military base in Lima.

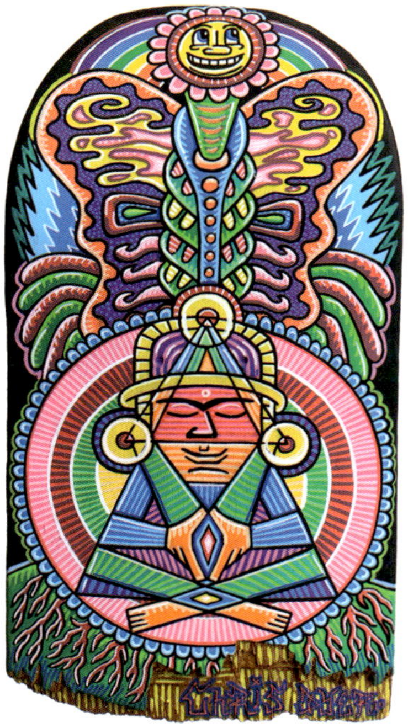

"Cocooning"
Paint Markers, 2020

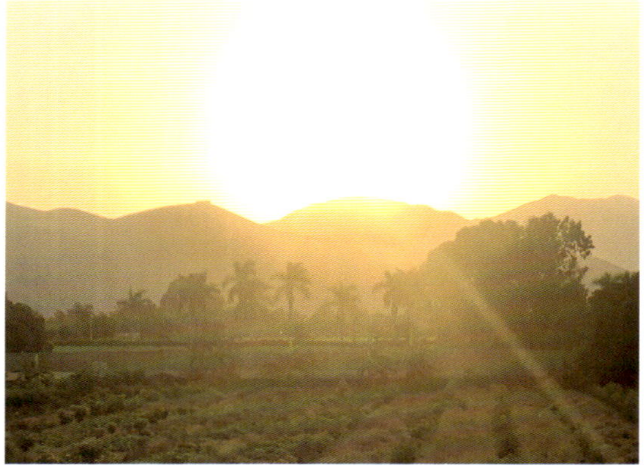
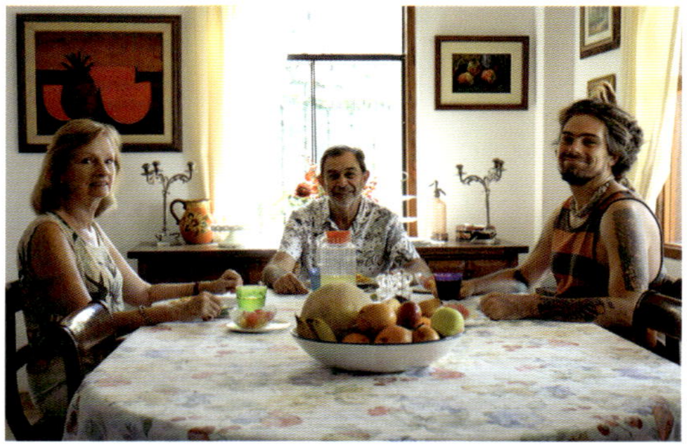
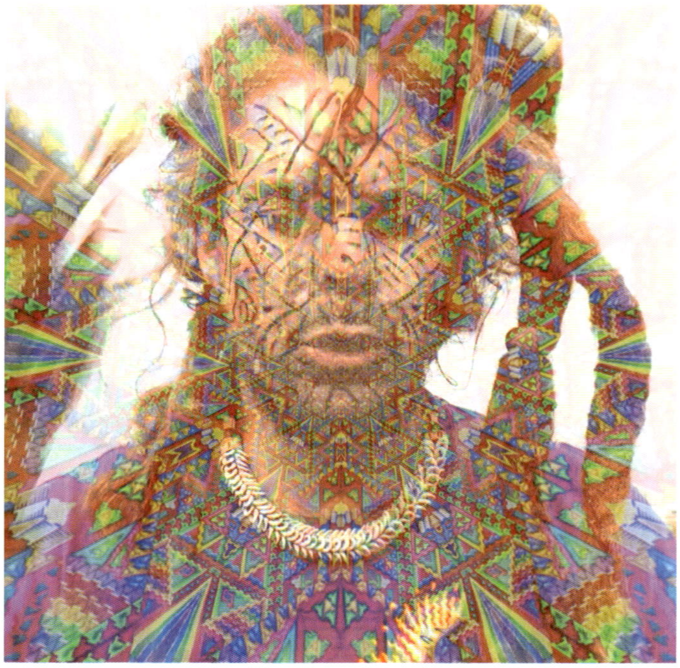

"Prayer for Humanity"
Video, collabo with **Burt Vera Cruz**, 2020

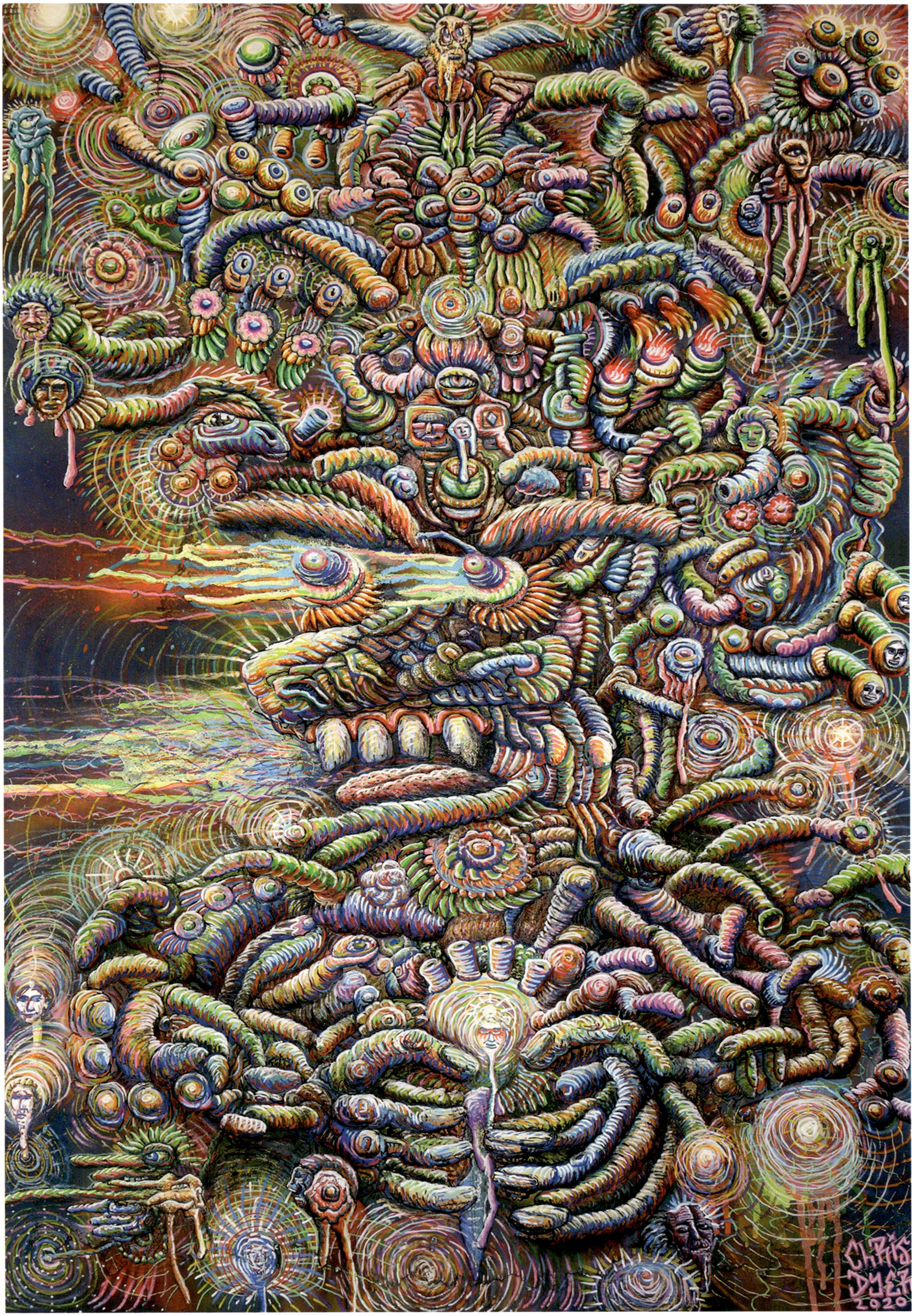

"Nobody Move, Nobody Get Hurt!" Spray paint and markers on wood, 2020

MONTREAL NEW NORMAL

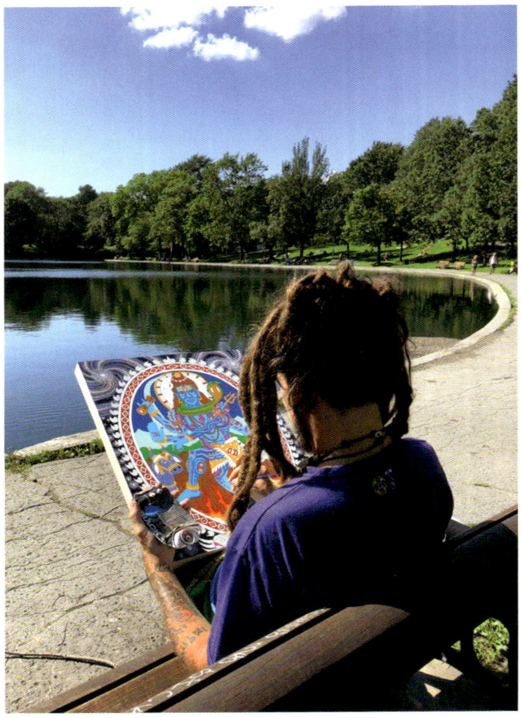

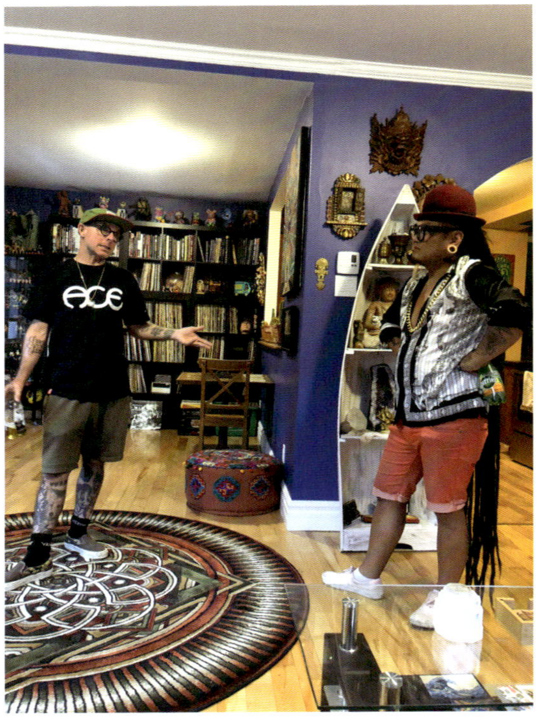

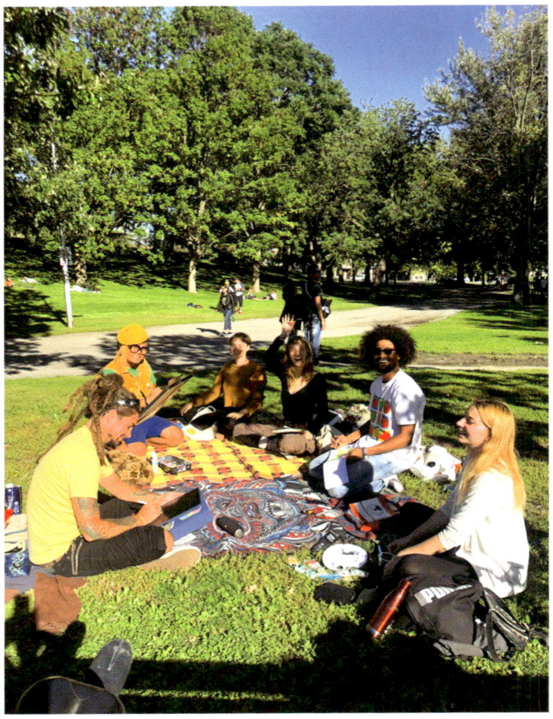

Being back home was weird, starting with the mandatory 2 week quarantine. My cool yet lonely apartment showed me how lucky I was to have missed winter there. Arianne was no longer my fiancée nor my girlfriend, yet her belongings and memories still filled my place. Covid laws didn't allow Americans into Canada for the rest of the year, so any hope for our relationship to rekindle slowly died. After a few painful months I finally accepted it was over and mailed back all her things to Florida. I was very sad and heartbroken about it all and spent a lot of time in my local (Lafontaine) park painting **"Nataraja Shiva"**. This was my own version of the classic Hindu depiction of God Shiva, who is dancing as he destroys the whole universe! I felt it was fitting, as it seemed like the world we all knew was getting erased. This icon also does remind us though that we are eternal beings and a new improved Creation period follows in the cycle.

Most people where socially distancing that summer, but I needed my friends close to me more than ever! I also started to organize weekly Art Jams in the park with anyone who'd be down to hang and create with me. It was through these fun gatherings that I met **Eloise**, a super nice French lady I dated for a couple of months. She was an artist, electronic music producer and a skater so we had so much fun together! I also started my **"Creative Friends"** Podcast project, which she helped me film. I am very grateful for all the healing my heart received those days, but as the weather cooled down and Lockdowns were coming back, we said goodbye. Spending another winter in Peru doing shamanic work and having family time in the sun made more sense to me!

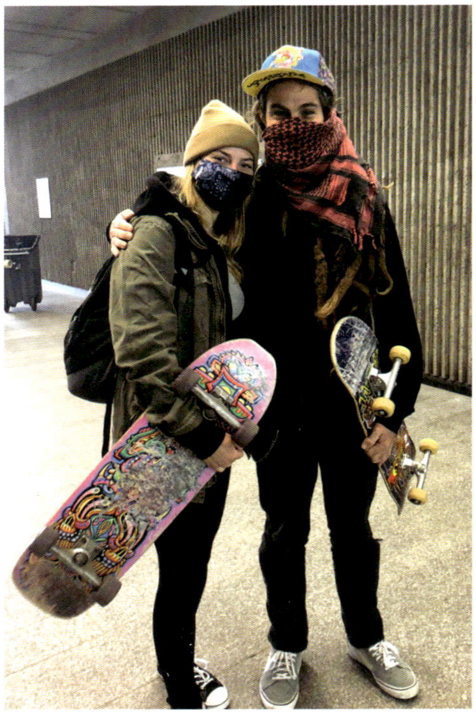

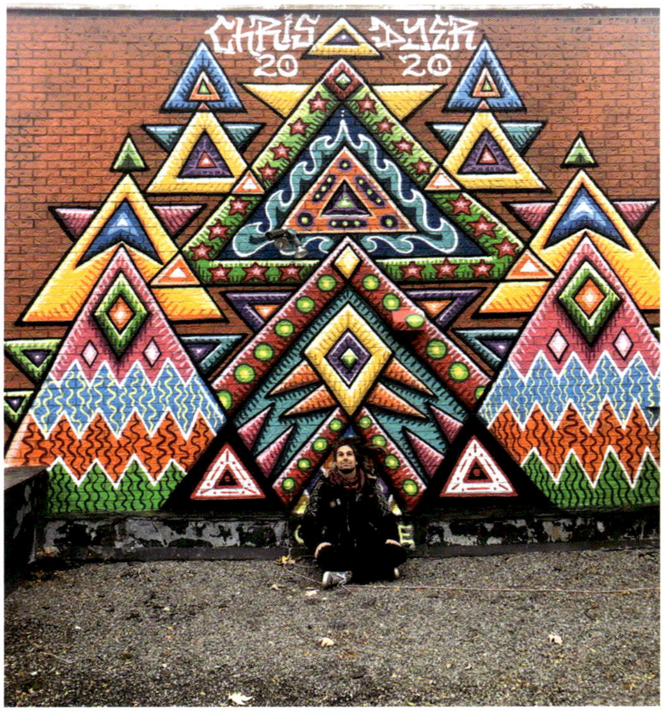

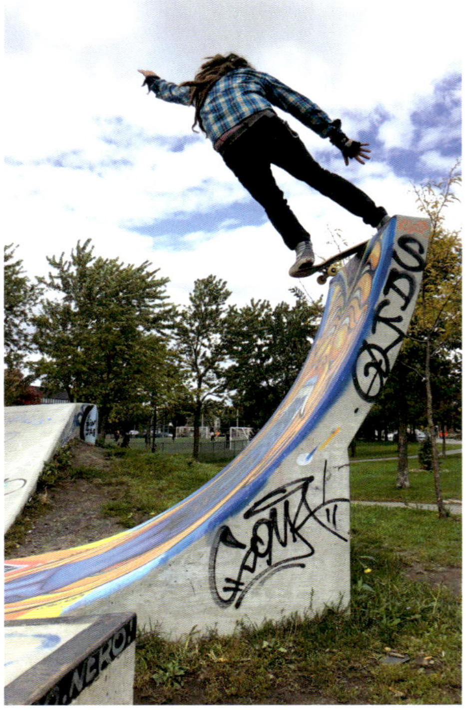

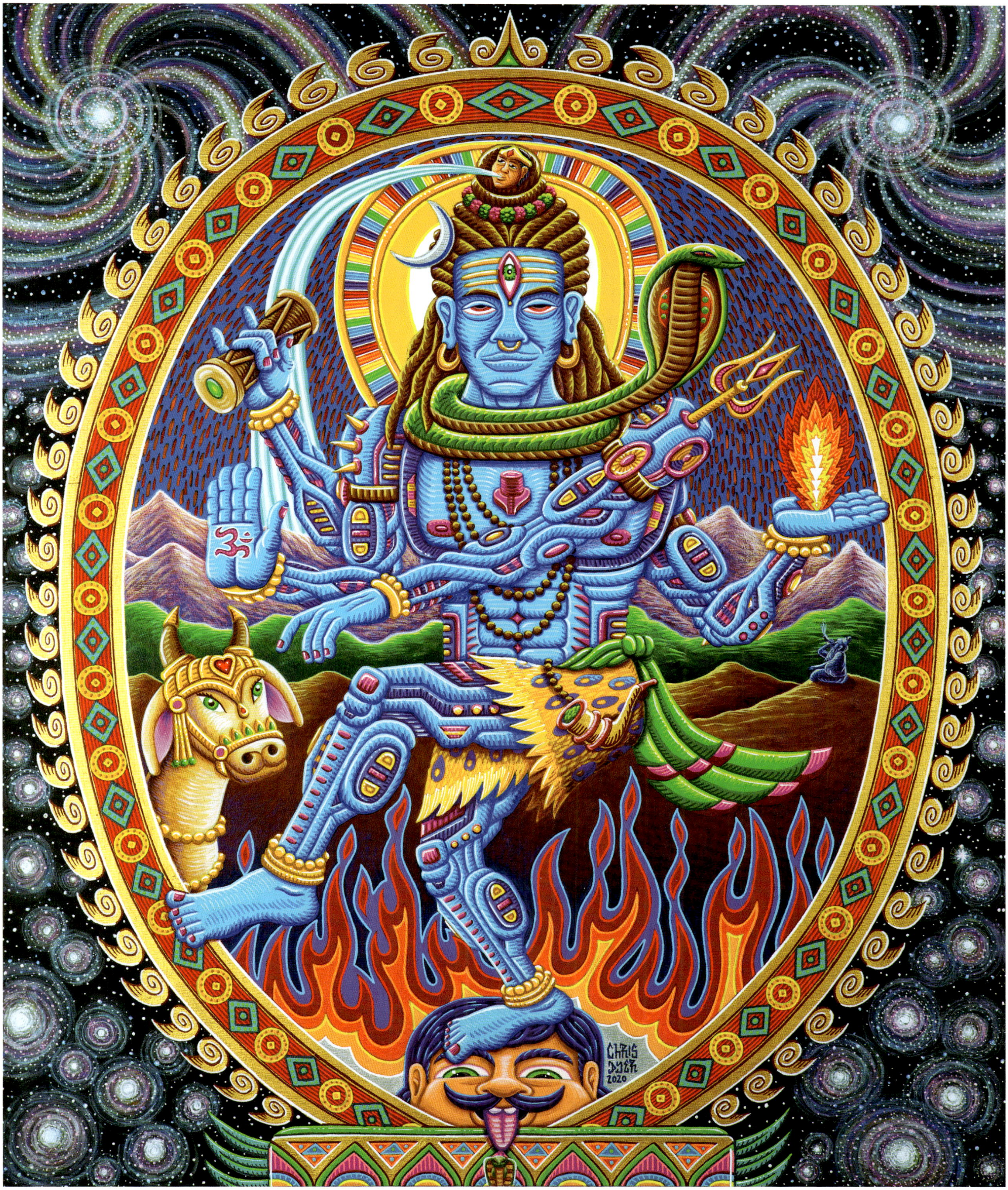

"Nataraja Shiva" Acrylics on canvas, 2020

SECOND QUILMANA QUARANTINE

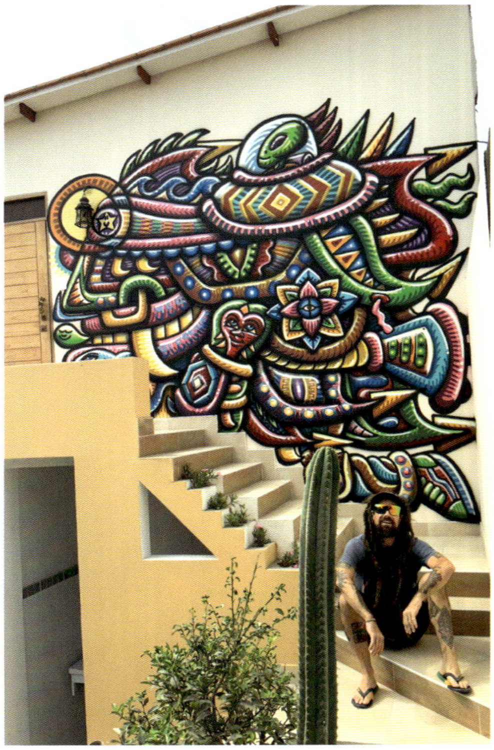

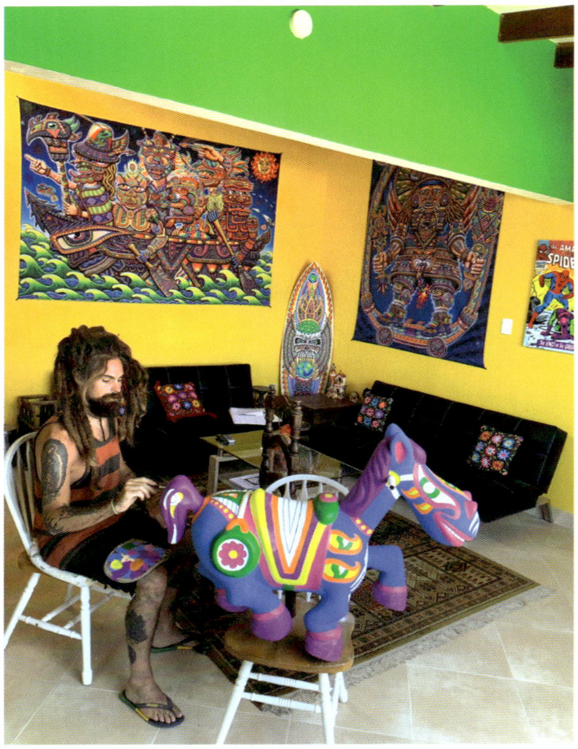

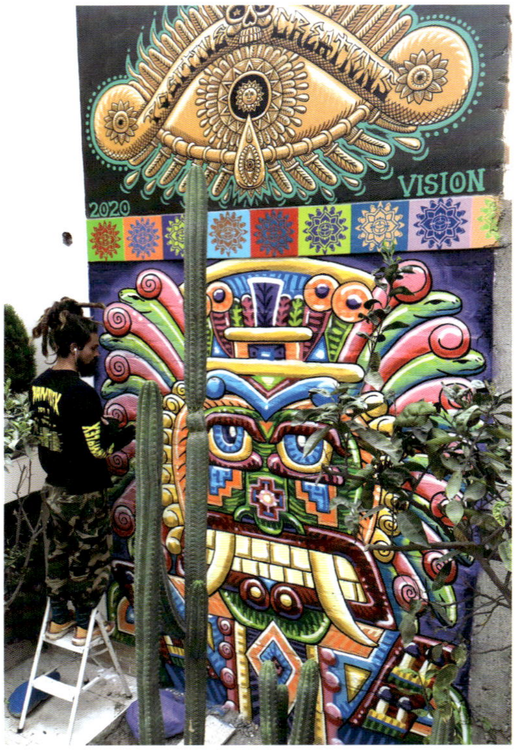

So I returned to my Peruvian home for five months, this time with enough art materials to stay productive through the second round of Lockdowns. My apartment was finally finished so I decorated it in my usual colorful style and started to use it as a wintertime creation studio. I also continued to add murals all around it for further activation. This sunny countryside Quarantine ended being quite enjoyable, especially since my dad bought a decent swimming pool and boxes of booze! I was happy and grateful. Also, again all odds, I did manage to hold my 2020 **"Healing Visions"** Art and Medicine Retreat in the jungle! With so many Covid hurdles in place, only two American students managed to make it though. Regardless, it still was a great time of painting in nature and healing with shamanic medicines. I even stayed an extra week to do my third "Master Plant Dieta". This diet was called **"Bachuja"**, which is a skinny yet strong tree whose consciousness would guide me to stand firm through life's challenges. It was quite the disgusting beverage I had to drink 3 times a day, making me vomit every time, but the lessons in Ayahuasca ceremony were magnified as potent as ever!

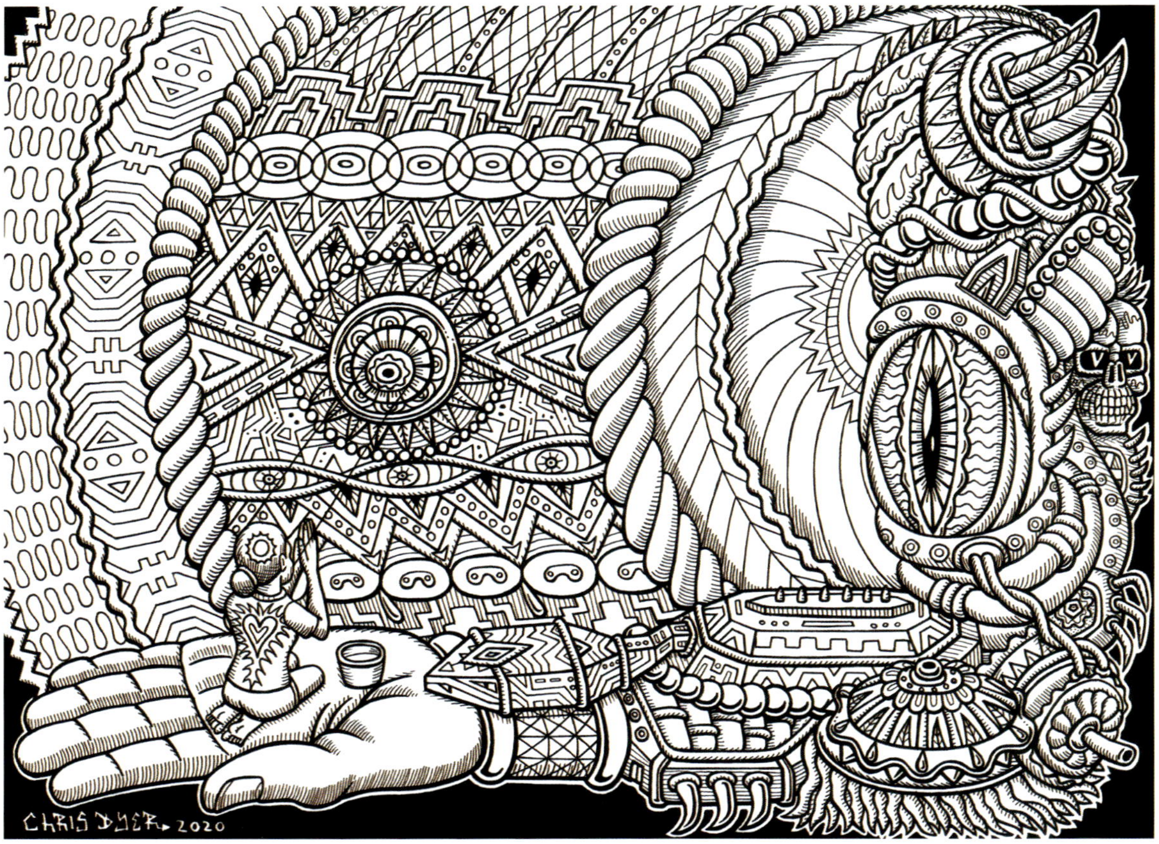

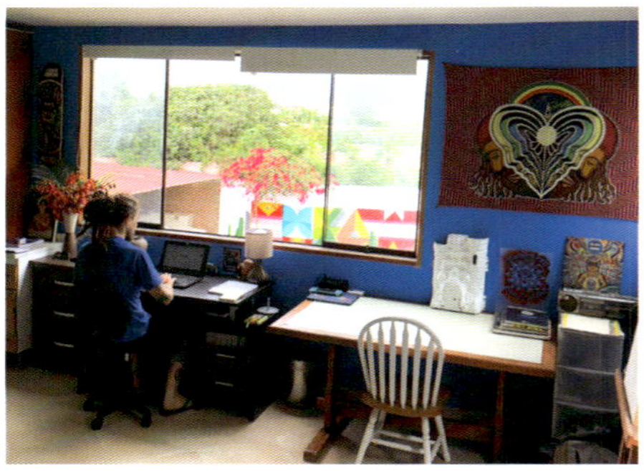

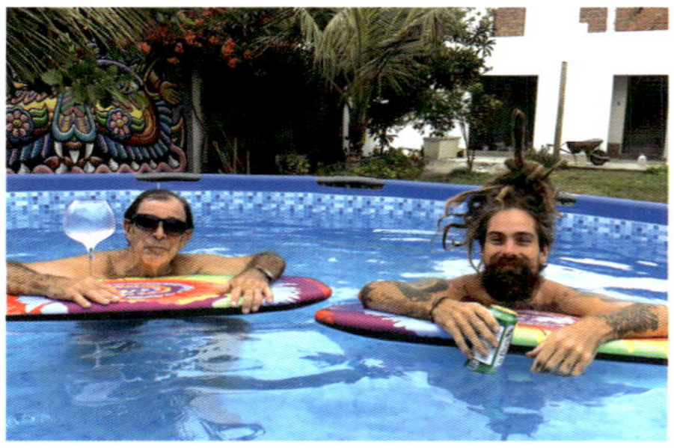

"Praying for Liberation"
Ink on paper, 2020

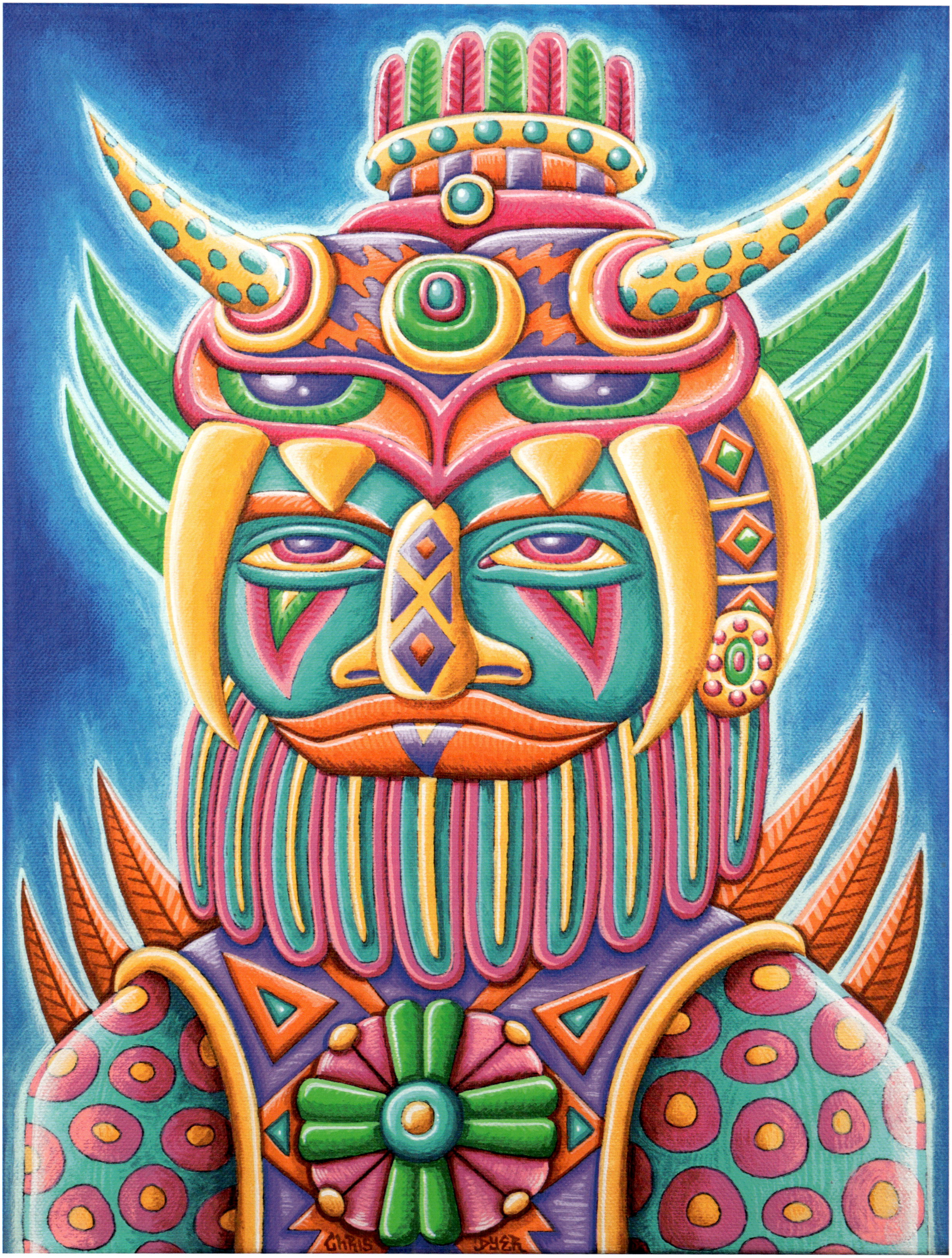

“Pachamago” Acrylics on canvas, 2021

SHAMANIC GRADUATION

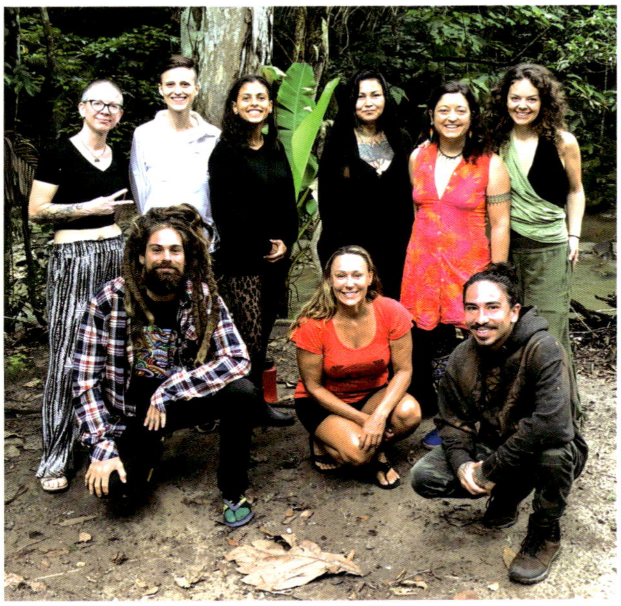

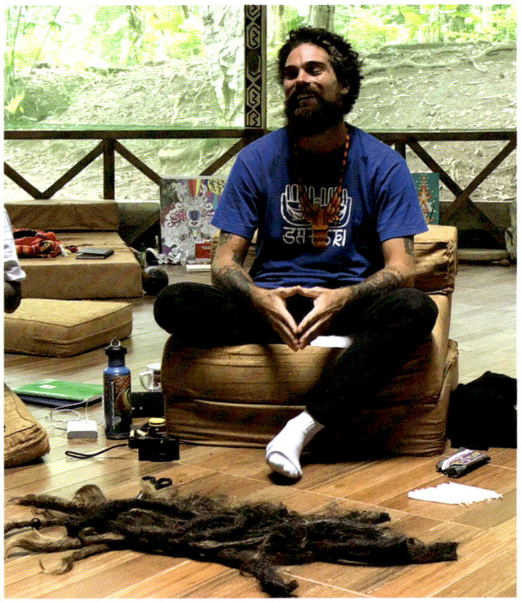

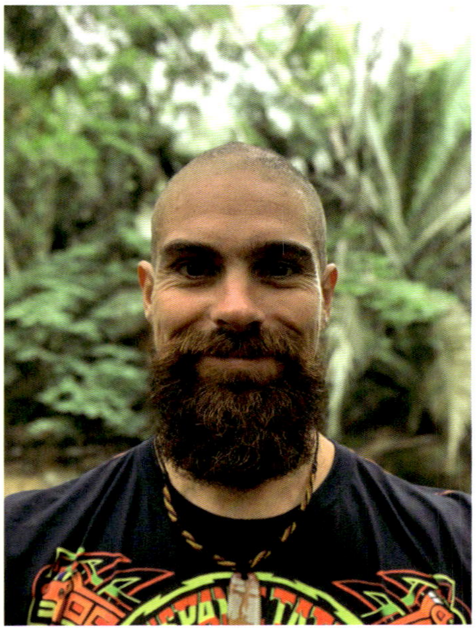

In March of 2021, right as I turned 42 years old, I returned to Katari Center in Tarapoto's jungle to hold my 6th **"Healing Visions"** Art and Healing Retreat. It was also my final one, but I didn't know that at the time. This Retreat actually had to last two weeks, instead of one, in order to count as the Quarantine foreigners arriving to Peru had to do. Despite the restrictions of the Covid-prudent world, an amazing group of nine artists made it down! This extended duration made it that we were able to fit in four Ayahuasca Ceremonies, each one more magical than the last! To intensify things, one of my students, **Judea Star**, was a super powerful psychic that was using her ceremony portals to help me repair an old sexual wound from my youth (when I unwillingly lost my virginity to a Lima prostitute at age 15). One of those Aya ceremonies was my **40th** and it took me very very deep! There was too much that I went through to recount here, but it revolved around a battle with an old squirmy parasite. At a moment of pure struggle, my new bestie Judea came over to play her singing bowl, turn me into pure light-energy, lure the "worm" out of my heart and pick it out (with her ethereal fingers). At that precise moment I finally vomited it out! Meanwhile, in my inner process, I was on a stairway to the Gates of Heaven, but the fear of judgement and of being fully myself was preventing me from entering my real enlightened state. So I begged God, one way or another, to Liberate me from giving a fuck about what anyone would ever think or say about me! I prayed to have so much Self-Love that nobody's judgement could ever touch me! But I had to jump in the water of Freedom, this self-chosen confidence with a clear action of commitment. The next morning during "Sharing Circle", I grabbed a pair of scissors and chopped off my 21 year-old Dreadlocks. I knew that I would look older, maybe less "cool" or pretty. But I wanted to love myself past my Identity, past what I look like, so I made a clear break with that strong superficial attachment! This was just the first step of my newest rebirth, as a week later my whole public identity would also be chopped off. But I didn't know that yet... I painted **"Chris-talization Codes"** during this retreat, as a reflection of the spiritual progress and growth I was building up all these hard years. Though I felt like a toddler in this newest stage of my path, so vulnerable and naked with my new bald head, I was also proud of this "graduation". I now felt a new kind of personal power, which probably would attract a new level of challenges to overcome it with. All worth it to go back home to Oneness!

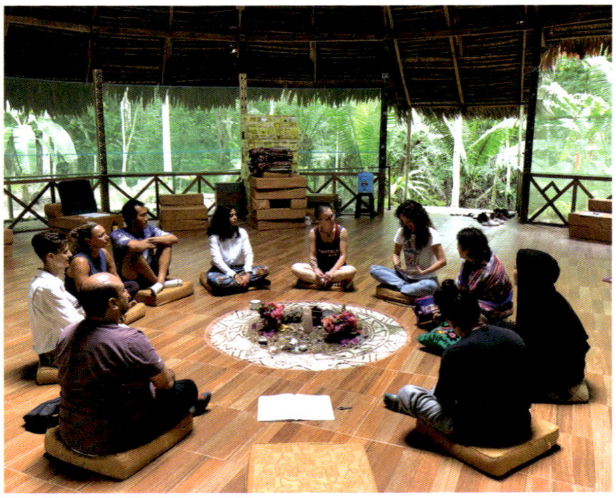

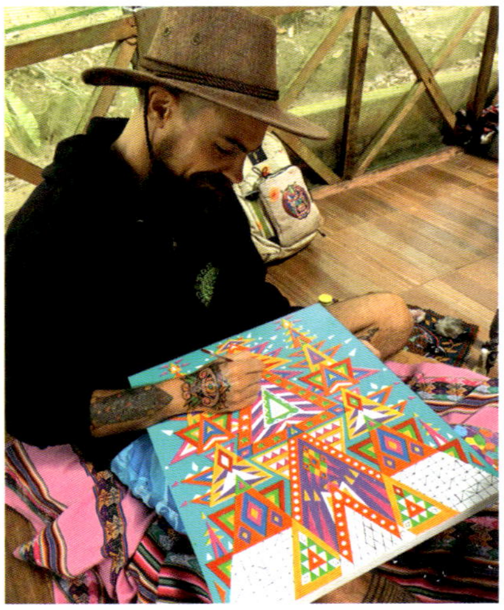

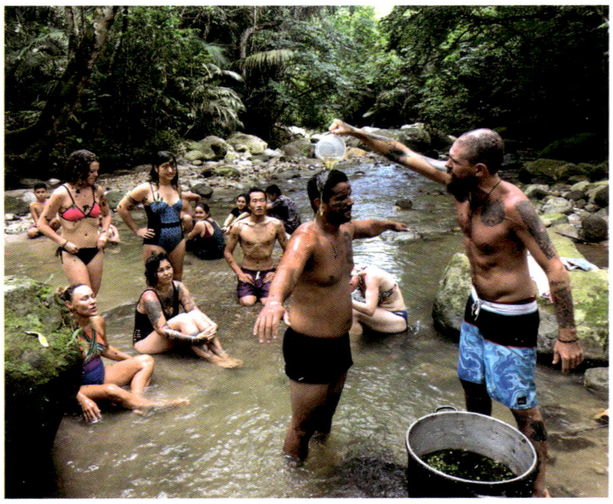

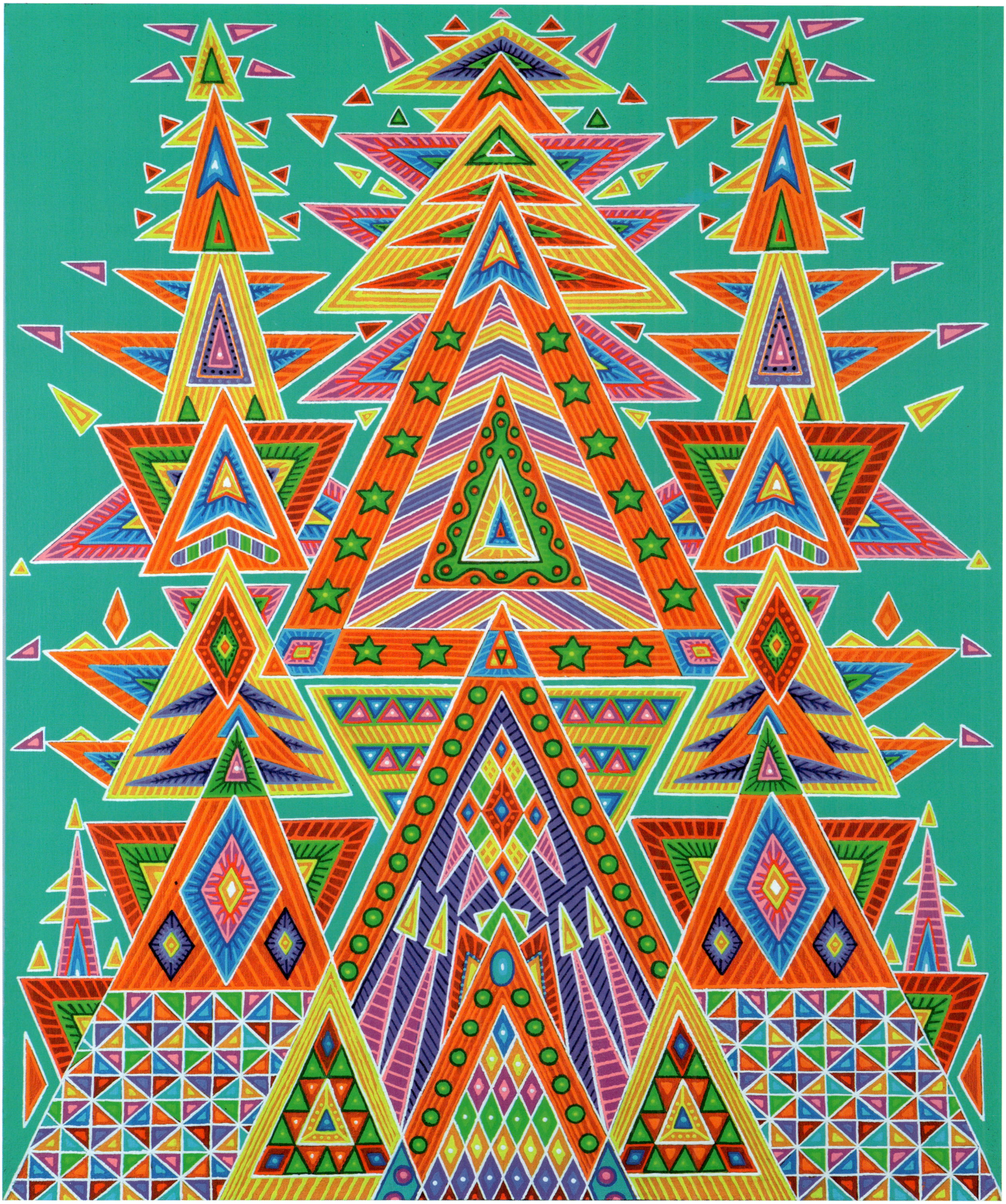

“Chris-taliation Codes” Acrylics on wood, 2021

ANDEAN INITIATION

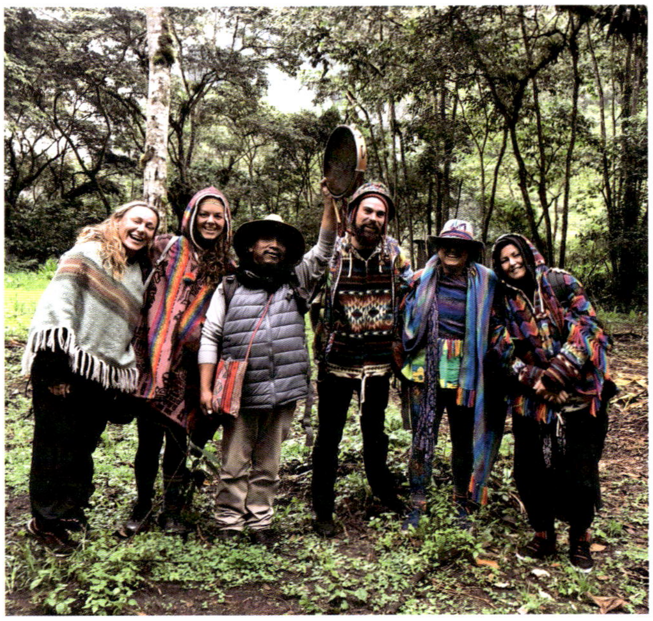
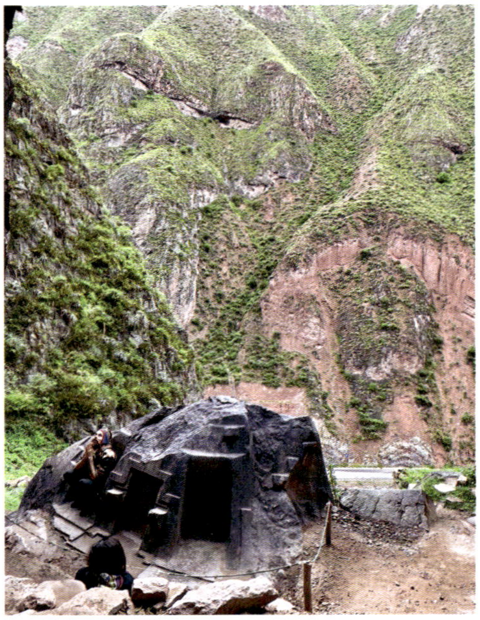
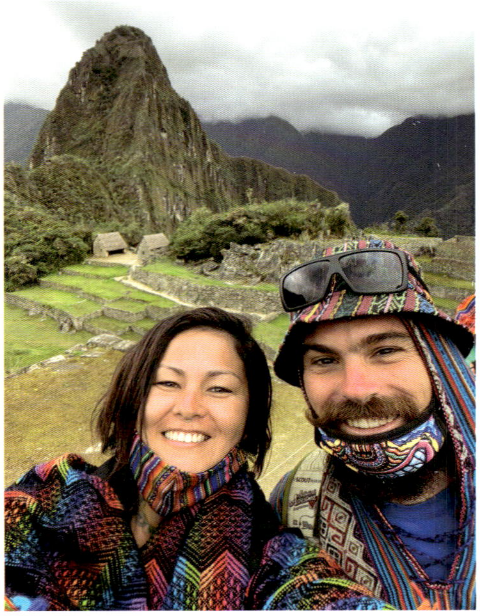

During the retreat, four of my female art students invited me to go to **Cuzco** with them for the following week. I had already been there many times before, but I felt it would be helpful if I served as their local escort and translator. Most importantly, on my final Ayahuasca ceremony, I saw that I somehow had to go to help Judea receive a psychic activation in Machu Picchu. On this trip to Cuzco we intended to continue our plant medicine work by teaming up with a local mystic guide called **Kucho**, who would serve us the sacred medicine of **Huachuma** (San Pedro). This whole trip was like a surreal movie, living the strangest days of my life!

One afternoon, as we where all departing on a ruin hike, I received some texts from a former student friend called **Sina**, from my 2019 jungle workshop. She informed me that in summer of 2020, which was seven months after my retreat, **Herbert** had manipulated her to masturbate over an online video-call. The news was shocking and painful on so many levels, especially since I had just departed from such a potent retreat at Katari. The idea that my healer, mentor and good friend of seven years was a predator and had hurt one of my students was more heartbreaking than I can explain.

Sina shared with me that Ayahuasca had requested her to tell the whole world that Herbert had sexually assaulted her. I honestly was too sensitive from the weeks of medicine to be ready for this. I was not in the place to give this situation its deserved attention, nor was I equipped with the necessary tools for navigating it in the best way. I requested she keep it private until my return home from Cuzco in a week, knowing that then I would be better able to give the situation my undivided attention. I needed this brief time to process the news as best as I could, while finishing my plant medicine work. I was also conflicted and worried for all the innocent people who would be hurt by this news going public. Not only would Herbert's wife, daughter and family be affected, but also Katari's workers whose livelihoods relied upon its success. I told her I didn't wan't them to suffer for what Herbert had done. She didn't like my responses and stopped communicating with me. Though I was very hurt and troubled, I continued to hold space for my friends on that journey through ancient ruins and cactus medicine. During an activation, I asked God what I should do. It responded that Love, Compassion and Forgiveness are the only ways this world will ever heal. I was hoping Sina would have some understanding on my personal process with the news, but Judea could already foresee a big storm about to hit my life... She said that no matter what or how I would respond, people were going to judge me and my life would be in shambles for some years. However, in the end this experience would teach me to be stronger and no longer care so much what people thought of me.

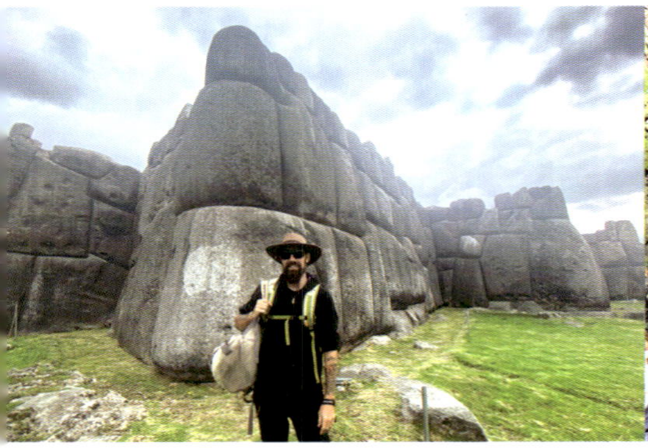
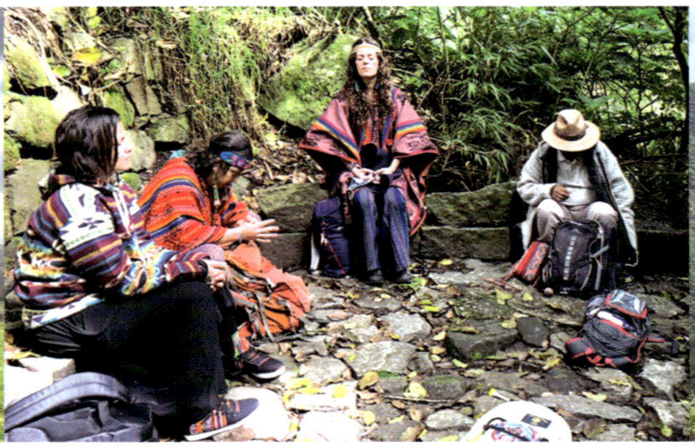
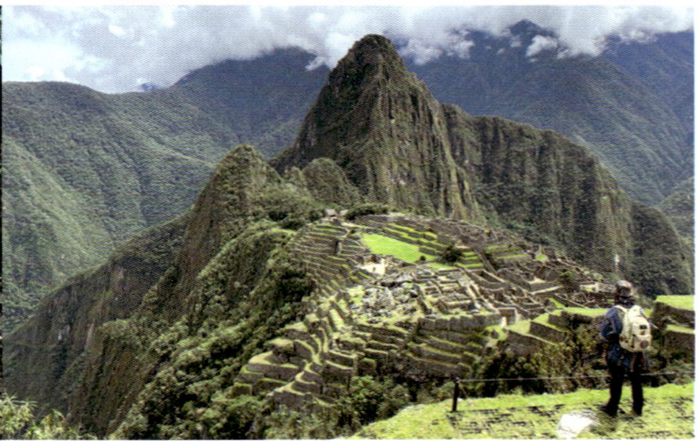

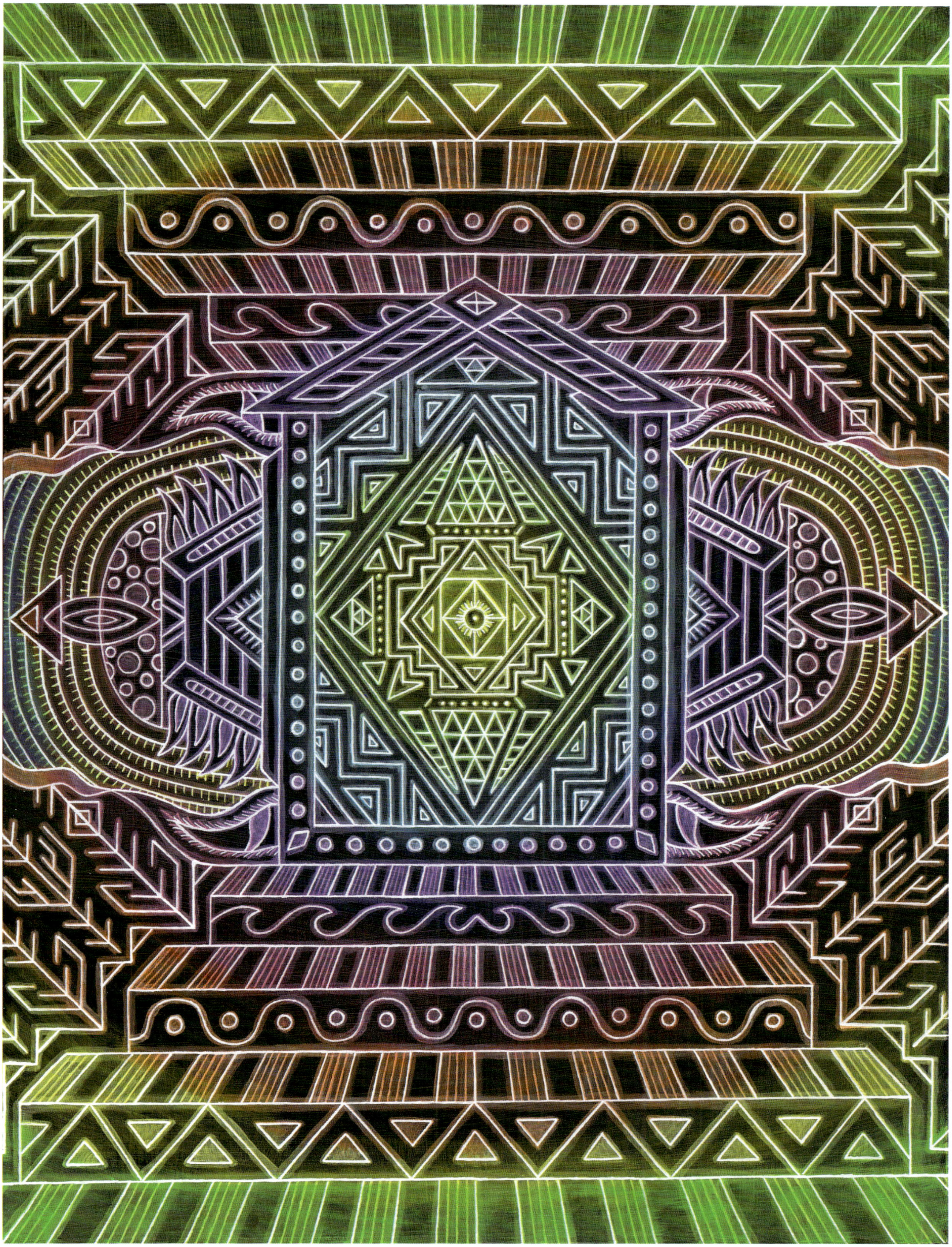

"Knocking on Heaven's Door" Acrylics on wood, 2023

DEATH OF ILLUSIONS

The day we visited **Machu Picchu** was so magical, especially since it was quite empty due to the Covid lack of tourism. Walking this sacred site was so potent under the influence of the cactus medicine, which helped us feel the energy beyond its physical structure. In the end **Judea** succeeded at finding an ancient stone library, where she received a big psychic activation from a tall grey alien guard! We had succeeded at our mission and I was so happy for her! But later that night, back at the hotel, Sina dropped her social media video about what happened with Herbert. In it she also accused me of silencing her, using fragments of my initial texts and audios as proof. The next day, as we where wrapping up our Cuzco journey, Sina's video was already going viral and the story quickly got twisted out of shape. Many misunderstood the story and believed that Sina was raped while attending my retreat and that I was shutting her down to save face. Others accused me of knowing about Herbert's perversions all along and even of bringing him victims through my workshop. Brutal misinformation. A giant wave of online hate mail started to hit me and all who worked with me.

My brand manager called me up by midnight to yell my head off. The situation affected the brand he had built up for us and he demanded I do an apology video at once! So I sat there in my hotel room, broken-hearted, confused, exhausted and filmed a response video. I could have said all of the politically correct things cancel culture wanted and in so doing, dodge some of the punishment coming at me, but it wouldn't have been sincere. Instead, I chose to do as I have always done and share honestly about the process from my heart. Though I said I would no longer work with Herbert or teach at Katari anymore, I also wished healing for both him and Sina, as both are souls of God. My words of compassion for my former mentor where interpreted as though I were defending or apologizing for him and thus supporting his actions. It was a disturbing wake up call as other women shared in the comments how he had also been inappropriate with them. This further made me realize that my mentor had lied and betrayed me all this time, crushing my heart even more...

From one day to the next my public image seemed to have been destroyed. Being that it was the end of the second Covid lockdowns, people where extra pent up and angry. Thousands of people publicly insulted me on all social medias over the next week, which was a huge psychic attack on my system. The judgement that hurt the worst came from friends and art colleagues, some who actually knew me pretty well. But the real ones, like my ex-wife Valerie also showed up online to fiercely defend me. Many others sent me private messages of support or personal perspectives to guide me on my path. It took me over a month to read all of my DMs and from them I learned a lot about how women feel in this world of aggressive men. No woman should feel unsafe.

As I returned to my family-home in Quilmana, I cried a lot. After conversations with a few good friends I realized that my honest first video had hurt the feelings of many abused women. They needed their art hero to strongly express support for the victim, as many related to her. So I filmed a second video apologizing for this and being more clear on my support for Sina. After that, I got off social media for a while. Just looking at the phone would hurt me. It was the break from my public persona I needed for so long. Now I was just me, no "famous artist" costume to carry, and I had to figure out if this was enough.

That month was the worst time of my life. I felt dead inside and drank every day to soften the edge. I didn't think I could go back to being a public artist nor help people any longer. I fell into a depression of despair and contemplated Suicide. My other option was to become a humble farmer hiding in my calm Peruvian valley. I knew I could find happiness again in the simple gift of living with some sun on my face. I thought of what happened, over and over again, to the point of torture. I knew I hadn't done any harm to anyone, but wished I would have responded differently. The shame was hard to shake. I felt I had let so many people down and was hard on myself for it. I was angry at all the friends who had betrayed me, but at least now I knew their true colors and was grateful to purge them out. In order to release some of my anger, I worked hard on my parent's land, as the earth could absorb my fury. I also painted different pieces including **"Death of Illusions"**. This intense self-portrait was my therapy and the expression of this difficult initiation. Part of the process was to paint it but not share it online, as this piece (and my life) was not for the public, it was for myself. Only now, years later am I sharing it with you in this book. I hope I don't hurt anyone's feelings with it.

Eventually, through some synchronicities, my Lima friend **Milagros** invited me to do a Huachuma ceremony with her. Though I felt hurt by Plant Medicines, who I knew had spiritually orchestrated this whole situation, I accepted. That ceremony was a really difficult one, which lasted ten hours of absolute physical pain and non-stop vomiting. Judea, who guided me so much those days, told me that the spirit of Huachuma had actually rinsed me clean of my accumulated negative feelings, so the struggles where well worth it. Now I was empty, like a seed ready to grow into a new being. So I decided to get back on the horse and return to my role as a public artist in service to humanity! Even if it seemed scary or daunting at the time, this was my destiny. I wasn't meant to hide in shame because of the sins of others! It was time to shine again, no matter what was said about me!

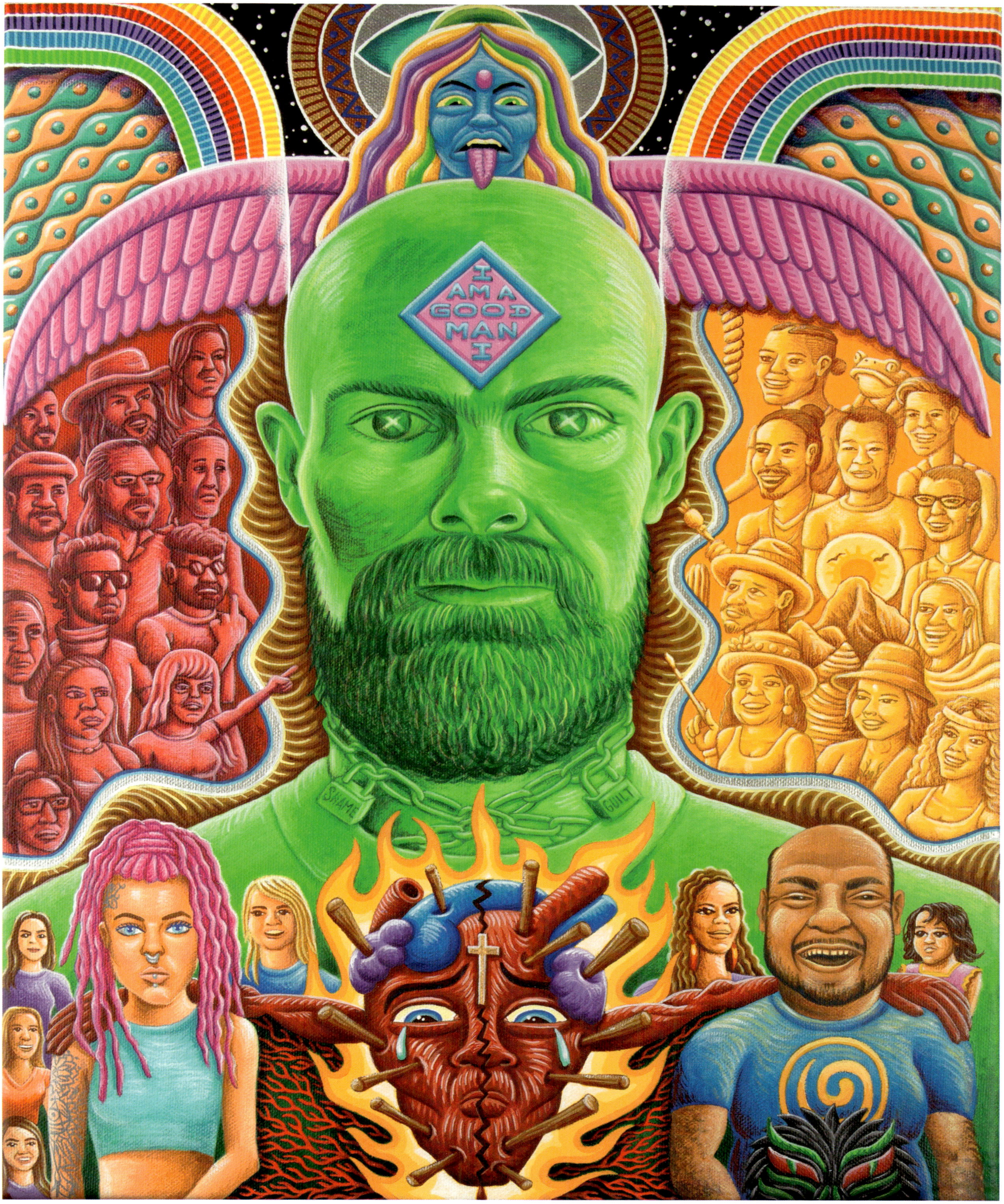

“Death of Illusions” Acrylics on canvas, 2021

MURAL TOUR 2021

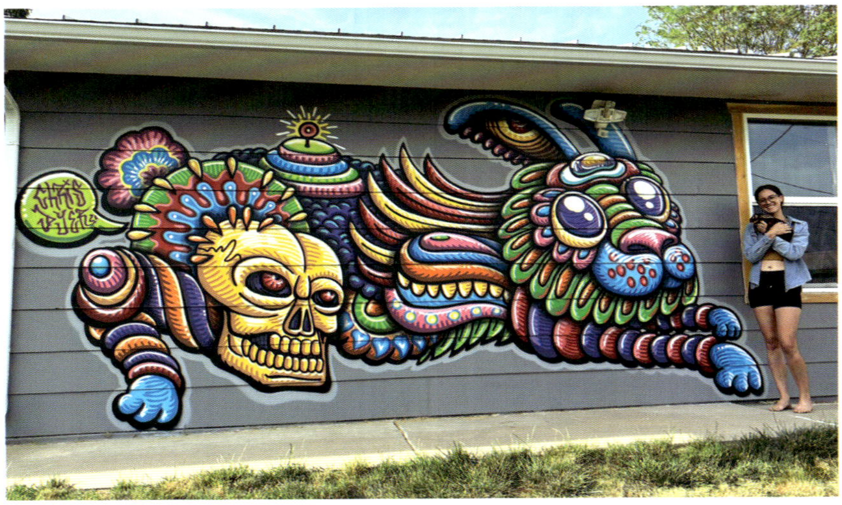

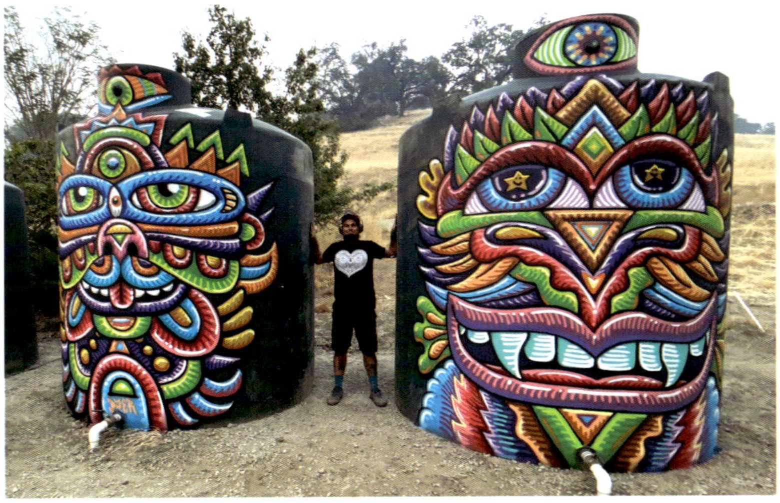

So I hit the road and got back in my flow. The whole temporary "Cancelation" had left me financially broke, as I still had to pay for the survival of my (freaked out) brand employees, but our sales were pretty dead. Luckily there were many nice people all over the United States who were very happy to hire me to paint murals for them. So I spent five months crushing these pieces non-stop in places like **New York, Oregon, Colorado, Austin, Tennessee, Las Vegas, Florida, Vermont** and all up and down **California**. It was very healing to hang out with so many people who knew I was a good person and supported me through my recuperation. Meanwhile online, my real fans showed me they were still there for me and happy to see my comeback. After so many years of being of service to the community, they knew I was a good person who deserved to make a living from his soul expressions, not some villain to be thrown away in the garbage (as some where proposing). I just put my head down and worked hard under the sun and dropped more murals than I can show you here!

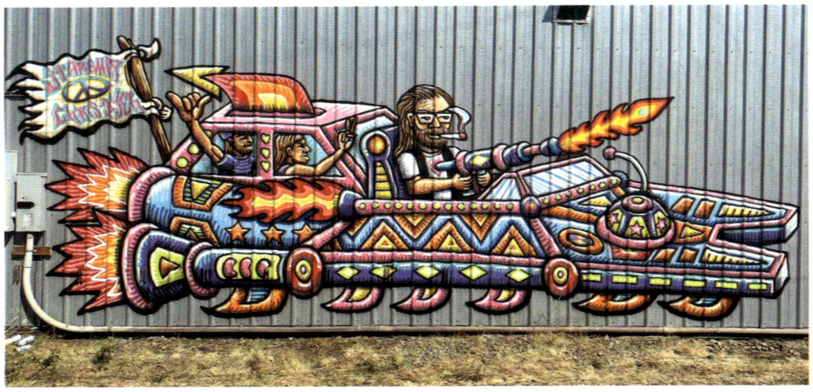

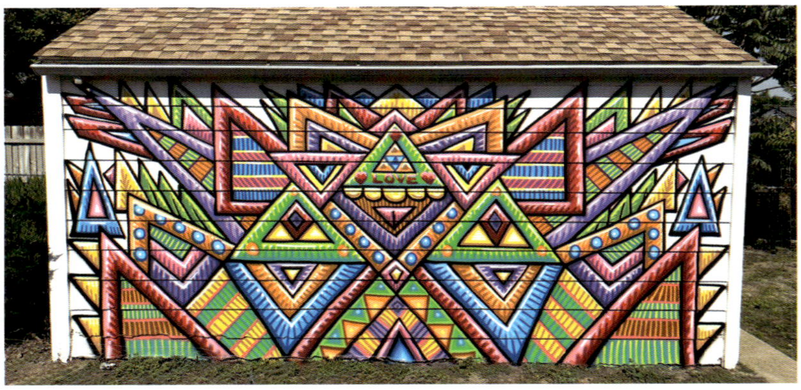

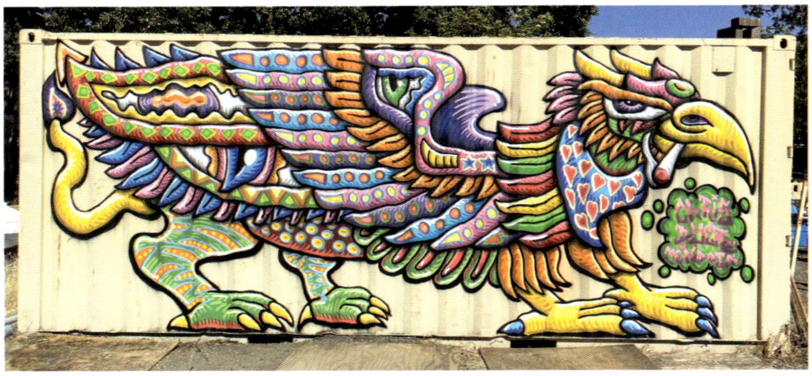

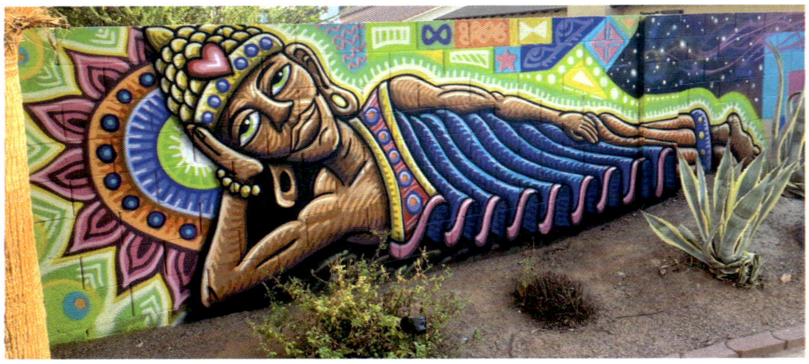

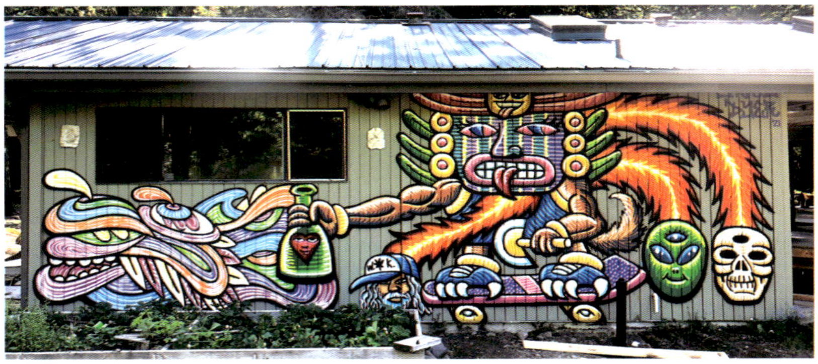

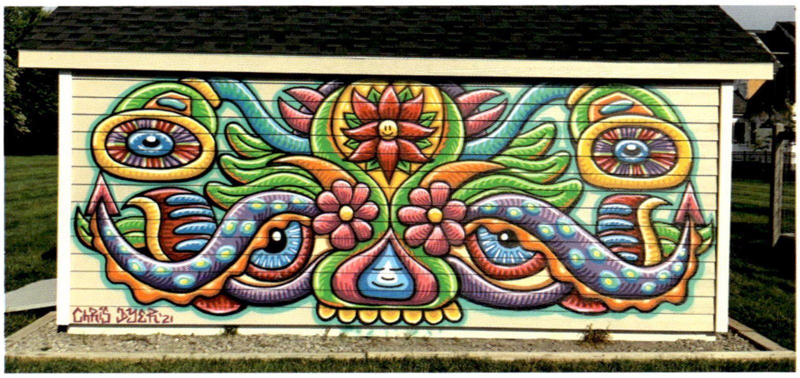

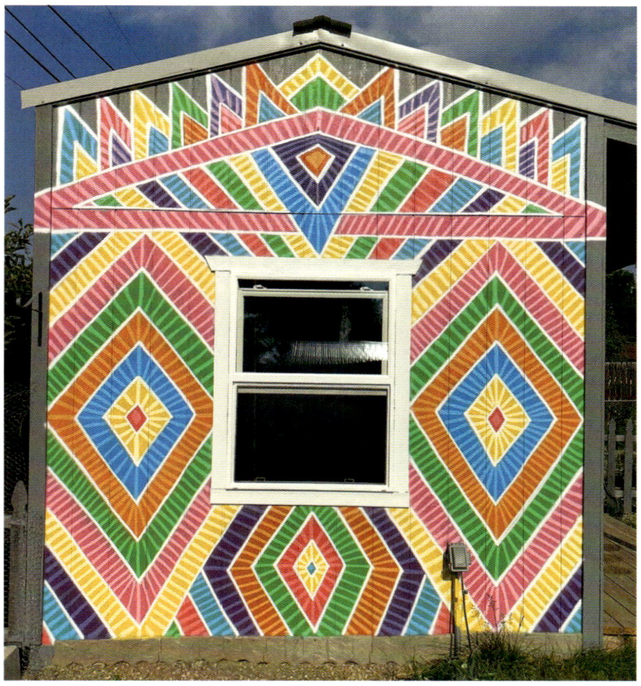

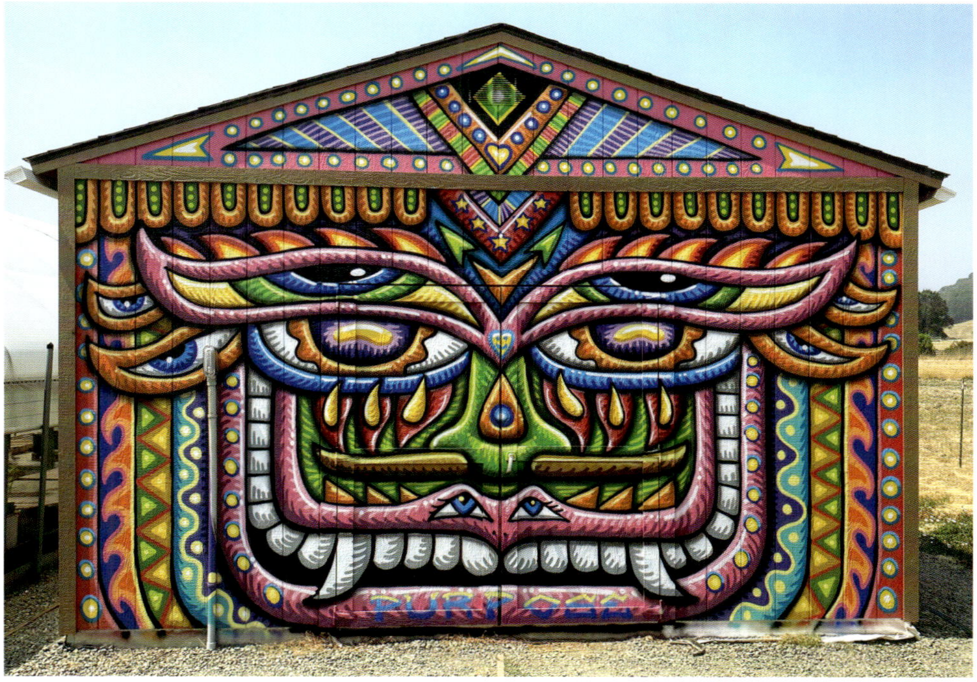

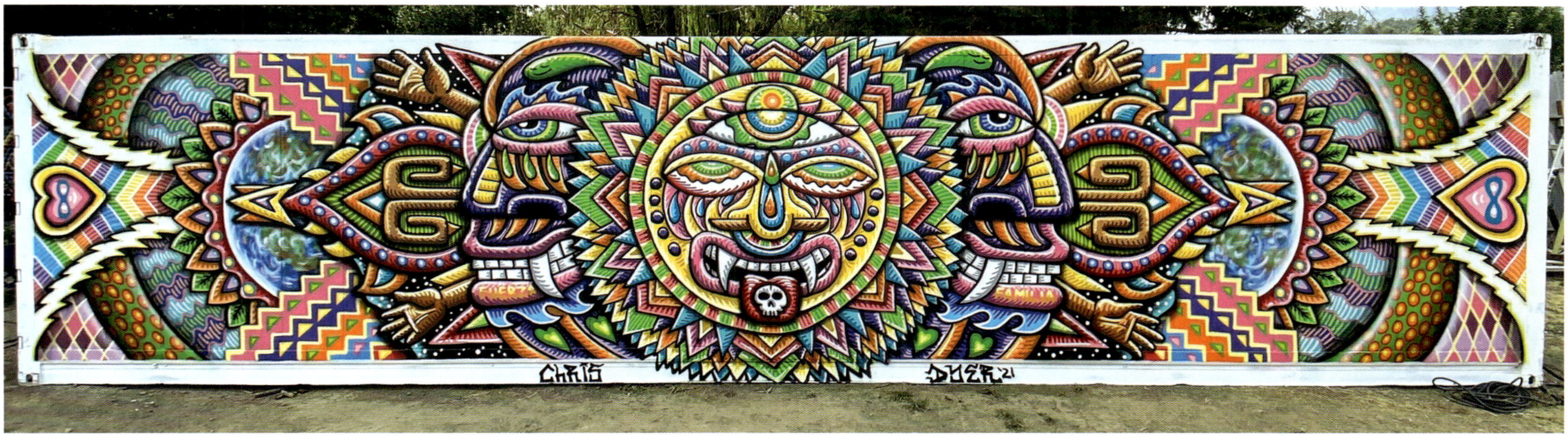
CHRIS
DYER'21

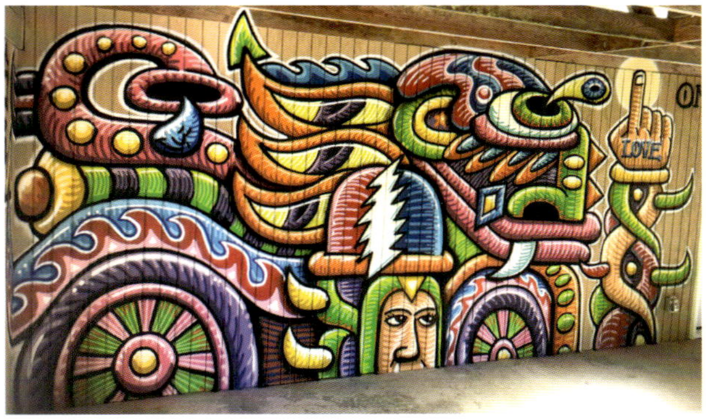

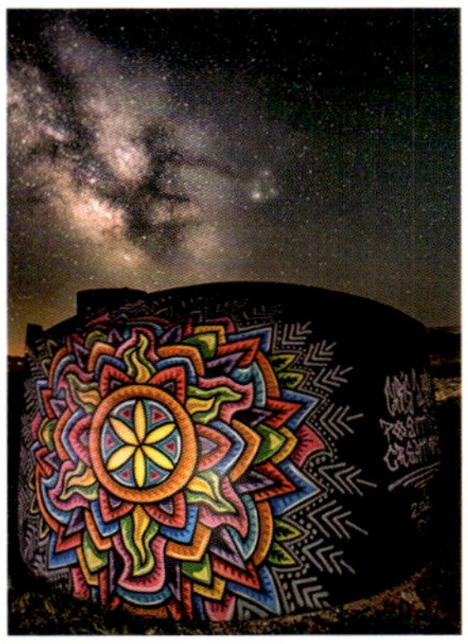

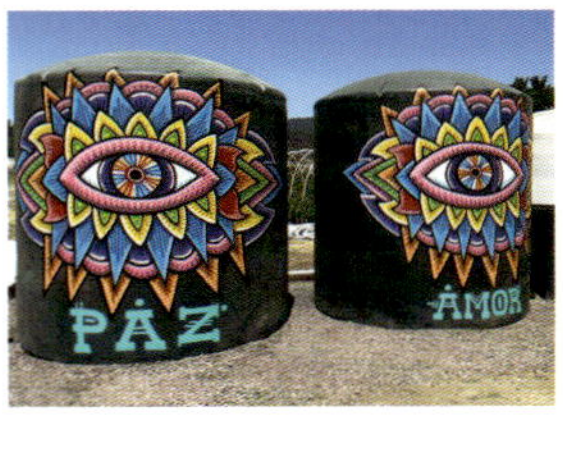
PAZ
AMOR

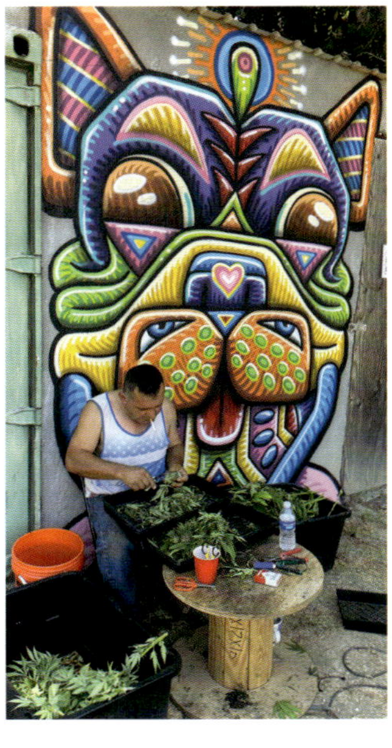

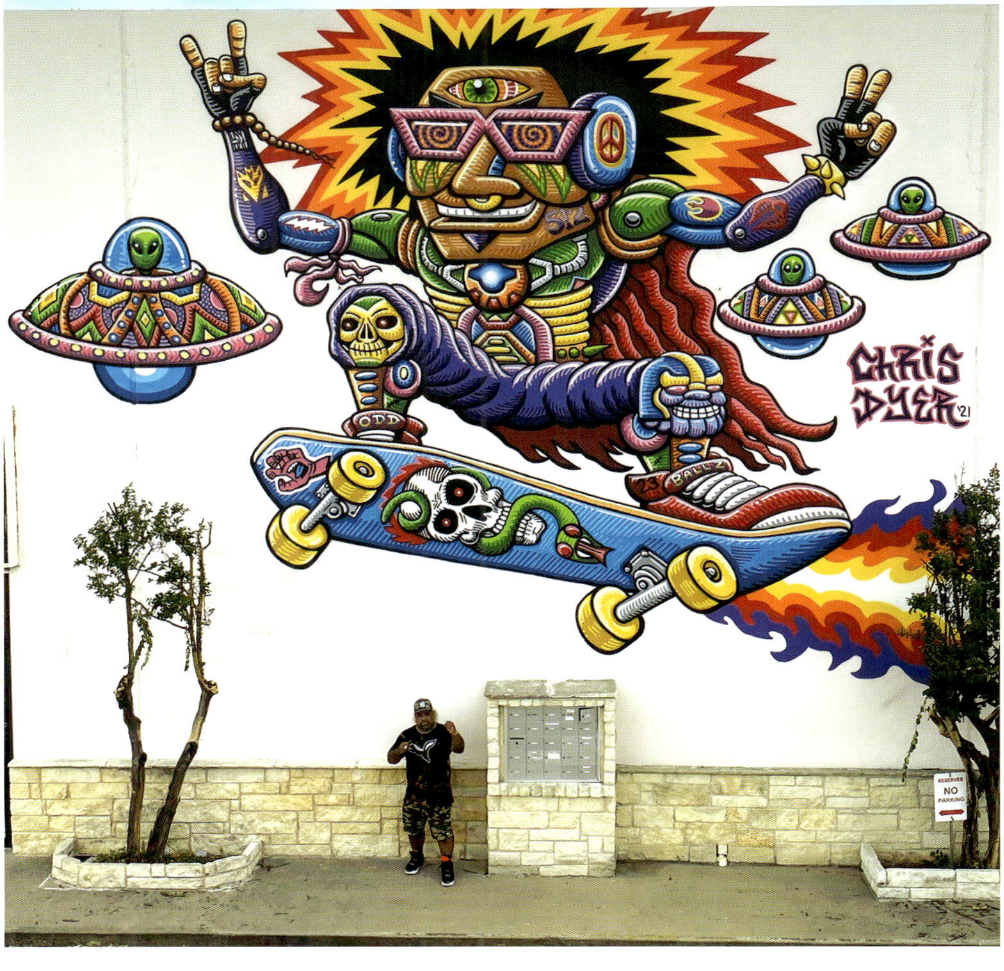
CHRIS
DYER '21

SPRAY PAINT CANVASES

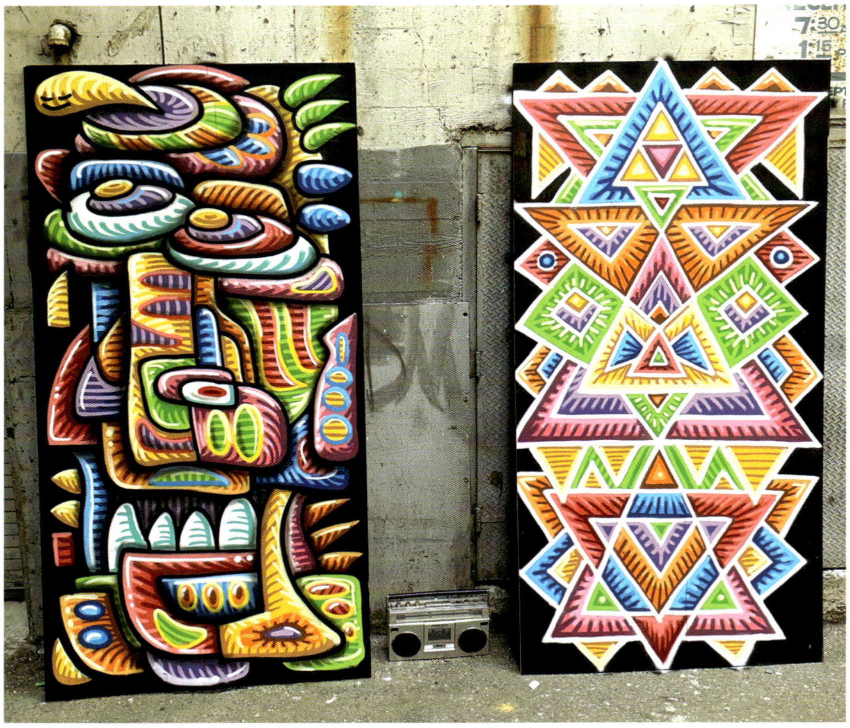

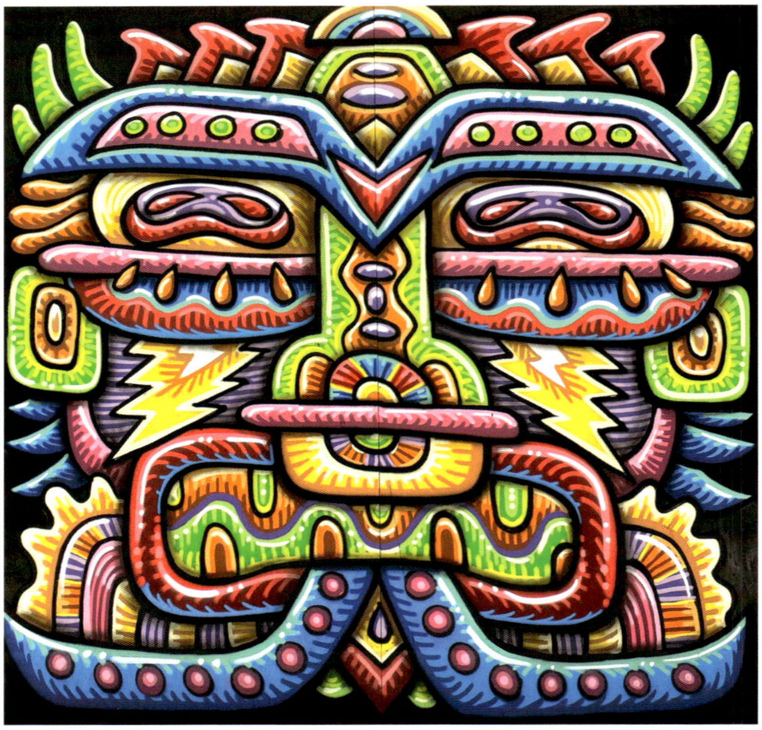

While on tour I was invited to have a partner exhibition with glassblower **Pinky Brewtz** at **Lifted Veil Gallery** in downtown **Los Angeles, California**. Since most of my art was far of reach in my Montreal home, I opted to spray paint a bunch of canvases and wooden panels. This felt like a combination between my mural and canvas work, that was fast enough to allow me to create a lot of work, but also kept my prices in a lower range. I was stoked to pretty much sell out the whole show! We also had legendary turntablist **Cut Chemist** DJ for the opening so I was very grateful for how everything turned out! Anyways, here are some of the canvases and panels I spray painted for that show, plus others I've done in other occasions.

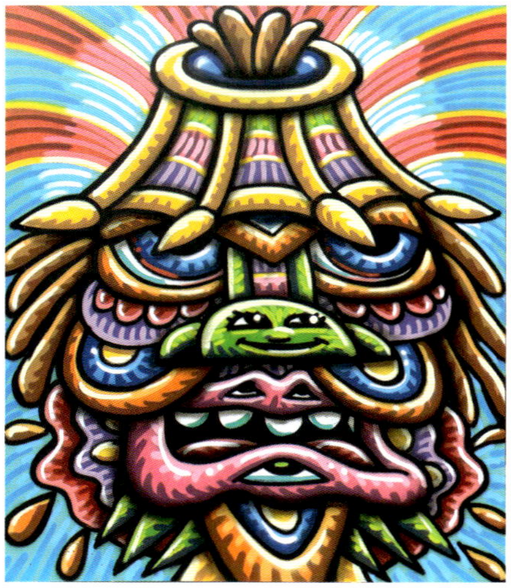

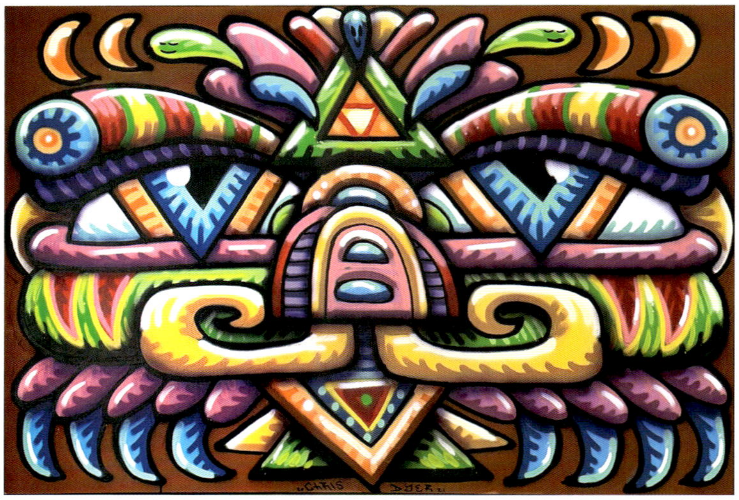

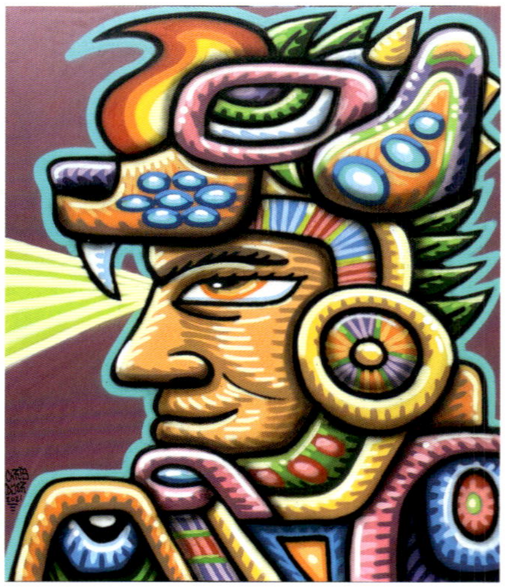

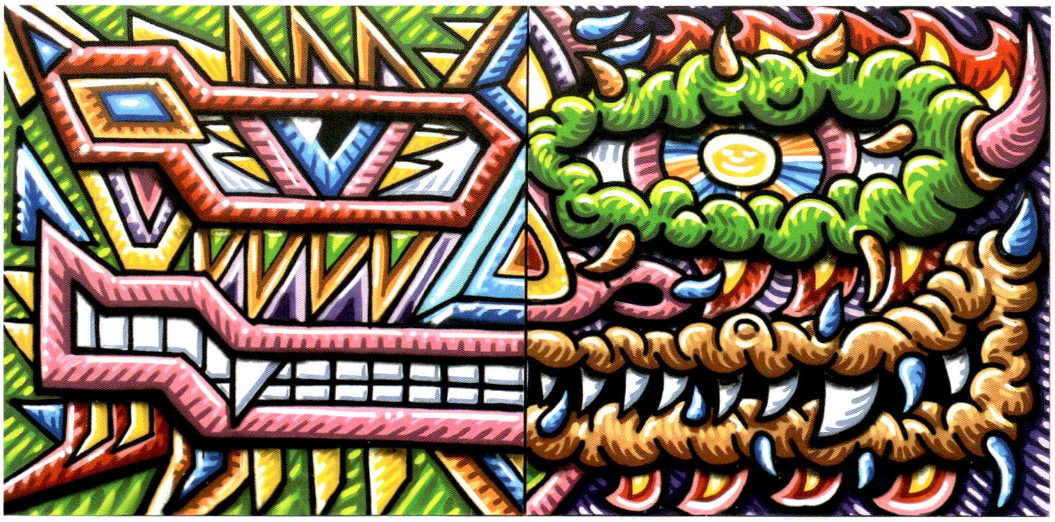

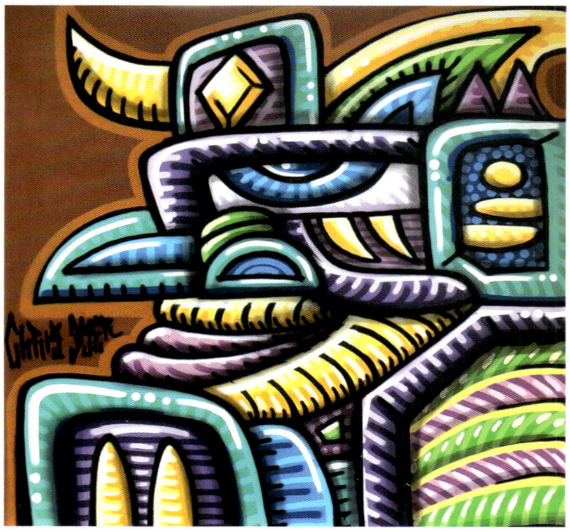

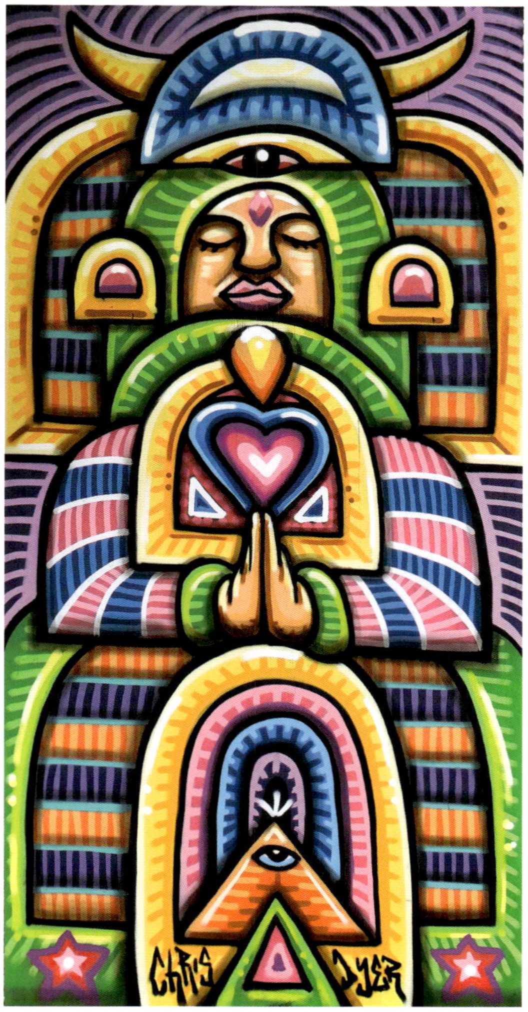
CHRIS DYER
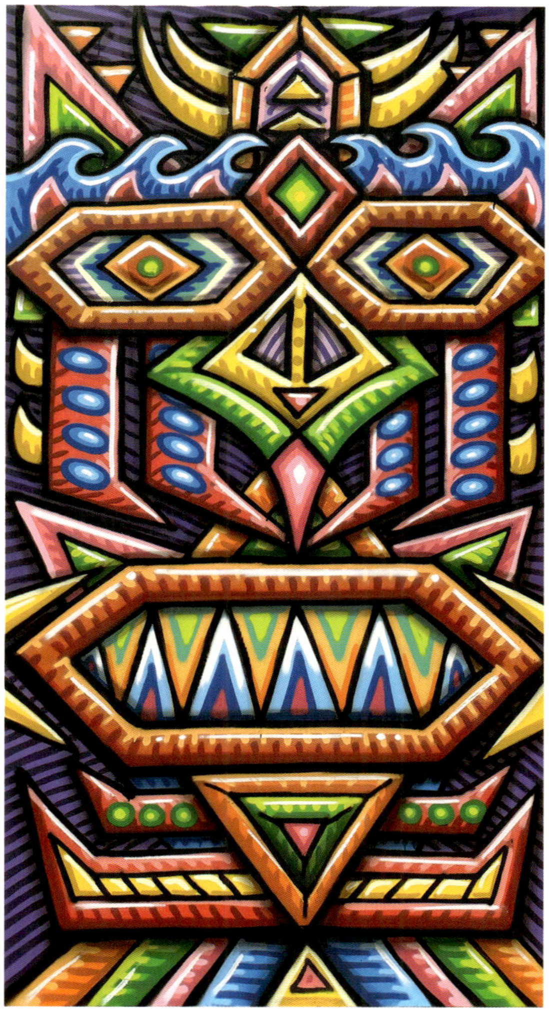
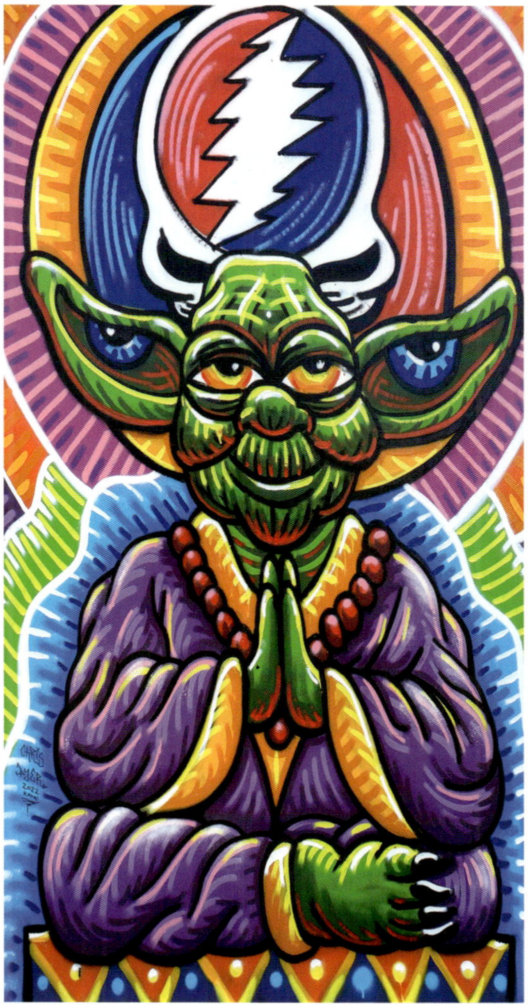
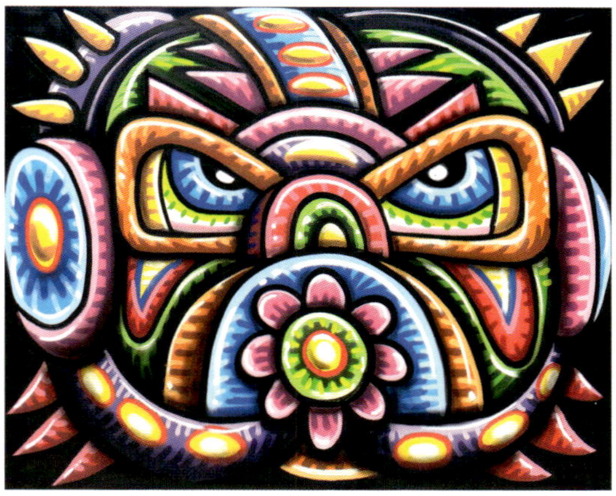
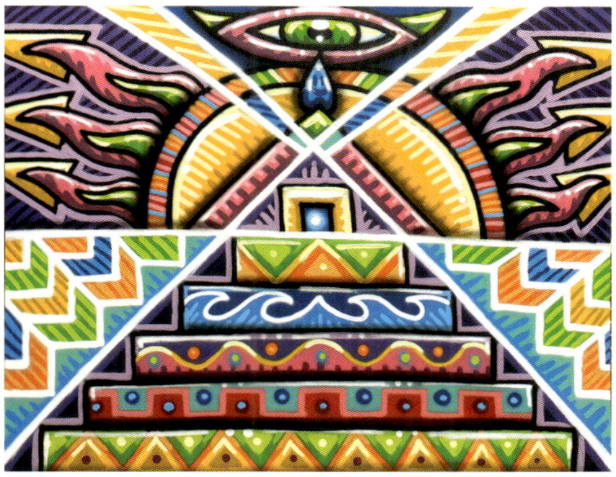
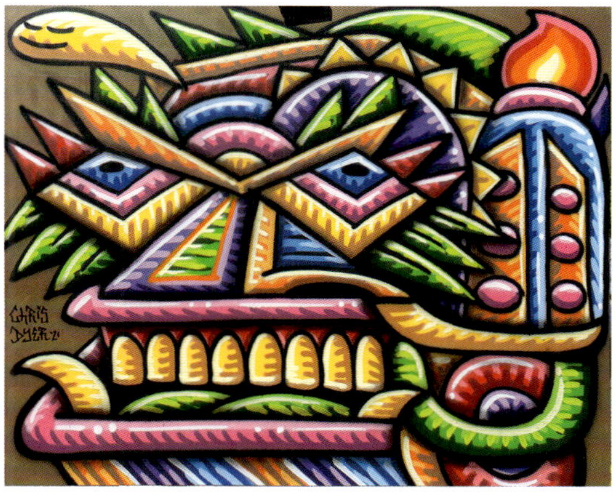
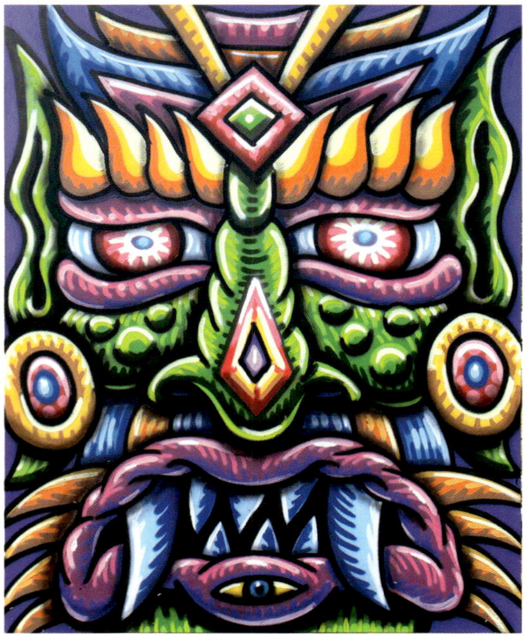
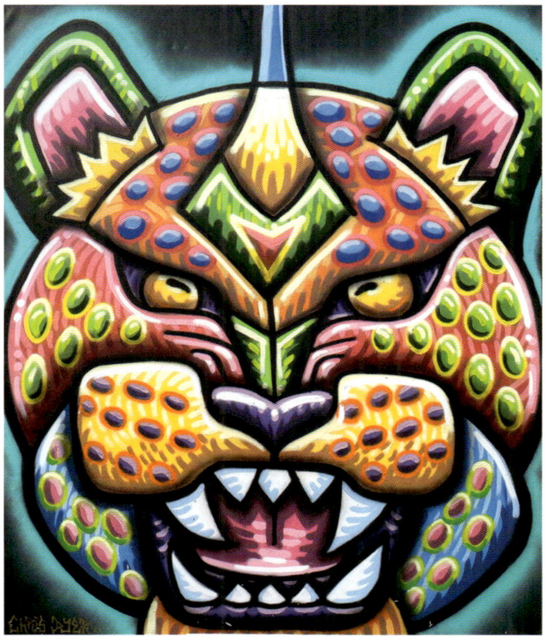
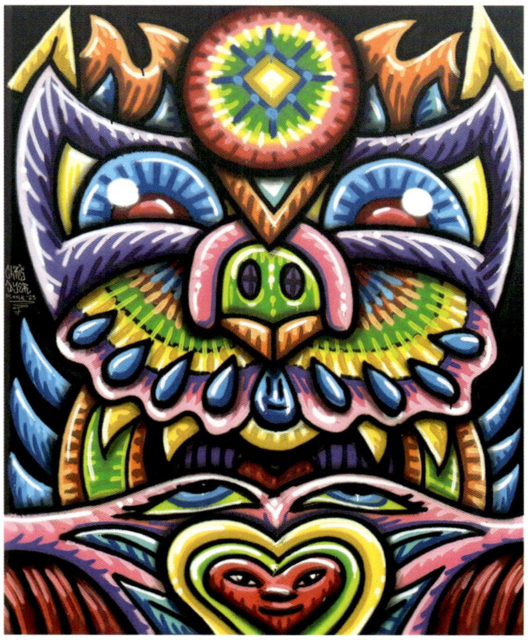

FRINGE MINORITY

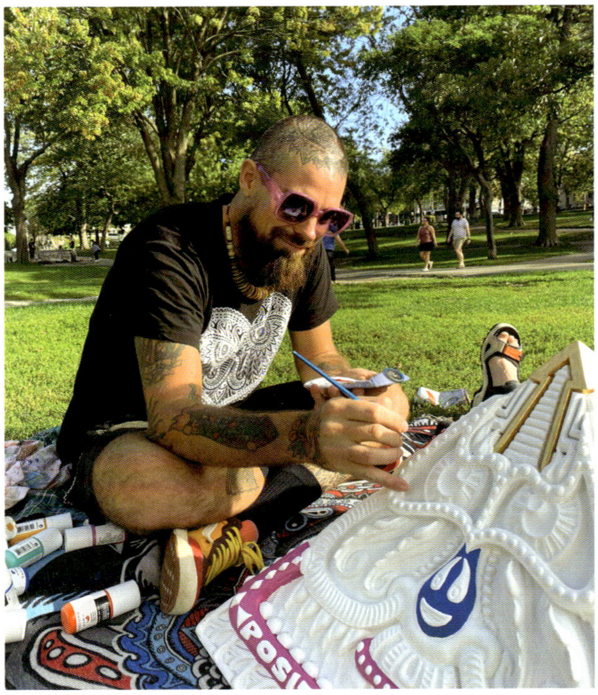

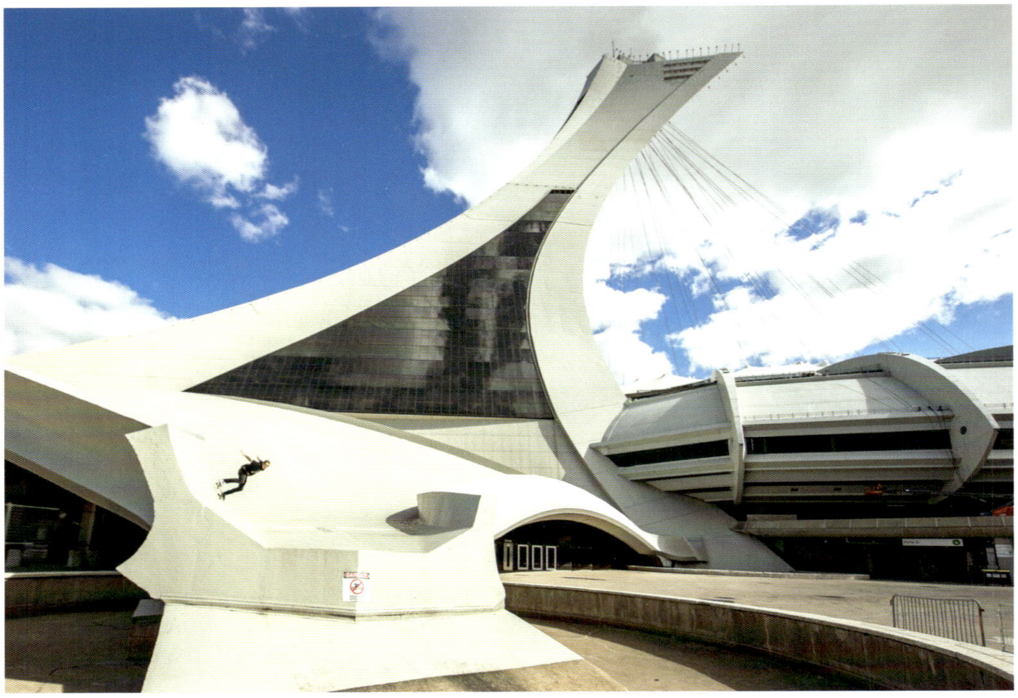

Getting back to my **Montreal** home after ten months away was really nice, but also really strange. While on tour, the Covid "Vaccine" (an experimental gene therapy) was rushed out by corporations, pushed by mainstream media and enforced by governments. I totally understood those who felt the need to take it, but my personal intuition told me stay clear of it. I felt I deserved the time to observe if this new medical treatment had any long term side-effects. It didn't take long before it was proven not to work as promised, but society had become very divided over the topic. It was so weird to now be in a Canada that no longer allowed me the freedom to eat at restaurants or enter public places without my **Vax-Passport App**. It was also surreal to be pushed away by good friends that now considered me forever-sick and dangerous to their families. The pressure got stronger when our Prime Minister **Justin Trudeau** started calling the "un-vaxed" a *"small fringe minority that where far-right extremists, misogynistic and racists who shouldn't be tolerated"*.
Most of my Montreal artist friends where also part of this 10% of Canadians who didn't trust this new "medicine". We all felt so stressed living in a society that was judging and shunning us so harshly. So I started organizing house parties at my place where everyone was welcome. I reached my tipping point with the situation when Trudeau announced that the Unvaxed would no longer be allowed on public transportation, including airplanes. So I decided to leave my beautiful apartment, friends and beloved city of over 20 years. I was heartbroken, but was not going to be locked in a golden cage, in a country loosing its freedom of choice. In a matter of two weeks I packed all of my possessions into boxes, stored them in one of my apartment's rooms and rented this spot to my dealer. Then I moved to the States on the last day I was legally allowed to do so.

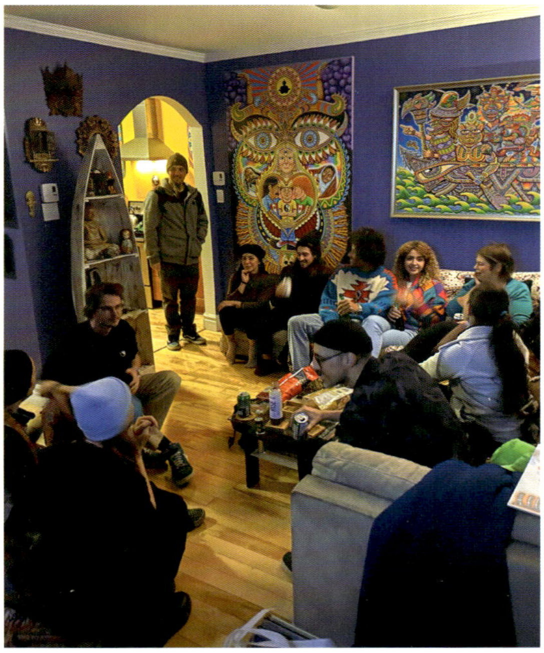

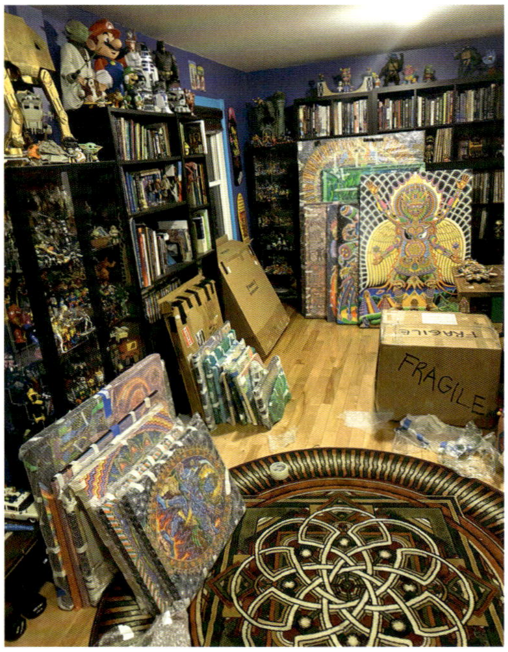

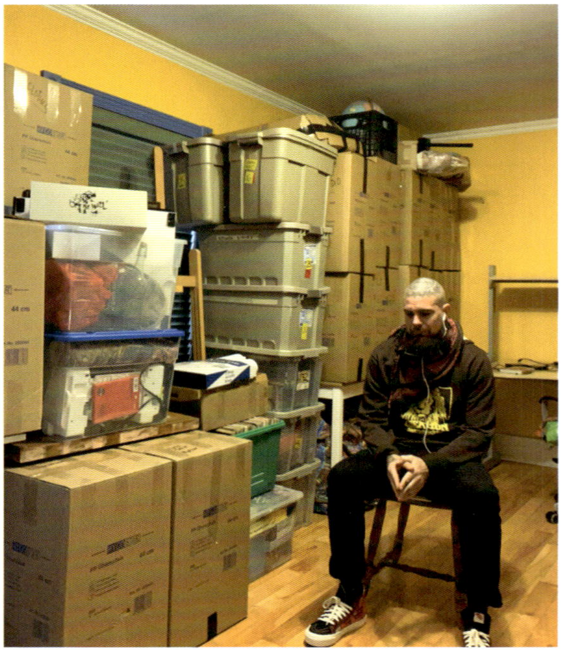

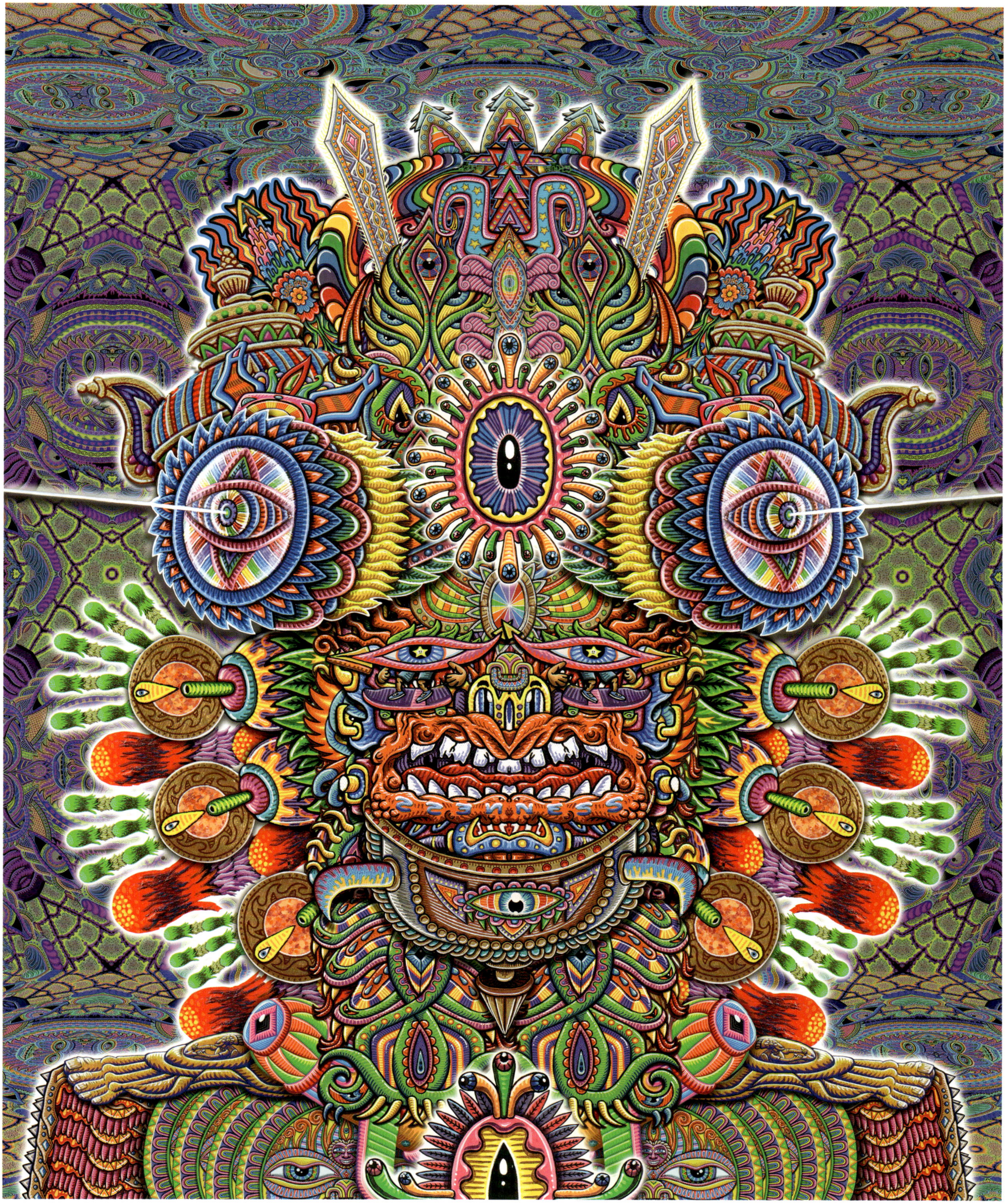

“Open your Eyes” NFT, 2021
animated by **Ryan Uhrich** with music by **The Gaslamp Killer**

EXILED IN DENVER

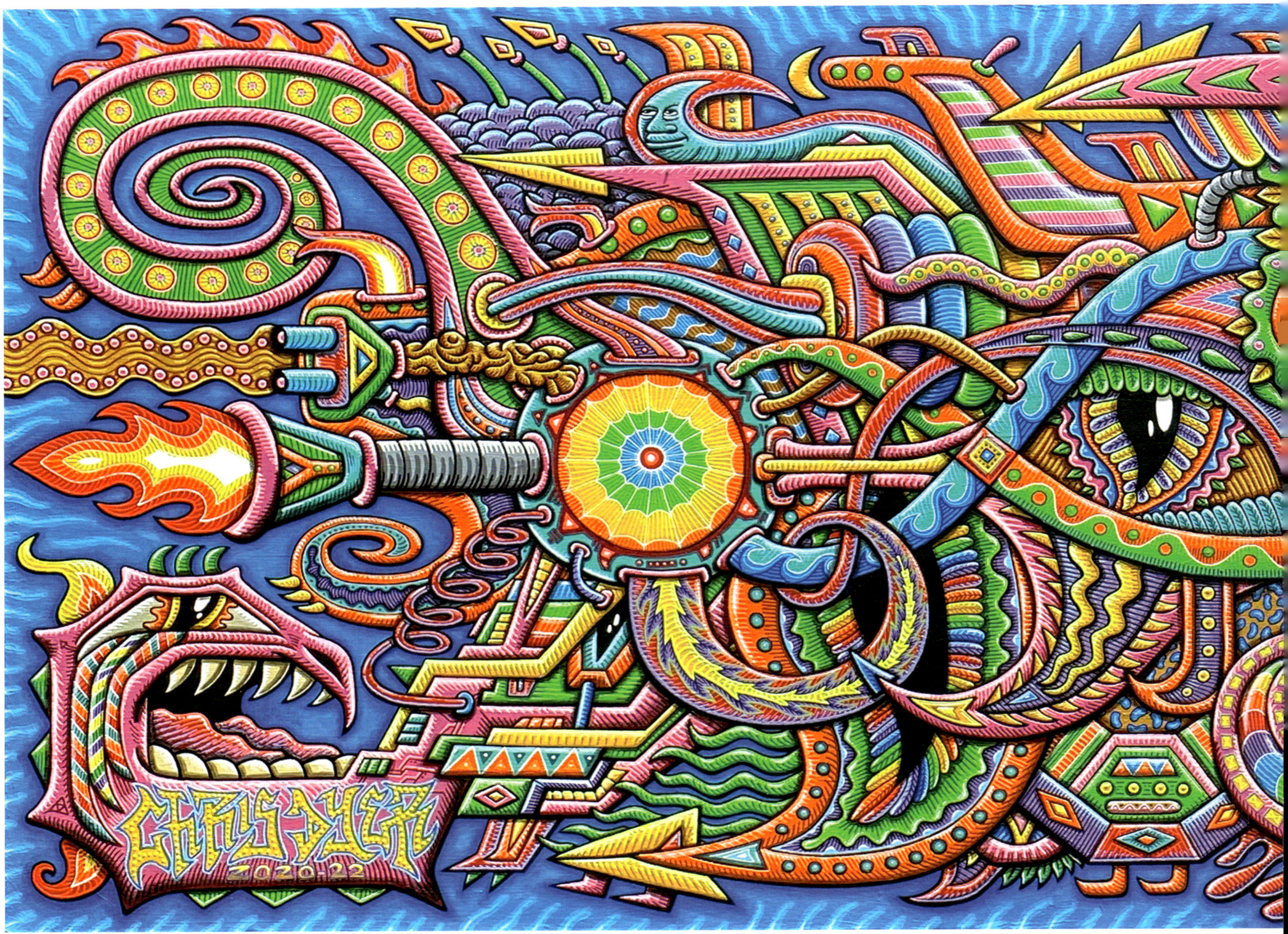

"The Process of Evolution" Acrylics on canvas, 2020-2022

The **Positive Creations** brand house in **Denver** had a small extra room in the basement so I moved there for a whole year. My brand manager **Cory Ponz** was happy to now have his artist in-house and put me to work on several projects.

After living by myself for so long it was challenging to share space with three roommates, especially since they had such different party lifestyles to my own. I did ok with few material possessions, but the small dark room was pretty depressing many days.

Denver had become a big city for **Visionary Art**, so I had lots of fans and some good old friends I would hang out with (mostly hiking and painting in Boulder). I also had quite a few haters there though, who badmouthed me constantly and blocked any opportunity I would get to do public events at galleries. It was so weird to be excluded from participating in the scene I helped create with my friends almost two decades before. All I wanted to do was share my art and vibration as service, but this ambitious city was too doggy dog to be a resonant community for me. My career still did well despite this energy though, so I remained Grateful.

In that year there I got the chance to finish painting **"The Process of Evolution"** which was a long ambitious mega-fishbomb canvas that expresses the chaos of the turbulent years it was created.

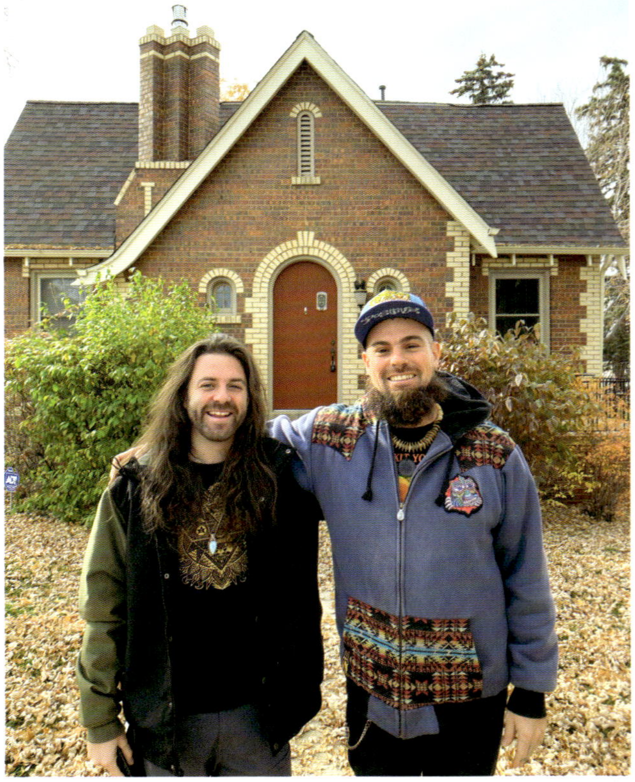

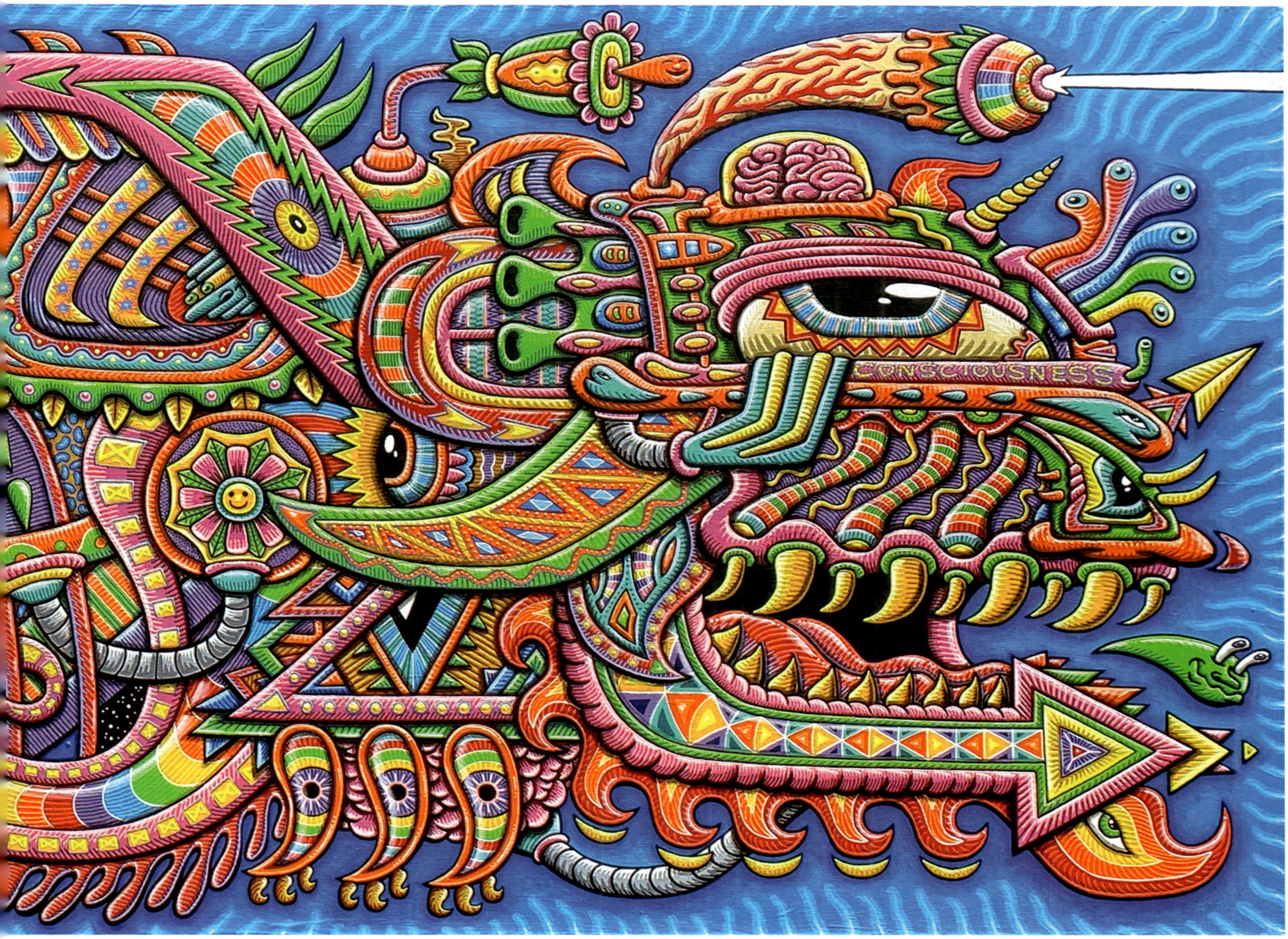
CONSCIOUSNESS

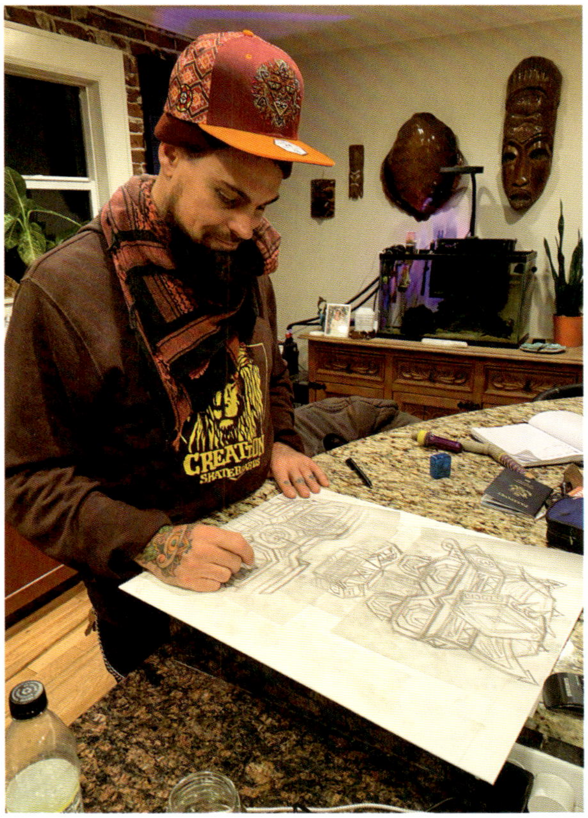
CREATION

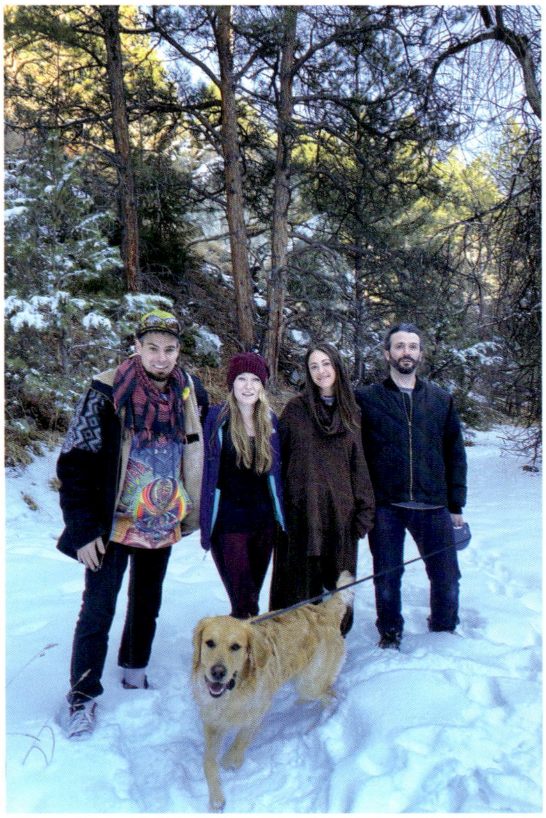

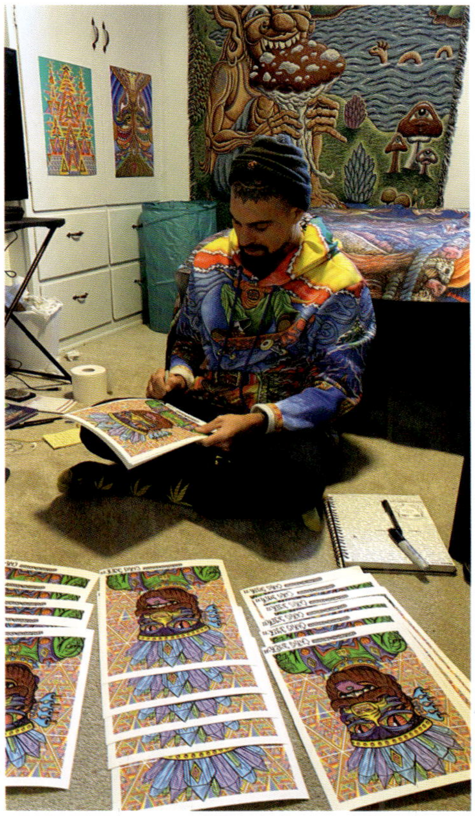

THE GALAKTIC GANG

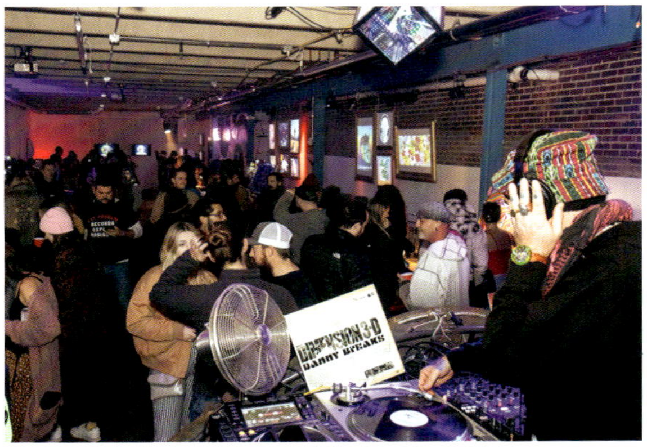

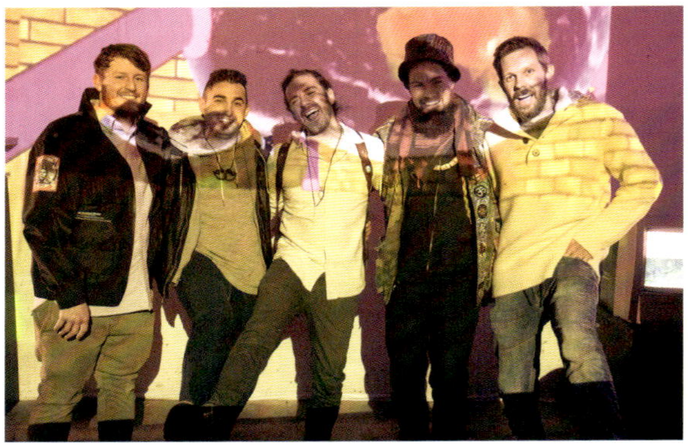

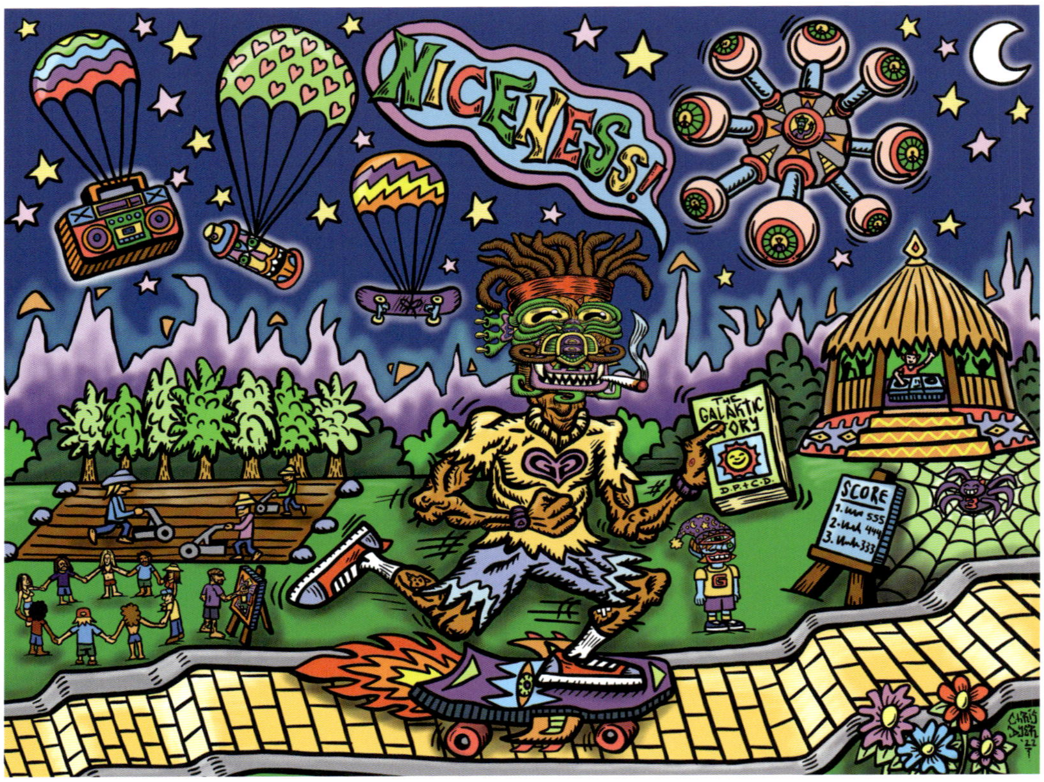

On the day I moved to Denver, Cory and I got together with our glassblower friends **Kyle Morton** and **Gabe Herrera**. At that brunch we decided to create an NFT Profile Picture (PFP) project called the **Galaktic Gang**! This required me to hand draw the traits of thousands of characters that our new community could mint at the end of the year. Observing a lot of mediocre art in the NFT world, I wanted to make sure I created high quality character puzzle pieces, which took me a while to draw. We worked with our **Fyresite Media** friends (Jason Turnquist and Travis Delly) who coded an algorithm that shuffled all of my traits, creating a wide variety of unique super trippy characters! Five-thousand five-hundred and fifty-five to be exact!

Once we launched the project I realized how I had gambled the power of my artist name, in the same way my new investors where gambling on the solidity of my NFTs. If the collection didn't sell out, people who did buy them would actually loose money and I would look terrible. A few days after we started our "Mint" we threw a big launch party for our Gang with free alcohol, food, music performances, live painters, video games, etc. It was super good vibes and I realized that we had formed a very special community, regardless if the NFTs sold out. This goal actually seemed impossible for some days, but by a winter solstice miracle, I woke up to the news that we had sold out all **5555** NFTs! It brought me to tears to know that my fans where still there to support my movement so passionately! It also was the most profit (by far) that I had ever made from any art project! I was so grateful and happy to keep my promise of working hard for this community for years to come!

Crypto and NFTs pretty much dropped hard after that peak we launched at, but regardless I spent most of 2022 creating "utilities" for my Gang. Along an awesome team of moderators, we have given away original paintings and prints, thrown different free IRL events, planted hemp trees in Kauai, built a Metaverse Party Spaceship to throw live VR parties, created a big line of exclusive merchandise, gave away several "Galaktic Gadgets" free mints, offered weekly events on our Discord, organized the "Galaktic Gold" rewards system with quests and contests, held frequent live conversations on Twitter, and much more! I also spent a long time drawing up the bodies of these interdimensional creatures that we hope to give away soon enough! All in all it's been a very fun experience and a good way to get closer to a lot of my core fans!

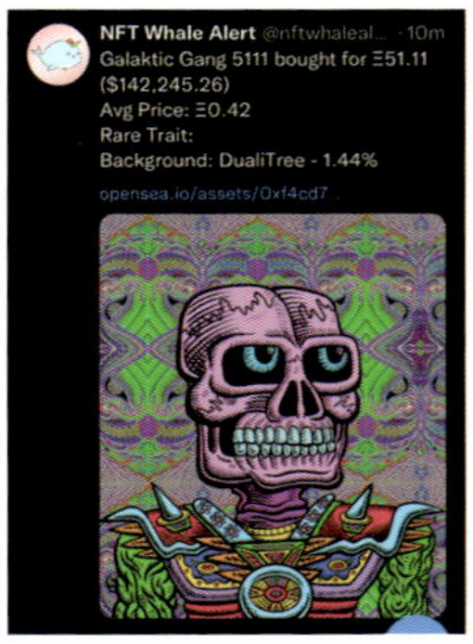

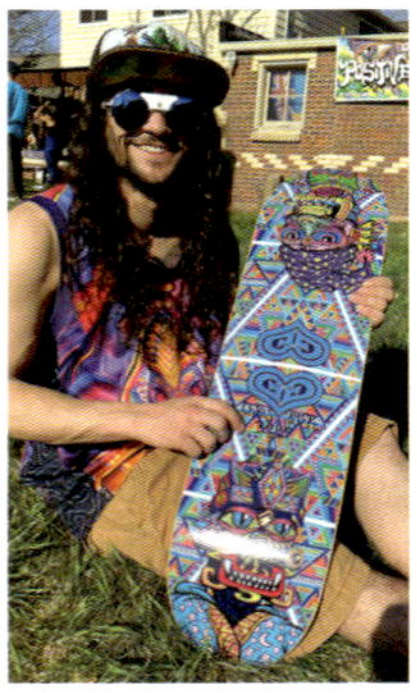

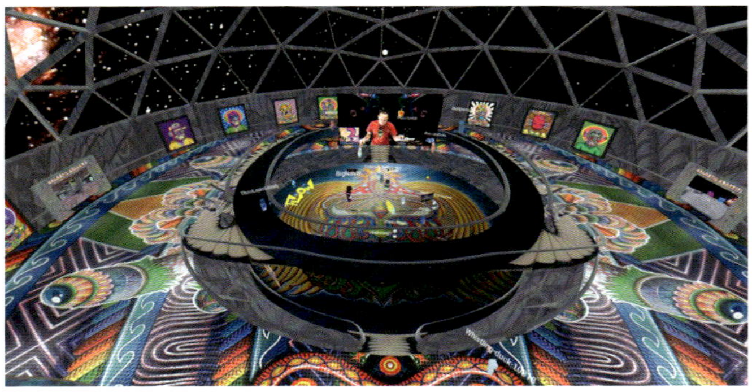

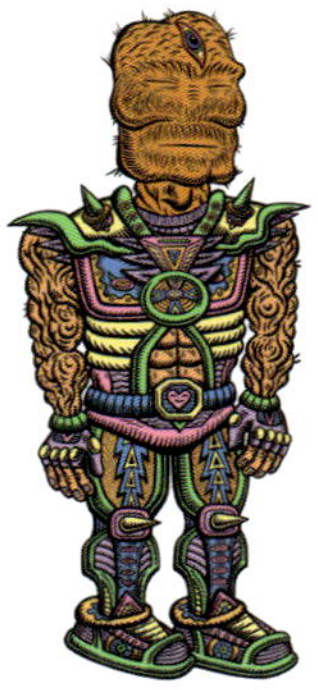

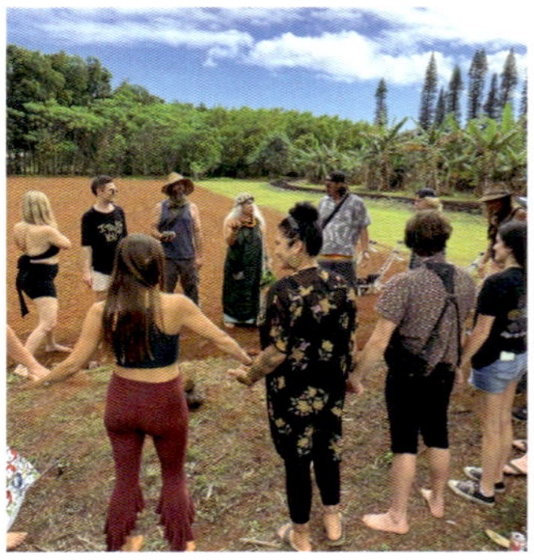

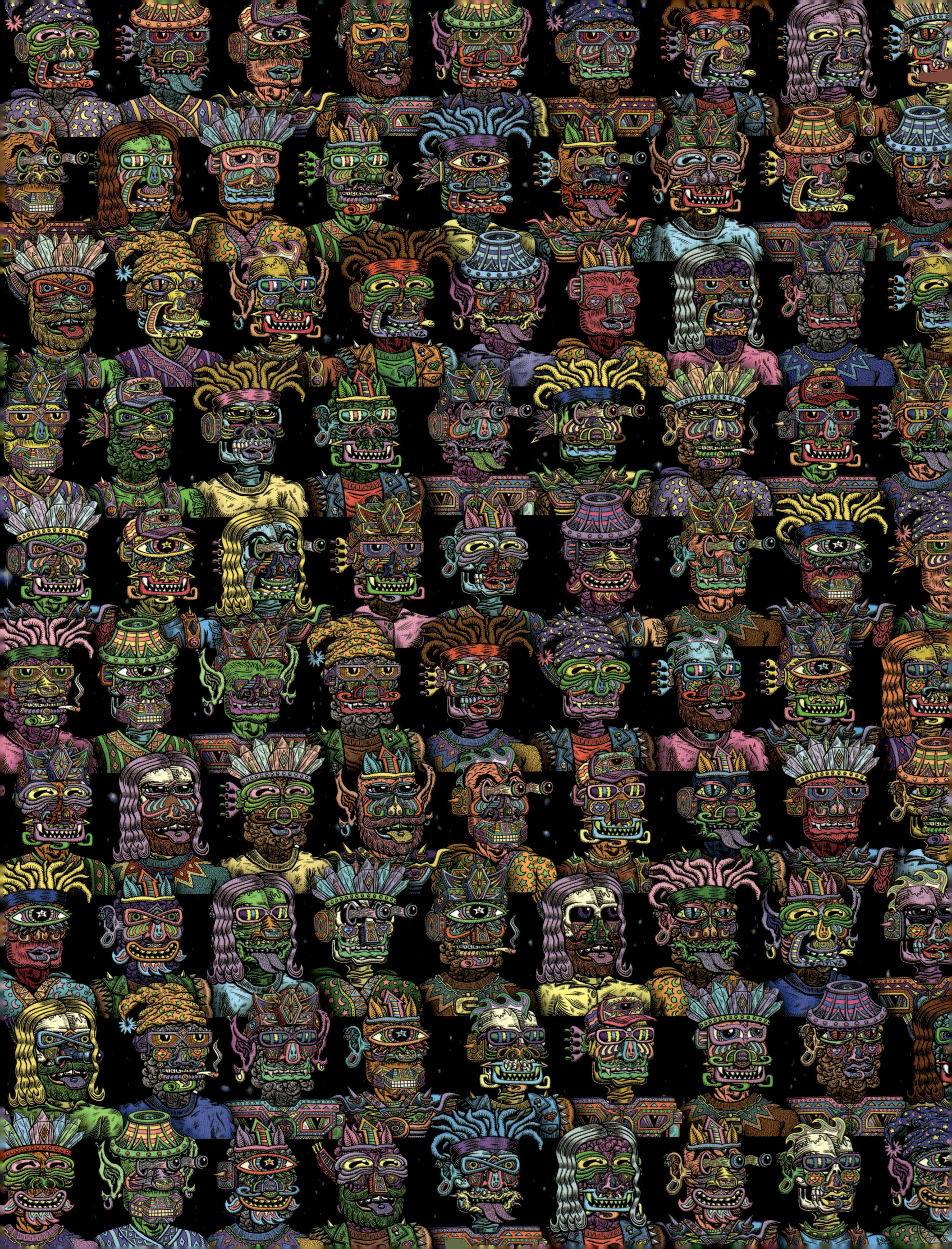

MURAL TOUR 2022

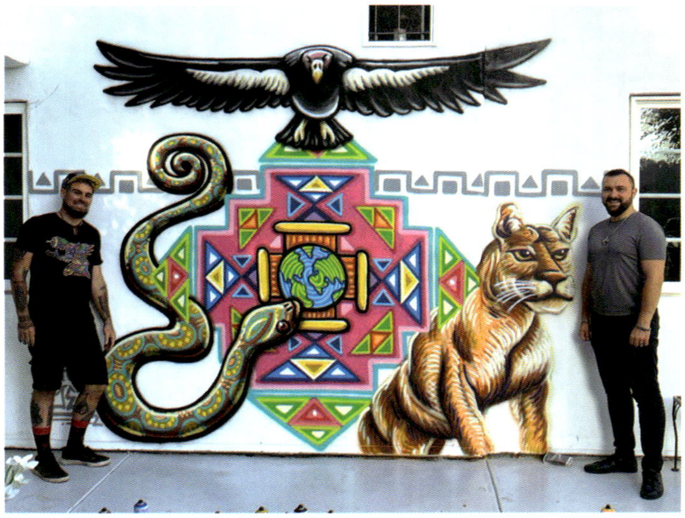

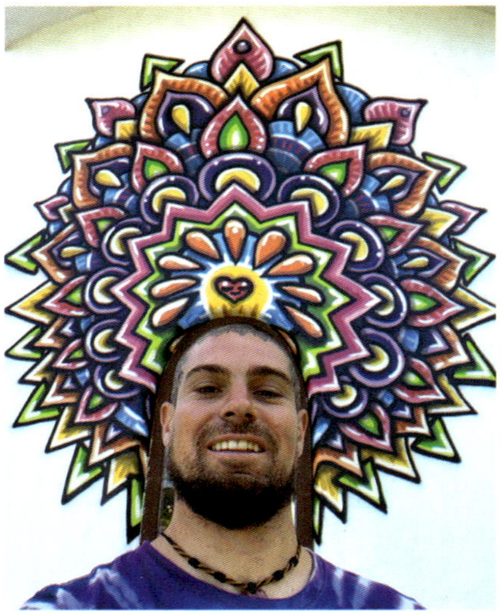

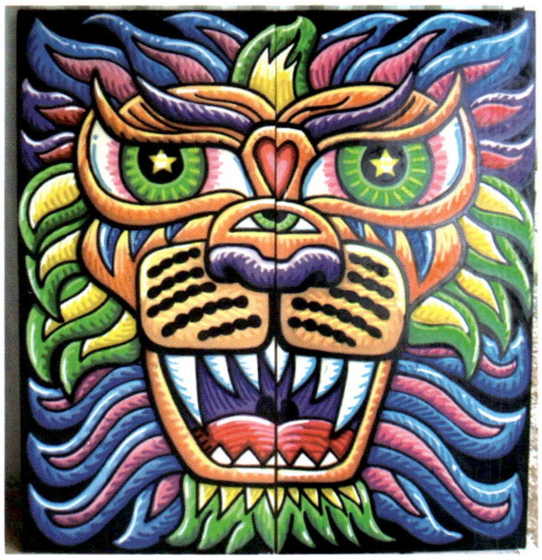

Summer came again so I organized a new mural tour, mostly through **California**. Though the roots Cannabis industry was struggling, there were still a few dispensaries and extracts brands that hired me to paint them murals. I was spray painting a lot of felines in my murals and I feel I attracted one too. Those days I started dating a lovely artist lady from Detroit called **Paulina Casati** who I quickly fell in Love with. So Grateful!

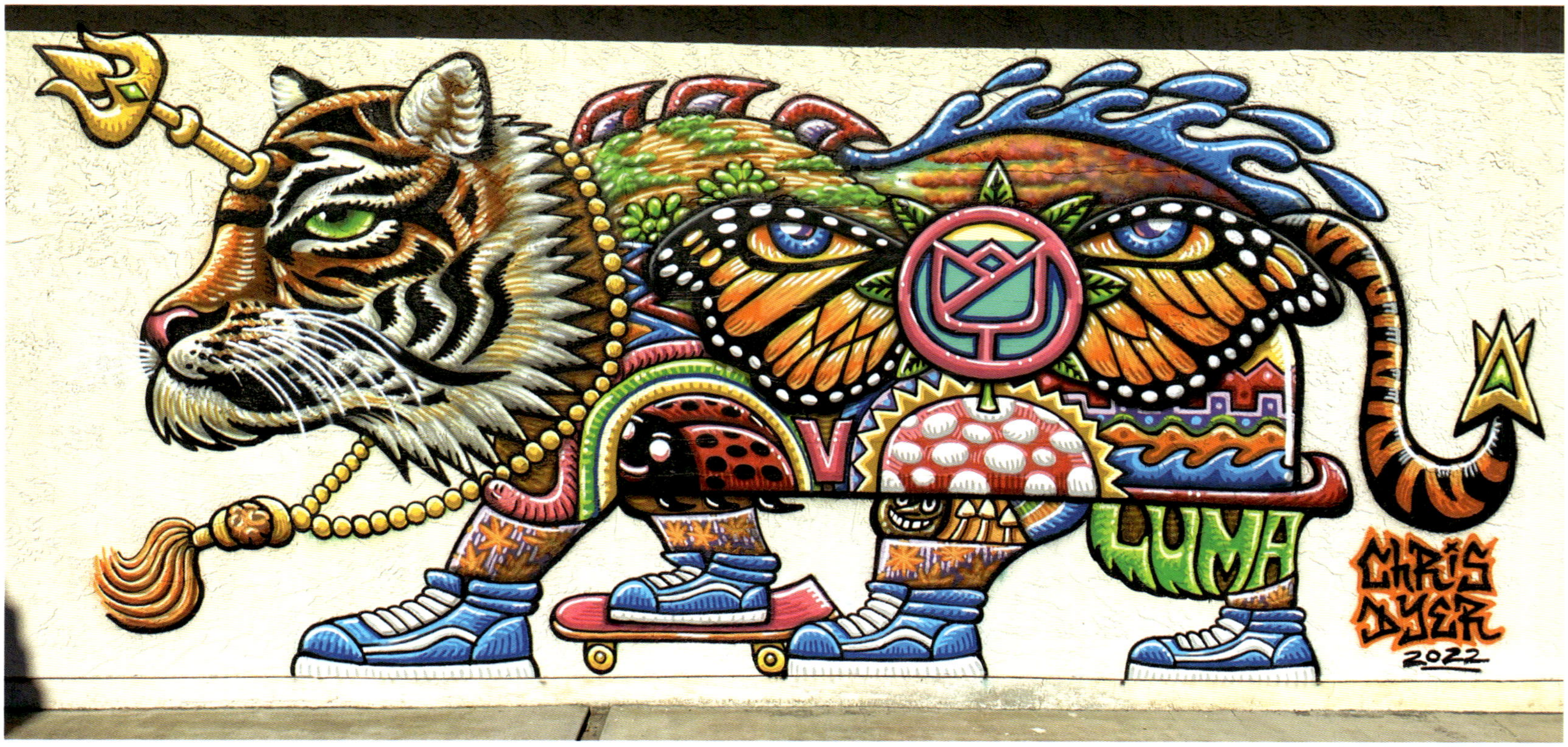

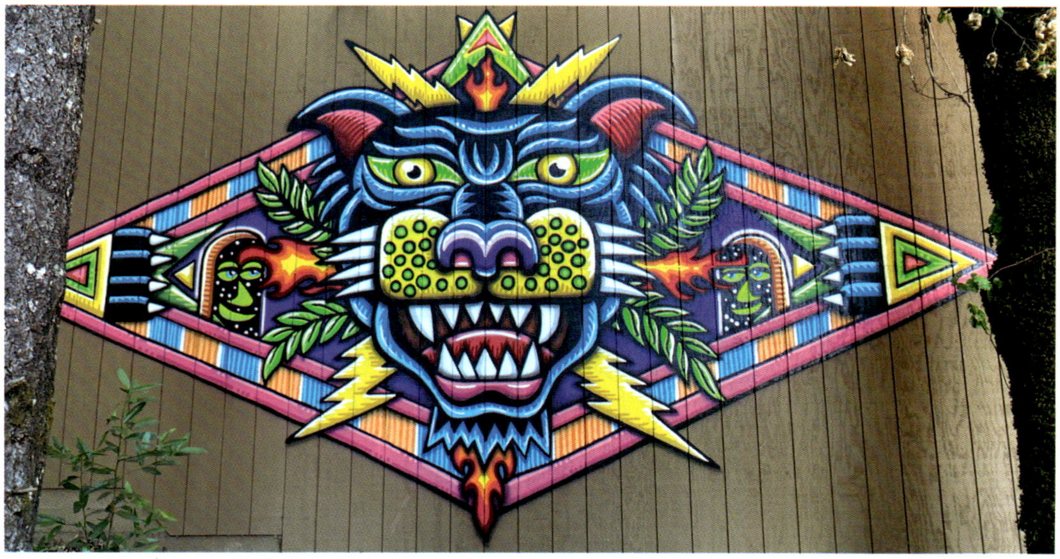

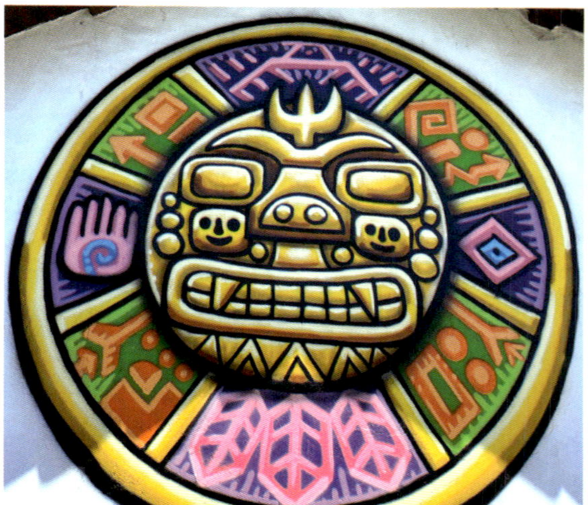

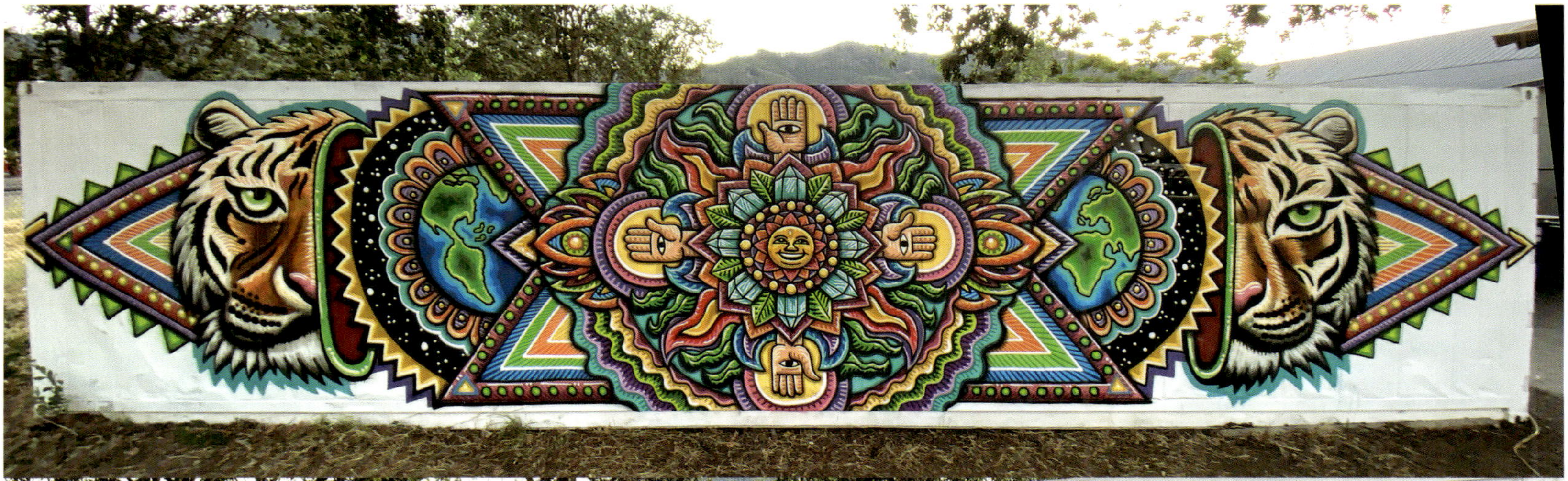
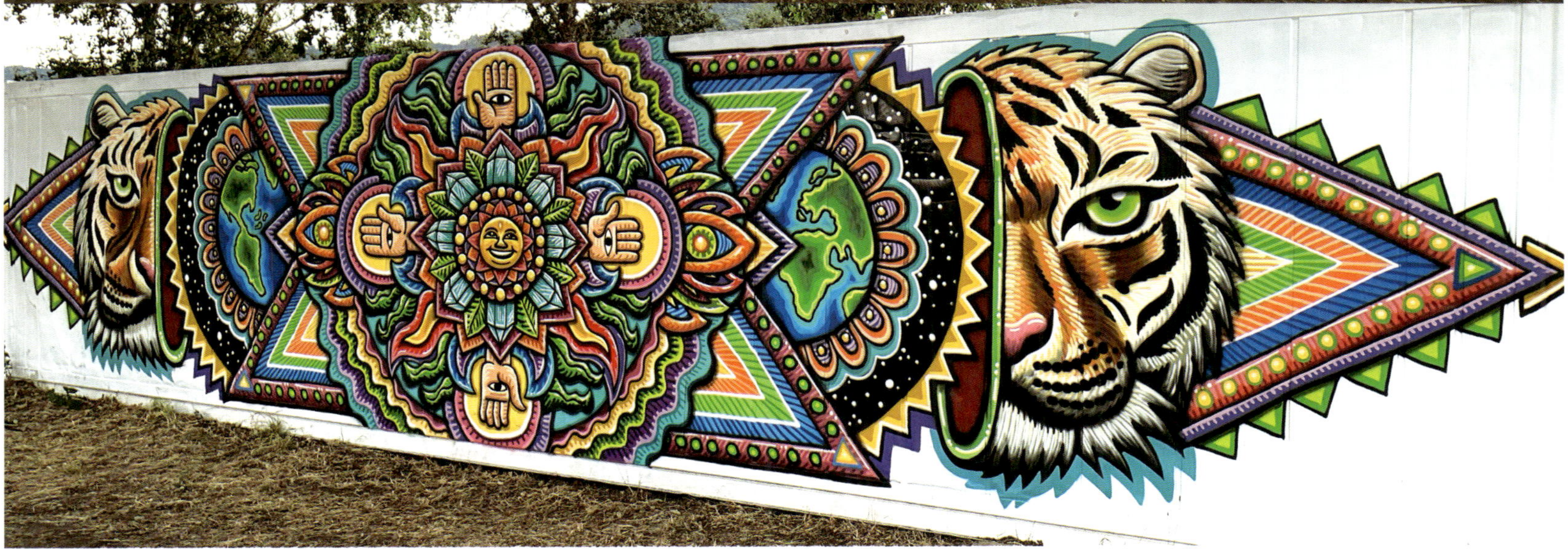
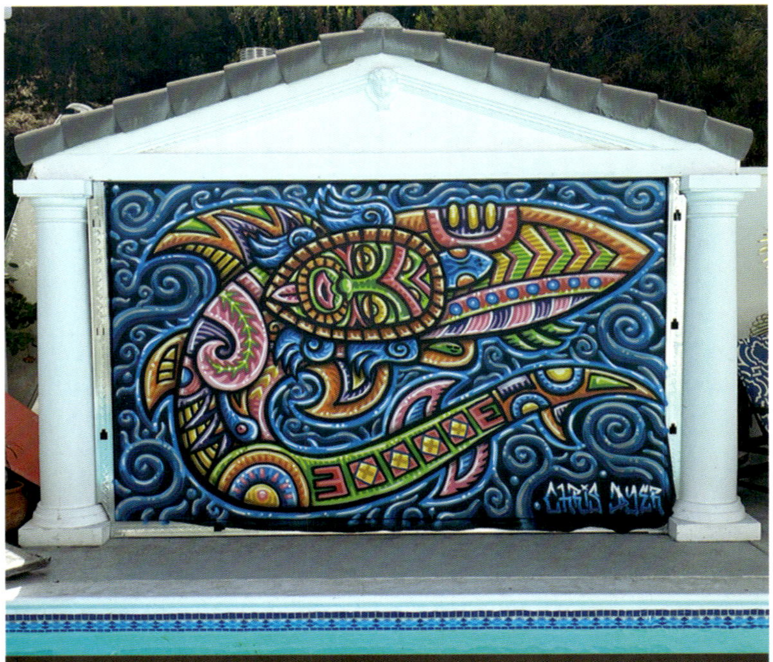
CHRIS DYER
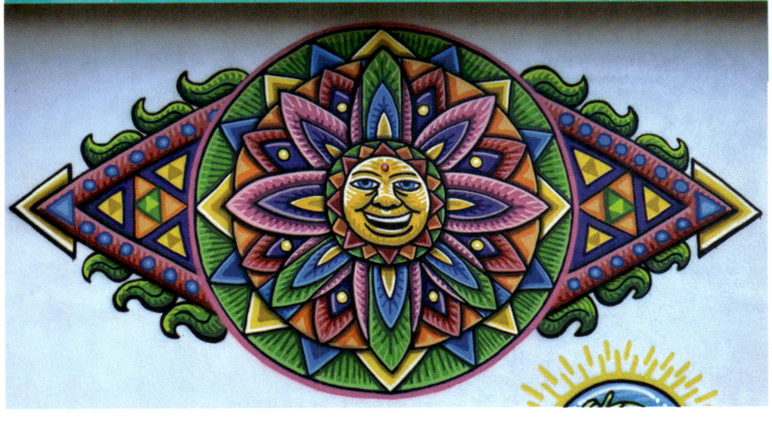
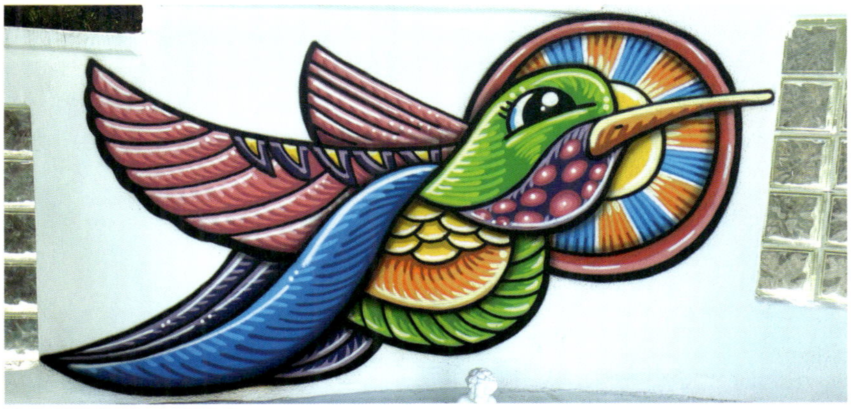
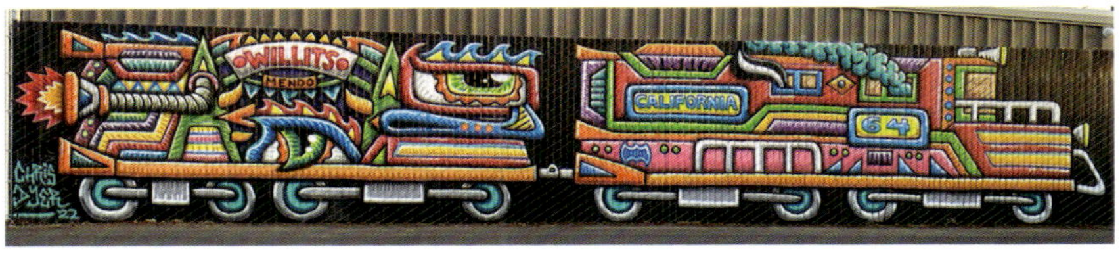
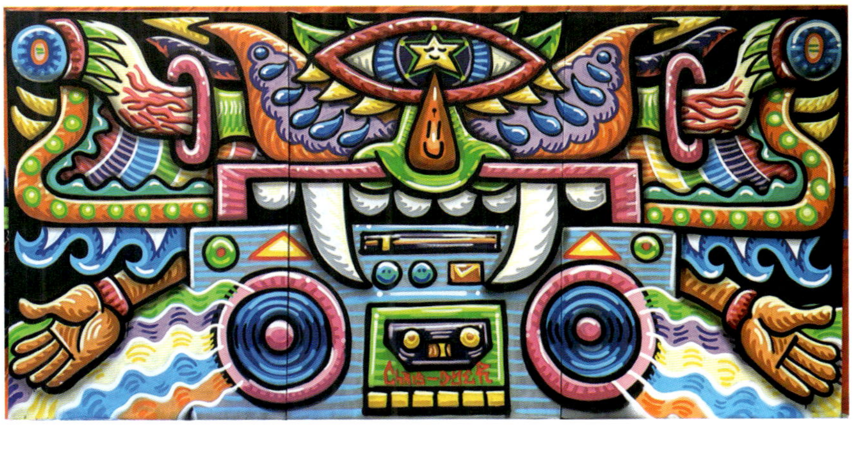

EXODUS

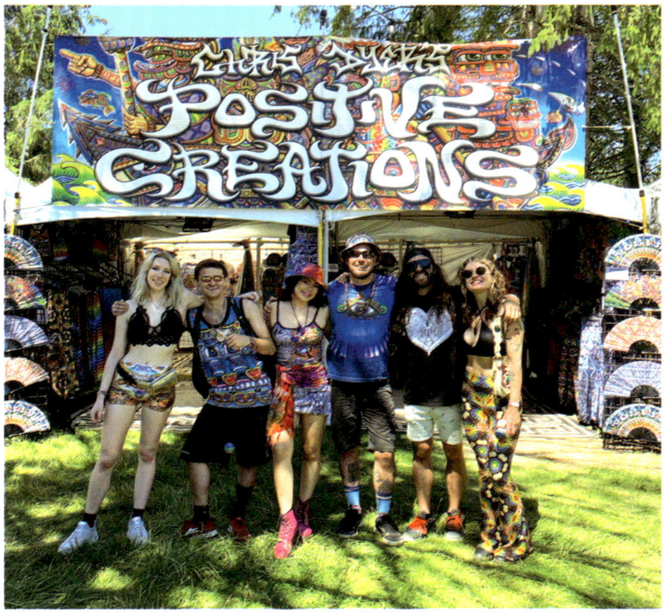

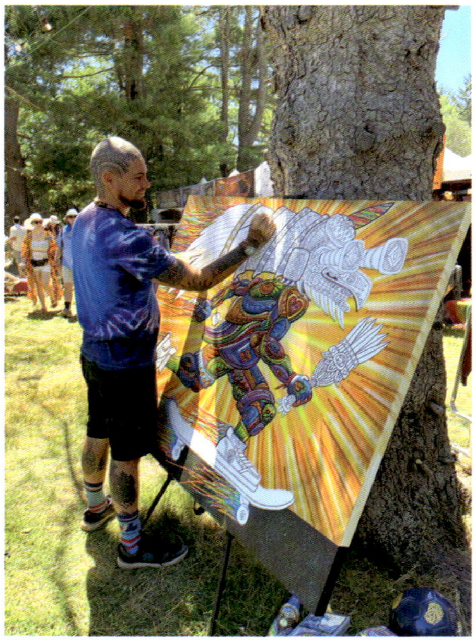

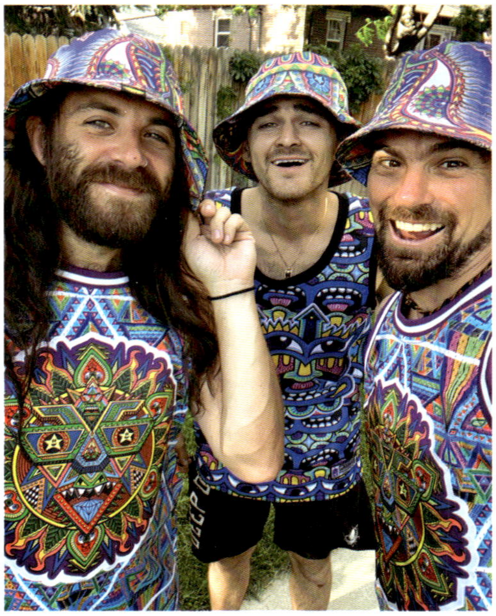

Earlier that summer, my brand manager **Cory** and I decided to invest into having a booth at a huge music festival called **"Electric Forest"**. Paying for the booth space and buying all the merch needed for it was a gamble that could kill the brand if we flopped. So to assure our success, I joined my team in the **Positive Creations** van and crossed the country with them! Once in **Michigan**, my main mission was to Live Paint in front of our booth for four whole days, and connect with hundreds of fans. To our relief and joy our booth sold very well, once again showing me that my community was still down with me and my work!

Even though Denver was a cool city full of opportunities, it wasn't really my vibe. So I finally made up my mind to move to Florida, buy a house and start a new chapter. Unfortunately my relationship with Cory came to an unexpected and abrupt end in those last months. We disagreed on the direction of the company and his attitude about it made me fall out of alignment with our partnership. This was a very sad and disappointing episode for me, but a purge that was meant to happen. I was calling for a clean energy slate and this breakup was part of it. My friends at **Grassroots California** carried the fulfillment of my brand after that, which ended giving me way less work, overhead and complications. Before leaving this Denver I made sure to drop some fun final murals, participated in a Psychedelic Panel Discussion and threw a Farewell BBQ Art Jam for my fans.

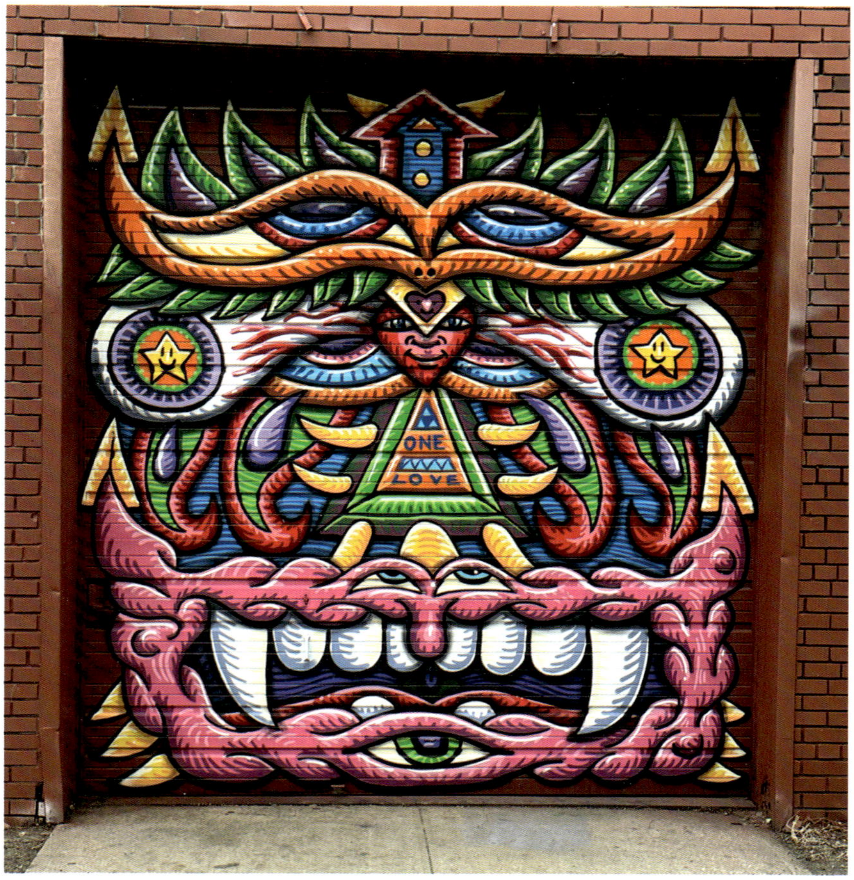

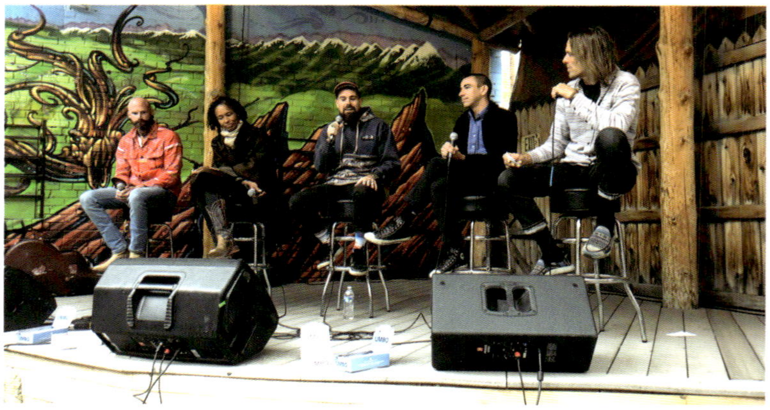

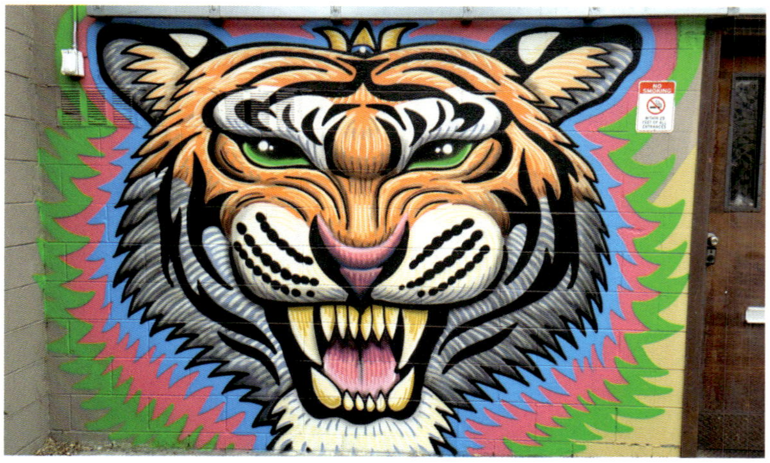

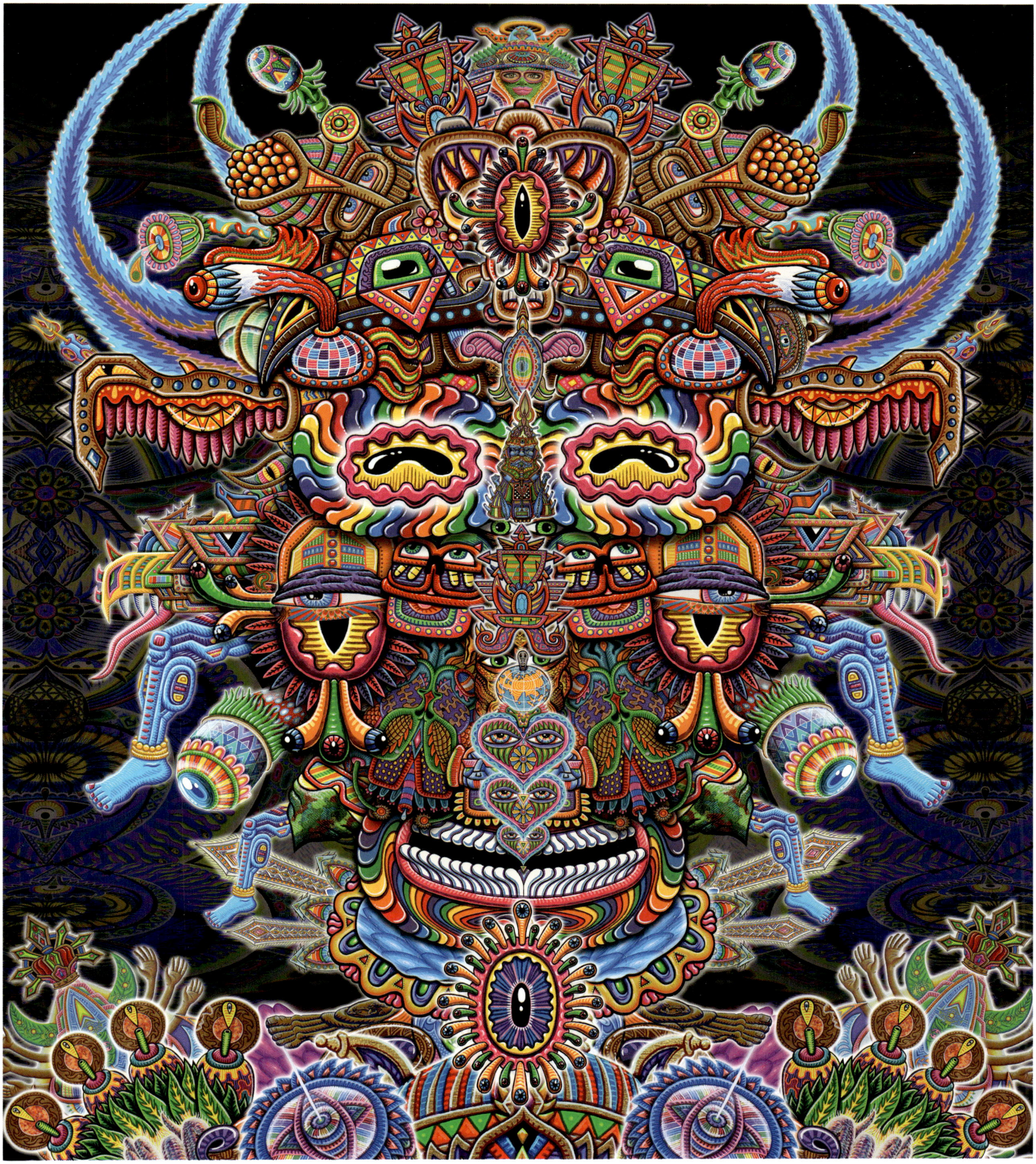

"Bullish" NFT , 2022

"Bullish" is a crypto term used to describe a period of economic optimism. As the world was continuously facing economic struggles, I called in this creature, in the shape of a digital collage, as a prayer for better times of abundance and blessings! Though we originally offered this as Limited Edition Prints, we also had **Phlerp** animate it so we could give it away as an NFT for holders of the **Galaktic Gang**. Chicago HipHop artist **Illuminati Congo** even made a whole song about our community to add vibration to this offering!

FLORIDA FRESH START

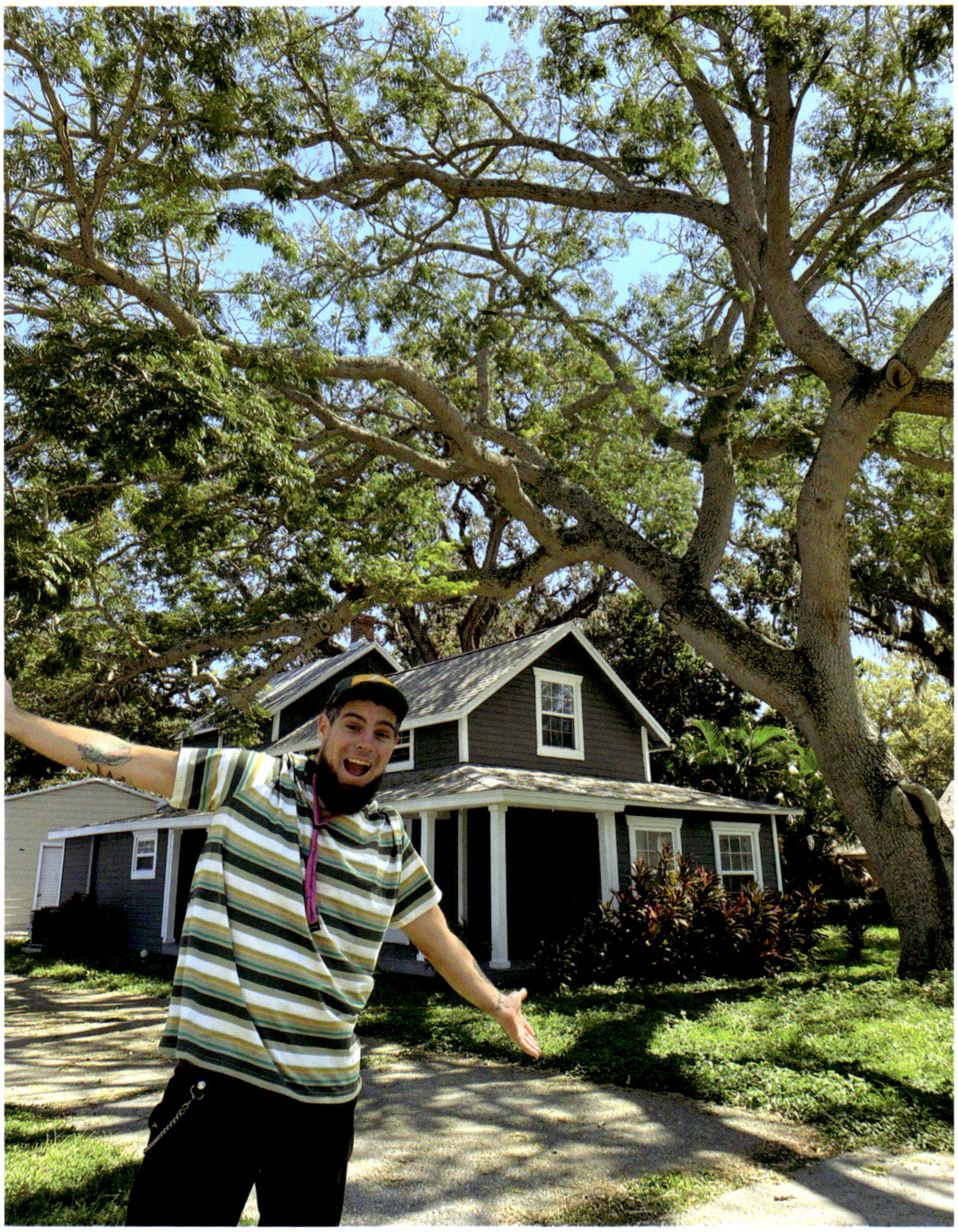

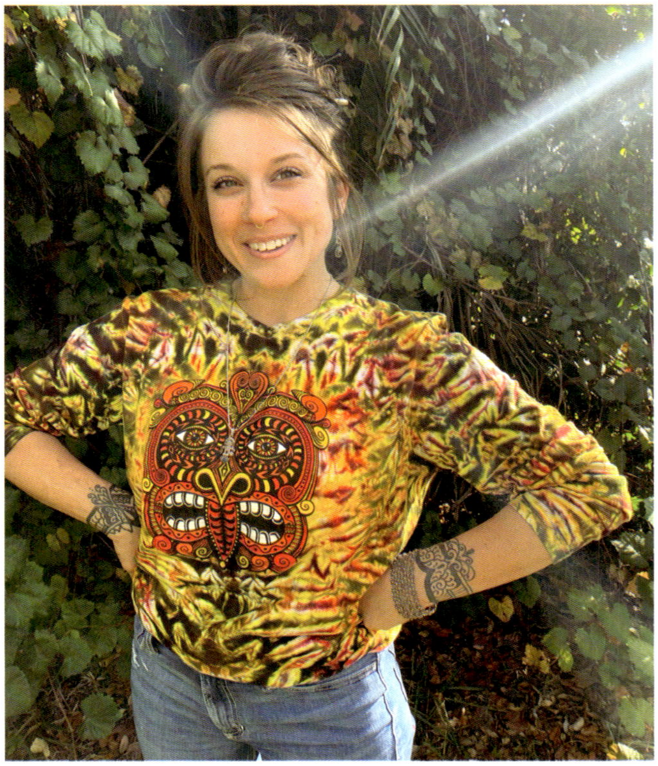

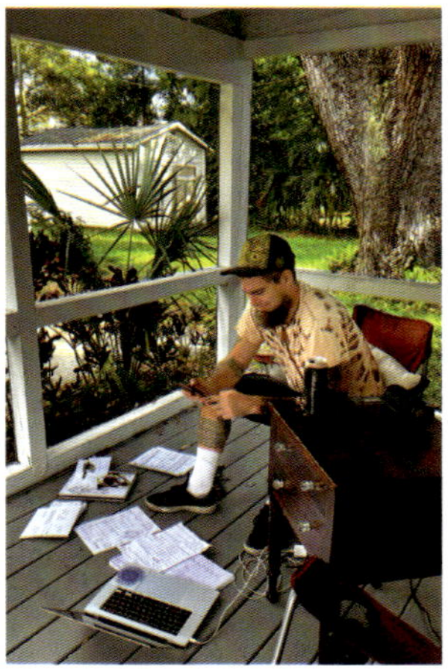

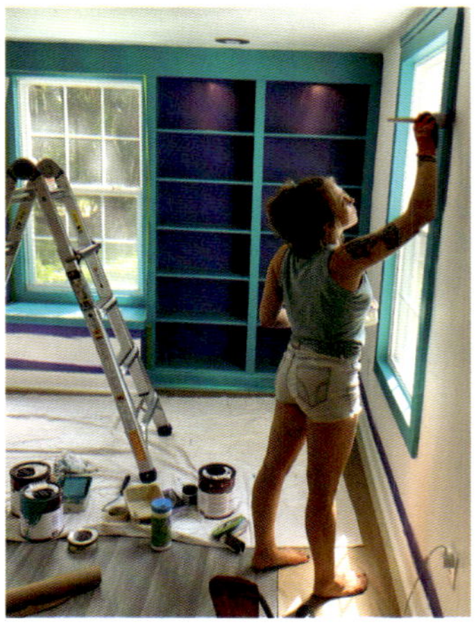

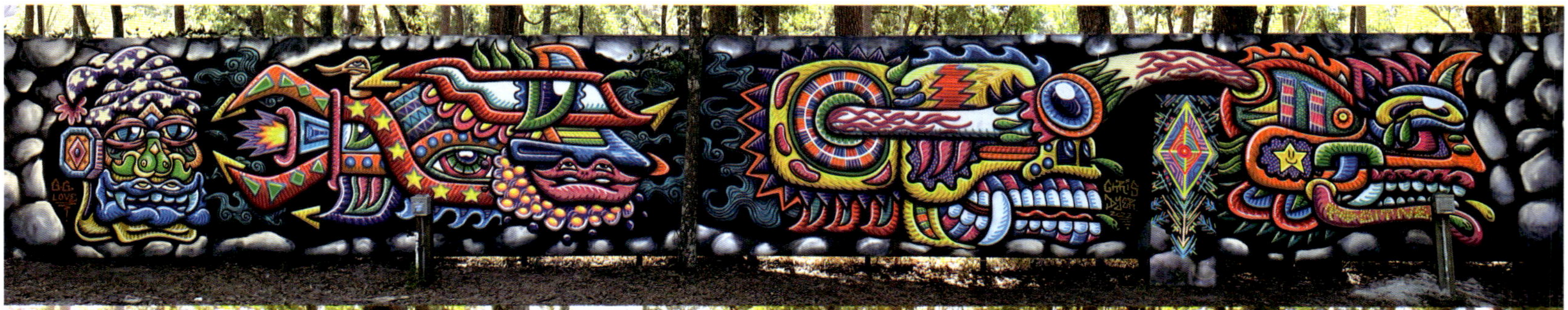

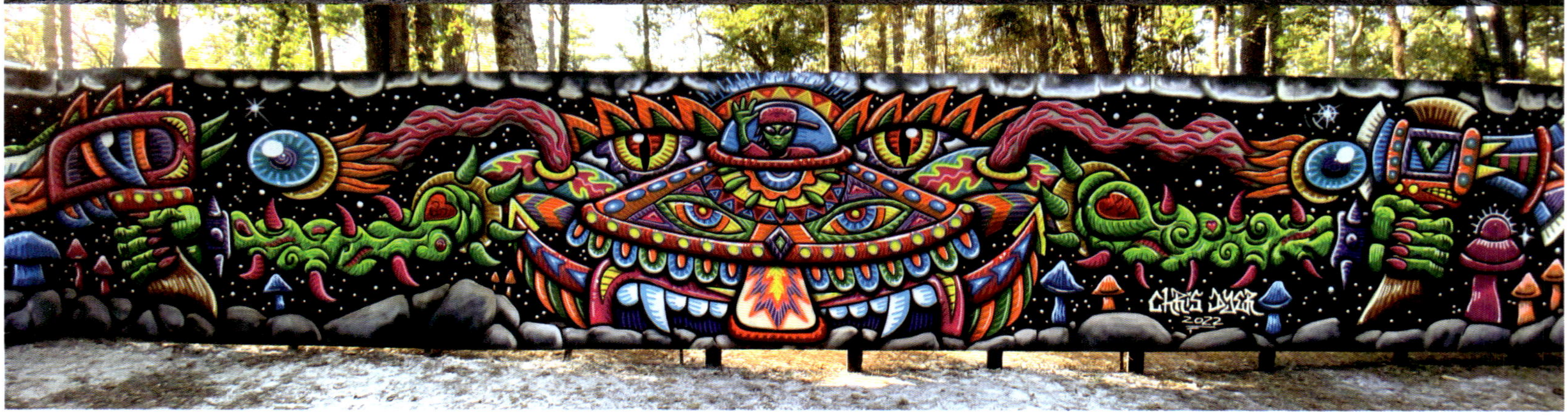

Murals for **Hullaween Music Festival** and **Mural Maze**, 2022

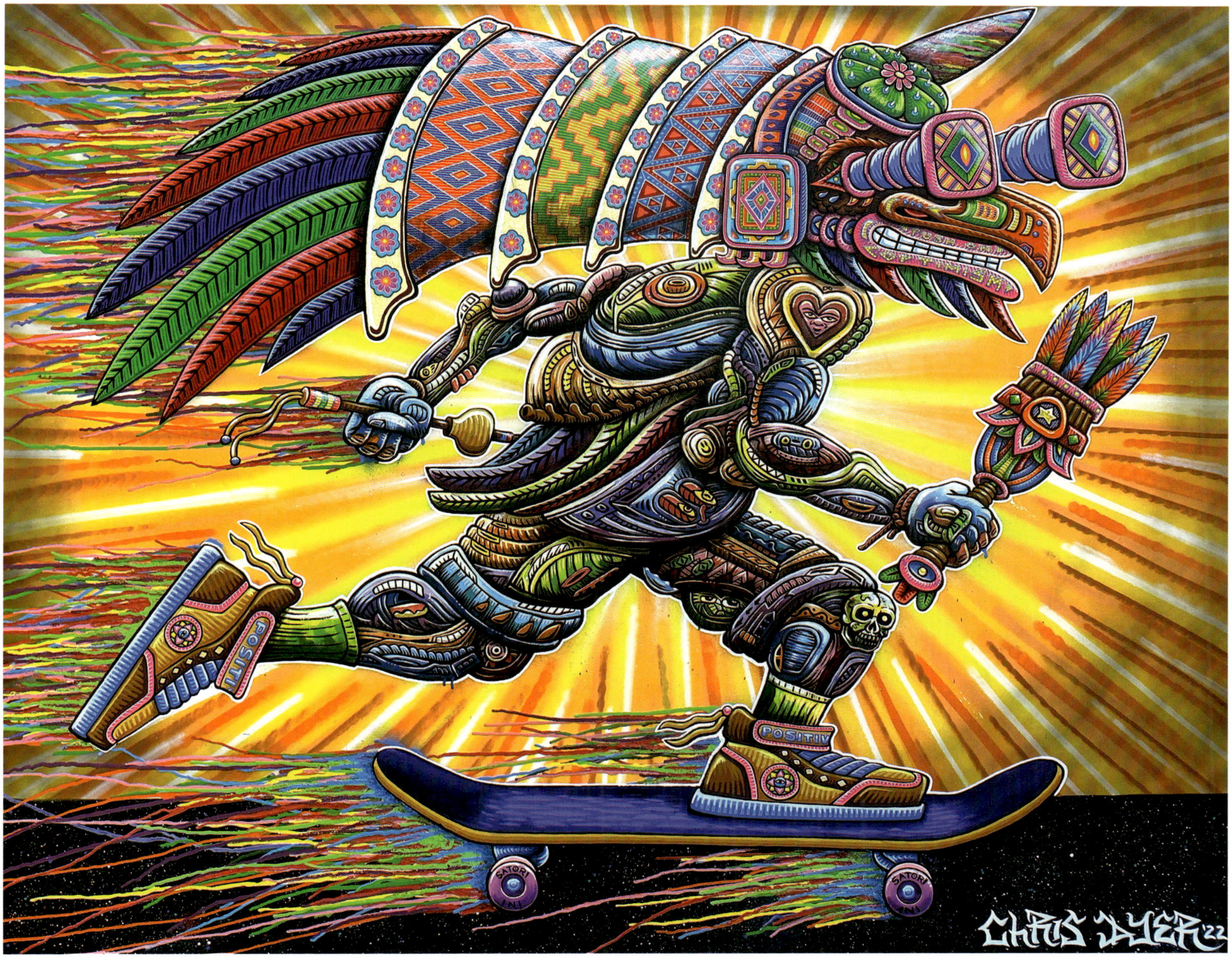

“Keep Pushing Forward” Acrylics and spray paint on canvas, 2022

After a few of years of life disillusions, I was due for a period of Pure Blessings! I chose **Saint Petersburg, Florida** to be my new home for many reasons, mostly the non-stop sunny weather, beautiful beaches, chill attitude and the healthy (yet unpretentious) art scene. Having a **Salvador Dali Museum** in town was also a sign that this place would be open to a trippy artist like myself!

I found my home on the first day of house-searching with my realtor, my Peruvian cousin Paulito. So I bought this cute 1910 house, framed in between two giant trees, close to the hippie bay neighborhood of **Gulfport**. My new girlfriend **Paulina** had also just closed a big episode of her own life in Detroit, so she moved down to live with me. This was the beging of a beautiful chapter of Love and Creation together! Yay!

As soon as the house was officially mine I had movers bring my possessions from Denver and the bigger load from Montreal. Months of decorating followed that.

The amount of office work I had those days setting up my new life was a bit overwhelming, but Paulina had my back covered. She painted the inside of the house and also helped renovate a few things to get it just right. It was a dream come true to own my first house and turn it into the best **“Positive Portal”** ever! The place had a big yard with lots of permaculture potential, a guest apartment in the back and a giant garage that I will eventually transform into a big art studio.

The local art scene was so welcoming on my arrival and I was instantly invited to be part of the magic happening here. As a way to Big Up the whole Florida community, I finally accepted to paint a mural for **Hullaween Music Festival** in **Suwanee**. It was a big beautiful piece that got extra trippy at night with projection mapping! The community was stoked and I was so Grateful!

BLESSED LANDING

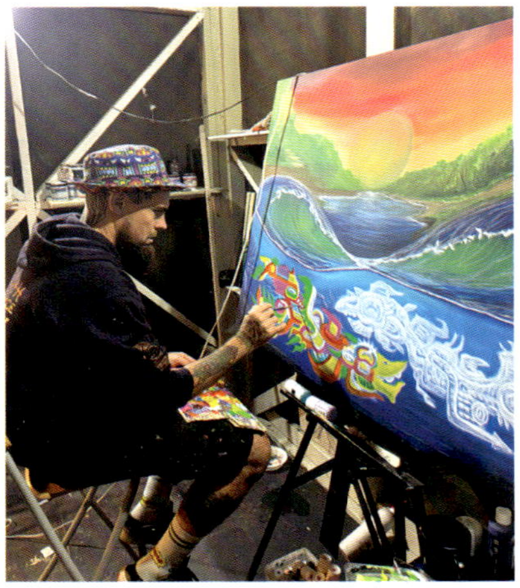
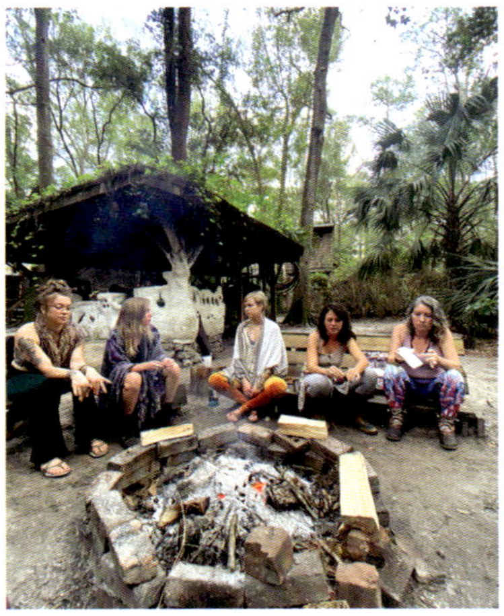
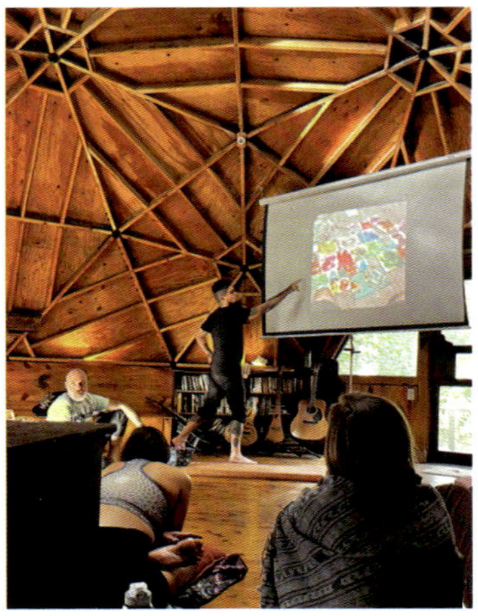
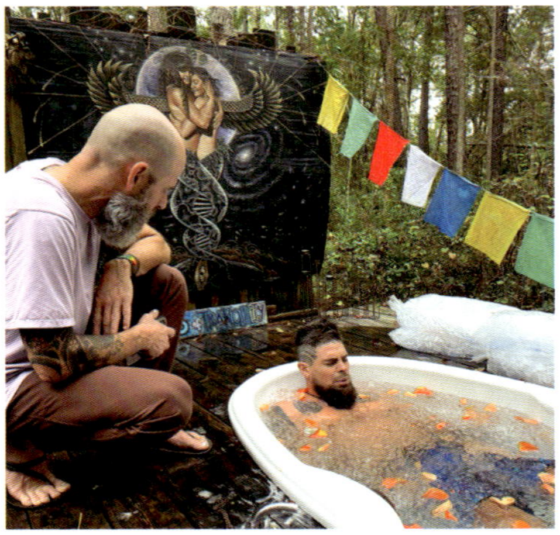

Though I just wanted to stay home and work on building that up, I decided to come in hot with a couple of potent local event offerings! One of them was **"Activate"**, which was my first Art Workshop since the letdown of my former shaman. False rumors still circulated a little bit about what had happened at my last Peruvian retreat, so my Badass artist friend **Ania Amador** backed up my teaching comeback by organizing this through her company **"Art in Session"**. It was a beautiful four day event at "Hostel in the Forest" in **Georgia**, where I got to teach art classes every day alongside my artist friends **Ania**, **Veronica Rose** and **Dome Moon**. On the spiritual healing side of things, instead of working with Plant Medicines, we did Yoga, Breath-work and Ice-baths, which were very powerful! This event was super healing for me and I was so grateful to go back to teaching, which is something I had missed a lot!

By the beginning of December 2022, **Basel** time was happening again in **Miami**. Since now I was only a few hours away, I decided to throw a big **Galaktic Gang** bash, to celebrate our first Anniversary! So I rented my friend Ray Orraca's **"Moksha Gallery"** and put together a solo exhibition of my art, along a group exhibition of different GG painters. Many of them also came to live paint for the Grand Opening. For that event, I played a vinyl DJ set as my alter-ego **"Selector El Flyer"** and also had some friends perform like **Illuminati Congo**! So many rad people joined us that night to add vibration, creativity and magic! I was so stoked and grateful!

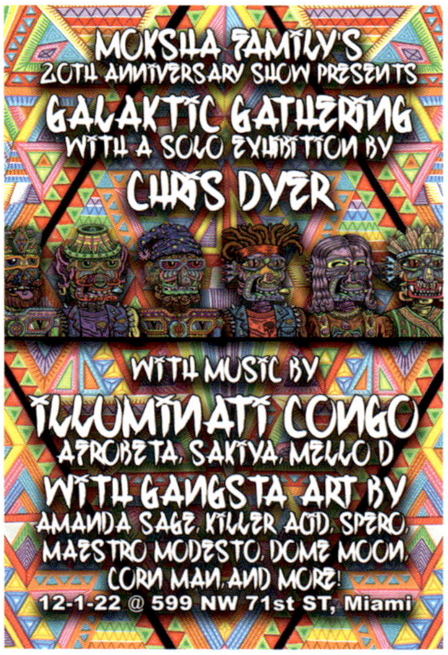

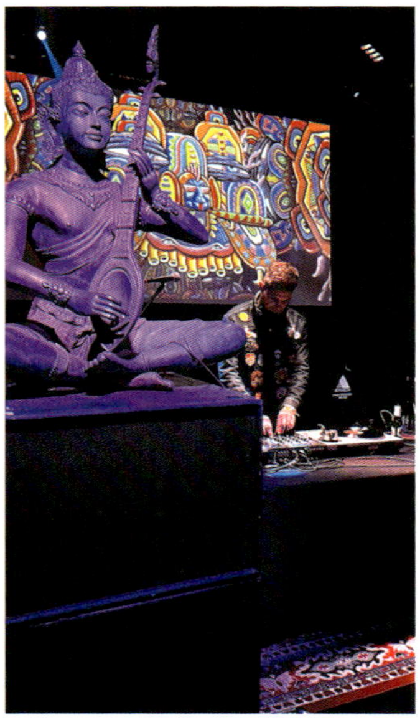
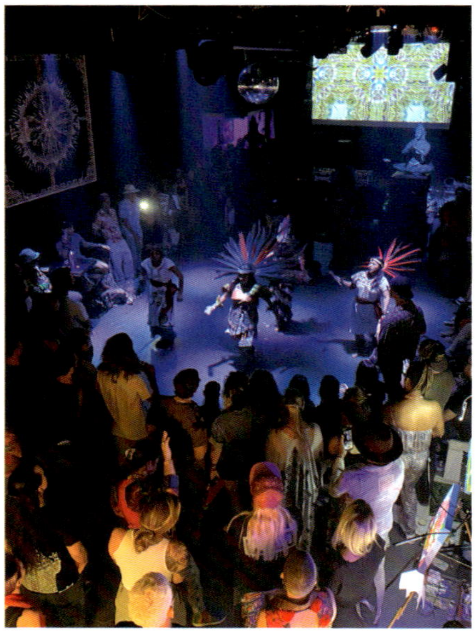
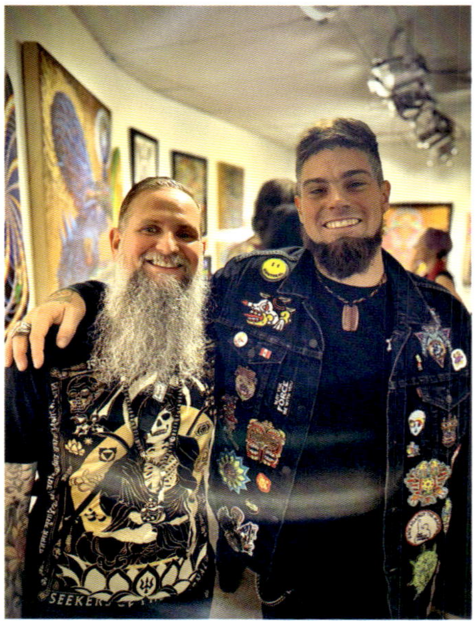

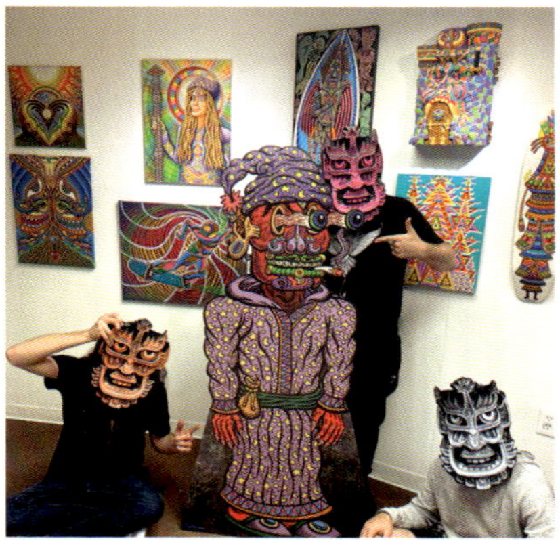
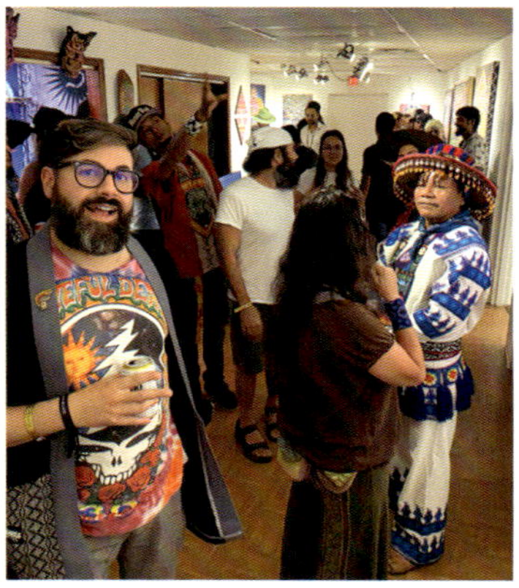
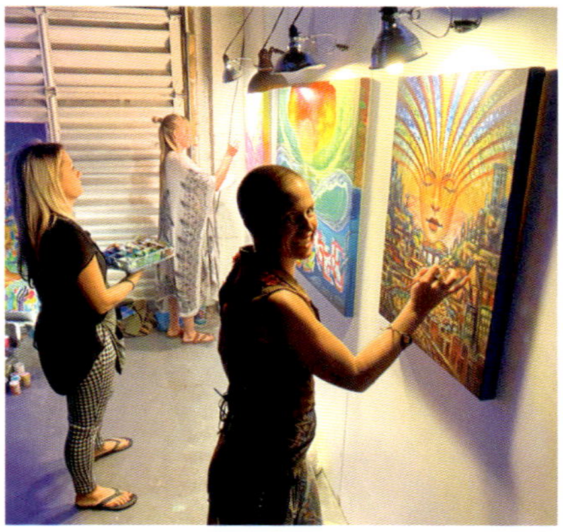
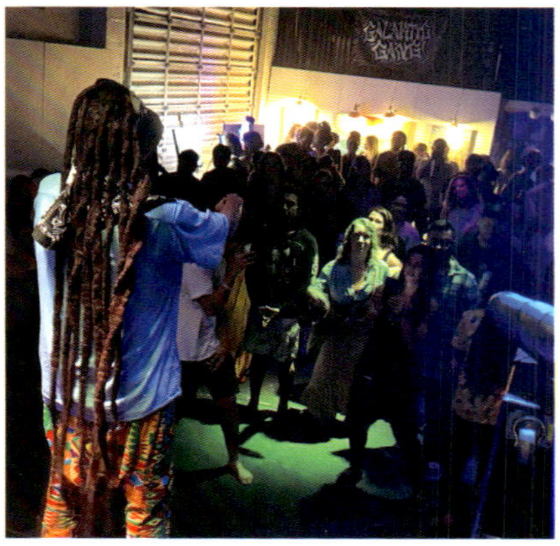

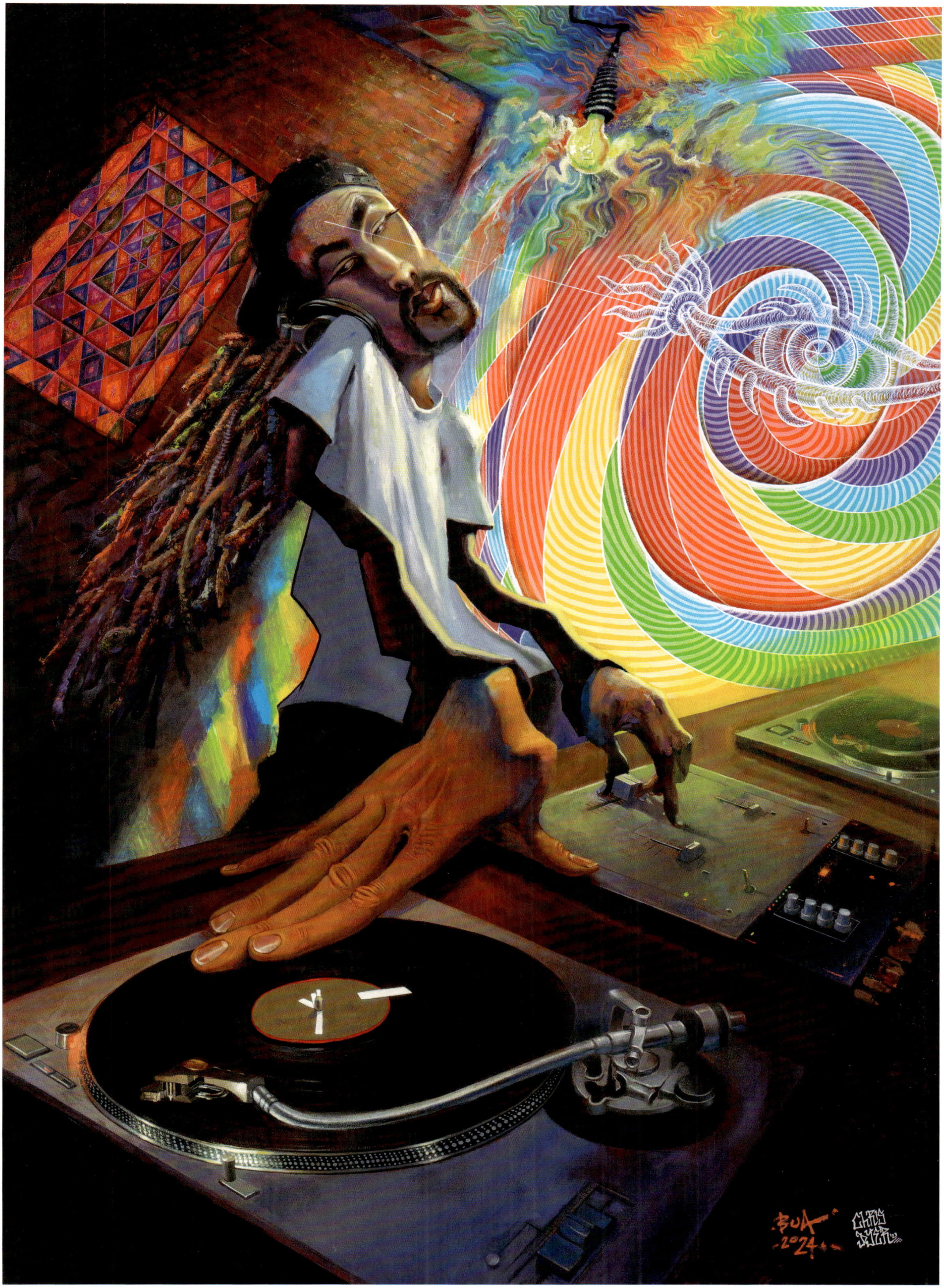

"The DJ" Collaboration with **Justin Bua**, Acrylics on canvas print, 2022

POSITIVE PORTAL 3

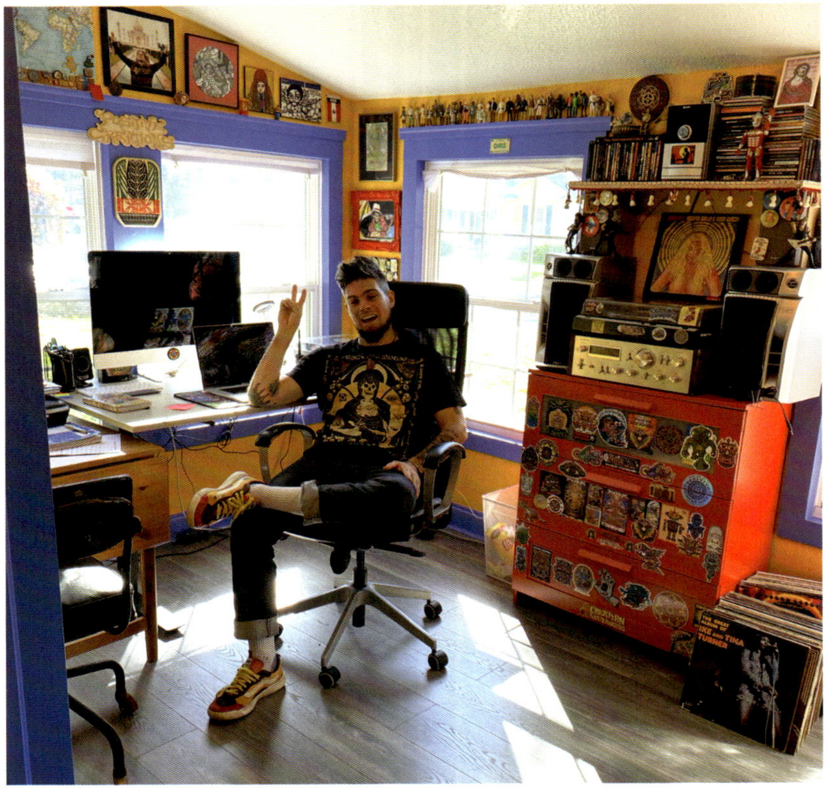

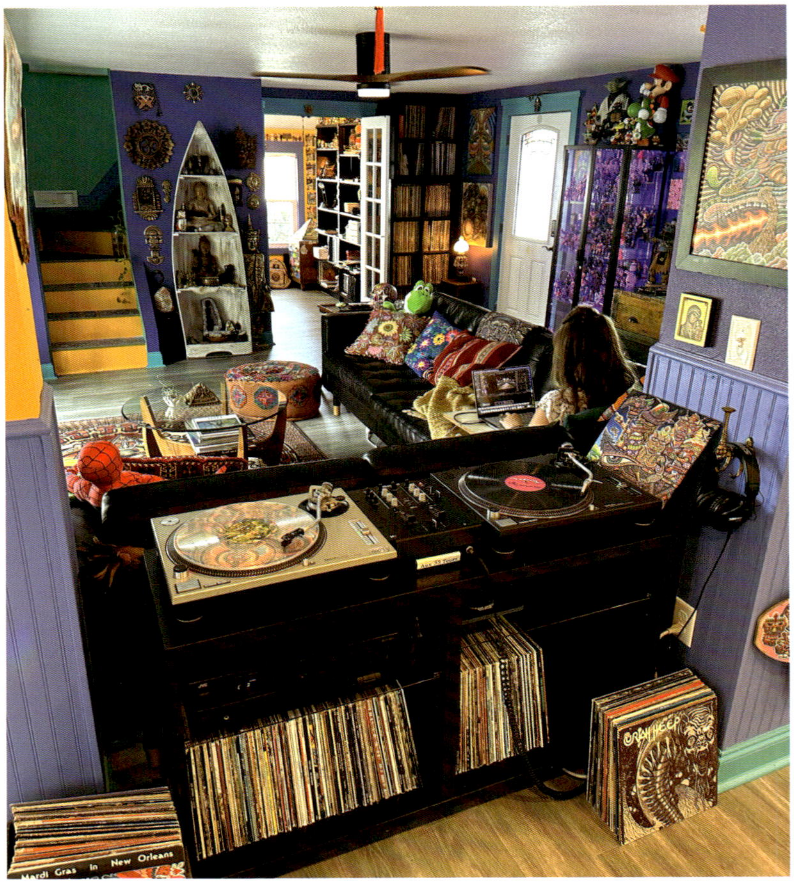

For me a home is my most crucial space for creation and recharging my energy. It is also one of my biggest art pieces, like a collage of my favorite cultural relics collected and created. I started up a few homes in the last decade, but between my divorce, the lockdowns abroad and my political exile, they didn't last so long. This new Florida house is a crystallization of the **"Positive Portal"** and one I hope I can enjoy more permanently! By now I have already successfully painted and decorated the inside of the house to a pretty satisfying level. I still have lots of permaculture work to shape up the yard and also ambitious plans for a proper art studio in the back structure. One step at a time. A bigger dream for the future is to eventually offer a Museum of my art, my friends' work and my cultural collections. Maybe this will be the place for that later project of my life?

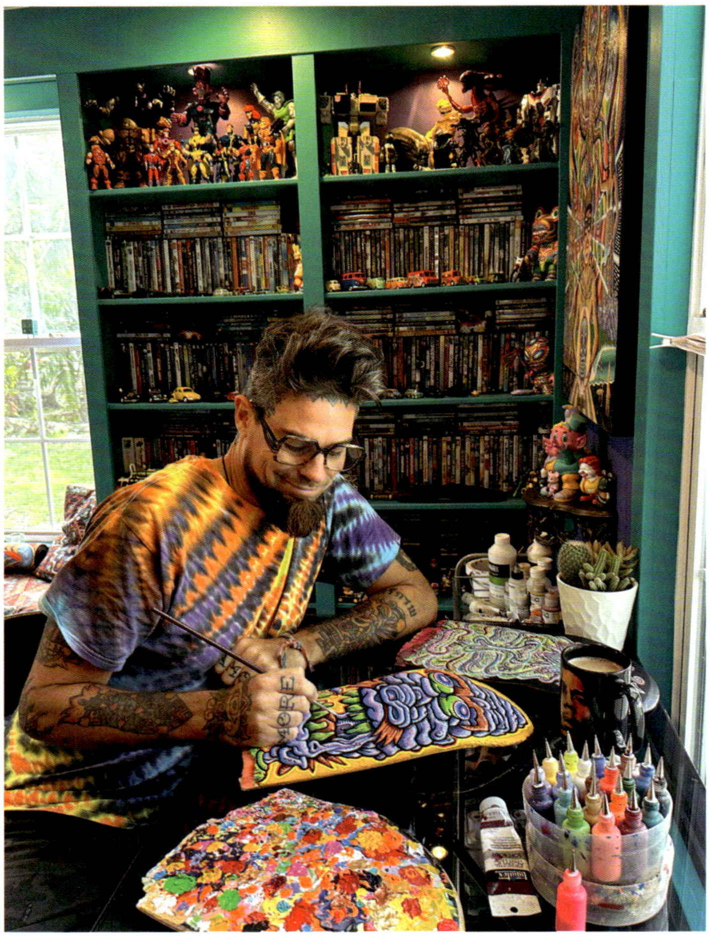

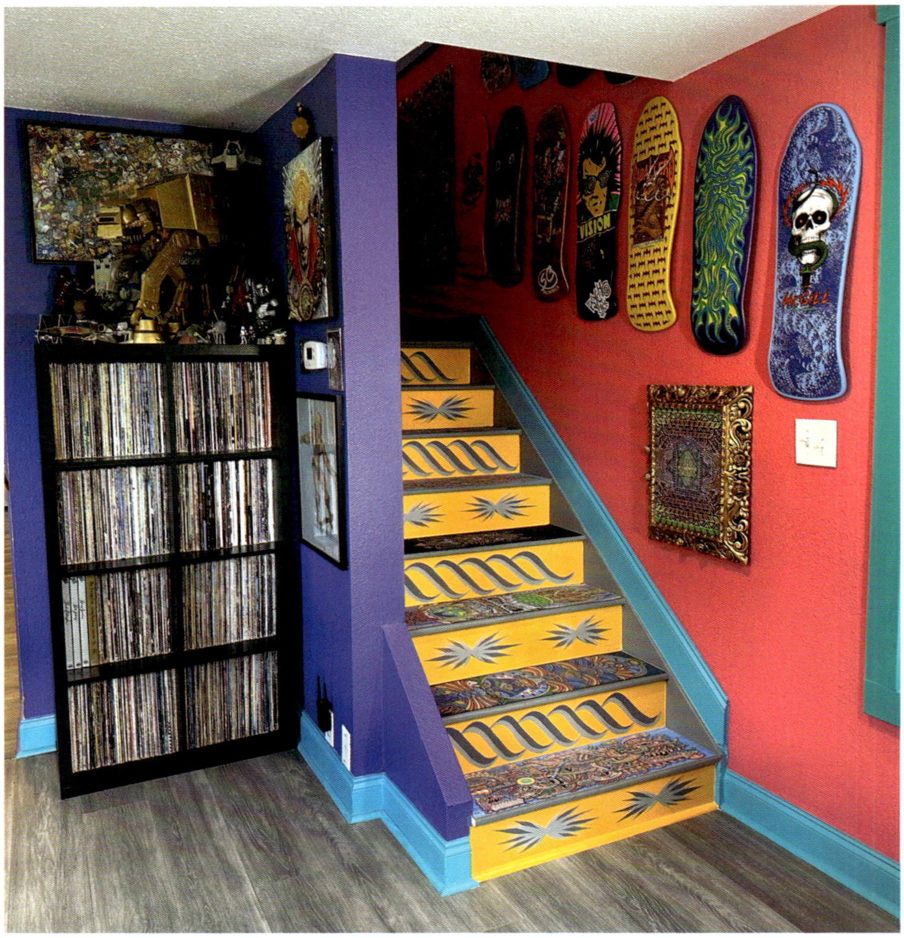

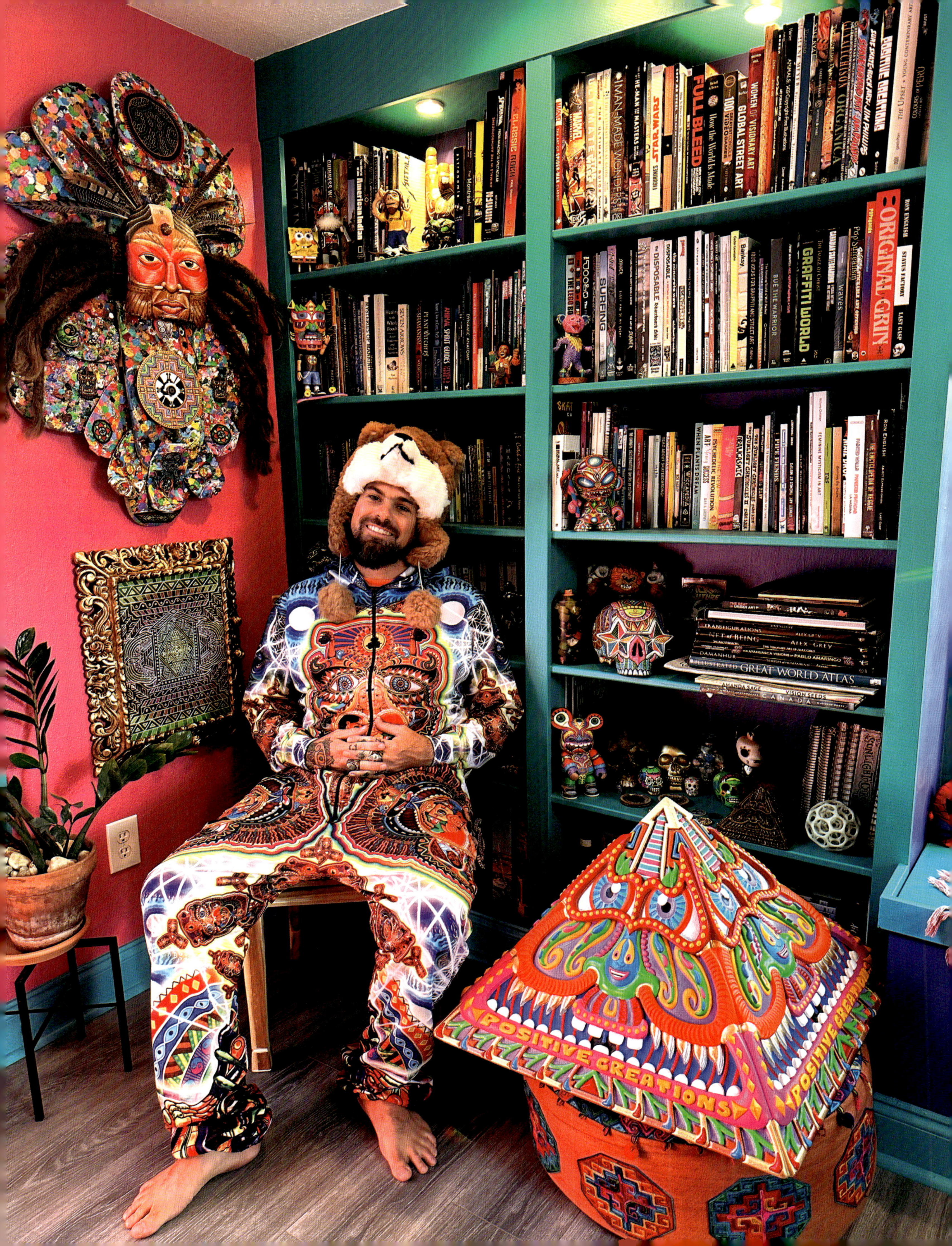
POSITIVE CREATIONS
POSITIVE CREATIONS
FULL BLEED
STAR WARS
GLOBAL STREET ART
WOMEN OF VISIONARY ART
CLASSIC ROCK
GRAFFITI WORLD
ORIGINAL GRIN
Banksy
SURFING
DISPOSABLE
TRANSFIGURATIONS
NET OF BEING
ALEX GREY
ILLUSTRATED GREAT WORLD ATLAS
AMANDA SAGE
VISION SEEDS

MURAL TOUR 2023

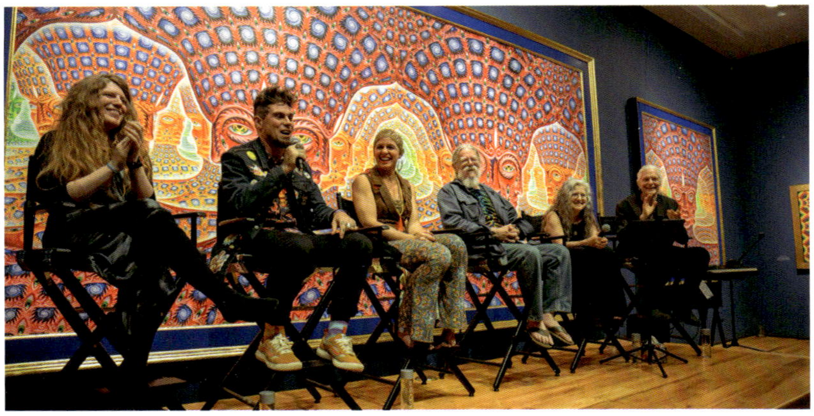

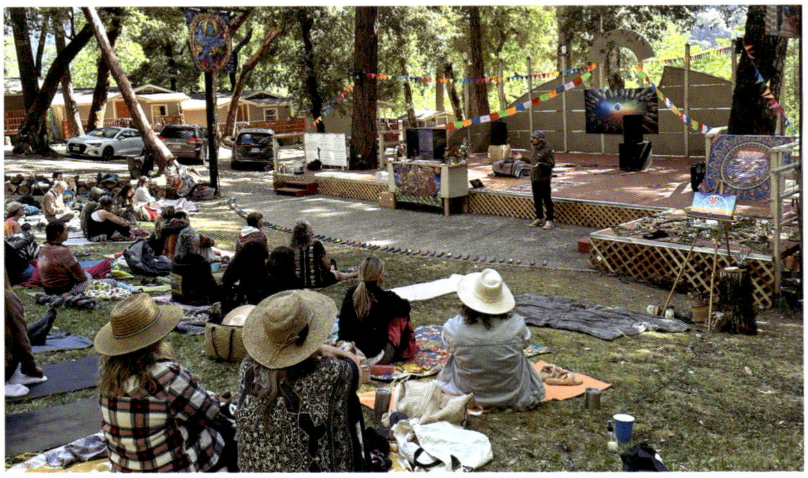

Spring arrived again and it was time to hit the road and spread the visual medicine all over the States! This tour was a lot more pleasant because I had sweet Paulina by my side to support me in so many ways! So we hopped around the country for some months, starting with **New York**. After years in it's making, it was crucial I attended the Grand Opening of **"Entheon"**, the Visionary Art Museum that my artist friends Alex and Allyson Grey finally completed! I was super stoked to have one of my paintings exhibited there and I also participated in the inaugural Artist Panel Discussion along the Greys, Mark Henson and Amanda Sage. My next stop was in **Detroit**, to paint a huge mural for the **Michigan Glass Project**, which is a fun charity event in benefit to art education for kids. A whole month in **California** followed, starting with a Retreat that my good friend **Judea Star** had organized along her psychic partner **Patty Davis**. Though the event revolved around spiritual and healing practices, I did get a whole afternoon to guide the 100 participants through some painting expressions! During that tour I also got to paint murals in **Colorado**, **Asheville**, **Ohio** and **Oregon**. I am pretty proud of the work I did during this time.

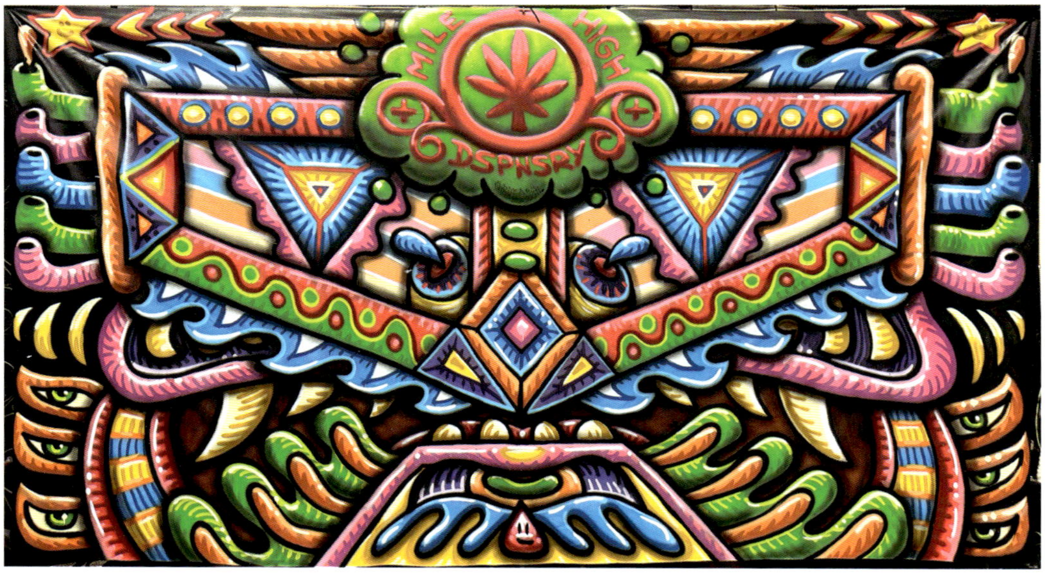

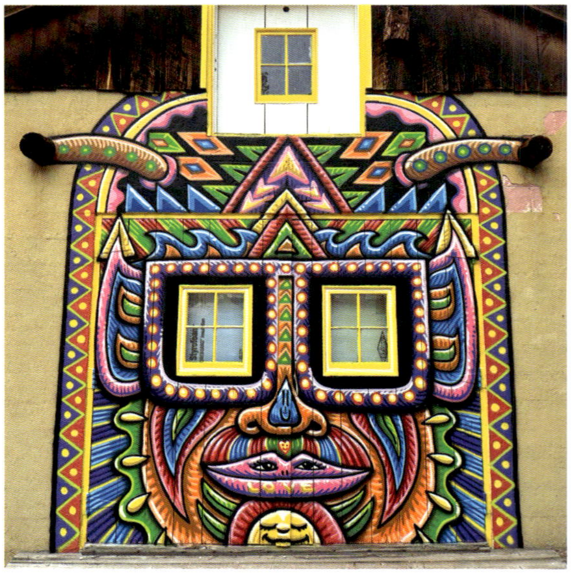

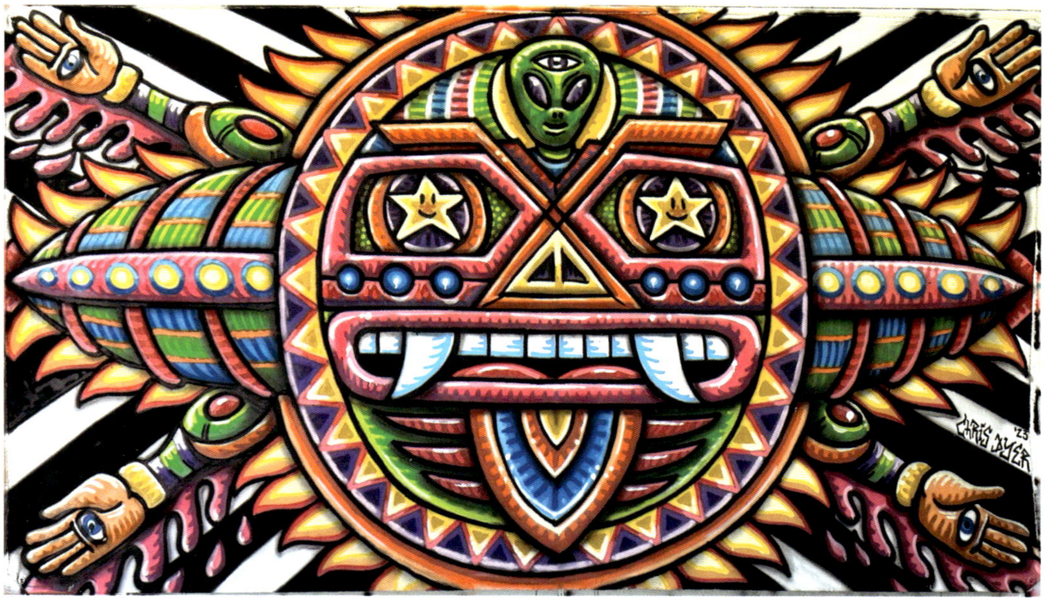

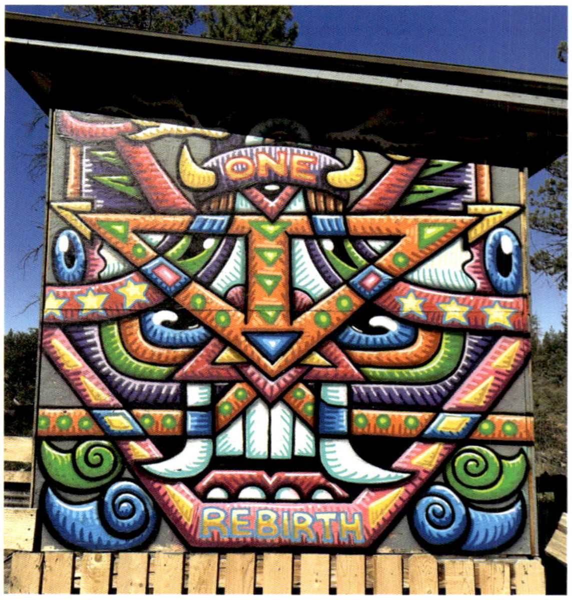

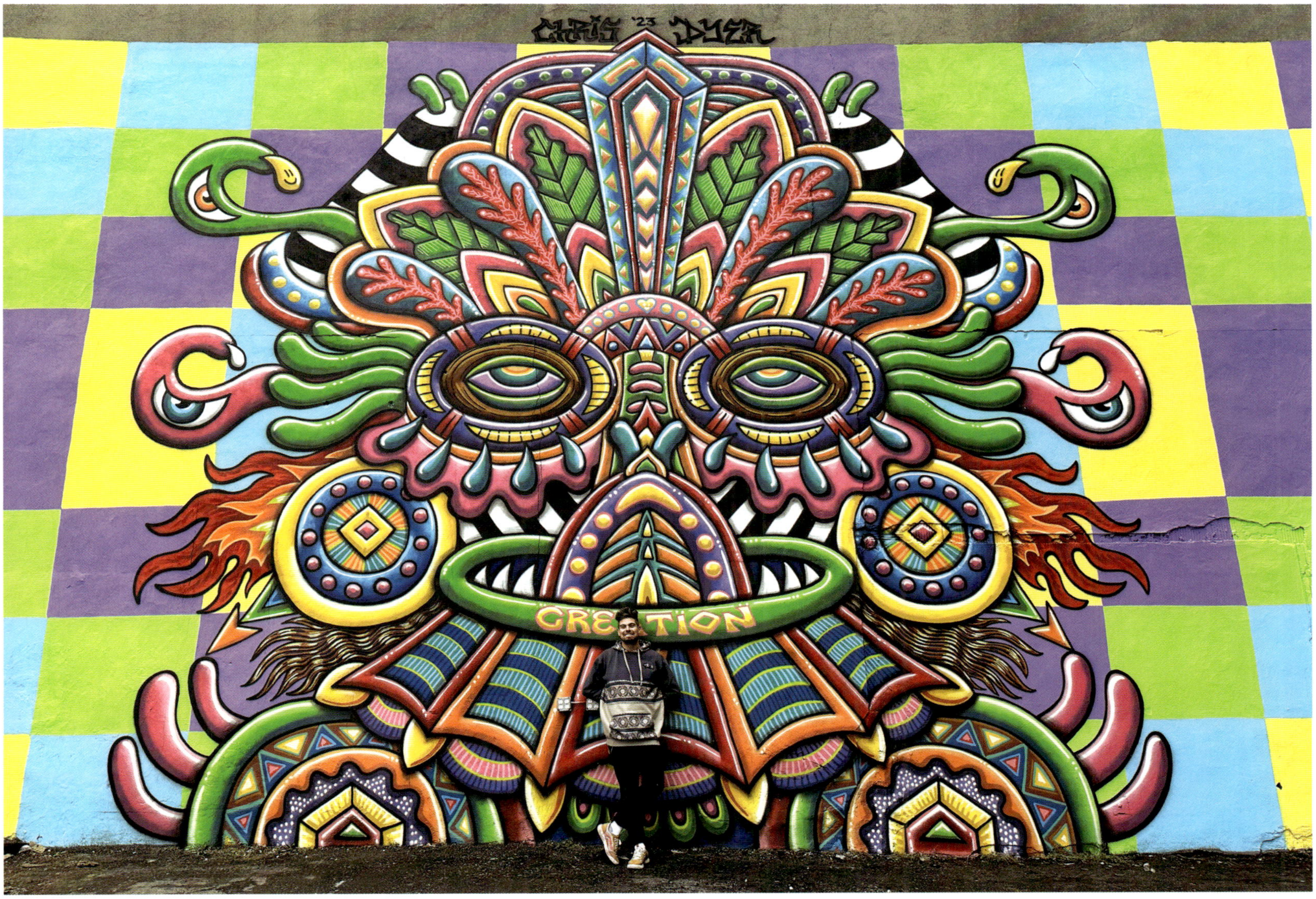
CREATION

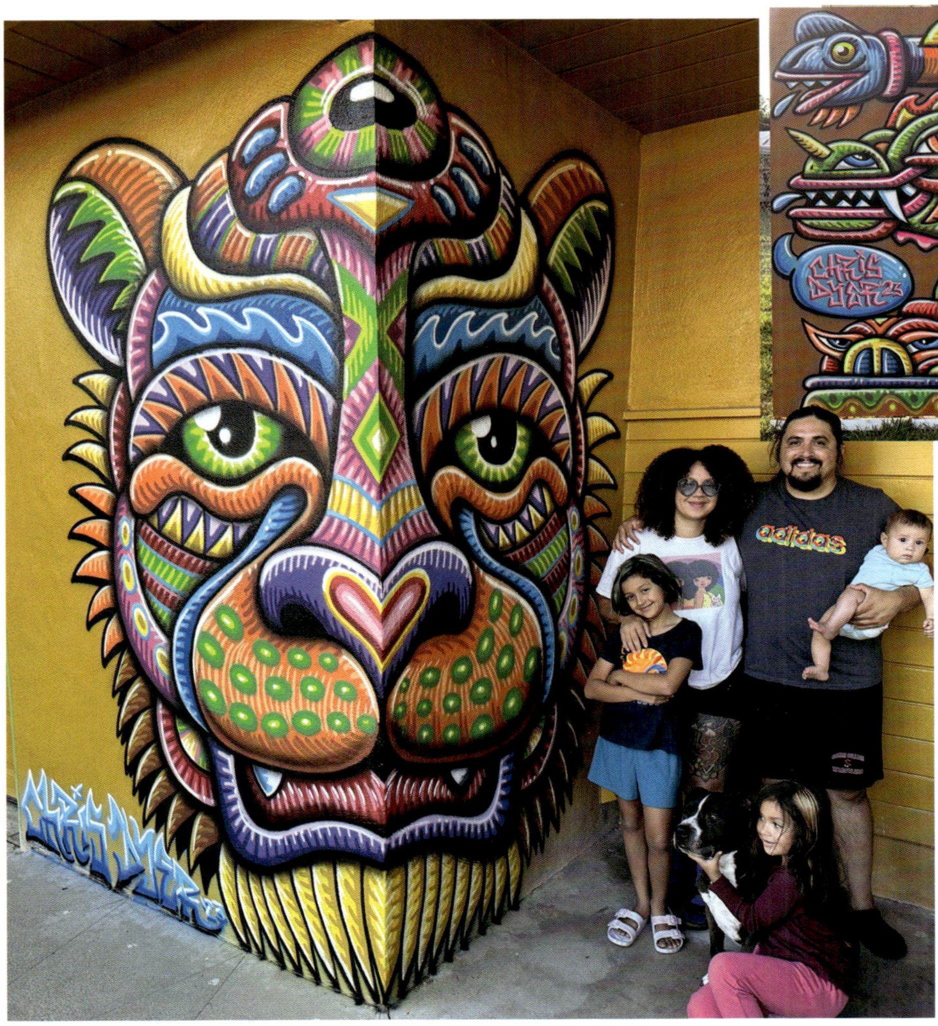
adidas

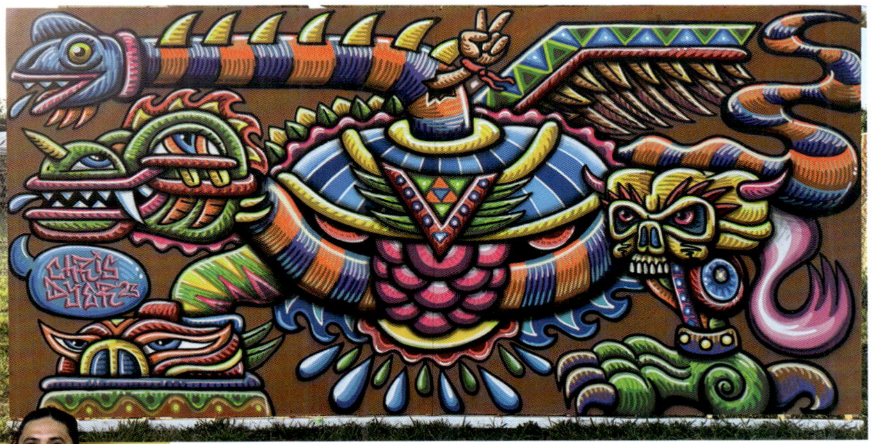

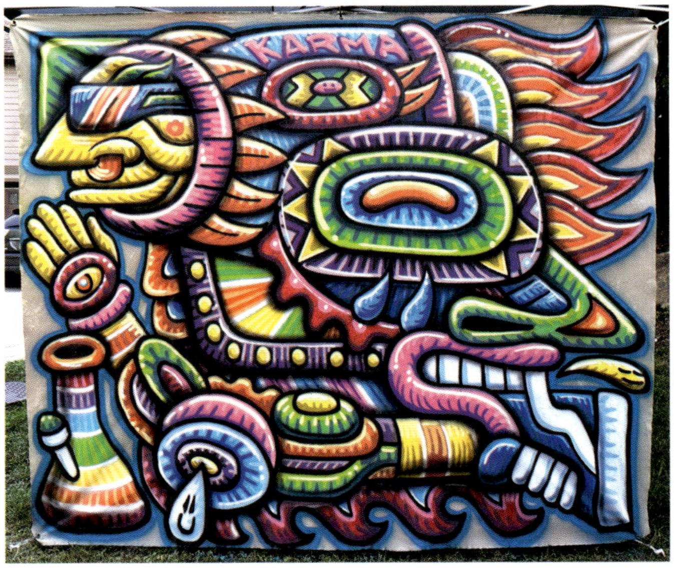
KARMA

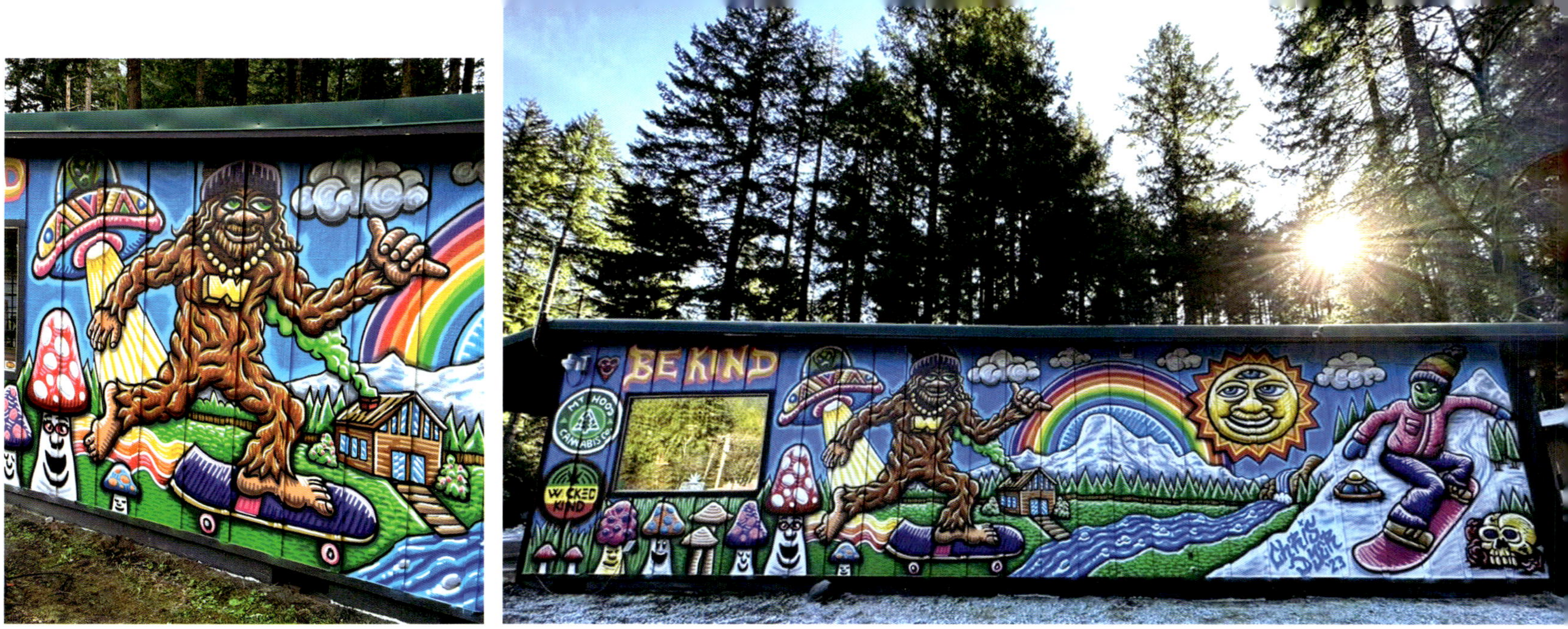

Mural for **“Mount Hood Cannabis”**, Oregon, 2023

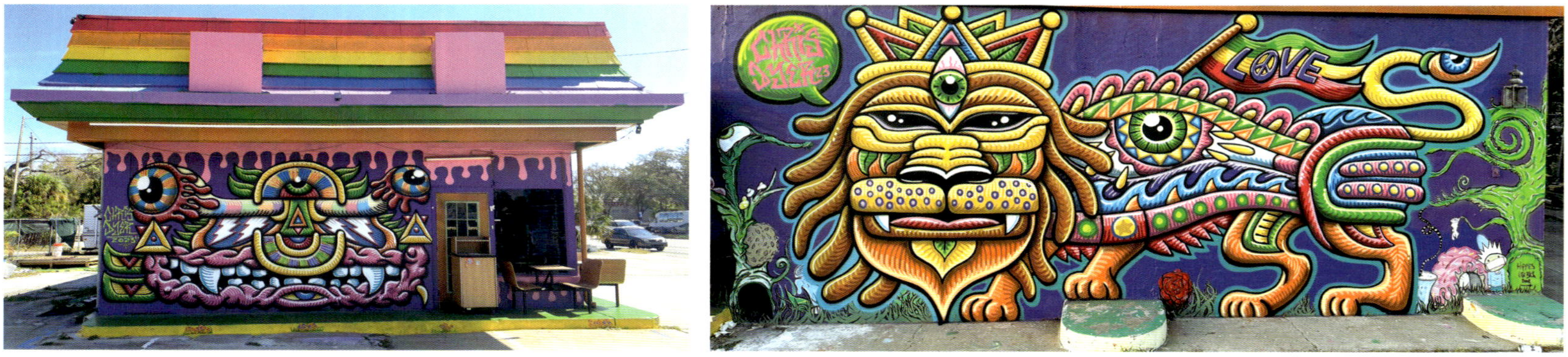

Murals for **“Zaza Smoke Shop”** in my neighborhood of Saint Petersburg, Florida, 2023

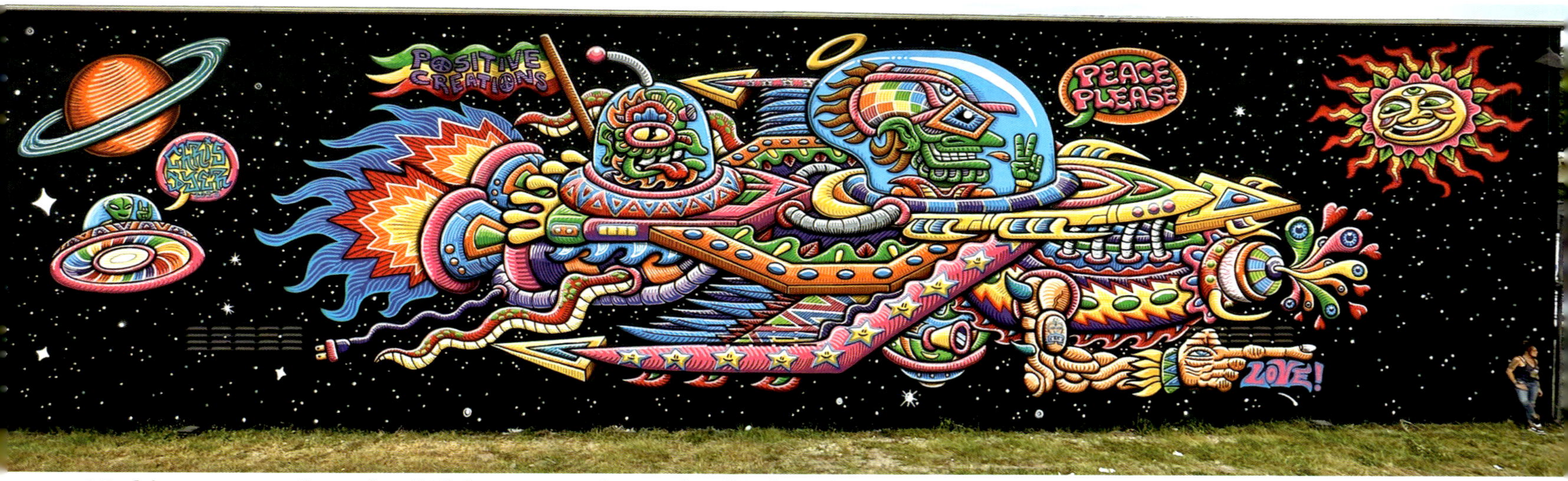

My biggest mural yet for **“Shine Mural Festival”** also close to my place in Saint Petersburg, Florida, 2023

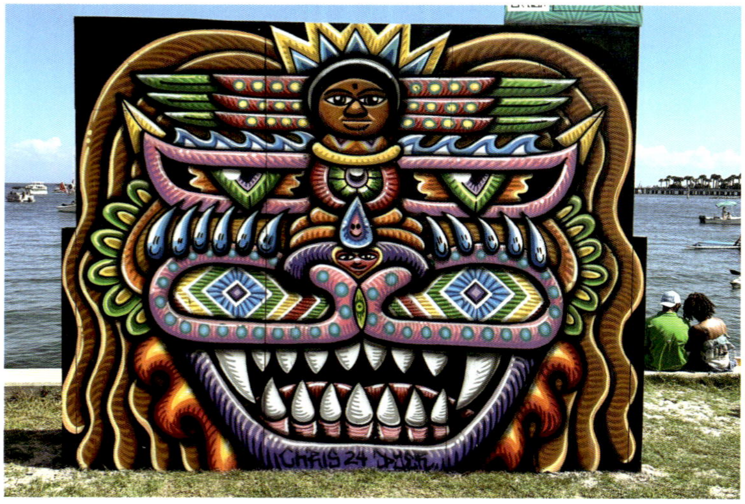

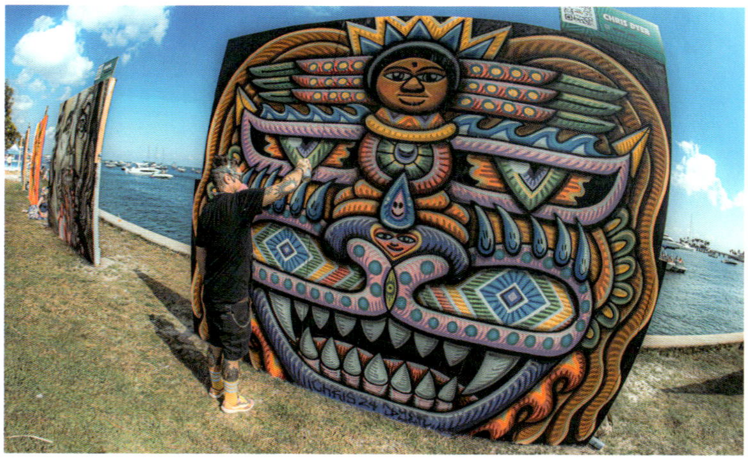

For **“Reggae Rise Up Festival”** Saint Pete, 2024

CDCF PODCAST

In the 2020 lockdown days I got interviewed so many times that I felt it was time I did a Podcast of my own. I am friends with so many positive creative magicians that highlighting them would be a resonant offering, especially in a world increasingly flooded with negative media and distorted narratives. So I started doing interviews in October of that year. People still felt nervous to have someone show up in person at their place. But doing these interviews IRL at their creative environments was a crucial part of the show's concept. So I started with my many Montreal artist friends and then my Peruvian ones, in the next Lockdown. After that the show would just happen wherever I would be traveling, kinda bringing back the vibes of the **"Artventures"** Travel Show I used to do back in the day. Though I worked with a couple of my usual editors for the first 60 episodes, I would say that the quality of the project really kicked in once my lady Paulina took over the production role, both filming and editing the conversations. As a collector, I get a thrill scoring these deep spiritual and artistic conversations with top-shelf souls! I am so honored and stoked to offer this nutritive media content to those hungry for inspiration!

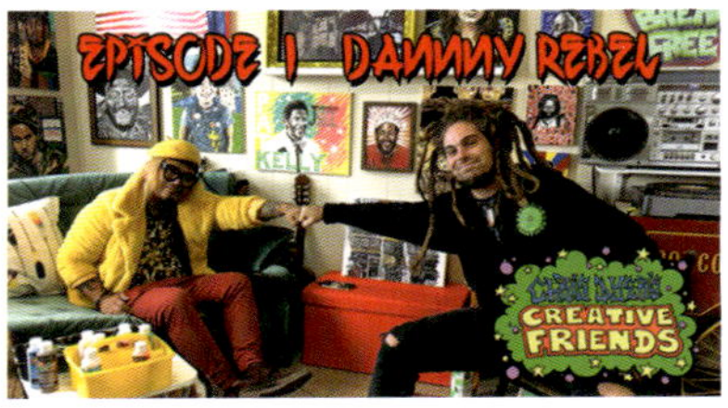

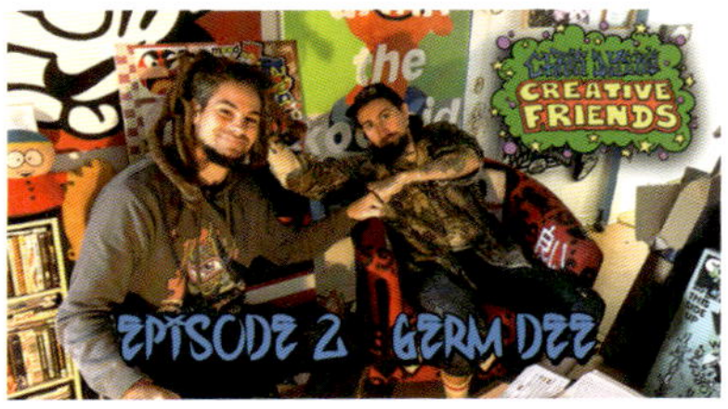

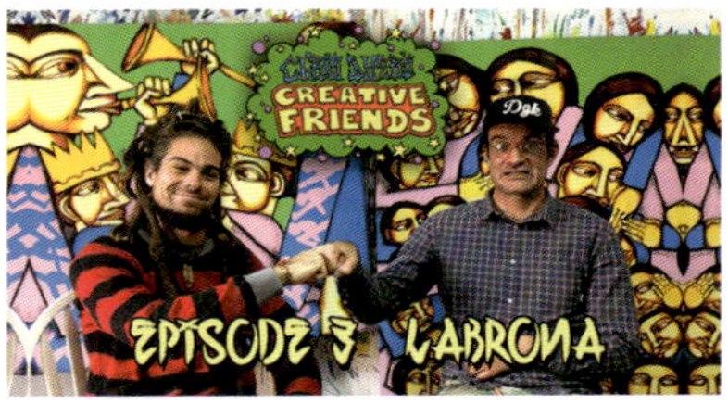

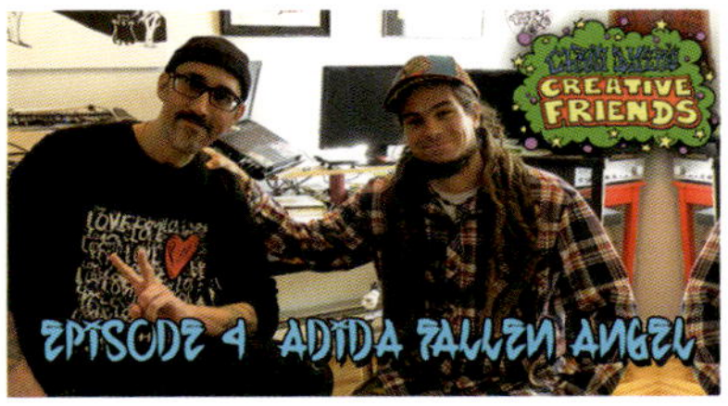

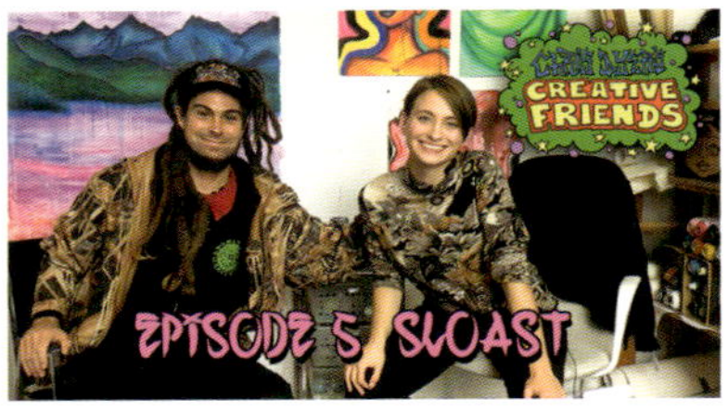

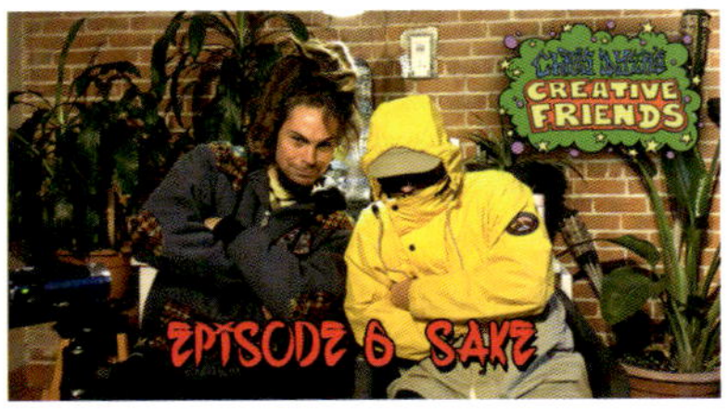

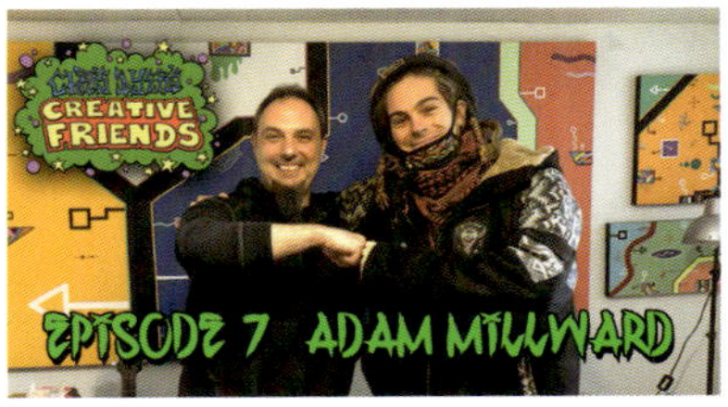

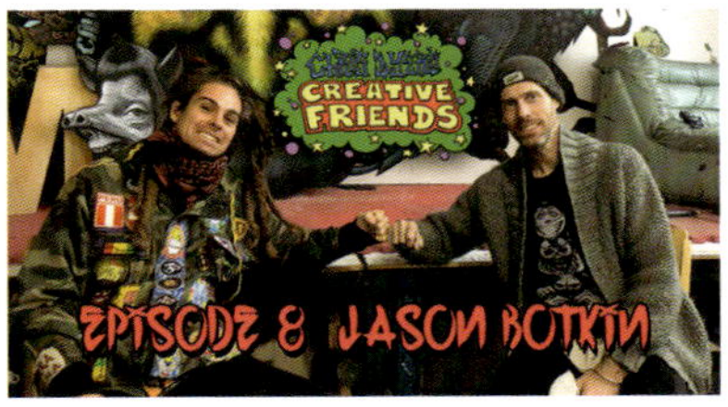

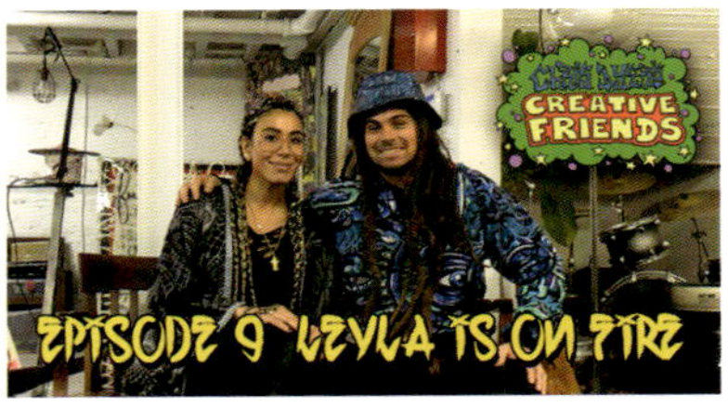

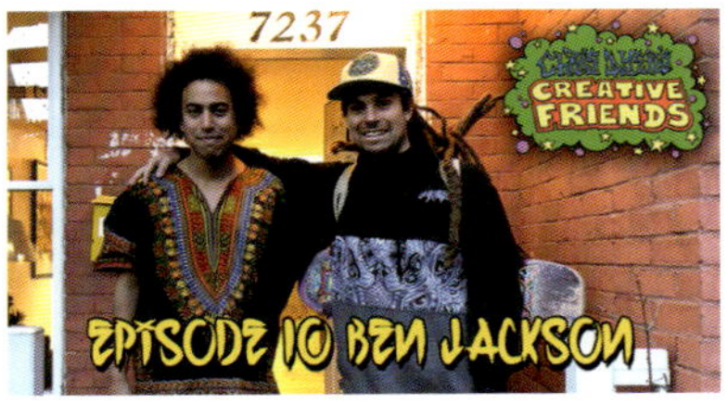

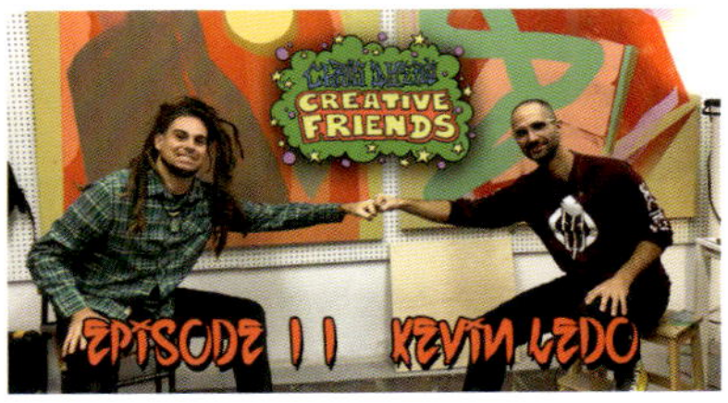

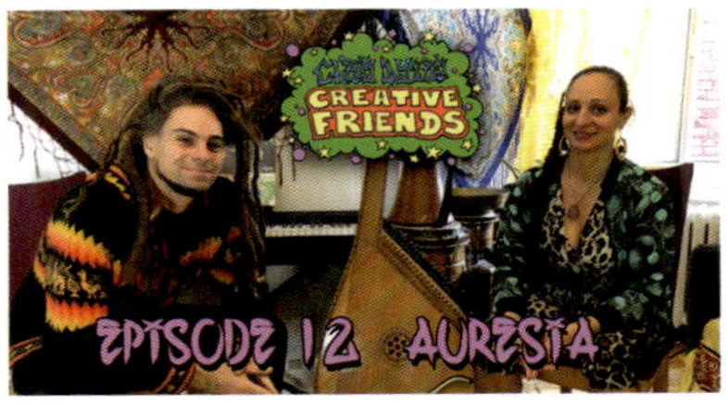

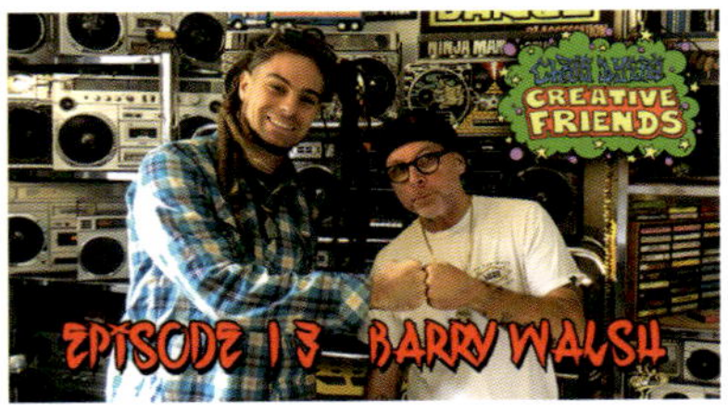

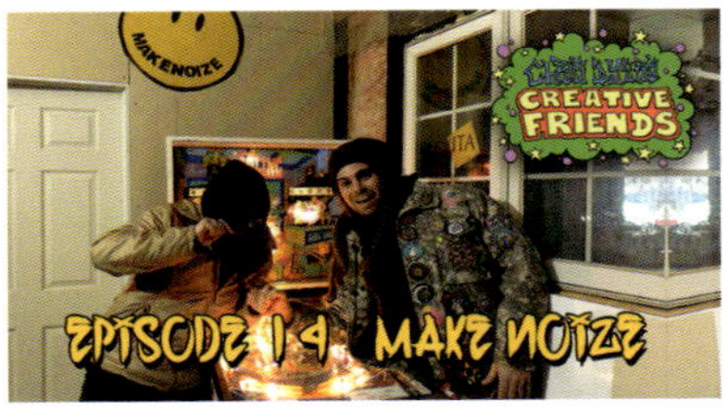

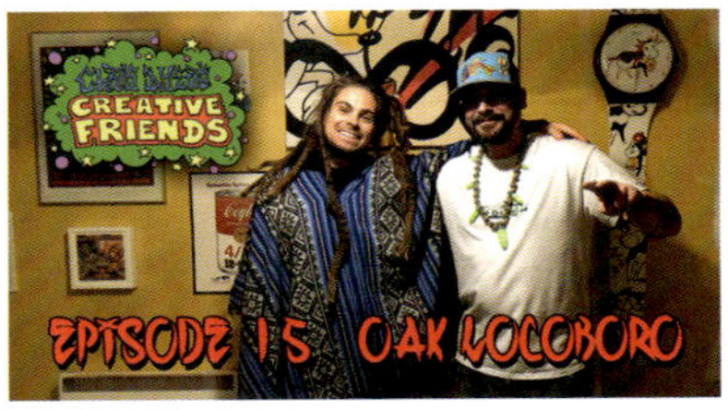

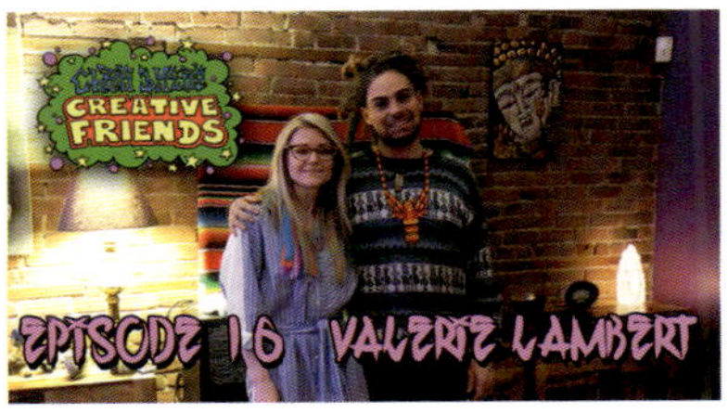

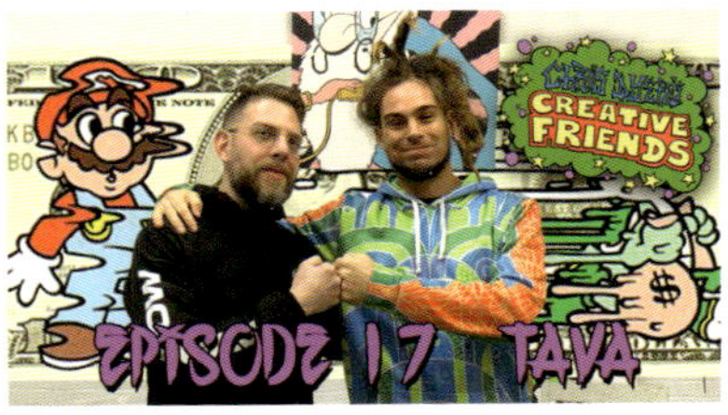

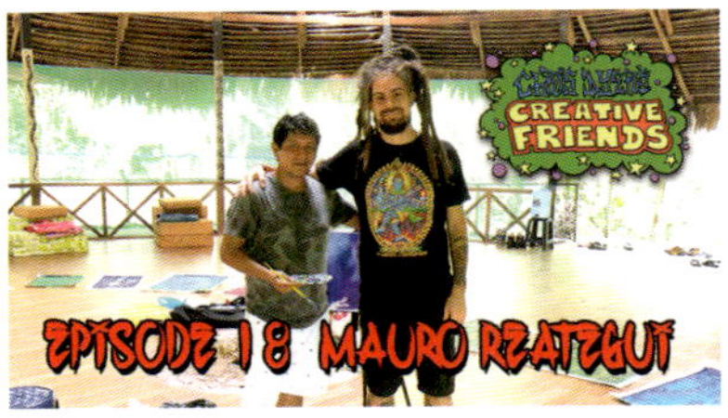

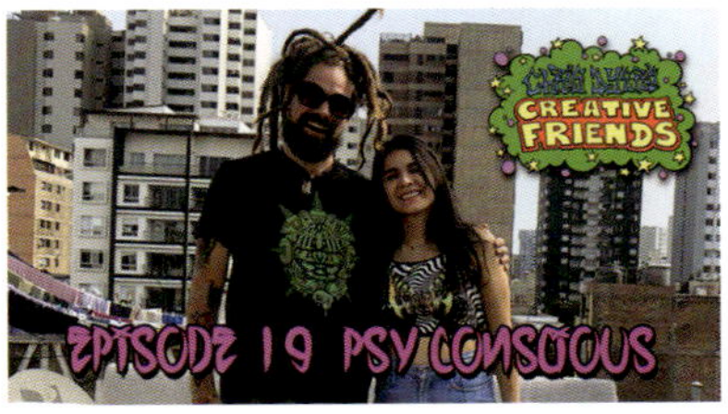

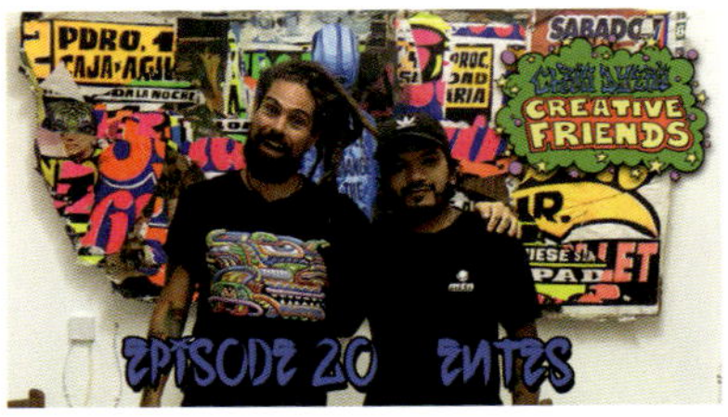

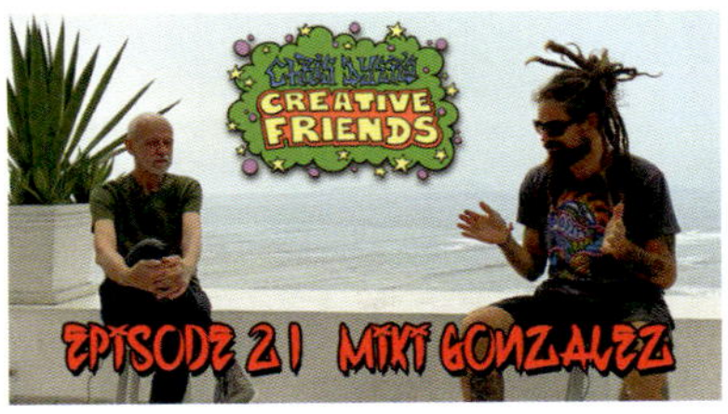

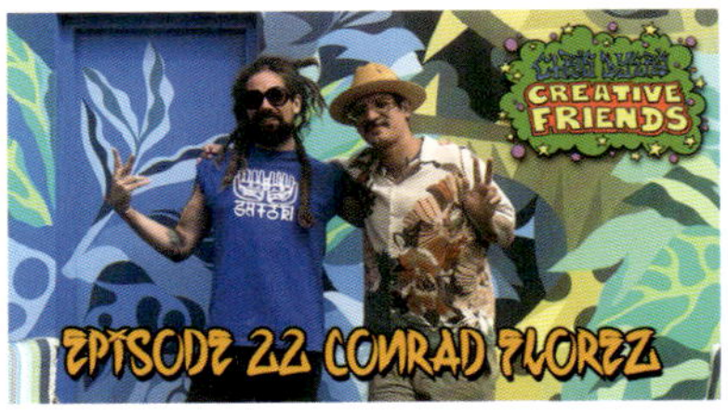

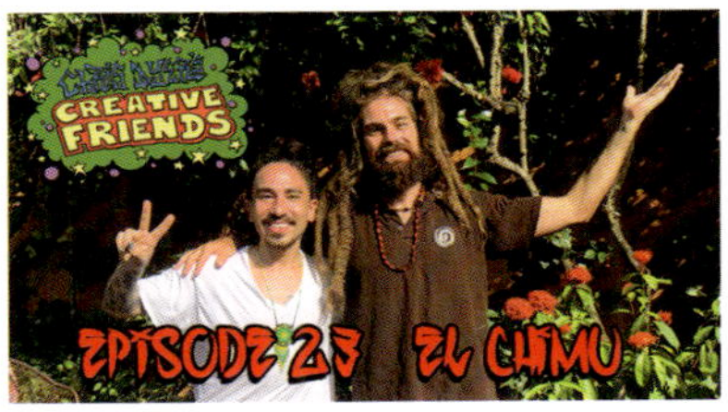

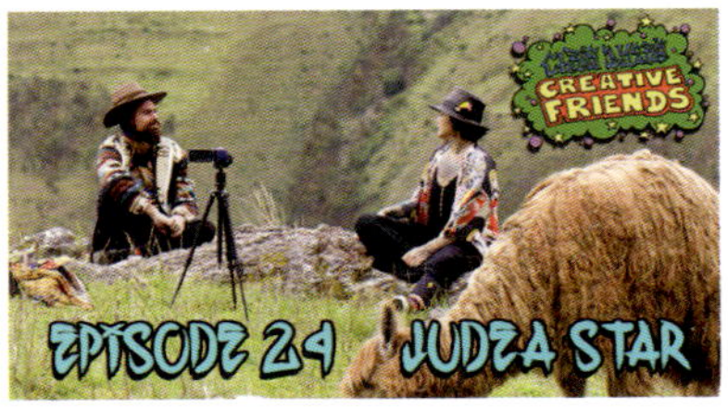

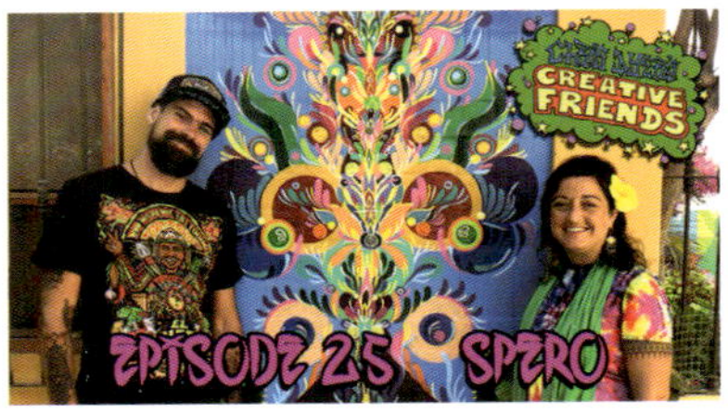

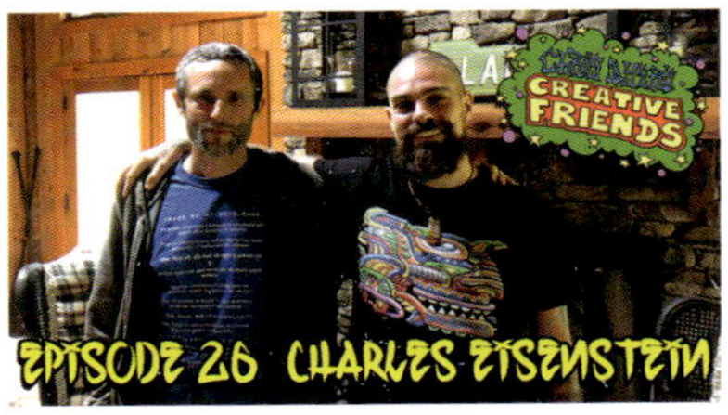

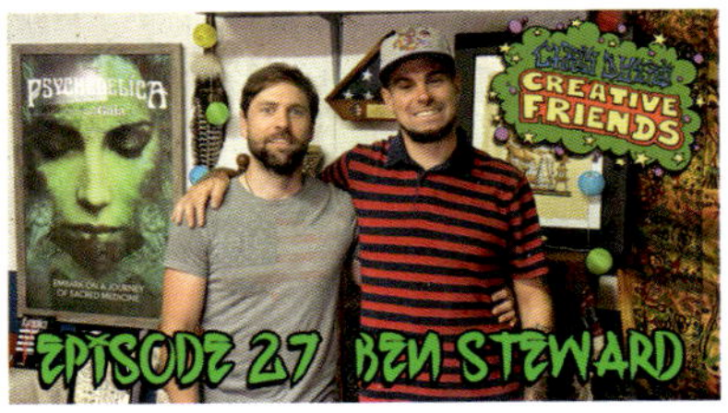

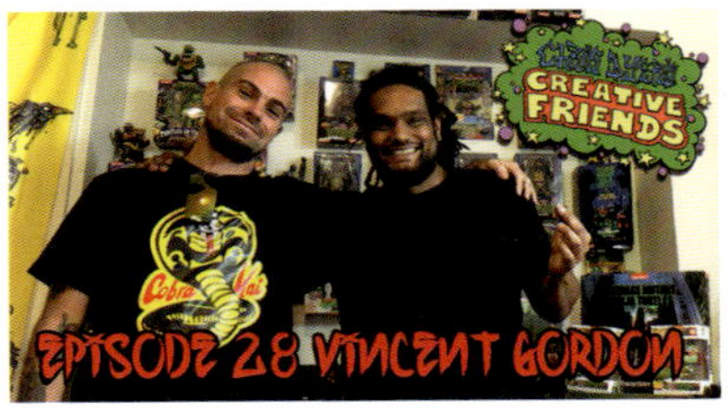

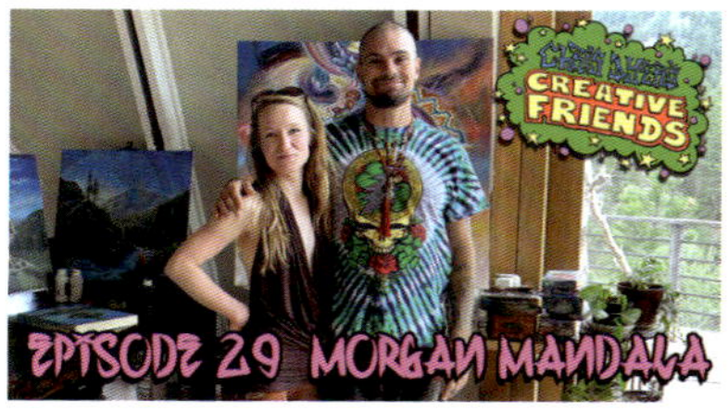
CREATIVE FRIENDS
EPISODE 29 MORGAN MANDALA
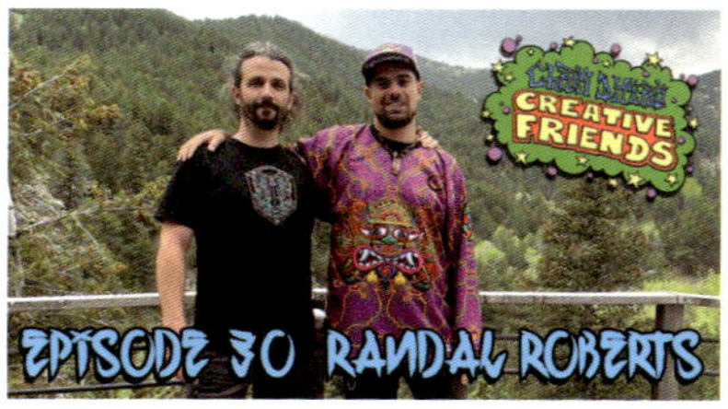
CREATIVE FRIENDS
EPISODE 30 RANDAL ROBERTS
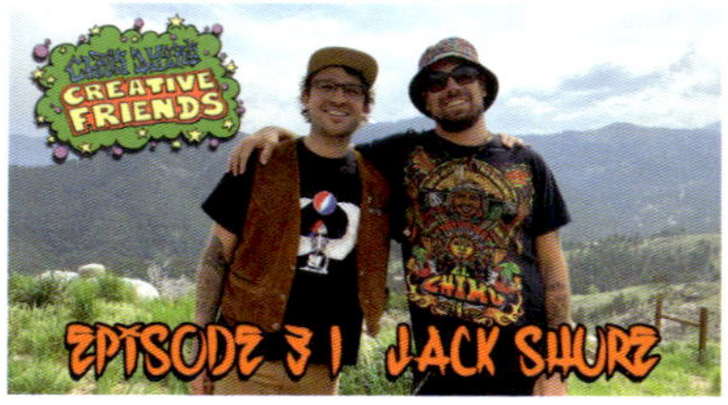
CREATIVE FRIENDS
EPISODE 31 JACK SHURE
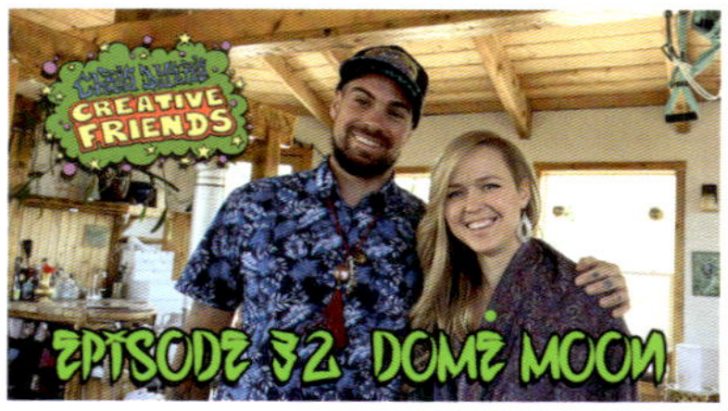
CREATIVE FRIENDS
EPISODE 32 DOME MOON
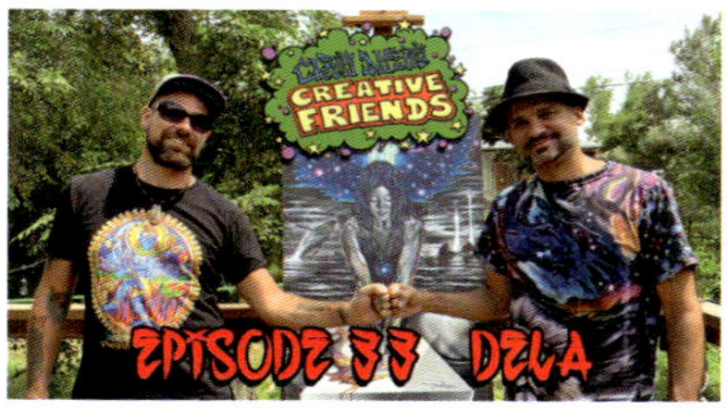
CREATIVE FRIENDS
EPISODE 33 DELA
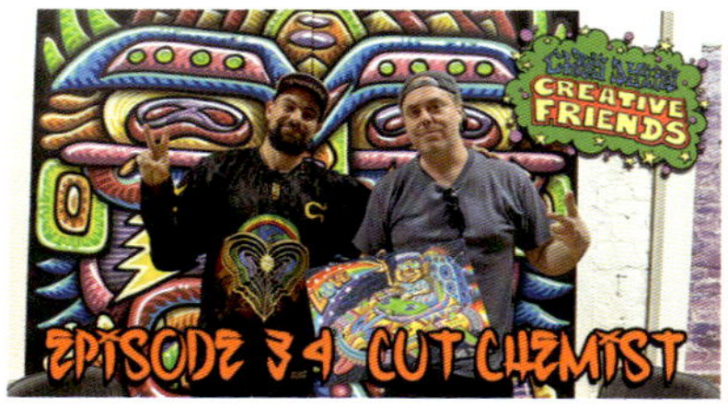
CREATIVE FRIENDS
EPISODE 34 CUT CHEMIST
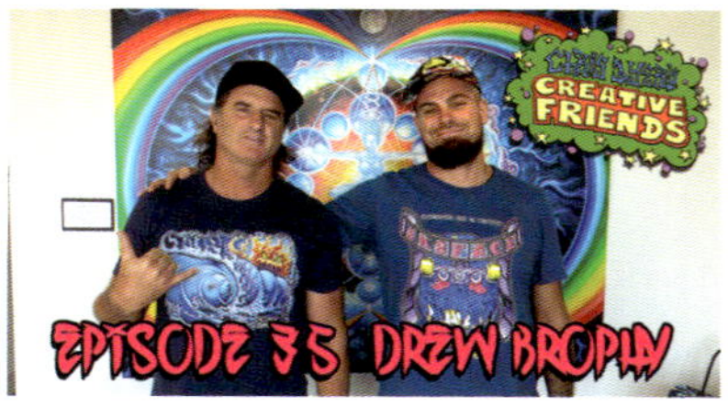
CREATIVE FRIENDS
EPISODE 35 DREW BROPHY
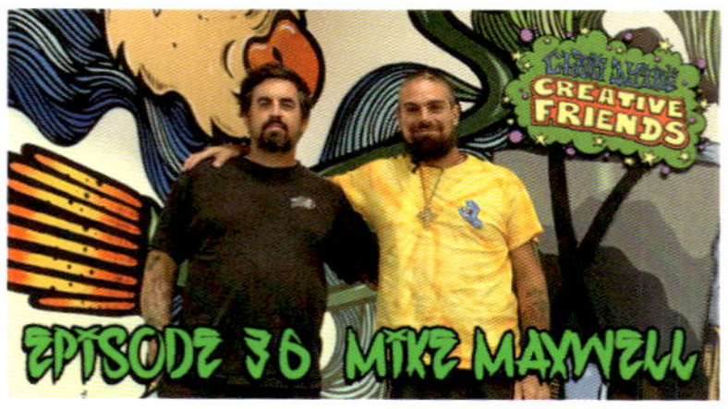
CREATIVE FRIENDS
EPISODE 36 MIKE MAXWELL
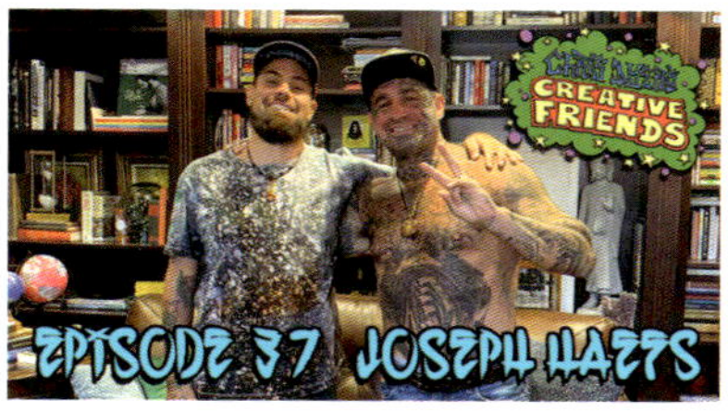
CREATIVE FRIENDS
EPISODE 37 JOSEPH HAEPS
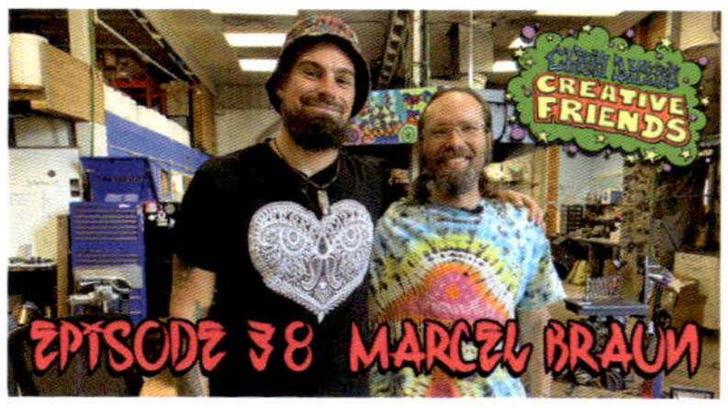
CREATIVE FRIENDS
EPISODE 38 MARCEL BRAUN
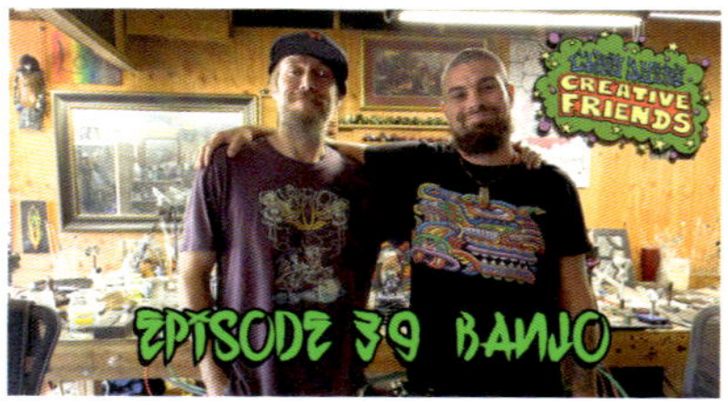
CREATIVE FRIENDS
EPISODE 39 BANJO
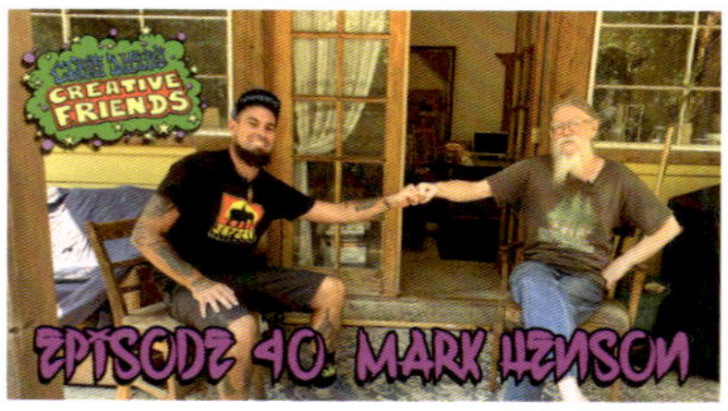
CREATIVE FRIENDS
EPISODE 40 MARK HENSON
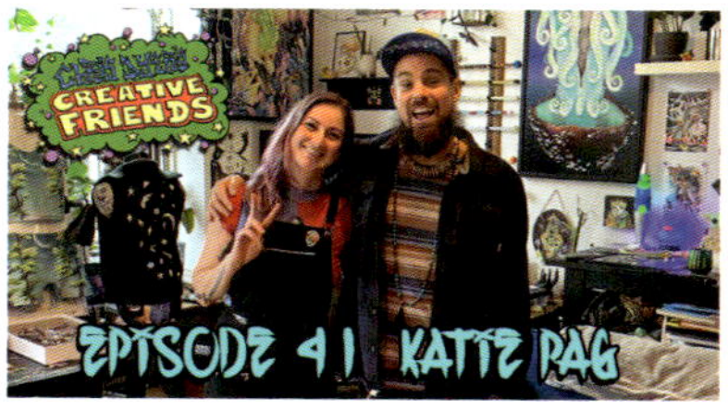
CREATIVE FRIENDS
EPISODE 41 KATIE RAG
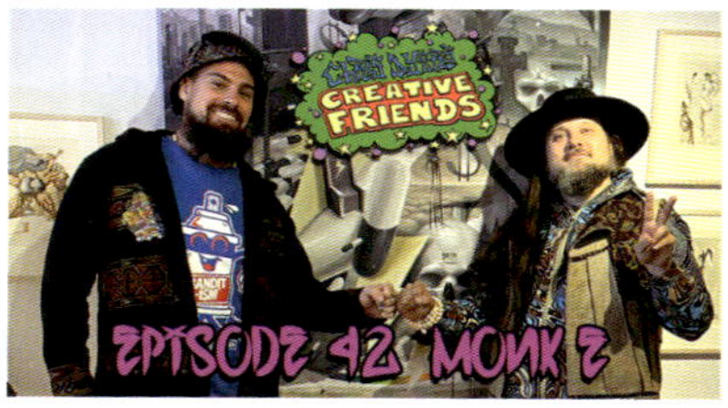
CREATIVE FRIENDS
EPISODE 42 MONK E
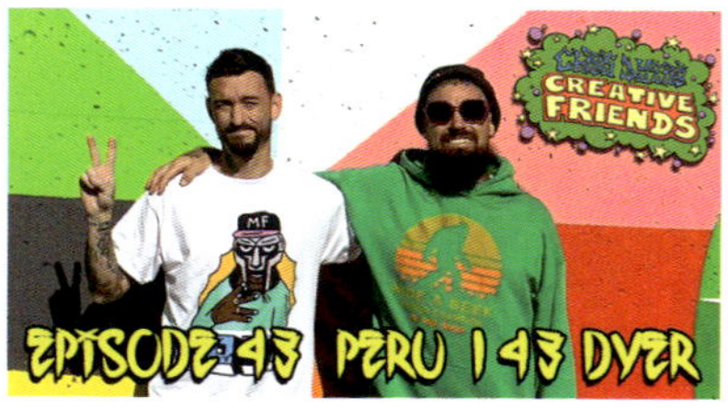
CREATIVE FRIENDS
EPISODE 43 PERU 143 DYER
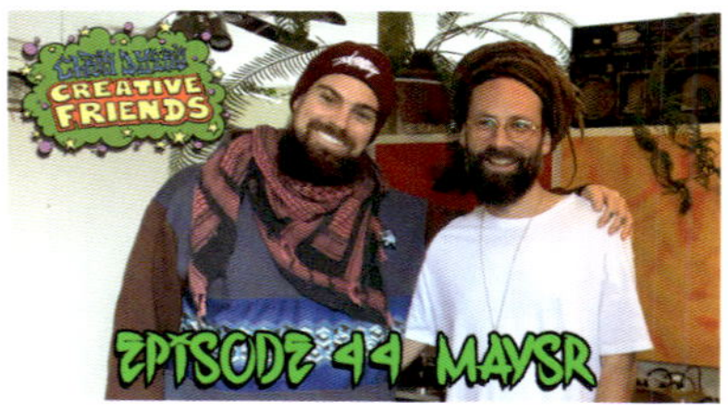
CREATIVE FRIENDS
EPISODE 44 MAYSR
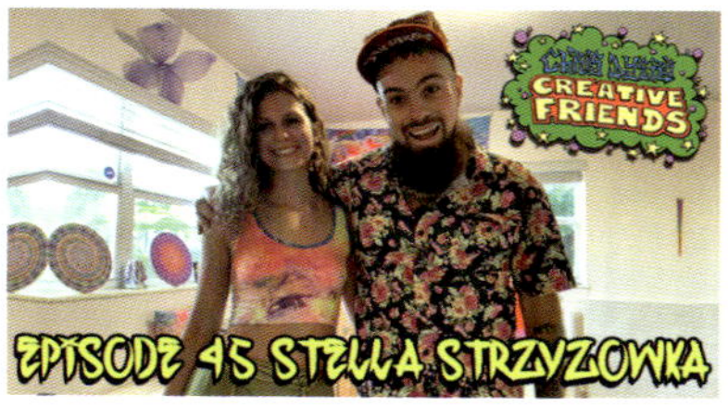
CREATIVE FRIENDS
EPISODE 45 STELLA STRZYZOWKA
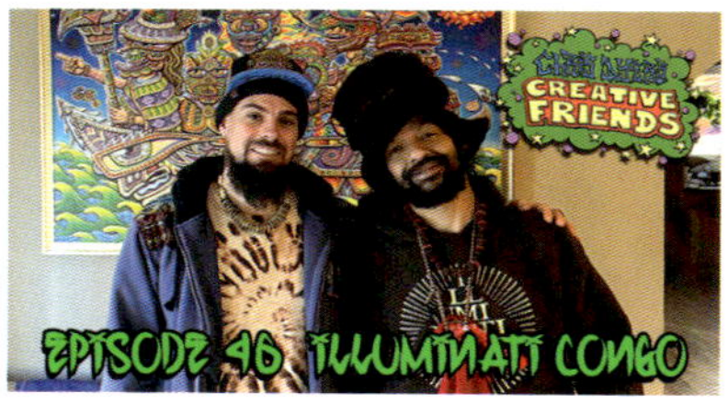
CREATIVE FRIENDS
EPISODE 46 ILLUMINATI CONGO
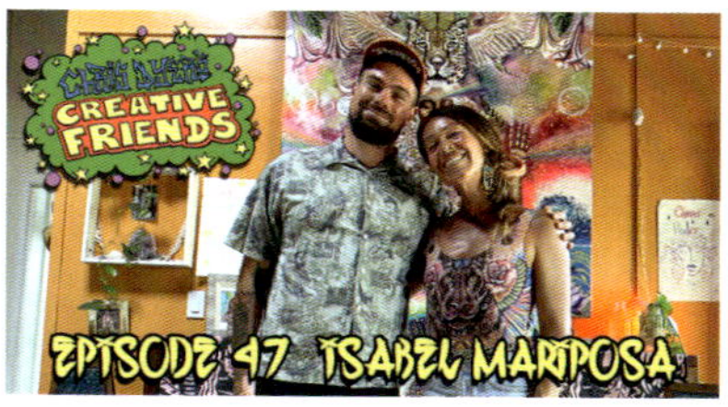
CREATIVE FRIENDS
EPISODE 47 ISABEL MARIPOSA
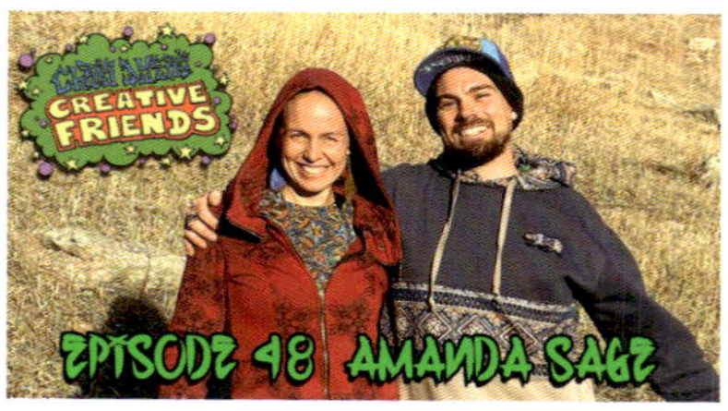
CREATIVE FRIENDS
EPISODE 48 AMANDA SAGE
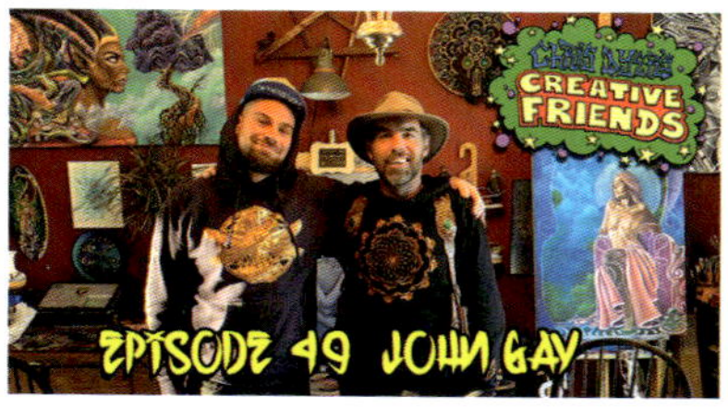
CHRIS DYER'S
CREATIVE FRIENDS
EPISODE 49 JOHN GAY
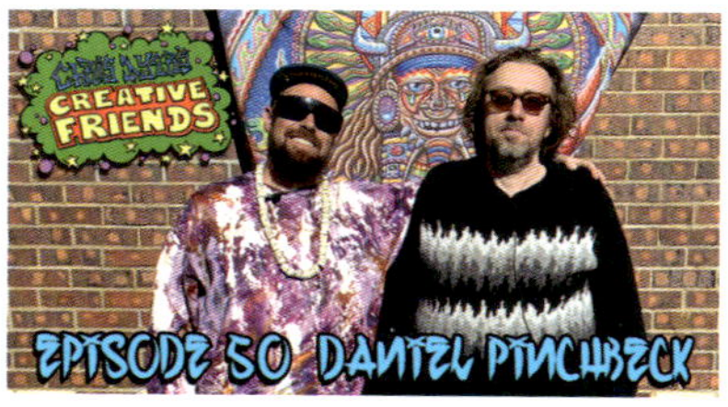
CREATIVE FRIENDS
EPISODE 50 DANIEL PINCHBECK
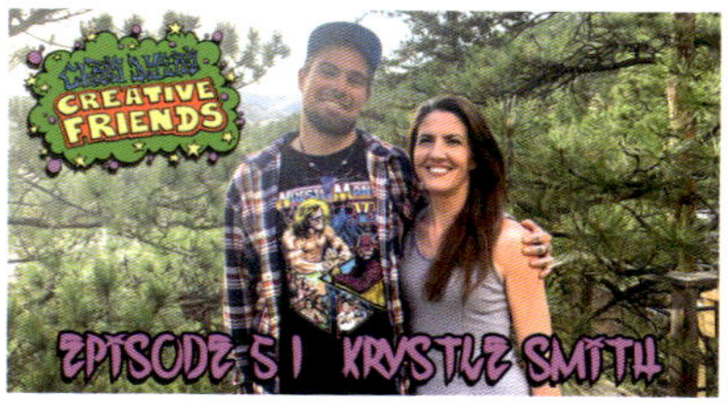
CREATIVE FRIENDS
EPISODE 51 KRYSTLE SMITH
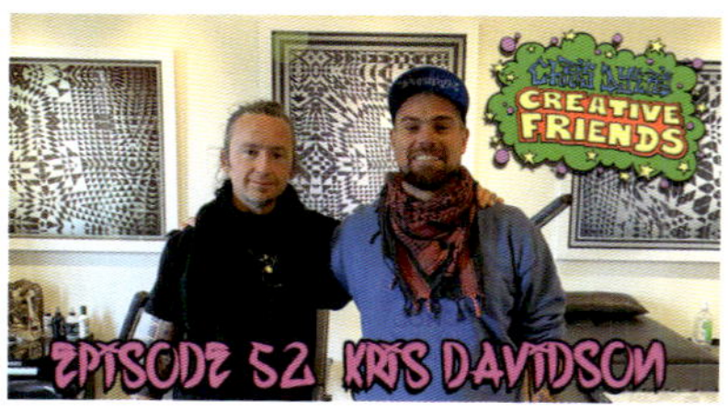
CREATIVE FRIENDS
EPISODE 52 KRIS DAVIDSON
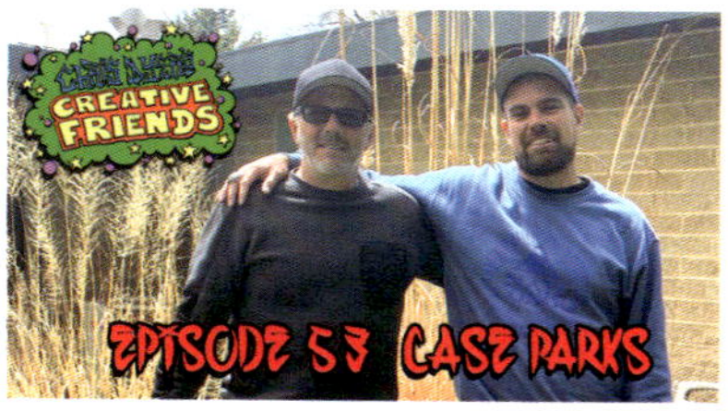
CREATIVE FRIENDS
EPISODE 53 CASE PARKS
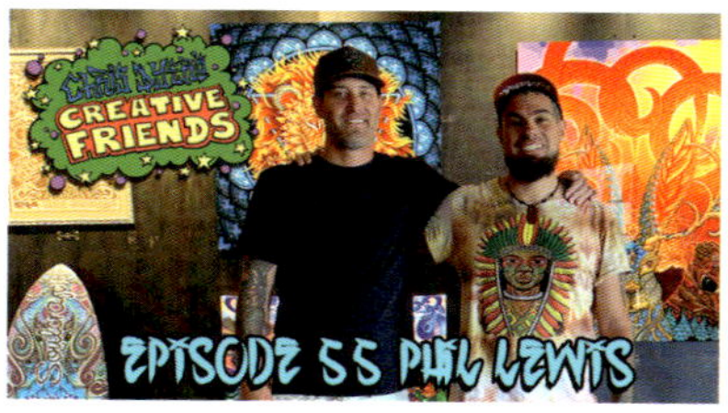
CREATIVE FRIENDS
EPISODE 55 PHIL LEWIS
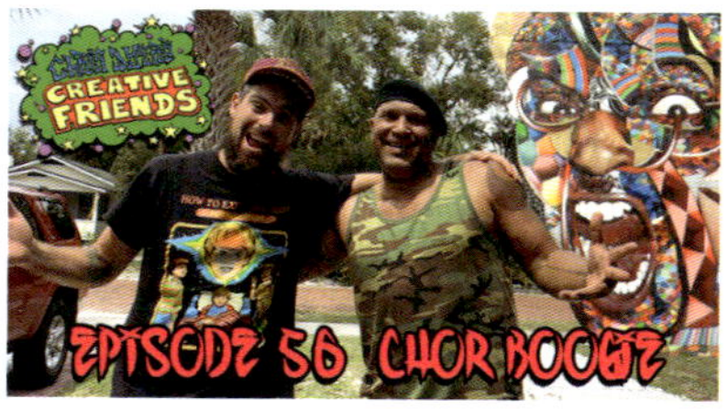
CREATIVE FRIENDS
EPISODE 56 CHOR BOOGIE
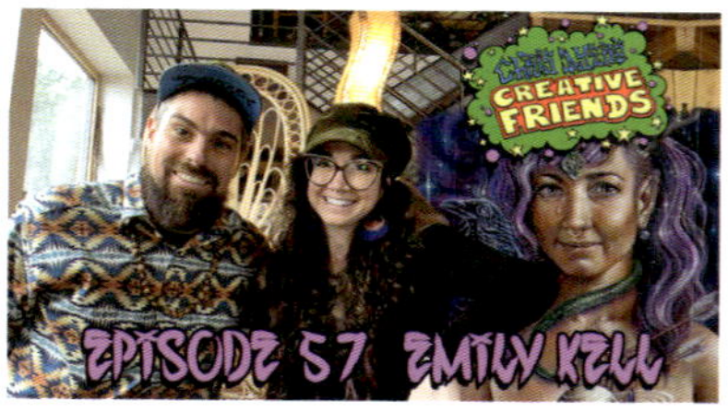
CREATIVE FRIENDS
EPISODE 57 EMILY KELL
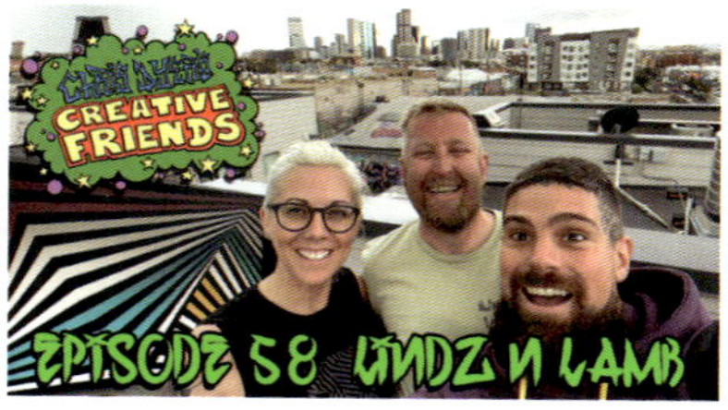
CREATIVE FRIENDS
EPISODE 58 LINDZ N LAMB
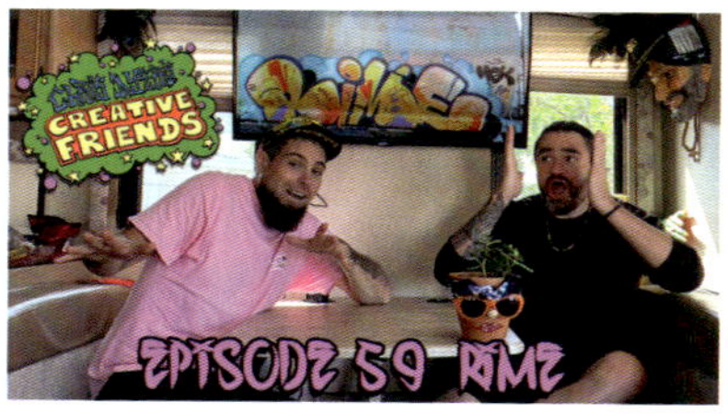
CREATIVE FRIENDS
EPISODE 59 RIME
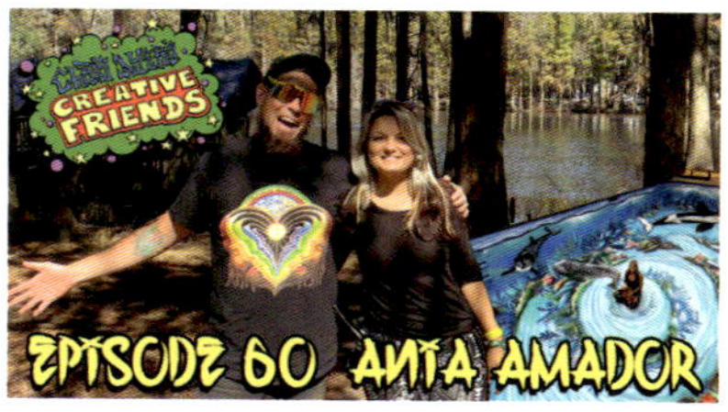
CREATIVE FRIENDS
EPISODE 60 ANITA AMADOR
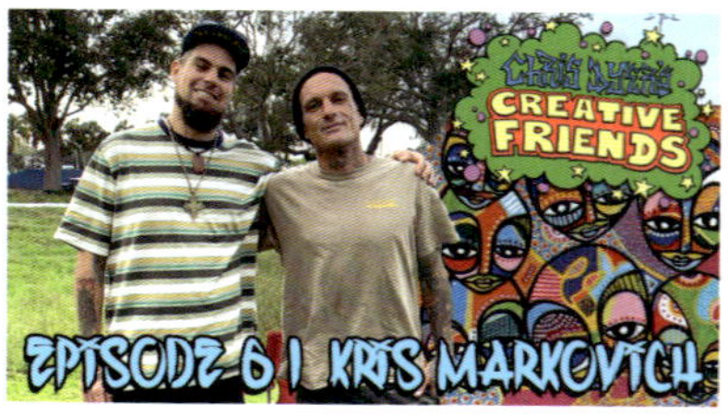
CREATIVE FRIENDS
EPISODE 61 KRIS MARKOVICH
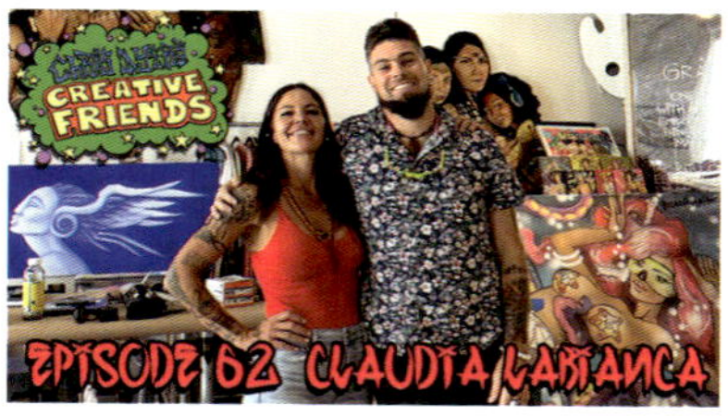
CREATIVE FRIENDS
EPISODE 62 CLAUDIA LARANCA
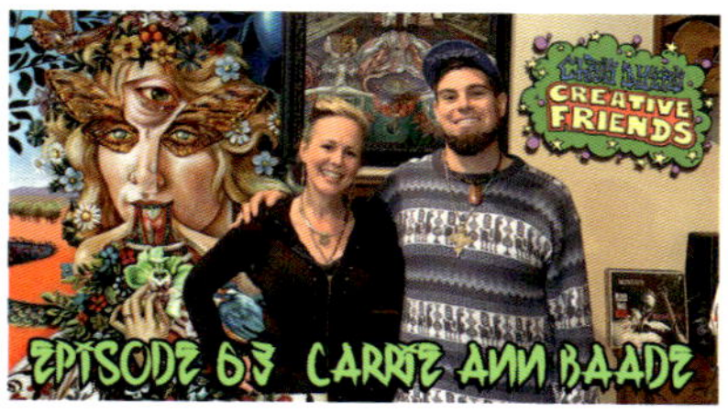
CREATIVE FRIENDS
EPISODE 63 CARRIE ANN BAADE
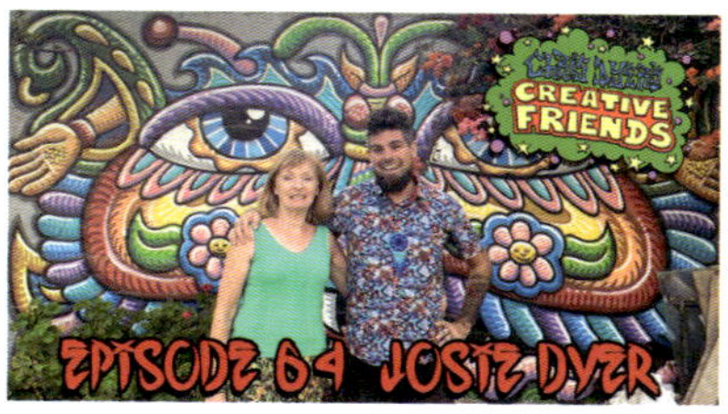
CREATIVE FRIENDS
EPISODE 64 JOSIE DYER
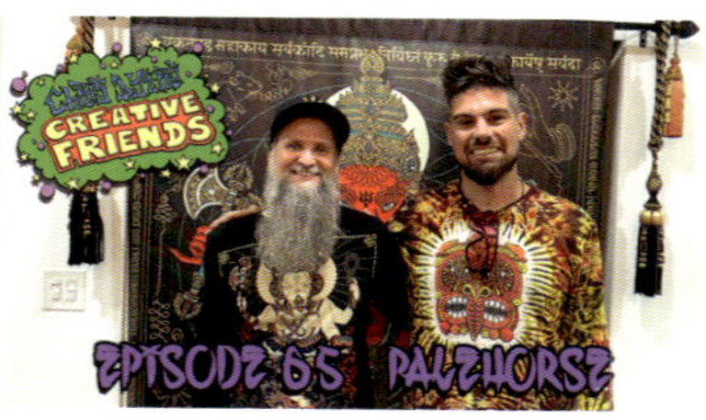
CREATIVE FRIENDS
EPISODE 65 PALEHORSE

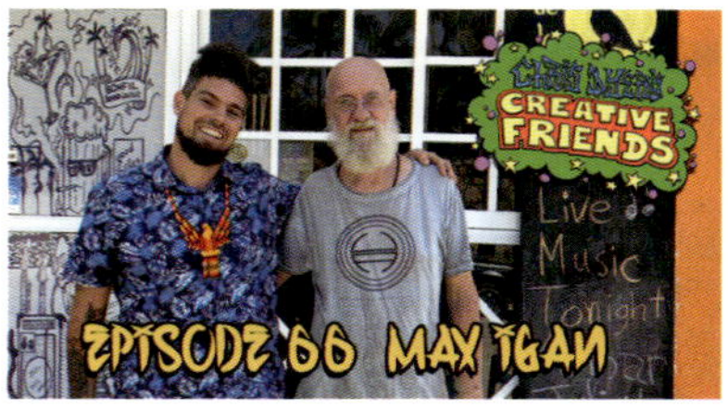

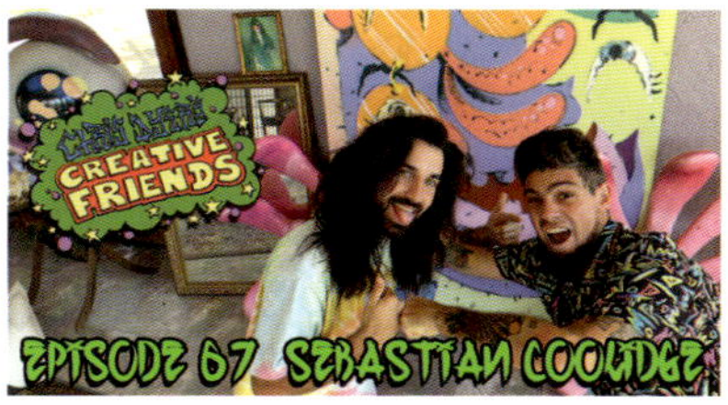

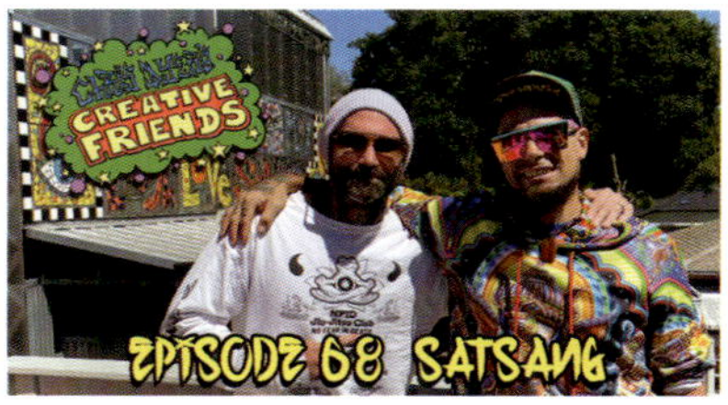

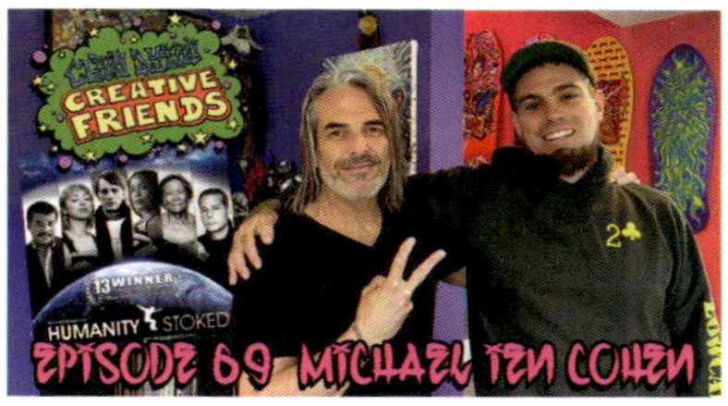

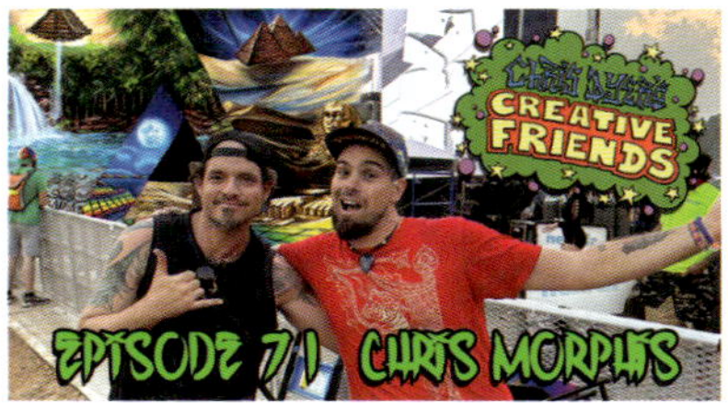

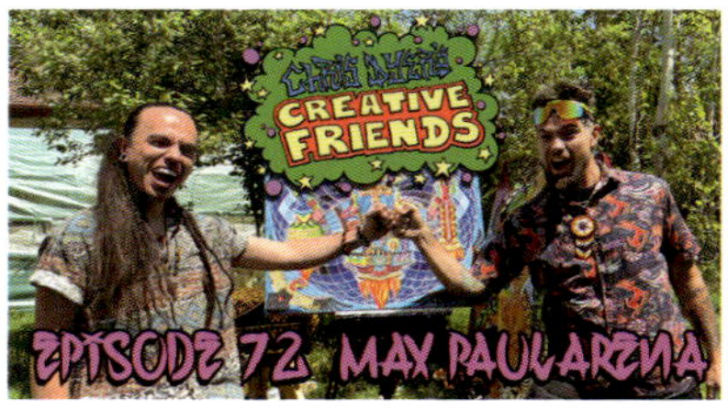

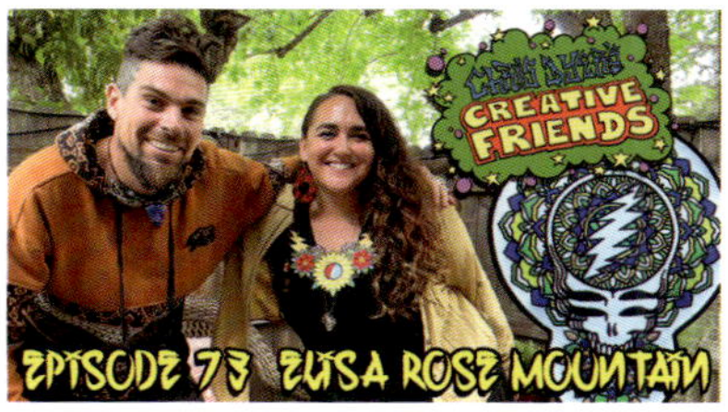

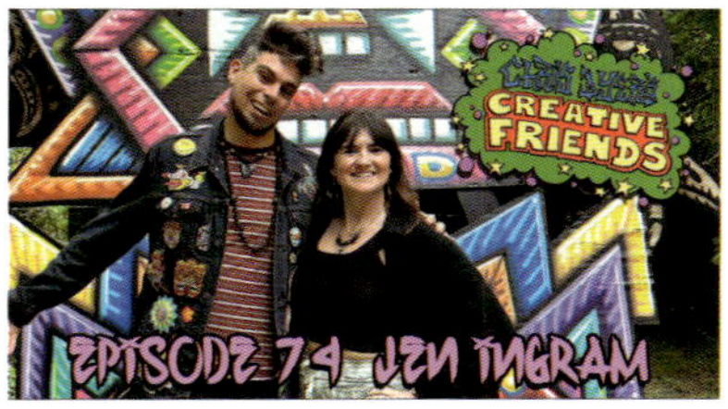

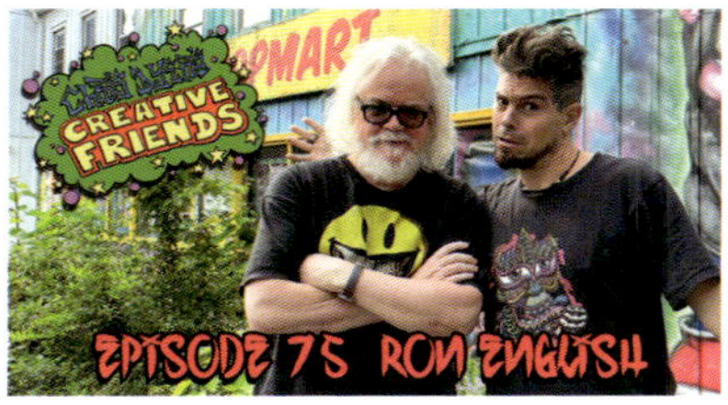

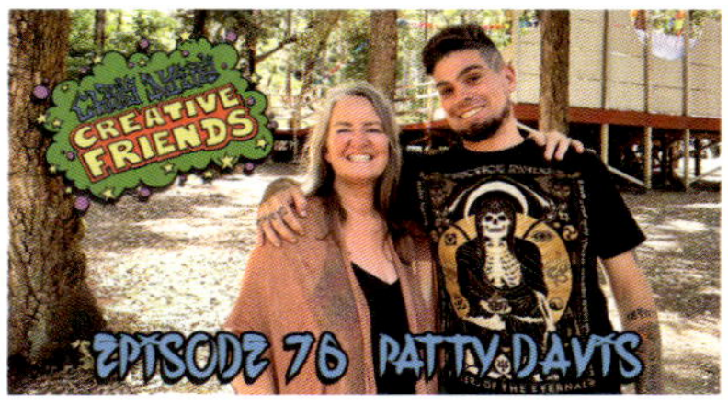

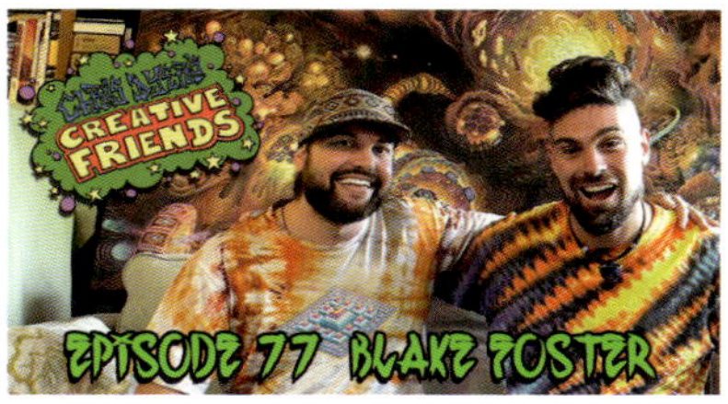

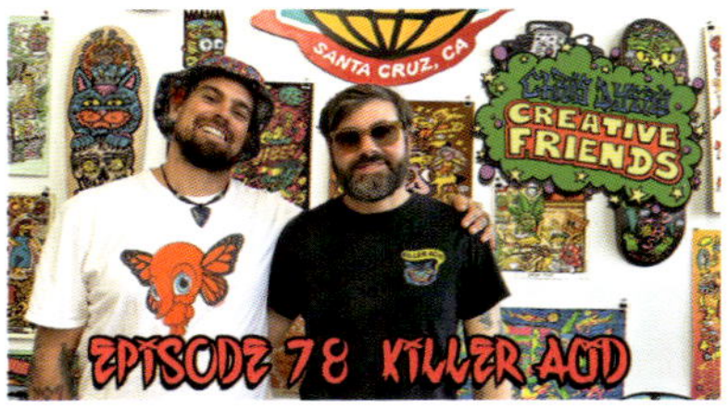

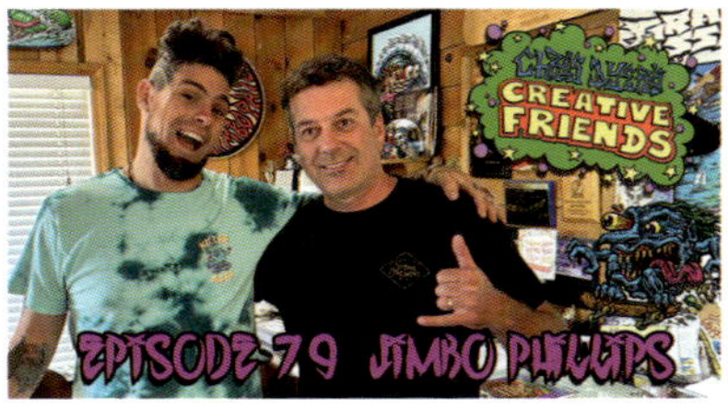

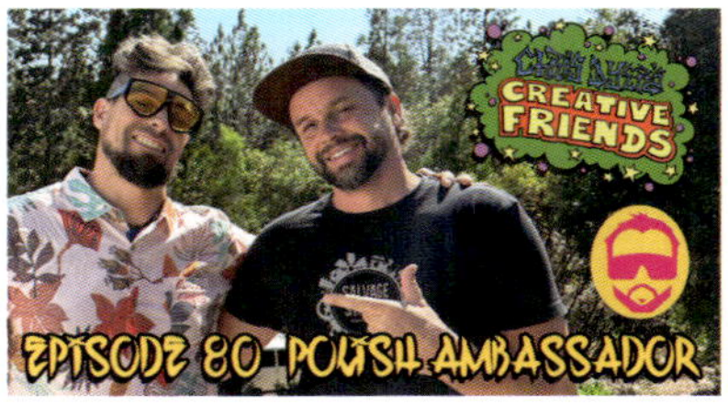

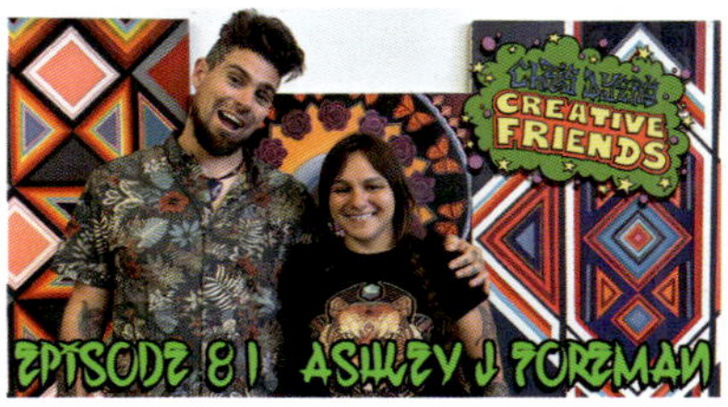

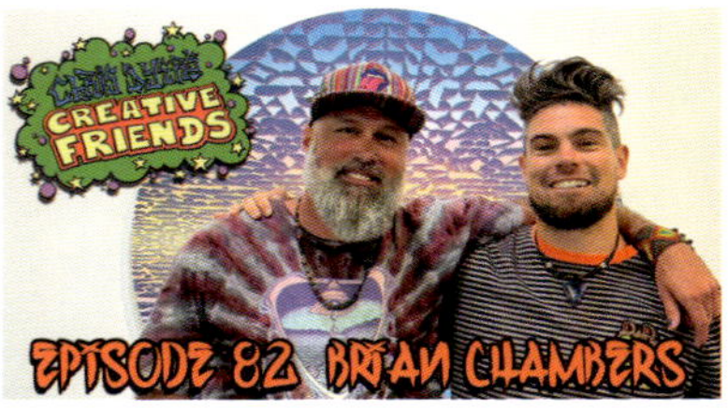

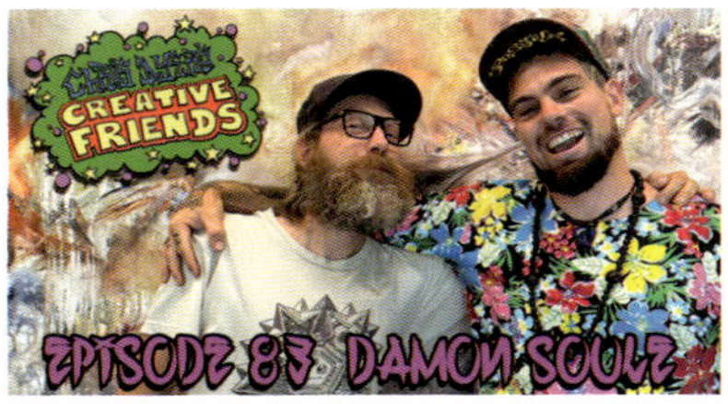

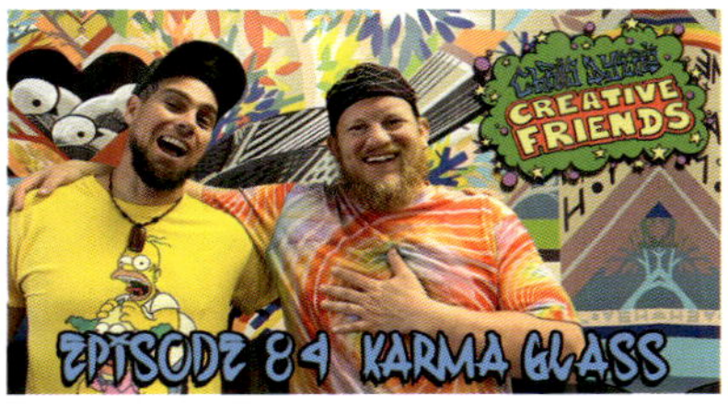

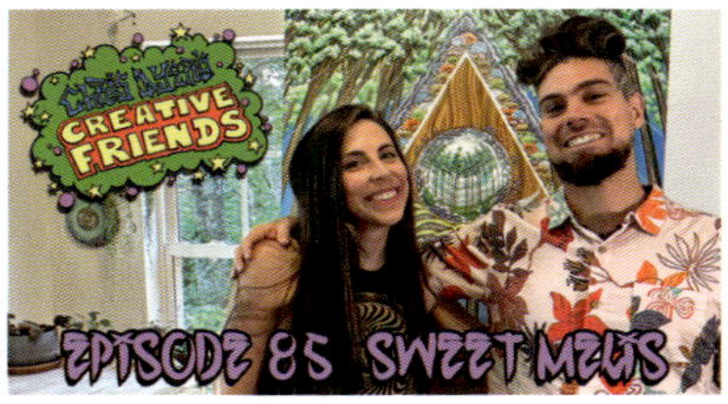

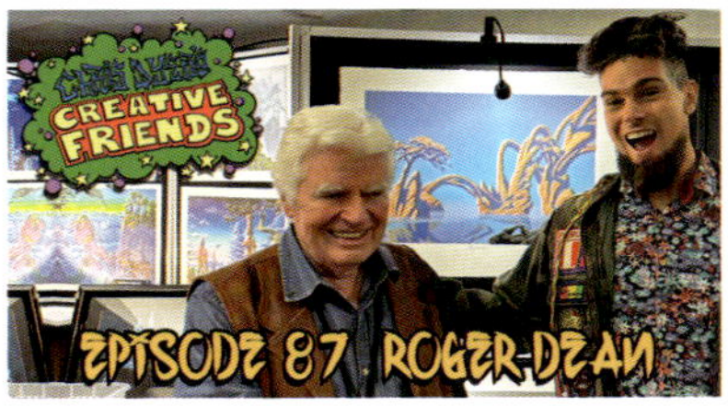

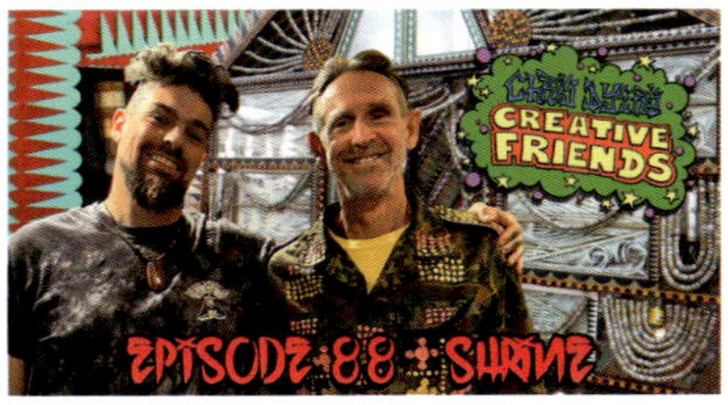

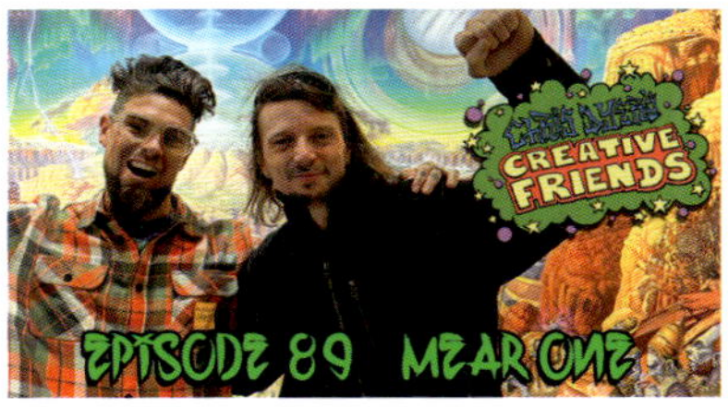

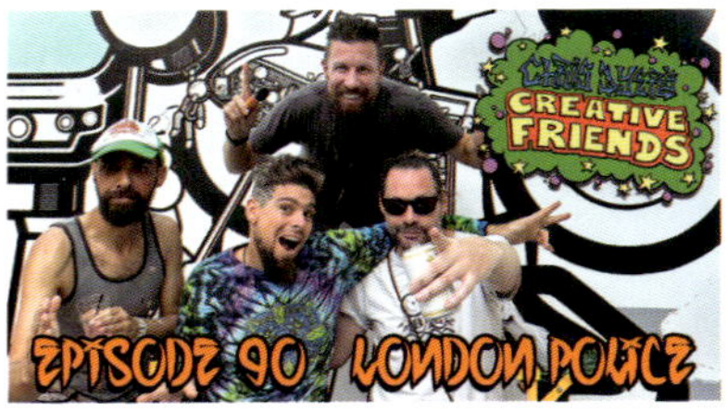

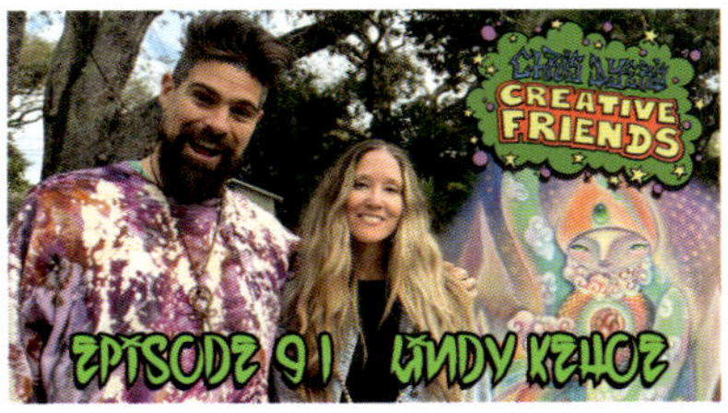

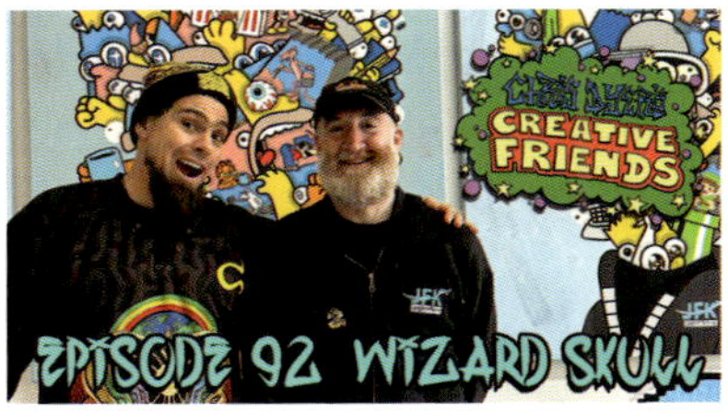

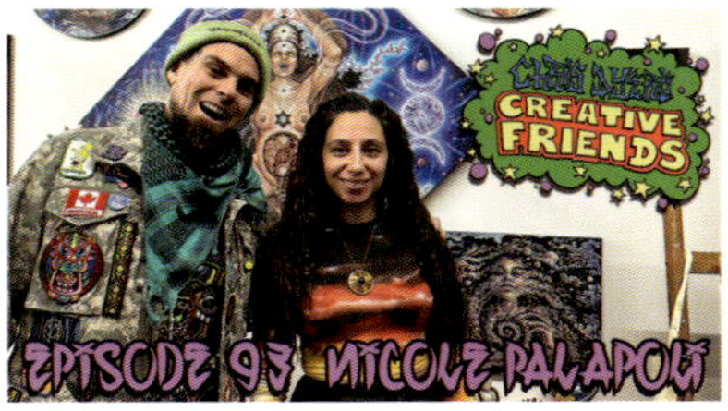

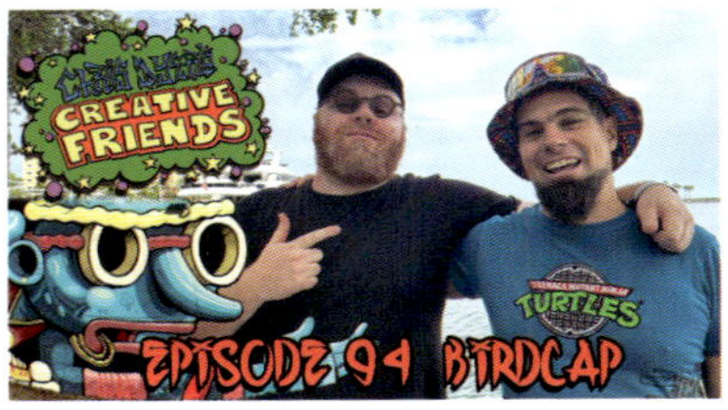

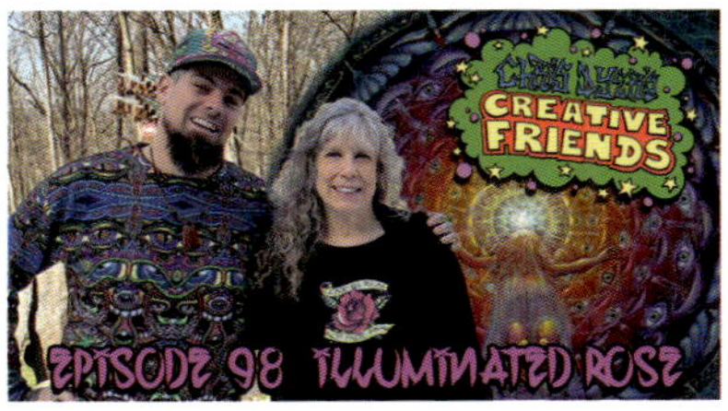

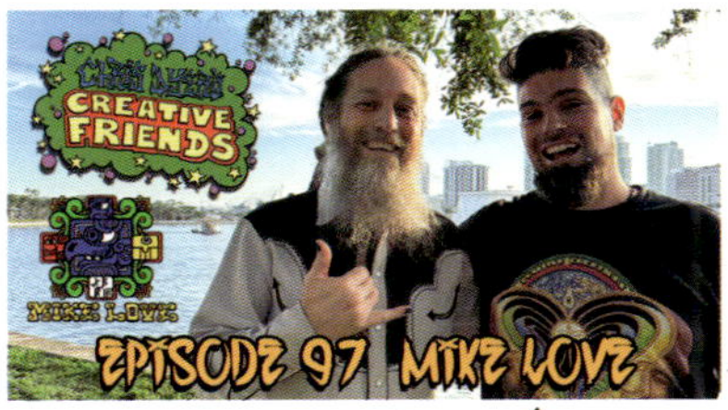

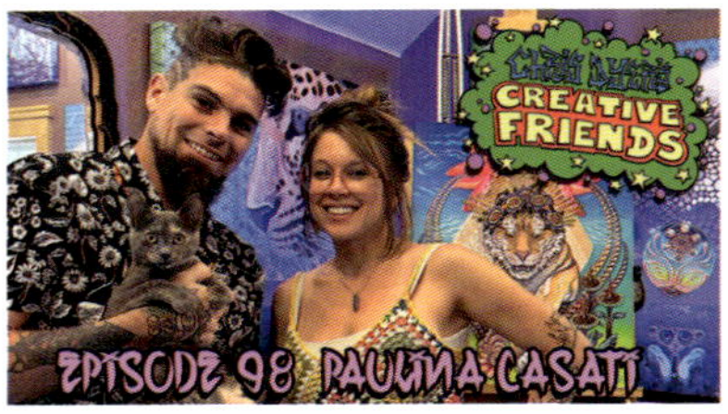

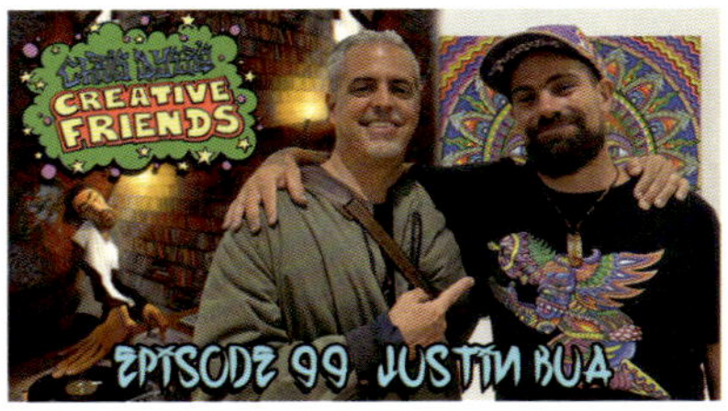

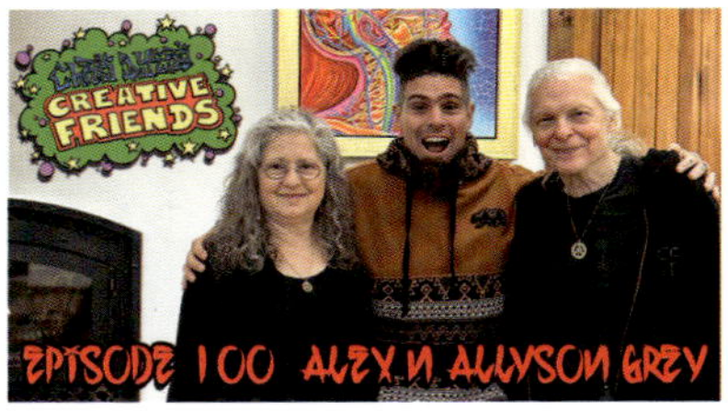

NEW EPISODES
EVERY 2 WEEKS

SUPERHEROES AND ROBOTS

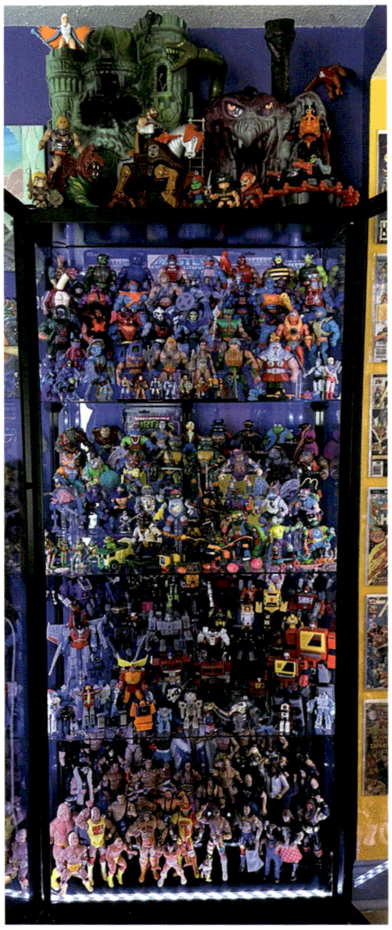

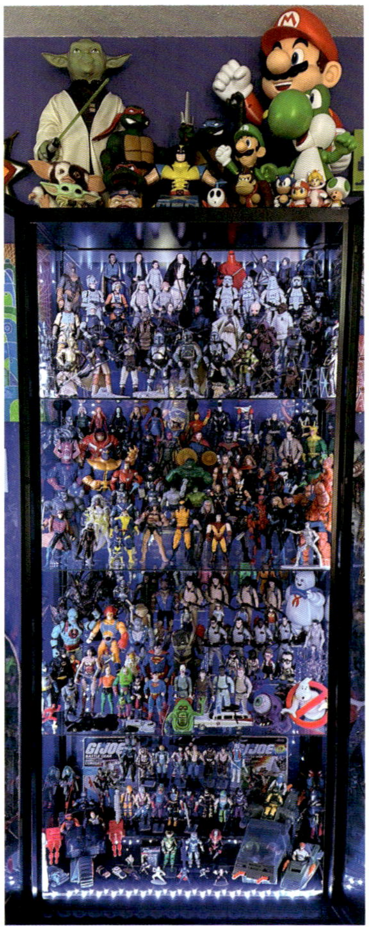

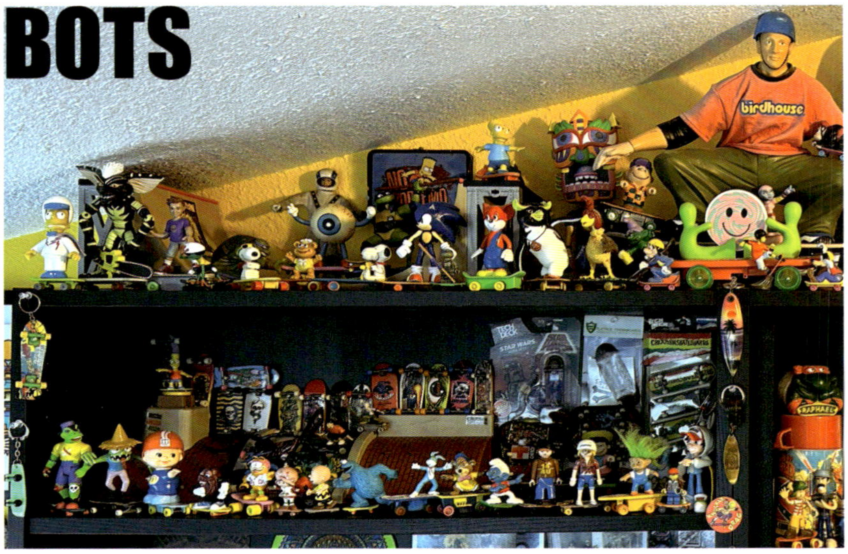

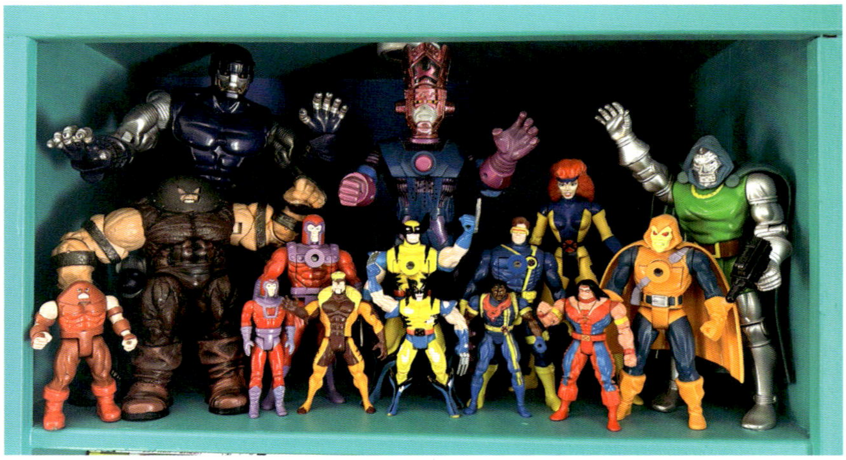

As an 80's kid and 90's teen, I can easily claim that I grew up with the best cartoons, movies and action figures! I've always been deeply fascinated by so many myths from the human imagination, perhaps because they remind me of planets and dimensions I've experienced in some past or future lives. I've been collecting action figures and toys since before I could afford them, the hunt alone is enjoyable! Each one of these colorful sculptures inspires me to express my own personal myths. If there will always be a battle between Good and Evil, might as well be a beautiful and fun one, no?

My watercolor painting **"Light Worker"** definitely borrowed colors from some of my favorite characters. When I began the piece I wanted to do a portrait of the Artificial Intelligence Artist that has entered our world recently. Since this new consciousness is doing such beautiful portraits of humans, I felt I had to do a portrait of it. But as I started to color it in, it didn't feel like it was the AI machine anymore. Instead I realized I was painting a modern Light Worker. A human who uses their creative gifts, Love and Magic to manifest a better world. The future is unknown and even scary, as technology is growing so quickly. But I have the faith that the spiritual potential of humanity is also quickly awakening. I believe we can be super heroes of our own stories and help Good overcome the imbalances of Evil! I believe our future can be Bright and Positive!

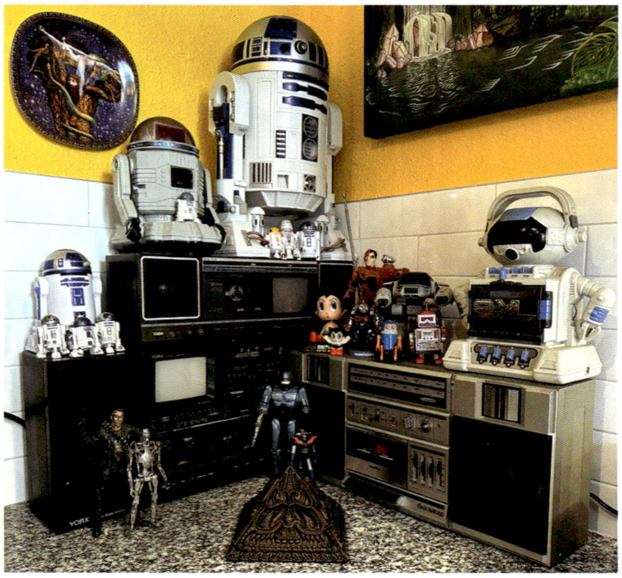

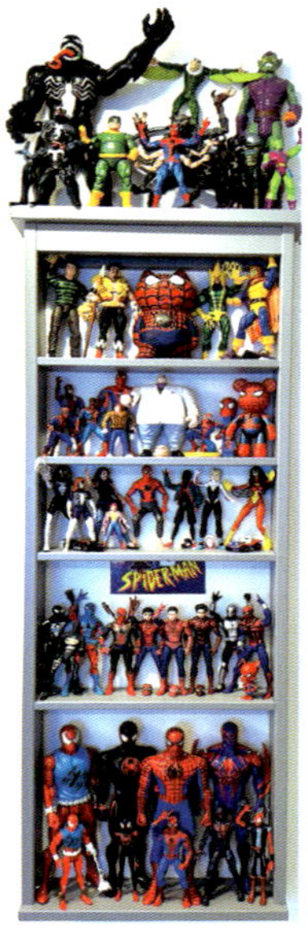

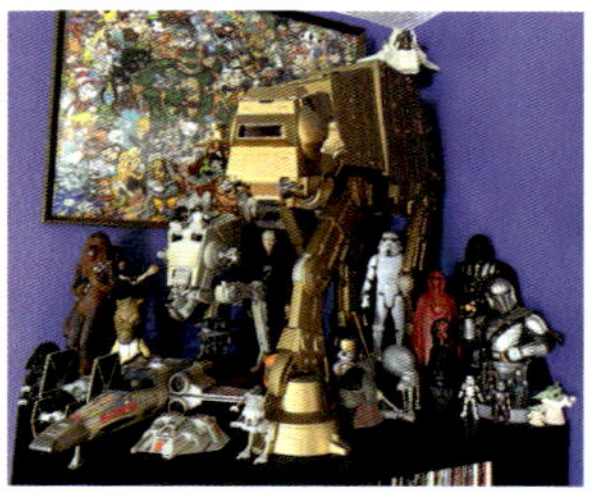

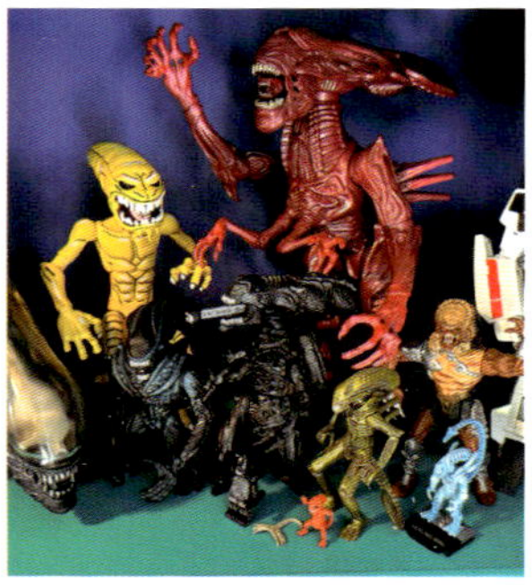

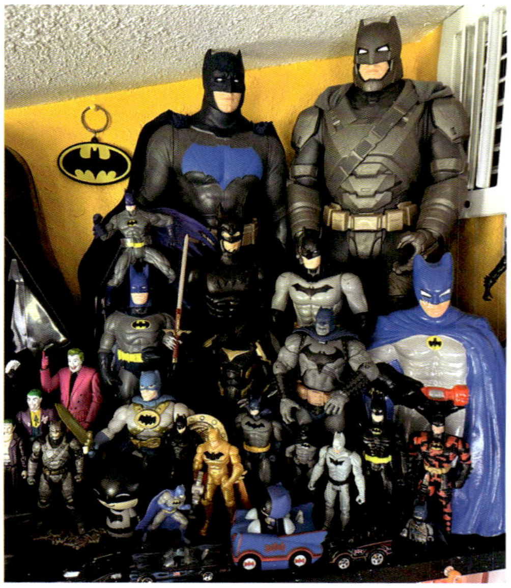

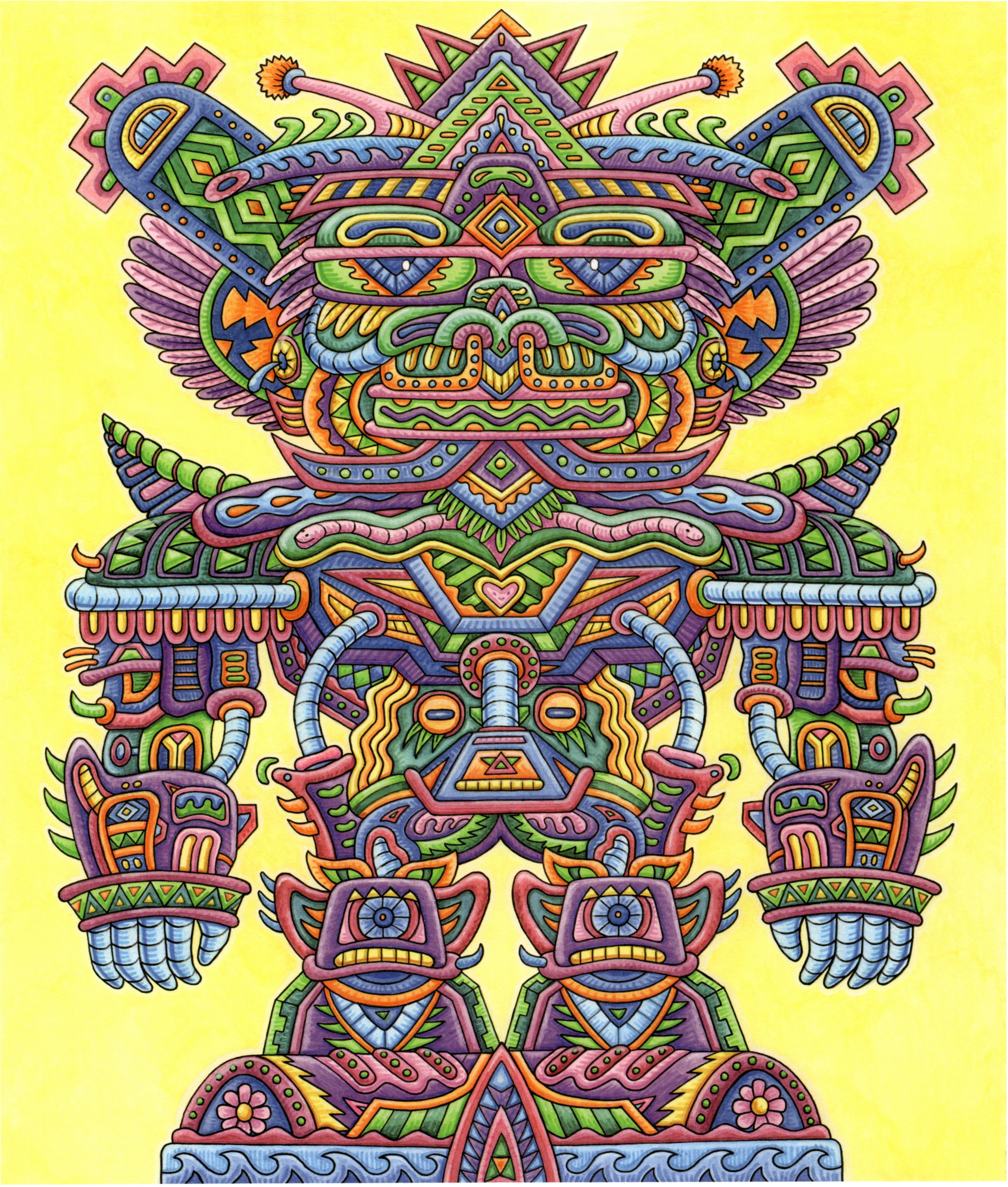

"Light Worker" Watercolours on paper, 2023

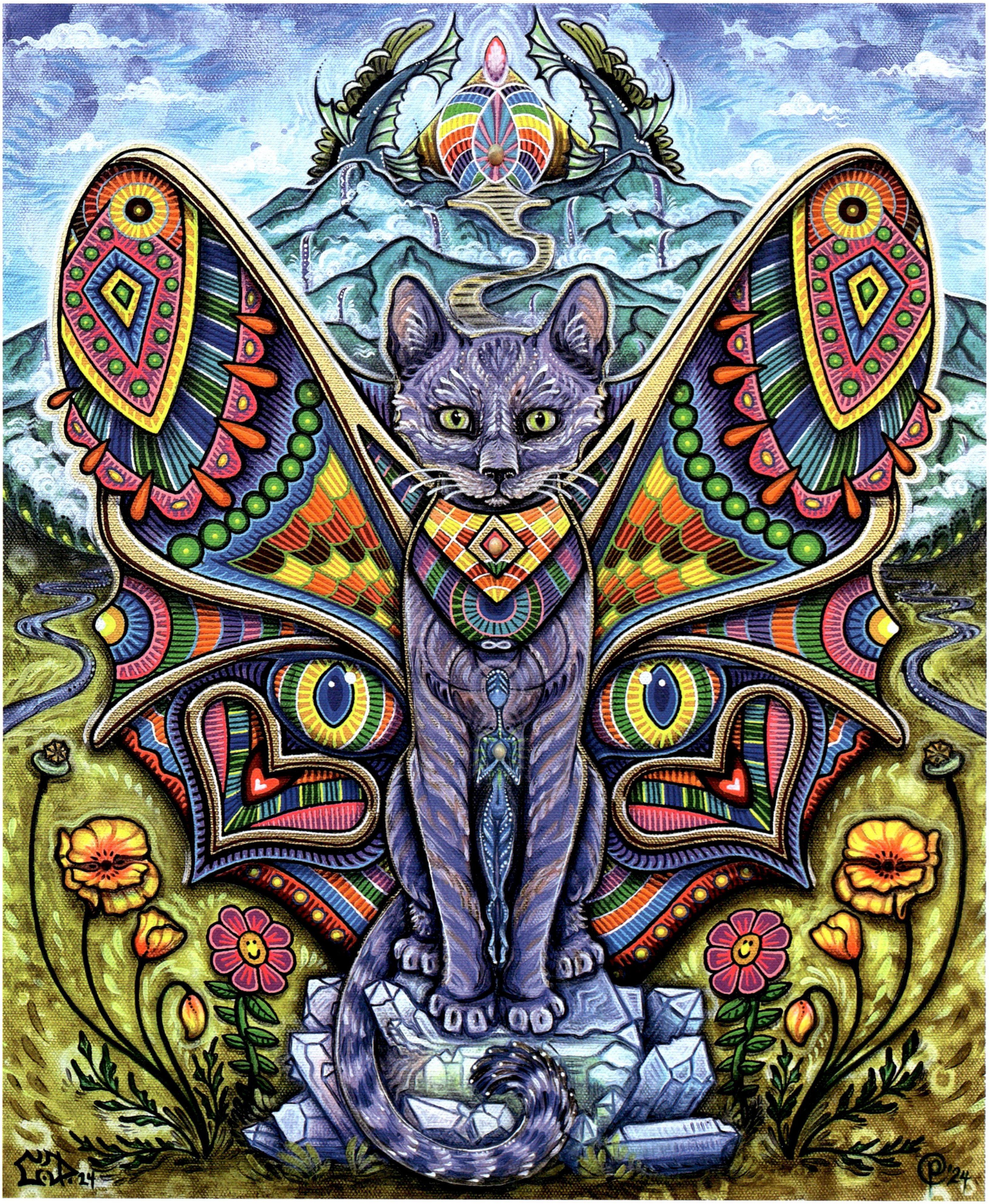

"Lyran Love"
collabo with **Paulina Casati**, Acrylics on canvas, 2024

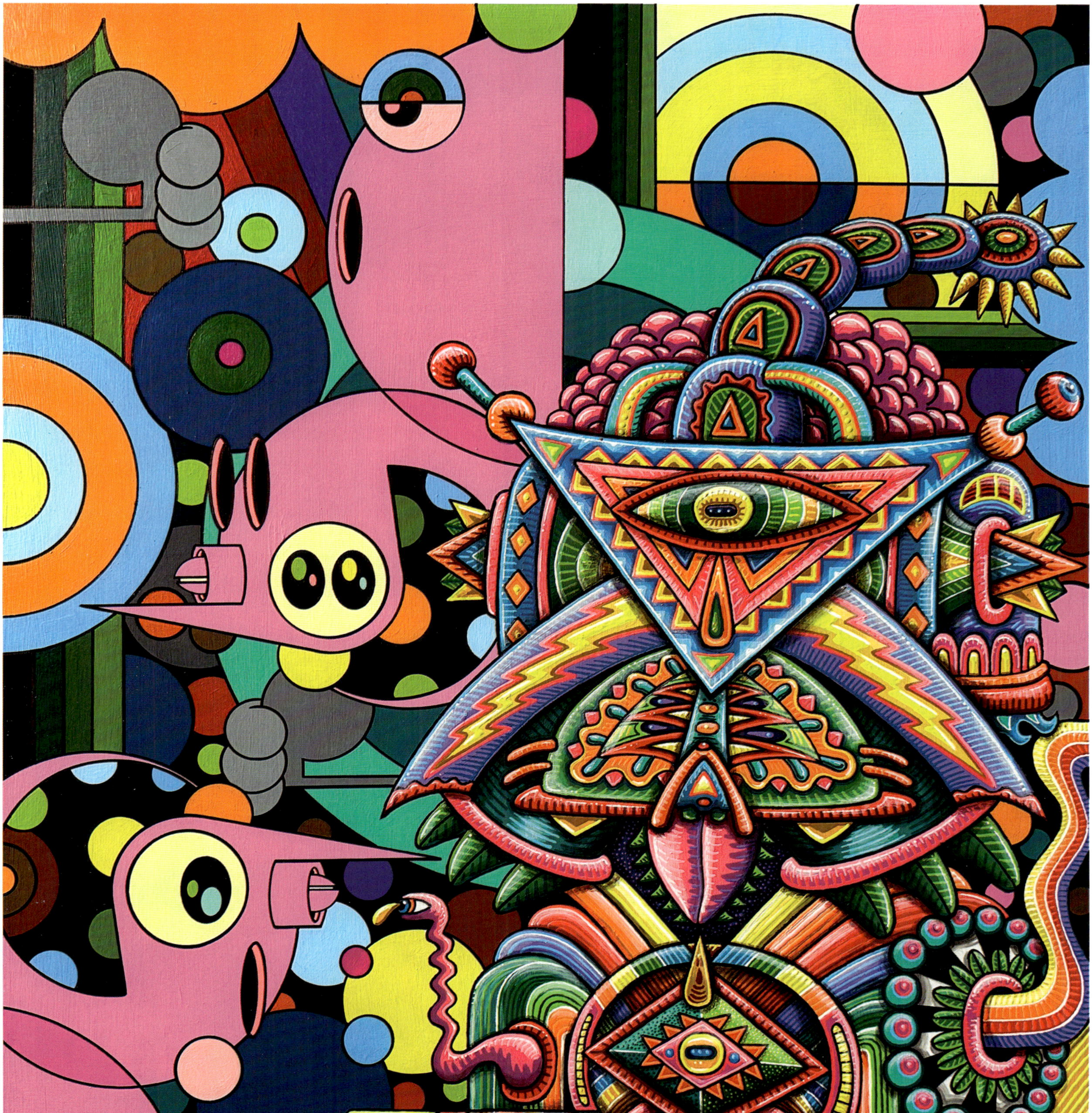

“Dalek Dimension” collabo with **James Marshall**, Acrylics on wood, 2023

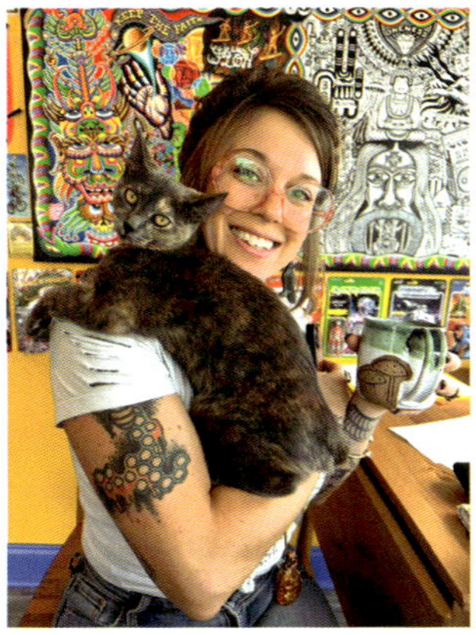
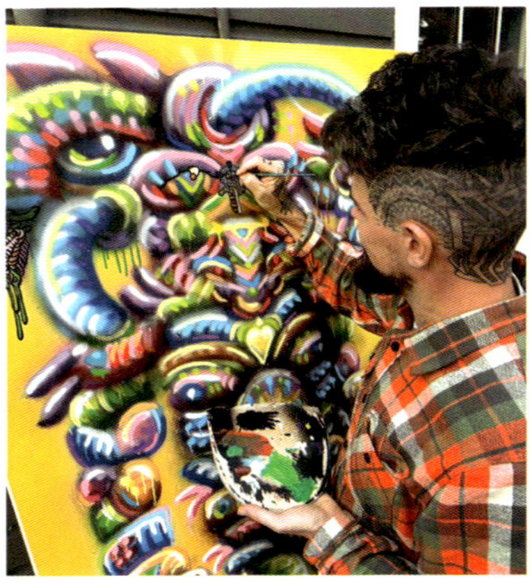
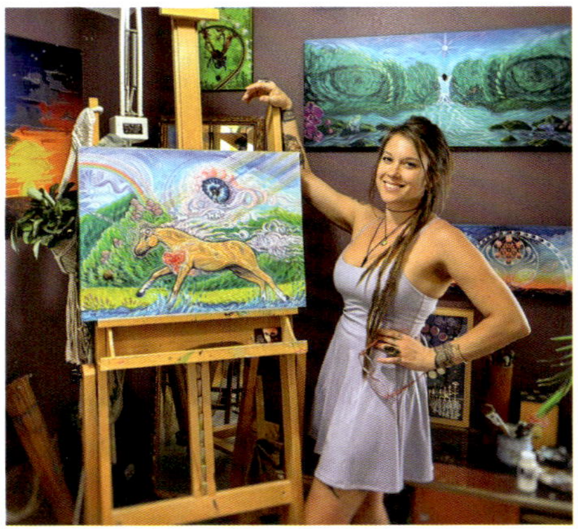
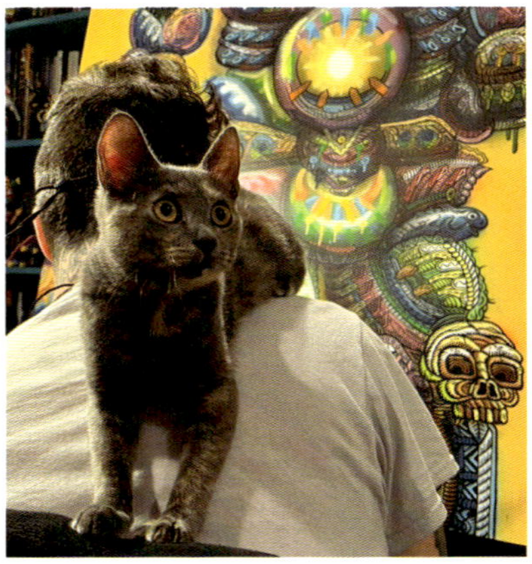

I really wanted to finish this book with some final banger pieces for you! In the previous couple of pages I share my newest collaboration paintings. The first one **"Lyran Love"** was done with my beloved lady **Paulina Casati**. It was a piece inspired on our new kitten Yoshima and about our past life connection as Lyran aliens. My entire current life chapter is a collaboration with Paulina, so it was a very easy flow to paint this.
The next collabo piece was done with the legendary artist **James "Dalek" Marshall**. We had been talking about doing a piece together for some years and we finally made it happen in time to get it into the pages of this book! I feel our colorful and psychedelic styles fused so well together, creating an interdimentional world of its own! Honoured to play with the "Space Monkey"!
Then the piece to the right here was a big wooden canvas I gave my all! I started the painting as a spray paint freestyle, then drew on top with acrylics, finally adding light and shadow glazes. I initially considered this being to be some Interdimensional Traveller but this concept soon developed deeper as I got a very interesting reading from a Psychic called **Elizabeth April**. In that reading she tapped into my latest Alien life before I chose to incarnate into Planet Earth as my many human lives. Elizabeth told me I used to be a Plaiedian alien called **"Ash"** who was the kind-hearted captain of a spaceship. His mission was to cruise out to planets on their lives' down-spiral, to reclaim cultural artifacts he could recycle. So I felt it would be fitting to add a collage as the landscape in the lower background. I really like how this vision turned out and it helps me connect with that version of my self that lives in some other strange reality.

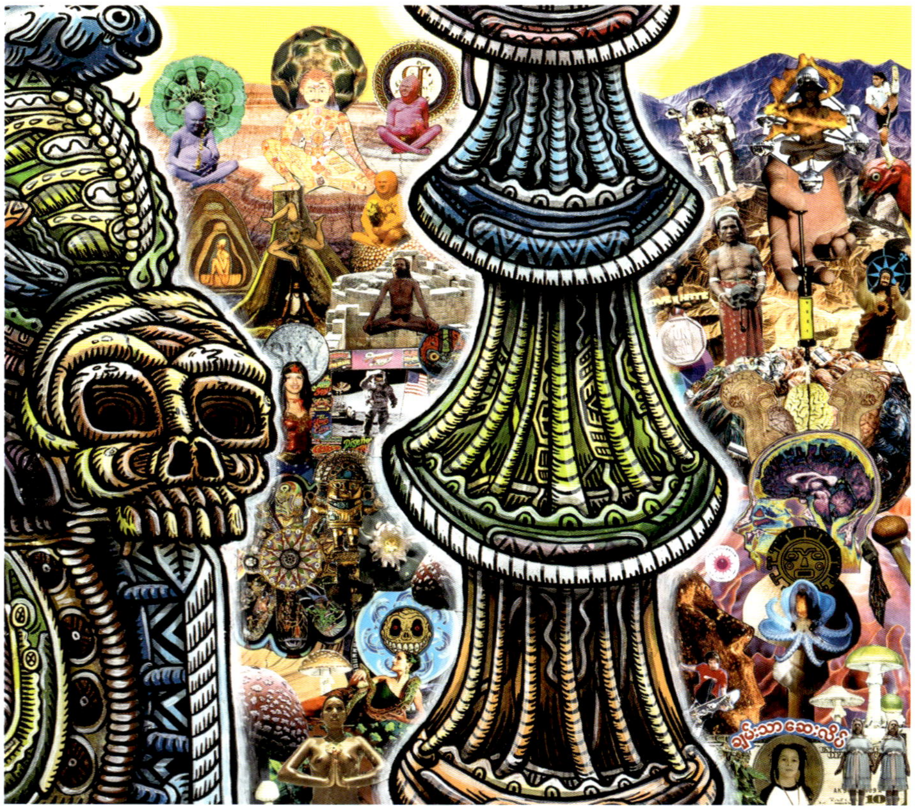

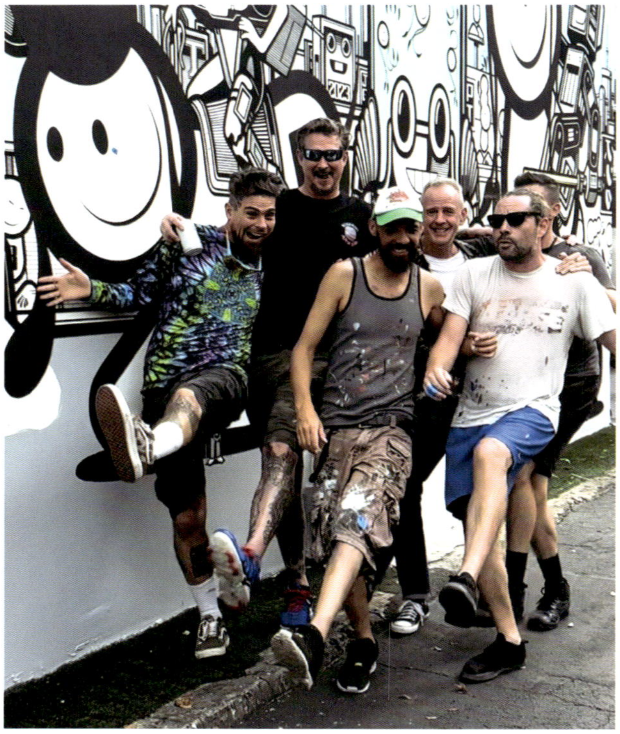

Dancing in Miami with Dalek, Fatboy Slim and The London Police, Basel 2023

I'VE KNOWN CHRIS' WORK FOR SOMETIME NOW. I'VE ALWAYS BEEN IMPRESSED WITH HIS VISION AND HIS ABILITY TO CONNECT AND COMMUNICATE WITH PEOPLE. HIS ART RADIATES HIS POSITIVE ENERGY AND GET IT DONE ATTITUDE. I HAVE A TON OF RESPECT FOR CHRIS AS AN ARTIST AND A PERSON. THE LOVE THAT HE SPREADS IS THE POSITIVITY THIS WORLD TRULY NEEDS. GETTING THE CHANCE TO FINALLY COLLABORATE WITH CHRIS WAS A REWARDING EXPERIENCE. I LOOK FORWARD TO MORE OPPORTUNITIES TO HANG OUT WITH AND WORK WITH HIM.

-JAMES "DALEK" MARSHAL, ARTIST

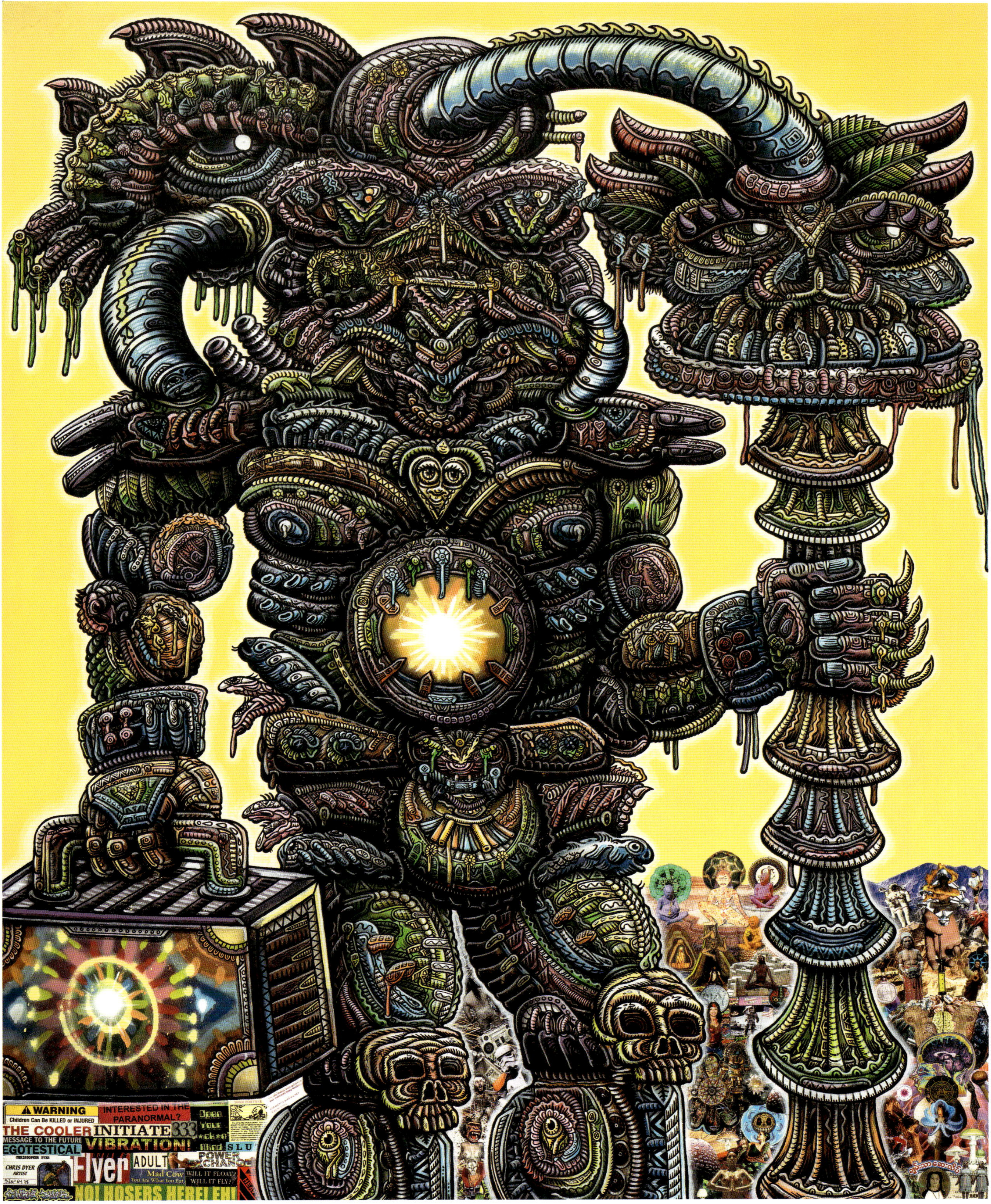

"Ash the Plaiedian Traveller"
Spray paint, acrylic and collage on wood, 2023

OUTRO

I wanted to finish this book with a painting that really wrapped up the 13 year process of evolution that has been covered within. So I painted a self portrait showing different versions of myself, peeling back to give birth to a higher vibration version. I called the painting **"I AM"** and this statement can be followed by: Love, Peace, Calmness, Self Love, Acceptance, God, Humanity, Unity, Consciousness, that I am, etc.

The Magnificent Eight creatures that are shown here, from bottom left:

A- Frida Kahlo-Was a soulful Mexican painter who expressed herself so strongly. A tortured person who died young and broken. I've always felt a great affinity with her, even before she blew up through the movie done about her in the early 2000s. More recently, a suspicion of mine was confirmed, when two different psychics told me I am one of the reincarnations of her. I don't remember that life, but if this is true, hopefully my life can be a chance to find happiness and harmony again.

B- Guadalupe Virgin- Not necessarily the Catholic symbol, but the archetype of the celestial mother, who has always been comforting to me. Painted in Green, she also represents the "Ayahuasca" motherly figure, who lives in me and guides my way when I listen enough. This character is also a low-key shout-out to my own (red hair) mother, Josie.

C- Chris Trinity- These are three different stages of my physical expression. On the left we have a fat, married, dreadlock version. To the right we see the shaved and tattooed head version from 2021-2022, a moment in transition, a sad chapter with many struggles. And in the middle we have a rainbow body, lighter version of me, full of Self Love. Perhaps closer to how I present myself today, yet this is always in flux.

D- Planet Earth- I placed our planet on the "Solar Plexus" of the more enlightened version of me, because I want our world to also grow into a higher frequency version. I am part of the earth, so I am the earth too.

E- Yeshua- Jesus has always been an important character in my life. I painted his skin blue because I didn't want him to be only one race (instead be part of all of them) and also because I believe he is connected to **Krishna**. That is also why I placed the Om symbol inside his Halo cross, marking the Trinity 333, numbers I am so connected to (I was born the 3 of the 3). The hand gesture is a blessing called the "Benediction". He was born into Jewish culture but I've read that in his "missing years" he studied under many different spiritual paths. Regardless of these human-cultural details, he incarnated in earth to help awaken the planet. Though very misunderstood, even today, I believe he did succeed in widely spreading a message of unconditional Love, raising the vibration of this planet. I resonate with him deeply, past the cultural religion structures that spanned from his stories. I believe the Christ Consciousness is still awakening inside each and every one of us, little by little, and is part of the new Positive era of humanity that we are just at the beginning of!

F- Sasquach- I've always had resonance with this mysterious and elusive "Bigfoot" creatures! According to the "Law of One" (information channelled in the early 80's), this "second density" race hosts entities from the planet **Maldek**, which was destroyed long ago (now where the asteroid belt is in our Solar System). These scarce creatures are here to work out karmic resolutions and dwell in deep underground passageways or uninhabited deep forests. This character is also a Low-key shout-out to my dad Teddy "el mono".

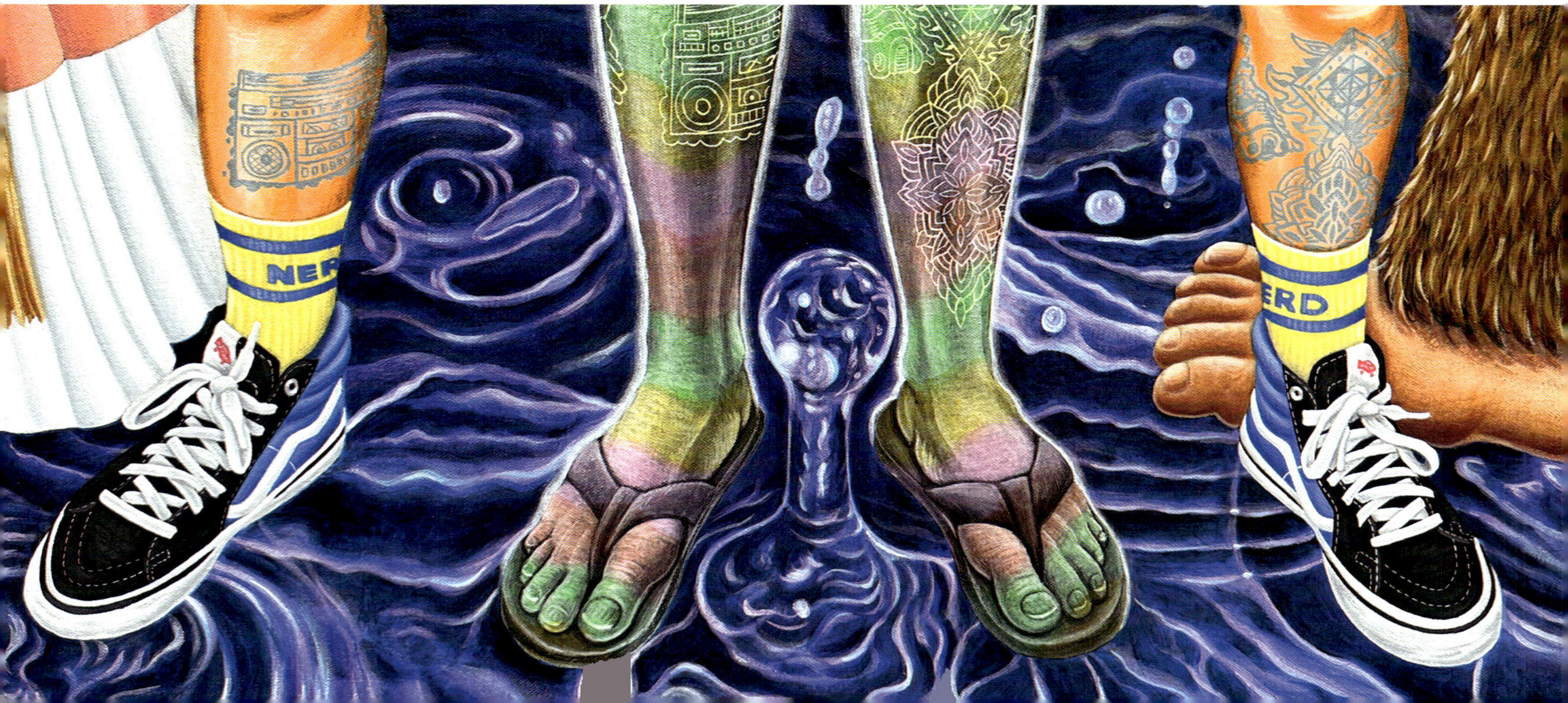

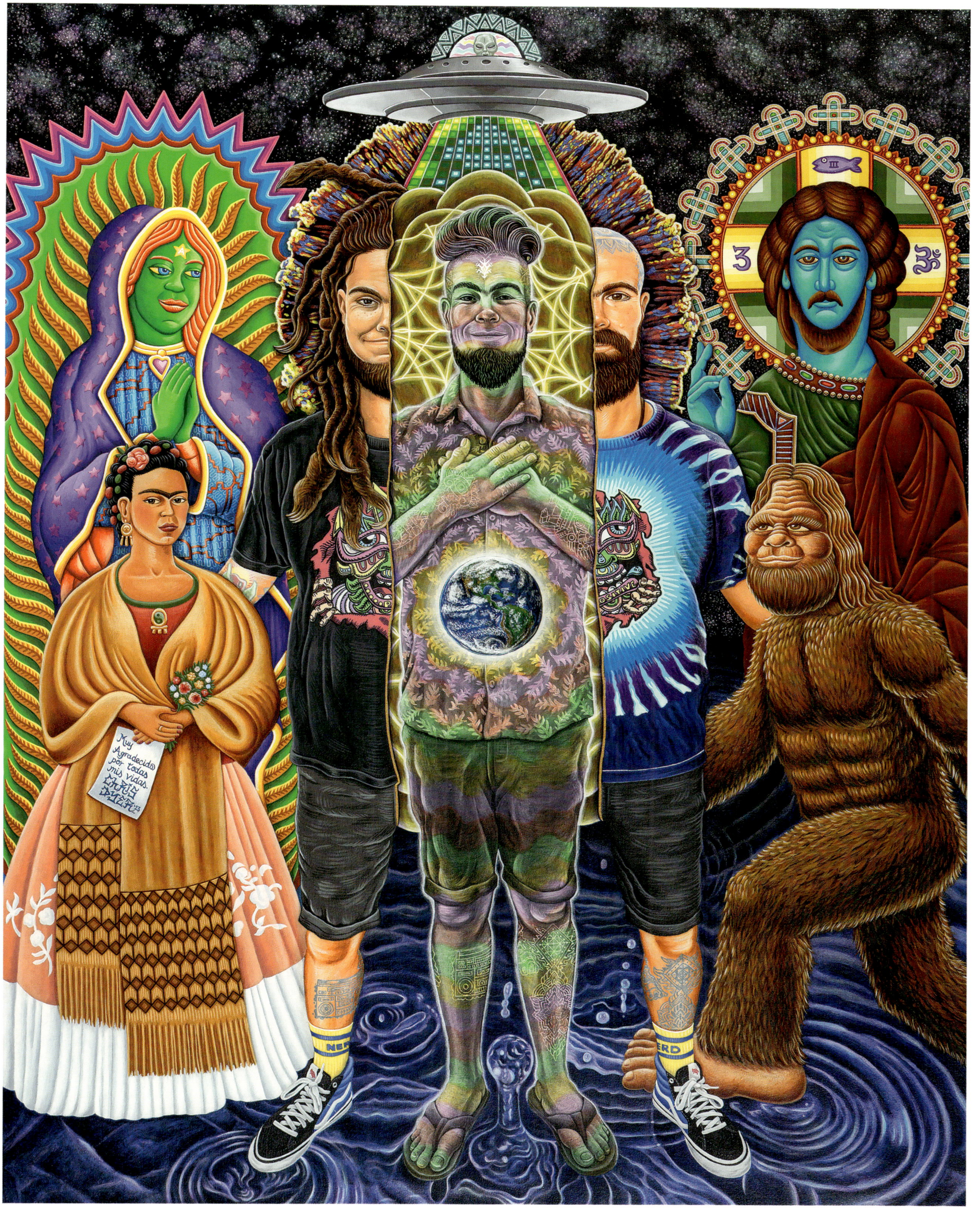

"I AM" Acrylics on canvas, 2023

GOODBYES AND GRATIT

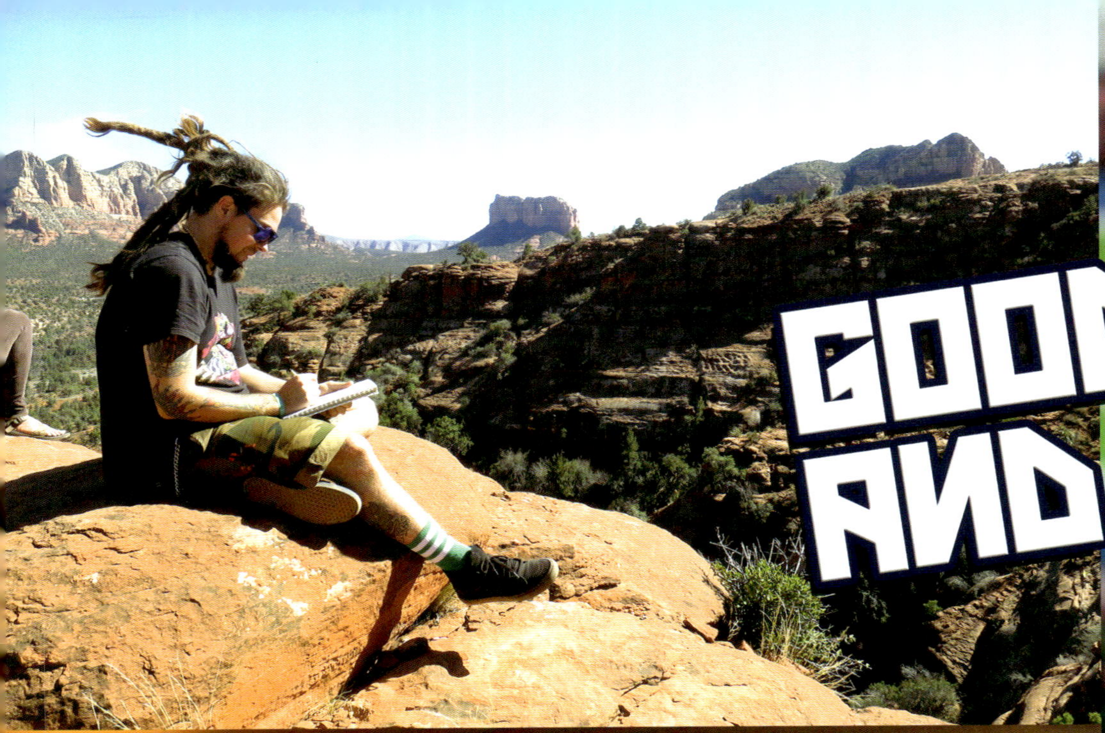

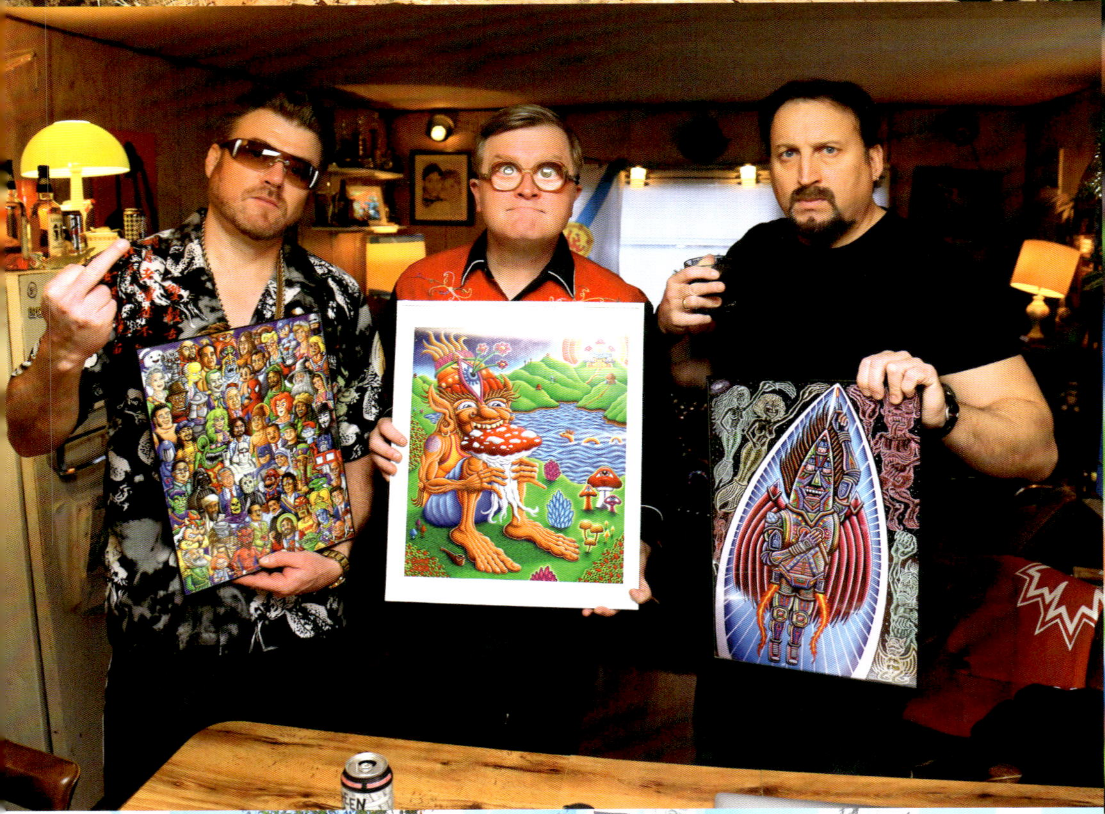

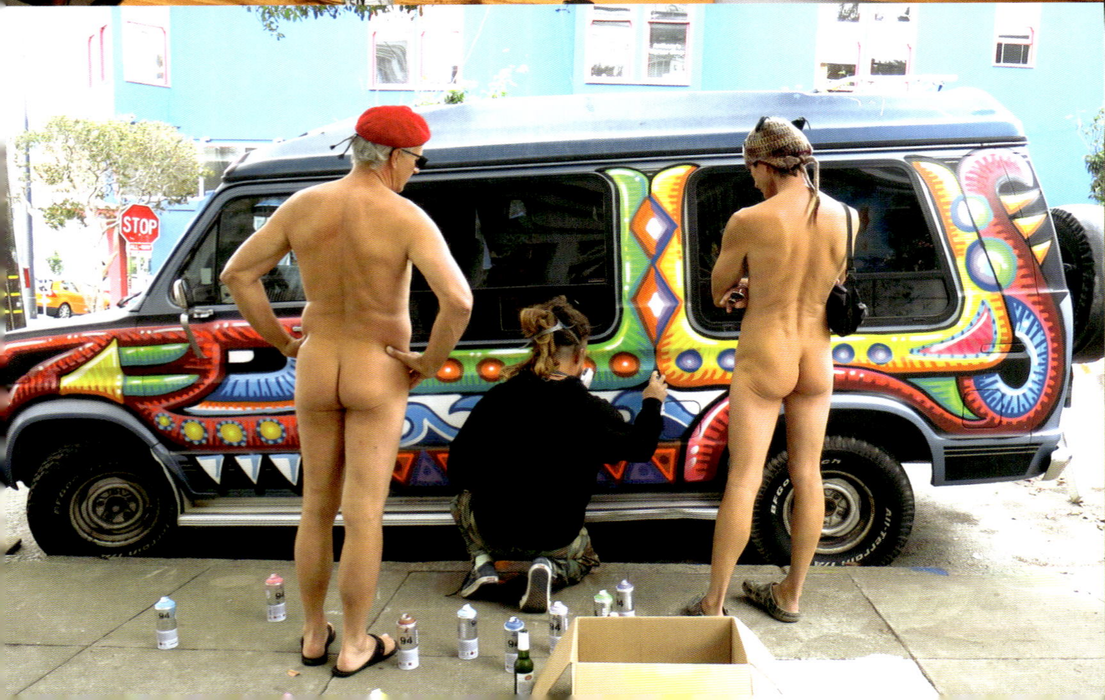

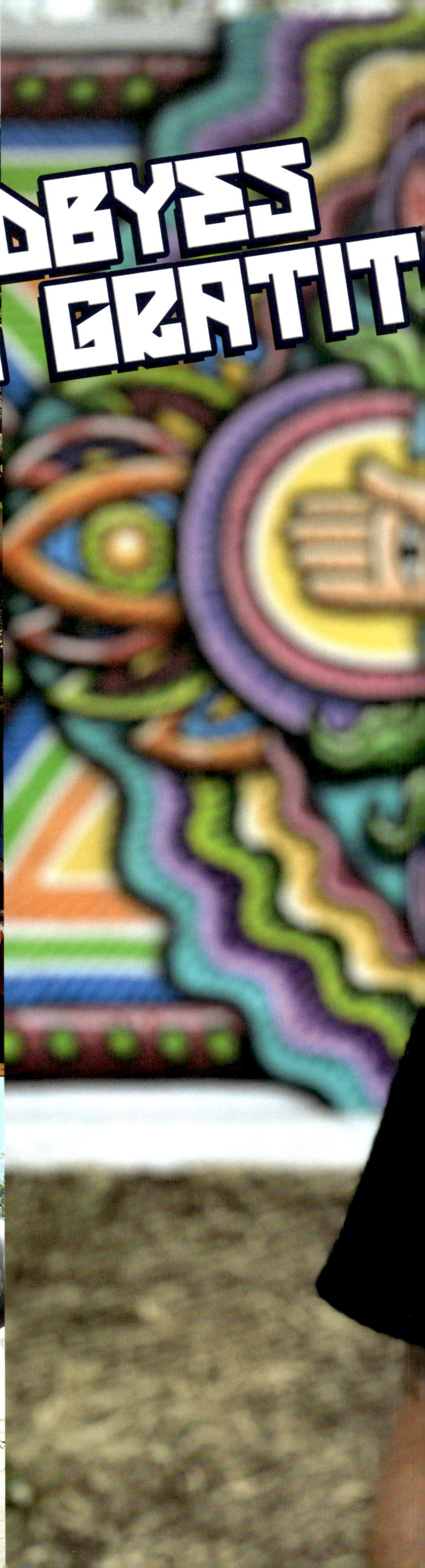

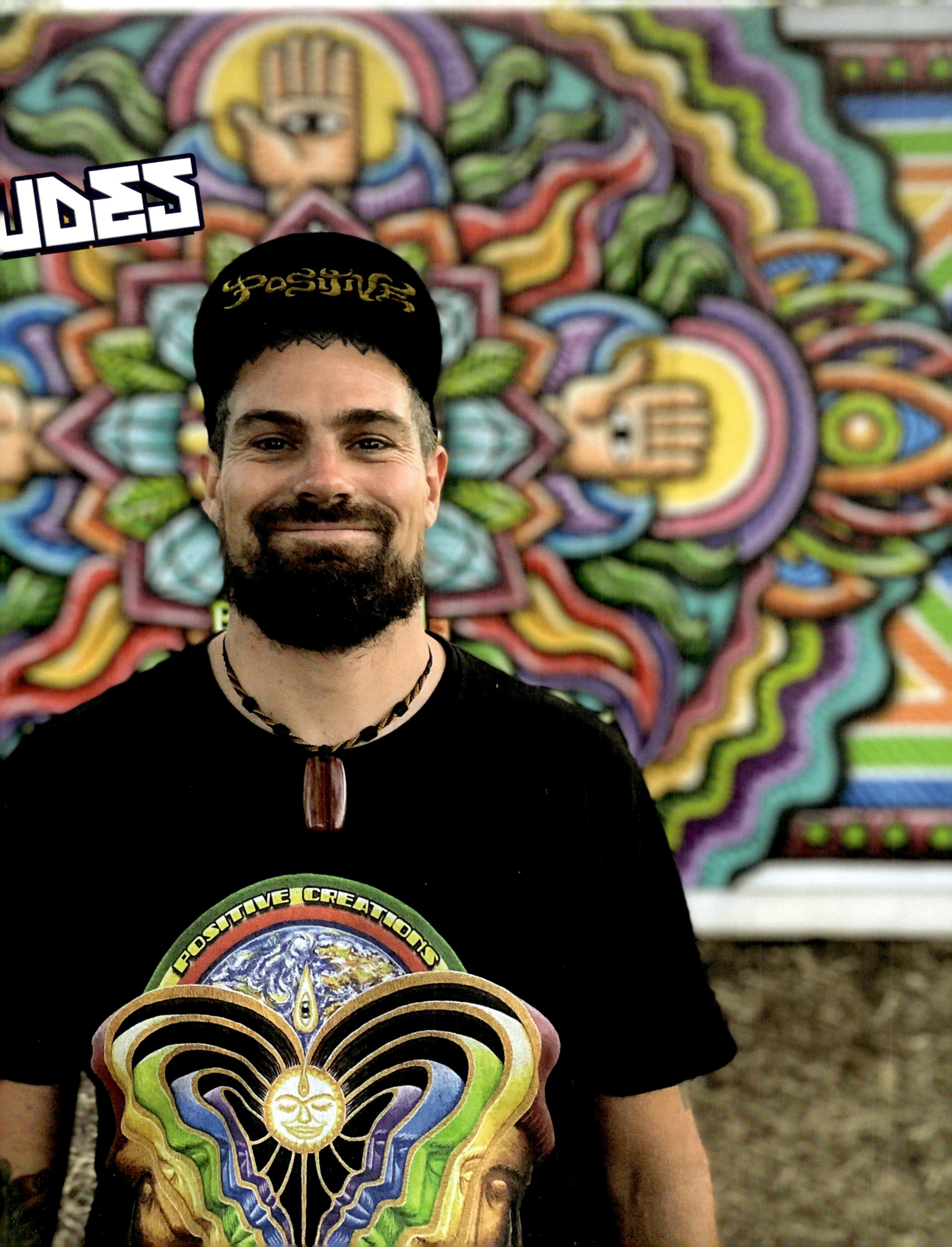
UDES
POSITIVE CREATIONS

FAN ART

There are so many people who have helped me in my life and art career that I can't possibly name you all! That said I wanted to shoutout anyone I didn't already previously in this book. Starting with my fans, which are such sweet people who have supported me so much throughout the years! Truly a **Positive Creations Tribe**! Here some fan art by them, followed by some portraits that artist friends have honored me with. So much Gratitude for you all!!!

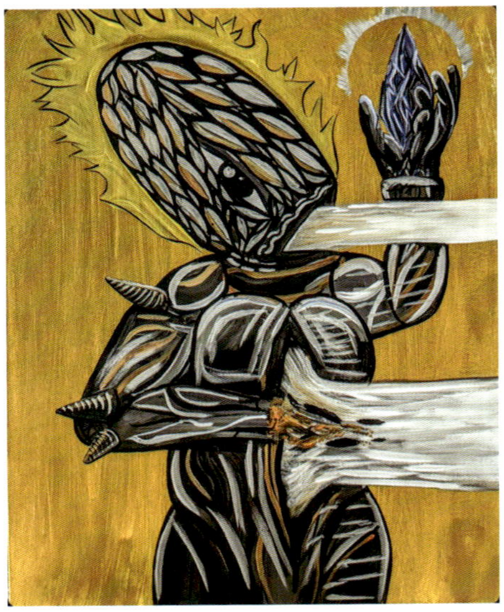
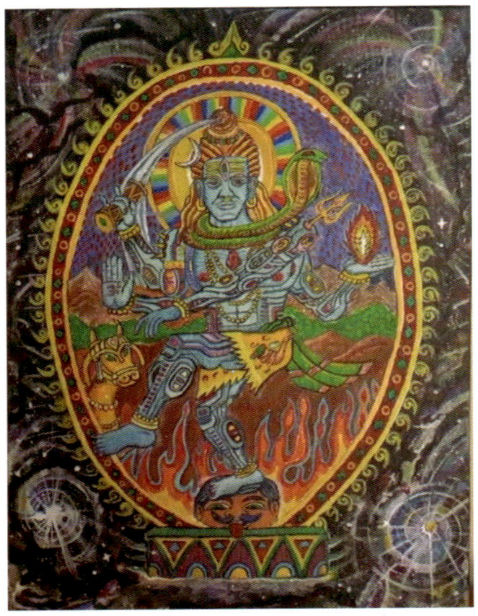
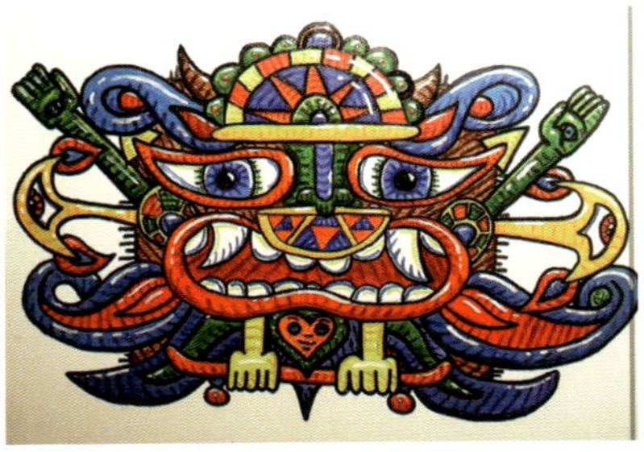
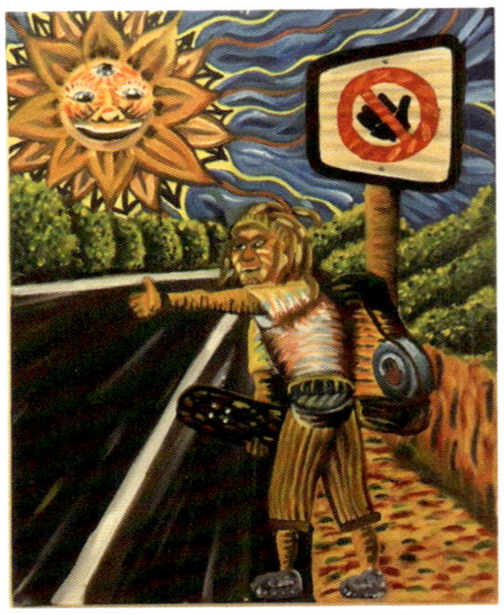
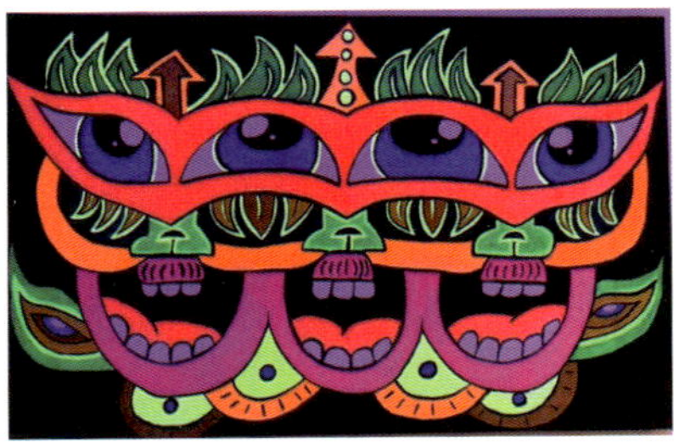
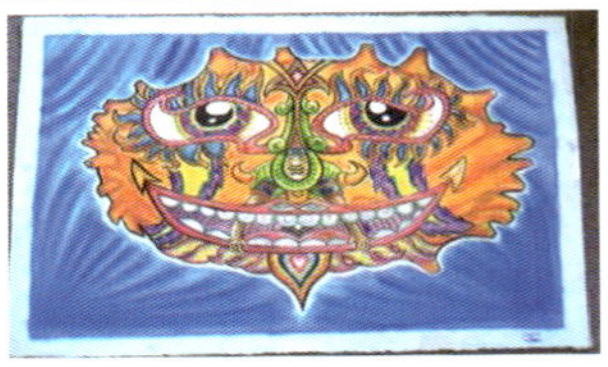
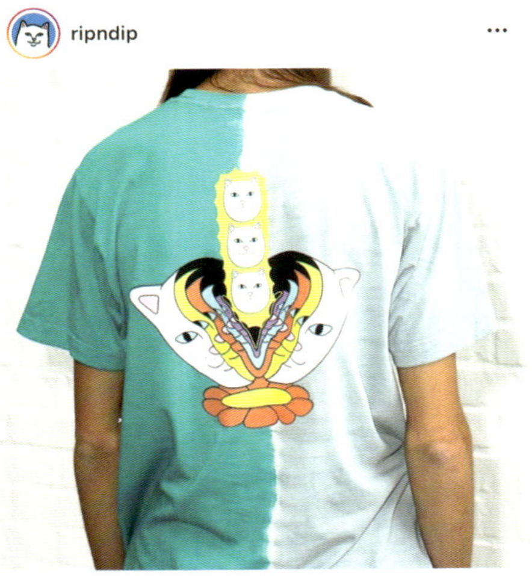

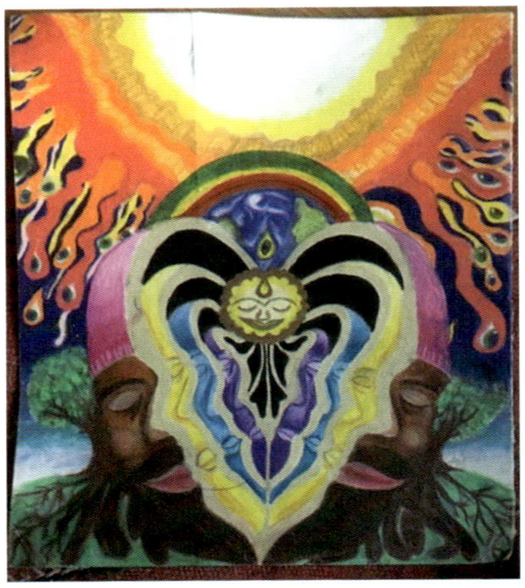
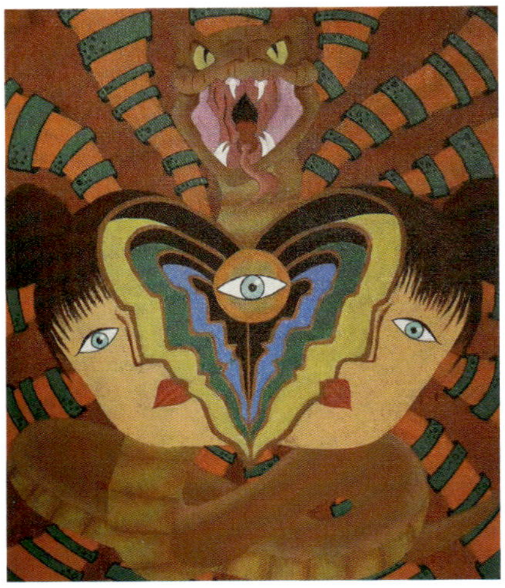
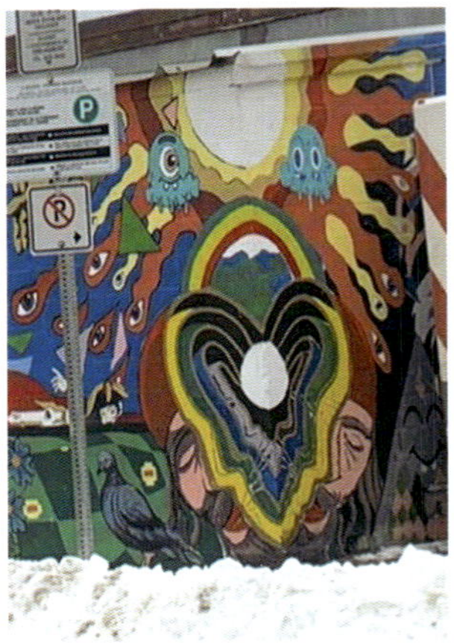
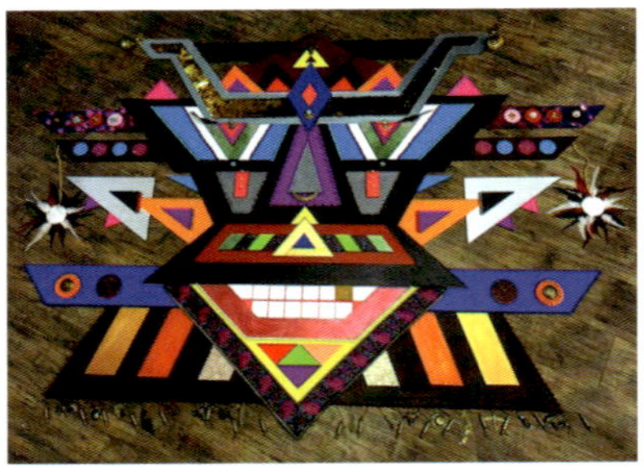
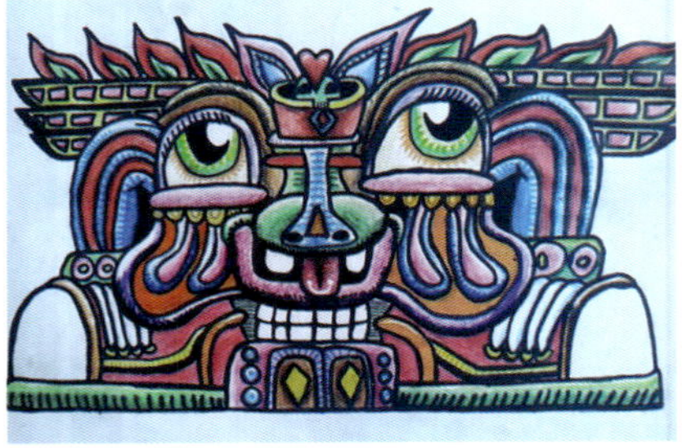
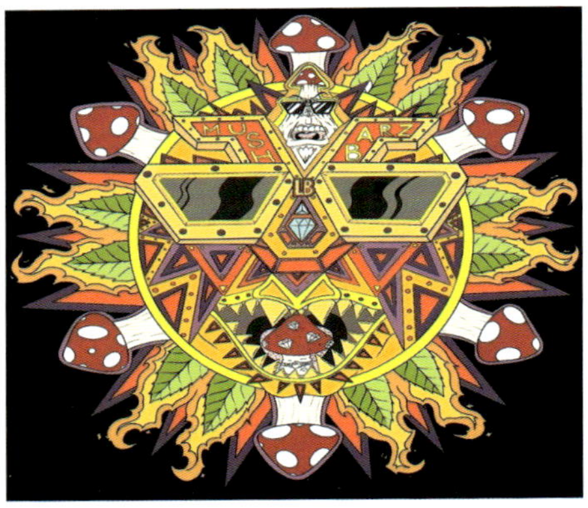
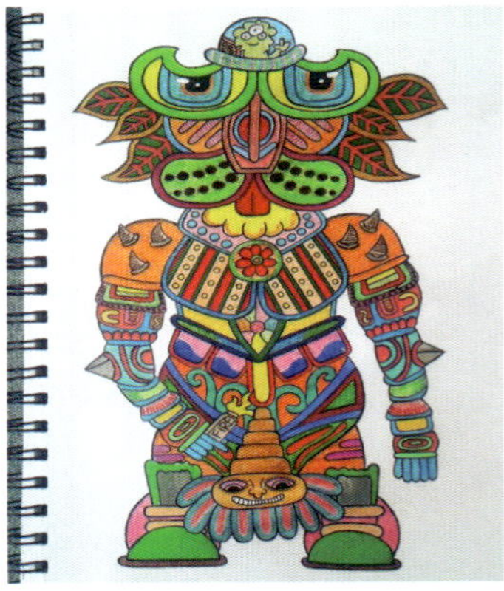
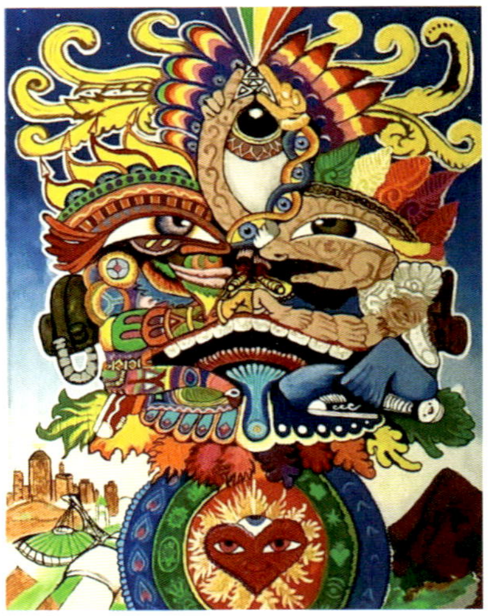
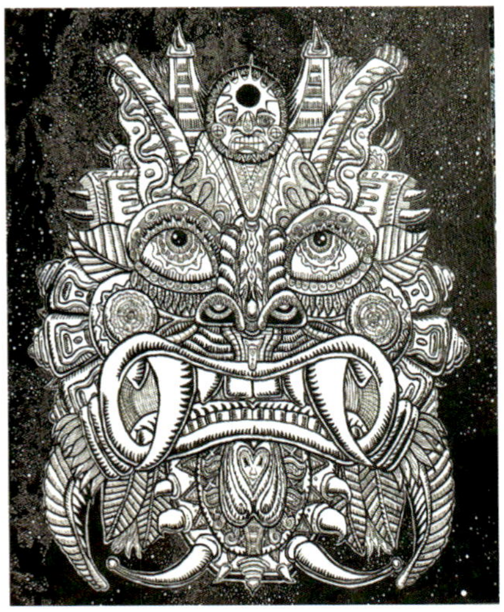
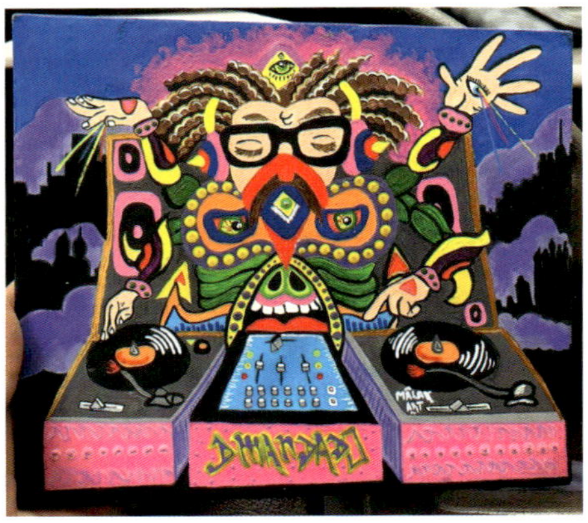
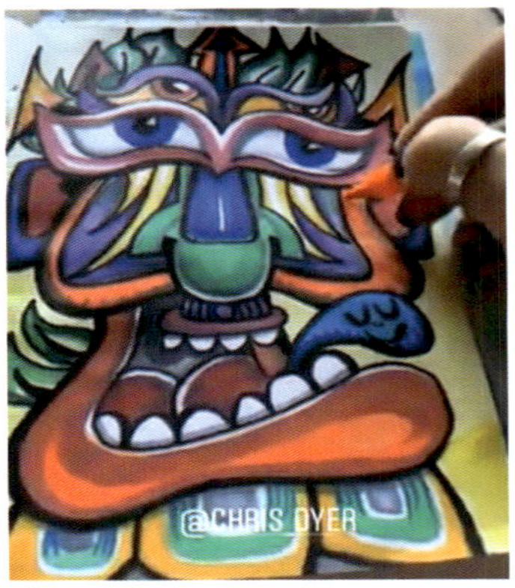

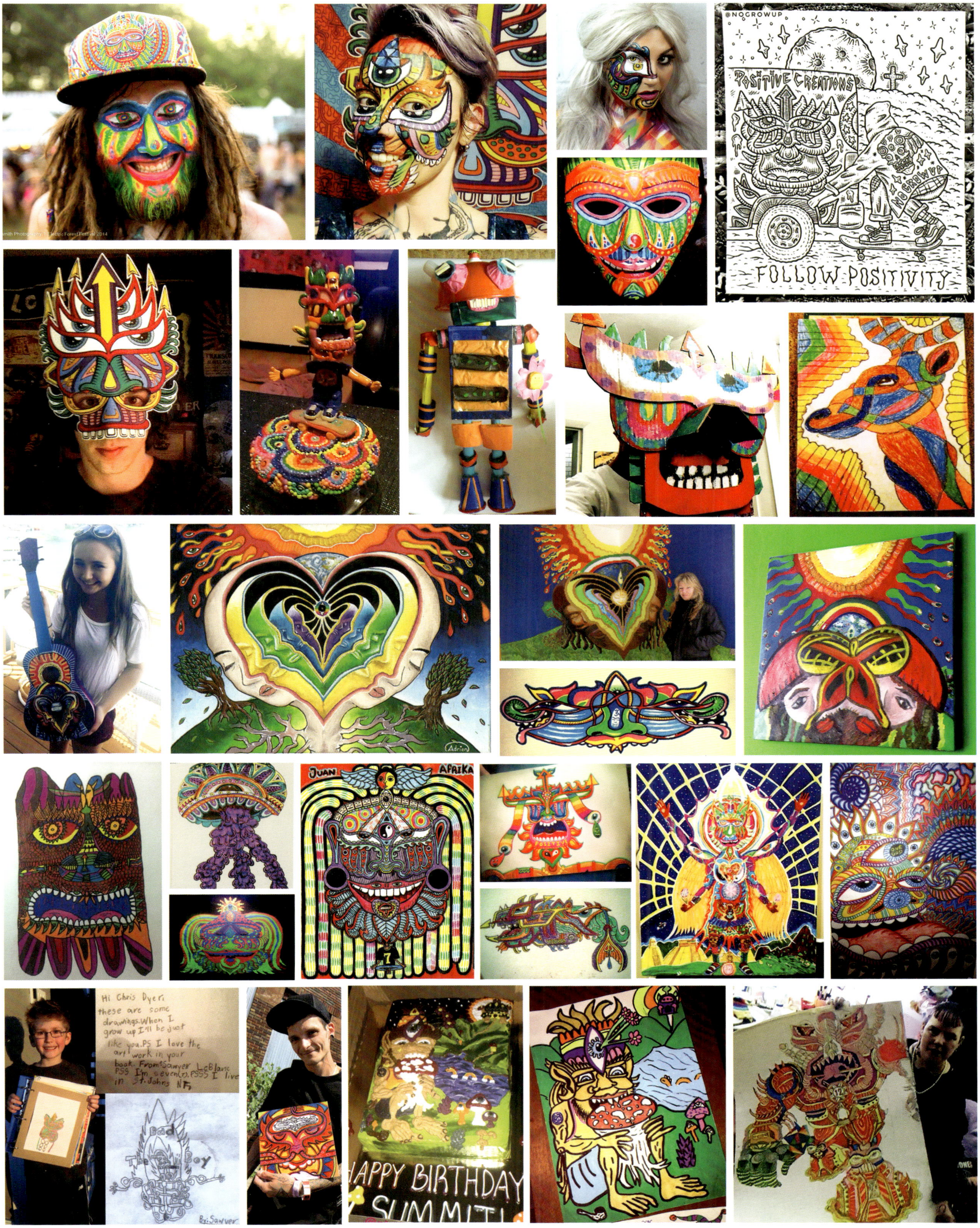
@NOGROWUP
POSITIVE CREATIONS
NO GROW UP
FOLLOW POSITIVITY
JUAN
AFRIKA
Hi Chris Dyer, these are some drawings. When I grow up I'll be just like you. PS I love the art work in your book. From Sawyer LeBlanc PSS I'm seven(7). PSSS I live in St. Johns NF
Bad
The Boy
By: Sawyer
APPY BIRTHDAY

FRIENDS' PORTRAITS

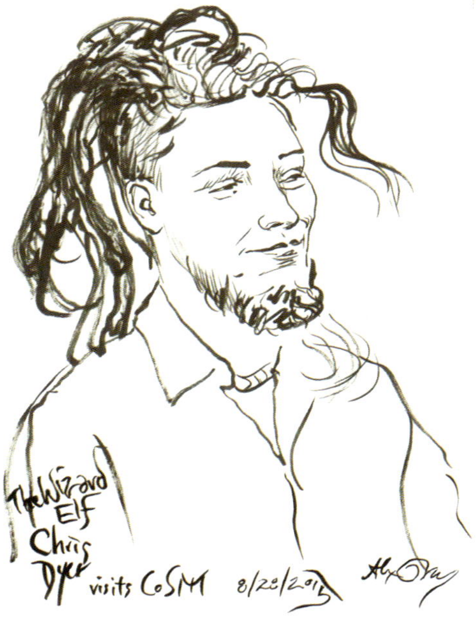

By Alex Grey

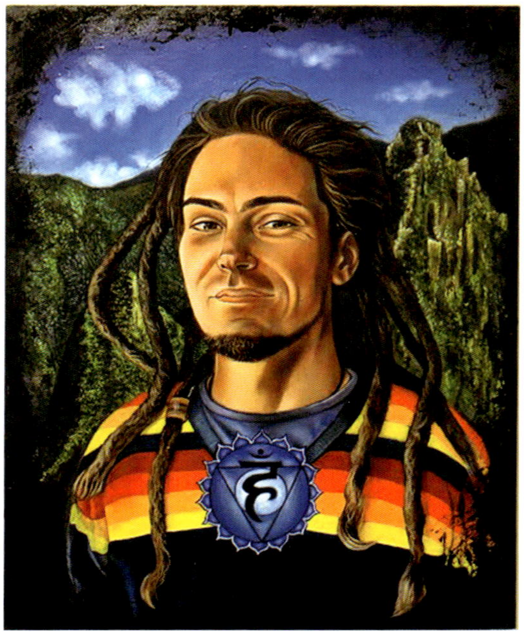

By Jennifer Mceuen

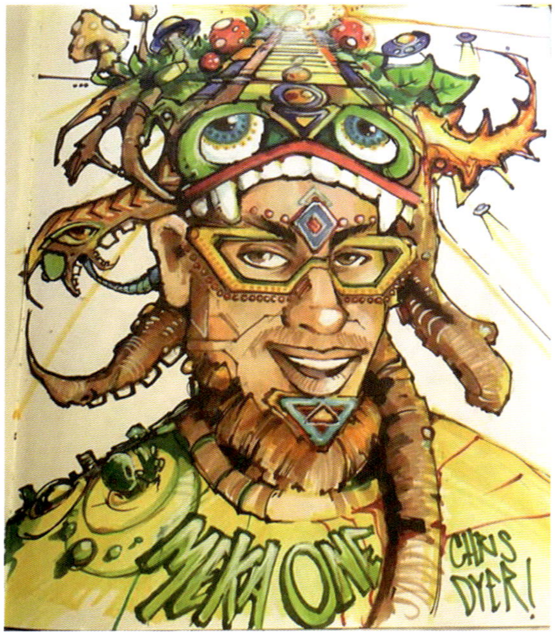

By Gabriel Welsh

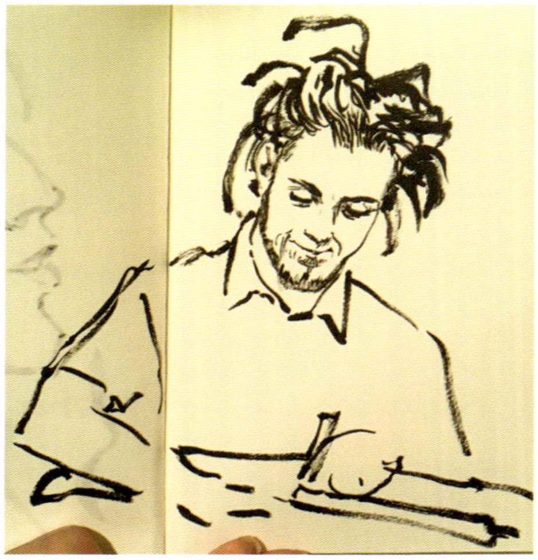

By Alex Grey

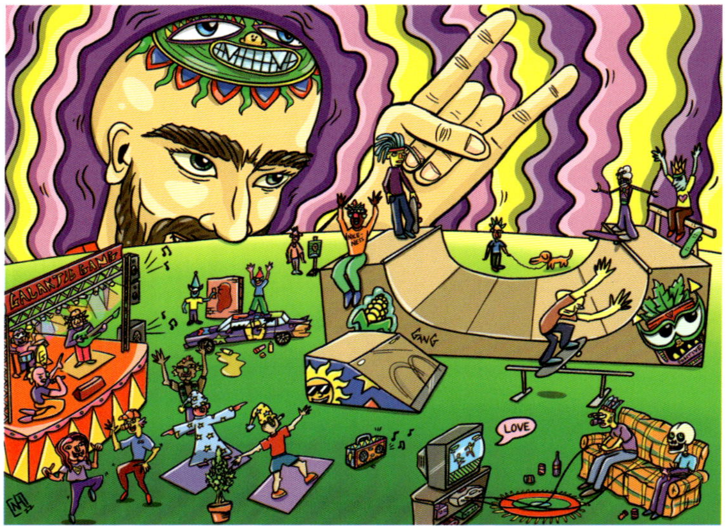

By Corn Man

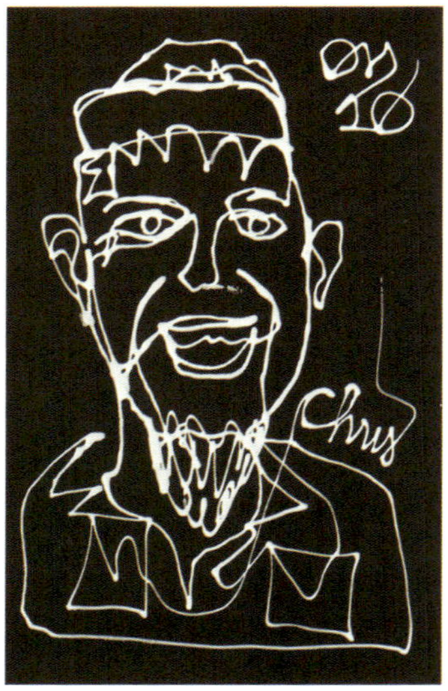

By Ohio Mike

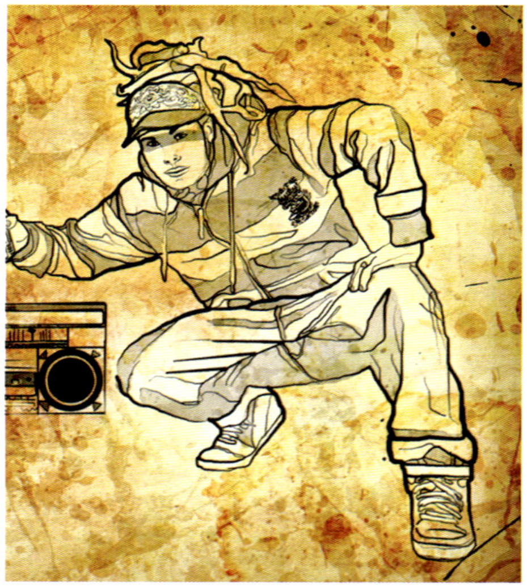

By Adida Fallen Angel

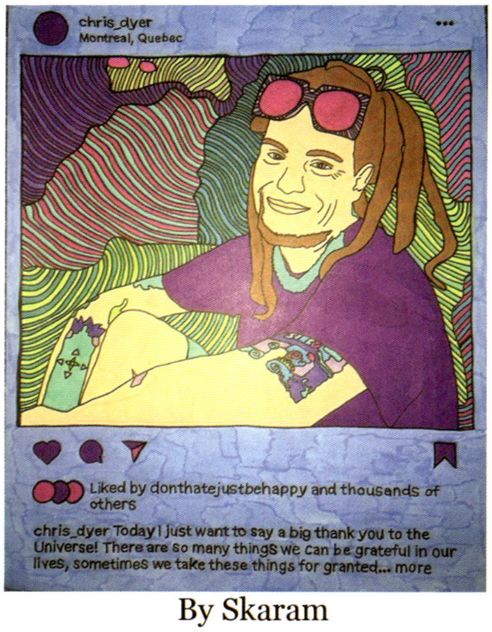

By Skaram

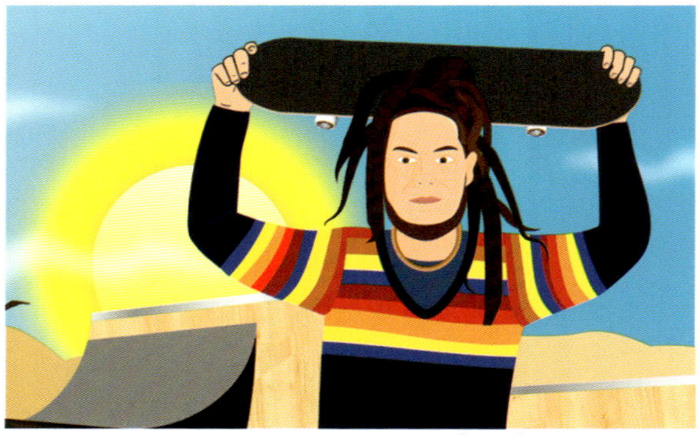

By Terren Overback

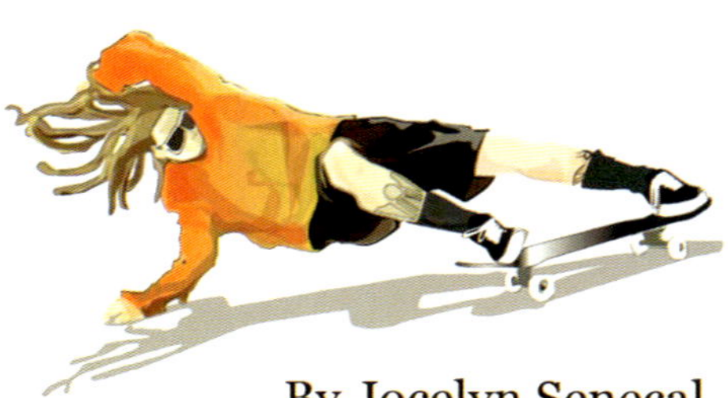

By Jocelyn Senecal

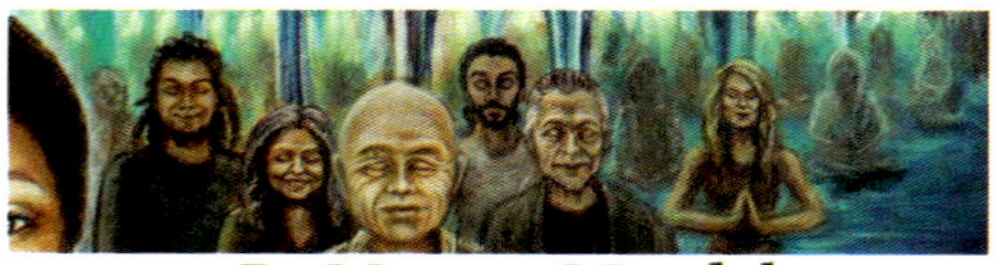

By Morgan Mandala

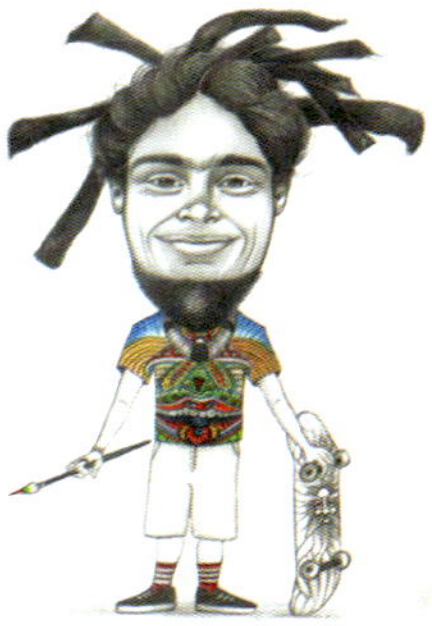

By Malsehevic Milica

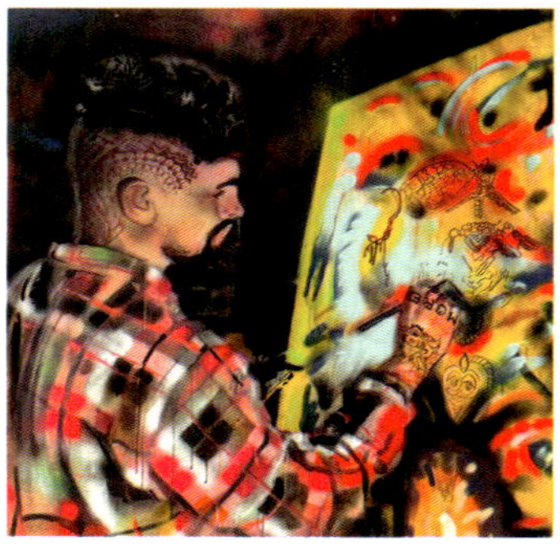

By Tony Kroll

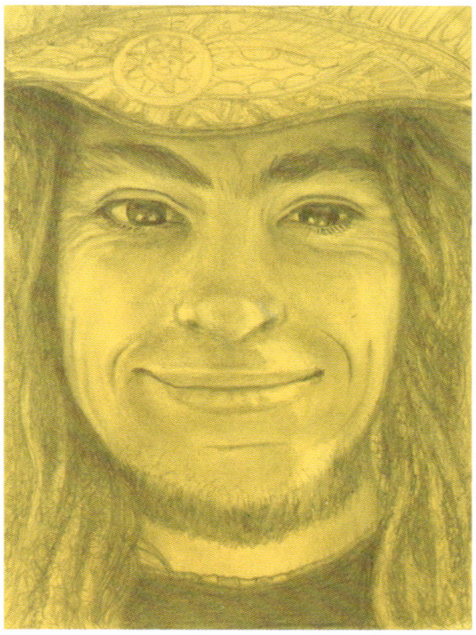
By Maritta Benjamin

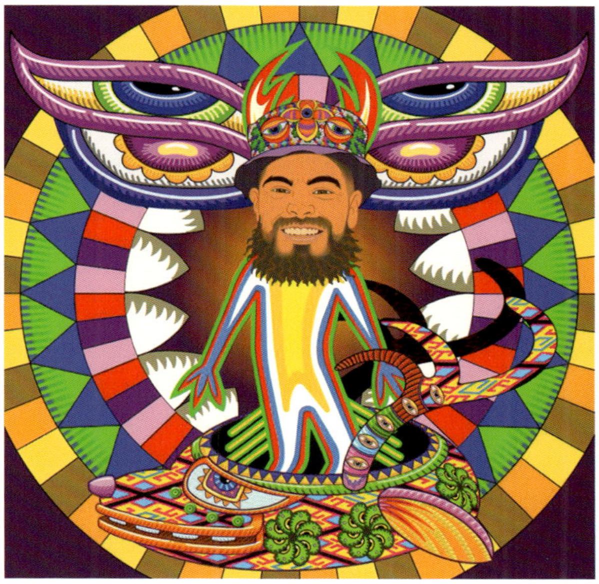
By Hidrogo

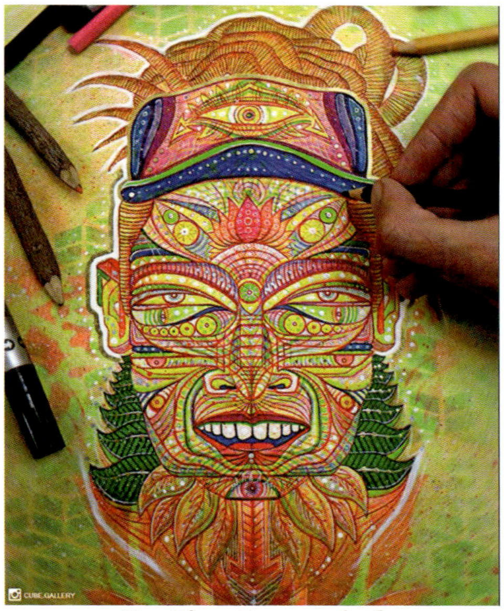
By Sina Irannejad

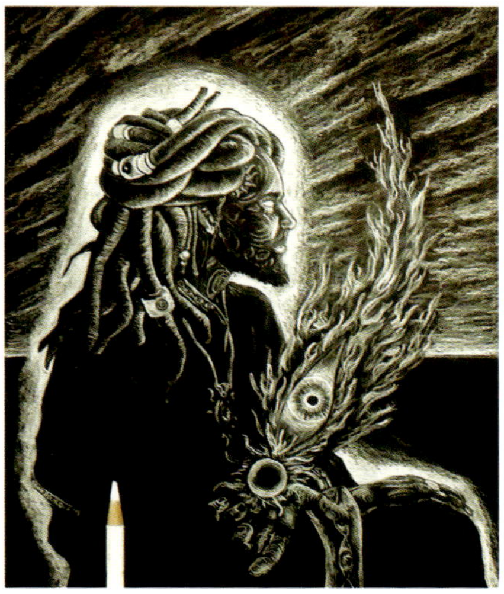
By Sean Bourque

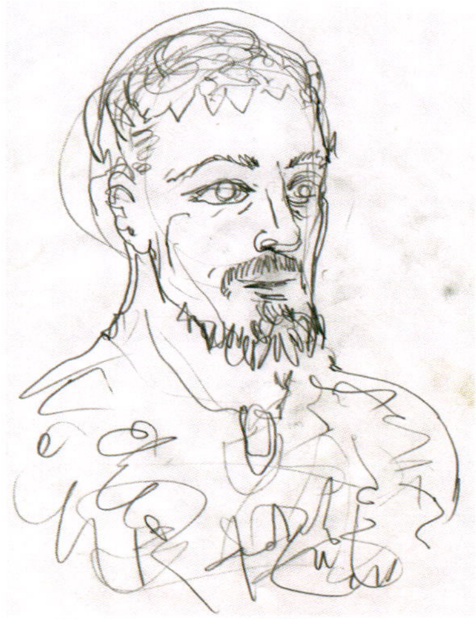
By Roman Villagrana

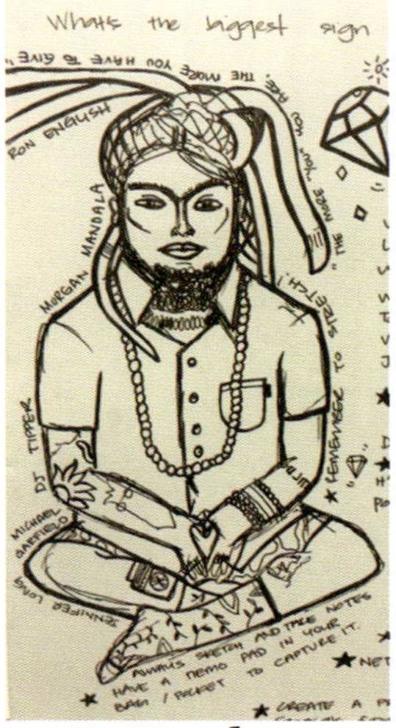

By Vondove

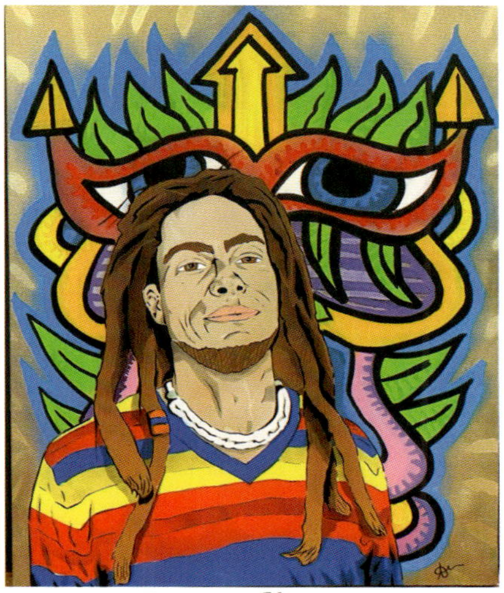
By Dredignsma

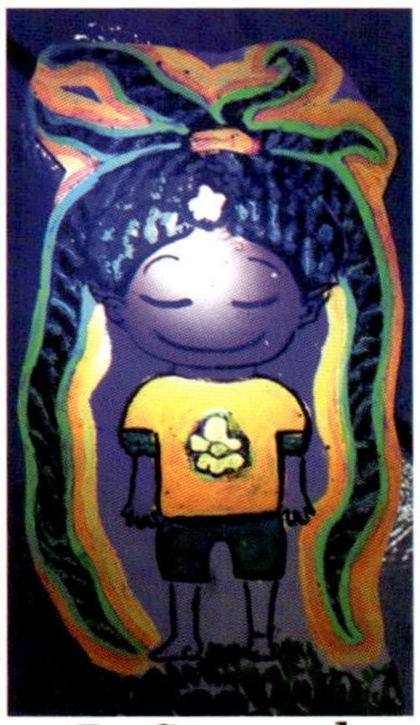
By Starseed

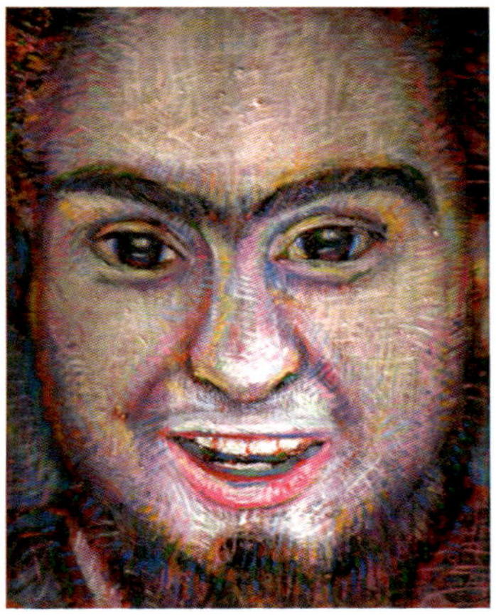
By Carlos Luis Sanchez Becerra

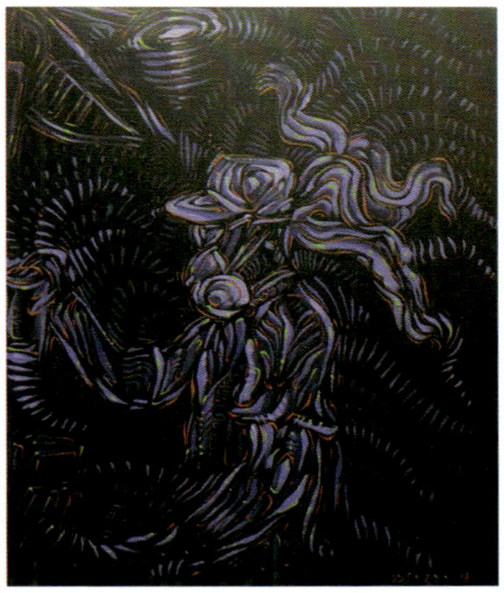
By Odenedo

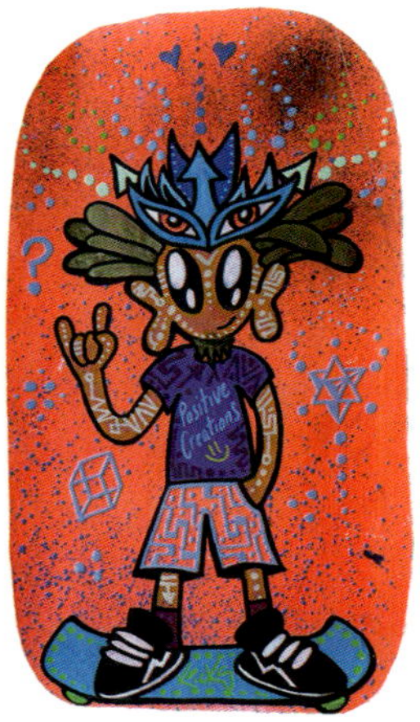
By Kicks

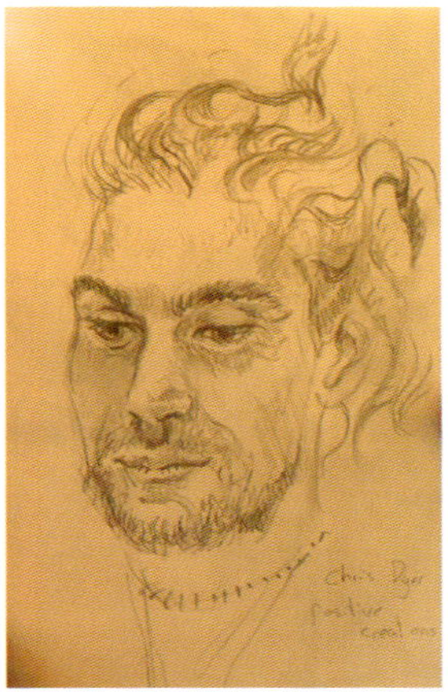
By Torus Energy

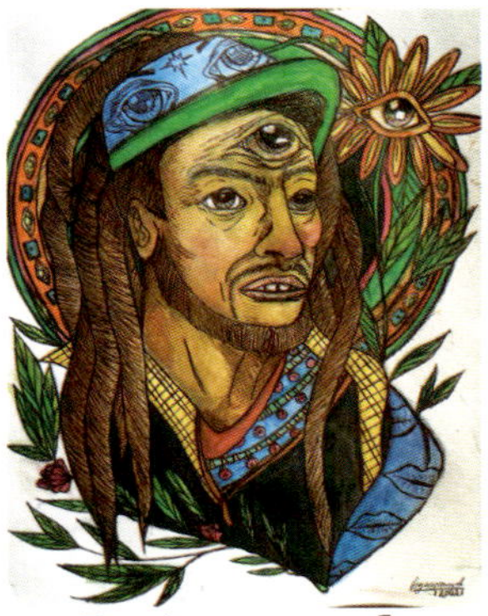
By Agaromad

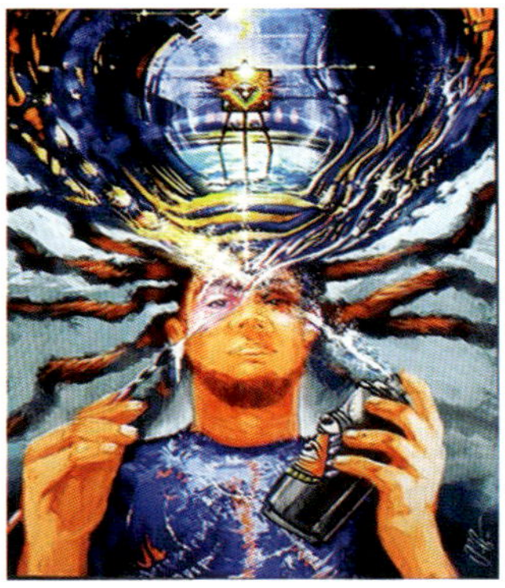
By Grant Lomman

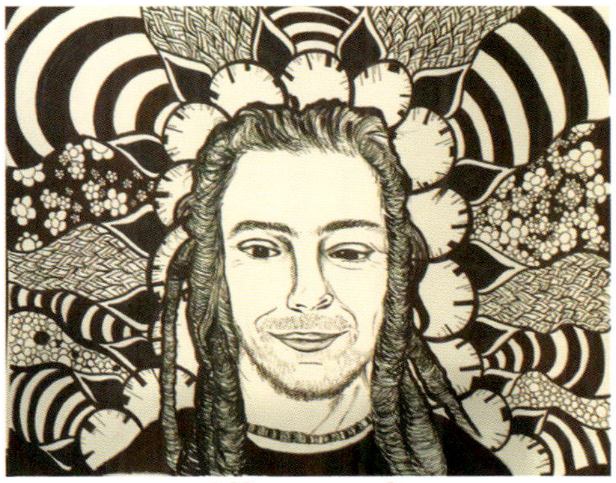
By Tiffany Molases

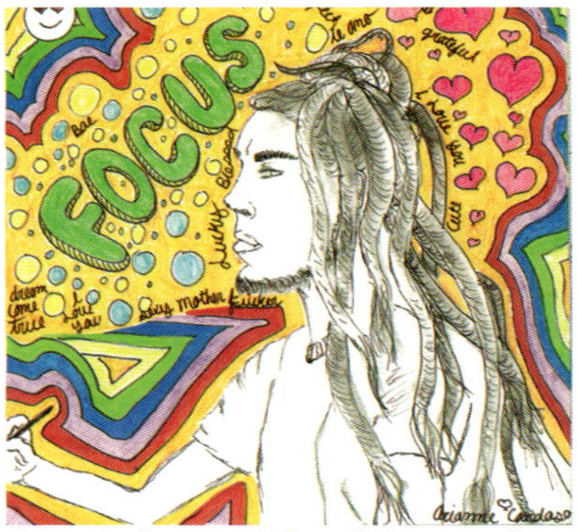

By Arianne The Metanoist

FAMILY

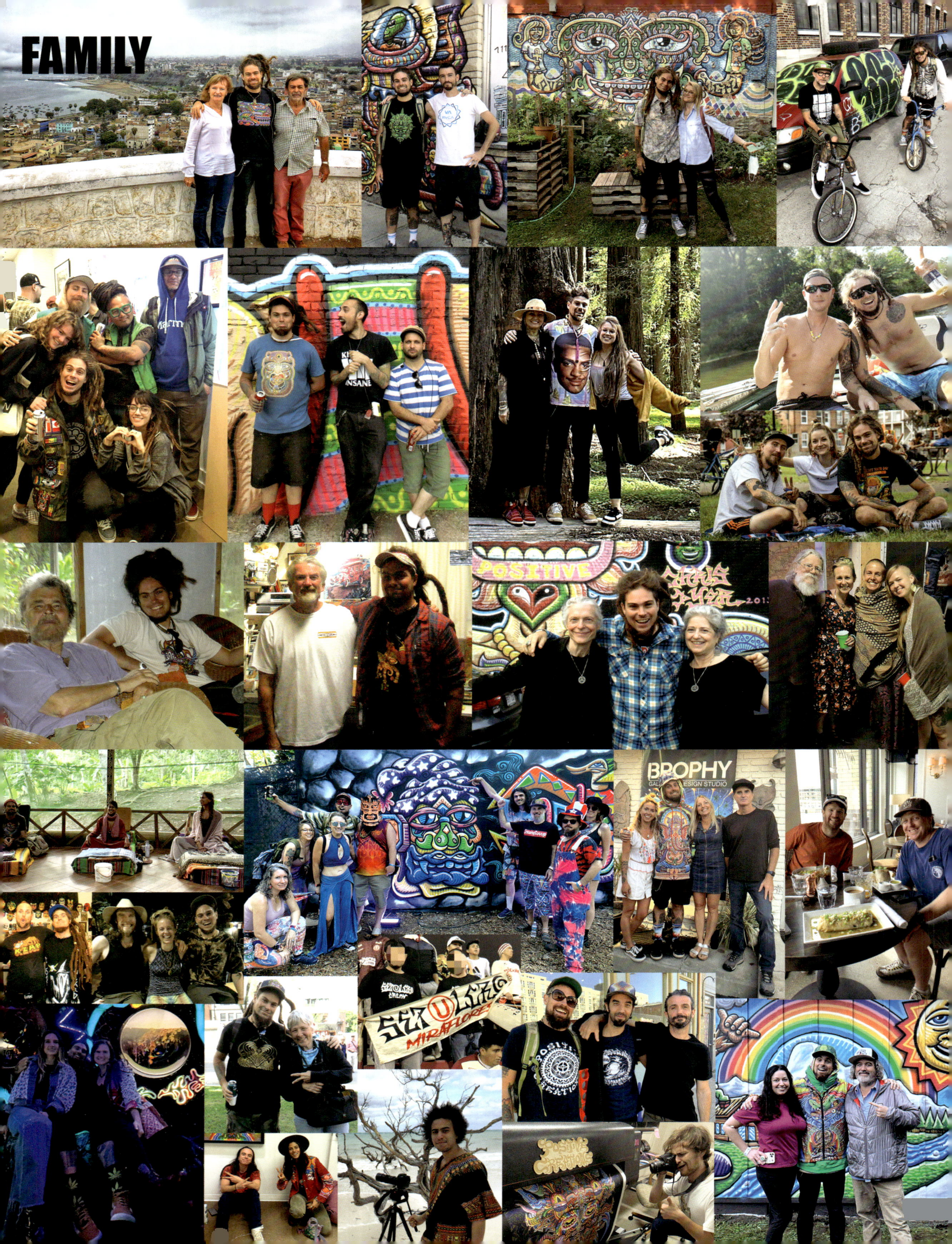

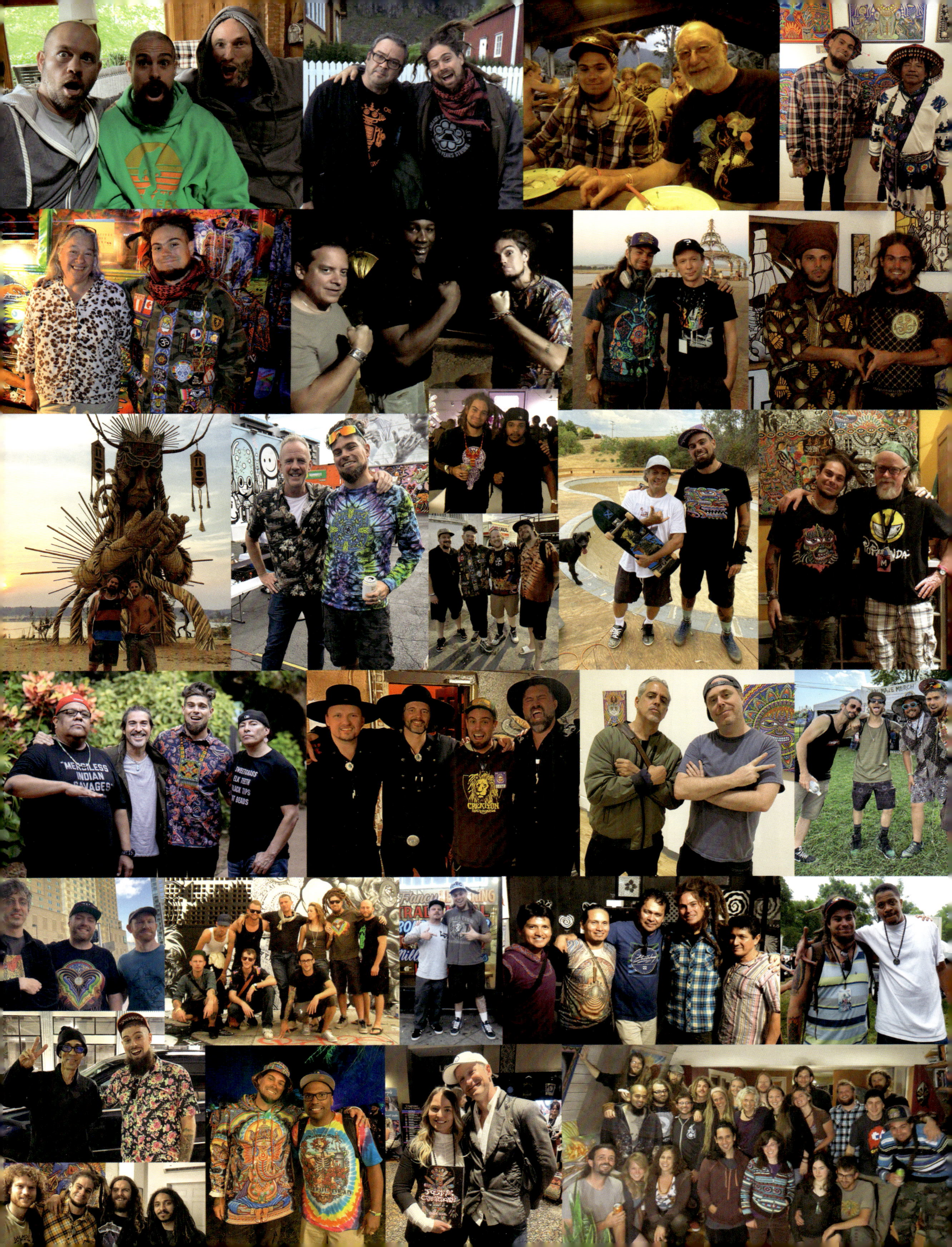
"MERCILESS
INDIAN
SAVAGES"

CLIENTS AND SPONSORS

I honestly wish money had nothing to do with the art that I create. Regardless of these desires of making Art for the sake of it, I have bills to cover in order to afford the time and space to keep producing my medicine. Luckily I have nice client friends who support my journey by buying my original work. Also, a Big Shoutout of Gratitude to all the brands that sponsored the printing of the thousands of copies of this book you hold in your hands!!

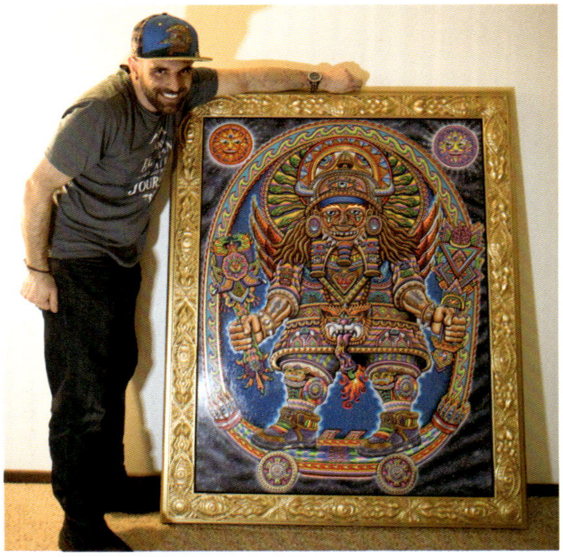
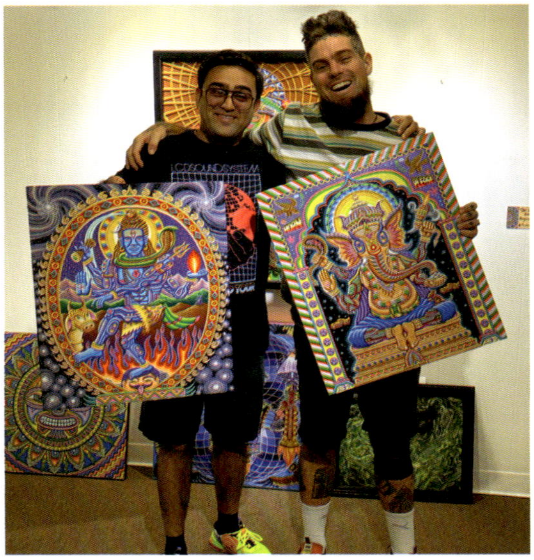
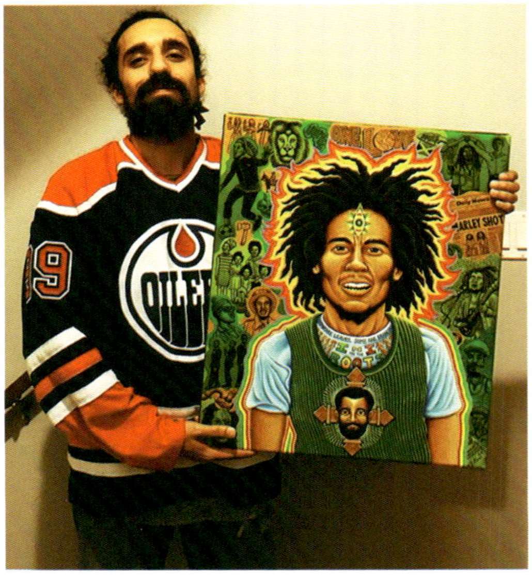
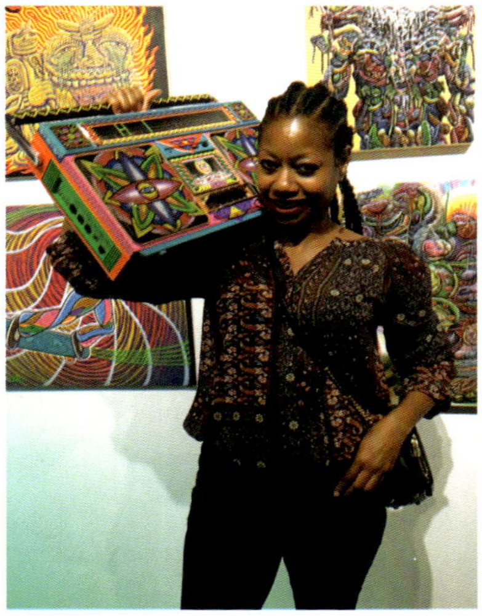
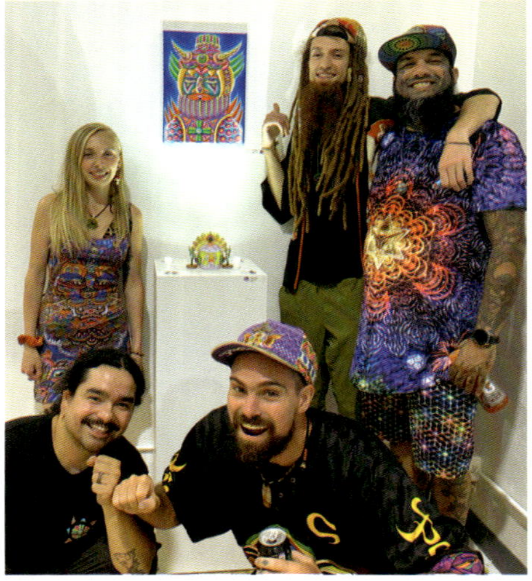
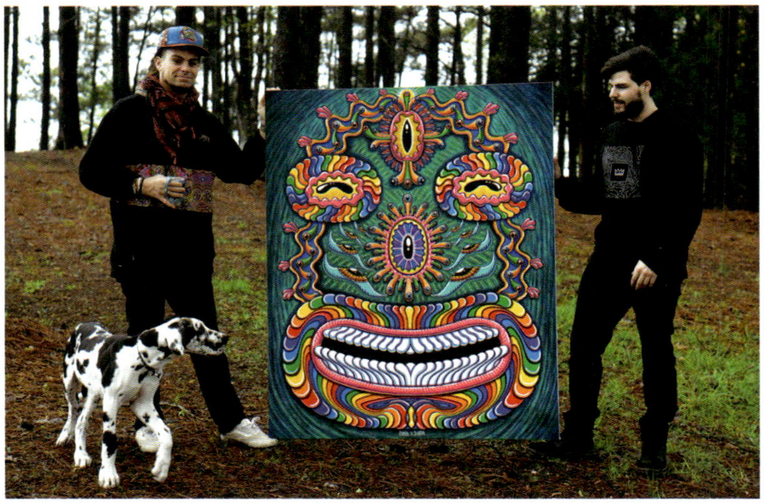
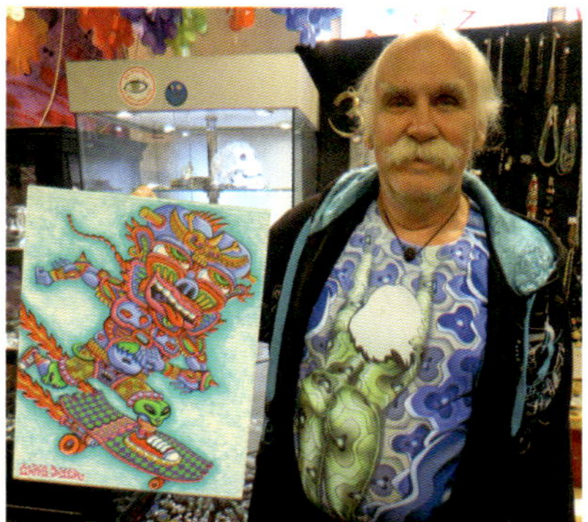
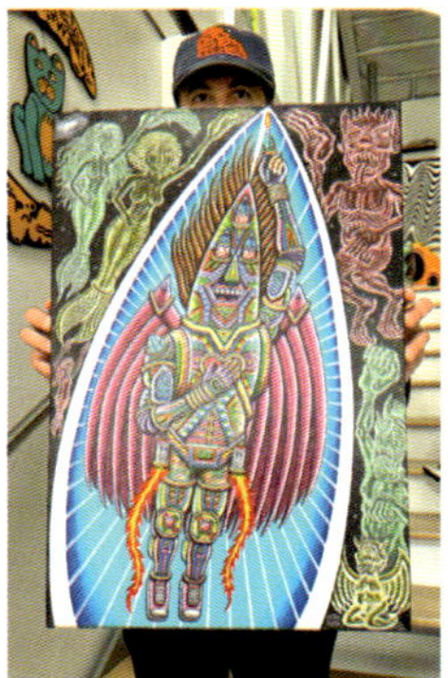
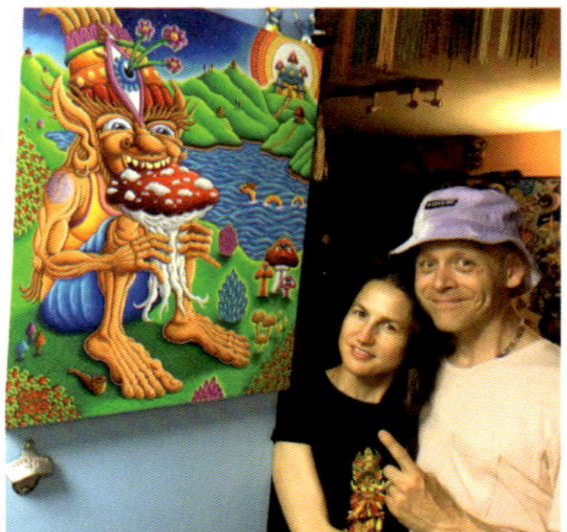
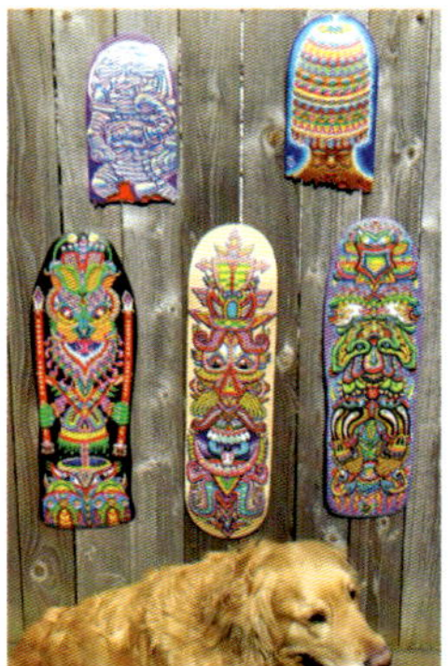
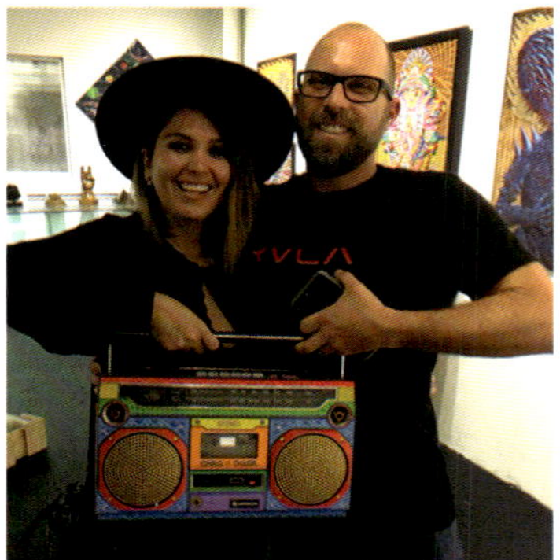
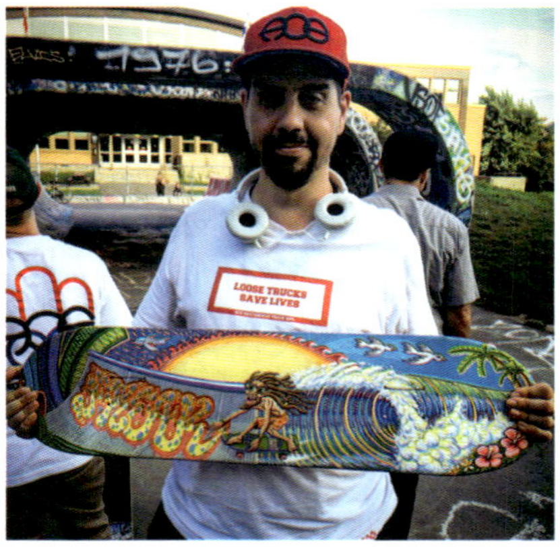
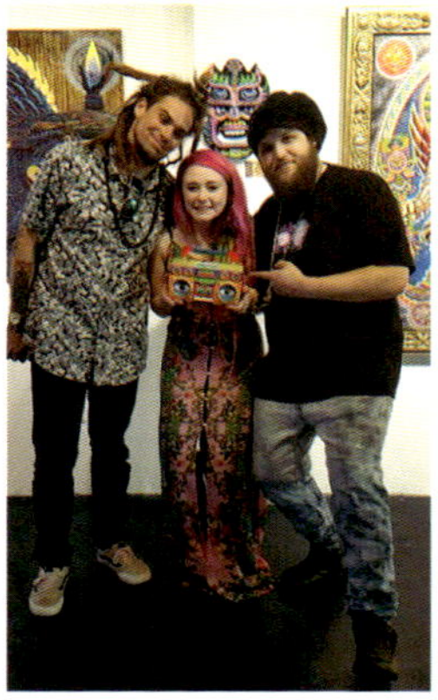
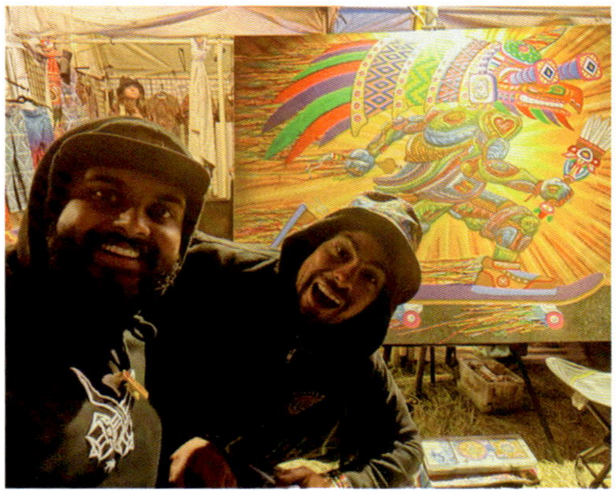
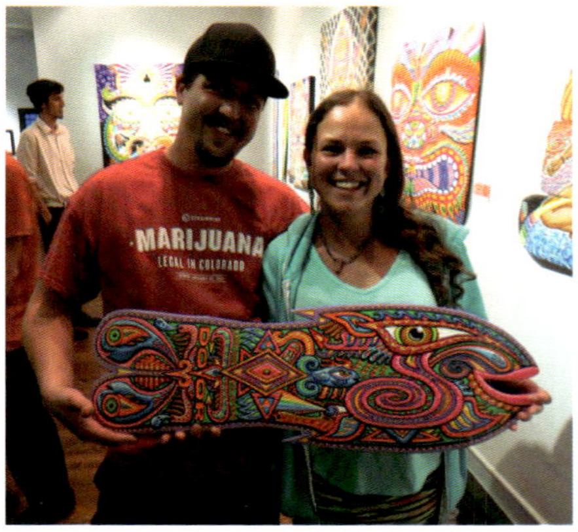

Photo Credits:
A. Comier, Pierre Gautier, Rico Michel, Adida Khavous, Dean Chamberlain, Melissa Robin, Jordana Clarke, Adrien Fumex, Zach Smith, Daniel Mathieu, Travis Knapp-Prasek, Nate Woodridge, Andrew Jimenez, Emily Behnke, Nathan Clough, Black Butterfly Photo, Marc A. Samson, Oskar Burman, Christina Covell, Ellie Paisley, Ben Jackson, Ambio, Heks FX, Jamie Zill, Johnathan Garza, Arianna Horton, T.J. Squires, Travis Feerkich, Ajai R. King, Pat Coyne and Kendralyn Liebeit. Blessings!

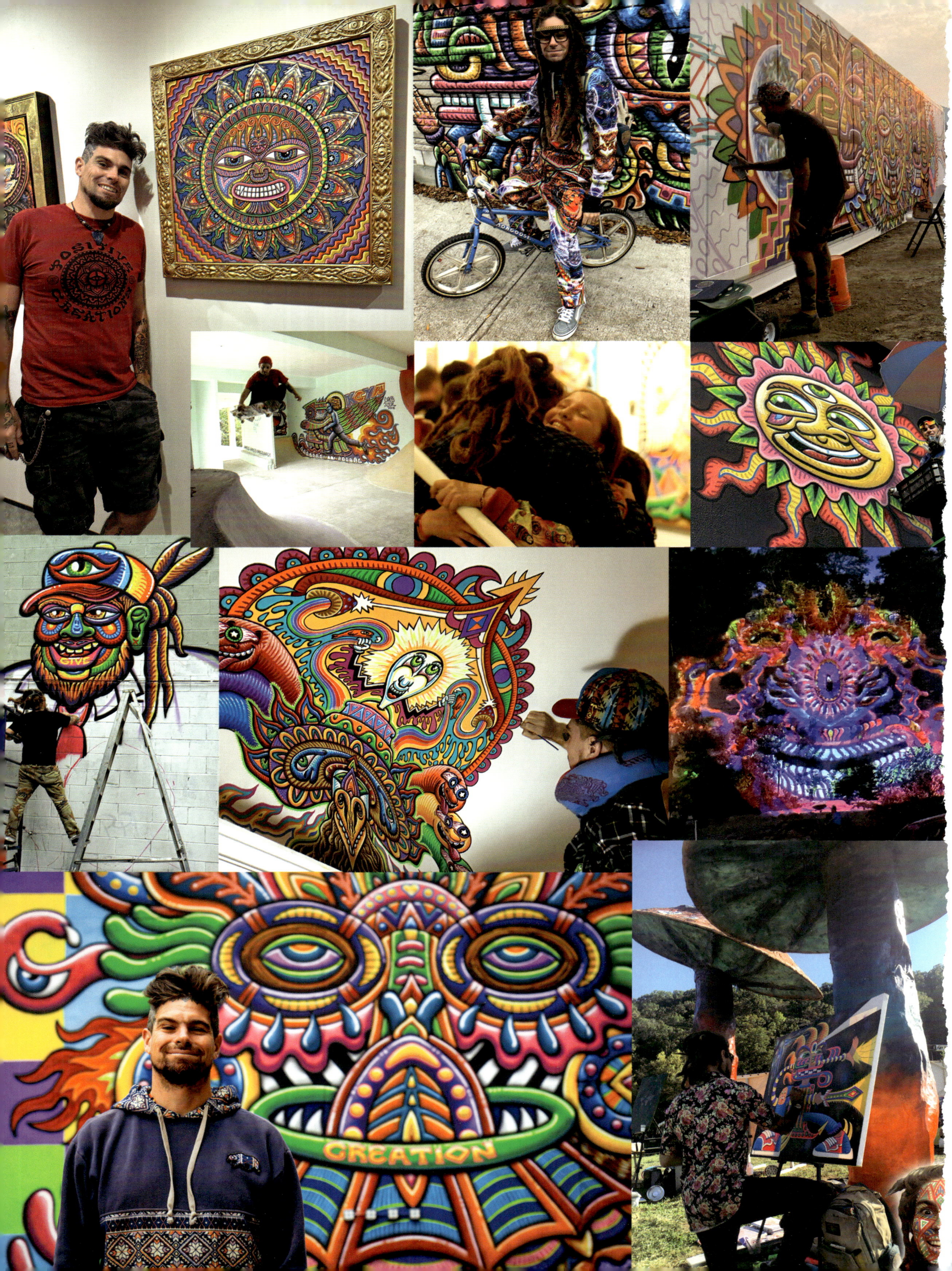
CREATION

SHAMANIC JOURNEY
CHRIS DYER

PUBLISHED BY POSITIVE CREATIONS AND LAST GASP

WWW.POSITIVECREATIONS.CA

LAST GASP
777 FLORIDA STREET, SAN FRANCISCO, CALIFORNIA, 94110
WWW.LASTGASP.COM

ISBN-13: 978-0-86719-928-4

COVER BACKGROUND IMAGE IS THE GALAXY MESSIER 83.
IMAGE CREDIT: ESO.

BOOK DESIGN: CHRIS DYER
COVER LAYOUT AND PRODUCTION: COLIN TURNER

FIRST PRINTING, 2024

PRINTED IN CANADA